AF334132

BIOINFORMATICS – TRENDS AND METHODOLOGIES

Edited by **Mahmood A. Mahdavi**

INTECHOPEN.COM

Bioinformatics – Trends and Methodologies
Edited by Mahmood A. Mahdavi

Published by InTech
Janeza Trdine 9, 51000 Rijeka, Croatia

Edition 2014

Publishing Process Manager Petra Nenadic

Technical Editor Teodora Smiljanic

Cover Designer InTech Design Team

Image Copyright Sashkin, 2011. Used under license from Shutterstock.com

Additional hard copies can be obtained from orders@intechopen.com

Bioinformatics – Trends and Methodologies, Edited by Mahmood A. Mahdavi
p. cm.
ISBN 978-953-307-282-1

Contents

Preface

Bioinformatics is a growing multidisciplinary field of science comprising biology, computer science, and mathematics. It is the theoretical and computational arm of modern biology. In other words, bioinformatics is a tool in the hands of biologists for analyzing huge amount of biological data available on mainstream public databases. Currently, bioinformatics has gained variety of applications in agriculture, medicine, engineering, and natural science. This book discusses a small portion of these applications along with basic concepts and fundamental techniques in bioinformatics.

The first section is a review of history of bioinformatics and the pace of its development in modern biology specifically in Europe. Section 2 and section 3 focus on fundamental principles of data integration and data mining as basic skills in bioinformatics. Data integration is now perceived a requirement in biology as the volume of biological data continues to grow. Section 2 provides an overview on integration of biomedical data using semantic web technologies and current efforts and challenges. Data mining is another basic tool to search databases for conserved regions, motifs, and regulatory modules effective in variety of diseases. Section 3 discusses these applications and basic approaches in data mining such as vector space information. Section 4 concentrates on another aspect of bioinformatics, sequence analysis. Sequences are analyzed to search for distribution of motifs, and search for domains. Basic tool for this analysis is sequence alignment which is discussed in this section in detail. Section 5 contains chapters on identification of specific structures in proteins such as endosomal sorting complex, chaperons, and human receptors. These structures are involved in different metabolic activities within the cell. Section 6 covers those chapters that discuss role of bioinformatics in genomic studies. Some applications of computational techniques in analysis of genomes such as SNP patterns, CPG islands, and virtual genomes have been described in this section. Section 7 focuses on regulatory machinery and the role micro RNAs in this system. Micro RNAs have recently been found to be important in regulatory networks. Some applications have been discussed in chapters within this section. Gene expression and system level understanding of expression process is one of the most interesting topics in bioinformatics. Section 8 contains fundamental principles of identification of differentially expressed genes from microarray data. The chapters in this section are suitable for those who seek basic information on gene expression and integration of this information into biological systems. Section 9 contains more advanced topics in bioinformatics including next generation sequencing. In this section the authors discuss more recent advances and technologies utilized in deep sequencing. The last section describes one of the growing practical applications of bioinformatics i.e. drug design. The ultimate goal of all theoretical analysis of biological data ought to be a product that improves lives of human. This section discusses one of thousands of efforts in designing a new drug for cancer treatment by means of bioinformatics.

Therefore, this book targets two types of readers: those who are new to bioinformatics and are interested in basic methods and fundamental principles and those who seek new approaches in bioinformatics. Both parties will benefit from studying this book.

In closing I wish to express my sincere sense of gratitude to all contributing authors, publishing process manager, Petra Nenadic and publishing staff.

Mahmood A. Mahdavi
Ferdowsi University of Mashhad (FUM), Mashhad
Iran

Part 1

Bioinformatics in Biology

Concepts, Historical Milestones and the Central Place of Bioinformatics in Modern Biology: A European Perspective

T.K. Attwood[1], A. Gisel[2], N-E. Eriksson[3] and E. Bongcam-Rudloff[4]
[1]*Faculty of Life Sciences & School of Computer Science, University of Manchester*
[2]*Institute for Biomedical Technologies, CNR*
[3]*Uppsala Biomedical Centre (BMC), University of Uppsala*
[4]*Department of Animal Breeding and Genetics,*
Swedish University of Agricultural Sciences
[1]*UK*
[2]*Italy*
[3,4]*Sweden*

1. Introduction

The origins of bioinformatics, both as a term and as a discipline, are difficult to pinpoint. The expression was used as early as 1977 by Dutch theoretical biologist Paulien Hogeweg when she described her main field of research as bioinformatics, and established a bioinformatics group at the University of Utrecht (Hogeweg, 1978; Hogeweg & Hesper, 1978). Nevertheless, the term had little traction in the community for at least another decade. In Europe, the turning point seems to have been *circa* 1990, with the planning of the *"Bioinformatics in the 90s"* conference, which was held in Maastricht in 1991. At this time, the National Center for Biotechnology Information (NCBI) had been newly established in the United States of America (USA) (Benson *et al.*, 1990). Despite this, there was still a sense that the nation lacked a *"long-term biology 'informatics' strategy"*, particularly regarding postdoctoral interdisciplinary training in computer science and molecular biology (Smith, 1990). Interestingly, Smith spoke here of 'biology informatics', not bioinformatics; and the NCBI was a 'center for biotechnology information', not a bioinformatics centre.

The discipline itself ultimately grew organically from the needs of researchers to access and analyse (primarily biomedical) data, which appeared to be accumulating at alarming rates simultaneously in different parts of the world. The rapid collection of data was a direct consequence of a series of enormous technological leaps that yielded what was considered, at the time, unprecedented quantities of biological *sequence* information. Hot on the heels of these developments was the concomitant wide-scale blossoming of algorithms and computational resources necessary to analyse, manipulate and store these growing quantities of data. Together, these advances gave birth to the field we now refer to as bioinformatics.

When we look back, it's clear that certain concepts and historical milestones were crucial to the evolution of this new field. Those we think most important, and consequently remember, depend largely on the perspective from which we view the emerging bioinformatics landscape. This chapter takes a largely European standpoint, while recognising that the development of bioinformatics in Europe was intimately coupled with parallel advances elsewhere in the world, and especially in the USA. The history is intricate. Here, we endeavour to recount the story as it unfolded along a number of tightly interwoven paths, including the rise and spread of some of the technological developments that spawned the data deluge and facilitated its world-wide propagation; of some of the databases that developed in order to store the rapidly accumulating data; and of some of the organisations and infrastructural initiatives that emerged to try to put some of those pivotal databases on a more solid financial footing.

2. The seeds of bioinformatics

It is hard to pinpoint where and when the seeds of bioinformatics were originally sown. Does the story start with Franklin and Gosling's foundational work towards the elucidation of the structure of DNA (Franklin & Gosling, 1953a, b, c), or with the opportunistic interpretation of their data by Watson and Crick (Watson & Crick, 1953)? Do we fast-forward to the ground-breaking work of Kendrew *et al.* (1958) and of Muirhead & Perutz (1963) in determining the first three-dimensional (3D) structures of proteins? Or do we step back, and focus on the painstaking work of Sanger, who, in 1955, determined the amino acid sequence of the first peptide hormone? Or again, do we jump ahead to the progenitors of the first databases of macromolecular structures and sequences in the mid-1960s and early '70s? This era clearly heralded some of the most significant advances in molecular biology, as witnessed by a string of Nobel Prizes at the time: *e.g.*, Sanger's Prize in Chemistry in 1958; Watson, Crick and Wilkins' shared Prize in Physiology or Medicine in 1962, following Franklin's death; and Perutz and Kendrew's Prize in Chemistry, also in 1962. Clearly, in its own way, each of these advances played an important part in the emergence of the vibrant new field that we recognise today as 'bioinformatics'.

As a humbling reference point, we have chosen to begin our story in the mid 1940s, with Fred Sanger's pioneering work on insulin. Sanger used a range of chemical and enzymatic techniques to elucidate, for the first time, the order of amino acids in the primary structure of a protein. Back then, this was a tremendously complex puzzle to tackle, and its completion required the successful resolution of many different challenges over several years. That this was a difficult incremental process is illustrated by the fact that, between 1945 and 1955, each step was published in a separate, stand-alone article. All in all, something like 10 papers detail the series of experiments that led to the eventual determination of the sequences of bovine insulin (*e.g.*, Sanger, 1945; Sanger & Tuppy, 1951a, b; Sanger & Thompson, 1953a,b; Sanger *et al.*, 1955; Ryle *et al.*, 1955) and of ovine and porcine insulins (Brown *et al.*, 1955). This was ground-breaking work, and had taken 10 years to complete. Incredibly, the 3D structure would not be known for another 14 years (Adams *et al.*, 1969). The primary and tertiary structures of this historical protein are illustrated in Figure 1.

Such was the enormity of manual sequencing projects that it was many years before the sequence of the first enzyme (ribonuclease) was determined. Work on this protein began in 1955. After preliminary studies in 1957 and 1958, the first full 'draft sequence' was published in 1960 (Hirs *et al.*, 1960). During the months that followed, the draft was meticulously refined, and a final version was published 3 years later (Smyth *et al.*, 1963). Crucially, this 8-

year project paved the way for the elucidation of the protein's 3D structure – indeed, without the sequence information, the electron density maps could not have been meaningfully interpreted (Wyckoff *et al.*, 1967). Knowledge of the primary structure of this small protein thus provided a vital piece of a 3D jigsaw puzzle that was to take a further 4

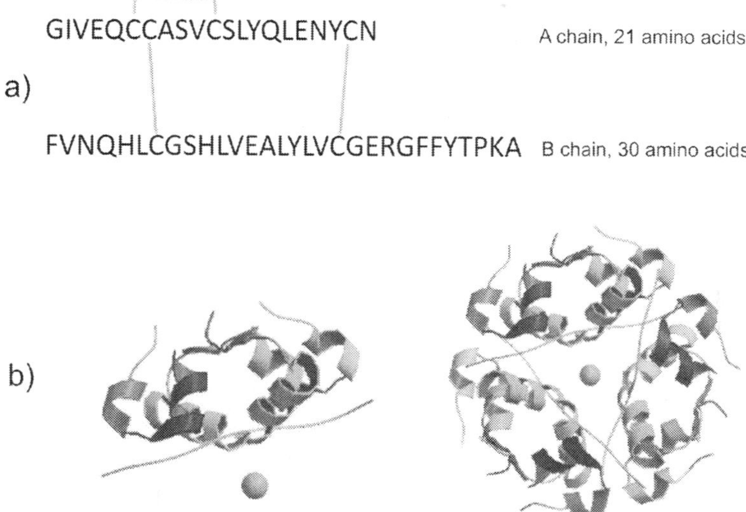

Fig. 1. Illustration of a) the primary structure of bovine insulin, showing intra- and interchain disulphide bonds connecting the a and b chains; and b) its zinc-coordinated tertiary structure (2INS), revealing two molecules in the asymmetric unit, and a hexameric biological assembly.

years to solve. Viewed in the light of the high-throughput sequence and structure determinations of today, these prolonged time-scales now seem almost inconceivable. Notwithstanding the challenges, however, the potential of peptide sequencing technology to aid our understanding of the biochemical functions and evolutionary histories of particular proteins, and to facilitate their structural analysis, was compelling. Consequently, the sequences of many other proteins were soon deduced. In the early '60s, amongst the first to appreciate the value of biological sequences, and particularly the ability to deduce evolutionary relationships from them, was Margaret Dayhoff. To facilitate her research and the work of others in the field, she began to collect all protein sequences then available, ultimately publishing them in book form – this was the first *Atlas of Protein Sequence and Structure* (Dayhoff *et al.*, 1965), often simply referred to as the *Atlas*. It may seem amusing to us now, but in a letter she wrote in 1967, she observed, *"There is a tremendous amount of information regarding the evolutionary history and biochemical function implicit in each sequence and **the number of known sequences is growing explosively** [our emphasis]. We feel it is important to collect this significant information, correlate it into a unified whole and interpret it"* (Dayhoff, 1967; Strasser, 2008). With the publication of the first *Atlas*, that 'explosive growth' amounted to 65 sequences!

In the decade that followed, time-consuming manual processes were gradually superseded with the advent of automated peptide sequencers, which increased the rate of sequence determination considerably. Meanwhile, another revolution was taking place, heralded by the elucidation of the 3D structures of the first proteins, those of myoglobin and haemoglobin, respectively (Kendrew *et al.*, 1958; Muirhead and Perutz, 1963). Building on the ongoing sequencing work, this advance set the scene for an exciting new era in which structure determination took centre stage in our quest to understand the biophysical mechanisms that underpin biochemical and evolutionary processes. In fact, so seductive was this approach that many more structural studies were initiated, and the numbers of deduced protein structures grew accordingly.

3. The development and spread of databases, organisations and infrastructures

Key to handling this burgeoning information was the recruitment of computers to help systematically analyse and store the accumulating sequence and structure data. At this time, the idea that molecular information could be collected within, and distributed from, electronic repositories was not only very new but also posed significant challenges. Just consider, for a moment, that concepts we take for granted today (email, the Internet, the World Wide Web) had not yet emerged; there was therefore no easy way to distribute data from a central database, other than by posting computer tapes and disks to individual users, at their request. This model of data distribution was clearly rather cumbersome and slow; it was also relatively costly, and led some of the first database pioneers to adopt pricing and/or data-sharing policies that threatened to drive away many of their potential users.

3.1 The Protein Data Bank (PDB)

One of the earliest, and hence now oldest, of scientific databases was established in 1965 at the Cambridge Crystallographic Data Centre (CCDC), under the direction of Olga Kennard (Kennard *et al.*, 1972; Allen *et al.*, 1991) – this was a repository of small-molecule crystal structures termed the Cambridge Structural Database, or CSD. The CSD, which originated as a traditional printed dissemination, ultimately assumed an electronic form so that Kennard could fulfill a dream, which she shared with J.D.Bernal, to be able to use data collections to discover new knowledge, above and beyond the results yielded by individual experiments (Kennard, 1997).

In 1971, a few years after the creation of the CSD, at a Cold Spring Harbor Symposium on the *"Structure and Function of Proteins at the Three Dimensional Level"*, Walter Hamilton and colleagues discussed the possibility of creating a similar kind of 'bank' for protein coordinate data. Key to their proposal was that this archive should be mirrored at sites in the UK and the USA (Berman, 2008). Consequently, Hamilton volunteered to set up the 'master copy' of the American bank at the Brookhaven National Laboratory (BNL), while Kennard subsequently agreed to host the European copy and to extend the CCDC small molecule format to accommodate protein structural data (Kennard *et al.*, 1972; Meyer, 1997). Thus was born the Protein Data Bank (PDB); this was to be operated jointly by the CCDC and BNL, and where possible, distributed on magnetic tape in machine-readable form. News of its establishment was announced in a short bulletin in October that year (Protein Data Bank, 1971); its first release held 7 structures (Berman *et al.*, 2000). Interestingly, Kennard viewed the PDB as a prototype for the EMBL data library, which was to materialise a decade later (Smith, 1990).

By 1973, the PDB was fully operational (Protein Data Bank, 1973). In August that year, the body of data it had been established to store amounted to 9 structures (see Table 1). Kennard and co-workers knew that the success of the resource was ultimately dependent on the support of the crystallography community in providing their data; but gaining sufficient community momentum to back the initiative was clearly a long, drawn-out process: note, for example, that the structure of ribonuclease, which had been determined 6 years earlier, was not yet listed amongst its holdings.

	Protein structures
1	Cyanide methaemoglobin V from sea lamprey
2	Cytochrome b_5
3	Basic pancreatic trypsin inhibitor
4	Subtilisin BPN (Novo)
5	Tosyl α-chymotrypsin
6	Bovine carboxypeptidase Aα
7	L-Lactate dehydrogenase
8	Myoglobin
9	Rubredoxin

Table 1. PDB holdings, August 1973.

Over the next 4 years, the number of structures acquired by the PDB grew slowly. By 1977, the archive also included the structure of a transfer RNA (tRNA), and hence the name *Protein Data Bank* was thought something of a misnomer (Bernstein *et al.*, 1977). Nevertheless, despite this reservation, the name stuck, and the resource (which today includes more than 5,000 nucleic acid and protein-nucleic acid complexes) is still referred to as the PDB. Interestingly, at that time, the database contained 77 sets of atomic coordinates relating to 47 macromolecules, highlighting a significant level of redundancy. Coupled with their ongoing concerns about the pace of growth of the archive, perhaps this explains why the Berstein *et al.* paper was published verbatim in May and November of 1977, and again in January 1978, in three different journals (Bernstein *et al.*, 1977a, b; 1978)? Whatever the real reasons, growth of the PDB compared to the CSD (~6,000 vs. ~150,000 structures in 1996) was slow (Kennard, 1997), and the number of unique structures remained relatively small – by 1992, the level of redundancy in the resource had been calculated to be ~7-fold (Berman, 2008; Hobohm *et al.*, 1992).

In 1996, shortly after the establishment of the European Bioinformatics Institute (EBI) near Cambridge, UK, a new database of macromolecular structures was created – this was the E-MSD (Boutselakis *et al.*, 2003). Building directly on PDB data, E-MSD was originally conceived as a pilot study to explore the feasibility of exploiting relational database technologies to manage structural data more effectively. In the end, the pilot project led to the creation of a database that was successful in its own right, and the E-MSD thereby became established as a major EBI resource.

During this period, a concerted effort was made to hasten the pace of knowledge acquisition from structural studies. Part of the motivation was to build on the still-limited number of structures available in the PDB, and partly also to address its growing level of redundancy. The idea was to establish a program of high-throughput X-ray crystallography – the so-called Structural Genomics Initiative (SGI) (Burley *et al.*, 1999). Several feasibility studies had already been launched and, in light of the broad-sweeping vision of the SGI, it had become clear that coping with high-throughput structure-determination pipelines would require new ways of gathering, storing, distributing and 'serving' the data to end users. One of the PDB's responses to this, and to the many challenges that lay ahead, was the formation of a new management structure. This was to be embodied in a 3-membered Research Collaboratory for Structural Bioinformatics (RCSB): the consortium included Rutgers, The State University of New Jersey; the San Diego Supercomputer Center at the University of California; and the Center for Advanced Research in Biotechnology of the National Institute of Standards and Technology (Berman *et al.*, 2000; Berman *et al.*, 2003). Once the consortium was established, the BNL PDB ceased operations and the RCSB formally took the helm on 1 July, 1999.

With the RCSB PDB in the USA, the E-MSD established in Europe, and a sister resource (PDBj) subsequently announced in Japan (Nakamura *et al.*, 2002), structure collection efforts had clearly taken on an international dimension. In consequence, in 2003, the 3 repositories were brought together beneath an umbrella organisation known as the worldwide Protein Data Bank (wwPDB), to streamline their activities and maintain a single, global, publicly available archive of macromolecular structural data (Berman *et al.*, 2003). By 2009, perhaps to align its nomenclature in a more obvious way with its consortium partners, E-MSD was renamed PDBe (Velankar *et al.*, 2009). Today, the RCSB remains the 'archive keeper', with sole write-access to the PDB, controlling its contents, and distributing new PDB identifiers to all deposition sites. In February 2011, the archive housed 71,415 structures.

3.2 The EMBL nucleotide sequence data library

Despite the advances in protein sequence- and structure-determination technologies between the mid-1940s and -'70s, sequencing nucleic acids had remained problematic. The key issues related to size and ease of molecular purification. It had proved possible to sequence tRNAs, largely because they're short (typically less than 100 nucleotides long) and individual molecules could, with some effort, be purified; but chromosomal DNA molecules are in a different league, containing many millions of nucleotides. Even if such molecules could be broken down into smaller chunks, purification was a major challenge. The longest fragment that could then be sequenced in a single experiment was ~500bp; and yields of potentially around half a million fragments per chromosome were simply beyond the technology of the day to handle.

During the mid '70s, however, Sanger had developed a technology (to become known as the 'Sanger method') that made it possible to work with much longer nucleotide fragments: this allowed completion of the sequencing of the 5,386 bases of the single-stranded bacteriophage φX174 (Sanger *et al.*, 1978), subsequently permitting rapid and accurate sequencing of even longer sequences – an achievement of sufficient magnitude to earn him his second Nobel Prize in Chemistry, in 1980. With this technique, he went on to sequence human mitochondrial DNA (Anderson *et al.*, 1981) and bacteriophage λ (Sanger *et al.*, 1982). These were landmark achievements (see Table 2), providing the first direct evidence of the phenomenon of overlapping gene sequences and of the non-universality of the genetic code (Sanger, 1988; Dodson, 2005). But it was automation of these techniques from the mid-'80s that significantly increased productivity, and began to make the human genome a realistic target.

Together, these advances prepared the way for a new revolution, one that would rock the foundations of molecular biology and make the gathered fruits of all sequencing efforts before it appear utterly inconsequential. Here, then, was a dramatic turning point: for the first time, it dawned on scientists that the new sequencing machines were shunting the bottlenecks away from data production *per se* and onto the requirements of data management: *"the rate limiting step in the process of nucleic acid sequencing is now shifting from data acquisition towards the organization and analysis of that data"* (Gingeras & Roberts, 1980). This realisation had profound consequences in both Europe and the USA, as a centralised data bank now seemed inescapable as a tool for managing nucleic acid sequence information efficiently.

Year	Protein	RNA	DNA	No. of residues
1935	Insulin			1
1945	Insulin			2
1947	Gramicidin S			5
1949	Insulin			9
1955	Insulin			51
1960	Ribonuclease			120
1965		tRNA$_{Ala}$		75
1967		5S RNA		120
1968			Bacteriophage λ	12
1977			Bacteriophage φX 174	5,375
1978			Bacteriophage φX 174	5,386
1981			Mitochondria	16,569
1982			Bacteriophage λ	48,502
1984			Epstein-Barr virus	172,282
2004			*Homo sapiens*	2.85 billion

Table 2. Sequencing landmarks.

So, the race was on to establish the first nucleotide sequence database. First past the post, in 1980, was the European Molecular Biology Laboratory (EMBL) in Heidelberg, who set up the EMBL data library. After an initial pilot period, the first release of 568 sequences was made in June 1982. The aim of this new resource was not only to make nucleic acid sequence data publicly available and encourage standardisation and free exchange of data, but also to provide a European focus for computational and biological data services (Hamm & Cameron, 1986).

From the outset, it was recognised that maintenance of such a centralised repository, and of its attendant services, would require international collaboration. In the UK, a copy of the EMBL library was being maintained at Cambridge University, together with its manual, indices and associated sequence analysis, and search and retrieval software. This integrated system also provided access to the library of sequences then being developed at Los Alamos, GenBank (Kanehisa *et al.*, 1984). It makes fascinating reading to learn that, *"this system is presently being used by over 30 researchers in eight departments in the University and in local research institutes. These users can keep in touch with each other via the MAIL command"*! With the support of the Medical Research Council (MRC), the Cambridge services were extended to the wider UK community on the Joint Academic network (JANET) (Kneale & Kennard, 1984). As with the PDB before it, it was important not only to push the data out to researchers, but also to pull their data in. Hence, a further planned development was to centralise collection of nucleic acid data from UK research groups, and to periodically transfer the information to the EMBL library. It was hoped that this would minimise both data-entry errors and the workload of EMBL staff at a time when the number of sequence determinations was predicted to *"increase greatly"* (Kneale & Kennard, 1984). Of course, the size of this 'great increase' could hardly have been predicted; in December 2010, the database contained 199,720,869 entries.

3.3 GenBank

The birth of GenBank, in December 1982, brought 606 sequences into the public domain. A consensus had emerged on the necessity of creating an international nucleic acid sequence repository at a scientific meeting at Rockefeller University in New York, in March 1979. At that time, several groups had expressed a desire to be a part of this endeavour, including those led by Dayhoff at the National Biomedical Research Foundation (NBRF); Walter Goad at Los Alamos National Laboratories; Doug Brutlag at Stanford; Olga Kennard and Fred Sanger at the MRC Laboratory in Cambridge; and Ken Murray and Hans Lehrach at the EMBL (Smith, 1990), all of whom had begun to create their own nucleotide sequence collections. However, it took the best part of 3 years for an appropriate funding model to emerge from the US National Institutes of Health (NIH), by which time the EMBL data library had already been publicly available for 6 months under the direction of Greg Hamm. By then, 3 proposals remained on the table for NIH support: 2 of these were from Los Alamos (one with Bolt, Beranek and Newman (BBN), the other with IntelliGenetics), and the third from NBRF. To the surprise of many, the decision was made in June 1982 to establish the new GenBank resource at Los Alamos (in collaboration with BBN, Inc.) rather than at the NBRF (Smith, 1990; Strasser, 2008).

Although there was a general sense of relief that a decision had finally been made, some members of the community (and doubtless Dayhoff herself) felt that the NBRF would have been a more appropriate home for GenBank, particularly given Dayhoff's successful track record as a curator of protein sequence data (Smith, 1990). Los Alamos, by contrast, although undoubtedly offering excellent computer facilities, was probably best known for its role in the creation of atomic weapons – this was not an obvious environment in which to establish the nation's first public nucleotide sequence database. The crux of the matter seemed to rest with the different philosophical approaches embodied in the NBRF and Los Alamos proposals, particularly as they related to scientific priority, data sharing/privacy and intellectual property policies. Dayhoff had intended to continue gathering sequences directly from literature sources and from bench scientists, and wasn't interested in matters of history or priority (Eck & Dayhoff, 1966); the Los Alamos team, on the other hand, advocated the collaboration of journal editors in making the publication of articles contingent on authors yielding their sequence data to the database. This latter approach was particularly compelling, as it would allow scientists to assert priority, and to keep their research results private until formally published and their provenance established; perhaps more importantly, it was unencumbered by proprietary interest in the data. Unfortunately, the fact that Dayhoff had prevented redistribution of NBRF's protein sequence library and sought revenues from its sales (albeit only to cover costs) worked against her – allowing the data to become the private hunting grounds of any one group of researchers was considered antithetical to the spirit of open access (Strasser, 2008). That the data and associated software tools should be free and open was thus paramount; it is perhaps ironic, then, that the site chosen for the database was within the secured area of what many in the community may have darkly perceived as 'The Atomic City' (en.wikipedia.org/wiki/The_Atomic_City).

As an aside, it's interesting that the vision of free data and programs was advocated so strongly at this time, not least because there was no funding model to support it! And precisely the same arguments are still being vehemently propounded today with regard to free databases, free software and free literature (*e.g.*, Lathrop *et al.*, 2011). But even now, database funding remains an unsolved and controversial issue: as Olga Kennard put it almost 15 years ago, *"Free access to validated and enhanced data worldwide is a beautiful dream. The reality, however, is more complex"* (Kennard, 1997).

Returning to our theme, perhaps the final nail in the coffin of Dayhoff's proposal was that the NBRF had only limited means of data distribution (via modems), whereas the Los Alamos outfit had the enormous benefit of being able to distribute their data via ARPANET, the computer network of the US Department of Defense. Together, these advantages were sufficient to swing the pendulum in favour of the Los Alamos team.

But the new GenBank did not, indeed could not, function in isolation. From its inception, it evolved in close collaboration with the EMBL data library and, from 1986 onwards, also with the DNA Data Bank of Japan. Although the databases were not identical (each with its own format, naming convention, and so on), the teams adopted common data-entry standards and data-exchange protocols in order to improve data quality and to manage both the growth of the resource and the annotation of its entries more effectively. Of this collaborative process, Temple Smith commented in 1990, *"By working out a division of labor with the EMBL and newer Japanese database efforts, and by involving the authors and journal editors, GenBank and the EMBL databases are currently keeping pace with the literature."* Today, the boot seems to be very much on the other foot, as the literature can no longer keep up with the data: by February 2011, GenBank contained 132,015,054 entries, presenting insurmountable annotation hurdles! (Note that this appears smaller than the size of the EMBL data library because GenBank doesn't report sequences from Whole Genome Shotgun projects in its total). Perhaps not surprisingly, the initial funding for GenBank was insufficient to adequately maintain this growing mass of data; hence, responsibility for its maintenance, with increased funding under a new contract, passed to IntelliGenetics in 1987; then, in 1992, it became the responsibility of the NCBI, where it remains today (Benson *et al.*, 1993; Smith, 1990).

3.4 The PIR-PSD

To some extent, the gathering momentum of nucleic acid sequence-collection efforts had begun to overshadow the steady progress being made in the world of protein sequences, most notably with the *Atlas*. By October 1981, this had run into its fifth volume, a large book with three supplements, listing more than 1,660 proteins. This information, as with all data collections, required constant updating and revision in the light both of new knowledge and of new data appearing in the literature. Moreover, as the community had become increasingly keen to harness the efficiency gains of central data repositories, and more databases were appearing on the horizon, making and maintaining cross-references to database entries, of necessity, had to become part of data-annotation and update processes if scientists were to be able to exploit new and existing sequence data fully. Under the circumstances, continued publication of the *Atlas* in paper form simply became untenable: the time was ripe to exploit the advances in computer technology that had given rise to the CSD, the PDB, the EMBL data library and GenBank. In 1984, the *Atlas* was consequently made available on computer tape as the Protein Sequence Database (PSD).

Later, in 1986, in order to facilitate protein sequence analysis more broadly, the NBRF established the Protein Identification Resource (PIR) (George *et al.*, 1986). This new online system included the PSD, several bespoke query and analysis tools (*e.g.*, the Protein Sequence Query (PSQ), SEARCH and ALIGN programs), and a new, efficient search program, FASTP. The latter was a modification of an earlier algorithm for searching protein and nucleic acid sequences (Wilbur & Lipman, 1983). Interestingly, given that the number of deduced sequences had, by that time, grown into the thousands, the great advantage of Wilbur and Lipman's method was considered to be its speed. Indeed, their paper reported a *"substantial reduction in the time required to search a data bank"*. Improving on this even further, the new FASTP algorithm was able to compare a 200-amino-acid sequence to the 2,677 sequences of the PSD in *"less than 2 minutes on a minicomputer, and less than 10 minutes on a microcomputer (IBM PC)"* (Lipman & Pearson, 1985). Looking back, such search times on such small numbers of sequences seem incredibly slow; at the time (when a contemporary algorithm required 8 hours for the same search), they were revolutionary.

As the PIR was built on NBRF's existing resources, it also made available its DNA databank (Dayhoff *et al.*, 1981a) and associated software tools, together with copies of GenBank and the EMBL data library; it also retained the NBRF's cost-recovery model, levying a charge for copies of its databases on magnetic tape and an annual subscription fee for use of its online services – in 1988, these amounted to $200 per tape release and $350 per annum respectively (Dayhoff *et al.*, 1981b; Sidman *et al.*, 1988). By 1992, the PSD had shown steady growth, with increasing contributions from European and Asian protein sequence centres – most notably, from MIPS (Martinsried, Germany) and from JIPID (Tokyo, Japan). Accordingly, a tripartite collaboration was established, termed PIR-International, to formalise these relationships and establish and disseminate a comprehensive set of protein sequences (Barker *et al.*, 1992). By this time, charging for access to the resource was no longer mentioned, possibly both as a consequence of this more formal distribution arrangement and the advent of browsers like Mosaic, which had suddenly and dramatically changed the way that information could be broadcast and received over the World Wide Web (or, simply, the Web). In 1997 PIR changed its name to the Protein Information Resource (George *et al.*, 1997) and, by 2003, with 283,000 sequences (Wu *et al.*, 2003), the PSD was the most comprehensive protein sequence database in the world.

3.5 Swiss-prot

While these events were taking place, a newly qualified Swiss student (who, as a teenager, had been interested in space exploration and the search for extraterrestrial life) attempted to embark on a Masters project involving both 'wet' and 'dry' work – this was Amos Bairoch. The experimental side of his project immediately hit problems when it was discovered that the new mass spectrometer he was to have used didn't work properly. He therefore set to work instead developing protein sequence analysis programs on the computer system running the spectrometer. These were the first steps towards creating the software system that was later to be known as PC/Gene, and was to become the most widely used PC-based sequence analysis package of its day (Bairoch, 2000).

Part of what made this software suite unique was its focus on proteins at a time when the analysis of nucleotide sequences was very much in vogue. In creating these tools, Bairoch entered >1,000 protein sequences into his computer by hand: some of these he gleaned from the literature; most were taken from the *Atlas*, which had not yet been released in electronic form. Of course, this was an immensely tedious process, and was also highly error-prone. Realising this, and anxious to avoid such problems for others in future, he wrote a letter to the *Biochemical Journal* recommending that researchers publishing protein and peptide sequences should compute checksums to *"facilitate the detection of typographical and keyboard errors"* (Bairoch, 1982). As part of the letter, he illustrated the computation of such a 'checking number' for an imaginary peptide, as shown in Figure 2. Although this recommendation was never widely adopted in publishing circles, Bairoch was at least able to ensure that it was implemented in his own database.

Peptide: H E L P I H A T E M A T H

$$CN \text{ computation: } CN = 1 \cdot 9 + 2 \cdot 7 + 3 \cdot 11 + 4 \cdot 15 + 5 \cdot 10 + 6 \cdot 9 + 7 \cdot 1 + 8 \cdot 17$$
$$+ 9 \cdot 7 + 10 \cdot 13 + 11 \cdot 1 + 12 \cdot 17 + 13 \cdot 9 = 788$$

$$COMP = A_2 R_0 N_0 D_0 C_0 Q_0 E_2 G_0 H_3 I_1 L_1 K_0 M_1 F_0 P_1 S_0 T_2 W_0 Y_0 V_0$$

$$NR = 13 \qquad MMP = 1186.66 \qquad CN = 788$$

Fig. 2. Computation of a 'checking number' (CN) for an imaginary peptide, as published in a letter to the *Biochemical Journal* in 1982. The journal editors either didn't notice, or chose to ignore, the hidden message in the peptide. Reproduced with permission, from Bairoch, A. (1982), *Biochemical Journal*, 203, 527-528. © the Biochemical Society

Several other important developments were to emerge from the work of this enthusiastic and industrious student. For the analysis software he was developing, he needed to distribute both a nucleotide and a protein sequence database. In 1983, he acquired a computer tape containing 811 sequences in version 2 of the EMBL data library; for his protein sequence database, he initially used the sequences he'd typed in for his Masters project. However, the following year, he received the first electronic copy of the *Atlas*. He was quick to appreciate the advantages and disadvantages of the PIR and EMBL formats, recognising that converting the manually annotated data of the former into something like the semi-structured format of the latter could produce a resource with the strengths of both – he called this PIR+ and released it side-by-side with his software package, PC/Gene, which by that time he'd commercialised through IntelliGenetics (Bairoch, 2000).
Use of the publicly available PIR data-set in this way was not without its problems. Amongst other, deeper, issues were the difficulty of parsing PIR files to extract specific information (*e.g.*, relating to post-translational modifications (PTMs), *etc.*); the lack of functional annotations for some of the newer entries; the lack of cross-referencing to the parent DNA of a given protein sequence; and so on. Somewhat ironically, given what he went on to achieve, Bairoch has written of this period, *"As I was not interested in building up databases I kept sending letters to PIR to ask them to remedy this situation"*. But his pleas met with little success. In the summer of 1986, in the face of increasing demand for unencumbered access to his database, he decided to release PIR+ independently of PC/Gene, to make it freely available to the entire research community. The new, public version of the database was released on 21 July 1986 and contained ~3,900 sequences (the exact number is unknown as the original floppy disks have been lost!) This new resource

was called Swiss-Prot (Bairoch & Boeckmann, 1991), and was to become the foremost manually annotated database of protein sequences in the world.

3.6 The European Molecular Biology Network (EMBnet)

It is interesting that, during this era, the distribution of databases like the EMBL data library, PIR, Swiss-Prot and so on, was still largely effected by the exchange of computer tapes and disks. By this time, a variety of computer networks had begun to evolve: the first such network, ARPANET (which began life with 4 nodes in late 1969), was the progenitor of the Internet, and was superseded by it in 1983 – recall, it was partly owing to the existence of ARPANET that GenBank was established at Los Alamos. Other networks that offered gateways into the Internet later merged with it, including Usenet and BITNET; commercial and educational networks, such as Telenet (or Sprintnet), Tymnet, Compuserve and JANET, were interconnected with it in the 1980s.

In 1988, Chris Sander at the EMBL helped to establish a new network, EMBnet, to disseminate data, knowledge and services, to support and advance molecular biology and biotechnology research across Europe. A major driver for creating EMBnet was the need for local access to databases such as the EMBL data library from centralised sources. Essentially, this is because scientists were now demanding to use client workstations with Graphical User Interfaces (GUIs) that provided real-time interaction with their back-end data/analysis servers. At the time, high-speed data communication across Europe was in its infancy, and access to remote computers using ordinary command-line oriented terminals was too slow. It was clear that communication delays could be eliminated if servers held copies of data locally; the sheer amount of compute resources needed for European research in this field also pointed to a distributed solution (note that computer cluster technology only gained widespread acceptance much later). Thus, an organised way of distributing data and resources from the EMBL to its member states had to be established.

The concept of a network of national 'nodes', each serving its country with up-to-date biological databases and also providing compute resources for data analysis, was formulated. It was given the name the European Molecular Biology network, EMBnet. The first practical steps were taken in the spring of 1988 to solicit feedback from scientists around Europe; and in July 1988, the first EMBnet Workshop was organised at EMBL, with participants from EMBL, Daresbury (UK), CITI2 (France), the CAOS/CAMM Centre (the Netherlands) and Hoffmann-La Roche. In November of that year, the EMBL Director General corresponded with EMBL Council members, encouraging them to stimulate local processes to identify regional EMBnet nodes. As more countries joined the network (France, Sweden, the UK, the Netherlands, Spain, Israel, Norway, Italy and Denmark, with Switzerland, West Germany, Austria, Greece and Finland waiting in the wings), EMBnet received its first European grant under the BRIDGE framework, in 1991.

The principal project objective was to promote EMBnet as a computer network for European bioinformatics. Service provision and knowledge sharing was to be orchestrated primarily by 'National Nodes', with government mandates to support their local communities, especially by providing access to bioinformatics data synchronised with the EMBL, GenBank and DDBJ central data repositories – in time, the network also attracted a number of 'Specialist' and 'Industrial' Nodes, whose resources and know-how were seen to complement those of its National Nodes (this arrangement of cooperating Nodes is illustrated in Figure 3).

Most EMBnet Nodes had VAX computers, and the original intention was to use DECNET as the underlying transport protocol. However, after a short, but expensive, period of using

X25/DataPak, this was replaced by a TCP/IP-package called MultiNet, which was licensed for all EMBnet Nodes from SRI (Stanford Research Institute). FTP-transmissions of database updates were often interrupted by network problems, and, to overcome the need for frequent re-transmissions, the NDT (Network Data Transfer, later xNDT for extended NDT) protocol was developed at the Swedish EMBnet Node at Uppsala Biomedical Centre, by Peter Gad. It was given a so-called 'systems well-known port' (embl-ndt, 394/udp,# EMBL Nucleic Data Transfer) by the Internet authorities, and is thus in good company with, for example, Telnet (port 23) and FTP (ports 20, 21). For a few years, (x)NDT, and its accompanying suite of client-server programs, was the method par preference, used at almost all EMBnet Nodes to keep their local databases updated. NDT took care of the transmission (database) entry by entry and didn't have to re-start following network interruptions. The Greek node, situated in Crete, only had a modem connection to the mainland, and benefited hugely from using the xNDT-suite. Indeed, at the time the European Bioinformatics Institute was established (when the EMBL Data Library moved from Heidelberg to Cambridge), most of the nucleotide sequence database update traffic in Europe was routed via the Swedish node using xNDT.

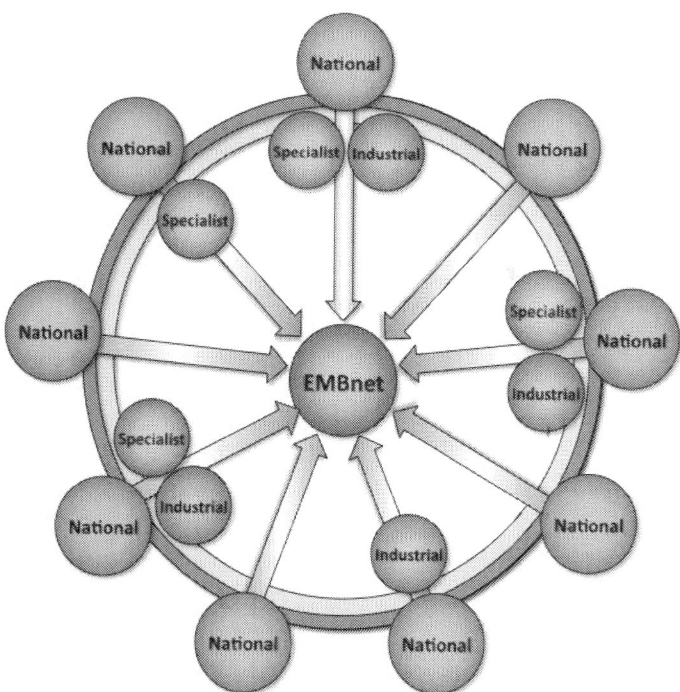

Fig. 3. Illustration of the relationship between the different Nodes of the early EMBnet: some National Nodes had either Specialist or Industrial Nodes affiliated with them; some had both; some had neither. Today, 31 National and Specialist Nodes contribute to the Network.

By the early '90s, biomolecular databases could be accessed across the Internet by means of the WAIS and Gopher network retrieval systems; and, under the auspices of EMBnet, Reinhard Doetlz had developed a new network access protocol, HASSLE, the Hierarchical Access System for Sequence Libraries in Europe (Doelz, 1994). But it was the advent of graphical Web browsers (first, Mosaic from the National Center for Supercomputing Applications in 1993, and then Netscape Navigator in 1994) that revolutionised the processes of database dissemination and information consumption – literally, at the click of a mouse button.

Of course, browsers allowed data and documents of all kinds to be instantly shared, and individuals and organisations across the globe were quick to establish their own unique 'Web presence'. EMBnet was no exception, and embraced the Web as a means of communicating more effectively with its widening community, in particular by publishing a regular newsletter, *EMBnet.news*. The newsletter was designed to provide reports and updates on its internal and international activities and achievements, together with technical and scientific papers on new developments in bioinformatics, computational biology and biocomputing. In 2000, the organisation provided an educational grant to help support the creation of the peer-reviewed journal *Briefings in Bioinformatics* (BiB) and, as a mark of its own success, *EMBnet.news* is also now in the process of transitioning to a peer-reviewed journal.

From the outset, EMBnet has promoted the development of distributed computing services to share workload among international servers; it has contributed to the development and maintenance of advanced database systems; it has been an advocate of the deployment of Grid technologies for the life sciences through its contributions to major European Grid projects; it developed, and continues to promote the use of, an e-learning system both to support distance learning in bioinformatics and to complement face-to-face bioinformatics teaching and training; and it is committed to bringing the latest software and algorithms to users, free of charge.

The combined expertise of its Nodes has allowed EMBnet to provide services to its local European life science communities with far greater effect than could be achieved by any of its individual Nodes in isolation. Following this success, a variety of Nodes world-wide have joined EMBnet such that, today, the network is global, with many countries from Asia, Africa and America joining in recent years (including Sri Lanka, Pakistan, Kenya and Costa Rica). Currently, the network connects 31 member Nodes extending over 27 countries; together, the Nodes continue to work to disseminate data, to share compute resources and to provide training support, reaching out to many thousands of users.

3.7 PROSITE

While EMBnet was being conceived, before the Internet had truly taken off, and while bioinformatics was still in the throes of been born, the computer savvy molecular biologists of the day were still busily swapping biomolecular databases on magnetic tapes and computer disks. Perhaps an inevitable consequence of the systematic collection of protein and nucleotide sequences in this way was the need to organise and classify these molecular entities in meaningful ways. The first endeavour to categorise protein sequences into evolutionarily related families, and to provide the diagnostic means to detect potential new family members, arose once again as a derivative of the PC/Gene suite. Inspired by the sequence analysis primer, *Of URFs and ORFs* (Doolittle, 1986), Bairoch began to amass examples of short sequences, characteristic of particular binding and active sites, and developed a program to scan his growing collection of sequence 'patterns'. This part-program, part-database chimera he named PROSITE (Bairoch, 1991). In March 1988, as part of PC/Gene, the first release of this new resource contained 58 entries.

As with Swiss-Prot before it, PROSITE swiftly gained popularity. Its growing band of users began not only to suggest additional patterns that could be included in the database, but also to pressure Bairoch into giving PROSITE an independent life of its own, outside PC/Gene. Consequently, the availability of a new public version was announced in October 1989, and formally released the following month with 202 entries (version 4.0). Diagnostically, it was clear that sequence patterns had certain limitations. In particular, matching a pattern is a binary 'match/no-match' event: even the most trivial difference (a single amino acid) results in a mis-match. As Swiss-Prot expanded and accommodated more and more divergent members of its various superfamilies, the more evident this particular weakness became. One solution to this problem emerged in the form of position-specific weight matrices, or profiles. Built from comprehensive sequence alignments, profiles are tolerant both of amino acid substitutions and of insertions/deletions; they therefore allow the relationships between families of sequences to be modelled more 'realistically'. Accordingly, with the help of Phillipp Bucher, Bairoch began to augment PROSITE with sequence profiles – the first release to include them came with version 12.0, in June 1994 (Bairoch & Bucher, 1994).

Another solution, which arose (at least methodologically) independently from PROSITE, was the development of protein family 'fingerprints'. Fingerprints are groups of conserved motifs, evident in multiple sequence alignments, whose unique inter-relationships provide distinctive signatures for particular protein families and structural/functional domains. They are diagnostically more powerful and flexible than patterns, because they can tolerate mis-matches at the level both of individual motifs and of the fingerprint as a whole. Fingerprints formed the basis of a database that began life as the Features Database, part of the SERPENT information storage and analysis resource for protein sequences established at the University of Leeds (Akrigg et al., 1992). Its first release, in October 1991, contained 29 entries: two thirds of these were linked to equivalent entries in PROSITE, which by then held 441 family descriptions.

Although disparate in size, the Features and PROSITE databases had various aspects in common; most notable amongst these was the principle of added-value through hand-crafted annotation of their diagnostic signatures. In March 1991, Bairoch met Terri Attwood for the first time at the British Crystallographic Association spring meeting in Sheffield. Faced with the same, relentlessly time-consuming, manual-annotation burdens, they shared their woes and discussed the wisdom of unifying the PROSITE and Features databases. Motivated by common ideals, they later formalised their ideas in the guise of their first European grant proposal to merge their databases into an integrated protein family annotation resource. This was 1992; they were not successful.

In the meantime, inspired by PROSITE, a range of other signature databases began to emerge. One of the earliest of these was Blocks, first described by Steve and Jorja Henikoff in December 1991 (Henikoff & Henikoff, 1991). Later came ProDom (Sonnhammer & Kahn, 1994), and later still Pfam (Sonnhammer et al., 1997). Initially linked closely to the annotation of predicted proteins from genomic sequencing of Caenorhabditis elegans, Pfam was to become one of the most widely used protein family databases across Europe and the USA.

3.8 The European Bioinformatics Institute (EBI)

Notwithstanding the proliferation of databases in the '80s, funding for their maintenance was becoming a significant problem. By the early '90s, supporting the EMBL data library was becoming increasingly difficult, and there was growing awareness that a more efficient European bioinformatics infrastructure would be needed to sustain it in future. In 1992, the EMBL concluded that the most robust solution would be to establish a new outstation, devoted to bioinformatics. The vision of creating a European Bioinformatics Institute (EBI) quickly took hold and, in December that year, the EMBL Governing Council published a call for proposals to host the new facility. The deadline was extremely short (February 1993); despite the interest of many countries, therefore, few were able to submit bids in time.

In a study by PA Consulting Group, commissioned by the EC's DGXII, a plan had been developed for a European Nucleotide Sequence Centre (ENSC). The EMBL Council decided to *"negotiate with the EC for the inclusion of the ENSC within the EBI"*; the EBI *"would provide bioinformatics services for European scientists, be a home for the Data Library, and include expansions in research and development necessary for long-term viability and strengthening of neglected areas such as user support"* (Philipson, 1992).

In EMBL's proposal for an EBI from October 1992, worries were expressed that Europe was lagging behind the USA: *"Over the last decade increments in US support for such resources have far outstripped those in Europe,"* and the EBI was conceived *"to ensure that European research needs are satisfied in a way which is appropriate to this global competitive context"* (EMBL, 1992). The need for supportive relations between EBI and the European scientific community was emphasised, as *"It would be impossible and undesirable for the EBI to be the sole bioinformatics resource in Europe"*. It was noted that support should be given to *"major European interest groups such as software developers, database hosts and other bioinformatics institutes"*; more specifically, *"In recognition of the need for strong national bioinformatics activities, the EBI will give technical and organisational support to the EMBnet Nodes, as is currently done by the EMBL Data Library"* (EMBL, 1992).

Among the bidders for the EBI were Germany, Sweden and the UK. Very favourable conditions were offered from all three. The Swedish bid for an EBI close to Uppsala Biomedical Centre, included, for example, sufficient office space, free of rent, and high-speed network connections. But Michael Ashburner led a more compelling UK bid. The proposal was to host the EBI on a park, newly purchased by the Wellcome Trust, at Hinxton, on the outskirts of Cambridge. The Trust and MRC had agreed each to fund half of the initial capital costs of creating a complete genomics infrastructure on this site, which would also include the newly established Sanger Centre (which, by then, had become embroiled in the HGP) and the Human Genome Mapping Project Resource Centre (Dickson & Abbott, 1993). With its *"clear commitment from all levels of the UK scientific community and Government"*, the UK bid won over both Uppsala and the alternative location in Heidelberg, directly adjacent to the EMBL; it was accepted by Council in March 1993. Paulo Zanella (who had directed the CERN Data Handling Division) was subsequently appointed as EBI's first director (Bairoch, 2000).

The EBI became fully operational after completion of the new building in September 1995 – this will no doubt have come as a great relief to the EMBL data library group, who had been accommodated in portable cabins on the Hinxton site since the end of 1994! The new facility had 3 broad divisions: research, industry and services, the latter being mostly devoted to provision and maintenance of the EMBL data library and Swiss-Prot (Bairoch, 2000). The EBI's mission was to ensure that the growing corpus of data from molecular biology and genome research was placed in the public domain and was freely accessible to the entire scientific community in order to promote scientific progress. Today, with its original 3-fold structure still largely in place, the Institute builds, maintains and disseminates databases and information services relevant to molecular biology, genetics, medicine and agriculture, and undertakes leading-edge research in bioinformatics and computational biology.

Despite its pivotal role as Europe's main bio-database provider, four years later, the EBI was in financial trouble. While the Wellcome Trust and MRC had financed the initial capital costs, the Institute relied on the EU for almost half its budget. In March 1999, however, the member states had advised the Commission that core funding and operational costs for infrastructure should not qualify for funding; the EBI's application for Framework funds was consequently rejected for being out of scope. Graham Cameron, by then joint Head of the Institute with Michael Ashburner, was quick to point out that without an immediate solution, *"we will have to abandon major projects like the DNA database, the draft human genome, the macromolecular structure database and the microarray expression database"* (Butler, 1999). The EBI was in a tricky situation, and Britain had shot itself in the foot: it could hardly contest the Commission's ruling against supporting the EBI because, a Commission official pointed out, *"it was among the countries most against funding infrastructure directly"* (Butler, 1999). The situation was neatly summed up in an editorial *Nature* ran at the time, *"If this Kafkaesque affair has any merit, it is that it has exposed the absence of a clear mechanism for the planning and support of research infrastructure at the European level"* (Nature Editorial, 1999). The cries for new mechanisms for infrastructural support, with stable partners, stable financing and long-term political commitment, doubtless helped to sew the seeds that in 2008 grew into the preparatory phase of ELIXIR, the European Life Science Infrastructure for Biological Information project.

3.9 Global data overload

The late '80s and early '90s were fertile years, giving rise to a flourishing number of new molecular structures and sequences, to new breeds of protein family signatures, and to new databases in which to store them. Looking back at this period of fervent activity, it's incredible to reflect that two major developments had yet to take place: together, these would not only seed an overwhelming explosion of biological data but would also spur their global dissemination – they were the advent of the Web and the arrival of high-throughput DNA sequencing. The latter made whole-genome sequencing practically feasible for the first time. Seizing this opportunity, there followed an unprecedented burst of sequencing activity, yielding, in quick succession, for example, the genomes of *Haemophilus influenzae* and *Mycoplasma genitalium* in 1995 (Fleischmann *et al.*, 1995; Fraser *et al.*, 1995), of *Methanococcus jannachii* and *Saccharomyces cerevisiae* in 1996 (Bult *et al.*, 1996; Goffeau *et al.*, 1996), of *Caenorhabditis elegans* in 1998 (*C.elegans* sequencing consortium, 1998), of *Drosophila melanogaster* in 2000 (Adams *et al.*, 2000) and, the ultimate prize, of *Homo sapiens* in 2001 (Lander *et al.*, 2001; Venter *et al.*, 2001; IHGSC, 2004). Hundreds of genomes have been sequenced since this fruitful dawn.

Hand-in-hand with these activities came the development of numerous organism-specific databases to store the emerging genomic data: for example, FlyBase (Ashburner & Drysdale, 1994), ACeDB (Eeckman & Durbin, 1995), SGD (Cherry *et al.*, 1998), TAIR (Huala *et al.*, 2001), Ensembl (Hubbard *et al.*, 2002), DictyBase (Kreppel *et al.*, 2004) and, of course, many more. For some, the value of this genomic 'gold rush' was not entirely clear: with much of the amassed data seemingly impossible to characterise, and vast amounts of it non-coding, the hoped-for treasure troves were beginning to look about as inspiring as large-scale collections of butterflies (Strasser, 2008), and perhaps suggested that molecular biology had entered a somewhat vacuous era of *"high-tech stamp collecting"* (Hunter, 2006). Arguments like this characterised some of the early opposition to the establishment of GenBank, and to the substantial resistance to the Human Genome Project (HGP) a few years later (Strasser, 2008).

Perhaps inevitably, then, the HGP was an extraordinarily high-profile affair. This was partly for the reasons outlined above, coupled with its considerable price-tag (estimated at $3 billion from 1990-2003), but in part also because of the public-private race between Francis Collins (who was directing the NIH National Human Genome Research Institute contributions to the HGP) and Craig Venter (then Head of Celera Genomics) to obtain the first rough draft of man's genetic blueprint. This intensely political 'drama' had been preceded by a similar struggle to be the first to sequence *Drosophila*, which served as a kind of 'warm up' battle for the human genome (Ashburner, 2006); it also had an intriguing parallel in the competition between two public-private corporations to sequence the genome of the commercially valuable *Agrobacterium tumefaciens* (Goodner *et al.*, 2001; Wood *et al.*, 2001; Harvey & McMeekin, 2004). The principal tension between these public and private, and public-private hybrid, enterprises arose not just from the race to be first to complete the sequencing: the struggle was as much about making the results public, on the one hand, and obtaining the property rights (for commercial exploitation, including gene patenting), on the other. Like the concerns in the early '80s surrounding NBRF's proprietary interest in protein sequences culled from the public domain, such conflicts raised serious questions about the duty of public science to ensure that genome sequences were made available for the public good; moreover, they challenged such wasteful competition, resulting in the acquisition of duplicate data-sets and, usually, back-to-back publications in high-profile journals (Harvey & McMeekin, 2004).

Another, more tangible, consequence of this intense orgy of genomic sequencing was the generation of more data than could realistically be managed and annotated by hand – and this was just the tip of an enormous future iceberg. As illustrated in Figure 4, with each

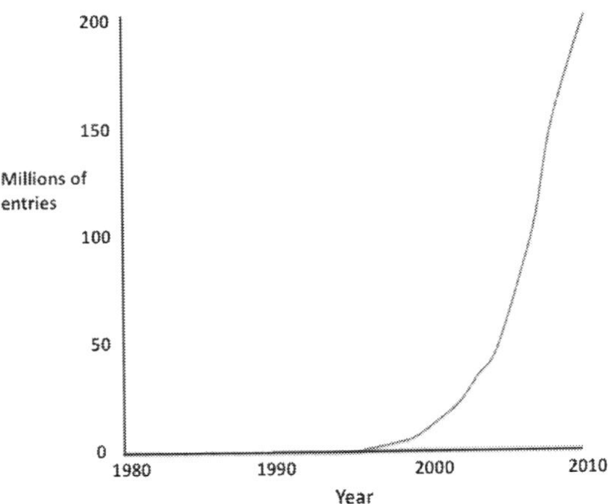

Fig. 4. Growth of the EMBL data library (millions of entries) since its inception (red curve). Also shown are the corresponding growth of the manually-annotated Swiss-Prot (green line), and of structures deposited in the PDB (this line is too small to be visible!).

passing year from the mid '90s, there was a widening gulf both between the volume of accumulating uncharacterised genomic sequence data and the fraction of this that it was possible to annotate, and between the quantities of deposited biomolecular sequence and structure data. Against this backdrop, Bairoch announced the development of a separate, automatically generated counterpart to augment Swiss-Prot, to help disseminate the fruits of the increasingly abundant genome projects more efficiently, without compromising the quality of Swiss-Prot by including within it substantial quantities of uncharacterised data.

3.10 TrEMBL

By 1996, the first shock-waves from the impact of whole genome sequencing were beginning to be felt. The aftermath was greatest for databases whose maintenance involved significant amounts of manual annotation. Some did not recover. Swiss-Prot did survive the quake, but to do so, new processes had to be put in place.

At the time, Swiss-Prot had the highest standard of annotation of any publicly available protein sequence database: from the outset, one of its leading goals was to provide critical analyses for all of its constituent sequences. To this end, each entry was accompanied by a significant amount of annotation, derived primarily from original publications and review articles by an expanding group of curators, with occasional input from an international panel of experts. This high degree of meticulous manual annotation had always been the rate-limiting step for each release of the resource; however, faced with the increased data flow from the growing number of genome projects, this hugely labour-intensive process simply became untenable.

To keep up, it was clear that a new approach was needed. The products of genomic sequences had to be made available more swiftly; but how could this be achieved without compromising the high quality of the existing Swiss-Prot data, or eroding the editorial standards of the database in future? The answer was to prepare a computer-generated supplement, with entries in a Swiss-Prot-like format, derived by translation of coding sequences in the EMBL library – this was TrEMBL, first released in October 1996 (Bairoch & Apweiler, 1996). TrEMBL 1.0 contained almost 105,000 entries, not far off twice the size of Swiss-Prot 34.0 (59,000 entries), with which it was released in parallel.

Initially, TrEMBL was an unannotated supplement to Swiss-Prot. Over the years, however, to accelerate the process of upgrading TrEMBL entries to the Swiss-Prot standard, automatic protocols have been established to annotate sequences with information about their potential functions, metabolic pathways, active sites, cofactors, binding sites, domains, subcellular location, and so on. Such information was derived from similarity and motif searches, initially using patterns, profiles, fingerprints and so on from databases like PROSITE, PRINTS and Pfam, and later using the amalgamated protein family resource, InterPro. By February 2011, with many millions of entries, TrEMBL was almost 26 times larger than Swiss-Prot, illustrating the vast disparity between manual and computer-assisted annotation strategies.

3.11 InterPro

Rolf Apweiler was to spearhead the development of TrEMBL at the EBI in collaboration with Bairoch at the Swiss Institute of Bioinformatics (SIB). In 1997, Michael Ashburner (then Director of the EBI) awarded Attwood an EBI Visiting Fellowship. This entailed weekly visits from London, and led to frequent discussions between Apweiler, Attwood and Bairoch about sequence annotation. The feasibility of uniting PROSITE and PRINTS again reared its head, but this time primarily as an instrument to help analyse and functionally annotate the growing numbers of uncharacterised genomic sequences. Compared to the original proposal in 1992, the case was much stronger, especially as there were now other related databases to bring into the picture: Daniel Kahn had released ProDom in 1994, and Richard Durbin had just announced Pfam. A new proposal was therefore submitted to the European Commission, and the vision of an integrated protein family database was finally funded.

In October 1999, a beta release of the unified resource was made with 2,423 entries (representing 615 domains, 1776 families, 27 repeats and 8 sites of PTM), based on Swiss-Prot 38.0 and TrEMBL 11.0 – this was InterPro (Apweiler *et al.*, 2001). By that time, PROSITE and the Features Database had both undergone significant changes: PROSITE had seen 3-fold growth to 1,370 entries (release 16.0); meanwhile, the Features Database had grown 40-fold to 1,157 entries (release 23.1) and had been renamed 'PRINTS' (Attwood *et al.*, 1994). The first release of InterPro therefore combined the contents of PROSITE 16.0 and PRINTS 23.1; it also incorporated descriptors from 241 profiles, together with 1,465 hidden Markov models from Pfam 4.0.

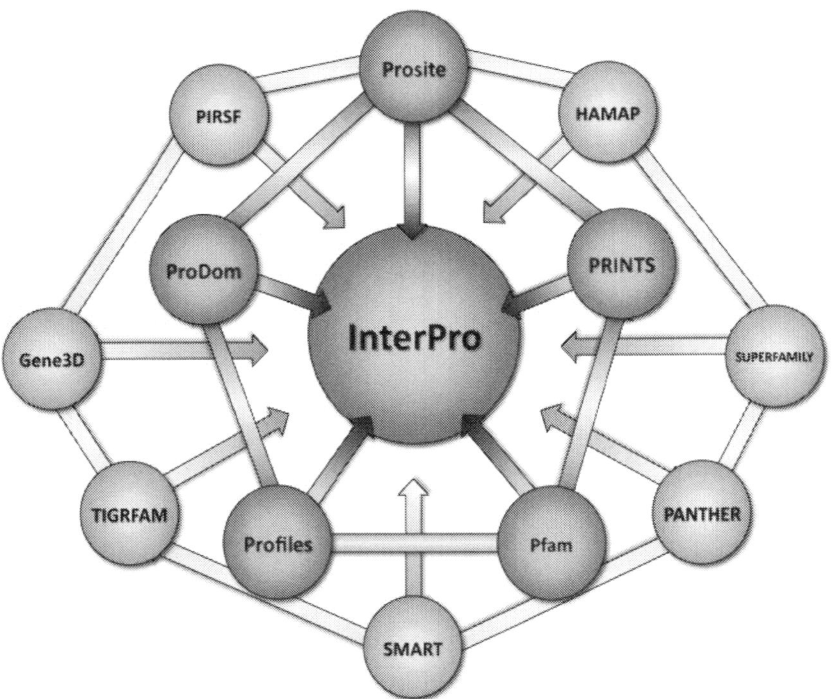

Fig. 5. Stylised illustration of the relationship between the InterPro integrating hub, its founding databases and its later additional partners, all of which contribute diagnostic signatures and, in some cases, protein family and domain annotation. The arrows indicate that information is shared both between satellite databases and between satellites and the central hub. See Table 3 for further details.

ProDom, although part of the original consortium (see Figure 5), was not included in the first release, initially because there was no obvious way of doing so. ProDom is built from automatically generated sequence clusters: it isn't a true signature database, in the sense that it doesn't exploit diagnostic discriminators; moreover, its sequence clusters need not have precise biological correlations, so can change between database releases. Assigning stable accession numbers to its entries was therefore impossible; this issue had to be addressed before it could be meaningfully included in InterPro. Other factors rendered a step-wise approach to the development of InterPro desirable. The scale of amalgamating just PROSITE, PRINTS and Pfam was immense. Trying to sensibly merge apparently equivalent database entries that, in fact, defined specific families, domains within those families, or even repeats within those domains, presented enormous challenges. In the beginning, InterPro therefore focused on amalgamating databases that offered some level of annotation, to facilitate the integration process.

Over the years, further partners joined the InterPro consortium, as illustrated in Figure 5. Today, with 12 primary sources, the integration challenges are legion (some of the complexity can be understood from the list of partners, and the numbers of their signatures that InterPro has incorporated, shown in Table 3)! With 21,185 entries in February 2011 (release 31.0), it is the most comprehensive integrated protein family database in the world (Hunter *et al.*, 2009).

Signature Database	Version	Signatures	Integrated Signatures
GENE3D	3.3.0	2,386	1,377
HAMAP	021210	1,675	1,429
PANTHER	7.0	80,933	1,777
PIRSF	2.74	3,248	2,791
PRINTS	41.1	2,050	2,009
PROSITE patterns	20.66	1,308	1,292
PROSITE profiles	20.66	901	877
Pfam	24.0	11,912	11,465
ProDom	2006.1	1,894	1,008
SMART	6.1	895	882
SUPERFAMILY	1.73	1,774	1,154
TIGRFAMs	9.0	3,808	3,796

Table 3. InterPro release 31.0, February 2011.

3.12 UniProt

The year 2004 marked a turning point for the way in which protein sequence data were to be collected and disseminated globally. The PIR-PSD, which had evolved from Dayhoff's *Atlas*, had been available online since 1986; Swiss-Prot, which originally built on PIR data, also became available in 1986; and TrEMBL had been released in 1996. The ongoing maintenance of these disparate resources over so many years had posed major funding headaches. For PIR, some of the difficulties were mitigated, at least in the early years, by charging for copies of their databases and for online access to their software; later, the international collaboration with MIPS and JIPID, supported by NSF and European grants, no doubt helped to sustain the resource.

Swiss-Prot, meanwhile, had had a rocky ride and had had to be rescued from the brink of closure, following a procedural 'catch-22' catastrophe: viewing Swiss-Prot as an international resource, the Swiss government declined to provide further support unless the database also gained a financial injection from a European Union (EU) grant; a joint proposal with the EBI for an EU infrastructure grant, however, was declined because Swiss-Prot was not being supported by the Swiss government! In May 1996, with only 2 months of salary remaining for the Swiss-Prot entourage, an Internet appeal was launched announcing the forthcoming closure, on 30 June, of Swiss-Prot and its associated databases and software tools, owing to lack of funding. This appeal stimulated a storm of protest on the Internet, in high-profile academic journals, and in the media. Such was the barrage that the Swiss government stepped in, offering interim funding until the end of the year. In the negotiations that followed, the need to create a stable vehicle for long-term funding both of Swiss-Prot and of the Swiss EMBnet Node was discussed, and resulted in the drafting of outline plans to establish a Swiss Institute of Bioinformatics (Bairoch, 2000).

Against this background, in 2002, with multinational funding from NIH, the NSF, the Swiss federal government and the EU, Swiss-Prot, TrEMBL and the PIR-PSD joined forces as the UniProt consortium. In forming the consortium, the idea was to build on the partners' many years of foundational work, by providing a stable, high-quality, unified database. This would serve as the world's most comprehensive protein sequence knowledgebase, replete with accurate annotations and extensive cross-references, and accompanied by freely-available, easy-to-use querying interfaces.

Under its hood, UniProt initially consisted of 3 separate database layers: the UniProt Archive (UniParc), to provide a complete, non-redundant collection of all publicly available protein sequence data; the UniProt Knowledgebase (UniProt), consisting of Swiss-Prot and TrEMBL, to act as the central database of protein sequences, with accurate, consistent and rich sequence and functional annotation; and the UniProt NREF databases (UniRef), to provide non-redundant subsets of the UniProt Knowledgebase, for efficient database searching (Apweiler *et al.*, 2004). By 2011, UniProt also included a Metagenomic and Environmental Sequence component, termed UniMES (The UniProt Consortium, 2011); by this time, UniProtKB:Swiss-Prot contained 525,207 entries, accompanied by UniProtKB:TrEMBL, with a staggering 13,499,622 entries.

3.13 The Swiss Institute of Bioinformatics (SIB)

Like the EBI, the need for which largely grew out of high-level negotiations to try to put the EMBL data library on a more stable financial footing, the Swiss Institute of Bioinformatics (SIB) grew out of similar high-level negotiations to establish long-term financial support for Swiss-Prot. At the time of the Swiss-Prot funding crisis, Bairoch was aware that the Swiss scientific authorities had been emphasising the need to establish centres of excellence in economically important, interdisciplinary areas that would be crucial for 'tomorrow's society'. Seizing upon this, together with Ron Appel, Philipp Bucher, Victor Jongeneel and Manuel Peitsch, he submitted a proposal to create a Swiss bioinformatics institute, whose goals were to:

- promote the development of bioinformatics software tools and databases;
- sustain high-quality bioinformatics research;
- collaborate with academic partners to provide a curriculum to train research scientists in the field of bioinformatics; and
- offer services to its user community through the Swiss Node of EMBnet.

After a lengthy period of consultation, the SIB was finally created as a non-profit foundation in March 1998, with Victor Jongeneel as the first director. The founders then went on to win funds for some of the SIB's activities from the Swiss Federal government: by law, only 50% of the Institute's work could be funded in this way – the rest had to come from other sources, preferably by commercial exploitation of its research.

Partly in response to this stipulation, but partly also because it had become clear that Swiss-Prot could not be reliably sustained solely with public funding, the decision was made to ask commercial users of the database to pay a licence fee. Various models for achieving this were tested; in the end, in 1997, Bairoch, Appel and Denis Hochstrasser decided that the best way forward was to set up a new company – this was Geneva Bioinformatics SA (GeneBio). Up to three quarters of the revenues now generated by GeneBio from sales of annual database and software licences are returned to SIB, thereby helping to bolster the work of the Swiss-Prot groups (Bairoch, 2000).

Today, the SIB leads and coordinates the field of bioinformatics in Switzerland: its vision, to help shape the future of the life sciences through excellence in bioinformatics services, research and education; its mission, to provide world-class core bioinformatics resources to both national and international research communities in fields spanning genomics, proteomics and systems biology. Many of its core activities, including maintenance of databases such as UniProt and InterPro, are carried out in close collaboration with the EBI.

3.14 The European Nucleotide Archive (ENA)

Meanwhile, with the advent of large-scale sequencing projects and the dawn of Next Generation Sequencing (NGS) technologies, a mounting tsunami of nucleotide sequence data was growing force across the globe; a number of important developments were to take place in its wake. By 2003, it was clear that there was a need to provide access not only to the most recent versions of sequences, but also to their historical artifacts – following the rush to patent genetic information, issues of priority became increasingly important, and it was vital to be able to see sequence entries exactly as they appeared in the past. Accordingly, the EBI established a Sequence Version Archive (Leinonen *et al.*, 2003), to store both current and earlier versions of entries in the EMBL data library (which, by then, had been dubbed EMBL-Bank).

By September 2004, EMBL-Bank had grown prodigiously, with more than 42 million entries (Kanz *et al.*, 2005) and, by 2007, was accompanied by the Ensembl Trace Archive (ETA) – the ETA was set up to provide a permanent archive for single-pass DNA sequencing reads (from whole-genome shotgun, EST and other large-scale sequencing projects) and associated traces and quality values. Together, EMBL-Bank and the ETA became known as ENA, the European Nucleotide Archive, Europe's primary nucleotide-sequence repository (Cochrane *et al.*, 2008). Throughout 2007, ENA continued to grow in terms both of its volume and of the nature of data it contained such that, by October of that year, it included more than 1.7 billion records (comprising ~1.7 trillion (1.7×10^{12}) base pairs of sequence) (Cochrane *et al.*, 2008). By 2010, ENA had embraced a third component – the Sequence Read Archive (SRA) – and now contained ~500 billion raw and assembled sequences, comprising 50×10^{12} base pairs; this is a phenomenal growth in just 3 years! During this period, NGS reads held in the SRA had become the largest and fastest growing source of new data, and accounted for ~95% of all base pairs made available by ENA (Leinonen *et al.*, 2011). Contributing to this mass of data were the completed genomes of more than 1,400 cellular organisms, and 3,000 viruses and phages.

But such enormous progress comes at a cost, challenging current IT infrastructures to the limit. Some of the oldest data in ENA date back to the early '80s, with the inception of the EMBL data library. As an aside, it is somewhat ironic that, even in those days, there were distribution headaches. Bairoch, for example, relates how difficult it was to transfer version 2 of the EMBL data library from computer tape to a mainframe computer and thence to his microcomputer, because the mainframe had no communication protocol to talk to a microcomputer – he therefore had to spend the night transferring the data, screen by screen, using a 300 baud acoustic modem (Bairoch, 2000). To put this in perspective, this version of EMBL-Bank contained 811 nucleotide sequences (with more than 1 million base pairs) – this is about the same amount of data that currently enters ENA every 2 seconds.

Today, ENA holds more than 20 terabases of nucleotide sequence data, which, combined with its annotation information, and so on, occupies more than 230 terabytes of disk space. The infrastructure required to store, maintain and service such a vast archive, and the cost of doing so, is beyond anything that either the originators of the first databases, or the developers of the new sequencing technologies could have conceived. Interestingly, in February 2011, the NCBI announced that it would be discontinuing its Sequence Read and Trace Archives for high-throughput sequence data, owing to budget constraints. The closure of the databases is to be phased, and completed within 12 months. The NCBI is still committed to supporting and developing information resources for biological data derived from NGS technologies (genotypes, variations, assemblies, gene expression data, and so on), but will need to find new funding strategies for access to and storage of the existing data.

3.15 ELIXIR

The opportunities NGS technologies present for advancing life science research (especially in areas such as healthcare, food security, energy diversification and environmental protection) are incredibly exciting; but these opportunities will be lost if they are not underpinned by a robust, effective and sustainable information infrastructure. The best estimates today suggest that, by 2020, NGS technologies will be producing data at up to a million times the current rate. Development of an appropriate infrastructure to manage the data deluge is therefore paramount.

The ELIXIR project is the realisation of this urgent need. Recognising that the task is of such magnitude that it cannot be tackled by a single organisation, it is a call to arms for international cooperation in building a pan-European infrastructure to help extract the maximum value from the investments that have already been made, and from those that will be made in future, in this area. The plan is for the ELIXIR infrastructure to be distributed across a variety of 'Nodes' hosted by centres of excellence across Europe, and for each of these to be connected to the EBI central 'Hub'. It is expected that some of the Nodes will act as national coordination centres to expedite interactions both with the Hub and with local funders; Nodes that perform similar functions will be expected to collaborate to form ELIXIR service networks, providing data or compute resources, or training, according to their speciality, as depicted in Figure 6.

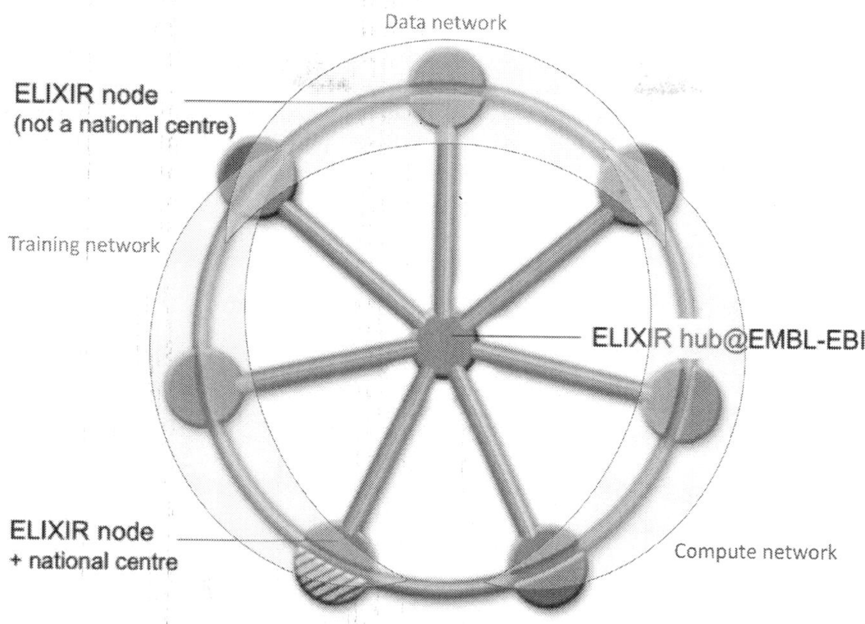

Fig. 6. Proposed topology of the ELIXIR Hub and Nodes. In an arrangement reminiscent of EMBnet 23 years before it, some of the Nodes are expected to serve as national bioinformatics centres; others, with similar functions, will collaborate as service networks, for example to provide data or compute resources, or training.

Initially, the numbers of Nodes is expected to be small, growing to ~20 during the first 5 years of the initiative (during the preparatory phase, more than 50 institutions submitted expressions of interest in becoming ELIXIR Nodes), at a cost of several hundred million euro. To garner support for the business case, governments of the European Member States have been invited to sign a non-binding Memorandum of Understanding (MoU) in order to initiate negotiations to construct ELIXIR; the MoU will become effective once 5 countries and the EMBL have signed. Europe's databases (estimated to number around 500), especially those hosted by the EBI, will become the foundation of the new ELIXIR infrastructure as part of its mission, *"to construct and operate a sustainable infrastructure for biological information in Europe to support life science research and its translation to medicine and the environment, the bio-industries and society"* (Thornton, 2011).

4. The development and spread of tools to keep pace with the new technologies

With the sequencing of biopolymers and subsequent organisation of the growing mass of biosequences in databases, visual comparison techniques became tedious, not least because *"the determination of the significance of a given result usually is left to intuitive rationalization"* (Needleman & Wunsch 1971). To reduce reliance on manual (often subjective) interpretation and put sequence analysis on a more systematic footing, algorithms to analyse and compare sequences began to emerge. As early as 1966, Fitch proposed computational analysis to study evolutionary homology, using mutation values to indicate how many nucleotides in the genomic code must change in order to introduce change (mutation) at the amino acid level. In 1970, Needleman and Wunsch described the first algorithm to quantify the similarity between two protein sequences (so-called global alignment) – today, this algorithm is still used to identify similarities between two sequences and infer likely ancestry. Years later, Smith and Waterman (1981) presented an algorithm to find local similarities: *"to find a pair of segments, one from each of two long sequences, such that there is no other pair of segments with greater similarity"*. In time, more efficient methods were required to compare newly sequenced proteins against the rapidly expanding databases. FASTP was the first 'fast' algorithm (Lipman & Pearson 1985).

Search algorithms like this afforded many of the earliest and most exciting discoveries attributable to 'bioinformatics'. For example, one of the first observations that gave a clue to the molecular mechanism of neoplastic transformation was provided by the finding of a near identity in amino acid sequence between the platelet-derived growth factor (PDGF) B-chain and a region in the transforming protein, p28sis, of simian sarcoma virus (SSV), an agent that causes sarcomas and gliomas in experimental animals (Waterfield *et al.*, 1983). This finding arose from computer searches using the Wilbur and Lipman algorithm on the, at the time (1983) available, NEWAT protein database created by Doolittle *et al.* This first success story, where simple sequence comparison led to the completely new concept of gene-oncogene, showed the medical community the enormous potential of computer techniques for sequence comparison and analysis.

In a similar way, DNA sequencing having been revolutionised by Sanger and by subsequent improvements of his technique, and having given rise to the growing number of nucleotide sequences being collected in data repositories like the EMBL data library and GenBank, so too algorithms to search these databases became a necessity. FASTA was a more sensitive modification of FASTP, and had the advantage of being able to search nucleotide sequence databases with either a nucleic acid or protein sequence by translating the DNA database during the search (Pearson & Lipman 1988). Later, somewhat overshadowing these developments, came the Basic Local Alignment Search Tool, BLAST (Altschul *et al.*, 1990); this offered an extended tool-set to apply any kind of sequence database search, and is still the most widely used tool in bioinformatics. The success of BLAST spawned a number of more specialised sequence search methods, such as PSI-BLAST, PHI-BLAST, BLAT, and so on, and is itself still in continuous development (Camacho *et al.*, 2009).

Aside from these very popular database search tools, many other sequence, annotation and expression analysis tools were developed for a broad range of applications: *e.g.*, for pattern recognition, for protein and RNA secondary structure prediction, for microarray data analysis, for proteome and genome annotation, and so on. In the early '90s, building on the existing University of Wisconsin Genetics Computer Group (UWGCG, or simply GCG) package, several such algorithms were collected at the EMBL and packaged as 'GCGEMBL Utilities', later known as 'Extended GCG'. However, GCG was then commercialised and its distribution policy changed. Reacting against the new policies, in 1998 several software developers founded EMBOSS, the European Molecular Biology Open Software Suite. Their aim was to develop new sequence analysis tools, by *"replacing popular but obsolete EGCG applications,"* and integrating with SRS, ACEDB, and a range of other publicly available software interfaces and tools. The idea was to encourage other developers to use the EMBOSS software libraries, and especially to harness the expertise and potential additional manpower at EMBnet Nodes (*e.g.,* in Germany, Italy, France, The Netherlands, Austria, Russia, Switzerland, Israel, Spain, Norway, and so on). Target users of the resource included those at the Sanger Centre, those served by EMBnet, and those in academic and pharmaceutical settings. Funded by the Wellcome Trust for 3 years, the project was a collaborative effort of the Sanger Centre, EMBnet UK (SEQNET), the EBI and CNRS Montpellier.

With the pivotal support of EMBnet, EMBOSS quickly became a comprehensive bioinformatics resource (Rice *et al.*, 2000). There are now several incarnations of the suite with different GUIs, including the EMBOSS team's Java-based interface, jEMBOSS; the Belgian and Argentinian EMBnet Nodes' wEMBOSS; and the EMBOSS GUI from the National Research Council of Canada. Today, EMBOSS is still being developed, adopting new specific file formats and algorithms in order to embrace the world of NGS data analysis.

Another important development driven by the EMBL was the Sequence Retrieval System (SRS), an information indexing system applied to flat-file databases, such as the EMBL data library, Swiss-Prot and PROSITE (Etzold and Argos, 1993). SRS became the most widely used data-retrieval system for flat-file systems, with an extended GUI to extract not only sequences but all related information, via an exhaustive sequence query and export system (Zdobnov *et al.*, 2002).

Europe-wide, there are vast numbers of other specialised biological data-analysis, data-visualisation and data-retrieval tools available: many of these are provided by the EBI; others by the SIB's ExPASy Proteomics Server; some are offered via the National and Specialist Nodes of EMBnet; others are available as Web services collected in the BioCatalogue (Bhagat *et al.*, 2010). The BioCatalogue evolved from the EMBRACE registry (Pettifer *et al.*, 2010), one of the end products of the EMBRACE project (European Model for Bioinformatics Research and Community Education) – this was a 5-year FP7 Network of Excellence, whose main goal was to orchestrate highly integrated access to a broad range of bio-molecular data and software packages. Achieving this required standardised access to tools and databases; to this end, the decision was to use Web services. In consequence, many of the project partners adapted their tools and database-access protocols, and logged their Web services in a common registry. At the end of EMBRACE, in 2010, the registry was handed over to the BioCatalogue, which is now being maintained in collaboration with myExperiment, myGrid, seekda and BioMoby, and hosts 2,053 services from 147 service providers and 505 members.

5. The central place of bioinformatics in modern biology

Clearly, we have travelled a very long way since Jensen and Evans positioned a single amino acid (a terminal phenylalanine) in insulin (Jensen & Evans, 1935; Sanger, 1945; Sanger, 1988) and Sanger elucidated its complete sequence, the first of any protein (recall Table 2). In a story spanning something like 70 years, bioinformatics has given us the first 'complete' catalogues of DNA and protein sequences, including the genomes and proteomes of organisms across the entire Tree of Life; it has furnished the requisite software to help analyse biological data on an unprecedented scale; it has hence yielded the possibilities to understand more about evolutionary processes in general, our place in the Tree of Life in particular, and ultimately, a great deal more about health, disease and disease processes. Figure 7 offers a summary of some of the most important landmarks that have charted the development of bioinformatics in Europe and helped to place it at the heart of 21st century biology.

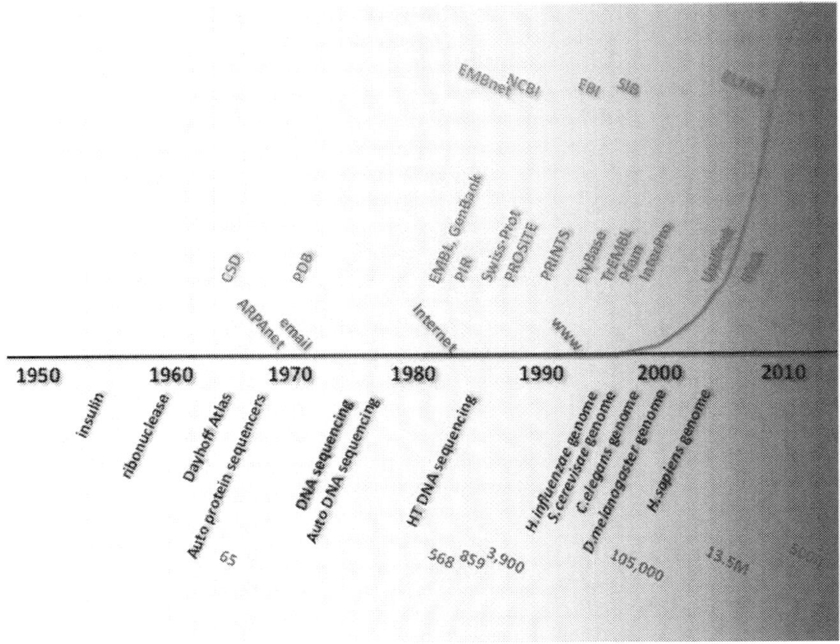

Fig. 7. Historical milestones that have placed bioinformatics at the heart of 21st century biology, from the determination of the first amino acid sequence, to the development of an archive of 500 billion nucleotide sequences. Some major milestones are denoted in black; key computing innovations are indicated in purple; example databases are indicated in blue; organisations and institutions in green; numbers of sequences in red, the growing mass of which is highlighted both in the red curve and the background gradient – the impact of genomic sequencing in the mid '90s is clear.

6. Conclusion – European bioinformatics goes global

The history of bioinformatics has clearly been a convoluted interplay between events in Europe, the USA, Japan and across the globe. Here, we have attempted to recount the story primarily from a European perspective as it unfolded largely from the point of view of sequence data: in terms of the technological innovations that spawned their extraordinary growth and dissemination, of the databases that grew up to manage and analyse them, and of the institutions and infrastructural initiatives that arose to try to give those databases some measure of financial stability. In so doing, we accept that we've only scratched the surface, and we regret any shortcomings that may have arisen from the necessary omission of so many of the other important details and perspectives.

Clearly, the evolution and impact of bioinformatics reaches far beyond Europe, and there are now many organisations world-wide with missions to bring life science data to their local communities, to make freely available easy-to-use software tools with which to analyse the data, and to provide training, both to users of bioinformatics databases and software, and to new generations of bioinformatics trainers (Schneider *et al.*, 2010). In this context, EMBnet, for example, which began life as the European Molecular Biology Network, is now a global bioinformatics network, maintaining fruitful cooperations with the Iberoamerican (SoIBio) and Asia Pacific (APBioNet) bioinformatics networks, as well as with the USA-based International Society for Computational Biology (ISCB); it has also established close ties with the African Society for Bioinformatics and Computational Biology (ASBCB), and synergies with other relevant groups in northern Africa are now developing. Interestingly, 33 years ago, Joshua Lederberg observed that, *"the claim of science to universal validity is supportable only by virtue of a strenuous commitment to global communication"* (Lederberg, 1978). Today, this is a commitment that EMBnet vigorously pursues; in a similar spirit, we can be quite sure that the contribution of Europe to the future evolution of bioinformatics will continue in a global arena.

7. Acknowledgement

We would like to thank Vicky Schneider for providing the inspiration (and the title) for this chapter.

8. References

Adams, M.J.; Blundell, T.L., Dodson, E.J., Dodson, G.G., Vijayan, M., Baker, E.N., Harding, M.M., Hodgkin, D.C., Rimmer, B. & Sheat, S. (1969) Structure of Rhombohedral 2 Zinc Insulin Crystals. *Nature*, 224, 49-495.

Adams, M.D.; Celniker, S.E., Holt, R.A., Evans, C.A., Gocayne, J.D. *et al.* (2000) The genome sequence of *Drosophila melanogaster*. *Science*, 287, 2185-2195.

Akrigg, D.A.; Attwood, T.K., Bleasby, A.J., Findlay, J.B.C., North, A.C.T., Parry-Smith, D.J., Perkins, D.N. & Wootton, J.C. (1992) SERPENT - An information storage and analysis resource for protein sequences. *CABIOS*, 8(3), 295-296.

Allen, F. H.; Davies, J.E., Galloy, J.J., Johnson, O., Kennard, O., Macrae, C.F., Mitchell, E.M., Mitchell, G.F., Smith, J.M. & Watson, D.G. (1991) The Development of Versions 3 and 4 of the Cambridge Structural Database System. *J. Chem. Inf. Comput. Sci.*, 31, 187-204.

Altschul, S.F., Gish, W., Miller, W. Myers, E.W. & Lipman, D.J. (1990) Basic local alignment search tool. J.Mol.Biol., 215, 403-410.

Anderson, S, Bankier, A.T., Barrell, B.G., de Bruijn, M.H., Coulson, A.R., Drouin, J., Eperon, I.C., Nierlich, D.P., Roe, B.A., Sanger, F., Schreier, P.H., Smith, A.J., Staden, R. and Young, I.G. (1981) Sequence and organization of the human mitochondrial genome. *Nature*, 290, 457-465.

Apweiler, R., Attwood, T.K., Bairoch, A., Bateman, A., Birney, E., Biswas, M., Bucher, P., Cerutti, L., Corpet, F., Croning, M.D., Durbin, R., Falquet, L., Fleischmann, W., Gouzy, J., Hermjakob, H., Hulo, N., Jonassen, I., Kahn, D., Kanapin, A., Karavidopoulou, Y., Lopez, R., Marx, B., Mulder, N.J., Oinn, T.M., Pagni, M., Servant, F., Sigrist, C.J. & Zdobnov, E.M. (2001) The InterPro database, an integrated documentation resource for protein families, domains and functional sites. *Nucleic Acids Res.*, 29(1), 37-40.

Apweiler, R.; Bairoch, A., Wu, C.H., Barker, W.C., Boeckmann, B., Ferro, S., Gasteiger, E., Huang, H., Lopez, R., Magrane, M., Martin, M.J., Natale, D.A., O'Donovan, C., Redaschi, N. & Yeh, L.S. (2004) UniProt: the Universal Protein knowledgebase. *Nucleic Acids Res.*, 32(Database issue), D115-119.

Ashburner, M. (1996) Won for all: how the Drosophila genome was sequenced. Cold Spring Harbor Laboratory Press, Cold Spring Harbor, New York, USA.

Ashburner, M. & Drysdale, R. (1994) FlyBase – the *Drosophila* genetic database. *Development*, 120(7), 2077-2079.

Bairoch, A. (1982) Suggestion to research groups working on protein and peptide sequence. *Biochem.J.*, 203(2), 527-528.

Bhagat, J., Tanoh, F., Nzuobontane, E., Laurent, T., Orlowski, J., Roos, M., Wolstencroft, K., Aleksejevs, S., Stevens, R., Pettifer, S., Lopez, R. & Goble, C.A. (2010) BioCatalogue: a universal catalogue of web services for the life sciences. Nucleic Acids Res., 38, W689-694

Bairoch, A. (2000) Serendipity in bioinformatics, the tribulations of a Swiss bioinformatician through exciting times! *Bioinformatics*, 16(1), 48-64.

Bairoch, A. & Boeckmann, B. (1991) The SWISS-PROT protein sequence data bank. *Nucleic Acids Res.*, 19 Suppl., 2247-2249.

Bairoch A. (1991) PROSITE: a dictionary of sites and patterns in proteins. *Nucleic Acids Res.*, 19 Suppl., 2241-2245.

Bairoch, A. & Apweiler, R. (1996) The SWISS-PROT protein sequence data bank and its new supplement TREMBL. *Nucleic Acids Res.*, 24(1), 21-25.

Bairoch, A. & Bucher, P. (1994) PROSITE: recent developments. *Nucleic Acids Res.*, 22(17), 3583-3589.

Barker, W.C.; George, D.G., Mewes, H.W. & Tsugita, A. (1992) The PIR-International Protein Sequence Database. *Nucleic Acids Res.*, 20 Suppl., 2023-206

Benson, D.; Boguski, M., Lipman, D.J. & Ostell, J. (1990) The National Center for Biotechnology Information. *Genomics*, 6, 389-391.

Benson, D.; Lipman, D.J. & Ostell, J. (1993) GenBank. *Nucleic Acids Res.*, 21(13), 2963-2965.

Berman, H.M.; Westbrook, J., Feng, Z., Gilliland, G., Bhat, T.N., Weissig, H., Shindyalov, I.N. & Bourne, P.E. (2000) The Protein Data Bank. *Nucleic Acids Res.*, 28(1), 235-242.

Berman, H.; Henrick, K. & Nakamura, H. (2003) Announcing the worldwide Protein Data Bank. *Nature Structural Biology*, 10, 980.

Berman, H. (2008) The Protein Data Bank: A historical perspective. *Foundations of Crystallography*, 64(1), 88-95.

Bernstein, F.C.; Koetzle, T.F., Williams, G.J., Meyer, E.F. Jr, Brice, M.D., Rodgers, J.R., Kennard, O., Shimanouchi, T. & Tasumi, M. (1977) The Protein Data Bank. A computer-based archival file for macromolecular structures. *J.Mol.Biol.*, 112(3), 535-

542. Reprinted in *Eur. J. Biochem.*, 80(2), 319-24 (1977); and *Archives of Biochemistry and Biophysics*, 185(2), 584-591 (1978).

Boutselakis, H.; Dimitropoulos, D., Fillon, J., Golovin, A., Henrick, K., Hussain, A., Ionides, J., John, M., Keller, P. A., Krissinel, E., McNeil, P., Naim, A., Newman, R., Oldfield, T., Pineda, J., Rachedi, A., Copeland, J., Sitnov, A., Sobhany, S., Suarez-Uruena, A., Swaminathan, J., Tagari, M., Tate, J., Tromm, S., Velankar, S. & Vranken, W. (2003) E-MSD: the European Bioinformatics Institute Macromolecular Structure Database. *Nucleic Acids Res.*, 31(1), 458-462.

Brown, H.; Sanger, F. & Kitai, R. (1955), The structure of pig and sheep insulins. *Biochemical Journal*, 60(4), 556–565.

Burley, S.K.; Almo, S.C., Bonanno, J.B., Capel, M., Chance, M.R., Gaasterland, T., Lin, D., Sali, A., Studier, F.W. & Swaminathan, S. (1999) Structural genomics: beyond the human genome project. *Nat. Genet.*, 23(2), 151-157.

Butler, D. (1999) Life science facilities in crisis as Brussels switches off funding. *Nature*, 402, 3-4. *C. elegans* Sequencing Consortium. (1998) Genome sequence of the nematode *C. elegans*: a platform for investigating biology. *Science*, 282, 2012-2018.

Camacho, C.; Coulouris, G., Avagyan, V., Ma, N., Papadopoulos, J., Bealer, K. & Madden, T.L. (2009) BLAST+: architecture and applications. BMC Bioinformatics, 10, 421.

Cherry, J.M.; Adler, C., Ball, C., Chervitz, S.A., Dwight, S.S., Hester, E.T., Jia, Y., Juvik, G., Roe, T., Schroeder, M., Weng, S. & Botstein, D. (1998) SGD: Saccharomyces Genome Database. *Nucleic Acids Res.*, 26(1), 73-79.

Cochrane, G.; Akhtar, R., Aldebert, P., Althorpe, N., Baldwin, A., Bates, K., Bhattacharyya, S., Bonfield, J., Bower, L., Browne, P., Castro, M., Cox, T., Demiralp, F., Eberhardt, R., Faruque, N., Hoad, G., Jang, M., Kulikova, T., Labarga, A., Leinonen, R., Leonard, S., Lin, Q., Lopez, R., Lorenc, D., McWilliam, H., Mukherjee, G., Nardone, F., Plaister, S., Robinson, S., Sobhany, S., Vaughan, R., Wu, D., Zhu, W., Apweiler, R., Hubbard, T. & Birney, E. (2008) Priorities for nucleotide trace, sequence and annotation data capture at the Ensembl Trace Archive and the EMBL Nucleotide Sequence Database. *Nucleic Acids Res.*, 36(Database issue), D5-D12.

Dayhoff, M.O.; Eck, R.V., Chang, M.A. & Sochard, M.R. (Eds.) (1965) *Atlas of protein sequence and structure*. National Biomedical Research Foundation, Silver Spring, Maryland, USA.

Dayhoff, M.O. to Berkley, C. (1967) Margaret O.Dayhoff Papers, Archives of the National Biomedical Research Foundation, Washington, D.C., USA.

Dayhoff, M.O.; Schwartz, R.M., Chen, H.R., Barker, W.C., Hunt, L.T. & Orcutt, B.C. (1981) Nucleic Acid Sequence Database. *DNA*, 1, 51-58; b) Dayhoff, M.O., Schwartz, R.M., Chen, H.R., Hunt, L.T., Barker, W.C. & Orcutt, B.C. (1981) Data Bank. *Nature*, 290, 8.

Dickson, D. & Abbott, A. (1993) Cambridge and Heidelberg compete for new European gene database. *Nature*, 361, 383.

Dodson, G. (2005) Fred Sanger: sequencing pioneer. *Biochem. J.*, doi:10.1042/BJ2005c013.

Doelz, R. (1994) Biocomputing on a Server Network. *EMBnet.news*, 1(2), 6-8.

EMBL (1992) The European Bioinformatics Institute (EBI): A Proposal

Eck, R.V. & Dayhoff, M.O. (1966) *Atlas of Protein Sequence and Structure*. National Biomedical Research Foundation, Silver Spring, Maryland, USA.

Doolittle, R.F. (1986) Of Urfs and Orfs: a primer on how to analyze derived amino acid sequences. University Science Books, 20 Edgehill Road, Mill Valley, CA 94941, USA. ISBN 0-935702-54-7

Etzold, T. & Argos, P. (1993) SRS – an indexing and retrieval tool for flat file data libraries. Comput.Appl. Biosci., 9, 49-57.

Eeckman, F.H. & Durbin, R. (1995) ACeDB and macace. *Methods Cell Biol.*, 48, 583-605.

Fitch, W.M. (1966) An improved method of testing for evolutionary homology. J.Mol.Biol., 16, 9-16.

Fleischmann, R.D.; Adams, M.D., White, O., Clayton, R.A., Kirkness, E.F. *et al.* (1995) Whole-genome random sequencing and assembly of *Haemophilus influenzae Rd. Science,* 269, 496-512.

Franklin, R.E. & Gosling, R.G. (1953) a) The structure of sodium thymonucleate fibres. I. The influence of water content. *Acta Cryst.,* 6, 673-677; b) The structure of sodium thymonucleate fibres. II. The cylindrically symmetrical Patterson function. *Ibid.,* 678-685; c) Molecular configuration in sodium thymonucleate. *Nature,* 171, 740-741.

Fraser, C.M.; Gocayne, J.D., White, O., Adams, M.D., Clayton, R.A. *et al.* (1995) The minimal gene complement of *Mycoplasma genitalium. Science,* 270, 397-403.

George, D.G.; Barker, W.C. & Hunt, L.T. (1986) The protein identification resource (PIR). *Nucleic Acids Res.,* 14(1), 11-15.

George, D.G.; Dodson, R.J., Garavelli, J.S., Haft, D.H., Hunt, L.T., Marzec, C.R., Orcutt, B.C., Sidman, K.E., Srinivasarao, G.Y., Yeh, L.S., Arminski, L.M., Ledley, R.S., Tsugita, A. & Barker, W.C. (1997) The Protein Information Resource (PIR) and the PIR-International Protein Sequence Database. *Nucleic Acids Res.,* 25(1), 24-28.

Gingeras, T.R. & Roberts, R.J. (1980) Steps towards computer analysis of nucleotide sequences. *Science,* 209, 1322-1328.

Goffeau, A.; Barrell, B.G., Bussey, H., Davis, R.W., Dujon, B. *et al.* (1996) Life with 6000 genes. *Science,* 274, 546-567.

Goodner, B.; Hinkle, G., Gattung, S., Miller, N., Blanchard, M. *et al.* (2001). Genome Sequence of the Plant Pathogen and Biotechnology Agent *Agrobacterium tumefaciens* C58. *Science,* 294, 2323-2328.

Hamm, G.H. & Cameron, G.N. (1986) The EMBL data library. *Nucleic Acids Res.,* 14(1), 5–9.

Harvey, M. & McMeekin, A. (2004) Public-private collaborations and the race to sequence *Agrobacterium tumefaciens. Nat. Biotechnol.,* 22(7), 807-810.

Henikoff, S. & Henikoff, J.G. (1991) Automated assembly of protein blocks for database searching. *Nucleic Acids Res.,* 19(23), 6565-6572.

Hirs, C.H.W.; Moore, S. & Stein, W.H. (1960) The Sequence of the Amino Acid Residues in Performic Acid-oxidized Ribonuclease. *J.Biol.Chem.,* 235, 633-647.

Hobohm, U.; Scharf, M., Schneider, R. & Sander, C. (1992) Selection of representative protein data sets. *Protein Sci.,* 1(3), 409-417.

Hogeweg, P. (1978) Simulating the growth of cellular forms. *Simulation,* 31, 90-96.

Hogeweg, P. & Hesper, B. (1978) Interactive instruction on population interactions. *Comput. Biol. Med.,* 8, 319-327.

Huala, E.; Dickerman, A.W., Garcia-Hernandez, M., Weems, D., Reiser, L., LaFond, F., Hanley, D., Kiphart, D., Zhuang, M., Huang, W., Mueller, L.A., Bhattacharyya, D., Bhaya, D., Sobral, B.W., Beavis, W., Meinke, D.W., Town, C.D., Somerville, C., Rhee & S.Y. (2001) The Arabidopsis Information Resource (TAIR): a comprehensive database and web-based information retrieval, analysis, and visualization system for a model plant. *Nucleic Acids Res.*, 29(1), 102-105.

Hubbard, T.; Barker, D., Birney, E., Cameron, G., Chen, Y., Clark, L., Cox, T., Cuff, J., Curwen, V., Down, T., Durbin, R., Eyras, E., Gilbert, J., Hammond, M., Huminiecki, L., Kasprzyk, A., Lehvaslaiho, H., Lijnzaad, P., Melsopp, C., Mongin, E., Pettett, R., Pocock, M., Potter, S., Rust, A., Schmidt, E., Searle, S., Slater, G., Smith, J., Spooner, W., Stabenau, A., Stalker, J., Stupka, E., Ureta-Vidal, A., Vastrik, I. & Clamp, M. (2002) The Ensembl genome database project. *Nucleic Acids Res.*, 30(1), 38-41.

Hunter, D.J. (2006) Genomics and proteomics in epidemiology: treasure trove or "high-tech stamp collecting"? *Epidemiology*, 17(5), 487-489.

Hunter, S.; Apweiler, R., Attwood, T.K., Bairoch, A., Bateman, A. *et al.* (2009) InterPro: the integrative protein signature database. *Nucleic Acids Res.*, 37 (Database Issue), D211-D215.

International Human Genome Sequencing Consortium. (2004) Finishing the euchromatic sequence of the human genome. *Nature*, 431, 931-945.

Jensen, H. & Evans Jr., E.A. (1935) Studies on crystalline insulin. XVIII. The nature of the free amino groups in insulin and the isolation of phenylalanine and proline from cyrstalline insulin. *J.Biol.Chem.*, 108, 1-12.

Kanehisa, M.; Fickett, J.W. & Goad, W.B. (1984) A relational database system for the maintenance and verification of the Los Alamos sequence library. *Nucleic Acids Res.*, 12(1), 149-158.

Kanz, C.; Aldebert, P., Althorpe, N., Baker, W., Baldwin, A., Bates, K., Browne, P., van den Broek, A., Castro, M., Cochrane, G., Duggan, K., Eberhardt, R., Faruque, N., Gamble, J., Diez, F.G., Harte, N., Kulikova, T., Lin, Q., Lombard, V., Lopez, R., Mancuso, R., McHale, M., Nardone, F., Silventoinen, V., Sobhany, S., Stoehr, P., Tuli, M.A., Tzouvara, K., Vaughan, R., Wu, D., Zhu, W. & Apweiler, R. (2005) The EMBL Nucleotide Sequence Database. *Nucleic Acids Res.*, 33(Database issue), D29-D33.

Kendrew, J.C.; Bodo, G., Dintzis, H.M., Parrish, R. G., Wyckoff, H. & Phillips, D. C. (1958) A three-dimensional model of the myoglobin molecule obtained by x-ray analysis. *Nature*, 181, 662-666.

Kennard, O.; Watson, D. G. & Town, W. G. (1972) Cambridge Crystallographic Data Centre. I. Bibliographic File. *J. Chem. Doc.*, 12(1), 14-19.

Kennard, O. (1997) From private data to public knowledge. In *The Impact of Electronic Publishing on the Academic Community*, an International Workshop organised by the Academia Europaea and the Wenner-Gren Foundation, Wenner-Gren Center, Stockholm, 16-20 April, 1997. Ian Butterworth, Ed. Published by Portland Press Ltd., London, UK. ISBN 1 85578 122 0

Kneale, G.G. & Kennard, O. (1984) The EMBL nucleotide sequence data library. *Biochem. Soc. Trans.*, 12, 1011–1014.

Kreppel, L.; Fey, P., Gaudet, P., Just, E., Kibbe, W.A., Chisholm, R.L. & Kimmel, A.R. (2004) dictyBase: a new Dictyostelium discoideum genome database. *Nucleic Acids Res.*, 32(Database issue), D332-D333.

Lander, E.S.; Linton, L.M., Birren, B., Nusbaum, C., Zody, M.C. *et al.* (2001) Initial sequencing and analysis of the human genome. *Nature*, 409, 860-921.

Lederberg, J. (1978) Digital Communications and the Conduct of Science; the New Literacy. *Proceedings of the IEEE*, 66, 1314-1319.

Leinonen, R.; Nardone, F., Oyewole, O., Redaschi, N. & Stoehr, P. (2003) The EMBL sequence version archive. *Bioinformatics*, 19(14), 1861-1862.

Leinonen, R.; Akhtar, R., Birney, E., Bower, L., Cerdeno-Tárraga, A., Cheng, Y., Cleland, I., Faruque, N., Goodgame, N., Gibson, R., Hoad, G., Jang, M., Pakseresht, N., Plaister, S., Radhakrishnan, R., Reddy, K., Sobhany, S., Ten Hoopen, P., Vaughan, R., Zalunin, V. & Cochrane, G. (2011) The European Nucleotide Archive. *Nucleic Acids Res.*, 39(Database issue), D28-31.

Lipman, D.J. & Pearson, W.R. (1985) Rapid and sensitive protein similarity searches. *Science*, 227, 1435-1441.

Meyer, E.F. (1997) The first years of the Protein Data Bank. *Protein Science, 6*, 1591-1597.

Muirhead, H. & Perutz, M. (1963) Structure of hemoglobin. A three-dimensional fourier synthesis of reduced human hemoglobin at 5.5 Å resolution. *Nature,* 199, 633–38.

Nakamura, H.; Ito. N. & Kusunoki, M. (2002) Development of PDBj: Advanced database for protein structures. *Tanpakushitsu Kakusan Koso.*, 47(8 Suppl), 1097-1101.

Nature Editorial. (1999) Vacuum at the heart of Europe. *Nature,* 402, 1.

Needleman, S.B. & Wunsch, C.D. (1971) A general method applicable to the search for similarities in the amino acid sequence of two proteins. J.Mol.Biol., 48, 443-453.

Pearson, W.R. & Lipman, D.J. (1988) Improved tools for biological sequence comparison. Proc.Natl. Acad.Sci. USA, 85, 2444-2448

Pettifer, S., Ison, J., Kalas, M., Thorne, D., McDermott, P., Jonassen, I., Liaquat, A., Fernandez, J.M., Rodriguez, J.M., Partners, I., Pisano, D.G., Blanchet, C., Uludag, M., Rice, P., Bartaseviciute, E., Rapacki, K., Hekkelman, M., Sand, O., Stockinger, H., Clegg, A.B., Bongcam-Rudloff, E., Salzemann, J., Breton, V., Attwood, T.K., Cameron, G. & Vriend, G. (2010) The EMBRACE web service collection. Nucleic Acids Res., 38, Suppl. W683-688

Philipson, L. (1992) Letter to EMBL Council Delegates, with annexes

Protein Data Bank (1971) *Nature New Biology*, 233, 223.

Protein Data Bank (1973) *Acta Crystallogr. sect. B*, 29, 1746.

Rice, P., Longden, I. & Bleasby, A. (2000) EMBOSS: the European Molecular Biology Open Software Suite. Trends Genet., 16, 276-277

Ryle, A.P.; Sanger, F., Smith, L.F. & Kitai, R. (1955) The disulphide bonds of insulin. *Biochem. J.*, 60(4), 541–556.

Sanger, F. (1945) The free amino groups of insulin. *Biochem. J.*, 39, 507-515.

Sanger, F. & Tuppy, H. (1951) a) The amino-acid sequence in the phenylalanyl chain of insulin. 1. The identification of lower peptides from partial hydrolysates. *Biochem. J.*, 49, 463–481; b) The amino-acid sequence in the phenylalanyl chain of insulin. 2. The investigation of peptides from enzymic hydrolysates. *Ibid.*, 481–490.

Sanger, F. & Thompson, E.O.P. (1953) a) The amino-acid sequence in the glycyl chain of insulin. 1. The identification of lower peptides from partial hydrolysates. *Biochem. J.*, 53, 353–366; b) The amino-acid sequence in the glycyl chain of insulin. 2. The investigation of peptides from enzymic hydrolysates. *Ibid.*, 366–374.

Sanger, F.; Thompson, E.O.P. & Kitai, R. (1955) The amide groups of insulin. *Biochem. J.*, 59(3), 509–518.

Sanger, F.; Coulson, A.R., Friedmann, T., Air, G.M., Barrell, B.G., Brown, N.L., Fiddes, J.C., Hutchison, C.A. 3rd, Slocombe, P.M. & Smith, M. (1978) The nucleotide sequence of bacteriophage phiX174. *J. Mol. Biol.*, 125(2), 225-246.

Sanger, F.; Coulson, A.R., Hong, G.F., Hill, D.F. & Petersen, G.B. (1982) Nucleotide sequence of bacteriophage lambda DNA. *J.Mol.Biol.*, 162(4), 729-773.

Sanger, F. (1988) Sequences, sequences, and sequences. *Ann.Rev.Biochem.*, 57, 1-28.

Sidman, K.E.; George, D.G., Barker, W.C. & Hunt, L.T. (1988) The protein identification resource (PIR). *Nucleic Acids Res.*, 16(5), 1869-1871.

Smith, T.F. & Waterman, M.S. (1981) Identification of common molecular subsequences. J.Mol.Biol., 147, 195-197

Smith, T.F. (1990) The history of the genetic sequence databases. *Genomics*, 6, 701-707.

Smyth, D.G.; Stein, W.H. & Moore, S. (1963) The Sequence of Amino Acid Residues in Bovine Pancreatic Ribonuclease: Revisions and Confirmations. *J.Biol.Chem.*, 238, 227-234.

Schneider, M.V.; Watson, J., Attwood, T., Rother, K., Budd, A., McDowall, J., Via, A., Fernandes, P., Nyronen, T., Blicher, T., Jones, P., Blatter, M.C., De Las Rivas, J., Judge, D.P., van der Gool, W. & Brooksbank, C. (2010) Bioinformatics training: a review of challenges, actions and support requirements. *Brief Bioinform.*, 11(6), 544-551

Sonnhammer, E.L. & Kahn, D. (1994) Modular arrangement of proteins as inferred from analysis of homology. *Protein Sci.*, 3(3), 482-492.

Sonnhammer, E.L.; Eddy, S.R. & Durbin, R. (1997) Pfam: a comprehensive database of protein domain families based on seed alignments. *Proteins*, 28(3), 405-420.

Strasser, B. (2008) *GenBank – Natural history in the 21st century?* Science, 322, 537-538.

Thornton, J. (2011) European Life Sciences Infrastructure for Biological Information, ELIXIR Business Case. European Bioinformatics Institute, Hinxton, Cambridge, UK.

UniProt Consortium. (2011) Ongoing and future developments at the Universal Protein Resource. *Nucleic Acids Res.*, 39(Database issue), D214-D219.

Velankar, S.; Best, C., Beuth, B., Boutselakis, C. H., Cobley, N., Sousa Da Silva, A.W., Dimitropoulos, D., Golovin, A., Hirshberg, M., John, M., Krissinel, E.B., Newman, R., Oldfield, T., Pajon, A. , Penkett, C. J., Pineda-Castillo, J., Sahni, G., Sen, S., Slowley, R., Suarez-Uruena, A., Swaminathan, J., van Ginkel, G., Vranken, W. F., Henrick, K. & Kleywegt, G. J. (2010) PDBe: Protein Data Bank in Europe. *Nucleic Acids Res.*, 38, D308–D317.

Venter, J.C.; Adams, M.D., Myers, E.W., Li, P.W., Mural, R.J. *et al.* (2001) The sequence of the human genome. *Science*, 291, 1304-1351.

Waterfield MD, Scrace GT, Whittle N, Stroobant P, Johnsson A, Wasteson A, Westermark B, Heldin CH, Huang JS, Deuel TF. Platelet-derived growth factor is structurally related to the putative transforming protein p28sis of simian sarcoma virus. Nature. 1983 Jul 7-13;304(5921):35-9.

Watson, J.D. & Crick, F.H.C. (1953) Molecular structure of nucleic acids. *Nature*, 171, 737-738.

Wilbur, W.J. & Lipman, D.J. (1983) Rapid similarity searches of nucleic acid and protein data banks. *Proc. Natl. Acad. Sci. USA.*, 80(3), 726-730.

Wood, D.W.; Setubal, J.C., Kaul, R., Monks, D.E., Kitajima, J.P. *et al.* (2001). The Genome of the Natural Genetic Engineer *Agrobacterium tumefaciens* C58. *Science*, 294, 2317-2323.

Wu, C.H.; Yeh, L.S., Huang, H., Arminski, L., Castro-Alvear, J., Chen, Y., Hu, Z., Kourtesis, P., Ledley, R.S., Suzek, B.E., Vinayaka, C.R., Zhang, J. & Barker, W.C. (2003) The Protein Information Resource. *Nucleic Acids Res.*, 31(1), 345-347.

Wyckoff, H.W.; Hardman, K.D., Allewell, N.M., Inagami, T., Johnson, L.N. & Richards, F.M. (1967). The structure of ribonuclease-S at 3.5 Å resolution. *J. Biol. Chem.*, 242, 3984–3988.

Zdobnov, E.M., Lopez, R., Apweiler, R. & Etzold, T. (2002) The EBI SRS server – new features. Bioinformatics, 18, 1149-1150.

Part 2

Data Integration

2

Data Integration in Bioinformatics: Current Efforts and Challenges

Zhang Zhang[1], Vladimir B. Bajic[1], Jun Yu[2],
Kei-Hoi Cheung[3,4,5,6] and Jeffrey P. Townsend[6,7]
*[1]Computational Bioscience Research Center (CBRC),
King Abdullah University of Science and Technology (KAUST), Thuwal*
*[2]CAS Key Laboratory of Genome Sciences and Information, Beijing Institute of Genomics,
Chinese Academy of Sciences, Beijing*
*[3]Center for Medical Informatics, [4]Department of Computer Science,
[5]Department of Genetics, [6]Program in Computational Biology and Bioinformatics,
[7]Department of Ecology and Evolutionary Biology, Yale University,
New Haven, Connecticut*
[1]Kingdom of Saudi Arabia
[2]China
[3,4,5,6,7]United States of America

1. Introduction

With the rapid advancements in next-generation sequencing (NGS) technologies and the consequently fast-growing volume of biological data, a diversity of data sources (databases and web servers) have been created to facilitate data management, accessibility, and analysis. A prerequisite of bioinformatics research has been the ability to find, maneuver and access data deposited in various data sources. For a given bioinformatic task, researchers often need to be skillful in interrogating these data sources, and in the use of extracted information for further data analysis/information search. For example, one must obtain data from one data source, reformat the data and submit to another data source for analysis, parse the analyzed result, and then combine the result with data obtained from the third data source, etc. Undisputedly, data integration becomes tedious and time-consuming, especially regarding the import and export of enormous files of modern NGS and other data. Thus, integration of data from distributed, heterogeneous and voluminous data sources turns out to be a significant obstacle to fully exploit the wealth of big biological data (Davidson, et al., 1995; Stein, 2002). The importance of the integration component of research stemming from studies based on high-throughput technologies (such as NGS), is twofold: (1) due to the great level of automation of the actual experimental procedures, the effort of obtaining the experimental data takes only about 20% or less of the overall research effort in an NGS project; approximately four fifths of the effort goes to the integration and analysis of a collection of the experimental data (Mardis, 2010); (2) the answers to the most important, complex biological questions today are rarely provided directly through the experimental results; to bring potential answers to the surface, downstream bioinformatics analysis often involves the integration of diverse data from multiple data sources.

The objective of data integration in bioinformatics is to establish automated and efficient ways to integrate large, heterogeneous biological datasets from multiple sources. However, this objective is challenged by data sources that are geographically distributed and heterogeneous in terms of their functions, structures, data access methods and dissemination formats. According to the 2010 update on the Bioinformatics Links Directory (Brazas, et al., 2010), there are almost 1500 unique publicly-available data sources. Based on their functions, data sources can be classified into diverse categories: (1) sequence databases, e.g., GenBank (Benson, et al., 2006), RefSeq (Pruitt, et al., 2009), CMR (Comprehensive Microbial Resource) (Davidsen, et al., 2010); (2) functional genomics databases, e.g., ArrayExpress (Parkinson, et al., 2011), FFGED (Filamentous Fungal Gene Expression Database) (Zhang and Townsend, 2010), GEO (Gene Expression Omnibus) (Barrett, et al., 2011); (3) protein-protein interaction databases, e.g., BIND (Biomolecular Interaction Network Database) (Bader, et al., 2003), DIP (Database of Interacting Proteins) (Salwinski, et al., 2004), IntAct (Aranda, et al., 2010), MINT (Molecular Interactions Database) (Ceol, et al., 2010); (4) pathway databases, e.g., KEGG (Kyoto Encyclopedia of Genes and Genomes) (Kanehisa, et al., 2010); (5) structure databases, e.g., CATH (Greene, et al., 2007), PDB (Protein Data Bank) (Rose, et al., 2011); (6) annotation databases, e.g., GO (Gene Ontology) (Ashburner, et al., 2000), NCBI Taxonomy (Sayers, et al., 2011). Moreover, data sources differ in data accessibility and dissemination. That is, different levels of provision are made by the data source managers for human-reading, computer-reading, or both. Certainly, data sources can also be classified by species of interest, such as, filamentous fungi (Zhang and Townsend, 2010), fly (Gilbert, 2007), mouse (Blake, et al., 2011), and yeast (Engel, et al., 2010).

Despite the challenges, the promise of data integration is high: heterogeneous data sources provide biological data encompassing a wide range of research fields. Therefore, data integration has the potential to facilitate a better and more comprehensive scope of inference for biological studies. Although efforts have been devoted to biological data integration over the past two decades, it remains challenging and laborious. Here we review current efforts and illustrate several approaches used for data integration. With a specific consideration of the exponentially-growing NGS data, we also describe challenges in this context and discuss potential trends.

2. Current efforts of data integration in bioinformatics

Several major approaches have been proposed for data integration, which can be roughly classified into five groups (Goble and Stevens, 2008; Zhang, et al., 2009): data warehousing, federated databasing, service-oriented integration, semantic integration and wiki-based integration. Across all of these groups, to a significant extent, an increasingly important component of data integration is the community effort in developing a variety of biomedical ontologies (see Section 3.2), to deal in a more specific manner with the technicality and globality of descriptors and identifiers of information that has to be shared and integrated across various resources (Antezana, et al., 2009; Maojo, et al., 2011; Rubin, et al., 2008).

2.1 Data warehousing

The data warehouse approach offers a "one-stop shop" solution to ease access and management of a large variety of biological data from different data sources. Data warehouses focus on data translation, fetching all accessible data from many disparate data sources, transforming the data and importing it into the data warehouse. Representative examples of data warehousing include:

- Atlas (Shah, et al., 2005) is a biological data warehouse that locally stores and integrates biological sequences, molecular interactions, homology information, functional annotations of genes, and biological ontologies. It includes data from BIND, DIP, Entrez Gene (Maglott, et al., 2011), GO, GenBank, HomoloGene, HPRD (Human Protein Reference Database) (Keshava Prasad, et al., 2009), IntAct, LocusLink (Pruitt and Maglott, 2001), MINT, RefSeq, OMIM (Online Mendelian Inheritance in Man) (Amberger, et al., 2009), Taxonomy, and UniProt (The UniProt Consortium, 2011).
- BioWarehouse (Lee, et al., 2006) is an open source toolkit for constructing data warehouses. It incorporates data from BioCyc (Karp, et al., 2005), CMR, ENZYME (Bairoch, 2000), GenBank, GO, KEGG, Taxonomy, and UniProt and integrates its component databases into a common representational framework within a single database management system.
- BIOZON (Birkland and Yona, 2006) is a unified biological resource on DNA sequences, proteins, complexes and cellular pathways. It relies on an extensive database schema that integrates information at the macro-molecular level as well as at the cellular level from a variety of data sources, including BIND, DIP, Genbank, InterPro (Hunter, et al., 2009), KEGG, PDB, RefSeq, Swiss-Prot (Bairoch, et al., 2004), UniGene (Sayers, et al., 2011), and UniProt.
- COLUMBA (Trissl, et al., 2005) is an integrated database of information on proteins, structures and annotations. It integrates twelve different databases, including CATH, ENZYME, GO, KEGG, PDB, SCOP (Andreeva, et al., 2008), and Swiss-Prot.
- VINEdb (Hariharaputran, et al., 2007) is a data warehouse for integration and interactive exploration of life science data. It manages diverse data from GO, IntAct, KEGG, OMIM, and UniProt and emphasizes the visualization of the integrated data in a comprehensible manner.

The data warehouse approach has several advantages. (1) The user does not need to access many web sites for multiple data sources. Data warehouses provide one single access point to conveniently manipulate a large variety of data. (2) All queries requested by users are executed within the data warehouse (rather than on distributed data sources) and therefore, data warehousing eliminates network bottlenecks and obtains high performance with fast response. (3) Due to data storage at a single managed point, data warehousing obtains benefits in data control, yielding easy customization to meet users' needs.

Despite its advantages, the data warehouse approach has a major problem; it requires continuous and often human-guided updates to keep the data comprehensive of the evolution of data sources, resulting in high costs for maintenance. In general, there are two kinds of changes. (1) Changes in data volume or revisions of data. Whenever extant data is revised or the volume of data in any data source is changed, the data warehouse must monitor for such remote changes and update the warehouse to store the new data. (2) Changes in data structure, including adding new data types and tables, changing database tables and their relationships, and changing output formats. Many biological data sources change their data structures roughly twice a year (Stein, 2003). Whenever the data sources change their data structures, consequent data translation into the data warehouse must be updated in response. Usually, modification of data translation is labor-intensive and expensive.

2.2 Federated databasing

Unlike data warehousing (with its focus on data translation), federated databasing focuses on query translation. The federated databasing approach executes all queries on the distributed sources by translating a query against the federated database into a query against many data sources. The federated database fetches the data from disparate data sources and then displays the fetched data for its user base. Representative examples for federated databasing include:

- BioMart (Haider, et al., 2009) is a query-oriented data integration system developed jointly by the Ontario Institute for Cancer Research (OICR) and the European Bioinformatics Institute (EBI). It provides a user-friendly and unified way to retrieve data from one or multiple data sources located at diverse geographical locations, including Ensembl (Flicek, et al., 2011), HGNC, Uniprot, Reactome (Croft, et al., 2011), Wormbase, and PRIDE (Jones, et al., 2008).
- DiscoveryLink (Haas, et al., 2001) developed by IBM is a system for integrated access to life sciences data from heterogeneous data sources, including GenBank, MedLine and Swiss-Prot. It features query optimization and cross-source queries that access relational databases and retrieve the data from diverse data sources.
- K2/Kleisli (Chung and Wong, 1999; Davidson, et al., 2001) is a federated database system, integrating data from EcoCyc (Keseler, et al., 2011), GenBank, GSDB (Harger, et al., 1998), dbEST (Boguski, et al., 1993), GDB (Letovsky, et al., 1998), KEGG and SRS-indexed databases. Kleisli uses a high-level query language called Collection Programming Language (CPL) as its query language, which was developed specifically for parsing, optimizing and executing queries. K2 is the newer version of Kleisli and replaces CPL by a powerful and easy-to-use SQL-like query language, Object Query Language (OQL).
- MRS (Hekkelman and Vriend, 2005) allows for very rapid queries in a large number of flat-file data banks, including EMBL, UniProt, OMIM, dbEST, PDB, KEGG. It combines a fast and reliable backend with a very user-friendly implementation of all the commonly used information retrieval facilities.
- QIS (Query Integrator System) is based on a set of distributed network-based servers, data source servers, integration servers, and ontology servers and relies on a combination of SQL-like syntax and XML (eXtensible Markup Language; a widely used standard for data description and exchange), to formulate a query (Marenco, et al., 2004). It stores diverse queries for data integration from continuously changing heterogeneous data sources in the biosciences, including CellPropDB (Crasto and Shepherd, 2007), Brain Architecture Management System (Bota and Swanson, 2010), Yale Microarray Database (Cheung, et al., 2002), a local Gene Annotation Database and GO.
- SRS (Sequence Retrieval System) is an index-based integration system and combines some features of data warehousing and federated databasing (Zdobnov, et al., 2002). SRS uses a keyword-based indexing language ICARUS to describe each integrated data source and locally creates a full-text index over all data sources. Meanwhile, it allows a single query to execute on multiple data sources based on local indexed entries. SRS contains a number of biological databases (see details in http://srs.ebi.ac.uk/ srsbin/cgi-bin/wgetz?-page+databanks+-noSession).
- TAMBIS (Transparent Access to Multiple Bioinformatics Information Sources) is an integration application to perform bioinformatics tasks over multiple data sources by

using an ontology of biological concepts (Stevens, et al., 2000). The prototype version of TAMBIS contains five data sources, viz., BLAST, CATH, ENZYME, PROSITE (Sigrist, et al., 2010) , and Swiss-Prot.

Queries in federated databases are executed within remote data sources and results displayed in federated databases are extracted remotely from the data sources. Due to this capability, federated databasing has two major advantages. (1) Federated databases can be regarded as an on-demand approach to provide immediate access to up-to-date data deposited in multiple data sources. (2) Compared with data warehousing, federated databasing does not replicate data in data sources; therefore, it presents relatively inexpensive costs for storage and curation. However, federated databasing still has to update its query translation to keep pace with data access methods at diverse remote data sources. In addition, since data is retrieved from remote data sources, federated databasing depends heavily on network connectivity and query complexity, which may lead to low efficiency and speed in data retrieval.

2.3 Service-oriented integration

Data warehousing and federated databasing both focus on centralizing data access, through data translation and query translation, respectively. They confront some similar problems stemming from data storage and curation, frequent updates, and high costs for data exchange and/or maintenance. In part to evade these issues, a decentralized approach has also been advanced, in which individual data sources agree to open their data via Web Services (WS). WS are designed for communication between computers over the Web and described by the Web Services Description Language (WSDL). There are several different protocols for WS, e.g., SOAP (Simple Object Access Protocol; a protocol for exchanging XML-based messages over computer networks), REST (REpresentational State Transfer; a simple protocol implemented using HTTP methods). WS support computer-to-computer interaction through Web Application Programming Interface (Web API) (Shi, 2007) and can perform a database query or computation. In the context of data integration, data can be programmatically accessed via WS and data sources serve as service providers. Therefore, this approach can be seen as a service-oriented approach. The service-oriented approach enables data integration from multiple heterogeneous data sources through computer interoperability. Several representative examples for service-oriented integration include:

- BioMOBY (Kawas, et al., 2006; Wilkinson and Links, 2002; Wilkinson, et al., 2008) is an open source ontology-based integration system for accessing distributed and heterogeneous data sources via WS. It implements a WS registry and uses standard ontology terms to annotate WS. BioMOBY adopts SOAP for data exchange and allows interoperability among different data sources to achieve automated data integration and sharing (Neerincx and Leunissen, 2005).
- DAS (Distributed Annotation System) is a client-server system to provide access to complete distributed genome annotations using SOAP-based WS (Dowell, et al., 2001; Katayama, et al., 2010; Olason, 2005). It allows a single machine to collect all annotations from multiple distributed data sources and display them to the user in a single view. DAS is widely used in the genome annotation community (http://en.wikipedia.org/wiki/Distributed_Annotation_System) and adopted by several systems, including Ensembl, WormBase, and the Berkeley Drosophila Genome Project (Jenkinson, et al., 2008; Messina and Sonnhammer, 2009; Olason, 2005).

- Taverna (Oinn, et al., 2004), a part of MyGrid (Stevens, et al., 2003), is a graphical workflow workbench application, aiming to integrate the growing number of molecular biology tools and databases (Hull, et al., 2006). Workflows in Taverna, written by a custom XML-based language called Simple Conceptual Unified Flow Language (SCUFL), can automatically record all data involved, provenance metadata, and results, facilitating complex data processing in a dynamic distributed environment.

The service-oriented approach features data integration through computer-to-computer communication via Web API and up-to-date data retrieval from diverse data sources. Thus, it befits well with the dynamic nature of bioinformatics. However, it remains challenging, primarily because its success in heterogeneous data integration requires that many data sources should become service providers by opening their data via WS and by standardizing data identities and nomenclature to ease data exchange and analysis. In addition, a unified WS registry is also necessitated, not only to establish standards for WS registration, but also to formulate standards for service-oriented workflows or pipelines (Zhang, et al., 2009).

2.4 Semantic integration

Most web pages in biological data sources are designed for human reading (e.g., HTML). The Semantic Web (Dibernardo, et al., 2008; Good and Wilkinson, 2006; Hendler, 2003; Lord, et al., 2004) aims to describe data in a way that computers can understand and to build an interconnected network that computers can easily and unambiguously process. According to the statement of definition from the World Wide Web Consortium (W3C), the purpose of the Semantic Web is to create a universal medium for the exchange of data using several standards, including Resource Description Framework (RDF; http://www.w3.org/RDF), RDF schema (RDFS—RDF Vocabulary Description Language; http://www.w3.org/TR/rdf-schema), Web Ontology Language (OWL; http://www.w3.org/owl), and standard Web query language SPARQL (http://www.w3.org/TR/rdf-sparql-query) for RDF. RDF provides standard formats (e.g, XML format) for data interchange and describes data as a simple statement, containing a set of triples: a *subject*, a *predicate* and an *object*. Any two statements can be linked by an identical *subject* or *object*. OWL builds on RDF and Uniform Resource Identifier (URI) and describes data structure and meaning based on ontology, which enables automated data reasoning and inferences by computers. The Semantic Web provides an machine-readable way for data representation and interoperability (Antezana, et al., 2009). Several studies have applied the Semantic Web technologies in data integration and representative examples of semantic integration are described below.

- Bio2RDF (Belleau, et al., 2008) is a mashup system that creates an integrated space of RDF documents linked together with normalized URIs. Bio2RDF applies the Semantic Web technologies to multiple data sources, such as Entrez Gene, HGNC, KEGG, MGI, OMIM PDB, PubMed and UniProt, and converts data into RDF format based on RDFizer (a set of tools for converting various data formats into RDF; http://simile.mit.edu/wiki/RDFizers), Sesame (an open source framework for storage, inference and querying of RDF data; http://www.openrdf.org) and OWL ontology. In Bio2RDF, each RDF document is expressed as a URI. When a query is requested to Bio2RDF for a given URI, for example, http://bio2rdf.org/go:0004396, the URI identifies RDF triples containing the GO term of Hexokinase (GO:0004396). Bio2RDF supports query via SPARQL.

- HCLS (The Health Care and Life Sciences Interest Group; http://www.w3.org/2001/sw/hcls/), established by W3C, aims to explore the potential benefits of the Semantic Web in the health care and life sciences domains (Cheung, et al., 2008) and advocates the application of the Semantic Web for advancing translational research (Ruttenberg, et al., 2007). The HCLS Knowledge Base (HCLS-KB; http://www.w3.org/TR/hcls-kb) is a Semantic Web system that imports data from many data sources in multiple domains of life sciences, including not only general sources, e.g., Entrez Gene, GO, HomoloGene, but also domain-specific sources, e.g., Allen Brain Atlas (an interactive, genome-wide image database of gene expression in the mouse brain; http://www.brain-map.org) (Lein, et al., 2007), SenseLab (a collection of neuroscience data; http://neuroweb.med.yale.edu/senselab) (Crasto, et al., 2007) and SWAN (Semantic Web Applications in Neuromedicine; aiming to organize and annotate scientific knowledge about Alzheimer disease and other neurodegenerative disorders) (Ciccarese, et al., 2008; Clark and Kinoshita, 2007; Kinoshita and Clark, 2007).
- YeastHub (Cheung, et al., 2005) is an integrated database in RDF format for the yeast community. It creates a RDF repository for RDF storage and provides a utility to convert tabular format into RDF format. YeastHub integrates different types of yeast data provided by different data sources (SGD, YGDP, MIPS, BIND, GO and TRIPLES) and supports RDF-based queries to retrieve and query the data.

Application of the Semantic Web technologies to biological data integration is a significant advancement for bioinformatics, enabling automated data processing and reasoning. The semantic integration uses ontologies for data description and thus represents ontology-based integration (Noy, 2004). However, the Semantic Web continues to evolve and its application in biological data integration has several limitations. The semantic integration locally stores a large collection of RDF documents, by copying data from multiple data sources and converting data into RDF format. From this view, the semantic integration can be regarded as a special data warehouse with data in RDF format. As a consequence, it inherits the pros and cons of data warehousing and is vulnerable to updates in data sources. To keep the RDF documents up-to-date, it requires tedious and periodical data retrieval and RDF conversion. In addition, once any data source changes data structure, the RDF conversion scripts must be updated consequently.

Currently, there is an ongoing project, the World Wide Web Consortium's SWEO (Semantic Web Education and Outreach) Linking Open Data Project (Bizer, 2009; Zhao, et al., 2009) that uses the Semantic Web technologies to connect related distributed data across the Web. Technically, linked data rely on RDF to create typed links between data from different data sources. Linked data is machine-readable, explicitly defined, and inter-linked to other data, promising to facilitate data integration, exposure, sharing, and connecting.

2.5 Wiki-based integration

A weakness common to all the above approaches is that the quantity of users' participations in the process is inadequate. With the increasing volume of biological data, data integration inevitably will require a large number of users' participations. A successful example that harnesses collective intelligence for data aggregation and knowledge collection is Wikipedia, an online encyclopedia (http://www.wikipedia.org) that allows any user to create and edit content. Wikipedia features collaborative integration, continuous and frequent update, up-to-date content, huge content coverage and low cost for maintenance

(McLean, et al., 2007). Although there are fears of inconsistency and inaccuracy since users can freely and anonymously change any content and/or add new content in the wiki (Arita, 2009; Bidartondo, 2008), it is testified that Wikipedia outperforms the traditional Encyclopedia in accuracy (Giles, 2005).

In consideration of the success of Wikipedia, a wiki-based approach has been on the horizon to store, manage and organize biological data (Giles, 2007; Salzberg, 2007; Waldrop, 2008; Yager, 2006). The wiki-based integration makes full use of collective intelligence and efforts for biological data integration. Representative examples include: WikiGenes (a wiki system that combines gene annotation with explicit authorship; Hoffmann, 2008), WikiProteins (a wiki-based system for protein annotation; Mons, et al., 2008), BOWiki (a ontology-based wiki for data annotation and knowledge integration; Hoehndorf, et al., 2009), Gene Wiki (a wiki for human gene annotation; Huss, et al., 2010; Huss, et al., 2008) and PDBWiki (a scientific wiki for the community annotation of protein structures; Stehr, et al., 2010). However, the wiki-based integration has its own shortcomings, including the unstructured data generated, the lack of a standard format for data exchange, the lack of credit for authorship and vulnerability to malicious editing (Lee, 2008; Potthast, et al., 2008).

3. Challenges ahead

Although a number of current efforts have been devoted to data integration, none of them have achieved a pre-eminent impact on their field yet. Since NGS data are growing at an exponential rate, the need for data integration is continually demanding and challenges for data integration are greatly increasing.

3.1 Data as a service

The low-cost and high-throughput NGS technologies can generate huge amounts of data at a relatively short period. To keep pace with the revolution of sequencing technologies, genome sequencing projects have transitioned from classical model organisms (e.g., fly, mouse, yeast), to other organisms (e.g., camel, dog, panda) and eventually, to sequencing individuals within populations, exemplified by the 1000 Genomes Project—a collection of the genomes of 1,000 humans (http://www.1000genomes.org) and the Genome 10K Project—a genomic zoo of genome sequences of 10,000 vertebrate species (http://www.genome10k.org). The era of $1000 personal genome sequencing is approaching within the following years and would produce unparalleled large-scale data, presenting considerable challenges for data integration.

It is infeasible to integrate such large amounts of data into a single point (such as a data warehouse). Data sources are developed for different purposes and fulfill different functions. Therefore, it is promising to establish an efficient way for data exchange among these distributed and heterogeneous data sources. However, a dozen of data sources are designed merely for data storage, but not for data exchange. The growing volume of biological data also requires "computer-readable" approaches for data integration. To ease data integration, data sources need to turn into service providers. In other words, data sources should not only serve as data providers that provide data for human reading with web interfaces (e.g., HTML), but also function as service providers that provide data for computer interoperability via WS. Service providers supply data as a WS, facilitating computer-to-computer interactions and thus enabling automated data integration from multiple data sources (Hansen, et al., 2003). As mentioned, there are several different protocols that can be used for creating WS. Among them, SOAP and REST have been widely adopted (Figure 1). SOAP is a well-defined standard with XML-structured messaging for request and response, whereas REST is relatively lightweight, relying on HTTP methods (viz., POST, GET, PUT or DELETE). Most commercial applications expose their services as RESTful Web APIs (Figure 1), largely due to its simplicity and easy implementation.

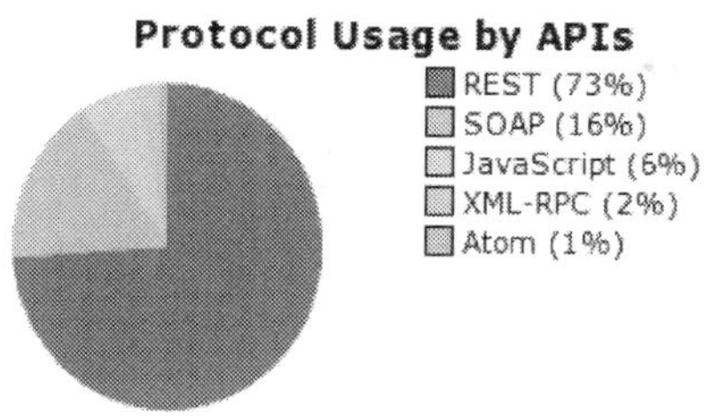

Fig. 1. Statistics of Web API protocols (obtained from http://www.programmableweb.com/apis, which collects more than 3,000 Web APIs; last access: February 27, 2011).

3.2 Standards for biological data

Due to the complex nature of biology, there are a wide variety of biological data types, e.g., sequence data, gene expression data, protein-protein interaction data, pathway data (Karasavvas, et al., 2004). Data sources store different data types as different formats (Li, 2006): flat file (e.g., tab-delimited file), sequence file (e.g., FASTA), structure file (e.g., PSF – Protein Structure File), and XML file (e.g., KGML – KEGG Markup Language for describing graph objects). Data sources often adopt their preferable data formats; even for a same data type, data formats in different sources are often incompatible. It is also noted that new data formats are often invented along with the development of related technologies. Examples of newly invented file formats include SAM (Sequence Alignment/MAP; a generic nucleotide alignment format that describes the alignment of query sequences or sequencing reads to a reference sequence or assembly; Li, et al., 2009), and GVF (Genome Variation Format; a simple tab-delimited format for describing genome variation data; Reese, et al., 2010). In addition, data sources output their data in diverse formats, such as HTML, raw file formats, and XML-based file formats. Taken together, diverse and heterogeneous data formats complicate data exchange, posing challenges for data integration.

Standards for biological data formats can ease data exchange and integration. There has been a successful attempt for standardizing biological pathway data. Pathway-related data sources differed in their data representation, making data integration difficult and inefficient. For this reason, BioPAX (Demir, et al., 2010) has been developed to deliver a compatible standard, facilitating integration, exchange, visualization and analysis of biological pathway data. Another effort related to cope with data incompatibilities of bioinformatics repositories has been devoted to the standardization issues of data exchange formats and WS (Katayama, et al., 2010). In short, establishing standard formats for biological data can realize efficient data exchange and integration. In return, standard data formats facilitate subsequent data analysis and visualization as well as downstream software development.

Equally important, data integration also requires standardizing nomenclature and ontologies for biological data (Rubin, et al., 2008). Suppose two data sources need to exchange gene annotations. They must share a standard regarding gene name. Otherwise, any ambiguity or inconsistency in nomenclature would bring a burden to data integration. Attention has been paid to standardizing nomenclature and ontologies for biological data, e.g., BioPortal (Noy, et al., 2009; Rubin, et al., 2006) for integrating and sharing biomedical ontologies in National Center for Biomedical Ontology, GO (Ashburner, et al., 2000) for standardizing the representation of gene and gene product attributes, HGNC (Seal, et al., 2011) for standardizing human gene symbols and names, OBO (Open Biomedical Ontologies) (Smith, et al., 2007) for creating a suite of orthogonal interoperable reference ontologies in the biomedical domain. However, a centralized system for nomenclature and ontologies standardization may not keep good pace with the rapid accumulation of biological data and any gap in standardization would provoke difficulties for data integration. A wiki-based system might be promising to harness all communities' efforts in standardizing nomenclature and ontologies collaboratively and efficiently.

3.3 WS-based pipelines

The goal of data integration is to enable combining information from different resources in an automated fashion without human intervention, so as to handle the increasing accumulation of biological data (Sarkar, et al., 2008). Towards this goal, data to be integrated should be re-defined in a broader manner, which include not merely sequences and other raw data, but also methods, tools, algorithms, analyzed results, discovered knowledge (see a paper for knowledge integration; Clark, 2007) and even connections among people (Zhang, et al., 2009). All kinds of data can be provided as a service. That is, raw data should be accessible via WS, methods, tools, and algorithms that are used to analyze data should be offered as WS (that is SaaS, Software as a Service), and analyzed results and discovered knowledge should be also delivered as WS (Zhang, et al., 2009). As a result, WS perform a variety of data manipulation, including data retrieval, integration, analysis, visualization, and sharing.

A pipeline with a combination of multiple WS can achieve data integration (Zhang, et al., 2009). Such WS-based pipelines lower technological entrance barriers and provide users with a lightweight programming environment. WS-based pipelines feature computer-to-computer data exchange, simplify data integration and analysis, maximize the scope of sharing and reuse, and function as a medium to link users located anywhere with similar research interests, and finally to form a scientific social community (SSC). SSC reflects several key elements of Web 2.0 and enables data integration, analysis and sharing with greater convenience, speed and efficiency (Zhang, et al., 2009). Any user may easily create WS-based pipelines (adding value), publish them online, and subscribe to pipelines created by other users. Consequently, pipelines may be widely shared, re-used and even integrated into other pipelines. As a result, communications and collaborations among users in SSC can be greatly increased, making knowledge discovery through collective intelligence possible. In addition, SSC can also serve as a registry for collecting WS (Bhagat, et al., 2010; Pettifer, et al., 2010).

3.4 Semantic Web Services

The ever-evolving next-generation Web (NGW), characterized as the Semantic Web, aims to provide information not only for human, but also for computers to semantically process large-scale data and automatically discover knowledge. From this view, the Semantic Web befits well with the exponential growth of biological data and promises in providing solutions for data integration and advancing translational research (Ruttenberg, et al., 2007). Semantic Web technologies have been applied for data integration as mentioned above. Nevertheless, these applications in essence belong to semantic warehouses and still have pains for integrating dynamic data. One potential solution is to combine WS with Semantic Web technologies and to provide Semantic WS (Matos, et al., 2010; Vandervalk, et al., 2009), namely, RDF-based WS for automated data processing and reasoning. As mentioned, WS are designed not only to perform a query, but also to conduct a computation. Considering that NGS technologies can swiftly generate hundreds of gigabases of sequencing data, WS would become increasingly data-intensive and computation-intensive (e.g., alignment of multiple large-scale sequences). Therefore, to deal with such large-scale data management and analysis, Semantic WS necessitate to adopt advances in high performance computing (Schadt, et al., 2010), such as, cloud/grid computing (Bateman and Wood, 2009; Stein, 2010) and Service-Oriented Computing (Papazoglou, et al., 2008). In addition, a Semantic WS framework (Wilkinson, et al., 2010) is also needed, in order to set up Semantic WS workflows or pipelines.

4. Conclusions

As a critical topic in bioinformatics, data integration bears fundamental significance for biological studies. Efforts have been devoted to this topic and the corresponding approaches for data integration have moved from traditional ones, e.g., data warehousing and federated databasing, to modern ones based on several advanced technologies, e.g., Web Service, Semantic Web and Wiki. The rapid development of sequencing technologies poses tremendous challenges for data integration. Integration of large-scale data not only requires adoption of informatics advances, but also needs communications and collaborations among people in related biological communities to maximize data openness via WS, set up standards for biological data, create Semantic WS-based pipelines and form a scientific social community. Such community harnesses collective intelligence and collaborative efforts for data integration, analysis and sharing, having the potential to be an ideal community of the people, by the people, and for the people.

5. References

Amberger, J., *et al.* (2009) McKusick's Online Mendelian Inheritance in Man (OMIM), *Nucleic Acids Res*, 37, D793-796.

Andreeva, A., *et al.* (2008) Data growth and its impact on the SCOP database: new developments, *Nucleic Acids Res*, 36, D419-425.

Antezana, E., *et al.* (2009) Biological knowledge management: the emerging role of the Semantic Web technologies, *Brief Bioinform*, 10, 392-407.

Aranda, B., *et al.* (2010) The IntAct molecular interaction database in 2010, *Nucleic Acids Res*, 38, D525-531.

Arita, M. (2009) A pitfall of wiki solution for biological databases, *Brief Bioinform*, 10, 295-296.

Ashburner, M., *et al.* (2000) Gene ontology: tool for the unification of biology. The Gene Ontology Consortium, *Nat Genet*, 25, 25-29.

Bader, G.D., *et al.* (2003) BIND: the Biomolecular Interaction Network Database, *Nucleic Acids Res*, 31, 248-250.

Bairoch, A. (2000) The ENZYME database in 2000, *Nucleic Acids Res*, 28, 304-305.

Bairoch, A., *et al.* (2004) Swiss-Prot: juggling between evolution and stability, *Brief Bioinform*, 5, 39-55.

Barrett, T., *et al.* (2011) NCBI GEO: archive for functional genomics data sets--10 years on, *Nucleic Acids Res*, 39, D1005-1010.

Bateman, A. and Wood, M. (2009) Cloud computing, *Bioinformatics*, 25, 1475.

Belleau, F., *et al.* (2008) Bio2RDF: towards a mashup to build bioinformatics knowledge systems, *J Biomed Inform*, 41, 706-716.

Benson, D.A., *et al.* (2006) GenBank, *Nucleic Acids Res*, 34, D16-20.

Bhagat, J., *et al.* (2010) BioCatalogue: a universal catalogue of web services for the life sciences, *Nucleic Acids Res*, 38, W689-694.

Bidartondo, M.I. (2008) Preserving accuracy in GenBank, *Science*, 319, 1616.

Birkland, A. and Yona, G. (2006) BIOZON: a hub of heterogeneous biological data, *Nucleic acids research*, 34, D235-242.

Bizer, C. (2009) The Emerging Web of Linked Data, *Ieee Intell Syst*, 24, 87-92.

Blake, J.A., *et al.* (2011) The Mouse Genome Database (MGD): premier model organism resource for mammalian genomics and genetics, *Nucleic Acids Res*, 39, D842-848.

Boguski, M.S., *et al.* (1993) dbEST--database for "expressed sequence tags", *Nat Genet*, 4, 332-333.

Bota, M. and Swanson, L.W. (2010) Collating and Curating Neuroanatomical Nomenclatures: Principles and Use of the Brain Architecture Knowledge Management System (BAMS), *Front Neuroinformatics*, 4, 3.

Brazas, M.D., *et al.* (2010) Providing web servers and training in Bioinformatics: 2010 update on the Bioinformatics Links Directory, *Nucleic Acids Res*, 38, W3-6.

Ceol, A., *et al.* (2010) MINT, the molecular interaction database: 2009 update, *Nucleic Acids Res*, 38, D532-539.

Cheung, K.H., *et al.* (2002) YMD: a microarray database for large-scale gene expression analysis, *Proc AMIA Symp*, 140-144.

Cheung, K.H., *et al.* (2005) YeastHub: a semantic web use case for integrating data in the life sciences domain, *Bioinformatics*, 21 Suppl 1, i85-96.

Cheung, K.H., *et al.* (2008) HCLS 2.0/3.0: health care and life sciences data mashup using Web 2.0/3.0, *J Biomed Inform*, 41, 694-705.

Chung, S.Y. and Wong, L. (1999) Kleisli: a new tool for data integration in biology, *Trends Biotechnol*, 17, 351-355.

Ciccarese, P., *et al.* (2008) The SWAN biomedical discourse ontology, *J Biomed Inform*, 41, 739-751.

Clark, T. (2007) Knowledge Integration in Biomedicine: Technology and Community, *Briefings in bioinformatics*, 8, E1-E3.

Clark, T. and Kinoshita, J. (2007) Alzforum and SWAN: the present and future of scientific web communities, *Briefings in bioinformatics*, 8, 163-171.

Crasto, C.J., *et al.* (2007) SenseLab: new developments in disseminating neuroscience information, *Brief Bioinform*, 8, 150-162.

Crasto, C.J. and Shepherd, G.M. (2007) Managing knowledge in neuroscience, *Methods Mol Biol*, 401, 3-21.

Croft, D., *et al.* (2011) Reactome: a database of reactions, pathways and biological processes, *Nucleic Acids Res*, 39, D691-697.

Davidsen, T., *et al.* (2010) The comprehensive microbial resource, *Nucleic Acids Res*, 38, D340-345.

Davidson, S.B., *et al.* (2001) K2/Kleisli and GUS: Experiments in integrated access to genomic data sources, *Ibm Syst J*, 40, 512-531.

Davidson, S.B., *et al.* (1995) Challenges in integrating biological data sources, *J Comput Biol*, 2, 557-572.

Demir, E., *et al.* (2010) The BioPAX community standard for pathway data sharing, *Nat Biotechnol*, 28, 935-942.

Dibernardo, M., *et al.* (2008) Semi-automatic web service composition for the life sciences using the BioMoby semantic web framework, *Journal of biomedical informatics*.

Dowell, R.D., *et al.* (2001) The distributed annotation system, *BMC bioinformatics*, 2, 7.

Engel, S.R., *et al.* (2010) Saccharomyces Genome Database provides mutant phenotype data, *Nucleic Acids Res*, 38, D433-436.

Flicek, P., *et al.* (2011) Ensembl 2011, *Nucleic Acids Res*, 39, D800-806.

Gilbert, D.G. (2007) DroSpeGe: rapid access database for new Drosophila species genomes, *Nucleic Acids Res*, 35, D480-485.

Giles, J. (2005) Internet encyclopaedias go head to head, *Nature*, 438, 900-901.

Giles, J. (2007) Key biology databases go wiki, *Nature*, 445, 691.

Goble, C. and Stevens, R. (2008) State of the nation in data integration for bioinformatics, *J Biomed Inform*, 41, 687-693.

Good, B.M. and Wilkinson, M.D. (2006) The Life Sciences Semantic Web is full of creeps!, *Briefings in bioinformatics*, 7, 275-286.

Greene, L.H., *et al.* (2007) The CATH domain structure database: new protocols and classification levels give a more comprehensive resource for exploring evolution, *Nucleic Acids Res*, 35, D291-297.

Haas, L.M., *et al.* (2001) DiscoveryLink: A system for integrated access to life sciences data sources, *Ibm Syst J*, 40, 489-511.

Haider, S., *et al.* (2009) BioMart Central Portal--unified access to biological data, *Nucleic Acids Res*, 37, W23-27.

Hansen, M., *et al.* (2003) Data integration using Web Services, *Lect Notes Comput Sc*, 2590, 165-182.

Harger, C., *et al.* (1998) The Genome Sequence DataBase (GSDB): improving data quality and data access, *Nucleic Acids Res*, 26, 21-26.

Hariharaputran, S., *et al.* (2007) VINEdb: a data warehouse for integration and interactive exploration of life science data, *Journal of Integrative Bioinformatics*, 4, 63.

Hekkelman, M.L. and Vriend, G. (2005) MRS: a fast and compact retrieval system for biological data, *Nucleic Acids Res*, 33, W766-769.

Hendler, J. (2003) Science and the semantic web, *Science (New York, N.Y*, 299, 520-521.

Hoehndorf, R., *et al.* (2009) BOWiki: an ontology-based wiki for annotation of data and integration of knowledge in biology, *BMC Bioinformatics*, 10 Suppl 5, S5.

Hoffmann, R. (2008) A wiki for the life sciences where authorship matters, *Nat Genet*, 40, 1047-1051.

Hull, D., *et al.* (2006) Taverna: a tool for building and running workflows of services, *Nucleic acids research*, 34, W729-732.

Hunter, S., *et al.* (2009) InterPro: the integrative protein signature database, *Nucleic Acids Res*, 37, D211-215.

Huss, J.W., 3rd, *et al.* (2010) The Gene Wiki: community intelligence applied to human gene annotation, *Nucleic Acids Res*, 38, D633-639.

Huss, J.W., 3rd, *et al.* (2008) A gene wiki for community annotation of gene function, *PLoS biology*, 6, e175.

Jenkinson, A.M., *et al.* (2008) Integrating biological data--the Distributed Annotation System, *BMC Bioinformatics*, 9 Suppl 8, S3.

Jones, P., *et al.* (2008) PRIDE: new developments and new datasets, *Nucleic Acids Res*, 36, D878-883.

Kanehisa, M., *et al.* (2010) KEGG for representation and analysis of molecular networks involving diseases and drugs, *Nucleic Acids Res*, 38, D355-360.

Karasavvas, K.A., *et al.* (2004) Bioinformatics integration and agent technology, *J Biomed Inform*, 37, 205-219.

Karp, P.D., *et al.* (2005) Expansion of the BioCyc collection of pathway/genome databases to 160 genomes, *Nucleic Acids Res*, 33, 6083-6089.

Katayama, T., *et al.* (2010) The DBCLS BioHackathon: standardization and interoperability for bioinformatics web services and workflows. The DBCLS BioHackathon Consortium*, *J Biomed Semantics*, 1, 8.

Kawas, E., *et al.* (2006) BioMoby extensions to the Taverna workflow management and enactment software, *BMC bioinformatics*, 7, 523.

Keseler, I.M., *et al.* (2011) EcoCyc: a comprehensive database of Escherichia coli biology, *Nucleic Acids Res*, 39, D583-590.

Keshava Prasad, T.S., *et al.* (2009) Human Protein Reference Database--2009 update, *Nucleic Acids Res*, 37, D767-772.

Kinoshita, J. and Clark, T. (2007) Alzforum, *Methods in molecular biology (Clifton, N.J*, 401, 365-381.

Lee, T.J., *et al.* (2006) BioWarehouse: a bioinformatics database warehouse toolkit, *BMC bioinformatics*, 7, 170.

Lee, T.L. (2008) Big data: open-source format needed to aid wiki collaboration, *Nature*, 455, 461.

Lein, E.S., *et al.* (2007) Genome-wide atlas of gene expression in the adult mouse brain, *Nature*, 445, 168-176.

Letovsky, S.I., *et al.* (1998) GDB: the Human Genome Database, *Nucleic Acids Res*, 26, 94-99.

Li, A. (2006) Facing the challenges of data integration in biosciences, *Engineering Letters*, 13, EL_13_13_13.

Li, H., *et al.* (2009) The Sequence Alignment/Map format and SAMtools, *Bioinformatics*, 25, 2078-2079.

Lord, P., *et al.* (2004) Applying Semantic Web services to bioinformatics: Experiences gained, lessons learnt, *Semantic Web - Iswc 2004, Proceedings*, 3298, 350-364.

Maglott, D., *et al.* (2011) Entrez Gene: gene-centered information at NCBI, *Nucleic Acids Res*, 39, D52-57.

Maojo, V., *et al.* (2011) Biomedical Ontologies: Toward Scientific Debate, *Methods Inf Med*, 50, [Epub ahead of print].

Mardis, E.R. (2010) The $1,000 genome, the $100,000 analysis?, *Genome Med*, 2, 84.

Marenco, L., *et al.* (2004) QIS: A framework for biomedical database federation, *J Am Med Inform Assoc*, 11, 523-534.

Matos, E.E., *et al.* (2010) CelOWS: an ontology based framework for the provision of semantic web services related to biological models, *J Biomed Inform*, 43, 125-136.

McLean, R., *et al.* (2007) The effect of Web 2.0 on the future of medical practice and education: Darwikinian evolution or folksonomic revolution?, *Medical Journal of Australia*, 187, 174-177.

Messina, D.N. and Sonnhammer, E.L. (2009) DASher: a stand-alone protein sequence client for DAS, the Distributed Annotation System, *Bioinformatics*, 25, 1333-1334.

Mons, B., *et al.* (2008) Calling on a million minds for community annotation in WikiProteins, *Genome Biol*, 9, R89.

Neerincx, P.B. and Leunissen, J.A. (2005) Evolution of web services in bioinformatics, *Brief Bioinform*, 6, 178-188.

Noy, N.F. (2004) Semantic integration: A survey of ontology-based approaches, *Sigmod Record*, 33, 65-70.

Noy, N.F., *et al.* (2009) BioPortal: ontologies and integrated data resources at the click of a mouse, *Nucleic Acids Res*, 37, W170-173.

Oinn, T., *et al.* (2004) Taverna: a tool for the composition and enactment of bioinformatics workflows, *Bioinformatics*, 20, 3045-3054.

Olason, P.I. (2005) Integrating protein annotation resources through the Distributed Annotation System, *Nucleic acids research*, 33, W468-470.

Papazoglou, M.P., *et al.* (2008) Service-oriented computing: a research roadmap, *International Journal of Cooperative Information Systems*, 17, 223-255.

Parkinson, H., *et al.* (2011) ArrayExpress update--an archive of microarray and high-throughput sequencing-based functional genomics experiments, *Nucleic Acids Res*, 39, D1002-1004.

Pettifer, S., *et al.* (2010) The EMBRACE web service collection, *Nucleic Acids Res*, 38, W683-688.

Potthast, M., *et al.* (2008) Automatic vandalism detection in Wikipedia, *Advances in Information Retrieval*, 4956, 663-668.

Pruitt, K.D. and Maglott, D.R. (2001) RefSeq and LocusLink: NCBI gene-centered resources, *Nucleic Acids Res*, 29, 137-140.

Pruitt, K.D., *et al.* (2009) NCBI Reference Sequences: current status, policy and new initiatives, *Nucleic Acids Res*, 37, D32-36.

Reese, M.G., *et al.* (2010) A standard variation file format for human genome sequences, *Genome Biol*, 11, R88.

Rose, P.W., *et al.* (2011) The RCSB Protein Data Bank: redesigned web site and web services, *Nucleic Acids Res*, 39, D392-401.

Rubin, D.L., *et al.* (2006) National Center for Biomedical Ontology: advancing biomedicine through structured organization of scientific knowledge, *OMICS*, 10, 185-198.

Rubin, D.L., *et al.* (2008) Biomedical ontologies: a functional perspective, *Brief Bioinform*, 9, 75-90.

Ruttenberg, A., *et al.* (2007) Advancing translational research with the Semantic Web, *BMC Bioinformatics*, 8 Suppl 3, S2.

Salwinski, L., *et al.* (2004) The Database of Interacting Proteins: 2004 update, *Nucleic Acids Res*, 32, D449-451.

Salzberg, S.L. (2007) Genome re-annotation: a wiki solution?, *Genome biology*, 8, 102.

Sarkar, I.N., *et al.* (2008) Automated simultaneous analysis phylogenetics (ASAP): an enabling tool for phlyogenomics, *BMC bioinformatics*, 9, 103.

Sayers, E.W., *et al.* (2011) Database resources of the National Center for Biotechnology Information, *Nucleic Acids Res*, 39, D38-51.

Schadt, E.E., *et al.* (2010) Computational solutions to large-scale data management and analysis, *Nat Rev Genet*, 11, 647-657.

Seal, R.L., *et al.* (2011) genenames.org: the HGNC resources in 2011, *Nucleic Acids Res*, 39, D514-519.

Shah, S.P., *et al.* (2005) Atlas - a data warehouse for integrative bioinformatics, *BMC Bioinformatics*, 6, 34.

Shi, X. (2007) Semantic Web Services: An Unfulfilled Promise, *IEEE IT Professional*, 9, 42-45.

Sigrist, C.J., *et al.* (2010) PROSITE, a protein domain database for functional characterization and annotation, *Nucleic Acids Res*, 38, D161-166.

Smith, B., *et al.* (2007) The OBO Foundry: coordinated evolution of ontologies to support biomedical data integration, *Nat Biotechnol*, 25, 1251-1255.

Stehr, H., *et al.* (2010) PDBWiki: added value through community annotation of the Protein Data Bank, *Database (Oxford)*, 2010, baq009.

Stein, L. (2002) Creating a bioinformatics nation, *Nature*, 417, 119-120.

Stein, L.D. (2003) Integrating biological databases, *Nat Rev Genet*, 4, 337-345.

Stein, L.D. (2010) The case for cloud computing in genome informatics, *Genome Biol*, 11, 207.

Stevens, R., *et al.* (2000) TAMBIS: transparent access to multiple bioinformatics information sources, *Bioinformatics*, 16, 184-185.

Stevens, R.D., *et al.* (2003) myGrid: personalised bioinformatics on the information grid, *Bioinformatics (Oxford, England)*, 19 Suppl 1, i302-304.

The UniProt Consortium (2011) Ongoing and future developments at the Universal Protein Resource, *Nucleic Acids Res*, 39, D214-219.

Trissl, S., *et al.* (2005) Columba: an integrated database of proteins, structures, and annotations, *BMC Bioinformatics*, 6, 81.

Vandervalk, B.P., *et al.* (2009) Moby and Moby 2: creatures of the deep (web), *Brief Bioinform*, 10, 114-128.

Waldrop, M. (2008) Big data: Wikiomics, *Nature*, 455, 22-25.

Wilkinson, M.D. and Links, M. (2002) BioMOBY: an open source biological web services proposal, *Briefings in bioinformatics*, 3, 331-341.

Wilkinson, M.D., *et al.* (2010) SADI, SHARE, and the in silico scientific method, *BMC Bioinformatics*, 11 Suppl 12, S7.

Wilkinson, M.D., *et al.* (2008) Interoperability with Moby 1.0--it's better than sharing your toothbrush!, *Briefings in bioinformatics*, 9, 220-231.

Yager, K. (2006) Wiki ware could harness the Internet for science, *Nature*, 440, 278.

Zdobnov, E.M., *et al.* (2002) The EBI SRS server--recent developments, *Bioinformatics*, 18, 368-373.

Zhang, Z., *et al.* (2009) Bringing Web 2.0 to bioinformatics, *Brief Bioinform*, 10, 1-10.

Zhang, Z. and Townsend, J.P. (2010) The filamentous fungal gene expression database (FFGED), *Fungal Genet Biol*, 47, 199-204.

Zhao, J., *et al.* (2009) Linked data and provenance in biological data webs, *Brief Bioinform*, 10, 139-152.

3

Semantic Data Integration on Biomedical Data Using Semantic Web Technologies

Roland Kienast and Christian Baumgartner
Institute of Electrical, Electronic and Bioengineering
University for Health Sciences, Medical Informatics and Technology
Austria

1. Introduction

Contemporary life sciences research requires an understanding of systems across wide ranges of scale and distribution. Therefore, there is an urgent need to integrate biomedical knowledge generated by different communities and separate subfields (Shadbolt et al., 2006). Scientific publications and curated databases together hold a vast amount of this useable knowledge. Additionally the number, size, and complexity of life science databases continues to grow (Kei-Hoi et al., 2009). Therefore scientists in the field of genomics, proteomics, metabolomics, clinical medicine and drug discovery need a concept to integrate their data, (Shadbolt et al., 2006) which is a prominent problem (Kei-Hoi et al., 2009). But to generate such a uniform data integration concept there are still some challenges to overcome such as handling the variety and amount of available data, inconsistency with data heterogeneity from the different sources, the autonomy and differing capabilities of the sources and a lack of standards for such an integration concept. Many heterogeneity conflicts remain in data integration due to the lack of semantics (Gagnon, 2007). In order, to efficiently exploit the knowledge from different resources, it will be important to connect the sources in a manner that machine processes can traverse and intelligently identify these links (Neumann et al., 2004). A promising approach to integrate heterogeneous data sources could be the use of *Semantic Web technologies*. They provide a framework to deal with the afore mentioned problems and fulfil the requirements for machine processing.

This book chapter provides an overview of data integration on biomedical data using Semantic Web technologies including existing techniques (standards, specifications and methods), challenges, approaches and projects.

2. Basics of data integration

Data integration is the task of "combining the data residing at different sources, and providing the user with a unified view of the data" (Calì et al., 2001; 2003). But to accomplish the task of combining different heterogeneous sources there are some challenges to be overcome.

2.1 Challenges in integrating information from heterogeneous data sources

In the dictionary[1] heterogeneity is defined as *"the quality of being diverse and not comparable in kind"*. In computer science this inability to compare can be divided into four different classes (Ouksel & Sheth, 1999):

---

[1] Webster's Online Dictionary http://www.websters-online-dictionary.org

- **System heterogeneity** is a result of different hardware platforms and operation systems.

- **Syntactic heterogeneity** is a difference of data representation formats.

- **Structural heterogeneity** rises from different data models or structure in various data sources.

- **Semantic heterogeneity** results from differences in the interpretation of the meaning of different resources.

This heterogeneity leads to some challenges in integrating information from multiple data sources. Some general problems are (Cheung et al., 2007):

- **Locating Resources:** To be able to integrate data it is important to find relevant and inter-operable data sources. But to find such sources it is beneficial to have a widely accepted standard for describing the content of data.

- **Different data formats:** Different resources often provide heterogeneous data formats. For example:
    - *structured data:* e.g. different databases
    - *semi-structured data:* e.g. HTML, XML data
    - *unstructured data:* e.g text documents, images

- **Identify Synonyms and Homonyms:** Before large scale databases where created, researchers independently named biological entities. As a consequence many synonyms exist. The ability to distinguish between synonyms and homonyms is very important for data integration.

- **Detect Ambiguity:** Different terms can be used to represent different concepts. For example the term *insulin* can represent the concept *hormone* or *drug*.

- **Recognize Granularity:** Different biological data sources may provide knowledge at different levels of granularity. For example one source provides information about different genetic diseases and their symptoms. Another source might only contain detailed information about haemophilia[2].

- **Scaling conflicts:** These conflicts occur when different reference systems are used to measure a value e.g., different date formats or size measures.

2.2 Different integration approaches

There are different approaches to integrate different data sources by using *warehousing*, *mediation* or a combination of both.

Warehouse integration consists in catalouging the data from multiple sources into a local database called the *warehouse*. All queries are executed on the data contained in the warehouse (Hernandez & Kambhampati, 2004; Kugler et al., 2008; Pfeifer et al., 2007). The task of importing data from a source into the warehouse is called the *ETL (Extract - Transform - Load)* process.

- *Advantages:* Warehousing eliminates various problems such as network bottlenecks, low response times, and temporarily unavailable sources. It allows to filter, validate, modify, and annotate the data obtained from the sources (Davidson et al., 1995).

---

[2] Haemophilia is a genetic disease which interferes with blood clotting.

- *Disadvantages:* It is necessary to build and maintain the warehouse and there is a danger of antiquated data. Therefore the warehouse system must regularly check the underlying sources for new or updated data and modify the local copy of the data if required (Davidson et al., 1995).

Mediator based integration concentrates on query translation. A mediator is a system which provides a query translation from a single mediated schema to the local schema of the underlying data source (Hernandez & Kambhampati, 2004). The data flow between mediators and data sources is provided by software components called *Wrappers*. Unlike warehousing, data is not centrally stored but it is accessed directly from the distributed sources.

- *Advantages:* The data is always up to date and there is no need to maintain a storage system.

- *Disadvantages:* Mediator based integration is sensitive to network bottlenecks, low response times and temporarily unavailable sources.

An other possibility is using Semantic Web technologies. The goal of the Semantic Web approach to data integration is to add machine readable metadata to resources and to define and describe relations among them. This makes it easier to automatically process and integrate information available within the different resources (W3C, 2004a) (see figure 1).

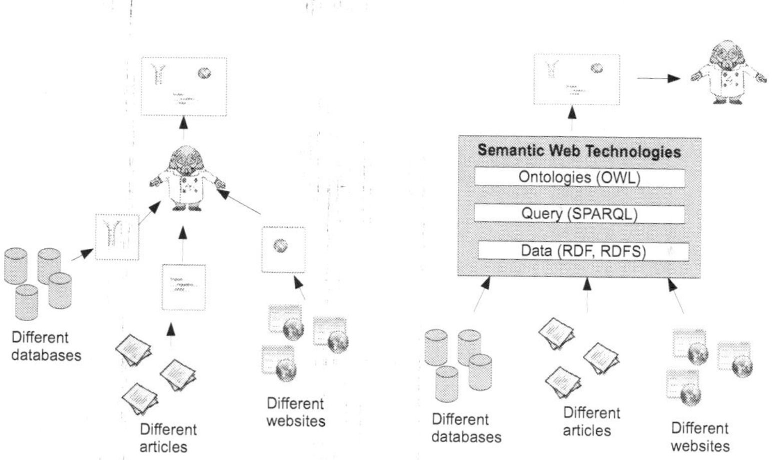

Fig. 1. The goal of data integration using Semantic Web technologies. *Right:* The user must consult several resources individually through different user interfaces to derive a result. *Left:* Semantic Web technology allows the integration of various heterogeneous resources. The system can process the data and provide the results to the user.

3. Semantic Web in a nutshell

Tim Berners-Lee , the director of the World Wide Web Consortium (W3C), coined the term Semantic Web (Berners-Lee et al., 2001) and it is mainly used to describe the model and technologies provided by the W3C which is the main international standards organization for the World Wide Web. The aim of the Semantic Web is to add structured meta-information to existing documents and data in order to give it a well defined semantic meaning. This enables machines to process semantic information but *"not human speech and writings"* (Berners-Lee et al., 2001). This semantic extension makes it easier for machines to automatically process and integrate information available on the Web (W3C, 2004a).

The basic idea behind the Semantic Web is to add machine readable metadata[3] to resources within the World Wide Web to define and describe relations among them. Semantic Web technologies are able to assimilate this gained information. Furthermore, they do not build a separate web, but function as an extension of the current web. The Semantic Web technology consists of a hierarchical use of various standards and technology in which each layer uses the capabilities of the layers below. The architecture of the semantic web is illustrated in figure 2. A brief description of each layer is summarized below:

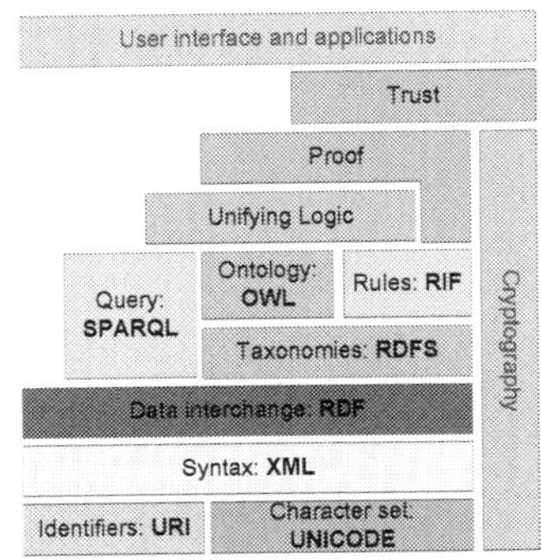

Fig. 2. Semantic Web stack

- **Character Set: UNICODE** defines a fundamental coding standard for data.

- **Identifiers: URI** is a standard for the identification of resources.

- **Syntax: XML** provides a fundamental syntax for structured documents.

- **Data interchange: RDF** is a data model for resources and relations between them. It uses the XML syntax.

- **Taxonomies: RDFS** is an extension of RDF and provides a vocabulary for describing RDF resources.

- **Rules: RIF** defines the rules of semantic data.

- **Ontologies: OWL** offers more opportunities to add semantic information to resources than RDFS.

- **Query: SPARQL** is a protocol and a query language for RDF.

- **Unifying Logic** allows to draw a conclusion.

- **Proof** attempts to verify the conclusions.

- **Trust** provides trusted principles and authentification methods between different agents.

---

[3] According to the Dictionary of Computing (`http://dictionary.reference.com/browse/meta-data`) metadata is *"definitional data that provides information about or documentation of other data managed within an application or environment."* In relation to the Semantic Web Tim Berners-Lee defines metadata as (Berners-Lee, 1997): *"machine understandable information about web resources or other thing"*. In short, metadata is data about data.

4. Semantic Web approach to data integration

The W3C defines the abilities of the Semantic Web as follows (W3C, 2011):
"The Semantic Web is about two things. It is about common formats for integration and combination of data drawn from diverse sources, where on the original Web mainly concentrated on the interchange of documents. It is also about language for recording how the data relates to real world objects. That allows a person, or a machine, to start off in one database, and then move through an unending set of databases which are connected not by wires but by being about the same thing."
Semantic Web approach to data integration can deal with heterogeneity by providing structured meta-information to existing documents and data. A key feature integrating information is the use of semantics which gives meaning to a word or concept (Gardner, 2005). Semantics can solve the problem of homonyms and synonyms between different sources because it is able to ensure the equivalence of two concepts which might have different names and forms (synonyms) or the dissimilarity of two concepts which might have the same name and form (homonyms). Semantics describe relationships between concepts. This enables a fully descriptive representation of the available information, showing the interaction between concepts and allows inferences. Semantic Web technologies provide a tool to describe such semantic: The use of *Ontologies*. In order to achieve a beneficial use of ontologies, it is important to link the data to its semantic knowledge. In other words, it is important to annotate instances to ontologies. But these data often have different data formats (relational databases, text files, web sites, etc.). Adding metadata can solve this problem. But to benefit from this metadata, it should be standardized and machine readable. Such a kind of metadata provided by the Semantic Web technology is based on the Extensible Markup Language (XML).

4.1 Important technologies for data integration in greater detail
This section describes the most important technologies which are needed for a semantic data integration based on Semantic Web technologies.

4.1.1 URI (Uniform Resource Identifiers)
A URI is defined in RFC3986 (Berners-Lee et al., 2005): *"A Uniform Resource Identifier (URI) is a compact sequence of characters that identifies an abstract or physical resource."* In the web URIs typically refer to websites or other data. But in general URIs can be used to generate unique identifiers for different resources. For example the namespaces of a XML (Extensible Markup Language) document are identified by URI references. Also, in RDF (Resource Description Framework), URIs are used to refer to resources (Hitzler et al., 2008).

4.1.2 XML (eXtensible Markup Language)
XML is a machine readable, standardized meta-language. It is an important basic technology for the Semantic Web (W3C, 2001) with which it is possible to create structured documents. These documents are text based and provide their data in a hierarchical and logically structured form which can be read by humans and by machines. It is an markup based language and uses tags for this purpose. In Informatics markup languages are used to extend parts of an document with additional information to describe it in more detail. This additional information is also called *metadata*.
Problems with XML and data integration:
XML is standardized, machine readable and defines the syntactical structure of a document. But in the view of the Semantic Web, XML tags are not much better than the natural language

(Hitzler et al., 2008). These tags can be ambiguous, their relationship is not clearly defined and they provide no meaning for machines.

4.1.3 RDF (Resource Description Framework)

Originally RDF was designed for adding metadata to web resources but it has become a framework for adding semantic information to resources. RDF is machine readable. Therefore it enables the encoding, exchange, and reuse of structured metadata and allows structured and semi-structured data to be mixed, exposed and shared across different applications(W3C, 2010a) which can make use of the semantic information (Fensel, 2004).

RDF provides a simple data model for describing relationships between resources in terms of named properties and their values. While XML can only describe documents in a tree structure, RDF is a framework for representing information about resources in the form of a directed graph. An edge of this graph describes the relationship between two resources. RDF documents can be written in Notation 3 (N3) (W3C, 2005), N-Triples (W3C, 2004d), Turtle (W3C, 2008c) syntax or in a XML syntax. This XML syntax is called RDF/XML (W3C, 2004f). But XML can only describe a tree structure whereas RDF represents a graph. Therefore it is necessary to *serialize* these complex data objects into strings. RDF uses so-called *"triples"* (3-tuples) to describe relationships between resources to serialize the graph. A RDF-triple consists of only three elements (W3C, 2004g):

1. *The subject:* Is a RDF URI reference or a blank node.

2. *The predicate:* Is a RDF URI reference.

3. *The object:* Is a RDF URI reference, a blank node or a literal.

A triple is conventionally written in the order subject, predicate, object and can be illustrated by a node and directed arc diagram (see figure 3). A set of these triples form a directed graph. A problem in RDF is that URI references can not describe a conclusive semantic interpretation

Fig. 3. Illustration of a triple

of RDF coded information (Hitzler et al., 2008) because a URI can also be a homonym or synonym of another URI. This principle is also known as *Non Unique Name Assumption*. A solution to this problem is to use thematic vocabularies such as FOAF (Friend of a Friend) vocabulary which can be used for linking people and information about them (Brickley & Miller, 2010).

4.1.4 Ontologies to share semantic information

(Gruber, 1993) defines an ontology as: *"An ontology is an explicit specification of a conceptualization."* This definition was slightly modified by (Studer et al., 1998): *"An ontology is a formal, explicit specification of a shared conceptualization."*

A *conceptualization* refers to an abstract model of a phenomenon in the world which identifies the relevant concepts of that phenomenon. *Explicit* correlates to the formed types of concepts and their limitations, which are defined explicitly. *Formal* is based on the fact that an ontology should be machine readable. *Shared* means that an ontology should cover matching knowledge. This knowledge is not limited to an individual and is accepted by a group (Fensel, 2004; Studer et al., 1998).

This abstract definition is understandable on the basis of a simple example. It contains a brief abstract of the ontology of animals (see figure 4).

The abstract model includes the terms *animal, fish, mammal* and *puma*. These terms come from

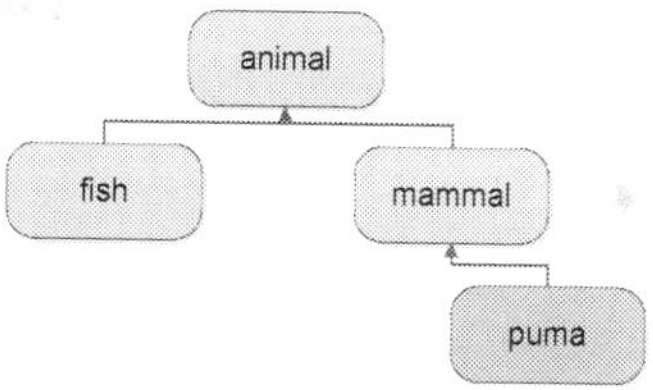

Fig. 4. A brief abstract of the ontology of animals.

the "phenomenon" of animals. Every term is explicit. The term puma is explicitly defined as a animal. It cannot be confused with the clothing brand Puma. Puma also have clear limitations: a puma is an organism which is a mammal and not a fish and belongs to the animals. An ontology is represented as a directed graph. A graph is formal and machine readable. The ontology is also shared because not only one individual can infer knowledge and it is accepted by a group of biologists.

The structure of an ontology is a directed acyclic graph. That makes it possible to support complex relationships which allow terms to have more than one parent. For example the Gene Ontology[4] term *GO:0070229 : negative regulation of lymphocyte apoptosis* is a subclass of *GO:2000107 : negative regulation of leukocyte apoptosis* and *GO:0070228 : regulation of lymphocyte apoptosis*. Ontologies are able to describe the semantic of the information sources in order to make their content explicit. A basic module of ontologies is the so called *"triple"*. Broadly defined, a triple contains two terms and a relation between them[5]. With these elements an ontology can be represented as a directed graph. The terms are the nodes and the relations are the edges of the graph (Smith et al., 2005).

4.1.5 RDFS (RDF Schema)

Like XML, RDF only provides a syntax for exchanging data. RDF properties can be considered as attributes of resources and also represent relationships between them. But it provides no mechanisms for adding a vocabulary to describing these attributes or relationships. RDFS, or also called *RDF Vocabulary Description Language*, extends RDF to describe such vocabularies (W3C, 2004c;e) and add terminological knowledge (schema knowledge) to this vocabulary. For that reason it can be seen as a semantic extension of RDF. RDF Schema vocabulary descriptions are written in RDF syntax (W3C, 2004e). It makes statements about the semantic relationship between terms within an arbitrarily defined vocabulary inside a RDFS document. This ability to define terminological knowledge allows RDFS to create *"light-weight"* ontologies (Hitzler et al., 2008; Volz et al., 2003) to describe semantic dependences within a domain.

Figure 4 shows a simple RDFS document in graph representation. RDFS organize RDF statements hierarchically into classes (terminological knowledge) and instances (assertional knowledge). Properties are used to describe relationships between classes. The terminological part includes the ontology while the assertional part presents conclusions about concrete

---

[4] see section 5.3.2

[5] see section 4.1.3 for a detailed description

qualities of the subject. This ontology describes, for example, that the class cell is a subclass of the class organ and that every cell consumes energy. Further, it is possible to derive implicit knowledge. If the muscle cell is an instance of the class cell and the ATP (Adenosine Tri-Phosphate) is an instance of high energy chemical bond, then it is possible to infer that a muscle cell is part of a human and ATP is a kind of energy.

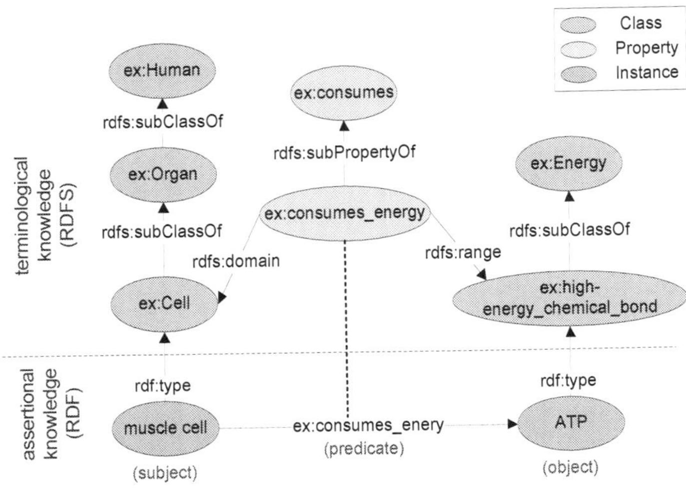

Fig. 5. Simple RDFS-Ontology in graph representation

4.1.6 OWL (Web Ontology Language)

OWL is designed to enable machine processing of information content. OWL can explicitly represent the meaning in terms of vocabularies and their relationship with each other to build an ontology. Since October 2009 the version OWL 2 is recommended from W3C(W3C, 2009a). In contrast to RDFS, OWL has more opportunities to expressing meaning and semantics. Therefore OWL can be seen as an extension of RDFS (W3C, 2004b). An OWL ontology is an RDF graph which consists as a set of triples. It also can be written in different syntactic forms but the most common syntax is RDF/XML for representing these triples.

OWL provides three increasingly expressive sub-languages (Alesso & Smith, 2006):

1. **OWL Lite** to generate a classification hierarchy and simplify constraints.   -> *Easily implementable*

2. **OWL DL** (description logic) supports maximum expressiveness while retaining computational completeness and decidability. -> *Mechanizable logic*

3. **OWL Full** provides maximum expression and syntactic freedom of RDF but with no computational guarantees. -> *Complete Logic*

Since OWL is an extension of RDFS and therefore also from RDF, any RDF document will generally be in OWL Full. OWL DL and OWL Lite also extend the RDF vocabulary, but they put restrictions on the use of this vocabulary (W3C, 2004a;b) for better machine processing. These restrictions guarantee computational completeness and decidability of reasoning systems like FaCT++ (Tsarkov & Horrocks, 2006) and the Pellet (Sirin et al., 2007) which are able to reason over OWL 2 ontologies (Grau et al., 2008). This is achieved because OWL Lite and DL are basically very expressive description logics (DL) where OWL DL is based on the $\mathcal{SHOIN}(D)DL$ (Hitzler et al., 2008) and OWL Lite to the slightly simpler $\mathcal{SHIF}(D)DL$.

Description Logics (DL) stem from semantic networks (Donini et al., 1996). They model *concepts* (equal to a class in OWL), *roles* (equal to a property in OWL) and *individuals* (equal to a object in OWL), and their *relationships*. Therefore they can be used to represent the knowledge of a specific domain in a formal and structured way. Here the context of ontologies is clearly visible. As described in 4.1.4 an ontology consists of axioms, which are used to provide information about classes and properties of a specific domain. The knowledge which is provided by DL is divided into a *TBox* and an *ABox* (Donini et al., 1996). The TBox (terminological box) contains sentences describing concept hierarchies and the ABox (assertional box) contains sentences about the individuals and where they are in the hierarchy (Van Harmelen et al., 2008). For example the statement *"Every protein is made of amino acids"* belongs to the TBox, while the statement *"Leucine is a amino acid"* belongs to the ABox.

The drawing of logical conclusions in OWL are based on the concept of the so-called *Open World Assumption (OWA)*. In contrast to the *Closed World Assumption (CWA)*, this assumption specifies that statements are neither true nor false if they can not be derived from a set of facts based on inference rules. The OWA does not assume that a answer is false unless it can be absolutely proven that the answer is false (Pollock, 2009). Listing 1 shows an example of both assumptions.

Listing 1. Example for the open- and closed world assumption

```
Knowledge Base:        The protein p53 is involved in apoptosis.
Query:                 Is the protein p53 involved in cell repair?
Answer:                    CWA: No.
                           OWA: Maybe or unknown.
```

4.1.7 SPARQL (Simple Protocol and RDF Query Language)

SPARQL is a protocol and query language for RDF which since January 2008 is an official W3C recommendation (W3C, 2008a). SPARQL queries often contain a set of triple patterns. These patterns, or also called basic graph patterns, look like RDF triples. The difference is that every subject, predicate or object, can be expressed as a variable. A match can be found by replacing variables through substituting RDF terms. If the result of the substitution is equivalent to a subgraph of the RDF data a match is found. For example, to find the meaning of the acronym *ATP* and where it is produced, the SPARQL query would look like Listing 2.

Listing 2. Simple SPARQL query

```
PREFIX ex: <http://example.com/>
SELECT ?longName ?part
WHERE
{ex:ATP ex:hasLongName   ?name.
?name    ex:producedIn    ?part}
```

The SELECT clause defines the variables which appear in the result and the WHERE clause provides the basic graph pattern. In this case the graph pattern consists of two triple patterns with two single variables.

As a simple knowledge basis following RDF data (see Listing3) in Turtle notation is used.

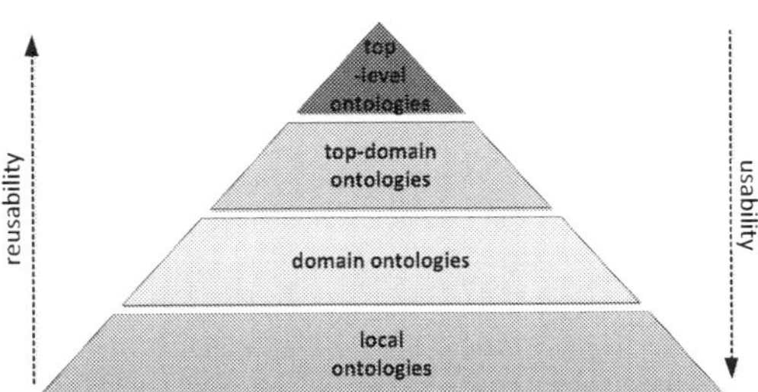

Fig. 6. Classification of ontologies. The reusability decreases with increasing specification. The availability behaves exactly opposite.

Listing 3. Simple RDF data

```
PREFIX ex: <http://example.com/cell>
ex:ATP   ex:hasLongName   "Adenosine_Tri-Phosphate"
ex:ATP   ex:producedIn    ex:mitochondrion
```

Querying this RDF 3 data with the SPARQL query 2 obtained the result shown in table 1. It

name	part
"Adenosine Tri-Phosphate"	*http://example.org/cell/mitochondrion/*

Table 1. Result of SPARQL Query 2 on RDF Data 3

is also possible to generate complex graph patterns out of a number of simple patterns or to define filters to restrict the result. SPARQL provides four query forms which form a result SELECT, ASK set or RDF graphs CONSTRUCT, DESCRIBE out of the pattern matching. To serialize a result from a SELECT or from an ASK query into a XML document the *SPARQL Variable Binding Results XML Format*(W3C, 2008b) can be used.

5. Using ontologies for data integration

Biomedical ontologies play an important role in the process of data integration and support both approaches for data integration: warehousing and meditation (Bodenreider, 2008). Ontologies are a type of controlled vocabulary that attempt to capture the knowledge of a specific domain. This is the standardization required from *warehousing approaches*, where different sources are transformed into a common format and converted to a common vocabulary. On the other hand, the *mediation-based approach* ontologies can be used for defining global schema and mapping between the global schema and local schemes of the sources to integrate. An example of a system using this approach is *ONTOFUSION* (Perez-Rey et al., 2006). The terminological part of ontologies, which contain a list of names for the entities represented in these ontologies, is also an important resource for natural language processing (Altman et al., 2008).

Based on their granularity, ontologies can be divided into four classes (see figure 6):

- **Top-level ontologies** describe very general concepts which are independent of a particular problem or domain (Guarino, 1998) and are highly reusable across specific domains.

- **Top-domain ontologies** contains core concepts of a given domain. For example: *Organism* or *Cell* for a biological domain. They work like an interface between top-level and domain ontologies (Stenzhorn et al., 2008).

- **Domain ontologies** include only domain specific concepts and therefore only describe a certain domain.

- **Local ontologies** describe the semantic of a single information resource.

The ability of ontologies to provide a map of concepts in relationships enables semantic data integration. In this context, ontologies are used to describe the semantics of the data sources in order to make their content explicit (Boury-Brisset, 2003). The integration can take place on an extremely granular level to map data from different resources, no mater if the resources contain structured or unstructured data (Gardner, 2005).

Ontology-based approaches to data integration usually provide a three-layer architecture where a semantic layer working as a mediator is between the presentation layer and the physical layer. This semantic mediator exploits mapping models and transforms queries into execution plans. Wrappers exploit the description of the data sources at the physical layer. This enables a transparent access to diverse data sources by using a unified query language (Boury-Brisset, 2003) like SPARQL. Ontologies are used in the mediator layer because they provide a common vocabulary for the integration of data, where each concept has a unique defined name, associated properties and clearly defined synonyms. Furthermore, an ontology is not a rigid structure, it can grow with time and can be connected to other ontologies. Wache (Wache et al., 2001) describes three approaches for ontology-based data integration:

- **Single ontology approach:** This approach uses only a single global ontology to integrate different sources. All information sources are related to the global ontology. The global ontology can be a combination of different specialized ontologies. This approach requires data sources with a similar view on the domain and a similar granularity. A disadvantage of this approach is that the integration of new information sources can lead to big changes in the used ontology.

- **Multiple ontologies approach:** The semantic of an source is described by its own local ontology. There is no common vocabulary and therefore inter-ontology mapping is required. An advantage of this approach is that new data sources, and their local ontologies, can be easily integrated. But the lack of common vocabulary can make the mapping between ontologies very difficult to define.

- **Hybrid approach:** This is a combination of the two preceding approaches. As with the multiple ontologies approach, resources are also described by local ontologies. But to avoid the disadvantages and to make these ontologies comparable, they are built from a shared global vocabulary. This vocabulary contains basic terms of a domain and allows querying through a shared vocabulary. The vocabulary can also be an ontology. Then it is also possible to dispense with the mapping between the local ontologies and only define mappings between the shared global ontology and the local ones. New sources can be easily added with no need to modify existing mappings.

An example of using ontologies for data integration in biomedicine is the Gene Ontology Annotation (GOA)[6] project run by the European Bioinformatics Institute (EBI). GOA is based on the single ontology approach and has as target to provide *"high quality electronic and manual"* annotations to the UniProt knowledgebase[7] (UniProtKB)(Barrell et al., 2009). For

---

[6] http://www.ebi.ac.uk/GOA
[7] http://www.ebi.ac.uk/uniprot

this purpose, GOA uses the standardized vocabulary of the Gene Ontology (GO) 5.3.2 and the International Protein Index (IPI) (Camon et al., 2004). The IPI offers complete, non redundant data sets representing the human, mouse and rat proteomes (Kersey et al., 2004).

Another advantageous feature of ontologies is that terms are organized in a hierarchical manner (Stein, 2003). That means more specific terms are specializations of more general terms. This could help to find the most specific common term shared by two data sources. An example of such a benefit could look like the following:

One research group might create a database in which gene products annotated to the *"negative regulation of T cell apoptosis"*-class of the Gene Ontology. Another group might identify gene products which negatively regulate the programmed cell death. If both groups use the terms of the GO, the two databases can be integrated by finding the most specific common term by traversing up the hierarchy (see figure 7). Without such an organized hierarchy of common concepts, the integration task comes down to tedious and error-prone work by hand (Stein, 2003).

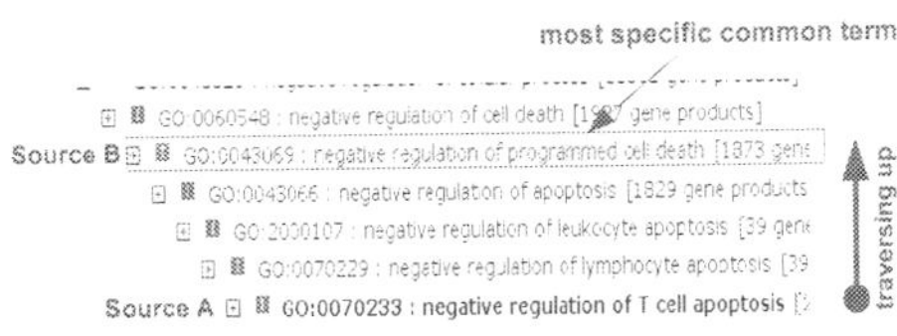

Fig. 7. Find the most specific common term by traversing up the hierarchy.
(This figure shows an extract of the Gene Ontology `http://www.geneontology.org`)

5.1 Examples of existing top-level ontologies

5.1.1 Descriptive Ontology for Linguistic and Cognitive Engineering (DOLCE)

DOLCE is the first module of the WonderWeb [8] foundational ontologies library. *"It aims at capturing the ontological categories underlying natural language and human commonsense."* (Masolo et al., 2003). The Dolce foundational ontology and its extensions provide a domain-independent framework to build ontologies on the basis of highly-reusable patterns.

5.1.2 Basic Formal Ontology (BFO)

The BFO is narrowly focused on the task of providing a genuine upper ontology which can be used in support of domain ontologies developed for scientific research, for example in biomedicine within the framework of the OBO Foundry (IFOMIS, Saarland University, 2010).

5.2 Examples of existing top-domain ontologies

5.2.1 The Unified Medical Language System (UMLS)

Having identified terminology is a key factor for data integration (Bodenreider, 2004) therefore the UMLS was developed by the National Library of Medicine (NLM)[9] and consists of three knowledge Sources which can be used separately or together (U.S. National Library of Medicine, 2010):

- **Lexical resources:** SPECIALIST lexicon: Intends to be a general English lexicon which includes many biomedical terms.

---

[8] `http://wonderweb.semanticweb.org`
[9] `http://www.nlm.nih.gov`

- **Terminological resources:** Metathesaurus: Includes biomedical and health related source vocabularies, concepts and the relationships between them.

- **Ontological resources:** Semantic Network: Contains categorization of all concepts represented in the UMLS Metathesaurus and relationships between these categories.

The *Semantic Network* (SN) can be seen as a collection of ontologies. In order to use these with Semantic Web technologies it is necessary to convert the SN to OWL DL. There are some approaches to map or convert UMLS SN to RDF (Zeng & Bodenreider, 2007), to OWL (Kashyap & Borgida, 2003; Schulz et al., 2009) or only parts to OWL (Chabalier et al., 2007). But there are formalism problems concerning this task like the complex semantics or the rich attribute set of the UMLS SN.

5.2.2 BioTop

BioTop is a top-domain ontology for the Life Sciences with the goal to provide *"an ontologically sound layer for linking and integrating various specific domain ontologies from the life sciences domain."* (Beisswanger et al., 2008).

5.3 Examples of existing domain ontologies
5.3.1 Open Biological and Biomedical Ontologies (OBO)

The OBO Foundry is a collaborative experiment involving science based ontology developers. The goal is to create orthogonal inter-operable reference ontologies in the biomedical domain (OBO Foundry, n.d.). These ontologies typically have the OBO flat file format. Like OWL, OBO is also an ontology representation languag (Richter, 2006). Ontologies based on the OBO flat file format can be bi-directionally converted to the OWL-DL format (Aranguren et al., 2007; Hoehndorf et al., 2010; Smith B. et al., 2007). The two most significant OBO are the Gene Ontology (GO), which contains the principle attributes of gene products, and the Sequence Ontology, which describes the features of biological sequences.

5.3.2 Gene Ontology (GO)

The GO project[10] contains defined terms which represent gene product properties. The GO covers three aspects of separate ontologies(Gene Ontology, n.d.):

- **Molecular function:** the elemental activities of a gene product at the molecular level, such as binding or catalysis.

- **Biological process:** operations or sets of molecular events with a defined beginning and end, pertinent to the functioning of integrated living units: cells, tissues, organs and organisms.

- **Cellular component:** the parts of a cell or its extracellular environment.

5.3.3 Sequence Ontology (SO)

The SO Project[11] contains defined terms which describe the features and properties of biological sequences. SO is a sister project of the GO and also part of OBO (Eilbeck et al., 2005).

---

[10] http://www.geneontology.org
[11] http://www.sequenceontology.org

6. Relational database integration using the Semantic Web Approach

A lot of biomedical data is available to the scientific community on the web. Much of this information is stored in a variety of different databases. The content of these databases differ from the type of biological data they provide (Baker & Cheung, 2007). For example:

- *Sequence databases* like EMBL Nucleotide Sequence Database (EBI, n.d.a) or NCBI's GenBank (NCBI, 2004).
- *Microarray gene expression databases* like the EMBL ArrayExpress Archive (EMBL-EBI, n.d.), NCBI's Gene Expression Omnibus (GEO)(NCBI, n.d.) or the Stanford Microarray Database (SMD) (Stanford University, n.d.).
- *Pathway databases* like KEGG (Kanehisa-Laboratories, n.d.) or the Human Protein Reference Database (HPRD) (Keshava Prasad et al., 2008).
- *Proteomic Databases* like the UniProt (EBI, n.d.b).

Computational analyses of biological data often require using multiple datasets. Currently, the integration of different data sets usually happens manually. This approach is very time consuming which requires integrated datasets with rich, flexible and efficient interfaces (Smith A. et al., 2007).

6.1 Problems of heterogeneous database integration

- **Technical heterogeneity** results from different access protocols, file formats, query languages and so on.
- **Data model heterogeneity** arises because of different models storing the same data.
- **Semantic heterogeneity** occurs during combination of different databases with various but related data. For example combine a gene database to a protein database. A gene may have gene products and therefore these two databases are related.

Resolving such heterogeneity and enabling database integration is a key problem which the Semantic Web aims to address (Baker & Cheung, 2007). Therefore a mapping language between RDF and relational databases called RDB2RDF is under development.

6.2 RDB2RDF

A workshop hosted by the W3C on *"RDF accesses to Relational Databases"* in October 2007 resulted in creating a RDB2RDF Incubator Group (W3C, 2010b), which operated from 2008 to 2009. The objective of this group was to create a group to develop a standardized mapping language between RDF and relational databases (W3C, 2009c). The resulting RDB2RDF working group started in 2009 with: *" The mission of the RDB2RDF Working Group, part of the Semantic Web Activity, is to standardize a language for mapping relational data and relational database schemas into RDF and OWL, tentatively called the RDB2RDF Mapping Language, R2RML."* (W3C, 2009b). The results of this working group are scheduled for release September 30th,2011.

The RDB2RDF mapping language could be used in two ways (see figure 8):

1. To extract the data from the relational database and store the content in RDF. In this case the data is physically converted to RDF in a ETL (Extract-Transform-Load) and then stored in a RDF triple store. An advantage of this approach is its easy implementation. A disadvantage is that there is always a separate copy of the relational data.

2. To generate virtual mapping between the Semantic Web technologies and the relational database. This virtual mapping queries via SPARQL which will be translated into SQL queries on the underlying relational data.

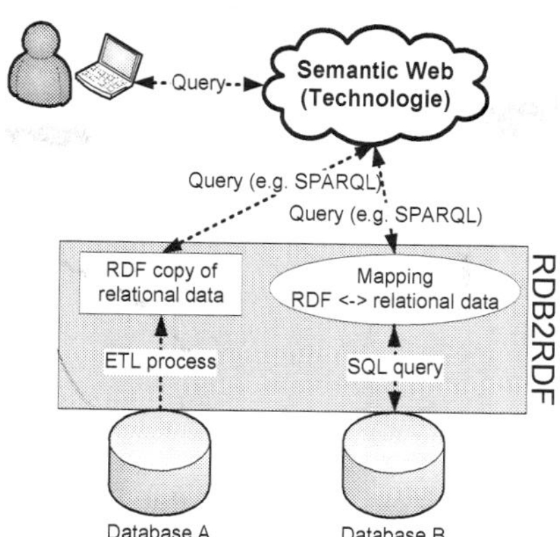

Fig. 8. Two approaches which use the RDB2RDF mapping language

7. Data integration and knowledge acquisition from biomedical literature

The quantity of biomedical literature is steadily growing with a rate of several thousand papers per week (Ananiadou et al., 2006). A large percentage of information is encoded in literature (Krallinger et al., 2008). But for a scientist it is next to impossible to read all relevant literature on a specific topic. Therefore it is important to extract semantic information out of literature to enable machine processing. This section provides an overview of how Semantic Web technologies support this task. Ontologies in particular are able to handle this influx of information and enable the data integration of biomedical literature (Spasic et al., 2005). Basic techniques to extract information from natural language are text mining (TM) and natural language processing (NLP).
Sections of TM are:

1. *Information retrieval (IR):* Retrieve of relevant documents.

2. *Information extraction (IE):* Extraction of relevant information from the document.

3. *Data mining (DM):* Discover of associations between information extracted by IE.

7.1 Information retrieval (IR)

The process of IR can be improved by adding a semantic layer. This layer formulates semantic queries, offering a higher expressive power than keyword matching (Spasic et al., 2005). However, adding semantic information to enhance the process of finding relevant information is generally a main part of Semantic Web technology. An example of such query systems are:

- **GoPubMed** (www.gopubmed.org): This system submits keywords to PubMed[12]. The resulting abstracts are matched against Gene Ontology and Medical Subject Headings (MeSH) (Doms & Schroeder, 2005) to be classified. To find a match, a term extraction algorithm based on local sequence alignment is used (Delfs et al., 2004). In other words GoPubMed organize the results of a PubMed search using the GO.

---

[12] PubMed (http://www.pubmed.gov) is a literature database provided by the National Library of Medicine and the National Institutes of Health.

- **Textpresso** (`http://www.textpresso.org`): A tool for neuroscience which has its own literature filled database. It uses a custom ontology to query nine different categories (Müller et al., 2008).

7.2 Information Extraction (IE), Data Mining (DM)

There are two ways to enhance the process of IE respectively, use TM and NLP supporting "literature data integration" based on Semantic Web technologies:

1. Ontology assisted extraction of meta-information from literature.

2. Semi-automatic or automatic engineering of ontologies by a specific domain based on information extracted from literature.

Generally, text mining is used to aid experts in extracting knowledge from a large volume of text by automatically filtering relevant information. A known problem is to find terms which represent specific classes of biomedical entities (e.g. protein names). This process is called *Named Entity Recognition* (NER). The integration of knowledge, supported by ontologies, can improve NER. The goal is to extract terms and map them to concepts of a domain specific ontology. A challenge in this process is the myriad variations of terms used to describe things in natural language. Approximately one third of term occurrences are variants (Jacquemin, 2001) and therefore only synonyms of known terms. Another problem is the specific terminology in biomedical texts. To have terminological knowledge is of vital importance to TM for characterizing knowledge in the domain. This knowledge is stored in ontologies and can enhance the process of IE by (Spasic et al., 2005):

- Using Ontology as a training set for NER by reducing it to a list of classified terms. This can be done in two ways:
    - *Passive ontology use (Ontology-based IE):* The goal of this approach is to map recognized terms in ontology concepts by look-up.
    - *Active ontology use(Ontology-driven IE):* involves ontologies directly in the process of term recognition.

- Using ontologies to improve machine learning approaches for TM tasks, such as term classification, term clustering and term relation extraction.

7.3 Semi-automatic or automatic ontology engineering

An advanced task is semi-automatic or automatic engineering of ontologies from a specific domain on the basis of information extracted from literature. Currently the development of ontologies *"is largely a manual process, based on personal experience and intuition"* (Alexopoulou et al., 2008). Two primary parts of this process are:

1. Extracting terms which represent a concept in the specific domain.

2. Finding relationships between different concepts.

For an automatic terminology development it is important to extract terms from a text. This automatic identification of possible candidates for terms is called *automatic term recognition (ATR)*. At the moment ATR is not able to fully automate the process of ontology design, but it can speed up this process by providing lists of useful domain-specific terms extracted from domain specific literature. Therefore it can support a semi-automatic creation of ontologies (Alexopoulou et al., 2008). Examples of frameworks which support ATR and further identify the semantic relations between them are:

- *Text2Onto:* This is a framework for ontology learning from textual resources. It is based on algorithms calculating the relative term frequency (Cimiano & Volker, 2005).

- *OntoLearn:* OntoLearn is based on a linguistic processor and a syntactic parser. It is able to extract syntactically plausible terminological noun phrases (Navigli & Velardi, 2004; Velardi et al., 2005).

8. Challenges in data integration using Semantic Web technologies

8.1 Uniform naming

A challenge faced by data integration is the individual naming of objects. For example a KEGG[13] entry refers to a collection of proteins involved in a pathway whereas a UniProt entry refers to a class of proteins, a class of variant proteins or some viral protein. To integrate these two resources mapping is required. One approach is to designate an authoritative names commission to manage the definitive list of such names (Stein, 2003). An example is the HUGO Gene Nomenclature Committee [14] for gene names and symbols (short-form abbreviation). But because of the dynamic in the field of biomedical research this approach rarely work in practice (Stein, 2003).

Another way could be the creation of globally unique biological identifiers. For this purpose URIs can be used which allows for the unique identifying of resources. This is central for the use of Semantic Web technologies. Therefore a process is needed which routinely assigns URIs to objects (Shadbolt et al., 2006) to create common, shared identities and names (Goble & Stevens, 2008).

8.2 Extraction of the semantic information out of existing knowledge

For efficient use of Semantic Web technologies, it would be useful to automatically or semi-automatically extract the semantic information from existing sources. Therefore a big challenge is to develop methods which support such a task. This would aid two main tasks in data integration using Semantic Web technologies:

1. **Annotate sources to existing ontologies:** This is a process which extracts information from the data source to automatically or semi-automatically annotate this source to an existing ontology.

2. **Creation process of ontologies:** This is a task which extracts information from different data sources belonging to a specific domain. The goal is to automatically or semi-automatically create an ontology based on the extracted domain information.

A large percentage of information encoded in literature (Krallinger et al., 2008) is in the form of natural language. Some approaches for such "semantic information extraction" from literature can be found in section 7.

8.3 Ontology development, maintenance and quality

Ontologies must be developed, managed and endorsed by committed practice communities (Shadbolt et al., 2006). Furthermore, an ontology is a "living structure" which means that concepts can change constantly because of new knowledge. They can be added, changed, replaced or removed. Therefore ontologies are not fixed for all time and must be constantly maintained. Another problem is the quality assurance (QA) of ontologies. According to Gruber (Gruber, 1995) design and quality criteria for ontologies should be:

---

[13] KEGG: Kyoto Encyclopedia of Genes and Genomes (`http://www.genome.jp/kegg/`)
[14] `http://www.hugo-international.org/comm_genenomenclaturecommittee.php`

1. *Clarity:* The intended meaning should be clearly defined and the definitions should be objective.

2. *Extendibility:* The effort needed to extend an ontology without invalidating it.

3. *Minimal encoding bias:* No particular symbol-level encoding should be used to specify terms.

4. *Minimal ontological commitment:* An ontology should use as few terms and relationships as possible to describe the domain being modeled.

5. *Coherence:* The content of the ontology should be coherent. In other words inferences should never contradicts a definition.

The quality of an ontology can be checked either collaboratively by users or centrally, by experts. To test the coherence of an ontology *Ontology-Reasoners* like Pellet[15] could be used. Ontology Reasoning is a process of automated logical inference of knowledge with ontologies. It is used to check the consistency of knowledge models and to infer new knowledge in accordance with the laws of logic.

8.4 Mapping, merging, alignment and integration of ontologies

Many individual ontologies are created and therefore the semantic mapping between different ontologies has become a core issue for the Semantic Web and data integration using its technology. To handle the increasing number of ontologies it is necessary to develop semi-automatic or automatic approaches (Ehrig & Sure, 2004).

The problem with the mapping of ontologies is their heterogeneity which can be divided into *metadata heterogeneity* and *instance heterogeneity* (Tang et al., 2006). Metadata heterogeneity is concerned with the intended meaning of the information held in different ontologies and deal with *structural conflicts* and *name conflicts*. Structural conflicts arise from ontologies which cover the same domain but have different taxonomies (Ehrig & Sure, 2004), and naming conflicts concern homonyms and synonyms between concepts of different ontologies. For instance heterogeneity referreds to the variation in notation different e.g. different date formats.

Merging, aligning and integration is an ontology reuse process to create a new ontology. The task of each process is as follows (Choi et al., 2006; Ding et al., 2002):

- **Merging** is the task of generating a single ontology by merging two or more different ontologies of the same domain.

- **Alignment** is a process of creating links between two ontologies when the sources are consistent but kept separate. This addresses the problem of mapping between ontologies.

- **Integration** generates a single ontology by combining two ore more different ontologies in different subjects.

Data which covers different domains can not often be described by only one ontology. Therefore it is necessary to map different ontologies. There are different strategies for mapping various ontologies:

- *Ontology mapping between a global ontology and local ontologies* (Beneventano et al., 2003): Defines mapping between concepts in local ontologies to global ontology.

- *Mapping between local ontologies:* These strategies define mapping between local ontologies.

---

[15] Pellet is a OWL 2 Reasoner for Java (`http://clarkparsia.com/pellet`).

8.5 Query RDF data

SPARQL overcomes the old problem of different, non standard query languages. Now it is possible to query RDF data using a standard query language (Quilitz & Leser, 2008). But it is important that content providers integrate SPARQL-endpoints to make their data available. Such endpoints provide a machine-friendly interface towards the knowledge base and enables queries using the SPARQL language. One challenge is to query more than just one endpoint at the same time with only one query. There are several approaches which can be divided into two groups (Haase et al., 2010; Kei-Hoi et al., 2009):

- **Warehousing:** This approach stores all RDF data from the different resources in one central database. This database is typically a *triple store* which is designed to efficiently store and handle RDF data.

- **Federated query**: A query engine decomposes a single query into sub-queries. Each of these queries can be answered by an individual endpoint. After that, all results are combined again into one and represented to the user.

Two examples of Java frameworks are *Sesame*[16] witch supports the warehouse approach and the *ARQ*[17] extension of the *Jena Ontology API*[18] which provides the federated query approach.

8.6 Visualization

The semantic integration of different resources results in increasing the amount of semantically linked data. Semantic Web technologies use RDF, defining links between data. Therefore the challenge is to create an interface to visualize and navigate a massive RDF graph without information overload. The visualization should help the user to easily explore and quickly find relevant information (Le Grand & Soto, 2002) in the structure.

8.7 Availability

There are two issues: The availability of ontologies and content. A key to integrating data using Semantic Web technologies is the availability of ontologies. Many ontologies are freely available but concerns arise if an ontology is commercial or only partially released. For example a license is necessary to access UMLS[19]. On the other side it is important to access content which is annotated to ontologies. But this may cause problems if this content is not available due to technical problems, deleted static web sites and legal restrictions, etc.

8.8 Different ontology formats

The Semantic Web defines ontologies in the OWL format. But other ontologies exists with different formats (for example the UMLS Rich Release Format (RRF) or the OBO format). Therefore, mapping must be defined to convert these different formats to OWL.

8.9 Multilingualism

A challenge is also multilingualism when using Semantic Web technologies (Börner, 2006). It plays a role in ontology development, annotation of data and representing multilingual informations in user interfaces (Benjamins et al., 2002). For example, a scenario that leads to a problem because of multilingualism:

User A annotates a document in French to *Term A* of an ontology designed in English. *User B*

---

[16] http://www.openrdf.org/

[17] http://jena.sourceforge.net/ARQ/

[18] http://jena.sourceforge.net

[19] This license is freely available for research purposes

searches for *Term A* in English and finds a document related to what he is interested in, but it is written in French.

9. Discussion

The idea behind the Semantic Web is to transform the Web into a global knowledge base (Kei-Hoi et al., 2009). The key to make this possible is data integration. Therefore Semantic Web technologies offer a more or less standardized hierarchical framework for data integration and enable a decentralized semantic integration of different heterogeneous data sources. For this integration, it is not necessary to change the structure of the data to assemble knowledge from structured and unstructured sources. This technology extends the source by adding machine readable semantic metadata using the Resource Description Framework (RDF). This metadata contains sets of relations between data and concepts. This will enable people to clearly and commonly define the concepts and logic within any document (Neumann et al., 2004). Furthermore, Semantic Web technologies support an automatic traverse of the connected resources. This queries the integrated sources or even infers new knowledge using the standard query language SPARQL. The prerequisite for meaningful semantic data integration is the presence of ontologies. They enable a unique identification of entities in heterogeneous information systems and provide semantic data integration on different granular levels. Semantic Web technologies provide standard languages including the RDF Schema (RDFS), and the Web Ontology Language (OWL) for creating ontologies. The quality of the data integration is tightly correlated with the quality of the used ontologies. But in recent years, many high quality open access biomedical ontologies have been created, such as the Gene Ontology, the Open Biological and Biomedical Ontologies.

In summary, Semantic Web technologies are a promising tool for data integration but there are still some challenges to be overcome such as uniform naming, extraction of the semantic information out of existing knowledge, ontology development, ontology maintenance or query RDF data (see section 8).

10. Additionally

A public available example software, termed *OBOBrowsA*, can be downloaded following the link `http://www.umit.at/page.cfm?vpath=departments/technik/iebe/tools/obobrowsa&switchLocale=en_US`. It is able to load and display OBO files[20] in tree or graph representation. The software further allows the user to interactively browse through the ontology, search for ontology classes and annotate textual data. The manual and application examples are included in the help function.

11. References

Alesso, H. & Smith, C. (2006). *Thinking on the Web: Berners-Lee, Gödel, and Turing*, Wiley-Interscience.

Alexopoulou, D., Wächter, T., Pickersgill, L., Eyre, C. & Schroeder, M. (2008). Terminologies for text-mining; an experiment in the lipoprotein metabolism domain, *BMC Bioinf* 9(Suppl 4): S2.

---

[20] Link to download OBO formated ontologies: `http://www.obofoundry.org`

Altman, R., Bergman, C., Blake, J., Blaschke, C., Cohen, A., Gannon, F., Grivell, L., Hahn, U., Hersh, W. & Hirschman, L. (2008). Text mining for biology-the way forward: opinions from leading scientists, *Genome Biol* 9(Suppl 2): S7.

Ananiadou, S., Kell, D. & Tsujii, J. (2006). Text mining and its potential applications in systems biology, *Trends Biotechnol* 24(12): 571–579.

Aranguren, M., Bechhofer, S., Lord, P., Sattler, U. & Stevens, R. (2007). Understanding and using the meaning of statements in a bio-ontology: recasting the gene ontology in owl, *BMC bioinformatics* 8(1): 57.

Baker, C. & Cheung, K. (2007). *Semantic Web: Revolutionizing knowledge discovery in the life sciences*, Springer Verlag.

Barrell, D., Dimmer, E., Huntley, R., Binns, D., O'Donovan, C. & Apweiler, R. (2009). The goa database in 2009–an integrated gene ontology annotation resource, *Nucleic Acids Res.* 37(Database issue): D396–D403.

Beisswanger, E., Schulz, S., Stenzhorn, H. & Hahn, U. (2008). Biotop: An upper domain ontology for the life sciences. a description of its current structure, contents and interfaces to obo ontologies, *Applied Ontology* 3(4): 205–212.

Beneventano, D., Bergamaschi, S., Guerra, F. & Vincini, M. (2003). Synthesizing an integrated ontology, *IEEE Internet Comput* 7(5): 42–51.

Benjamins, V., Contreras, J., Corcho, Ó. & Gómez-Pérez, A. (2002). Six challenges for the semantic web, *KR2002 Semantic Web Workshop*.

Berners-Lee, T. (1997). Metadata architecture, URL: http://www.w3.org/DesignIssues/Metadata. 18.03.2011.

Berners-Lee, T., Fielding, R. & Masinter, L. (2005). Uniform resource identifier (uri): Generic syntax, URL: http://tools.ietf.org/rfc/rfc3986.txt. 18.03.2011.

Berners-Lee, T., Hendler, J. & Lassila, O. (2001). The semantic web, *Sci. Am.* 284(5): 28–37.

Bodenreider, O. (2004). The unified medical language system (umls): integrating biomedical terminology, *Nucleic Acids Res.* 32(Database Issue): D267.

Bodenreider, O. (2008). Ontologies and data integration in biomedicine: Success stories and challenging issues, *in* A. Bairoch, S. Cohen-Boulakia & C. Froidevaux (eds), *Data Integration in the Life Sciences*, Vol. 5109 of *Lecture Notes in Computer Science*, Springer Berlin / Heidelberg, pp. 1–4.

Börner, K. (2006). Semantic association networks: Using semantic web technology to improve scholarly knowledge and expertise management, *in* V. Geroimenko & C. Chen (eds), *Visualizing the Semantic Web*, Springer London, pp. 183–198.

Boury-Brisset, A. (2003). Ontology-based approach for information fusion, *Proceedings of the Sixth International Conference on Information Fusion*, pp. 522–529.

Brickley, D. & Miller, L. (2010). Foaf vocabulary specification 0.98, URL: http://xmlns.com/foaf/spec/. 18.03.2011.

Calì, A., Calvanese, D., De Giacomo, G. & Lenzerini, M. (2001). Accessing data integration systems through conceptual schemas, *Conceptual Modeling - ER 2001*, Vol. 2224 of *Lecture Notes in Computer Science*, Springer Berlin / Heidelberg, pp. 270–284.

Calì, A., Calvanese, D., De Giacomo, G. & Lenzerini, M. (2003). On the expressive power of data integration systems, *in* S. Spaccapietra, S. March & Y. Kambayashi (eds), *Conceptual Modeling - ER 2002*, Vol. 2503 of *Lecture Notes in Computer Science*, Springer Berlin / Heidelberg, pp. 338–350.

Camon, E., Magrane, M., Barrell, D., Lee, V., Dimmer, E., Maslen, J., Binns, D., Harte, N., Lopez, R. & Apweiler, R. (2004). The gene ontology annotation (goa) database:

sharing knowledge in uniprot with gene ontology, *Nucleic Acids Res.* 32(Database Issue): D262–D266.

Chabalier, J., Dameron, O. & Burgun, A. (2007). Integrating and querying disease and pathway ontologies: building an owl model and using rdfs queries, *ISMB conference*, Citeseer.

Cheung, K., Smith, A., Yip, K., Baker, C. & Gerstein, M. (2007). Semantic web approach to database integration in the life sciences, *in* C. J. O. Baker & K.-H. Cheung (eds), *Semantic Web*, Springer US, pp. 11–30.

Choi, N., Song, I. & Han, H. (2006). A survey on ontology mapping, *SIGMOD Rec.* 35(3): 34–41.

Cimiano, P. & Volker, J. (2005). A framework for ontology learning and data-driven change discovery, *Proceedings of the 10th International Conference on Applications of Natural Language to Information Systems (NLDB)*, Springer, pp. 227–238.

Davidson, S., Overton, C. & Buneman, P. (1995). Challenges in integrating biological data sources, *J. Comput. Biol.* 2(4): 557–572.

Delfs, R., Doms, A., Kozlenkov, A. & Schroeder, M. (2004). Gopubmed: ontology-based literature search applied to geneontology and pubmed, *Proceedings of German Bioinformatics Conference. LNBI*, pp. 169–178.

Ding, Y., Fensel, D., Klein, M. & Omelayenko, B. (2002). The semantic web: yet another hip?, *Data Knowl Eng* 41(2-3): 205–227.

Doms, A. & Schroeder, M. (2005). Gopubmed: exploring pubmed with the gene ontology, *Nucleic Acids Res.* 33(Web Server Issue): W783–W786.

Donini, F., Lenzerini, M., Nardi, D. & Schaerf, A. (1996). *Reasoning in description logics*, Center for the Study of Language and Information, Stanford, CA, USA.

EBI (n.d.a). Embl nucleotide sequence database, URL: http://www.ebi.ac.uk/embl. 18.03.2011.

EBI (n.d.b). Uniprot, URL: http://www.ebi.ac.uk/uniprot. 18.03.2011.

Ehrig, M. & Sure, Y. (2004). Ontology mapping - an integrated approach, *in* C. Bussler, J. Davies, D. Fensel & R. Studer (eds), *The Semantic Web: Research and Applications*, Vol. 3053 of *Lecture Notes in Computer Science*, Springer Berlin / Heidelberg, pp. 76–91.

Eilbeck, K., Lewis, S., Mungall, C., Yandell, M., Stein, L., Durbin, R. & Ashburner, M. (2005). The sequence ontology: a tool for the unification of genome annotations, *Genome Biol* 6(5): R44.

EMBL-EBI (n.d.). Array express archive, URL: http://www.ebi.ac.uk/microarray-as/ae. 18.03.2011.

Fensel, D. (2004). *Ontologies: A Silver Bullet for Knowledge Management and Electronic Commerce*, Springer.

Gagnon, M. (2007). Ontology-based integration of data sources, *10th international Conference on Information Fusion, Quebec, Canada*.

Gardner, S. (2005). Ontologies and semantic data integration, *Drug Discov Today* 10(14): 1001–1007.

Gene Ontology (n.d.). An introduction to the gene ontology, URL: http://www.geneontology.org/GO.doc.shtml. 18.03.2011.

Goble, C. & Stevens, R. (2008). State of the nation in data integration for bioinformatics, *Journal of biomedical informatics* 41(5): 687–693.

Grau, B., Horrocks, I., Motik, B., Parsia, B., Patel-Schneider, P. & Sattler, U. (2008). Owl 2: The next step for owl, *Web Semantics: Science, Services and Agents on the World Wide Web* 6(4): 309–322.

Gruber, T. (1993). A translation approach to portable ontology specifications, *Knowl Acquis* 5: 199–220.

Gruber, T. (1995). Toward principles for the design of ontologies used for knowledge sharing, *Int J Hum-Comput St* 43(5): 907–928.

Guarino, N. (1998). Formal ontology in information systems, *Formal ontology in information systems: proceedings of the first international conference (FOIS'98), June 6-8, Trento, Italy*, IOS Press.

Haase, P., Mathäß, T. & Ziller, M. (2010). An evaluation of approaches to federated query processing over linked data, *Proceedings of the 6th International Conference on Semantic Systems*, ACM, pp. 1–9.

Hernandez, T. & Kambhampati, S. (2004). Integration of biological sources: current systems and challenges ahead, *SIGMOD Rec.* 33(3): 51–60.

Hitzler, P., Krötzsch, M., Rudolph, S. & Sure, Y. (2008). *Semantic Web: Grundlagen*, Springer.

Hoehndorf, R., Oellrich, A., Dumontier, M., Kelso, J., Rebholz-Schuhmann, D. & Herre, H. (2010). Relations as patterns: bridging the gap between obo and owl, *BMC Bioinf* 11(1): 441.

IFOMIS, Saarland University (2010). Basic formal ontology (bfo), URL: http://www.ifomis.org/bfo. 18.03.2011.

Jacquemin, C. (2001). *Spotting and discovering terms through natural language processing*, MIT press Cambridge, MA.

Kanehisa-Laboratories (n.d.). Kegg: Kyoto encyclopedia of genes and genomes, URL: http://www.genome.jp/kegg). 18.03.2011.

Kashyap, V. & Borgida, A. (2003). Representing the umls semantic network using owl, *The SemanticWeb - ISWC 2003*, Vol. 2870 of *Lecture Notes in Computer Science*, Springer Berlin / Heidelberg, pp. 1–16.

Kei-Hoi, C., Robert, F., Scott, M., Matthias, S., Jun, Z. & Adrian, P. (2009). A journey to semantic web query federation in the life sciences, *BMC Bioinf* 10(Suppl 10): S10.

Kersey, P., Duarte, J., Williams, A., Karavidopoulou, Y., Birney, E. & Apweiler, R. (2004). The international protein index: an integrated database for proteomics experiments, *Proteomics* 4(7): 1985–1988.

Keshava Prasad, T., Goel, R., Kandasamy, K., Keerthikumar, S., Kumar, S., Mathivanan, S., Telikicherla, D., Raju, R., Shafreen, B., Venugopal, A. et al. (2008). Human protein reference database–2009 update, *Nucleic Acids Res.* 37(Database issue): D767–D772.

Krallinger, M., Valencia, A. & Hirschman, L. (2008). Linking genes to literature: text mining, information extraction, and retrieval applications for biology, *Genome Biol* 9(Suppl 2): S8.

Kugler, K., Tejada, M., Baumgartner, C., Tilg, B., Graber, A. & Pfeifer, B. (2008). Bridging data management and knowledge discovery in the life sciences, *Open Bioinformatics Journal* 2: 28–36.

Le Grand, B. & Soto, M. (2002). Visualisation of the semantic web: Topic maps visualisation, *Sixth International Conference on Information Visualisation, 2002. Proceedings*, pp. 344–349.

Masolo, C., Borgo, S., Gangemi, A., Guarino, N. & Oltramari, A. (2003). Wonderweb deliverable d18, URL: http://www.loa-cnr.it/Papers/DOLCE2.1-FOL.pdf. 18.03.2011.

Müller, H., Rangarajan, A., Teal, T. & Sternberg, P. (2008). Textpresso for neuroscience: searching the full text of thousands of neuroscience research papers, *Neuroinformatics* 6(3): 195–204.

Navigli, R. & Velardi, P. (2004). Learning domain ontologies from document warehouses and dedicated web sites, *Comput Linguist* 30(2): 151–179.

NCBI (2004).   Genbank overview, URL: `http://www.ncbi.nlm.nih.gov/genbank/GenbankOverview.html`. 18.03.2011.

NCBI (n.d.).   Gene expression omnibus, URL: `http://www.ncbi.nlm.nih.gov/geo`. 18.03.2011.

Neumann, E., Miller, E. & Wilbanks, J. (2004). What the semantic web could do for the life sciences, *Drug Discov Today* 2(6): 228–236.

OBO Foundry (n.d.). The open biological and biomedical ontologies, URL: `http://www.obofoundry.org`. 18.03.2011.

Ouksel, A. & Sheth, A. (1999).   Semantic interoperability in global information systems, *SIGMOID Rec.* 28(1): 5–12.

Perez-Rey, D., Maojo, V., Garcia-Remesal, M., Alonso-Calvo, R., Billhardt, H., Martin-Sanchez, F. & Sousa, A. (2006).   Ontofusion: Ontology-based integration of genomic and clinical databases, *Comput Biol Med* 36(7-8): 712–730.

Pfeifer, B., Aschaber, J., Baumgartner, C., Dreiseitl, S., Modre-Osprian, R., Schreier, G. & Tilg, B. (2007). A life science data warehouse system to enable systems biology in prostate cancer, *4th International Workshop, p 9ff DILS 2007, Pennsylvania, USA.*

Pollock, J. (2009). *Semantic Web for Dummies*, For Dummies.

Quilitz, B. & Leser, U. (2008).   Querying distributed rdf data sources with sparql, *ESWC'08: Proceedings of the 5th European semantic web conference on The semantic web*, Springer-Verlag, Berlin, Heidelberg, pp. 524–538.

Richter, J. (2006).   The obo flat file format specification, version 1.2, URL: `http://www.geneontology.org/GO.format.obo-1_2.shtml`. 18.03.2011.

Schulz, S., Beisswanger, E., Van Den Hoek, L., Bodenreider, O. & Van Mulligen, E. (2009). Alignment of the umls semantic network with biotop: methodology and assessment, *Bioinformatics* 25(12): i69–i76.

Shadbolt, N., Hall, W. & Berners-Lee, T. (2006). The semantic web revisited, *IEEE Intell Syst App* 21(3): 96–101.

Sirin, E., Parsia, B., Grau, B., Kalyanpur, A. & Katz, Y. (2007).   Pellet: A practical owl-dl reasoner, *Web Semantics: science, services and agents on the World Wide Web* 5(2): 51–53.

Smith, A., Cheung, K., Yip, K., Schultz, M. & Gerstein, M. (2007). Linkhub: a semantic web system that facilitates cross-database queries and information retrieval in proteomics, *BMC Bioinf* 8(Suppl 3): S5.

Smith, B., Ashburner, M., Rosse, C., Bard, J., Bug, W., Ceusters, W., Goldberg, L., Eilbeck, K., Ireland, A., Mungall, C. & others (2007). The obo foundry coordinated evolution of ontologies to support biomedical data integration, *Nat Biotechnol* 25(11): 1251–1255.

Smith, B., Ceusters, W., Klagges, B., Köhler, J., Kumar, A., Lomax, J., Mungall, C., Neuhaus, F., Rector, A. & Rosse, C. (2005). Relations in biomedical ontologies, *Genome Biol* 5: R46.

Spasic, I., Ananiadou, S., McNaught, J. & Kumar, A. (2005). Text mining and ontologies in biomedicine: making sense of raw text, *Brief Bioinform* 6(3): 239–251.

Stanford University (n.d.). Stanford microarray database, URL: `http://smd.stanford.edu`. 18.03.2011.

Stein, L. (2003). Integrating biological databases, *Nat Rev Genet* 4(5): 337–345.

Stenzhorn, H., Schulz, S., Beißwanger, E., Hahn, U., Van Den Hoek, L. & Van Mulligen, E. (2008). Biotop and chemtop–top-domain ontologies for biology and chemistry, *7th International Semantic Web Conference (ISWC)*, Vol. 401, Citeseer.

Studer, R., Benjamins, V. & Fensel, D. (1998). Knowledge engineering: Principles and methods, *Data Knowl Eng* 25: 161–197.

Tang, J., Li, J., Liang, B., Huang, X., Li, Y. & Wang, K. (2006). Using bayesian decision for ontology mapping, *Web Semantics: Science, Services and Agents on the World Wide Web* 4(4): 243–262.

Tsarkov, D. & Horrocks, I. (2006). Fact++ description logic reasoner: System description, *in* U. Furbach & N. Shankar (eds), *Automated Reasoning*, Vol. 4130 of *Lecture Notes in Computer Science*, Springer Berlin / Heidelberg, pp. 292–297.

U.S. National Library of Medicine (2010). About the umls, URL: `http://www.nlm.nih.gov/research/umls/about_umls.html`. 18.03.2011.

Van Harmelen, F., Lifschitz, V. & Porter, B. (2008). *Handbook of knowledge representation*, Elsevier Science Ltd.

Velardi, P., Navigli, R., Cucchiarelli, A., Neri, F., Buitelaar, P., Cimiano, P. & Magnini, B. (2005). *Evaluation of OntoLearn, a methodology for automatic learning of domain ontologies*, IOS Press.

Volz, R., Oberle, D. & Studer, R. (2003). Implementing views for light-weight web ontologies, *Database Engineering and Applications Symposium, International* 0: 160–169.

W3C (2001). Xml in 10 points, URL: `http://www.w3.org/XML/1999/XML-in-10-points.html.en`. 18.03.2011.

W3C (2004a). Owl web ontology language overview, URL: `http://www.w3.org/TR/2004/REC-owl-features-20040210`. 18.03.2011.

W3C (2004b). Owl web ontology language reference, URL: `http://www.w3.org/TR/owl-ref`. 18.03.2011.

W3C (2004c). Rdf primer, URL: `http://www.w3.org/TR/2004/REC-rdf-primer-20040210`. 18.03.2011.

W3C (2004d). Rdf test cases, URL: `http://www.w3.org/TR/rdf-testcases`. 18.03.2011.

W3C (2004e). Rdf vocabulary description language 1.0: Rdf schema, URL: `http://www.w3.org/TR/rdf-schema`. 18.03.2011.

W3C (2004f). Rdf/xml syntax specification (revised), URL: `http://www.w3.org/TR/rdf-syntax-grammar`. 18.03.2011.

W3C (2004g). Resource description framework (rdf): Concepts and abstract syntax, URL: `http://www.w3.org/TR/2004/REC-rdf-concepts-20040210`. 18.03.2011.

W3C (2005). Primer: Getting into rdf & semantic web using n3, URL: `http://www.w3.org/2000/10/swap/Primer`. 18.03.2011.

W3C (2008a). Sparql protocol for rdf, URL: `http://www.w3.org/TR/rdf-sparql-protocol`. 18.03.2011.

W3C (2008b). Sparql query results xml format, URL: `http://www.w3.org/TR/rdf-sparql-XMLres`. 18.03.2011.

W3C (2008c). Turtle - terse rdf triple language, URL: `http://www.w3.org/TeamSubmission/turtle`. 18.03.2011.

W3C (2009a). Owl 2 web ontology language document overview, URL: `http://www.w3.org/TR/owl2-overview`. 18.03.2011.

W3C (2009b). Rdb2rdf working group charter, URL: `http://www.w3.org/2009/08/rdb2rdf-charter.html`. 18.03.2011.

W3C (2009c). W3c rdb2rdf incubator group report, URL: `http://www.w3.org/2005/Incubator/rdb2rdf/XGR-rdb2rdf-20090126`. 18.03.2011.

W3C (2010a). Resource description framework (rdf), URL: `http://www.w3.org/RDF`. 18.03.2011.

W3C (2010b). W3c rdb2rdf incubator group, URL: `http://www.w3.org/2005/Incubator/rdb2rdf)`. 18.03.2011.

W3C (2011). W3c semantic web activity, URL: http://www.w3.org/2001/sw. 18.03.2011.

Wache, H., Voegele, T., Visser, U., Stuckenschmidt, H., Schuster, G., Neumann, H. & Hübner, S. (2001). Ontology-based integration of information-a survey of existing approaches, *IJCAI-01 Workshop: Ontologies and Information Sharing*, Vol. 2001, Citeseer, pp. 108–117.

Zeng, K. & Bodenreider, O. (2007). Integrating the umls into an rdf-based biomedical knowledge repository, *AMIA Annu Symp Proc.*, p. 1170.

Part 3

Data Mining and Applications

4

Vector Space Information Retrieval Techniques for Bioinformatics Data Mining

Eric Sakk and Iyanuoluwa E. Odebode
Department of Computer Science, Morgan State University, Baltimore, MD
USA

1. Introduction

Information retrieval (IR) can be defined as the set of processes involved in querying a collection of objects in order to extract relevant data and information Dominich (2010); Grossman & Frieder (2004). Within this paradigm, various models ranging from deterministic to probabilistic have been applied. The goal of this chapter is to invoke a mathematical structure on bioinformatics database objects that facilitates the use of vector space techniques typically encountered in text mining and information retrieval systems Berry & Browne (2005); Langville & Meyer (2006).

Several choices and approaches exist for encoding bioinformatics data such that database objects are transformed and embedded in a linear vector space Baldi & Brunak (1998). Hence, part of the key to developing such an approach lies in invoking an algebraic structure that accurately reflects relevant features within a given database. Some attention must therefore be devoted to the numerical encoding of bioinformatics objects such that relevant biological and chemical characteristics are preserved. Furthermore, the structure must also prove useful for operations typical of data mining such as clustering, knowledge discovery and pattern classification. Under these circumstances, the vector space approach affords us the latitude to explore techniques analogous to those applied in text information retrieval Elden (2004); Feldman & Sanger (2007); Grossman & Frieder (2004).

While the methods presented in this chapter are quite general and readily applicable to various categories of bioinformatics data such as text, sequence, or structural objects, we focus this work on amino acid sequence data. Specifically, we apply the BLOCKS protein sequence database Henikoff et al. (2000); Pietrokovski et al. (1996) as the template for testing the applied techniques. It is demonstrated that the vector space approach is consistent with pattern search and classification methodologies commonly applied within the bioinformatics literature Baldi & Brunak (1998); Durbin et al. (2004); Wang et al. (2005). In addition, various subspace decomposition approaches are presented and applied to the pattern search and pattern classification problems.

To summarize, the main contribution of this work is directed towards bioinformatics data mining. We demonstrate that information measures derived from the vector space approach are consistent with and, in many cases, reduce to those typically applied in the bioinformatics literature. In addition, we apply the BLOCKS database in order to demonstrate database search and information retrieval techniques such as

- Pattern Classification

- Compositional Inferences from the Vector Space Models
- Clustering
- Knowledge Discovery

The chapter is outlined in Figure 1 as follows. Section 2 provides basic background regarding information retrieval and bioinformatics techniques applied in this work. Given this foundation, Section 3 presents various approaches to encoding bioinformatics sequence data. Section 4 then introduces the subspace decomposition methodology for the vector space approach. Finally, Section 5 develops the approach in the context of various applications listed in Figure 1.

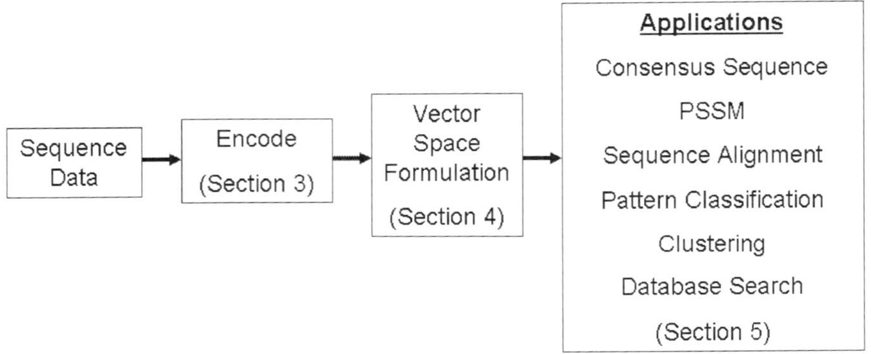

Fig. 1. Flowchart for the chapter

2. Overview and notation

Part of the goal of this chapter is to phrase the bioinformatics database mining problem in terms of vector space IR (information retrieval) techniques; hence, this section is devoted toward reviewing terms and concepts relevant to this work. In addition, definitions, mathematical notation and conventions for elements such as vectors and matrices are introduced.

2.1 Vector space approach to information retrieval

Information retrieval can be thought of as a collection of techniques designed to search through a set of objects (e.g. contained within a database, on the internet, etc) in order to extract information that is relevant to the query. Such techniques are applicable, for example, to the design of search engines, as well as performing data mining, text mining, and text categorization Berry & Browne (2005); Elden (2004); Feldman & Sanger (2007); Hand et al. (2001); Langville & Meyer (2006); Weiss et al. (2005). One specific category of this field that has proven useful for the design of search engines and constructing vector space models for text retrieval is known as Latent Semantic Indexing (LSI) Berry et al. (1999; 1995); Deerwester et al. (1990); Salton & Buckley (1990). Using the LSI approach, textual data is transformed (or *'encoded'*) into numeric vectors. Matrix analysis techniques Golub & Van Loan (1989) are then applied in order to quantify semantic relationships within the textual data.

	Document 1	Document 2	Document 3	Document 4
Term 1	1	0	1	0
Term 2	0	1	1	0
Term 3	1	1	0	1
Term 4	1	1	0	1
Term 5	1	0	1	0

Table 1. Example of a 5 × 4 term-document matrix.

Consider categorizing a set of m documents based upon the presence or absence of a list of n selected terms. Under these circumstances, an $n \times m$ term-document matrix can be constructed where each entry in the matrix might reflect the weighted frequency of occurrence of each term of interest. Table 1 provides an example; in this case, a matrix column vector defines the frequency of occurrence of each term in a given document. Such a construction immediately facilitates the application of matrix analysis for the sake of quantifying the degree of similarity between a query vector and the document vectors contained within the term-document matrix.

Given an $n \times m$ term-document matrix A, consider an $n \times 1$ vector q constructed from a query document whose components reflect the presence or absence of entries in the same list of n terms used to construct the matrix A. The question then naturally arises how one might quantify the similarity between the query vector q and the term-document matrix A. Defining such a similarity measure would immediately lead to a scoring scheme that can be used to order results from most relevant to least relevant (ie induce a *'relevance score'*).

Given the vector space approach, a natural measure of similarity arises from the inner product. Assuming an ℓ_2-norm, if both q and the columns of A have been normalized to unit magnitude, then the inner product between q and the jth column vector of A becomes

$$q^T a_j = ||q|| \, ||a_j|| \cos \theta_j = \cos \theta_j \tag{1}$$

(where the $'T'$ superscript denotes the transpose). Since all components of q and A are non-negative, all inner products will evaluate to a value such that $0 \leq \cos \theta_j \leq 1$. Similar queries approach a value of one indicating a small angle between the query and column vector, dissimilar queries approach a value of zero indicating orthogonality. This specific measure is called the *'cosine similarity'* and is abbreviated as

$$\cos \theta = q^T A \tag{2}$$

where $\cos \theta$ represents a row vector whose components quantify the *relevance* between the query and each column vector of A.

Given the vector space approach, LSI (latent semantic indexing) goes a step further in order to infer semantic dependencies that are not immediately obvious from the raw data contained in the term-document matrix. In terms of linear algebra, the LSI methodology translates into characterizing the column space of A based upon some preferred matrix decomposition. A tool commonly applied in this arena is the Singular Value Decomposition (SVD) Golub & Van Loan (1989) where the term-document matrix is factored as follows:

$$A = U \Sigma V^T \tag{3}$$

where U is an $n \times n$ orthogonal matrix (i.e. $U^{-1} = U^T$), V is an $m \times m$ orthogonal matrix (i.e. $V^{-1} = V^T$). Furthermore, Σ is an $n \times m$ diagonal matrix of singular values such that

$$\sigma_1 \geq \sigma_2 \geq \cdots \geq \sigma_r > 0 \tag{4}$$

where $r = rank(A)$ and $\sigma_i \equiv \Sigma_{ii}$. It turns out that the first r columns of U define an orthonormal basis for the column space of the matrix A. This basis defines the underlying character of the document vectors and can be used to infer linear dependencies between them. Furthermore, it is possible to expand the matrix A in terms of the SVD:

$$A = \sum_{j=1}^{r} \sigma_j u_j v_j^T \tag{5}$$

where u_j and v_j represent the jth columns of U and V. This expansion weights each product $u_j v_j^T$ by the associated singular value σ_j. Hence, if there is a substantial decreasing trend in the singular values such that $\sigma_j / \sigma_1 << 1$ for all $j > L$, one is then led to truncate the above series in order to focus on the first L terms that are responsible for a non-negligible contribution to the expansion. This truncation is called the *low rank approximation* to A:

$$A \approx \sum_{j=1}^{L} \sigma_j u_j v_j^T \tag{6}$$

The low rank approximation describes, among other aspects, the degree to which each basis vector in U contributes to the matrix A. Furthermore, the subspace defined by the first L columns of U is useful for inferring linear dependencies in the original document space.

2.2 Bioinformatics

Given this abbreviated overview of vector space approaches to information retrieval, we now put it in the context of bioinformatics research. In particular, the SVD has been applied in many contexts as it can be thought of as a deterministic version of principal component analysis Wall et al. (2003). One specific area of honorable mention is pioneering work dealing with the analysis of microarray data Alter et al. (2000a;b); Kuruvilla et al. (2004).

With regard to information retrieval and LSI in bioinformatics Done (2009); Khatri et al. (2005); Klie et al. (2008), research in this area devoted to phylogenetics and multiple sequence alignment Couto et al. (2007); Stuart & Berry (2004); Stuart, Moffett & Baker (2002) has been reported. Much of this work can be traced back to initial foundations where the encoding of protein sequences has been performed using the frequency of occurrence of amino acid k-grams Stuart, Moffett & Leader (2002). Using the k-gram approach, column vectors in the data matrix (i.e. what was previously referred to as the 'term-document matrix') are encoded amino acid sequences and their components are the frequency of occurrence of each possible k-gram within each sequence. For example, if amino acids are taken $k = 3$ at a time, then there exist $n = 20^k = 8000$ possible 3-grams. Assuming there are m amino acid sequences, the associated data matrix will be $n \times m = 8000 \times m$. For each amino acid sequence, a sliding, overlapping window of length k is used to count the frequency of occurrence of each k-gram and entered into the data matrix A.

The goal of this chapter is to build upon the IR and bioinformatics foundation in order to introduce novel perspectives on operations and computations commonly encountered in bioinformatics such as the consensus sequence, position specific scoring matrices (PSSM), database searches, pattern classification, clustering and multiple alignments. In doing so, it is our intent that the reader's view of these tools will be expanded toward novel applications beyond those presented here.

3. Sequence encoding

Many choices exist for the encoding of and weighting of entries within the term-document matrix; in addition, there exist a wide range of possibilities for matrix decompositions as well as the construction of similarity and scoring measures Elden (2004); Feldman & Sanger (2007); Hand et al. (2001); Weiss et al. (2005). The goal of this chapter is not to expand on the set of choices for the sake of text retrieval and generic data mining; instead, we must focus on techniques and approaches that are relevant to bioinformatics. Specifically, our attention in this section is devoted toward developing and presenting novel encoding schemes that preserve relevant biological and chemical properties of genomic data.

An assortment of methods have been proposed and studied for converting a protein from its amino acid sequence space into a numerical vector Bacardit et al. (2009); Baldi & Brunak (1998); Bordo & Argos (1991); Stuart, Moffett & Leader (2002). Scalar techniques generally assign a real number that relates an amino acid to some physically measurable property (e.g. - volume, charge, hydrophobicity) Andorf et al. (2002); Eisenberg et al. (1984); Kyte & Doolittle (1982); Wimley & White (1996). On the other hand, orthogonal or 'standard' vector encoding techniques Baldi & Brunak (1998) embed each amino acid into a k dimensional vector space where k is the number of symbols. For example, if $k = 20$ (as it would be for the complete amino acid alphabet), the jth amino acid where $1 \leq j \leq 20$ is represented by a 20 dimensional vector that is assigned a one at the jth position and zero in every other position. In general, standard encoding transforms a sequence of length L into an $n = Lk$ dimensional vector. As an example consider the DNA alphabet $\mathcal{A} = \{A, G, C, T\}$. In this case $k = 4$ and standard encoding transforms the alphabet symbols as

$$A = \begin{pmatrix} 1 \\ 0 \\ 0 \\ 0 \end{pmatrix}, \ G = \begin{pmatrix} 0 \\ 1 \\ 0 \\ 0 \end{pmatrix}, \ C = \begin{pmatrix} 0 \\ 0 \\ 1 \\ 0 \end{pmatrix}, \ T = \begin{pmatrix} 0 \\ 0 \\ 0 \\ 1 \end{pmatrix}. \tag{7}$$

Therefore, for an example sequence $s = AT$ with $L = 2$, this encoding method yields the following vector of dimension $n = Lk = 8$:

$$x^T = \begin{pmatrix} 1\,0\,0\,0\,0\,0\,0\,1 \end{pmatrix}.$$

Observe that, for typical values of L, assuming a data set of m sequences, standard encoding leads to an $n \times m$ data matrix that is sparse.

In bioinformatics, given the limitations on biological measurement, the number of experimental observations tends to be limited and values of m are often small with respect to n. Under these conditions, it is often the case that vector encoding methodologies lead to sparse data matrices (as is the case for text retrieval applications) in high dimensional vector spaces. Observe, for example, that the k-gram method reviewed in Section 2.2 fits this description.

We can expand upon the standard encoding approach by categorizing the standard amino acid alphabet into families that take into account physical and chemical characteristics derived from the literature Andorf et al. (2002); Baldi & Brunak (1998). In addition, entries within the data matrix can be weighted based upon their hydrophobicity Eisenberg et al. (1984); Kyte & Doolittle (1982). Table 2 introduces alphabet symbols used to group amino acids according to hydrophobicity, charge and volume. Tables 3-5 show examples of various encoding schemes that we apply for this analysis.

Hydrophobicity	R=hydrophobic, H=hydrophilic
Charge	P=positive, N=negative, U=uncharged
Volume	S=smal, M=medium, ML=medium-large, L=medium

Table 2. Encoding symbols applied in Tables 3-5

R	1	A, I, L, M, F, P, W, V, D, E
H	3	R, H, K, N, C, Q, G, S, T, Y

Table 3. Hydrophobic/Hydrophilic Encoding

RU	1	A, I, L, M, F, P, W, V
HN	2	D, E
HP	3	R, H, K
HU	4	N, C, Q, G, S, T, Y

Table 4. Charged Hydrophobic/Hydrophilic Encoding

RUS	1	A
RUM	2	F
RUML	3	I, L, M, V
RUL	4	F, W
HPML	5	R, H, K
HNM	6	D
HNML	7	E
HUS	8	G, S
HUM	9	N, C, V
HUML	10	Q
HUL	11	Y

Table 5. Volume/Charged Hydrophobic/Hydrophilic Encoding

4. Subspace decompositions for pattern classification

LSI techniques necessarily require the application of matrix decompositions such as the SVD to infer column vector dependencies in the data matrix. Decompositions of this kind can lead to the construction of subspaces that can mathematically categorize subsets of sequences into families. Furthermore, since these families define specific classes of data, they can be used as training data in order to perform database searches and pattern classification. The application of linear subspaces for the sake of pattern classification Oja (1983) consists of applying orthogonal projection operators based upon the training classes (an orthogonal projection operator P obeys $P = P^T$ and $P^2 = P$).

4.1 Orthogonal projections

To begin, let us assume there are training sequences of known classification that can be categorized into M distinct classes and that the ith class contains m_i encoded vectors of dimension n. For each class, an $n \times m_i$ matrix A_i can be constructed (assuming the training vectors are column vectors). To characterize the linear subspace generated by each class, we can apply the singular value decomposition (SVD) Golub & Van Loan (1989). In addition to providing us with an orthonormal basis for each class, we can also glean some information about the influence of the singular values and singular vectors from the rank approximants. Class data matrices are therefore decomposed as

$$A_i = U_i \Sigma_i V_i^T \tag{8}$$

where U_i is $n \times n$ orthogonal matrix, Σ_i is $n \times m_i$ whose diagonal contains the singular values and V_i is an $m_i \times m_i$ orthogonal matrix. Assume the rank of each data matrix A_i is r_i and let Q_i denote the $n \times r_i$ matrix formed from first r_i columns of U_i. Given the properties of the SVD, the columns of Q_i define an orthonormal basis for the column space of A_i. Hence, an orthogonal projection operator for the ith class is established by computing

$$P_i = Q_i Q_i^T. \tag{9}$$

(given that the SVD induces $U_i^T = U_i^{-1}$, it is straightforward to check that $P_i^2 = P_i$ and $P_i^T = P_i$).

Consider an $n \times 1$ query vector x whose classification is unknown. The class membership of x can be ascertained by identifying the class yielding the maximum projection norm:

$$C(x) \equiv \underset{i=1,\cdots,M}{\arg\max} ||P_i x||. \tag{10}$$

One computational convenience of constructing the orthonormal bases Q_i is that it is not necessary to compute the projections when making this decision. Given any Q with orthonormal columns and orthogonal projection $P = QQ^T$ such that $P^2 = P$ and $P = P^T$, observe that

$$||Px||^2 = x^T P^T P x = x^T P^2 x$$

$$= x^T P x = x^T Q Q^T x \tag{11}$$

$$= ||Q^T x||^2 = ||x^T Q||^2.$$

Under these circumstances, to decide class membership, Equation (10) reduces to

$$C(x) \equiv \underset{i=1,\cdots,M}{\arg\max} ||x^T Q_i||. \tag{12}$$

Furthermore, the values $||x^T Q_i||$ immediately yield relevance scores and confidence measures for each class.

4.2 Characterization of the orthogonal complement

It is important to note that the union of all the class subspaces *need not* be equal to the n dimensional vector space from which all data vectors are derived. To perform a complete orthogonal decomposition of the n dimensional vector space in terms of the data, we first define the matrix

$$A \equiv [A_1 \cdots A_M].\tag{13}$$

The goal then is to characterize the null space $\mathcal{N}(A^T)$, the subspace which is orthogonal to the column space of A. Assuming the rank of A is r_A, computing the SVD

$$A = U_A \Sigma_A V_A^T \tag{14}$$

and forming the matrix Q_A from the the first r_A columns of U_A yields an orthogonal decomposition of the subspace generated by **all** class vectors. Hence, a projection operator for this subspace is constructed as

$$P_A = Q_A Q_A^T.\tag{15}$$

In addition, a projection for the orthogonal complement $\mathcal{N}(Q_A^T)$ of A is then easily formed via

$$P_{A\perp} = I_n - P_A \tag{16}$$

where I_n is the $n \times n$ identity matrix. A complete orthogonal decomposition Lay (2005) of a vector $x \in \mathcal{R}^n$ can then be determined from

$$x = P_A x + P_{A\perp} x.\tag{17}$$

4.3 Information retrieval

Before attempting to decide the class membership of a vector $x \in \mathcal{R}^n$ based upon Equation (12), it is sensible to characterize the portion of the vector that contributes to the class subspace defined by Q_A. Given Equation (17), this is most easily done by comparing $||P_A x||$ with $||P_{A\perp} x||$ as

$$\tan(\phi) = \frac{||P_{A\perp} x||}{||P_A x||}\tag{18}$$

where ϕ is the angle between x and the subspace defined by Q_A. Ideally, if the class subspaces have been completely characterized, $\tan(\phi)$ should be small. Conversely, larger values of $\tan(\phi)$ would indicate that x is a member of a class subspace that has not yet been defined. Under these circumstances, the orthogonal complement would have to be further characterized and partitioned in order to define more classes beyond the known M existing classes.

It is also possible to phrase the tangent measure as a scalar version of the more familiar cosine similarity defined above in Equation (2). If $||x|| = 1$, the cosine similarity measure takes on a convenient form

$$\cos(\phi) = ||x^T Q_A||.\tag{19}$$

To see why, consider the inner product

$$x^T(P_A x) = x \cdot P_A x = ||x|| \, ||P_A x|| \cos(\phi).\tag{20}$$

If $||x|| = 1$, then

$$\cos(\phi) = \frac{x^T P_A x}{||P_A x||}.\tag{21}$$

However, since P_A is an orthogonal projection

$$||P_A x|| = \sqrt{x^T P_A^T P_A x} = \sqrt{x^T P_A x} \tag{22}$$

and Equation (21) can therefore be rewritten as

$$\cos(\phi) = \sqrt{x^T P_A x}. \tag{23}$$

On the other hand, by applying Equation (11) to Equation (22), it follows that

$$||x^T Q_A|| = \sqrt{x^T P_A x} \tag{24}$$

as well; hence, the equality of Equations (23) and (24) establishes Equation (19). Equation (19) should also be clear from the geometric fact that

$$\cos(\phi) = \frac{||P_A x||}{||x||}. \tag{25}$$

Assuming $||x|| = 1$, Equation (19) then easily follows by applying Equation (11) to Equation (25). Equations (23) and (24) are presented in order to offer additional insight by relating the inner product to the projection operator.

Of central focus in the next section will be to apply the above projection framework to information retrieval in bioinformatics. Since the classification problem will be of significance, we note that, given the identity in Equation (19), Equation (12) can be rephrased in term of the cosine similarity measure

$$C(x) \equiv \arg\max_{i=1,\cdots,M} \cos(\phi_i) \tag{26}$$

where

$$\cos(\phi_i) \equiv ||x^T Q_i||. \tag{27}$$

In addition, this measure of class membership becomes more reliable if the contribution of x to the orthogonal complement of the data set is small. For instance, when ϕ is small, $cos(\phi)$ in Equation (19) approaches unity. Therefore, $\cos(\phi)$ can be applied as a measure of data set reliability while $\cos(\phi_i)$ can be used to produce relevance scores for $i = 1, \cdots, M$. These conclusions are summarized in Table 6.

Similarity Measure	Purpose	Reference
$\cos(\phi)$	Data Set Reliability	Equation (19)
$\cos(\phi_i)$	Relevance Score	Equations (26) - (27)

Table 6. Reliability and relevance measures to be applied in Section 5

.

5. Applications

In bioinformatics, families with similar biological function are often formed from sets of protein or nucleic acid sequences. For example, databases such as Pfam Finn et al. (2010), PROSITE Sigrist et al. (2010) and BLOCKS Pietrokovski et al. (1996) categorize sequence domains of similar function into distinct classes. Given the encodings discussed in Section 3, we seek to demonstrate how Equations (19) and (26) can applied in order to perform sequence modeling, pattern classification and database search computations typically encountered in bioinformatics Baxevanis & Ouellette (2005); Durbin et al. (2004); Mount (2004).

5.1 Consensus sequence

A set of m sequences of length L having some related function (e.g. DNA promoter sites for a common sigma factor) is often represented in the form of an $m \times L$ matrix where each column refers to a common position in each sequence. A consensus sequence s_C of length L is constructed by extracting the symbol having the highest frequency in each column. This approach to sequence model construction, while quite rudimentary, is often useful for visualizing obvious qualitative relationships amongst sequence elements.

Using the vector space approach, it is possible to recover the consensus sequence. Assuming each sequence symbol is encoded into a k dimensional vector, each sequence will be encoded into a vector of length $n = Lk$ (see Section 3). Hence the original $m \times L$ matrix of sequences will be transformed into an $n \times m$ data matrix of the form described in Section 2.1. In this case, each column vector in the data matrix represents an encoded amino acid sequence.

To recover the consensus, it is useful to introduce notation for describing an empirically derived average vector μ_A from an $n \times m$ data matrix A as follows:

$$\mu_A \equiv \left(\frac{1}{m}\right) A \mathbf{e} \tag{28}$$

where $\mathbf{e}$ and $m \times 1$ vector of ones. Then, μ_A is an $n \times 1$ column vector made up of L contiguous 'subvectors' of dimension k where the value of k depends upon the encoding method applied. Let v_i for $i = 1, \cdots, L$ represent each subvector in μ_A; then, the ith symbol in the consensus sequence $s_C(i)$ can be inferred by associating the component of v_i yielding the highest average with the originally encoded symbol. To be precise, let the alphabet of k sequence symbols (e.g. DNA, amino acids, structural, text, etc) be defined as

$$\mathcal{A} \equiv \{a_1, a_2, \cdots, a_k\} \tag{29}$$

and let the jth component of v_i be written as v_{ij} for $j = 1, \cdots, k$. The subscript index of the component with the maximum average in v_i can therefore be extracted as

$$J = \arg\max_{j=1,\cdots,k} v_{ij} \tag{30}$$

and the associated alphabet symbol is entered into the ith position of the consensus sequence as

$$s_C(i) = a_J \tag{31}$$

where $a_J \in \mathcal{A}$. The algorithm for recovering the consensus sequence can be summarized as follows:

1. Given the $n \times m$ encoded data matrix A, compute μ_A.

2. For each v_i where $i = 1, \cdots, L$, apply Equation (30).

3. Given the alphabet $\mathcal{A}$, apply Equation (31) in order to construct the consensus sequence s_C.

5.2 Position specific scoring matrix

The consensus sequence, while qualitatively useful, is an incomplete sequence model in that it does not consider cases where two or more symbols in a given position are close to equiprobable. Under these circumstances, one is forced to arbitrarily choose one symbol for the consensus at the expense of loosing information about the other symbols. In contrast, the position specific scoring matrix (PSSM) is a sequence model that considers the frequency of occurrence of all symbols in each position. Furthermore, the PSSM can be used to score and rank sequences of unknown function in order to quantify their similarity to the sequence model.

Given an $m \times L$ matrix of of m related sequences of length L and an alphabet of k symbols, a $k \times L$ 'profile' matrix of empirical probabilities is first constructed by computing the symbol frequency for each position. The profile matrix can be thought of as the preimage of the PSSM. While it can provide important statistical details regarding the sequence model, it does not have the capability to score sequences in an additive fashion position by position. To do this requires converting the profile into a $k \times L$ PSSM of additive information scores. Given a sequence s of length L, the PSSM can then be used to compute a score for s in order to determine its relationship to the sequence model.

Recovering the PSSM from the vector space approach is straightforward. Given an $n \times m$ data matrix of encoded sequences, the ith subvector v_i in the average vector μ_A computed from Equation (28) is equivalent to the ith column in the $k \times L$ profile matrix. Simply reshaping the $kL \times 1$ vector μ_A into a $k \times L$ matrix recovers the profile. However, since the goal is to score sequences of unknown function, we are more interested in showing how μ_A can be applied to recover a PSSM score. Assume that the components of μ_A have been transformed by applying the same information measure $\mathcal{I}_{PSSM}$ used to convert the profile to the PSSM. Assuming an encoding alphabet with k symbols, a query sequence s of length L can be encoded to form a $kL \times 1$ vector x. The PSSM score S_{PSSM} of x can then be recovered via the inner product:

$$S_{PSSM} = x^T \mathcal{I}_{PSSM}(\mu_A) \tag{32}$$

where $\mathcal{I}_{PSSM}(\mu_A)$ represents the conversion of a probability vector into an vector of additive information scores.

The similarity of Equation (32) with Equation (2) is worth noting. Assume several families of sequences of equal length L are encoded into separate data matrices A_i where $i = 1, \cdots, M$ and M is the number of families. It should be clear that the relevance score for the query vector x can be produced using the cosine similarity according to

$$S_{PSSM} = x^T \mathcal{I}_{PSSM} \tag{33}$$

where

$$\mathcal{I}_{PSSM} = \left[\mathcal{I}_{PSSM}(\mu_{A_1}) \; \mathcal{I}_{PSSM}(\mu_{A_2}) \; \cdots \; \mathcal{I}_{PSSM}(\mu_{A_M}) \right] \tag{34}$$

is the $n \times M$ information matrix that describes the sequence families.

It is of important theoretical interest that the vector space approach recovers both the PSSM and its information capacity to score sequences. However, it is more useful to observe that invoking an algebraic structure on a set of sequences induces a spectrum of novel possibilities. For instance, the SVD can be applied to the data matrix and a scoring scheme can be derived from the computed orthogonal basis. In addition, as mentioned at the end of Section 3, it is possible to weight both the data matrix and the encoded sequence according to more biologically significant measures such as hydrophobicity. Finally, and probably most importantly, the vector space formulation allows for powerful optimization techniques Golub & Van Loan (1989); Luenberger (1969) to be applied in order to maximize the scoring capacity of the sequence model.

5.3 Clustering

Our goal in this section is to investigate how clustering encoded sets of vectors will partition an existing set of data. While there are several approaches to performing data clustering Theodoridis & Koutroumbas (2003), we choose to invoke techniques that characterize the mean behavior of a data cluster. Specifically, we analyze one supervised method (Section 5.3.2) and one unsupervised method (Section 5.3.3). As we shall see, these approaches will enable us to construct 'fuzzy' regular expressions capable of algebraically describing the behavior of a given data set. It will become clear that this approach will offer additional insight to sequence clustering techniques typically encountered in the literature Henikoff & Henikoff (1991); Smith et al. (1990). As the BLOCKS database Henikoff et al. (2000); Pietrokovski et al. (1996) has been constructed from sequence clusters using ungapped multiple alignment, we choose to apply this database as the template in order to compare it against the vector space model.

5.3.1 The BLOCKS database

The BLOCKS database consists of approximately 3000 protein families (or 'blocks'). Each family has a varying number of sequences that have been derived from ungapped alignments. Therefore, while sequence lengths between two different families may differ, sequences contained within each family, by the definition of a 'block', must all have the same length. Furthermore, the number of sequences in each family can vary and there is can be a considerable degree of redundancy within some families; hence, it is sensible to analyze how the data is distributed with respect to each BLOCKS family.

The histogram in Figure 2 illustrates the number of BLOCKS families as function of sequence length. For example, there are 90 families containing sequences of length $L = 40$. From this figure, we can conclude that it is generally possible to find at least 40 families containing nominal sequence lengths. It is also important to characterize how the number of sequences contained within each family is distributed throughout the database. The histogram in Figure 3 illustrates the number of BLOCKS families as function of the number of sequences contained within each family. From this figure, we observe that many families contain somewhere between 9 and 20 representative sequences. Finally, for the sake of clarity, we restrict our attention to sequences having the same lengths. The extension of these results to variable length sequences is the subject of current research based upon existing methodologies cited in the literature Couto et al. (2007); T. Rodrigues (2004). The histogram in Figure 4 illustrates the number of BLOCKS families as function of the number of sequences contained within in each family; however, observe that this representative sample has been restricted to those families containing sequences of equal length (in this case $L = 30$). The behavior in this graph is typical in that most families contain on the order of 10-12 sequences of equal length. For the purposes of illustration and without loss of generality, we choose to demonstrate the techniques in the upcoming sections using families containing sequences of equal length.

5.3.2 Centroid approach

In this section, we cluster sequences whose BLOCKS classification is known a priori in order to algebraically characterize each family. To do this, each family in the analysis is encoded separately and Equation (28) is applied to each family data matrix in order to derive a family centroid. Since the families are already partitioned, this approach is a supervised clustering technique that will enable us to derive symbol contributions from the centroid vectors.

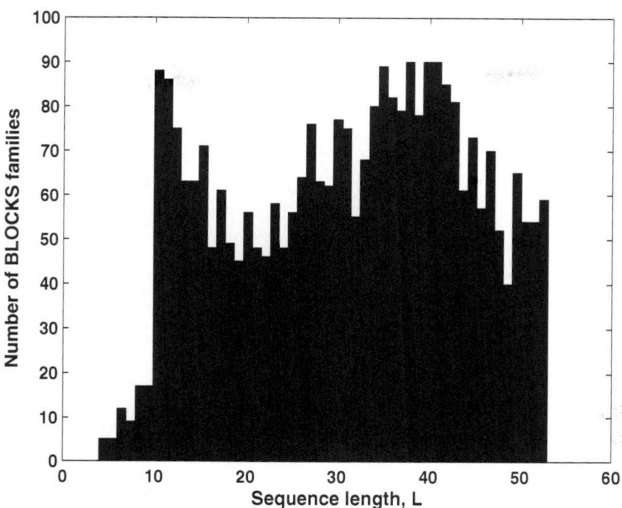

Fig. 2. Histogram of the number of BLOCKS families as function of sequence length.

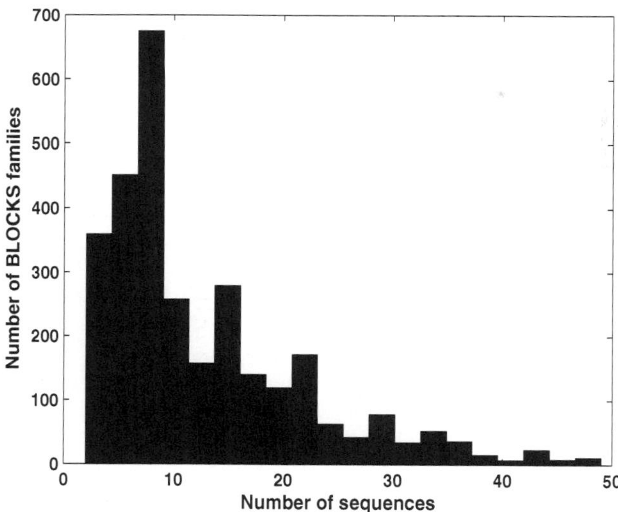

Fig. 3. Histogram of the number of BLOCKS families as function of the number of sequences contained in each family.

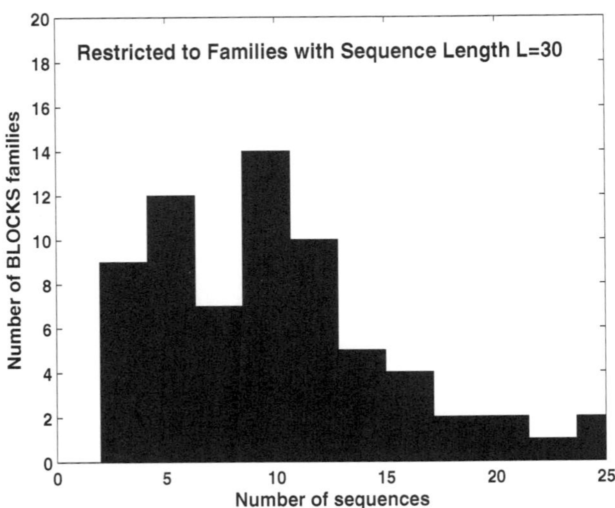

Fig. 4. Histogram of the number of BLOCKS families as function of the number of sequences contained in each family (restricted to families with sequences of length L=30)

For this numerical experiment, we apply Table 5 as the encoding scheme and choose the BLOCKS family sequence length to be $L = 30$. Under these conditions, sequences will be encoded into column vectors of dimension $n = (30)(11) = 330$. In addition, all encoded data vectors are normalized to have unit magnitude.

There are 73 families in the BLOCKS database that have block length $L = 30$. Furthermore, there are a total of 910 sequences distributed amongst the 73 families. As mentioned above, there is a small degree of sequence redundancy within some BLOCKS families. After removing redundant sequences, a total of $J = 755$ sequences of length $L = 30$ are distributed amongst $I = 73$ families. Given the encoding method, the dimensions of the non-redundant data matrix A will be 330×755.

Figure 5 shows the results of computing the distance between all centroids. From this histogram, we observe that database families are fairly well-separated since the minimum distance between any two centroids is greater than 0.6.

In order to analyze the performance of the encoding method, we apply the inner product. Specifically, each data vector v_j is classified by choosing the family associated with the centroid yielding the largest inner product:

$$C(v_j) \equiv \arg\max_{i=1,\cdots,I} v_j^T \mathcal{M}. \tag{35}$$

where $j = 1, \cdots, J$ and

$$\mathcal{M} = \begin{bmatrix} \mu_{A_1} & \mu_{A_2} & \cdots & \mu_{A_I} \end{bmatrix} \tag{36}$$

For standard encoding (i.e. $k = 20$, $n = 600$), all 755 data vectors were classified correctly using Equation (35). On the other hand, when applying the encoding method in Table 5, there

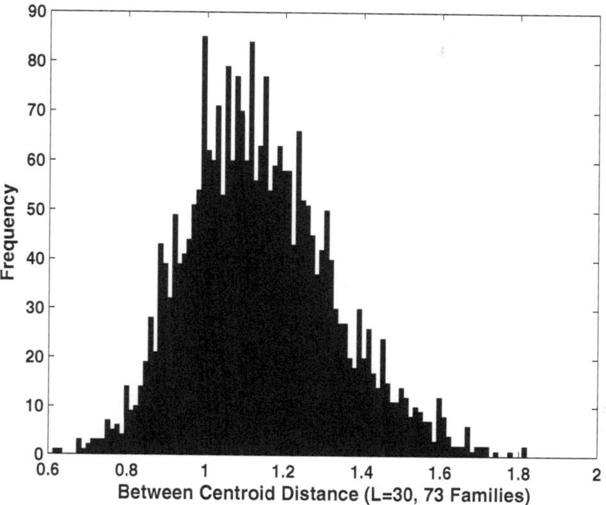

Fig. 5. Histogram of between centroid distance.

was one misclassification. Figure 6 illustrates that data vector number 431 (which as member of family 30, 'HlyD family secretion proteins') was misclassified into family 54 (Osteopontin proteins). So, while the vector dimension is reduced from 600 to 330 (because k is reduced from 20 to 11), a minor cost in classification accuracy is incurred. At the same time, we observe a substantial reduction in dimensionality.

We note one final application of the centroid approach for deriving 'fuzzy' regular expressions extracted from the vector components of the centroid vectors. Consider the sum normalized i^{th} family centroid

$$\mathcal{N}_{A_i} \equiv \left(\frac{1}{\sum_{j=1}^{n} (\mu_{A_i})_j} \right) \mu_{A_i}. \tag{37}$$

For each subvector associated with each sequence position in $\mathcal{N}_{A_i}$, it is then possible to write an expression describing the percentage contribution of each symbol to analytically characterize the ith sequence family.

5.3.3 K-means approach

In contrast to the supervised approach, we now wish to take all sequences of length L in the database and investigate how they are clustered when the unsupervised K-means algorithm is applied. When this algorithm is applied to small numbers of families (e.g. < 10), our results indicate that this algorithm will accurately determine the sequence families for the encoding method presented. However, as the number of data vectors grow, the high-dimensionality of the encoding method tends to obscure distances and, hence, can obscure the clusters. We briefly address this issue in the conclusions section of this chapter.

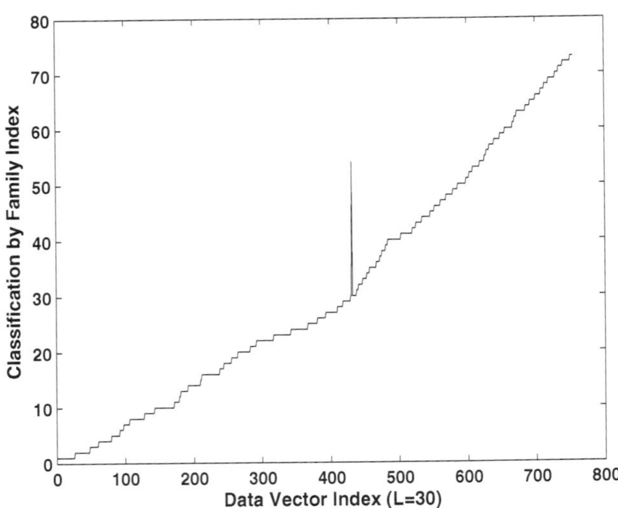

Fig. 6. Family classification of each data vector.

5.4 Database search and pattern classification

We now come to what is arguably one of the most important applications in this chapter. In this section, we will apply the reliability and relevance measures summarized in Table 6 to perform BLOCKS database searches and pattern classification Bishop (2006); Hand et al. (2001).

5.4.1 Characterization of BLOCKS orthogonal complement

When constructing a database, it is critical to understand and analytically characterize the spectrum of objects *not* contained within the database. This task is easily achieved by considering the orthogonal complement. As first step, we consider families with sequence lengths $L = 15$ (70 families) and $L = 30$ (73 families). Furthermore, we compare encodings from Table 3 and Table 5 with standard encoding. Specifically, for each encoding method, an $n \times m$ non-redundant data matrix A consisting of all data vectors of from all families with sequence length L is constructed. The SVD is then applied to construct an orthogonal basis Q_A for the column space of A. The rank r of A ($r=\mathcal{D}[Q_A]$) and the dimension of the null space of A are then compared ($\mathcal{D}[\mathcal{N}(Q_A^T)]$). Using this approach, it is then possible to assess the quantity $n - \mathcal{D}[Q_A]$ to determine the size of the subspace left uncharacterized by the database. Table 7 summarizes the results. From this table, it is clear that, after redundant encoded vectors are removed, the BLOCKS database thoroughly spans the pattern space. Furthermore, the histogram in Figure 5 further indicates that, while the sequence subspace is well represented, there is also a good degree of separation between the family classes.

5.4.2 Pattern classification

Another important database characterization is to examine how the projection method classifies data vectors after the class subspace bases have been constructed using the SVD.

renewcommand11.2

Sequence Length	Encoding Method	n	m	$\mathcal{D}[Q_A]$	$\mathcal{D}[\mathcal{N}(Q_A^T)]$
$L = 15$	Standard	300	949	286	14
$L = 15$	Table 5	165	949	165	0
$L = 15$	Table 3	30	936	30	0
$L = 30$	Standard	600	785	576	13
$L = 30$	Table 5	330	785	330	0
$L = 30$	Table 3	60	774	60	0

Table 7. Characterization of BLOCKS orthogonal complement for various sequence lengths and encodings

In a manner similar to Figure 6, we classify all encoded data vectors in order to determine their family membership by applying Equation (26). Figures 7 - 8 show results where the $L = 15$ and $L = 30$ cases have been tested. For the $L = 15$ case, as the vector space dimension decreases more classification errors arise since a reduced encoding will result in more non-unique vectors. The $L = 30$ case leads to longer vectors, hence, it is more robust to reduced encodings.

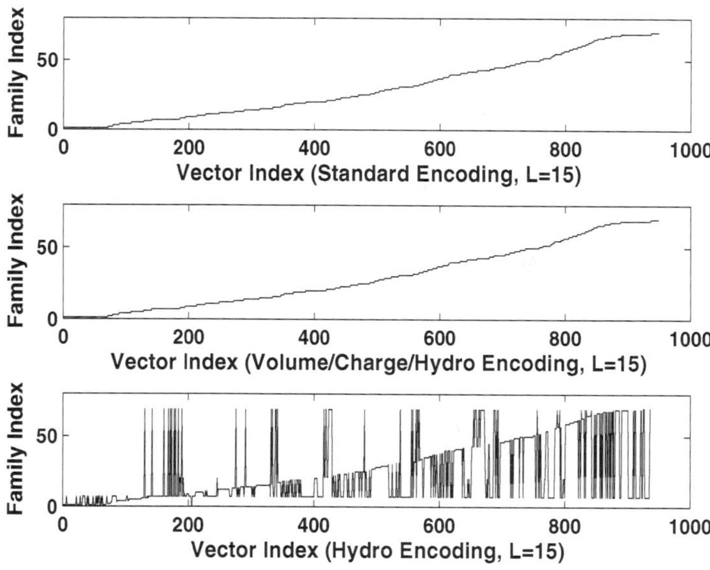

Fig. 7. Family classification of each data vector.

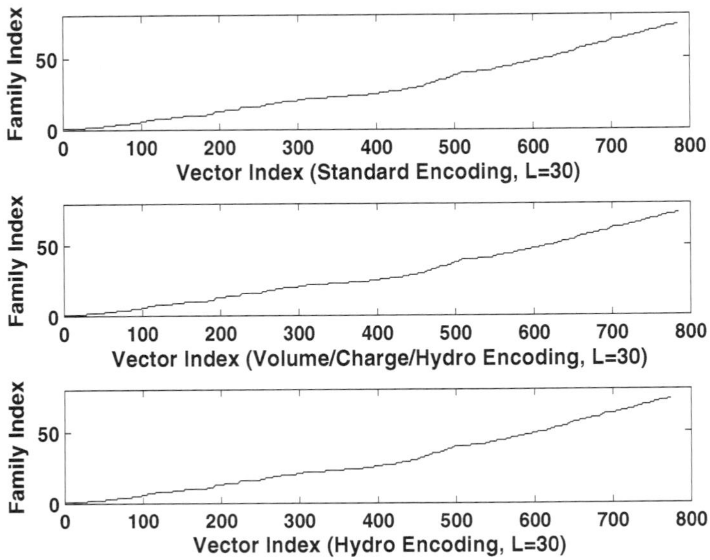

Fig. 8. Family classification of each data vector.

5.4.3 BLOCKS database search

In this section, we demonstrate how to perform database searches using the relvance and reliability equations summarized in Table 6. Database search examples have been reported using the BLOCKS database Henikoff & Henikoff (1994). In this work, we analyze the effect of randomly mutating sequences within the BLOCKS database to analyze family recognition as a function sequence mutation. For the purposes of illustration, we consider a test sequence from the Enolase protein family (BL00164D) in order to examine relevancy and database reliability. For this test sequence with $L = 15$, amino acids are randomly changed where the number of positions mutated is gradually increased from 0 to 12. Furthermore, encodings from Table 3 are compared with standard encoding.

For this series of tests, the reliability always gives a value of $\cos(\phi) = 1$, implying that the randomization test did not result in a vector outside the subspace defined by the database. This corroborates conclusions drawn in Section 5.4.1. Figure 9 shows that the classification remains stable for both encodings until about 5-6 positions out of 15 have been mutated (the family index for the original test sequence is 10). In addition, the relevance can be summarized by computing the *difference* between the maximum value of $\cos(\phi_i)$ and the second largest value. For the sake of illustration, if the BLOCKS family with index 10 does not yield the maximum projection, then the relevance difference is assigned a negative value. Figure 10 show the results of this computation. In this test, we observe a consistent decrease in the relevance difference indicating that secondary occurrences are gaining influence against the family class of the test sequence.

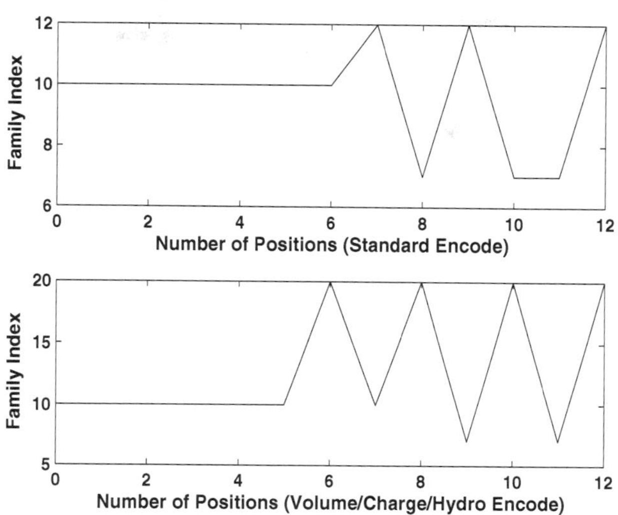

Fig. 9. Family classification as a function of the number of positions randomized.

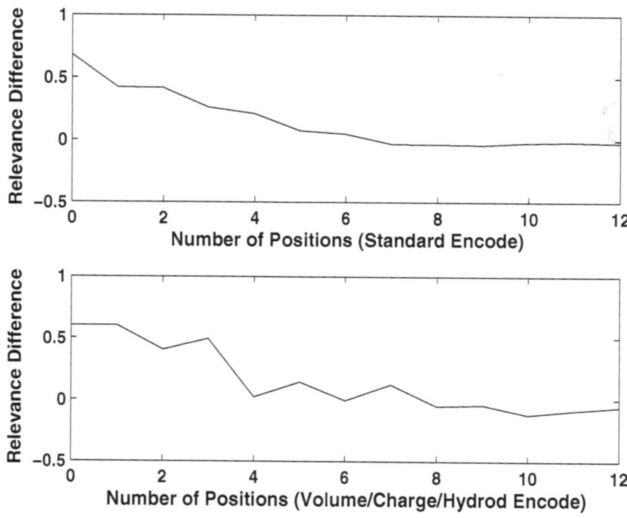

Fig. 10. Relevance differential as a function of the number of positions randomized.

6. Conclusions

This chapter has elaborated upon the application of information retrieval techniques to various computational approaches in bioinformatics such as sequence modeling, clustering, pattern classification and database searching. While extensions to multiple sequence alignment have been alluded to in the literature Couto et al. (2007); Stuart, Moffett & Baker (2002), there is a need to include and model gaps in the approaches proposed in this body of work. Extensions to the vector space methods outlined in this chapter might involve including a new symbol to represent a gap. Regardless of the symbol set employed, it is clear that the approach described can lead to sparse elements embedded in high dimensional vector spaces. While data sets of this kind can be potentially problematic Beyer et al. (1999); Hinneburg et al. (2000); Houle et al. (2010); Steinbach et al. (2003), subspace dimension reduction techniques are derivable from LSI approaches such as the SVD.

The IR techniques introduced above are readily applicable in any setting where bioinformatics data (sequence, structural, symbolic, etc) can be encoded. This work has focused primarily on amino acid sequence data; however, given existing structural encoding techniques Bowie et al. (1991); Zhang et al. (2010), future work might be directed toward vector space approaches to structural data. The methods outlined in this chapter allow for novel biologically meaningful weighting schemes, algebraic regular expressions, matrix factorizations for subspace reduction as well as numerical optimization techniques applicable to high dimensional vector spaces.

7. Acknowledgements

This work was made possible by funding from grant DHS 2008-ST-062-000011, "Increasing the Pipeline of STEM Majors among Minority Serving Institutions". The authors would like to thank David J. Schneider of the USDA-ARS for many helpful discussions.

8. References

Alter, O., Brown, P. O. & Botstein, D. (2000a). Generalized singular value decomposition for comparative analysis of genome-scale expression data sets of two different organisms, *PNAS* 100: 3351–3356.

Alter, O., Brown, P. O. & Botstein, D. (2000b). Singular value decomposition for genome-wide expression data processing and modeling, *PNAS* 97: 10101–10106.

Andorf, C. M., Dobbs, D. L. & Honavar, V. G. (2002). Discovering protein function classification rules from reduced alphabet representations of protein sequences, *Proceedings of the Fourth Conference on Computational Biology and Genome Informatics*, Durham, NC, pp. 1200–1206.

Bacardit, J., Stout, M., Hirst, J. D., Valencia, A., Smith, R. E. & Krasnogor, N. (2009). Automated alphabet reduction for protein datasets, *BMC Bioinformatics* 10(6).

Baldi, P. & Brunak, S. (1998). *Bioinformatics: The Machine Learning Approach*, MIT Press, Cambridge, MA.

Baxevanis, A. D. & Ouellette, B. F. (2005). *Bioinformatics: A practical guide to the analysis of genes and proteins*, Wiley.

Berry, M. W. & Browne, M. (2005). *Understanding Search Engines: Mathematical Seacrh Engines and Text Retrieval*, SIAM.

Berry, M. W., Drmac, Z. & Jessup, E. R. (1999). Matrices, vector spaces, and information retrieval, *SIAM Rev.* 41: 335–362.

Berry, M. W., Dumais, S. T. & OŠBrien, G. W. (1995). Using linear algebra for intelligent information retrieval, *SIAM Rev.* 37: 573–595.

Beyer, K., Goldstein, J., Ramakrishnan, R. & Shaft, U. (1999). When is "nearest neighbor" meaningful?, *In Int. Conf. on Database Theory*, pp. 217–235.

Bishop, C. M. (2006). *Pattern Recognition and Machine Learning*, Springer.

Bordo, D. & Argos, P. (1991). Suggestions for safe residue substitutions in site-directed mutagenesis, *Journal of Molecular Biology* 217: 721–729.

Bowie, J. U., Luthy, R. & Eisenberg, D. (1991). A method to identify protein sequences that fold into a known three-dimensional structure, *Science* 253: 164–170.

Couto, B. R. G. M., Ladeira, A. P. & Santos, M. A. (2007). Application of latent semantic indexing to evaluate the similarity of sets of sequences without multiple alignments character-by-character, *Genetics and Molecular Research* 6: 983–999.

Deerwester, S., Dumais, S. T., Furnas, G. W., Landauer, T. K. & Harshman, R. (1990). Indexing by latent semantic analysis, *Journalof the American Society for Information Science* 41: 391–407.

Dominich, S. (2010). *The Modern Algebra of Information Retrieval*, Springer.

Done, B. (2009). Gene function discovery using latent semantic indexing, *Wayne State University (Ph.D.. Thesis)* .

Durbin, R., Eddy, S., Krogh, A. & Mitchison, G. (2004). *Biological Sequence Analysis,* Cambridge University.

Eisenberg, D., Schwarz, E., Komaromy, M. & Wall, R. (1984). Analysis of membrane and surface protein sequences with the hydrophobic moment plot, *Journal of Molecular Biology* 179: 125–142.

Elden, L. (2004). *Matrix Methods in Data Mining and Pattern Recognition,* SIAM.

Feldman, R. & Sanger, J. (2007). *The Text Mining Handbook,* Cambridge.

Finn, R. D., Mistry, J., Tate, J., Coggill, P., Heger, A., Pollington, J. E., Gavin, O., Gunesekaran, P., Ceric, G., Forslund, K., Holm, L., Sonnhammer, E., Eddy, S. & Bateman, A. (2010). The Pfam protein families database, *Nucl. Acids Res.* 38: D211–222.

Golub, G. H. & Van Loan, C. F. (1989). *Matrix Computations,* Johns Hopkins University Press, Baltimore, MD.

Grossman, D. A. & Frieder, O. (2004). *Information Retrieval: Algorithms and Heuristics,* Springer.

Hand, D., Mannila, H. & Smyth, P. (2001). *Principles of Data Mining,* MIT Press.

Henikoff, J. G., Greene, E. A., Pietrokovski, S. & Henikoff, S. (2000). Increased coverage of protein families with the blocks database servers, *Nucl. Acids Res.* 28: 228–230.

Henikoff, S. & Henikoff, J. G. (1991). Automated assembly of protein blocks for database searching, *Nucleic Acids Research* 19: 6565–6572.

Henikoff, S. & Henikoff, J. G. (1994). Protein family classification based on searching a database of blocks, *Genomics* 19: 97–107.

Hinneburg, E., Aggarwal, C., Keim, D. A. & Hinneburg, A. (2000). What is the nearest neighbor in high dimensional spaces?, *In Proceedings of the 26th VLDB Conference,* pp. 506–515.

Houle, M., Kriegel, H., Kröger, P., Schubert, E. & Zimek, A. (2010). Can shared-neighbor distances defeat the curse of dimensionality?, *in* M. Gertz & B. Ludascher (eds), *Scientific and Statistical Database Management,* Vol. 6187 of *Lecture Notes in Computer Science,* Springer, pp. 482–500.

Khatri, P., Done, B., Rao, A., Done, A. & Draghici, S. (2005). A semantic analysis of the annotations of the human genome, *Bioinformatics* 21: 3416–3421.

Klie, S., Martens, L., Vizcaino, J. A., Cote, R., Jones, P., Apweiler, R., Hinneburg, A. & Hermjakob, H. (2008). Analyzing large-scale proteomics projects with latent semantic indexing, *Journal of Proteome Research* 7: 182–191.

Kuruvilla, F. G., Park, P. J. & Schreiber, S. L. (2004). Vector algebra in the analysis of genome-wide expression data, *Genome Biology* 3(3).

Kyte, J. & Doolittle, R. F. (1982). A simple method for displaying the hydropathic character of a protein, *Journal of Molecular Biology* 157: 105–132.

Langville, A. N. & Meyer, C. D. (2006). *Google's PageRank and Beyond: The Science of Search Engine Rankings*, Princeton University Press.

Lay, D. C. (2005). *Linear Algebra and Its Applications*, Wiley.

Luenberger, D. G. (1969). *Optimization by Vector Space Methods*, Wiley.

Mount, D. W. (2004). *Bioinformatics: Sequence and Genomic Analysis*, Cold Spring Harbor Laboratory Press.

Oja, E. (1983). *Subspace Methods of Pattern Recognition*, Wiley, New York, NY.

Pietrokovski, S., Henikoff, J. G. & Henikoff, S. (1996). The blocks database - a system for protein classification, *Nucl. Acids Res.* 24: 197–200.

Salton, G. & Buckley, C. (1990). Improving retrieval performance by relevance feedbackl, *J. Amer. Soc. Info. Sci.* 41: 288–297.

Sigrist, C. J. A., Cerutti, L., de Castro, E., Langendijk-Genevaux, P. S., Bulliard, V., Bairoch, A. & Hulo, N. (2010). PROSITE: a protein domain database for functional characterization and annotation, *Nucl. Acids Res.* 38: D161–166.

Smith, H., Annau, T. & Chandrasegaran, S. (1990). Finding sequence motifs in groups of functionally related proteins, *PNAS* 87: 826–830.

Steinbach, M., Ertöz, L. & Kumar, V. (2003). The challenges of clustering high-dimensional data, *In New Vistas in Statistical Physics: Applications in Econophysics, Bioinformatics, and Pattern Recognition*, Springer-Verlag.

Stuart, G. W. & Berry, M. W. (2004). An SVD-based comparison of nine whole eukaryotic genomes supports a coelomate rather than ecdysozoan lineage, *BMC Bioinformatics* 5(204).

Stuart, G. W., Moffett, K. & Baker, S. (2002). Integrated gene and species phylogenies from unaligned whole genome protein sequences, *Bioinformatics* 18: 100–108.

Stuart, G. W., Moffett, K. & Leader, J. J. (2002). A comprehensive vertebrate phylogeny using vector representations of protein sequences from whole genomes, *Mol. Biol. Evol.* 19: 554–562.

T. Rodrigues, L. Pacífico, S. T. (2004). Clustering and artificial neural networks: Classification of variable lengths of Helminth antigens in set of domains, *Genetics and Molecular Biology* 27: 673–678.

Theodoridis, S. & Koutroumbas, K. (2003). *Pattern Recognition*, Elsevier.

Wall, M. E., Rechtsteiner, A. & Rocha, L. M. (2003). *Singular value decomposition and principal component analysis*, KLuwer, pp. 91–109.

Wang, J. T. L., Zaki, M. J., Toivonen, H. T. T. & Sasha, D. (eds) (2005). *Data Mining in Bioinformatics*, Spinger.

Weiss, S. M., Indurkhya, N., Zhang, T. & Damerau, F. J. (2005). *Text Mining: Predictive Methods for Analyzing Unstructured Information*, Springer.

Wimley, W. C. & White, S. H. (1996). Experimentally determined hydrophobicity scale for proteins at membrane interfaces, *Nature Structural Biology* 3: 842–848.

Zhang, Z. H., Lee, H. K. & Mihalek, I. (2010). Reduced representation of protein structure: implications on efficiency and scope of detection of structural similarity, *BMC Bioinformatics* 11(155).

5

Massively Parallelized
DNA Motif Search on FPGA

Yasmeen Farouk[1], Tarek ElDeeb[2] and Hossam Faheem[1]
[1]Faculty of Computer and Information Sciences, Ain Shams University,
[2]Faculty of Engineering, Cairo University,
Egypt

1. Introduction

Understanding the mechanisms that regulate gene expression is a major challenge in biology. Motif finding problem is considered an important task in this challenge. Addressing the complexity nature of the problem together with being very data intensive has encouraged introducing field programmable gate arrays (FPGAs) to the problem. FPGAs are very powerful in such computationally intensive tasks.

Many Algorithms are introduced to solve this problem. They can be categorized into pattern-based and profile-based algorithms [1]. Pattern-based algorithms include PROJECTION[4], MULTIPROFILER[6], and MITRA[3]. Profile-based algorithms includes CONSENSUS[7], MEME[2] and Gibbs sampling[5]. Although these algorithms show good performance, they still can fail to identify all the possible motifs in the sequences. They also show poor performance when trying to solve the challenge problem presented by Pvzner and Sze[8]. Some of them fail due to local search, others which are based on statistical measures fail to separate the motif from the background sequences.

We can also categorize Motif finding algorithms due to the solution they provide. Some algorithms provide exact solution others provide approximate one. Brute Force algorithm is an exact algorithm but it suffers from the intractability of its running time. It increases exponentially with the size of the required motif. This makes the Brute Force unsuitable for long motifs.

Our enhanced Brute Force algorithm, skip Brute Force, can predict the quality of the computed motif. The algorithm skips those iterations which will lead to a poor scored motif, thus leads to a better running time than the original Brute Force. This enhancement guarantees the same exactness of the Brute Force. But, it still suffers from the intractable running time for long motifs.

Many approaches can be applied to speed up the running time of any algorithm using hardware; examples include chip multiprocessors, graphics processing units (GPUs) and (FPGAs). GPUs are inexpensive, commodity parallel devices and have already been employed as powerful coprocessors for a large number of applications. However, GPUs have limited instructions and limited parallelism relative to FPGA's configurability. The research in [10] employed acceleration using GPU. Another approach uses clusters of workstations [12]. However, clusters typically have high maintenance and energy costs when compared to single node solutions. Others use special hardware [9][11], where a cost performance ratio would be fairer for comparison [9].

The repetitive nature of the algorithm and the locality of the data encourage the use of FPGAs. Many operations can be done concurrently to enhance the running time. FPGAs proved to successfully accelerate sequential algorithms minimum by one or two orders of magnitude. They also have been widely used to accelerate bioinformatics problems such as Smith-Waterman and BLAST algorithms. This research offers an enhanced Brute Force algorithm hardware accelerated using Field Programmable Gate Arrays (FPGAs). Our research leads to a speed up by 1.5MX and thus boosting the running time without sacrificing the accuracy.

The rest of this chapter is organized as follows: In Section 2 we describe the motif finding problem and presents our enhanced Brute Force algorithm; skip Brute Force. Section 3 presents the hardware implementation of our novel approach with a detailed view to its components. Performance evaluation is presented in section 4. Finally, section 5 concludes our work and presents future enhancements.

2. Skip brute force algorithm

Brute-force search or exhaustive search, also known as generate and test, is a very general problem solving technique that consists of systematically enumerating all possible candidates for the solution and checking whether each candidate satisfies the problem's statement.

The motif finding problem can be summarized as follows:

Planted *(l,d)*- Motif Problem: Find the motif consensus M which is a fixed but unknown nucleotide sequence of length l. Suppose that M occurs once in each of t background sequences of common length n. Each occurrence of M is mutated by exactly d point substitutions in positions chosen independently at random. Given the t sequences, recover the motif occurrences and the consensus M.

Pevzner and Sze[8] presented the challenge problem(15,4) which makes a particular parameterization to the panted motif problem. The motif we are searching for is of length l=15, the allowed mutations d=4 and the number of sequences we are searching in is t=20 each of size n=600. The parameters of the challenge problem are typical values for finding transcription factor binding sites in co-regulated gene promoter regions yeast [4].

The Brute Force algorithm solves the motif finding problem by considering the set of all 4^l possible l-mers. It computes the total distance of each l-mer in that set to all other l-mers in all t sequences. The correct motif is the one that have the smallest total distance along all the other l-mers. The run time of this algorithm is O($4^l nt$). The running time for finding a motif of l=11 is about 5hrs and it fails to handle longer motifs in reasonable time. To solve the challenge problem, the running time of the Brute Force algorithm would obviously be too slow.

The idea behind our skip Brute Force algorithm is that it skips all the iterations that will not lead to a correct solution. The algorithm is forced to skip over the remaining iterations in two cases. The algorithm generates all possible 4^l l-mers. It then iterates over all the sequences examining that generated l-mer with all the windows in each sequence. For each sequence iteration, the current score is initialized with the allowed mutation and then the score of each window is computed; i.e. the hamming distance between that window and the current l-mer. If this distance beats the current score then we would suspect the current window to be an implanted motif until another window in the same sequence with a higher score beats it.

The planted motif problem guarantees to find the motif in each sequence. Based on this fact the skip algorithm skips the iterations over the remaining sequences if it reached the end of the current sequence without finding any window that matches the current l-mer (this l-mer can not be the motif) and jumps to the next l-mer. Assuming a single solution, the algorithm also skips the iterations over the remaining l-mers if it reaches the last sequence (t=20) without skipping any iteration (the solution is found).

A pseudo code of the skip Brute Force algorithm is shown below in Figure 1.

```
1.     for L = 0 to 4^L_motifSize - 1 do  % examine all possible l-mers
2.        for Ti = 1 to t_sequences do % loop on all t sequences
3.           motif_found   = 0;
4.         current_score  = d_mutations;
5.        for W = 1 to n_seqSize-l_motifSize+1 do % loop on all windows
6.           dist = compute_distance ( L , W );
7.          if dist <= current_score
8.             solution.motif    = Li; % this can be the motif
9.             solution.posit(Ti)  = W; % save its position
10.            motif_found      = 1; % a suspected motif was found
11.                    current_score  =  dist;
12.                       if Ti = t_sequences   % we reached the last sequence
13.               solution_found     = 1;
14.            end
15.            %% break; %% (does not guarantee to find best solution)
16.          end
17.        if motif_found  == 0
18.          break; % Skip that Li, it is not the Motif
19.        end
20.          end
21.     end
22.      if solution_found
23.        break;
24.      end
25.   end
```

Fig. 1. Pseudo Code of the skip Brute Force Algorithm. If the commented break command is applied, then algorithm will skip-more.

2.1 Skip-more brute force

In our early implementation of the skip algorithm, we did not consider scores for the motifs found. We forced to skip the current sequence if a single motif is found that has d mutations within the allowed range (line 15). Here the algorithm fails to find the best motif as more windows in the current sequence can reveal occurrences of motifs with lower mutations. The complexity of this algorithm is $O(4^l nt)$ at its worst case, just as the Brute Force.

3. Hardware implementation of skip brute force

Our design benefits from the concurrent nature of the FPGAs as a hardware platform; control, multiplexing, matching and decision making are all occurring on the same clock edge. We used VHDL to model our design preserving its extendibility for more complex challenging problems in future. Figure 2 shows the system block diagram.

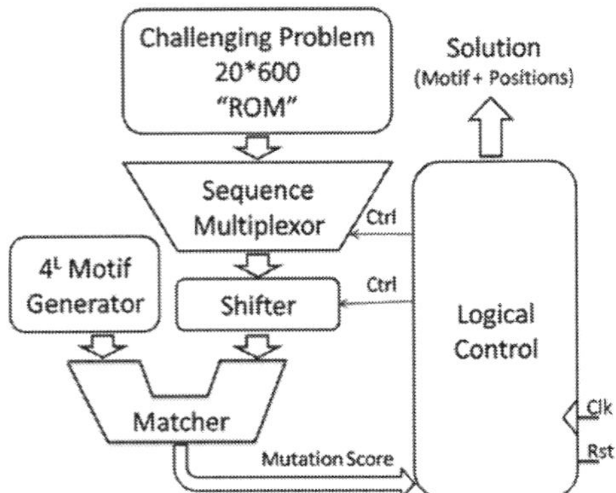

Fig. 2. Block diagram of the skip Brute Force - running on an FPGA with one matching unit.

All t-sequences are first loaded into an on-chip read-only memory 'ROM' as shown in Figure 3. On the contrary, the set of all 4^l l-mers are not stored, but locally generated. Gaining from encoding each nucleotide into 2-bit symbol, the 4^l Motif Generator is a simple controlled binary counter. The shifter block is fed by the currently needed sequence and only reveals a sliding l-sized window of it at a time. The matching block compares the revealed window to the generated l-mer and outputs the hamming distance as the mutation score. The logical control unit synchronizes the system to properly implement the skip Brute Force algorithm. More details are found in the following subsections.

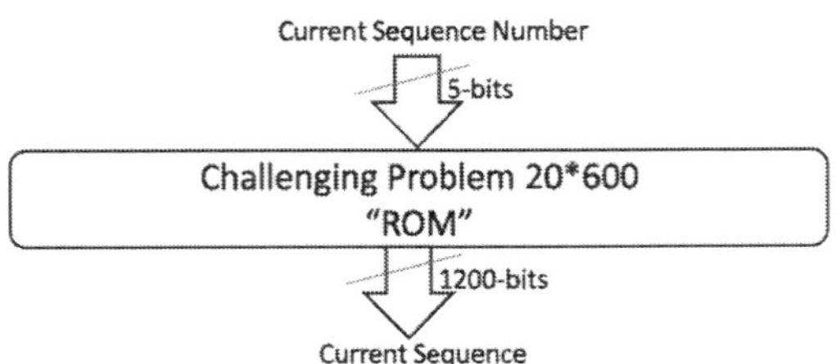

Fig. 3. The ROM Block holding the challenging problem sequence.

3.1 Sequence multiplexor

The sequence multiplexor gets one sequence at a time. The Logical control issues the signal to the multiplexor to load the sequence from the ROM and feed the shifter.

3.2 Sequence shifter

The sequence shifter block has the following inputs: clk, reset and the sequence to be shifted. The shifter outputs an l-sized motif each clock cycle through a windowing approach.

The shifter outputs (n-l+1) motifs for each sequence unless it is interrupted by resetting it. Our skip Brute Force resets the shifter in one case; when the shifter has generated all the (n-l+1) l-mers for this sequence. The shifter is reset to be fed with new sequence to generate the newly suspected motifs (l-mers) from this sequence.

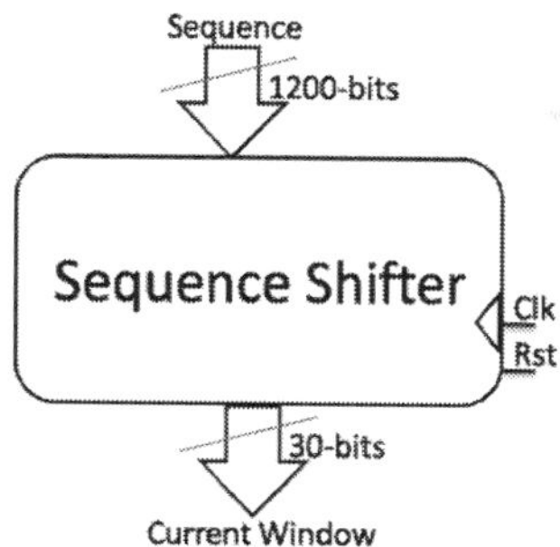

Fig. 4. Sequence Shifter block diagram.

The skip-more algorithm resets the shifter in two cases. The first case is the one previously explained. The second case happens when the matching unit finds an l to be within the d allowed mutations. In this case the system resets the shifter as the motif is considered to be found. Block diagram of Sequence Shifter is shown in Figure 4.

3.3 Motif generator

The set of all 4^l l-mers starting with AA ... A to TT ...T is not stored in the system. The four DNA nucleotides {A,C,G,T} are easily encoded into the 2-bit symbols 00,01,10 and 11 respectively. The system locally generates all the possible l-mers by a simple controlled binary counter of size l bits.

That is, in a system with l=3 we would like to generate AAA, AAC, AAG, AAT, ...,TTT. According to the encoding mentioned above; we would like to generate a series of 6-bits each as follows 000000, 000001, 000010, 000011, ..., 111111. The relation between these encoded bits can be obtained by a simple binary counter of size l bits.

3.4 Matching block

The matching block consists of many sub-blocks; xoring units, an l-bit adder and a comparison block. The matching block takes two l-sized sequences and compares them. If the difference between the two sequences is less than or equal to the allowed mutation (the two sequences have less than or equal to d different nucleotides), it outputs a match signal.

The matching block uses a series of xoring gates to determine if two l nucletoids are identical. The l-bit adder is used to count the differences between them. Finally, a comparison block is used to compare the value obtained from the adder with the d allowed mutation.

The matching block also outputs the score of the matching process. This score is used by the logical control to determine the quality of the motif obtained. The Matching block diagram is shown in Figure 5. Detailed Matching block diagram is shown in Figure 6.

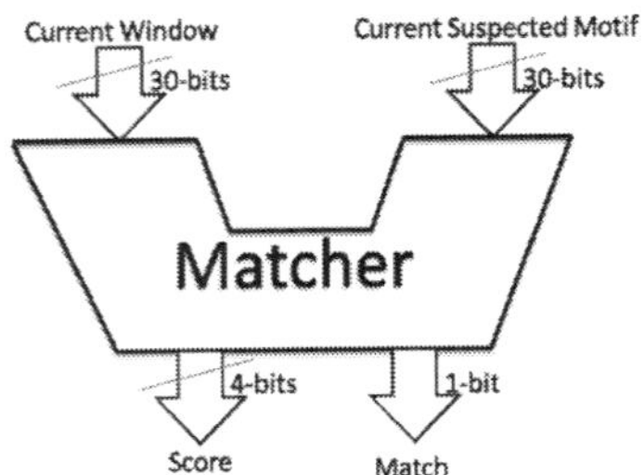

Fig. 5. Matching block diagram.

Our design is meant to be extendible by instantiating more of the matching units. Thus, its circuit implementation has to be highly optimized. Classical hamming distance circuits start with an array of XOR gates to determine matching nucleotides, followed by l sequential adders to compute the required distance. This approach leads to long circuit delays that will cause the system maximum frequency to drop, degrading the performance.

Our design replaces the sequential adders with a specially designed adders tree. For the (15, 4) problem, the proposed design shortens the critical path from fifteen 4-bit adders to only four full adders and two half adders. Figure 7 shows the optimized adder tree.

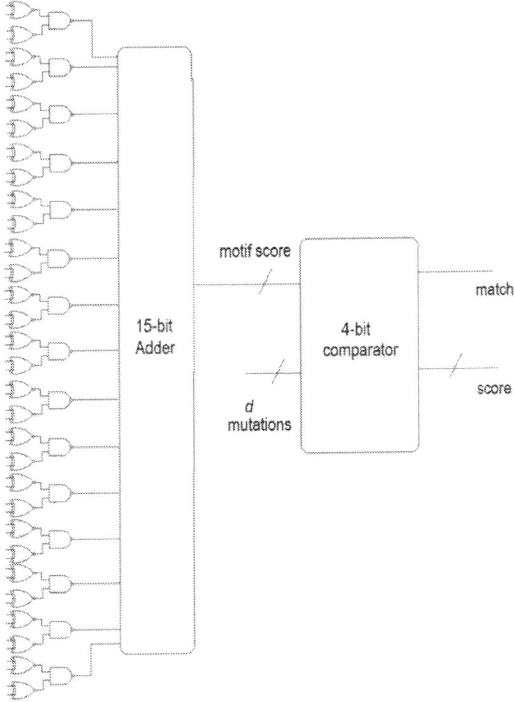

Fig. 6. Matching block components - xoring units are double the size of the motif.

3.5 Adder tree

The l-bit adder takes a pattern of size l, calculates the number of ones in this pattern and outputs the count in a $\log_2 l$ bits. For $l=15$, the adder would accept a 15 bit input signal and ouputs a 4-bit output signal. A 15-bit input signals needs five full adders; this would be stage 0. Stage 0 outputs 5 sum signals and 5 carry signals. Stage 1 needs 1 full adder and 1 half-adder for the output sum signals and the same for the output carry signals. Accordingly, stage 2 needs only 4 half adders, stage 3 needs 2 full adder and stage 4 needs 1 half adder. The final stage needs 1 full adder.

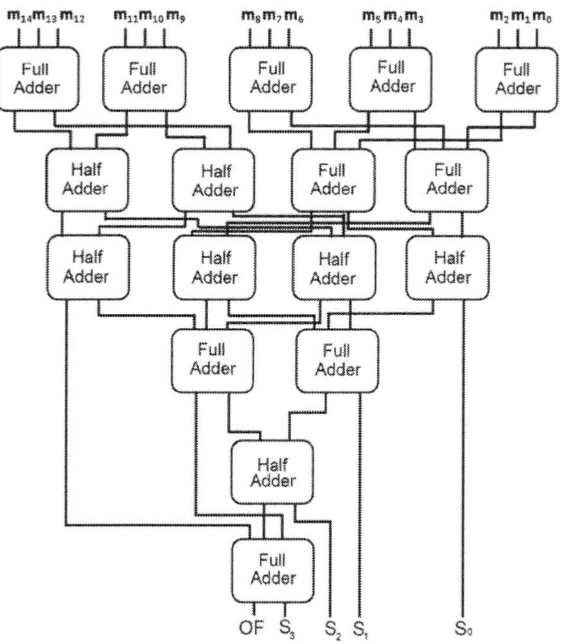

Fig. 7. The six stages adder tree - The critical path involves 4 full adders and 2 half adders.

3.6 Logical control

The system is managed by the logical control. Reset signals are issued to the motif generator and to the sequence shifter to control the flow of the sequences to be compared. As explained earlier, the logical control issues this signal under certain events. The logical control outputs the best motif which is determined by the scoring function.

3.7 Multiple matching units

It is clear that scaling up the design by utilizing more matching units in parallel will speed up the overall performance by the factor of extra units. Slight modifications and some logic duplication will be introduced for proper functionality and synchronization. The only limiting factor to the performance boost is the FPGA resources.

Figure 8 shows the block diagram of the skip Brute force running on an FPGA with multiple matching units. All t sequences are also loaded into an on-chip read-only memory ROM as the previous architecture. The sequence multiplexor feeds n series of sequence shifter followed by a matching unit. The matching unit takes its two l-sized sequences one from the shifter and the other from the logical unit which contains the motif generator. The outputs of the matching unit in each series are ANDed to determine the value of solution found. The number of the series of sequence shifter followed by matching unit is equal to n, where n is the number of the examined sequences. In the previous architecture, the system has to loop over all the sequences for each generated motif. This corresponds to $n.t.4^l$ loops. In this enhanced architecture, the system loops only $n . 4^l$.

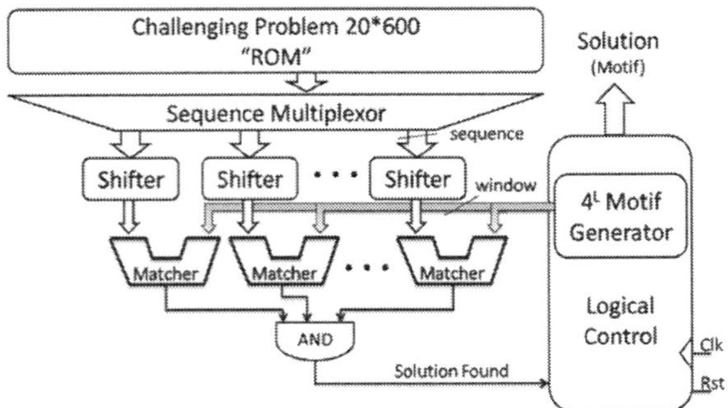

Fig. 8. Block diagram of the skip Brute Force - running on an FPGA with multiple matching units.

4. Performance evaluation and results

We tested the performances of Brute Force algorithm and skip Brute Force on synthetic problem instances generated according to the planted (l,d)-motif model. We followed the FM model described by Pvzner and Sze [8] to generate synthetic data to test our work. We produced problem instances as follows:

First, a motif consensus M of length l is chosen by picking l bases at random. Second, $t= 20$ occurrences of the motif are created by randomly choosing d positions per occurrence (without replacement) and mutating the base at each chosen position to a different, randomly chosen base. Third, we construct t background sequences of length $n=600$ using $n*t$ bases chosen at random. Finally, we assign each motif occurrence to a random position in a background sequence, one occurrence per sequence. All random choices are made uniformly and independently with equal base frequencies.

The skip Brute Force achieves an average speedup of 9.11X. Both Brute Force and skip Brute Force algorithms were modelled and implemented on MatlabR2006b[15]. All the experiments ran on an AMD 5500 X2+ processor with 2GB RAM. For fair comparison, it is reported in literature that the Matlab platform is about 5 to 6 times slower than an optimized C coded program.

To evaluate the hardware implementation; we need to define the expected number of matching operations. First, we define the probability to find a random l-mer in a given sequence with up to d mutations as:

$$P_d = \sum_{i=0}^{d} \binom{l}{i} \left(\frac{3}{4}\right)^i \left(\frac{1}{4}\right)^{l-i}$$

Additionally, we define the expected number of required matching operations to find the correct implanted motif as:

$$E(l, d) = \frac{4^l}{2}(n - l + 1)\left(1 + \sum_{i=1}^{t-1} P_d^i\right)$$

We then deduce for a problem of size $n=600$, $t=20$, the expected matching operations to be as shown in table 1.

L	D	Expected Matching Operations
9	2	7.7699×10^7
11	3	1.2388×10^9
12	3	4.9428×10^9
13	4	1.9750×10^{10}
14	4	7.8813×10^{10}
15	4	3.1464×10^{11}
17	5	5.0170×10^{12}

Table 1. Expected matching operations for different (l,d) problems.

We synthesized our design for multiple matching units (MU). Synthesis results of one, five, ten and twenty matching units need further analysis. Figure 9 shows the area utilization of the FPGA. The FPGA utilization increases almost linearly with increasing the number of MUs.

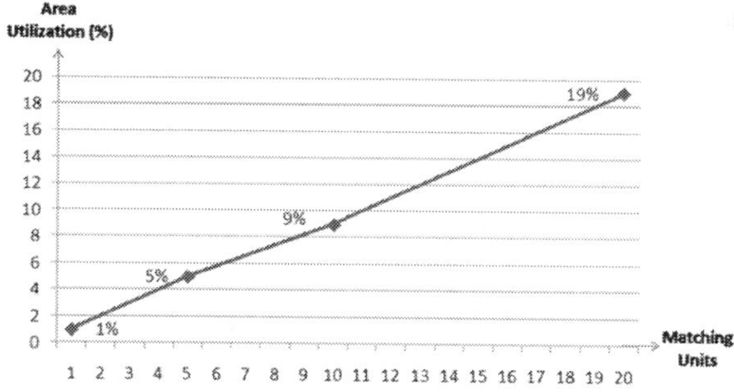

Fig. 9. FPGA area utilization - increases almost linearly.

The design of multiple MUs inherits parallelization; this means the system critical path remains the same even after increasing the number of MUs. Unfortunately, the system maximum frequency decreases with increasing the number of MUs. This is due to the increased complexity of the FPGA interconnects. Over 80% of transistors inside the FPGA are dedicated to the programmable routing network as programmable switches and buffers. The increased complexity of the interconnects leads to FPGA resource starvation.

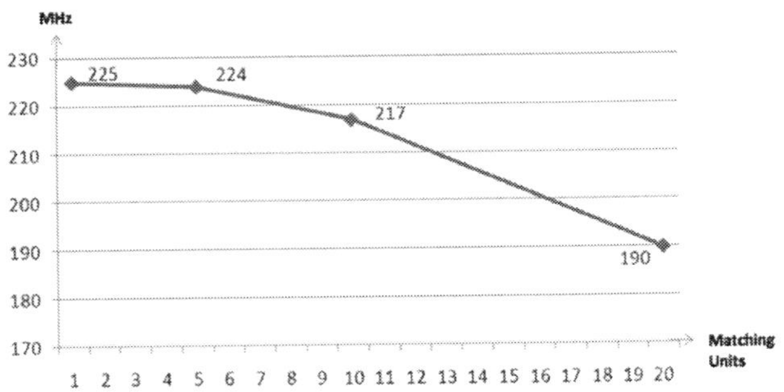

Fig. 10. Maximum system frequency - decreases due to interconnects complexity.

Furthermore, It is well known that interconnects in FPGA dominate the system performance and power consumption.
Depending on the architecture, 60% to 80% of the FPGA critical path delay is due to the routing between logic blocks. Long interconnects exhibit a substantial delay and often lead to timing violation and require further optimizations. In a recent study [13], it was found that FPGA interconnects is poorly scaled. Based on the extrapolation of future device performance, interconnects will become the performance bottleneck, of which the clock rate will be slowed down to 17 MHz in a 13 nm process. Figure 10 shows degradation in the maximum frequency of the system with increasing the number of matching units.
We define the system throughput as the number of matching operations per second. Figure 11 shows the curve of the system throughput. The throughput increases by increasing the number of MUs. The curve tends to be linear but the degradation in the maximum frequency alters this linearity.

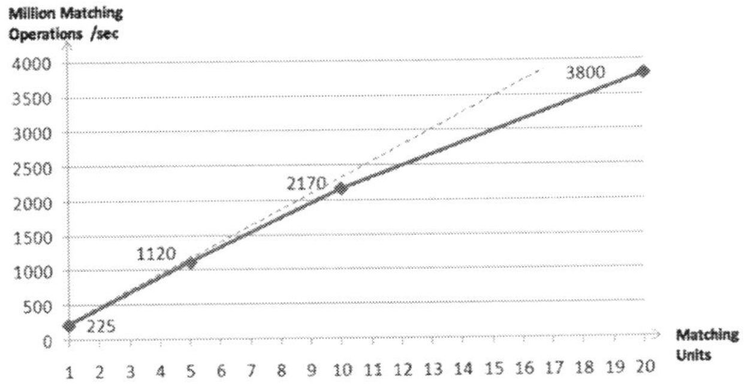

Fig. 11. System throughput - increases almost linearly.

Figure 12 compares the running time of Brute Force, skip Brute Force, skip Brute Force running on FPGA with one matching unit and with 20 matching units of different challenge problems. The running time of Brute Force in all challenge problems is the highest. Our skip Brute Force algorithm running on an FPGA has the best running time.

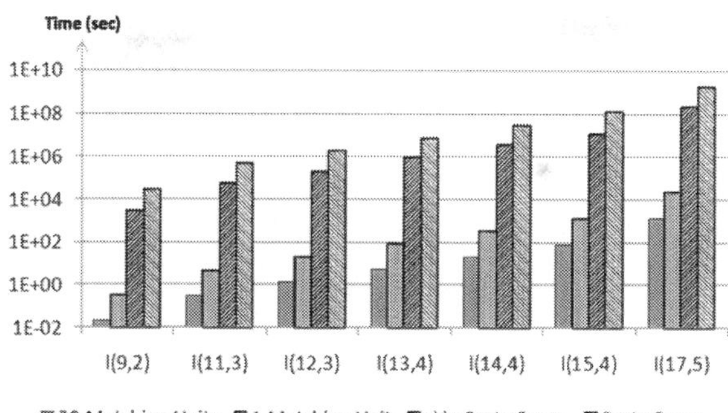

Fig. 12. Running time of various challenge problems - skip Brute Force running on an FPGA based architecture with 20 matching units has the fastest running time.

Utilizing one matching unit leads to a speedup by 9800X over pure software running time of skip Brute Force. It is clear that scaling up the design by utilizing more matching units in parallel will speed up the overall performance nearly by the factor of extra units. We used 20 matching units and achieved a speed up factor 16.88X over one matching unit.

Thus, applying the skip Brute Force (9.11X) on 20 matching units (16.88X) running on an FPGA-based architecture (9800X) would offer 1.5MX boosting in the performance.

Figure 13 illustrates these observations.

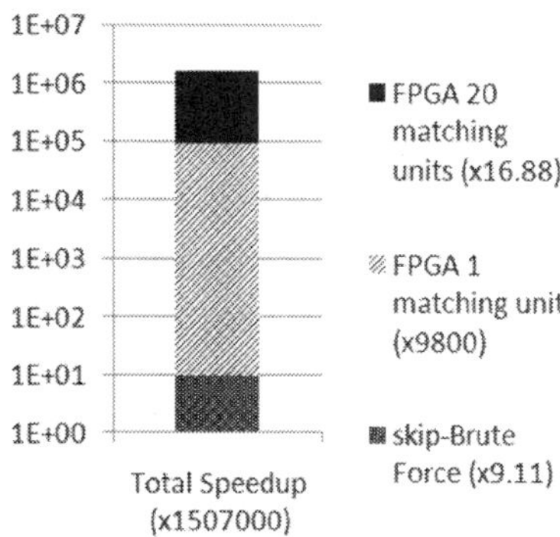

Fig. 13. Speedup factors of our accelerating designs - Total speedup is 1.5MX.

RTL synthesis and Place and route were accomplished using Quartus tool on the Stratix III FPGA technology, a product from Altera[14]. The skip Brute Force FPGA design does not use any of the FPGA memory blocks. The PowerPlay tool showed a total of power consumption of 400mW.

5. Conclusion and future work

This chapter presents a proof-of-concept parallization of motif finding on FPGA to achieve high performance at low cost. Among all Motif Finding Algorithms, Brute Force is known to be the most accurate. This is mainly because it searches the space of all possible motifs. The major drawback of Brute Force is the intractability of its running time. The algorithm running time grows exponentially with the length of the motif. This makes the Brute Force unsuitable for long motifs. The algorithm can not be used to solve the (15,4) challenge problem in a reasonable time.

In order to find the correct solution for the planted motif problem; we have to over-come two main problems. We have to be able to identify the motif from background sequences by applying an exact algorithm such as the Brute Force that guarantees to always find the correct motif. We also have to overcome its running time and memory complexities through acceleration by enhancement in the algorithm itself and by hardware implementation. Our research presented here addresses these two issues.

We presented an enhanced Brute Force algorithm; skip Brute Force, which can predict the quality of the obtained motif. The algorithm skips those iterations which will lead to a poor scored motif, thus leads to a better running time. This enhancement guarantees the same exactness of the Brute Force. Our enhanced algorithm showed a speedup factor of average 9.11X.

The repetitive nature of the algorithm and the locality of the data encourage the use of FPGAs. Many operations can be done concurrently to enhance the running time. FPGAs proved to successfully accelerate sequential algorithms minimum by one or two orders of magnitude. They also have been widely used to accelerate bioinformatics problems such as Smith-Waterman and BLAST algorithms. This research offers an enhanced Brute Force algorithm hardware accelerated using Field Programmable Gate Arrays (FPGAs).

We designed an FPGA-based architecture to accelerate our skip Brute Force algorithm. The core of the skip Brute Force algorithm is its matching unit. Utilizing one matching unit leads to a speedup by 9800X over pure software running time of skip Brute Force. It is clear that scaling up the design by utilizing more matching units in parallel will speed up the overall performance nearly by the factor of extra units. We used 20 matching units and achieved a speed up factor 16.88X over one matching unit.

Thus, applying the skip Brute Force (9.11X) on 20 matching units (16.88X) running on an FPGA-based architecture (9800X) would offer 1.5MX boosting in the performance.

Obviously, the real boosting in the performance (9800X) is achieved by introducing FPGA to the algorithm. It is neither the effect of enhancing the Brute Force algorithm, nor the effect of applying more matching units.

Many motif finding algorithms achieves better running time on the expense of the motif accuracy obtained. We succeeded to accelerate the motif finding problem without sacrificing the accuracy by applying an exact algorithm; skip Brute Force.

Our work can be extended to accelerate other motif finding algorithms that have shown better performance to solve the motif finding problem. Algorithms such as Projection [4] and MEME [2] proved to have high accuracy and much better running time. Introducing these algorithms to hardware acceleration will offer more boosting to its running time.

An embedded processor can be added on the FPGA to run the algorithm on chip. This approach will eliminate the communication overheads which is the bottleneck in most hardware-software co-designs.

Furthermore, our approach can be applied to other biological applications. One of the most important problems in the biological research is the tertiary structure prediction of a protein using amino acid information. This is particularly important in the context of designer proteins in the area of drug discovery. Graph analysis of biological networks is also computationally intensive.

6. References

[1] Rajasekaran, S., Balla, S. and Huang, C.H.: Exact algorithm for planted motif challenge problems, Proceedings of Asia-Pacific Bioinformatics Conference, 249–259 (2005)

[2] Bailey, T.L., Williams, N., Misleh, C., Li, W.W.: MEME: discovering and analyzing DNA and protein motifs. Nucleic Acid Research 34, W369–W373 (2006)

[3] A. Brazma, I. Jonassen, J. Vilo, and E. Ukkonen, Predicting gene regulatory elements in silico on a genomic scale, Genome Research 15, 1202-1215(1998)

[4] Buhler, J., Tompa, M.: Finding motifs using random projections. J. Comput. Biol. 9, 225–242 (2002)

[5] Lawrence, C.E., Altschul, S.F., Boguski, M.S., Liu, J.S., Neuwald, A.F., Wootton, J.C.: Detecting subtle sequence signals: a Gibbs sampling strategy for multiple alignment. Science 262, 208–214 (1993)

[6] E. Eskin and P. Pevzner, Finding composite regulatory patterns in DNA sequences, Bioinformatics S1, 354-363(2002)

[7] Hertz, G., Stormo, G.: Identifying DNA and protein patterns with statistically significant alignments of multiple sequences. Bioinformatics 15(7-8), 563–577 (1999)

[8] Pevzner, P., and Sze, S.-H.: Combinatorial approaches to finding subtle signals in DNA sequences. Proc. 8th Int. Conf. Intelligent Systems for Molecular Biology, 269–78(2000)

[9] Jan SchrOder, Lars Wienbrandt, Gerd Pfeiꞓer, and Manfred Schimmler: Massively Parallelized DNA Motif Search on the Reconfigurable Hardware Platform COPACOBANA. PRIB 2008 LNBI 5265, 436-447(2008)

[10] Chen Chen, Bertil Schmidt, Liu Weiguo, and Wolfgang Müller-Wittig: GPU-MEME: Using Graphics Hardware to Accelerate Motif Finding in DNA Sequences. PRIB 2008 LNBI 5265, 448-459(2008)

[11] Sandve, G.K., Nedland, M., Syrstad, B., Eidsheim, L.A., Abul, O., Drablas, F.: Accelerating motif discovery: Motif matching on parallel hardware. In: Bücher, P., Moret, B.M.E. (eds.) WABI 2006. LNCS (LNBI), vol. 4175, pp. 197–206. Springer, Heidelberg (2006)

[12] Grundy, W.N., Bailey, T.L., Elkan, C.P.: ParaMEME: A parallel implementation and a web interface for a DNA and protein motif discovery tool. Computer Applications in the Biological Sciences (CABIOS) 12, 303–310 (1996)

[13] Terrence Mak The Future Looks Gloomy for FPGA Interconnects Technical Report Series NCL-EECE-MSD-TR-2009-145, 2009.

[14] Altera Inc., http://www.altera.com/

[15] Matlab Product Family. http://www.mathworks.com.

6

A Pattern Search Method for Discovering Conserved Motifs in Bioactive Peptide Families

Feng Liu[1], Liliane Schoofs[2], Geert Baggerman[2],
Geert Wets[1] and Marleen Lindemans[2]
[1]Data Analysis & Modeling Group, Transportation Research Institute, Hasselt University
[2]Functional Genomics and Proteomics, Department of Biology, K.U. Leuven
Belgium

1. Introduction

Bioactive peptides play critical roles in regulating most biological processes in animals, and they have considerable biological, medical and industrial importance. Peptides belonging to the same family are often characterized by a typical short sequence motif (pattern) that is highly functionally preserved among the family members. In this chapter, we design a pattern search method to facilitate the detection of such conserved motifs. First, all known bioactive peptides annotated in Uniprot are collected and classified, and the program Pratt is used to search these unaligned peptide sequences in each family for conserved patterns. The obtained patterns are then refined by taking into account the information on amino acids at important functional sites collected from literature, and are further tested by scanning them against all the Uniprot proteins. The diagnostic power of the patterns is demonstrated by the fact that, while the false positive is kept to zero to ensure that the signatures are exclusive to peptides and their precursors, nearly 94% of all known peptide family members accommodate one or several of the identified patterns.

In total, we brought to light 155 novel peptide patterns in addition to the 56 established ones in the PROSITE database. All the patterns represent 110 peptide families; among which 55 are not characterized by PROSITE and 12 are also dismissed by other existing motif databases, such as Pfam. Using the newly uncovered peptide patterns as a search tool, we predicted 95 hypothetical proteins as putative peptides or peptide precursors.

2. Problem statement and background

Whole genome sequencing projects have made available immense sequence data at a pace that far supersedes their rate of annotation. As a result, out of 1.7 million protein sequences, which are currently available for all the completely sequenced metazoan genomes, nearly 15% could not be assigned to any putative function. Although several tools/algorithms are available to contribute towards the putative functional assignments of the proteins, yet large numbers of proteins remain un-elucidated. In most cases this is due to the low degrees of sequence similarities with known proteins; alternatively, the existing similarities can be confined to only very small part(s) of the entire protein. The latter is especially true for precursor proteins coding for bioactive peptides. Consequently, there is still a need for bioinformatic tools to predict the function of the enormously large number of the unknown protein sequences.

Bioactive peptides occur in the whole animal kingdom, from the least evolved phyla to the highest vertebrates (Filipsson et al., 2001; Masashi et al., 2001). They play key roles as signaling molecules in many, if not all physiological processes, for instance as a peptidergic neurotransmitter or neurohormone, as a peptidergic toxin, or as a growth factor (Boonen et al., 2007; Boonen et al., 2010). They are synthesized in the cell in the form of large preproproteins (precursors), which are a special class of proteins as they undergo extensive post-translational processing prior to producing final mature bioactive peptides (Schoofs & Baggerman, 2003). Peptides and their precursors that are structurally and functionally related have been classified into peptide families; each family of proteins is assumed to be derived from a common ancestor (Husson et al., 2009). During the evolutionary process, the protein sequences may have much diverged, but the essential amino acids involved in the biologically important activities are still present. These conserved amino acids along with their particular sequential order form the functional foundation and represent the motif (pattern) of a peptide family.

However, over the course of natural adaptation, different peptide families have diverged at different rates. While for some peptide families, the similarity extends over a much longer region even over the entire peptide precursor sequences; for many others, a short highly conserved motif is responsible for the function of the precursor proteins throughout the family members, and the sequence fragments outside the conserved regions often display no significant similarities (Baggerman et al., 2005). The latter conserved sequence characteristics can be further exposed by many short but biologically important functional peptides released from known large precursors as annotated in Uniprot, such as the 3-amino-acid thyroliberin peptide 'QHPamide' (Vandenborne et al., 2005) and 4-amino-acid neuropeptides 'FMRFamide' (Baggerman et al., 2002). For some mature peptides, the precursor proteins (genes) are unknown, such as the 2-amino-acid neuropeptide 'GWamide' (P83570) from *Sepia officinalis* (Henry et al., 1997) and the human growth-modulating peptide 'GHK' (P01157) (Schlesinger et al., 1977). The existence of numerous short bioactive peptides within the precursor proteins implies that only a very small conserved peptide motif may be a biologically important functional portion of the precursors.

Due to the fact that only short sequence regions are conserved, peptides or their precursors are sometimes not identified by existing sequence alignment algorithms e.g. BLAST or by motif search methods. While BLAST programs (Altschul et al., 1997) are very suitable to scan databases for homologous proteins, they are far less efficient at finding similarities to short conserved regions which can be only a few amino acids in length, when the whole genome sequence is scanned. For large precursors which are usually a few hundred amino acids in length and for which the biologically conserved regions are limited, the important domains are often masked by long randomly unrelated sequence regions. This is because for any two random large protein sequences, BLAST usually can find a relative long local alignment, at least longer than the short conserved peptide motif, and BLAST tends to assign a higher score to a longer alignment (Durbin et al., 1998). In addition, if a pair of homologues involves a short independent peptide molecule, which may be either an unknown peptide sequence as query or a known mature peptide as target from a protein database, it is difficult for BLAST to detect the pair of homologues, because the involvement of a short sequence makes the pairwise sequence alignment less likely to obtain a significant BLAST score (e.g., e-value < 0.01).

Like BLAST, motif search methods are important tools to search for a protein in a database, nevertheless, they are also limited to detect all members from a characterized peptide family. Most of the motifs in the existing databases, e.g. PROSITE (Hulo et al., 2004) and Pfam (Finn et al, 2010), cover the entire precursor sequences or sequence domains which are much longer than the conserved bioactive peptide regions. Therefore, the database motifs show their weakness when they are used to detect short mature peptides for which the precursors are unknown and the information on the sequences outside the peptide regions is thus missing. In addition, the construction of these motifs requires a good multiple protein sequence alignment in order to produce an accurate signature. This works well when the sequences are easy to align. However, for some peptide families for which the conserved regions are very short and the bulk of peptide precursor sequences is not very well preserved, the multiple alignment is very difficult to obtain or evaluate. The overall precursor protein sequence identity, especially in distantly related homologues, may be too low for an accurate alignment. In some cases, the short conserved regions are repeated within a precursor, making it even more challenging to build a unique alignment that truly reflects the evolutionary relationship.

In this chapter, we have followed an alternative approach, taking unaligned sequences as a starting point. We then used a pattern search program to look for conserved patterns. We first collected all currently annotated peptides and peptide precursor proteins in Metazoa through a search in Uniprot and classified them into peptide families. Next, we extracted peptide sequences in each family and used the program Pratt to search the sequences for representative patterns. Such patterns consist of highly conserved positions that can be separated by fixed or variable spacing. The patterns are then refined by incorporating the information that is available in literature on the important amino acids contained within the biologically active site(s) of the peptides. The specificity of the generated patterns are further verified by scanning them against Uniprot in order to ascertain that proteins picked up by the patterns are either annotated as peptides or peptide precursor proteins or have an unknown function.

3. Data collection

3.1 Peptide precursor collection and classification

A protein was collected into a peptide-precursor database if it is annotated in the Uniprot protein database (release 6.6) consisting of Swiss-Prot (release 48.6) and TrEMBL (release 31.6) with one of the following keywords: hormone, antimicrobial, toxin. The hormone includes bombesin, bradykinin, cytokine, glucagon, growth factor, hormone, hypotensive agent, insulin, neuropeptide, neurotransmitter, opioid peptide, pyrokinin, tachykinin, thyroid hormone, vasoactive, vasoconstrictor and vasodilator (the definition of the keywords can be referred to in this database). The antimicrobial consists of antibiotic, antiviral defense, defensin and fungicide; while the toxin includes naturally produced and secreted poisonous proteins that damage or kill other cells. However, when the protein is also characterized by non-peptide keywords, such as receptor, signal-anchor, transmembrane, binding protein, DNA binding, nuclear protein, transport, collagen, enzyme or words ending in 'ase' (excluding 'disease'), it is excluded, in order to avoid the selection of proteins which are not peptides or peptide precursors.

Stand-alone PSI-BLAST (ftp://ftp.ncbi.nih.gov/blast/executables/) is then used to align all the assembled sequences with all the Uniprot proteins except the ones which are already in the peptide-precursor database. Based on the conserved sequence characteristics of peptide families, the score matrix PAM30 is used and the word size is set to 2, allowing for the search for short but strong similarities. The proteins, which show significant similarities (e-value <0.01) with the known peptides or precursors, are retained. The obtained list is then checked manually in terms of the proteins' cellular location, molecular function and biological process as stated by GO (gene ontology) terms or in literature. As a result, 1345 more proteins which have as yet not been annotated in Uniprot are added to the peptide-precursor database.

Proteins collected in this database are automatically classified into peptide families if their family classification information is available in Uniprot that is based on a significant match to an existing motif or based on sequence similarities. Otherwise, proteins that display sequence similarities with a significant BLAST score, are clustered into the same family. A protein can also be assigned to a particular family based on its molecular function described in literature.

3.2 In silicon extraction of peptides

From each precursor protein in a peptide family, the bioactive peptide sequences are extracted in silicon from the beginning and ending positions of the subsequences that are annotated as 'peptide' or 'chain' in 'feature' line in the corresponding protein file in Uniprot. The conserved basic cleavage sites flanking the peptides, which contribute to the endoproteolytic cleavage process of the peptides from their precursors, such as the monobasic site (G)R or (G)K, the dibasic sites (G)KR, (G)RR, (G)KK or (G)RK, or a combination of consecutive K or R, are also withdrawn along with the subsequences (Liu & Wets, 2005; Rouille et al., 1995).

Entries in the family that only constitute the peptide sequence, i.e. in those cases where the precursor is unknown, are also retained. Proteins less than 200aa (amino acids) in length, which contain an N-terminal signal peptide and for which no mature peptides have as yet been identified, presumably contain a single peptide and are therefore also deposited after in silicon removal of the N-terminal signal peptide. According to the statistics on all annotated bioactive peptide sequences in Uniprot, 97% are no longer than the 200aa threshold value. The presence of a signal peptide is assumed when it is indicated in Uniprot; in other cases, it is forecasted by the signal peptide prediction program signalP (http://www.cbs.dtu.dk/services/SignalP/).

In total, 110 datasets of peptide families are formed with each including at least 10 peptide sequences. All the extracted peptide sequences in each of the families were scanned independently for patterns conserved in the corresponding family.

4. Method

Different software available on the internet provides users the tools to search for patterns conserved in a set of unaligned protein sequences. Pratt (http://www.ebi.ac.uk/pratt/#) (Jonassen et al., 1995) is a flexible pattern search tool in the number of parameters that can be controlled by users. It allows searching for patterns of conserved positions with limited variable length spacing, which is important because even in well-conserved peptide regions, variable loop sizes can occur. Pratt is run on each of the peptide family datasets, and the searching parameters are set based on maximum pattern length and pattern flexibilities found in the existing peptide patterns in PROSITE.

For each Pratt run which starts with the minimum percentage of sequences to match the pattern (the parameter C%) equal to 90%, the most significant pattern, which is the one with the highest fitness in the Pratt output list, is retained. The obtained pattern is then refined by integrating the information on the important functional sites in the matched peptide sequences depicted in literature. The amino acids occurring at these sites are added to the pattern if they are absent at the corresponding sites in the pattern.

The pattern is further verified by scanning it against all the Uniprot proteins using the ScanProsite tool (http://www.expasy.org/tools/scanprosite/). Two possible cases occur: (1) If the pattern is not contained in any known non-peptide protein, it is retained as a conserved peptide pattern. (2) Otherwise, if the pattern is matched by both peptide and non-peptide proteins (further referred to as true and false positive hits, respectively), it is subsequently processed as follows. (2a)If the pattern does not include any wildcard region where any amino acid is accepted, the positions where the pattern is located in all matching protein sequences are checked. If the pattern exclusively occurs at the N- or C-terminus of the true positive hits, or if the peptide proteins are all small molecules, the pattern is retained with a constraint ('<' or '>') imposed at the N- or C-terminus of the pattern to limit the maximum distance between the conserved pattern region and the N- or C-terminus of the peptide or precursor protein. If the pattern with such a restriction cannot distinguish the true positives from the false ones, the pattern is eliminated. (2b)Or, if the pattern has wildcard regions, the sequence fragments corresponding to the pattern in all the matching sequences are extracted and aligned. If the two groups of amino acids in a wildcard region X in this alignment have different physicochemical properties between the true and the false positive hits, the region X is replaced by the group of amino acids distinctively occurring in the true positive proteins. In the other case, when the two groups of amino acids share identical physicochemical properties, the pattern is discarded. The amino acid symbol sets: DE, KRH, NQ, ST, ILV, FWY, AG, C, M and P, which are classified based on the physiochemical nature of the side groups (Smith & Smith), are used.

If a conserved pattern cannot be obtained, the parameter C% is reduced by 10%, and Pratt is re-run against the same dataset. As the percentage of sequences to match the pattern decreases, a pattern which is usually longer and contains more sites than the previously one is shown up and processed by similar refinement and verification. The procedure is repeated until a pattern, which represents the majority of a group of related peptide sequences and rules out any known non-peptide proteins, is discovered.

Once a conserved pattern is identified in the peptide family dataset, the program ps-scan (ftp://ftp.expasy.org/databases/prosite/tools/ps_scan/sources/) is run locally on the pattern against this dataset. The sequence regions which match the pattern are removed from the original peptides. Each of the two remaining parts of the peptide sequences at their N- and C-terminus is left to form an independent sequence if it is not less than 4aa in length, given the assumption that the minimum length of the peptide pattern we search for is not less than this value. Thus, a reduced dataset is created including not only the peptides which are not covered by the identified pattern, but also the remaining sequences of the original peptides that match the pattern. This methodology is based on the fact that a peptide precursor protein may contain several conserved regions, and that our extracted peptide sequences include long peptide chains which may contain a few shorter, unrelated, bioactive peptides. The reduced peptide family dataset is then scanned by Pratt to discover the next pattern. The search procedure is repeated until the parameter C% is less than 50%.

This means that the remaining dataset contains no more patterns representing the majority of the sequences.

Fig. 1 represents the scheme of the described pattern searching procedure which is aimed to examine short bioactive peptide sequences rather than their large precursor molecules, and to take into account not only the biologically functional sites of each individual peptide discussed in literature, but also the general information which is extracted by the computational tool Pratt from all related peptides in a family.

5. Results

5.1 'PeptideMotif' database

We have built a peptide-precursor database consisting of 11,688 peptides and precursor proteins originated from 1420 metazoan organisms; of which 11,437 proteins (98%) are categorized into 110 distinctive peptide families. Based on bioactive peptide sequences drawn from the peptide families, we uncovered in total 211 conserved patterns which are assembled into the peptide motif database 'PeptideMotif'.

All the patterns range between 4 and 52 amino acids (column) in length with 78 (37%) no longer than 10aa. While each of the patterns covers most of the peptides or precursors belonging to the corresponding family, the false positives are kept to zero because it is guaranteed by the criterion that a known protein matching the pattern is indeed a peptide or precursor protein from this family.

5.2 Comparison with the other motif databases

The PROSITE database (http://ca.expasy.org/prosite) is a motif database of protein families and domains. It consists of biologically significant sites, patterns and profiles that help to reliably identify to which known protein family (if any) a new sequence belongs. Its 19.9 release contains 56 entries (patterns) describing 55 peptide families in Metazoa (the omega-atracotoxin family has two patterns) belonging to categories of cytokines and growth factors, hormones and active peptides, and toxins. All the 55 families are also covered by patterns in the 'PeptideMotif' database, and these peptide patterns (Table 1) share the similar length to their PROSITE counterparts. However, in terms of conserved sequence characteristics revealed in both database motifs, more amino acids are imposed at the conserved sites or wildcard regions in the 'PeptideMotif' patterns. This is due to the fact that the identified peptide patterns are not only trained by running them against the Swiss-Prot protein database which is also used as the test dataset by PROSITE, but also against the TrEMBL database, in which many proteins are also annotated by keywords or literature. In addition, for 25 of the 56 families, we have found 34 additional novel patterns and they are marked as 'new' in Table 1.

The remaining 121 'PeptideMotif' patterns presented in Table 2 allow the identification of 55 peptide families that are untouched by PROSITE signatures; they cover 3866 bioactive peptide sequences cleaved from 3572 precursors. Among the patterns, 28 representing 12 families are also not characterized by any other motif database, such as Pfam (Bateman et al., 2004) and CDD (Marchler-Bauer et al., 2005). The sequence reminiscence for these families is short and often occurs repeatedly within a same precursor protein. The sequences outside the conserved region are not well preserved, and thus a probability model based on protein sequence alignments cannot efficiently characterize such peptide families.

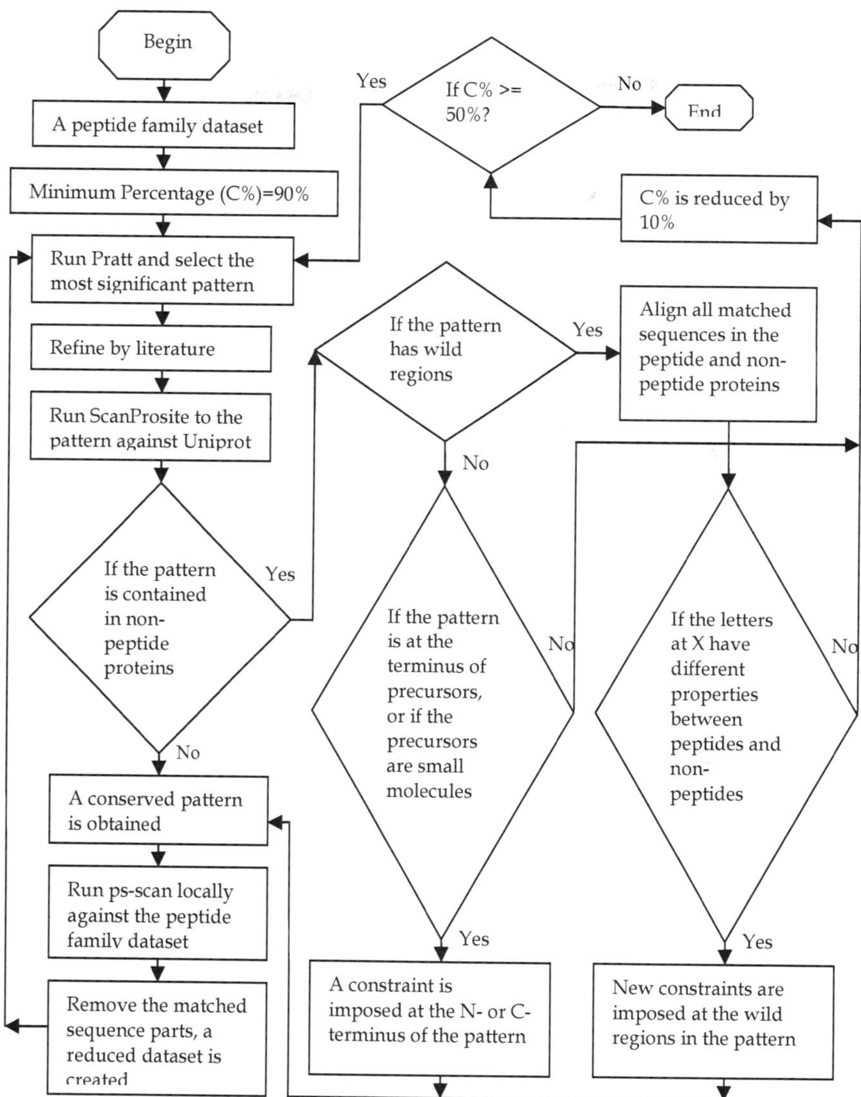

Fig. 1. Procedure for searching patterns in peptide sequences.
Note: The parameters are set as follows: the maximum pattern length (PL) is 52, the maximum length of a wildcard (PX) is 15, the maximum number of flexible wildcards (FN) is 3, the maximum flexibility of a flexible wild card (FL) is 8, the upper limit on the product of flexibilities for a pattern (FP) is 48, the minimum percentage of sequences to match the pattern (C%) is 90, 80, 70, 60 and 50%, respectively, and all other parameters are at default.

Cytokines and growth factors
(1) Granulins; (1) C-x-D-x(2)-H-C-C-{LIVM}-x(4)-C; {42, 241, 2}; {Q616A1, Q7JKP2, Q9U362}
(2)HBGF/FGF; (1) G-x-[LIVM]-{AGNP}-[STAGP]-{AGC}-{C}-x-{KRHNDE}-{WPC}-x-[STAGDENKRHQ](0,1)-[AGST](0,1)-[DENA]-C-{QP}-[FYLIVM]-{C}-[EQH]-x-{P}-{C}-{LIVM}-[DENKRHL]-{PLIVMDE}-[YHF]; (2) [GR]-[LIVM]-[LIVM]-{CWPDE}-[LIVM]-{PST}-{QLIVM}-x-[KRDEVIAGQFYNCS]-[STAGLMHQ]-{CP}-{AGDEN}-[FY]-[LIVM]-[AGSC]-[MLIV]-[NSTDEK]-[GAKRSTNDEQ]-[EDNKRHSTQA]-G(new); (3) G-S-[RHKQ]-[LIVM]-{CWPDE}-[LIVM]-{PST}-{QLIVM}-x-[KRDEVIAGQFYNCS]-[STAGLMHQ]-{CP}-{AGDEN}-[FY]-[LIVM]-[AGSC]-[MLIV]-[NSTDEK]-[GAKRSTNDEQ]-[EDNKRHSTQA]-G (new); {300,530,44}
(3) PTN/MK heparin-binding; (1) S-[DE]-C-x-[DE]-W-x-W-x(2)-C-x-P-x-[SN]-x-D-C-G-[LIVMA]-G-x-R-E-G (identical); (2) C-[KR]-[YF]-x-[KRFY]-x(2)-W-[AGST]-x-C-[DENST] (new); {51, 84, 1}
(4) Nerve growth factor; (1) [GSRAED]-[CR]-[KRLIVM]-G-[LIVAT]-[DE]-{C}-x(2)-[YW]-{P}-S-x-[CR]; (2) [SAP]-[LIVA]-C-[DEY]-[SAG]-{WM}-[STDENC]-x-W-[VE]-[AGSTNI] (new); {321, 471, 12}
(5)Platelet-derived growth factor (PDGF); (1) P-[PSRAKQGL]-C-[LIVMFYAGST]-x(3)-[RQ]-C-[AGSTMLIVN]-G-S(0,1)-[CN]-C; {158, 158, 23}
(6)Small cytokines C-x-C; (1) C-x-C-{CFYW}-{CW}-x(3)-{P}-x(2)-{C}(8)-x(5,8)-C-x(2,3)-[EQMA]-[LIVMTE]-[LIVMF]-x(9,14)-C-[LIVMRK]-[DENH]; {206, 206, 18}; { Q6DUZ6, Q6GLX8, Q4T8B9}
(7) Small cytokines (intercrine/chemokine) C-C; (1) C-C-[LIVMFYSTQRKHDE]-{P}(2)-{CDE}-{C}(7)-x(2,5)-{P}-[FYWAC]-{C}(2)-x(3,6)-C-{KM}-{C}(1,3)-[SAG]-[LIVMTS]-[LIVMRTDE]-[FYLIVDE]-{C}(7,10)-C-[STAGVILM]; {234, 234,27}; { Q3ZBN3, Q32L58}
(8)TGF-beta; (1) [WFYSTKRHL]-[LIVM]-[LIVMKRHF]-{CPNL}-P-{FY}-{PCW}-[FYILVA]-{C}-{QCWKRH}-{PA}-{PAGC}-C-{C}-[GE]-{C}-C; {766, 766, 59}
(9)interferon alpha, beta and delta; (1) [FYH]-[FY]-{CP}-[GNRKCDSTI]-[LIVM]-{W}-{AGC}-[KRN](0,1)-[FYLVIMN]-L-{PAG}-{C}-{PST}-{PFYW}-[FYHDEN]-x-{QY}-[CYQE]-[AT]-W; (2) L-{QKR}-x(0,4)-[GAEDVI]-[LVI]-[QHNDEFY]-[RQ]-[QH]-[LMIV]-[DENQVSTR]-x-L-[DENKRQ]-x-C-[LIVMKRQG] (new); {272, 442, 29}
(10)Granulocyte-macrophage colony-stimulating factor; (1) C-P-[LP]-T-{ST}-E-x-{QLIVMT}-C; {25, 25, 1}; {Q4G094}
(11) Interleukin-1; (1) [LIVSTNDEFH]-[YESTMVIR]-[LFC]-{AGCFYL}-[SA]-[ASLV]-{CFY}-[CFYWH]-[PKRST]-{FYLC}-[WHLIVM]-[FYL]-[LI]-[SCA]-[TSVG]-x(6)-[PKRHCLIVMT]-x(0,2)-[LIVM]-[AGSTCVINDE]; {128, 128, 24}
(12) Interleukin_2; (1) [ST]-E-[LF]-x(2)-L-x-C-L-x-[EDN]-E-L; {74, 74, 14}
(13) Interleukin_4_13; (1) [LI]-x-E-[LIVM](2)-{Q}(4)-x(0,1)-[LIVM]-[TL]-x(5,7)-C-x(2)-[LMIVST]-x-[IV]-x-[DNS]-[LIVMA]; (2) [KREV]-N-[STA]-[STED]-[DEAG]-{C}(3,4)-C-[RKT]-[AV]-x(11,17)-C (new); {73, 119, 4}
(14) Interleukin_6; (1) C-x(9)-C-[FYLIVM]-x(5)-G-L-x(2)-[FY]-x(3)-L; {69, 69, 8}
(15) Interleukin_7_9; (1) N-[DAT]-[LAPS]-[SCT]-F-L-K-{AGDE}-L-L; {20, 20, 2}
(16) Interleukin_10; (1)[KQSN]-{C}(4)-C-[QYCH]-x(4)-[LIVM](2)-x-[FL]-[FYT]-[LMVRT]-x-[DERST]-[IV]-[LMF]; {75,75,12}
(17) LIF / OSM; (1) [PSTA]-x(4)-F-[NQ]-x-K-x(3)-[CG]-x-[LF]-L-x(2)-Y-[HK] ; {24, 24, 4}
(18) Osteopontin; (1) P-x(1,5)-[KQ]-x-[TA]-x(2)-[GA]-S-S-E-E-K; {27, 27, 0}
Hormones
(19) Adipokinetic (1) [AGC]-Q-[LVI]-[NT]-[FY]-[ST]-[PASTKR]-[AGWSDEN]-W-[AGNDEST]; (2) <Q-[LVI]-[NT]-[FY]-[ST]-[PASTKR]-[AGWSDEN]-W-[AGNDEST>] (new); {45, 45, 0} {Q5TTQ9}
(20) Bombesin-like peptides (1) [HLIVMQ]-W-A-[STIVRK]-G-[SH]-[LF]-M; {42, 42, 1}
(21) Calcitonin/CGRP/IAPP (1) [KR]-R-x(0,1)-C-[SAGDNT]-[STNG]-x(0,1)-[STAGVIL]-[TS]-C-[VMALI]-x(3)-[LYF]-x(3)-[LYFVI]; (2) <x(0,1)-C-[SAGDNT]-[STNG]-x(0,1)-[STAGVIL]-[TS]-C-[VMALI]-x(3)-[LYF]-x(3)-[LYFVI] (new); {83, 84, 7}

(22) Corticotropin-releasing factor (1) [KR]-R-x(0,28)-[PQASLVIG]-[STPI]-[LIVM]-S-[LIVM]-x-[LIVMNAG]-[PST]-[LIVMFT]-x-[LIVM]-[LM]-[RN]-x(2)-[LIVMWF]; (2) <x(0,8)-[PQASLVIG]-[STPI]-[LIVM]-S-[LIVM]-x-[LIVMNAG]-[PST]-[LIVMFT]-x-[LIVM]-[LM]-[RN]-x(2)-[LIVMWF] (new); (3) T-R-[PQASLVIG]-[STPI]-[LIVM]-S-[LIVM]-x-[LIVMNAG]-[PST]-[LIVMFT]-x-[LIVM]-[LM]-[RN]-x(2)-[LIVMWF] (new); {64, 64, 9}; {Q4RWF4}

(23) Arthropod CHH/MIH/GIH neurohormones (1) [LIVM]-{C}-x(2)-C-[KR]-{FY}-[DENGRKHQ]-C-[FY]-{C}-{AGKRC}-{C}(2)-[FYILVM]-{C}-{CP}-C; {135, 135, 5} {Q23247}

(24) Erythropoietin/thrombopoeitin (1) P-x(4)-C-D-x-R-[LIVM](2)-x-[KRH]-x(14)-C; {34, 34, 8, 0}

(25)Granins   (1){DEF}-[DE]-[SN]-L-[SAN]-[AD]-[LIMVKR]-[DE]-[AGLSTQ]-E-L;   (2)   [LIVM]-x-[KHR]-C-[LIVM](2)-[ED]-[LIVM](2)-x(5)-[KRH]-[STP]-x(3)-[PST]-x(4)-C   (new);   (3)   K-R-[STAG]-[NDEST]-[ED]-x(2)-[DE]-[DEGA]-[QKR]-Y-[AGST]-P-Q   (new);   {63, 96, 5};   {Q86T07, Q4RYY8, Q566G8}

(26) Galanin (1) G-W-[ST]-L-N-[ST]-[AG]-[AG]-[FY]-[LIVM]-[LIVM]-G-P; (2) <L-N-[ST]-[AG]-[AG]-[FY]-[LIVM]-[LIVM]-G-P (new); {31, 31, 1}

(27) Gastrin/cholecystokinin (1) [FY]-x(0,2)-[GADN]-[AS](0,1)-[WH]-[MFLIV]-[DR]-F-G-[KR]-[RS]; (2) Y-x(0,2)-[GA]-[AS](0,1)-[WH]-[MFL]-[DR]-F> (new); {88, 102, 4}

(28)Glucagon/GIP/secretin/VIP   (1)   [YH]-[STAIVGD]-[DENQ]-[AGF]-[LIVMSTE]-[FY]-{QLPAGDEKR}-[DENSTAK]-[DENSTA]-[LIVMFYG]-[RKSTDEN]-x(3)-{P}-{P}-x(2)-[AGSTLIVMQ]-[KREQL]-[KRDENQL]-[LVFYWG]-[LIVQ]; {202, 305, 8}

(29) Glycoprotein hormones alpha chain (1) C-x-G-C-C-[FY]-S-x-A-[FY]-P-T-P; {109, 109, 4}

(30) Glycoprotein hormones beta chain (1)C-{C}(2)-[CW]-{C}(7,9)-C-[STAGMLIVED]-G-[HFYLRS]-C-{C}-[STA]; (2) <x(0,8)-C-[STAGMDEVLI]-G-[HFYL]-C-{CKRH}-[ST] (new); (3) <x-[CW]-{C}(7,9)-C-[STAGDEVLIM]-G-[HFYL]-C-{C}-[ST] (new); {341, 341, 13}

(31) Gonadotropin-releasing hormones (1) Q-[HY]-[FYW]-S-x(4)-P-G-G-[KR]-R; (2) Q-[HY]-[FYW]-S-x(4)-P-G> (new); {178, 188, 4}

(32) Insulin (1){C}(2)-[IVLMPSTAFYR]-{CNE}-x-{C}-C-C-{CPM}-{P}-{CHW}-C-[STDNEKIGQ]-{C}(2)-{CPAG}-[LIVMFSQ]-{CD}-{CPW}-{CHDEP}-C; (2) <x(0,205)-C-G-{FYILVMQW}-{CWPSTLIVM}-[LIVFY]-[VILMASTPH]-{AGHCFYPQW}-{CPQSW}-[LIVMRKHQWF]-{CNP}-{WCQP}-[LVIMATC]-C-{LM}-x(0,204)> (new);{507, 877, 52} {Q32L79, Q621L6, Q61VN2, Q61GN7, Q4T1R8}

(33) Natriuretic peptides (1) C-F-G-x(3)-[DEA]-[RH]-I-x(3)-[ST]-x(2)-G-C; {155, 155,10}

(34) Neurohypophysial hormones (1) C-[LIFY]-[LIFYV]-x-N-C-P-x-G; (2) C-x(2,6)-[CW]-G-x(4,6)-C-[FYAGLIVM]-x(3)-[LIVFY]-C-C (new); {112, 259, 4}

(35) Neuromedin U and S (1) [FY]-[LIVMF]-[FY]-R-P-R-N-G-[KR]; (2) [FY]-[LIVMF]-[FY]-R-P-R-N> (new); {24, 24, 3}

(36) Pancreatic (1)   [FY]-x(2)-{LIVM}-[LIVM]-x(2)-[YK]-x(3)-[LIVMFYRHK]-x-R-[PQVH]-R-[YF]-[GD]-[KR]-[RS];   (2)   [FY]-x(3)-[LIVM]-x(2)-[YK]-x(3)-[LIVMFYRHK]-x-R-[PQVH]-R-[YF]-x(0,1)> (new); {118, 118, 7}

(37) Parathyroid hormone (1) [KR]-R-x-[VI]-[STAGFYN]-[EH]-x-Q-x(2)-H-[DEN]-x-[GR]; {54, 54, 3}

(38) Pyrokinins (1) [AGHNQDEST]-{FYST}-[PQVIWFYED]-[FY]-[AGST]-P-R-[LI]-G-[KR]-R; (2) [AGHNQDEST]-{FYST}-[PQVIWFYED]-[FY]-[AGST]-P-R-[LI]> (new); {72, 89, 4} {Q7PTL2, Q5TV14}

(39) Somatotropin (1) C-{KRAG}-[STNRAC]-x(2)-[LIVMFYSRNW]-x-[LIVMSTAGY]-P-x(2)-{FYW}-x(2)-[TALIVMSHN]-x(7)-[LIVMFYP]-x(2)-{QHKR}-{KRHP}-{NW}-x-[LIVMFYR]-[LIVMSTC]-x-[STACVLMIG]-W;   (2)   C-[LIVMFG]-x-[KHRSNDEQVI]-[DEN]-{CNDEPQ}-{AGLMVI}-[KRMT]-{DENKRHPQ}-x-[STNALIVMF]-[FYLIVMKS]-[LIMVT]-x-{NDEKRH}-[LIVMATE]-[KRNEQTA]-C (new); (3) [ED]-K-L-L-[DE]-R-[VIA]-[IV]-x-H-[AT]-E-L (new); (4) C-F-[KRH](2)-[DEN]-[LIVMAG]-[HKR](2)-[LIVM]-[DEQ]-[ST]-[FYLIVM]-x(0,1)> (new); {633, 1093, 45}

(40) Tachykinin (1) [AGSTQKRFY]-[SF]-[IVFYTHQ]-G-[LVIM]-M-G-[KR]-[RS]; (2) [AGSTQKRFY]-F-[IVLMFYSHQ]-G-[LVIMS]-R-G-K-R (new); (3) <x(0,9)-F-[IVLMFYTHQ]-G-[LVIMSTAG]-[RM]> (new); {104, 124,6}

(41) Urotensin II (1) C-F-W-K-Y-C (identical); {30, 30,1}
(42) Endothelin (1) C-{C}-C-{C}(4)-D-{C}(2)-C-{C}(2)-[FY]-C; {50, 104, 2}
(43) Agouti (1) C-{C}(6)-C-{C}(6)-C-C-{C}(2)-C-{C}(2)-C-{C}-C-{C}(5,6)-C-{C}-C-{C}(6,9)-C; (2) C-{C}(6)-C-{C}(6)-C-C-{C}(2)-C-{C}(2)-C-{C}-C-{C}(5,6)-C-{C}-C-{C}(0,8)> (new); (3) C-{C}(6)-C-{C}(6)-C-C-{C}(2)-C-{C}(2)-C> (new); (4) C-{C}(6)-C-{C}(6)-C-C-{C}(2)-C-{C}(2)-C-{C}-C-{C}(5,6)-C(0,1)> (new); {37, 37, 7}
Antimicrobial
(44) Cecropin (1) W-[KDN]-{QNDEGAKRW}-[FYGA]-K-[KRE]-[LIVM]-E-[RKHAGN]-x-[AGVI]; (2) [GS]-[WRKHG]-[LIVMST]-[KRST]-K-{QNDEGAKRW}-[FYGA]-K-[KRED]-[LIVM]-E-[RKHAGN]-x-[AGVI] (new); {96, 96, 3} {Q5TWE5}
(45) Mammalian defensins (1) C-{C}-C-{C}(3,5)-C-{C}(6)-{CP}-[GARKSTW]-x-[SC]-{C}(6,10)-C-C; (2) C-[PR]-x-C-x(2,5)-C-x(2)-C-[PQ]-x-C-[PQ]-x-C (new); {119, 145, 5}
(46) Arthropod defensins (1) [CG]-x(0,1)-{C}-{CQ}-[HNSEDRY]-C-x(3)-{C}(0,1)-[GR]-{A}-x-[GRQAY]-[GAL]-x-C-{FY}-x(3,4)-C-{C}-C; (2) [CG]-x(0,1)-{C}(2)-[HNSEDRY]-C-x(3)-{C}(0,1)-[GR]-{A}-x-[GRQAY]-[GAL]-x-C-{FY}-x(6)-C-{C}-C (new); {103, 105, 7}; {Q6XD83}
(47) Cathelicidins (1) Y-{LIVM}-[EDQN]-[AVI]-[LMVI]-{HKRG}-[RKHQ]-A-[LIVMA]-[DQGEN]-x-[LIVMFY]-N-[DEQ]; {58, 58, 0}
Toxin
(48) Snake toxins (1) C-{CKRPL}-x(0,2)-C-[PRTFG]- {C}(5)-x(0,6)-C-C-{P}-x-[PDEN]-x-C-[NDEY]; {352, 352, 20}
(49) Myotoxins (1) K-x-C-H-x-K-x(2)-H-C-x(2)-K-x(3)-C-x(8)-K-x(2)-C; {15, 15, 0}
(50) Scorpion short toxin 1 (1) C-{C}(4,5)-C-{PC}-{CQ}-{C}-C-x(3)-{C}-{CPWA}-x(1,4)-[GASEDN]-[KRAVISNDE]-C-[VIMQTDK]-[NG]-x(1,2)-{P}-C-[HKRDENVI]-C; {77, 77, 6}
(51) Alpha-conotoxin (1) < x(0,35)-{C}(15)-C-C-[SHYNDE]-{C}(2,3)-C-{C}(3,7)-C-{C}(0,12)>; (2) <{C}(0,14)-C-C-[SHYNDE]-{C}(2,3)-C-{C}(3,7)-C-[G>]> (new); {34, 34, 1}
(52) I-superfamily conotoxin (1) C-{C}(6)-C-{C}(5)-C-C-{C}(1,3)-C-C-{C}(2,4)-C-{C}(3,10)-C (identical); {37, 37, 0}
(53) Mu-agatoxin and spider toxin SFI (1) C-{C}(2)-[DEKR]-{C}(3)-C-{C}(4,7)-C-C-{C}(2,4)-C-{C}-C-{C}(4,15)-C-{C}-C-x(0,10)>; {36, 36, 2}
(54) Omega-atracotoxin (ACTX) (1)C-[IT]-P-S-G-Q-P-C (identical); (2)C-C-[GE]-[ML]-T-P-x-C (identical); {13, 13, 0}
(55) Ergtoxin (1) C-{C}(5)-C-x(8)-C-{C}(2)-C-C-x(9)-C-x(4)-C-{C}-C {25, 25, 0}

Table 1. The conserved peptide patterns similar to PROSITE signatures.

Cytokines and growth factors
(1) Interferon gamma (1) [RHSG]-[KRQ]-A-[AGFYLIVM]-x-[DE]-[LIVFY]-{QPAG}-x-[VI]-[VMLIY]-{LVIM}-x(1,4)-L-[STAGPKRLIVM]-{Q}-x(1,9)-[AGKR]-[KR]-R; (2) [RHSG]-[KRQ]-A-[AGFYLIVM]-x-[DE]-[LIVFY]-{QPAG}-x-[VI]-[VMLIY]-{LVIM}-x(1,4)-L-S-P-x(1,7)>; {91, 91, 44}
(2) Interleukin_3 (1) [CVLIM]-[LIVM]-P-x-[AGPST]-x(2)-[STAGDENRKH]-x(12,14)-[DE]-F-[RKQ]-{NDEAGQST}-K-L; {20, 20, 0}
(3) Interleukin_5 (1) [HDE]-x(2)-C-x(3)-[IVLM]-F-x-G-[LIVMST]-x(2)-L-x-[NST]; {23, 23, 1}
(4) Interleukin_12 alpha (1) [KRHE]-[LM]-C-x(2)-[LM]-[KRHQ]-[AG]-x(3)-R-x(2)-T-x(2)-[KR]-x(3)-Y-[LMIV]; {34, 34, 7}
(5) Interleukin_15(1)C-{C}(4)-[LM]-{C}-C-[FY]-[LIVFYQ]-x-[DE]-[LIVM]-x(2)-[LIVM]-x(2)-[ED]; {44, 44, 1}

(6) Interleukin_17 (1) [RLM]-{QKR}-[PS]-{P}-x-[LIVMFY]-{RKH}-{CP}-[AS]-x-Cx-[CHKRNDESTFY]-x-[GRKHFY]-C-[LIVM]; {47, 47, 4}

(7) Interleukin_18 (1) [EQ]-[SY]-S-[SL]-x(2)-[GS]-x-[FY]-L-[AST]-[CF]; {41, 41, 3}

(8) Receptivity factor (1) L-[LIVMPAG]-x(2)-[YF]-[LIVM]-x(2)-[QLIVM]-[GA]-x-P-[LIVMFY]-x-[DENHKRLIVM]-[PAG]-[DEAGST]-[FY]; {204, 204, 0}

(9) GMF-beta (1) [FY]-[LIVM](2)-x-[STAG]-[FYWH]-x(5)-[DE]-x(5)-P-[LIVM]-x(2)-[LIVM]-[FYWN]-x(2)-P; {29, 29, 1}; {Q9VJL6, Q29NM1}

Hormones

(10) ACTH_domain and opioid neuropeptides (1) K-R-[YF]-G-G-F-[LIVMT]-[STGKRIV]-[AGKRSTLIVMPY]; (2) K-R-[YF]-G-G-F-[LIVMT]>; (3) K-[KN]-[YF]-G-G-F-M-[KR]; (4) <[YF]-G-G-F-[LIVMT]-[STGKRIV]-[AGKRSTLIVMPY]; (5){CFYWHM}-Y-x-[MIVSTFY]-{FY}-H-F-R-W; (6) <Y-x-[MIVSTFY]-{FY}-H-F-R-W; {397, 1045, 4}

(11) FMRFamide and related neuropeptides (1){LCFY}-{LCFYQWST}-{LCFYQWH}-{LCDEFYKRQW}-[LVMI]-[MLIV]-R-F-G-K-R;(2){LCFY}-{LCFYQWSTLIVM}-{LCFYQWHKR}-{LCDEFYKRQWLIVM}-[LM]-[MIV]-R-F-GR-[ASPD]-{LCFYHKR}-{LCQST};(3)<x(0,8)-[LVMI]-[MLIV]-R-F>;(4){CLIVM}-{CAGLIVMW}-{QCFYLW}-[FY]-[MLIV]-R-F-G-K-R; (5){CHIV}-x-{CQN}-{HIV}-{CLIVMY}-{CAGLIVMW}-{QCFYLWIV}-[FY]-[MLIV]-R-F-G-R-[DNESTAG];(6)<x(0,9)-[FY]-[MLIV]-R-F>;(7)[AGED]-[LIVMFY]-Q-G-R-F-G-R-[DEN];(8)P-[AGST]-[LIVM]-R-[MLIV]-R-F>;(9)N-Q-[VI]-R-F-G-K-R; (10) [STG]-[LVMI]-F-R-F-G-K-R; (11)[RD]-[QPH]-F-[FY]-R-F-G-[KR]-{FWYL}; (12)[RD]-[QPH]-F-[FY]-R-F>; (13)R-P-[VI]-G-R-F-G-[KR]-[RS]; (14)S-A-[LM]-A-R-F-G-[KR]-[RS]; (15)[PQ]-[HL]-[LMFY]-R-G-R-F-G-R; (16)[STNFYH]-[LQ]-PQ-R-F-G-[KR]-{LC}; (17)F-M-[NH]-F-G-K-R; (18)[AGNQ]-[GLE]-P-[LI]-R-F-G-[KR]-{QLIVMAG}; (19)P-[RK]-P-L-R-F-G>; (20)[FL]-G-T-M-R-F-G-[KR]-[RS]; (21)Q-[WL]-[LMIV]-[AGKRST]-G-R-F-G-[KR]; (22)[GA]-[GA]-[FY]-[ST]-[FY]-R-F-G-[RK]; (23)[GA]-[GA]-F-[ST]-[FY]-R-F>; {214,605,2}; {Q7YWT6, Q622X3,Q61P51, Q616K2, Q613X6, Q21656, P34405, Q60ZQ9, Q618S3, Q620F8, Q620P9, Q7PUD4, Q618T6, Q705J7, Q3SXL4, Q3KNG4, Q60YH4, Q622X1, Q28Z02, Q297C5, Q28Z02}

(12) Neuropeptide-like protein* (1) G-M-Y-G-G-[FYW]-G-R; (2) A-Q-[FW]-G-Y-G-[GY]-x(2)-[KRFYG]; (3) G-[FYW]-G-G-Y-G-G-Y-G-R-G; (4) P-L-Q-F-GK-R; (5) [STRIV]-M-S-F-G-K-R; (6) [AGIV]-M-[AG]-F-G-K-R; (7) [DE]-K-R-G-G-A-R-A-[FYLIVM]; (8) R-x-G-[FML]-R-PG-K-R; (9) [RFYM]-[AGTR]-F-A-F-A-K-R; {33, 84, 7}; {Q60NA1, Q619H9, Q624T4, Q61BN3, Q627I5, Q60MJ8, Q625G9, Q622L1, Q622L2}

(13) Wamide neuropeptides* (1) [QRKED]-{P}-[KRPQN]-[IVP]-G-[LM]-W-G-R-[RDESA]; (2) [ANPRKQ]-x-[AGLQP]-[RHKLIVP]-G-[LM]-W-G-K-R; (3) K-[KR]-x(1,5)-W-x(6)-W-G-[KR]-R; {10, 86, 1} {Q7Q4X3, Q8T3G1, Q60TK2, Q2LZG9}

(14) Thyroliberin (1)[KR]-[HKR]-Q-H-P-G-[KR]-R; {12, 78, 1}

(15) Neurotensin/neuromedin N (1)[KR]-[IVTRK]-P-Y-I-L-K-R; (2) [KR]-[IVTRK]-P-Y-I-L>; {14, 24, 0}

(16) Allatostatin* (1) [KR]-R-{NCKRFY}-x(0,11)-[FY]-[DENAGST]-[FY]-G-[LIVM]-G-[KR]-R; (2) <x(0,11)-[FY]-[DENAGST]-[FY]-G-[LIVM]>; (3) [KR]-R-x(0,3)-[FY]-[DENAGST]-[FY]-G-[LIVM]>; {52, 222, 3}; {Q7QAG2, Q29BZ8}

(17) Egg-laying hormone (1) K-R-R-[LIVM]-R-F-[HNY]-[KR]-R; (2) P-R-[LIVM]-R-F-[HNY]-[PSTDEN]-x-[KRG]-[KR]-[KR]; (3) P-R-[LIVM]-R-F-[HNY]-[PSTDEN]-x(1,2)>; {21, 32, 2}

(18) Periviscerokinin (1)<x(0,1)-[AG]-x(0,3)-[GS]-[LIVM]-[LIFY]-x-[FYAMV]-[AGPM]-R-x>;{59, 59, 0}

(19) Somatostatin (1) C-[KRM]-[NSIV]-[FY]-[FY]-W-[KRDE]-[STG]-x-[ST]-x-C; {71, 71, 2}

(20) Orcokinin* (1) [KR]-R-N-F-[DE]-[DE]-[IV]-[DE]-[KR]; (2) <N-F-[DE]-[DE]-[IV]-[DE]-[KR]; {3, 22, 0}; {Q7Q025, Q7QNH4, Q9W1F8, Q292P8}

(21) Allatotropin* (1)N-x(4)-[STIV]-A-R-G-[FY]-G-[KR]-R; (2)N-x(4)-[STIV]-A-R-G-[FY]>; {15, 18, 1}; {Q7QKW9, Q7PZX1}

(22) Ghrelin and Motilinrelated peptide (1) G-[STL]-[ST]-F-[LIVM]-[ST]-P-x(0,1)-[AGSTDE]-[FYQHM]-[QRK]; (2) [FY]-[VILM]-P-x-[FY]-[TS]-x(2)-[DE]-[LIVM]-[QRK]-[RK]-x-[QRK]-[ED]-[KR]; {68, 68, 12}
(23) ADM (1) [AG]-C-{P}-x-[AGFY]-[STMLIV]-C-[AGQIVT]-[VMLIFYHKR]-[QH]-x-[LIVM]; {23, 23, 1}; {Q4RDH7, Q6IFS9}
(24) Hepcidin* (1) C-[CGW]-x-C-C-{C}(4,5)-[CG]-G-x-C-C; {44, 44, 1}; {Q4RUL1, Q4RUL2}
(25) Achatin* (1) K-R-G-F-[AGF]-[DG]-K-R; (2) <G-F-[AGF]-[DG]>; {5, 20, 0}
(26) Cocaine- and amphetamineregulated transcript protein (1) C-x-C-x(5)-C-x(3)-[LIVM]-L-K-[C>]; {11, 11, 2}; {Q4RMR3, Q568S2, Q68EU1, Q4SGG2, Q4T695, Q4TBI3}
(27)Bradykinin (1) P-[PAT]-G-[FW]-[ST]-P-[FL]-R; {58, 84, 7}; {Q5XJ76}
(28) GBP/PSP1/paralytic (1) N-[FY]-x(2)-[GA]-C-x(2)-[GA]-[FY]-x-[RK]-[TS]-x-[DE]-[GA]-[RK]-C-[KR]-x-[TS]; {18, 18, 0}
(29) Stanniocalcin (1) C-L-x(2,6)-[GA]-C-x(2,5)-F-x-C-x(4)-[ST]-[CS]; {45, 45, 1}
(30) Resistin (1) C-x-C-x(3)-C-x(2)-W-x(7)-C-x-C-x-C-x(4)-W-x(4)-C-C; {22, 22, 2}
(31) Pro-MCH (1) [RK]-R-x(2,6)-[LMIV]-x-C-[MLIV](2)-[GA]-[RK]-[VLIM]-[FY]-x(2)-C-W; (2) R-[ED]-x(2)-[DE](3)-N-[ST]-[AG]-x-[FY]-[PK]-[IV]-[GD]-[RK]-R; {29, 39, 4}
(32) Pigment dispersing hormone (1) K-R-N-[ST]-[DEGA]-[LIVM](2)-N-[STAG]-[LIVM](2); (2) <N-[ST]-[DEGA]-[LIVM](2)-N-[STAG]-[LIVM](2); {21, 21, 1}; {Q298P6}
(33) Orexin (1) [HQ]-A-A-G-[IV]-L-T-[LIVM]-G-[KR]-R; (2) [HQ]-A-AG-[IV]-L-T-[LIVM]>; {11, 18, 0}
(34)Leucokinin* (1) [PQAGSTKRH]-x-F-[HYN]-[AGSP]-W-[GA]-G-K-R; (2) <x-[PQAGSTKRH]-x-F-[HYN]-[AGSP]-W-[GA]>; {11, 11, 0}; {Q60MR3, Q8MNU5}
(35)Myomodulin* (1) [LIVM]-[HQPST]-M-L-R-L-G-K-R; {3, 29, 0}
(36)Nitrophorin (1) C-[ST]-x(9,10)-[KRH]-x(2)-[FYW](2)-x(3,4)-[FYW](2)-x-[TS]-x-[FY]-x(4,5)-[PTS]; {11, 11, 1}
(37)Prokineticin (1) Q-C-x(4)-[CFY]-C-x(2)-[ST]-x(3)-[KR]-x-[LIVM]-[RK]-x-C-x-P-x-[GA]-x(2)-[GA]-x(2)-C-[HYF]-P; {35, 35, 1}
(38) Leptin (1)L-x-[VIT]-[FY]-[QRH]-[QKA]-[IV]-[LIVMH]-x-[SNG]-[LM]-[PHQS]; {68, 68, 13}
Antimicrobial
(39)Bombinin (1) K-R-[LIVM](2)-G-P-[LIVM](2)-x(2)-[VILM]-[STG]-x(2)-[LIVM]-x(2)-[LIVM](2); (2) <[LIVM](2)-G-P-[LIVM](2)-x(2)-[VILM]-[STG]-x(2)-[LIVM]-x(2)-[LIVM](2); (3) [SG]-IG-x(0,3)-[LIV]-x(2,7)-K-[STAGIV]-[AGFYIV]-[LIVF]-[KR]-[GAC]-[AGFYL]-[AGLVIM]-[KRN]; {59, 110, 0}
(40) Brevinin, Dermaseptin, Aurein, Caeridin, Caerin, Dahlein, Temporin Ponericin and Uperin (1) <x(7)-{C}(2)-x(0,68)-C-[KSTAGLVE]-[LIVA]-[STAKYD]-[KRYGN]-[KRDESTQLG]-C>; (2) C-[KSTAGLVE]-[LIVA]-[STAKYD]-[KRYGN]-[KRDESTQLG]-C-R-x>; (3) <[DGA]-[LIVF]-[LIVMFW]-[DNESAGQKPLM]-[STLIVMKFAGDN]-[LVIMAGTF]-[KRAGSTVIL]-[KRHDENGASTQ]-[LIVMAGKFYSTW]-[IVLMAGFKRH]-[AGKRHSTDENQLIV]-{W}-x(0,2)>; (4) <[DGA]-[LIVF]-[LIVMFW]-[DNESAGQKPLM]-[STLIVMKFAGDN]-[LVIMAGTF]-[KRAGSTVIL]-[KRHDENGASTQ]-[LIVMAGKFYSTW]-[IVLMAGFKRH]-[AGKRHSTDENQLIV]-{W}-{CP}(2)-x(0,35)>; (5) <x(0,45)-{QAGR}-{FYLQKRST}-K-R-[DGA]-[LIVFW]-[LIVMFW]-[DNESAGQKPLFM]-[STLIVMKFAGDN]-[LVIMAGTFY]-[KRAGSTVIL]-[KRHDENGASTQ]-[LIVMAGKFYSTW]-[IVLMAGFYKRH]-[AGKRHSTDENQLIV]-{W}-x(0,37)>; (6) <x(0,1)-[FIVLM]-[LIVMFYST]-[PGAQ]-x-[LIVMFY]-[AGSTIVLM]-[KRSTNDEMLIV]-[LIVMAGFY](0,1)-[LIVMAG](0,1)-x(0,2)-[GKRDEST]-[LIVM](2)>; (7) K-R-[FIVLM]-[LIVMFYST]-[PGAQ]-x-[LIVMFY]-[AGSTIVLM]-[KRSTNDEMLIV]-[LIVMAGFY](0,1)-[LIVMAG](0,1)-x(0,2)-[GKRDEST]-[LIVM](2)-G-K>; {278, 310, 25}
(41) Dermorphin (1) K-R-Y-A-F-x-[YVLI]-[PVILM]-x-[RG];(2) <Y-A-F-x-[YVLI]-[PVILM]-x>; {6, 22, 0}
(42)Termicin* (1) C-x(4)-C-W-x(2)-C-x(12)-C-x(4)-C-x-C; {21, 21, 0}

(43)Liver-expressed antimicrobial (1) [KR]-P-x(4)-C-x(5)-C-x(3)-[LIVM]-C-[KR]-x(2)-[RKHQ]-[CQ]; {15, 15, 0}; {Q4SXZ9, Q5M9I7}
(44) Penaeidin (1) [CR]-x(1,3)-C-{C}(2)-[LIVM]-{C}(7)-[CYF]-[CST]-{C}(3)-[GA]-x-C-C; {40, 40, 0}
(45) Ceratotoxin* (1) [ST]-[LIVM]-[GA]-[ST]-[AG]-x-[KR]-[KR]-[AG]-[LIVM]-P-[LIVM]-[AG]-[KR](2); {10, 10, 3}
(46)Attacin (1) [GTS]-[AGVMLI]-[AGFYST](0,1)-[FYLIV]-[AGDEL]-{GMQWKRHNDE}-{PKR}-[NKG]-[ADENHIV](0,1)-[NDEKR](0,1)-[GSR]-[HFL]-[GAS]-[GAL]-[STAED]-[LIVM]-[TSMQ]-[KRHDNEGA]-[TSEAG]-[HKRQGT] (2) Y-x-Q-[KRH]-L-[PG]-G-P-Y-G-N-S-x-P; {50, 50, 1}; {Q290V6, Q291C0, Q295K8, Q29QF8, Q29QG5}
(47)Beta-defensin (1) <x(0,79)-{WP}-x-C-{C}-{CP}-{CW}-{CA}-{C}(0,4)-C-{CP}-{C}-{CW}-{C}(0,2)-C-{C}(3)-{CP}(2)-{C}(2)-{CP}-{C}(1,5)-C-{C}(0,3)-{C}(4)-C-C-{CDENFWYP}-x(0,128)>; {326, 326, 13}; {Q32P86, Q2XXN6, Q2XXN7, Q2XXN8, Q2XXN9}
(48) 4 kDa defensin* (1) G-[CGA]-P-x(2)-[HQP]-x(2)-[CRK]-[DE]-x-[HP]-[CRWK]-[KR]-G-[MLIVEDN]; {27, 27, 0}
Toxin
(49)Conotoxin scaffold III/IV, muconotoxin and M conotoxin (1) <x(0,62)-{C}-x(2)-{C}(10)-C-C-{C}(2,6)-C-{C}(2,5)-C-{C}(1,5)-C-{C}(0,3)-C-{C}(0,3)>; (2) <{C}(0,9)-C-C-{C}(2,6)-C-{C}(2,5)-C-{C}(1,5)-C-{C}(0,1)-C-{C}(0,3)>; {62, 62, 0}
(50)Conotoxin scaffold IX and tau conotoxin (1) <x(0,49)-{C}(12)-{CDEFY}-{C}(2)-C-C-{C}(4,7)-C-{C}(0,2)-C-{C}(0,9)>; (2) <{C}(0,14)-C-C-{C}(4,7)-C-{C}(0,2)-C-{C}(0,9)>; {80, 80, 1}
(51)Conotoxin scaffold VI/VII, four-loop conotoxin, Spider potassium channel inhibitory toxin, O superfamily (1) <x-{PA}-x(0,17)-{C}(0,21)-{C}(2)-{CQ}-{C}(11)-{CI}-{CP}-{C}-{CH}-C-{C}(3,6)-C-{QC}-{C}(3,9)-C-C-{C}(2,8)-C-{CQ}-{C}(2,9)-C-{C}(0,9)>;(2)<{C}(0,16)-{CQ}-C-{CI}-{C}(2,5)-C-{QPC}-{C}-{CY}(2)-{C}(0,6)-C-C-{C}(2,8)-C-{CQ}-{C}(2,9)-C-{C}(0,9)>; (3) <C-{CI}-{C}(2,5)-C-{QPC}-{C}-{CY}(2)-{C}(0,6)-C-C-{C}(2,8)-C-{CQ}-{C}(2,9)-C-{C}(0,9)>; {408, 408, 25}
(52) Scorpion toxin (1) [CKDEN]-{C}(3)-[CI]-{CDEN}-{C}(2)-C-{C}(3)-C-{C}(6,10)-G-{C}(1,2)-[CF]-x-{C}(3,11)-C-[WYF]-C; (2) [CKDEN]-{C}(3)-[CI]-{CDEN}-{C}(4,9)-C-{C}(3)-C-{C}(6,10)-G-{C}(1,2)-[CF]-x-{C}(3,11)-C-[WYF]-C; {223, 223, 14}; {Q2TSD9}
(53) Scorpion short toxin 2 (1) C-x-P-C-x(10)-C-x(2)-C-C-x(5,7)-C-x(2,3)-Q-C-LIVM]-C; {14, 14, 0}
(54) Anenome neurotoxin (1) C-x-C-{C}(4)-P-x(6,8)-G-x(5,13)-C-x(6,9)-C-x(6,9)-C-C; {25, 25, 0}
(55) Melittin (1) [LIVM]-[GA]-x(2)-[LIVM]-[KR]-[LIVM]; (2)-x(3)-[LIVM]-P-x-[LIVM](2)-x-W-[LIVM]; {11, 11, 0}

Table 2. The novel conserved peptide patterns.
Note: each family is described in the following items: (1) the name of the family; (2) all identified patterns; patterns marked with 'identical' are completely identical to their PROSITE counterpart and the ones marked as 'new' are novel to PROSITE in Table 1; (3) the number of true positive peptide or precursor proteins, the number of matches to the pattern, and the number of false negative hits, all these numbers are in a bracket; (4) if there are novel putative peptides or precursors predicted by the patterns of the family, they are listed in a second bracket.

6. Case study

Patterns respectively representing the family of opioid and POMC-derived peptides as well as the FMRFamide and related neuropeptides (FARPs) are here shown as test cases in order to provide insights into the conserved sequence characteristics in many know peptide families and how the peptide patterns deduced based on these characteristics perform.

6.1 Opioid and POMC-derived peptides

The family includes subfamilies of opioid peptides and pro-opiomelanocortin (POMC) proteins, and proteins in this family vary in length ranging from large precursors with a few hundred amino acids, e.g. Q805B5 in *Chimaera phantasma* (325aa), to short peptides or partial sequence fragments, e.g. Q7M2Z6 in Sheep (13aa).

6.1.1 The subfamily of opioid peptides

Opioid peptides are neuropeptides that are involved in pain control mechanisms in vertebrates, and they consist of proenkephalin (PENK), nociceptin (PNOC) and prodynorphin (PDYN) (Comb et al., 1982). The 41-column PROSITE pattern PS01252 'C-x(3)-C-x(2)-C-x(2)-[KRH]-x(6,7)-[LIF]-[DNS]-x(3)-C-x-[LIVM]-[EQ]-C-[EQ]-x(8)-W-x(2)-C' matches 39 Uniprot proteins. However, 92 remaining sequences from the subfamily are disregarded; including nine full peptide precursors e.g. zebrafish Q7T3L0 and 83 peptides or sequence fragments e.g. human Q9BYY3.

The subfamily is also described by a 71-column Pfam motif PF01160. When querying this motif against all proteins in the subfamily by means of 'both global (ls) and fragment (fs)' search modes (http://www.sanger.ac.uk/Software/Pfam/search.shtml), 78 precursors are singled out. But, the other 53 opioid proteins, e.g. cat Q28409, zebrafish Q8AX66 and Q9W687 from *Acipenser transmontanus*, cannot be recognized by the Pfam motif with a score higher than a gathering threshold.

A further investigation into the proteins missed by the Pfam motif is conducted by comparing them with all proteins in the non-redundant protein sequence database nr using BLAST (http://www.ncbi.nlm.nih.gov/BLAST). The alignments with Q28409 (Fig. 2) reveal that, while the similarities between the two Mammal precursors Q28409 and P01210 are conserved along the entire sequences, the resemblances between Q28409 and Q8AX66/Q4RIZ7 from the remote phylum of Actinopterygii are confined to a limited region identified as '[KR]-[KR]-Y-G-G-F-[ML]-[KR]-[KR]'. The few highly conserved amino acids are also observed from the alignments between Q9W687 and Q5Y3C6 from Chondrichthyes and Q6SYA7 from Dipnoi (Fig. 3). However, this conserved region is too short to produce a significant score, and therefore BLAST comparison alone will fail to detect the limited similarity preserved among the distant homologues with a critical confidence level.

The existing PROSITE pattern and the Pfam motif both characterize only the conserved N-terminal region of the peptide precursors, they are thus not sufficient in identifying all short bioactive opioid peptides or sequence fragments which are cleaved from their large precursors and do not carry the N-terminal part of the proteins, but nevertheless bring the crucial conserved peptide sequence region with them and preserve the fundamental function of the peptide subfamily. Therefore, although the sequences, e.g. Q28409, Q8AX66 and Q9W687, cannot be identified by the existing motifs, they all share the pattern '[KR]-[KR]-Y-G-G-F-[ML]-[KR]-[KR]' from our 'PeptideMotif' database. The pattern, which is derived from the bioactive peptide sequences, could be more functionally conserved and more performable in identifying opioid peptides or entire precursor proteins.

6.1.2 The subfamily of POMC-derived peptides

The subfamily shares similar peptide sequences with opioid precursors, but also contains other non-opioid peptides such as ACTH and alpha-MSH, which are involved in the stress response and stimulate corticosteroid release (Arends et al., 1998).

```
Query=Q28409|PENK_FELCA Proenkephalin A-Felis silvestris catus(Mammalia) Length=187

> P01210|PENK HUMAN   Proenkephalin A precursor - Homo sapiens (Mammalia)
Length=267   Score =  429 bits (1004),  Expect = 1e-118

Query   WETCKEFLKLSQLEIPQDGTSALRESS-PEESHALRKKYGGFMKRYGGFMKKMDELYPQE
        WETCKE L+LS+ E+PQDGTS LRE+S PEESH L K+YGGFMKRYGGFMKKMDELYP E
Sbjct   WETCKELLQLSKPELPQDGTSTLRENSKPEESHLLAKRYGGFMKRYGGFMKKMDELYPME

Query   PEEEAP-AEILAKRYGGFMKKDAEEEEDALASSSDLLKELLGPGETETAAAPRGR-----
        PEEEA +EILAKRYGGFMKKDAEE+ D+LA+SSDLLKELL  G+       R R
Sbjct   PEEEANGSEILAKRYGGFMKKDAEED-DSLANSSDLLKELLETGDN------RERSHHQD

Query   ---DDEDVSKSHGGFMRALKGSPQLAQEAKMLQKRYGGFMRRVGRPEWWMDYQKRYGGFL
        ++E+VSK +GGFMR LK SPQL  EAK LQKRYGGFMRRVGRPEWWMDYQKRYGGFL
Sbjct   GSDNEEEVSKRYGGFMRGLKRSPQLEDEAKELQKRYGGFMRRVGRPEWWMDYQKRYGGFL

Query   KRFADSLPSDEEGESYS
        KRFA++LPSDEEGESYS
Sbjct   KRFAEALPSDEEGESYS

> Q8AX66|Q8AX66_BRARE Proenkephalin (Fragment) - Brachydanio rerio (Actinopterygii)
Length=216  Score =  140 bits (324),  Expect = 9e-32

Query   KKYGGFMKRYGGFMKKMDELYPQEPEEEAPAEILAKRYGGFMKKDAE----EEED-----
        KKYGGFMKR                +E L KRYGGFMKK AE    E ED
Sbjct   KKYGGFMKR-------------------SESLIKRYGGFMKKAAEFYGLESEDVDQGR

Query   ALASSSDLLKELLGP-----GETETAAAPRGRDDED-VSKSHGGFMR-----ALKGSPQL
        A+ ++ D+ E+L        GE E AA R + E+ +K +GGFMR     AL
Sbjct   AILTNHDV--EMLANQVEADGEREEAALTRSKGGEEGTAKRYGGFMRRGGLYAL------

Query   AQEA--KMLQKRYGGFMRRVGRPEWWMDYQ--KRYGGFLKRFADSLPSDEEGE
          E+  + LQKRYGGFMRRVGRP+WW   Q  KRYGGFLKR      S E+ E
Sbjct   --ESGVRELQKRYGGFMRRVGRPDWW---QESKRYGGFLKR------SQEQDE

> Q4RIZ7|Q4RIZ7_TETNG Chromosome undetermined SCAF15040 - Tetraodon nigroviridis
(Actinopterygii)  Length=246 Score =  123 bits (283),  Expect = 2e-26

Query   KKYGGFMKRYGGFMKKMD------ELYPQEPEEEA--PAEIL-----------------
        KKYGGFMKRYGGFM + D      E +P +P+EE     EIL
Sbjct   KKYGGFMKRYGGFMSRRDVPEGALE-HPSDPDEEENIRLEILKILNAAAVHGSEGGGKAG

Query   --AKRYGGFMKKDAEEEEDALASSSDLLKELLGPGETETAAAPRGRDDEDVSKSHGGFMR
          KRYGGFM++ AEE     A+  DLL+ +LG                          R
Sbjct   EEGKRYGGFMRR-AEEG----AAQGDLLEAVLG---------------------------R

Query   ALKGSPQLAQEAKMLQKRYGGFMRRVGRPEW-------------WM---DYQKRYGGFL
        LK          KRYGGFMRRVGRPEW             W   D QKRYGGF+
Sbjct   GLK------------KRYGGFMRRVGRPEWLVDSSKRGGVLKRAWGSDNDLQKRYGGFM
```

Fig. 2. Sequence alignments between Q28409 and P01210/Q8AX66/Q4RIZ7 by BLAST.
Notes: the conserved opioid peptide sequence similarities are in bold.

No signature represents the subfamily in PROSITE; three Pfam motifs explain the proteins including PF08384 (45 columns), PF00976 (41 columns) and PF08035 (31 columns). These motifs capture separate conserved regions located respectively at the N-ternimus of the precursors after the removal of the signal peptide, at the sequences coding for ACTH and for 'beta-endorphin' peptides. However, the remaining parts of the precursors encoding for peptides of gamma-MSH (12aa) and beta-MSH (17aa) are left untouched. As a result, 27 mature peptides or sequence fragments, e.g. Q9PRN3 from the *Sea lamprey*, horse P01202 and leech P41989, cannot be detected by any of these Pfam motifs.


```
Query= Q9W687|Q9W687_ACITR Proenkephalin (Fragment)-Acipenser
transmontanus (Actinopterygii)   Length=45

> Q5Y3C6|Q5Y3C6_HETPO Proenkephalin - Heterodontus portusjacksoni
 (Chondrichthyes)  Length=264 Score = 39.2 bits (85),  Expect = 0.032

Query  14    RYDGFSKQ------PEHTDSKEITSEEV---EKRYGGFM  43
             RY GF K+      P   D  EI S+EV   EKRYGGFM
Sbjct  225   RYGGFMKRWNDILVPSDEDG-EIYSKEVPELEKRYGGFM  262


Score = 31.2 bits (66),  Expect = 8.7

Query  14    RYDGFSKQPEHTDSKE--ITSEEVE----------KRYGGFM  43
             RY GF K+     DS +  I+  EV+         KRYGGFM
Sbjct  105   RYGGFMKK---ADSGDMYIS--EVDDENKGREILSKRYGGFM  141

> Q6SYA7|Q6SYA7_PROAN Prodynorphin (Fragment) - Protopterus annectens
 (Dipnoi)  Length=191 Score = 33.7 bits (72),  Expect = 1.5

Query  33    EEVEKRYGGFM  43
             EE++KRYGGFM
Sbjct  169   EELQKRYGGFM  179
```

Fig. 3. Sequence alignments between Q9W687 and Q5Y3C6/Q6SYA7 by BLAST.
Note: the conserved opioid peptide sequence similarities are in bold.

The BLAST alignment between Q9PRN3 and all proteins in the nr database unveils that, although Q9PRN3 cannot be identified by the Pfam motifs, it shares the highly conserved 'PeptideMotif' pattern 'Y-x-[MV]-x-H-F-R-W' with other POMC subfamily members, e.g., Q2L6A9 from Hyperoartia, P01193 and Q53WY7 from Mammalia, and Q32U15 from Amphibia (Fig. 4). This 8-column peptide pattern is a part of the 41-column Pfam motif PF00976. While the sequence region, which is described by this Pfam motif, may be an entire functional or structural domain, this peptide pattern contained within the longer domain is probably the most essentially functional part.

In total, our procedure identifies six novel peptide patterns in the combination of these two subfamilies. Among all the 397 proteins in this family, 113 were found to contain two of the peptide patterns, and the rest match one of them. These patterns characterize conserved domains located at different regions of a precursor sequence, and each of them can exclusively represent an opioid or POMC peptide or its precursor protein.

6.2 FMRFamide and related neuropeptides (FARPs)

It is widely known that FARPs occur throughout the whole animal kingdom and therefore this family is an ideally suited test case to check whether the disclosed pattern is capable of retrieving FARPs from all metazoan species (Ubuka et al., 2009). In total, 23 conserved peptide patterns have been uncovered from the family, and they match 214 FARPs sequences with 605 hits due to the presence of multiple copies of the conserved patterns within some precursor proteins. The identified FARPs distribute among a wide range of phyla, including Nematoda (85), Arthropoda (50), Mollusca (24), Annelida (9), Platyhelminthes (1), Cnidaria (10) and Chordata (35).

An 11-column Pfam motif PF01581 characterizes FARPs from all above-mentioned phyla except Chordata, e.g. human Q9HCQ7 and mouse Q9WVA8. In addition, conversely to the 'PeptideMotif' patterns, 49 FARP peptides or precursor proteins in these characterized phyla, e.g., Q9TWD2 from *Lymnaea stagnalis* and Q95QP2 from *Caenorhabditis elegans*, cannot be revealed by the Pfam motif with a significant score (e-value <0.01).

```
Query= Q9PRN3|Q9PRN3_PETMA Melanotropin MSH-B - Petromyzon marinus
(Hyperoartia)  Length=20

> Q2L6A9|Q2L6A9_MORMR Proopiomelanotropin (Fragment) - Mordacia mordax
(Hyperoartia)  Length=154 Score = 51.5 bits (114),  Expect = 5e-06

Query  2    QESADGYRMQHFRWGQPLP  20
            QE+ D YR+QHFRWG+PLP
Sbjct  11   QENPDAYRIQHFRWGEPLP  29

> P01193|COLI_MOUSE Corticotropin-lipotropin precursor(Pro-
opiomelanocortin) (POMC) - Mus musculus (Mammalia)  Length=235
Score = 32.5 bits (69),  Expect = 2.4

Query  8    YRMQHFRWGQP  18
            Y M+HFRWG+P
Sbjct  125  YSMEHFRWGKP  135

Score = 30.8 bits (65),  Expect = 7.7

Query  3    ESADG-YRMQHFRWGQP  18
            E  DG YR++HFRW  P
Sbjct  183  EKDDGPYRVEHFRWSNP  199

Score = 22.3 bits (45),  Expect =  2753

Query  8    YRMQHFRW  15
            Y M HFRW
Sbjct  77   YVMGHFRW  84

> Q53WY7|Q53WY7_HUMAN Proopiomelanocortin (Fragment) - Homo sapiens
(Mammalia)  Length=30 Score = 22.3 bits (45),  Expect =  2753

Query  8    YRMQHFRW  15
            Y M HFRW
Sbjct  3    YVMGHFRW  10

> Q32U15|Q32U15_9NEOB Proopiomelanocortin A (Fragment) - Trachycephalus
jordani (Amphibia)  Length=82 Score = 23.1 bits (47),  Expect =  1529

Query  8    YRMQHFRW  15
            Y M HFRW
Sbjct  23   YVMSHFRW  30
```

Fig. 4. Sequence alignments between Q9PRN3 and P01193/Q53WY7/Q32U15 by BLAST.
Note: the conserved peptide sequence similarities are in bold.

The Clustal-W multi-alignment of all these FARP sequences together or within each of the seven phyla using default parameters (http://www.ebi.ac.uk/clustalw/) shows that the FARP precursors display sequence similarities within the mature peptide regions, particularly in the area containing the conserved peptide patterns, and that the remaining parts of the precursor sequences display rather low similarities. The FARP peptide precursors also differ from each other by the number of peptide repeat units within the sequences, which is thought to have arisen by unequal crossover events (Lee et al., 1998). In addition, we also observed that most of the mature FARP peptides share common C-terminal sequences but have much mutated N-terminal extensions. All these make it problematic to construct an accurate multiple alignment in order to derive a statistical model which represents distantly related proteins from various phyla throughout the evolutionary history of the FARP peptide family.

7. Conclusion

Protein domains are highly conserved throughout evolution and there are several databases available that catalogue protein families and domains. Such motif and domain databases are very useful in assigning a putative function to an unknown protein. Peptide precursor proteins are a distinctive class of molecules because they undertake various posttranslational modifications in order to ultimately synthesize stabilized and functional mature peptides, making the annotation of peptides and peptide precursor proteins challenging. This is illustrated by the fact that many metazoan peptides and peptide precursors are not represented by the motifs currently present in the widely used motif database such as PROSITE.

Because of the tremendously increasing number of protein sequences and because of the wide range of peptide families, a comprehensive database of conserved patterns typical for endogenously occurring mature peptides is of great value in identifying new peptides and precursor proteins to catch up with their sequencing rate. We therefore have designed a searching procedure to find conserved patterns within the known peptides, and as a result, we have constructed a 'PeptideMotif' database that is representative of most currently known peptide families.

Many peptides have been isolated and sequenced as mature peptides and their precursor proteins are often unknown as yet. Therefore, these small peptides are difficult to be identified by other motif databases. Motifs in databases such as Pfam contain two Hidden Marcov Models (HMMs) for each family based on a multiple protein sequence alignment, one built to find complete domains (ls mode) and the other to match fragments of domains (fs mode) (Durbin et al., 1998). These motifs are sensitive at identifying complete domains and thus they can efficiently detect the proteins which have similarities that cover the full length protein sequence or at least contain a complete domain. However, these motifs do not work very well when they encounter short peptides which lack information on amino acids at the sites outside the peptide sequences, or when the conserved regions are limited, especially in distantly related proteins where the overall-length sequence similarity may be not well preserved. In contrast, the patterns derived directly from the mature peptide sequences grasp the highly preserved region of the precursor proteins and thus are able to identify not only the peptide precursor molecules but also the fully processed peptides.

Conservative peptide sequence patterns correspond to functionally and structurally important parts of the peptides, i.e. the binding site to specific receptors, the disulphide bonds for stability and tertiary structure. The discovery of peptide motifs will be undoubtedly of great value for any peptide-related studies ranging from the identification of putative peptides and precursor proteins to the annotation of critical functional residues (Husson et al., 2010), to the complement of peptidomic research in detecting and verifying peptides in vitro (Baggerman et al., 2004; Boonen et al., 2008; Menschaert et al., 2010). For example, scanning the peptide patterns against Uniprot revealed 95 proteins (listed in Tables 1 and 2) which are not as yet annotated as putative peptides or precursor proteins.

When determining short functional patterns for peptide sequences, we have to evaluate how representative the peptide motifs are in the 110 characterized peptide families. Short motifs often have some degree of degeneracy and the presence of a motif in a protein may reflect a conserved functional role, a yet to be discovered structural functional role or a non-functional role. When using the short currently identified peptide patterns, while the false positives are kept to zero, we observe that 440 (3.8%) of the mature peptides or sequence fragments and 282 (2.5%) of the peptide precursor proteins in these described families cannot be recognized by the peptide patterns. Many of them could be determined by combining the peptide pattern search procedure with the structural hallmarks of bioactive peptides and their precursors (Liu et al., 2006), such as the length of a peptide precursor which is usually not longer than 500 amino acids, the presence of a signal peptide which directs a precursor protein into the secretary pathway of the cell, and the presence of typical cleavage sites flanking the mature peptides. To be even more successful in identifying all false negatives while eliminating all false positives because of the short length and degeneracy of most short motifs, it may be possible to make use of 3D structural patterns when they become available for peptide precursor proteins. Patterns that integrate 3D structural information of the sequences will be more sensitive in identifying peptides and peptide precursors (Gribskov et al., 1988; Taylor et al., 2004).

While the majority of known peptide families have been profiled by the established peptide patterns, the remaining ones accounting for in total 251 peptides and precursor proteins (2% of all the proteins in the peptide-precursor database) are not processed by the pattern search procedure. They are from small peptide families, such as eclosion hormones, ecdysis-triggering hormones and apelin, which have only a few homologies so far. A pattern based on the small number of peptides usually cannot gain enough confidence in representing the family, and also cannot sufficiently reflect the sequence divergence accumulated in the evolutionary course of the family member. As more peptides and precursor proteins are sequenced, our patterns search procedure can be applied to the corresponding families and the 'PeptideMotif' database will be updated accordingly, keeping the peptide pattern database widely applicable for the identification of critical functional residues and for the annotation of hypothetical molecules in various peptide families.

8. References

Altschul, S.F.; Madden, T.L.; Schaffer, A.A.; Zhang, J.; Zhang, Z.; Miller, W. & Lipman, D.J. (1997). Gapped BLAST and PSI-BLAST: a new generation of protein database search programs. *Nucleic Acids Res*, Vol. 25, No. 17, pp. 3389-3402, ISSN 0305-1048

Arends, R.J.; Vermeer, H.; Martens, G.J.; Leunissen, J.A.; Wendelaar Bonga, S.E. & Flik G. (1998). Cloning and expression of two proopiomelanocortin mRNAs in the common carp (Cyprinus carpio L.). *Mol Cell Endocrinol*, Vol.143, No. 1-2, (August 1998), pp. 23–31, ISSN 0303-7207

Baggerman, G.; Cerstiaens, A.; De Loof, A. & Schoofs, L. (2002). Peptidomics of the larval Drosophila melanogaster central nervous system. *J. Biol. Chem*, Vol. 277, pp. 40368-40374, ISSN 0021-9258

Baggerman, G.; Liu, F.; Wets, G. & Schoofs, L. (2005). Bioinformatic analysis of peptide precursor proteins. *Ann N Y Acad Sci*, Vol.1040, pp. 59–65, ISSN 0077-8923

Baggerman, G.; Verleyen, P.; Clynen, E.; Huybrechts, J.; De Loof, A. & Schoofs, L. (2004). Peptidomics. *J Chromatogr B Analyt Technol Biomed Life Sci*, Vol. 803, No. 1, pp. 3-16, ISSN 1570-0232

Bateman, A.; Coin, L.; Durbin, R.; Finn R.D.; Hollich, V.; Griffiths-Jones, S.; Khanna, A.; Marshall, M.; Moxon, S.; Sonnhammer, E.L.L.; Studholme, D.J.; Yeats, C. & Eddy, S.R. (2004). The Pfam protein families database. *Nucl Acids Res*, Vol. 32, No. suppl 1, pp. D138–41, ISSN 0305-1048

Boonen, K.; Baggerman, G.; D'Hertog, W.; Husson, S.J.; Overbergh, L.; Mathieu, C. & Schoofs, L. (2007). Neuropeptides of the islets of Langerhans: a peptidomics study. *Gen Comp Endocrinol*, Vol. 152, No. 2-3, pp. 231-241, ISSN 0016-6480

Boonen, K.; Landuyt, B.; Baggerman, G.; Husson, S.J.; Huybrechts, J. & Schoofs, L. (2008). Peptidomics: the integrated approach of MS, hyphenated techniques and bioinformatics for neuropeptide analysis. *J Sep Sci*, Vol. 31, No. 3, pp. 427-445, ISSN 1615-9306

Boonen, K.; Husson, S.J.; Landuyt, B.; Baggerman, G.; Hayakawa, E.; Luyten, W.H. & Schoofs, L. (2010). Identification and relative quantification of neuropeptides from the endocrine tissues. *Methods Mol Biol*, Vol. 615, pp. 191-206, ISSN 1940-6029

Comb, M.; Seeburg, P.H.; Adelman, J.; Eiden, L. & Herbert, E. (1982). Primary structure of the human Met- and Leu-enkephalin precursor and its mRNA. *Nature*, Vol. 295, pp. 663-666, ISSN 0028-0836

Durbin, R.; Eddy, S.; Krogh, A. & Mitchison, G. (1998). *Biological sequence analysis: probabilistic models of proteins and nucleic acids*, Cambridge University Press, ISBN 9780521629713, Cambridge, UK

Filipsson, K.; Kvist-Reimer, M. & Ahren, B. (2001). The neuropeptide pituitary adenylate cyclase-activating polypeptide and islet function. *Diabetes*, Vol.50, No.9, pp. 1959–1969, ISSN 0012-1797

Finn, R.D.; Mistry, J.; Tate, J.; Coggill, P.; Heger, A.; Pollington, J.E.; Gavin, O.L.; Gunasekaran, P.; Ceric, G.; Forslund, K.; Holm, L.; Sonnhammer, E. L. L.; Eddy S. R. & Bateman A. (2010). The Pfam protein protein families database. *Nucleic Acids Res*, Vol.38, No. suppl 1, pp. D211-D222, ISSN 0305-1048

Gribskov, M.; Homyak, M.; Edenfield, J. & Eisenberg, D. (1988). Profile scanning for three-dimensional structural patterns in protein sequences. *Comput Appl Biosci*, Vol. 4, No. 1, pp. 61–66, ISSN 0266-7061

Henry, J.; Favrel, P. & Boucaud-Camou, E. (1997). Isolation and identification of a novel Ala-Pro-Gly-Trp-amide-related peptide inhibiting the motility of the mature oviduct in the cuttlefish, Sepia officinalis. *Peptides*, Vol.18, No. 10, pp. 1469–1474, ISSN 0196-9781

Hulo, N.; Sigrist, C.J.; Le, S.V.; Langendijk-Genevaux, P.S.; Bordoli, L.; Gattiker, A.; De Castro, E.; Bucher, P. & Bairoch, A. (2004). Recent improvements to the PROSITE database. *Nucl Acids Res*, Vol. 32, pp. D134–D137, ISSN 0305-1048

Husson, S.J.; Clynen, E.; Boonen, K.; Janssen, T.; Lindemans, M.; Baggerman, G. & Schoofs, L. (2010). Approaches to identify endogenous peptides in the soil nematode Caenorhabditis elegans. *Methods Mol Biol*, Vol. 615, pp. 29-47, ISSN 1940-6029

Husson, S.J.; Landuyt, B.; Nys, T.; Baggerman, G.; Boonen, K.; Clynen, E.; Lindemans, M.; Janssen, T. & Schoofs, L. (2009) Comparative peptidomics of Caenorhabditis elegans versus C. briggsae by LC-MALDI-TOF MS. *Peptides*, Vol. 30, No. 3, pp. 449-457, ISSN 0196-9781

Jonassen, I.; Collins, J.F. & Higgins, D.G. (1995). Finding flexible patterns in unaligned protein sequences. *Protein Sci*, Vol. 4, No. 8, pp. 1587–1595, ISSN 0961-8368

Lee, H.S.; Simon, J.A. & Lis, J.T. (1998). Structure and expression of ubiquitin genes of Drosophila melanogaster. *Mol Cell Biol*, Vol. 8, No. 11, pp. 4727–4735, ISSN 0898-7750

Liu, F.; Baggerman, G.; D'Hertog, W.; Verleyen, P.; Schoofs, L. & Wets, G. (2006). In silico identification of new secretory peptide genes in Drosophila melanogaster. *Mol Cell Proteomics*, Vol. 5, No. 3, pp. 510–522, ISSN 1535-9476

Liu, F. & Wets, G. (2005). A Neural Network Method for Prediction of Proteolytic Cleavage Sites in Neuropeptide Precursors. *Proceedings of the 2005 IEEE Engineering in Medicine and Biology 27th Annual Conference*, Vol. 3, pp. 2805-2808, ISSN 1557-170X, ShangHai, China, September 1-4, 2005

Marchler-Bauer, A.; Anderson, J.B.; Cherukuri, P.F.; Weese-Scott, C.; Geer, L.Y.; Gwadz, M.; He, S.; Hurwitz, D.I.; Jackson, J.D.; Ke, Z.; Lanczycki, C.J.; Liebert, C.A.; Liu, C.; Lu, F.; Marchler, G.H.; Mullokandov, M.; Shoemaker, B.A.; Simonyan, V.; Song, J.S.; Thiessen, P.A.; Yamashita, R.A.; Yin, J.J.; Zhang, D. & Bryant, S.H. (2005). CDD: a conserved domain database for protein classification. *Nucl Acids Res*, Vol. 33, pp. D192–196, ISSN 0305-1048

Masashi, Y.; Watanobe, H. & Terano, A. (2001). Central regulation of hepatic function by neuropeptides. *J Gastroenterol*, Vol. 36, pp. 361–367, ISSN 0002-9270

Menschaert, G.; Vandekerckhove, T.T.; Baggerman, G.; Schoofs, L.; Luyten, W. & Van Criekinge, W. (2010). Peptidomics coming of age: a review of contributions from a bioinformatics angle. *J Proteome Res*, Vol. 9, No. 5, pp. 2051-2061, ISSN 1535-3893

Rouille, Y.; Duguay, S.J.; Lund, K.; Furuta, M.; Gong, Q.; Lipkind, G.; Oliva AA, J., Chan, S.J. & Steiner, D.F. (1995). Proteolytic processing mechanisms in the biosynthesis of neuroendocrine peptides: the subtilisin-like proprotein convertases. *Front Neuroendocrinol*, Vol. 16, No. 4, pp. 322–361, ISSN 0091-3022

Schlesinger, D.H.; Pickart, L. & Thaler, M.M. (1977). Growth-modulating serum tripeptide is glycyl-histidyl-lysine. *Experientia*, Vol. 33, No. 3, pp. 324–325, ISSN 0014-4754

Schoofs, L. & Baggerman, G. (2003). Peptidomics in Drosophila melanogaster. *Brief Funct Genomic Proteomic*, Vol. 2, No. 2, pp. 114-120, ISSN 2041-2647

Taylor, W.R. & Jonassen, I. (2004). A structural pattern-based method for protein fold recognition. *Proteins*, Vol. 56, No. 2, pp. 222–234, ISSN 0887-3585

Vandenborne, K.; Roelens, S.A.; Darras, V.M.; Kuhn, E.R. & Van der, G.S. (2005). Cloning and hypothalamic distribution of the chicken thyrotropin-releasing hormone precursor cDNA. *J Endocrinol*, Vol. 186, No. 2, pp. 387–396, ISSN 0022-0795

Smith, R.F. & Smith, T.F. (1990). Automatic generation of primary sequence patterns from sets of related protein sequences. *Proc Natl Acad Sci USA*, Vol. 87, No. 1, pp. 118–122, ISSN 1091-6490

Ubuka, T.; Morgan, K.; Pawson, A.J.; Osugi, T.; Chowdhury, V.S.; Minakata, H.; Tsutsui, K.; Millar, R.P. & Bentley, G.E. (2009). Identification of human GnIH homologs, RFRP-1 and RFRP-3, and the cognate receptor, GPR147 in the human hypothalamic pituitary axis. *PLoS ONE*, Vol. 4, No. 12, e8400, ISSN 1932-6203

7

Database Mining: Defining the Pathogenesis of Inflammatory and Immunological Diseases

Fan Yang, Irene Hwa Yang, Hong Wang and Xiao-Feng Yang
*Department of Pharmacology, Cardiovascular Research Center, Temple University
School of Medicine, Philadelphia,
U.S.A.*

1. Introduction

Cardiovascular disease (CVD) is a leading cause of mortality in developed countries (Jan et al., 2010; Yang et al., 2008). Despite a long held understanding and strong characterization of the traditional and non-traditional risk factors for CVD, some mechanisms of CVD onset have only recently been uncovered. As a chronic inflammatory autoimmune disease, atherosclerosis and its progression involve innate and adaptive immune systems. Using new concepts and technologies to improve the current understandings of the molecular pathogenesis of inflammatory and immune responses would lead to the future development of novel therapeutics for these diseases.

Biomedical literature and databases, available in electronic forms, contain a vast amount of knowledge resulting from experimental research (Ishii et al., 2007; Palakal et al., 2007). In the past decade, both traditional hypothesis-driven research and discovery-driven "-omics" research, including genomics, transcriptomics (Liang et al., 2005), proteinomics, metabolomics, glycomics, lipidomics, localizomics, protein-DNA interactomics, protein-protein interactomics, fluxomics, phenomics (Joyce & Palsson, 2006), and antigen-omics (http://www.cancerimmunity.org/links/databases.htm) (Houle et al., 2010; Shimokawa et al., 2010; Weinstein, 1998;2002), has generated a tremendous amount of data and established many experimental data-based searchable databases. These databases include PubMed, nucleotide database, protein database, and other databases generated by the National Institutes of Health (NIH)/National Center for Biotechnology Information (NCBI) (see the NCBI handbook at http://www.ncbi.nlm.nih.gov/books/NBK21101/) and other institutions. This development has not only provided resources, but also raised unprecedented challenges and opportunities for biomedical scientists to develop more systemic and panoramic approaches to analyze the data contained in the databases and generate new hypotheses. The inconsistency between the vast amount of experimental data, various searchable databases, and relatively smaller numbers of database-mining research papers (< 50 papers on database mining in inflammation and immune responses listed in the PubMed) indicate the challenges that experimental biomedical scientists face, which include both technical/methodological difficulties and out-of-date concepts.

Traditionally, medical literature search using the Index Medicus was the major approach for biomedical scientists to identify knowledge gaps and preparing new hypotheses. However, this approach has been significantly enhanced by more systemic approaches such as *1)*

NCBI-PubMed search and Google Scholar search; 2) experimentally screening cDNA libraries and various arrays (nucleic acid arrays, antibody arrays, protein arrays and metabolic arrays) (King et al., 2005; Loza et al., 2007; Pandey et al., 2004; Warner & Dieckgraefe, 2002); and 3) mining experimental databases (Chen et al., 2010; Jan et al., 2010; Ng et al., 2004; Yang et al., 2006a; Yang et al., 2006b; Yin et al., 2009). The screening analysis of microarray data often requires bioinformatic methods, algorithms, and expertise. In comparison, database mining offers many advantages. First, database mining requires much less bioinformatic assistance in each laboratory when compared to the generation of algorithms required in microarray analyses, since the purpose of generating databases is to use bioinformatic approaches to mine easily organize the experimental data for biomedical scientists to mine (Spasic et al., 2005). Second, database mining enables full-value extraction from costly experimental data, and third, it provides panoramic analyses on existing knowledge gaps by generating new hypotheses for further experimental research. However, database mining requires biomedical scientists to have more conceptual advances than technical assistances. The purpose of database mining is to analyze experimental data deposited by various research projects, rather than predicting theoretic results based on pure theoretical bioinformatic studies. Thus, database mining is not limited to sequence comparisons of nucleic acids and proteins (Mount, 2004), sequence alignments, analysis of hydrophobicity index and functional domain prediction of proteins. Additionally, database mining has not generally been listed as a required course for graduate and postdoctoral studies, which presents a challenge of properly training young biomedical scientists with essential database mining techniques. On top of these aforementioned challenges, reviewers from peer-reviewed database mining publications often mistakenly regard the experimental data in electronic forms deposited in databases as "non-experimental or theoretical" and demand ridiculous additional verifying experiments to be performed, even requiring the use of outdated experimental techniques or methods. To overcome these difficulties, bioinformatic scientists will have to work together with biomedical colleagues and delve into the biological significance of database mining projects, rather than sticking to an argument of "no algorithms means no bioinformatics". Already, more and more database mining papers have been published as scientists put aside their differences. For example, the 2011 (18th) database issue of the journal "Nucleic Acid Research" features descriptions of 96 new and 83 updated online databases covering various areas of molecular biology (Galperin & Cochrane, 2011). The Nucleic Acids Research online Database Collection, available at: http://www.oxfordjournals.org/nar/database/a/, now lists 1330 carefully selected molecular biology databases. In addition, 32 databases and analysis resources of immunological interest have been established (Salimi et al., 2010). Moreover, our recent invited review lists 11 B cell antigen epitope databases and 13 T cell antigen epitope analysis resources (Jan et al., 2010). These progresses suggest that a data mining approach has gradually been accepted as mainstream practice in analyzing experimental data and generating new hypotheses for various projects (Salimi et al., 2010).

Our lab has successfully pioneered major advances in database mining in the fields of adaptive immune reactions, innate immune responses, and inflammation (Chen et al., 2010; Jan et al., 2010; Ng et al., 2004; Virtue, 2011; Yang et al., 2006a; Yang et al., 2006b; Yin et al., 2009). In this chapter, we will summarize the general approaches, principles, and databases used and new working models proposed in our database mining research. This discussion will prove to be important and useful for most biomedical scientists, since many are not often involved in the bioinformatic algorithm generation, but may want to use database mining methods in their research either as parts of existing experimental studies or as free-standing projects. Of note, the database mining concept is not "brand new". Medical research has a long history in full-value extraction from costly data. For example, a meta-analysis uses a statistical approach to combine the results of several epidemiological studies that address a set of related research hypotheses. This practice started well over 100 years ago and has been widely used in various disease-related researches (http://en.wikipedia.org/wiki/Meta-analysis) (Egger & Smith, 1997; Egger et al., 1997). We believe that the practice of database mining will become a routine exercise to identify existing knowledge gaps and to generate new hypotheses.

2. Principles of database mining

In recent years, many databases regarding immune responses and inflammation have been established (Jan et al., 2010; Yang et al., 2006a), which have expanded the scope and depth of a publicly searchable online repertoire of tools. The results derived from the database mining analyses have become parts of many research papers or free-standing papers. Although projects may vary in format, database mining approaches follow the same set of principles (Fig. 1): 1) Hypothesis: A clearly-presented hypothesis based on the current biomedical literature search in a given field and previous experimental data in the lab is required to carry on a database mining project as we reported (Ng et al., 2004; Yan et al., 2004), which is similar to that of experimental projects. Of note, the database mining referred here focuses on database mining as a free standing project rather than as a part of experimental research; 2) Scope: Database mining scopes in terms of gene numbers are far more than that examined in experimental approaches. For example, our own research will examine mRNA transcript expressions of about 30 genes including all the reported toll-like receptors, NOD-like receptors, and inflammatory caspases in more than ten tissues. This scope allows us to obtain a panoramic view on the expressions of inflammatory pathways without focusing on a single gene in many tissues (Yin et al., 2009); 3) Suitable databases: Databases that are suitable for examining the hypothesis are available for online analytic search, which is also similar to the methods and reagents for experimental projects; 4) Sizable experimentally verified data for generating confidence intervals with statistical significance: To consolidate the results generated from database mining, the experimentally verified data are published by various laboratories, which can be used to generate statistically significant confidence intervals by using the same online analysis tools as we reported (Virtue, 2011). In this study, our analysis in the TargetScan yielded 524 microRNAs, which were predicted to participate in 1368 unique interactions with the 33 inflammatory gene mRNAs. To ensure relevance, we examined the context value and percentage of experimentally verified microRNAs. Confidence intervals were generated from 45 interactions between 28 experimentally verified human microRNAs and 36 genes found within the Tarbase, an online database of experimentally verified microRNAs (http://diana.cslab.ece.ntua.gr/tarbase/) (Papadopoulos et al., 2009; Sethupathy et al., 2006). These experimental interactions were also selected based on their confirmation by luciferase reporter assays and single site specificity. The 45 microRNA-mRNA interactions that met these criteria were then evaluated in TargetScan to determine the microRNA

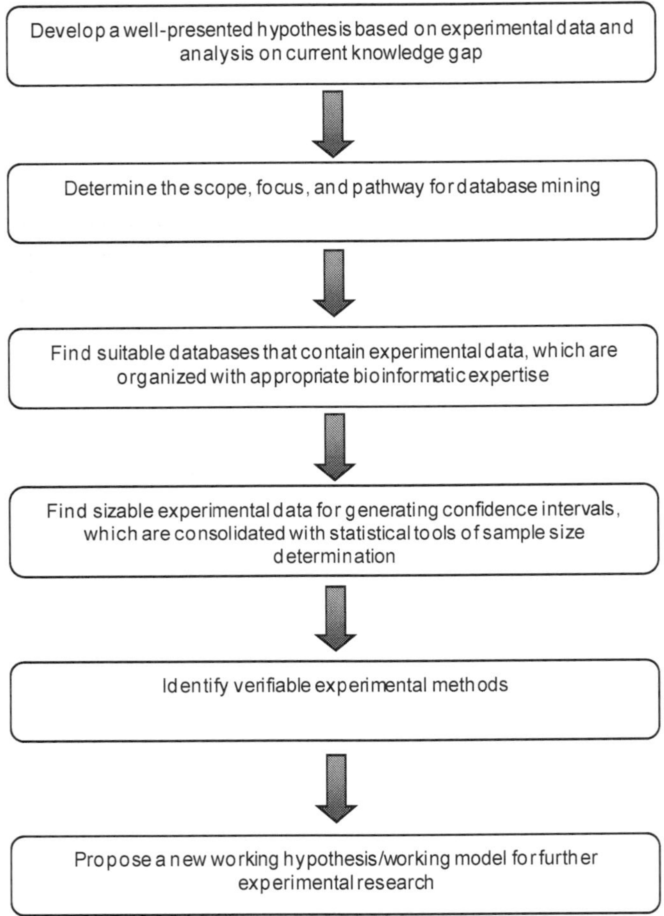

Fig. 1. Detabase mining flow-chart and principles.

context values and percentages. Analysis of this data yielded a mean and standard deviation (SD) of -0.25 ± 0.12 and 76.07 ± 19.07 for context value and context percentage, respectively. The intervals were then constructed and the lower limits (the mean - 2 x standard deviations) were calculated for context percentage (76.07-1.96 (19.07/SQRT (46)) = 76.07 - 5.51 = 70.56) and context value (-0.25-1.96(0.12/SQRT (46) = - 0.25 - 0.04= -0.22). All predicted microRNAs interactions with a context value ≤-0.22 and context percentage ≥70 were accepted. Using the lower limit thresholds for context value and percentage, 297 out of the 524 predicted microRNAs met the criteria and were considered equivalent to the experimentally verified microRNAs. In order to generate valid confidence intervals, sample sizes have to be estimated with statistical tools of sample size determination (Rosner, 2000) as we reported (Ng et al., 2004); 5) Verifiable methods: Experimental methods are available to verify the data generated by the database mining (Yan et al., 2004); and *6)* A new working model/hypothesis: Through database mining, a new knowledge gap will be identified, and a new hypothesis will be proposed to test fewer, much more-focused genes in further experiments. The following sections will illustrate these principles in our own publications (Chen et al., 2010; Jan et al., 2010; Ng et al., 2004; Virtue, 2011; Yang et al., 2006a; Yang et al., 2006b; Yin et al., 2009).

3. Database mining example 1: Stimulation-responsive alternative splicing is an important mechanism in generating self-antigen epitopes (Ng et al., 2004; Xiong et al., 2006; Yan et al., 2004; Yang et al., 2006a; Yang, 2007)

In our invited review, we pointed out that the identification and molecular characterization of self-antigens expressed by human malignancies, that are capable of elicitation of anti-tumor immune responses in patients, have been an active field in tumor immunology (Yang & Yang, 2005). More than 2,000 tumor antigens have been identified, and most of these antigens are self-antigens (Yang & Yang, 2005). Despite this, the important question of how non-mutated self-protein antigens, generated from normal cells and tumor cells, gain immunogenicity and trigger immune recognition remained unanswered (Yang & Yang, 2005). Mutations may be responsible for some aspects of elevated immunogenicity underlying certain tumor-specific antigens (p53 and Ras), while chromosome translocations and abnormalities, such as expression of the fusion oncogene Bcr-Abl in chronic myelogenous leukemia (Clark et al., 2001; Pinilla-Ibarz et al., 2000; Yotnda et al., 1998; Zorn, 2001) (Yang et al., 2002; Yang et al., 2001) are responsible for other aspects. However, the mechanism underlying the immunogenicity of most non-mutated self-tumor antigens is their aberrant overexpression in tumors (Yang & Yang, 2005). Zinkernagel *et al* (Zinkernagel & Hengartner, 2001) suggested that the overexpression of self-antigens or novel antigenic structure, overcomes the threshold of antigen concentration at which an immune response is initiated (Shlomchik et al., 2001). This threshold might be lower for certain untolerized regions of certain antigen epitopes. Overexpressed genes, often encode tumor antigens up to 100 fold. These genes are identified by serological identification of self-antigens by screening a cDNA library with patients' sera (SEREX) (Sahin et al., 1995), which may reflect the inherent methodological bias for the detection of abundant transcript (Preuss et al., 2002). The overexpression of tumor antigens in tumors may result from transcriptional and post-transcriptional mechanisms. We recently demonstrated that overexpression of tumor antigen CML66L in leukemia cells and tumor cells via alternative splicing is the mechanism for its immunogenicity in patients with tumors (Yan et al., 2004; Yang et al., 2001). This not only illustrates the principle of overexpression of tumor antigen, but also elucidated alternative splicing as its molecular mechanism (Yan et al., 2004). A significant proportion of the SEREX-defined self-tumor antigens are autoantigens (Chen, 2004), for example, CML28 that we identified is autoantigen Rrp46p (Yang et al., 2002). Using this information gathered from SEREX, we hypothesized that alternative splicing is a general mechanism for the overexpression of untolerized self-antigen epitopes in tumors and autoimmune diseases. In order to test this hypothesis, we database mined the NIH-NCBI AceView database to examine the potential mechanisms of how non-mutated self-proteins gain new untolerized structures that trigger immune recognition (Ng et al., 2004). The AceView database provides a curated, comprehensive, and non-redundant sequence representation of all public mRNA sequences (mRNAs from GenBank or RefSeq, and single pass cDNA sequences from dbEST and Trace). These experimental cDNA sequences are first co-aligned on the genome, and then clustered into a minimal number of alternative transcript variants and grouped into genes (http://www.ncbi.nlm.nih.gov/IEB/Research/Acembly/). Our results showed that alternative splicing occurs in 100% of autoantigen transcripts. This is significantly higher than the approximately 42% rate of alternative splicing observed in the 9554 randomly selected human gene transcripts ($p<0.001$). Within the isoform-specific regions of the autoantigens, 92% and 88% encoded MHC class I and class II-restricted T-cell antigen epitopes, respectively, and 70% encoded antibody binding domains. Alternative splicing can be canonical or non-canonical. Canonical splicing removes introns that have 5′GT and 3′AG consensus flanking sequences (GT-AG rule) (Lewin, 2000). Our results demonstrated that 80% of the autoantigen transcripts undergo non-canonical alternative splicing, which is significantly higher than the less than 1% rate in randomly selected gene transcripts ($p<0.001$). These studies suggest that non-canonical alternative splicing may be an important mechanism for the generation of untolerized epitopes that may lead to autoimmunity. Furthermore, the product of a transcript that does not undergo alternative splicing is unlikely to be a target antigen in autoimmunity (Ng et al., 2004). To consolidate this finding, we also examined the effect of proinflammatory cytokine tumor necrosis factor-α (TNF-α) on the prototypic alternative splicing factor (ASF)/SF2 in the splicing machinery. Our results show that TNF-α downregulates ASF/SF2 expression in cultured muscle cells. This result correlates with our finding of reduced expression of ASF/SF2 in inflamed muscle cells from patients with autoimmune myositis (Xiong et al., 2006). Based on our and others' data, we recently proposed a new model of stimulation-responsive splicing for the selection of autoantigens and self-tumor antigens (Yang et al., 2006a) [also see Fig. 1 at (http://preview.ncbi.nlm.nih.gov/pubmed/16890493)]. Our new model theorizes that the significantly higher rates of alternative splicing of autoantigen and self-tumor antigen transcripts that occur in response to stimuli, such as proinflammatory cytokines, could induce extra-thymic expression of untolerized antigen epitopes to elicit autoimmune and anti-tumor responses. By using B lymphocyte (B cell) antigen epitope analysis databases and T cell antigen epitope analysis databases listed in Tables in our recent invited review (http://www.ncbi.nlm.nih.gov/pmc/articles/PMC2858284/pdf/JBB2010-459798.pdf) (Jan et al., 2010), we showed that protein sequences encoded by alternatively spliced exons are sufficient to equip antibody-binding antigen epitopes and major histocompatibility complex (MHC) class I- and MHC II-restricted T cell antigen epitopes to stimulate B lymphocytes and T lymphocytes, respectively (Ng et al., 2004). Of note, our model not only applies to non-mutated self-tumor antigens associated tumors and autoantigens associated with various autoimmune diseases, but also to the composition and expansion of the self-antigen repertoire of stem cells. Our additional database mining study has generated a new model of differential epitope processing for MHC class I-restricted viral antigen epitopes and tumor antigen epitopes (Yang et al., 2006b). Our reports have demonstrated the principles of database mining in adaptive immune responses.

4. Database mining example 2: Three-tier model for inflammasome/caspase-1 activation and inflammation privilege of tissues are important mechanisms underlying the differences in the readiness of inflammation initiation in tissues

Atherosclerosis is the leading cause of morbidity and mortality in industrialized society. Several "traditional" risk factors have been identified for atherosclerosis including hyperlipidemia, oxidized low density lipoprotein, cigarette smoking, diabetes, hypertension, obesity (Ross, 1992), and hyperhomocysteinemia (HHcy), etc. Chronic vascular inflammation is an essential requirement for the progression of atherosclerosis in patients (Hansson, 2005). Recent progress in characterizing pathogen-associated molecular patterns' (PAMPs) receptor families (PAMP-Rs) and inflammasomes (the protein complex for activation of caspase-1) has further emphasized the importance of proinflammatory cytokine interleukin-1β (IL-1β) signaling in bridging proatherogenic risk factors to initiate inflammation (Yang et al., 2008). However, constitutive expression levels and expression readiness of PAMP-Rs, inflammasome components and proinflammtory caspases in tissues remained poorly defined. We hypothesized that PAMP-Rs, inflammasome components, proinflammatory caspases, IL-1, and IL-18 are differentially expressed in cardiovascular tissues. To examine this hypothesis, we mined the NCBI-UniGene database, analyzed cDNA cloning and DNA sequencing data from tissue cDNA libraries and studied expression profiles of Toll-like receptors (TLRs), cytosolic nucleotide binding and oligomerization domain (NOD)-like receptors (NLRs), inflammasome components, inflammatory caspases, and caspase-1 cleavable inflammatory cytokines. The UniGene database provides an organized view of the transcriptome with information on protein similarities, gene expression, cDNA clone reagents, and genomic location (http://www.ncbi.nlm.nih.gov/unigene), in which each UniGene entry is a set of transcript sequences that appear to come from the same transcription locus (gene or expressed pseudogene). After analyzing the data from the UniGene database, we made several important findings: (1) Among 11 tissues examined, vascular tissues and heart express fewer types of TLRs and NLRs than immune system tissues including blood, lymph nodes, thymus, and trachea; (2) Brain, lymph nodes, and thymus do not express proinflammatory cytokines IL-1β and IL-18 constitutively, suggesting that these two cytokines need to be upregulated in response to inflammatory stimuli in the tissues; and (3) based on the expression data of three characterized inflammasomes (NALP1, NALP3 and IPAF inflammasomes), the examined tissues can be classified into three tiers: the first tier tissues including brain, placenta, blood, and thymus express inflammasome(s) in constitutive status; the second tier tissues have inflammasome(s) in nearly-ready expression status (with the requirement of upregulation of one component); and the third tier tissues like heart and bone marrow, require upregulation of at least two components in order to assemble functional inflammasomes. Based on the expression readiness of inflammasomes in tissues, we propose a new working model of three-tier responsive expression of inflammasomes in tissues and suggest a new concept of third tier tissues' inflammatory privilege, which provides an insight on the differences of tissues in initiating acute inflammations. This model suggests that (a) first-tier tissues with constitutively expressed inflammasomes initiate inflammation quicker than second and third-tier tissues; and (b) second tier tissues (requiring one component of upregulation) including vascular tissue, and third tier tissues including heart (requiring more than one component upregulation) are in an inducible expression status of inflammasomes. The inducible expressions of inflammasomes are presumably mediated through various signal pathways that initiate inflammation, and the interplay between the signal pathways, may take a longer time and overcome a higher threshold than first tier tissues. Traditional concepts of immune privilege suggests a protective mechanism from autoimmune destruction based on the lack of expression of antigen-presenting self-major compatibility complex (MHC) molecules in tissues (Yang & Yang, 2005). The lack of expression of self-MHCs in immune privileged tissues including testis results in the failure of self-antigen presentation that stimulates the hosts' immune system, thereby protecting immune privileged tissues from autoimmune destruction. Similarly, we proposed a new concept of tissues' inflammatory privileges that emphasize a protective mechanism against tissue destruction mediated by inflammasome/IL-1β-based innate immune responses. In our new concept of tissues' inflammatory privilege, vascular tissue and heart disproportionally express fewer types of TLRs and NLRs and may only inducibly express inflammasomes, thus preventing against uncontrolled inflammatory destruction mediated by inflammasome-based innate immune responses (Streilein & Stein-Streilein, 2000). Our new concept and model may also explain the potential differences between cardiovascular tissues and other tissues in initiating acute inflammation. The first-tier tissues may have a higher probability of experiencing acute inflammation than the second-tier and third-tier tissues.

We and others showed that elevated levels of plasma homocysteine (Hcy), termed hyperhomocysteinemia (HHcy), is an independent risk factor, equivalent to hyperlipidemia, for cardiovascular diseases (CVD) including coronary heart disease and stroke (Maron & Loscalzo, 2009; Wang et al., 2003; Zhang et al., 2009). Recently, we performed an additional database mining study using to examine the expression of more than 20 homocysteine metabolic enzymes and methylation enzymes in >20 tissues in humans and mouse (Chen et al., 2010). We generated a new model of how hypomethylation (a post-translational protein modification) modulates the expressions of homocysteine-metabolizing enzymes (Chen et al., 2010). Taken together, our studies have demonstrated the principles of database mining in innate immune reactions.

5. Database mining example 3: A group of anti-inflammatory microRNAs may play critical roles in inhibiting the expression of proatherogenic molecules

Previous research has established that numerous genes are upregulated in atherogenesis through epigenetic or genetic transcriptional mechanisms (Turunen et al., 2009). However, transcription-independent mechanisms have received far less scrutiny. Recent publications suggest that microRNAs, a newly characterized class of short (18-24 nucleotide long), endogenous, non-coding RNAs (Bartel, 2009), contribute to the development of particular disease states by regulating diverse biological processes such as cell growth, differentiation, proliferation, and apoptosis (Zhang, 2008). This biological control is accomplished by post-transcriptional gene silencing (Naeem et al., 2010) through Watson and Crick base-pairing predominately at the 3'-untranslated region (3'UTR) of messenger RNAs (mRNAs) (Cordes et al., 2009; Rasmussen et al., 2010). This pairing can be further characterized as "perfect" or "near perfect", leading to target mRNA cleavage and degradation, or "imperfect", causing the inhibition of mRNA translation (Naeem et al., 2010). With the identification and sequencing of more than 800 human microRNAs thus far, it is thought that up to 30% of human genes may be regulated by microRNAs (Cheng et al., 2010; Zhang, 2008). Supporting evidence suggests that microRNAs function as key players during critical stages of cellular development and finely tune gene expression in the maintenance of routine cellular functioning (Baek et al., 2008). Furthermore, microRNAs can act on transcription factors, which lead to a broad indirect cellular effect as a result of their widespread gene modulating nature. In addition, the recent research has demonstrated that changes in microRNAs expression patterns are connected to several pathological conditions including cardiovascular disease and atherosclerosis. These studies primarily focused on characterizing microRNAs in atherosclerosis disease models, which had been previously reported to have elevated expression in disease conditions (Haver et al., 2010; Rink & Khanna, 2010). Thus, current microRNAs research has failed to provide a panoramic view of how microRNAs regulate proatherogenic inflammatory genes in a panoramic view and whether upregulation of proatherogenic inflammatory genes is the result of anti-inflammatory microRNA downregulation. To address these issues, we hypothesized that a group of anti-inflammatory microRNAs may regulate the expressions of proatherogenic molecules (Virtue, 2011). We then developed a novel database mining approach using three types of databases including the online microRNA target prediction software TargetScan (http://www.targetscan.org/) (Dong et al., 2010; Rosero et al., 2010; Vickers & Remaley, 2010), the Tarbase, an online database of experimentally verified microRNAs (http://diana.cslab.ece.ntua.gr/tarbase/) (Papadopoulos et al., 2009; Sethupathy et al., 2006), and the online microRNA.org expression database (http://www.microrna.org/ microrna/home.do) (Betel et al., 2008), in concert with a statistical analysis strategy established in our previous database mining publications (Chen et al., 2010; Ng et al., 2004; Shen et al., 2010; Yang et al., 2006b; Yin et al., 2009). Our unique research using database mining yielded several key findings. First, we discovered that the expression of 33 inflammatory genes (mRNAs) is upregulated in atherosclerotic lesions and second, that the mRNAs of those genes contain structural features in their 3'UTR for potential regulation by microRNAs. Furthermore, these structural features are statistically identical to experimentally verified 3'UTR microRNAs binding sites. Third, 21 out of the 33 inflammatory genes (64%) are targeted by highly expressed microRNAs while the remaining 12 inflammatory genes (36%) are targeted by normally expressed microRNAs. Fourth, it was also established that 10 of the 21 highly expressed microRNA-targeted inflammatory genes (48%) were targeted by a single microRNA, suggesting the specificity of microRNA regulation. Meanwhile, 12 out of the 25 highly expressed microRNAs (48%) targeted single inflammatory genes while the other 13 microRNAs targeted multiple inflammatory genes. Finally, it was determined that the microRNAs targeting atherosclerotic inflammatory genes use statistically higher numbers of "poorly conserved" binding interactions than the control group of microRNAs from the confidence interval. These results suggest that the microRNAs regulating atherosclerotic inflammatory genes possess special features (Virtue, 2011).

Previous research has shown that microRNAs participate in modulating atherosclerosis-related processes including hyperlipidemia (microRNA-33, microRNA-125a-5p), hypertension (microRNA-155), plaque rupture (microRNA-222, microRNA-210), and atherosclerosis itself (microRNA-21, microRNA-126) (Rink & Khanna, 2010). However, whether certain microRNAs play a role in preventing the disease development remains unknown. One of the most interesting findings from our study is that the 25 microRNAs that are highly expressed under normal untreated conditions target 21 out of the 33 (64%) atherosclerosis-upregulated inflammatory genes. The important result suggests a novel mechanism where a group of highly expressed anti-inflammatory microRNAs suppress the upregulation of proatherogenic inflammatory genes under normal physiological conditions. It has been well established that microRNAs play important roles in fine-tuning developmental processes and participate in the development of diseases such as cancer. Our results are the first to suggest that microRNAs may play a protective role by suppressing proatherogenic genes to maintain healthy arteries. Our conclusion is supported by other publications, which show that 7 out of the 20 microRNAs identified in this study were downregulated in the experimental studies by various proatherogenic factors (Chen et al., 2009; Elia et al., 2009; Ji et al., 2007). Together, our studies have demonstrated the principles of database mining in inflammation.

6. Conclusion

Active research in human and mouse genomes, transcriptomes, microRNAs transcriptomes, proteomes, and antigen-omes in the past decade has generated a tremendous amount of data and established many experimental data-based searchable databases. This provides unprecedented opportunities for biomedical scientists to develop more systemic and panoramic approaches to analyze the databases and generate new hypotheses. In this chapter, we briefly summarize our pioneering efforts in using our new database mining methods to address important questions in inflammatory and immunological diseases. The new principles and basic methodologies of database mining developed in our laboratories are elucidated in the following studies: 1) stimulation-responsive alternative splicing model for the generation of untolerized autoantigen epitopes; 2) a three-tier model for inflammasome/caspase-1 activation and inflammatory privileges of tissues; and 3) a group of anti-inflammatory microRNAs in inhibiting proatherogenic gene expression during atherogenesis. With recent technological breakthroughs, database mining has provided significant new insights and hypotheses in specifying the novel directions for experimental research.

7. Acknowledgements

This work was partially supported by the National Institutes of Health Grants HL094451 and HL108910 (XFY), HL67033, HL82774, and HL77288 (HW). FY and IHY contribute equally to this work. Correspondence: Prof. Yang at xfyang@temple.edu.
Disclosures: none declared.

8. References

Baek, D., J. Villen, C. Shin, F. D. Camargo, S. P. Gygi, and D. P. Bartel. "The Impact of MicroRNAs on Protein Output." *Nature* 455, no. 7209 (2008): 64-71.

Bartel, D. P. "MicroRNAs: Target Recognition and Regulatory Functions." *Cell* 136, no. 2 (2009): 215-33.

Betel, D., M. Wilson, A. Gabow, D. S. Marks, and C. Sander. "The MicroRNA.Org Resource: Targets and Expression." *Nucleic Acids Res* 36, no. Database issue (2008): D149-53.

Chen, N. C., F. Yang, L. M. Capecci, Z. Gu, A. I. Schafer, W. Durante, X. F. Yang, and H. Wang. "Regulation of Homocysteine Metabolism and Methylation in Human and Mouse Tissues." *Faseb J* 24, no. 8 (2010): 2804-17.

Chen, T., Z. Huang, L. Wang, Y. Wang, F. Wu, S. Meng, and C. Wang. "MicroRNA-125a-5p Partly Regulates the Inflammatory Response, Lipid Uptake, and Orp9 Expression in oxLDL-Stimulated Monocyte/Macrophages." *Cardiovasc Res* 83, no. 1 (2009): 131-9.

Chen, YT. "Serex Review." *Cancer Immunity* http://www.cancerimmunity.org/SEREX/ (2004).

Cheng, Y., N. Tan, J. Yang, X. Liu, X. Cao, P. He, X. Dong, S. Qin, and C. Zhang. "A Translational Study of Circulating Cell-Free MicroRNA-1 in Acute Myocardial Infarction." *Clin Sci (Lond)* 119, no. 2 (2010): 87-95.

Clark, R. E., I. A. Dodi, S. C. Hill, J. R. Lill, G. Aubert, A. R. Macintyre, J. Rojas, A. Bourdon, P. L. Bonner, L. Wang, S. E. Christmas, P. J. Travers, C. S. Creaser, R. C. Rees, and J. A. Madrigal. "Direct Evidence That Leukemic Cells Present HLA-Associated Immunogenic Peptides Derived from the Bcr-Abl B3a2 Fusion Protein." *Blood* 98, no. 10 (2001): 2887-93.

Cordes, K. R., N. T. Sheehy, M. P. White, E. C. Berry, S. U. Morton, A. N. Muth, T. H. Lee, J. M. Miano, K. N. Ivey, and D. Srivastava. "MiR-145 and MiR-143 Regulate Smooth Muscle Cell Fate and Plasticity." *Nature* 460, no. 7256 (2009): 705-10.

Dong, H., M. Paquette, A. Williams, R. T. Zoeller, M. Wade, and C. Yauk. "Thyroid Hormone May Regulate Mrna Abundance in Liver by Acting on Micrornas." *PLoS One* 5, no. 8 (2010).

Egger, M., and G. D. Smith. "Meta-Analysis. Potentials and Promise." *Bmj* 315, no. 7119 (1997): 1371-4.

Egger, M., G. D. Smith, and A. N. Phillips. "Meta-Analysis: Principles and Procedures." *Bmj* 315, no. 7121 (1997): 1533-7.

Elia, L., M. Quintavalle, J. Zhang, R. Contu, L. Cossu, M. V. Latronico, K. L. Peterson, C. Indolfi, D. Catalucci, J. Chen, S. A. Courtneidge, and G. Condorelli. "The Knockout of MiR-143 and -145 Alters Smooth Muscle Cell Maintenance and Vascular Homeostasis in Mice: Correlates with Human Disease." *Cell Death Differ* 16, no. 12 (2009): 1590-8.

Galperin, M. Y., and G. R. Cochrane. "The 2011 Nucleic Acids Research Database Issue and the Online Molecular Biology Database Collection." *Nucleic Acids Res* 39, no. Database issue (2011): D1-6.

Hansson, G. K. "Inflammation, Atherosclerosis, and Coronary Artery Disease." *N Engl J Med* 352, no. 16 (2005): 1685-95.

Haver, V. G., R. H. Slart, C. J. Zeebregts, M. P. Peppelenbosch, and R. A. Tio. "Rupture of Vulnerable Atherosclerotic Plaques: MicroRNAs Conducting the Orchestra?" *Trends Cardiovasc Med* 20, no. 2 (2010): 65-71.

Houle, D., D. R. Govindaraju, and S. Omholt. "Phenomics: The Next Challenge." *Nat Rev Genet* 11, no. 12 (2010): 855-66.

Ishii, N., K. Nakahigashi, T. Baba, M. Robert, T. Soga, A. Kanai, T. Hirasawa, M. Naba, K. Hirai, A. Hoque, P. Y. Ho, Y. Kakazu, K. Sugawara, S. Igarashi, S. Harada, T. Masuda, N. Sugiyama, T. Togashi, M. Hasegawa, Y. Takai, K. Yugi, K. Arakawa, N. Iwata, Y. Toya, Y. Nakayama, T. Nishioka, K. Shimizu, H. Mori, and M. Tomita. "Multiple High-Throughput Analyses Monitor the Response of E. Coli to Perturbations." *Science* 316, no. 5824 (2007): 593-7.

Jan, M., S. Meng, N. C. Chen, J. Mai, H. Wang, and X. F. Yang. "Inflammatory and Autoimmune Reactions in Atherosclerosis and Vaccine Design Informatics." *J Biomed Biotechnol* 2010 (2010): 459798.

Ji, R., Y. Cheng, J. Yue, J. Yang, X. Liu, H. Chen, D. B. Dean, and C. Zhang. "MicroRNA Expression Signature and Antisense-Mediated Depletion Reveal an Essential Role of Microrna in Vascular Neointimal Lesion Formation." *Circ Res* 100, no. 11 (2007): 1579-88.

Joyce, A. R., and B. O. Palsson. "The Model Organism as a System: Integrating 'Omics' Data Sets." *Nat Rev Mol Cell Biol* 7, no. 3 (2006): 198-210.

King, J. Y., R. Ferrara, R. Tabibiazar, J. M. Spin, M. M. Chen, A. Kuchinsky, A. Vailaya, R. Kincaid, A. Tsalenko, D. X. Deng, A. Connolly, P. Zhang, E. Yang, C. Watt, Z. Yakhini, A. Ben-Dor, A. Adler, L. Bruhn, P. Tsao, T. Quertermous, and E. A. Ashley. "Pathway Analysis of Coronary Atherosclerosis." *Physiol Genomics* 23, no. 1 (2005): 103-18.

Lewin, Benjamin. "Nuclear Splicing." In *Genes Vii*, edited by Benjamin Lewin. Cambridge: Oxford University Press Inc., New York, 2000.

Liang, M., A. W. Cowley, Jr., M. J. Hessner, J. Lazar, D. P. Basile, and J. L. Pietrusz. "Transcriptome Analysis and Kidney Research: Toward Systems Biology." *Kidney Int* 67, no. 6 (2005): 2114-22.

Loza, M. J., C. E. McCall, L. Li, W. B. Isaacs, J. Xu, and B. L. Chang. "Assembly of Inflammation-Related Genes for Pathway-Focused Genetic Analysis." *PLoS One* 2, no. 10 (2007): e1035.

Maron, B. A., and J. Loscalzo. "The Treatment of Hyperhomocysteinemia." *Annu Rev Med* 60 (2009): 39-54.

Mount, DW. "Historical Introduction and Overview." In *Bioinformatics. Sequence and Genome Analysis*, edited by DW Mount, 1-27. Cold Spring Harbor, New York: Cold Spring Harbor Laboratory Press, 2004.

Naeem, H., R. Kuffner, G. Csaba, and R. Zimmer. "Mirsel: Automated Extraction of Associations between Micrornas and Genes from the Biomedical Literature." *BMC Bioinformatics* 11 (2010): 135.

Ng, B., F. Yang, D. P. Huston, Y. Yan, Y. Yang, Z. Xiong, L. E. Peterson, H. Wang, and X. F. Yang. "Increased Noncanonical Splicing of Autoantigen Transcripts Provides the Structural Basis for Expression of Untolerized Epitopes." *J Allergy Clin Immunol* 114, no. 6 (2004): 1463-70.

Palakal, M., J. Bright, T. Sebastian, and S. Hartanto. "A Comparative Study of Cells in Inflammation, Eae and Ms Using Biomedical Literature Data Mining." *J Biomed Sci* 14, no. 1 (2007): 67-85.

Pandey, R., R. K. Guru, and D. W. Mount. "Pathway Miner: Extracting Gene Association Networks from Molecular Pathways for Predicting the Biological Significance of Gene Expression Microarray Data." *Bioinformatics* 20, no. 13 (2004): 2156-8.

Papadopoulos, G. L., M. Reczko, V. A. Simossis, P. Sethupathy, and A. G. Hatzigeorgiou. "The Database of Experimentally Supported Targets: A Functional Update of Tarbase." *Nucleic Acids Res* 37, no. Database issue (2009): D155-8.

Pinilla-Ibarz, J., K. Cathcart, and D. A. Scheinberg. "CML Vaccines as a Paradigm of the Specific Immunotherapy of Cancer." *Blood Rev* 14, no. 2 (2000): 111-20.

Preuss, K. D., C. Zwick, C. Bormann, F. Neumann, and M. Pfreundschuh. "Analysis of the B-Cell Repertoire against Antigens Expressed by Human Neoplasms." *Immunol Rev* 188 (2002): 43-50.

Rasmussen, K. D., S. Simmini, C. Abreu-Goodger, N. Bartonicek, M. Di Giacomo, D. Bilbao-Cortes, R. Horos, M. Von Lindern, A. J. Enright, and D. O'Carroll. "The MiR-144/451 Locus Is Required for Erythroid Homeostasis." *J Exp Med* 207, no. 7 (2010): 1351-8.

Rink, C., and S. Khanna. "MicroRNA in Ischemic Stroke Etiology and Pathology." *Physiol Genomics* (2010).

Rosero, S., V. Bravo-Egana, Z. Jiang, S. Khuri, N. Tsinoremas, D. Klein, E. Sabates, M. Correa-Medina, C. Ricordi, J. Dominguez-Bendala, J. Diez, and R. L. Pastori. "MicroRNA Signature of the Human Developing Pancreas." *BMC Genomics* 11, no. 1 (2010): 509.

Rosner, B. "Estimation of Sample Size and Power for Comparing Two Means." In *Fundamentals of Biostatistics*, edited by B. Rosner, 307-29. Australia, Canada, Mexico, Singapore, Spain, United Kingdom, United States, 2000.

Ross, R. "Atherosclerosis." In *Cecil Textbook of Medicine*, edited by JB Wyngaarden, Smith, LH, Bennett, JC., 293-98. Philadelphia, London, Toronto, Montreal, Sydney, Tokyo: W.B. Saunders Company, 1992.

Sahin, U., O. Tureci, H. Schmitt, B. Cochlovius, T. Johannes, R. Schmits, F. Stenner, G. Luo, I. Schobert, and M. Pfreundschuh. "Human Neoplasms Elicit Multiple Specific Immune Responses in the Autologous Host." *Proc Natl Acad Sci U S A* 92, no. 25 (1995): 11810-3.

Salimi, N., W. Fleri, B. Peters, and A. Sette. "Design and Utilization of Epitope-Based Databases and Predictive Tools." *Immunogenetics* 62, no. 4 (2010): 185-96.

Sethupathy, P., B. Corda, and A. G. Hatzigeorgiou. "Tarbase: A Comprehensive Database of Experimentally Supported Animal Microrna Targets." *Rna* 12, no. 2 (2006): 192-7.

Shen, J., Y. Yin, J. Mai, X. Xiong, M. Pansuria, J. Liu, E. Maley, N. U. Saqib, H. Wang, and X. F. Yang. "Caspase-1 Recognizes Extended Cleavage Sites in Its Natural Substrates." *Atherosclerosis* 210, no. 2 (2010): 422-29.

Shimokawa, K., K. Mogushi, S. Shoji, A. Hiraishi, K. Ido, H. Mizushima, and H. Tanaka. "Icod: An Integrated Clinical Omics Database Based on the Systems-Pathology View of Disease." *BMC Genomics* 11 Suppl 4 (2010): S19.

Shlomchik, M. J., J. E. Craft, and M. J. Mamula. "From T to B and Back Again: Positive Feedback in Systemic Autoimmune Disease." *Nat Rev Immunol* 1, no. 2 (2001): 147-53.

Spasic, I., S. Ananiadou, J. McNaught, and A. Kumar. "Text Mining and Ontologies in Biomedicine: Making Sense of Raw Text." *Brief Bioinform* 6, no. 3 (2005): 239-51.

Streilein, J. W., and J. Stein-Streilein. "Does Innate Immune Privilege Exist?" *J Leukoc Biol* 67, no. 4 (2000): 479-87.

Turunen, M. P., E. Aavik, and S. Yla-Herttuala. "Epigenetics and Atherosclerosis." *Biochim Biophys Acta* 1790, no. 9 (2009): 886-91.

Vickers, K. C., and A. T. Remaley. "MicroRNAs in Atherosclerosis and Lipoprotein Metabolism." *Curr Opin Endocrinol Diabetes Obes* 17, no. 2 (2010): 150-5.

Virtue, A, J. Mai, Y. Yin, S. Meng, T. Tran, X. Jiang, H. Wang, and X-F Yang. "Structural Evidence of Anti-Atherogenic MicroRNAs. " *Frontiers in Bioscience* 17 (2011): 3133-45.

Wang, H., X. Jiang, F. Yang, J. W. Gaubatz, L. Ma, M. J. Magera, X. Yang, P. B. Berger, W. Durante, H. J. Pownall, and A. I. Schafer. "Hyperhomocysteinemia Accelerates Atherosclerosis in Cystathionine Beta-Synthase and Apolipoprotein E Double Knock-out Mice with and without Dietary Perturbation." *Blood* 101, no. 10 (2003): 3901-7.

Warner, E. E., and B. K. Dieckgraefe. "Application of Genome-Wide Gene Expression Profiling by High-Density DNA Arrays to the Treatment and Study of Inflammatory Bowel Disease." *Inflamm Bowel Dis* 8, no. 2 (2002): 140-57.

Weinstein, J. N. "Fishing Expeditions." *Science* 282, no. 5389 (1998): 628-9.

— — — . "'Omic' and Hypothesis-Driven Research in the Molecular Pharmacology of Cancer." *Curr Opin Pharmacol* 2, no. 4 (2002): 361-5.

Xiong, Z., A. Shaibani, Y. P. Li, Y. Yan, S. Zhang, Y. Yang, F. Yang, H. Wang, and X. F. Yang. "Alternative Splicing Factor Asf/Sf2 Is Down Regulated in Inflamed Muscle." *J Clin Pathol* 59, no. 8 (2006): 855-61.

Yan, Y., L. Phan, F. Yang, M. Talpaz, Y. Yang, Z. Xiong, B. Ng, N. A. Timchenko, C. J. Wu, J. Ritz, H. Wang, and X. F. Yang. "A Novel Mechanism of Alternative Promoter and Splicing Regulates the Epitope Generation of Tumor Antigen Cml66-L." *J Immunol* 172, no. 1 (2004): 651-60.

Yang, F., I. H. Chen, Z. Xiong, Y. Yan, H. Wang, and X. F. Yang. "Model of Stimulation-Responsive Splicing and Strategies in Identification of Immunogenic Isoforms of Tumor Antigens and Autoantigens." *Clin Immunol* 121, no. 2 (2006a): 121-33.

Yang, F., and X. F. Yang. "New Concepts in Tumor Antigens: Their Significance in Future Immunotherapies for Tumors." *Cell Mol Immunol* 2, no. 5 (2005): 331-41.

Yang, X. F. "Immunology of Stem Cells and Cancer Stem Cells." *Cell Mol Immunol* 4, no. 3 (2007): 161-71.

Yang, X. F., D. Mirkovic, S. Zhang, Q. E. Zhang, Y. Yan, Z. Xiong, F. Yang, I. H. Chen, L. Li, and H. Wang. "Processing Sites Are Different in the Generation of HLA-A2.1-Restricted, T Cell Reactive Tumor Antigen Epitopes and Viral Epitopes." *Int J Immunopathol Pharmacol* 19, no. 4 (2006b): 853-70.

Yang, X. F., C. J. Wu, L. Chen, E. P. Alyea, C. Canning, P. Kantoff, R. J. Soiffer, G. Dranoff, and J. Ritz. "CML28 Is a Broadly Immunogenic Antigen, Which Is Overexpressed in Tumor Cells." *Cancer Res* 62, no. 19 (2002): 5517-22.

Yang, X. F., C. J. Wu, S. McLaughlin, A. Chillemi, K. S. Wang, C. Canning, E. P. Alyea, P. Kantoff, R. J. Soiffer, G. Dranoff, and J. Ritz. "CML66, a Broadly Immunogenic Tumor Antigen, Elicits a Humoral Immune Response Associated with Remission of Chronic Myelogenous Leukemia." *Proc Natl Acad Sci U S A* 98, no. 13 (2001): 7492-7.

Yang, X. F., Y. Yin, and H. Wang. "Vascular Inflammation and Atherogenesis Are Activated Via Receptors for Pamps and Suppressed by Regulatory T Cells." *Drug Discov Today Ther Strateg* 5, no. 2 (2008): 125-42.

Yin, Y., Y. Yan, X. Jiang, J. Mai, N. C. Chen, H. Wang, and X. F. Yang. "Inflammasomes Are Differentially Expressed in Cardiovascular and Other Tissues." *Int J Immunopathol Pharmacol* 22, no. 2 (2009): 311-22.

Yotnda, P., H. Firat, F. Garcia-Pons, Z. Garcia, G. Gourru, J. P. Vernant, F. A. Lemonnier, V. Leblond, and P. Langlade-Demoyen. "Cytotoxic T Cell Response against the Chimeric P210 Bcr-Abl Protein in Patients with Chronic Myelogenous Leukemia." *J Clin Invest* 101, no. 10 (1998): 2290-6.

Zhang, C. "Micrornas: Role in Cardiovascular Biology and Disease." *Clin Sci (Lond)* 114, no. 12 (2008): 699-706.

Zhang, D., X. Jiang, P. Fang, Y. Yan, J. Song, S. Gupta, A. I. Schafer, W. Durante, W. D. Kruger, X. Yang, and H. Wang. "Hyperhomocysteinemia Promotes Inflammatory Monocyte Generation and Accelerates Atherosclerosis in Transgenic Cystathionine Beta-Synthase-Deficient Mice." *Circulation* 120, no. 19 (2009): 1893-902.

Zinkernagel, R. M., and H. Hengartner. "Regulation of the Immune Response by Antigen." *Science* 293, no. 5528 (2001): 251-3.

Zorn, E., Orsini, E., Wu, CJ., Stein, B., Chillemi, A., Canning, C., Alyea, EP, Soiffer, RJ., and Ritz, J. "A CD4+ T Cell Clone Selected from a Cml Patient after Donor Lymphocyte Infusion Recognizes Bcr-Abl Breakpoint Peptides but Not Tumor Cells." *Transplantation* 71, no. 8 (2001): 1131-7.

8

Data Mining Pubmed Identifies Core Signalings and miRNA Regulatory Module in Glioma

Chunsheng Kang[1] et al. *
[1]Department of Neurosurgery, Laboratory of Neuro-Oncology, Tianjin Medical University
General Hospital, Tianjin Key Laboratory of Nerve Injury, Variation and Regeneration,
Tianjin,
China

1. Introduction

Glioblastoma multiforme (GBM) is the most common form of malignant brain cancer and persist as serious clinical and scientific problems. The current standard of therapy for GBM patients, include surgery, radiotherapy and chemotherapy with temozolomide, produces a median survival of only 14.6 months (Stupp et al., 2005). Now, new intervention is increasingly being tested, particularly with inhibitors of neo-angiogenesis and growth factor receptors, and high throughout profiling studies are leading to the discovery of novel genetic alterations and signaling pathways. The Cancer Genome Atlas Network recently catalogs recurrent genomic abnormalities in GBM, and proposes a molecular classification of GBM into Proneural, Neural, Classical, and Mesenchymal subtypes and integrates multidimensional genomic data to establish patterns of somatic mutations and DNA copy number (Verhaak et al., 2010). In recent years, microRNAs (miRNAs), small noncoding RNA molecules, have been identified in the progression of various human cancers and used to a notable molecular label to cancers. In glioma, miR-21, miR-221, miR-222, miR-181a and miR-125b have been proven to play critical roles in gliomagenesis and proposed as novel targets for antiglioma therapies (Shi et al., 2008; Shi et al., 2010; Zhang et al., 2009b; Zhang et al., 2010c; Zhou et al., 2010a; Zhou et al., 2010b). Thus, molecular regulation of glioma is comprehensive and still unclear and under further investigation.

Biomedical literature is growing at a double-exponential pace, with approximately 20 million publications in MEDLINE. Up to now, there have been more than 50 thousand of glioma-related publications in MEDLINE (Pubmed with: glioma). Thus, a massive wealth of information is embedded in the literature and waiting to be discovered and extracted. Literature mining is a promising strategy to utilize this untapped information for knowledge discovery and has been applied successfully to various biological problems including the discovery and characterization of molecular interactions (protein-protein, gene-protein, gene-drug, protein sorting and molecular binding) (Friedman et al., 2001;

* Junxia Zhang[1], Yingyi Wang[2], Ning Liu[2], Jilong Liu[3], Huazong Zeng[3], Tao Jiang[4], Yongping You[2] and
Peiyu Pu[1]
[2]Department of Neurosurgery, Jiangsu Provincial People's Hospital, Nanjing, China , [3]Shanghai Sensichip Co Ltd,
Shanghai, China, [4]Department of Neurosurgery, Tiantan Hospital, Capital Medical University, Beijing, China

Rindflesch et al., 2000; Sekimizu et al., 1998). As no searchable records are available to efficiently retrieve information relevant to molecular network in glioma, we extracted glioma-related genes and miRNAs by data mining Pubmed abstracts and established glioma associated network based on these genes and miRNAs to identify key signalings and miRNA regulatory module in glioma.

2. Results

2.1 Identification of glioma-related genes and miRNAs

For glioma we queried Pubmed with: glioma[title] AND ("1980/01/01"[PDAT] : "2010/04/01"[PDAT]). It led to the identification a total of 670 genes and 14 miRNAs that interacted with glioma. The top 10 glioma-related genes were listed in Table 1. These 14 glioma-related miRNAs were miR-21, miR-34a, miR-221, miR-222, miR-10b, miR-125b, miR-128, miR-146b, miR-15b, miR-181a, miR-196a, miR-26a, miR-451 and miR-9. Additionally, we score the journals describing these genes and miRNAs, and the top 10 journals were listed in Table 2.

Gene	PubMed Count
EGFR	130
VEGF	123
GFAP	87
TRAIL	71
CD95	52
JNK	52
ERK	49
IFN	48
PTEN	47
NGF	47

Table 1. The top 10 glioma-related genes.

Journal	Count
Cancer Res.	133
J. Neurooncol.	103
Oncogene	53
J. Neurochem.	46
J. Neurosurg.	38
Int. J. Cancer	37
J. Biol. Chem.	36
Biochem. Biophys. Res. Commun.	33
Clin. Cancer Res.	33

Table 2. The top 10 journals describing glioma-related genes and miRNAs.

2.2 Biological function of glioma-related genes

To better understand the biological role of glioma-related genes, the catalogued genes were visualized using Gene Ontology (GO) terms and pathway analysis. The Gene Ontology (GO) provides a structured and controlled ontology for describing gene products in terms of their associated molecular function, biological process, or cellular component in a species-independent manner. The molecular function enrichment revealed that 22 GO terms appeared to be significantly enriched and most glioma-associated genes encode for protein binding. In the biological process category, the genes mainly participated in signaling transduction, response stress, cell differentiation and regulation of cell proliferation. Finally, the cellular component category found that products of these genes were active mainly in cytoplasm membrane (Table 3).

Category	GO term
molecular function	protein binding, protein dimerization activity, signal transducer activity, cytokine activity, enzyme binding, growth factor activity, growth factor binding, receptor activity, protein kinase activity, glycosaminoglycan binding, kinase binding, enzyme regulator activity, G-protein-coupled receptor binding, carbohydrate binding, peptide receptor activity, collagen binding, polysaccharide binding, kinase activity, ATP binding, enzyme inhibitor activity, transmembrane receptor protein tyrosine kinase activity, adenyl nucleotide binding
biological process	response to stress, regulation of cell proliferation, cell differentiation, regulation of phosphorylation, regulation of immune system process, negative regulation of cell proliferation, cell proliferation, anti-apoptosis, apoptosis, neurogenesis, response to hormone stimulus, hemopoiesis, regulation of protein kinase activity, immune response, signal transduction, inflammatory response, cell migration, angiogenesis, cell communication, phosphorylation, gliogenesis, cell cycle process
cellular component	intrinsic to plasma membrane, integral to plasma membrane, plasma membrane, extracellular region, cell projection, vesicle, nucleoplasm, cytosol, cell soma, secretory granule, platelet alpha granule, transcription factor complex, apical plasma membrane

Over-represented GO terms were identified after multiple testing adjustments (P-value<0.05).

Table 3. Set of GO terms with highly enriched genes.

To further explore the pathway involved in these genes, we searched KEGG database for their pathway information. 16 pathways whose P-value was less than 0.01 were kept (Table 4). The most top enriched pathway is p53 signaling pathway, including 27 genes and Toll-like receptor signaling pathway including 33 genes.

2.3 Interaction network of glioma-related genes

To uncover the potential interaction networks or synergistic effects of these glioma-related genes, we employed each gene set as queries and searched for their interaction partners by accessing the database STRING. STRING integrates different public databases containing information on direct and indirect functional protein–protein associations by benchmarking them against the common reference set, KEGG pathway database. 204 genes had interactions in the database STRING. We next tried to connect these genes into a network to identify biologically informative linker genes which were statistically enriched for connections to member of glioma-related gene list. Figure 1A summarized PIK3CA, PIK3CB and JAK2 three queries served as "hubs" (label with red circle), which has high connection and was an indicator for essentialness in a network. Surprisingly, further analysis found that PIK3CA, PIK3CB and JAK2 were associated with signaling transduction, MAPK pathway, growth factor, cell apoptosis, cell proliferation, cell adhesion and cell migration (Figure 1B). Given that PIK3CA and PIK3CB encode the protein PI3K subunit p110α and p110β, respectively, these data suggested that PI3K and JAK2 signalings provided excellent biomarkers for glioma aggressiveness.

Pathway	Count	Enrichment P-value
p53 signaling pathway	27	0
Toll-like receptor signaling pathway	33	0
Apoptosis	30	9.80E-10
Cytokine-cytokine receptor interaction	65	2.48E-09
Glioma	23	8.80E-08
MAPK signaling pathway	51	1.24E-06
ErbB signaling pathway	24	1.02E-05
Focal adhesion	40	1.12E-05
Cell cycle	28	1.28E-05
T cell receptor signaling pathway	27	1.47E-05
Adipocytokine signaling pathway	20	3.11E-05
Chemokine signaling pathway	38	3.22E-05
Neurotrophin signaling pathway	29	4.10E-05
VEGF signaling pathway	18	0.003731
Adherens junction	18	0.003731

Over-represented KEGG pathways were identified after multiple testing adjustments (P-value<0.05).

Table 4. Set of signaling pathways with highly enriched genes.

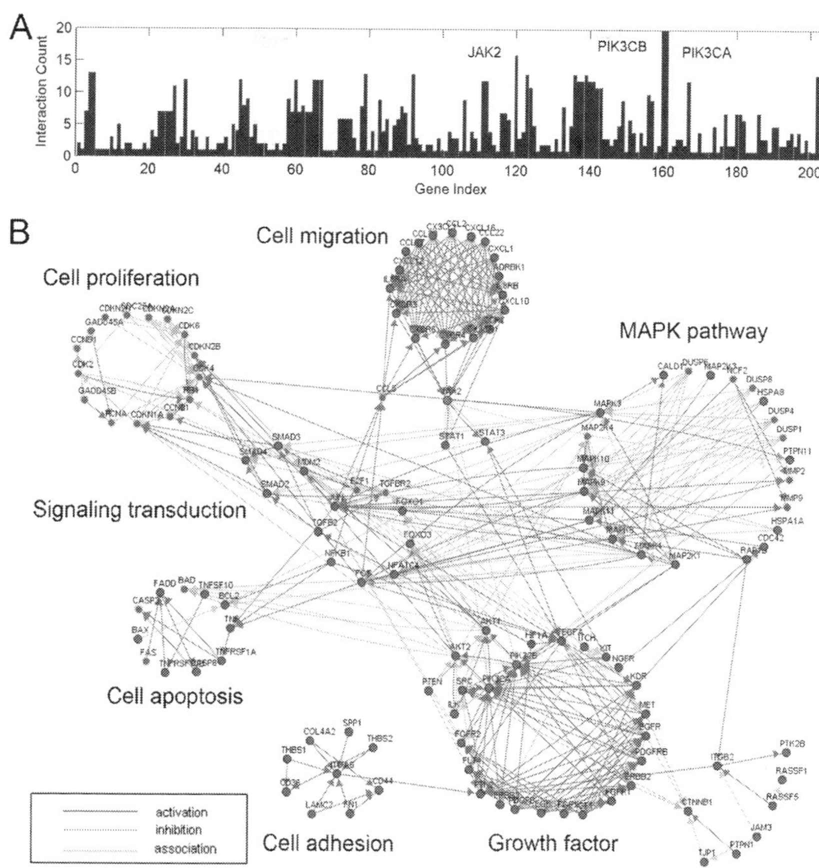

Fig. 1. Visualization of glioma-related gene interaction network.
(A) Connectivity analysis was performed using the Search Tool for the Retrieval of Interacting Genes/Proteins (STRING) to generate glioma-related gene knowledge-driven network, as described in Methods. Analysis revealed PI3KCA, PI3KCB and JAK2 are hub genes with P-value<0.001, which had an influential role in network stability.
(B) PI3K and JAK2 hub signalings located at the key status of glioma-related gene knowledge-driven network, and exerted a wide effect on kinds of biological functions and pathways, including signaling transduction, MAPK pathway, growth factor, cell apoptosis, cell proliferation, cell adhesion and cell migration. Purple lines correspond to activation, blue lines to inhibition, and yellow lines to association. Red circles (PI3KCA, PI3KCB and JAK2) are indicated for hub genes.

2.4 Glioma-related miRNA pathway

Because each miRNA target prediction program uses a different computer-aided algorithm for prediction, encompassing all these methods will probably produce a more reliable model of target prediction. Thus, a union target gene list of 14 glioma-related miRNAs was generated from 3 target prediction programs (PicTar, TargetScan and miRanda). To further explore the signaling pathway in these target genes, pathway analysis was performed. Table 5 showed that p53 signaling pathway, Apoptosis, Focal adhesion, MAPK signaling pathway, Toll-like receptor signaling pathway and Cell cycle pathways were significantly over-represented. Actually, these 6 pathways were included in the pathways of glioma-related genes. These findings imply that glioma-related genes and miRNAs prefer a common set of signaling pathways.

Pathway	Count	Enrichment P-value
p53 signaling pathway	19	8.67E-09
Apoptosis	21	2.4E-08
Focal adhesion	26	0.000123
MAPK signaling pathway	30	0.000499
Toll-like receptor signaling pathway	15	0.005773
Cell cycle	16	0.006547

Over-represented KEGG pathways were identified after multiple testing adjustments (P-value<0.05).

Table 5. Set of signaling pathways with highly enriched microRNA targets.

In order to construct the network between glioma-related miRNAs and the signaling pathway, integrated analysis of the targets of glioma-related miRNAs was performed. This procedure obtained 6 miRNA-pathway networks. For instance, p53 signaling pathway network contained 12 miRNAs (miR-21, miR-34a, miR-221, miR-222, et al) and 19 genes (PTEN, CDK6, BBC3, et al) (Fig.2).

Fig. 2. Visualization of miRNA-p53 pathway network in glioma.

The network was visualized with Medusa software. Blue quadrangles represent glioma-related miRNAs. Red circles represent miRNA targets that were overlapped by glioma-related geges.

3. Discussion

The overall utility of our data mining approach, including the strategy for constructing interaction networks, is to explore biological mechanisms involved in glioma progression. In this study, we obtained 670 genes and 14 miRNAs that interacted with glioma and generated interaction networks from abstract-based text mining. Importantly, our analysis identified PI3K and JAK2 hub signalings and miRNA regulatory module in glioma.

3.1 Core signalings in glioma

By integration of PubMed text mining, homology prediction, gene neighbor, protein-protein interaction, gene fusion and other data sources, we constructed glioma-related genes knowledge-driven network. Further analysis revealed that PI3K and JAK2 hub signalings that had an influential role in network stability, located at the key status of glioma-related genes knowledge-driven network. These signaling exerted a wide effect on kinds of biological functions and pathways, including signaling transduction, MAPK pathway, growth factor, cell apoptosis, cell proliferation, cell adhesion and cell migration. Further, integrating GO and pathway analysis, data revealed that proliferation without control and invasive growth were the essential characteristic of glioma.

PI3Ks are heterodimers comprised of a regulatory subunit (p85) and a catalytic subunit (p110). Activated receptor tyrosine kinases recruit the PI3 kinase complex to the membrane via the p85 regulatory subunit, thereby activating the catalytic subunit p110, which then phosphorylates phosphatidylinositol-4,5-bisphosphate (PIP2) to phosphatidylinositol-3,4,5-trisphosphate (PIP3). PIP3 recruits protein AKT to the plasma membrane where AKT is phosphorylated at Thr308 and Ser473 (Cheng et al., 2009). A high frequency of mutations in PIK3CA, the gene encoding the p110alpha subunit of PI3K, was found in glioblastoma (Gallia et al., 2006; Kita et al., 2007). Our recent data showed that PI3K activity were greatly increased with the ascending of tumor grade and correlated positively with AKT2 expression (Wang et al., 2010). Activation of PI3K/Akt signaling cascade results in cell survival and proliferation as well as inhibition of cell apoptosis through regulating downstream targets. AKT contributes to glioma cell migration and invasion by regulating the formation of cytoskeleton, influencing adhesion and MMP2/9 expression (Pu et al., 2004; Zhang et al., 2009a; Zhang et al., 2010d). AKT promotes the cell cycle progression by suppression of cyclin-dependent kinase inhibitors p21 and p27 and increase of Cyclin D1 (Guillard et al., 2009; Koul et al., 2010; Pu et al., 2006). AKT inhibits cell apoptosis by inactivation of caspase pathway, and activation of BCL2, NFκB and mTOR signaling cascade (Jiang et al., 2009; Ruano et al., 2008; Zhang et al., 2010d). Further, prosurvival signaling by PI3K contributes to therapeutic resistance in the setting of established antiglioma therapies. Several studies have shown that PI3K inhibition sensitizes glioma cells to radiation and chemical therapy (Opel et al., 2008; Prevo et al., 2008). Additionally, our study recently has showed that co-suppression of PI3K and AKT exerts significant proliferation and invasion inhibition effects on glioma cells (Fu et al., 2009). In the current study, we found that is PI3K is a molecular hub in glioma-related genes knowledge-driven network, and associated with a wide variety of cell biological functions and signaling pathways. Therefore, it is urgent to develop novel therapies for targeting PI3K/AKT signaling in glioma treatment.

In our case, network analysis also identifies a new candidate hub gene JAK2 in glioblastoma. JAKs, which have four members, JAK1, JAK2, JAK3 and Tyrosine kinase 2 (Tyk2) in mammals, are non-receptor tyrosine kinases involved in upstream intracellular signaling pathways that become activated after extracellular ligand binding to a variety of cytokine and growth-factor receptors (Pesu et al., 2008). JAK2 is known to be able to phosphorylate members of the signal transducers and activators of the transcription (STAT) protein family, subsequently leading them to translocate to the nucleus and bind to specific DNA sequences in the promoters of multiple responsive genes (Ghoreschi et al., 2009; Rane and Reddy, 2000). STAT family has been reported to be involved in the development of glioma. Of note, STAT3, is aberrantly activated in human glioblastoma tissues, and this activation is implicated in controlling critical cellular events thought to be involved in gliomagenesis, such as cell cycle progression, apoptosis and angiogenesis (Brantley and Benveniste, 2008). Recently, a glioma-specific regulatory network has revealed the transcriptional module that activates expression of mesenchymal genes in malignant glioma and STAT3 is one of key transcription factors necessary in human glioma cells for mesenchymal transformation (Carro et al., 2010). Additionally, nuclear staining of phospho-STAT5 is overexpressed in glioma tissues, and cytoplasm staining of STAT5b is markedly increased in glioblastoma multiforme compared with that in normal brain (Kondyli et al., 2010; Liang et al., 2009). Reduction of STAT5b inhibits glioma cell growth, cell cycle progression, invasion and migration through regulation of gene expression, such as Bcl-2, p21, p27 and VEGF (Liang et al., 2009). As another member of STAT family, STAT1 is up-regulated in the majority of glioblastomas (Haybaeck et al., 2007). Little evidence exists to show the mechanism of JAK2 (upstream regulator of STAT family) involved in glomagenesis. However, data mining analysis displays that JAK2 occupies a core regulatory node of glioma-related genes knowledge-driven network. These data indicate that modulation of the mechanism responsible for JAK2 in glioma would help us to elucidate the development of glioma and inhibition of JAK2/STAT signaling could be used as a new therapeutic strategy to treatment glioma. The JAK/STAT pathway plays a central role in principal cell fate decisions, regulating the processes of innate immunity, adaptive immunity, cell proliferation, differentiation, and apoptosis.

In addition, we found the gene CTNNB1 (encoding β-catenin) at the lower right corner of Fig.1 would warrant further investigation. β-catenin and Tcf-4 are the core components of the canonical Wnt/β-catenin/Tcf pathway, which is a crucial factor in the development of many cancers (MacDonald et al., 2009; Ying and Tao, 2009). β-catenin accumulates in the nucleus, where it interacts with coregulators of transcription including Tcf-4 and Lef-1 to form a β-catenin/Tcf/Lef complex. This complex regulates transcription of multiple genes involved in cellular proliferation, differentiation, survival and apoptosis, including Fra-1, c-myc and Cyclin D (Wang et al., 2002; Yochum et al., 2008). Recently several reports have showed that aberrant activation of Wnt/β-catenin/Tcf signaling pathway is an important contributing factor in gliomas (Liu et al., 2010; Pu et al., 2009; Sareddy et al., 2009). β-catenin and Tcf-4 were up-regulated in glioma tissues in comparison to normal brain tissues. Knockdown of β-catenin by siRNA in human glioma cells inhibited cell proliferation and invasive ability, induced apoptotic cell death and delayed the tumor growth (Pu et al., 2009). However, up to now, little direct evidence exists to show the mechanism of β-catenin and Tcf-4 involved in gliomagenesis.

Actually, our data doses not well confirm the update results of The Cancer Genome Atlas Network (TCGA) (Verhaak et al., 2010). TCGA catalogs recurrent genomic abnormalities in

GBM, and describes a gene expression-based molecular classification of GBM into Proneural, Neural, Classical, and Mesenchymal subtypes. Aberrations and gene expression of EGFR, NF1, and PDGFRA/IDH1 each define the Classical, Mesenchymal, and Proneural subtypes, respectively. Despite of the differences of two studies, our data showed another approach to explore the mechanism involved in glioma using existing data.

3.2 MiRNA regulatory module in glioma

miRNAs are a new class of small, non-coding RNAs located in noncoding regions or the introns of the genome, and regulate gene expression by binding to the 3′-untranslated region (3′-UTR) of specific mRNAs. Extensive studies have indicated that miRNAs could function as oncogenic miRNAs or tumor suppressor miRNAs, playing crucial roles in carcinogenesis. Expression profiling of glioma has unveiled miRNA signatures that not only distinguish glioma from normal tissues, but can also differentiate histotypes or molecular subtypes with altered genetic pathways (Ciafre et al., 2005; Lavon et al., 2010). Our data mining analysis showed that 6 pathways involved in 14 glioma-related miRNAs, in line with the pathway analysis of glioma-related genes, indicating that glioma-related genes and miRNAs exert an effect on a common set of signaling pathways. Moreover, we found that the pathway regulatory control mediated by miRNAs differs from pathway to pathway and the targets of a specific miRNA are significantly enriched in multiple pathways. In p53 signaling pathway network, 12 miRNAs and 19 genes are involved. Among these miRNA and target gene relationships, MDM2, CDK6, CDKN2A and CCNE1 are successfully identified as direct targets of miR-221, miR-34a, miR-125b and miR-15b, respectively (Kim et al., 2010; Pogue et al., 2010; Sun et al., 2008; Xia et al., 2009). Our data recently showed that miR-221 and miR-222 directly modulate PTEN expression via targeting PTEN 3′-UTR (Zhang et al., 2010a). In addition, we have also evidenced that BBC3, also named p53 up-regulated modulator of apoptosis (PUMA), is a new target of miR-221, consistent with bioinformatics analysis (Zhang et al., 2010b). Further, a recent publication revealed that miR-21 can impair p53-mediated apoptosis in response to chemotherapeutic (doxorubicin)-induced DNA damage, therefore contributing to drug resistance in glioblastoma cells (Papagiannakopoulos et al., 2008). Thus, modulation of these p53-related targets by miR-21 may potentially explain previous observation that p53 signaling pathway were up-regulated in response to miR-21 knockdown (Frankel et al., 2008). These exciting results prompt us to further elucidate the intricacy of the interaction between miRNAs and the signaling pathway.

In conclusion, using data mining analysis, we construct glioma-related genes knowledge-driven network and show that PI3K and JAK2 hub signalings are key steps leading to oncogenesis in glioma, and further propose miRNA regulatory module in glioma. These data demonstrate the power of data mining strategies as tools for biological discovery and identify core signalings and miRNA regulatory module in glioma, suggesting that the application of this strategy to consolidate all existing data for other diseases may yield important discoveries in disease pathogenesis.

4. Experimental procedures

4.1 Natural language processing (NLP) system

Medline/PubMed is used as information source for bioinformatics text mining. Medline abstracts were retrieved using National Center for Biotechnology Information (NCBI)

PubMed portal. We queried Pubmed with: glioma[title] AND ("1980/01/01"[PDAT] : "2010/04/01"[PDAT]). All abstracts were downloaded as HTML text without images and then converted into XML documents. Sentence tokenization was performed with Lingpipe tools. Subsequent analysis is based on the sentence as the basic units. Gene mentions were tagged using ABNER (Settles, 2005). To solve the matter of plethora of gene aliases, all gene mentions were normalized to Entrez gene (http://www.ncbi.nlm.nih.gov/Entrez/) official gene symbols. Only sentences with glioma, the genes were selected.

In order to test the null hypothesis 'the relationship between glioma and the gene is random', hypergeometric distribution test was employed. Let N be the total number of PubMed abstracts and m, n be the number mentions in PubMed for glioma and a related gene, respectively.

$$p = 1 - \sum_{i=0}^{k-1} p(i \mid n,m,N)$$

Where

$$p(i \mid n,m,N) = \frac{n!(N-n)!m!(N-m)!}{(n-i)!i!(n-m)!(N-n-m+i)!N!}$$

The "glioma-gene" relations with P-value<0.05 were then summarized and subjected to a relational database for further analysis.

4.2 Gene ontology analysis

Gene ontology analysis was performed by GSEA Base package of BioConductor (http://www.bioconductor.org/). The glioma-related genes were performed a gene set enrichment analysis based on the gene ontology (GO) categories.

4.3 Pathway analysis

Expression Analysis Systematic Explorer (EASE) (Hosack et al., 2003) was used to analyze KEGG pathways. Over representation of genes in a KEGG pathway is present if a larger fraction of genes within that pathway is differentially expressed compared with all genes in the genome. The "glioma-gene" relationships retrieved by our NLP system were filtered by pathway enrichment analysis. The links between glioma and related genes were then visualized in Cytoscape software (Cline et al., 2007) (http://www.cytoscape.org/). Genes were grouped according to pathways. Genes that involves in multiple pathways are assigned to a single pathway with the smallest enrichment P-value.

4.4 Gene network analysis

Integrating PubMed text mining, homology prediction, gene neighbor, protein-protein interaction, gene fusion and other data sources through the Search Tool for the Retrieval of Interacting Genes/Proteins (STRING), we created glioma-related genes knowledge-driven network (von Mering et al., 2005). Linker genes below a P-value threshold of 0.01 were identified as "hubs". The results from the search are saved in data files describing links between two genes and then handled in Medusa software.

4.5 Target gene prediction and pathway analysis of miRNAs

Three computational tools: TargetScan v5.1 (http://www.targetscan.org/), miRanda v5 (http://microrna.sanger.ac.uk/), PicTar ver. March 26, 2007 (http://pictar.mdc-berlin.de/) were utilized to identify miRNA targets in 3'-UTR of genes. The union of these results was listed for further analysis. These targets were used to analyze KEGG pathways.

4.6 MiRNA-target network analysis

The overlap of target genes of glioma-related miRNAs predicted by computational tools and glioma related genes derived from NLP analysis was calculated. A bipartite network of microRNAs and corresponding target genes was constructed. The network was displayed in separated pathways.

5. Acknowledgments

This work was supported by China National Natural Scientific Fund (30971136, 30872657, 81072078), Tianjin Science and Technology Committee (09JCZDJC17600), Program for New Century Excellent Talents in University (NCET-07-0615), Jiangsu Province's "333" Key Talent Foundation (0508RS08).

6. References

Brantley, EC, Benveniste, EN. (2008). Signal transducer and activator of transcription-3: a molecular hub for signaling pathways in gliomas. *Mol Cancer Res.* Vol.6, NO.5, pp. 675-684.

Carro, MS, Lim, WK, Alvarez, MJ, Bollo, RJ, Zhao, X, Snyder, EY, Sulman, EP, Anne, SL, Doetsch, F, Colman, H, Lasorella, A, Aldape, K, Califano, A, Iavarone, A. (2010). The transcriptional network for mesenchymal transformation of brain tumours. *Nature.* Vol.463, NO.7279, pp. 318-325.

Cheng, CK, Fan, QW, Weiss, WA. (2009). PI3K signaling in glioma--animal models and therapeutic challenges. *Brain Pathol.* Vol.19, NO.1, pp. 112-120.

Ciafre, SA, Galardi, S, Mangiola, A, Ferracin, M, Liu, CG, Sabatino, G, Negrini, M, Maira, G, Croce, CM, Farace, MG. (2005). Extensive modulation of a set of microRNAs in primary glioblastoma. *Biochem Biophys Res Commun.* Vol.334, NO.4, pp. 1351-1358.

Cline, MS, Smoot, M, Cerami, E, Kuchinsky, A, Landys, N, Workman, C, Christmas, R, Avila-Campilo, I, Creech, M, Gross, B, Hanspers, K, Isserlin, R, Kelley, R, Killcoyne, S, Lotia, S, Maere, S, Morris, J, Ono, K, Pavlovic, V, Pico, AR, Vailaya, A, Wang, PL, Adler, A, Conklin, BR, Hood, L, Kuiper, M, Sander, C, Schmulevich, I, Schwikowski, B, Warner, GJ, Ideker, T, Bader, GD. (2007). Integration of biological networks and gene expression data using Cytoscape. *Nat Protoc.* Vol.2, NO.10, pp. 2366-2382.

Frankel, LB, Christoffersen, NR, Jacobsen, A, Lindow, M, Krogh, A, Lund, AH. (2008). Programmed cell death 4 (PDCD4) is an important functional target of the microRNA miR-21 in breast cancer cells. *J Biol Chem.* Vol.283, NO.2, pp. 1026-1033.

Friedman, C, Kra, P, Yu, H, Krauthammer, M, Rzhetsky, A. (2001). GENIES: a natural-language processing system for the extraction of molecular pathways from journal articles. *Bioinformatics.* Vol.17 Suppl 1, S74-82.

Fu, Y, Zhang, Q, Kang, C, Zhang, J, Zhang, K, Pu, P, Wang, G, Wang, T. (2009). Inhibitory effects of adenovirus mediated Akt1 and PIK3R1 shRNA on the growth of malignant tumor cells in vitro and in vivo. *Cancer Biol Ther.* Vol.8, NO.11, pp. 1002-1009.

Gallia, GL, Rand, V, Siu, IM, Eberhart, CG, James, CD, Marie, SK, Oba-Shinjo, SM, Carlotti, CG, Caballero, OL, Simpson, AJ, Brock, MV, Massion, PP, Carson, BS, Sr., Riggins, GJ. (2006). PIK3CA gene mutations in pediatric and adult glioblastoma multiforme. *Mol Cancer Res*. Vol.4, NO.10, pp. 709-714.

Ghoreschi, K, Laurence, A, O'Shea, JJ. (2009). Janus kinases in immune cell signaling. *Immunol Rev*. Vol.228, NO.1, pp. 273-287.

Guillard, S, Clarke, PA, Te Poele, R, Mohri, Z, Bjerke, L, Valenti, M, Raynaud, F, Eccles, SA, Workman, P. (2009). Molecular pharmacology of phosphatidylinositol 3-kinase inhibition in human glioma. *Cell Cycle*. Vol.8, NO.3, pp. 443-453.

Haybaeck, J, Obrist, P, Schindler, CU, Spizzo, G, Doppler, W. (2007). STAT-1 expression in human glioblastoma and peritumoral tissue. *Anticancer Res*. Vol.27, NO.6B, pp. 3829-3835.

Hosack, DA, Dennis, G, Jr., Sherman, BT, Lane, HC, Lempicki, RA. (2003). Identifying biological themes within lists of genes with EASE. *Genome Biol*. Vol.4, NO.10, pp. R70.

Jiang, H, Shang, X, Wu, H, Gautam, SC, Al-Holou, S, Li, C, Kuo, J, Zhang, L, Chopp, M. (2009). Resveratrol downregulates PI3K/Akt/mTOR signaling pathways in human U251 glioma cells. *J Exp Ther Oncol*. Vol.8, NO.1, pp. 25-33.

Kim, D, Song, J, Jin, EJ. (2010). MicroRNA-221 regulates chondrogenic differentiation through promoting proteosomal degradation of slug by targeting mdm2. *J Biol Chem*.

Kita, D, Yonekawa, Y, Weller, M, Ohgaki, H. (2007). PIK3CA alterations in primary (de novo) and secondary glioblastomas. *Acta Neuropathol*. Vol.113, NO.3, pp. 295-302.

Kondyli, M, Gatzounis, G, Kyritsis, A, Varakis, J, Assimakopoulou, M. (2010). Immunohistochemical detection of phosphorylated JAK-2 and STAT-5 proteins and correlation with erythropoietin receptor (EpoR) expression status in human brain tumors. *J Neurooncol*.

Koul, N, Sharma, V, Dixit, D, Ghosh, S, Sen, E. (2010). Bicyclic triterpenoid Iripallidal induces apoptosis and inhibits Akt/mTOR pathway in glioma cells. *BMC Cancer*. Vol.10, NO.1, pp. 328.

Lavon, I, Zrihan, D, Granit, A, Einstein, O, Fainstein, N, Cohen, MA, Zelikovitch, B, Shoshan, Y, Spektor, S, Reubinoff, BE, Felig, Y, Gerlitz, O, Ben-Hur, T, Smith, Y, Siegal, T. (2010). Gliomas display a microRNA expression profile reminiscent of neural precursor cells. *Neuro Oncol*. Vol.12, NO.5, pp. 422-433.

Liang, QC, Xiong, H, Zhao, ZW, Jia, D, Li, WX, Qin, HZ, Deng, JP, Gao, L, Zhang, H, Gao, GD. (2009). Inhibition of transcription factor STAT5b suppresses proliferation, induces G1 cell cycle arrest and reduces tumor cell invasion in human glioblastoma multiforme cells. *Cancer Lett*. Vol.273, NO.1, pp. 164-171.

Liu, X, Wang, L, Zhao, S, Ji, X, Luo, Y, Ling, F. (2010). beta-Catenin overexpression in malignant glioma and its role in proliferation and apoptosis in glioblastma cells. *Med Oncol*.

MacDonald, BT, Tamai, K, He, X. (2009). Wnt/beta-catenin signaling: components, mechanisms, and diseases. *Dev Cell*. Vol.17, NO.1, pp. 9-26.

Opel, D, Westhoff, MA, Bender, A, Braun, V, Debatin, KM, Fulda, S. (2008). Phosphatidylinositol 3-kinase inhibition broadly sensitizes glioblastoma cells to death receptor- and drug-induced apoptosis. *Cancer Res*. Vol.68, NO.15, pp. 6271-6280.

Papagiannakopoulos, T, Shapiro, A, Kosik, KS. (2008). MicroRNA-21 targets a network of key tumor-suppressive pathways in glioblastoma cells. *Cancer Res*. Vol.68, NO.19, pp. 8164-8172.

Pesu, M, Laurence, A, Kishore, N, Zwillich, SH, Chan, G, O'Shea, JJ. (2008). Therapeutic targeting of Janus kinases. *Immunol Rev*. Vol.223, 132-142.

Pogue, AI, Cui, JG, Li, YY, Zhao, Y, Culicchia, F, Lukiw, WJ. (2010). Micro RNA-125b (miRNA-125b) function in astrogliosis and glial cell proliferation. *Neurosci Lett.* Vol.476, NO.1, pp. 18-22.

Prevo, R, Deutsch, E, Sampson, O, Diplexcito, J, Cengel, K, Harper, J, O'Neill, P, McKenna, WG, Patel, S, Bernhard, EJ. (2008). Class I PI3 kinase inhibition by the pyridinylfuranopyrimidine inhibitor PI-103 enhances tumor radiosensitivity. *Cancer Res.* Vol.68, NO.14, pp. 5915-5923.

Pu, P, Kang, C, Li, J, Jiang, H. (2004). Antisense and dominant-negative AKT2 cDNA inhibits glioma cell invasion. *Tumour Biol.* Vol.25, NO.4, pp. 172-178.

Pu, P, Kang, C, Li, J, Jiang, H, Cheng, J. (2006). The effects of antisense AKT2 RNA on the inhibition of malignant glioma cell growth in vitro and in vivo. *J Neurooncol.* Vol.76, NO.1, pp. 1-11.

Pu, P, Zhang, Z, Kang, C, Jiang, R, Jia, Z, Wang, G, Jiang, H. (2009). Downregulation of Wnt2 and beta-catenin by siRNA suppresses malignant glioma cell growth. *Cancer Gene Ther.* Vol.16, NO.4, pp. 351-361.

Rane, SG, Reddy, EP. (2000). Janus kinases: components of multiple signaling pathways. *Oncogene.* Vol.19, NO.49, pp. 5662-5679.

Rindflesch, TC, Tanabe, L, Weinstein, JN, Hunter, L. (2000). EDGAR: extraction of drugs, genes and relations from the biomedical literature. *Pac Symp Biocomput.* 517-528.

Ruano, Y, Mollejo, M, Camacho, FI, Rodriguez de Lope, A, Fiano, C, Ribalta, T, Martinez, P, Hernandez-Moneo, JL, Melendez, B. (2008). Identification of survival-related genes of the phosphatidylinositol 3'-kinase signaling pathway in glioblastoma multiforme. *Cancer.* Vol.112, NO.7, pp. 1575-1584.

Sareddy, GR, Panigrahi, M, Challa, S, Mahadevan, A, Babu, PP. (2009). Activation of Wnt/beta-catenin/Tcf signaling pathway in human astrocytomas. *Neurochem Int.* Vol.55, NO.5, pp. 307-317.

Sekimizu, T, Park, HS, Tsujii, J. (1998). Identifying the Interaction between Genes and Gene Products Based on Frequently Seen Verbs in Medline Abstracts. *Genome Inform Ser Workshop Genome Inform.* Vol.9, 62-71.

Settles, B. (2005). ABNER: an open source tool for automatically tagging genes, proteins and other entity names in text. *Bioinformatics.* Vol.21, NO.14, pp. 3191-3192.

Shi, L, Cheng, Z, Zhang, J, Li, R, Zhao, P, Fu, Z, You, Y. (2008). hsa-mir-181a and hsa-mir-181b function as tumor suppressors in human glioma cells. *Brain Res.* Vol.1236, 185-193.

Shi, L, Zhang, J, Pan, T, Zhou, J, Gong, W, Liu, N, Fu, Z, You, Y. (2010). MiR-125b is critical for the suppression of human U251 glioma stem cell proliferation. *Brain Res.* Vol.1312, 120-126.

Stupp, R, Mason, WP, van den Bent, MJ, Weller, M, Fisher, B, Taphoorn, MJ, Belanger, K, Brandes, AA, Marosi, C, Bogdahn, U, Curschmann, J, Janzer, RC, Ludwin, SK, Gorlia, T, Allgeier, A, Lacombe, D, Cairncross, JG, Eisenhauer, E, Mirimanoff, RO. (2005). Radiotherapy plus concomitant and adjuvant temozolomide for glioblastoma. *N Engl J Med.* Vol.352, NO.10, pp. 987-996.

Sun, F, Fu, H, Liu, Q, Tie, Y, Zhu, J, Xing, R, Sun, Z, Zheng, X. (2008). Downregulation of CCND1 and CDK6 by miR-34a induces cell cycle arrest. *FEBS Lett.* Vol.582, NO.10, pp. 1564-1568.

Verhaak, RG, Hoadley, KA, Purdom, E, Wang, V, Qi, Y, Wilkerson, MD, Miller, CR, Ding, L, Golub, T, Mesirov, JP, Alexe, G, Lawrence, M, O'Kelly, M, Tamayo, P, Weir, BA, Gabriel, S, Winckler, W, Gupta, S, Jakkula, L, Feiler, HS, Hodgson, JG, James, CD, Sarkaria, JN, Brennan, C, Kahn, A, Spellman, PT, Wilson, RK, Speed, TP, Gray, JW,

Meyerson, M, Getz, G, Perou, CM, Hayes, DN. (2010). Integrated genomic analysis identifies clinically relevant subtypes of glioblastoma characterized by abnormalities in PDGFRA, IDH1, EGFR, and NF1. *Cancer Cell*. Vol.17, NO.1, pp. 98-110.

von Mering, C, Jensen, LJ, Snel, B, Hooper, SD, Krupp, M, Foglierini, M, Jouffre, N, Huynen, MA, Bork, P. (2005). STRING: known and predicted protein-protein associations, integrated and transferred across organisms. *Nucleic Acids Res*. Vol.33, NO.Database issue, pp. D433-437.

Wang, G, Kang, C, Pu, P. (2010). Increased expression of Akt2 and activity of PI3K and cell proliferation with the ascending of tumor grade of human gliomas. *Clin Neurol Neurosurg*. Vol.112, NO.4, pp. 324-327.

Wang, HL, Wang, J, Xiao, SY, Haydon, R, Stoiber, D, He, TC, Bissonnette, M, Hart, J. (2002). Elevated protein expression of cyclin D1 and Fra-1 but decreased expression of c-Myc in human colorectal adenocarcinomas overexpressing beta-catenin. *Int J Cancer*. Vol.101, NO.4, pp. 301-310.

Xia, H, Qi, Y, Ng, SS, Chen, X, Chen, S, Fang, M, Li, D, Zhao, Y, Ge, R, Li, G, Chen, Y, He, ML, Kung, HF, Lai, L, Lin, MC. (2009). MicroRNA-15b regulates cell cycle progression by targeting cyclins in glioma cells. *Biochem Biophys Res Commun*. Vol.380, NO.2, pp. 205-210.

Ying, Y, Tao, Q. (2009). Epigenetic disruption of the WNT/beta-catenin signaling pathway in human cancers. *Epigenetics*. Vol.4, NO.5, pp. 307-312.

Yochum, GS, Cleland, R, Goodman, RH. (2008). A genome-wide screen for beta-catenin binding sites identifies a downstream enhancer element that controls c-Myc gene expression. *Mol Cell Biol*. Vol.28, NO.24, pp. 7368-7379.

Zhang, B, Gu, F, She, C, Guo, H, Li, W, Niu, R, Fu, L, Zhang, N, Ma, Y. (2009a). Reduction of Akt2 inhibits migration and invasion of glioma cells. *Int J Cancer*. Vol.125, NO.3, pp. 585-595.

Zhang, C, Kang, C, You, Y, Pu, P, Yang, W, Zhao, P, Wang, G, Zhang, A, Jia, Z, Han, L, Jiang, H. (2009b). Co-suppression of miR-221/222 cluster suppresses human glioma cell growth by targeting p27kip1 in vitro and in vivo. *Int J Oncol*. Vol.34, NO.6, pp. 1653-1660.

Zhang, CZ, Han, L, Zhang, AL, Fu, YC, Yue, X, Wang, GX, Jia, ZF, Pu, PY, Zhang, QY, Kang, CS. (2010a). MicroRNA-221 and microRNA-222 regulate gastric carcinoma cell proliferation and radioresistance by targeting PTEN. *BMC Cancer*. Vol.10, NO.1, pp. 367.

Zhang, CZ, Zhang, JX, Zhang, AL, Shi, ZD, Han, L, Jia, ZF, Yang, WD, Wang, GX, Jiang, T, You, YP, Pu, PY, Cheng, JQ, Kang, CS. (2010b). MiR-221 and miR-222 target PUMA to induce cell survival in glioblastoma. *Mol Cancer*. Vol.9, NO.1, pp. 229.

Zhang, J, Han, L, Ge, Y, Zhou, X, Zhang, A, Zhang, C, Zhong, Y, You, Y, Pu, P, Kang, C. (2010c). miR-221/222 promote malignant progression of glioma through activation of the Akt pathway. *Int J Oncol*. Vol.36, NO.4, pp. 913-920.

Zhang, J, Han, L, Zhang, A, Wang, Y, Yue, X, You, Y, Pu, P, Kang, C. (2010d). AKT2 expression is associated with glioma malignant progression and required for cell survival and invasion. *Oncol Rep*. Vol.24, NO.1, pp. 65-72.

Zhou, X, Ren, Y, Moore, L, Mei, M, You, Y, Xu, P, Wang, B, Wang, G, Jia, Z, Pu, P, Zhang, W, Kang, C. (2010a). Downregulation of miR-21 inhibits EGFR pathway and suppresses the growth of human glioblastoma cells independent of PTEN status. *Lab Invest*. Vol.90, NO.2, pp. 144-155.

Zhou, X, Zhang, J, Jia, Q, Ren, Y, Wang, Y, Shi, L, Liu, N, Wang, G, Pu, P, You, Y, Kang, C. (2010b). Reduction of miR-21 induces glioma cell apoptosis via activating caspase 9 and 3. *Oncol Rep*. Vol.24, NO.1, pp. 195-201.

Part 4

Sequence Analysis and Evolution

9

Significance Score of Motifs in Biological Sequences

Grégory Nuel
Institute for Mathematical Sciences (INSMI), CNRS, Paris
Department of Applied Mathematics (MAP5), University of Paris Descartes
France

1. Introduction

In Bioinformatics, it is common to search biological sequences (DNA, RNA, proteins) for functional motifs such as cross-over hotspot instigators (chi), restriction sites, regulation motifs, binding sites, active sites in proteins, etc. (Beaudoing et al., 2000; Brazma et al., 1998; El Karoui et al., 1999; Frith et al., 2002; Hampson et al., 2002; Karlin et al., 1992; Leonardo Marino-Ramírez & Landsman, 2004; van Helden et al., 1998). Due to evolution pressure, functional motifs are likely to be more conserved than non-functional motifs. As a consequence, it is a natural strategy to search biological sequences for motifs which are statistically exceptional (ex: over- or under-represented).

Given $\mathcal{M}$ a motif of interest (from simple strings to complex regular expressions), a recurrent question is: "how surprising is it to observe n occurrences of $\mathcal{M}$ in my dataset ". In statistical terms, this is equivalent to compute the p-value of observation n in respect with a relevant reference model. More precisely, if $X_{1:\ell} = X_1 \ldots X_\ell$ is a length ℓ random sequence generated by our reference model, and if N denotes the random number of occurrences of $\mathcal{M}$ in $X_{1:\ell}$, for any $n \geqslant 0$ our objective is to compute the significance score of observation n:

$$S(n) = \begin{cases} + \log_{10} \mathbb{P}(N \leqslant n) & \text{if } n \leqslant \mathbb{E}[N] \\ - \log_{10} \mathbb{P}(N \geqslant n) & \text{if } n > \mathbb{E}[N] \end{cases} \tag{1}$$

this score representing the p-value in a decimal log-scale, negative (resp. positive) values being associated to under- (resp. over-) representation events.

In order to compute such a score for a given motif $\mathcal{M}$ and a given dataset, one needs two essential steps:

1) **Counting:** count the observed number n of occurrences of motif $\mathcal{M}$ in the dataset;

2) **Significance:** compute the p-value of observation n with respect to a reference model.

In this chapter, we give all the necessary details to perform these two steps using state of the art approaches including some unpublished results.

2. Counting motifs

2.1 Biological motifs

We can see on Fig. 1 various examples of the kind of biological motifs we usually deal with in Bioinformatics. In most cases, these motifs are built from a set of active sequences (putative

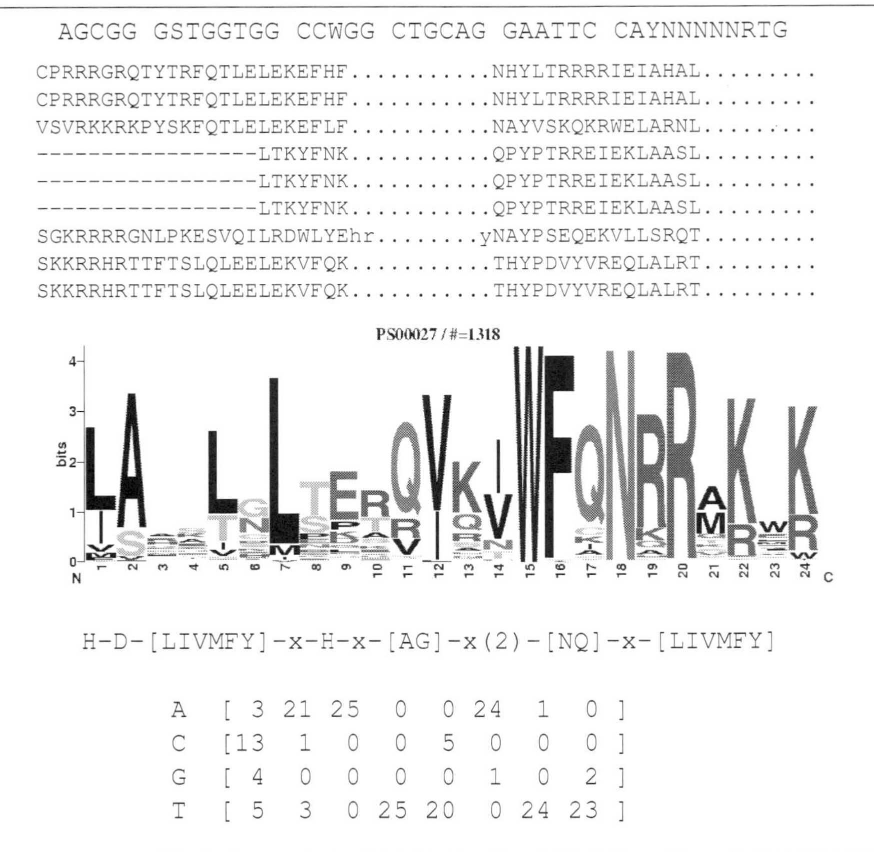

Fig. 1. Various kind of biological motifs. From top to bottom: strings in IUPAC (Cornish-Bowden, 1985) alphabet (DNA), multiple alignment (proteins), sequence logo (proteins), consensus pattern (proteins), and frequency matrix (DNA). Various sources including ReBase (Roberts et al., 2010), PROSITE (Sigrist et al., 2010), and JASPAR databases (Bryne et al., 2008).

or confirmed by experiments) in the form of a multiple alignment or a frequency matrix from which can be derived a consensus. This consensus could sometimes be a simple string (ex: AGCGG the chi site of *B. subtilis*) but in most cases it is a degenerated pattern (ex: CAYNNNNNRTG a restriction site in the IUPAC alphabet, PROSITE signatures). In all cases however, it is possible to consider our biological motif $\mathcal{M}$ as a (possibly large) set of strings.

Formally, let $\mathcal{M}$ be a finite set of strings over a finite alphabet $\mathcal{A}$. Ex: $\mathcal{A} = \{A, C, G, T\}$ for DNA sequences; this is the alphabet we are going to use from now on in our examples. Let $X_{1:\ell} = X_1 \ldots X_\ell$ be an observed sequence of length ℓ over $\mathcal{A}$. Then the number $N(\mathcal{M}; X_{1:\ell})$ of

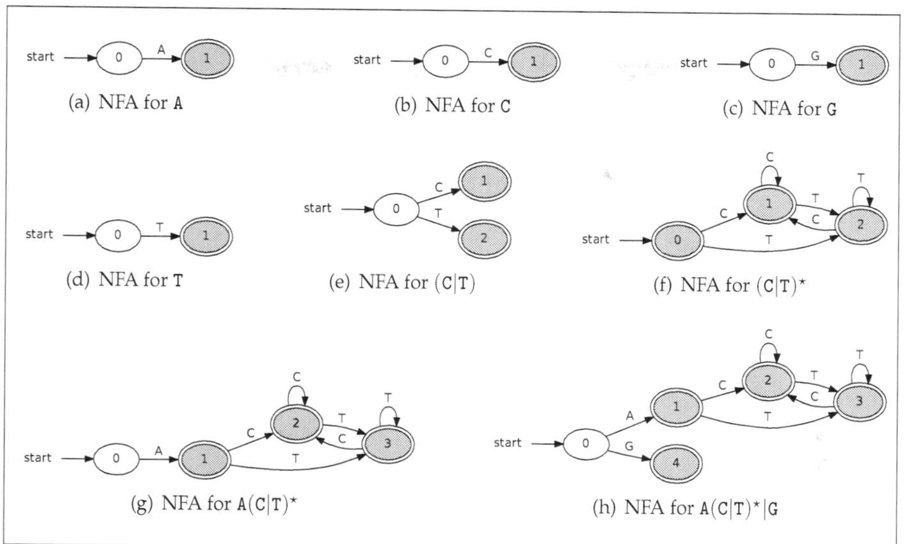

Fig. 2. Glushkov's construction for $A(C|T)^*|G$. (a), (b), (c), and (d) are singletons; (e) results from the union of (b) and (d); (f) results from the Kleene's closure of (e); (g) results from the concatenation of (a) and (f); (h) results from the union of (g) and (c).

matching positions of $\mathcal{M}$ in $X_{1:\ell}$, is defined by

$$N(\mathcal{M}; X_{1:\ell}) = \sum_{i=1}^{\ell} \mathbf{1}_{X_{1:i} \in \mathcal{A}^* \mathcal{M}} \qquad (2)$$

$\mathcal{A}^*\mathcal{M}$ being the set of all finite sequences over $\mathcal{A}$ ending with one element of $\mathcal{W}$ (this notation will be explained in the next section), and where $\mathbf{1}_A$ is the indicator function of event A.

In the particular case where $\mathcal{M}$ contains no strings that are included into each other (which is a common assumption), the number N of matching position corresponds exactly to the number of occurrences. However, there is no need to put any restriction on $\mathcal{M}$ as long as we are interested in the number of matching positions like we do.

From now on, if the sequence $X_{1:\ell}$ is observed, we denote by the number of matching positions by n, and if the sequence $X_{1:\ell}$ is random, we simply denote by N the random number of matching positions.

2.2 Regular languages

Let us denote by $\mathcal{A}^*$ the set of all finite sequences over $\mathcal{A}$. Any subset $\mathcal{L} \subset \mathcal{A}^*$ is then called a *language* over $\mathcal{A}$. We denote by $\mathcal{P}(\mathcal{A}^*)$ the set of all possible languages over $\mathcal{A}$. We denote by $\varepsilon \in \mathcal{A}^*$ the empty sequence, and for the sake of simplicity, the singletons of $\mathcal{P}(\mathcal{A}^*)$ will be simply denoted by their element. Ex: A instead of {A}, TGC instead of {TGC}, ε instead of {ε}. We define on these languages three *regular operations*:

Union (|): for all $\mathcal{L}_1, \mathcal{L}_2 \in \mathcal{P}(\mathcal{A}^*)$, $\mathcal{L}_1|\mathcal{L}_2 = \mathcal{L}_1 \cup \mathcal{L}_2$. The neutral element of the binary operator | is $\emptyset$. Ex: {AT, GA}|{T, GA, TT} = {AT, T, GA, TT}.

Require: remove first all states that are not reachable from σ or that cannot reach any element
   of $\mathcal{F}$
1: $\mathcal{W} \leftarrow \{\mathcal{F}, \mathcal{Q} \setminus \mathcal{F}\}$ and $\mathcal{P} \leftarrow \{\mathcal{F}, \mathcal{Q} \setminus \mathcal{F}\}$
2: **while** $\mathcal{W}$ is not empty **do**
3:    select and remove $\mathcal{V}$ from $\mathcal{W}$
4:    **for all** $a \in \mathcal{A}$ **do**
5:      $\mathcal{S} = \{q \in \mathcal{Q}, \delta(q,a) \in \mathcal{V}\}$
6:      **for all** $\mathcal{R} \in \mathcal{P}$ such as $\mathcal{R} \cap \mathcal{S} \neq \varnothing$ and $\mathcal{R} \nsubseteq \mathcal{S}$ **do**
7:        replace $\mathcal{R}$ in $\mathcal{P}$ by $\mathcal{R}_1 \leftarrow \mathcal{R} \cap \mathcal{S}$ and $\mathcal{R}_2 \leftarrow \mathcal{R} \setminus \mathcal{R}_1$
8:        **if** $\mathcal{R} \in \mathcal{W}$ **then**
9:          replace $\mathcal{R}$ in $\mathcal{P}$ by $\mathcal{R}_1$ and $\mathcal{R}_2$
10:       **else**
11:         **if** $|\mathcal{R}_1| \leqslant |\mathcal{R}_2|$ **then** add $\mathcal{R}_1$ to $\mathcal{W}$ **else** add $\mathcal{R}_2$ to $\mathcal{W}$ **end if**
12:       **end if**
13:     **end for**
14:   **end for**
15: **end while**

Algorithm 1. Performs Hopcroft's reduction on NFA $(\mathcal{A}, \mathcal{Q}, \sigma, \mathcal{F}, \delta)$. $\mathcal{W}$ (working set) and $\mathcal{P}$
(partition set) are two sets of set of NFA states. The resulting complexity is $O(|\mathcal{Q}| \log |\mathcal{Q}|)$.

Concatenation ($\cdot$): for all $\mathcal{L}_1, \mathcal{L}_2 \in \mathcal{P}(\mathcal{A}^*)$, $\mathcal{L}_1 \cdot \mathcal{L}_2 = \{xy, x \in \mathcal{L}_1, y \in \mathcal{L}_2\}$. The neutral
   element of the binary operator $\cdot$ is ε. For all $\mathcal{L} \in \mathcal{P}(\mathcal{A}^*)$, $\mathcal{L}^0 = \varepsilon$ (convention), $\mathcal{L}^1 = \mathcal{L}$,
   $\mathcal{L}^2 = \mathcal{L} \cdot \mathcal{L}$ and the notation extends recursively to $\mathcal{L}^k$ for any $k \geqslant 3$. Ex: $\{\text{G}, \text{GA}\} \cdot \{\text{AT}, \text{T}\} =$
   $\{\text{GAT}, \text{GT}, \text{GAAT}\}$; $\{\text{G}, \text{GA}\}^3 = \{\text{GGG}, \text{GGGA}, \text{GGAG}, \text{GGAGA}, \text{GAGG}, \text{GAGGA}, \text{GAGAG}, \text{GAGAGA}\}$. For the
   sake of simplicity, $\cdot$ is implicitly used when the operator is omitted.. Ex: $\mathcal{A}\mathcal{L}$ means $\mathcal{A} \cdot \mathcal{L}$.

Kleene's closure (*): For all $\mathcal{L} \in \mathcal{P}(\mathcal{A}^*)$, $\mathcal{L}^* = \sum_{k \geqslant 0} \mathcal{L}^k$. Ex: $\{\text{AT}\}^* = \{\varepsilon, \text{AT}, \text{ATAT}, \text{ATATAT}, \ldots\}$.

The precedence rule of these operations is: $|$ (lowest precedence), $\cdot$ (associative operator), *
(highest precedence). Ex: $\text{A}|\text{C} \cdot \text{T}^* = (\text{A}|(\text{C}(\cdot\text{T}^*)))$, $\text{TT} \cdot \text{A}|\text{C}^* \cdot \text{G} = ((\text{TT} \cdot \text{A})|((\text{C}^*) \cdot \text{G}))$.
We call *regular expression* over $\mathcal{A}$ any algebric expression over $\mathcal{P}(\mathcal{A}^*)$ defined from singleton
elements and a finite number of regular operations. The resulting language is called a
regular language. Ex: any finite language is a regular language, $\mathcal{A}^*$ is a regular language,
$(\text{A}|\text{C}|\text{G}|\text{T})^*\text{GGATG}$ is a regular language, $\{\text{AG}, \text{AAGG}, \text{AAAGGG}, \ldots\}$ is <u>not</u> a regular language.

2.3 Non-deterministic finite automaton

A *Non-deterministic Finite Automaton* (NFA) is defined as a 5-tuple $(\mathcal{A}, \mathcal{Q}, \sigma, \mathcal{F}, \delta)$ where: $\mathcal{A}$ is a
finite alphabet, $\mathcal{Q}$ is a finite *state space*, $\sigma \in \mathcal{Q}$ is the *starting state*, $\mathcal{F} \subset \mathcal{Q}$ is the set of *final states*,
and $\delta : \mathcal{Q} \times \mathcal{A} \to \mathcal{P}(\mathcal{Q})$ is the *transition function*. An element $X_{1:\ell} \in \mathcal{A}^*$ is *accepted* by this NFA
if and only if it exists a *path* from the starting state to one of the final state that sequentially
use the letters $X_{1:\ell}$ in the transitions. More formally, it means that it exists a sequence of states
(ie: elements of $\mathcal{Q}$) $q_0 = \sigma, q_1, q_2 \ldots, q_{\ell-1}, q_\ell \in \mathcal{F}$ such as $q_i \in \delta(q_{i-1}, X_i)$ for all $1 \leqslant i \leqslant \ell$. The
language of a NFA is the set of all elements of $\mathcal{A}^*$ it accepts.

Theorem 1. For any language $\mathcal{L} \in \mathcal{P}(\mathcal{A}^*)$: $\mathcal{L}$ regular $\iff$ it exists a NFA whose language is
$\mathcal{L}$.

We admit that the language of a NFA is always regular (see Hopcroft et al., 2001, for the
formal proof) but we will prove the reciprocal with the Glushkov's construction (Allauzen &

Mohri, 2006). This construction provides a simple way to build the NFA directly from the regular expression of the language. The idea is to treat the regular expression as any algebraic expression with a stack of operands (NFAs) and a stack of operators (regular operations). Since a regular expression is by definition built from singleton elements of $\mathcal{A}^\star$ and the three regular operations, we only need to give the construction of a NFA corresponding to singleton elements, and the constructions corresponding to the regular operations.

Singleton: for any $X_{1:\ell} \in \mathcal{A}^\star$ we build the NFA $(\mathcal{A}, \mathcal{Q}, \sigma, \mathcal{F}, \delta)$ with $\mathcal{Q} = \{0, 1, \ldots, \ell\}$, $\sigma = 0$, $\mathcal{F} = \{\ell\}$, and $\delta(i - 1, X_i) = \{i\}$ for all $1 \leqslant i \leqslant \ell$.

Union: the union $(\mathcal{A}, \mathcal{Q}, \sigma, \mathcal{F}, \delta)$ of two NFAs $(\mathcal{A}, \mathcal{Q}_1, \sigma_1, \mathcal{F}_1, \delta_1)$ and $(\mathcal{A}, \mathcal{Q}, \sigma_2, \mathcal{F}_2, \delta_2)$ is given by: $\mathcal{Q} = \mathcal{Q}_1 \cup \mathcal{Q}_2 \setminus \{\sigma_2\}$, $\sigma = \sigma_1$, $\mathcal{F} = \mathcal{F}_1 \cup \mathcal{F}_2$ and

$$\delta(q, a) = \begin{cases} \delta_1(\sigma_1, a) \cup \delta_1(\sigma_2, a) & \text{if } q = \sigma_1 \\ \delta_1(q, a) & \text{if } q \in \mathcal{Q}_1 \setminus \{\sigma_1\} \\ \delta_2(q, a) & \text{if } q \in \mathcal{Q}_2 \setminus \{\sigma_2\} \end{cases} \tag{3}$$

Concatenation: the concatenation $(\mathcal{A}, \mathcal{Q}, \sigma, \mathcal{F}, \delta)$ of two NFAs $(\mathcal{A}, \mathcal{Q}_1, \sigma_1, \mathcal{F}_1, \delta_1)$ and $(\mathcal{A}, \mathcal{Q}, \sigma_2, \mathcal{F}_2, \delta_2)$ is given by: $\mathcal{Q} = \mathcal{Q}_1 \cup \mathcal{Q}_2 \setminus \{\sigma_2\}$, $\sigma = \sigma_1$, $\mathcal{F} = \mathcal{F}_2$ and

$$\delta(q, a) = \begin{cases} \delta_1(q, a) & \text{if } q \in \mathcal{Q}_1 \setminus \mathcal{F}_1 \\ \delta_2(\sigma_2, a) & \text{if } q \in \mathcal{F}_1 \\ \delta_2(q, a) & \text{if } q \in \mathcal{Q}_2 \setminus \{\sigma_2\} \end{cases} \tag{4}$$

Kleene's closure: the Kleene's closure $(\mathcal{A}, \mathcal{Q}, \sigma, \mathcal{F}, \delta)$ of NFA $(\mathcal{A}, \mathcal{Q}_1, \sigma_1, \mathcal{F}_1, \delta_1)$ is given by: $\mathcal{Q} = \mathcal{Q}_1$, $\sigma = \sigma_1$, $\mathcal{F} = \mathcal{F}_1 \cup \{\sigma_1\}$ and

$$\delta(q, a) = \begin{cases} \delta_1(q, a) & \text{if } q \in \mathcal{Q}_1 \setminus \mathcal{F}_1 \\ \delta_1(\sigma_1, a) & \text{if } q \in \mathcal{F}_1 \end{cases} \tag{5}$$

Using Glushkov's construction, it is then possible to build a NFA whose language correspond to the regular expression of our choice. However in general, this construction is not optimal in terms of number of states. Fortunately, the reduction algorithm (Algorithm 1) due to Hopcroft provides a (partial) solution to this problem. Note that finding a minimal NFA for a given regular expression is a difficult task in general, but that Hopcroft's reduction is a good heuristic (we will see later that in the case of DFA, Hopcroft's reduction is indeed a minimization).

2.4 Counting with NFA

NFAs provide with Algorithm 2 an extremely efficient way to look for matching positions of any motif $\mathcal{M}$ (in fact, any regular expression) in a sequence $X_{1:\ell}$. The algorithm directly results from the definition of the language of a NFA.

Let us illustrate this algorithm with a toy example: how to find all matching positions of $\mathcal{M} = G(G|C)G$ in $X_{1:12} = \text{AGCGGTGGGCGA}$? We first use Glushkov's construction and Algorithm 1 to obtain on Fig. 3 a minimal NFA whose language is $(A|C|G|T)^\star G(G|C)G$. Then we directly apply Algorithm 2 starting with $\mathcal{S} = \{0\}$:

- $i = 1$, $X_1 = \text{A}$, $\mathcal{S} \leftarrow \delta(\{0\}, \text{A}) = \{0\}$;

- $i = 2$, $X_2 = \text{G}$, $\mathcal{S} \leftarrow \delta(\{0\}, \text{G}) = \{0, 1\}$;

> **Require:** $(\mathcal{A}, \mathcal{Q}, \sigma, \mathcal{F}, \delta)$ be a (minimal) NFA whose language is $\mathcal{A}^\star \mathcal{M}$
> 1: $\mathcal{S} \leftarrow \{\sigma\}$
> 2: **for** $i = 1 \ldots \ell$ **do**
> 3: $\mathcal{S} \leftarrow \cup_{q \in \mathcal{S}} \delta(q, X_i)$
> 4:   **if** $\mathcal{S} \cap \mathcal{F} \neq \varnothing$ **then**
> 5:   report i as a matching position
> 6:   **end if**
> 7: **end for**

Algorithm 2. NFA pattern matching. Returns all matching positions of motif $\mathcal{M}$ in $X_{1:\ell}$. Complexity is $O(|\mathcal{Q}| \times \ell)$.

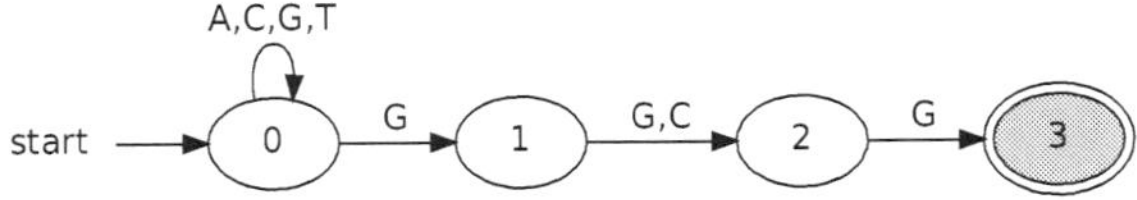

Fig. 3. Minimal NFA whose language is $(\texttt{A}|\texttt{C}|\texttt{G}|\texttt{T})^\star\texttt{G}(\texttt{G}|\texttt{C})\texttt{G}$.

- $i = 3, X_3 = \texttt{C}, \mathcal{S} \leftarrow \delta(\{0,1\}, \texttt{C}) = \{0,2\}$;
- $i = 4, X_4 = \texttt{G}, \mathcal{S} \leftarrow \delta(\{0,2\}, \texttt{G}) = \{0,1,3\}$, matching position;
- $i = 5, X_5 = \texttt{G}, \mathcal{S} \leftarrow \delta(\{0,1,3\}, \texttt{G}) = \{0,1,2\}$;
- $i = 6, X_6 = \texttt{T}, \mathcal{S} \leftarrow \delta(\{0,1,2\}, \texttt{T}) = \{0\}$;
- $i = 7, X_7 = \texttt{G}, \mathcal{S} \leftarrow \delta(\{0\}, \texttt{G}) = \{0,1\}$;
- $i = 8, X_8 = \texttt{G}, \mathcal{S} \leftarrow \delta(\{0,1\}, \texttt{G}) = \{0,1,2\}$;
- $i = 9, X_9 = \texttt{G}, \mathcal{S} \leftarrow \delta(\{0,1,2\}, \texttt{G}) = \{0,1,2,3\}$, matching position;
- $i = 10, X_{10} = \texttt{C}, \mathcal{S} \leftarrow \delta(\{0,1,2,3\}, \texttt{C}) = \{0,2\}$.
- $i = 11, X_{11} = \texttt{G}, \mathcal{S} \leftarrow \delta(\{0,2\}, \texttt{G}) = \{0,1,3\}$, matching position;
- $i = 12, X_{12} = \texttt{A}, \mathcal{S} \leftarrow \delta(\{0,1,3\}, \texttt{A}) = \{0\}$.

We hence return three matching positions: 4, 9 and 11.

One should note in this example that in twice occasions, we need to recompute a previously computed transition ($i = 7$ and $i = 11$). Obviously, this kind of event is likely to appear very often when working with longer sequences. It is hence a natural idea to store in memory previously computed transitions. This approach, known as *lazy determinization* (Green et al., 2004), speeds up considerably pattern matching (reducing the complexity from $O(|\mathcal{Q}| \times \ell)$ to $O(\ell)$) at the expense of a higher memory usage. We will see later that the amount of memory needed can increase exponentially with the NFA size $|\mathcal{Q}|$; this problem is usually addressed by allocating a fixed amount of memory to a buffer of computed transitions which is flushed when full.

3. Significance

Since we now have efficient algorithms to count the number of occurrence of a motif $\mathcal{M}$ in a sequence $X_{1:\ell}$, let us deal with the significance of an observation n.

3.1 Reference model

The choice of a reference model is obviously a key point. Since biological sequences like DNA or proteins are known to have unbalanced letter compositions, it is hence clear that our model should at least take into account this source of bias. A natural parametric approach [1] is hence to model $X_{1:\ell}$ as a i.i.d. sequence with $\mathbb{P}(X_i = a) = \pi(a) \; \forall a \in \mathcal{A}$ with all $\pi(a) \in [0,1]$ and $\sum_{a \in \mathcal{A}} \pi(a) = 1$. This model is called model M0 with parameter π.

For example, in the complete genome of HIV1 (Genbank AF033819) we observe the following counts: 3272 A, 1642 C, 2225 G, and 2042 T. The maximum likelihood estimates of a M0 model based on this observation is then: $\widehat{\pi}(A) = 3272/9181 \simeq 35.64\%$, $\widehat{\pi}(C) = 1642/9181 \simeq 17.88\%$, $\widehat{\pi}(G) = 2225/9181 \simeq 24.23\%$, and $\widehat{\pi}(T) = 2042/9181 \simeq 22.24\%$.

But if we look now to the frequencies of di-nucleotides on the same HIV1 genome, we observe considerable bias as well:

AA 1087	AC 524	AG 971	AT 690
CA 754	CC 378	CG 82	CT 427
GA 769	GC 425	GG 625	GT 406
TA 662	TC 315	TG 546	TT 519

For example, we observe $971/3272 = 29.68\%$ of G after a A, but a G occurs after a C only $82/1641 = 16.41\%$ of the time. This phenomenon is directly explained by the fact that the di-nucleotide CG tend to be easily methylated (see CpG island, Fatemi et al., 2005). Is hence tempting to take into account the frequencies of di-nucleotides in our reference model, or tri-nucleotides, or more, which naturally leads to Markov models.

For any $d \geqslant 0$, we denote by Md the (homogeneous) Markov model of order d defined for any $i \geqslant d + 1$, $a \in \mathcal{A}^d$, and $b \in \mathcal{A}$ by:

$$\mathbb{P}(X_i = b | X_{i-d:i-1} = a) = \pi(a,b) \tag{6}$$

where π denotes the *transition matrix* of Md. This model is clearly defined conditionally to $X_{1:d}$.

The maximum likelihood estimator $\widehat{\pi}$ is then given for all $a \in \mathcal{A}^d$, and $b \in \mathcal{A}$ by:

$$\widehat{\pi}(a,b) = \frac{n_{ab}}{\sum_{b' \in \mathcal{A}} n_{ab'}} \tag{7}$$

where n_{ab} are the observed counts of word ab in the training dataset.

When working with Markov model and biological sequences, a recurrent question is: what order d should I choose for my reference model ? This is a classical model selection problem which can easily be solved using penalized likelihood criteria like BIC or AIC (Liddle, 2007). For example, using the BIC criterion, one would select $d = 1$ for the complete genome of HIV1 ($\ell \simeq 10$kb), and $d = 5$ for the complete genome of E. coli ($\ell \simeq 4.6$Mb). However, since our objective is the significance of motifs counts rather than the modelization of biological sequence in itself, we suggest a different approach.

First, it is critical to realize than working with a model Md as reference model allows to take into account the sequence composition bias in $(d+1)$-mers. Hence, with $d = 1$ one takes into account the composition bias in di-nucleotides, and with $d = 5$, one takes into account the composition bias in hexa-nucleotides. The decision could then be based on the information one wishes to include in the reference model; working on coding sequences, one might wish to take into account at least the codon bias hence resulting in the choice of $d \geqslant 2$. On the other

---

[1] An alternative non-parametric approach, the *shuffling*, consists in performing uniformly a random permutation of the original sequence; this approach is not treated here.

> **Require:** $(\mathcal{A}, \mathcal{Q}_1, \sigma, \mathcal{F}_1, \delta_1)$ a NFA
> 1: $q_0 \leftarrow \{\sigma\}$, $L \leftarrow 1$, $\mathcal{Q}_2 \leftarrow \{q_0\}$, $\mathcal{F}_2 \leftarrow \varnothing$
> 2: **for** $i = 0 \dots L - 1$ **do**
> 3:   **for all** $a \in \mathcal{A}$ **do**
> 4: $\mathcal{S} \leftarrow \delta_1(q_i, a)$
> 5:   **if** $\exists j, q_j = \mathcal{S}$ **then**
> 6: $\delta_2(q_i, a) = q_j$
> 7:   **else**
> 8: $q_L \leftarrow \mathcal{S}$, $L \leftarrow L + 1$, $\mathcal{Q}_2 \leftarrow \mathcal{Q}_2 \cup \{q_L\}$
> 9:   **if** $\mathcal{S} \cap \mathcal{F}_\infty$ **then** $\mathcal{F}_2 \leftarrow \mathcal{F}_2 \cup \{q_L\}$ **end if**
> 10:   **end if**
> 11:   **end for**
> 12: **end for**
> **Output:** return $(\mathcal{A}, \mathcal{Q}_2, q_0, \mathcal{F}_2, \delta_2)$

Algorithm 3. Determinization. Build a DFA which recognizes the same language than the original NFA.

hand, it would obviously be pointless to use a reference model of order $d = 7$ to study a motif of length 8 or less.

Another critical point to keep in mind is that motif significance is by nature very sensitive to the parameters of the reference model. In order to convince us, let us a consider the following simple example with $\mathcal{M} = \mathtt{GGATG}$, a reference model M0 of parameter π, and $\ell = 1,000,000$. If $\pi(\mathtt{A}) = \pi(\mathtt{T}) = 0.10$ and $\pi(\mathtt{C}) = \pi(\mathtt{G}) = 0.40$ we get $\mathbb{E}[N_\ell] = \ell \times 0.40^3 \times 0.10^2 \simeq 640.0$. Now if $\pi(\mathtt{A}) = \pi(\mathtt{T}) = 0.08$ and $\pi(\mathtt{C}) = \pi(\mathtt{G}) = 0.42$ then $\mathbb{E}[N_\ell] = \ell \times 0.42^3 \times 0.08^2 \simeq 474.2$. If we admit that the standard deviation of N_ℓ is roughly equal to $\sigma = 25$ (we will see later on how to perform such computation), an observation of $n = 550$ could be interpreted as a significant over-representation with the first parameters, and a significant under-representation with the second parameters (observation n deviates from the expectation by more than three standard deviations in both cases). The reason behind this is that parameter values are typically involved in complex products when evaluating the significance of an observation, and that such operations usually increase small variations rather than averaging them (like with sums). This problem have been investigated in Nuel (2006c) where it is shown that unwise choices of d might lead to many false positive results.

3.2 Monte-Carlo simulations

Since the theoretical distribution of N not easy to obtain, it is tempting to study it from the empirical point of view by performing simple simulations. The approach is quite straightforward:

1) generate a random dataset i according to the reference model;

2) count the number of occurrence n_i of $\mathcal{M}$ in the dataset;

3) repeat 1) and 2) until we have a sample $n_1, n_2, \dots, n_r$.

Once a reference sample have been obtained, we can derive the empirical p-value of the observation n using:

$$\widehat{\mathbb{P}}(N \leqslant n) = \frac{\sum_{i=1}^{r} \mathbf{1}_{n_i \leqslant n}}{r} \quad \text{or} \quad \widehat{\mathbb{P}}(N \geqslant n) = \frac{\sum_{i=1}^{r} \mathbf{1}_{n_i \geqslant n}}{r} \tag{8}$$

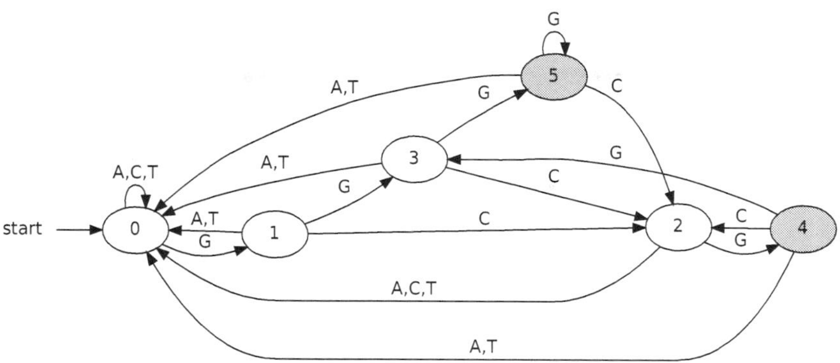

Fig. 4. Minimal DFA whose language is $(A|C|G|T)^{\star}G(G|C)G$.

or, alternatively, one might use this sample to derive empirical expectation, variance, and z-score:

$$\widehat{Z}(n) = \frac{n - \widehat{\mu}}{\sigma} \quad \text{with} \quad \widehat{\mu} = \frac{1}{r}\sum_{i=1}^{r} n_i \quad \text{and} \quad \widehat{\sigma}^2 = \frac{1}{r}\sum_{i=1}^{r}(n_i - \widehat{\mu})^2. \tag{9}$$

If this approach is quite simple, it suffers several drawbacks: 1) it is slow; 2) sample size must be large to obtain accurate results. Indeed, if the true p-value is p, then $\widehat{p} \sim \mathcal{B}(r, p)$ where r is the sample size. The following table gives a 90% upper bound confidence for $\widehat{p}$ for several value of r in the case where $p = 10^{-5}$:

r	10^3	10^4	10^5	10^6	10^7	10^8
bound	1.00×10^{-3}	1.00×10^{-4}	3.00×10^{-5}	1.50×10^{-5}	1.14×10^{-5}	1.04×10^{-5}

we clearly see that it requires at least $r = 10^6$ samples to obtain the first accurate digit in $\widehat{p}$, and a prohibitive $r = 10^8$ samples for the second digit. Considering that very small p-value are easily encountered in motif significance (ex: $10^{-20}, 10^{-50}, 10^{-100}$), it is clear that empirical p-value have a limited interest in this context.

Empirical z-score does not suffer the same drawback but makes the implicit assumption that N has a Gaussian distribution which is highly questionable as we will see later on.

For completeness, let us point out that *importance sampling* techniques might solve the estimation problem by sampling N using a tailored dataset distribution (Chan et al., 2010). However, these sophisticated numerical techniques are slow and requires a good skills to be implemented.

3.3 Markov chain embedding

The key to perform any motif significance computation if first to embed the original problem into an order 1 Markov chain taking into account all the combinatoric complexity. This technique, called *Markov chain embedding* have been used by many authors in the context of motif significance Antzoulakos (2001); Boeva et al. (2005); Chang (2005); Fu (1996); Nuel (2006a), but it is only recently that its connexion to NFA and Deterministic Finite Automata (DFA) have been pointed out (Crochemore & Stefanov, 2003; Lladser, 2007; Nicodème et al., 2002; Nuel, 2008a; Nuel & Prum, 2007; Ribeca & Raineri, 2008).

We start with a NFA whose language is $\mathcal{A}^{\star}\mathcal{M}$ from which we build a DFA $(\mathcal{A}, \mathcal{Q}, q_0, \mathcal{F}, \delta)$ using the determinization algorithm (Algorithm 3). A DFA differs from an NFA only by the definition of its transition function: $\delta : \mathcal{Q} \times \mathcal{A} \to \mathcal{P}(\mathcal{Q})$ for a NFA, and $\delta : \mathcal{Q} \times \mathcal{A} \to \mathcal{Q}$ for a DFA. For example, we can see on Figure 4, a (minimal) DFA whose language is $(\mathtt{A}|\mathtt{C}|\mathtt{G}|\mathtt{T})^{\star}\mathtt{G}(\mathtt{G}|\mathtt{C})\mathtt{G}$. This DFA has more states (6) than the corresponding NFA (4). In fact, since the state space $\mathcal{Q}_2$ of a DFA corresponds to a subset of the parts of the original NFA state space $\mathcal{Q}_1$, we have $|\mathcal{Q}_2| \leqslant 2^{|\mathcal{Q}_1|}$. Fortunately, this upper bound is seldom reached in practice.

Theorem 2 (Markov chain embedding for Model M0). Let $(\mathcal{A}, \mathcal{Q}, \sigma, \mathcal{F}, \delta)$ be a (minimal) DFA whose language is $\mathcal{A}^{\star}\mathcal{M}$. Let $X_{1:\ell}$ be a random sequence generated by the M0 model of parameter π. We consider the sequence $Z_{0:\ell}$ recursively defined by $Z_0 = \sigma$, and $Z_i = \delta(Z_{i-1}, X_i)$ for all $1 \leqslant i \leqslant \ell$. Then $Z_{0:\ell}$ is an order 1 Markov chain whose transition matrix $\mathbf{T}$ is defined for all $p, q \in \mathcal{Q}$ by:

$$\mathbf{T}(p, q) = \sum_{a \in \mathcal{A}, \delta(p,a)=q} \pi(a) \tag{10}$$

and having the following property for all $1 \leqslant i \leqslant \ell$: $X_{1:i} \in \mathcal{A}^{\star}\mathcal{M} \iff Z_i \in \mathcal{F}$.

For example, if we consider the DNA motif $\mathtt{G}(\mathtt{G}|\mathtt{C})\mathtt{G}$ and the corresponding DFA of Figure 4, we get the following transition matrix:

$$\mathbf{T} = \begin{pmatrix} \pi(\mathtt{A}) + \pi(\mathtt{C}) + \pi(\mathtt{T}) & \pi(\mathtt{G}) & 0 & 0 & 0 & 0 \\ \pi(\mathtt{A}) + \pi(\mathtt{T}) & 0 & \pi(\mathtt{C}) & \pi(\mathtt{G}) & 0 & 0 \\ \pi(\mathtt{A}) + \pi(\mathtt{C}) + \pi(\mathtt{T}) & 0 & 0 & 0 & \pi(\mathtt{G}) & 0 \\ \pi(\mathtt{A}) + \pi(\mathtt{T}) & 0 & \pi(\mathtt{C}) & 0 & 0 & \pi(\mathtt{G}) \\ \pi(\mathtt{A}) + \pi(\mathtt{T}) & 0 & \pi(\mathtt{C}) & \pi(\mathtt{G}) & 0 & 0 \\ \pi(\mathtt{A}) + \pi(\mathtt{T}) & 0 & \pi(\mathtt{C}) & 0 & 0 & \pi(\mathtt{G}) \end{pmatrix}.$$

In order to extend Theorem 2 to order Md with $d > 0$ it is necessary to build DFA $(\mathcal{A}, \mathcal{Q}, \sigma, \mathcal{F}, \delta)$ be a (minimal) DFA whose language is $\mathcal{A}^{\star}\mathcal{M}$ and with the property that for all $q \in \mathcal{Q}$, $\mathrm{past}(q) = \{a \in \mathcal{A}^d, \exists p \in \mathcal{Q}, \delta(p, a) = q\}$ is either empty or a singleton. A DFA having this property is called a order d DFA by Lladser (2007), and is called non d-ambiguous by Nuel (2008a). The construction of such a (minimal) DFA is not very complicated but is a bit technical. A possible approach suggested by Nuel (2008a) consists in starting from a DFA without this property and duplicating any "ambiguous" state. Another more straightforward approach consists in adding the elements of $\mathcal{A}^{\star}\mathcal{A}^d$ to the original language with a specific label for the final states corresponding to each elements of $\mathcal{A}^d$, and to keep these labels during minimization and determinization algorithms.

Theorem 3 (Markov chain embedding for Model Md). Let $(\mathcal{A}, \mathcal{Q}, \sigma, \mathcal{F}, \delta)$ be a (minimal) order d DFA whose language is $\mathcal{A}^{\star}\mathcal{M}$. Let $X_{1:\ell}$ be a random sequence generated by the Md model of parameter π. We consider the sequence $Z_{d:\ell}$ recursively defined by $Z_d = \delta(\sigma, X_{1:d})$, and $Z_i = \delta(Z_{i-1}, X_i)$ for all $1 \leqslant i \leqslant \ell$. Then $Z_{d:\ell}$ is an order 1 Markov chain whose transition matrix $\mathbf{T}$ is defined for all $p, q \in \mathcal{Q}$ by:

$$\mathbf{T}(p, q) = \sum_{a \in \mathcal{A}, \delta(p,a)=q} \pi(\mathrm{past}(p), a) \tag{11}$$

and having the following property for all $1 \leqslant i \leqslant \ell$: $X_{1:i} \in \mathcal{A}^{\star}\mathcal{M} \iff Z_i \in \mathcal{F}$.

One should note that $Z_{d:\ell}$ is defined on $\delta(\sigma, \mathcal{A}^d \mathcal{A}^{\star})$ which could be slightly smaller than $\mathcal{Q}$. This subset corresponds to the states of $\mathcal{Q}$ having a order d past. If we consider the DFA

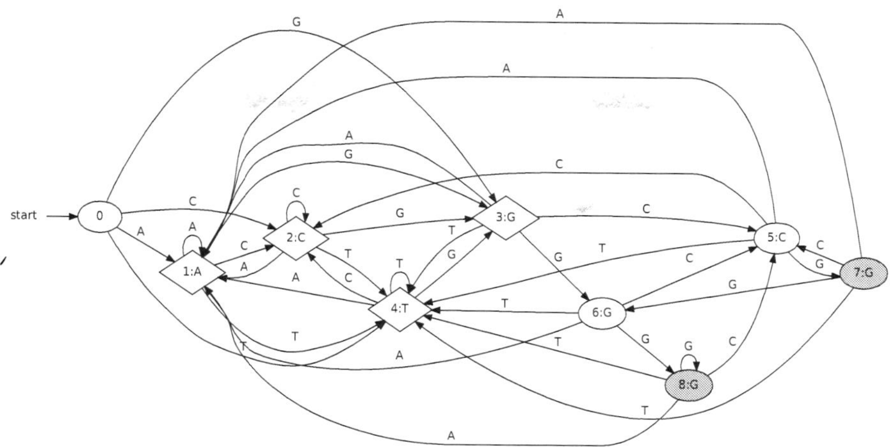

Fig. 5. Minimal order 1 DFA whose language is $(\mathtt{A}|\mathtt{C}|\mathtt{G}|\mathtt{T})^{\star}\mathtt{G}(\mathtt{G}|\mathtt{C})\mathtt{G}$. The order 1 past of each state is indicated in the state itself. Diamond-shaped states correspond to the elements of $\delta(0, \mathcal{A}^1)$.

of Figure 5, $d = 1$, and with $X_1 = \mathtt{A}$, we see that the Markov chain $Z_{d:\ell}$ is defined on $\{1, 2, 3, 4, 5, 6, 7, 8\}$ by $Z_1 = 1$ and the following transition matrix:

$$\mathbf{T} = \begin{pmatrix} \pi(\mathtt{A},\mathtt{A}) & \pi(\mathtt{A},\mathtt{C}) & \pi(\mathtt{A},\mathtt{G}) & \pi(\mathtt{A},\mathtt{T}) & 0 & 0 & 0 & 0 \\ \pi(\mathtt{C},\mathtt{A}) & \pi(\mathtt{C},\mathtt{C}) & \pi(\mathtt{C},\mathtt{G}) & \pi(\mathtt{C},\mathtt{T}) & 0 & 0 & 0 & 0 \\ \pi(\mathtt{G},\mathtt{A}) & 0 & 0 & \pi(\mathtt{G},\mathtt{T}) & \pi(\mathtt{G},\mathtt{C}) & \pi(\mathtt{G},\mathtt{G}) & 0 & 0 \\ \pi(\mathtt{T},\mathtt{A}) & \pi(\mathtt{T},\mathtt{C}) & \pi(\mathtt{T},\mathtt{G}) & \pi(\mathtt{T},\mathtt{T}) & 0 & 0 & 0 & 0 \\ \pi(\mathtt{C},\mathtt{A}) & \pi(\mathtt{C},\mathtt{C}) & 0 & \pi(\mathtt{C},\mathtt{T}) & 0 & 0 & \pi(\mathtt{C},\mathtt{G}) & 0 \\ \pi(\mathtt{G},\mathtt{A}) & 0 & 0 & \pi(\mathtt{G},\mathtt{T}) & \pi(\mathtt{G},\mathtt{C}) & 0 & 0 & \pi(\mathtt{G},\mathtt{G}) \\ \pi(\mathtt{G},\mathtt{A}) & 0 & 0 & \pi(\mathtt{G},\mathtt{T}) & \pi(\mathtt{G},\mathtt{C}) & \pi(\mathtt{G},\mathtt{G}) & 0 & 0 \\ \pi(\mathtt{G},\mathtt{A}) & 0 & 0 & \pi(\mathtt{G},\mathtt{T}) & \pi(\mathtt{G},\mathtt{C}) & 0 & 0 & \pi(\mathtt{G},\mathtt{G}) \end{pmatrix}.$$

From now on, we assume that our motif problem with Md reference model is embedded into the Markov chain $Z_{d:\ell}$ whose transition matrix is decomposed into $\mathbf{T} = \mathbf{P} + \mathbf{Q}$ where matrices $\mathbf{P}$ and $\mathbf{Q}$ are defined for all p, q by: $\mathbf{P}(p,q) = \mathbf{T}(p,q)\mathbf{1}_{q \notin \mathcal{F}}$, and $\mathbf{Q}(p,q) = \mathbf{T}(p,q)\mathbf{1}_{q \in \mathcal{F}}$.

3.4 Main results

We present here the main results that are then used to derive exact computations and various approximations of $S(n)$. In all this section, we assume that N is the random number of occurrences of $\mathcal{M}$ in $X_{1:\ell}$, a sequence generated by a Md model ($X_{1:d}$ being fixed) with $d \geqslant 0$. we denote by $\mathbf{T} = \mathbf{P} + \mathbf{Q}$ be the transition $(L \times L)$ matrix of the Markov chain embedding of the corresponding problem. We also introduce two vectors: $\mathbf{u}$ a $1 \times L$ vector filled with '0' and having a '1' in the position corresponding to $X_{1:d}$, and $\mathbf{v}$ a $L \times 1$ vector of '1'.

Proposition 4 (probability generating function). If we denote by $G(y) = \mathbb{E}[y^N]$ the probability generating function (pgf) of N, then we have:

$$G(y) = \sum_{n \geqslant 0} \mathbb{P}(N = n)y^n = \mathbf{u}(\mathbf{P} + y\mathbf{Q})^{\ell-d}\mathbf{v}. \tag{12}$$

Proof. The first equality derives directly from the definition of $G(y)$. For the second equality now, it is clear that $\mathbf{u}(\mathbf{P}+\mathbf{Q})^{\ell-d}$ gives the marginal distribution of Z_ℓ. We then connect this distribution to N by counting the number of times we use the transitions of $\mathbf{Q}$ with the dummy variable y so that $\mathbf{u}(\mathbf{P}+y\mathbf{Q})^{\ell-d}$ gives the joint distribution of (Z_ℓ, N). Finally, we sum up the contributions of all states using the product with $\mathbf{v}$. $\square$

For example, let us consider $\mathcal{M} = \mathtt{G(G|C)G}$ and $X_{1:12}$ generated by a M0 model with parameters $\pi(\mathtt{A}) = \pi(\mathtt{T}) = 0.10$ and $\pi(\mathtt{C}) = \pi(\mathtt{G}) = 0.40$. Proposition 4 hence gives:

$$G(y) = \begin{pmatrix} 1 & 0 & 0 & 0 & 0 & 0 \end{pmatrix} \times \begin{pmatrix} 0.6 & 0.4 & 0 & 0 & 0 & 0 \\ 0.2 & 0 & 0.4 & 0.4 & 0 & 0 \\ 0.6 & 0 & 0 & 0 & 0.4y & 0 \\ 0.2 & 0 & 0.4 & 0 & 0 & 0.4y \\ 0.2 & 0 & 0.4 & 0.4 & 0 & 0 \\ 0.2 & 0 & 0.4 & 0 & 0 & 0.4y \end{pmatrix}^{12} \times \begin{pmatrix} 1 \\ 1 \\ 1 \\ 1 \\ 1 \\ 1 \end{pmatrix} \tag{13}$$

$$= 0.33369 + 0.31148y + 0.19357y^2 + 0.09681y^3 + 0.04140y^4 + 0.01569y^5$$
$$+ 0.00528y^6 + 0.00157y^7 + 0.00042y^8 + 0.00008y^9 + 0.00002y^{10}. \tag{14}$$

From this result, we have the whole distribution of N: support is $\{0, 1, \ldots, 10\}$, $\mathbb{P}(N = 0) = 0.33369$, $\mathbb{P}(N = 1) = 0.31148, \ldots, \mathbb{P}(N = 10) = 0.00002$. We can also easily derive moments of N from this distribution: $\mathbb{E}[N] = 1.28$, $\sigma[N] = 1.29$.

Lemma 5 (derivatives of the pgf). For any $k \leqslant 0$, the order k derivative of the pgf G is given by:

$$G^{(k)}(y) = k![z^k]\mathbf{u}(\mathbf{P}+y\mathbf{Q}+z\mathbf{Q})^{\ell-d}\mathbf{v} \tag{15}$$

where the $[z^k]$ operator denotes the extraction of the coefficient of z^k in the expression.

Proof. The formal proof can be found in Nuel (2010) in a slightly less general case. Here we prove it only for the first two derivatives in the particular case where $\ell - d = 3$. Starting from $G(y) = \mathbf{u}(\mathbf{P}+y\mathbf{Q})^3\mathbf{v}$ we get:

$$G'(y) = \mathbf{u}\left(\mathbf{Q}(\mathbf{P}+y\mathbf{Q})^2 + (\mathbf{P}+y\mathbf{Q})\mathbf{Q}(\mathbf{P}+y\mathbf{Q}) + (\mathbf{P}+y\mathbf{Q})^2\mathbf{Q}\right)\mathbf{v} \tag{16}$$

and

$$G''(y) = 2\mathbf{u}\left(\mathbf{Q}^2(\mathbf{P}+y\mathbf{Q}) + \mathbf{Q}(\mathbf{P}+y\mathbf{Q})\mathbf{Q} + (\mathbf{P}+y\mathbf{Q})\mathbf{Q}^2\right)\mathbf{v} \tag{17}$$

which are easily connected to the terms coefficients of z^1 and z^2 in $\mathbf{u}(\mathbf{P}+y\mathbf{Q}+z\mathbf{Q})^{\ell-d}\mathbf{v}$. $\square$

If we denote for all $k \geqslant 0$ the k-th *factorial moment* of N by $F_k = \mathbb{E}[N!/(N-k)!]$, then, by the definition of the pgf, it is clear that $F_k = G^{(k)}(0)$, and thanks to Lemma 5 we get:

$$F_k = k![z^k]\mathbf{u}(\mathbf{T}+z\mathbf{Q})^{\ell-d}\mathbf{v}. \tag{18}$$

And if we now denote the moment generating function (mgf) of N by $M(t) = \mathbb{E}[e^{tN}] = G(e^t)$, and the cumulant generating function (cgf) of N by $\Lambda(t) = \log\mathbb{E}[e^{tN}] = \log M(t) = \log G(e^t)$, we get directly the k-th moment of N: $\mathbb{E}[N^k] = M^{(k)}(0)$; and the k-th cumulant of N: $\kappa_k = \Lambda^{(k)}(0)$.

Corollary 6 (characteristics moments). *If we denote by $\mu = \kappa_1$ the expectation of N, by $\sigma = \sqrt{\kappa_2}$ the standard deviation of N, by $\gamma_1 = \kappa_3/\sigma^3$ the skewness of N, and by $\gamma_1 = \kappa_4/\sigma^4$ the excess kurtosis of N, then we get: $\mu = F_1$, $\sigma^2 = F_2 + F_1 - F_1^2$,*

$$\gamma_1 = \frac{3F_2 - 3F_1^2 + F_3 - 3F_1 F_2 + 2F_1^3 + F_1}{\sigma^3}, \tag{19}$$

and

$$\gamma_2 = \frac{7F_2 - 7F_1^2 + 6F_3 - 18F_1 F_2 + 12F_1^3 + F_4 - 4F_1 F_3 - 3F_2^2 + 12F_1^2 F_2 - 6F_1^4 + F_1}{\sigma^4}. \tag{20}$$

Proof. On just need to compute the derivatives $\Lambda^{(1)}(0)$, $\Lambda^{(2)}(0)$, $\Lambda^{(3)}(0)$, and $\Lambda^{(4)}(0)$. $\qquad\square$

If we consider again $\mathcal{M} = \mathsf{G(G|C)G}$ and $X_{1:12}$ generated by a M0 model with parameters $\pi(\mathsf{A}) = \pi(\mathsf{T}) = 0.10$ and $\pi(\mathsf{C}) = \pi(\mathsf{G}) = 0.40$. Eq. (18) hence gives:

$$\sum_{k \leqslant 0} \frac{F_k}{k!} = \left(1\ 0\ 0\ 0\ 0\ 0\right) \times \begin{pmatrix} 0.6 & 0.4 & 0 & 0 & 0 & 0 \\ 0.2 & 0 & 0.4 & 0.4 & 0 & 0 \\ 0.6 & 0 & 0 & 0 & 0.4+0.4y & 0 \\ 0.2 & 0 & 0.4 & 0 & 0 & 0.4+0.4y \\ 0.2 & 0 & 0.4 & 0.4 & 0 & 0 \\ 0.2 & 0 & 0.4 & 0 & 0 & 0.4+0.4y \end{pmatrix}^{12} \times \begin{pmatrix} 1 \\ 1 \\ 1 \\ 1 \\ 1 \\ 1 \end{pmatrix} \tag{21}$$

$$= 1 + 1.28y + 1.01683y^2 + 0.61211y^3 + 0.29709y^4 + 0.11835y^5$$
$$+ 0.03845y^6 + 0.00992y^7 + 0.00193y^8 + 0.00025y^9 + 0.00002y^{10}. \tag{22}$$

From this result, we can get all factorial moments of N: $\mathbb{E}(1) = F_0 = 1$, $\mathbb{E}(N) = F_1 = 1.28$, $\mathbb{E}(N(N-1)) = F_2 = 2.033664$, $\mathbb{E}(N(N-1)(N-2)) = F_3 = 3.6726374$, $\mathbb{E}(N(N-1)(N-2)(N-3)) = F_4 = 7.1302266, \ldots, \mathbb{E}(N!/(N-10)!) = F_{10} = 60.881161$. Thanks to Corollary 6 we get the following characteristic moments: $\mu = 1.28$, $\sigma = 1.294320$, $\gamma_1 = 1.163783$, $\gamma_2 = 1.492661$.

3.5 Exact computations

As we have seen above, Proposition 4 provides a way to obtain the whole distribution of N by computing $G(y) = \mathbf{u}(\mathbf{P} + y\mathbf{Q})^{\ell-d}\mathbf{v}$ from which we can easily derive $S(n)$ for any $n \geqslant 0$:

$$S(n) = \begin{cases} +\log_{10}\left(\sum_{k=0}^{n}[y^k]G(y)\right) & \text{if } n \leqslant \mathbb{E}[N] \\ -\log_{10}\left(\sum_{k=n}^{+\infty}[y^k]G(y)\right) & \text{if } n > \mathbb{E}[N] \end{cases}.$$

From the algorithmic point of view, there are basically two approaches to compute $S(n)$ using Expression (12). The first one, called *power*, consists in computing $(\mathbf{P} + y\mathbf{Q})^{\ell-d}$ using the power method and a binary decomposition of $\ell - d$. Ex: if $\ell - d = 1097$ then $\ell - d = 2^{10} + 2^6 + 2^3 + 2^0$. We then just have to recursively compute $\mathbf{D}_k(y) = (\mathbf{P} + y\mathbf{Q})^{2^k}$ using the relation $\mathbf{D}_{k+1}(y) = \mathbf{D}_k(y) \times \mathbf{D}_k(y)$ for all $k \geqslant 0$. Since in the computation of $S(n)$ we are only interested in terms of degree n or less (or n or more), we can easily truncate [2] all polynomials at degree n thus dramatically reducing the computational costs of polynomial products. We end

---

[2] In the case of over-representation, all contributions of degree n or more are summed into the term of degree n.

up with a $O(\log_2 \ell \times n^2 \times L^3)$ complexity in time where L is the order of the transition matrix $\mathbf{T} = \mathbf{P} + \mathbf{Q}$. The corresponding memory complexity is $O(\log_2 \ell \times n \times L^2)$. Since the length ℓ of the dataset appears in a logarithmic scale in these complexity, the power approach is obviously suitable for large datasets (ex: $\ell = 10^6$ or $\ell = 10^9$). Unfortunately, the cubic complexity with L (quadratic in memory) prevents the approach to deal with complex motifs with high L. One should also note that the quadratic complexity in n could really be a problem when dealing with frequent motifs and/or large datasets. In order to overcome this problem, Ribeca & Raineri (2008) suggested to use fast Fourier transforms (FFT) to perform all polynomial product hence replacing n^2 by $n \log_2 n$ in the time complexity. However appealing at first glance, this approach is not recommended in practice since the FFT products in floating-point arithmetics induce numerical instabilities that make totally unreliable the smallest coefficients of the polynomials. And unfortunately, these coefficients are precisely the one needed to study the tail distribution of N.

Another interesting approach called *full recursion*, consists in computing $\mathbf{v}_i = (\mathbf{P} + y\mathbf{Q})^i \mathbf{v}$ for all $0 \leqslant i \leqslant \ell - d$ recursively using the relation $\mathbf{v}_{i+1} = (\mathbf{P} + y\mathbf{Q})\mathbf{v}_i$. There are two main interests for this approach: 1) we have only products between polynomials of degree 1 and polynomials of degree n (by dropping terms of degree greater than n like in the power approach); 2) we can take full advantage of the sparse structure (only $L \times |\mathcal{A}|$ non-zero terms in the worst case) of the transition matrix $\mathbf{T} = \mathbf{P} + \mathbf{Q}$. The resulting complexity is $O(\ell \times L \times |\mathcal{A}| \times n)$ in time, and $O(L \times n)$ in memory. Since these complexities are linear with L, this approach is able to handle very complex motifs. The drawback is that the approach can be very slow when dealing with large ℓ and n. It exists a sophisticated version of this recursion called *partial recursion* (see Nuel & Dumas, 2010) which allows to replace $\ell \times n$ by $\log \ell \times n^2$ in the time complexity. However, the quadratic complexity in n and numerical instabilities in floating-point arithmetic restrains its use to small n (ex: $n \leqslant 10$).

For completeness, let us point out another approach to the problem. The idea is that we can derive from Expression (12) the following expression:

$$G(y, z) = \sum_{n \geqslant 0} \sum_{\ell \geqslant d} \mathbb{P}(N_\ell = n) y^n z^\ell = \mathbf{u} z^d (\mathbf{I} - \mathbf{P}z + yz\mathbf{Q})^{-1} \mathbf{v} \tag{23}$$

where $\mathbf{I}$ is the identity matrix and N_ℓ the number of matching position in $X_{1:\ell}$. It is then possible to obtain $\mathbb{P}(N_\ell = n)$ for any ℓ and n using (fast) Taylor expansions of $G(y, z)$. For the mathematician, this approach is so "natural" that it is often referred as the "golden" approach to the problem of motif significance (Nicodème et al., 2002). However, this approach suffers several severe drawbacks that dramatically limits its practical interest: 1) the approach needs sophisticated computer algebra systems to be implemented (rather than simple floating point arithmetic for the previous approaches); 2) the explicit computation of $(\mathbf{I} - \mathbf{P}z + yz\mathbf{Q})^{-1}$ could be very time (and memory) consuming; 3) even if the explicit computation of the inverse matrix is avoided (which is highly advisable), the coefficient extraction using state of the art techniques (like high-order lifting for example) is often slower than the much simpler alternative developed above (see Nuel & Dumas, 2010, for details).

Considering either the power or the recursion approaches we obtain easy to implement algorithms allowing to compute the exact value of $S(n)$ in all cases except when dealing with high complexity motifs (large L) and/or frequent motifs (large n). But even if we stick to more tractable cases, exact computations could be slow. The question hence is: is it possible to compute fast and reliable approximations of $S(n)$?

ℓ	expectation	std. dev.	skewness	e. kurtosis	time (s)
12	1.280000	1.294320	1.163783	1.492661	0.01
120	15.104000	4.585724	0.361328	0.149974	0.02
1200	153.344000	14.648033	0.113920	0.014936	0.03
12000	1535.744000	46.367282	0.036014	0.001492	0.04
120000	15359.744000	146.640798	0.011394	-0.000410	0.05

Table 1. Characteristic moments the number N of occurrences of motif $\mathcal{M} = \mathrm{G(G|C)G}$ in a sequence $X_{1:\ell}$ generated by a M0 model with parameters $\pi(\mathrm{A}) = \pi(\mathrm{T}) = 0.10$ and $\pi(\mathrm{C}) = \pi(\mathrm{G}) = 0.40$. Computation performed using the power approach.

3.6 Near-Gaussian approximations

Since the random count N is basically defined by Eq. (2) as large sum of Bernouilli variables, the idea of approximating the distribution of N using Gaussian approximation sounds appealing. Indeed, Gaussian approximations are historically the first ones to have been suggested for this problem (Cowan, 1991; Kleffe & Borodovski, 1997; Pevzner et al., 1989; Prum et al., 1995). From the theoretical point of view, Central Limit Theorems (CLT) for weakly dependent variables ensure that N is asymptotically normal distributed. On Table 1, we can see the characteristic moments of N for motif $\mathcal{M} = \mathrm{G(G|C)G}$ and various value of the sequence lengths ℓ. According to theory, we observe that the skewness and excess kurtosis both decease toward 0 when ℓ grows (a normal distribution has null skewness and excess kurtosis). But it is also clear that N is not normally distributed for small values of ℓ. As a consequence, the quality of a Gaussian approximation for $S(n)$ is expected to be questionable at finite distance.

In order to overcome this issue, Nuel (2010) suggested to consider near Gaussian approximations instead of simple Gaussian approximations for this problem. The idea is simply to perform a higher order asymptotic development that exploits more than the two first moments of N. This technique is known as the Edgeworth's expansion. Blinnikov & Moessner (1998) gives a general (and rather complicated) formula for this expansion. For practical purpose, we present the result only up to order 3 expansions.

Proposition 7 (Edgeworth's expansion). If we denote by $\varphi(z) = \exp(-z^2/2)/\sqrt{2\pi}$ the probability distribution function (pdf) of a standard Gaussian, then for all $n \geqslant 0$ we have the following approximation:

$$\mathbb{P}(N = n) \simeq \frac{\varphi(z)}{\sigma} \left(C_0(z) + \sigma C_1(z) + \sigma^2 C_2(z) + \sigma^3 C_3(z) \right) \tag{24}$$

with

$$C_0(z) = 1 \quad C_1(z) = \frac{S_3}{6} H_3(z) \quad C_2(z) = \frac{S_4}{24} H_4(z) + \frac{S_3^2}{72} H_6(z) \tag{25}$$

$$C_3(z) = \frac{S_5}{120} H_5(z) + \frac{S_3 S_4}{144} H_7(z) + \frac{S_3^3}{1296} H_9(z) \tag{26}$$

where $\mu = \mathbb{E}[N]$, $\sigma = \sqrt{\mathbb{V}[N]}$, $z = (n - \mu)/\sigma$, $S_k = \kappa_k/\sigma^{2k-2}$ for all $k \geqslant 1$, and where $H_k(z)$ are the Hermite polynomials defined recursively by $H_0(z) = 1$ and $H_k(z) = z H_{k-1}(z) - H'_{k-1}(z)$ for all $k \geqslant 1$.

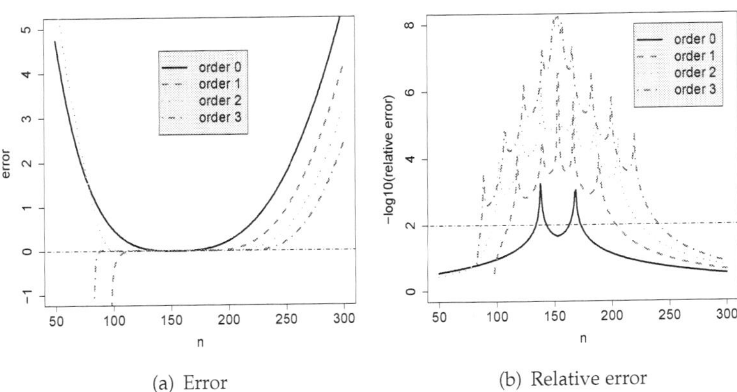

(a) Error   (b) Relative error

Fig. 6. Reliability of NG approximations for $\mathcal{M} = \text{G(G|C)G}$ on a random sequence $X_{1:\ell}$ generated by a M0 model with parameters $\pi(\text{A}) = \pi(\text{T}) = 0.10$ and $\pi(\text{C}) = \pi(\text{G}) = 0.40$, and with $\ell = 1200$. The error $\text{NG}_h(n) - S(n)$ is given on Figure (a); and the relative error (log-scale) $- \log_{10} |\text{NG}_h(n) - S(n)| / |S(n)|$ on Figure (b). The horizontal rule indicates the null error on Figure (a), and the threshold corresponding to two correct digits on Figure (b).

For $h \in \{0,1,2,3\}$ we define the Near Gaussian (NG) approximation of order h of $S(n)$ by:

$$
\text{NG}_h(n) =
\begin{cases}
+ \log_{10} \left(\displaystyle\sum_{k=0}^{n} \frac{1}{\sigma} \varphi \left(\frac{k - \mu}{\sigma} \right) \sum_{j=0}^{h} \sigma^j C_j \left(\frac{k - \mu}{\sigma} \right) \right) & \text{if } n \leqslant \mathbb{E}[N] \\[2em]
- \log_{10} \left(\displaystyle\sum_{k=n}^{+\infty} \frac{1}{\sigma} \varphi \left(\frac{k - \mu}{\sigma} \right) \sum_{j=0}^{h} \sigma^j C_j \left(\frac{k - \mu}{\sigma} \right) \right) & \text{if } n > \mathbb{E}[N]
\end{cases}
\tag{27}
$$

We can see on Figure 6 the reliability of NG approximations. In solid black, the order 0 approximation corresponds to the classical Gaussian approximation. Unsurprisingly, this central limit approximation is accurate for the center of the distribution (n close to the expectation $\mu = 153.3$), the reliability quickly deceases when $|n - \mu|$ increases.

Central limit theorems (CLT) for N have established long ago that N should be asymptotically Gaussian distributed. The problem however with CLT theorems is that the quality of the resulting approximation dramatically decreases at finite distance when considering tail distribution events. Here we try to overcome the issue by considering Near-Gaussian approximations that exploits higher moments of N to improve the quality of the approximations. In order to do this, a critical problem is first to obtain the first k-th moments of N. Of course we can access these moments by computing the full distribution of N, but if it is possible to do so, why bothering with approximations. We hence need an method to compute the moments of N whose complexity should be somehow significantly smaller than the complete exact computations. With higher order approximation, we can see a dramatic improvement of reliability of the results, with a noticeable increase of the region where at least two digits are correct (up to $n \in [80; 240]$ for NG_3).

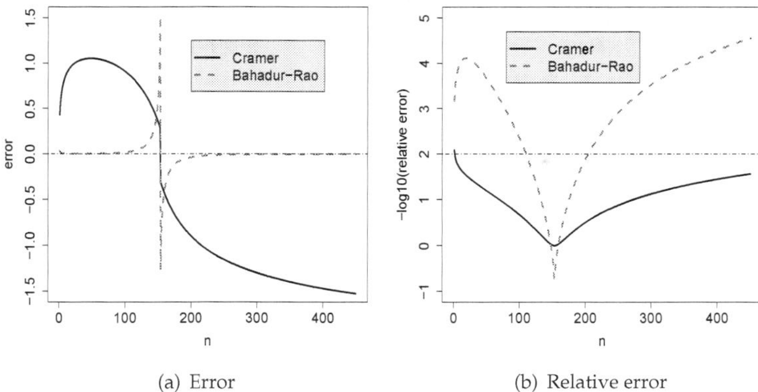

(a) Error   (b) Relative error

Fig. 7. Reliability of CB and BR approximations for $\mathcal{M} = \mathtt{G}(\mathtt{G}|\mathtt{C})\mathtt{G}$ on a random sequence $X_{1:\ell}$ generated by a M0 model with parameters $\pi(\mathtt{A}) = \pi(\mathtt{T}) = 0.10$ and $\pi(\mathtt{C}) = \pi(\mathtt{G}) = 0.40$, and with $\ell = 1200$. The error $\mathrm{CB}(n) - S(n)$ or $\mathrm{BR}(n) - S(n)$ is given on Figure (a); and the relative error (log-scale) $- \log_{10} |\mathrm{CB}(n) - S(n)| / |S(n)|$ or $- \log_{10} |\mathrm{BR}(n) - S(n)| / |S(n)|$ on Figure (b). The horizontal rule indicates the null error on Figure (a), and the threshold corresponding to two correct digits on Figure (b).

From the computational point of view, the order h approximation requires the cumulants of N up to order $h + 2$. Using the power approach, the resulting complexity is hence $O(\log_2 \ell \times h^2 \times L^3)$ in time and $O(\log_2 \ell \times (h + 2) \times L^2)$ in memory. Using the recursion, the complexity resulting complexity is $O(\ell \times L \times |\mathcal{A}| \times h)$ in time, and $O(L \times h)$ in memory. In both cases, the computational time drops significantly from the exact computations.

Thanks to NG approximations, we hence have a fast and reliable way to compute an approximation of $S(n)$ when n falls in the center of the distribution (ex: $|S(n)| \leqslant 3.0$), but NG approximations unfortunately remain totally unreliable for tail distribution events (ex: $|S(n)| > 3.0$), which are moreover often precisely the event of interest. Fortunately we have a solution to this problem.

3.7 Bahadur-Rao

We want here to study specifically the tail distribution of N with events on the form $\mathbb{P}(N \geqslant n)$ with large n (or $\mathbb{P}(N \leqslant n)$ with small n). For all $t > 0$ let us first notice that we can use the Markov inequality to write: $\mathbb{P}(N \geqslant n) = \mathbb{P}(e^{tN} \geqslant e^{tn}) \leqslant \mathbb{E}[e^{tN}]/e^{tn} = \exp(\Lambda(t) - tn)$. By taking the smallest of these bounds for $t > 0$ we hence get: $\log \mathbb{P}(N \geqslant n) \leqslant \Lambda(\tau) - \tau n$ with τ defined by $\Lambda'(\tau) = n$. This upper bound, known as the Chernoff's Bound (CB), is often surprisingly sharp for events located in the tail distribution. By dealing symmetrically with $\mathbb{P}(N \leqslant n)$ and $t < 0$ we hence obtain the following approximation for $S(n)$:

$$\mathrm{CB}(n) = \delta_n \frac{\tau n - \Lambda(\tau)}{\log(10)} \tag{28}$$

where $\delta_n = -1$ if $n \leqslant \mathbb{E}[N]$, and $\delta_n = +1$ if $n > \mathbb{E}[N]$.

From the computational point of view, the solution τ of $\Lambda'(\tau) = n$ can be easily determined numerically using (for example) using the Newton-Raphson sequence (Press et al., 1992). Starting for a first guess t_0 (ex: $t_0 = 0$), one performs $t_{i+1} = t_i + (n - \Lambda'(t_i))/\Lambda''(t_i)$ for $i \geqslant 0$ until convergence to τ. The computation of Λ, Λ', and Λ'' being possible thanks to Lemma 5 and the following formulas:

$$\Lambda(t) = G(e^t) \quad \Lambda'(t) = \frac{e^t G'(e^t)}{G(e^t)} \quad \Lambda''(t) = \frac{e^{2t} G''(e^t)}{G(e^t)} - \frac{e^{2t} G'(t)^2}{G(e^t)^2} + \frac{e^t G'(e^t)}{G(e^t)} \tag{29}$$

with $G(e^t) = [z^0]\mathbf{u}(\mathbf{P} + e^t\mathbf{Q} + z\mathbf{Q})^{\ell-d}\mathbf{v} = \mathbf{u}(\mathbf{P} + e^t\mathbf{Q})^{\ell-d}\mathbf{v}$, $G'(e^t) = [z^1]\mathbf{u}(\mathbf{P} + e^t\mathbf{Q} + z\mathbf{Q})^{\ell-d}\mathbf{v}$, and $G''(e^t) = 2[z^2]\mathbf{u}(\mathbf{P} + e^t\mathbf{Q} + z\mathbf{Q})^{\ell-d}\mathbf{v}$.

Moreover, this bound can be further refined using the Bahadur-Rao Theorem (Bahadur & Rao, 1960) and gives the following approximation for $S(n)$:

$$\mathrm{BR}(n) = \mathrm{CB}(n) + \delta_n \log 10 \left((1 - e^{-|\tau|})\sqrt{2\pi\Lambda''(\tau)} \right). \tag{30}$$

From the computational point of view, $\mathrm{CB}(n)$ and $\mathrm{BR}(n)$ can be computed either with the power approach with complexities $O(\log_2 \ell \times L^3)$ in time and $O(\log_2 \ell \times L^3)$ in memory; or with the recursion approach with complexities $O(\ell \times L \times |\mathcal{A}|)$ in time and $O(L \times |\mathcal{A}|)$ in memory.

On Figure 7 we can see the reliability of the approximations $\mathrm{CB}(n)$ and $\mathrm{BR}(n)$. Unsurprisingly, the farther from the center of the distribution, the better are both approximations. We also observe that $\mathrm{BR}(n)$ is a dramatic improvement over $\mathrm{CB}(n)$ since it obtains at least two correct digits of $S(n)$ for all n but on $[120, 200]$. At the end of previous section, we have seen that the order 3 NG approximation achieves the same precision for region $[80; 240]$, hence, by combining both $\mathrm{NG}_3(n)$ (for the center of the distribution) and $\mathrm{BR}(n)$ (for the tail distributions), one can achieve at least two correct digits of $S(n)$ on the whole bulk of the distribution for a modest computational cost.

4. Discussion

Obtaining the distribution of motif count in random sequences is a very challenging problem that has attracted considerable attention from mathematicians and computer scientists in the last fifty years. Recently however, a significant advance has been obtained by connecting the well-known theory of pattern matching and automata to the Markov chain embedding technique Lladser (2007); Nuel (2008a); Nuel & Prum (2007). Thanks to this finding, it is now possible to deal with simple (runs of 1 in binary sequences, single words, etc.) or complex motifs (PROSITE signature, gapped motifs, etc.) using the same general framework.

Using exact approaches, it is possible to obtain efficiently the first moments of any motif count N, and even the complete distribution of N. As a consequence, the computation of $S(n)$ is now tractable for a wide range of motif problems including large datasets or complex motifs. However, the case of complex frequent motifs in large datasets remains an open problem (Nuel & Dumas, 2010).

As an alternative to exact computations, a wide range of approximations have been developed (see Lothaire, 2005; Nuel, 2006b; Reignier, 2000, for a review). We can basically classify these approximations in three categories: 1) Gaussian approximations (Cowan, 1991; Kleffe & Borodovski, 1997; Nuel, 2010; Pevzner et al., 1989; Prum et al., 1995); 2) Poisson approximations Erhardsson (2000); Geske et al. (1995); Godbole (1991); Reinert & Schbath (1999); Roquain & Schbath (2007); 3) large deviations approximations Denise et al. (2001); Nuel (2004).

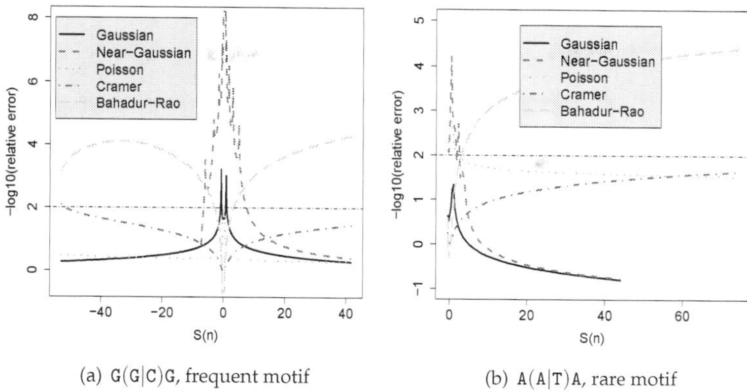

(a) G(G|C)G, frequent motif

(b) A(A|T)A, rare motif

Fig. 8. Relative error in log-scale for various approximations of $S(n)$ ($n = 0, \ldots, 200$) in a sequence $X_{1:\ell}$ generated by a M0 model with parameters $\pi(\text{A}) = \pi(\text{T}) = 0.10$ and $\pi(\text{C}) = \pi(\text{G}) = 0.40$.

In this chapter we deliberately left aside the Poisson-based approximations and considered only two of these approximations: the (Near-) Gaussian approximations with $\text{NG}_h(n)$, and the large deviations based approximations with $\text{CB}(n)$ and $\text{BR}(n)$. The reason why Poisson-based approximations are not considered here is basically practical, these approximations cannot be directly derived from the formalism of this manuscript and require the introduction of many tedious notions like clumps, overlapping words and so on. However, we compare here the performance of all these approximations (including compound Poisson approximations) in the case where $X_{1:\ell}$ generated by a M0 model with parameters $\pi(\text{A}) = \pi(\text{T}) = 0.10$ and $\pi(\text{C}) = \pi(\text{G}) = 0.40$ i.i.d. DNA sequence, and for two motifs: the frequent G(G|C)G, and the rare A(A|T)A.

We can see on Figure 8 the relative error (in log-scale) for all approximations. For Gaussian approximations, performances are only good in the very center of the distribution (for n very close to $\mathbb{E}(n)$) for the frequent motif G(G|C)G, and performances are poor almost everywhere for the rare motif T(A|T)T. This observation to consistent with the well known claim that "Gaussian approximations a more suitable for frequent motif" (Lothaire, 2005). It has however to be pointed out that even in the most favorable case (with highly frequent motif), Gaussian approximations totally fail to capture the tail distribution of N and hence not suitable for the highly significant observations we usually encounter in biological sequences (Nuel, 2006b). If we consider now the near-Gaussian approximation, taking into account more moments of N dramatically improve the result for both motifs, but the failure to deal with extreme distribution events remains.

Compound Poisson approximations are known to be extremely sensitive to the relative abundance of the motif of interest in the sequence, being more accurate for rare motifs (Lothaire, 2005; Roquain & Schbath, 2007). It is hence not a surprise to see that Poisson approximations are totally unreliable for the frequent motif G(G|C)G. For the rare motif T(A|T)T we naturally obtain much better results but like for Gaussian approximations, and even in this favorable case, reliability decreases in the tail distribution. Considering that Poisson approximations are not easily generalizable to motifs defined by regular expressions, that their computations could be complicated and time consuming, and that their reliability is highly questionable in some configurations, it seems advisable to avoid their use is most cases.

With large deviations based approximations, we unsurprisingly get a low reliability in the center of the distribution, but a high reliability in the tail distribution. With Bahadur-Rao precise approximations, the improvement over the classical Chernoff's bound is quite impressive, and the complementarity with Near-Gaussian approximations clearly shows that a combination of both approaches could be a very efficient way to obtain reliable approximations of $S(n)$ for all n.

In this chapter we gave all the necessary ingredients to assess the significance score of motif in a biological sequence using state of the art results, including several unpublished ones: Lemma 5 which is an extension of the results of Nuel (2010), and the complete "Bahadur-Rao" Section which provides interesting improvements over previous large deviations work (Denise et al., 2001; Nuel, 2004).

Let us finally point out that for the sake of compactness, we have left aside some interesting questions and extensions like: approximate matching Hopcroft et al. (2001), renewal occurrences (Nuel, 2006b; Roquain & Schbath, 2007), joint distributions (Nuel, 2008b; Stefanov & Szpankowski, 2007), dataset with many sequences (Nuel et al., 2010), and sensitivity to parameter estimation (Nuel, 2006c). Even if some results are already available for these problems, many questions still have to be answered in the exciting and challenging field of the distribution of motifs in random sequences.

5. References

Allauzen, C. & Mohri, M. (2006). A unified construction of the glushkov, follow, and antimirov automata, *in* R. KrA?lovic & P. Urzyczyn (eds), *Mathematical Foundations of Computer Science 2006*, Vol. 4162 of *Lecture Notes in Computer Science*, Springer Berlin / Heidelberg, pp. 110–121.

Antzoulakos, D. L. (2001). Waiting times for patterns in a sequence of multistate trials, *J. Appl. Prob.* 38: 508–518.

Bahadur, R. R. & Rao, R. R. (1960). On deviations of the sample mean, *The Annals of Math. Statistics.* 31(4): 1015–1027.

Beaudoing, E., Freier, S., Wyatt, J., Claverie, J.-M. & Gautheret, D. (2000). Patterns of variant polyadenylation signal usage in human genes, *Genome Res.* 10(7): 1001–1010.

Blinnikov, S. & Moessner, R. (1998). Expansions for nearly Gaussian distributions, *Astron. Astrophys. Suppl. Ser.* 130: 193–205.

Boeva, V., ClA©ment, J., RA©gnier, M. & Vandenbogaert, M. (2005). Assessing the significance of sets of words, *Combinatorial Pattern Matching 05, Lecture Notes in Computer Science, vol. 3537*, Springer-Verlag.

Brazma, A., Jonassen, I., Vilo, J. & Ukkonen, E. (1998). Predicting gene regulatory elements in silico on a genomic scale, *Genome Res.* 8(11): 1202–1215.

Bryne, J., Valen, E., Tang, M., Marstrand, T., Winther, O., da Piedade, I., Krogh, A., Lenhard, B. & Sandelin, A. (2008). JASPAR, the open access database of transcription factor-binding profiles: new content and tools in the 2008 update., *Nucleic Acids Res.* 36: 102–106.

Chan, H. P., Zhang, N. R. & Chen, L. H. Y. (2010). Importance sampling of word patterns in dna and protein sequences, *J. of Comput. Biol.* 17(12): 1697–1709.

Chang, Y.-M. (2005). Distribution of waiting time until the rth occurrence of a compound pattern, *Statistics and Probability Letters* 75(1): 29–38.

Cornish-Bowden (1985). IUPAC-IUB symbols for nucleotide nomenclature, *Nucl. Acids Res.* 13: 3021–3030.

Cowan (1991). Expected frequencies of dna patterns using whittle's formula, *J. Appl. Prob.* 28: 886–892.

Crochemore, M. & Stefanov, V. (2003). Waiting time and complexity for matching patterns with automata, *Info. Proc. Letters* 87(3): 119–125.

Denise, A., RA©gnier, M. & Vandenbogaert, M. (2001). Assessing the statistical significance of overrepresented oligonucleotides, *Lecture Notes in Computer Science* 2149: 85–97.

El Karoui, M., Biaudet, V., Schbath, S. & Gruss, A. (1999). Characteristics of chi distribution on different bacterial genomes, *Res. Microbiol.* 150: 579–587.

Erhardsson, T. (2000). Compound Poisson approximation for counts of rare patterns in Markov chains and extreme sojourns in birth-death chains, *Ann. Appl. Probab.* 10(2): 573–591.

Fatemi, M., Pao, M., Jeong, S., Gal-Yam, E., Egger, G., Weisenberger, D. & Jones, P. (2005). Footprinting of mammalian promoters: use of a cpg dna methyltransferase revealing nucleosome positions at a single molecule level, *Nucleic Acids Res* 33(20): 176.

Frith, M. C., Spouge, J. L., Hansen, U. & Weng, Z. (2002). Statistical significance of clusters of motifs represented by position specific scoring matrices in nucleotide sequences, *Nucl. Acids. Res.* 30(14): 3214–3224.

Fu, J. C. (1996). Distribution theory of runs and patterns associated with a sequence of multi-state trials, *Statistica Sinica* 6(4): 957–974.

Geske, M. X., Godbole, A. P., Schaffner, A. A., Skrolnick, A. M. & Wallstrom, G. L. (1995). Compound poisson approximations for word patterns under markovian hypotheses, *J. Appl. Probab.* 32: 877–892.

Godbole, A. P. (1991). Poissons approximations for runs and patterns of rare events, *Adv. Appl. Prob.* 23.

Green, T. J., Gupta, A., Miklau, G., Onizuka, M. & Suciu, D. (2004). Processing xml streams with deterministic automata and stream indexes, *ACM Trans. Database Syst.* 29: 752–788.

Hampson, S., Kibler, D. & Baldi, P. (2002). Distribution patterns of over-represented k-mers in non-coding yeast DNA, *Bioinformatics* 18(4): 513–528.

Hopcroft, J. E., Motwani, R. & Ullman, J. D. (2001). *Introduction the automata theory, languages, and computation, 2d ed.*, ACM Press, New York.

Karlin, S., Burge, C. & Campbell, A. (1992). Statistical analyses of counts and distributions of restriction sites in DNA sequences, *Nucl. Acids. Res.* 20(6): 1363–1370.

Kleffe, J. & Borodovski, M. (1997). First and second moment of counts of words in random texts generated by markov chains, *Bioinformatics* 8(5): 433–441.

Leonardo Marino-Ramírez, John L. Spouge, G. C. K. & Landsman, D. (2004). Statistical analysis of over-represented words in human promoter sequences, *Nuc. Acids Res.* 32(3): 949–958.

Liddle, A. R. (2007). Information criteria for astrophysical model selection, *Monthly Notices of the Royal Astronomical Society: Letters* 377: 74–78.

Lladser, M. E. (2007). Mininal markov chain embeddings of pattern problems, *Information Theory and Applications Workshop*, pp. 251–255.

Lothaire, M. (ed.) (2005). *Applied Combinatorics on Words*, Cambridge University Press, Cambridge.

Nicodème, P., Salvy, B. & Flajolet, P. (2002). Motif statistics, *Theoretical Com. Sci.* 287(2): 593–617.

Nuel, G. (2004). Ld-spatt: Large deviations statistics for patterns on markov chains, *J. Comp. Biol.* 11(6): 1023–1033.

Nuel, G. (2006a). Effective p-value computations using Finite Markov Chain Imbedding (FMCI): application to local score and to pattern statistics, *Algorithms for Molecular Biology* 1(1): 5.

Nuel, G. (2006b). Numerical solutions for patterns statistics on markov chains, *Stat. App. in Genet. and Mol. Biol.* 5(1): 26.

Nuel, G. (2006c). Pattern statistics on markov chains and sensitivity to parameter estimation, *Algorithms for Molecular Biology* 1(1): 17.

Nuel, G. (2008a). Pattern Markov chains: optimal Markov chain embedding through deterministic finite automata, *J. of Applied Prob.* 45(1): 226–243.

Nuel, G. (2008b). Waiting time distribution for pattern occurrence in a constrained sequence: an embedding markov chain approach, *Discrete Mathematics and Theoretical Computer Science* 10: 3.

Nuel, G. (2010). On the first k moments of the random count of a pattern in a multi-states sequence generated by a markov source, *Journal of Applied Probability* 47: 1–19.

Nuel, G. & Dumas, J.-G. (2010). Sparse approaches for the exact distribution of patterns in long multi-states sequences generated by a markov source, *submitted to J. Applied. Prob.* . arXiv:1006.3246v1.

Nuel, G. & Prum, B. (2007). Analyse statistique des séquences biologiques: modélisation markovienne, alignements et motifs, *Hermes editions, Paris*.

Nuel, G., Regad, L., Martin, J. & Camproux, A.-C. (2010). Exact distribution of a pattern in a set of random sequences generated by a markov source: applications to biological data, *Algorithms for Molecular Biology* 5: 15.

Pevzner, P., Borodovski, M. & Mironov, A. (1989). Linguistic of nucleotide sequences: The significance of deviation from mean statistical characteristics and prediction of frequencies of occurrence of words, *J. Biomol. Struct. Dyn.* 6: 1013–1026.

Press, W. H., Teukolsky, S. A., Vetterling, W. T. & Flannery, B. P. (1992). *Numerical Recipes in C*, Cambridge University Press.

Prum, B., Rodolphe, F. & de Turckheim, E. (1995). Finding words with unexpected frequencies in dna sequences, *J. R. Statist. Soc. B* 11: 190–192.

Reignier, M. (2000). A unified approach to word occurrences probabilities, *Discrete Applied Mathematics* 104(1): 259–280.

Reinert, G. & Schbath, S. (1999). Compound poisson and poisson process approximations for occurrences of multiple words in markov chains, *J. of Comp. Biol.* 5: 223–254.

Ribeca, P. & Raineri, E. (2008). Faster exact Markovian probability functions for motif occurrences: a DFA-only approach, *Bioinformatics* 24(24): 2839–2848.

Roberts, R., Vincze, T., Posfai, J. & Macelis, D. (2010). REBASE – a database for dna restriction and modification: enzymes, genes and genomes, *Nucl. Acids Res.* 38: 234–236.

Roquain, E. & Schbath, S. (2007). Improved compound poisson approximation for the number of occurrences of any rare word family in a stationary markov chain, *Adv. in Appl. Probab.* 39(1): 128–140.

Sigrist, C., Cerutti, L., de Castro, E., Langendijk-Genevaux, P., Bulliard, V., Bairoch, A. & Hulo, N. (2010). PROSITE, a protein domain database for functional characterization and annotation, *Nucleic Acids Res.* 38.

Stefanov, V. T. & Szpankowski, W. (2007). Waiting Time Distributions for Pattern Occurrence in a Constrained Sequence, *Discrete Mathematics and Theoretical Computer Science* 9(1): 305–320.

van Helden, J., André, B. & Collado-Vides, J. (1998). Extracting regulatory sites from the upstream region of yeast genes by computational analysis of oligonucleotide frequencies, *J. Mol. Biol.* 281(5): 827–842.

10

A Systematic and Thorough Search for Domains of the Scavenger Receptor Cysteine-Rich Group B Family in the Human Genome

Alexandre M. Carmo[1] and Vattipally B. Sreenu[2]
[1]IBMC – Instituto de Biologia Molecular e Celular and ICBAS – Instituto de Ciências Biomédicas de Abel Salazar, Universidade do Porto
[2]The Weatherall Institute of Molecular Medicine, University of Oxford
[1]Portugal
[2]UK

1. Introduction

The biological function of proteins is largely determined by their individual component domains, which are segments within the protein sequence that are self-contained and spatially arranged. These can be catalytic or structural, and define a number of different features of proteins such as their enzymatic activity, interactions with other proteins, sugars or lipids, and determine the cellular localization of the proteins that contain them. A number of intracellular three-dimensionally-arranged domains, such as Src-homology (SH) or Pleckstrin-homology (PH) domains, define the nature of protein interactions with other components of the cell, and enable them to interact with their substrates or binding partners. The specificity of interactions that is given by the domain is unique to its protein. Similarly, the extracellular part of most membrane-bound or secreted proteins of eukaryotic cells is also organized in semi-autonomously-arranged blocks that potentially confer multiple diverse functions to a particular protein. These domains have been classified and grouped into protein superfamilies depending on the similarity they have with domains of prototypical proteins, for example immunoglobulin, fibronectin or C-type lectin domains. Members of these groups are believed to be homologous and to have arisen by divergent evolution from a common ancestor. Many membrane-bound or extracellular proteins are comprised of several domains of the same type, but it is not uncommon to find mosaic proteins containing domains from different superfamilies.

The scavenger receptor cysteine-rich (SRCR) superfamily comprises a group of proteins that contain one or multiple domains structurally similar to the membrane distal domain of the type I scavenger receptor expressed by human macrophages (Freeman et al., 1990). Proteins classified as belonging to this superfamily may contain other types of domains additionally to the dominant SRCR modules, such as EGF, CUB, LCCL, or other domains. In mammals, SRCR proteins are typically expressed in cells of the immune system (Resnick et al., 1994), although some members can be also expressed in non-immune cells and organs, including liver, kidney, placenta, stomach, brain and heart (Sarrias et al., 2004). Group A domain-containing SRCR proteins are present in phyla from the most primitive metazoan to vertebrates, whereas group B domain containing SRCR proteins are only found in vertebrates. Intriguingly, although SRCR proteins can include other domains, no proteins have been reported to contain group A and B domains simultaneously.

In mammalian species, SRCR group B orthologs are usually very well conserved and regarding some of the proteins, a high level of conservation is extended to birds and fish. However, in some cases a human SRCR protein apparently has no corresponding ortholog in some mammals, and conversely, there are examples of SRCR group B proteins that are well characterized in a few mammalian species, that have not been described in humans. By analyzing the human genome, we can now identify all the remaining, still undescribed genes encoding SRCR group B domains, which will allow us to perform phylogenetic analysis of the complete set of group B domains. By comprehensive and systematic whole genome analysis we have found two new putative transcriptional units containing clusters of potential SRCR domains, and additionally a further putative gene that contains a single domain. After our thorough search, we are now confident that all proteins containing group B SRCR domains in the human genome have been identified.

2. The scavenger receptor cysteine-rich group B family

2.1 Biological function of SRCR group B proteins

The cell surface antigens CD5 and CD6, which function in T lymphocytes, are probably the most well characterized of the family, each containing three extracellular SRCR domains (Aruffo et al., 1991; Jones et al., 1986). CD5 and CD6 co-associate with each other at the surface of T cells (Castro et al., 2003; Gimferrer et al., 2003), and are involved in the regulation of T cell receptor-mediated activation. The extensive characterization of the interaction of CD6 with its ligand CD166, expressed by antigen presenting cells (Aruffo et al., 1997), and the identification of different binding partners for CD5 (Biancone et al., 1996; Calvo et al., 1999; Pospisil et al., 2000; Van de Velde et al., 1991), had initially suggested that SRCR group B domains participate in intercellular contacts *via* protein-protein interactions. Also, the three SRCR domain-containing soluble protein Spα (Gebe et al., 1997) has been reported to bind to cells of myeloid and lymphoid origin. Also known as AIM (apoptosis inhibitor expressed by macrophages), API6 (apoptosis inhibitor 6) or CD5L (CD5-like molecule), Spα is best known for promoting macrophage survival. Therefore, this sub-group of small SRCR-containing proteins may be described as having a role in cellular communication, differentiation and activation. However, for most of the remaining members of the family no such clear function has been established. In particular the lack of cellular ligands for most of these proteins raises the possibility that a totally different function for SRCR domains may exist, if indeed SRCR domain proteins share any common function.

In addition to CD5, CD6 and Spα, the group B SRCR family presently contains five other proteins, of which two, CD163 and M160, are membrane bound and expressed by macrophages. CD163 (Law et al., 1993) and M160 (CD163L1) (Gronlund et al., 2000), which were both identified in human monocytes, are considered a subgroup of the SRCR group B molecules. No definitive function has been established for these molecules, although CD163 has been described as binding to, and internalizing, tumor necrosis factor-like weak inducer of apoptosis (TWEAK), thus having a potential role in atherosclerosis (Moreno et al., 2009). Additionally, CD163 has a detoxifying role in iron metabolism, where by binding to hemoglobin-complexed haptoglobin it is able to remove hemoglobin from the plasma

(Graversen et al., 2002; Kristiansen et al., 2001). The remaining three members of the group B SRCR family are secreted glycoproteins of different sizes and structural complexity. DMBT1, which was identified on the basis of its deletion in a medulloblastoma cell line, is the largest member of the family, comprising 14 SRCR domains separated by SRCR-interspacing domains (Mollenhauer et al., 1997). Apart from being secreted, DMBT1 is also found in association with the plasma membrane of macrophages, although it is not clear whether there is a specific receptor or the poorly characterized DMBT1 gene may encode a transmembrane sequence. Once in the membrane, DMBT1 is a ligand for Surfactant protein D (SP-D), a C-type lectin that binds to exposed carbohydrates (Holmskov et al., 1999). The SRCR soluble proteins S4D-SRCRB and SSc5D have four and five group B domains, respectively, and little is known of their functional or binding properties (Gonçalves et al., 2009; Padilla et al., 2002).

However, it has been recently suggested that Spα (Sarrias et al., 2005), DMBT1 (Bikker et al., 2002), CD163 (Fabriek et al., 2009), CD5 (Vera et al., 2009) and CD6 (Sarrias et al., 2007) are capable of detecting microbe-associated molecular patterns, and could bind and clear bacteria or fungi, reaffirming a scavenger-like role for this group of molecules. These developments notwithstanding, SRCR superfamily proteins may prove to have very diverse functions, to the extent that the structural properties of the highly conserved SRCR domains may be the only unifying feature of the family.

2.2 Structure and organization of SRCR domains

Typically, the 100-110 amino acid-long SRCR domains possess a characteristic pattern of cysteine residues that establish intra-domain disulfide bridges and contribute to the overall architecture of the compact domain. The number of cysteine residues and their distribution, together with the organization of the genomic sequence encoding each domain, divide the SRCR family into two groups, A and B. Group A domains are encoded by split exons, and typically have six cysteine residues establishing three disulfide bonds. Group B domains, on the other hand, are encoded by a single exon and have eight cysteine residues, whose distribution is remarkably conserved in nearly all known domains (Fig. 1).

So far, eight human SRCR group B proteins have been described, Spα, CD5, CD6, S4D, SSc5D, CD163, M160 and DMBT1 that contain three to fourteen SRCR domains. Their encoding genes are dispersed throughout the genome, however a few highly similar pairs such as CD5-CD6 and CD163-M160 are located on the same chromosome. The identity between individual domains of different SRCR group B proteins varies from 20 to 80%, and phylogenetic analysis suggests that they have evolved by sequential intragene duplication, although there are examples that suggest they may have evolved in some cases by inter-protein domain shuffling. Only four SRCR domains have been characterized by X-ray crystallography, and of these three are group A SRCR domains, those of hepsin, a cell surface serine protease involved in cell growth and maintenance of cellular morphology (Somoza et al., 2003), M2bp, a tumor associated antigen and matrix protein (Hohenester et al., 1999), and MARCO, a trimeric SRCR group A protein expressed by macrophages and dendritic cells that recognizes polyanionic particles and pathogens (Ojala et al., 2007). The crystal structure of the membrane proximal domain of CD5 (Rodamilans et al., 2007), together with an NMR solution structure of domain 1 of CD5 (Garza-Garcia et al., 2008) constitute the only sources of structural information of SRCR group B domains. Comparing the structures, it is however apparent that the 3D assembly of the different domains in the two groups is overall conserved, all displaying a very similar fold.

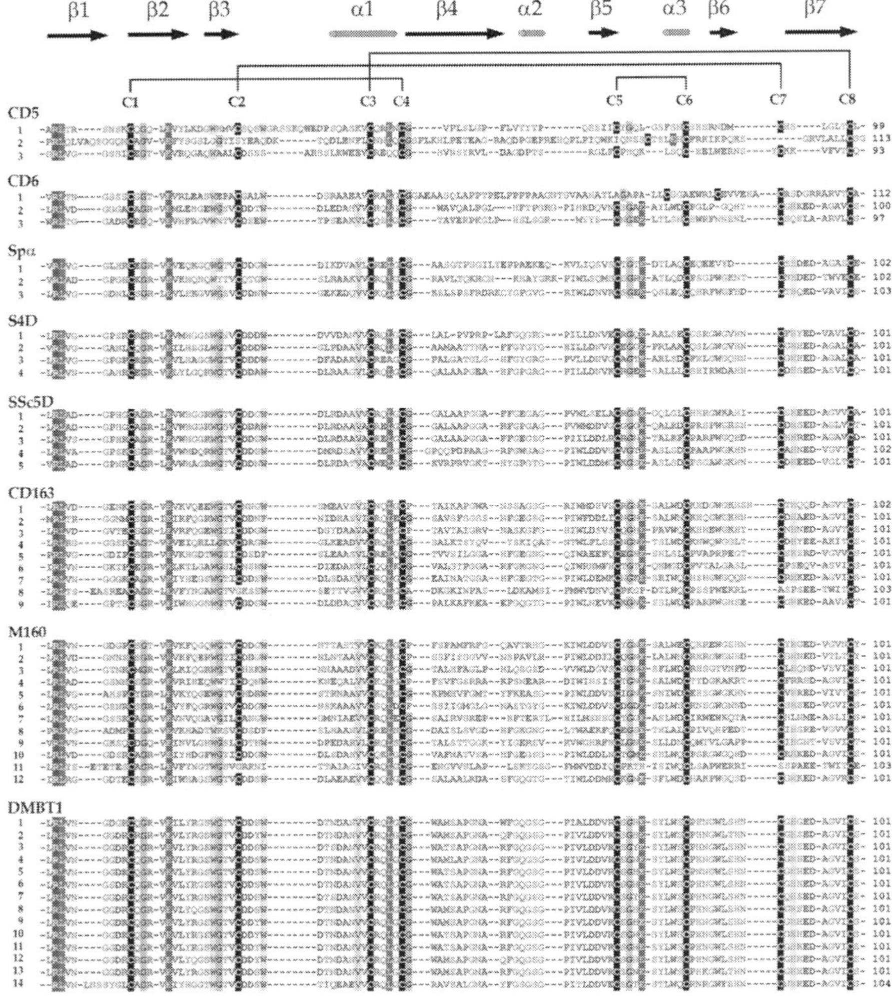

Fig. 1. Sequence alignment of domains from group B SRCR superfamily members.

SRCR domains are typically sequences of 100-110 amino acids in length compacted into a heart-shaped fold, where a six/seven-stranded β-sheet cradles an α-helix. Strands β1, β3 and β4, together with β7, form a curved sheet that wraps around the core α1 helix. From β4 onwards, the structures start to diverge. It is the sequence of amino acids between the beginning of the domain and the β4 strand that is best conserved between group A and group B domains, and that roughly corresponds in the group A proteins to the first of two exons that encode a full SRCR A domain, and in group B proteins to the first 50 amino acids of the domain.

2.3 Homology between SRCR domains

The level of amino acid identity among human SRCR group B domains from different molecules varies from 20% to 80%, but within the same molecule this level can be higher and even be identical in some domains (e.g. domains 3 and 7, and 10 and 11 of DMBT1). Similarly, some molecules are remarkably conserved between species, especially among mammals, although it appears that some level of conservation can be extended to birds, fish and amphibians in a few specific cases. There are good indications for there being orthologs of CD6 in the genomes of *T. guttata* and *D. rerio*, and some other examples. Nevertheless, the structure of SRCR group B-containing molecules is best preserved in mammalian species. The strong homology of SSc5D domains dates back to the divergence of egg- and non-egg-laying mammals, while CD163 has clearly conserved orthologs in all mammals, including non-placental species (Table 1).

	D1	D2	D3	D4	D5	D6	D7	D8	D9
P. troglodytes	99	99	98	97	97	99	99	99	100
C. jacchus	94	87	88	87	95	93	98	89	99
O. cuniculus	90	82	84	81	85	84	73	47	63
R. norvegicus	78	75	82	75	83	81	84	70	79
M. musculus	78	76	77	75	83	76	81	70	79
C. familiaris	88	87	88	90	93	89	92	81	86
E. caballus	85	84	89	87	94	87	92	87	87
B. taurus	82	86	90	87	91	85	89	77	85
M. domestica	51	58	51	45	58	51	76	60	70
O. anatinus	36	28	36	ND	40	57	64	40	70

Table 1. Homology between human and other mammalian CD163 domains. Numbers represent percentage of identity between each domain, compared to the human sequence.

The significantly conserved homology of some SRCR orthologs is suggestive of profound functional constraints acting on these proteins. On the other hand, it appears that not all human SRCR B group molecules have described orthologs in all mammalian species, and conversely, that there are some SRCR proteins described in different animals that have not been reported in man.

Noticeably, bovine WC1 (Wijngaard et al., 1992) does not have a human counterpart, nor do the mouse SCART molecules (Kisielow et al., 2008). Similarly, the human macrophage specific receptor M160 is not found in all mammalian species, while the closely related molecule CD163, also specific to the monocytic/macrophage lineage, is clearly present in all genomes that we have examined. We have compared the similarity between individual domains of known and characterized members of the SRCR B group, and the corresponding domains in the bovine proteins (Table 2). While proteins such as S4D, SSc5D and CD163 show high levels of identity between human and bovine sequences, others like CD5 and Spα are more distantly related. M160 does not have a straightforward ortholog in cattle, so the bovine sequence used was of the related molecule M160-like, that is related in turn to the SCART 1 and 2 molecules present in the mouse.

	CD5	CD6	Spα	S4D	SSc5D	CD163	M160	DMBT1
D1	48	52	ND	99	96	82	ND	ND
D2	48	83	62	95	97	86	ND	ND
D3	66	81	72	97	95	90	32	ND
D4				96	ND	87	ND	86
D5					89	91	28	ND
D6						85	38	86
D7						89	38	ND
D8						77	ND	86
D9						85	32	85
D10							55	88
D11							47	84
D12							69	82
D13								85
D14								83

Table 2. Similarity between human and bovine corresponding SRCR domains. Percentage identity between each domain is indicated.

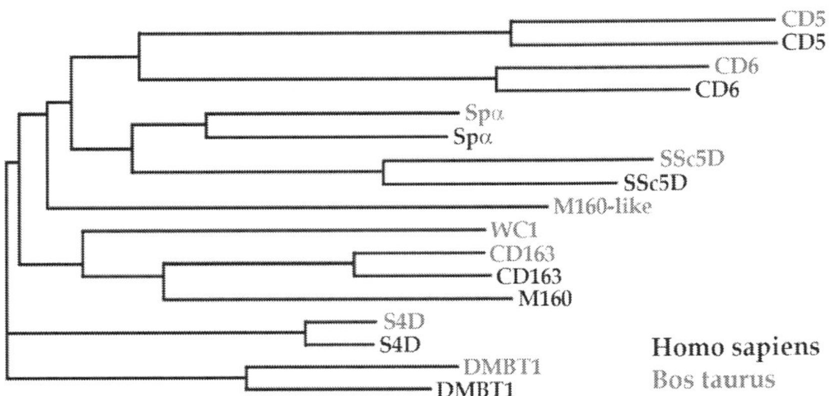

Fig. 2. Relationships between human and bovine SRCR molecules.

There are three groups of genes in the CD163 family: CD163 itself (CD163a), present in all mammals; M160 (CD163b), so far only found in the genomes of primates and in horses; and

SCART (CD163c), of which there are two genes found in the mouse, and the bovine gene M160-like (Herzig et al., 2010). These sets of genes are related to WC1 genes expressed in cattle, sheep and swine. To obtain a better idea of the relationship between these families of genes, we aligned the full sequences of known human and bovine proteins containing SRCR group B domains using ClustalW and drew the corresponding phylogram (Fig. 2). As can be seen, there are no direct links between human M160, bovine M160L and bovine WC1, raising the possibility that either some genes were lost during mammalian evolution, or that the complete characterization and annotation of the genomes has still not been fully achieved. Clearly, either hypothesis does not exclude the other.

3. A systematic and thorough search for SRCR domains in the genome

Our hope is that the evolution and function of SRCR domains would emerge when all members of this protein family have been identified. The advent of the human genome sequence has allowed us to screen, using bioinformatics-based approaches, for new SRCR proteins still not described or characterized. We decided to focus on group B molecules, given that proteins of this type are more conserved, restricted in number, and their specialized function, in this case immune-related, seems better defined. We performed searches for new members of the SRCR-SF in the completed human genome sequence by interrogating the genome using TBLASTN 2.2.20+ (Altschul et al., 1997; http://www.ncbi.nlm.nih.gov/BLAST). Initially, we screened for new sequences exhibiting similarity with any or all of the SRCR domains comprising the then known SRCR superfamily proteins (Gonçalves et al., 2009). We expected that, for a given TBLASTN run, *bona fide* new SRCR domains would have smaller E values than the best matches of the search sequence with Group A SRCR domains. According to this criterion, the search identified the sequences encoding domains within already known and characterized proteins *i.e.* CD5, CD6, Spα, S4D, CD163, M160 and DMBT1. Additionally, we identified a cluster of five new SRCR domains, which we further investigated and that later resulted in the cloning and characterization of SSc5D, a molecule secreted by macrophages and that comprises five SRCR group B domains (Gonçalves et al., 2009).

A *caveat* in our methodology was that not all group B domains were identified using this strategy. The most divergent domains, namely those of CD5, were not retrieved in all searches, and in particular CD5-d1 was rarely identified as having a clear homology with any other group B domain. Sequence alignment of all group B domains (Fig. 1) highlights the striking differences of CD5 sequences, and also to some extent of the CD6 domains, when compared with other sequences that are remarkably similar to each other. In order to perform a more rigorous search for all putative SRCR group B domains, we conducted a comprehensive systematic search using PSI-BLAST (Altschul et al., 1997) to find distant homologs. All known SRCR domains were used as queries to search iteratively against human non-redundant database with the target sequence length set to 250. BLOSUM62 amino acid substitution matrix with gap open penalty 11, and extension penalty 1, was used. Sequence masking was disabled and the PSI-BLAST threshold was set to 0.005. While searching, each PSI-BLAST query was iterated including new hits from the previous search until it converged, i.e. no new hits were found in subsequent searches. After each search iteration, results were checked for new SRCR proteins. This meticulous and robust method picked up all known SRCR domain-containing proteins along with novel proteins (Table 3).

Protein	Number of SRCR Domains	Chromosome
Spα	3	3
S4D	4	7
DMBT1	17*	10
CD5	3	11
CD6	3	11
CD163	9	12
M160	12	12
SSc5D	5	19
8D	8	10
D11#	11	10
HHIPL1	1	14

Table 3. List of SRCR-containing proteins. * - DMBT1 has been described as containing 14 SRCR domains; # - annotated as a pseudogene; in red denotes new SRCR domains from uncharacterized proteins.

From this genome-wide search we obtained a total of 76 SRCR group B domains distributed in 11 genes, each putatively encoding a varying number of SRCR domains. The eleven genes are spread across the genome on seven different chromosomes: chromosome 10 contains three SRCR group B-encoding genes, chromosomes 11 and 12 contain two each, and chromosomes 1, 7, 14 and 19 each contain a copy of just one SRCR-encoding gene. Among these genes and in addition to known domains from characterized genes, our search has uncovered 23 new putative group B domains, three of which represent previously unreported domains localized within the DMBT1 gene. The DMBT1 gene thus putatively encodes a maximum of 17 SRCR domains. Some controversy has existed on the number of SRCR domains within the DMBT1 molecule. Like other SRCR-containing proteins (Castro et al., 2007; Padilla et al., 2002), DMBT1 can be expressed as different isoforms arising by alternative splicing, which include or exclude individual SRCR domains (Mollenhauer et al., 1999). It is possible that the new DMBT1 domains have not been previously reported because they are not expressed in the tissues or cells investigated, however it is also plausible that the exons coding for these domains have been silenced during evolution and are now non-functional.

The remaining new domains belong to 3 new putative genes, one 8 domain-encoding gene (8D), one gene, annotated as a DMBT1-like pseudo-gene, that encodes 11 fragments of SRCR domains of variable lengths (D11), and a gene encoding a putative Hedgehog interacting protein-like 1 molecule (HHIP-like 1), which contains a single SRCR domain.

In order to analyze the sequence conservation and diversity of SRCR domains, we aligned all individual 76 SRCR group B domains using ClustalW2 (Thompson et al., 1994) with the default substitution matrix (Gonnet series) and gap opening and extension penalties of 10 and 0.2 respectively. Due to the sequence diversity in SRCR domains, several insertions and deletions were found in the multiple sequence alignment (Fig. 3).

To locate sequence patterns as well as conserved amino acids, the multiple sequence alignment was used to create a WebLogo (Crooks et al., 2004; http://weblogo.berkeley.edu).

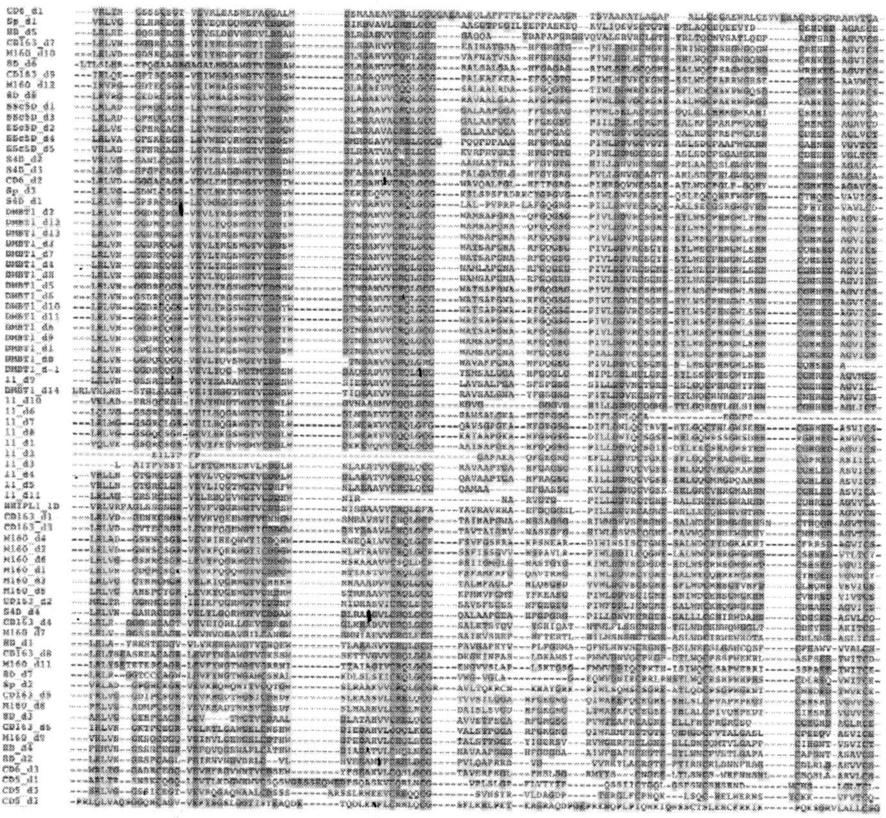

Fig. 3. Multiple sequence alignment of all SRCR domains.

The overall height of the stack indicates the sequence conservation at that position, while the height of symbols within the stack indicates the relative frequency of each amino acid at that position. It is apparent from the WebLogo that, although sequences vary substantially between SRCR domains, all cysteine residues (colored in red) are conserved across the family (Fig. 4).

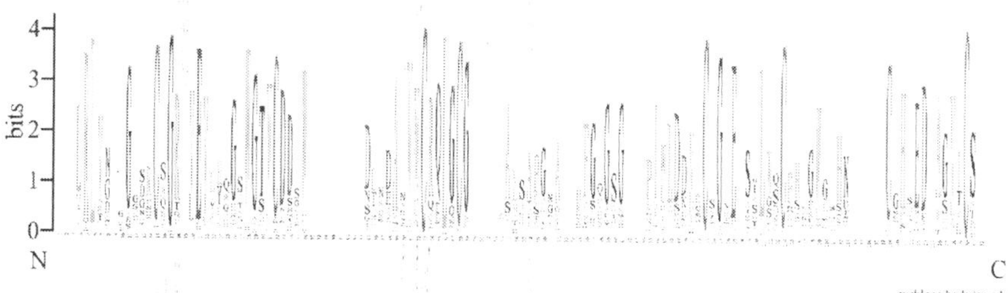

Fig. 4. Multiple sequence alignment of SRCR domains in WebLogo format.

In order to estimate evolutionary relationships among SRCR domains, we performed a phylogenetic analysis utilizing the maximum likelihood phylogenetic reconstruction method (proml) available in the phylip phylogenetic package (Felsenstein, 1989). Gaps were trimmed from the SRCR multiple sequence alignment prior to tree building and the Jones-Taylor-Thornton probability model employed with constant rate of change among sites. The reliability of internal branches was subsequently evaluated using 100 bootstrap samplings. SRCR domains exhibit very complex evolutionary relationships (Fig. 5). In the reconstructed phylogenetic tree, intra-protein domain clustering as well as inter-protein domain clusters were observed. Intra-domain clustering, as in the case of DMBT1, strongly suggests the evolution of these domains via sequential intragenic duplication. At the same time it is difficult to understand the inter-protein domain similarities. CD5, CD6, Spα, M160 and CD163 exhibit more diverse relationships. Among them, SRCR domains show greater inter than intra protein similarities. Given their low sequence similarities, it is uncertain whether the domains evolved through gene duplication and accumulated mutations have reduced sequence similarity, or if it is through a convergent evolution mechanism subsequent to domain shuffling. The similarities of domain pairs M160_d4-CD163_d1, M160_d7-CD163_d4 M160_d8-CD163_d5, M160_d9-CD163_d6, M160_d10-CD163_d7, M160_d11-CD163_d8, M160_d12–CD163_d9, CD5_d1-CD6_d3 and CD5_d2-S4D_d4 are strongly suggestive of inter-protein domain shuffling.

4. Concluding remarks - the completion of the SRCR group B family

In contrast to the complexity and variety of large protein families such as the G protein coupled receptor (GPCR) superfamily, which has nearly 800 genes in the human genome, corresponding to roughly 4% of the full protein-encoding genome, group B of the scavenger receptor cysteine-rich superfamily appears to be much more limited. So far it includes only 8 members in the entire human genome, although there are additionally 3 proteins described in other mammalians; SCART1 and SCART2 initially found in mice, and the 11 SRCR domain-containing protein WC1 expressed in cattle, sheep and swine. Also, the function of mammalian SRCR proteins seems to be restricted to the immune system, although the exact nature or biological role of the family is still to be fully determined.

In this study we set out to identify the remaining members of the SRCR group B family in order to obtain a clear understanding of the biological significance of this important group of proteins and to clarify some as yet unresolved questions regarding their evolution in mammalian species. We searched the human genome for the presence of SRCR-encoding genes using as probes the amino acid sequence of all reported human SRCR domains. Interestingly, one of the new members we have identified, HHIP-like 1, contains a single SRCR domain, which is unknown in the family. Moreover, the amino acid sequence corresponding to the SRCR domain constitutes only a small fraction of the total of the putative protein (13%). This is in contrast with most other members, whose amino acid content corresponding to SRCR domains relative to the whole of the protein is significantly higher, varying between 32% (SSc5D) and 92% (Spα). HHIP-like 1 is related to Hedgehog interacting protein, a regulatory component of the Hedgehog signaling pathway (Chuang and McMahon, 1999). However, unlike HHIP-like 1, HHIP does not contain an SRCR domain.

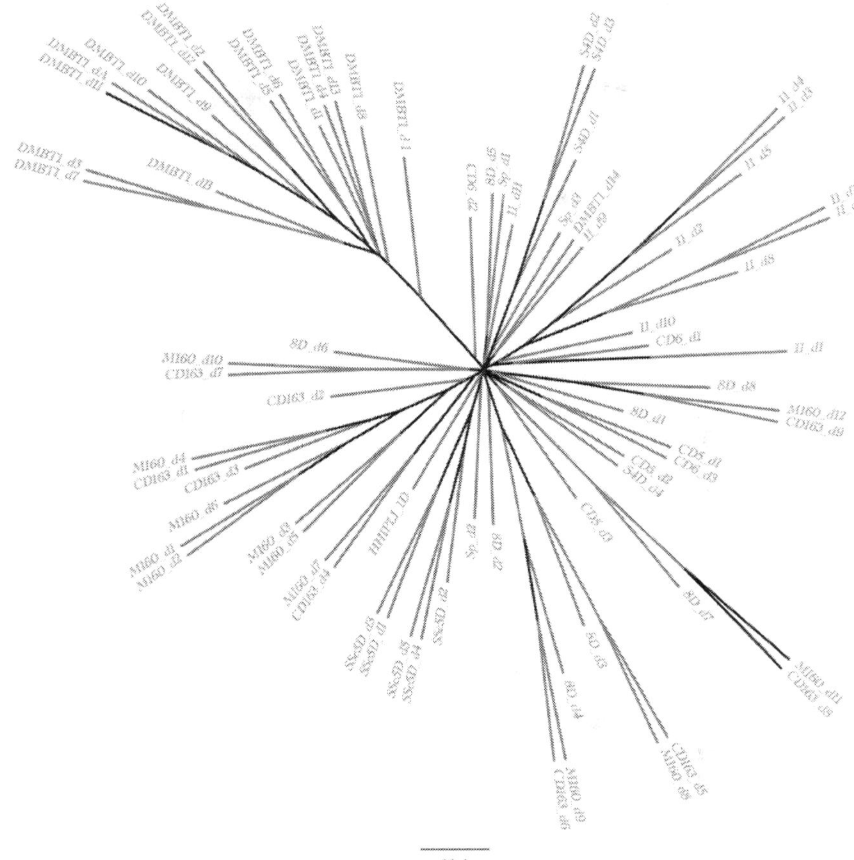

50.0

Fig. 5. Maximum likelihood phylogenetic estimation of human SRCR domains. Internal branch reliability was assessed using bootstrapping method (100 bootstrap replicates). Branches observed in more than 75 of 100 bootstrapped re-sampling are shown in red.

The second cluster of SRCR domains we have uncovered is located on chromosome 10 and includes 8 such domains, thus we provisionally termed it 8D. Using the predicted exon-derived protein sequence, we BLAST-searched other mammalian genomes and the proteins that we retrieved which were most similar to human 8D were mouse SCART1, bovine M160L, and mouse SCART2, whose ClustalW alignment scores were 70, 66 and 57, respectively (Fig. 6). Human 8D and mouse SCART1 have 64% identity for the entire sequence, while some individual SRCR domains share identities of close to, and even above 80%. We thus believe that 8D is the human ortholog of mouse SCART1. It remains to be seen whether human 8D can be expressed and produce a mature and functional protein, although we have detected several 8D transcripts of different sizes (C Gonçalves and A Carmo, unpublished).

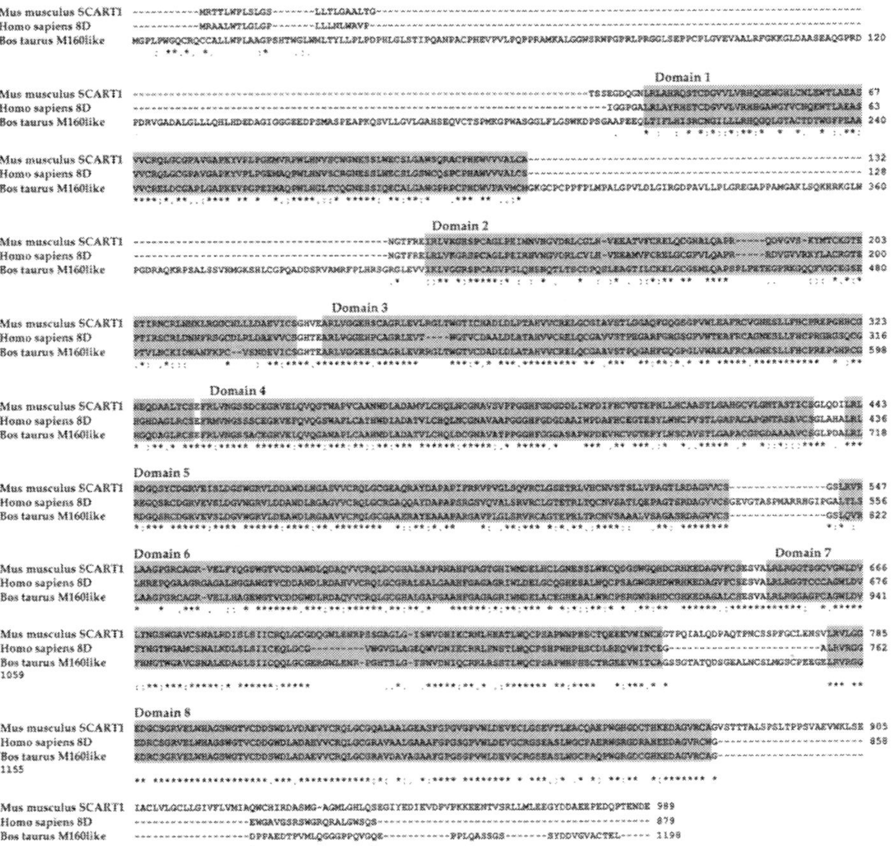

Fig. 6. Sequence alignment of mouse SCART1, human 8D and bovine M160-like protein.

The last new set of domains we have identified is located in a gene also on chromosome 10, but has been annotated as a non-coding pseudogene. Analysis of its putative sequence derived from the exon-like sequences in fact reveal that some stretches of several of the SRCR domains are missing, adding to a number of frameshifts and premature stop codons. Curiously, 11 SRCR-like domains can be identified, exactly the same number as the typical bovine WC1 protein. Comparison between the two sequences has failed however to definitely determine whether these two genes have the same evolutionary origin, as individually identifiable SRCR or SRCR-type domains seem to have already drifted apart significantly.

With the recognition of the three new genes, albeit none of them proven to be functional as yet together with the detection of three new putative SRCR-encoding sequences present in the DMBT1 gene, we are confident that we have completed the identification of the full set of scavenger receptor cysteine-rich group B domains in the human genome.

5. Acknowledgements

We thank Dr. Simon Lee for reviewing this manuscript. The work in Alexandre Carmo's laboratory is funded by FEDER through the Programa Operacional Factores de Competitividade – COMPETE, and by FCT – Fundação para a Ciência e a Tecnologia. Vattipally Sreenu is funded by the University of Oxford.

6. References

Altschul, S.F., Madden, T.L., Schäffer, A.A., Zhang, J., Zhang, Z., Miller, W., and Lipman, D.J. (1997). Gapped BLAST and PSI-BLAST: a new generation of protein database search programs. Nucleic Acids Res 25, 3389-3402.

Aruffo, A., Bowen, M.A., Patel, D.D., Haynes, B.F., Starling, G.C., Gebe, J.A., and Bajorath, J. (1997). CD6-ligand interactions: a paradigm for SRCR domain function? Immunol Today 18, 498-504.

Aruffo, A., Melnick, M.B., Linsley, P.S., and Seed, B. (1991). The lymphocyte glycoprotein CD6 contains a repeated domain structure characteristic of a new family of cell surface and secreted proteins. J Exp Med 174, 949-952.

Biancone, L., Bowen, M.A., Lim, A., Aruffo, A., Andres, G., and Stamenkovic, I. (1996). Identification of a novel inducible cell-surface ligand of CD5 on activated lymphocytes. J Exp Med 184, 811-819.

Bikker, F.J., Ligtenberg, A.J., Nazmi, K., Veerman, E.C., van't Hof, W., Bolscher, J.G., Poustka, A., Nieuw Amerongen, A.V., and Mollenhauer, J. (2002). Identification of the bacteria-binding peptide domain on salivary agglutinin (gp-340/DMBT1), a member of the scavenger receptor cysteine-rich superfamily. J Biol Chem 277, 32109-32115.

Calvo, J., Places, L., Padilla, O., Vilà, J.M., Vives, J., Bowen, M.A., and Lozano, F. (1999). Interaction of recombinant and natural soluble CD5 forms with an alternative cell surface ligand. Eur J Immunol 29, 2119-2129.

Castro, M.A.A., Nunes, R.J., Oliveira, M.I., Tavares, P.A., Simões, C., Parnes, J.R., Moreira, A., and Carmo, A.M. (2003). OX52 is the rat homologue of CD6: evidence for an effector function in the regulation of CD5 phosphorylation. Journal of Leukocyte Biology 73, 183-190.

Castro, M.A.A., Oliveira, M.I., Nunes, R.J., Fabre, S., Barbosa, R., Peixoto, A., Brown, M.H., Parnes, J.R., Bismuth, G., Moreira, A., et al. (2007). Extracellular Isoforms of CD6 generated by alternative splicing regulate targeting of CD6 to the immunological synapse. Journal of Immunology 178, 4351-4361.

Chuang, P.T., and McMahon, A.P. (1999). Vertebrate Hedgehog signalling modulated by induction of a Hedgehog-binding protein. Nature 397, 617-621.

Crooks, G.E., Hon, G., Chandonia, J.M., and Brenner, S.E. (2004). WebLogo: a sequence logo generator. Genome Res 14, 1188-1190.

Fabriek, B.O., van Bruggen, R., Deng, D.M., Ligtenberg, A.J., Nazmi, K., Schornagel, K., Vloet, R.P., Dijkstra, C.D., and van den Berg, T.K. (2009). The macrophage scavenger receptor CD163 functions as an innate immune sensor for bacteria. Blood 113, 887-892.

Felsenstein, J. (1989). Mathematics vs. Evolution: Mathematical Evolutionary Theory. Science 246, 941-942.

Freeman, M., Ashkenas, J., Rees, D.J., Kingsley, D.M., Copeland, N.G., Jenkins, N.A., and Krieger, M. (1990). An ancient, highly conserved family of cysteine-rich protein domains revealed by cloning type I and type II murine macrophage scavenger receptors. Proc Natl Acad Sci USA *87*, 8810-8814.

Garza-Garcia, A., Esposito, D., Rieping, W., Harris, R., Briggs, C., Brown, M.H., and Driscoll, P.C. (2008). Three-dimensional solution structure and conformational plasticity of the N-terminal scavenger receptor cysteine-rich domain of human CD5. J Mol Biol *378*, 129-144.

Gebe, J.A., Kiener, P.A., Ring, H.Z., Li, X., Francke, U., and Aruffo, A. (1997). Molecular cloning, mapping to human chromosome 1 q21-q23, and cell binding characteristics of Spalpha, a new member of the scavenger receptor cysteine-rich (SRCR) family of proteins. J Biol Chem *272*, 6151-6158.

Gimferrer, I., Farnós, M., Calvo, M., Mittelbrunn, M., Enrich, C., Sánchez-Madrid, F., Vives, J., and Lozano, F. (2003). The accessory molecules CD5 and CD6 associate on the membrane of lymphoid T cells. J Biol Chem *278*, 8564-8571.

Gonçalves, C.M., Castro, M.A.A., M., Henriques, T., Oliveira, M.I., Pinheiro, H.C., H., Oliveira, C., Sreenu, V.B., Evans, E.J., Davis, S.J., Moreira, A., *et al.* (2009). Molecular cloning and analysis of SSc5D, a new member of the scavenger receptor cysteine-rich superfamily. Molecular Immunology *46*, 2585-2596.

Graversen, J.H., Madsen, M., and Moestrup, S.K. (2002). CD163: a signal receptor scavenging haptoglobin-hemoglobin complexes from plasma. Int J Biochem Cell Biol *34*, 309-314.

Gronlund, J., Vitved, L., Lausen, M., Skjodt, K., and Holmskov, U. (2000). Cloning of a novel scavenger receptor cysteine-rich type I transmembrane molecule (M160) expressed by human macrophages. J Immunol *165*, 6406-6415.

Herzig, C.T., Waters, R.W., Baldwin, C.L., and Telfer, J.C. (2010). Evolution of the CD163 family and its relationship to the bovine gamma delta T cell co-receptor WC1. BMC Evol Biol *10*, 181.

Hohenester, E., Sasaki, T., and Timpl, R. (1999). Crystal structure of a scavenger receptor cysteine-rich domain sheds light on an ancient superfamily. Nat Struct Biol *6*, 228-232.

Holmskov, U., Mollenhauer, J., Madsen, J., Vitved, L., Gronlund, J., Tornoe, I., Kliem, A., Reid, K.B., Poustka, A., and Skjodt, K. (1999). Cloning of gp-340, a putative opsonin receptor for lung surfactant protein D. Proc Natl Acad Sci USA *96*, 10794-10799.

Jones, N.H., Clabby, M.L., Dialynas, D.P., Huang, H.J., Herzenberg, L.A., and Strominger, J.L. (1986). Isolation of complementary DNA clones encoding the human lymphocyte glycoprotein T1/Leu-1. Nature *323*, 346-349.

Kisielow, J., Kopf, M., and Karjalainen, K. (2008). SCART scavenger receptors identify a novel subset of adult gammadelta T cells. J Immunol *181*, 1710-1716.

Kristiansen, M., Graversen, J.H., Jacobsen, C., Sonne, O., Hoffman, H.J., Law, S.K., and Moestrup, S.K. (2001). Identification of the haemoglobin scavenger receptor. Nature *409*, 198-201.

Law, S.K., Micklem, K.J., Shaw, J.M., Zhang, X.P., Dong, Y., Willis, A.C., and Mason, D.Y. (1993). A new macrophage differentiation antigen which is a member of the scavenger receptor superfamily. Eur J Immunol *23*, 2320-2325.

Mollenhauer, J., Holmskov, U., Wiemann, S., Krebs, I., Herbertz, S., Madsen, J., Kioschis, P., Coy, J.F., and Poustka, A. (1999). The genomic structure of the DMBT1 gene: evidence for a region with susceptibility to genomic instability. Oncogene *18*, 6233-6240.

Mollenhauer, J., Wiemann, S., Scheurlen, W., Korn, B., Hayashi, Y., Wilgenbus, K.K., von Deimling, A., and Poustka, A. (1997). DMBT1, a new member of the SRCR superfamily, on chromosome 10q25.3-26.1 is deleted in malignant brain tumours. Nat Genet *17*, 32-39.

Moreno, J.A., Muñoz-García, B., Martín-Ventura, J.L., Madrigal-Matute, J., Orbe, J., Páramo, J.A., Ortega, L., Egido, J., and Blanco-Colio, L.M. (2009). The CD163-expressing macrophages recognize and internalize TWEAK: potential consequences in atherosclerosis. Atherosclerosis *207*, 103-110.

Ojala, J.R., Pikkarainen, T., Tuuttila, A., Sandalova, T., and Tryggvason, K. (2007). Crystal structure of the cysteine-rich domain of scavenger receptor MARCO reveals the presence of a basic and an acidic cluster that both contribute to ligand recognition. J Biol Chem *282*, 16654-16666.

Padilla, O., Pujana, M.A., López-de la Iglesia, A., Gimferrer, I., Arman, M., Vilà, J.M., Places, L., Vives, J., Estivill, X., and Lozano, F. (2002). Cloning of S4D-SRCRB, a new soluble member of the group B scavenger receptor cysteine-rich family (SRCR-SF) mapping to human chromosome 7q11.23. Immunogenetics *54*, 621-634.

Pospisil, R., Silverman, G.J., Marti, G.E., Aruffo, A., Bowen, M.A., and Mage, R.G. (2000). CD5 is a potential selecting ligand for B-cell surface immunoglobulin: a possible role in maintenance and selective expansion of normal and malignant B cells. Leuk Lymphoma *36*, 353-365.

Resnick, D., Pearson, A., and Krieger, M. (1994). The SRCR superfamily: a family reminiscent of the Ig superfamily. Trends Biochem Sci *19*, 5-8.

Rodamilans, B., Muñoz, I.G., Bragado-Nilsson, E., Sarrias, M.R., Padilla, O., Blanco, F.J., Lozano, F., and Montoya, G. (2007). Crystal structure of the third extracellular domain of CD5 reveals the fold of a group B scavenger cysteine-rich receptor domain. J Biol Chem *282*, 12669-12677.

Sarrias, M.R., Roselló, S., Sánchez-Barbero, F., Sierra, J.M., Vila, J., Yélamos, J., Vives, J., Casals, C., and Lozano, F. (2005). A role for human Sp alpha as a pattern recognition receptor. J Biol Chem *280*, 35391-35398.

Sarrias, M.R., Farnós, M., Mota, R., Sánchez-Barbero, F., Ibáñez, A., Gimferrer, I., Vera, J., Fenutría, R., Casals, C., Yélamos, J., *et al.* (2007). CD6 binds to pathogen-associated molecular patterns and protects from LPS-induced septic shock. Proc Natl Acad Sci USA *104*, 11724-11729.

Sarrias, M.R., Grønlund, J., Padilla, O., Madsen, J., Holmskov, U., and Lozano, F. (2004). The Scavenger Receptor Cysteine-Rich (SRCR) domain: an ancient and highly conserved protein module of the innate immune system. Crit Rev Immunol *24*, 1-37.

Somoza, J.R., Ho, J.D., Luong, C., Ghate, M., Sprengeler, P.A., Mortara, K., Shrader, W.D., Sperandio, D., Chan, H., McGrath, M.E., *et al.* (2003). The structure of the extracellular region of human hepsin reveals a serine protease domain and a novel scavenger receptor cysteine-rich (SRCR) domain. Structure *11*, 1123-1131.

Thompson, J.D., Higgins, D.G., and Gibson, T.J. (1994). CLUSTAL W: improving the sensitivity of progressive multiple sequence alignment through sequence weighting, position-specific gap penalties and weight matrix choice. Nucleic Acids Res 22, 4673-4680.

Van de Velde, H., von Hoegen, I., Luo, W., Parnes, J.R., and Thielemans, K. (1991). The B-cell surface protein CD72/Lyb-2 is the ligand for CD5. Nature 351, 662-665.

Vera, J., Fenutría, R., Cañadas, O., Figueras, M., Mota, R., Sarrias, M.R., Williams, D.L., Casals, C., Yelamos, J., and Lozano, F. (2009). The CD5 ectodomain interacts with conserved fungal cell wall components and protects from zymosan-induced septic shock-like syndrome. Proc Natl Acad Sci USA 106, 1506-1511.

Wijngaard, P.L., Metzelaar, M.J., MacHugh, N.D., Morrison, W.I., and Clevers, H.C. (1992). Molecular characterization of the WC1 antigen expressed specifically on bovine CD4-CD8- gamma delta T lymphocytes. J Immunol 149, 3273-3277.

11

Assessing Multiple Sequence Alignments Using Visual Tools

Catherine L. Anderson[1], Cory L. Strope[2] and Etsuko N. Moriyama[2,3]
[1]Department of Computer Science and Engineering
[2]School of Biological Sciences and
[3]Center for Plant Science Innovation
University of Nebraska-Lincoln,
U.S.A.

1. Introduction

Bioinformatics and molecular evolutionary analyses most often start with comparing DNA or amino acid sequences by aligning them. Pairwise alignment, for example, is used to measure the similarities between a query sequence and each of those in a database in BLAST similarity search, the most used bioinformatics tool (Altschul *et al.*, 1990; Camacho *et al.*, 2009). Evolutionary history among sequences can be reflected better when more than two sequences are aligned, in a multiple sequence alignment (MSA). When building an MSA, we assume that the sequences compared are derived from a common ancestral sequence. Then the process of MSA building is to infer homologous positions between the input sequences and place gaps in the sequences in order to align these homologous positions. These gaps represent evolutionary events of their own. Gaps (also called indels) are caused by either insertions or deletions of characters (nucleotides or amino acids) on a particular lineage of sequences during the evolution. Building an MSA is, therefore, to reconstruct the evolutionary history of the sequences involved. While it is easy to understand that the quality of MSAs affects the quality of phylogenetic tree reconstruction, the effect of MSA quality reaches far beyond this. Some examples of bioinformatics methods that utilize information extracted from MSAs include: profile building in similarity search (*e.g.*, PSI-BLAST: Altschul *et al.*, 1997), motif/profile recognition (*e.g.*, PROSITE: Hulo *et al.*, 2008), profile hidden Markov models for protein families/domains (*e.g.*, Pfam: Finn *et al.*, 2010), and protein secondary-structure prediction (for review, see Pirovano & Heringa, 2010). There are numerous bioinformatics and molecular evolutionary analyses that are affected by MSA quality and they can be benefited by having reliable MSAs.

Despite the significance of having good MSAs, assessing MSA quality is far from straightforward. Measuring the quality of MSAs requires two components: a benchmark dataset and a scoring method. A benchmark dataset includes *reference alignments*. These alignments are considered to represent the evolutionary history of the sequences truthfully. The same set of sequences included in a reference alignment is then aligned using the MSA methods to be tested. The *reconstructed* MSA can be compared with the reference MSA using a scoring method and the quality of the reconstructed MSA is assessed compared to the reference MSA. Problems exist both in benchmark MSA datasets as well as in the methods used to measure the MSA quality.

The majority of benchmark MSA datasets are built on real sequences by aligning structural elements and in some cases with hand-curation (*e.g.*, PREFAB: Edgar, 2004b; OXBench: Raghava *et al.*, 2003; HOMSTRAD: Stebbings & Mizuguchi, 2004; BAliBASE: Thompson *et al.*, 2005; Thompson *et al.*, 2011; SABmark: Van Walle *et al.*, 2005). Since the true evolutionary history of the sequences included in these datasets is unknown, positional homologies among sequences are unknown and the accuracy of these reference MSAs is subjective (some issues on benchmark datasets, see Edgar, 2010). Some other benchmark datasets are generated by simulating sequence evolution based on specific molecular evolutionary models (*e.g.*, IRMBASE: Subramanian *et al.*, 2005). The advantage of these simulated datasets is that the evolutionary history of sequences (the guide tree) is known and the *true* alignment is given as an outcome of the simulation. Since the evolutionary history is known, these datasets can be used to assess the quality of both MSAs as well as phylogenetic reconstruction methods. The disadvantage is that the biological correctness of the simulation relies solely on the evolutionary models used.

Issues also exist in the methods used to measure the quality of MSAs. While a number of statistics has been proposed (*e.g.*, Position Shift Error score: Cline *et al.*, 2002; sum-of-pairs score and column score: Thompson *et al.*, 1999), there is no definite answer how to measure 'biological correctness' of MSAs. It remains for the end user to incorporate the statistics into their evaluation of this 'biological correctness'.

Due to its significant impact on many bioinformatics and molecular evolutionary studies, MSA is one of the most scrutinized bioinformatics fields (Kemena & Notredame, 2009; Thompson *et al.*, 2011). However, assessment of MSAs is usually reserved for power users. Often regular users simply run one MSA method and proceed to the next analysis without examining their alignment output (Morrison, 2009b). Considering how MSA quality affects the outcomes of further analysis, assessment of MSAs, however, should be included as regular part of sequence analysis. In order to facilitate comparative analysis of MSAs, we recently developed a software package called SuiteMSA (Anderson *et al.*, 2011). SuiteMSA provides several alignment-viewing tools that allow the user to compare MSAs both visually and quantitatively. SuiteMSA also includes a feature-rich biological sequence simulator, indel-Seq-Gen v2.1 (Strope *et al.*, 2009), with a user-friendly graphical interface, allowing the users to generate their own benchmark alignments for testing various MSAs.

In this chapter, we first review some of the statistics used to assess the quality of MSAs focusing on those used in SuiteMSA. We then describe how MSA comparison can be actually performed using various MSA viewers available in SuiteMSA. Five examples are chosen from diverse types of alignment problems: proteins with secondary structures, transmembrane proteins, proteins with length variation, simulated protein sequences, and ribosomal DNAs. These comparisons illustrate how various MSA methods perform differently based on their underlying assumptions. We also discuss how different alignment statistics should be used for assessing MSAs and their limitations.[1]

---

[1] All input files and alignments shown in this chapter are available from the following website:
http://bioinfolab.unl.edu/~canderson/SuiteMSA/supplement.html

2. Statistics used to assess multiple sequence alignments

There are two types of alignment statistics. The first type of statistics is used to characterize a single alignment for the level of conservation in each alignment position and for various gap measures. These are descriptive measures for a specific alignment and should not be interpreted as a measure of the alignment quality. The second type of statistics can be used to compare any two alignments containing the same sequences.

2.1 Descriptive statistics on a single multiple sequence alignment

We describe the following two descriptive statistics: information content and average hydrophobicity. Both are calculated on a per column basis.

2.1.1 Information content

The Shannon entropy is a measure of the amount of uncertainty (Shannon, 1948). When it is applied to MSA analysis, it is interpreted as a measure of the diversity of characters within a given alignment column (Schneider & Stephens, 1990). The amount of information conveyed, or information content, is given by the decrease in this uncertainty and represents the level of sequence conservation within a column.

Formally defined, the entropy for the kth column of an alignment is given as:

$$H(k) = -\sum_{s \in k} f(s,k) \log_2 f(s,k),\qquad(1)$$

where s is any character contained in column k and $f(s,k)$ is the frequency of s as it appears in column k. If there are x_s of the character s in the column that has x of non-gap characters, $f(s,k)$ is calculated as x_s/x. The information content in the kth column is given as:

$$I(k) = \log_2 S - H(k),\qquad(2)$$

where S is the number of character types for an alignment (4 for a nucleotide alignment and 20 for an amino acid alignment). Both $H(k)$ and $I(k)$ have their units in bits.

It can be seen from these equations that the higher the number of distinct characters within a column, the higher the entropy value (H) and thus, the lower the information content (I) in the column. For a completely conserved column c, one which contains only one type of characters, the entropy $H(c)$ is 0; thus it contains the maximum amount of information. For a nucleotide alignment this maximum value is 2, while for an amino acid alignment it is 4.32.

Note that gaps are not considered in calculating $f(s,k)$ in equation (1). Excluding gaps from calculation could inflate the information content for a column that contains many gaps. A single character in a column of gaps, for example, can be erroneously attributed a maximum information content. In order to compensate for this situation, the column information calculation is normalized by multiplying each column's information content by the proportion of non-gap characters present in the column (Schneider & Stephens, 1990).

While the information content is a measure applicable to a single alignment, it can be useful to compare the information statistics among alternate alignments for trends.

2.1.2 Average hydrophobicity

Hydrophobicity is one of the most useful properties of amino acid residues, which is directly related to the function and structure of proteins. Many different types of hydrophobicity indices are available (Kawashima *et al.*, 2008). By plotting hydrophobicity values along the sequence, the presence of functional/structural regions (*e.g.*, membrane-spanning regions in transmembrane proteins or core regions in globular proteins) can be predicted. For MSA analysis, comparing the distribution of hydrophobicity along the alignment among different MSAs can provide a visual aid for evaluating the consistency between alignments. Equation (3) below shows how the average hydrophobicity for column k, $h(k)$, is calculated for an alignment containing N sequences:

$$h(k) = \frac{\left(\sum_{i=1}^{N} h_i\right)}{N}, \tag{3}$$

where h_i is the hydrophobicity index value of ith residue of column k. In SuiteMSA, the hydrophobicity index provided by Kyte and Doolittle (1982) is used and the value of 0 is assigned for a gap.

2.2 Measuring the similarity between two multiple sequence alignments

As mentioned earlier, many statistics have been proposed to compare two MSAs. The sum-of-pairs score (SPS) and the column score (CS) are the two used most often. Both scores were proposed by Thompson *et al.* (1999). The values of these two scores react differently to varying inconsistency between MSAs compared.

When comparing two alignments, one is referred to as the *reference alignment* and the other the *test alignment*. The test alignment is compared against the reference. If the reference alignment is known to be 'correct', these statistics can be used to measure the alignment quality. As mentioned before, however, the 'correctness' of an alignment can be highly subjective in the case of many available benchmark datasets. An alignment can be said to be truly 'correct' only if its exact evolutionary history is known and if the alignment reflects it correctly. Usually it is possible only if the alignment was generated by a sequence evolution simulator. Even if the 'true' alignment can be obtained by sequence simulation, however, 'biological realism' of the evolutionary model used with the simulation becomes an issue. In this chapter, SPS and CS are thus used more as general comparison measures.

2.2.1 Sum-of-pairs score (SPS)

To calculate the SPS for a test MSA against the reference MSA, each pair of characters within an alignment column is treated as an alignment unit. The per-column SPS is the number of alignment units within a specific column of the test alignment that are also aligned in the same column of the reference alignment. The total of all per-column scores from the entire alignment is obtained and normalized by dividing by the total number of character pairs. This is formally defined as follows:

i.   Let an alignment of length M containing N sequences be an N by M array, **A**. Then the character in the ith sequence and k^{th} column of the alignment is identified as A_{ik}.

ii. Let there be two alignments for comparison: alignment $\mathbf{A_r}$ (referred to as the reference alignment) of length M_r containing N sequences and alignment **A** (referred to as the test alignment) of length M containing N sequence, where M_r and M can be but are not required to be equal.

iii. To examine the kth column of **A**, consisting of elements $A_{1k}, A_{2k}, \ldots A_{nk}$, let p_{ijk} be defined as:

$$\begin{cases} p_{ijk} = 1 \text{ if } A_{ik} \text{ and } A_{jk} \text{ of alignment } \mathbf{A} \text{ are in the same column of } \mathbf{A}_r, \\ p_{ijk} = 0 \text{ otherwise.} \end{cases} \quad (4)$$

iv. Then the score for k^{th} column of $\mathbf{A}$ is defined as:

$$S_k = \sum_{i=1}^{N} \sum_{j=i+1}^{N} p_{ijk}. \quad (5)$$

v. The score for the full alignment $\mathbf{A}$ is given as:

$$SPS = \frac{\left(\sum_{k=1}^{M} S_k \right)}{\left(\sum_{k=1}^{M_r} S_{rk} \right)}, \quad (6)$$

where S_{rk} is the score for the reference alignment, $\mathbf{A}_r$. This reference score is calculated as $S_{rk} = x(x-1)/2$ where x is the number of characters in column k excluding gaps. The maximum possible SPS is a value of 1.0 when $\mathbf{A} = \mathbf{A}_r$. The SPS is not symmetric in that the score will be different if the reference and test alignments are switched.

2.2.2 Column score (CS)

To calculate the CS, the test and reference alignments are compared column-wise. The column score is the number of 'matched' columns between the test alignment and the reference alignment divided by the total number of 'considered' columns in the test alignment. This is formally defined as follows:

i. For the kth column of $\mathbf{A}$:

$$\begin{cases} C_k = 1 \text{ if all the characters in the column } k \text{ of alignment } \mathbf{A} \text{ are matched in alignment } \mathbf{A}_r, \\ C_k = 0 \text{ otherwise.} \end{cases} \quad (7)$$

ii. The column score for the full alignment $\mathbf{A}$ is given as:

$$CS = \frac{\left(\sum_{k=1}^{M} C_k \right)}{M}. \quad (8)$$

In SuiteMSA, two types of CS are calculated: un-gapped and gapped.

Un-gapped CS: This score considers only un-gapped columns (columns that have no gaps), where M of equation (8) equals the number of un-gapped columns in the alignment (shown in red in Fig. 1). For example, if an alignment has 500 columns and only 200 contain no gaps and of these 200, 150 columns are exactly as they appear in the reference alignment, then the un-gapped CS is given as 150/200 = 0.75. The disadvantage to these criteria is that very gappy alignments with very few un-gapped columns can still produce a high column score if those un-gapped columns are all 'matched'. For instance, a test alignment of any length, even if only one column is un-gapped and matches a column in the reference alignment, will yield a column score of 1.0.

```
        Reference alignment              Test alignment
                 11                               11
         12345678901                      12345678901
    T1   A-WCD-EFG-X                  T1  A-WCD-EFG-X
    T2   AW-CD-EFG-X                  T2  AW-C-DEF-GX
    T3   AW-CDEF--GX                  T3  AW-C-DEF-GX
    T4   AW-CDEF--GX                  T4  AW-C-DEF-GX
    T5   A-WCD-EF-GX                  T5  A-WC-DEF-GX
    T6   A-WCD-EFG-X                  T6  A-WC-DEFGX-
    T7   A-WCD-EFG-X                  T7  A-WC-DEFG-X
                                          ++++
```

Fig. 1. Illustration of the column score calculation. In the Test alignment, 'un-gapped' columns are shown in red. 'Un-gapped matched' columns are indicated with red '+' under the alignment. For 'gapped' CS, all but 5th column of the Test alignment are considered and these columns are shown in blue as well as red. However, only those columns indicated with '+' (both red and blue) are counted as 'matched' against the Reference alignment. In this example, 'un-gapped' CS is 0.5 (2 out of 4 columns are matched) and 'gapped' CS is 0.4 (4 out of 10 columns are considered to be matched).

Gapped CS: This score considers columns that contain more than 20% non-gap characters. To be 'matched' the characters that appear in a column of the test alignment must appear in a column of the reference alignment with no additional characters. For example, in Fig. 1, all but 5th column of the Test alignment are considered. The columns 6-11 are not counted as 'matched'. This is because, for example, while in the Test alignment, 'G' of T1 position 9 is aligned only with 'G' of T6 and T7, in the Reference alignment, 'G' of T1 position 9 is aligned with 'G' of T2 as well as T6 and T7. The advantage to 'gapped' CS is that it allows more columns to be considered; columns with gaps can be matched if the same non-gap characters (but no other characters) are aligned in the reference alignment. This does offset the disadvantage of the potentially inflated un-gapped CS mentioned before.

Exclusion of any alignment columns that include gaps can be justified since gaps represent evolutionary events that are often not traceable. They are either the insertion of new characters, the deletion of existing characters, or a combination of the two. Therefore, while they are represented by the same gap symbol in the alignment, they are not equivalent. It is often not possible to infer if a gap in one alignment was generated by the same event as a gap in the second alignment. On the other hand, excluding all alignment positions with gaps even for those containing only a small number of gaps may not be desirable. In SuiteMSA, as described above, a column is considered as long as it contains a number of non-gap characters above the 20% threshold. A third column score is also provided in SuiteMSA as '% consistency', which considers all columns regardless of the number of gaps. Comparing these values can help assessing the difference between two alignments.

2.2.3 Implementation of SPS and CS

In addition to SuiteMSA, several implementations of SPS and CS are available as listed in Table 1. Note that not all of these programs generate the same value for the same alignment. The difference is caused by different criteria used to define, for example, 'matched' columns and which columns should be 'considered' for counting. When comparing scores, due to this inconsistency among programs, it is necessary to use the same implementation of scoring methods.

Program	Reference	Note
bali_score	(Thompson *et al.*, 1999)	standalone; C program; MSF format.
qscore	(Edgar, 2004b)	standalone; C++ program; calculates Q score (SPS), TC (CS), Modeler score, and Shift scores; fasta format.
VerAlign		available from http://www.ibi.vu.nl/programs/veralignwww MSF format.
SuiteMSA	(Anderson *et al.*, 2011)	part of the GUI software; fasta format.

Table 1. Programs available to calculate SPS and CS. The actual SPS and CS values for alignments discussed in this chapter given by different programs are available from our website (see footnote 1).

3. Visual inspection of MSAs

In the following sections, using various examples, we will show how MSAs can be compared using SuiteMSA's visual tools and statistics. See Anderson *et al.* (2011) and SuiteMSA User's Manual for detailed description of various tools available in SuiteMSA. Among the numerous MSA methods currently available, we chose seven MSA methods listed in Table 2 for comparative analysis. We chose these methods based on their general popularity in various bioinformatics analyses, their availability, and some of their features useful for aligning particular types of proteins (*e.g.*, transmembrane proteins).

Method (version)	Reference	Description
ClustalW2 (2.1)	(Larkin *et al.*, 2007)	Progressive alignment; weights sequences based on branch lengths and adjusts gap penalties; one of the earliest methods implemented. http://www.clustal.org/
MUSCLE (3.8.31)	(Edgar, 2004a, 2004b)	Progressive alignment; fast distance estimation using kmer counting; iterative refinement using tree-dependent restricted partitioning. http://www.drive5.com/muscle/
MAFFT (6.843)	(Katoh & Toh, 2008)	Progressive alignment; L-INS-i method is used for iterative refinement incorporating local pairwise alignment information in this study. http://mafft.cbrc.jp/alignment/software/
Probalign (1.4)	(Roshan & Livesay, 2006)	Uses partition function posterior probability estimates to compute maximum expected accuracy alignments. [eProbalign] http://probalign.njit.edu/probalign/login
PRANK (web version)	(Löytynoja & Goldman, 2005, 2008)	Phylogeny-aware gap handling; not meant for divergent sequences; recognizes insertions and deletions as distinct evolutionary events. [webPRANK] http://www.ebi.ac.uk/goldman-srv/webprank/

Method (version)	Reference	Description
PRALINE (web version)	(Pirovano *et al.*, 2008)	Progressive alignment with profile pre-processing; incorporates secondary structure and transmembrane information; PSIPRED and Phobious (for GPCR alignment) chosen for this study. http://www.ibi.vu.nl/programs/pralinewww/
PROMALS (web version)	(Pei & Grishin, 2007)	Progressive alignment enhanced with profiles and secondary structure information; a hidden Markov model using a combined scoring of amino acids and secondary structures. http://prodata.swmed.edu/promals/

Table 2. The seven MSA methods compared in this study. All methods are used with the default options unless noted otherwise.

3.1 Examining a protein MSA with secondary structure prediction

When protein sequences are aligned, it is useful to identify the location of their functional or structural landmarks to determine if such landmarks are aligned properly. Useful landmarks include secondary structures, transmembrane regions, and conserved domains or motifs. Color-coding MSAs based on properties of amino acids also helps determine if the distribution of different types of amino acids is consistent or varied among sequences.

3.1.1 Inspecting a single MSA

In Fig. 2, eight protein sequences of the lipocalin family (Pfam PF00061; Finn *et al.*, 2010) are aligned. The lipocalin family proteins are highly divergent at the sequence level yet highly conserved at the structure level (Flower *et al.*, 2000). The common structural feature among these proteins is a single eight-stranded antiparallel beta-barrel. The MSA shown in Fig. 2 was originally produced using PROMALS3D (Pei *et al.*, 2008) with manual adjustment (Strope *et al.*, 2009). Using SuiteMSA's secondary structure viewer, we aligned the lipocalin MSA with the secondary structures predicted from the eight sequences using PSIPRED (Jones, 1999). It can be seen in Fig. 2 that eight beta-strand regions (shown as brown-colored clusters of 'E' letters) are clearly well aligned with very few gaps.

Fig. 2 also shows the per-column information content displayed as a blue bar chart below the MSA. The information content reflects the level of conservation for each column. This display is especially useful when dealing with alignments containing a large number of sequences and/or long sequences. When comparing such large alignments, the information content display can be used to quickly scan along the alignment to search for, *e.g.*, high conservation areas (indicated as high information content regions). In Fig. 2, fully conserved columns (positions 51, 53, 148, 150, and 179 are readily identifiable by the full-height bars. In fact, these positions are part of the three conserved motifs shared among lipocalin proteins. These motifs (indicated as M1, M2, and M3 in Fig. 2) are described as "structurally conserved regions" (SCR1, 2, and 3, respectively) by Flower *et al.* (2000). SCR1 corresponds to PROSITE lipocalin motif (PS00213; Hulo *et al.*, 2008).

Several summary statistics are given at the top of MSA Viewer window (Fig. 2). The following statistics are available:

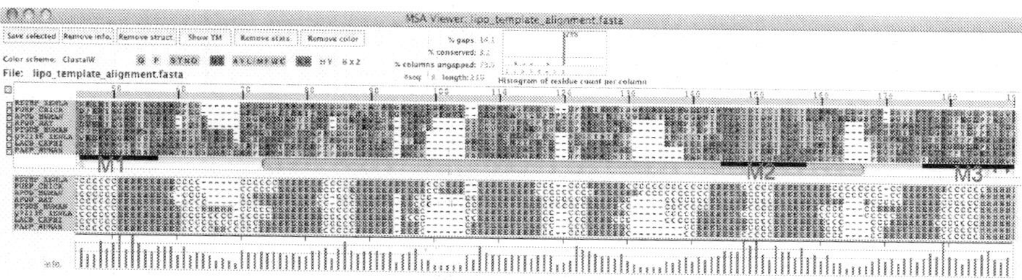

Fig. 2. The alignment of eight protein sequences from the lipocalin family. The MSA Viewer is used to display the MSA aligned with the predicted secondary structures. Black thick lines marked with M1, M2, and M3 indicate the locations of the three conserved motifs. Symbols used for the secondary structure prediction are: H (green) for helix, C (cream) for coil, and E (brown) for beta-strand. The alignment statistics are shown above the MSA. The column information content is displayed as a blue bar chart at the bottom indicating the level of conservation for each column.

- % gaps. The number of gap symbols within the alignment divided by the total number of characters within the alignment (alignment length times number of sequences). This should not be confused with the number of insertion/deletion events in the alignment since an individual event can span multiple positions.
- % conserved. The number of completely conserved columns divided by the total number of columns. A conserved column is defined as an un-gapped column containing a single type of characters.
- % columns un-gapped. The number of un-gapped columns divided by the total number of columns.
- The histogram of character count per column. This histogram represents the gappiness of the MSA using a non-gap character frequency distribution (the inverse of gap frequency distribution). For the lipocalin MSA, 73% of the columns have no gap (this is also shown as % columns un-gapped).

3.1.2 Comparing two MSAs

In Fig. 3A, we compared the previously shown lipocalin MSA (listed as 'Reference') with the MSA generated by ClustalW2 using the MSA Comparator. Under the blue selection bar and the green range bar, alignment positions are color-coded for the consistency with respect to the reference MSA. Blue characters illustrate where completely consistent columns are, and red characters depict those inconsistently aligned. Compared against the reference, ClustalW2 MSA is more compacted with very few gaps, making the alignment shorter (201 positions compared to 219 in the reference). We further examined the ClustalW2 MSA using the secondary structure display function of the MSA Viewer. As illustrated in Fig. 3B, the ClustalW2 MSA does not have the beta-strand regions (shown as brown-colored clusters of 'E' letters) aligned as well as the reference MSA does.

As mentioned earlier, the information content is the indicator of sequence divergence within a single MSA, and not a direct comparison between two alignments. However, as shown in Fig. 3A, the information content distributions (blue and green bar charts) can be compared between the alignments. It is especially useful when dealing with large alignments containing

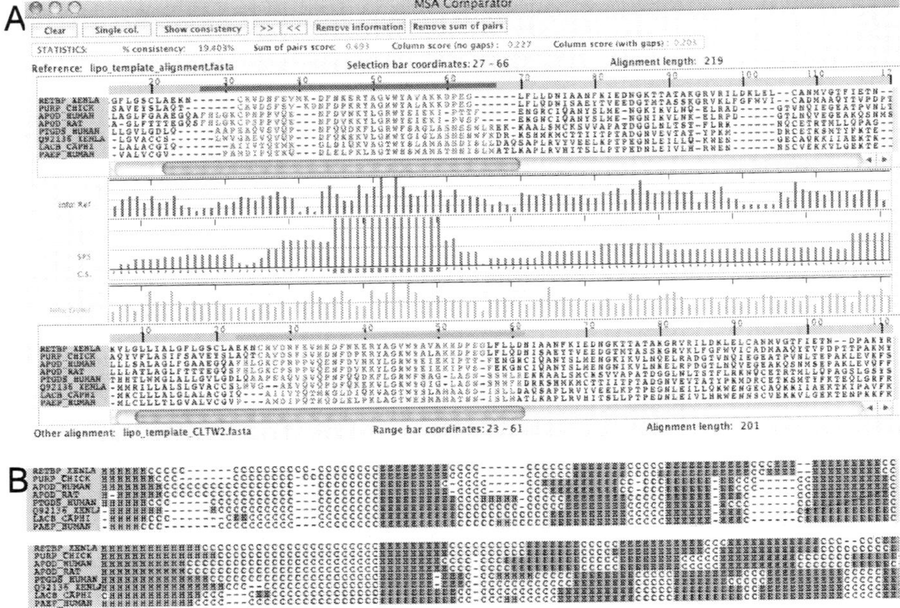

Fig. 3. Comparison of the ClustalW2 MSA with the reference alignment of the lipocalin family. A. The two MSAs are compared using the MSA Comparator (the reference and ClustalW2 alignments shown at the top and bottom, respectively). The column SPS display (brown bar chart) is positioned between the two MSAs and is aligned to the ClustalW2 alignment. At the bottom of the column SPS display is the column score (CS) indicator. The un-gapped CS uses those columns marked with purple squares, and the gapped CS uses columns marked with both purple and red squares (small and large squares indicate 'considered' and 'matched' columns, respectively). Summary statistics shown above the reference alignment include: % consistency, SPS, and two types of CS. B. The MSA Viewer is used to generate the secondary structure representation for the reference and ClustalW2 MSAs (shown at the top and bottom, respectively). Symbols used for the secondary structure prediction are: H (green) for helix, C (cream) for coil, and E (brown) for beta-strand.

many/long sequences. On the other hand, SPS is the result of a direct comparison between two MSAs. The per-column SPS (brown bar chart) displayed in Fig. 3A clearly shows where the test alignment (ClustalW2 in this case) is consistent (and to what degree) with the reference.

3.1.3 Comparing multiple MSAs

In Fig. 4, we compared MSAs produced by four methods against the reference lipocalin family MSA (MSA 1). Using the Pixel Plot, we can clearly see different patterns among the MSAs. The magenta-highlighted areas illustrate how the corresponding characters are aligned (or not) in each MSA. The PRALINE MSA (MSA 2) is fairly consistent compared to the reference MSA. This is expected since PRALINE uses secondary structure information when optimizing the alignments. On the other hand, MAFFT, MUSCLE, and ClustalW2 MSAs show a similar displacement of the same sequences, apparent from the ragged edges

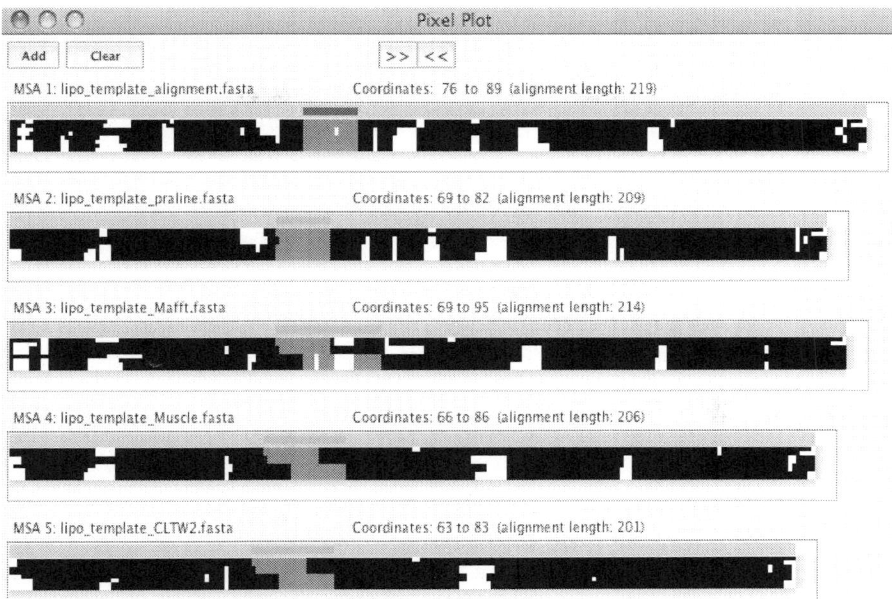

Fig. 4. Comparison of the lipocalin family reference MSA (MSA 1) with four reconstructed MSAs (PRALINE, MAFFT, MUSCLE, and ClustalW2). The Pixel Plot is used to show the alignment patterns with each non-gap character represented with a solid colored pixel and a gap with a blank pixel. Characters corresponding to those under the blue selection bar for the reference MSA are highlighted in magenta in all MSAs. The green range bars for MSAs 2-5 show the column ranges where corresponding characters are located.

of the magenta areas. Alignments generated by MAFFT, MUSCLE, and ClustalW2 (MSAs 3-5) are roughly consistent to each other, but not consistent with the reference and PRALINE alignments. All four MSA methods tested produced shorter alignments (201-214 positions) compared to the reference alignment (219 positions). The shortest alignment was obtained from ClustalW2 (201 positions).

4. Aligning transmembrane protein sequences

In the previous section, we showed that comparing MSAs and secondary structure predictions help us assess the quality of MSAs. In this section, we will examine alignments of another type of proteins, transmembrane proteins.

4.1 G-protein coupled receptors

G protein-coupled receptor (GPCR) proteins contain seven transmembrane (TM) regions. They constitute a large protein superfamily grouped into three major and several minor classes (Horn *et al.*, 2003; Vroling *et al.*, 2011). Although the TM regions are relatively constant in length (22~24 amino acids or aa), the lengths of the N-/C-terminal and loop regions are highly varied especially among different classes (Inoue *et al.*, 2004; Wistrand *et al.*, 2006). GPCR sequences are also highly divergent. These features make aligning GPCR sequences a challenge. We sampled 25 protein sequences from three major classes of GPCRs (Classes A, B, and C). The lengths of these GPCR sequences vary from 201 to 972 aa.

4.2 Alignment of GPCR sequences

Fig. 5 shows the alignment of the 25 GPCRs generated by PRALINE (showing only the first three TM area). Since PRALINE incorporates information from secondary structure, TM structure, as well as profiles based on PSI-BLAST similarity search (Table 2), it is expected to perform well in aligning TM regions. In order to confirm this, TM regions were predicted for each of the 25 GPCR sequences using MEMSAT3 (http://bioinf.cs.ucl.ac.uk/psipred/; Nugent & Jones, 2009). The predicted TM structural information was then aligned with the PRALINE MSA. Fig. 5 shows that the predicted TM regions (depicted with 'X' in green color) are clearly well aligned and visualized as green-colored clusters. The 'hydrophobicity' color scheme used for the MSA display as well as the average column hydrophobicity plot also confirm that more hydrophobic amino acids are found in predicted TM regions.

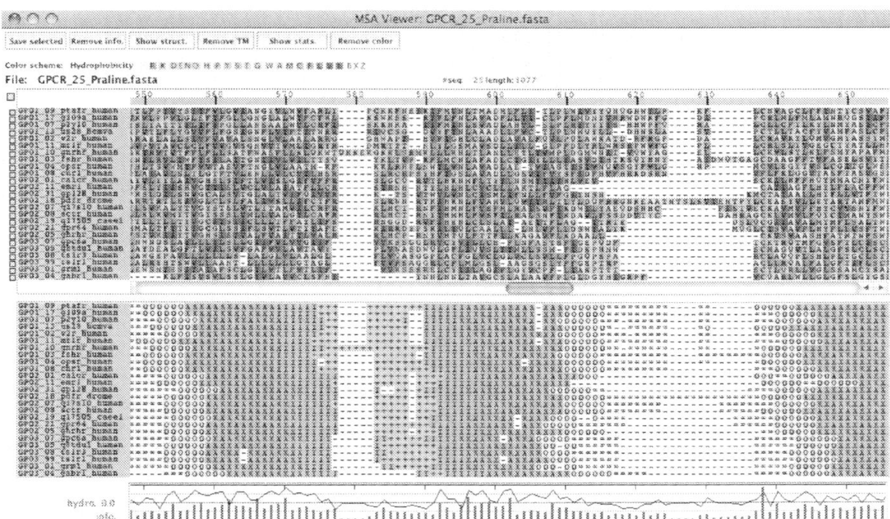

Fig. 5. Alignment of 25 GPCR proteins generated by PRALINE compared with TM structural predictions. Using the MSA Viewer, the PRALINE MSA is displayed using the 'hydrophobicity' color scheme showing hydrophobic amino acids more toward red and hydrophilic amino acids more toward blue. The predicted TM structure corresponding to each sequence of the MSA is aligned below. The symbols (based on MEMSAT3 prediction) used to show different TM structural components are as follows: 'X' (green) for the TM region, '+' (light brown) for the inside loop, 'I' (brown) for the inside helix cap, '=' (cream) for the outside loop, and 'O' (yellow) for the outside helix cap. The first three TM regions are depicted as three clusters of green letter X's. At the bottom of the display is the information content for each column (blue bar) and the average hydrophobicity for each column (black line plot). The average hydrophobicity (see equation (3)) is based on the index given by Kyte and Doolittle (1982).

4.3 Comparison of GPCR MSAs reconstructed by seven methods

We aligned the 25 GPCR protein sequences using seven methods. The seven MSAs produced were compared using Pixel Plot in Fig. 6. Compared to the terminal or loop regions, seven TM regions are expected to have fewer gaps. Using the Pixel Plot we can confirm such patterns. Approximate areas predicted to have TM regions can be located as clusters of solid colored pixels. In Fig. 7, the seven MSAs are represented in the predicted TM structures. The area includes the first five TM regions shown as the green-colored clusters. Both PRALINE and PROMALS utilize information from secondary structure prediction (also TM prediction for PRALINE) as well as profiles based on PSI-BLAST similarity search (Table 2). As expected, in the MSAs reconstructed by these two methods, predicted TM structures are aligned better than other methods. Other methods with the exception of PRANK also generated MSAs that aligned the area containing the first three TM regions relatively well. The rest of the sequences were more difficult for alignment. Probalign had a difficulty in reconstructing also the third TM region. With all MSA methods, all positions after the third TM region were not well reconstructed in terms of conservation of TM regions. The difficulty in aligning the second half of the protein sequences is likely caused by the large length variation found among GPCR classes, especially in the fourth and fifth loops (between TM4 and TM5, and TM5 and TM6, respectively) (Wistrand et al., 2006).

In order to gain more insights on the difference among GPCR protein MSAs quantitatively, we gathered SPS values from all pairwise comparisons among the seven MSAs. Each of the seven MSAs was used as the reference and other six MSAs were tested against. Fig. 8 clearly shows that SPS is not symmetric. As expected, PRALINE and PROMALS, both of which utilize secondary structure and TM prediction information, had very high SPS' when they are compared to each other (0.546 and 0.543). Interestingly, using PRALINE or PROMALS as the reference, MAFFT was found to perform very well although MAFFT does not incorporate secondary structure nor profile information. It should be also noted that SPS' are among the highest when Probalign was compared to MAFFT (either as the reference or the test MSA).

The most drastic difference between the row and column averages of SPS' is found in PRANK. The SPS' obtained when the PRANK MSA was used as the reference (shown in the PRANK column) are all higher than those obtained when the PRANK MSA was tested against others (shown in the PRANK row). This can be explained by the gappy nature of the PRANK MSA (see Figs. 6 and 7). The PRANK MSA tends to have more gaps because of the underlying design of the method. It attempts to identify distinct insertions and deletions and tries not to collapse such independent events into the same column. For the same set of sequences, the reference alignment that has more gaps has a fewer number of character-pairs available (denominator in equation (6)) when averaging the total SPS, which tends to generate a higher SPS. Note also that the phylogeny-aware algorithm used with PRANK cannot perform well when sequences are too diverged (Löytynoja & Goldman, 2008). With extremely diverged GPCR sequences, PRANK was not expected to perform very well, which was indicated by constantly low SPS' obtained with PRANK. Although in the absence of 'true' reference alignment, low SPS values do not necessarily indicate incorrect alignment but rather inconsistency between the alignments, virtually no TM region was conserved in the PRANK MSA (Figs. 6 and 7). We will examine more on PRANK in the next section.

Fig. 6. Comparison of seven GPCR protein MSAs. The characters corresponding to the second TM (TM2) regions are highlighted with magenta-colored pixels. It shows that the TM2 region is reconstructed well in the MSAs by PRALINE (MSA 1) and PROMALS (MSA 2), relatively well by MAFFT (MSA 3), MUSCLE (MSA 4) and ClustalW2 (MSA 5), and not very well by Probalign (MSA 6) and PRANK (MSA 7). For the PRALINE MSA, the positions for the seven TM regions are as follows: 555-572, 595-611, 641-663, 683-703, 738-756, 813-830, and 854-875, which roughly correspond to solid-colored regions.

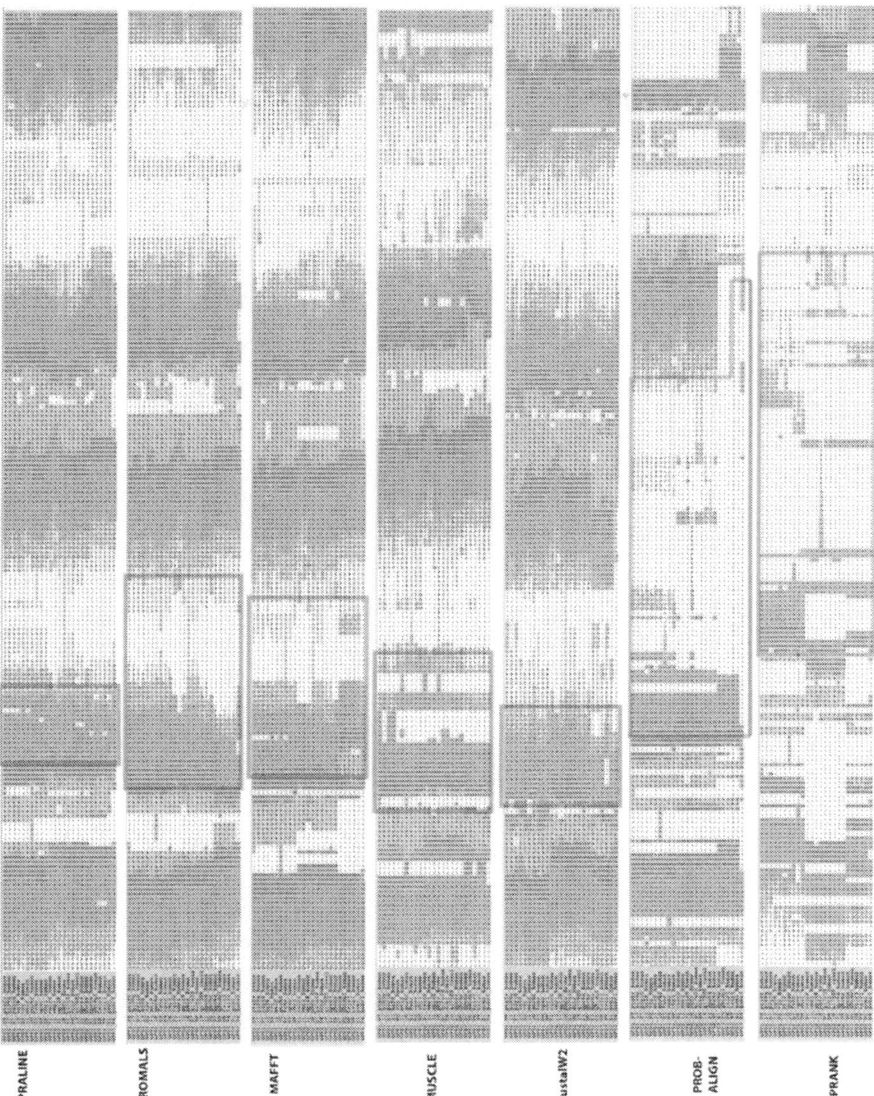

Fig. 7. Seven GPCR protein MSAs represented in TM structures predicted by MEMSAT3. The areas covering the first five predicted TM regions are shown. The red boxes indicate the areas containing amino acids predicted for the second TM regions. Wider red boxes in reconstructed MSAs indicate TM regions with a higher number of gaps (*e.g.*, Probalign and PRANK). The symbols representing amino acids predicted for different TM structural components are as follows: 'X' (green) for the TM region, '+' (light brown) for the inside loop, 'I' (brown) for the inside helix cap, '=' (cream) for the outside loop, and 'O' (yellow) for the outside helix cap.

Test \ Reference	PRALINE	PROMALS	Probalign	MAFFT	MUSCLE	ClustalW2	PRANK	[Average]
PRALINE	(1,077)	0.543	0.563	**0.592**	0.474	**0.381**	0.351	**0.484**
PROMALS	0.546	(1,078)	0.538	0.568	**0.500**	0.345	0.344	0.474
Probalign	0.477	0.455	(1,111)	0.520	0.457	0.324	**0.362**	0.433
MAFFT	**0.569**	**0.546**	**0.590**	(1,081)	0.498	0.346	0.357	**0.484**
MUSCLE	0.462	0.487	0.526	0.505	(1,445)	0.325	0.322	0.438
ClustalW2	0.383	0.346	0.384	0.362	0.335	(1,041)	0.283	0.349
PRANK	0.231	0.227	0.227	0.245	0.218	0.186	(2,419)	0.232
[Average]	0.445	0.434	0.471	**0.465**	0.414	0.318	0.337	

Fig. 8. Pairwise comparison of the sum-of-pairs scores (SPS) between GPCR protein MSAs reconstructed by the seven methods. The numbers in parentheses are the alignment lengths (the number of columns in each alignment). The highest score in each comparison is shown in boldface.

5. A different perspective on gaps

In this section we highlight the alignment method PRANK, which is unique in emphasizing a different perspective on the evolutionary process producing insertions and deletions. As shown in the previous section, it tends to produce more gaps in alignments compared to other methods. We compare the alignment generated by PRANK with four other methods.

5.1 Viral envelope glycoprotein, gp120

Löytynoja and Goldman (2008) used the viral exterior envelope glycoprotein, gp120, from human and simian immunodeficiency viruses (HIVs and SIVs, respectively) as an example to demonstrate how PRANK works. In this section, we used the same set of sequences they used (the seed alignment of Pfam Family GP120, PF00516, excluding SIVGB, SIVV1, and SIVG1). The entry of HIVs and SIVs into the host requires the interaction of the viral gp120 with the cell-surface proteins of the host. In order to avoid the host's immune system, several regions of the gp120 proteins evolve fast. Fig. 9 shows the MSA of gp120 proteins compared with the predicted secondary structures.

5.2 Gap treatment

The 'gap' within an alignment is a general expression for two very different types of evolutionary events. It represents either an insertion of one or more characters or the deletion of one or more. Both types of events are unobservable, and as such it is difficult to distinguish which event creates a gap in an alignment. For example, the 'gappy' section of an alignment, such as the V1 section of HIV/SIV gp120 (Fig. 9), can be interpreted either as the result of a high substitution rate along with frequent independent deletions or as the result of frequent independent short insertions and deletions. Optimization functions used in most MSA methods over-infer the former scenario, stacking independent insertions in the same column and potentially erroneously inflating substitution rates in such regions. Using phylogenetic information, PRANK, on the other hand, allows for the inference of both deletions and insertions as separate events.

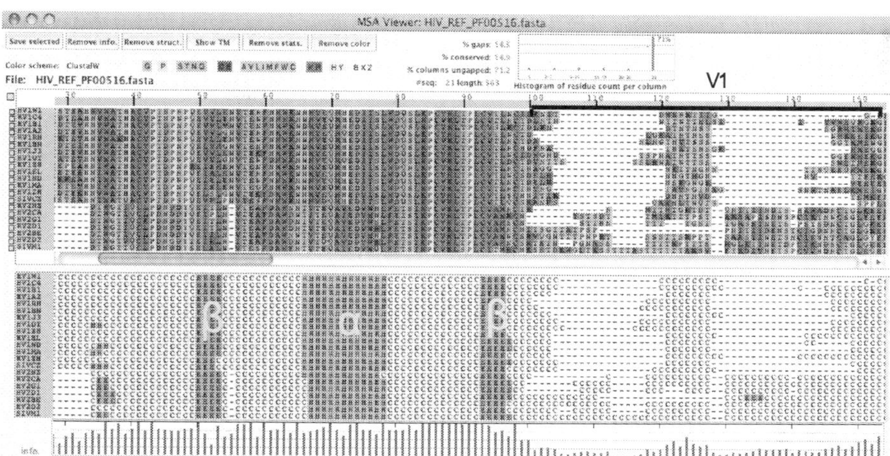

Fig. 9. Reference MSA of HIV/SIV gp120 proteins. The reference alignment was based on the seed alignment of Pfam Family GP120 (PF00516). The secondary structure is predicted for each sequence by PSIPRED (Jones, 1999) and is displayed using the MSA Viewer. The symbols depicting different secondary structures are as follows: H (green): alpha-helix, E (brown): beta-strand, and C (cream): coil. The MSA region shown above contains the N-terminal conserved area and the V1 variable region (positions 100-150). The predicted regions of the beta-strands (positions 50-53 and 93-96) and the alpha-helix (positions 66-78) correspond to the known HIV gp120 protein structure.

Progressive alignment methods such as ClustalW2, MAFFT, and MUSCLE build an alignment based on aligning the profiles of previously aligned sequences. The presence of a gap in the profiles is not checked to determine if the addition of another gap is parsimonious with the guide tree. The decision of whether adding a gap or not is based on the optimization function score. Since the inference of additional gaps penalizes the optimization function score, it often results in incorrectly matching potentially independent insertions, creating incorrect homologies.

PRANK attempts to avoid the above-mentioned pit-falls in progressive alignments by utilizing "phylogeny-aware" handling of gaps and treating insertions and deletions differently. The overall effect of the PRANK method compared to other progressive alignment methods is that the alignment is extended due to the separation of the independent insertions. As Löytynoja and Goldman (2008) stated, "the resulting alignments may be fragmented by many gaps and may not be as visually beautiful as the traditional alignments, but if they represent correct homology, we have to get used to them."

5.3 Comparison of the PRANK MSA with others

We aligned the set of 21 gp120 sequences using PRANK and other five alignment methods. For PRANK, we reconstructed the phylogeny using PhyML 3.0 (Guindon et al., 2010) and used it as the input phylogeny (with rooting between HIV1 and HIV2 clusters, the topology was identical with the one given in Löytynoja & Goldman, 2008). As shown in Fig. 10, the

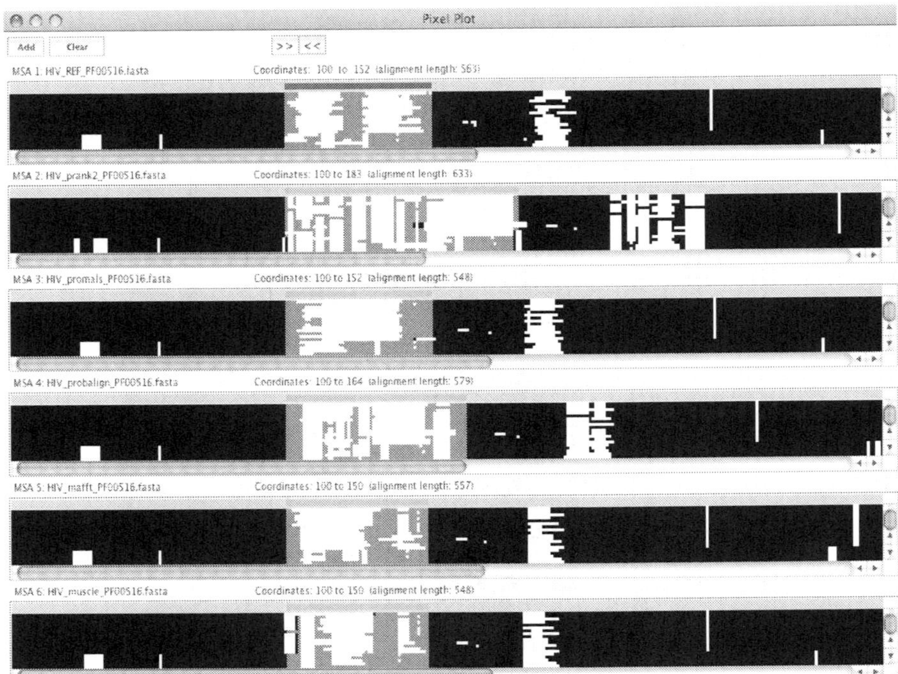

Fig. 10. Comparison of gp120 MSAs. The Pixel Plot is used to compare five reconstructed MSAs (MSA 2: PRANK, MSA 3: PROMALS, MSA 4: Probalign, MSA 5: MAFFT, and MSA 6: MUSCLE) with the reference alignment (MSA 1, based on the seed alignment of Pfam Family GP120, PF00516). The area highlighted in magenta color is part of the V1 variable region, where the patterns show that the PRANK MSA is highly inconsistent with other MSAs.

major differences among MSAs are found starting at the first highly variable area, V1. Within this area, PRANK infers far more insertions than the other methods. The number of sites covered by the blue selection bar in the reference alignment (MSA 1) is 53. The corresponding sites in the other alignments are spread over from 51 columns with MAFFT (MSA 5) to 84 columns in PRANK (MSA 2).

Table 3 summarizes alignment statistics. As expected, PRANK generated the longest alignment. This is indicated in the PRANK MSA having a higher % gaps, lower % consistency, and lower % no-gap columns. Note also that the reference alignment used was the Pfam seed alignment, which in principle was generated using an alignment strategy similar to methods other than PRANK. These comparisons clearly illustrate the point made by Löytynoja and Goldman (2008). Depending on the MSA method used, a very different evolutionary mechanism would be emphasized to explain fast evolving gp120 sequences: either accelerated substitution rates or extremely high rate of short insertions or deletions. Another important point is that scores devised for MSA comparison (*e.g.*, SPS) should be used with the knowledge of the assumption underlying the design of the method used as well as the nature of the reference alignment.

Method	SPS	CS with no-gap	CS with gaps	% consistency	MSA length (aa)	% conserved	% gaps	% no-gap columns
Reference	-	-	-	-	563	14.90	14.50	71.20
PRANK	0.872	0.845	0.702	53.08	633	13.60	**23.90**	61.30
PROMALS	0.919	0.855	**0.775**	**68.24**	548	15.30	12.10	76.60
Probalign	**0.920**	0.838	0.761	62.50	579	15.00	16.80	72.70
MAFFT	0.907	0.827	0.727	63.90	557	15.40	13.60	74.70
MUSCLE	0.910	**0.926**	0.750	66.20	548	**15.50**	12.10	**77.60**

Table 3. Alignment statistics for gp120 MSAs. SPS, CS, and % consistency are obtained against the reference alignment. The highest value in each comparison is shown in boldface.

Fig. 11 illustrates a comparison between the MSAs generated by MAFFT (top) and PRANK (bottom). In Fig. 11A, the region under the blue selection bar for the MAFFT MSA (positions 104 to 128; 25 aa long) is more compact than the region covered by the corresponding amino acids in the PRANK MSA as indicated by the long green range bar (ranging from positions 106 to 159; 54 aa long). In this region, PRANK shows, for example, two independent insertions marked with light blue boxes ('GL' and 'MIR') both happening in SIV/HIV2 sequences. In the MAFFT MSA, these two sequences are part of a much longer insertion region unique to SIV/HIV2, implying that frequent deletion events shortened this region in various HIV2. Another insertion found in HIV1 by PRANK, 'SSSLR' (in a light green box), is shown to be almost independent. However, in the MAFFT MSA, the corresponding region appears to have experienced many deletion events instead. This shows the "gap magnet" phenomenon found in many progressive-alignment methods. Fig. 11B from the same MSA area highlights another possible artifact often found in MSAs generated by progressive alignment methods. In the red area in the MAFFT MSA, all sequences are aligned (matched) generating the "collapsed insertions", implying homologous relationships among these sequences. However, in the PRANK MSA, the corresponding sequences are spread out in a wide range of columns. These examples show that the inferred evolutionary scenarios can be completely different depending on the alignment methods used to analyze sequences.

6. Using simulated sequences for testing MSA methods

In this section we will discuss the use of simulation data in the comparison of alignment methods. The advantage of using simulated sequences is the availability of the 'true' alignment. In the simulation example discussed in this section, we simulate two sets of eight lipocalin sequences described in Section 3. The lipocalin protein family has a common structural feature, a single eight-stranded antiparallel beta-barrel. They also share three conserved motifs. We will use the simulation program indel-Seq-Gen version 2.1 (iSGv2.1; Strope *et al.*, 2009) to simulate this lipocalin family proteins. iSGv2.1 is included in the SuiteMSA package and the simulation can be done using its graphical user interface.

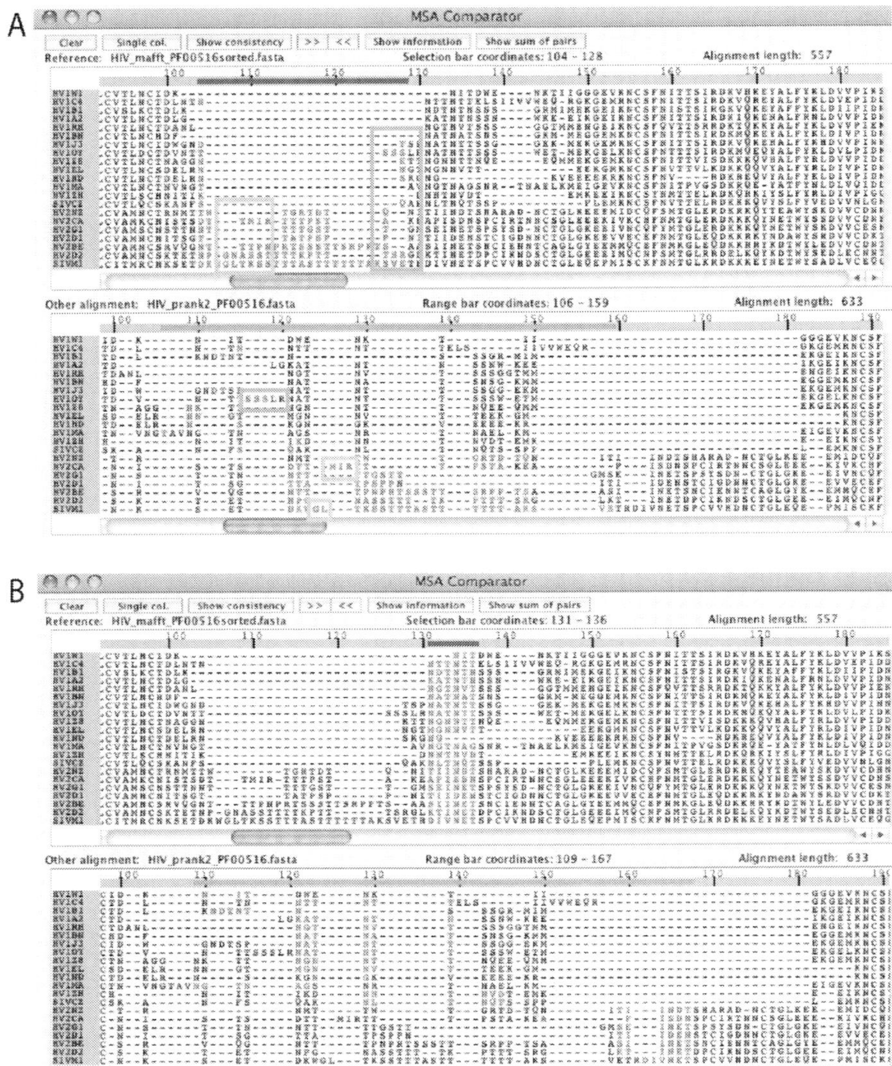

Fig. 11. Comparison of gp120 alignment regions generated by MAFFT and PRANK. For both panels A and B, the MAFFT MSA is used as the reference (top) and the PRANK MSA (bottom) is compared against. The blue selection bar for the MAFFT MSA shows the alignment area selected, and the green range bar for the PRANK MSA shows the column range where corresponding amino acids are found in the MSA. The corresponding amino acids in the two MSAs are shown with red color ('red' indicates that the alignment of these characters is inconsistent between the MSAs). See the main text for the description on the sequences marked with light blue and light green boxes.

6.1 Setting up the iSGv2.1 simulation

iSGv2.1 simulation requires a guide tree and a root sequence or MSA. By providing a root MSA, instead of generating a random root sequence, the site-specific amino acid (or nucleotide) frequency distribution derived from each MSA column can be used to generate a simulation root sequence (for details, refer to iSG user manual). For the root MSA, we used the 8-protein alignment of the lipocalin family we described in Section 3. The evolutionary parameters chosen to simulate the lipocalin protein family are listed below. We performed two simulations: the second more divergent than the first. For any parameters not mentioned, default values were used. Three input files are prepared: a guide tree file, a lineage file, and a root MSA file. For details on preparing the guide tree, the three motifs used, and how to set up the length-limitation template, refer to Strope *et al.* (2009) as well as Anderson *et al.* (2011). All input files used for this simulation are available from: http://bioinfolab.unl.edu/~canderson/SuiteMSA/supplement.html.

i.   Basic parameters
- Guide tree file: lipo8_3.tre (provides the guide tree and option parameters listed below)
- Substitution model: PAM

ii.   Advanced parameters
- Lineage file: lipo8_3.spec (provides the motif and template information)
- Branch scale: 0.5 (first simulation), 2.0 (second simulation)
- Random number seed: 6262

iii.   Guide tree options (information included in the guide tree file)
- Use root msa file: lipo8_3template.root_in
- Maximum indel length: 10
- Insertion probability = deletion probability = 0.02 (first simulation), 0.025 (second simulation)
- Indel length distribution = deletion length distribution: file name = inDL (provides indel length distribution)

After running each simulation, we obtained a set of eight simulated sequences, the true alignment of the eight sequences, and a record of all insertion and deletion events. As shown in Fig. 12, the 'true' alignments from both simulations (the first more conserved and the second more diverged) maintained the three conserved lipocalin motifs (M1, M2, and M3) specified in the simulations. As expected, the second MSA derived from the simulated sequences with a higher rate of substitutions (longer branch lengths) and a higher rate of indel probability is about 100 aa longer (Fig. 12B, 303 aa) than the first MSA (Fig. 12A, 215 aa). We used these 'true' alignments as the references for the next analysis.

6.2 Comparison of MSA reconstruction using simulated sequences

We used four MSA methods (MAFFT, MUSCLE, Probalign, and PRANK) to align both sets of the eight simulated sequences. For PRANK, the simulation guide trees (with branch lengths scaled for the 'more conserved' and 'more divergent' simulations) were used as the input phylogenies. In Fig. 13, the Pixel Plot is used to compare the reconstructed MSAs against the reference MSAs (the true alignments obtained from the two simulations). Tables 4 and 5 summarize the alignment statistics for the two sets of simulated data.

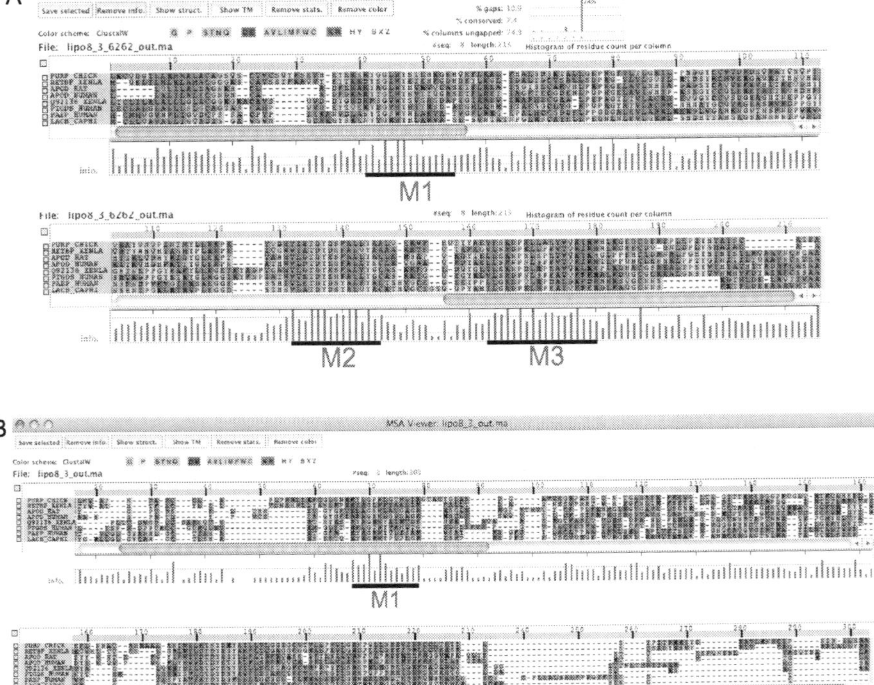

Fig. 12. 'True' alignments of the two sets of simulated lipocalin protein sequences (A: more conserved and B: more divergent simulations). Both alignments clearly show that the three motifs (M1, M2, and M3) are conserved among these two sets of simulated protein sequences.

Fig. 13. Comparison of simulated lipocalin protein MSAs. The Pixel Plot is used to compare four reconstructed MSAs with the reference alignments (A: more conserved and B: more divergent simulations). The 'true' alignments obtained from the simulations are used as the reference alignment (MSA 1). M1 (red box), M2 (blue box), and M3 (green box) show the location of three conserved regions. The regions highlighted in magenta show an example of inconsistent alignments found in reconstructed alignments relative to the true reference alignments. MSA methods used are MAFFT (MSA 2), MUSCLE (MSA 3), Probalign (MSA 4), and PRANK (MSA 5).

Fig. 13A shows that all four methods produced highly consistent MSAs for the sequences obtained from the more conserved simulation. While two of the three conserved motifs were identified correctly in all MSAs, in the region of the first motif (M1), all reconstructed MSAs contained gaps. Consistently very high SPS' (0.91~0.93, Table 4) indicate that all methods performed very well. The proportion of gaps is also consistent between all reconstructed MSAs and the reference (~10%, Table 4).

Method	SPS	CS with no-gap	CS with gaps	% consistency	MSA length (aa)	% conserved	% gaps	% no-gap columns
Reference	-	-	-	-	215	7.4	10.9	74.9
MAFFT	**0.933**	**0.850**	**0.782**	**72.77**	213	7.0	10.0	75.1
MUSCLE	0.921	0.817	0.751	70.28	212	7.1	9.6	**77.4**
Probalign	0.912	0.787	0.704	63.76	218	**7.8**	**12.1**	73.9
PRANK	0.932	0.826	0.776	71.5	215	7.5	10.5	75.2

Table 4. Alignment statistics for the simulated 'more conserved' lipocalin family MSAs. SPS, CS, and % consistency are obtained against the reference alignment. The highest value in each comparison is shown in boldface.

Method	SPS	CS with no-gap	CS with gaps	% consistency	MSA length (aa)	% conserved	% gaps	% no-gap columns
Reference	-	-	-	-	303	2.00	**39.70**	39.60
MAFFT	0.533	**0.481**	0.263	20.64	252	2.40	27.50	42.90
MUSCLE	0.532	0.421	0.314	**28.11**	219	2.70	16.60	**63.00**
Probalign	**0.585**	0.465	**0.321**	23.56	258	2.30	29.20	49.20
PRANK	0.504	0.395	0.264	24.88	213	**2.80**	14.30	60.60

Table 5. Alignment statistics for the simulated 'more divergent' lipocalin family MSAs. SPS, CS, and % consistency are obtained against the reference alignment. The highest value in each comparison is shown in boldface.

In Fig. 14, we compared PRANK and MAFFT alignments more in detail using the MSA Comparator. This is the same region highlighted in magenta color in Fig. 13A. The alignment columns that are fully consistent between the reference and PRANK (Fig. 14A) or MAFFT (Fig. 14B) are shown with blue color. Black characters, on the other hand, indicate inconsistently aligned columns. For example, the characters contained in the red square in the reference MSA are aligned exactly the same in the PRANK MSA. However, as shown in Fig. 14B for the MAFFT MSA, the gap in column 35 (in the reference) is filled with the characters shifted from the left. The Pixel Plot in Fig. 13 shows that the same shifting and filling of the gap happened in all but the PRANK MSA. This demonstrates the "gap magnet" phenomenon described in the previous section. Using the simulated data, we know the origins of gaps. In Fig. 14, '-' in yellow cells are derived from deletion events. Characters in green cells, on the other hand, are derived by insertion events. Therefore, stacking up the 'QVD' sequences and avoiding inserting gaps as done by MAFFT (Fig. 14B) is evolutionary incorrect. With commonly used affine-gap penalty systems, opening new gaps is highly penalized as opposed to extending an existing gap. This is reinforced with progressive alignment methods. This situation is clearly illustrated in the example shown in Fig. 14B. Using its "phylogeny-aware" gap handling, PRANK was able to correctly align these gaps.

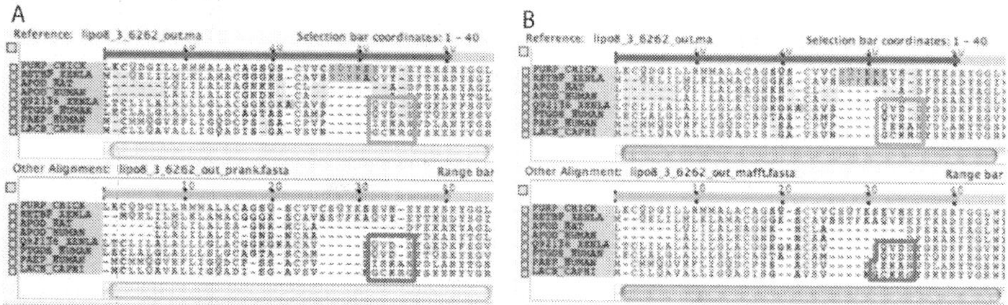

Fig. 14. Comparisons of PRANK (A) and MAFFT (B) alignments against the reference alignment (the simulated 'true' alignment). The region is taken from the area highlighted in magenta in Fig. 13A. The MSA Comparator is used to show the actual insertion (marked with green) and deletion (marked with yellow) events in the reference alignment. These events are traced during the iSGv2.1 simulation.

When the divergence level was much higher, as shown in Fig. 13B, all methods could still identify all of the three conserved motif sites. However, all MSAs were highly inconsistent within the unconstrained areas. SPS' are significantly lower (0.50-0.59, Table 5). For this dataset, PRANK produced the most inconsistent MSA, which was expected as PRANK is recommended for aligning closely related sequences. It should also be noted that there is little agreement among the alignments. This indicates that regardless of the statistics used, no one method can be concluded as ideal. Using multiple methods is recommended so that a selection of alignment hypotheses can be used to generate a more robust hypothesis.

7. Aligning ribosomal DNA sequences

We have so far concentrated our discussion on protein sequence alignments. In order to obtain the full picture of alignment issues, in this section, we will examine the alignment of ribosomal DNA (rDNA) sequences.

7.1 Small-subunit ribosomal DNA sequences and secondary structure

The ribosomal RNA genes contain large stretches of highly conserved sites (stem or knot binding sites) interspersed with regions of varying sites (loop regions). These two types of regions within the gene have different information content due to strong selective constraints on the secondary structures and function within the stem and knot areas *versus* very weak constraints on the loop area. Fig. 15 shows a predicted secondary structure of the small-subunit ribosomal RNA (or 18S rRNA) from a parasitic protozoa *Toxoplasma gondii*, a member of the family Sarcocystidae (Phylum Apicomplexa; Class Conoidasida; Subclass Coccidia).

Figs. 16 and 17 show part of the 18S rDNA MSA of 60 Coccidia species (D. A. Morrison personal communication; Morrison, 2009a). As shown in Fig. 16, stem regions are highly conserved. This alignment illustrates the high level of conservation found in approximately 45% of the 18S rDNA alignment. On the other hand, large loop regions as the one shown in Fig. 15 have much lower functional constraints. As shown in Fig. 17, sequences of such regions are highly variable and alignment reconstruction of such regions often requires laborious manual adjustment, iteratively incorporating information from the predicted rRNA secondary structures (Morrison, 2009a).

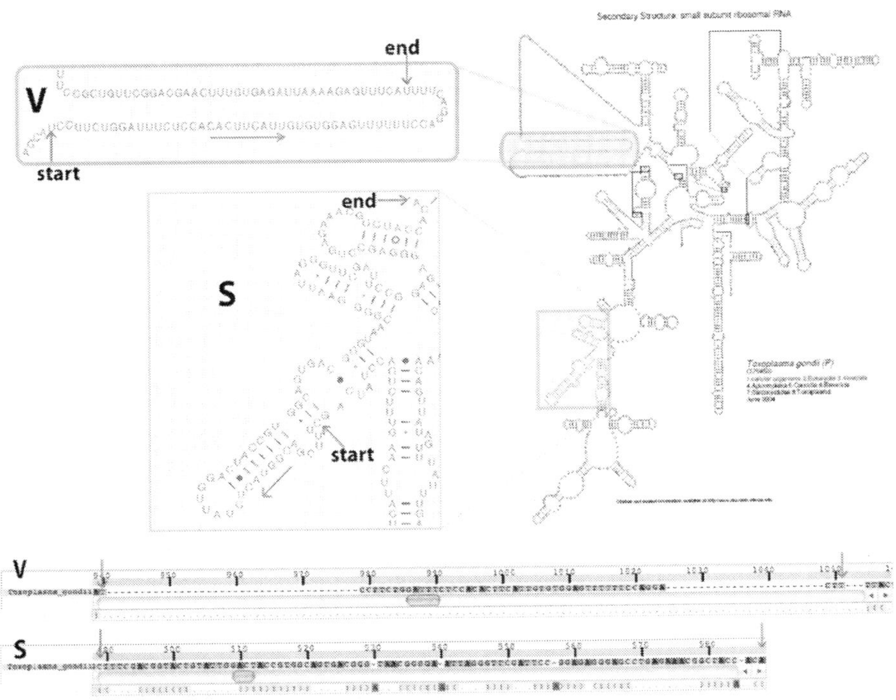

Fig. 15. Predicted secondary structure of the *Toxoplasma gondii* 18S rRNA. The secondary structure was obtained from Comparative RNA Web Site (http://www.rna.ccbb.utexas.edu/; Cannone *et al.*, 2002). The callouts 'S' and 'V' show the 'stem' and the large 'loop' regions, respectively. Their sequence-structure alignments are shown at the bottom (the orange arrows pointing to the beginning and ending of the regions).

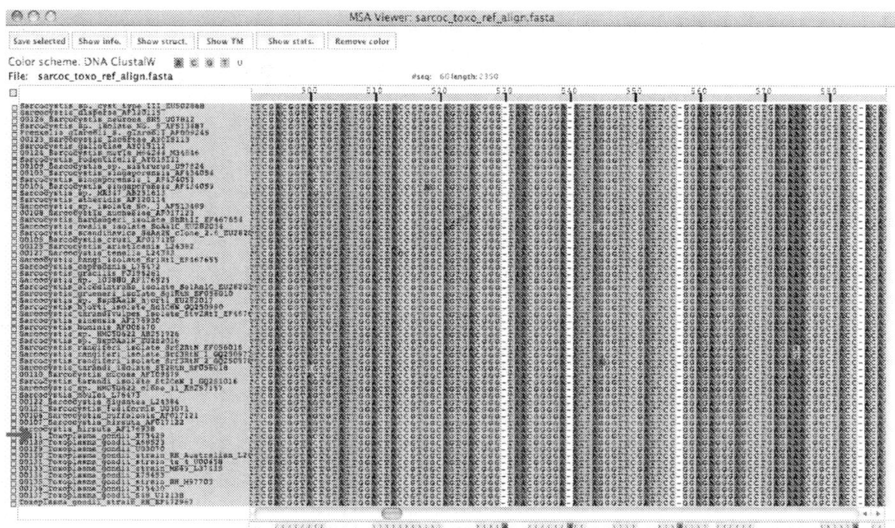

Fig. 16. Alignment of a highly conserved stem region of 18S rDNA from 60 Coccidia species. Using the MSA Viewer, the rRNA secondary structure information from *T. gondii* is displayed below the alignment. This alignment corresponds to the region in the callout 'S' shown in Fig. 15. The sites that are considered to be ambiguously aligned for this family are indicated by a red 'A' in the structural representation. These positions do not appear in the *T. gondii* structure. The alignment was provided by D. A. Morrison.

7.2 Comparison of 18S rDNA MSA reconstruction

We generated the alignments of full 18S rDNA sequences using four MSA methods. Using the above-mentioned alignment provided by D. A. Morrison as the reference, we compared the performance of the MSA methods. The alignment statistics are summarized in Table 6.

Method	SPS	CS with no gap	CS with gaps	% consistency	MSA length (nuc)	% conserved	% gaps	% no-gap columns
Reference	-	-	-	-	2095	50.60	15.80	62.40
Probalign	**0.953**	0.919	0.863	65.96	2389	44.30	**26.10**	55.60
MAFFT	0.950	0.898	0.844	73.08	2088	50.10	15.50	**64.10**
MUSCLE	0.950	0.917	**0.867**	73.77	2116	50.20	16.60	63.00
ClustalW2	0.948	**0.946**	0.855	**75.23**	2055	**51.40**	14.10	62.50

Table 6. Alignment statistics for the 18S rDNA MSAs. SPS, CS, and % consistency are obtained against the reference alignment. The highest value in each comparison is shown in boldface.

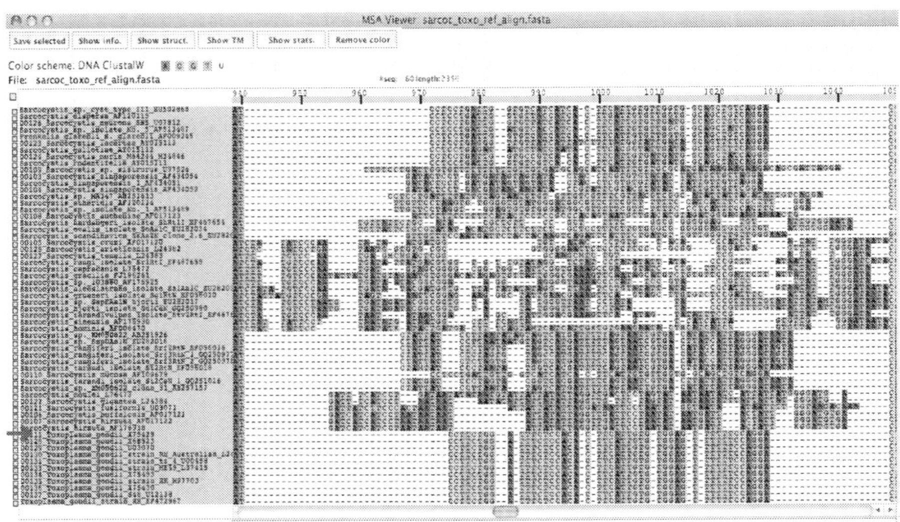

Fig. 17. Alignment of a highly variable loop region of 18S rDNA from 60 Coccidia species. One of the secondary structures used to refine the alignment was from *T. gondii*. This structure is displayed below the alignment. This alignment corresponds to the region in the callout 'V' shown in Fig. 15. The alignment was provided by D. A. Morrison.

All four methods appear to have produced alignments highly consistent with the reference. This must be owing to highly conserved stem or functional regions that cover almost 50% of the sequence regions. Such consistency is reflected by the high CS values particularly when gapped columns are excluded (CS with no gap) and also the small differences in CS values among MSAs. ClustalW2 has the highest un-gapped CS, indicating that ClustalW2 has the highest number of columns that match the reference alignment, and likewise, the highest % consistency. While the ClustalW2 MSA is the shortest (2,055 nucleotides), the longest and most 'gappy' MSA was obtained by Probalign. Similar trends are found in the other examples described in this chapter. Note, however, that the Probalign MSA had the highest SPS (0.953) and second highest 'CS with gaps' (0.863; MUSCLE had a slightly better score, 0.867).

Now let us visually examine these alignments. Keep in mind that the sequences are highly conserved, and that phylogenetic information will be derived mainly from the regions that are sufficiently variable. In Fig. 18, the Pixel Plot was used to compare the four reconstructed MSAs against the reference MSA. The selected area of the reference MSA under the blue selection bar includes the subsequence shown in the callout 'V' of Fig. 15 (Fig. 16 also shows the same area of the reference MSA). The magenta-colored pixels show the distribution of characters included in this selected area. In the reference MSA, the magenta-colored area has relatively small amount of gaps, providing the largest aligned overlap, putatively the most phylogenetically informative region, within this large loop region. However, in the alternative MSAs (MSAs 2-5), magenta-colored corresponding characters are spread over much wider regions (green bars show the ranges covered by corresponding characters). Note that each MSA method found a few conserved subsequences (matched columns) within this region.

However, each method also introduced a large number of gaps, affecting the consistency in the alignments of the surrounding areas immediately before and after the selected region. In spite of the high SPS' observed with these MSAs and the degree of conservation within the alignments, there is little consensus among the MSAs of this phylogentically critical area. Through visual comparisons among alternative MSAs it becomes possible to recognize that very different hypotheses could emerge depending on the MSA chosen. Such significant differences among the MSAs are, and should be, alarming to researchers, since such inconsistency in MSAs could affect phylogenetic hypotheses.

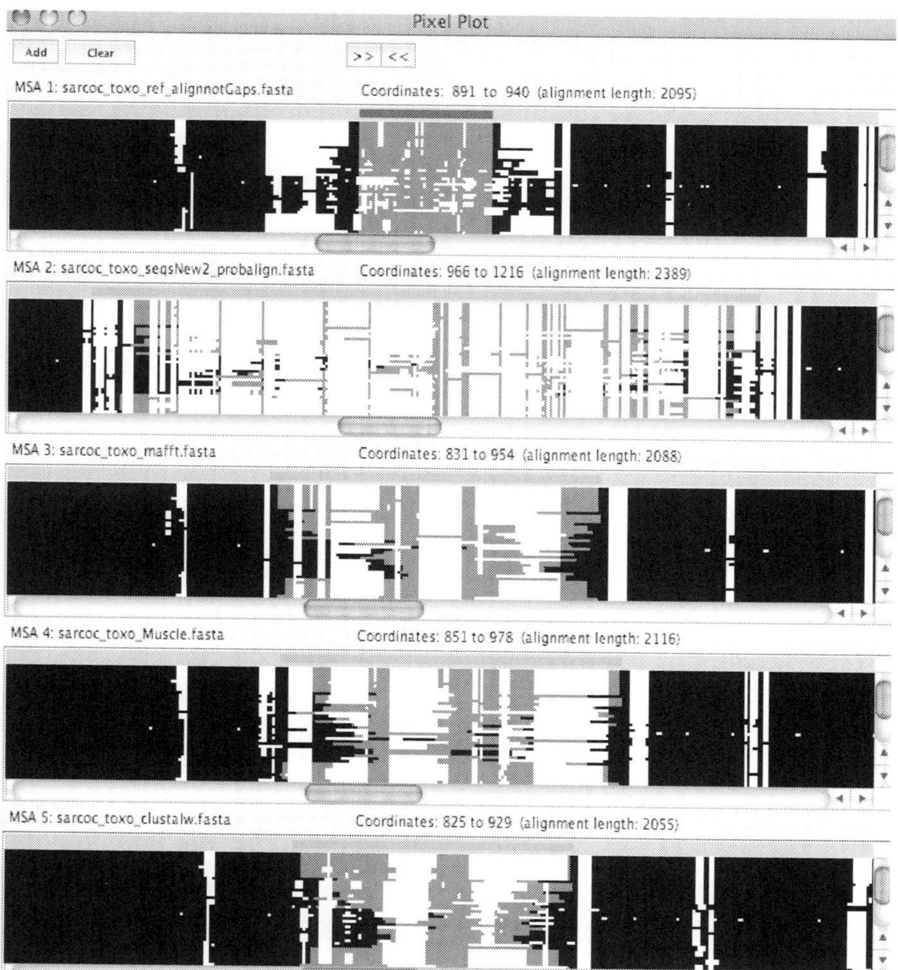

Fig. 18. Comparison of 18S rDNA MSAs. Pixel Plot is used to compare four reconstructed MSAs with the reference. The alignment provided by D. A. Morrison was used as the reference and compared with MSAs generated by Probalign, MAFFT, MUSCLE, and ClustalW2.

8. Conclusion

Advancements in the field of bioinformatics and molecular evolution have resulted in many different methods for reconstructing MSAs. While each MSA method has a different objective function and different heuristics to maximize the objective function for building the alignment, if they were in fact meant to reconstruct alignments that reflect the evolutionary history of sequences, we would expect some level of consensus between them. Such is not the case in reality. We used five types of alignment problems in this chapter. Using seven different MSA methods, we discussed the similarity and difference among MSAs built by these methods. We have shown that assessment of MSAs can be performed using a combination of descriptive statistics both for individual alignments and the comparison of two alternate alignments. We have also shown that using visual tools provided by SuiteMSA, we can examine MSAs based on the alignment of structural features such as secondary structure and transmembrane predictions. We further demonstrated how the sequence simulator included in SuiteMSA can be used to produce benchmark alignments.

We should keep in mind that alignments reconstructed by any MSA methods are only hypotheses on the evolutionary relation of the sequences. Furthermore, while these alignments can be assessed as consistent (or not) with the accepted model for the given sequences (the reference alignment), this reference is itself a hypothesis unless generated by a simulation program and may not be 'correct'. It is important for the researcher to understand the underlying assumptions of the alignment methods as well as the characteristics of the biological sequences to be aligned and to assess the resulting alignments. User friendly graphical tools such as SuiteMSA can assist in the critical assessment of MSAs prior to their use in further studies.

9. Acknowledgements

We would like to thank Dr. David A. Morrison (Swedish University of Agricultural Sciences) for providing us 18S rDNA alignments and discussion. This work has been partially supported by NSF AToL grant 0732863 to ENM.

10. References

Altschul, S. F., Gish, W., Miller, W., Myers, E. W., & Lipman, D. J. (1990). Basic local alignment search tool. *Journal of molecular biology*, Vol. 215, No. 3, pp. 403-410.

Altschul, S. F., Madden, T. L., Schaffer, A. A., Zhang, J., Zhang, Z., Miller, W., & Lipman, D. J. (1997). Gapped BLAST and PSI-BLAST: a new generation of protein database search programs. *Nucleic acids research*, Vol. 25, No. 17, pp. 3389-3402.

Anderson, C. L., Strope, C. L., & Moriyama, E. N. (2011). SuiteMSA: Visual tools for multiple sequence alignment comparison and molecular sequence simulation. *BMC bioinformatics*, Vol. 12, pp. 184.

Camacho, C., Coulouris, G., Avagyan, V., Ma, N., Papadopoulos, J., Bealer, K., & Madden, T. L. (2009). BLAST+: architecture and applications. *BMC bioinformatics*, Vol. 10, pp. 421.

Cannone, J. J., Subramanian, S., Schnare, M. N., Collett, J. R., D'Souza, L. M., Du, Y., Feng, B., Lin, N., Madabusi, L. V., Muller, K. M., Pande, N., Shang, Z., Yu, N., & Gutell, R. R. (2002). The comparative RNA web (CRW) site: an online database of comparative sequence and structure information for ribosomal, intron, and other RNAs. *BMC bioinformatics*, Vol. 3, pp. 2.

Cline, M., Hughey, R., & Karplus, K. (2002). Predicting reliable regions in protein sequence alignments. *Bioinformatics,* Vol. 18, No. 2, pp. 306-314.

Edgar, R. C. (2004a). MUSCLE: a multiple sequence alignment method with reduced time and space complexity. *BMC bioinformatics,* Vol. 5, No. 1, pp. 113.

Edgar, R. C. (2004b). MUSCLE: multiple sequence alignment with high accuracy and high throughput. *Nucleic acids research,* Vol. 32, No. 5, pp. 1792-1797.

Edgar, R. C. (2010). Quality measures for protein alignment benchmarks. *Nucleic acids research,* Vol. 38, No. 7, pp. 2145-2153.

Finn, R. D., Mistry, J., Tate, J., Coggill, P., Heger, A., Pollington, J. E., Gavin, O. L., Gunasekaran, P., Ceric, G., Forslund, K., Holm, L., Sonnhammer, E. L., Eddy, S. R., & Bateman, A. (2010). The Pfam protein families database. *Nucleic acids research,* Vol. 38, No. Database issue, pp. D211-222.

Flower, D. R., North, A. C., & Sansom, C. E. (2000). The lipocalin protein family: structural and sequence overview. *Biochimica et biophysica acta,* Vol. 1482, No. 1-2, pp. 9-24.

Guindon, S., Dufayard, J.F., Lefort, V., Anisimova, M., Hordijk, W., & Gascuel, O. (2010). New algorithms and methods to estimate maximum-likelihood phylogenies: assessing the performance of PhyML 3.0. *Systematic biology,* Vol. 59, No. 3, pp. 307-321.

Horn, F., Bettler, E., Oliveira, L., Campagne, F., Cohen, F. E., & Vriend, G. (2003). GPCRDB information system for G protein-coupled receptors. *Nucleic acids research,* Vol. 31, No. 1, pp. 294-297.

Hulo, N., Bairoch, A., Bulliard, V., Cerutti, L., Cuche, B. A., de Castro, E., Lachaize, C., Langendijk-Genevaux, P. S., & Sigrist, C. J. (2008). The 20 years of PROSITE. *Nucleic acids research,* Vol. 36, No. Database issue, pp. D245-249.

Inoue, Y., Ikeda, M., & Shimizu, T. (2004). Proteome-wide classification and identification of mammalian-type GPCRs by binary topology pattern. *Computational biology and chemistry,* Vol. 28, No. 1, pp. 39-49.

Jones, D. T. (1999). Protein secondary structure prediction based on position-specific scoring matrices. *Journal of molecular biology,* Vol. 292, No. 2, pp. 195-202.

Katoh, K. & Toh, H. (2008). Recent developments in the MAFFT multiple sequence alignment program. *Briefings in bioinformatics,* Vol. 9, No. 4, pp. 286-298.

Kawashima, S., Pokarowski, P., Pokarowska, M., Kolinski, A., Katayama, T., & Kanehisa, M. (2008). AAindex: amino acid index database, progress report 2008. *Nucleic acids research,* Vol. 36, No. Database issue, pp. D202-205.

Kemena, C. & Notredame, C. (2009). Upcoming challenges for multiple sequence alignment methods in the high-throughput era. *Bioinformatics,* Vol. 25, No. 19, pp. 2455-2465.

Kyte, J. & Doolittle, R. F. (1982). A simple method for displaying the hydropathic character of a protein. *Journal of molecular biology,* Vol. 157, No. 1, pp. 105-132.

Larkin, M. A., Blackshields, G., Brown, N. P., Chenna, R., McGettigan, P. A., McWilliam, H., Valentin, F., Wallace, I. M., Wilm, A., Lopez, R., Thompson, J. D., Gibson, T. J., & Higgins, D. G. (2007). Clustal W and Clustal X version 2.0. *Bioinformatics,* Vol. 23, No. 21, pp. 2947-2948.

Löytynoja, A. & Goldman, N. (2005). An algorithm for progressive multiple alignment of sequences with insertions. *Proceedings of the National academy of sciences of the United States of America,* Vol. 102, No. 30, pp. 10557-10562.

Löytynoja, A. & Goldman, N. (2008). Phylogeny-aware gap placement prevents errors in sequence alignment and evolutionary analysis. *Science,* Vol. 320, No. 5883, pp. 1632-1635.

Morrison, D. A. (2009a). Evolution of the Apicomplexa: where are we now? *Trends in parasitology,* Vol. 25, No. 8, pp. 375-382.

Morrison, D. A. (2009b). Why would phylogeneticists ignore computerized sequence alignment? *Systematic biology,* Vol. 58, No. 1, pp. 150-158.

Nugent, T. & Jones, D. T. (2009). Transmembrane protein topology prediction using support vector machines. *BMC bioinformatics,* Vol. 10, pp. 159.

Pei, J. & Grishin, N. V. (2007). PROMALS: towards accurate multiple sequence alignments of distantly related proteins. *Bioinformatics,* Vol. 23, No. 7, pp. 802-808.

Pei, J., Kim, B. H., & Grishin, N. V. (2008). PROMALS3D: a tool for multiple protein sequence and structure alignments. *Nucleic acids research,* Vol. 36, No. 7, pp. 2295-2300.

Pirovano, W., Feenstra, K. A., & Heringa, J. (2008). PRALINETM: a strategy for improved multiple alignment of transmembrane proteins. *Bioinformatics,* Vol. 24, No. 4, pp. 492-497.

Pirovano, W. & Heringa, J. (2010). Protein secondary structure prediction. *Methods in molecular biology,* Vol. 609, pp. 327-348.

Raghava, G. P., Searle, S. M., Audley, P. C., Barber, J. D., & Barton, G. J. (2003). OXBench: a benchmark for evaluation of protein multiple sequence alignment accuracy. *BMC bioinformatics,* Vol. 4, pp. 47.

Roshan, U. & Livesay, D. R. (2006). Probalign: multiple sequence alignment using partition function posterior probabilities. *Bioinformatics,* Vol. 22, No. 22, pp. 2715-2721.

Schneider, T. D. & Stephens, R. M. (1990). Sequence logos: a new way to display consensus sequences. *Nucleic acids research,* Vol. 18, No. 20, pp. 6097-6100.

Shannon, C. E. (1948). A mathematical theory of communication. *Bell system technical journal,* Vol. 27, pp. 379-423.

Stebbings, L. A. & Mizuguchi, K. (2004). HOMSTRAD: recent developments of the Homologous Protein Structure Alignment Database. *Nucleic acids research,* Vol. 32, No. Database issue, pp. D203-207.

Strope, C. L., Abel, K., Scott, S. D., & Moriyama, E. N. (2009). Biological sequence simulation for testing complex evolutionary hypotheses: indel-Seq-Gen version 2.0. *Molecular biology and evolution,* Vol. 26, No. 11, pp. 2581-2593.

Subramanian, A. R., Weyer-Menkhoff, J., Kaufmann, M., & Morgenstern, B. (2005). DIALIGN-T: an improved algorithm for segment-based multiple sequence alignment. *BMC bioinformatics,* Vol. 6, pp. 66.

Thompson, J. D., Koehl, P., Ripp, R., & Poch, O. (2005). BAliBASE 3.0: latest developments of the multiple sequence alignment benchmark. *Proteins,* Vol. 61, No. 1, pp. 127-136.

Thompson, J. D., Linard, B., Lecompte, O., & Poch, O. (2011). A comprehensive benchmark study of multiple sequence alignment methods: current challenges and future perspectives. *PloS one,* Vol. 6, No. 3, pp. e18093.

Thompson, J. D., Plewniak, F., & Poch, O. (1999). BAliBASE: a benchmark alignment database for the evaluation of multiple alignment programs. *Bioinformatics,* Vol. 15, No. 1, pp. 87-88.

Van Walle, I., Lasters, I., & Wyns, L. (2005). SABmark--a benchmark for sequence alignment that covers the entire known fold space. *Bioinformatics,* Vol. 21, No. 7, pp. 1267-1268.

Vroling, B., Sanders, M., Baakman, C., Borrmann, A., Verhoeven, S., Klomp, J., Oliveira, L., de Vlieg, J., & Vriend, G. (2011). GPCRDB: information system for G protein-coupled receptors. *Nucleic acids research,* Vol. 39, No. Database issue, pp. D309-319.

Wistrand, M., Kall, L., & Sonnhammer, E. L. (2006). A general model of G protein-coupled receptor sequences and its application to detect remote homologs. *Protein science,* Vol. 15, No. 3, pp. 509-521.

12

Optimal Sequence Alignment and Its Relationship with Phylogeny

Atoosa Ghahremani and Mahmood A. Mahdavi
Department of Chemical Engineering, Ferdowsi University of Mashhad,
Azadi Square, Pardis Campus, Mashhad,
Iran

1. Introduction

The main motivation for predicting functions of hundreds of thousands of genes and proteins found across genomes and proteomes is variations within a family of related nucleic acid or protein sequences that provide an unreliable source of information for evolutionary biology. Protein molecules are more diverse in structure and function than any other kind of molecule. Then if nucleic acid sequences undergo mutations, insertions, crossing-over and some another changes, these variations have a direct effect on the coded protein molecules (Fitch, 1970; Pearson et al., 1997). If a protein sequence is present in many different organisms or be conserved along evolution, it is predicted that it might have a similar function in all the organisms. Two molecules of related function usually have similar sequences reciprocally two molecules of similar sequence usually have related functions (Dardel, 2006). The objective of bioinformatics is to detect such similarities, using computer methods to draw biological conclusions. Collecting available wealth of sequence information, help to track ancient genes and back trough the tree of life then to discover new organisms based on their sequences (Fitch, 1966). Searching diverse genes may show different evolutionary histories that reflecting transfers of genetic material between species. If we recognize the function and/or structure of a member of an evolutionary family then we can predict the function of all the other members and even identify the important functional groups. For this, we need to identify which proteins are belonging to the same family and then distinguish proteins that are evolved from the same ancestor after a set of accepted mutation events. Such proteins have amino acid sequences that are likely to be more similar than expected for unrelated protein sequences. When two or more than two sequences share a common evolutionary ancestor they called homologous (Fitch, 1970). There is no homology degree, sequences are either homologues or not (Reeck et al., 1987; Tautz, 1998). These types of proteins almost always share a significantly related tree-dimentional structure. An example for very similar structures which is determined by x-ray crystallography is RBP and β-lactoglobulin (Fig. 1). Once the homology between some related sequences is inferred, identity and similarity are the quantities for describing the relatedness of sequences. In one type of homology, two sequences may be homologous but without sharing statistically significant identity. In general, three dimensional structures differ much more slowly than amino acid identity between two proteins (Chothia & Lesk,

1986). There are two types of homology, orthology and paralogy. Orthologs are homologous sequences that are in different species but arose from a common ancestral gene during speciation event. It has been predicted that orthologous sequences have similar biological functions (In Fig. 2, human and rat RBPs both transport vitamin A in serum). Paralogs are homologous sequences evolved from gene duplication mechanism. An example for paralogous sequences is human RBP plasma to the other carrier protein human apolipoprotein D (Fig. 3). It is predicted that paralogous sequences have distinct functions but their functions are related together (Pevsner, 2003a; Mount, 2001a).

Homology inference heavily relies on alignment of primary structure of proteins and DNA sequences. This is a procedure for identifying the matching residues within the sequences sharing the same functional and/or structural role in the different members of the family (Xu & Miranker, 2003). After performing alignment and evaluating alignment scores, the most closely related sequence pairs become apparent and may be placed in the outer branches of an evolutionary tree. With continuing alignment procedure for different sequences of particular gene, a predicted pattern of evolution for that particular gene is generated and a tree has been found for inferring the changes that have taken place in the tree branches. Therefore, the first step for making a phylogenetic tree is a sequence alignment (Feng, 1985). An indication for each pair of sequences is the sequence similarity score. A tree is derived based on the best accounts for the numbers of changes (distances) between the sequences of these scores.

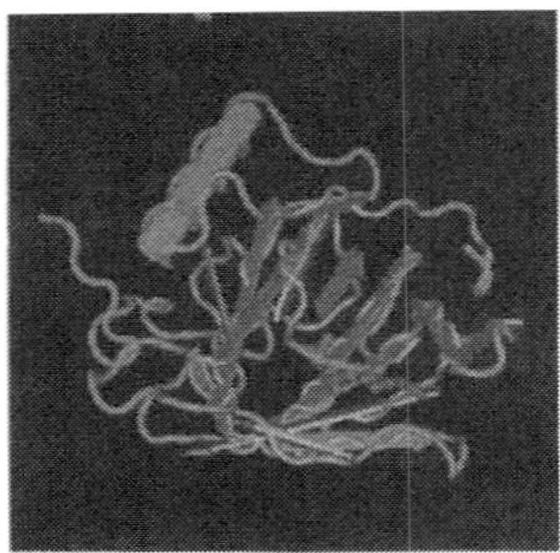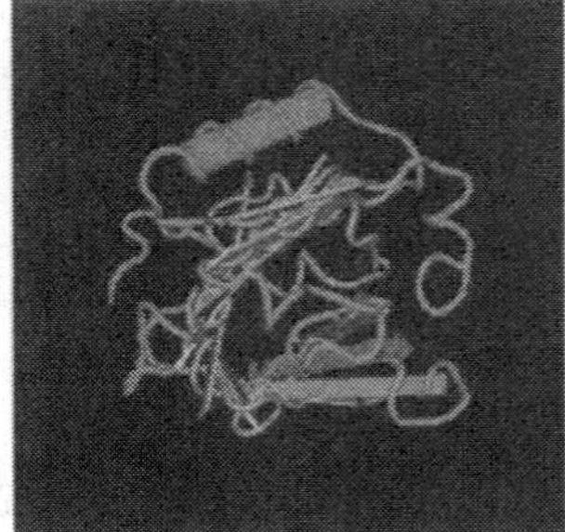

Fig. 1. Tree-dimentional structure of two lipocalins: bovine RBP (left side), bovin β-lactoglobuline (right side). These two proteins are homologous (evolve from a common ancestor), and they share very similar tree-dimensional structure consisting of a binding pocket for a ligand and eight antiparallel beta sheets.

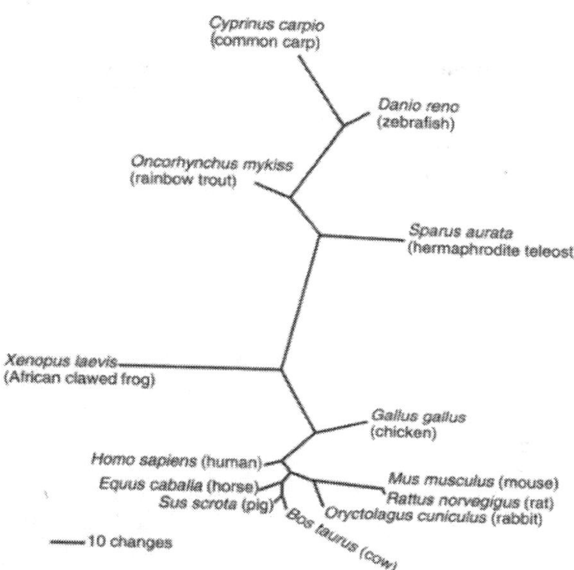

Fig. 2. Orthologous RBPs. In this tree, sequences that are more closely related to each other are grouped closer.

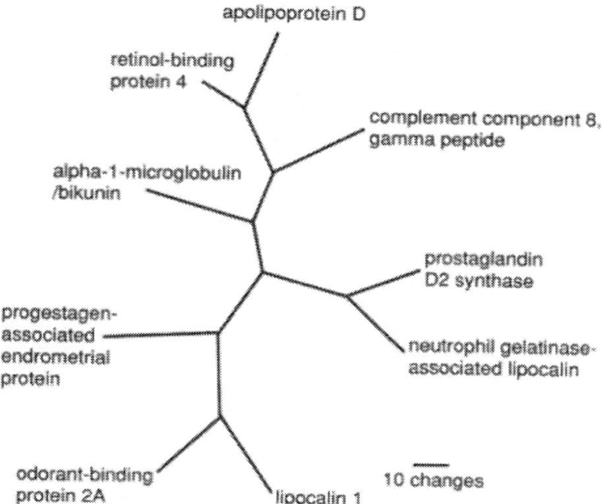

Fig. 3. Paralogous of human lipocalin proteins. Each of them is a member of protein family.

2. Alignment approaches

Sequence alignment is a way for comparing two (pair-wise alignment) or more than two (multiple alignment) sequences. This procedure looks for a series of particular residues or patterns that are in the same order. It is useful for discovering functional, structural, and evolutionary information in biological sequences (Wen et al., 2005; Berezin et al., 2003; Smoot, 2003). After sequence analysis if very much alike or similar sequences are found, they will probably have the same or similar biochemical functions and tree-dimensional structures (for protein sequences). If two sequences from different organisms are similar, there may have evolved from a common ancestor and the sequences are then defined to be homologous (Doolittle, 1981; Fitch & Smith, 1983; Feng & Doolittle, 1985). There are two approaches for sequence alignment: multiple sequence alignment and pair-wise sequence alignment.

2.1 Multiple sequence alignment

Multiple sequence alignment is a widely used method for comparing subsequences or entire length of more than two sequences and discovering the relations of their host organisms (Fig. 4). If two sequences are very close in terms of evolution, most of their residues remain unchanged and it will be rather difficult to detect important residues. On the other hand, if two sequences are evolutionarily distant, a reliable alignment of their sequences will be much more difficult to obtain. With aligning highest number of sequences of homologous proteins the aforementioned problem will be solved. Performing alignment the highly conserved residues that define structural and functional domains in protein families will be identified. New members of these families with the same domains can be found by searching sequence databases. A multiple sequence alignment implies a pair-wise alignment for each pair of sequences. The score of the multiple sequence alignment is the sum of scores of all implied pair-wise alignments. Multiple sequence alignment often tells us more than pair-wise alignment because it is more informative about evolutionary conservation (Edgar & Sjolander, 2004). The most common algorithm for multiple sequence alignment is BLAST. This algorithm has some programs like CLUSTALW for performing alignment and CLUSTALX for preparing graphical representation of the alignment (Larkin et al., 2007)

2.2 Pair-wise sequence alignment

In pair-wise alignment, two sequences are placed directly next to each other in two rows. For aligning protein sequences, the single-letter amino acid code is used. Identical or similar residues are placed in the same columns and non-identical residues can be placed either in the same column as a mismatch or opposite to a gap in the other sequences. The gaps are introduced to the sequences for shifting the residues (without disturbing its order) and obtaining the most possible matched residues, also for generating sequences with the same lengths. Some similar not identical residues are identified by pair-wise sequence alignment. Similar pairs of residues are related to each other because they share similar biochemical properties and are related functionally and structurally. When two similar residues are aligned, it is a representation of a conservative substitution that occurred during evolution. Amino acids with similar properties are comprised acidic amino acids like "D, E", basic amino acids like "K, R, H", hydroxylated amino acids "S, T", and hydrophobic amino acids "W, F, Y, L, I, V, M, A" (Pevsner, 2003a).

```
fly        GAKKVIISAP  SAD.APM..F  VCGVNLDAYK  PDMKVVSNAS  CTTNCLAPLA
human      GAKRVIISAP  SAD.APM..F  VMGVNHEKYD  NSLKIISNAS  CTTNCLAPLA
plant      GAKKVIISAP  SAD.APM..F  VVGVNEHTYQ  PNMDIVSNAS  CTTNCLAPLA
bacterium  GAKKVVMTGP  SKDNTPM..F  VKGANFDKY.  AGQDIVSNAS  CTTNCLAPLA
yeast      GAKKVVITAP  SS.TAPM..F  VMGVNEEKYT  SDLKIVSNAS  CTTNCLAPLA
archaeon   GADKVLISAP  PKGDEPVKQL  VYGVNHDEYD  GE.DVVSNAS  CTTNSITPVA

fly        KVINDNFEIV  EGLMTTVHAT  TATQKTVDGP  SGKLWRDGRG  AAQNIIPAST
human      KVIHDNFGIV  EGLMTTVHAI  TATQKTVDGP  SGKLWRDGRG  ALQNIIPAST
plant      KVVHEEFGIL  EGLMTTVHAT  TATQKTVDGP  SMKDWRGGRG  ASQNIIPSST
bacterium  KVINDNFGII  EGLMTTVHAT  TATQKTVDGP  SHKDWRGGRG  ASQNIIPSST
yeast      KVINDAFGIE  EGLMTTVHSL  TATQKTVDGP  SHKDWRGGRT  ASGNIIPSST
archaeon   KVLDEEFGIN  AGQLTTVHAY  TGSQNLMDGP  NGKP.RRRRA  AAENIIPTST

fly        GAAKAVGKVI  PALNGKLTGM  AFRVPTPNVS  VVDLTVRLGK  GASYDEIKAK
human      GAAKAVGKVI  PELNGKLTGM  AFRVPTANVS  VVDLTCRLEK  PAKYDDIKKV
plant      GAAKAVGKVL  PELNGKLTGM  AFRVPTSNVS  VVDLTCRLEK  GASYEDVKAA
bacterium  GAAKAVGKVL  PELNGKLTGM  AFRVPTPNVS  VVDLTVRLEK  AATYEQIKAA
yeast      GAAKAVGKVL  PELQGKLTGM  AFRVPTVDVS  VVDLTVKLNK  ETTYDEIKKV
archaeon   GAAQAATEVL  PELEGKLDGM  AIRVPVPNGS  ITEFVVDLDD  DVTESDVNAA
```

Fig. 4. Multiple sequence alignment of the portion of the glyseraldehyde 3-phosphate dehydrogenase (GAPDH) protein from six organisms.

For homology inference, after aligning two sequences some quantities must be calculated including percent identity and percent similarity. The percent similarity or positive of two protein sequences is the sum of both identical and similar matches divided by length of alignment and characterized with mark (:) in the alignment. The percent identity is concluded from the number of identical residues divided by the length of alignment and is shown with (|) mark in the alignment (Fig. 5). Since the similarity measure is calculated based upon a variety of definitions for identifying the degree of related residues, then it is more useful to consider the degree of identity shared by two protein sequences. In aligning sequences with different lengths, there must be no column with merely gap characters. In an optimal alignment, mismatched residues and gaps are placed in positions where bring as many as possible identical and similar residues.

2.2.1 Gaps and gap penalties

For obtaining the best possible alignment, introducing gaps in alignment and gap penalties for calculating alignment score is necessary. The addition of gaps in an alignment may be biologically relevant because the gaps reflect evolutionary changes that have occurred. They also allow full alignment of two proteins. The gaps represent two of tree types of common mutations occurred during evolution and caused divergence of the sequences of the two proteins. Insertions and deletions occur when residues are added or removed during evolution relative to the ancestor protein sequence and cause entering null characters or gaps to one of the sequences while aligning. There are two types of gap penalties: gap opening penalty for any gap (g) and gap extension penalty for each element in the gap (r) (Resee, 2002; Edgar, 2009). Thus, the total gap score w_x can be calculated.

$$w_x = g + rx \tag{1}$$

where, x is the length of the gap. There are several forms of gap penalty, including: 1-constant penalty, the simplest form where each gap is given a constant penalty independent of the length of the gap, 2-proportional penalty where the penalty is proportional to the length of the gap. With this form, longer gaps are given higher penalties than shorter ones, 3-affine gap penalty that is the most complex form of gap penalty (Fig. 6). It has both constant and proportional contributions. The motivation for using affine gap penalty is that opening a gap should be strongly penalized, but once a gap is opened it should cost less to extend it. If the used gap penalty is too high relative to the range of scores in the substitution matrix, gap will never appear in the alignment, but conversely if the gap penalty is too low compared to the matrix scores, gaps will appear everywhere in the alignment in order to align as much same residues as possible.

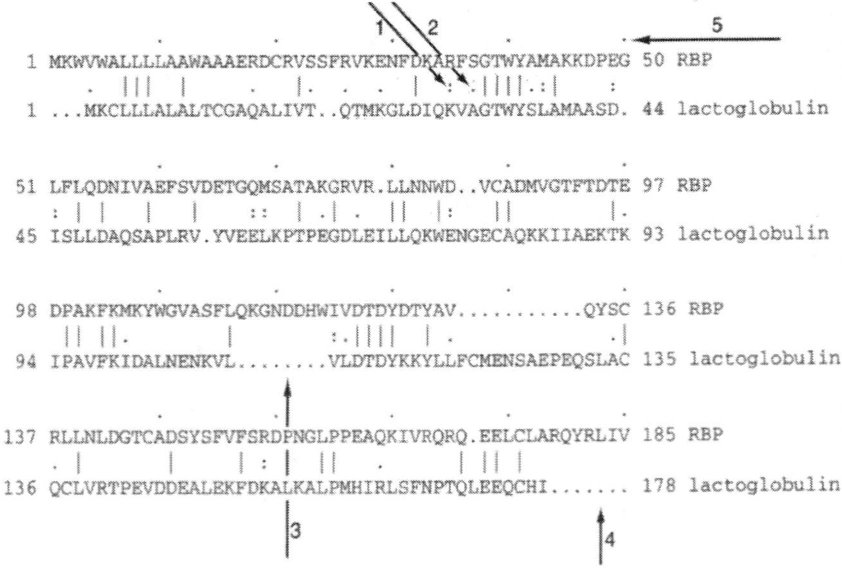

Fig. 5. Pair-wise alignment of human RBP and β-lactoglobulin. The alignment is global (the entire lengths of each protein is aligned) and there are many positions of identity between two sequences (shown with |). Dots are different. (1) The pair dots indicating different amounts of similarity (like R and K that share similar biochemical properties). (2) Single dots also indicate similarity, but less than paired dots. (3, 4) Dots in the place of alphabetic characters along the sequences show internal and external gaps. (5) A dot indicated above the sequences entered for marking every 10 residues.

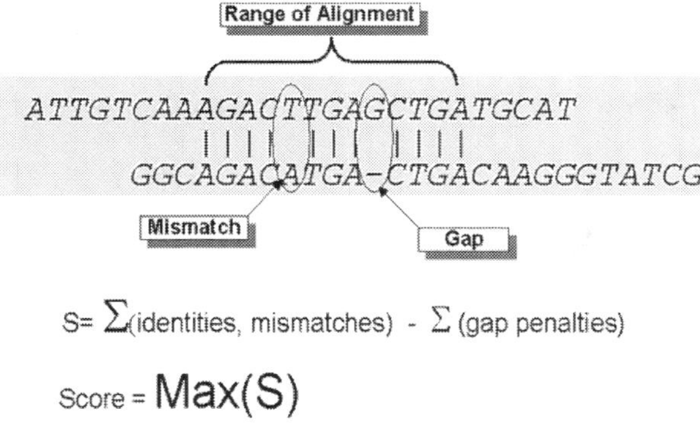

$$S = \sum (\text{identities, mismatches}) - \sum (\text{gap penalties})$$

$$\text{Score} = \text{Max}(S)$$

Fig. 6. A typical illustration of calculating gap affine penalty.

2.3 Alignment algorithms

For short and very closely related sequences, finding the best alignment is easy. However, in cases where sequences are long and not closely related finding the best alignment is rather difficult. If gaps are introduced in the alignment to account for deletions or insertions in the two sequences, the number of possible alignments increases exponentially. In these cases, computational methods are required. The known computational methods for this task are called dynamic programming algorithms. Such algorithms take two input sequences and produce the best alignment between them as output (Sankoff, 1972).

In general, there are two approaches for aligning sequences, global alignment and local alignment. In global alignment, the entire length of the sequence is subject to alignment. Sequences that are quite similar and their lengths are approximately the same are suitable for global alignment. In local alignment, the subsequences with the highest number of identical or similar residues are aligned and generate an alignment that is terminated at the ends of the regions with strong similarity. This type of alignment is a suitable way for aligning sequences that are similar along some regions of their length but dissimilar in others, sequences with different length, and those sequences share conserved regions. In sequence similarity analysis two dynamic programming algorithms are commonly used, the Needleman-Wunsch algorithm and the Smith-Waterman algorithm. These algorithms are closely related, but the main difference is that the Needleman-Wunsch algorithm finds global similarity between sequences while the Smith-Waterman algorithm finds local similarity. The Smith-Waterman algorithm is the most used, because in reality biological sequences are not often similar over their entire lengths, but are similar only in particular regions (Pearson, 1992; Smith & Waterman, 1981a; Smith et al., 1981b).

2.3.1 Global sequence alignment

Needleman-Wunsch algorithm is one of the first and most important algorithms for aligning two protein sequences based upon dynamic programming. The importance of this algorithm is from the point that it produces an optimal alignment of protein or DNA sequences even with entering the gaps. Generating global sequence alignment using this algorithm undergoes tree steps: 1-setting up identity matrix, 2-scoring the matrix, and 3-identifying the optimal alignment. In the first step, the two sequences are placed in a two-dimensional matrix (Fig. 7). The first sequence of length "m" is arranged horizontally along x axis so that each amino acid residue correspond to a column. The second sequence of length "n" is listed vertically along the y axis so that each amino acid residue corresponds to a row. For generating an amino acid identity matrix, simply each cell takes a value of +1 if the corresponding residues in row and column are identical and zero otherwise. Thus, for two identical sequences, in this matrix the +1 value would describe a diagonal line from top left to bottom right.

In the second step, a scoring matrix is generated. The assignment of scores starts from the bottom right of the matrix, corresponding to the carboxy termini of the proteins, and proceeds to the top. For moving through the matrix, to define a path corresponding to the sequence alignment, there are several rules. Briefly, for setting up the scoring matrix in the second step, at position i and j, take the value of the cell plus the maximum score obtained from any of the following three values:

1. The score diagonally down (at position $i+1, j+1$), without including any gaps.
2. The highest score may find in position $i+1, j+2$ to the end of row j. Finding the highest score in this position cause to the addition of a gap in the column. The number of gap can be greater than 1.
3. The highest score may find in position $i+2, j+1$ to the end of column of i. This finding corresponds to the addition of a gap in the row.

The third step is identifying the optimal alignment, i.e. the path through the matrix that maximizes the score. Thus, a path through as many positions of identity as possible while introducing as few gaps as possible must be found exploiting a trace-back strategy. We begin at the upper left of the matrix (amino termini of the proteins) with the highest value (in Fig. 7 this value is "+8" corresponding to an alignment of residues A to A). Then we find the path down and to the right with the highest numbers along the diagonal. Going off the diagonal implies automatically the insertion of a gap in one of the sequences and entering some penalty. There may be more than one optimal alignment where all of them have an equally high score (Fig. 7). In such cases that uses unitary scoring scheme, multiple optimal alignment is obtained, but the introduction of a sophisticated scoring matrix like series of BLOSUM and PAM, it is unlikely to find multiple optimal alignments. For evaluating the obtained global alignment, the percent identity and similarity shared by two proteins, the length of the alignment, and the number of gaps which is introduced to the alignment is calculated (Needleman & Wunsch, 1970).

2.3.2 Local sequence alignment

Local alignment, a modified dynamic programming algorithm, seeks the highest scoring local match between two sequences. This algorithm proposed by smith and waterman (1981) is a very strong method for finding the high scoring subsets of two protein or DNA sequences. It is very useful in a variety of applications such as database searching. In general, this algorithm generates a matrix by two protein sequences and then finds the optimal path along a diagonal like global algorithm, but the alignment does not necessarily extend to the ends of the two sequences and for starting the alignment from some internal position, there is no penalty.

The Smith-Waterman algorithm constructs a matrix with an extra row along the top and an extra column on the left side. Thus, for two sequences of lengths "m" and "n", the matrix dimension is m+1 by n+1. The score of each cell is selected as the maximum score in the

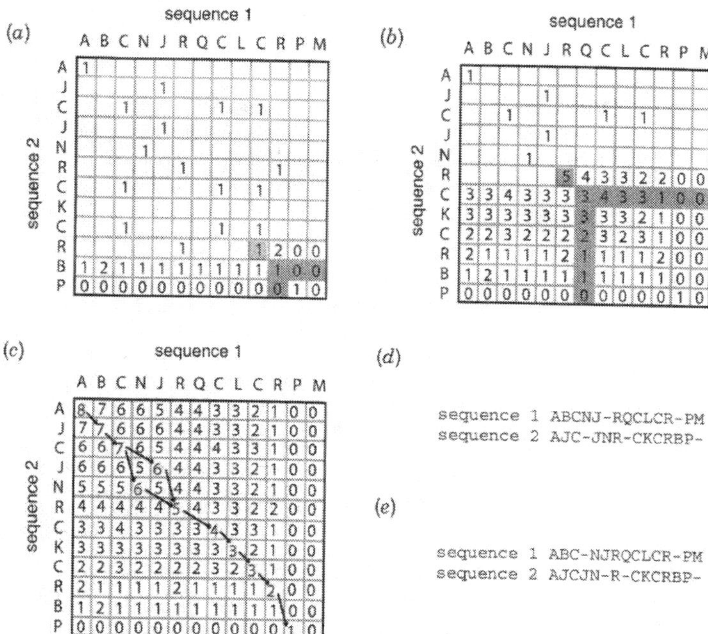

Fig. 7. Global pair-wise alignment of two amino acid sequences using a dynamic programming algorithm. Generating the scoring matrix and using the trace-back procedure for obtaining the optimal alignment path is shown and ultimately the alignment of the two equally optimal path are shown in section d (the upper path) and e (the lower path).

preceding diagonal or the score obtained from the introduction of a gap, but the score cannot be negative. In this algorithm if a negative value is generated in each cell, a zero is inserted in the cell, instead (Fig. 8). The score of each cell like i, j or $H(i, j)$ is given as the maximum of four possible values:

1. The score which is located at position $i-1, j-1$ (the score diagonally up to the left). This score is added to the new score in position $s(i, j)$ which consists of either a match (1) or a mismatch (-0.3).
2. $s(i, j-1)$, located at one cell to the left minus a gap penalty.
3. $s(i-1, j)$, immediately above the new cell, minus a gap penalty.
4. zero. Assures that there is no negative value in the matrix.

For two sequences, $a = a_1\ a_2\ \dots\ a_n$, and $b = b_1\ b_2\ \dots\ b_m$, where $H_{i,j} = H\ (a_1\ a_2\ \dots a_i,\ b_1\ b_2\ \dots b_j)$, then:

$$H_{i,j} = \max\{H_{i-1,j} - 1 + s(a,b), \max(H_{i-x,j} - w_x), \max(H_{i,j-y} - w_y), 0\} \tag{2}$$

$$H_{x0} = H_{0y} = 0 \quad \text{for} \quad 0 \le x \le n \quad \text{and} \quad 0 \le y \le m$$

$$1 \le i \le n \quad \text{and} \quad 1 \le j \le m$$

$$w_x = 1 + \frac{1}{3 \times x} \quad \text{and} \quad w_y = 1 + \frac{1}{3 \times y} \tag{3}$$

In equation (2), $H_{i,j}$ is the score at position i in sequence a and position j in sequence b, $s(a_i, b_j)$ is the score for aligning the characters at positions i and j. In equation (3), w_x is the penalty for a gap of length x in sequence a, and w_y is the penalty for a gap of length y in sequence b.

The maximal alignment can begin and end everywhere in the matrix so that the linear order of the two amino acid sequences cannot be violated. The trace-back procedure finds the highest value in the matrix and begins the alignment from the position of the highest number. It proceeds diagonally up to the left until a cell is reached with a value of zero. The zero value defines the start of the alignment, and is not necessarily at the extreme top left of the matrix (Smith & Waterman, 1981).

	Δ	C	A	G	C	C	U	C	G	C	U	U	A	G
Δ	0·0	0·0	0·0	0·0	0·0	0·0	0·0	0·0	0·0	0·0	0·0	0·0	0·0	0·0
A	0·0	0·0	1·0	0·0	0·0	0·0	0·0	0·0	0·0	0·0	0·0	0·0	1·0	0·0
A	0·0	0·0	1·0	0·7	0·0	0·0	0·0	0·0	0·0	0·0	0·0	0·0	1·0	0·7
U	0·0	0·0	0·0	0·7	0·3	0·0	1·0	0·0	0·0	0·0	1·0	1·0	0·0	0·7
G	0·0	0·0	0·0	1·0	0·3	0·0	0·0	0·7	1·0	0·0	0·0	0·7	0·7	1·0
C	0·0	1·0	0·0	0·0	2·0	1·3	0·3	1·0	0·3	2·0	0·7	0·3	0·3	0·3
C	0·0	1·0	0·7	0·0	1·0	3·0	1·7	1·3	1·0	1·3	1·7	0·3	0·0	0·0
A	0·0	0·0	2·0	0·7	0·3	1·7	2·7	1·3	1·0	0·7	1·0	1·3	1·3	0·0
U	0·0	0·0	0·7	1·7	0·3	1·3	2·7	2·3	1·0	0·7	1·7	2·0	1·0	1·0
U	0·0	0·0	0·3	0·3	1·3	1·0	2·3	2·3	2·0	0·7	1·7	2·7	1·7	1·0
G	0·0	0·0	0·0	1·3	0·0	1·0	1·0	2·0	3·3	2·0	1·7	1·3	2·3	2·7
A	0·0	0·0	1·0	0·0	1·0	0·3	0·7	0·7	2·0	3·0	1·7	1·3	2·3	2·0
C	0·0	1·0	0·0	0·7	1·0	2·0	0·7	1·7	1·7	3·0	2·7	1·3	1·0	2·0
G	0·0	0·0	0·7	1·0	0·3	0·7	1·7	0·3	2·7	1·7	2·7	2·3	1·0	2·0
G	0·0	0·0	0·0	1·7	0·7	0·3	0·3	1·3	1·3	2·3	1·3	2·3	2·0	2·0

Fig. 8. A typical example for pair-wise local sequence alignment using smith-waterman algorithm.

3. Rapid and heuristic versions of smith-waterman: FASTA and BLAST

Theoretically sequence alignment techniques are based upon two different backgrounds (Pearson, 1996, 1988): Dot matrix analysis (Gibbs & McIntyre, 1970) and the dynamic programming analysis such as Needleman-Wunsch and Smith-Waterman. The dot matrix analysis is used when the sequences are known to be very much alike and this similarity is clearly observed by displaying any possible alignments as diagonals on the matrix. This analysis reveals readily any insertions, deletions, direct and inverted repeats that are found with difficulty by the other methods. However, major limitation of this analysis is that most of these programs do not show an actual alignment. For comparing sequences based on this analysis, one sequence (A) is listed across the top of a page and the other sequence (B) is listed down the left side. Starting with the first character in sequence B and then move across the page to the end of the first row and placing a dot in any column where the character in sequence A is the same. This continues until the page is filled with dots representing all the possible matches of A characters with B characters. Any region of similar residues is identified by a string of dots located on the diagonal. Other dots, located on the positions everywhere other than diagonal represent random matches that are probably not related to any significant alignment.

There are tree types of variations for analysis of two protein sequences by the dot matrix method. First, one can use chemical similarity of the amino acid R group or some other features for detecting similarity score. Second, one can apply the specific scoring matrices such as PAM and BLOSUM. These matrices provide scores for matches that have occurred based on aligning the protein families (these matrices will be described in section 4) (States & Boguski, 1991). Finally, it can be analyzed by producing several different matrices, each of them with a different scoring system and with average of different scores. This method is suitable for more distantly related proteins.

Although the alignment algorithms based on dynamic programming analysis such as Smith and Waterman guaranteed to find the optimal alignment(s) between two sequences, it is relatively slow. For pairwise alignment, the speed is not a problem but when it is used for database searching, that is, comparing one sequence as a query to an entire database, the speed of the algorithm becomes an important factor. In most algorithms there is a parameter called N that refers to the number of data items need to be processed. The required time for the algorithm to perform a task is greatly affected by this parameter. If the running time is proportional to N, then doubling N doubles the running time. For both algorithms based on dynamic programming, Needleman-Wunsch and Smith-Waterman, the memory space and the time required for aligning two sequences is proportional to the product of the length of two queries, m×n, and for the search of a database of size N, that is, m×n×N. The modified algorithm of Smith-Waterman was developed to provide rapid alternative algorithms such as FASTA (Pearson and Lipman, 1988) and BLAST (Basic Local Alignment Search Tool) (Altschul et al., 1990). Both of these algorithms require less time to perform an alignment. These algorithms are heuristic and since they restrict the search by scanning a database for likely matches before performing the actual alignment they require less time, but it is not guaranteed to find optimal alignments.

3.1 FASTA heuristic algorithm

This algorithm, divides the query sequence as well as the considered database into subsequences with arbitrary lengths (for protein sequences two or three amino acid length), so called "words". Then, the positions of the words in the query sequence and database sequences are calculated. The ktup value or the length of the words is a value which determines how many consecutive identities are required for a match to be declared. The lesser the ktup value, the more sensitive the alignment. Often, ktup = 2 is taken for proteins, and ktup=6 for nucleotides. The same word can appear more than once in the sequence without affecting the algorithm (Pearson, 2000). After dividing sequences according to ktup value to consecutive subsequences, the relative position of each word in the two sequences is calculated by subtracting the position of the word in the query from each of the database sequences. Those words that have the same offset, they can be part of the same alignment without insertions or deletions. Therefore, by constructing a look-up table, all dense regions of identities between two sequences are identified. Next, the score of each aligned regions is calculated using PAM250 matrix selecting the 10 highest scoring regions for each database sequence. The sum of the scores of the 10 regions is called the best initial regions (init1) and used to rank the matches for further analysis. The longer regions of identity are generated by joining initial regions (initn) with scores greater than a certain threshold. The initn score is the sum of the scores of these aligned regions after subtracting a penalty accounting for the gaps. In later versions of FASTA, an optimization step is added. When the initn score reaches to a certain threshold value, the score of the region is recalculated for producing an OPT score by performing a full local alignment of the region using Smith-Waterman dynamic programming algorithm. This optimization increases the sensitivity but decreases the selectivity of the search (pearson, 1990, 1991,1998; Tramontano, 2006; Mahdavi, 2010). These scores (initn and OPT) are the basis to rank database matches.

3.2 BLAST heuristic algorithm

The BLAST algorithm was established as a new tool to perform a sequence similarity search based on an algorithm that is faster than FASTA, but is as sensitive as FASTA. The BLAST web server (http://www.ncbi.nlm.nih.gov) is the most widely used for sequence database searches and is backed up by a powerful computer system. The original version of the BLAST looks for contiguous similarity regions between the query and database sequences (without using gaps). The speed of the algorithm like FASTA increases by initially searching common words or k-tuples in the query sequence and each database sequence. While FASTA searches for all possible words of same length, BLAST searches the words that are most significant. The word length for this algorithm is fixed at 3 for proteins and 11 for nucleic acids. This length is the minimum length required to achieve a word score that is high enough to be significant but not so long to miss short but significant patterns. There are several steps involved for searching a protein sequence database for a query protein sequence by BLAST algorithm (Altschul et al., 1990, 1994, 1997). In similarity searching by BLAST program, three steps need to be taken. The program compiles a preliminarily list of pair-wise alignment called "word pairs". Then the algorithm scans a database for word pairs that meet some threshold score T and extends the word pairs to find those sequences that scores better than the cutoff score S. Scores are calculated from scoring matrices (such as BLOSUM62) along with gap penalties.

In preprocessing stage, the query string is divided into words of length 3. The goal of the preprocessing stage is to build a hash table, which is called query index. The keys of the hash table are the 20×20×20=8000 possible tree-letter words. The value associated with each word is the position of that word in the list of all query words that gain a high score when aligned against the key word. The threshold for high-score that is defined by default in BLOSUM62 scoring matrix is 11. Threshold score or neighborhood word score threshold (T) is selected for reducing the number of possible matches. For example, if a three-letter word PQG occurs in the query sequence, the match score of this word to itself is calculated by the log-odds BLOSUM62 matrix as P-P match, plus that for a Q-Q match, plus that for a G-G match that equals to 7+5+6=18. Similarly, the PQG match to PEG scores 15, to PGR 14, to PSG 13, and to PQA 12. For DNA words, the score for a match is +5 and for a mismatch is -4. With selecting the threshold score, the list of possible matching words is shortened from 8000 (for w (word length) = 3) to the highest scoring words that satisfy the threshold score. The preprocessing stage is repeated for each three- letter word in the query sequence. The remaining high-scoring words that include possible matches to each three-letter position in the query sequence are listed in a table called the query index in order to create an efficient rapidly comparing search to the database sequences. In the second step, each database sequence is scanned for identifying an exact match to one of the words listed in the query index. If a match is found, this match is used to seed a possible ungapped alignment between the query and database sequences. In the last step, an attempt is made for extending an alignment from the matching words in each direction along the sequences. The extending process is continued as long as the score is increased and is stopped once the accumulated score did not increase and begun to fall a small amount below the best score found for shorter extensions (Dawid, 2001; Pevsner, 2003b). In this condition, a longer stretch of sequence (called the HSP or high-scoring segment pair) with a greater score than the original word is found. In order to determining a suitable value for S, the range of scores found by comparing random sequences is examined and significant values are selected. In the later version of BLAST, called BLAST2 or gapped BLAST (Altschul et al., 1997; Brenner, et al., 1998), a list of high-scoring matching words is made similar to the original method with the exception that a lower value of T, the word cutoff score, is used. The lower cutoff score produces longer word list and matches to lower scoring words in the database sequences.

In order to remove the low-complexity regions that are not useful for producing meaningful sequence alignments, the filtering programs is used. Filtering masks portions of the query sequence that have commonly found stretch of amino acids or nucleotides with limited information content. For protein sequence queries, the SEG program is used and for nucleic acid sequences, the DUST program is employed. Using Filtering programs, low complexity residues are replaced with a string of characters with the letter X (for protein sequences) or N (for nucleic acid sequences). In general, filtering is useful to avoid receiving spurious database matches, but in some cases authentic matches may be missed.

3.2.1 An example

Let the following query sequence:

$$\text{C I N C I N N A T I} \quad (w=3, n=10, T=11, \text{BLOSUM62 matrix})$$

where, the number of words with length 3 (w=3) is calculated as follows:

$$N = n - w + 1 \tag{4}$$

Then, for the given query sequence, N=8. The three-letter words of the query sequences are:

C I N (1)   I N C (2)   N C I (3)   C I N (4)   I N N (5)   N N A (6)   N A T (7)   ATI (8)

Using BLOSUM62 matrix, 54 words of 8000 key words in the hash table obtain score 11 or greater when aligned with the C I N word which is located at positions 1 and 4.

CAN CCN CDN CEN CFN CGN CHN CIA CID CIE CIG CIH CIK CIM CIN CIP CIQ CIR CIS CIT CIY CKN CLD CLE CLG CLH CLK CLN CLQ CLR CLS CLT CMD CMH CMN CMS CNN CPN CQN CRN CSN CTN CVD CVE CVG CVH CVK CVN CVQ CVR CVS CVT CWN CYN

Similarly, only three pairs obtain score 11 or greater when aligned with A T I at position 8. Overall, preprocessing of the query sequence assigns 204 entries of the 8000 possible keys. After preprocessing stage, the next step is scanning the target string (reference sequence) successively for finding exact matches to one of the words in the query index. Suppose, following sequence as a target string:

$$\text{P R E C I N C T S}$$

For this sequence N=7, then the three-letter words along their locations are:

PRE(1), REC(2), ECI(3), CIN(4), INC(5), NCT(6), CTS(7)

Looking up NCT at position 6 of the target string, the search generates hits (3,6) and (7,6). This means that similar words to position 6 at the reference sequence are at positions 3 and 7 of the query sequence. After finding the location of the exact matches, each hit is extended to the right and to the left to increase the alignment's score. The alignment is extended until the overall alignment score maximizes. In this example, the corresponding alignment for the hit at query position 3 and target position 6 is:

$$- - - c i\, N C I\ N n a t i$$

$$p r e\ c i\, N C T\ S ----$$

Hence, the final local alignment is:

$$C I N C I N$$

$$C I N C T S$$

The score of this local alignment is calculated as follows:

$$S_{CC} + S_{II} + S_{NN} + S_{CC} + S_{IT} + S_{NS} = 9 + 4 + 6 + 9 + (-1) + 1 = 28$$

Another hit at query position 7 and target position 6 is:

$$c i\ n c i\ n N A T I$$

$$- p r e c i\ N C T s$$

The score of this alignment can no longer be increased by further extending it to either left or right (Dwyer, 2003).

4. Representation of different substitution matrices

4.1 Amino acid substitution matrices

Amino acid arrangement of proteins and nucleic acids change due to mutations occur over the course of evolution. Amino acids are substituted by other amino acids during mutation and these substitutions cause variations in phenotype of the related species. There are some regions in the sequence that undergo massive mutations and some other regions remain conserved over a long period of time in evolution. The alignment outcome demonstrates conserved regions in related protein sequences that represent functions of the proteins (Campanella et al., 2003). Additionally, it shows some amino acid substitutions commonly occur in related proteins from different species. Substituted amino acids are compatible with protein structure and function and are chemically similar to amino acids which are changed. Some substitutions are rare or least common and some of them are most common. Sequence alignment is a useful tool for understanding the type of changes occurred in related protein sequences. Based on the type of substitution different matrices were built such as PAM and BLOSUM. Substitution matrices are used in sequence alignments while they are built out of aligning carefully selected sequences. In the following the detail description of PAM and BLOSUM substitution matrices is presented.

4.1.1 PAM (point accepted mutation) matrices

Margaret Dayhoff (1978) developed a method for determining the most likely amino acid changes that occurred during evolution by assessing ancestral relationship among a group of proteins (Kim & Kececioglu, 2008). The analysis was performed based on multiple sequence alignment of 34 closely related protein superfamilies which were grouped in 71 phylogenetic trees (such as: cytochrome c, hemoglobin, myoglobin, virus coat proteins, chymotrypsinogen, glyceraldehydes 3-phosphate dehydrogenase, clupeine, insulin and ferredoxin). The studied groups of proteins ranged from very well conserved (like, histones and glutamate dehydrogenase) to proteins with high rate of point mutations (like immunoglobin chains and carrier proteins). In this model for creating the mutation data matrix (MDM), the sequences of all of the nodal common ancestors in each tree were generated by multiple sequence alignment of each protein family, then counting the most frequent amino acids for inferring the common ancestor of each family from those most frequent amino acids. The matrix of accepted point mutation was calculated for each protein family separately from the constructed phylogenetic tree which was inferred for each studied protein family. In this matrix it was assumed that the likelihood of amino acid X replacing Y is the same as that of Y replacing X, and hence 1 was entered in cell YX as well as in cell XY (Dayhoff, 1972). Dayhoff assumed that by considering this symmetry, the frequency of occurrence of an amino acid in any large group of studied proteins appears to have been relatively constant with time. The accumulated accepted point matrix for closely related sequences was generated by summing the number of corresponding elements of each separately accepted point matrix, which was computed for each protein family sequences together. Next, the relative mutability of the 20 amino acids in sequences of each studied protein family was calculated. Relative mutability was simply calculated as the number of observed changes of an amino acid divided by its frequency of occurrence in the aligned sequences. Mutability was normalized with respect to the basic unit of evolutionary distance as being a single accepted point mutation in a sequence of length 100. Consequently, the average relative mutability of an amino acid was therefore the total number of changes observed for this amino acid in all the families of studied proteins, divided by the total sum of all local frequencies of occurrence of the amino acid multiplied by the numbers of mutations per 100 residues in each of the branches of all the family trees. The mutation probability matrix was then constructed (Fig. 9). An element of this matrix, M_{ij}, gives the probability that the amino acid in column j would be replaced by the amino acid in row i after a given evolutionary interval. The values of the non diagonal elements of this matrix were computed by following equation (Dayhoff, 1972):

$$M_{ij} = \frac{\lambda m_j A_{ij}}{\sum\limits_i A_{ij}} \tag{5}$$

Where, A_{ij} is an element of the accepted point mutation matrix, λ is proportionality constant, and m_j is the mutability of the jth amino acid. The values of diagonal elements are calculated as follows:

$$M_{ij} = 1 - \lambda m_j \tag{6}$$

In mutation probability matrix, the ratio of the individual non-diagonal terms within each column has the same ratio of the observed mutation in the mutation data matrix. The proportionality constant λ is the same for all columns of the matrix and is calculated by following equation for 1PAM evolutionary interval in which 1% of amino acids have changed (Higgs & Attwood, 2005):

$$\lambda = 0.01 \frac{N_{tot}}{A_{tot}} \qquad (7)$$

where, N_{tot} is the total number of amino acids in the data set, and A_{tot} is the total number of elements in the A_{ij} matrix.

In mutation probability matrix, the diagonal elements are all slightly less than one, and off diagonal elements are very small. The number of unchanged amino acids, when a 100-residue protein sequence (of average composition) is exposed to the evolutionary changes, is computed as follows:

$$100 \times \sum_i f_i M_{ii} \qquad (8)$$

ORIGINAL AMINO ACID

| | | A | R | N | D | C | Q | E | G | H | I | L | K | M | F | P | S | T | W | Y | V |
		Ala	Arg	Asn	Asp	Cys	Gln	Glu	Gly	His	Ile	Leu	Lys	Met	Phe	Pro	Ser	Thr	Trp	Tyr	Val
A	Ala	9730	0	31	24	5	34	37	42	5	3	5	18	19	5	54	99	45	0	0	32
R	Arg	0	9881	5	0	0	13	0	0	17	0	0	23	18	2	0	1	0	0	0	0
N	Asn	14	7	9701	36	0	20	7	10	24	4	2	19	1	0	10	51	17	0	0	4
D	Asp	13	0	45	9757	0	27	96	8	6	0	2	8	1	0	1	26	2	0	0	4
C	Cys	1	0	0	0	9928	0	0	1	0	2	0	0	11	0	0	12	3	0	0	6
Q	Gln	12	14	15	16	0	9736	24	4	14	4	2	9	11	0	11	13	10	0	0	5
E	Glu	21	0	9	95	0	40	9726	13	4	4	4	13	1	0	17	15	12	0	0	7
G	Gly	40	0	22	13	3	11	22	9870	1	0	2	5	0	0	17	42	8	0	0	7
H	His	2	19	20	4	0	15	3	0	9865	4	3	6	0	3	0	10	5	11	4	1
I	Ile	1	0	3	0	3	4	3	0	4	9703	22	4	22	14	2	3	14	0	0	70
L	Leu	4	0	3	3	0	4	7	2	6	52	9899	6	99	19	0	5	7	0	0	24
K	Lys	17	65	37	13	0	23	21	5	14	9	6	9845	11	0	6	22	14	0	4	13
M	Met	2	7	0	0	5	4	0	0	0	7	14	2	9672	5	0	5	2	0	0	12
F	Phe	2	3	0	0	0	0	0	0	4	18	10	0	18	9879	0	5	2	30	74	2
P	Pro	23	0	9	1	0	13	13	7	0	3	0	3	0	0	9850	11	5	0	0	4
S	Ser	59	2	67	28	27	22	16	26	17	4	3	14	23	6	15	9598	69	0	0	7
T	Thr	30	0	25	3	8	20	14	6	8	24	5	10	11	3	8	76	9759	0	0	20
W	Trp	0	0	0	0	0	0	0	0	4	0	0	0	0	8	0	0	0	9941	7	0
Y	Tyr	0	0	0	0	0	0	0	0	4	0	0	2	0	51	0	0	0	17	9909	0
V	Val	27	0	7	5	18	12	10	6	3	156	22	12	82	3	8	9	25	0	0	9783

(REPLACEMENT AMINO ACID — row labels at left)

Fig. 9. Mutation probability matrix for the evolutionary distance of 2PAMs. Each element of this matrix gives the probability that the amino acid in column j will be replaced by the amino acid in row i after a given evolutionary interval, in this case 2 accepted point mutations per 100 amino acids. Values are multiplied by 10000 for convenience.

Other PAM matrices are calculated from multiplying PAM1 matrix by itself with respect to the characteristic number of the PAM matrix (e.g. PAM250 matrix is produced when the PAM1 matrix is multiplied by itself 250 times). A scoring system has been developed for converting the elements of a PAM mutation probability matrix into a scoring matrix or log-odd matrix as follows (Pevsner, 2003a):

$$S(a,b) = 10\log_{10}\left(\frac{M_{ab}}{P_b}\right) \tag{9}$$

where, M_{ab} is the probability that the aligned pair of amino acid residues a and b represent an authentic alignment and P_b is the normalized frequency representing the probability that the residue b was aligned by chance.

The PAM1 matrix is recalculated (Jones et al., 1992) using updated data, called PET91. This dataset was generated from Release 15.0 of the SWISS-PROT protein sequence database (Bairoch, 1996), containing 16941 sequences. Also, a mutation data matrix has been calculated for transmembrane proteins (Jones et al., 1993). It was found that this new mutation data matrix is very different from matrices calculated from general sequence sets which are biased towards water-soluble globular proteins. The differences are discussed in the context of specific structural requirements of membrane spanning segments. Calculating the mutation data matrix for each protein family and hence creating specific PAM scoring matrix for each protein family will help to improve the accuracy of the protein sequence alignment results.

4.1.2 BLOSUM matrices (Blocks Amino Acid Substitution Matrices)

BLOSUM scoring matrices are improved alternatives to PAM. These series of scoring matrices are widely used for scoring protein sequence alignments. The BLOSUM matrices are derived from the database for storing the sequence alignments of the most conserved regions of protein families, BLOCK database (S. Henikoff & J.G. Henikoff, 1996). This database of blocks is consisted of over 500 groups of local multiple alignments of distantly related proteins. The BLOSUM matrix values are obtained by the same method applied to PAM matrices. The values are computed from the observed amino acid substitutions in a large set of about 2000 conserved amino acid patterns. The constructed blocks from patterns of amino acids in each protein family, derived ungapped multiple alignments. For deriving BLOSUM matrices from blocks, not all the sequences are used but a percentage of identity higher than a certain threshold are merged and considered (S. Henikoff & J.G. Henikoff, 1992). Therefore, different BLOSUM matrices are produced for each threshold. For example, BLOSUM62 matrix (Fig. 10) is derived from merging several alignments with 62%, 80%, and 95% identity. This matrix is useful for scoring proteins that share less than 62% identity. By increasing the clustering percentage, the ability of the resulting matrix to distinguish actual from random alignments also increased. The numbers associated with BLOSUM matrices do not have the same interpretation as those for PAM matrices. BLOSUM matrices with smaller numbers represent more evolutionary distances while BLOSUM matrices with higher numbers represent closer evolutionary distances. Consequently, BLOSUM matrices are obtained based on entirely different type of sequence analysis and a much larger data set than the Dayhoff's PAM matrices. The values of the BLOSUM scoring matrix are obtained based on similar procedure applied to PAM matrices. However, BLOSUM scoring matrices are calculated from 2 times the log base 2 of the odds ratio, as follows:

$$S_b(a,b) = 2\log_2\left(\frac{M_{ab}}{P_b}\right) \tag{10}$$

4.1.3 Comparison of the PAM and BLOSUM amino acid substitution matrices

Methods of computing PAM and BLOSUM scoring matrices have several important differences. The PAM matrices are computed based on a mutational model of evolution which assumes each amino acid change at a specific position is independent of the previous changes at that position (based on Markov model).

	A	R	N	D	C	Q	E	G	H	I	L	K	M	F	P	S	T	W	Y	V
A	4																			
R	-1	5																		
N	-2	0	6																	
D	-2	-2	1	6																
C	0	-3	-3	-3	9															
Q	-1	1	0	0	-3	5														
E	-1	0	0	2	-4	2	5													
G	0	-2	0	-1	-3	-2	-2	6												
H	-2	0	1	-1	-3	0	0	-2	8											
I	-1	-3	-3	-3	-1	-3	-3	-4	-3	4										
L	-1	-2	-3	-4	-1	-2	-3	-4	-3	2	4									
K	-1	2	0	-1	-1	1	1	-2	-1	-3	-2	5								
M	-1	-2	-2	-3	-1	0	-2	-3	-2	1	2	-1	5							
F	-2	-3	-3	-3	-2	-3	-3	-3	-1	0	0	-3	0	6						
P	-1	-2	-2	-1	-3	-1	-1	-2	-2	-3	-3	-1	-2	-4	7					
S	1	-1	1	0	-1	0	0	0	-1	-2	-2	0	-1	-2	-1	4				
T	0	-1	0	-1	-1	-1	-1	-2	-2	-1	-1	-1	-1	-2	-1	1	5			
W	-3	-3	-4	-4	-2	-2	-3	-2	-2	-3	-2	-3	-1	1	-4	-3	-2	11		
Y	-2	-2	-2	-3	-2	-1	-2	-3	2	-1	-1	-2	-1	3	-3	-2	-2	2	7	
V	0	-3	-3	-3	-1	-2	-2	-3	-3	3	1	-2	1	-1	-2	-2	0	-3	-1	4

Fig. 10. BLOSUM62 scoring matrix.

By predicting the phylogenetic tree of the studied sequences of each protein family, the early changes that occur as protein diverge from a common ancestor during evolution is identified. In order to derive matrices used for more distantly related proteins, short term changes are extrapolated. In contrast, BLOSUM matrices are derived based on all observed changes in an aligned region of a related family of proteins without considering the global similarity between the considered protein sequences. Since these related proteins in the family are known to be related biochemically, they should be derived from a common ancestor. Generally, PAM model is designed to track the evolutionary origins of proteins but the BLOSUM model is designed to find their conserved domains. Both use log-odd values in their scoring systems (Vogt, 1995).

4.2 Nucleic acid scoring matrices

There are scoring matrices for DNA sequence alignments as amino acid scoring matrices. A series of nucleic acid PAM matrices are calculated in similar way that amino acid PAM scoring matrices are generated. To derive DNA PAM matrices first a PAM1 mutation matrix which is representing 99% sequence conservation or 1% mutations across evolutionary distance is calculated. It is upon the assumption that the frequencies of four nucleotides in studied sequences are equal. Also all mutations from any nucleotide to any other are equally likely. Thus, the four diagonal elements of the PAM1 matrix representing no changes are equal to 0.99, but the other elements of the matrix representing changes are 0.00333. For converting substitution matrix to scoring matrix just as amino acid matrices, the values of the this matrix is used for producing log-odds scoring matrices which is representing the frequency of substitutions expected to occur at increasing evolutionary distances. For scoring DNA alignments with DNA PAM scoring matrices, the lower numbered DNA PAM matrices is used for more alike DNA sequences and the high numbered DNA PAM matrices are used for more diverge DNA sequences along evolutionary distance (States et al., 1991).

5. Statistical analysis of alignments

One of the main challenges of the sequence similarity searches is to detect weather an identified sequence similarity between DNA or protein sequences are statistically significant. For two proteins that are quite similar and clearly grouped in the same family, assessing the significance is not necessary. However, when we are dealing with two sequences with no clear similarity, once the alignment is performed statistical analysis becomes important. In such cases, biologists would like to know if the observed similarity resulted from the alignment is obtained by chance or is authentic. A statistical test assists biologists to identify the more distant related protein or DNA sequences from unrelated. The assessing test is performed on the basis of the assumption that the alignment scores follow a normal distribution. For evaluating the distribution of alignment scores, some random sequences are generated by sequence shuffling technique. Analysis of the alignment scores of random sequences reveal that the scores follow a type of normal distribution called Gumbel extreme value distribution (Altschul & Gish, 1996; Altschul & Bouguski, 1994). Generally, the statistical analysis of alignment scores for local alignments is better understood than global alignments. Since, the Smith-Waterman algorithm reveals regions of conserved or closely matching with a positive score, in random or unrelated sequence alignments these regions are rarely found. Therefore, presence of such regions in real sequences is significant while the probability of occurrence of such regions by chance is close to zero. P-value is a suitable parameter which is used for identifying the probability that a score of S or greater is obtained by chance between two unrelated matched sequences of similar composition and length. Hence, very low p-value corresponds to significant matches meaning that it is improbable the obtained score occurred by chance. It is more probable that the high score occurred as a consequence of a real biological or evolutionary relationship. However, a more common statistical parameter which is reported by most softwares for quantifying the statistical significance of an identified similarity is E-value or expected value. E-value is the expected frequency of scores "S" occurred by chance. P and E values can be calculated for the two matched sequences separately (calculating the probability of obtaining score between the two sequences at least as high by chance) or for the database similarity searches. It must be noted that, when the p-value for two matched sequences is low, E-values for searching a large database can be quite large.

Assessing the statistical significance of a global alignment is very difficult, because performing a global alignment using Needleman-Wunch algorithm and a suitable scoring system produces many different alignments with quite similar scores. In aligning random or unrelated sequences using global alignment method, the aligned sequences have very high scores. Such investigations show that the tendency of global algorithm is to match as many characters as possible. Regardless of this difficulty, a way is developed for assessing the significance of a Needleman-Wunsch global alignment score. In this test the random or unrelated sequences are created by shuffling the reference sequence(s) and the query sequence(s) is aligned against random sequences in pairwise fashion, then the average of scores of alignments is taken and is compared with the score of the real alignment in Z-score parameter assuming that the overall distribution of the randomized score is normal:

$$z = \frac{x - \mu}{\sigma} \tag{11}$$

Where, x is the current score of two aligned sequences, μ is the mean score of many randomized sequence comparisons, and σ is standard deviation of those measurements obtained with random sequences. For evaluating the statistical significance of the two aligned sequences the obtained Z-score is related to probability value. If all random alignments have a score less than the authentic score, this indicates that the p-value is less than 0.01 i.e. the probability of occurrence by chance is less than 0.01. As a result, the studied sequences are significantly related.

Evaluation of statistical significance of local alignment scores of two sequences or a sequence against a database of sequences (like BLAST and FASTA algorithms) is based on E-value. In aligning sequences locally, the high scoring segment pairs (HSPs) are identified. For BLAST algorithm, E-value is the most important statistics associated with BLAST output describing the number of hits expected to occur by chance. Statistical evaluation of locally aligned sequences is somewhat similar to that of global alignments, but the random sequence alignment scores follow extreme value distribution which approximately resembles a normal distribution with a positively skewed tail in the higher score range. The goal is to evaluate the probability of obtaining a random alignment with a score equal or higher than real sequences of interest. Thus, E-value is calculated as follows:

$$E = Kmne^{-\lambda s} \tag{12}$$

Where, K is a constant value, m is the effective length of the query sequence, n is the effective length of the random sequences, λ is the scaling factor, and S is the score that reflects the similarity of each pairwise comparison. The K and λ parameters are described by Karlin and Altschul (1990) and calculated by aligning 10000 random amino acid sequences of variable lengths using Smith-Waterman method and a combination of the scoring matrix and a suitable set of gap penalties for the matrix. Then values of the K and λ were estimated for each combination by fitting the data to the predicted extreme value distribution as reported in Table 1.

Setting a threshold for E-value and p-value in database similarity searches, the sequence similarities with scores lower than the threshold are considered significant. The sequences with significant similarities are called "hits". Based on the results of the search, the database is grouped into two subsets called hits (positives) and non-hits (negatives). These subsets conceptually grouped into true and false positives and true and false negatives. A true positive is a hit enforced by a real biological pressure while a false positive is a hit without a real biological relationship to the query sequence. A true negative is a non-hit with no biological background to the query sequence and a false negative is also non-hit with a biological relationship in reality.

Scoring matrix	Gap opening penalty	Gap extension penalty	K	λ
BLOSUM50	∞	0-∞	0.11	0.232
BLOSUM50	15	8-15	0.09	0.222
BLOSUM50	11	8-11	0.05	0.197
BLOSUM50	11	1	--	--
BLOSUM62	∞	0-∞	0.13	0.318
BLOSUM62	1	3-12	0.1	0.305
BLOSUM62	8	7-8	0.06	0.27
BLOSUM62	7	1	--	--
PAM250	∞	0-∞	0.09	0.229
PAM250	15	5-15	0.06	0.215
PAM250	1	8-10	0.031	0.175
PAM250	11	1	--	--

Table 1. Statistical parameters (K, λ) based on different scoring matrices and different suitable affine gap penalties.

Evaluation of the results of a database search is performed by two complementary measurements, known as sensitivity and specificity (Westhead et al., 2002). The sensitivity (S_n) is the proportion of the real biological relationships in the database that are detected as hits and are calculated as follows:

$$S_n = \frac{n_{tp}}{(n_{tp} + n_{fn})} \tag{13}$$

where, n_{tp} is the number of true positives, and n_{fn} is the number of false negatives. The specificity of the search is the proportion of hits corresponding to the real biological relationships and is obtained as follows:

$$S_p = \frac{n_{tp}}{(n_{tp} + n_{fp})} \tag{14}$$

where, n_{fp} is the number of false positives. To obtain more accurate results from database searching, both sensitivity and specificity must be as close as possible to 1, but in practice this is not possible. By increasing the threshold, the sensitivity is likely to increase (i.e. obtaining more true positives and less false negatives), but the specificity is probably decreased (i.e. more false positives). Hence, there is a trade off between these two quantities for increasing the accuracy of the results. It should be noted that analysis of sensitivity and specificity is only possible if the real biological relationships in the database is already known and categories of true and false positives and negatives are created. The categories are created from experimental determination of protein structure and function (Karlin et al., 1991; Pearson, 1998).

6. Summary and conclusion

In this chapter, the sequence alignment methods and their basic concepts are described. Alignment is the tool for inferring homology. Two types of sequence alignments including global and local are studied that align a query sequence against a reference sequence. Both methods guarantee to find an alignment with the highest scores based on the choice of suitable scoring matrices. These matrices such as PAM and BLOSUM are computed based on substitution matrices. Phylogeny is the core data upon which substitution matrices are constructed. Evolutionary relationships between sequences come from the fact that species undergo mutations over time. In mutated species amino acid sequences of proteins change so that some residues are substituted by other biochemically similar residues. Substitution matrices are built upon the close examination and quantitative analysis of mutations that has been extensively described in this chapter. In order to align a query sequence against a database the same basic concepts for two sequences (query vs. reference) are applied, but faster algorithms are needed. The modified Smith-Waterman algorithms (BLAST and FASTA) are presented for this purpose and are described in full detail. Ultimately, for evaluating the statistical significance of the resulted alignments, these algorithms use parameters such as P- and E-values. Using these values, real relationships are distinguished from random relationships. The statistical analysis of alignment outputs are discussed in detail in this chapter.

7. References

Altscul, S.F. (1991). Amino acid substitution matrices from an information theoretic perspective. *J. Mol. Biol*, Vol. 219, No. 3, (June 1991), pp. (555-565)

Altscul, S.F.; Gish, W.; Miller, W.; Myers, E.W. & Lipman D.J. (1990). Basic Local Alignment Search Tool. *J. Mol. Biol*, Vol. 215, (15 May 1990), pp. (403-410)

Altscul, S.F. & Gish, G. (1996). Local alignment statistic. *Method Enzymol*, Vol. 266, pp. (460-480)

Altscul, S. F.; Boguski, M.S.; Gish, W. & Wotton, J.C. (1994). Issues in searching molecular sequence databases. *Nat. Genet.*, Vol. 6, pp. (119-129)

Altscul, S.F.; Madden T.L.; Schäffer, A.A.; Zhang, J.; Zhang, Z.; Miller, W. & Lipman, D.J., (1997). Gapped BLAST and PSI-BLAST: A new generation of protein databas search programs. *Nucleic Acid Res,*Vol. 25, No. 17, (July 1997), pp. (3389-3402).

Barioch, A. & Apweiler, R. (1996). The SWISSPROT Protein Sequence Data Bank and its New Supplement TREMBLE. *Nucleic Acids Research*, Vol. 24, No. 1, pp. (21-25)

Berezin, C.; Glaser, F.; Rosenberg, J.; Paz, I.; Pupko, T.; Fariselli, P.; Casadio, R. & Ben-Tal, N., (2003). ConSeq: the identification of functionally and structurally important residues in protein sequences. *Bioinformatics*, Vol. 20, No. 8, (September 2003), pp. (1322-1324).

Brenner, S.E. (1998). Practical database searching. *Trends Guide to Bioinformatics*, Vol. 16, No. 1, (November 1998), pp. (9-12)

Campanella, J.J.; Bitincka, L. & Smalley J. (2003). MatGAT: An application that generates similarity/identity matrices using protein or DNA sequences. *BMC Bioinformatics*, Vol. 4, No. 29 (10 July 2003)

Chothia, C. & Lesk, A.M. (1986). The relation between the divergence of sequence and structure in proteins. *Embo J.*, Vol. 5, No. 4, (April 1986), pp. (823-826)

Dayhoff, M.O. (1972). *Atlas of Protein Sequence and Structure Vol. 5*, Silver Spring, USA

Dardel, F. & Kepes, F. (2006). Sequence comparison, In: *Bioinformatics: Genomics and Post-Genomics*, pp. (25-50), John Wiley & Sons, ISBN13: 978-0-470-02001-2, USA

Doolittle, R.F. (1981). Similar amino acid sequences: chance or common ancestry. *Science*, Vol. 214, No. 4517, (October 1981), pp. (149-159)

Edgar, R.C. (2009). Optimizing substitution matrix choice and gap parameters for sequence alignment. *BMC Bioinformatics*, Vol. 10, No. 396, (2 December 2009)

Edgar, R.C. & Sjolander, K. (2004). COACH: profile–profile alignment of protein families using hidden Markov models. *Bioinformatics*, Vol. 20, Issue 8, pp. (1309–1318)

Feng, D.F. & Doolittle, R. F. (1987). Progressive sequence alignment as prerequisite to correct phylogenetic trees. *J. Mol. Evol*, Vol. 25, No. 4, pp. (351-360)

Feng, D.F.; Johnson M. S. & Doolittle R. F. (1985). Aligning amino acid sequences: Comparison of commonly used methods. *J. Mol. Evol*, Vol. 21, No. 9, pp. (112-125)

Fitch, W.M. (1966). An improved method of testing for evolutionary homology. *J. Mol. Biol.*, Vol. 16, No. 1, (March 1966), pp. (9-16)

Fitch, W.M. (1970). Distinguishing homologous from analogous proteins. *Syst. Zool*, Vol. 19, No. 2, (June 1970), pp. (99-113)

Fitch, W.M. (1970). An improved method for determining codon variability in a gene and its application to the rate of fixation of the mutations in evolution. *Biochem. Genet.*, Vol. 4, No. 5, (October 1970), pp. (579-593)

Fitch, W.M. & Smith, T.F. (1983). Optimal sequence alignments. *Proc. Natl. Acad. Sci.*, Vol. 80, No. 5, (March 1983), pp. (1382-1386)

Gibbs, A.J. & McIntyre, G.A. (1970). The Diagram, a method for comparing sequence. Its use with amino acid and nucleotide sequences. *Eur. J. Biochem.*, Vol. 16, No. 1, (September, 1970), pp. (1-11)

Henikoff, S. & Henikoff, J.G. (1992). Amino acid substitution matrices from protein blocks. *Proc. Natl. Acad. Sci.*, Vol. 89, (November 1992), pp. (10915-10919)

Henikoff, S. & Henikoff, J.G. (1996). Blocks Database and its Applications. *Methods Enzymol.*, Vol. 266, pp. (88-105)

Higgs, P.G. & Attwood, T.K. (2005). Model of Sequence Evolution, In: *Bioinformatics and Molecular Evolution*, pp. (58-80), Blackwell Science Ltd, ISBN: 978-1-4051-0683-2, UK

Jones, D.T.; Taylor, W.R. & Thornton, J.M. (1992). The rapid generation of mutation data matrices from protein sequences. *CABIOS*, Vol. 8, No. 3, pp. (275-282).

Jones, D.T.; Taylor W.R. & Thornton, J.M. (1993). A mutation data matrix for transmembrane proteins. *FEBS Letters*, Vol. 339, pp. (269-275)

Karlin, S. & Altschul S.F. (1990). Methods for assessing the statistical significance of molecular sequence features by using general scoring schemes. *Proc. Natl. Acad. Sci.*, Vol. 87, No. 6, (March 1990), pp. (2264-2268)

Karlin, S.; Bucher, P. & Brendel, P. (1991). Statistical methods and insights for protein and DNA sequences. *Annu. Rev. Biophys. Chem.*, Vol. 20, (June 1991), pp. (175-203)

Kim, E. & Kececioglu, J. (2008). Learning scoring schemes for sequence alignment from partial examples. *IEEE/ACM Trans Comput. Biol. Bioinform.*, Vol. 5, No. 4, (June 2008), pp. (546-556)

Larkin, M.A.; Blackshields, G.; Brown, N.P.; Chenna, R.; McGettigan, P.A..; McWilliam H.; Valentin, F.; Wallace, I.M.; Wilm, A.; Lopez, R.; Thompson, J.D.; Gibson, T.J. & Higgins, D.G. (2007). ClustalW and ClustalX version 2.0. *Bioinformatics*, Vol. 23, No. 21, (November 2007), pp. (2947-8)

Mahdavi, M.A. (2010). Medical informatics: transition from data acquisition to data analysis by means of bioinformatics tools and resources. *Int. J. Data Mining and Bioinformatics*, Vol. 4, No. 2, pp. (158-174)

Mount, D.W. (2001a) Alignment of Pairs of Sequences, In: *Bioinformatics: Sequence and Genome Analysis*, pp. (53-137), Cold Spring Harbor Laboratory Press, ISBN: 0-87969-597-8, USA

Mount, D.W. (2001b). Database Searching For Similar Sequences, In: *Bioinformatics: Sequence and Genome Analysis*, pp. (282-335), Cold Spring Harbor Laboratory Press, ISBN: 0-87969-597-8, USA

Needleman, S.B. & Wunsch, C.D. (1970). A general method applicable to the search for similarities in the amino acid sequence of two proteins. *J. Mol. Biol.*, Vol. 48, pp. (443-453)

Pearson, W.R. (1990). Rapid and sensitive sequence comparison with FASTP and FASTA. *Method Enzymol.*, Vol. 183, pp. (63-98)

Pearson, W.R. (1991). Searching protein sequence libraries: Comparison of the sensitivity and selectivity of the Smith-Waterman and FASTA algorithms. *Genomics*, Vol. 11, No. 3, (November 1991), pp. (635-650)

Pearson, W.R. (1995). Comparison of methods for searching protein sequence databases. *Protein Sci.*, Vol. 4, pp. (1145-1160)

Pearson, W.R. (1996). Effective protein sequence comparison. *Methods Enzymol.*, Vol. 266, pp. (227-258)

Pearson, W.R. (1998). Empirical statistical estimates for sequence similarity searches. *J. Mol. Biol.*, Vol. 276, No. 1, (February 1998), pp. (71-84)

Pearson, W.R. (2000). Flexible sequence similarity searching with FASTA3 program package. *Methods Mol. Biol.*, Vol. 132, No. 2, pp. (185-219)

Pearson, W.R. & Lipman, D.J. (1988). Improved tools for biological sequence comparison. *Proc. Natl. Acad. Sci., USA,* Vol. 85, No. 8, (April 1988), pp. (2444-2448)

Pesrson, W.R. & Miller, W. (1992). Dynamic programming algorithm for biological sequence comparison. *Method Enzymol.,* Vol. 210, PP. (575-601).

Pesrson, W.R.; Wood, T.; Zhang, Z. & Miller, W. (1997). Comparison of DNA sequences with protein sequences. *Genomics,* Vol. 46, No. 1, (November 1997), pp. (24-36)

Pevsner, J. (2003a). Pairwise Sequence Alignment, In: *Bioinformatics and Functional Genomics,* pp. (41-84), John Wiley & Sons, ISBN: 0-471-21004-8, USA

Pevsner, J. (2003b). Basic Local Aligment Search Tool, In: *Bioinformatics and Functional Genomics,* pp. (87-126), John Wiley & Sons, ISBN: 0-471-21004-8, USA

Reeck, G.R.; Haën, C.; Teller, D.C.; Doolittle, R. F.; Fitch, W. M.; Dickerson, R. E.; Chambon, P.; McLachlan, A. D.; Margoliash, E.; Jukes, T. H. & Zuckerk, E. (1987). Homology in Proteins and nucleic acids: A terminology muddle and a way out of it. *Cell,* Vol. 50, (August 1987), pp. (667)

Reese, J.C. & Pearson, W.R. (2002) Empirical determination of effective gap penalties for sequence comparison. *Bioinformatics,* Vol. 18, No. 11, (April 2002), pp. (1500-1507).

Dwyer, R.A. (2003). Local Alignment and the BLAST Heuristic, In: *Genomic Perl from Bioinformatics Basics to Working Code,* pp. (93-108), Cambridge University Press, ISBN: 0-521-80177, UK

Sankoff, D. (1972). Matching sequences under deletion/insertion constraints. *Proc. Natl. Acad. Sci.,* Vol. 69, No. 1, (January 1972), pp. (4-6)

Smith, T.F. & Waterman, M.S. (1981). Identification of Common Molecular Subsequences. *J. Mol. Biol.,* Vol. 147, pp. (195-197)

Smith, T.F. & Waterman, M.S. (1981a). Comparison of bio-sequences. *Adv. Appl. Math.,* Vol. 2, No. 4, (December 1981), pp. (482-489)

Smith, T.F.; Wterman, M.S. & Fitch, W.M. (1981b). Comparative bio-sequence metrics. *J. Mol. Evol.,* Vol. 18, No. 1, pp. (38-46).

Smoot, M.E.; Guerlain, S.A. & Pearson W.R. (2003) Visualization of near-optimal sequence alignments. *Bioinformatics,* Vol. 20, No. 6, (July 2003), pp. (953-958).

States, D.J. & Boguski, M.S. (1991).Similarity and homology. In: *Sequence analysis prime,* (ed. Gribskov, M. & Devereux, J.), pp. (92- 124), Stockton Press, New York

States, D.J.; Gish, W. & Altschul, S.F. (1991). Improved sensitivity of nucleic acid database searches using application –specific scoring matrices. *Methods,* Vol. 3, PP. (66-70)

Tramontano, A. (Ed(s). Etheridge, A. M.; Gross, L.J.; Lenhart, S.; Miani, P.K.; Ranganathan, S.; Safer, H.M. & Voit, E.O.).(2006). *Introduction to Bioinformatics,* Chapman & Hall/ CRC, ISBN: 1-58488-569-6, UK

Vogt, G.; Etzold, T. & Argos, P. (1995). An Assessment of Amino Acid Exchange Matrices in Aligning Protein sequences: The Twilight Zone Revisited. *J. Mol. Biol.,* Vol. 249, pp. (816–831).

Wen, Z.N.; Wang, K.; Li, M.; Nie, F. & Yangc, Y. (2005). Analyzing functional similarity of protein sequences with discrete wavelet transform. *Computational Biology and Chemistry,* Vol. 29, pp. (220–228)

Westhead, D.R.; Parish, J.H. & Twyman, R.M. (2002). *Bioinformatics.* 2nd Edition, BIOS Scientific Publisher, ISBN: 1- 85996-272-6, UK

Xu, W. & Miranker, D.P. (2003). A metric model of amino acid substitution. *Bioinformatics*, Vol. 20, No. 8, (November 2003), pp. (1214–1221)

13

Predicting Virus Evolution

Tom Burr
Los Alamos National Laboratory
USA

1. Introduction

Viruses are an important cause of human disease, often because they are highly transmittable from human to human. A key tool from population genetics that can be applied to the study of viruses is coalescent theory. Coalescent theory predicts genealogical tree shapes as a function of how the studied organisms are evolving. Therefore, under its model assumptions, coalescent theory can be used to infer aspects of the demographic history of evolving organisms. For example, there are characteristics of tree shapes that imply whether the organism population has been constant, growing, or shrinking in size over time.

This chapter reviews some of the successes of coalescent theory in the context of inferring aspects of virus evolution, using human immunodeficiency (HIV) and influenza viruses as case studies. Next, the chapter describes limitations of coalescent theory, even as extended to allow some forms of selection, population subdivision, and viral recombination. The relatively new goal to predict influenza virus evolution (rather than infer past evolution) is used to emphasize modeling needs beyond standard or extended coalescent theory models. A new small-scale simulation that combines viral fitness with demographic population structures such as family and work groups is then described as an example extension to coalescent theory models.

Prediction goals include early detection of highly lethal new strains and improved vaccine designs that anticipate future evolutionary directions. Regardless which evolutionary model is used to predict virus evolution, because real virus evolution is complex beyond current understanding, there will be substantial model error. Model error, model parameter estimation error, and purely random effects can combine to make some forecast goals unattainable. In these cases the most appropriate prediction is similar to what is often said about stock markets: there will be change.

2. Background

Humans are susceptible to many viral pathogens, including the human immunodeficiency virus (HIV) and the influenza virus. Although it is a relatively new goal in population genetics, predicting virus evolution can help with vaccine design and with other mitigation strategies (Bush et al., 1999; Ferguson and Anderson, 2002; Plotkin et al., 2002; Rambaut et al., 2008). Using estimated phylogenetic (genealogical) tree shapes to infer aspects of evolution such as organism growth rates has received far more attention to date (Felsenstein et al., 1999; Innan and Stephan, 2000; Pybus et al., 2000; Stephens and Connelly, 2000; Ewing et al., 2004)

This chapter focuses on HIV and the influenza virus in the context of what might be predicted about virus evolution. Influenza is a highly transmittable disease that infects millions each year, resulting in many deaths. HIV is also transmittable through risky behaviors and it too results in many deaths each year.

In population genetics, coalescent theory (Kingman, 1982; Stephens and Donnelly, 2000; Burr et al., 2001; Ewing et al., 2004;) is a key tool that predicts genealogical tree shapes as a function of how the studied organisms (taxa) are evolving. Therefore, under its model assumptions, coalescent theory can be used to infer aspects of the demographic history of evolving organisms. For example, there are characteristics of tree shapes that imply whether the organism population has been constant, growing, or shrinking in size over time (Pybus et al., 2000).

This chapter will first review some of the successes of coalescent theory in the context of inferring aspects of virus evolution, using HIV (Rodrigo et al., 1999; Burr et al., 2001; Rambaut et al., 2001) and influenza viruses (Ferguson and Anderson, 2002; Plotkin et al., 2002, Burr et al., 2002) as case studies. Next, the chapter describes limitations of coalescent theory, even as extended to allow some forms of serial sampling, selection, population subdivision, and viral recombination (Excoffier and Foll, 2011). The relatively new goal to predict influenza virus evolution (rather than infer past evolution) is used to emphasize modeling needs beyond standard or extended coalescent theory models. A new small-scale simulation that combines viral fitness with demographic population structures such as family and work groups is then described as an example extension to coalescent theory models.

Most genetic data analyses rely on a forward model that specifies evolutionary forces and associated probabilities describing how offspring are generated. Evolutionary forces include drift, mutation, recombination, migration, and selection. Drift refers to random change over successive generations due to finite population sizes. In the absences of mutation and selection, the fraction of a population of size N having a given trait drifts randomly somewhat like the number of heads in a set of N coin tosses. Mutations are changes in the DNA sequence that occur for many reasons. Recombination ("reassortment" in the case of influenza) refers to sections of genome that are broken and then recombined, resulting in large genetic differences between offspring and parents, and complicating phylogenetic analyses because different genome sections can have different genealogies. Migration refers to exchange of genetic material among partly isolated subpopulations. There are many other evolutionary forces, too many to describe here.

For simulating DNA sequences from a population, the state of art invokes coalescent theory, which uses simplified models of the forward evolutionary process. These simplifications allow inverse analytical solutions and corresponding simulation software, but with questionable assumptions. This is done in order to avoid having to simulate directly from the forward model and track the evolutionary histories. Sample genealogies can instead be simulated by running time from the present toward the past and tracking probabilistically when lineages coalesce to share a common ancestor. An example genealogy of a sample taken at a single time from a population that is maintaining a constant population size is given in Figure 1. These coalescent-based simulated sample units are then used to infer how a population is evolving using features of the associated phylogenetic tree (Pybus et al., 2000). In addition, analytical approximations used in inference invoke the same model assumptions used in coalescent theory.

Agent-based models (Eubank et al., 2004) provide a richer framework than classical epidemiology models of disease spread, such as the susceptible-infected-recovered (SIR) model. Because agent-based models track individual rather than aggregate behavior, they are believed to more reliably predict, for example, the impact of candidate mitigation strategies such as vaccinations and isolation. In an analogous way, we describe predictions for virus evolution that probably will require a higher-fidelity modeling framework than coalescent theory and its extensions.

The following sections include HIV and influenza examples of using coalescent theory to infer aspects of prior evolution, limitations of coalescent theory to infer future HIV and influenza evolution, introduces the new small-scale simulation that combines viral fitness with demographic features, and discusses limitations of our current ability to predict viral evolution.

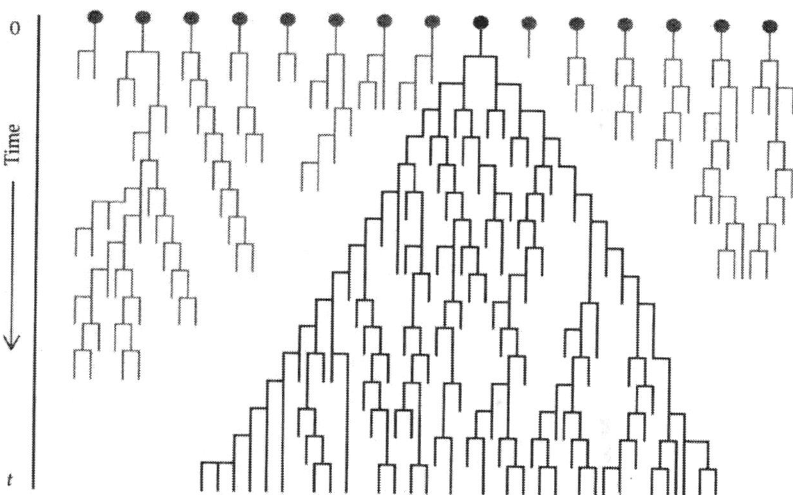

Fig. 1. The most recent common ancestor and sample genealogy from an evolving population. At time t a sample is collected, and at time 0 in the past, all individuals in the sample coalesce to share a common ancestor. For simplicity here, the population size is assumed to be constant over time, with each individual at time 0 represented by a dot (not all individuals are shown).

3. HIV and influenza examples

3.1 Example 1: HIV

Within host. A coalescent model within individuals has been applied (Rodrigo et al., 1999) to analyze HIV-1 viral load data from infected individuals after the administration of an HIV-1 inhibitor to estimate the HIV generation time in vivo. The estimate was 1-2 days, which agreed well with an estimate based on a different approach (Perelson et al, 1996), although it assumed nonrecombining DNA sequences from a population of constant effective size N. Consider samples from two sample times, separated by d days. The number of days per generation is estimated as $dn(n-c)/2Nc$ where c is the number of coalescent events that have occurred, d is the number of days between samples. The method assumed: (a) the population size N is constant; (b) the estimated phylogeny is the same as the true genealogy of the sampled individuals, and (c) the exchangeability assumption that each individual virus has the same propensity to reproduce. Implicit in (b) is the further assumption that recombination, migration, and selection do not interfere with the ability to estimate the true phylogeny. Further, an approximate technique for accommodating serial samples is required, which has recently become available (Excoffier and Foll, 2011).

Between host. An example (Burr et al., 2001) involves whether the 8 to 10 approximately equidistant subtypes of HIV-1 (type M) could have arisen under available models of how HIV is evolving (Fig. 1). To examine this, coalescent theory was used to simulate DNA data from a very simplified forward model of how HIV is evolving at both the macro and micro levels (see Section 4.1). This provided a reference distribution against which to compare the data. If features of the observed data (such as the ratio of the between-subtype to within-subtype genetic distance) are in the tail of the coalescent-theory-based reference distribution of those same features, then the forward model used to simulate the data is not credible. Examples of phylogenetic trees estimated from coalescent-based simulated data are given in the right box of four subplots in Figure 2. Notice that subtypes are expected to arise in examples (b), (c), and (d), but not in (a). Subplot (a) is the classic "star phylogeny" that arises when the underlying population size is growing rapidly, forcing most coalescent events to occur early in the growth period, and all at nearly the same time.

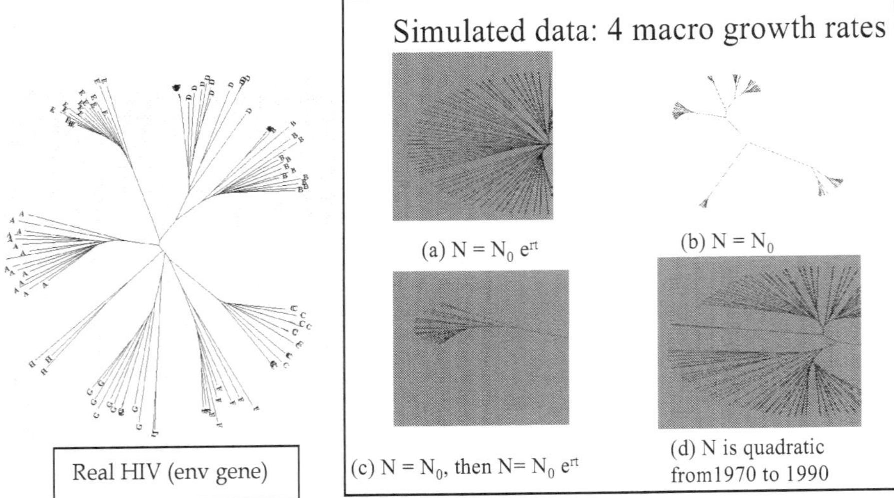

Fig. 2. **HIV, env region.** Consensus trees (of 100 bootstrap samples) using maximum likelihood for real (the left plot) HIV (env gene) sequences and for coalescent-based simulated (the four right plots) sequences under different assumptions about the time behavior of the number of infecteds N.

3.2 Example 2: Influenza

Figure 3 shows a principal coordinate (PC) plot (Venables and Ripley, 1999) of a 129-by-129 distance matrix based on the nucleoprotein (NP) region of 129 influenza viruses isolated from humans, swine, and avian hosts. PCs provide a low dimensional way to represent a distance matrix. For this data, all pairs of distances can be quite accurately reproduced using only the first two PCs as in Figure 3. It is known that the NP region maintains a type of "species signature" such as depicted in Figure 3 (Burr et al., 1999, 2002; Chen et al., 2006). A key aspect of influenza evolution is the fact that avian and swine hosts occasionally act as "reassortment vessels" for human influenza, resulting in dramatically different strains that evade effective human immune response. As an aside, the term "reassortment" seems to be applied only to influenza, presumably because its genome consists of eight distinct segments. For our purposes, "reassortment" is the same as recombination, in which sections of the genome get recombined (Forrest and Webster, 2010).

Figure 4 shows a PC plot of a distance matrix based on the hamagglutinin (HA) region of influenza viruses. Figure 5 is a phylogenetic tree built using neighbor joining (Swofford et al., 2000) of the same HA sequences.

Figures 4 and 5 illustrate (Nelson and Holmes, 2007) that the HA region appears to display the effects of positive selection due to the cactus-like structure with most lineages dying out. This cactus shape is unlike the classic "star-like" shape HIV trees of type M as in Figure 2. Such a cactus shape can also arise without positive selection from a combination of serially sampled taxa and sequential random population bottlenecks (which can occur in influenza due to its strong seasonality). Therefore, the cactus shape by itself can indicate but does not prove that positive selection is in effect. More formally, the statistical notion of identifiability probably does not hold in this context. Model identifiability implies that as sample size increases toward infinity, model parameters can be uniquely estimated (see Section 6).

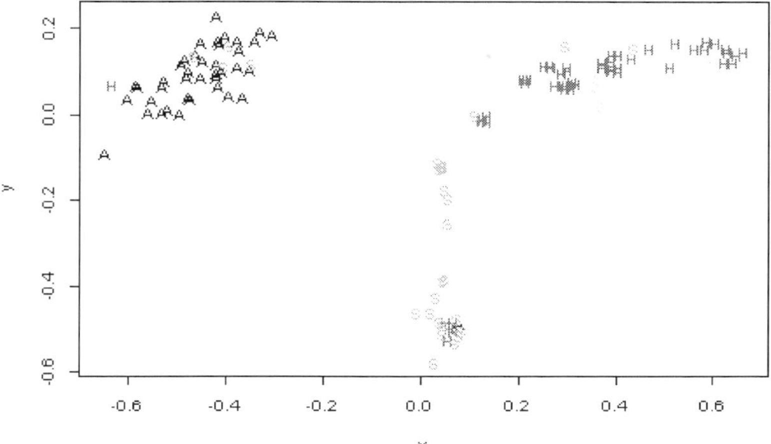

Fig. 3. Principal coordinate plot of the evolutionary distances among 129 influenza viruses extracted from human (H), avian (A), and swine (S) hosts. Distances are computed for the Nucleoprotein region of the virus, which exhibits species signatures. Among the 129, there are 14 "misidentified" taxa. However,the human (H) that is clustered with the avian group was known to have been infected by poultry. There are 44 avian, 57 humans, and 28 swine, all available from www.flu.lanl.gov.

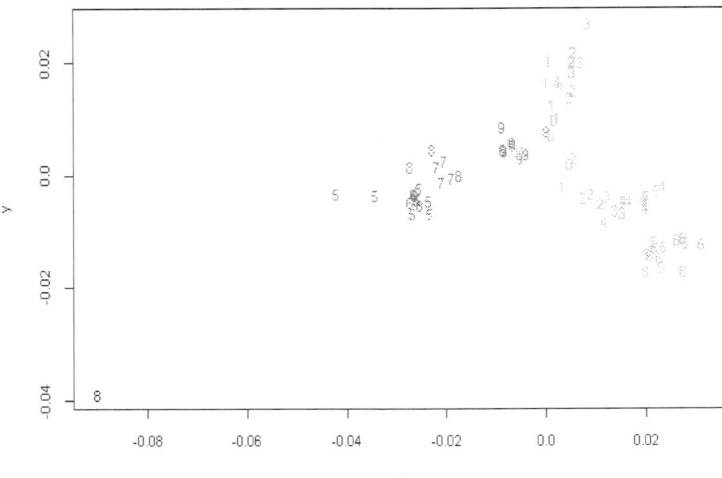

Fig. 4. Principal coordinate plot of the influenza viruses (HA region) found in humans. Digit = year, Black = 1960's, Red = 1980's, Green = 1990's. Genetic drift and strain extinctions are known to occur (cactus shape of typical tree).

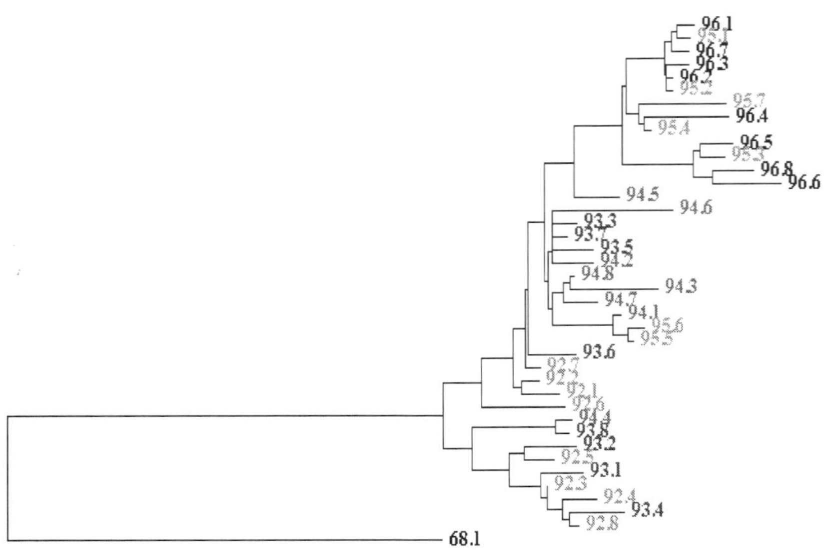

Fig. 5. Neighbor joining tree of the same HA sequences in humans that was used in Fig. 3.

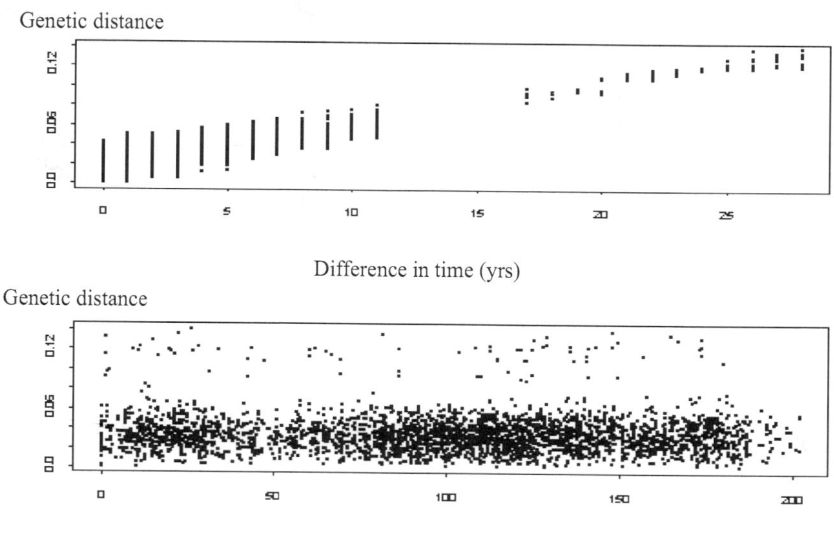

Fig. 6. Genetic distance versus time (top) and versus difference in space (bottom) for the HA region.

4. Limitations of coalescent theory for predicting HIV and influenza evolution

Coalescent theory leads to tremendous insights and powerful simulation and inference tools. However, limitations of coalescent techniques include (a)-(d) as follows:

a. Little is known concerning accuracy and robustness of coalescent theory's restrictive assumptions in many settings, although some forward models are known not to be well approximated by any coalescent model (depending on the relative time scales of various evolutionary effects such as drift, migration, and selection) (Sjodin et al., 2005);

b. Inference methods (Pybus et al., 2000; Stephens and Donnelly, 2000) invoke coalescent approximations to estimate the probability of candidate branching orders as part of the inference process. This leads to the undesirable situation of forcing a zero mismatch between the inference method's assumptions and the assumptions regarding how the population is evolving;

c. Coalescent theory is expanding along with associated software for implementation, but no current coalescent-based software includes all extensions to the original coalescent theory. However, one new option (Excoffier and Foll, 2011) for coalescent-based software includes many of the standard evolutionary features such as serial sampling, recombination, and geographic isolation;

d. Building trees supports inferences regarding, for example, whether a virus strain appears to be a natural branch from historical strains, or whether the strain seems to have made an unnatural leap indicating bioengineering. However, key coalescent assumptions that are violated by both HIV and influenza viruses are that all subtypes are equally transmissible and there is no recombination. Therefore, although to a limited extent and under restrictive assumptions, extensions to coalescent theory have been made to accommodate recombination, selection, overlapping generations, and population subdivision, there are cases where the theory is either inadequate or the sensitivity of its conclusions to its assumptions is unknown. The corresponding inference quality using estimated trees is also unknown; the state of the art is therefore to quantify precision, but not accuracy.

The forward model is a key component of total uncertainty associated with population genetics inferences. The current approach is: specify an amenable-to-coalescent-theory forward model for how a population is evolving that includes for example, population size, structure, and selection effects; identify the coalescent effective population size N_e (Sjodin et al., 2005) in the nearest available coalescent model, which is often a complicated task. Then, use the closest coalescent model to simulate sample genealogies under restrictive assumptions about the population and the sampling process. The $N_{effective}$ notion arose from coalescent theory by mapping the actual population size N in a population that violates some coalescent assumptions (such as nonoverlapping generations) to a different size $N_{effective}$ such that in some aspects, the actual and model populations evolve probabilistically in approximately the same manner. Coalescent theory was originally applied to macroscopic populations such as plants and animals (for example, Innan and Stephan, 2000); it has also been applied to microscopic populations such as DNA sequences from virus populations (for example, Rodrigo et al, 1999).

Coalescent theory will continue to provide insight into evolutionary processes; however, it is currently unknown how robust associated inferences are with respect to model violations. For example, Innan and Stephan [5] assumed the wild plant Arabidopsis thaliana (useful for genetic studies because of its well known demographic history and genome) consists of many isolated colonies, each having negligible genetic variation within a colony. They applied a coalescent model (correcting for the growing population size of A. thalina) to simulate the probability distribution of Tajima's D statistic against which to compare the observed D in real samples, as a test for selection. Tajima's D statistic is based on the difference between two estimates of the amount of variation (one using the number of sites having genetic variation and the other based on pairwisedifferences between individuals). They concluded that there was evidence for selection (distinguishing the type of selection, such as balancing or purifying is a separate challenge). Because of the simplifications inherent in the coalescent approach, it is currently unknown how robust the evidence for selection is in this for A. thalina.

4.1 Example 1: HIV

Coalescent models of HIV reproduction within an individual might be adequate (Rodrigo et al., 1999); however, these would become prohibitively unwieldy if all HIV-infected humans were modeled. For example, all models must specify the macro components such as the reproductive rate in susceptible populations and/or subpopulations.

As mentioned in Section 3.1, an investigation into the development of the HIV subtypes led to an application of coalescent theory to model the population dynamics of HIV (Burr et al., 2001). Figure 2 illustrates the approach taken. Various features (such as the ratio of the between-subtype to within-subtype genetic distance) involving the subtypes of real HIV sequences (env gene) were compared to the same features in corresponding coalescent-based simulated data. However, it became apparent that it would be necessary to implement a model that made less restrictive assumptions than coalescent theory (Burr et al., 2001).

One possible new way to simulate sequences is to track each HIV case by geographic region including all known transmission routes such as sex, needles, blood transfusions, and mother-to-child, and track the genealogy of each case. One would then sample ~100 simulated sequences from around the world or in specified regions at a snapshot in time, or distributed in time, and distributed spatially in either case. With careful bookkeeping one could deduce the sample genealogy (which 2 samples coalesced first to their most recent common ancestor (MRCA), which samples coalesced next, etc.) back in time until all 100 sequences coalesced to the single MRCA. This would produce 99 coalescent times and sample identities, which define the genealogy of the sample. This genealogy could also be thought of as the true evolutionary tree for the sample to be compared to coalescent-based genealogies.

Related to the origin of the HIV subtypes is the goal to predict the stability of the subtypes because current vaccine design approaches rely on "mosaic" pseudo-HIV viruses that exploit the known characteristic or representative sequence of each subtype (Barouch et al., 2010). Although a few new subtypes have been defined since the original, the M clade trees with 8-10 subtypes have been remarkably stable over time (Korber and Myers, 1992; Burr et al., 2001). Both within-host and between-host modeling efforts should allow for multiple viral sequence types within hosts, because within-host variation in contemporaneous HIV sequences isolated from various regions of the genome exhibit substantial variation, easily up to 10% differences.

4.2 Example 2: Influenza

Imagine a particularly bad flu season. Not only does it appear that more people are infected than normal by early November, but there are anomalous deaths. Could this be a bio attack or perhaps a another human-to-human transmittable version of the swine-origin influenza A (H1N1) virus?

As Figure 6 suggests, there is empirical evidence that a time gap of three or more years is sufficient for a temporal signature. For example, strains isolated in 1993 should be genetically distinct from strains in 1996 or later (Burr et al., 1999). Therefore, we might be suspicious in 2012 if the strain looks like a 2008 strain. However, the empirical evidence assumes a constant population size because the genetic distance between two samples depends on the coalescent time since they evolved from the same ancestral sequence. And the time since the two samples shared a common ancestor depends on several factors, including how the population is structured and the size and growth rate of the population. If some of these factors change dramatically, then the three-year rule would become either shorter or longer. Currently, coalescent methods either hold these factors constant over time, or extensions to the approximations have not been implemented. Therefore, empirical reconstructions of phylogenetic trees such as those in Burr et al. (1999) are incomplete for assessing the robustness of candidate signatures. The corresponding inferences thus have unknown reliability.

The $N_{effective}$ concept is part of the success of coalescent theory, including in the influenza context Bedford et al (2010) estimate $N_{effective}$ for influenza A using a coalescent model that includes subdivision and migration. Bayesian Evolutionary Analysis Sampling Trees (BEAST, Pybus et al., 2007) was used to estimate μ assuming both N and μ are constant over time. In this example, it could be important that observed and reported influenza mutation rates need not be stable over time for several reasons, including the fact that $N_{effective}$ changes with time.

In influenza, genome reassortment, selection, the presence of multiple strains and multiple hosts, and host immunity all complicate matters. Given what is known about influenza evolution, what might we predict today about influenza evolution? Two related prediction goals to consider for influenza are: (1) in a given year, predict which new strains are most likely to be in the surviving lineage, and (2) predict the prevalent strains in the next year, so that vaccine design can be most effective.

Concerning prediction goal (1), Bush et al (1999) proposed a prediction method that involved whether influenza isolates on lineages having the most changes in positively selected codes were "more fit" that other isolates. At least 18 of the 329 AA codons in H3 HA1 are thought to experience positive selection, with mutations favoring new variants that can escape host immunity. An AA sequence was defined as "more fit" if it is more closely related to surviving lineages than another contemporary strain.

Concerning prediction goal (2) the world health organization (WHO) recommends three strains to target in the vaccine for each flu season. Plotkin et al. (2002) use non-hierarchical clustering over time to evaluate the number of HA1 sequences within each cluster over time. This leads to a sequence-based algorithm to choose vaccine strains and the recommended strains differed from the WHO recommendation in 9 of 16 years in the study period from 1985 to 2000. A limitation of the Plotkin et al (2002) study is the biased sampling used by WHO in which novel strains are deliberately overrepresented in the database.

The new small-scaled agent-based simulation described in Section 5 addresses both prediction goals 1 and 2.

5. New small-scale agent-based simulation for influenza

In choosing/developing an evolutionary model it is of course important to consider the modeling goals. What are the prediction goals? How should the dynamic host/pathogen system be modeled? Which hosts should be included? Human, swine, avian, other? Is it sufficient to use a detailed model of a region such as New York state and a less detailed model of the outside region?

The basic susceptible-infected-recovered (SIR) model in classical epidemiology mathematically describes average population behavior using differential equations to move from S to I to R. This SIR model has been extended in various ways including structures such as contact groups and stochastic effects such as varying contact rates (Burr and Chowell, 2008,2009). Figure 7 gives examples of different simulated outbreak shapes in a small population of 1000 individuals. The number of newly infected is plotted each day for the simulated data. The small population is either (a) an unstructured population with all individuals equally in contact with all other individuals; (b) a randomly generated network model in which individuals are only exposed to member of their own clique, but some individuals belong to multiple cliques. (c) A network model with cliques assigned to nodes in a lattice; (d) a more realistic spatial network in which cliques belong to small geographic regions. A clique is a small group of individuals for which the contact probability is relatively high and assumed to be the same between each member of the clique. Various signatures of non-homogeneity using the shape of typical outbreak curves were developed for such network models, which were then shown to be detectably different from outbreak curves from the basic SIR model with homogeneous individuals all equally mutually exposed (Burr and Chowell, 2008). One concept that arose in Burr and Chowell (2008) is that predictions of the total number of infected based on the basis SIR model were often quite wrong in the structured population. This is an example of using failed predictions to determine that more fidelity is needed than the SIR model provides.

There has been progress toward merging SIR models with viral fitness. Minayev and Ferguson (2009a, 2009b) extended SIR models by including two key notions: cross immunity to similar strains in a host that has been previously infected by a similar strain, and transient strain-transcending immunity.

At least two related empirical studies have been published, both previously mentioned (Bush et al., 1999; Plotkin et al, 2002) In Bush et al. (1999), the number of AA changes in a lineage appeared to convey a selective advantage in the following sense. The lineage for which the most AA changes occurred were more likely to be represented in the surviving lineages. That is, mutation conveys selective advantage, which is believed to be the case simply because the human host has some immunity to prior strains. At this point, "strain" will be defined following Plotkin et al. (2002) as arising from cluster analyses bases on the Manhattan metric that counts the number of AA differences between pairs of sequences. With that definition of a strain, and using 2 AA changes as the threshold above which a new strain is defined, Plotkin et al. (2002) reported empirical assessment of the number of strains by calendar year in influenza samples.

5.1 Evidence of departures from standard models

Graves and Picard (1999) report evidence of violations of the classic SIR model for influenza. Signatures of departure from SIR (Burr et al., 2006) characterize departures from the "one season fits all" assumption (which assumes each flu season occurs like clockwork, peaking in the winter during the same weeks, etc) using a hierarchical model that captures year-to-year variation in baseline, and peak onset and duration (Burr et al., 2006). Burr and Chowell (2008) use a reference distribution of simulated outbreak curve shapes to assess whether a collection of simulated and real outbreak curves follow SIR-type models. On that basis, many real outbreaks do not follow SIR-type models.

5.2 Description of the new small-scale simulation

In the context of predicting viral evolution as considered here, the SIR-type model must be extended include population demographics and characteristics of the virus. Minayev and Ferguson (2009a,b) develop one approach to include viral characteristics. Our approach to be described in this section is similar, but is entirely stochastic and allows for demographic structure. With the present implementation, population sizes of approximately 10,000 can complete in reasonable (tens of minutes) run times, so the simulation is "small-scale."

Here is pseudo code to describe the new simulation. In some cases, parameter names such as "average.duration.of.infection" are used to clarify.

Pseudo-simulation code (Example R (R, 2004) code named `flu1()`)

1.   Initialize the population matrix and the matrix of AA sequence.

pop.matrix is N rows (individuals) and 30 columns with:

Column 1 is current age.

Column 2 is infection status (0 = susceptible, 1 = infected, 2 = recovered and not susceptible).

Column 3 is the number of times the individual has been infected.

Column 4 is the family group. Column 5 is the work group. Column 6 is the "other group."

Column 7 is the time of first infection. Column 8 is an integer denoting the AA sequence of infection 1. Column 9 is the donor ID for infection 1.

No. of newly infected individuals each day

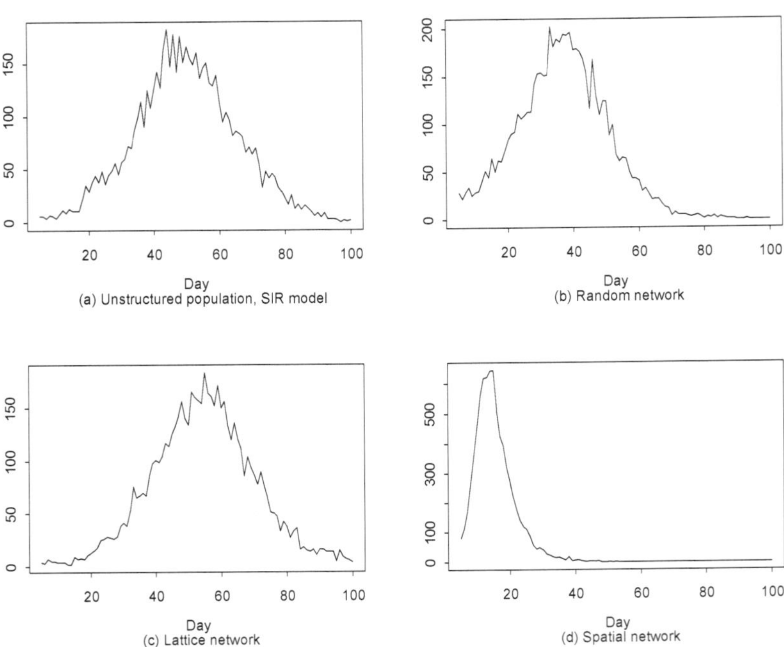

Fig. 7. Example time series of newly infected individuals in simulated SIR models of populations of 1000 individuals. (a) basic SIR model; (b) a randomly generated network model in which individuals are only exposed to member of their own clique, but some individuals belong to multiple cliques. (c) A network model with cliques assigned to nodes in a lattice; (d) a more realistic spatial network in which cliques belong to small geographic regions.

Columns 10-12 are the same as columns 7-9, but for the second infection by the individual. A maximum of 30 infections is allowed and then each new infection is recorded in the last 3 columns by writing over the previous data.

AA. seq.matrix begins with 2 rows (by default) and 329 AA sites (columns).

The default is to being with two random but distinct AA sequences.

At each time step (the default time step is 1 day), any of several events can occur:

2. There is a probability for each individual to change status from S (0) to I (1), or from I (1) to R (2), or from R back to S.

Any susceptible (S) individuals that an infect (I) individual contacts in the respective family, work, and other groups leads to a probability of infection determined by two parameters. First, there is a force of infection parameter for each of the three group types that characterizes how strongly individuals in the three group types interact. Second, the similarity of the infected individual's current strain to the closest strain of a given susceptible is computed and the cross-immunity function γ is calculated.

The value of the function γ in Minayev and Ferguson (2009b) alters the transmission probability accordingly. Cross immunity modeled by γ decreases to zero as a smooth function of time (examples given below), with an average of 10 year total immunity from identical strains. And, values of $\gamma.a$ and $\gamma.b$ in γ can be altered to decease or increase the degree of cross-immunity as a function of the Manhattan distance between strains. The cross-immunity concept is that S individuals who have had the strain of the potential donor I are less susceptible to infection. As Plotkin et al (2002) describe, ideally a distance measure between two sequences should somehow reflect immuniological properties of the corresponding viral proteins. Although steps have been taken in that direction (Lapedes and Farber, 2001), more research is required before similar metrics can be defensibly applied in modeling contexts such as our new small-scale simulation.

Any newly infected host will have the donor strain, but the simulation allows for mutation to a new strain. There are 329 H3 HA1 (Bush et al., 1999) amino acid (AA) sites with one estimate of the effective mutation rate $N\mu$ being 0.0057 nucleotide substitutions per site per year. Of the 329 AA sites, at least 18 have exhibited positive selection effects (Plotkin et al., 2002). Here we will not consider estimation error in $N\mu$, so the simulation default value is $N\mu = 0.0057 \times 3 = 0.171$ per AA site per year. A technical issue arises here because we use the actual popluation size N rather than the effective size $N_{\text{effective}}$. It would be more appropriate to use $N_{\text{effective}}$, but that value is currently unknown in the context of this model population. In future work, $N_{\text{effective}}$ could be defined and estimated on the basis of the number of observed distinct sequences during outbreak.

If a newly infected incurs any mutations, add the new strain to AA.seq.matrix, increasing the number of rows by one. Columns in pop.matrix identify which strains each host has had in the sequence matrix of all strains ever experienced in the model population

3.   Any infected can recover.

The per-step recovery probability is 1/(average.duration .of. infection). The time to recovery is therefore a geometric random variable with average duration average.duration.of.infection.

4.   Any recovered can lose immunity.

The time t from recovery to immunity is random, with t ~ Normal(avg.time.to.immunity,σ). The default simulation values are avg.time.to.immunity=10 years and σ = 1 year.

If at any time step (day) the number of infected is 0, then the infection would die out. Therefore, a reintroduction of new infected occurs at a random time with a user-specified average value with default value of 1 year, representing the typical time gap between outbreaks.

Figure 8 plots the percent currently infected at each time step for one 7-year realization of 10,000 individuals. A key output of `flu1` is the current strain of each infected individual at each time step. This allows us to consider strategies in Bush et al (1999) and in Plotkin et al. (2002) for prediction goals (1) and (2) described earlier in this section. Figure 9 plots four of the eight strains that emerged during the 7 simulated years. Following Plotkin et al. (2002), sequences were regarded as being the same strain if the number of AA differences among the 18 positively-selected AA sites is 2 or less. Equivalently, sequences were regarded as being distinct strains if the number of AA differences is 3 or more. Figures 8 and 9 used the values $\gamma.a = 0.4$, $\gamma.b = 0.95$.

Experimentation with `flu1` to generate multiple realizations of outbreaks having identical parameter values allows us to examine the role of chance in our models. Experimentation with `flu1` with different parameter values allows us to examine the effects of parameter changes. Small numerical experiments with `flu1` to date has lead to the following following conclusions:

1. The $\gamma.a$ and $\gamma.b$ in γ are as critical to the size of each outbreak as the overall transmission probabilities within the family, group, and other groups. For example, the function γ takes values 0.990, 0.891, 0.792, 0.693, 0.594, 0.495, 0.396, 0.297, 0.198, 0.099, 0.000,... for distances of 1, 2, ..., 11,... respectively, for $\gamma.a = 0.1$, $\gamma.b = 0.99$, and takes values 0.8, 0.4, and 0.0, for distances of 1, 2, 3 ..., respectively for $\gamma.a = 0.5$, $\gamma.b = 0.8$. The modeled transmission probability is multiplied by $1\text{-}\gamma$ so for $\gamma.a = 0.1$, $\gamma.b = 0.99$ there is very little chance of a susceptible individual acquiring influenza from a host having an AA sequence that differs in only 1 position among 18 positions from a strain the susceptible has had within the duration of immunity (10 years on average for example). This means that a single AA mutation can have dramatically different effects on transmission probability depending on $\gamma.a$ and $\gamma.b$. Qualitatively, this is anticipated because if immunity to a new strain is very high in individuals with previous infection by a similar older strain, then the average outbreak size will be small if previous outbreaks due to the older strain were large.

2. The values of $\gamma.a$ and $\gamma.b$ in γ are also critical to the typical number of strains maintained in the population and to whether change occurrence of a large number of mutations in a newly infected will have strong selective advantage by avoiding the collective immune experiences of available human hosts. It is currently unknown whether the observed number of strains could adequately provide a model such as `flu1` with estimates of $\gamma.a$ and $\gamma.b$ (See section 6).

3. As expected, the group structures can lead to outbreak shapes that differ from classic SIR outbreak shapes (Burr and Chowell, 2008). This is evident in comparing the outbreak shapes in Figure 8 to the SIR-model outbreak in Figure 7a for example. The shapes in Figure 8 fall off very sharply, more like the spatial network in Figure 7d.

4. In population genetics, the composite parameter $\theta = 2N_{\text{effective}}\mu$ where μ is the mutation rate determines the rate of genetic changes and the expected amount of diversity in a random sample (see Section 6). The $N_{\text{effective}}$ concept for influenza sequences was addressed in Bedford et al. (2010), but as mentioned in Section 4, observed genetic diversity is interpreted in the context of idealized evolutionary models that are amenable to coalescent theory. More experiments with `flu1` are planned, and if possible, an approximate coalescent model as implemented in available software will be applied so that the adequacy of coalescent-based approximations can be evaluated in the context of simulated flu outbreaks. We caution that many genetic effects of influenza evolution are omitted from `flu1` and from any available coalescent-based simulation.

6. Model Identifiability and Inference

Model identifiability is a key statistical concept. A model is identifiable if its parameters can be accurately and precisely estimated as the sample size increases toward infinity. In population genetics, a key parameter that arises from coalescent theory considerations is the composite parameter $\theta = 2N_{\text{effective}}\mu$, which determines the rate of genetic changes. Many studies address methods to estimate θ but because $N_{\text{effective}}$ and the mutation rate μ enter θ as a product, they are confounded, leading to a lack of identifiability unless auxiliary data is used to separately estimate $N_{\text{effective}}$ or μ and a strict evolutionary clock is assumed, meaning that μ is constant over time and lineages.

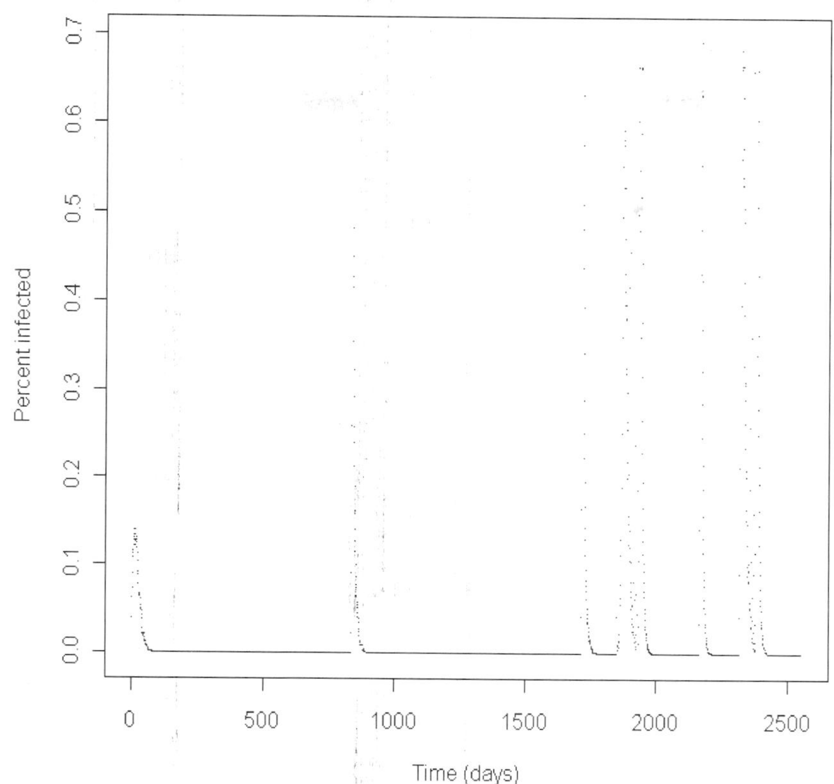

Fig. 8. Example simulated outbreaks from `flu1`. The number currently infected is plotted by day for years.

For a particular evolutionary model, inference is possible using Bayesian evolutionary analysis, for example, by using BEAST (Pybus et al., 2000) that relies on Markov Chain Monte Carlo, resulting in a posterior distribution on model parameters. The Bayesian approach allows one to repeatedly sample from the posterior probability of model parameters, and then generate hypothetical future genetic data for each set of model parameter values. This approach provides an envelope of possible future multivariate time series of genetic data from each sampled subject. It is computationally challenging even for a given model of evolution.

In Burr and Chowell (2008), in simulated data from models with demographic structure but no host immunity or viral strain information, predictions from SIR models with parameters estimated from the early portion of an outbreak were often badly wrong. Such bad prediction errors can indicate model violations, perhaps eventually leading to more appropriate models. To our knowledge, using prediction quality to assess model adequacy in this context is new. However it is possible that multiple wrong models provide adequate predictions, so model identifiability remains a research topic in this area.

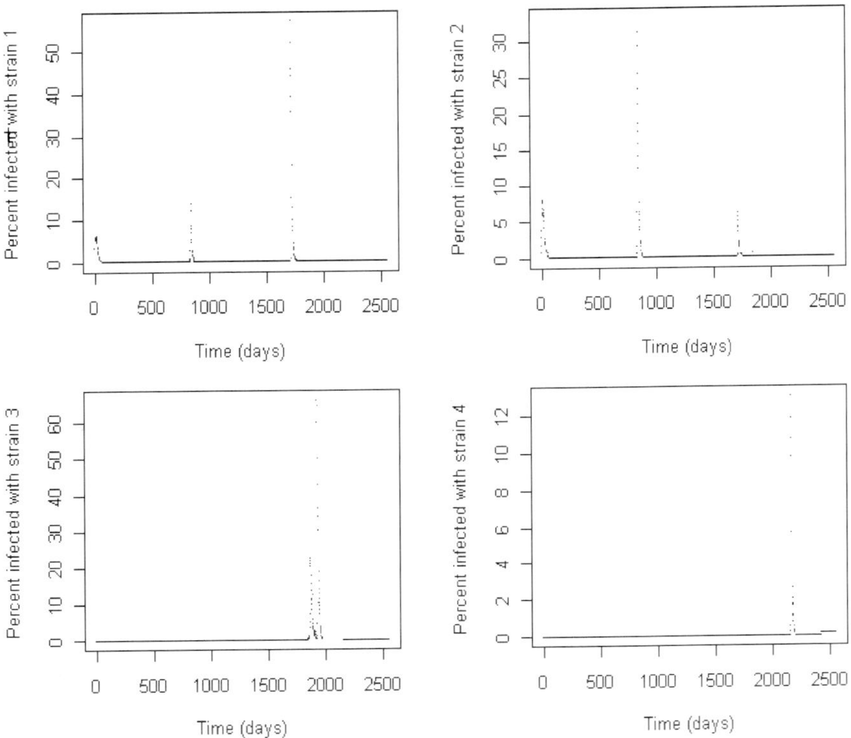

Fig. 9. Percent infected by day with strain 1, 2, 3 or 4 for the same simulated 7 years as in Figure 8.

7. Conclusions/summary

Coalescent theory and its success in some contexts at inferring aspects of past virus evolution were described. Then the argument was made that relatively new goals to predict aspects of virus evolution will require higher fidelity modeling that is anticipated to be available via coalescent theory or its extensions.

As a step toward high fidelity modeling, a small-scale agent based simulation was described and example results presented. For influenza, two prediction goals were considered: (1) in a given year, predict which new strains are most likely to be in the surviving lineage, and (2) predict the prevalent strains in the next year, so that vaccine design can be most effective. The new small-scale simulation code `flu1` in R can provide insight into the feasibility of meeting these goals, but it too makes restrictive modeling assumptions with unknown accuracy. A related concept was described that involves using prediction quality on simulated data that follows an assumed model to assess whether prediction performance on corresponding real data indicates model violations. Model violations that are evident from poor prediction quality can help prioritize future upgrades to the models.

8. References

Barouch, D. et al., (2010). Mosaic HIV-1 Vaccines Expand the Breadth and Depth of Cellular Immune Responses in Rhesus Monkeys, *Nature Medicine* 16, 319-323.

Bedford, T; Cobey, S; Peerli, P., & Pascual, M. (2010). Global Migration Dynamics Underlie Evolution and Persistence of Human Influenza A (H3N2), *PloS Pathogens* 6(5), 1-9, 2010.

Burr, T.; Skourikhine A.; Bruno, W., & Macken, C. (1999). Confidence Measures for Evolutionary Trees: Applications to Molecular Epidemiology. *Proc. IEEE Inter. Conf. on Information, Intelligence and Systems, Genetics and Evolution Section* ; 107-114. Burr, T. (2000). Quasi-Equilibrium Theory for the Distribution of Rare Alleles in a Subdivided Population: Justification and Implications. *Theoretical Population Biology*, 57(3): 297-306.

Burr, T. ; Myers, G., & Hyman, J. (2001). The Origin of AIDS – Darwinian or Lamarkian? *Phil. Trans. R. Soc. Lond. B* 356:877-887.

Burr, T.; Gattiker, J., & LaBerge G. (2002). Genetic Subtyping using Cluster Analysis. *Special Interest Group on Knowledge Discovery and Data Mining Explorations* 3:33-42.

Burr, T.; Gattiker, J., & Gerrish,P. (2003). An Investigation of Error Sources and Their Impact in Estimating the Time to the Most Recent Ancestor of Spatially and Temporally Distributed HIV Sequences. *Statistics in Medicine* 22(9):1495-1516

Burr ,T.; Graves, T.; Klaman, R.; Michalek, S.; Picard ,R., & Hengartner, N. (2006). Accounting for Seasonal Patterns in Syndromic Surveillance Data for Outbreak Detection, *BioMedCentral, Medical Informatics and Decision Making*, 6:40.

Burr, T., & Chowell, G. (2008). Signatures of non-homogeneous mixing in disease outbreaks. *Mathematical and Computer Modelling* 48:122-140, 2008

Burr, T., & Chowell, G. (2009) The Reproduction Number R(t) in Structured and Non-structured Populations. *Mathematical Biosciences and Engineering* . 6(2) 239-259.

Bush, R.; Bender, C.; Subbarao, K; Cox, N; & Fitch, W. (1999). Predicting the Evolution of Human Influenza A, *Science* 286: 1921-1925.

Chen, G. et al, (2006). Genomic Signatures of Human versus Avian Influenza A Viruses, *Emerging Infectious Diseases* 12(9): 1353-1360.

Eubank, S.; Goclu, H.; Kumar, A.; Marathe, M.; Srinivasan, A.; Totoczkal, Z., & Wang, N. (2004). Modelling Disease Outbreaks in Realistic Urban Social Networks. *Nature*, 429:180-184.

Ewing, G.; Nicholls, G., & Rodrigo A. (2004). Using Temporally Spaced Sequences to Simultaneously Estimate Migration Rates, Mutation Rage and Population Sizes in Measurably Evolving Populations. *Genetics* 168:2407-2420.

Excoffier, L., & Foll, M. (2011). fastsimcoal: a Continuous-time Coalescent Simulator of Genomic Diversity under Arbitrarily Complex Evolutionary Scenarios, *Bioinformatics* Advance Access, March 2011.

Felsenstein, J.; Kuhner, M.; Yamato, J., & Beerli P. (1999). Likelihoods on Coalescents: a Monte Carlo Sampling Approach to Inferring Parameters from Population Samples of Molecular Data. pp. 163-185 in *Statistics in Molecular Biology and Genetics*, ed. Francoise Seillier-Moiseiwitsch. IMS Lecture Notes-Monograph Series, volume 33. Inst. of Math. Statistics and American Mathematical Society, Hayward, California.

Ferguson, N., & Anderson, R. (2002). Predicting Evolutionary Change in the Influenza A Virus, *Nature Medicine* 8(6): 562-563.

Forrest, H., & Webster, R. (2010). Perspectives on Influenza Evolution and the Role of Research, *Animal Health Research Reviews* 11(1): 3-18.

Grassley, N.; Harvey, P., & Holmes, E. (1999) Population Dynamics of HIV-1 Inferred from Gene

Sequences. *Genetics* 151: 427-438.

Graves, T., & Picard, R. (2003) Predicting the Evolution of P&I Mortality During A Flu Season, Los Alamos National Laboratory Unrestricted Release Report, LAUR02-4717.

Innan, H., & Stephan, W. (2000). The Coalescent in an Exponentially Growing Metapopulation and Its Application to Arabidopsis thaliana, *Genetics* 155, 2015-2109.

Kingman, J. (1982). On the Genealogy of Large Populations. *J. Appl. Probability* 19: 27-43.

Korber, B., & Myers, G. (1992) Signature Pattern Analysis: a Method for Assessing Viral Sequence Relatedness. *AIDS Res. Hum. Retro.*, 8, 1549–1560.

Lapedes, A., & Farber R. (2001). The Geometry of Shape Space: Application to Influenza, *Journal of Theoretical Biology* 212(1), 57-69.

Minayev, P., & Ferguson, N. (2009a). Improving the Realism of Deterministic Multi-strain Models: Implications for Modelling Influenza A, *J. R. Society Interface* 6, 509-518, 2009.

Minayev, P., & Ferguson, N. (2009b) Incorporating Demographic Stochasticity into Multi-strain Epidemic Models: Application to Influenza A, *J. R. Society Interface* 6, 989-996.

Nelson, M., & Holmes, E. (2007). The Evolution of Epidemic Influenza, *Nature Reviews Genetics* 8, 196-205.

Perelson, A. et al. (1996). HIV-1 Dynamics in Vivo: Virion Clearance Rate, Infected Cell Life-Span, and Viral Generation Time *Science* 271, 1582-1586.

Plotkin, J.; Dushoff, J., & Levin, S. (2002). Hemagglutinin Sequence Clusters and the Antigenic Evolution of Influenza A, *Proc. Nat. Acad. Sci, USA* 2002; 99: 6263-6268

Pybus, O.;Rambaut, A., & Harvey, P. (2000). An Integrated Framework for the Inference of Viral Population History From Reconstructed Genealogies. *Genetics* 155: 1429-1437.

R: a Language and Environment for Statistical Computing, R Development Core Team, www.R-project.org.

Rambaut, A.; Pybus, O.; Nelson, M.; Viboud, C.; Taubenberger, J., & Holmes, E. (2008).The Genomic and Epidemiological Eynamics of Human Influenza A Virus. *Nature* 453:615-9

Rambaut, A.; Robertson, D.; Pybus, O.; Peeters, M., & Holmes ,E. (2001). Phylogeny and the Origin of HIV-1. *Nature*,410:1047-8

Rodrigo et al. (1999). Coalescent Estimates of HIV-1 Generation Time in Vivo. *Proc. Nat. Acad. Sci USA* 96:2187-2191.

Sjodin, P.; Kaj, K.; Krone, S.; Lascoux, M., & Nordborg, M. (2005). On the Meaning and Existence of an Effective Population Size. *Genetics* 169: 1061-1070.

Swofford, D.; Olsen, G.; Waddell, P., & Hillis, D., Phylogenetic Inference, Chapter 11 in Molecular Systematics, Edited by Hillis, D.; Moritz. C., & Mable, B, SInaer, Sunderland, Mass. 1996.

Stephens, M., & Donnelly P. (2000). Inference in Molecular Population Genetics. *J. Royal Statistical Soc* B 62(4); 605-655.

Venables, W., & Ripley, B. (1999) Modern Applied Statistics with Splus, Springer: New York.

Part 5

Protein Structure Analysis

14

A Bioinformatical Approach to Study the Endosomal Sorting Complex Required for Transport (ESCRT) Machinery in Protozoan Parasites: The *Entamoeba histolytica* Case

Israel López-Reyes[1], Cecilia Bañuelos[1],
Abigail Betanzos[2] and Esther Orozco[2,3]
[1]*Instituto de Ciencia y Tecnología del Distrito Federal,*
[2]*Centro de Investigación y de Estudios Avanzados del Instituto Politécnico Nacional,*
[3]*Universidad Autónoma de la Ciudad de México,*
México

1. Introduction

1.1 The potential of bioinformatics for the study of protein structure and function

Proteins are macromolecules formed by amino acid polymers that regulate cellular functions. Each protein is composed by the repetition and combination of 20 different amino acids, whose order is determined by the genetic code. To perform their biological functions, proteins fold into one or more specific spatial conformations, determined by non-covalent interactions such as hydrogen bonding, ionic interactions, Van der Waals forces and hydrophobic packing, and covalent interactions, such as disulfide bonds (Chiang et al., 2007).

Determining the structure and function of a protein is a milestone of many aspects of modern biology to understand its role in cell physiology. Bioinformatics is the research, development or application of computational approaches for expanding the use of biological, medical, behavioral or health-related data. It also includes those tools to acquire, store, organize, archive, analyze or visualize infomation. Over the past years, bioinformatical tools have been widely used for the prediction and study of protein biology. Moreover, bioinformatical tools have revealed the existence of protein "interactomes", demonstrating the interaction among distinct biomolecules (protein-protein, protein-lipids, protein-carbohydrates, etc.) to perform cellular processes (Kuchaiev & Przulj, 2011).

During the last decades, genome sequencing projects together with bioinformatics programs and algorithms have enormously contributed to understand protein structure, protein interactions and protein functions. At present, over six million unique protein sequences have been deposited in public databases, and this number is increasing rapidly. Meanwhile, despite the progress of high-throughput structural genomics initiatives, just over 50,000 protein structures have been experimentally determined (Kelley & Sterberg, 2009). The greatest challenge the molecular biology community is facing today is to analyze the wealth of data that has been produced by the genome sequencing projects, where bioinformatics has been fundamental. Traditionally, molecular biology research has been carried out entirely at the laboratory bench, but the huge increase in the amount of data has made necessary to incorporate computers and sophisticated software into research.

Additionally, availability of genome databases for distinct organisms has improved our knowledge on the way to elucidate the last universal common ancestor. In conclusion, analyzing and comparing the genetic material of different species is an increasingly important approach for studying the numbers, locations, biochemical functions and evolution of genes and proteins.

In this review, we selected a particular scientific case to emphasize the usefulness and potential of bioinformatics in addressing a biological problem.

Most cellular processes use scaffold proteins to recruit other proteins and to facilitate their correct interaction and functioning. Thus, we focused on the very little studied scaffold proteins that form the Endosomal Sorting Complexes Required for Transport (ESCRT) machinery during protozoan endocytosis, a fundamental process for cell survival. Here, as a study case, we aimed to highlight the possible identity, function and interactions of ESCRT complexes in *Entamoeba histolytica*, as determined by the use of bioinformatical tools.

1.2 Role of the ESCRT in endocytosis

Endocytosis is a crucial process in multiple cellular and physiological events, including nutrient uptake, virus budding, cell surface receptor downregulation and cell signaling. It involves the internalization of molecules or particles of different sizes from the external environment, through membrane remodeling and vesicle formation events (de Souza et al., 2009). In endocytosis, a huge number of interactomes are involved. In the study of the highly complex endocytosis process, bioinformatics databases and computational tools have been of enormous value.

Several plasma membrane proteins interact with target molecules (cargo) to internalize and transport them along the endocytic pathway. Depending on their function, membrane proteins are recycled back to the cell surface or degraded at lysosomal compartments together with cargo. Delivery of endocytosed cargo for degradation occurs through the fusion of intracellular vesicles called early and late endosomes that finally reach lysosomes.

In the majority of cell types, late endosomes fuse among them to form multivesicular bodies (MVB), which are essential intermediates for nutrient, ligand and receptor trafficking (Williams & Urbé, 2007). The best characterized signal for entering cargo molecules into the degradative MVB pathway is ubiquitination. Ubiquitination is a conjugation event in which a highly conserved 76 amino acid protein called ubiquitin, is covalently attached for cargo labeling. Most of the cargo proteins that accumulate in MVB are marked by a single ubiquitin, which is recognized by a specific and conserved protein machinery termed "Endosomal Sorting Complex Required for Transport (ESCRT)" and whose function is fundamental during endocytosis (Williams & Urbé, 2007).

The ESCRT machinery was first characterized in yeast. It consists of a group of vacuolar protein sorting factors (some of them called Vps), which form different multimeric complexes (ESCRT-0, -I, -II and -III) that bind among them but also associate to accesory proteins and endosomal membrane lipids to perform the whole endocytic process (Fig. 1) (Hurley & Emr, 2006).

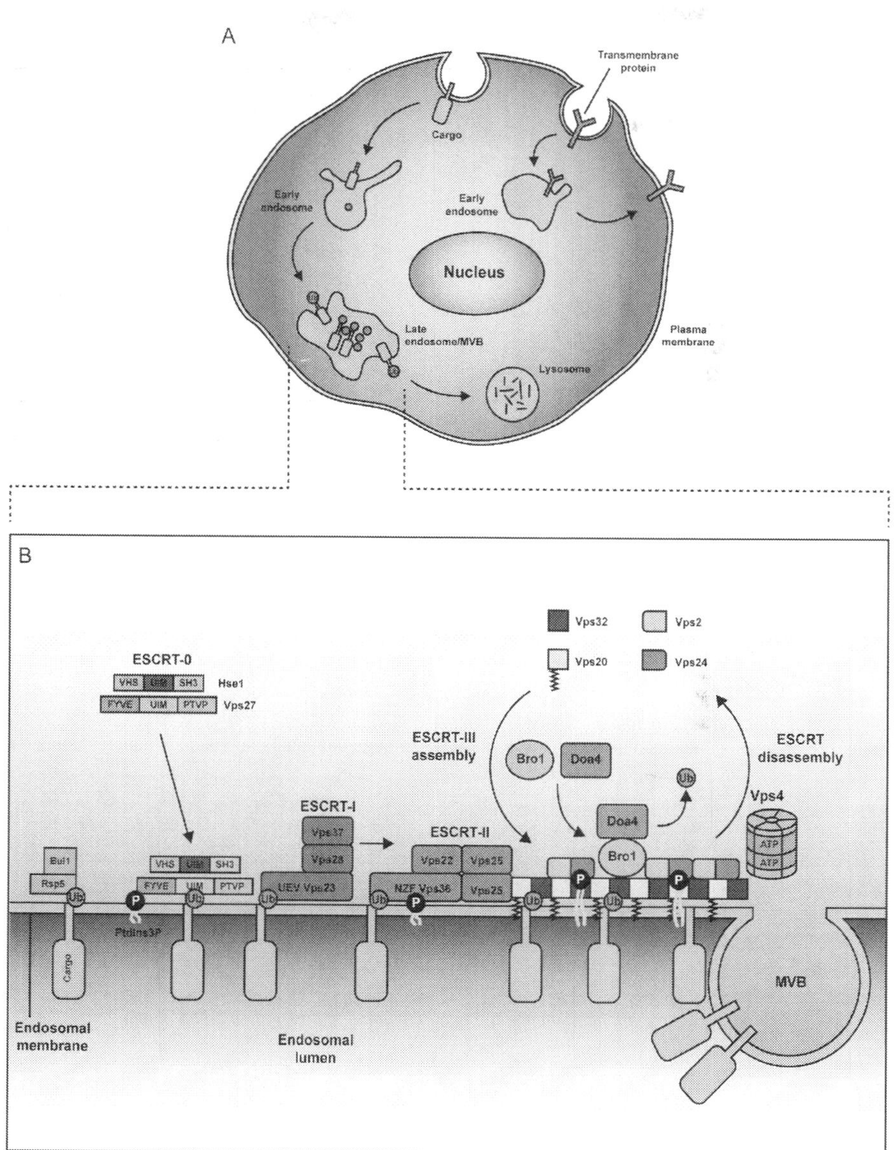

Fig. 1. The ESCRT machinery involved in the endosomal MVB pathway.

(A) Eukaryotic cells internalize cargo molecules from the external environment by endocytic processes. These molecules transit along several compartments for surface recycling or degradation. The degradation pathway involves an endomembrane system constituted of membrane bound organelles called endosomes that mature from early to late endosomes/MVB for finally cargo delivering into lysosomes. According to (B), at late endosome level, molecules to be incorporated into the degradation pathway should be tagged with ubiquitin. In yeast, ubiquitination of cargo proteins is mediated by the ubiquitin ligase Rsp5 and by Bul1. Then, the ESCRT-0 complex initiates the MVB sorting process by endosomal membrane binding through the Vps27 domain, and ubiquitin recognition of cargo by UIM domains present in Vps27 and Hse1 proteins. Subsequently, Vps27 activates the ESCRT-I complex through its interaction with Vps23. Ubiquitinated cargo is recognized by ESCRT-I (via the UEV domain of Vps23) and by ESCRT-II (via the NZF domain of Vps36). Vps36 has an extensive positively charged region with high affinity to phosphoinositides, allowing ESCRT-II attachment to endosomal membranes. Then, ESCRT-III concentrates cargo proteins into MVB. ESCRT-III also associates to accessory proteins such as Bro1 and Doa4. Importantly, the Vps4 ATPase catalyzes the dissociation of ESCRT complexes to initiate new cycles of cargo sorting and transport. Together, ESCRT-0 to -III and -accessory proteins direct cargo sorting, vesicle fusion, and MVB biogenesis (modified from Hurley & Emr, 2006).

Cargo ubiquitination is mediated by the Rsp5 ubiquitin ligase and Bul1 protein. Then, cargo sorting through the MVB pathway initiates with the association of Vps27 and Hse1 proteins to make up the ESCRT-0 complex. Vps27 has a FYVE (Fab1, YOTB, Vac1, EEA1) domain, which binds to membrane lipids, and an UIM (Ubiquitin Interaction Motif) domain that determines an important role for ESCRT-0 in the initial selection of ubiquitinated cargo at the endosomal membrane (Hurley & Emr, 2006; Williams & Urbé, 2007). Then, ESCRT-0 recruits ESCRT-I, formed by Vps23, Vps28, Vps37 and Mvb12 proteins (Curtiss et al., 2007; Katzmann et al., 2001). Vps23 also recognizes and binds ubiquitinated proteins through its terminal UEV (Ubiquitin E2 Variant) domain. ESCRT-I binds to ESCRT-II formed by Vps22, Vps25 and Vps36 proteins (Babst et al., 2002a). This later protein also displays an ubiquitin-interacting domain and a recognition region for phosphoinositides binding. Next, ESCRT-II binds to the ESCRT-III complex composed of Vps2, Vps20, Vps24 and Vps32 proteins (Babst et al., 2002b). Vps32 associates to Bro1, which recruits Doa4, an ubiquitin hydrolase that removes ubiquitin from cargo proteins prior to their incorporation into MVB (Kim et al., 2005; Odorizzi et al., 2003). One of the main functions of ESCRT-III is to concentrate the MVB cargo in the endosomal inward membrane, and to recruit Vps4, an ATPase that catalyzes the disassembly of ESCRT complexes from the endosomal membrane to initiate new rounds of cargo sorting and trafficking, and vesicle formation, and vesicle formation (Hurley & Emr, 2006; Hurley & Hanson, 2010; Williams & Urbé, 2007).

Accessory proteins such as Vta1 and Ist1, regulate Vps4 function (Dimaano et al., 2008; Shiflett et al., 2004), whereas Vps46 and Vps60 have also been suggested to bind ESCRT-III, although their precise functions have yet to be determined (Babst et al., 2002b).

1.3 Evolution of the ESCRT machinery

During the evolution from prokaryotic to eukaryotic organisms, some properties were lost while others were acquired. Among the latter is the ability of eukaryotic cells to incorporate macromolecules, complexes and other cells through endocytosis (de Souza et al., 2009). Comparative genomics and phylogenetic studies have determined that the basic features of intracellular trafficking systems arose very early in eukaryotic evolution (Dacks & Field,

2007). Similarly, evidence for the existence of MVB-like organelles in diverse primitive eukaryotes has also been reported (Allen et al., 2007; Tse et al., 2004; Yang et al., 2004).

Lysosomal targeting of ubiquitinated cargo by ESCRT complexes is conserved in animals and fungi (Leung et al., 2008). Extensive experimental and bioinformatical comparative analysis of genomic data indicate that ESCRT factors are well conserved across the eukaryotic lineage (Williams & Urbé, 2007). ESCRT-I, -II and –III as well as -accessory proteins are almost completely retained in all studied taxa, indicating an early evolutionary origin and a near-universal system for cargo trafficking through the MVB pathway. Particularly, all eukaryotic organisms studied to date have at least an ESCRT-III protein, suggesting that the minimal ESCRT necessary for MVB formation might be ESCRT-III (Williams & Urbé, 2007). In addition, the number of components of ESCRT-III is greatly expanded in mammals in comparison to yeast, being Vps46 the most frequent ESCRT-III multicopy gene product (Dacks et al., 2008).

A common ancestry within the same ESCRT complexes or among them, has been reported for Vps20, Vps32 and Vps60 proteins (sharing a Snf7 domain), and Vps2, Vps24 and Vps46 proteins (sharing a Vps24 domain). All these proteins are highly similar at sequence level and are encoded by multicopy genes, probably due to gene amplification events (Leung et al., 2008). In terms of biological conservation, it seems that several ESCRT components had to be expanded to provide functional redundancy. Thus, this redundancy would preserve ESCRT functions in the endocytic MVB pathway even if losses of components were presented along evolution.

Significantly, the Vps4 ATPase responsible for recycling ESCRT components, is present in all taxa, indicating a highly conserved mechanism for delivering energy in the system. This is consistent with recent evidence for an archael origin for Vps4 (Obita et al., 2007).

The most prominent evolutionary variation in the MVB pathway is the restriction of ESCRT-0 to animals and fungi, suggesting that a distinct mechanism for ubiquitin labeling, signal recognition and endosomal membrane binding likely operates in the rest of eukaryotic organisms (Leung et al., 2008).

1.4 Endocytosis and the MVB pathway in parasitic protozoa

Protozoa are a diverse group of single cell eukaryotic organisms, in some of them are pathogens. Parasitic infections due to protozoa affect millions of people worldwide, causing a wide range of diseases, high rates of morbidity and mortality each year and an immense economic burden for public health (Geoff, 1997).

In pathogenic protozoa, endocytosis is a basic mechanism for ingesting host macromolecules and it has thus been associated to parasite virulence. Previous work based on ultrastructural, cytochemical, biochemical and molecular studies has shown that protozoan parasites possess the structural compartments and proteins necessary to perform endocytosis (de Souza et al., 2009). The extent of endocytic activity varies among different protozoa and even across various developmental stages. In addition, in trypanosomatids, the endocytic process is highly active in a well-defined region of the parasite cell surface called the flagellar pocket (Ghedin et al., 2001). However, only very few studies have been published to characterize the endocytic MVB pathway in protozoan parasites, some of them are summarized below.

Giardia lamblia is a protozoan parasite that causes diarrheal infections. It is also one of the most primitive organisms, with a substantially different endomembrane morphology as compared to higher eukaryotes. Although the morphology of membrane-bound vesicles in *Giardia* has been previously described, there exists few information about vesicle budding and fusion (Lanfredi-Rangel et al., 1998). Recently, it was reported that a putative gene encoding a FYVE domain-containing protein homologous to yeast Vps27 is expressed in *G. lamblia*. This protein binds to endosomal membrane phospholipids suggesting the presence of a MVB pathway in this parasite (Sinha et al., 2010). However, very little is known about the ESCRT machinery in *Giardia* (Leung et al., 2008).

Leishmania major, a flagellated parasite provoking leishmaniasis disease, presents a plasma membrane invagination (flagellar pocket) where the flagellum emerges. This site contains a complex and highly polarized MVB-like network where endocytosis and exocytosis occur for crucial exchanges such as nutrient uptake. In this parasite, a Vps4 homologue (LmVps4) has been characterized using a Vps4 dominant negative mutant in which the highly conserved E residue required for ATP hydrolysis was substituted by a Q amino acid at position 235. The LmVps4 mutant protein was accumulated around endocytic vesicular structures and this provoked a defect in cargo protein transport to the MVB-lysosomes, as it has been reported for yeast and mammalian Vps4 mutants (Babst et al, 1998; Fujita et al., 2003). Additionally, LmVps4 is probably involved in *Leishmania* pathogenicity, since the Vps4 mutant protein also impaired parasite differentiation and virulence (Besteiro et al., 2006).

Trypanosomes infect a variety of hosts and cause several diseases, including the fatal human diseases known as sleeping sickness and Chagas disease. In this group of flagellate protozoa, the trafficking system has been previously characterized (Field et al., 2007). Trypanosomes contain glycosil-phosphatidylinositol-anchored proteins and morphologically-related MVB structures, and also exhibit ubiquitin-dependent internalization of transmembrane proteins for degradation (Allen et al., 2007; Chung et al., 2004). The functional conservation of the ESCRT system has been confirmed in *Trypanosome brucei*. Despite extreme sequence divergence, epitope-tagged *Trypanosome* TbVps23 and TbVps28 proteins localize to the endosomal pathway. Knockdown of TbVps23 partially prevents degradation of ubiquitinated proteins. Therefore, despite the absence of an ESCRT-0 complex, the MVB pathway seems to function in this parasite, similarly to the yeast and human systems (Leung et al., 2008).

Members of the *Apicomplexan* phylum of intracellular parasites, such as *Plasmodium falciparum* and *Toxoplasma gondii*, responsible for malaria and toxoplasmosis, respectively, contain morphologically unique secretory organelles termed rhoptries that are essential for host cell invasion, and also display internal membrane-resembling MVB structures (Coppens & Joiner, 2003; Hoppe et al., 2000). In *T. gondii*, it has been hypothesized that the MVB pathway could intersect with the rhoptry biogenesis one. To explore this, wild type (PfVps4) and mutant (PfVps4E214Q) *P. falciparum* Vps4 proteins were independently overexpressed in *T. gondii*. As expected, PfVps4 was located in *T. gondii* vesicular structures, whereas PfVps4E214Q was found in aberrant organelles where rhoptries proteins were also present, indicating that the secretion pathway could be disrupted by the altered Vps4 protein. These findings suggest that MVB formation may occur in *T. gondii* and *P. falciparum* and that it could be affecting the secretory route too (Yang et al., 2004).

During host cell infection, *P. falciparum* lives within a special compartment known as the parasitophorous vacuole. For the parasite to survive and multiply, molecules from the host cell cytoplasm cross the parasitophorous vacuole membrane and trigger signals for the endocytic process. Despite the scarce information being available for supporting a feasible relationship between the MVB pathway and the mechanism of nutrient uptake and intracellular phagotrophy (the ability to ingest portions of host cytoplasm) through the parasitophorous vacuole, it may be possible that these two processes are related (de Souza et al., 2009).

E. histolytica, which causes amoebiasis, destroys almost all human tissues through macromolecules participating in adherence, contact-dependent cytolysis and proteolytic and phagocytic activities. A well-characterized protein involved in these key events is EhADH112 (García-Rivera et al., 1999). Interestingly, this protein is located at MVB-like structures in *E. histolytica* trophozoites and is structurally related to Bro1 (Bañuelos et al., 2005), an accessory protein that interacts with the ESCRT-III complex in yeast. Recently, our research group reported the presence of a set of 19 putative ESCRT proteins in this parasite and characterized a yeast Vps4 homologue by analyzing its ATPase function and relationship to parasite virulence in wild type and mutant cells (López-Reyes et al., 2010). Results derived from these studies strongly suggest that *E. histolytica* possesses a well conserved ESCRT machinery.

2. Experimental approaches for the identification and characterization of ESCRT proteins

The ESCRT components involved in mediating endosomal MVB sorting of ubiquitinated proteins have been identified and characterized by several methodologies.

Initially, over 70 *vps* genes required for the vacuolar transport of proteins were identified by genetic screening in yeast (Bonangelino et al., 2002; Bowers et al., 2004). At this moment, only 20 of these genes are known to be functionally involved in yeast MVB formation.

In addition, the structure and function of putative binding domains present in ESCRT components have been characterized using recombinant proteins and site-directed mutagenesis. In particular, ubiquitin recognition and binding to ESCRT complexes by proteins such as Hse1 and Vps27, Vps23 or Vps36 were elucidated by using crystallographic structures of recombinant proteins that associate or not, to ubiquitin. The same methodologies have been used for characterizing lipid binding domains such as the FYVE motif, present in Vps27, and for positively charged regions with affinity to phosphoinositides, such as those exhibited by Vps36 and Vps24 (Misra & Hurley, 1999; Pornillos et al., 2002; Stahelin et al., 2002; Sundquist et al., 2004).

The yeast two-hybrid system is an assay to examine protein interactions. This system includes the construction of a bait protein containing a DNA binding domain, which hybridizes to a prey protein with an activation domain. The expression of the reporter gene means that the proteins of interest interact with each other since the activation domain promotes the transcription of the reporter gene (Gietz et al., 1997). On the other hand, pull-down assays are performed either to prove a suspected interaction between two proteins or to investigate unknown proteins or molecules that may bind to a protein of interest (Kaltenbach et al., 2007). Alternatively, affinity purification of histidine- or glutathione-succinyl-transferase-(GST)-tagged bait proteins can be performed via immobilized affinity chromatography. The bait protein (or ligand) is captured to a solid support (beads) by covalent attachment to an activated beaded support or through an affinity tag that binds to a receptor molecule on the support (Pandeya & Thakkar, 2005).

In yeast, Bro1 binding to Vps32 was discovered by two-hybrid experiments, whereas Bro1 association to Vps4 was revealed by GST pull-down experiments. Additionally, using both methodologies, interactions between Vps20 and Vps28; Vps20 and Vps22; and Vps22 and

Vps28, were identified. Moreover, protein-protein interactions for ESCRT assembly have been evidenced by yeast-two-hybrid assays, affinity purification or both methods (Vps20 with Vps25 and Vps36; Vps27 with Hse1; Vps4 with Vps32; Vps22 with Vps25; and Vps22 with Vps36) (Bowers et al., 2004).

Another strategy to study protein functions is via dominant negative (DN) mutants. Mutations are changes in a genomic sequence and sometimes their expression is dominant over the wild-type protein synthesis in the same cell. Usually, DN mutants can still interact with the normal partner proteins thus blocking the functions of the wild-type protein. To improve our knowledge on the ESCRT model, several DN mutants for Vps proteins have been generated, including Hrs, Vps27, Vps23, Vps20 and Vps4 (Kanazawa et al., 2003; Li et al., 1999; Fujita et al., 2003).

Research using such strategies has increased our knowledge on the identity, structure, function and biological relationships of several molecules participating in the protein sorting through the endosomal MVB pathway. However, complementary experimental efforts need to be performed to better understand this cellular process.

3. Computational research on protein biology

One of the most familiar applications of bioinformatics is the comparison of the amino acid sequence from a query protein against the amino acid sequence of a protein previously characterized in structure and function, to theoretically elucidate whether they are related. This approach gives insights into functional similarities and evolutionary relationships deduced from the presence of common structural features (Söding, 2005).

Similarity and homology are two important concepts in the bioinformatical analysis of protein sequences. Similarity is a quantitative measure between two or more related amino acid sequences. By contrast, homology is a qualitative measure which indicates if two or more proteins are evolutionarily related or derived from a common ancestor (Claverie & Notredame, 2006). Protein sequences are usually submitted, annotated and stored in databases that allow their comparison and analysis by certain software.

In general, a database is a digital system that organizes, stores and easily retrieves large amounts of data. Currently, several genome and proteome databases are freely available for studying protein biology. However, the sheer amount of data makes highly difficult to manually interpret it. Therefore, databases require supplementary and incisive computational tools in order to understand the information.

One of the most recognized databases is the UniProt Knowledgebase (UniProtKB, http://www.uniprot.org/). The UniProtKB is the central hub for the collection of functional information on annotated proteins. The UniProtKB consists of a section containing manually-annotated records with information extracted from literature and curator-evaluated computational analysis (UniProtKB/Swiss-Prot), and a section with computationally analyzed records that await full manual annotation (UniProtKB/TrEMBL). Manual annotation consists of a critical and continuously updated review of experimentally proven or computer-predicted data about each protein by an expert team of biologists.

The UnipProtKB captures the mandatory core data for each entry (amino acid sequence, protein name, description, taxonomic data and citation information) and supplementary information derived from experimental evidence or computational data.

More than 99% of the protein sequences provided by UniProtKB comes from coding
sequences translation and related data submitted to the public nucleic acid databases,
including the European Molecular Biology Laboratory (EMBL) Bank, the GenBank (USA)
and the DNA DataBank of Japan (DDBJ). Taking advantage of the information as much as
possible, there are a number of computational tools to finally interpret databases, some of
them are briefly described below.

The Expert Protein Analysis System (ExPaSy) is a proteomics server from the Swiss Institute
of Bioinformatics that analyzes protein sequences and structures and contains genome
databases for several organisms ranging from *Archae* to human (http://expasy.org/
tools/#proteome). It has several tools useful to depict primary, secondary and tertiary
protein structures and to determine putative postranslational modifications, among others.

The Basic Local Alignment Search Tool (BLAST) is an algorithm for comparing primary
biological sequence information, such as amino acid sequences of different proteins or
nucleotides of distinct DNA sequences. A BLAST search enables a researcher to compare a
query sequence with data existing in sequence libraries or databases, and to identify the
sequences that resemble the query sequence above a certain threshold. The main idea of
BLAST is that there are often high-scoring segment pairs (HSP) contained in a statistically
significant alignment. BLAST searches for high scoring sequence alignments between the
query sequence and sequences from genome databases, using a heuristic approach that
approximates the Smith-Waterman algorithm (Altschul et al., 1990). The BLASTP program,
which compares protein queries to protein databases, is a heuristic model that attempts to
optimize a specific similarity measure. The goal of this tool is to find regions of sequence
similarity. These regions can yield clues about the structure and function of the novel
sequence and its evolutionary history and homology by comparison to other sequences in
databases (Henikoff & Henikoff, 2000). To produce a multiple sequence alignment from the
BLASTP output, this program simply collects all database sequence segments that have been
aligned to the query with an expectation value (*E*-value) below a threshold by a default set
to 0.001. Thus, the lower the *E*-value, the greater the similarity between the input and the
match sequences will be. An *E-value* < e-3 of an alignment means that the alignment is
highly unique and not due to error (http://bips.u-strasbg.fr/fr/Tutorials/Comparison/
Blast/blastall.html). As an alternative for accurate searches of query sequences, the Position
Specific Iterative (PSI)-BLAST program iteratively searches for one or more proteins
databases to find sequences similar to one or more protein query sequences.

ClustalW is also a widely used multiple sequence alignment computer program
(http://align.genome.jp/). In many cases, the input set of query sequences is assumed to
have an evolutionary relationship, share a lineage and descend from a common ancestor.
This algorithm is usually supplemented by the BOXSHADE application
(http://www.ch.embnet.org/software/BOX_form.html). BOXSHADE is a program for
creating good looking printouts from multiple-aligned protein or DNA sequences.
BOXSHADE does not produce alignments by itself, it has to take as input a file preprocessed
by a multiple alignment program or a multiple file editor such as ClustalW. In the standard
BOXSHADE output, identical and similar residues in the multiple-alignment chart are
represented by different colors or shadings.

3.1 Computational tools for predicting protein domains

Protein domains, defined as the independent folding units within a polypeptide, are also
understood as the functional and evolutionarily conserved modules of protein families.

The Pfam protein family database is a large collection of multiple sequence alignments that is generated by probabilistic models known as hidden Markov models (HMM) (http://www.sanger.ac.uk/resources/databases/pfam.html). The Pfam database contains information about protein domains and families. For each family in Pfam, one can look at multiple alignments, view protein domain architectures, examine species distribution, and follow links to other databases and view known protein structures.

Despite the increasing volume of biochemical and molecular literature on protein data, Pfam contains the essential information about major protein domains for the understanding of the ever more complicated biological landscape.

Since the ClustalW and BOXSHADE programs could be useful to identify conserved residues and similar regions among amino acid sequences, they also allow the prediction of putative domains in a protein or group of proteins of interest.

3.2 Computational approaches for predicting secondary protein structure

Secondary structure refers to highly regular local sub-structures within a molecule. The secondary structure of a protein is defined by patterns of hydrogen bonds between the main-chain peptide groups, leading to several recognizable protein domains, such as alpha (α) helices and beta (β) sheets (Offer et al., 2002).

So far, several algorithms have been described for predicting secondary protein structures, one of them being Jpred (Cole et al., 2008). Jpred uses a 3-iteration PSI-BLAST search to obtain sequences from existing databases for predicting secondary structures. Jpred now includes Jnet, a neural network method also for secondary structure prediction. The Jnet algorithm works by applying multiple sequence alignments, alongside PSI-BLAST and HMM profiles (Cuff & Barton, 1999). The updated Jnet algorithm provides α-helix and β-sheet predictions at an accuracy of 81.5% (Cole et al., 2008).

3.3 Computational algorithms for predicting tertiary protein structure

The tertiary structure of a protein refers to the three-dimensional arrangement of a single protein molecule. The α-helices and β-sheets are folded into a compact structure due to non-specific hydrophobic interactions. However, this structure is stable only when the parts of a protein domain are locked into place by specific tertiary interactions, such as salt bridges, hydrogen bonds, and the tight packing of side chains and disulfide bonds (Peng & Kim, 1994).

The Protein Data Bank (PDB) contains information about experimentally-determined structures of proteins and nucleic acids, and complex assemblies (http://www.pdb.org/pdb/home/home.do). The Resource for Studying Biological Macromolecules curates and annotates the PDB data according to agreed upon standards and also provides a variety of tools and resources. Interestingly, the PDB is a repository for three dimensional structural data of proteins (typically obtained by X-ray crystallography or Nuclear Magnetic Resonance spectroscopy) submitted by biologists and biochemists from around the world.

The PDB is a key resource in areas of structural biology, such as structural genomics. Contents of the PDB are thought to be primary data, and currently there are hundreds of derived databases that categorize data differently.

The Phyre (Protein homology/analogy recognition engine) webserver is a powerful computational tool that uses profile-profile matching algorithms to considerably improve protein predictions (Kelley & Stenberg, 2009). The Phyre platform follows the most successful general approaches for predicting the structure of proteins, which involve the detection of homologues of a known three dimensional structure, the so-called template-based homology modeling and fold-recognition. Practical applications from three dimensional protein structure predictions include guidance on functional hypothesis, the selection of mutagenesis sites and the design of rational drugs, among others.

The Phyre server uses a library of known protein structures taken from the SCOP (Structural classification of proteins) database and augmented with newer depositions in the PDB. Sequences of each of these structures are scanned against a non-redundant sequence database and a profile is constructed and deposited in a "fold" library. The known and predicted secondary structures of these proteins are also stored in the fold library. A user-submitted sequence follows the same process. Five iterations of PSI-BLAST are used to gather both close and remote sequence homologues. The pairwise alignments generated by PSI-BLAST are combined into a single alignment with the query sequence as the master. Following the profile construction, the secondary structure of the query is predicted using three distinct programs (Psi-Pred, SSPro and Jnet). Subsequently, both profile and secondary structure, are scanned against the fold library using a profile-profile algorithm that returns a score. Scores are fitted to an extreme value distribution to generate an E-value. The top ten highest scores are then used to construct full three-dimensional models for the query. Where possible, missing or inserted regions caused by deletions or insertions in the alignment are repaired using a loop library and reconstruction procedures.

An alternative program widely used to model tertiary protein structures is SWISS-MODEL. SWISS-MODEL is a fully automated protein structure homology-modeling server accessible via the ExPASy web server or from the DeepView program (http://swissmodel.expasy.org/). The purpose of this server is to make protein modeling accessible to all biochemists and molecular biologists worldwide by providing tools for protein structure accurate predictions.

Once a tertiary structure has been modeled, it is sometimes necessary to get access into a model viewer. Jmol is a free open-source viewer for chemical three dimensional structures that is written in Java (so it runs on Windows, Mac OS X, Linux and UNIX systems). Jmol returns a representation of a molecule that may be used as a teaching tool, or for research e.g. in chemistry and biochemistry. The most notable feature is an applet that can be integrated into web pages to display molecules in a variety of models: "ball and stick", "space filling", "ribbon", etc. (http://jmol.sourceforge.net/download/).

4. ESCRT protein survey in protozoan parasites with bioinformatical tools

By using a bioinformatical screening and comparative genomic analysis, we confirmed in this work the presence of ESCRT representatives in unrelated groups of unicellular parasites of medical importance belonging to the following taxa: *Entamoebidae (Entamoeba)*, *Diplomonadida (Giardia)*, *Alveolata* of the phyllum *Apicomplexa (Toxoplasma* and *Plasmodium)*, and *Kinetoplastida (Trypanosoma* and *Leishmani*a).

First, we obtained yeast or mammalian amino acid sequences for ESCRT-0 to -III and - associated proteins from the UniProtKB database. Then, the retrieved sequences were used as probes to screen the Eukaryotic Pathogen database (EuPathDB version 2.9, http://eupathdb.org/eupathdb/). The EuPathDB has been developed as a Bioinformatics Resource Center and constitutes an integrated genome database covering eukaryotic pathogens of the genera *Cryptosporidium, Giardia, Entamoeba, Leishmania, Plasmodium, Toxoplasma, Trichomonas* and *Trypanosoma,* among others. This portal offers an entry point to all these resources, and the opportunity to leverage orthology (structural correspondence or similarity of genes or proteins in different species due to a common ancestor origin) for searches across genera in an interface that is functional, user-friendly and sophisticated.

Using yeast ESCRT protein sequences as queries in the EuPathDB resource for each parasite genome, the BLASTP program reported several amino acid sequences for each pathogen. When no matches were found, human corresponding ESCRT protein sequences were used as queries. Putative parasite ESCRT homologous sequences were selected with the following criteria: *i)* at least 20% identity and 35% similarity to the query sequence, *ii)* E-value lower than 0.002, and *iii)* absence of stop codons in the coding sequence. Furthermore, all recovered sequences were subjected to reverse BLAST analysis in the ExPaSy server to identify related proteins from genome databases. A candidate was taken into consideration if reverse BLAST recovered the original query within the top five hits. Failure to complete these tests resulted in a "not determined" assignment.

BLAST results showed that all parasites studied here contain putative protein sequences representing the ESCRT-0 to -III and -accessory proteins involved in the endocytic MVB pathway. In Table 1, we summarized the results derived from our parasite ESCRT genomic survey in comparison to ESCRT members previously reported in yeast or human. The major noticeable feature was the high conservation of ESCRT components in all taxa, as previously reported (Leung et al., 2008). As noticed, *Entamoeba histolytica* and *Leishmania major* contain the most represented and conserved ESCRT machinery among parasites, with 19 ESCRT components. Meanwhile, *Trypanosoma cruzi* and *Plasmodium falciparum* displayed 15 and 14 ESCRT putative proteins, respectively. By contrast, we only found 9 out of the 20 ESCRT proteins in *Toxoplasma gondii* and *Giardia lamblia.*

Ubiquitin-label recognition is the signal for cargo protein entrance towards degradation through the endosomal pathway (Bowers et al., 2004). Rsp5 and Bul1 proteins mediate ubiquitin-attachment to cargo proteins in yeast. Here, bioinformatical approaches revealed that ubiquitination seems to be mediated by Rsp5 rather than Bul1 homologues, since Rsp5-like proteins were present in all protozoan genomes.

Unlike preceding work, we found at least one ESCRT-0 representative for each parasite, indicating that proteins recognizing ubiquitin signals could be participating in cargo sorting in these protozoa. ESCRT-I and -II were the least represented complexes among all parasites, suggesting that some taxa members could have lost specific components along ESCRT evolution. However, we cannot exclude that the lack of individual ESCRT components might be the result of malfunctionings in gene or protein detection, more than a real absence of the protein. In particular, failures have been frequently reported for *Giardia* due to difficulties to recover candidate orthologues in its extremely divergent genome.

To the best of our knowledge, there is no sequenced eukaryotic genome without an ESCRT-III-related gene. Moreover, the size of the subset of ESCRT-III-related genes is greatly expanded in higher eukaryotes such as mammals, compared to yeast. As a consequence, it has been hypothesized that the ESCRT-III complex might be the minimal ESCRT unit for MVB formation (Williams & Urbé, 2007). Consistently, our results revealed at least two ESCRT-III representatives in each parasite genome analyzed.

Regarding the ESCRT-accesory proteins, the most conserved sequences among all parasites were the Rsp5, Vps4, Vps46, Doa4, Vta1 and Bro1 homologues, in contrast to Ist1, which was only present in trypanosomatids.

Taken together, our *in silico* results support the existence of a seemingly conserved ESCRT machinery for endosomal protein trafficking through the MVB pathway in protozoan parasites.

	Saccharomycetales / Primates	Amoebida	Diplomonadida	Eucoccidiorida	Haemosporida	Trypanosomatida	
ESCRT complex	Saccharomyces cerevisiae/ Homo sapiens	Entamoeba histolytica	Giardia lamblia	Toxoplasma gondii	Plasmodium falciparum	Leishmania major	Trypanosoma cruzi
ESCRT-0	Hse1	+	-	-	-	+	+
	Vps27	+	+	+	+	+	+
ESCRT-I	Vps23/Tsg101	+	-	-	-	+	+
	Vps28	+	-	-	+	+	-
	Vps37/hVps37D	+	-	-	+	+	-
	Mvb12	-	-	-	-	-	-
ESCRT-II	Vps22/EAP30	+	+	-	-	+	-
	Vps25/EAP20	+	+	-	-	-	-
	Vps36	+	-	-	-	+	+
ESCRT-III	Vps2	+	+	-	+	+	-
	Vps20	+	-	-	+	+	+
	Vps24	+	+	+	+	+	+
	Vps32	+	-	+	+	+	+
Upstream ESCRT- accessory proteins	Bul1	-	-	-	-	-	-
	Rsp5	+	+	+	+	+	+
Downstream ESCRT- accessory proteins	Vps4	+	+	+	+	+	+
	Ist1	-	-	-	-	+	+
	Vta1	+	-	+	+	+	+
	Vps46	+	+	+	+	+	+
	Vps60	+	-	-	+	+	+
	Doa4	+	+	+	+	+	+
	Bro1	+	-	+	+	+	+

Table 1. Comparison of ESCRT machineries from parasitic protozoa.
The presence (+) of homologous proteins is based on data obtained by BLAST searches from protein sequence databases at NCBI, UniProtK and EuPathDB, as described in the text.
Proteins apparently absent (-) from complete genome sequencing projects are indicated.

4.1 Characterization of the ESCRT machinery in *E. histolytica*

Our previous work, using comparative genomics for predicting ESCRT proteins in *E. histolytica*, provided valuable insights into the existence of a highly conserved ESCRT machinery in this parasite. López-Reyes et al. (2010) reported a set of 19 putative ESCRT proteins representing from ESCRT-0 to -III and -associated proteins (Table 2). Moreover, earlier characterization of ubiquitin genes and -transcripts and demonstration of an ubiquitin-conjugating system, together with our finding of a putative Rsp5 ubiquitin ligase (EhRsp5) *E. histolytica* provided additional support for the presence of at least one candidate that possibly mediates ubiquitin attachment to cargo molecules prior to their internalization into endosomes (Wöstmann et al., 1996).

Previous work has provided knowledge into the architecture, membrane recruitment and functional interactions of the ESCRT machinery through multiple domains that have been shaped along evolution. These scaffolds serve as gripping tools for recognizing cargo proteins, membrane lipids, ESCRT components and accessory proteins along the MVB route (Hurley & Emr, 2006).

To dissect the presence of putative ubiquitin and phosphoinositide binding domains in *E. histolytica* ESCRT-like components, we selected ESCRT-0 to -III representatives (EhVps27, EhVps23, EhVps36 and EhVps24, respectively) presumably containing these structural features according to their yeast and human homologues and performed multiple sequence alignments with the ClustalW program.

Putative complex	*Entamoeba histolytica* Predicted protein	Accesion number	*Homo sapiens* Protein	Accesion number	E-value	S (%)	I (%)	*Saccharomyces cerevisiae* Protein	Accesion number	E-value	S (%)	I (%)
ESCRT-0	EhHse1	C4M9E1	STAM1	Q92783	9e-08	72	50	Hse1	P38753	2e-10	70	62
	EhVps27	C4LYX5	HRS	O14964	----	---	---	Vps27	P40343	1e-11	61	49
ESCRT-I	EhVps23	C4LUR9	TSG101	Q99816	1.4e-10	51	33	Vps23	P25604	0.0052	31	25
	EhVps28	C4M842	hVps28	Q9UK41	----	---	---	Vps28	Q02767	0.00057	45	28
					----	---	---	Vps37	Q99176	0.00084	46	21
	EhVps37D	C4M6J5	hVps37D	Q6P2C3	3.8e-06	50	35	nd	----	----	---	---
	----	----	nd	----	----	---	---	Mvb12	P42939	----	---	---
ESCRT-II	EhVps22	C4LXI0	EAP30	Q96H20	9e-22	47	30	Vps22	Q12483	3.4e-15	48	25
	EhVps25	C4LZE7	EAP20	Q9BRG1	9e-08	52	28	Vps25	P47142	0.00038	46	19
	EhVps36	C4LTE5	EAP45	Q86VN1	1.8e-15	49	25	Vps36	Q06696	1.1e-09	48	26
ESCRT-III	EhVps2	C4LZV3	CHMP2A	O43633	8.9e-24	55	29	Vps2	P36108	2e-05	50	29
			CHMP2B	Q9UQN3	7.9e-16	48	25	----	----	----	---	---
	EhVps20	C4MAC7	CHMP6	Q96FZ7	----	---	---	Vps20	Q04272	0.00015	54	26
	EhVps24	C4M2Y2	CHMP3	Q9Y3E7	----	---	---	Vps24	P36095	2.2e-05	48	22
	EhVps32	C4M1A5	CHMP4A	Q9BY43	0.0012	48	24	Vps32	P39929	2.5e-12	48	25
			CHMP4B	Q9H444	9.6e-07	43	20	----	----	----	---	---
			CHMP4C	Q96CF2	1.4e-06	43	20	----	----	----	---	---
Upstream ESCRT-accessory proteins	----	----	nd	----	----	---	---	Bul1	P48524	----	---	---
	EhRsp5	C4M9I9	NEDD4	P46934	1.6e-50	53	33	Rsp5	P39940	7.8e-57	57	36
Downstream ESCRT-accessory proteins	EhVps4	C4LYN8	hVps4A	Q9UN37	1.1e-114	69	52	Vps4	P52917	3e-114	78	60
			hVps4B	O75351	3e-114	78	60	----	----	----	---	---
	----	----	hIst1	P53990	----	---	---	Ist1	P53843	----	---	---
	EhVta1	C4M0R8	hVta1	Q9NP79	2.8e-05	44	23	Vta1	Q06263	----	---	---
	EhVps46	C4LYH6	CHMP1A	Q9HD42	----	---	---	Vps46	P69771	0.00032	48	18
			CHMP1B	Q7LBR1	----	----	---	----	----	----	---	---
	EhVps60	C4M7T5	CHMP5	Q9NZZ3	5.6e-15	45	28	Vps60	Q03390	9e-06	46	19
	EhDoa4	C4LTM2	UBP4	Q13107	1e-77	58	36	Doa4	P32571	2e-27	50	31
	EhADH112	Q9U7F6	Alix	Q9UKL5	1e-21	40	20	Rim20	Q12033	2e-12	38	21
								BRO1	P48582	0.003	50	32

Table 2. Comparison of *E. histolytica, H. sapiens* and *S. cerevisiae* ESCRT machineries. Data of conserved ESCRT proteins from yeast and human were obtained at NCBI and UniProtKB databases. Putative *E. histolytica* ESCRT proteins were retrieved by BLAST searches at EupathDB and corresponding UniProtKB accession numbers were obtained. Putative ESCRT proteins of *E. histolytica* exhibited significant E-values (1.1e-114 to 0.00032) and high similarity (20 to 62%) to yeast and human ESCRT orthologues. nd, not determined; ----, non-significant similarity or identity and E-values; S, similarity; I, identity (Modified from López-Reyes et al., 2010).

Our computational comparative analysis showed that the ESCRT-0 complex, lacks the characteristic VHS (Vps27, Hrs and STAM) domain of yeast Vps27, required for the protein interaction with ubiquitin (Williams & Urbé, 2007). However, EhVps27 displayed a (R/K)(R/K)HHCR motif usually found within conserved FYVE domains and necessary for phosphatidylinositol 3-phosphate (PtdIns3P) binding (Misra & Hurley, 1999). This finding was also supported by the Pfam database, which reported the presence of a putative FYVE domain in the EhVps27 amino acid sequence.

Membrane phospholipids such as PtdIns3P, have been previously implicated in the regulation of endocytosis and phagocytosis and 12 FYVE-domain containing proteins have been identified in *E. histolytica* (Nakada-Tsukui et al., 2009).

The UEV domain present in yeast Vps23 and its human homologue Tsg101 is necessary to recognize ubiquitin signals in proteins to be sorted into MVB (Pornillos et al., 2002; Sundquist et al., 2004). Despite a less conserved similarity among analyzed sequences, our bioinformatics approach suggested the presence of a putative UEV domain at the N-terminus of EhVps23, also supported by Pfam domain predictions.

According to our current investigation, EhVps36 lacks the yeast NZF and human GLUE domains previously reported in Vps36 homologues. Both domains have been implicated in ubiquitin and PtdIns3P binding, respectively. Instead, EhVps36 conserves a N-terminal positively charged amino acid region. Similarly, the EhVps24 protein exhibits a positively charged amino acid tract present in almost its full sequence. Since specific binding to phosphoinositides requires electrostatic interactions between negatively charged phosphates on lipids and positively charged amino acids in proteins, it is feasible that EhVps36 and EhVps24 associate to phosphoinositides present at endosomal membranes (Whitley et al., 2003).

Secondary structure assignments for putative ESCRT proteins of *E. histolytica* were achieved by using the Jpred program. In agreement with our previous findings, EhVps27, EhVps36 and EhVps24, and EhVps23 proteins resulted in similar arrangements to yeast Vps27, Vps36 and Vps24 proteins, and human Tsg101, respectively. Furthermore, according to both Phyre and SWISS-MODEL tertiary structure predictions, the three-dimensional structures of EhVps27 and EhVps36 matched to yeast Vps27 (PDB code: 1vfy) and Vps36 (PDB code: 1u5t) crystalline structures, respectively. In addition, the Phyre software predicted a conformational arrangement similar to human Tsg101 (PDB code: 1s1q) and CHMP3 (PDB code: 2gd5) proteins for EhVps23 and EhVps24, respectively.

Altogether, our results indicate the presence of putative structural and conformational features for ubiquitin and lipid binding in representative proteins from the *E. histolytica* ESCRT-0, -I, -II and -III complexes.

To determine the identity of putative ESCRT-accesory proteins, we first focused on EhADH112, a protein widely studied by our group and involved in *E. histolytica* adherence to and phagocytosis of host cells (García-Rivera et al., 1999). *In silico* analysis of the primary sequence of EhADH112 together with Pfam protein domain predictions, revealed that EhADH112 is structurally related to yeast Bro1 and its human homologue Alix. EhADH112 has a conserved Bro1 domain at its N-terminus. In Bro1 and Alix proteins, the Bro1 domain constitutes the interacting site for Vps32 or CHMP4B, respectively, both components of the ESCRT-III complex. Experimental approaches demonstrated that *E. histolytica* parasites overexpressing only a part of the EhADH112 Bro1 domain, reduced dramatically their ability to ingest cells, thus providing additional evidence for EhADH112 participation in phagocytosis (our unpublished results). Furthermore, immunolocalization of EhADH112 and truncated EhADH112 proteins in parasites, using both transmission electron and laser confocal microscopy, revealed that besides its detection at the plasma membrane and cytoplasmic vacuoles, EhADH112 is also in MVB-like organelles, whereas the EhADH112 mutant version accumulates in cytoplasmic vesicles. These findings led us to assign a putative role for the EhADH112 Bro1 domain to recruit proteins to the endosomal membranes forming MVB. Possibly, Vps proteins from the ESCRT-III complex or some other molecules could be involved in this event, thus affecting the *E. histolytica* phagocytosis process. In order to identify putative interacting partners for EhADH112, we used a computational survey for yeast Vps32 or human CHMP4B homologous sequences in the *E. histolytica* genome. We found a putative EhVps32 protein whose existence in *E. histolytica* was confirmed by further experimental data (Bañuelos et al., 2007). According to multiple sequence analysis and Pfam database predictions, EhVps32 contains a Snf7 domain, present in all members of the Snf7 family. Additionally, the predicted EhVps32 secondary structure using the Jpred program, suggested that EhVps32 conserves the characteristic five α-helices present in the Snf7 family protein (Fig. 2A). Using the Phyre program, the tertiary structure for EhVps32 was modeled. Results showed that the predicted structure of EhVps32 is related to human CHMP3, a Snf7 family member (Fig. 2B). Since the crystal structure for CHMP4B has not yet been solved, the program uses by default the CHMP3 crystal structure as template due to the presence of the highly conserved Snf7 domain. Thus, tertiary structures for CHMP4B and Vps32 were also modeled using CHMP3 as template (Fig. 2B). Retrieved results showed that EhVps32 adopts a conformational structure and folding more similar to CHMP4B than to yeast Vps32 and this is in agreement with the highest similarity reported for EhVps32 to the human sequence of CHMP4B by BLAST analysis (Table 2).

To confirm the predicted interaction between EhADH112 and EhVps32 proteins, pull down experiments were perfomed. Assays demonstrated that EhADH112 binds through its N-terminus to a recombinant protein of EhVps32 fused to GST (our unpublished data).

Since yeast Vps4 and its orthologues have been previously described as key molecules for ESCRT dissociation and recycling, López-Reyes et al., (2010) characterized the EhVps4 protein in more detail. Protein domain predictions, as well as tertiary structure modeling and phylogenetic trees assayed for EhVps4 suggest, that it conserves a typical Vps4 architecture (Babst et al., 1998) and is more related to protozoan Vps4 homologues than to that of higher eukaryotes. Biochemical experiments using an EhVps4 recombinant protein and ATP as substrate, evidenced the ATPase activity of EhVps4 *in vitro*. As expected, when using a mutant version of EhVps4, in which an E residue was substituted by a Q amino acid, the ATPase activity was reduced. Furthermore, *E. histolytica* parasites overexpressing the EhVps4 mutant protein displayed reduced virulence properties, suggesting a role for EhVps4 in parasite pathogenicity, probably related to its participation in the endocytic pathway.

5. Challenges and perspectives

Our previous results obtained via bioinformatical tools and biochemical experiments, allow us to propose a model for the ESCRT machinery in *E. histolytica* (Fig. 3). Since we found the EhVps27 component of the ESCRT-0 complex, we suggest that it may initiate the MVB sorting process. Additionally, EhVps27 has a FYVE domain that possibly mediates protein binding to the endosomal membrane. However, EhVps27 lacks the UIM domain, important for the initial selection of ubiquitinated cargo, probably by EhRsp5. Perhaps, EhVps23, through its UEV motif, or another unidentified protein could be recruiting cargo proteins to endosomes. Furthermore, the EhVps23 UEV domain could associate toEhVps27 and other components of the ESCRT-I complex, which includes the EhVps28 and EhVps37 proteins. Then, ESCRT-I binds to ESCRT-II (formed by EhVps22, EhVps25 and EhVps36 proteins). Although EhVps36 does not exhibit an ubiquitin-interacting domain as yeast homologues, this protein contains a recognition region for phosphoinositides that presumably would allow ESCRT-II attachment to the endosomal membrane. Next, ESCRT-II binds to the ESCRT-III complex, which contains the overall components previously described for yeast. Interestingly, similarly to yeast Vps20, EhVps20 has a myristoylated modification that facilitates ESCRT-III insertion into the endosomal membrane. Then, ESCRT-III interaction

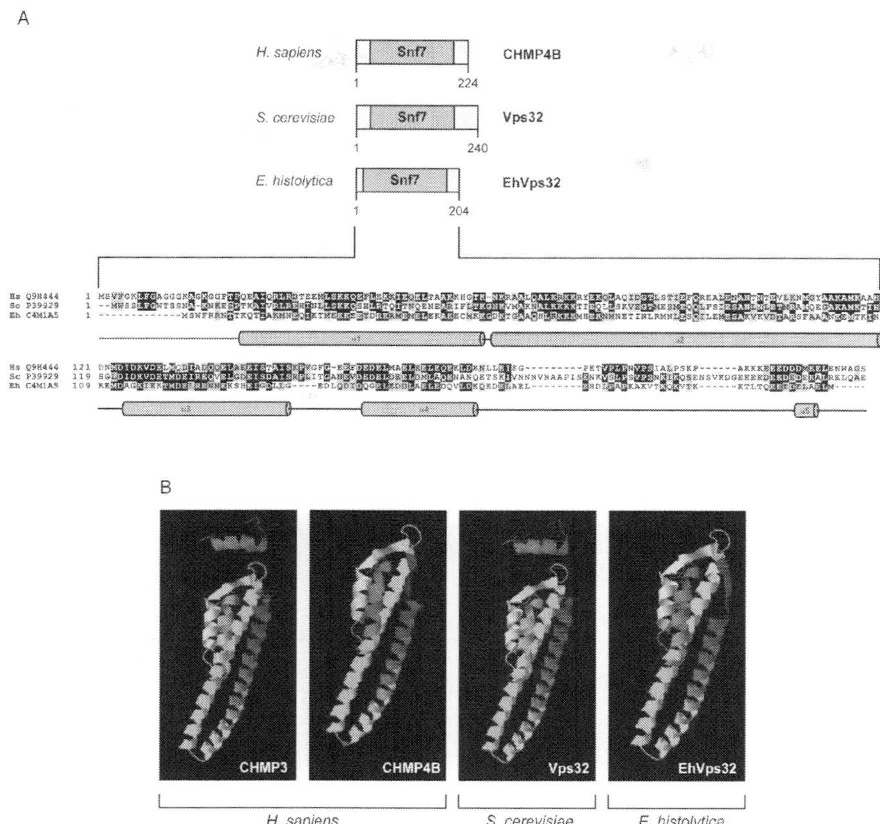

Fig. 2. Structural comparison of Vps32 homologues.
(A) At the top, a schematic representation for human CHMP4B, yeast Vps32 and *E. histolytica* EhVps32 proteins is shown. Numbers indicate amino acids for each protein. All proteins contain conserved Snf7 domains, present in the Snf7 family proteins. Vps32 orthologues belong to the ESCRT-III complex and have been described as the interacting partners of Bro1 domain-containing proteins. At the bottom, a multiple sequence alignment for Vps32 homologues is shown. Hs, *H. sapiens*; Sc, *S. cerevisiae*; and Eh, *E. histolytica*. Black boxes, identical amino acids; grey boxes, conserved substitutions; and open boxes, different residues. Numbers at left are relative to the position of the start codon in each protein. The Jpred secondary structure prediction program revealed that EhVps32 folds into five α-helices (green horizontal cylinders) as it has been reported for Vps32 homologues. (B) Tertiary protein structure for *H. sapiens, S. cerevisiae* and *E. histolytica* Vps32 homologues. Modeling was done using the Phyre program with the crystal structure of human CHMP3 as template.

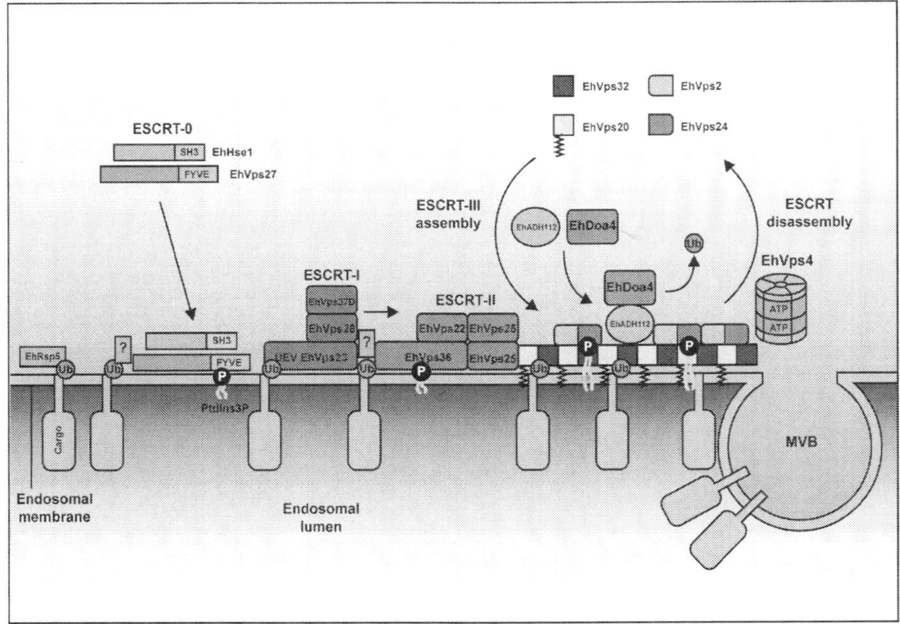

Fig. 3. Model for the role of the ESCRT machinery in *E. histolytica* within the endosomal MVB pathway.

In *E. histolytica*, the EhRsp5 protein could be responsible for cargo protein ubiquitination. Then, the EhVps27 protein could initiate the MVB process. Similar to yeast Vps27, EhVps27 has a FYVE domain that binds PtdIns3P allowing endosomal membrane attachment. However, EhVps27 lacks the UIM domain, important for ubiquitin recognition in cargo proteins. Instead, EhVps23 could be mediating this event through its UEV motif. Subsequently, EhVps27 binds to the ESCRT-I complex through EhVps23. Then, EhVps36 by its positively charged region binds to PtdIns3P, facilitating the ESCRT-II attachment to endosomal membranes. *E. histolytica* contains all ESCRT-III components which belong to the Snf7 family of proteins. In addition, it has several accessory proteins, including the EhADH112 (a Bro1 domain-containing protein), EhDoa4 (deaubiquitinating enzyme that removes ubiquitin from cargo) and EhVps4 (an ATPase) proteins. Finally, as in yeast, EhVps4 may play a critical role in catalyzing the dissociation of ESCRT from the endosomal membrane in order to start new rounds of cargo protein sorting through MVB.

with accessory proteins could be mediated by EhVps32. In fact, EhVps32 could associate to EhADH112 through its putative N-terminal Bro1 domain (our unpublished data). Besides, EhADH112 could also be recruiting another accessory molecule, the EhDoa4 ubiquitin hydrolase, removing ubiquitin from cargo prior MVB internalization. Finally, the EhVps4 ATPase might catalyze the disassembly of the ESCRT complex from the endosomal

membrane to initiate new rounds of cargo sorting and vesicle formation. Possibly, EhVta1
may have a role in regulating EhVps4 function.

Of note, *E. histolytica* possesses a conserved ESCRT machinery. However, the study related
to ESCRT functions and putative interactions along the MVB pathway needs to be
corroborated by experimental approaches.

6. Conclusions

Bioinformatics, the application of statistics and computer sciences to molecular biology,
entails the creation and advancement of databases, algorithms, computational and statistical
techniques and theory to solve formal and practical problems arising from the management
and analysis of biological data. In this chapter, we used bioinformatics to analyze the ESCRT
protein machinery possibly participating in parasitic protozoa endosomal pathways, with
particular attention on the *E. histolytica* case.

The ESCRT machinery comprises a set of protein complexes that regulate recognition,
sorting and trafficking of monoubiquitinated proteins into MVB compartments towards
lysosome degradation. Previous work has shed light on molecular details underlying the
assembly and regulation of ESCRT in yeast and human. Here, we took advantage from
eukaryotic pathogen genome database availability and bioinformatics tools to identify
proteins representing putative ESCRT components in protozoan parasites of medical
importance. We found representative proteins for ESCRT-0, -I, -II, -III and -accesory proteins
in almost all protozoa examined, being *E. histolytica* and *L. major* the parasites in which
ESCRT components were the most represented. Despite these findings, several issues need
to be experimentally addressed to finely determine the structure and function of ESCRT
proteins and their putative role during endocytosis in these parasites.

In *E. histolytica*, we found a highly conserved ESCRT machinery with 19 putative
components representing all complexes. These findings have been experimentally confirmed
by determining the expression of most ESCRT gene transcripts (López-Reyes, et al., 2010).
Furthermore, our current *in silico* results suggest that some *E. histolytica* ESCRT-0 to -III
components contain putative FYVE or ubiquitin binding domains, both important to recruit
cargo molecules to endosomal membranes. In addition, our computational analysis together
to previous functional characterization of putative *E. histolytica* ESCRT-accessory proteins,
strongly suggest the presence of a Bro1-domain containing protein (EhADH112), its putative
interacting partnership, EhVps32, and an ATPase (EhVps4) that may be responsible for
energy-dependent ESCRT disassembly. Of note, tertiary structure modeling of EhVps32
supported our experimental findings on EhADH112 binding to EhVps32, proving the value
of bioinformatical approaches. Therefore, our overall results provide significant evidence for
a conserved role of the *E. histolytica* ESCRT machinery in the MVB endocytic pathway.

In summary, bioinformatics and experimental approaches can improve our understanding
on evolutionary implications of the MVB sorting pathway in *E. histolytica*, *L. major*, *T. cruzi*,
P. falciparum, *T. gondii* and *G. lamblia* and also for elucidating its possible relationship to
parasite pathogenicity and virulence.

Although some limitations exist due to incompleteness of experimental data, we conclude
that computational methods have a reasonable prediction accuracy and provide invaluable
basis for further experimental validation.

7. Acknowledgements

Authors would like to thank Dra. Rossana Arroyo, Dr. Jaime Ortega and Dr. Michael Schnoor for providing their comments on the manuscript and Alfredo Padilla-Barberi for efforts in the artwork.

8. References

Allen, C.L., Liao, D., Chung, W.L. & Field, M.C. (2007). Dileucine signal-dependent and AP-1-independent targeting of a lysosomal glycoprotein in *Trypanosoma brucei*. *Molecular and Biochemical Parasitology*, Vol. 156, pp. 175–190, ISSN 0166-6851

Altschul, S.F., Gish, W., Miller, W., Myers, E.W., & Lipman, D.J. (1990). Basic local alignment search tool. *Journal of Molecular Biology*, Vol. 215, No. 3, pp. 403-410, ISSN 0022-2836

Babst, M., Katzmann, D.J., Estepa-Sabal, E.J., Meerloo, T., & Emr, S.D. (2002a). ESCRT-III: an endosome-associated heterooligomeric protein complex required for MVB sorting. *Developmental Cell*, Vol. 3, pp. 271–282, ISSN 1534-5807

Babst, M., Katzmann, D.J., Snyder, W.B., Wendland, B., & Emr, S.D. (2002b). Endosome-associated complex, ESCRT-II, recruits transport machinery for protein sorting at the multivesicular body. *Developmental Cell*, Vol. 3, pp. 283–289, ISSN 1534-5807

Babst, M., Wendland, B., Estepa, E.J., & Emr, S.D. (1998). The Vps4p AAA ATPase regulates membrane association of a Vps protein complex required for normal endosome function. *The EMBO Journal*, Vol. 17, pp. 2982–2993, ISSN 0261-4189

Bañuelos, C., García-Rivera, G., López-Reyes, I., & Orozco, E. (2005). Functional characterization of EhADH112: an Entamoeba histolytica Bro1 domain-containing protein. *Experimental Parasitology*, Vol. 110, No. 3, pp. 292-297, ISSN 0014-4894

Bañuelos, C., López-Reyes, I., García-Rivera, G., González-Robles, A. and Orozco, E. (2007). The presence of a Snf7-like protein strenghtens a role for EhADH in the *Entamoeba histolytica* multivesicular bodies pathway. *Proceedings of the 5th European Congress on Tropical Medicine and International Health*, Boeree, M.J. (ed), Vol. 978, pp. 31–35, Amsterdam, The Netherlands

Besteiro, S., Williams, R.A., Morrison, L.S., Coombs, G.H., & Mottram, J.C. (2006). Endosome sorting and autophagy are essential for differentiation and virulence of Leishmania major. *The Journal of Biological Chemistry*, Vol. 281, No. 16, pp. 11384-11396, ISSN 0021-9258

Bonangelino, C.J., Chavez, E.M., & Bonifacino, J.S. (2002). Genomic screen for vacuolar protein sorting genes in *Saccharomyces cerevisiae*. *Molecular Biology of the Cell*, Vol. 13, pp. 2486–2501. ISSN 1059-1524

Bowers, K., Lottridge, J., Helliwell, S.B., Goldthwaite, L.M., Luzio, J.P. & Stevens, T.H. (2004). Protein–Protein Interactions of ESCRT Complexes in the Yeast *Saccharomyces cerevisiae*. *Traffic*, Vol. 5, pp.194–210, ISSN 1398-9219

Chiang, Y.S., Gelfand, T.I., Kister, A.E. & Gelfand, I.M. (2007). New classification of supersecondary structures of sandwich-like proteins uncovers strict patterns of strand assemblage. *Proteins*, Vol. 68, No. 4, pp. 915–921, ISSN 0887-3585

Chung, W.L., Carrington, M. & Field, M.C. (2004). Cytoplasmic targeting signals in transmembrane invariant surface glycoproteins of trypanosomes. *The Journal of Biological Chemistry*, Vol. 279, pp. 54887-54895, ISSN 1067-8816

Claverie, J.M. & Notredame, C. (2006). *Bioinformatics for Dummies* (2nd ed). Wiley Publishing, Inc. ISBN: 978-0-470-08985-9 Indianapolis, IN

Cole, C., Barber, J.D. & Barton, G.J. (2008). The Jpred 3 secondary structure prediction server. *Nucleic Acids Research*, Vol. 35, No. suppl. 2, pp. W197-W201, ISSN 0305-1048

Coppens, I. & Joiner, K.A. (2003). Host but not parasite cholesterol controls *Toxoplasma* entry by modulating organelle discharge. *Molecular Biology of the Cell*, Vol. 14, pp. 3804-3820, ISSN 1059-1524

Cuff, J.A. & Barton, G.J. (1999). Evaluation and improvement of multiple sequence methods for protein secondary structure prediction. *Proteins*, Vol. 34, No. 4, pp. 508-519, ISSN 0887-3585

Curtiss, M., Jones, C. & Babst, M. (2007). Efficient cargo sorting by ESCRT-I and the subsequent release of ESCRT-I from multivesicular bodies requires the subunit Mvb12. *Molecular Biology of the Cell*, Vol. 18, No. 2, pp. 636-645, ISSN 1059-1524

Dacks, J.B. & Field MC. (2007). Evolution of the eukaryotic membrane-trafficking system: origin, tempo and mode. *Journal of Cell Science*, Vol. 120, pp. 2977–2985, ISSN 0021-9533

Dacks, J.B., Poon, P.P. & Field, M.C. (2008). Phylogeny of endocytic components yields insight into the process of non-endosymbiotic organelle evolution. *Proceedings of the National Academy of Sciences of the United States of America*, Vol. 105, pp. 588–593, ISSN 0027-8424

de Souza, W., Sant'Anna, C. & Cunha-e-Silva, N.L. (2009). *Progress in Histochemistry and Cytochemistry*, Vol. 44, No. 2, pp. 67-124, ISSN 0079-6336

Dimaano, C., Jones, C.B., Hanono, A., Curtiss, M. & Babst, M. (2008). Ist1 regulates Vps4 localization and assembly. *Molecular Biology of the Cell*, Vol. 19, No. 2, pp. 465-474, ISSN 1059-1524

Field, M.C., Gabernet-Castello, C. & Dacks, J.B. (2007). Reconstructing the evolution of the endocytic system: insights from genomics and molecular cell biology. *Advances in experimental medicine and biology*, Vol. 607, pp. 84–96, ISSN 0065-2598

Fujita, H., Yamanaka, M., Imamura, K., Tanaka, Y., Nara, A., Yoshimori, T., Yokota, S. & Himeno, M. (2003). A dominant negative form of the AAA ATPase SKD1/VPS4 impairs membrane trafficking out of endosomal/lysosomal compartments: class E vps phenotype in mammalian cells. *Journal of Cell Science*, Vol. 116, Pt 2, pp. 401-414, ISSN 0021-9533

García-Rivera, G., Rodríguez, M.A., Ocádiz, R., Martínez-López, M.C., Arroyo, R., González-Robles, A. & Orozco, E. (1999). *Entamoeba histolytica*: a novel cysteine protease and an adhesin form the 112 kDa surface protein. *Molecular Microbiology*, Vol. 33, No. 3, pp. 556-68, ISSN 0950-382X

Geoff, H. (1997). The Molecular Epidemiology of Parasites, In: *Principles of Medical Biology, Microbiology*, Edward Bittar (ed), pp. 597-614, JAI Press Inc., ISBN: 1-55938-814-5. Greenwich, Conn

Ghedin, E., Debrabant, A., Engel, J.C. & Dwyer, D.M. (2001). Secretory and endocytic pathways converge in a dynamic endosomal system in a primitive protozoan. *Traffic*, Vol, 2, pp. 175–188, ISSN 1398-9219

Gietz, R.D., Triggs-Raine, B., Robbins, A., Graham, K. & Woods, R. (1997). Identification of proteins that interact with a protein of interest: Applications of the yeast two-hybrid system. *Molecular and Cellular Biochemistry*, Vol. 172, No. 1-2, pp. 67–79, ISSN 0300-8177

Henikoff, S. & Henikoff, J.G. (2000). Amino acid substitution matrices. *Advances in Protein Chemistry*, Vol, 54, pp. 73-97, ISSN 0065-3233

Hoppe, H.C., Ngo, H.M., Yang, M. & Joiner, K.A. (2000). Targeting to rhoptry organelles of *Toxoplasma gondii* involves evolutionarily conserved mechanisms. *Nature Cell Biology*, Vol. 2, pp. 449-456, ISSN 1465-7392

http://align.genome.jp/

http://bips.u-strasbg.fr/fr/Tutorials/Comparison/Blast/blastall.html

http://eupathdb.org/eupathdb/

http://expasy.org/tools/#proteome

http://jmol.sourceforge.net/download/

http://swissmodel.expasy.org/

http://www.ch.embnet.org/software/BOX_form.html

http://www.pdb.org/pdb/home/home.do

http://www.sanger.ac.uk/resources/databases/pfam.html

http://www.uniprot.org/

Hurley, J.H. & Emr, S.D. (2006). The Escrt Complexes: Structure and Mechanism of a Membrane-Trafficking Network. *Annual Review of Biophysics Biomolecular Structure*, Vol. 35, pp. 277–298, ISSN 1056-8700

Hurley, J.H. & Hanson, P.I. (2010). Membrane budding and scission by the ESCRT machinery: it's all in the neck. *Nature Reviews. Molecular Cell Biology*, Vol. 11, No. 8, pp. 556-566, ISSN 1471-0072

Kaltenbach, L.S., Romero, E., Becklin, R.R., Chettier, R., Bell, R., Phansalkar, A., Strand, A., Torcassi, C., Savage, J., Hurlburt, A., Cha, G.H., Ukani, L., Chepanoske, C.L., Zhen, Y., Sahasrabudhe, S., Olson, J., Kurschner, C., Ellerby, L.M., Peltier, J.M., Botas, J. & Hughes, R.E. (2007) Huntingtin interacting proteins are genetic modifiers of neurodegeneration. *PLoS Genetics*, Vol. 3, No. 5, pp. e82, ISSN 1553-7390

Kanazawa, C., Morita, E., Yamada, M., Ishii, N., Miura, S., Asao, H., Yoshimori, T., & Sugamura, K. (2003). Effects of deficiencies of STAMs and Hrs, mammalian class E Vps proteins, on receptor downregulation. *Biochemical Biophysical Research Communication*, Vol. 309, No. 4, pp. 848-856, ISSN 0006-291X

Katzmann, D.J., Babst, M., & Emr, S.D. (2001). Ubiquitin-dependent sorting into the multivesicular body pathway requires the function of a conserved endosomal protein sorting complex, ESCRT-I. *Cell*, Vol. 106, pp. 145–155, ISSN 0092-8674

Kelley, L.A. & Sternberg, M.J. (2009). Protein structure prediction on the Web: a case study using the Phyre server. *Nature protocols*, Vol. 4, No. 3, pp. 363-371, ISSN 1754-2189

Kim, J., Sitaraman, S., Hierro, A., Beach, B.M., Odorizzi, G. & Hurley, J.H. (2005). Structural basis for endosomal targeting by the Bro1 domain. *Developmental Cell*, Vol. 8, No. 6, pp. 937-947, ISSN 1534-5807

Kuchaiev, O. & Przulj, N. (2011). Integrative Network Alignment Reveals Large Regions of Global Network Similarity in Yeast and Human. *Bioinformatics*. Vol. Mar 16, [Epub ahead of print], ISSN 1367-4803

Lanfredi-Rangel, A., Attias, M., de Carvalho, T.M., Kattenbach, W.M. & de Souza, W. (1998). The peripheral vesicles of trophozoites of the primitive protozoan *Giardia lamblia* may correspond to early and late endosomes and to lysosomes. *Journal of Structural Biology*, Vol. 123, pp. 225–235, ISSN 1047-8477

Leung, K.F., Dacks, J.B. & Field, M.C. (2008). Evolution of the Multivesicular Body ESCRT Machinery; Retention Across the Eukaryotic Lineage. *Traffic*, Vol. 9, pp. 1698–1716, ISSN 1398-9219

Li, Y., Kane, T., Tipper, C., Spatrick, P. & Jenness, D.D. (1999). Yeast mutants affecting possible quality control of plasma membrane proteins. *Molecular Cell Biology*, Vol. 19, No. 5, pp. 3588-3599, ISSN 1471-0072

López-Reyes, I., García-Rivera, G., Bañuelos, C., Herranz, S., Vincent, O., López-Camarillo, C., Marchat, L.A, & Orozco, E. (2010). Detection of the endosomal sorting complex required for transport in *Entamoeba histolytica* and characterization of the EhVps4 protein. *Journal of Biomedicine & Biotechnology*, Vol. 2010, pp. 890674, ISSN 1110-7243

Misra, S. & Hurley, J.H. (1999). Crystal structure of a phosphatidylinositol 3-phosphate-specific membrane-targeting motif, the FYVE domain of Vps27p. *Cell*, Vol. 97, No. 5, pp. 657-666, ISSN 0092-8674

Nakada-Tsukui, K., Okada, H., Mitra, B.N. & Nozaki, T. (2009) Phosphatidylinositol-phosphates mediate cytoskeletal reorganization during phagocytosis via a unique modular protein consisting of RhoGEF/DH and FYVE domains in the parasitic protozoan *Entamoeba histolytica*. *Cellular Microbiology*, Vol. 11, No. 10, pp. 1471-1491, ISSN 1462-5814

Obita, T., Saksena, S., Ghazi-Tabatabai, S., Gill, D.J., Perisic, O., Emr, S.D. & Williams, R.L. (2007). Structural basis for selective recognition of ESCRT-III by the AAA ATPase Vps4. *Nature*, Vol. 449, pp. 735–739, ISSN 0028-0836

Odorizzi, G., Katzmann, D.J., Babst, M., Audhya, A. & Emr, S.D. (2003). Bro1 is an endosome-associated protein that functions in the MVB pathway in *Saccharomyces cerevisiae*. *Journal of Cell Science*, Vol. 116, pp. 1893–1903, ISSN 0021-9533

Offer, G., Hicks, M.R. & Woolfson, D.N. (2002). Generalized Crick equations for modeling noncanonical coiled coils. *Journal of Structural Biology*, Vol. 137, No. 1-2, pp. 41-53, ISSN 1047-8477

Pandeya, S.N. & Thakkar, D. (2005). Combinatorial chemistry: A novel method in drug discovery and its application. *Indian Journal of Chemistry*, Vol. 44B, pp. 335-348, ISSN 0019-5103

Peng, Z.Y. & Kim, P.S. (1994). A protein dissection study of a molten globule. *Biochemistry*, Vol. 33, No. 8, pp. 2136-2141, ISSN 0006-2960

Pornillos, O., Alam, S.L., Rich, R.L., Myszka, D.G., Davis, D.R. & Sundquist, W.I. (2002). Structure and functional interactions of the Tsg101 UEV domain. *The EMBO Journal*, Vol. 21, No. 10, pp. 2397-2406, ISSN 0261-4189

Shiflett, S.L., Ward, D.M., Huynh, D., Vaughn, M.B., Simmons, J.C. & Kaplan, J. (2004) Characterization of Vta1p, a class E Vps protein in *Saccharomyces cerevisiae*. *The Journal of Biological Chemistry*, Vol. 279 No. 12, pp. 10982-10990, ISSN 0021-9258

Sinha, A., Mandal, S., Banerjee, S., Ghosh, A., Ganguly, S., Sil, A.K. & Sarkar, S. (2010). Identification and Characterization of a FYVE Domain from the Early Diverging Eukaryote *Giardia lamblia*. *Current Microbiology*, Vol. Dec 17, [Epub ahead of print], ISSN 0343-8651

Söding, J. (2005). Protein homology detection by HMM-HMM comparison. *Bioinformatics*. Vol. 21, No. 7, pp. 951-60, ISSN 1367-4803

Stahelin, R.V., Long, F., Diraviyam, K., Bruzik, K.S., Murray, D. & Cho, W. (2002). Phosphatidylinositol 3-phosphate induces the membrane penetration of the FYVE domains of Vps27p and Hrs. *The Journal of Biological Chemistry*, Vol. 277, pp. 26379, ISSN 0021-9258

Sundquist, W.I., Schubert, H.L., Kelly, B.N., Hill, G.C., Holton, J.M. & Hill, C.P. (2004). Ubiquitin recognition by the human TSG101 protein. *Molecular Cell*, Vol. 13, No. 6, pp. 783-789, ISSN 1097-2765

Tse, Y.C., Mo, B., Hillmer, S., Zhao, M., Lo, S.W., Robinson, D.G. & Jiang, L. (2004). Identification of multivesicular bodies as prevacuolar compartments in *Nicotiana tabacum* BY-2 cells. *The Plant Cell*, Vol. 16, pp. 672–693, ISSN 1040-4651

Whitley, P., Reaves, B.J., Hashimoto, M., Riley, A.M., Potter, B.V. & Holman, G.D. (2003). Identification of mammalian Vps24p as an effector of phosphatidylinositol 3,5-bisphosphate-dependent endosome compartmentalization. *The Journal of Biological Chemistry*, Vol. 278, No. 40, pp. 38786-38795, ISSN 0021-9258

Williams, R.L. & Urbé, S. (2007). The emerging shape of the ESCRT machinery. *Nature Reviews. Molecular Cell Biology*, Vol. 8, pp. 355-368, ISSN 1471-0072

Wöstmann, C., Liakopoulos, D., Ciechanover, A. & Bakker-Grunwald, T. (1996) Characterization of ubiquitin genes and -transcripts and demonstration of a ubiquitin-conjugating system in *Entamoeba histolytica*. *Molecular and Biochemical Parasitology*, Vol. 82, No.1, pp. 81-90, ISSN 0166-6851

Yang, M., Coppens, I., Wormsley, S., Baevova, P., Hoppe, H.C., & Joiner, K.A. (2004). The *Plasmodium falciparum* Vps4 homolog mediates multivesicular body formation. *Journal of Cell Science*, Vol. 117, Pt 17, pp. 3831-3838, ISSN 0021-9533

15

Structural Bioinformatics Analysis of Acid Alpha-Glucosidase Mutants with Pharmacological Chaperones

Sheau Ling Ho
Chinese Culture University
Taiwan

1. Introduction

Most lysosomal storage disorders (LSDs) are usually inherited, caused by the deficiency of a single lysosomal hydrolase, leading to the accumulation of the corresponding substrate. LSDs can also result from mutations in proteins involved in the intracellular trafficking of lysosomal enzymes (Carrell & Lomas, 1997, Kopito & Ron, 2000, Selkoe, 2003, and Arakawa et al., 2006). Indeed, LSDs are considered as a group of more than sixty diverse inherited disorders. Each of the diseases is due to a specific enzymatic defect (Hodges & Cheng, 2006, Raben et al., 2009). Pompe disease is one of these LSDs through point mutations (single wild type amino acid substitutions) in the gene that encodes for acid α-glucosidase (GAA). The resulting total or partial deficiency of lysosomal acid α-glucosidase triggers glycogen to accumulate in lysosomes (Alberts et al., 2002, Raben et al., 2002, Bernier et al., 2004, Kroos et al., 2008).

Recently, various small molecule pharmacological chaperones have been discovered to increase stability of such mutant proteins and facilitate their efficient trafficking of lysosomal enzymes. As such, it pointed the way to a new therapeutic approach in LSDs treatment. In this study, we are concerned with revealing the mechanism and accurate structures underlying the defects in the folding behaviors of the involved enzymatic protein mutants, also the way in which they interact with small molecule pharmacological chaperones.

The pharmacological chaperone 1-deoxynojirimycin (DNJ) showed improvement in the treatment of Pompe disease. Yet, experimental data had shown that only a number of GAA mutants responded well to this pharmacological chaperone (Hirschhorn & Reuser 2001, Petsko & Ringe, 2004, and Chaudhuri & Paul 2006, Sugawara et al., 2009, Flanagan et al., 2009). In an effort to improve the stability of mutant enzymes, the understanding on the molecular interaction between the enzyme and the chaperones is very important. Since neighboring residues share physical characteristics, we undertook a detailed study of the surroundings of GAA variants in the structures (Zvelebil, et al., 1987). Thus, we herein aim at discriminating between structural, as opposed to, GAA mutants, based on analysis of their local environments.

Despite the absence of crystallographic data of human acid alpha-glucosidase, we reviewed recently published papers to construct a structural model of human maltase-glucoamylase

(MGAM) through homology modeling using the structural information (PDB ID: 2QLY) as a template. Note that there are approximate 44% amino acid sequence identities between the GAA and template. Based on the sequence alignment and the structural mode, our structural model, GAA residues (84-952) were threaded on to the MGAM template. The active site region for both GAA and MGAM overlaid well and the key catalytic residues had high similar spatial alignment (D518/D616 and D445/D542 in GAA and template respectively).

This study involved active site analysis that we applied the proposed model to reveal whether any conformational changes take place at the active site of GAA mutants and molecular docking studies on DNJ which we presented the geometry of the binding site of the complexes of GAA/DNJ and GAA mutants/DNJ. These were done by visual inspection of the atomic models looking at the interaction between the human GAA variants and chaperones, in terms of both binding energy and spatial orientation of the active site. Structural studies should be useful in improving our understanding of enzyme protein stability, molecular recognition and binding and then will help us to further elucidate the molecular basis of Pompe diseas.

2. Methodology

2.1 Structural modelling of the wild-type and mutant human acid α-glucosidase

A structural model of wild-type human acid α-glucosidase was built using molecular modeling software, MIFit (a cross-platform interactive graphics application for molecular modelling), and Molecular Operating Environment, MOE (CCG-Chemical Computing Group Inc.), by means of homology modeling. The structural of human intestinal maltase-glucoamylase (PDB: 2QLY) was used as a template and then energy minimization was carried out. The root-mean-square gradient (RMSD) was computed in terms of all the atoms in a protein backbone and the value was less than 0.6 Å which is indicative of considerable structural similarity.

More than hundred different GAA mutations know to cause Pompe disease are predicted to produce full-length proteins corresponding to a single amino acid substitution. Thus, based on the wild-type human acid α-glucosidase model, the structural models of mutants incorporating the amino acid substitutions were constructed using MIFiT. And the initial model was further refined by energy minimization. However, because of the low amino acids sequence identity between the human acid α-glucosidase and template, the investigations were restricted to a limited region of the enzyme protein.

2.2 Molecular docking

2.2.1 Preparation of ligand

The initial structure of the pharmacological chaperone 1-deoxynojirimycin (DNJ) (Figure 1) for the docking was generated using ChemDraw Ultra Version 9.0 (CambridgeSoft Corp.). And then geometry optimized ligands were prepared using MOE.

2.2.2 Docking

According to the effect of DNJ on responsive GAA mutants, six severe effects of GAA variants (G377R, A445P, L552P, Y575S, E579K, and H612Q) and wild-type GAA were chosen as the receptor for docking (Flanagan et al., 2009). Enzyme proteins and ligand structures were imported into MOE 2010.10 where three-dimensional structures were generated using a course energy minimization protocol and the MMFF94x force field (Halgren, 1996, 1999).

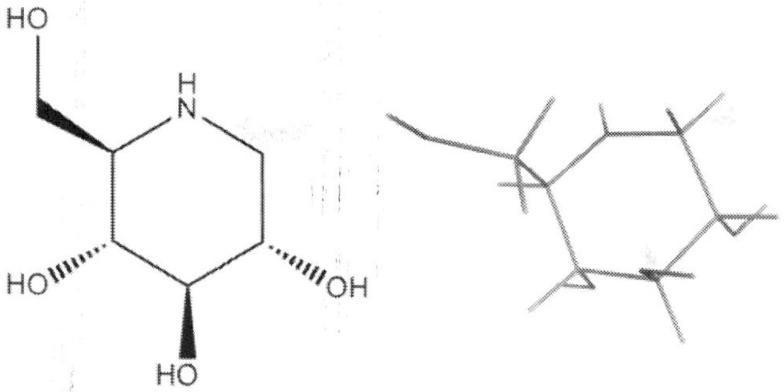

Fig. 1. 3D and 2D visualization of DNJ.

2.2.3 Structural analysis of GAA mutation

To exam the effect of atoms, each mutant model was superimposed on the wild-type structure on the basis of the Cα atom by the least-square-mean fitting method (Matsuzawa et al., 2005 and Saito et al., 2008). We assumed that the structure was influenced by an amino acid substitution when the position of an atom in a mutant differed from that in the wild-type structure, thus, such substations were expected to affect neighboring residue and to locally affect the electrostatic surface of the enzyme.

3. Results and discussion

3.1 Structure modelling of human GAA
3.1.1 Wild-type

As the results showed, our constructed wild-type model of GAA appears to be composed of five domains: a trefoil type-Π domain (residues 89–135), an N-terminal b-sandwich domain (residues 136–346), a catalytic $(\beta/\alpha)_8$ barrel domain (residues 347–723) with two inserted loops, which include insert 1 (residues 444–491) and insert 2 (residues 522–567) protruding out between β3 and α3, and between β4 and α4, respectively, a proximal C-terminal domain (residues 724–818) and a distal C-terminal domain (residues 819–952) (Figure 2). The key catalytic activity (D518 and D616) (Hermans et al., 1991, Sugawara et al., 2008 and Sugawara et al., 2009) and sequence motifs of family 31 glycosyl hydrolases were well conserved (Davies & Henrissat, 1995, and Lovering et al., 2005).

The proposed active-site pocket here was composed to residues of residues W376, W402, D404, I441, D443, W481, W516, D518, M519, F525, R600, W613, D616, D645, F649, and H674 (see Figure 3). Like many other sugar-binding enzymes, there were a lot of hydrophobic residues lining the active-site pocket, including W376, W402, I441, W481, W516, F525, W613, and F649.

3.1.2 Wild-type vs. mutants

The six mutant forms of GAA which responded to DNJ severely were superposed with wild-type. After the structure was superimposed, RMSD was computed in terms of the active-site pocket between the wild-type and mutants and the value were found to be less than 0.8 Å respectively in between. These varied situations were illustrated in Figure 3.

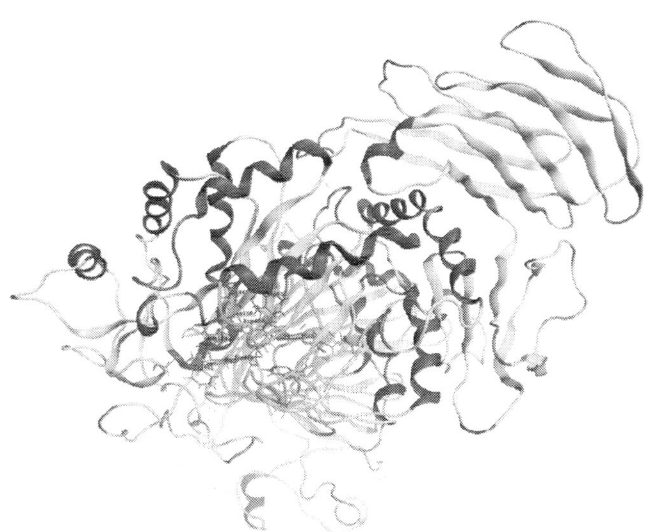

Fig. 2. GAA structural model. A ribbon diagram of GAA structural model. The orange shallow circle area represents the active-site pocket.

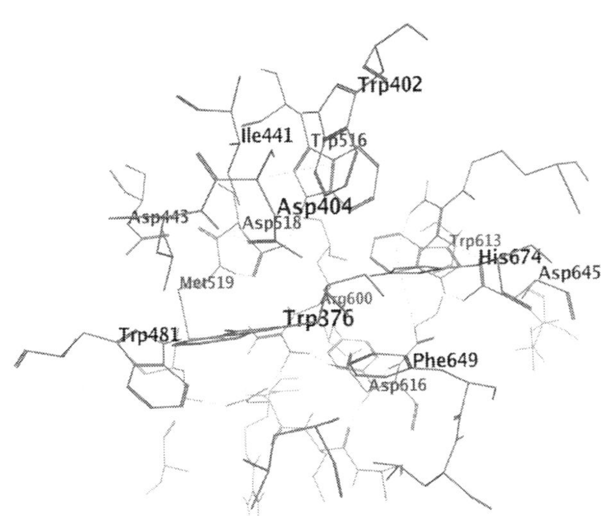

Fig. 3. A close-up view of the active-site pocket (W376, W402, D404, I441, D443, W481, W516, D518, M519, F525, R600, W613, D616, D645, F649, and H674).

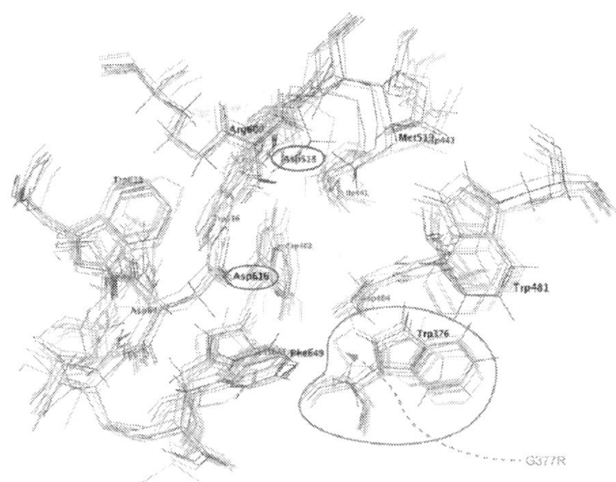

Fig. 4. Superimposed with the corresponding active-site pocket of the wild-type and six mutant variants GAA. The conserved catalytic residues D518/D616 are circled in red. Of GAA variant (G377R), Try turned forwards in the active site.

The comparison results were shown that no significant changes in the conformations of amino acid residues that comprise the active site and mutations of the key catalytic residues were conserved but when mutated as G377R, Try veered forward in active site. This might imply that new drugs can be designed or existing drugs can be modified based on its interaction with the new tyrosine residue (see Figure 4). This observation rules out the possibility of a conformational difference between the mutant and the wild-type enzyme as the derivation cause for the reduction of catalytic activity.

3.2 Docking

Molecular docking is utilized for the prediction of protein-ligand complexes which creates possible protein-ligand complex geometries. To understand the interaction between the enzyme and the pharmacological chaperone DNJ, we examined the binding affinity of the DNJ to the enzyme based on the complex geometry and binding energy. In the complex of the DNJ and enzyme model (either wild-type or mutants), the DNJ molecule fitted into the active-site pocket well.

Of the wild-type, residues D404, D518 and D616 were predicted to bind to the hydroxyl groups and the nitrogen of DNJ through hydrogen bonding inside the active-site pocket. Residues W376, I441, W481, W516, M519, W613, and F649 might be involved in the hydrophobic interaction of the DNJ. It is assumed that these residues contribute to the substrate binding specificity. The active-site pocket was apt for DNJ as to both space and binding. We also observed that the interactions between DNJ and the active-site pocket residues of wild-type and mutants; the nitrogen of DNJ was interacted with D518 through hydrogen bonding. (Figure 5 and Figure 6)

The DNJ fit into the active-site pocket well and a limit space between the nitrogen atom of DNJ and the wall of the active-site pocket of wild-type GAA and mutant variants respectively were observed (Figure 7, Figure 8 and Figure 9).

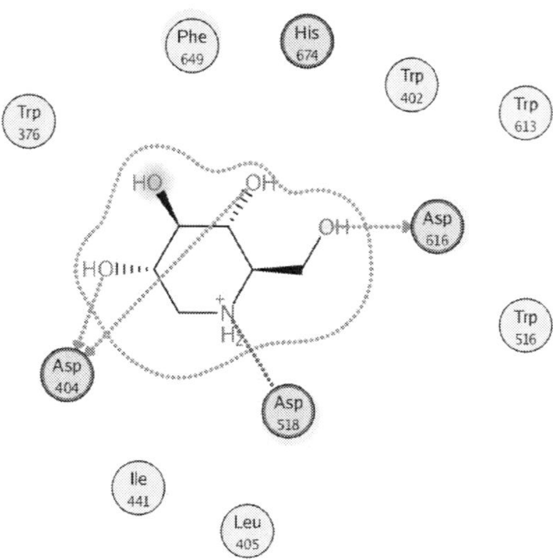

Fig. 5. The interaction diagram between DNJ and the wild-type GAA inside the active-site pocket

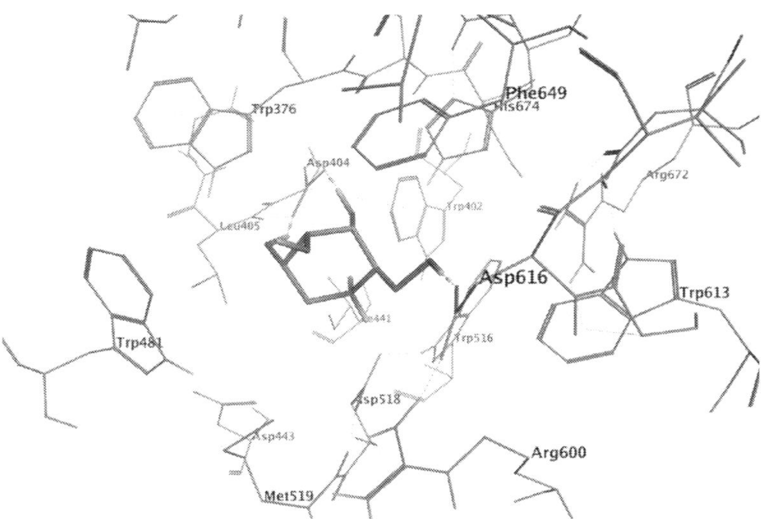

Fig. 6. Structure of wild-type GAA bound to DNJ.

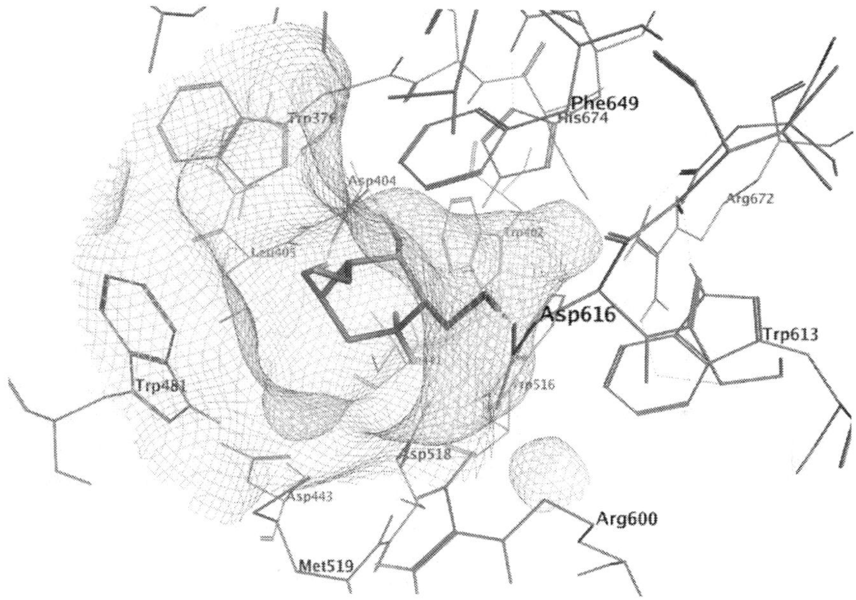

Fig. 7. Surface representation of the active-site pocket of wild-type GAA with bound DNJ.

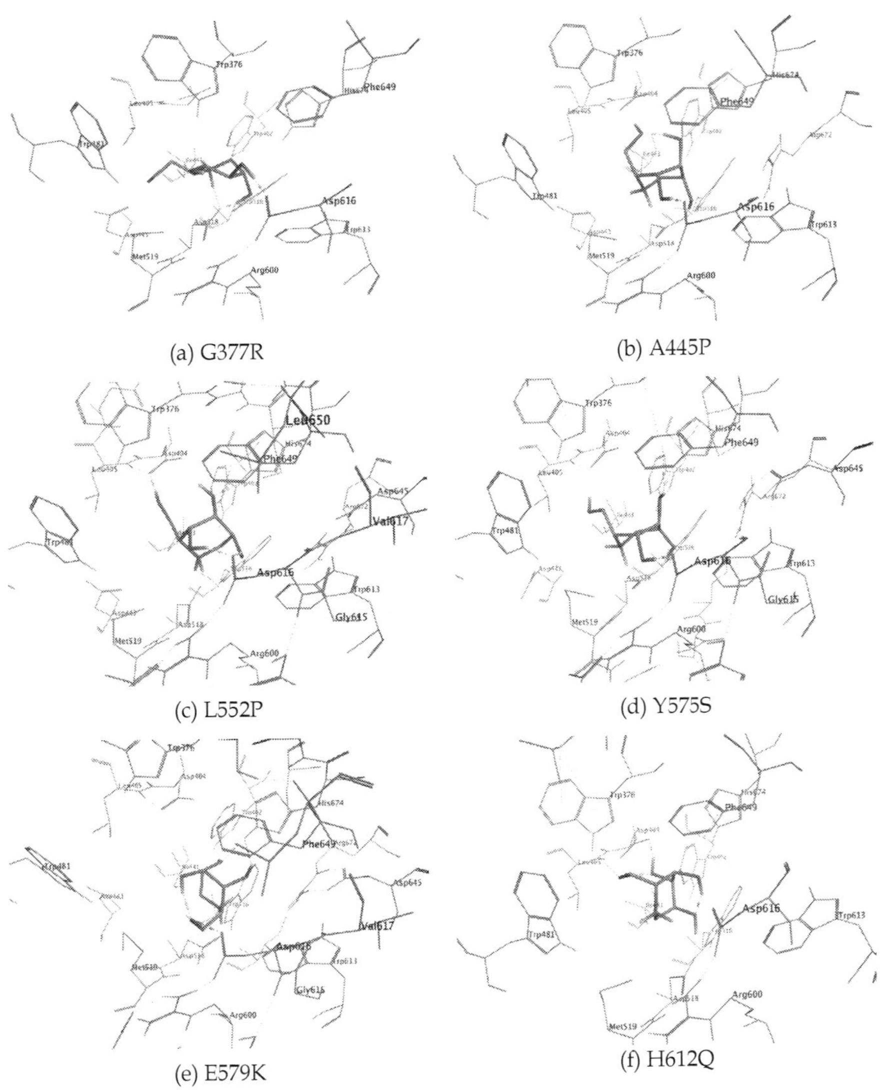

(a) G377R

(b) A445P

(c) L552P

(d) Y575S

(e) E579K

(f) H612Q

Fig. 8. Structure of GAA mutant variants bound to DNJ.

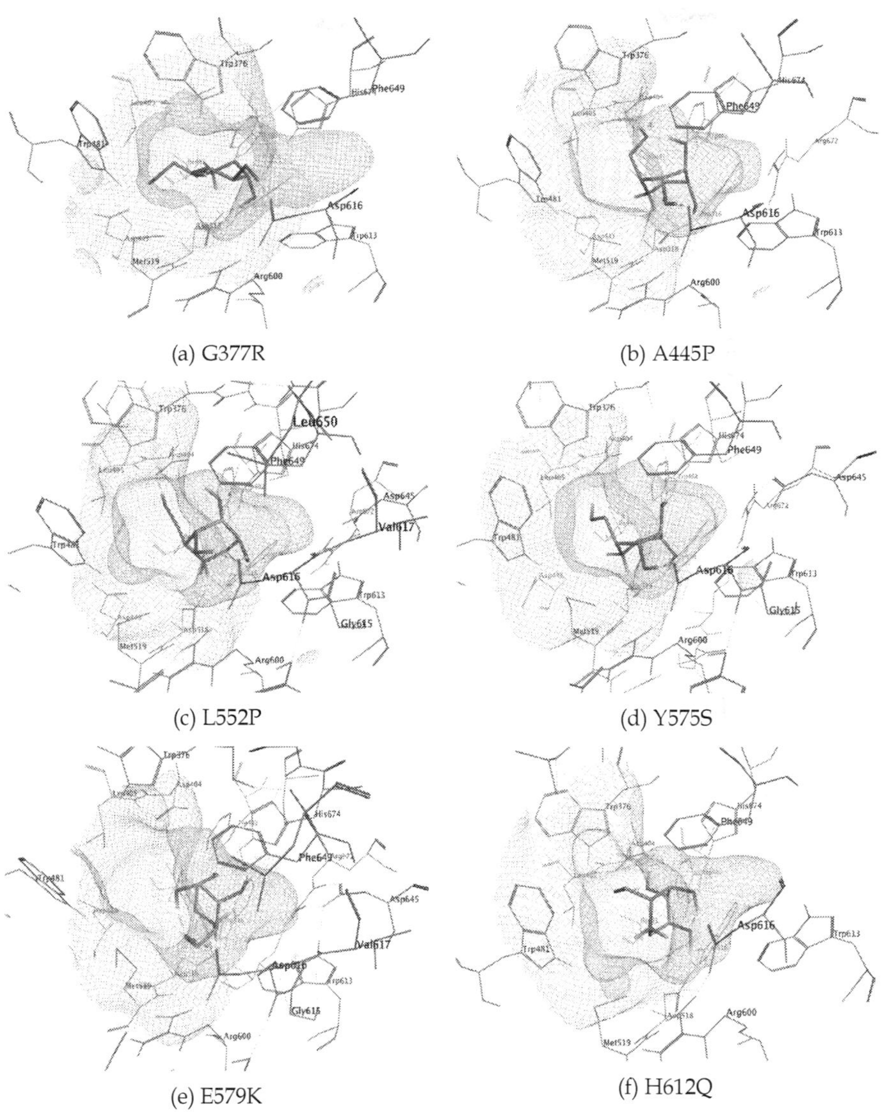

Fig. 9. Surface representation of the active-site pocket of GAA variants with bound DNJ. G377R variant shows a larger narrow funnel-shaped region of the active-site cavity.

We noticed that a narrow funnel-shaped region of the active-site cavity of wild-type GAA was smaller compared with that of other mutant variants. Especially, not only G377R variant showed a larger narrow funnel-shaped region of the active-site cavity compared with that of wild-type GAA or other mutant variants but also of GAA variant (G377R), Try turned forwards in the active site. Thus, it should be possible to modify this molecule to develop a novel derivative suitable for Pompe disease.

The theme of molecular docking is a vital aspect in drug discovery and development. Molecular docking is utilized for the prediction of protein–ligand complexes which predicts the binding affinity of the ligand to the protein based on the complex geometry. The binding energies also reflect the binding affinity of a ligand. The docking results were described in Table 1. The values showed that the binding energy of mutated complex (GAA variants) was higher than that of wild-type complex. Thus, it is interesting to speculate that increase in binding energy due to mutation might decrease the binding affinity of GAA towards DNJ, stabilizing GAA, and modulating its activity.

Ligand (DNJ)	*wild-type*	*Mutants (GAA variants)*					
		G377R	A445P	L552P	Y575S	E579K	H612Q
Binding Energy (kcal/mol)	-149.782	-107.416	-99.904	-130.414	-102.599	-109.852	-95.383

Table 1. Energy values obtained in docking calculation.

Still, these binding energies might not yet sufficient for determining binding affinity of ligands or drug candidates associations, some other physical effects such as electrostatics, van der waals, hydrogen bonding, and hydrophobic could affect the binding affinity; those are also needed to be evaluated.

4. Conclusions

This work involved active site analysis, molecular docking and binding energy studies. We revealed the mechanism in the folding behaviors of the involved enzymatic protein mutants, and the way they interacted with small molecule pharmacological chaperones based on spatial schematics which provided a basis for experimental validation. The validity of this approach was supported by the identification of some known GAA mutants. Therefore, the conformational changes detected in the distribution of various residues and their constituents around various GAA mutants should be useful in improving our understanding of enzyme protein stability, molecular recognition and binding. Effectively we have demonstrated the corresponding structural conformations associated with GAA wild-type and mutants in their three-dimensional environment. The difference in binding energies might rise due to mutations which could affect the binding affinity of DNJ. And then, it turns out that the complex structures and energy results presented here may provide useful consideration in the therapeutic approaches to these diseases as well as in the design of novel inhibitors associated with sucrose degradation.

5. Acknowledgments

The author is grateful to Dr. Wei-Chieh Cheng for his expert advice and useful discussion and Dr. Cheng-Yuan Huang acknowledged for exchanging information.

6. References

Alberts B., Bray D., Hopkin K., Johnson A., Lewis J., Raff M., Roberts K., & Walter P. (2002). *Essential Cell Biology*. Garland Science Textbooks, London.

Arakawa T., Ejima D., Kita Y., & Tsumoto K. (2006). Small molecule pharmacological chaperones: From thermodynamic stabilization to pharmaceutical drugs. *Biochim Biophys Acta*. Vol. 764:1677-1687.

Bernier V., Lagace M., Bichet D.G.,,& Bouvier M. (2004). Pharmacological chaperones: potential treatment for conformational diseases. *TRENDS in Endocrinology and Metabolism* Vol. 15(5): 222-228.

Carrell R.W. & Lomas, D.A. (1997). Conformational disease, *The Lancet* Vol. 350: 134-138.

Chaudhuri T.K. & Paul S. (2006). Protein-misfolding diseases and chaperone-based therapeutic approaches. *FEBS J*. Vol. 273:1331-1349.

Davies G. & Henrissat B. (1995). Structures and mechanism of glycosyl hydrolases. Structure. Vol. 3:853-859.

Flanagan JJ., Rossi B., Tang K., Wu X., Mascioli K., Donaudy F., Tuzzi MR., Fontana F., Cubellis MV., Porto C., Benjamin E., Lockhart DJ., Valenzano KJ., Andria G., Parenti G., & Do HV. (2009). The pharmacological chaperone 1-deoxynojirimycin increases the activity and lysosomal trafficking of multiple mutant forms of acid alpha-glucosidase. *Hum Mutat*. Vol. 30(12):1683-92.

Halgren T.A. (1996). Merck molecular force field.1. Basis, form, scope, parameterization, and performance of MMFF94. *J. Comp. Chem*. Vol. 17(5-6):490-519.

Halgren T.A. (1999a). MMFF VI. MMFF94s Option for Energy Minimization Studies. *J. Comp. Chem*. Vol. 20:720-729.

Halgren T.A. (1999b). MMFF VII. Characterization of MMFF94, MMFF94s, and Other Widely Available Force Fields for Conformational Energies and for Intermolecular-Interaction Energies and Geometries. *J. Comp. Chem*. Vol. 20:730-748.

Hermans Monique M.P., Kroos Marian A., Beeurnen Jos van, Oostra Ben A., & Reuser Arnold J.J. (1991). Human Lysosomal α-Glucosidase characterization of the catalytic site. *J. Biol. Chem*. Vol. 266(21): 13507-13512.

Hirschhorn R. & Reuser A.J.J. (2001). Glycogen Storage Disease type II; acid α-Glucosidase (Acid Maltase) deficiency. *The Metabolic and Molecular Bases of Inherited Disease*. D.V. M.D., Editor, Mc Graw-Hill: New York.

Hodges B.L. & Cheng S.H. (2006). Cell and gene-based therapies for the lysosomal storage diseases. *Curr Gene Ther*. Vol. 6:227-241.

Kopito R.R. & Ron D. (2000). Conformational disease. *Nat. Cell Biol*. Vol. 2: E207-E209.

Kroos M., Pomponio RJ., van Vliet L., Palmer RE., Phipps M., Van der Helm R., Halley D., & Reuser A. (2008). GAA Database Consortium. Update of the Pompe disease mutation database with 107 sequence variants and a format for severity rating. *Hum Mutat*. Vol. 6: E13-E26.

Lovering A.L., Lee S. S., Kim Y-W, Withers S.G., & Strynadka N.C.J. (2005). Mechanistic and Structural Analysis of a Family 31 Glycosidase and Its Glycosyl-enzyme Intermediate. *J. Biol. Chem*. Vol. 280(3):2105-2115.

Matsuzawa F., Aikawa S., Doi H., Okumiya T., & Sakuraba H. (2005). Fabry disease: correlation between structural changes in alpha-galactosidase, and clinical and biochemical phenotype. *Hum. Genet*. Vol. 117:317-328.

Molecular Operating Environment (MOE) 2010.10. (2010.) *Chemical Computing Group,* Inc; Montreal, Quebec.

Petsko GA. & Ringe D. (2004). From structure to function. *In Protein Structure and Function.* London; New Science Press.

Raben N., Shea L., & Hill V. (2009). Monitoring Autophagy in Lysosomal Storage Disorders. *Methods in Enzymology* Vol. 453:417-449.

Raben N., Plotz P., & Byrne BJ. (2002). Acid alpha-glucosidase deficiency (glucogenosis type II, Pompe disease). *Curr Mol Med.* Vol. 2:145-166.

Saito S., Ohno K., Sugawara K., & Sakuraba H. (2008). Structural and clinical implications of amino acid substitutions in N-acetylgalactosamine-4-sulfatase: insight into mucopolysaccharidosis type VI. *Mol. Genet. Metab.* Vol. 93:419–425.

Selkoe D.J. (2003). Folding proteins in fatal ways. *Nature* Vol. 426:900–904.

Sugawara K., Ohno K., Saito S., & Sakuraba H. (2008). Structural characterization of mutant alpha-galactosidases causing Fabry disease. *J. Hum. Genet.* Vol. 53:812–824.

Sugawara K., Saito S., Sekijima M., Ohno K., Tajima Y., & Kroos M.A. (2009). Structural modeling of mutant α-glucosidases resulting in a processing/transport defect in Pompe disease. *J. Hum. Genet.* Vol. 54:324-330.

Zvelebil M.J., Barton G.J., Taylor W.R., & Sternberg M.J. (1987). Prediction of Protein Secondary Structure and Active Sites Using the Alignment of Homologous Sequences. *J. Mol Biol.* Vol. 195(4):957-961.

16

Bioinformatics Domain Structure Prediction and Homology Modeling of Human Ryanodine Receptor 2

V. Bauerová-Hlinková[1] et al.*
[1]*Institute of Molecular Biology, Slovak Academy of Sciences, Bratislava, Slovakia*

1. Introduction

Ryanodine receptors (RyRs) are homotetrameric intracellular calcium release channels in the membranes of the endoplasmic (ER) and sarcoplasmic reticulum (SR) (George et al. 2005, Meissner 2002, 2004). Each subunit consists of ~5000 amino acid residues (George et al. 2005). There are three isoforms of the ryanodine receptor: the RyR1 isoform is expressed predominantly in skeletal muscle, the RyR2 isoform predominates in cardiac muscle, and the RyR3 isoform is expressed in a variety of tissues (Sorrentino 1995). In the mammalian heart, the RyR2 isoform is a principal component of the excitation-contraction (E-C) coupling process. Action potential depolarization of the cardiac cell results in injection of calcium ions into the cell via calcium channels (dihydropyridine receptors, DHPRs). This small calcium influx then drives the release of calcium from intracellular calcium stores by triggering the opening of RyR2 channels (Fabiato 1985). The released calcium causes contraction by binding to troponin C (Ebashi and Ogawa 1988). Consequently, precise regulation of RyR activity during heartbeat is essential to proper cardiac function.

In several cardiac diseases, such as heart failure and the genetic diseases CVPT (catecholaminergic polymorphic ventricular tachycardia) and ARVD2 (arrhythmogenic right ventricular dysplasia), the function of RyR is compromised. In heart failure, the release of calcium in response to the action potential is decreased, while RyR remains more active during the diastole (Durham et al. 2007, Yano et al. 2006). In CPVT and ARVD2, RyRs contain mutations that lead to altered RyR activity which may result in premature calcium release in the absence of an action potential (Durham et al. 2007, Yano et al. 2006).

In this work we present a bioinformatics analysis of the whole of human RyR2 (hRyR2) in context with the available functional information, in order to locate individual domains for further biochemical and structural studies. The reliability of the predictions in the N-terminal region (Bauerova-Hlinkova et al. 2010) was verified experimentally by expressing and characterizing the domains identified. We also describe the results of a CD-

* J. Bauer[1], E. Hostinová[1], J. Gašperík[1], K. Beck[3], Ľ. Borko[1], A. Faltínová[2], A. Zahradníková[2] and J. Ševčík[1]
[2]*Institute of Molecular Physiology and Genetics, Slovak Academy of Sciences, Bratislava, Slovakia*
[3]*School of Dentistry, Cardiff University, Heath Park, Cardiff, Wales, UK*

spectroscopy study we carried out in order to determine the domain organization of RyR2; this study also included an analysis of the secondary structure elements of the N-terminal part of RyR2. Finally, we present a homology model of the N-terminal part of RyR2 which is based on the recently determined X-ray structure of rabbit RyR1. The amino-acid sequence identity of these two proteins is more than 80%, which suggests that predictions made from this model will most likely be reliable. The homology model agrees with our bioinformatics analysis and also with the results of our CD-spectroscopy study. This model should help to locate and identify the mutations and the residues in their proximity that are responsible for the cardiac diseases CPVT1 and ARVD2.

2. Physiological function of RyR2

Calcium release from intracellular stores is mediated by two types of calcium release channels – ryanodine receptors (RyRs) and inositol trisphosphate receptors (IP3Rs) (Berridge 1994). These channels are expressed in most tissues. RyRs play a primary role in skeletal and cardiac muscle cells, where they mediate muscle contraction. In these tissues IP3Rs play only a modulatory role. In contrast, smooth muscle, neurons and non-excitable tissues rely on IP3R to play the primary role in calcium release, while RyRs play a modulatory role (Berridge 1994). The study of RyRs is therefore mostly concerned with understanding their role in the activation of skeletal and cardiac muscle contraction.

2.1 Ion permeation

The physiological role of the RyR is to allow permeation of Ca^{2+} ions from the lumen of the SR into the cytosol. Although the calcium gradient between these two compartments is high (the diastolic free Ca^{2+} concentration is only ~100 nM in the cytosol but ~1–2 mM in the SR lumen (Shannon et al. 2003)), concentrations of other ions are much larger (~150 mM K^+) or comparable (~1 mM Mg^{2+}) on both sides of the SR membrane. During the systole, >70% of the Ca^{2+} ions are released from the SR in several milliseconds. Therefore the conductance, which determines the rate of transport, and the permeability of the channel for Ca^{2+} ions, which enables selective transport of Ca^{2+} in the presence of high concentrations of other ions, have to be sufficiently high.

The properties of RyRs have been investigated in planar bilayers by fusion of SR vesicles (Meissner and Henderson (1987), reviewed by Meissner (2002)) and by incorporation of purified ryanodine receptors (Lai et al. (1988), reviewed by Meissner (2002, 2004)) into bilayer membranes. RyRs are characterised by their high conductance and relatively low ion selectivity. Their monovalent cation conductance is very high (200–700 pS), highest for the RyR2 isoform and lowest for the RyR1 isoform, and they are half-saturated at ~10–50 mM concentrations for all monovalent cations. Despite their differences in conductance, their permeability to all monovalents is approximately equal. The channel is 6.5-fold more permeable for divalent than for monovalent ions, and their conductance (90–200 pS) (Williams 1992) increases with the size of the divalent ion. Half-saturation is achieved at ~0.5 mM divalent ion concentration, i.e., at much lower concentrations than for monovalent ions. These properties of the RyR channel enable effective transport of Ca^{2+} ions. The large conductance ensures a sufficient transport rate, while the high calcium affinity ensures that under normal conditions, the rate of Ca^{2+} transport will be close to maximal. The unitary Ca^{2+} current under physiological conditions has been estimated to be

0.4–0.6 pA (Mejia-Alvarez et al. 1999, Kettlun et al. 2003). The permeation properties are conferred on the RyR by the amino acids forming the pore, which are close to the C-terminal end of the RyR (Du et al. 2001, Zhao et al. 1999), and where aa. GGIG were proposed to form the selectivity filter (Balshaw et al. 1999, Gao et al. 2000).

2.2 Regulation by Ca^{2+}

Ca^{2+} ions are the most important regulator of RyR activity (Fabiato 1985). They act at several Ca^{2+} binding sites, leading to activation as well as inactivation of RyR. From the physiological point of view it is important to note that Mg^{2+} ions, present at millimolar concentrations in the cytosol and the SR lumen, are also capable of binding to all RyR Ca^{2+} binding sites. The existence of two activation sites and two inactivation sites has been proposed (Laver 2007, Laver 2009).

2.2.1 Cytosolic activation

Cytosolic Ca^{2+} is the physiological activator of the RyR2 and RyR3 isoforms and contributes to the activation of the RyR1 isoform. In the cardiac myocyte, diastolic Ca^{2+} is ~ 50–100 nM (Baartscheer et al. 1998, Kagaya et al. 1995). Ca^{2+} ions activate RyR channels in the concentration range relevant for excitation-contraction coupling (0.3–100 μM). The probability that RyR channels are open in the absence of other modulators increases with increasing calcium concentration with half-activation at ~1 μM (Chu et al. 1993, Coronado et al. 1994, Gyorke et al. 1994, Meissner 2004, Zahradnikova et al. 1999).

The time course of both RyR activation (Gyorke and Fill 1993, Schiefer et al. 1995, Zahradnikova and Zahradnik 1999, Zahradnikova et al. 1999, Zahradnikova et al. 2003) and deactivation (Schiefer et al. 1995, Velez et al. 1997) is very rapid; the activation rate is dependent on Ca^{2+} concentration (Schiefer et al. 1995, Zahradnikova et al. 1999) while the deactivation rate is not (Schiefer et al. 1995). The fast activation and deactivation kinetics should allow RyRs to respond to physiological calcium signals that last only a few milliseconds. The response of the ryanodine receptor to rapid and brief calcium elevations, mimicking physiological stimuli, has shown that RyR has several Ca^{2+} binding sites. In wild-type RyRs, binding of at least 4 Ca^{2+} ions precedes channel activation (Zahradnikova et al. 1999). RyR channels containing subunits mutated in the putative Ca^{2+} binding sites are less sensitive to activation by cytosolic Ca^{2+} (Li and Chen 2001). Analysis of the calcium dependence of RyR tetramers containing both wild-type and mutated monomers confirmed the presence of a single Ca^{2+} binding site on each of the monomers and revealed that activation by Ca^{2+} proceeds by allosteric interaction between Ca^{2+} binding and channel opening (Zahradnik et al. 2005). The cytosolic Ca^{2+} binding activation site is located in the C-terminal part of the channel (Chen et al. 1998, Li and Chen 2001). The C-terminal part of the RyR sequence (amino acids 3661–5037) is capable of forming an ion channel that can be activated by calcium (Bhat et al. 1997, Xu et al. 2000).

Due to competition between Ca^{2+} and Mg^{2+} ions, the apparent sensitivity of RyR2 channels *in situ* to activation by calcium is decreased about 10 times by Mg^{2+} binding to the activation site (Meissner 1994). The calcium dependence of *in situ* RyR activity enabled elucidation of the mechanism of the differences between the effect of Mg^{2+} and Ca^{2+} on RyR. While binding of Ca^{2+} to the activation site has a strong positively allosteric effect, the binding of Mg^{2+} has a weak negatively allosteric effect (Zahradnikova et al. 2010). At diastolic calcium concentrations, more than 75% of the cytosolic activation sites are occupied by Mg^{2+}

(Zahradnikova et al. 2010). Since Mg^{2+} dissociation from this site is relatively slow (Zahradnikova et al. 2003, 2010), it limits the rate at which RyRs can respond to physiological Ca^{2+} elevations, which might play an important role in the physiological regulation of RyRs.

2.2.2 Luminal activation

Calcium ions also affect RyR activity from the side of the SR lumen. At low cytosolic Ca^{2+} concentrations, when RyR activity is low, the presence of Ca^{2+} at the luminal side increases RyR activity by prolonging channel opening if calcium current flows from the lumen to the cytosol, i.e., by binding to the cytosolic calcium binding site (Laver 2007, Laver 2009, Xu and Meissner 1998). Luminal Ca^{2+} also affects RyR activity by binding to a luminal binding site which may be located either on the channel or on an associated protein (Gaburjakova and Gaburjakova 2006, Gyorke and Gyorke 1998, Gyorke et al. 2004, Qin et al. 2008). The action of luminal Ca^{2+} is complicated by the fact that the SR lumen contains a large amount of calsequestrin, a low-affinity Ca^{2+} buffer, which, in addition to its buffering effect, also interacts with RyR and modulates its activity (see below). In planar lipid bilayers, the effect of luminal Ca^{2+} on RyR activity can be explained by a combination of direct binding to the luminal activation site and of action at the cytosolic sites via "feed-through" of Ca^{2+} that passes through the channel pore to the cytosolic side of the channel (Laver 2007, 2009). Mg^{2+} inhibits the luminal effect of Ca^{2+} by competing with it at the luminal activation site (Laver and Honen 2008).

2.2.3 Inactivation

Their low sensitivity to Ca^{2+}-induced inactivation distinguishes RyR2 and RyR3 from the skeletal isoform, which is half-inactivated by ~100 μM Ca^{2+} (Chu et al. 1993, Lamb 1993, Smith et al. 1988). The identity of the inactivating calcium binding site is unknown. Because of the differences between RyR1 on one hand and RyR2/RyR3 on the other, it is assumed that the differences in sensitivity to calcium-dependent inactivation may be partially due to the divergent region DR1, which differs between these RyR isoforms (Du et al. 2000). The inhibitory site has low specificity—the affinity of Mg^{2+} and Ca^{2+} to this binding site is similar (Gyorke and Gyorke 1998, Laver and Honen 2008, Laver et al. 1997, Xu et al. 1996).

2.2.4 Activation by ATP

ATP increases the probability that the RyR channel will be open (EC_{50} = ~100 μM) without markedly affecting its calcium dependence (Xu et al. 1996). The activity of the RyR1 isoform is potentiated more strongly than that of RyR2 (Zimanyi and Pessah 1991). Although most ATP in the cell is present in the form of $Mg \cdot ATP$, it seems that the activating species is free ATP^{2-} (Copello et al. 2002). Other nucleosides are much less effective than ATP. ADP is a partial agonist with a lower affinity (EC_{50} = ~1 mM). Adenosine and adenine have a still lower effect. CTP, GTP, ITP and UTP do not activate the channel at all (Meissner 2002). The existence of the adenine ring is necessary for ATP binding, and the large effectiveness of channel activation by ATP appears to be caused by the presence of the negatively charged phosphate groups (Chan et al. 2000, 2003).

2.2.5 Modulation by associated proteins

Calmodulin (CaM) is a small Ca^{2+}-binding protein that affects many enzymes, receptors and channels. CaM with four bound calcium ions and apo-CaM without bound Ca^{2+} ions have different conformations and therefore also different effects. CaM inhibits all RyR isoforms. Apo-CaM has a stimulatory effect on the activity of RyR1 and RyR3, but, depending on conditions, it either does not affect or inhibits the RyR2 isoform. The effects of CaM are mediated by its high-affinity binding to a binding site (amino acids 3583–3603 in RyR2) on each of the monomers, which is conserved in all RyR isoforms. The different CaM effects on the different isoforms are apparently due to differences in the isoforms in a region outside the CaM binding site (Meissner 2004). The locations of bound CaM and apo-CaM on the binding site are different (Meissner 2004), and a calcium-dependent physical relocation of CaM on the RyR molecule has also been observed by cryoelectron microscopy (cryo-EM) (Samso and Wagenknecht 2002). Modulation of RyR activity by calmodulin may therefore involve conformational changes in more distant parts of the RyR protein.

FKBP (FK506-binding protein) belongs to the immunophilins, cytosolic receptors for imunosuppresants such as rapamycin and FK506. Each RyR monomer contains a binding site for either FKBP12 (in RyR1) or FKBP12.6 (in RyR2). The interaction of FKBP with the channel stabilizes the protein complex and supports coordinated gating of all four subunits. It is thought that FKBP also plays a role in coupled gating of neighbouring RyR channels (Williams et al. 2001).

In addition to RyR channels, the SR membrane of terminal cisternae also contains the proteins triadin and junctin (Bers 2004) which associate with RyRs from the luminal side. In the lumen of the terminal cisterna there is also a large quantity of the protein calsequestrin (CSQ), a low-affinity calcium-binding protein that serves as a calcium buffer and also modulates RyR activity in a calcium-dependent manner (Bers 2004). CSQ most probably interacts with the RyR channel through interactions with triadin and junctin, so that for correct luminal regulation all three accessory proteins are necessary (Gyorke et al. 2004, Terentyev et al. 2008).

2.2.6 Modulation by phosphorylation

Ryanodine receptors have several conserved regions that are putative phosphorylation sites. Furthermore, kinases (PKA) and phosphatases (PP1 and PP2A) are directly attached to the channel, suggesting that regulation by phosphorylation may have physiological significance (Marx et al. 2001). The first phosphorylation site discovered on the RyR2 molecule (Witcher et al. 1991) was S2809 (S2843 in RyR1), which can be phosphorylated by the Ca^{2+}/calmodulin-dependent protein kinase II (CaMKII) and to some extent also by PKA. Other kinases, such as PKG and PKC, affect RyRs as well (Takasago et al. 1991), e.g. by changing their ability to bind the alkaloid ryanodine. The mechanisms by which phosphorylation and dephosphorylation induce changes in RyR activity are not clearly understood, however. An increase in RyR activity due to an increase in calcium sensitivity (Marx and Marks 2002), as well as an increase in the rate of adaptation after a rapid calcium increase (Valdivia et al. 1995) have both been observed after phosphorylation.

2.2.7 Interdomain interactions

Most of the mutations that affect RyR2 function in CPVT and ARVD2 are located in either of four domains: the N-terminal domain, the central domain, the cytoplasmic I-domain, and the transmembrane domain. This clustering, as well as the similarity between the effects of mutations at different positions within these domains (hyperactivation of the channel and increased sensitivity to agonists) led to the postulation of the interdomain hypothesis (Yamamoto et al. 2000). It was hypothesized that there is an interaction between the N-terminal and the central domain that stabilizes the channel in the closed state. Mutations within these domains would then weaken this interdomain interaction (Ikemoto and Yamamoto 2000, Yamamoto et al. 2000) and these changes might play a key role in the regulatory mechanisms of the channel. The experimental strategy to test this hypothesis was based on the assumption that if an interaction between two regions functions as a regulatory mechanism, then a synthetic domain peptide with a sequence identical to that of one of the interacting regions should destabilize the interaction and disturb RyR regulation in a way similar to that observed in the mutations. Several domain peptides from the N-terminal and central region of RyR1 or RyR2 (H163–S195, L590–C609 and L601–C620, L2442–P2477 and G2460–P2495, D2380–A2411) were indeed able to activate RyR and increase its sensitivity to agonists (El-Hayek et al. 1999, Faltinova et al. 2011, Tateishi et al. 2009, Yamamoto and Ikemoto 2002, Yang et al. 2006). The group of Yamamoto and Ikemoto further postulated, based results of George et al. (2004), that the interaction between the I-domain and another, undefined domain also plays a role in stabilizing the closed state of RyR2. A domain peptide from the I-domain (P4090–E4123) did indeed activate RyR2 (Tateishi et al. 2009). Furthermore, mutations in the N-terminal and central domains destabilized the interaction of RyR2 with its regulator calmodulin (Ono et al. 2010). Two RyR-stabilizing drugs that act on the central (K201) and N-terminal domains (dantrolene) antagonized the effect of the central and N-terminal mutations, respectively, and restored calmodulin binding (Ono et al. 2010, Xu et al. 2010). Transmission between the interdomain interaction, calmodulin binding, and channel opening is believed to be mediated by a calmodulin-like domain (residues 4064–4210 in RyR1; (Xiong et al. 2006)) and its interaction with the calmodulin binding domain of RyR (Ono et al. 2010). The effect of CPVT and ARVD2 mutations on the extent of interdomain interaction may be manifested as a change in the intrinsic opening tendency of the channel or in the allosteric effect between calcium binding and channel opening (Zahradnikova et al. 2010).

2.3 Excitation-contraction coupling

The RyRs are located at tubulo-reticular junctions, special calcium release sites, where they face the adjacent calcium channels (DHPRs) of the plasma membrane. The release sites in both skeletal and cardiac muscle contain clusters of RyRs and DHPRs, and their structures are quite similar. However, DHPRs and RyRs are positioned very precisely adjacent to one another in skeletal muscle but not in cardiac muscle (Protasi 2002). Therefore, in contrast to skeletal muscle, where RyR1 is activated by conformational changes in the DHPR protein (Rios and Brum 1987, Rios et al. 1993), in cardiac cells RyRs are activated by calcium ions that flow into the dyadic space during single-channel openings of DHPRs (Fabiato 1985).

Calcium sparks, calcium release events of individual calcium release units (Cheng et al. 1993), raise local cytosolic Ca^{2+} concentrations by ~200 nM (Cannell et al. 1994, Cannell et al. 1995, Cheng et al. 1993, Lopez-Lopez et al. 1995). They can be discerned when release probability is low (Cheng et al. 1993). Although the probability of spontaneous sparks in a rat ventricular myocyte is low (about 100 s^{-1}) (Cheng et al. 1993), openings of L-type Ca^{2+} channels greatly increase this probability during a voltage step depolarization (Cannell et al. 1995, Lopez-Lopez et al. 1995). Ca^{2+} sparks are stereotypical, i.e., their amplitudes and spatio-temporal properties appear to be independent of their trigger signal (Cannell et al. 1995, Lopez-Lopez et al. 1995). This indicates that the amplitude and time course of a Ca^{2+} spark is largely governed by the properties of the participating RyRs. Thus, Ca^{2+} sparks can be considered to be the elementary Ca^{2+} release events underlying E-C coupling, and gradation of calcium release in response to I_{Ca} can be explained by the summation of variable numbers of Ca^{2+} sparks being activated (Cheng et al. 1996).

Under normal conditions, Ca^{2+} sparks are unable to activate additional Ca^{2+} sparks in adjacent regions, although the local free Ca^{2+} concentration associated with a Ca^{2+} spark is much larger than the global increase in free Ca^{2+} concentration produced by Ca^{2+} current activation ((Cannell et al. 1995), but see Parker et al. (1996)). This observation can be explained by the fact that SR Ca^{2+} release channels are situated very close to the L-type Ca^{2+} channel (the "local control model"; (Stern 1992)), where they sense the > 100-fold increase in local free Ca^{2+} concentration upon opening of a nearby L-type Ca^{2+} channel. The sensitivity of this local control is most clearly seen in the evidence that a single DHPR channel opening can elicit a Ca^{2+} spark (Cannell et al. 1995, Lopez-Lopez et al. 1995, Santana et al. 1996). A detailed analysis revealed that the probability of Ca^{2+} activation depends on the square of the single sarcolemmal Ca^{2+} channel current and on the square of the local free Ca^{2+} concentration (Santana et al. 1996) and that it is quite sensitive to the duration of the DPHR openings (Zahradnikova et al. 1999). Theoretical calculations (Cannell and Soeller 1997) as well as experimental data (Zahradnikova et al. 1999) suggest that RyRs can respond rapidly to calcium influx via DHPRs; the responsiveness of RyRs *in situ* depends on the geometrical arrangement of channels in the narrow dyadic space, in which high Ca^{2+} levels rapidly develop near the SR membrane. Such high Ca^{2+} levels lead to a rapid rate of binding of calcium to the RyR calcium sensitive sites, thereby reducing the latency between DHPR opening and SR calcium release to ~1 ms, in correspondence with the experimentally observed DHPR mean open times. However, direct measurements of the latency between long (~20-ms) calcium channel openings and spark activation (Wang et al. 2001) indicated a much longer latency (~7 ms). Since the binding of Mg^{2+} (Zahradnikova et al. 2010, Zahradnikova et al. 2003) has not been included in the model (Cannell and Soeller 1997), it may be inferred that only RyR channels that do not have Mg^{2+} bound are able to respond rapidly to DHPR openings (Zahradnikova et al. 2010, Zahradnikova et al. 2003).

It is not clear how many RyR channels contribute to a Ca^{2+} spark. While there are 5-9 RyRs per DHPR in cardiac myocytes, individual Ca^{2+} sparks may reflect activation of up to 20 RyRs (Bridge et al. 1999, Lukyanenko et al. 2000). This means that the majority of RyRs are activated by neighbouring RyRs and not by adjacent DHPR channels. A quantitative model of spark activation based on the allosteric action of Ca^{2+} and Mg^{2+} on RyR2 opening (Zahradnikova et al. 2010) predicts the opening of 1–8 RyR2 channels per spark, in agreement with experimental findings (Wang et al. 2001).

3. Structure of ryanodine receptors

3.1 Overall structural features determined by cryoelectron microscopy (cryo-EM)

RyR channels are the largest ion channels known so far, which makes structural studies of them very challenging. So far, the structure of a whole RyR has been determined only by cryo-EM. Most of these studies, including sub-nanometer EM (Samso et al. 2009,

Serysheva et al. 2008) have focused on the skeletal RyR1 isoform, but some studies have been performed on RyR2 (Liu et al. 2002, Sharma et al. 1998) and RyR3 (Liu et al. 2001, Sharma et al. 2000) as well. In agreement with the high sequence homology of RyRs, which reaches ~65%, EM structures of all three isoforms are very similar (Wagenknecht and Samso 2002). The RyR2 (Sharma et al. 1998) and RyR3 (Sharma et al. 2000) isoforms differ slightly from the RyR1 isoform in several structural domains (called divergent regions) that map to segments of reduced homology between the RyR isoforms (Zhang et al. 2003), though the overall structure of the RyR isoforms is very well conserved (Wagenknecht and Samso 2002). The complete channel is made from a combination of four monomers to yield a tetramer with a fourfold axis of symmetry. The divergent regions have been suggested to play a role in calcium-dependent inactivation (DR1) (Du and Maclennan 1999), in signal transmission between DHPR and RyR1 (DR2) (Perez et al. 2003), and in conformational changes of the RyR and RyR-RyR interactions (DR3) (Zhang et al. 2003).

Each subunit of the RyR homotetramer consists of two main parts: a cytoplasmic part and a transmembrane part. The cytoplasmic part of the whole receptor, also called the "foot", is very large (280 × 280 × 120 Å) and interacts with many modulators which affect channel gating (Yano et al. 2006). It is composed of several structural segments: the clamp and the handle at the perimeter, the central rim surrounding the putative pore, and the column connecting the cytoplasmic and transmembrane parts (Fig. 1). These segments have been further subdivided into 15 subdomains (Lanner et al. 2010). The clamps are located at the corners of the cytoplasmic part and are likely to participate in intermolecular interactions with neighboring RyR molecules and other RyR modulators. They undergo large changes during the opening and closing of the channel (Orlova et al. 1996, Samso et al. 2009, Serysheva et al. 1999). Like the cytoplasmic domain, the transmembrane part undergoes large structural changes during the opening and closing of the RyR2 channel (Orlova et al. 1996, Samso et al. 2009, Serysheva et al. 1999).

3.2 Bioinformatics domain prediction

To find the putative individual structural entities of hRyR2, we analyzed the whole hRyR2 amino acid sequence using the PFAM domain database (Finn et al. 2008). Fourteen probable domains were found in the hRyR2 monomer. Eight of them are located in the N-terminal region (residues 1–~1561) and were identified as Ins145_P3_rec, MIR, RIH, SPRY and two RyR domains. The central region (residues 1562–3000) contains the RIH domain and two RyR domains. The C-terminal part (residues 3001–4995) contains an RIH associated domain, a RR_TM4-6 domain and an Ion_Trans domain, Fig. 2. The beginnings and ends of each domain are numbered according to the PFAM search results. Mutations of specific residues involved in ARVD2 and CPVT1 are shown (Yano et al. 2006; www.fsm.it/cardmoc). LIZ1-3 (amino acid residues 554–585, 1603–1631, and 3003–3039) represent leucine-isoleucine zipper areas. The proposed binding partners, SPI, PR130, mKAP, PP1, PP2A, PKA, D, K201, FKBP, and CaM represent spinophilin, protein 130, muscle specific kinase anchoring protein, protein phosphatases 1 and 2A, protein kinase A, dantrolene, 1,4-benzothiazepine derivative K201 (JTV519), FK-binding protein, and calmodulin, respectively. Binding partners for hRyR2 and their positions were adapted from Wang et al. (2011), Yamamoto et al. (2008), and Yano et al. (2006).

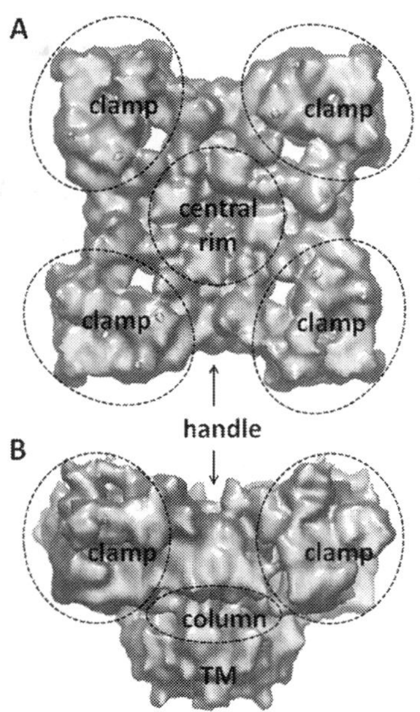

Fig. 1. A cryo-EM density map of RyR1 (accession no. 1274, http://www.ebi.ac.uk/emdb-srv/atlas/1274_summary.html) in the in closed state. A. Cytopasmic view. B. Side view. The cytoplasmic (clamp, handle, central rim and column) and transmembrane regions (TM) are indicated.

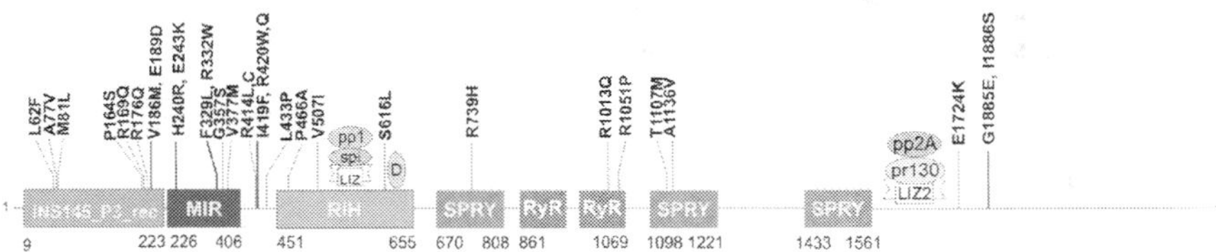

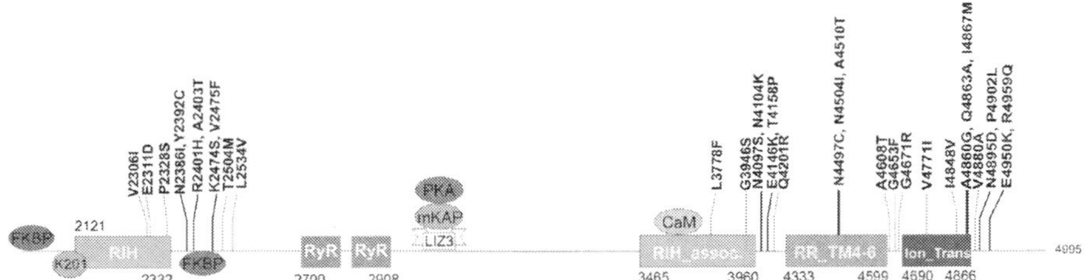

Fig. 2. Analysis of the human cardiac ryanodine receptor using the PFAM database. The position and type of mutations resulting in CVPT or ARVD2, as reported at www.fsm.it/cardmoc/, are indicated above the sequence regions.

3.3 X-ray analysis

To date, X-ray structures have been determined for several N-terminal fragments of rabbit RyR1 (residues ~12–210 (Amador et al. 2009, Lobo and Van Petegem 2009); residues 12–532 (Tung et al. 2010)); and murine RyR2 (residues 12–217, wt and mutants A77V and V186M) (Lobo and Van Petegem 2009). The overall structures of all isoforms, including those containing mutations, are very similar (superposition results in r.m.s.d. of 0.69 Å for 150 C_α atoms), Fig. 3, which is not surprising due to their close sequence homology and physiological function. The longest fragment, residues 12–532, is composed of three structural domains, which have been designated as A (1–205), B (206–394) and C (395–532) (Tung et al. 2010). Domains B and C are homologous respectively with the β-trefoil and α-helical domains of the IP3R binding core. Domain A is homologous with the IP3 binding suppressor domain of IP3R (Yuchi and Van Petegem 2011). The central motif of domains A and B is a β-trefoil core consisting of 12 β-strands which are held together by hydrophobic interactions. In the A domain, a 10-residue α-helix is inserted between strands β4 and β5 (Lobo and Van Petegem 2009). Domain C consists of five α-helices. Most of the secondary structure elements are connected by flexible loops, which were proposed to be located at the interfaces with other RyR domains or at the interfaces with proteins interacting with RyR (Tung et al. 2010, Yano et al. 2006). The X-ray crystal structures allowed the precise mapping of several mutations which are associated with CPVT and ARVD2 (Lobo and Van Petegem 2009), as well as the homologous mutations in RyR1 which are responsible for malignant hyperthermia (MH) and central core disease (CCD) (Tung et al. 2010).

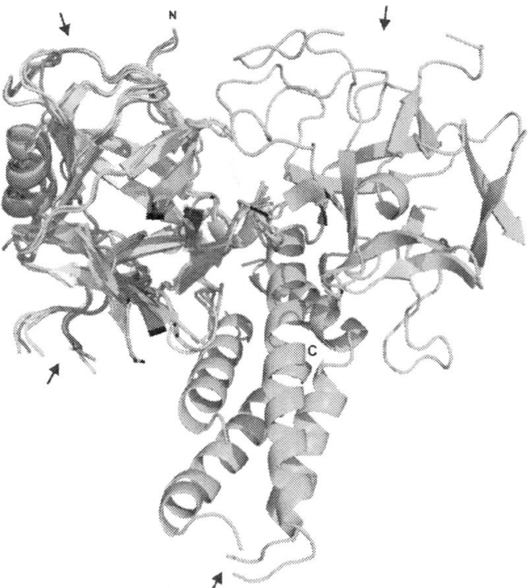

Fig. 3. Comparison of X-ray structures of the N-terminal domains of RyR1 (PDB ID 2XOA green, 3HSM pink, 3ILA magenta) and RyR2 (PDB ID 3IM5 blue, 3IM6 yellow, 3IM7 purple). The superposition was performed using the program Multiprot (Shatsky et al. 2004), through 150 C_α atoms with a r.m.s.d. of 0.69 Å. Arrows indicate flexible loops.

3.4 Relationships between domain structure, 3D structure and RyR function
3.4.1 The Ins145_P3_rec domain

The Ins145_P3_rec domain is found in RyRs and IP3Rs (Ponting C. P. 2000). In IP3R, it participates in forming the ligand binding suppressor region (Bosanac et al. 2005). In the structure of RyR1, it is equivalent to the first N-terminal domain A (Tung et al. 2010). The PFAM prediction assigned this domain to residues 9–223, while in the RyR1 structure it corresponds to the equivalent RyR2 amino acids 12–228. This domain contains two closely spaced clusters of mutations associated with CPVT and ARVD in the region of residues 62–81 and 164–189 (http://www.fsm.it/cardmoc), which belong to the first mutation cluster CPVT-I (George et al. 2007). The domain consists of 12 β-strands, arranged into a β-trefoil motif (see below). Superposing the ligand-binding suppressor domain of the IP3R (PDB ID 1XZZ; (Serysheva et al. 2008)) and the X-ray structure of the N-terminal portion of RyR1 into the cryo-EM density map of RyR1 (Tung et al. 2010) indicates that this domain should lie in the clamp or on the central rim of the ion channel, respectively.

3.4.2 The MIR domain

MIR domains are found in a number of proteins (George et al. 2007, Hamada et al. 1996, Strahl-Bolsinger and Scheinost 1999), including IP3Rs (Bosanac et al. 2005, Bosanac et al. 2002), and RyRs (Amador et al. 2009, Lobo and Van Petegem 2009, Ponting 2000, Tung et al. 2010). They usually consist of several ~50-residue MIR motifs with a β-trefoil fold (Murzin et al. 1992), and form β-barrel structures with hairpin triplets and internal pseudo-threefold symmetry (Bosanac et al. 2005). In RyR1, the MIR domain is equivalent to the second N-terminal domain, domain B (Tung et al. 2010). In PMT1 mannosyltransferases, MIR motifs are located in the luminal loops of the enzyme and are essential for transferase activity (Stahl-Bolsinger et al., 1999). In IP3R, the first two of the β-trefoil motifs were found to belong to the suppressor region (Ins145_P3_rec, (Bosanac et al. 2002), see above), while the latter two (parts of the MIR domain) belong to the ligand binding region (Bosanac et al. 2005). Similar β-trefoil motifs were predicted to be present in the N-terminal region of the RyR1 isoform (Bosanac et al. 2002), and were later found in its crystal structure (Amador et al. 2009), although the sequence similarity between IP3R and RyR is relatively low. PFAM predicted this domain to lie between residues 226–406 of RyR2, and in the RyR1 structure it corresponds to the equivalent RyR2 amino acids 228–411. This region contains a large number of CPVT/ARVD2 mutations (Fig. 2) (http://www.fsm.it/cardmoc/), which belong to the first mutation cluster CPVT-I (George et al. 2007). Docking of the ligand-binding domain of IP3R (PDB ID 1N4K, (Serysheva et al. 2005); PDB ID 1XZZ and PDB ID 1N4K, (Serysheva et al. 2008)) into the cryo-EM structure of RyR1 predicts that this domain will lie in the clamp region while doing a similar docking using the X-ray structure of the N-terminal sequence of RyR1 (Tung et al. 2010) indicates that the MIR domain should lie on the central rim.

3.4.3 The RIH domains

Two RIH domains were found in both RyRs and IP3Rs. The X-ray structure of a major part of the first RIH domain of both IP3R (Bosanac et al. 2002) and RyR1 (Tung et al. 2010) has been determined. In the case of RyR1, this corresponds to domain C and the structure extends out to residue 532, which corresponds to residue 543 in hRyR2. Structurally, RIH is composed of α-helices. In IP3R, this domain forms the binding site for inositol 1,4,5-

trisphosphate (Bosanac et al. 2002). By superposing the ligand suppressor domain (PDB ID 1XZZ) and the ligand binding core (PDB ID 1N4K) on the N-terminal part of RyR1 (PDB ID 2XAO), it was proposed that all three domains of IP3R, i.e. Ins145_P3_rec, MIR and RIH, interact together, as predicted by Chan et al. (2007), and are arranged similarly as in the N-terminal part of RyR1 (Yuchi and Van Petegem 2011). The PFAM prediction placed this domain between residues 451–655, while in the RyR1 structure its beginning corresponds to the equivalent RyR2 amino acid 410. In RyR2, the RIH domain was reported to contain a leucine–isoleucine zipper between amino acid residues 554 and 585 that mediates binding of the phosphatase PP1 via the spinophilin targeting protein (Marx et al. 2001). This domain was also proposed to contain the binding site for dantrolene (residue 626 in hRyR2), and it contains several of the CPVT/ARVD2 mutations (http://www.fsm.it/cardmoc/), which belong to the first mutation cluster CPVT-I (George et al. 2007). It was located in the clamp region by cryo-EM (Wang et al. 2011). However, docking of the X-ray structure of the N-terminal sequence of RyR1 into the cryo-EM structure of RyR1 predicts that this domain lies in the central rim (Tung et al. 2010).

PFAM predicted that the second RIH domain lies between residues 2121-2332. This domain and its C-terminally adjacent region contain the central cluster of CPVT/ARVD mutations (CPVT-II, (George et al. 2007), http://www.fsm.it/cardmoc/) and is flanked by putative binding sites for the protein FKBP 12.6. Cryo-EM places this region in the clamp (Liu et al. 2005, Wang et al. 2011).

3.4.4 The SPRY domains

The SPRY domain (**sp**1A kinase and the **ry**anodine receptors) (Ponting et al. 1997) structurally consists of several antiparallel β-strands connected with flexible loops. The precise function of the SPRY domain (and the related B30.2 domain) is unknown; however, it is believed to act as a protein–protein interaction module capable of binding multiple targets by recognizing the conformation of a partner protein rather than a consensus sequence motif (Woo et al. 2006, Yao et al. 2006). The B30.2/SPRY domain has been identified in numerous and diverse proteins across bacterial and eukaryotic species (e.g. pyrin/marenostrin and other butyrophilin-like homologues, ryanodine receptors and midin1), including over 150 proteins in humans (Rhodes et al. 2005), suggesting that the specific function of the B30.2/SPRY domain within a given protein may heavily rely on the other domains in their neighbourhood (Kleiber and Singh 2009). PFAM predicted that RyR2 contains three SPRY domains, corresponding to residues 670–808, 1098–1221, and 1433–1561. The first two domains contain three CPVT/ARVD mutations: R739H, T1107M and A1136V (Medeiros-Domingo et al. 2009), Fig. 2, which lie outside of the four mutation clusters.

3.4.5 The RyR domains

Four copies of the RyR domain are present in the ryanodine receptor, of which two belong to the N-terminal and two to the central regions. The function of this domain is unknown (Ponting 2000). In the second RyR domain, two isolated CPVT mutations, which lie outside of the four mutation clusters, have been found to date: R1013Q and R1051P, Fig. 2 (Marjamaa et al. 2009, Medeiros-Domingo et al. 2009).

3.4.6 The RIH_associated and RR_TM4-6 domains

According to PFAM, the RIH_associated domain should lie between residues 3465–3960. This domain contains the calmodulin binding site, which was localized to the column region of RyR according to cryo-EM (Samso and Wagenknecht 2002). The adjacent RR_TM4-6 domain was predicted to lie between residues 4333–4599 by PFAM. It contains the divergent region DR1 (Liu et al. 2002), the putative calcium sensor that is responsible for the physiological activation of RyR2 (Chen et al. 1998, Li and Chen 2001), and also the calmodulin-like domain (Xiong et al. 2006). The end of the RIH_associated domain together with the RR_TM4-6 domain (aa. 3722–4610) were identified as a separate functional domain (called the I-domain) (George et al. 2004), which contains a third cluster of CPVT/ARVD mutations (CPVT-III, (George et al. 2007), http://www.fsm.it/cardmoc/); cryo-EM locates this domain in the column of RyR1 (Wang et al. 2011).

3.4.7 The Ion_Trans domain

The Ion_Trans (ion transport) domain covers the transmembrane region of the ryanodine receptor. This domain is found in most voltage-dependent ion channels as well as in RyRs and IP3Rs. The domain usually has six transmembrane helices, the final two of which flank a loop that determines ion selectivity (Unnerstale et al. 2009). The tetrameric ion channels (potassium channels, IP3Rs and RyRs) contain one Ion_Trans domain per monomer, while the sodium and calcium channels contain four Ion_Trans domain repeats. This domain is located in the transmembrane region, embedded in the membrane of the SR, Fig. 1A,B, and contains the ion conducting pore. It has been proposed that the pore includes the GVRAGGGIGD amino acid sequence (Du et al. 2001, Zhao et al. 1999), where the amino acids GGIG were proposed to form a selectivity filter (Balshaw et al. 1999, Gao et al. 2000). The fourth cluster of CPVT/ARVD2 mutations (CPVT-IV, (George et al. 2007), http://www.fsm.it/cardmoc/) occurs in this domain and in the flanking regions on both its sides.

3.4.8 Regions without a known domain structure

Two of the three regions of isoform sequence diversity (DR2 and DR3; (Perez et al. 2003, Zhang et al. 2003)) are located outside of the PFAM-predicted domains. DR2 is located between the second and the third SPRY domains (residues 1353-1397, Liu et al. 2004), while DR3 (residues 1852-1890) is located between SPRY3 and RIH2. Both DR2 and DR3 are found in the clamp region of RyR1 (Wang et al. 2011). DR3 contains two isolated CPVT/ARVD2 mutations, G1885E and G1886S (Milting et al. 2006), which lie outside of the four mutation clusters.

The second and third leucine-isoleucine zipper (aa. 1604–1644 and 3004–3041), that were found to bind PP2A and PKA with the help of the adapter proteins PR130 and mAKAP, respectively (Marx et al. 2001), are also located outside the PFAM-predicted domains. The location of these motifs in the 3D structure of the RyR2 is unknown.

4. Cloning, expression and characterization of predicted N-terminal hRyR2 domains

In our previous work we concentrated on the production and characterization of recombinant N-terminal domains of hRyR2 (residues 1–759) in *Escherichia coli* expression systems ((Bauerova-Hlinkova et al. 2010); unpublished results). Based on the bioinformatics analysis described above, we assumed that the predicted domains would form individual entities and might behave as stable proteins. We designed several constructs covering the predicted first three N-terminal domains (Ins145_P3_rec, MIR, RIH) with various starting and terminating residues, Table 1, taking into consideration the predicted secondary structure elements and the known structure of the related IP3R domains. All fragments were designed not to disrupt the predicted secondary structure elements, Fig. 6. In this study we obtained three authentic recombinant hRyR2 fragments with good expression yields and solubility: 1–606 (involves first three putative N-terminal domains), 391–606 and 409–606 (involves the core of the predicted RIH domain) and several hRyR2 fragments expressed with a fusion partner, either thioredoxin or Nus A protein, Table 1.

hRyR2 fragment	Calculated $M_w \times 10^3$	Protein Expression
1–247.His$_6$	27.9	++
1–606.His$_6$	68.6	++
391–606.His$_6$	25.2	++
409–606.His$_6$	23.2	+++
Nus.1–606	128.6	++
Nus.230–606	104.0	++
Trx.384–606.His$_6$	43.3	+++
Trx.391–606.His$_6$	42.5	+++
Trx.409–606.His$_6$	40.5	+++

Table 1. Designed fragments of the N-terminal part of hRyR2 with good expression and solubility. The fragment 1–247.His6 contains the Ins145_P3_rec domain. The longest N-terminal hRyR2 fragment 1–606.His6 involves all three putative N-terminal domains. The hRyR fragments 384–606, 391–606 and 409–606 involve the core of the RIH domain. To improve solubility, some fragments were expressed with fusion partners – Nus A protein and thioredoxin. Quantification of expression: ++ 1–5 mg/g expressed cells, +++ more than 5 mg/g expressed cells. The amount of the protein was determined after IMAC purification (Bauerova-Hlinkova et al. 2010).

The folding and thermal stability of these expressed fragments was assessed by circular dichroism (CD) spectroscopy (Fig. 4) and a thermofluor shift assay (Fig. 5). The secondary structure content of the fragments was derived from the CD spectra using the CDsstr algorithm (Johnson 1999) with an extensive set of reference databases (Whitmore and Wallace 2004). For the longest fragment, 1–606, the amount of α-helices and β-strands resulted in *ca.* 23 and 29%, respectively (Fig. 4A; (Bauerova-Hlinkova et al. 2010). For the C-terminal domain covering residues 409 to 606 (Fig. 4B), a higher degree of α-helicity (*ca.* 50%) was found. This value is lower than expected from the model for this region (62%, see section 4.1.), which indicates that the expected N-terminal helix might be only partially folded. Such disorder within the terminal regions is frequently observed in NMR and X-ray derived structures of protein fragments. The spectra of the thioredoxin fusion protein fragments 384–606 (Fig. 4C) and 409–606 (Fig. 4D) indicated α-helix and β-strand contents of *ca.* 40 and 10%, respectively.

With temperature increasing up to 35°C, only small changes of the CD signal could be observed for fragment 1–606 (Fig. 5A), but further heating resulted in irreversible precipitation under our experimental conditions (Bauerova-Hlinkova et al. 2010). A similar behaviour was observed for the fragment 409–606, which was stable up to 37°C (Fig. 4B) and started to precipitate at T > 42°C (data not shown). When the fragment 409–606 was fused with thioredoxin A, its CD signal indicated a gradual loss of α-helicity (*ca.* 25% at 95°C) that was fully recovered upon cooling (data not shown).

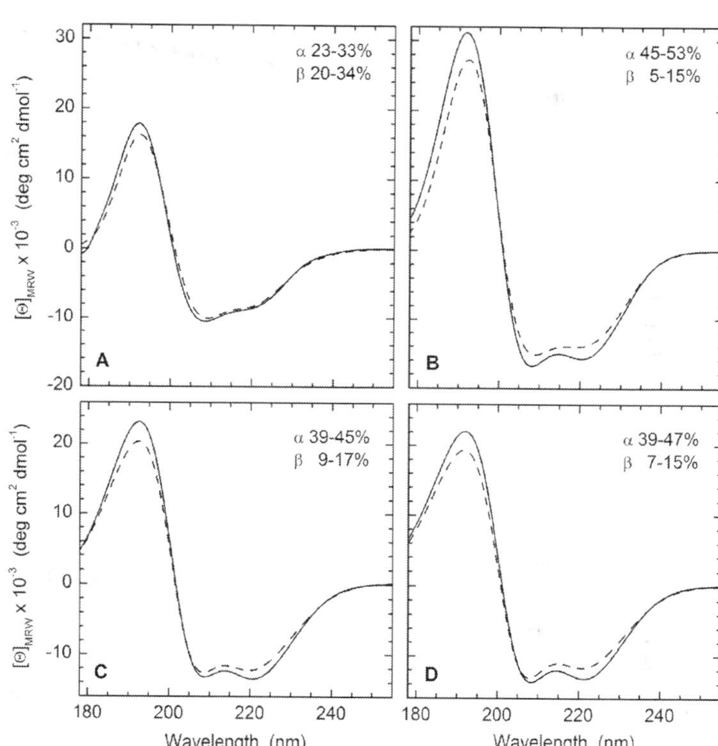

Fig. 4. Far-UV CD spectra of recombinant hRyR2 fragments 1–606 (A) and 409-606 (B), and as fusion proteins with thioredoxin A at the N-terminus Trx-384-606 (C) and Trx-409-606 (D). Spectra were recorded in an 0.02-cm cell at 4°C (solid line) and 37°C (dashed line; 35°C for hRyR2 1–606). Samples were dialyzed into 100 mM NaF, 20 mM Tris SO$_4$ pH 7.5 or 8.0, including either 0.1% Tween-20 (A-C) or sulfobetaine SB14 (D). Deconvolution of the 4°C spectra using the CDsstr algorithm as implemented in Dichroweb with various reference databases ((Whitmore and Wallace 2004); http://dichroweb.cryst.bbk.ac.uk/) results in the amount of α-helix and β-strand shown at the top right of each panel.

The results of the thermofluor shift assay, performed with the longest hRyR2 fragment 1–606, were in good agreement with the temperature dependence of the circular dichroism spectra. The thermal stability of the fragment was tested in a wide range of buffers (Tris, Hepes, MES, citrate, Na/K phosphate, Bicine, Tricine; pH range 5.0–9.0), Fig. 5, and in the presence or absence of 1 and 5 mM Ca^{2+}, Mg^{2+}, ATP and 5–20% glycerol. The fragment is the most stable in neutral-basic pH (7.0–8.0) with a T$_m$ of ~45°C, Fig. 5B, C. The presence of Ca^{2+}

or ATP did not change the T_m significantly, suggesting that the fragment does not contain binding sites for these ligands.

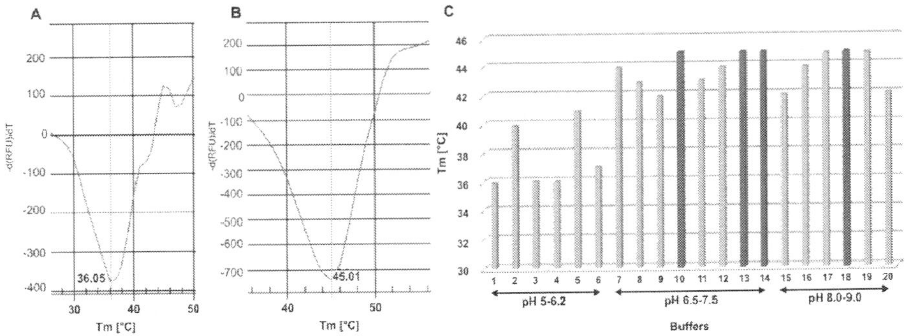

Fig. 5. The first derivative of the thermal denaturation curve of recombinant 1–606 hRyR2 fragment obtained by thermofluor shift assay, measured in 200 mM Na-citrate, pH 5.5 (A), and 200 mM Na-phosphate, pH 7.5 (B). C. T_m of the recombinant hRyR2 fragment 1-606 obtained by the thermofluor shift assay in different buffers and pH (1 – K-phosphate 5.0; 2 – Na-phosphate 5.5; 3 – Na-citrate 5.5; 4 – MES 5.8; 5 – K-phosphate 6.0; 6 – MES 6.2; 7 – Na-phosphate 6.5; 8 – Na-cacodylate 6.5; 9 – MES 6.5; 10 – K-phosphate 7.0; 11 – HEPES 7.0; 12 – Na-acetate 7.3; 13 – Na-phosphate 7.5; 14 – Tris 7.5; 15 – Imidazol 8.0; 16 – HEPES 8.0; 17 – Tris 8.0; 18 – Bicine 8.0; 19 – Tris 8.5; 20 – Bicine 9.0). The conditions under which RyR2 1-606 was the most stable are in red. For each measurement 8 µg of protein were used.

4.1 Model structure of the N-terminal part of hRyR2

The amino-acid sequence of the recently determined structure of the N-terminal region of rabbit RyR1 (PDB ID 2XOA (Tung et al. 2010)) is 63% identical and 77% similar to the corresponding sequence of hRyR2 (similarity is here defined as having a Gonnet Pam250 matrix score > 0.5 as determined by ClustalX 2.1). The 2XOA structure therefore represents an excellent template for constructing a homology model of the N-terminal region of hRyR2. The structure covers residues 12–543 of the hRyR2 sequence. The homology model was constructed using Modeller 9v8 (Sali and Blundell 1993). The hRyR2 sequence was first aligned with the template structure using the alignment.align2d command of Modeller and then manually edited to improve the alignment (Fig. 6). This alignment was used to build a homology model using the automodel class. Residues 90–107 of the human sequence, which had been disordered in the template structure, were constrained to form an α-helix in accordance with the secondary structure predictions, see below. The structure was thoroughly refined using automodel.library_schedule = autosched.slow and automodel.max_var_iterations = 300 for the initial optimization step, which was then followed by molecular dynamics refinement using automodel.md_level = refine.slow. The whole process was repeated twice. The refinement target function (objective function) minimized the geometry restraints and Charmm energy terms enforcing proper stereochemistry (described in (Sali and Blundell 1993)).

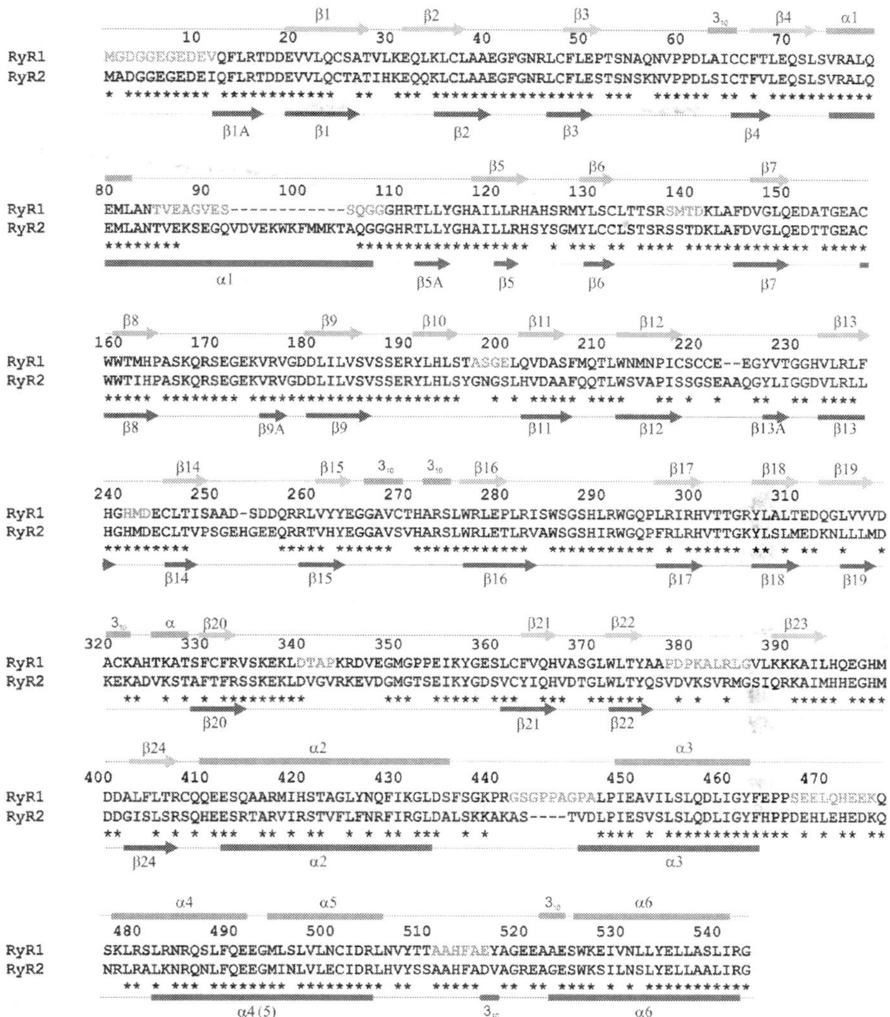

Fig. 6. The sequence alignment of hRyR2 and rabbit RyR1 (PDB ID 2XOA) sequences which was used as a template for the homology modeling of the hRyR2 tertiary structure. The alignment was performed using the alignment.align2d command of Modeller 9v8 (Sali and Blundell 1993). The secondary structure elements of hRyR2 (α-helices and β-strands are shown as red bars and blue arrows, respectively) were predicted by Jpred (Cole et al. 2008). The numbering of predicted secondary structure elements of hRyR2 corresponds to those found in the RyR1 template structure (α-helices and β-strands are shown as pink bars and light blue arrows, respectively). The alignment covers residues 1–543 of the human RyR2 protein. Residues in grey are missing in the RyR1 structure and correspond to flexible loops. Identical residues (~64%) in both sequences are labelled by asterisks.

Twenty trial structures were generated and the best one was chosen by first discarding all those with unreasonable geometry in the loop regions, and then selecting the one with the lowest objective function score. The loops in this structure were then refined using the functions found in the Modeller loopmodel class (described in Fiser et al. (2000)). This was done in two stages. First, the loop containing helix α1A (see below) was refined to give five different positions. Second, for each of these positions an additional five structures were generated with different positions for all of the loops. The final structure was selected based on the lowest objective function. The final structure was inserted into the RyR1 crystal packing arrangement to check for possible clashes with neighbouring molecules, which might indicate unlikely loop conformations; none were found. The final model is shown in Fig. 7A,B.

The hRyR2 model contains three domains, aa. 12–219 (Ins145_P3_rec), 228–408 (MIR) and 411–543 (RIH; residue numbers refer to the hRyR2), analogous to those of the template structure (Tung et al. 2010). The RyR1 template structure and hRyR2 homology model are in agreement with the PFAM predictions shown in Fig. 2; however, the beginning of the third domain, RIH, is shifted by about 40 aa. residues towards the N-terminus.

With a few exceptions, the hRyR2 homology model (Fig. 7) confirmed the secondary structure predictions, nearly all of the β-strands (22 out of 27) were found in the predicted positions in the template structure, although with a minor shift of one to three residues, Fig. 6.

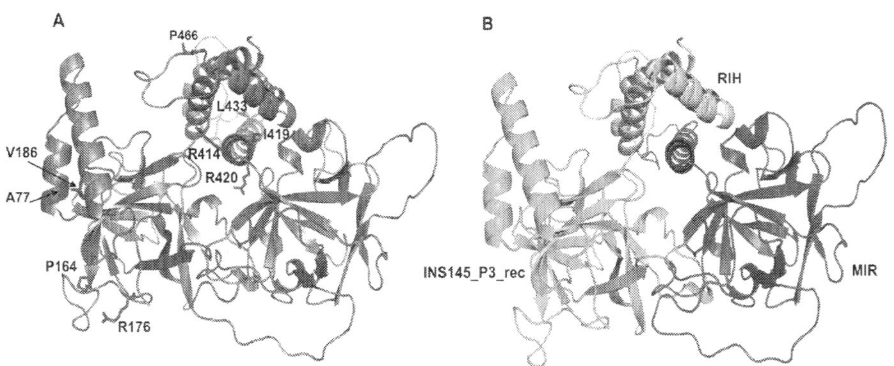

Fig. 7. (A) hRyR2 homology model constructed by Modeller 9v8 (Sali and Blundell 1993) using the alignment with rabbit RyR1, shown in Fig. 6. Loops which were disordered in the template structure and the modelled α1A-helix are in orange. Residues which cause physiological dysfunction of hRyR2 when mutated are indicated. (B) The RyR2 homology model coloured according to the domains predicted using the PFAM database. The colour scheme is the same as in Fig. 2; Ins145_P3_rec is green, MIR is red, and RIH is yellow. The grey α-helix, α2 (aa. 409–436), according to the PFAM results, precedes the RIH domain, but is not part of the MIR domain.

The beginning of the first β-strand (β1A; aa. 11–16) was missing in the template structure so that its presence could not be verified. The short β-strands β5A, β9A, and β13A were not present in the RyR1 structure. β23 was present in the template and the modelled structure but was not predicted by JPred. Three long α-helices (α2, α3, and α6) were correctly predicted by JPred with small variations at the beginnings or the ends in the model. In the region of the predicted helix α4, two shorter α-helices were modelled which are separated from each other only by a two-residue turn, as found in the template structure. Neither the shortest α-helix (aa. 325–328) nor four out of the five 3_{10} helices were predicted.

The first predicted α-helix (α1) deserves additional consideration. In comparison to RyR1, the RyR2 sequence contains a 12-residue insertion, Fig. 6, suggesting that the structure of this region differs in these two proteins. In hRyR2, helix α1 was predicted to be 33 residues long (residues 75–107). However, the Ins145_P3_rec domain, which includes the helix α1, was determined independently three times in RyR2 and contains only the first ten residues of this helix, followed by a gap (Lobo and Van Petegem 2009). This indicates that the predicted helix α1 cannot span the whole range. Instead, most likely, this region forms a helix-turn-helix motif (aa. 75–110), as found in the structure of the IP3R ligand binding suppressor domain (Bosanac et al. 2005). The motif has to be rather flexible to explain its absence in the previously solved RyR structures as well as the conformational flexibility predicted by (Bosanac et al. 2005). Inclusion of an 18-residue α1A, separated from the helix α1 observed in the template structure by a six-residue linker, resulted in five different conformations, which shows that the modelled motif has sufficient mobility to explain its absence in the solved structures. Most likely, this motif will be stabilized in the whole RyR2 protein by interaction with a binding partner (another RyR2 domain or an interacting ligand).

Between the helix α1A and the long disordered loop containing residues 464–477, there is a very large cavity, which suggests the existence of a large binding pocket. The helix α1A and the loop 464–477, which sit atop of this cavity, both contain several aromatic residues (W98, F100, H469, H472). The presence of the aromatic residues in the surface, three of which are exposed to the cavity (F100, H469, H472) may indicate protein-protein binding events with a putative ligand. The P466A mutant, located at the beginning of the loop, is known to substantially disrupt the proper physiological function of RyR2, causing syncope (Tester et al. 2005). Proline residues have lower conformational flexibility than other residues, so the most likely reason for the importance of P466 would be a necessity to decrease the flexibility of the loop containing residues 464–477. In addition to the P466A mutant, two other mutants in this area are also known to cause RyR2 dysfunction: A77V, causing CPVT and ARVD2 (d'Amati et al. 2005), and V186M, causing CPVT (Tester et al. 2006). All three mutations in this area induce only small changes in the surface shape of the protein. Taken together, all this implies that this part of the structure might be involved in the binding of RyR2 to other interacting proteins or its own domains. This is consistent with the results seen in RyR1, where the docking of the first three N-terminal domains into the full-length cryo-EM density map revealed that the loop involving P455 (P466 in hRyR2) as well as the beginning of helix α4 belong to interface 6 (Tung et al. 2010).

The reliability of the hRyR2 homology model is further confirmed by the CD-spectroscopy of hRyR2 fragment 1–606, Fig. 4A, which revealed 23% α-helices and 29% β-strands in the fragment. This is in good agreement with the hRyR2 model structure, in which the content of α-helices and β-strands was 23% and 24%, respectively.

5. Conclusion

In this work, bioinformatics analysis of the whole human RyR2 is presented. The analysis shows that the protein is composed of 14 domains. We were concerned particularly with the first three N-terminal domains of the protein (Ins145_P3_rec, MIR, RIH). Verification that the domains identified can behave as separate, independent protein units was provided by their successful expression in *E. coli* and subsequent characterization. CD-spectroscopy was used to determine the domain organization and to identify the secondary structure elements of the N-terminal part of hRyR2. The amino acid sequence identity of hRyR2 with that of rabbit RyR1, the X-ray structure of which is known, is higher than 60%, which allowed the construction of a reliable homology model of the N-terminal part of hRyR2. Its reliability was further strengthened by its conformity with the bioinformatics analysis and the CD-spectroscopy study. This model should allow a clearer insight to be gained into the possible influence of mutations on the cardiac diseases CPVT1 and ARVD2.

6. Acknowledgment

This work was supported by VEGA grants 2/0131/10 and 2/0190/10 and by APVV-0628-10 and APVV-0721-10. VB would like to thank Dr. Elena Hlinková for encouragement and support during the writing of the chapter.

7. References

Amador FJ, Liu S, Ishiyama N, Plevin MJ, Wilson A, MacLennan DH, Ikura M. 2009. Crystal structure of type I ryanodine receptor amino-terminal beta-trefoil domain reveals a disease-associated mutation "hot spot" loop. Proc Natl Acad Sci U S A 106: 11040-11044.

Baartscheer A, Schumacher CA, Fiolet JW. 1998. Cytoplasmic sodium, calcium and free energy change of the Na+/Ca2+-exchanger in rat ventricular myocytes. J Mol Cell Cardiol 30: 2437-2447.

Balshaw D, Gao L, Meissner G. 1999. Luminal loop of the ryanodine receptor: a pore-forming segment? Proc Natl Acad Sci U S A 96: 3345-3347.

Bauerova-Hlinkova V, Hostinova E, Gasperik J, Beck K, Borko L, Lai FA, Zahradnikova A, Sevcik J. 2010. Bioinformatic mapping and production of recombinant N-terminal domains of human cardiac ryanodine receptor 2. Protein Expr Purif 71: 33-41.

Berridge MJ. 1994. The biology and medicine of calcium signalling. Mol Cell Endocrinol 98: 119-124.

Bers DM. 2004. Macromolecular complexes regulating cardiac ryanodine receptor function. J Mol Cell Cardiol 37: 417-429.

Bhat MB, Zhao J, Takeshima H, Ma J. 1997. Functional calcium release channel formed by the carboxyl-terminal portion of ryanodine receptor. Biophys J 73: 1329-1336.

Bosanac I, Alattia JR, Mal TK, Chan J, Talarico S, Tong FK, Tong KI, Yoshikawa F, Furuichi T, Iwai M, Michikawa T, Mikoshiba K, Ikura M. 2002. Structure of the inositol 1,4,5-trisphosphate receptor binding core in complex with its ligand. Nature 420: 696-700.

Bosanac I, Yamazaki H, Matsu-Ura T, Michikawa T, Mikoshiba K, Ikura M. 2005. Crystal structure of the ligand binding suppressor domain of type 1 inositol 1,4,5-trisphosphate receptor. Mol Cell 17: 193-203.

Bridge JH, Ershler PR, Cannell MB. 1999. Properties of Ca2+ sparks evoked by action potentials in mouse ventricular myocytes. J Physiol (Lond) 518: 469-478.

Cannell MB, Soeller C. 1997. Numerical analysis of ryanodine receptor activation by L-type channel activity in the cardiac muscle diad. Biophys J 73: 112-122.

Cannell MB, Cheng H, Lederer WJ. 1994. Spatial non-uniformities in [Ca2+]i during excitation-contraction coupling in cardiac myocytes. Biophys J 67: 1942-1956.

Cannell MB, Cheng H, Lederer WJ. 1995. The control of calcium release in heart muscle. Science 268: 1045-1049.

Chan J, Whitten AE, Jeffries CM, Bosanac I, Mal TK, Ito J, Porumb H, Michikawa T, Mikoshiba K, Trewhella J, Ikura M. 2007. Ligand-induced conformational changes via flexible linkers in the amino-terminal region of the inositol 1,4,5-trisphosphate receptor. J Mol Biol 373: 1269-1280.

Chan WM, Welch W, Sitsapesan R. 2000. Structural factors that determine the ability of adenosine and related compounds to activate the cardiac ryanodine receptor. Br J Pharmacol 130: 1618-1626.

Chan WM, Welch W, Sitsapesan R. 2003. Structural characteristics that govern binding to, and modulation through, the cardiac ryanodine receptor nucleotide binding site. Mol Pharmacol 63: 174-182.

Chen SR, Ebisawa K, Li X, Zhang L. 1998. Molecular identification of the ryanodine receptor Ca2+ sensor. J Biol Chem 273: 14675-14678.

Cheng H, Lederer WJ, Cannell MB. 1993. Calcium sparks: elementary events underlying excitation-contraction coupling in heart muscle. Science 262: 740-744.

Cheng H, Lederer MR, Lederer WJ, Cannell MB. 1996. Calcium sparks and [Ca2+]i waves in cardiac myocytes. Am J Physiol 270: C148-C159.

Chu A, Fill M, Stefani E, Entman ML. 1993. Cytoplasmic Ca2+ does not inhibit the cardiac muscle sarcoplasmic reticulum ryanodine receptor Ca2+ channel, although Ca(2+)-induced Ca2+ inactivation of Ca2+ release is observed in native vesicles. J Membr Biol 135: 49-59.

Cole C, Barber JD, Barton GJ. 2008. The Jpred 3 secondary structure prediction server. Nucleic Acids Res 36: W197-201.

Copello JA, Barg S, Sonnleitner A, Porta M, Diaz-Sylvester P, Fill M, Schindler H, Fleischer S. 2002. Differential activation by Ca2+, ATP and caffeine of cardiac and skeletal muscle ryanodine receptors after block by Mg2+. J Membr Biol 187: 51-64.

Coronado R, Morrissette J, Sukhareva M, Vaughan DM. 1994. Structure and function of ryanodine receptors. Am J Physiol 266: C1485-1504.

d'Amati G, Bagattin A, Bauce B, Rampazzo A, Autore C, Basso C, King K, Romeo MD, Gallo P, Thiene G, Danieli GA, Nava A. 2005. Juvenile sudden death in a family with polymorphic ventricular arrhythmias caused by a novel RyR2 gene mutation: evidence of specific morphological substrates. Hum Pathol 36: 761-767.

Du GG, Maclennan DH. 1999. Ca(2+) inactivation sites are located in the COOH-terminal quarter of recombinant rabbit skeletal muscle Ca(2+) release channels (ryanodine receptors). J Biol Chem 274: 26120-26126.

Du GG, Khanna VK, MacLennan DH. 2000. Mutation of divergent region 1 alters caffeine and Ca(2+) sensitivity of the skeletal muscle Ca(2+) release channel (ryanodine receptor). J Biol Chem 275: 11778-11783.

Du GG, Guo X, Khanna VK, MacLennan DH. 2001. Functional characterization of mutants in the predicted pore region of the rabbit cardiac muscle Ca(2+) release channel (ryanodine receptor isoform 2). J Biol Chem 276: 31760-31771.

Durham WJ, Wehrens XH, Sood S, Hamilton SL. 2007. Diseases associated with altered ryanodine receptor activity. Subcell Biochem 45: 273-321.

Ebashi S, Ogawa Y. 1988. Ca2+ in contractile processes. Biophys Chem 29: 137-143.

El-Hayek R, Saiki Y, Yamamoto T, Ikemoto N. 1999. A postulated role of the near amino-terminal domain of the ryanodine receptor in the regulation of the sarcoplasmic reticulum Ca(2+) channel. J Biol Chem 274: 33341-33347.

Fabiato A. 1985. Time and calcium dependence of activation and inactivation of calcium-induced release of calcium from the sarcoplasmic reticulum of a skinned canine cardiac Purkinje cell. J Gen Physiol 85: 247-289.

Faltinova A, Gaburjakova J, Zahradnikova A. 2011. Activation of the rat cardiac ryanodine receptor by its domain peptide DPcpvt-C. Physiol Res 60: *in press*.

Finn RD, Tate J, Mistry J, Coggill PC, Sammut SJ, Hotz HR, Ceric G, Forslund K, Eddy SR, Sonnhammer EL, Bateman A. 2008. The Pfam protein families database. Nucleic Acids Res 36: D281-288.

Fiser A, Do RK, Sali A. 2000. Modeling of loops in protein structures. Protein Sci 9: 1753-1773.

Gaburjakova J, Gaburjakova M. 2006. Comparison of the effects exerted by luminal Ca2+ on the sensitivity of the cardiac ryanodine receptor to caffeine and cytosolic Ca2+. J Membr Biol 212: 17-28.

Gao L, Balshaw D, Xu L, Tripathy A, Xin C, Meissner G. 2000. Evidence for a role of the lumenal M3-M4 loop in skeletal muscle Ca(2+) release channel (ryanodine receptor) activity and conductance. Biophys J 79: 828-840.

George CH, Yin CC, Lai FA. 2005. Toward a molecular understanding of the structure-function of ryanodine receptor Ca2+ release channels: perspectives from recombinant expression systems. Cell Biochem Biophys 42: 197-222.

George CH, Jundi H, Thomas NL, Fry DL, Lai FA. 2007. Ryanodine receptors and ventricular arrhythmias: emerging trends in mutations, mechanisms and therapies. J Mol Cell Cardiol 42: 34-50.

George CH, Jundi H, Thomas NL, Scoote M, Walters N, Williams AJ, Lai FA. 2004. Ryanodine receptor regulation by intramolecular interaction between cytoplasmic and transmembrane domains. Mol Biol Cell 15: 2627-2638.

Gyorke I, Gyorke S. 1998. Regulation of the cardiac ryanodine receptor channel by luminal Ca2+ involves luminal Ca2+ sensing sites. Biophys J 75: 2801-2810.

Gyorke I, Hester N, Jones LR, Gyorke S. 2004. The role of calsequestrin, triadin, and junctin in conferring cardiac ryanodine receptor responsiveness to luminal calcium. Biophys J 86: 2121-2128.

Gyorke S, Fill M. 1993. Ryanodine receptor adaptation: Control mechanism of Ca2+-induced Ca2+ release in heart. Science 260: 807-809.

Gyorke S, Velez P, Suarez-Isla B, Fill M. 1994. Activation of single cardiac and skeletal ryanodine receptor channels by flash photolysis of caged Ca2+. Biophys J 66: 1879-1886.

Hamada T, Tashiro K, Tada H, Inazawa J, Shirozu M, Shibahara K, Nakamura T, Martina N, Nakano T, Honjo T. 1996. Isolation and characterization of a novel secretory protein, stromal cell-derived factor-2 (SDF-2) using the signal sequence trap method. Gene 176: 211-214.

Ikemoto N, Yamamoto T. 2000. Postulated role of inter-domain interaction within the ryanodine receptor in Ca(2+) channel regulation. Trends Cardiovasc Med 10: 310-316.

Johnson WC. 1999. Analyzing protein circular dichroism spectra for accurate secondary structures. Proteins 35: 307-312.

Kagaya Y, Weinberg EO, Ito N, Mochizuki T, Barry WH, Lorell BH. 1995. Glycolytic inhibition: effects on diastolic relaxation and intracellular calcium handling in hypertrophied rat ventricular myocytes. J Clin Invest 95: 2766-2776.

Kettlun C, Gonzalez A, Rios E, Fill M. 2003. Unitary Ca2+ current through mammalian cardiac and amphibian skeletal muscle ryanodine receptor channels under near-physiological ionic conditions. J Gen Physiol 122: 407-417.

Kleiber ML, Singh SM. 2009. Divergence of the vertebrate sp1A/ryanodine receptor domain and SOCS box-containing (Spsb) gene family and its expression and regulation within the mouse brain. Genomics 93: 358-366.

Lai FA, Erickson HP, Rousseau E, Liu QY, Meissner G. 1988. Purification and reconstitution of the calcium release channel from skeletal muscle. Nature 331: 315-319.

Lamb GD. 1993. Ca2+ inactivation, Mg2+ inhibition and malignant hyperthermia. J Muscle Res Cell Motil 14: 554-556.

Lanner JT, Georgiou DK, Joshi AD, Hamilton SL. 2010. Ryanodine receptors: structure, expression, molecular details, and function in calcium release. Cold Spring Harb Perspect Biol 2: a003996.

Laver DR. 2007. Ca2+ stores regulate ryanodine receptor Ca2+ release channels via luminal and cytosolic Ca2+ sites. Biophys J 92: 3541-3555.

Laver DR. 2009. Luminal Ca(2+) activation of cardiac ryanodine receptors by luminal and cytoplasmic domains. Eur Biophys J 39: 19-26.

Laver DR, Honen BN. 2008. Luminal Mg2+, a key factor controlling RYR2-mediated Ca2+ release: cytoplasmic and luminal regulation modeled in a tetrameric channel. J Gen Physiol 132: 429-446.

Laver DR, Baynes TM, Dulhunty AF. 1997. Magnesium inhibition of ryanodine-receptor calcium channels: Evidence for two independent mechanisms. J Membr Biol 156: 213-229.

Li P, Chen SR. 2001. Molecular basis of Ca(2)+ activation of the mouse cardiac Ca(2)+ release channel (ryanodine receptor). J Gen Physiol 118: 33-44.

Liu Z, Zhang J, Li P, Chen SR, Wagenknecht T. 2002. Three-dimensional reconstruction of the recombinant type 2 ryanodine receptor and localization of its divergent region 1. J Biol Chem 277: 46712-46719.

Liu Z, Zhang J, Wang R, Wayne Chen SR, Wagenknecht T. 2004. Location of divergent region 2 on the three-dimensional structure of cardiac muscle ryanodine receptor/calcium release channel. J Mol Biol 338: 533-545.

Liu Z, Wang R, Zhang J, Chen SR, Wagenknecht T. 2005. Localization of a disease-associated mutation site in the three-dimensional structure of the cardiac muscle ryanodine receptor. J Biol Chem 280: 37941-37947.

Liu Z, Zhang J, Sharma MR, Li P, Chen SR, Wagenknecht T. 2001. Three-dimensional reconstruction of the recombinant type 3 ryanodine receptor and localization of its amino terminus. Proc Natl Acad Sci U S A 98: 6104-6109.

Lobo PA, Van Petegem F. 2009. Crystal structures of the N-terminal domains of cardiac and skeletal muscle ryanodine receptors: insights into disease mutations. Structure 17: 1505-1514.

Lopez-Lopez JR, Shacklock PS, Balke CW, Wier WG. 1995. Local calcium transients triggered by single L-type calcium channel currents in cardiac cells. Science 268: 1042-1045.

Lukyanenko V, Gyorke I, Subramanian S, Smirnov A, Wiesner TF, Gyorke S. 2000. Inhibition of Ca(2+) sparks by ruthenium red in permeabilized rat ventricular myocytes. Biophys J 79: 1273-1284.

Marjamaa A, Laitinen-Forsblom P, Lahtinen AM, Viitasalo M, Toivonen L, Kontula K, Swan H. 2009. Search for cardiac calcium cycling gene mutations in familial ventricular arrhythmias resembling catecholaminergic polymorphic ventricular tachycardia. BMC Med Genet 10: 12.

Marx SO, Marks AR. 2002. Regulation of the ryanodine receptor in heart failure. Basic Res Cardiol 97 Suppl 1: I49-51.

Marx SO, Reiken S, Hisamatsu Y, Gaburjakova M, Gaburjakova J, Yang YM, Rosemblit N, Marks AR. 2001. Phosphorylation-dependent regulation of ryanodine receptors: a novel role for leucine/isoleucine zippers. J Cell Biol 153: 699-708.

Medeiros-Domingo A, Bhuiyan ZA, Tester DJ, Hofman N, Bikker H, van Tintelen JP, Mannens MM, Wilde AA, Ackerman MJ. 2009. The RYR2-encoded ryanodine receptor/calcium release channel in patients diagnosed previously with either catecholaminergic polymorphic ventricular tachycardia or genotype negative, exercise-induced long QT syndrome: a comprehensive open reading frame mutational analysis. J Am Coll Cardiol 54: 2065-2074.

Meissner G. 1994. Ryanodine receptor/Ca2+ release channels and their regulation by endogenous effectors. Annu Rev Physiol 56: 485-508.

Meissner G. 2002. Regulation of mammalian ryanodine receptors. Front Biosci 7: d2072-2080.

Meissner G. 2004. Molecular regulation of cardiac ryanodine receptor ion channel. Cell Calcium 35: 621-628.

Meissner G, Henderson JS. 1987. Rapid calcium release from cardiac sarcoplasmic reticulum vesicles is dependent on Ca2+ and is modulated by Mg2+, adenine nucleotide, and calmodulin. J Biol Chem 262: 3065-3073.

Mejia-Alvarez R, Kettlun C, Rios E, Stern M, Fill M. 1999. Unitary Ca2+ current through cardiac ryanodine receptor channels under quasi-physiological ionic conditions. J Gen Physiol 113: 177-186.

Milting H, Lukas N, Klauke B, Korfer R, Perrot A, Osterziel KJ, Vogt J, Peters S, Thieleczek R, Varsanyi M. 2006. Composite polymorphisms in the ryanodine receptor 2 gene associated with arrhythmogenic right ventricular cardiomyopathy. Cardiovasc Res 71: 496-505.

Murzin AG, Lesk AM, Chothia C. 1992. beta-Trefoil fold. Patterns of structure and sequence in the Kunitz inhibitors interleukins-1 beta and 1 alpha and fibroblast growth factors. J Mol Biol 223: 531-543.

Ono M, et al. 2010. Dissociation of calmodulin from cardiac ryanodine receptor causes aberrant Ca(2+) release in heart failure. Cardiovasc Res 87: 609-617.

Orlova EV, Serysheva II, van Heel M, Hamilton SL, Chiu W. 1996. Two structural configurations of the skeletal muscle calcium release channel. Nat Struct Biol 3: 547-552.

Parker I, Zang WJ, Wier WG. 1996. Ca2+ sparks involving multiple Ca2+ release sites along Z-lines in rat heart cells. J Physiol (Lond) 497: 31-38.

Perez CF, Mukherjee S, Allen PD. 2003. Amino acids 1-1,680 of ryanodine receptor type 1 hold critical determinants of skeletal type for excitation-contraction coupling. Role of divergence domain D2. J Biol Chem 278: 39644-39652.

Ponting C, Schultz J, Bork P. 1997. SPRY domains in ryanodine receptors (Ca(2+)-release channels). Trends Biochem Sci 22: 193-194.

Ponting CP. 2000. Novel repeats in ryanodine and IP3 receptors and protein O-mannosyltransferases. Trends Biochem Sci 25: 48-50.

Protasi F. 2002. Structural interaction between RYRs and DHPRs in calcium release units of cardiac and skeletal muscle cells. Front Biosci 7: d650-658.

Qin J, Valle G, Nani A, Nori A, Rizzi N, Priori SG, Volpe P, Fill M. 2008. Luminal Ca2+ regulation of single cardiac ryanodine receptors: insights provided by calsequestrin and its mutants. J Gen Physiol 131: 325-334.

Rhodes DA, de Bono B, Trowsdale J. 2005. Relationship between SPRY and B30.2 protein domains. Evolution of a component of immune defence? Immunology 116: 411-417.

Rios E, Brum G. 1987. Involvement of dihydropyridine receptors in excitation-contraction coupling in skeletal muscle. Nature 325: 717-720.

Rios E, Karhanek M, Ma J, Gonzalez A. 1993. An allosteric model of the molecular interactions of excitation-contraction coupling in skeletal muscle. J Gen Physiol 102: 449-481.

Sali A, Blundell TL. 1993. Comparative protein modelling by satisfaction of spatial restraints. J Mol Biol 234: 779-815.

Samso M, Wagenknecht T. 2002. Apocalmodulin and Ca2+-calmodulin bind to neighboring locations on the ryanodine receptor. J Biol Chem 277: 1349-1353.

Samso M, Feng W, Pessah IN, Allen PD. 2009. Coordinated movement of cytoplasmic and transmembrane domains of RyR1 upon gating. PLoS Biol 7: e85.

Santana LF, Cheng H, Gomez AM, Cannell MB, Lederer WJ. 1996. Relation between the sarcolemmal Ca2+ current and Ca2+ sparks and local control theories for cardiac excitation-contraction coupling. Circ Res 78: 166-171.

Schiefer A, Meissner G, Isenberg G. 1995. Ca2+ activation and Ca2+ inactivation of canine reconstituted cardiac sarcoplasmic reticulum Ca(2+)-release channels. J Physiol (Lond) 489: 337-348.

Serysheva, II, Hamilton SL, Chiu W, Ludtke SJ. 2005. Structure of Ca2+ release channel at 14 A resolution. J Mol Biol 345: 427-431.

Serysheva, II, Schatz M, van Heel M, Chiu W, Hamilton SL. 1999. Structure of the skeletal muscle calcium release channel activated with Ca2+ and AMP-PCP. Biophys J 77: 1936-1944.

Serysheva, II, Ludtke SJ, Baker ML, Cong Y, Topf M, Eramian D, Sali A, Hamilton SL, Chiu W. 2008. Subnanometer-resolution electron cryomicroscopy-based domain models for the cytoplasmic region of skeletal muscle RyR channel. Proc Natl Acad Sci U S A 105: 9610-9615.

Shannon TR, Guo T, Bers DM. 2003. Ca2+ scraps: local depletions of free [Ca2+] in cardiac sarcoplasmic reticulum during contractions leave substantial Ca2+ reserve. Circ Res 93: 40-45.

Sharma MR, Jeyakumar LH, Fleischer S, Wagenknecht T. 2000. Three-dimensional structure of ryanodine receptor isoform three in two conformational states as visualized by cryo-electron microscopy. J Biol Chem 275: 9485-9491.

Sharma MR, Penczek P, Grassucci R, Xin HB, Fleischer S, Wagenknecht T. 1998. Cryoelectron microscopy and image analysis of the cardiac ryanodine receptor. J Biol Chem 273: 18429-18434.

Shatsky M, Nussinov R, Wolfson HJ. 2004. A method for simultaneous alignment of multiple protein structures. Proteins 56: 143-156.

Smith JS, Imagawa T, Ma J, Fill M, Campbell KP, Coronado R. 1988. Purified ryanodine receptor from rabbit skeletal muscle is the calcium-release channel of sarcoplasmic reticulum. J Gen Physiol 92: 1-26.

Sorrentino V. 1995. The ryanodine receptor family of intracellular calcium release channels. Adv Pharmacol 33: 67-90.

Stern MD. 1992. Theory of excitation - contraction coupling in cardiac muscle. Biophys J 63: 497-517.

Strahl-Bolsinger S, Scheinost A. 1999. Transmembrane topology of pmt1p, a member of an evolutionarily conserved family of protein O-mannosyltransferases. J Biol Chem 274: 9068-9075.

Takasago T, Imagawa T, Furukawa K, Ogurusu T, Shigekawa M. 1991. Regulation of the cardiac ryanodine receptor by protein kinase-dependent phosphorylation. J Biochem 109: 163-170.

Tateishi H, Yano M, Mochizuki M, Suetomi T, Ono M, Xu X, Uchinoumi H, Okuda S, Oda T, Kobayashi S, Yamamoto T, Ikeda Y, Ohkusa T, Ikemoto N, Matsuzaki M. 2009. Defective domain-domain interactions within the ryanodine receptor as a critical cause of diastolic Ca2+ leak in failing hearts. Cardiovasc Res 81: 536-545.

Terentyev D, Kubalova Z, Valle G, Nori A, Vedamoorthyrao S, Terentyeva R, Viatchenko-Karpinski S, Bers DM, Williams SC, Volpe P, Gyorke S. 2008. Modulation of SR Ca release by luminal Ca and calsequestrin in cardiac myocytes: effects of CASQ2 mutations linked to sudden cardiac death. Biophys J 95: 2037-2048.

Tester DJ, Kopplin LJ, Will ML, Ackerman MJ. 2005. Spectrum and prevalence of cardiac ryanodine receptor (RyR2) mutations in a cohort of unrelated patients referred explicitly for long QT syndrome genetic testing. Heart Rhythm 2: 1099-1105.

Tester DJ, Arya P, Will M, Haglund CM, Farley AL, Makielski JC, Ackerman MJ. 2006. Genotypic heterogeneity and phenotypic mimicry among unrelated patients referred for catecholaminergic polymorphic ventricular tachycardia genetic testing. Heart Rhythm 3: 800-805.

Tung CC, Lobo PA, Kimlicka L, Van Petegem F. 2010. The amino-terminal disease hotspot of ryanodine receptors forms a cytoplasmic vestibule. Nature 468: 585-588.

Unnerstale S, Lind J, Papadopoulos E, Maler L. 2009. Solution structure of the HsapBK K+ channel voltage-sensor paddle sequence. Biochemistry 48: 5813-5821.

Valdivia HH, Kaplan JH, Ellis-Davies GC, Lederer WJ. 1995. Rapid adaptation of cardiac ryanodine receptors: modulation by Mg2+ and phosphorylation. Science 267: 1997-2000.

Velez P, Gyorke S, Escobar AL, Vergara J, Fill M. 1997. Adaptation of single cardiac ryanodine receptor channels. Biophys J 72: 691-697.

Wagenknecht T, Samso M. 2002. Three-dimensional reconstruction of ryanodine receptors. Front Biosci 7: d1464-1474.

Wang R, Zhong X, Meng X, Koop A, Tian X, Jones PP, Fruen BR, Wagenknecht T, Liu Z, Chen SR. 2011. Localization of the dantrolene-binding sequence near the FK506-binding protein-binding site in the three-dimensional structure of the ryanodine receptor. J Biol Chem 286: 12202-12212.

Wang SQ, Song LS, Lakatta EG, Cheng H. 2001. Ca2+ signalling between single L-type Ca2+ channels and ryanodine receptors in heart cells. Nature 410: 592-596.

Wang SQ, Stern MD, Rios E, Cheng H. 2004. The quantal nature of Ca2+ sparks and in situ operation of the ryanodine receptor array in cardiac cells. Proc Natl Acad Sci U S A 101: 3979-3984.

Whitmore L, Wallace BA. 2004. DICHROWEB, an online server for protein secondary structure analyses from circular dichroism spectroscopic data. Nucleic Acids Res 32: W668-673.

Williams AJ. 1992. Ion conduction and discrimination in the sarcoplasmic reticulum ryanodine receptor/calcium-release channel. J Muscle Res Cell Motil 13: 7-26.

Williams AJ, West DJ, Sitsapesan R. 2001. Light at the end of the Ca(2+)-release channel tunnel: structures and mechanisms involved in ion translocation in ryanodine receptor channels. Q Rev Biophys 34: 61-104.

Witcher DR, Kovacs RJ, Schulman H, Cefali DC, Jones LR. 1991. Unique phosphorylation site on the cardiac ryanodine receptor regulates calcium channel activity. J Biol Chem 266: 11144-11152.

Woo JS, Imm JH, Min CK, Kim KJ, Cha SS, Oh BH. 2006. Structural and functional insights into the B30.2/SPRY domain. EMBO J 25: 1353-1363.

Xiong L, Zhang JZ, He R, Hamilton SL. 2006. A Ca2+-binding domain in RyR1 that interacts with the calmodulin binding site and modulates channel activity. Biophys J 90: 173-182.

Xu L, Meissner G. 1998. Regulation of cardiac muscle Ca2+ release channel by sarcoplasmic reticulum lumenal Ca2+. Biophys J 75: 2302-2312.

Xu L, Mann G, Meissner G. 1996. Regulation of cardiac Ca2+ release channel (ryanodine receptor) by Ca2+, H+, Mg2+, and adenine nucleotides under normal and simulated ischemic conditions. Circ Res 79: 1100-1109.

Xu X, Bhat MB, Nishi M, Takeshima H, Ma J. 2000. Molecular cloning of cDNA encoding a drosophila ryanodine receptor and functional studies of the carboxyl-terminal calcium release channel. Biophys J 78: 1270-1281.

Xu X, et al. 2010. Defective calmodulin binding to the cardiac ryanodine receptor plays a key role in CPVT-associated channel dysfunction. Biochem Biophys Res Commun 394: 660-666.

Yamamoto T, Ikemoto N. 2002. Peptide probe study of the critical regulatory domain of the cardiac ryanodine receptor. Biochem Biophys Res Commun 291: 1102-1108.

Yamamoto T, El-Hayek R, Ikemoto N. 2000. Postulated role of interdomain interaction within the ryanodine receptor in Ca(2+) channel regulation. J Biol Chem 275: 11618-11625.

Yamamoto T, Yano M, Xu X, Uchinoumi H, Tateishi H, Mochizuki M, Oda T, Kobayashi S, Ikemoto N, Matsuzaki M. 2008. Identification of target domains of the cardiac ryanodine receptor to correct channel disorder in failing hearts. Circulation 117: 762-772.

Yang Z, Ikemoto N, Lamb GD, Steele DS. 2006. The RyR2 central domain peptide DPc10 lowers the threshold for spontaneous Ca2+ release in permeabilized cardiomyocytes. Cardiovasc Res 70: 475-485.

Yano M, Yamamoto T, Ikeda Y, Matsuzaki M. 2006. Mechanisms of Disease: ryanodine receptor defects in heart failure and fatal arrhythmia. Nat Clin Pract Cardiovasc Med 3: 43-52.

Yao S, Liu MS, Masters SL, Zhang JG, Babon JJ, Nicola NA, Nicholson SE, Norton RS. 2006. Dynamics of the SPRY domain-containing SOCS box protein 2: flexibility of key functional loops. Protein Sci 15: 2761-2772.

Yuchi Z, Van Petegem F. 2011. Common allosteric mechanisms between ryanodine and inositol-1,4,5-trisphosphate receptors. Channels (Austin) 5: 120-123.

Zahradnik I, Gyorke S, Zahradnikova A. 2005. Calcium activation of ryanodine receptor channels--reconciling RyR gating models with tetrameric channel structure. J Gen Physiol 126: 515-527.

Zahradnikova A, Zahradnik I. 1999. Analysis of calcium-induced calcium release in cardiac sarcoplasmic reticulum vesicles using models derived from single-channel data. Biochim Biophys Acta 1418: 268-284.

Zahradnikova A, Valent I, Zahradnik I. 2010. Frequency and release flux of calcium sparks in rat cardiac myocytes: a relation to RYR gating. J Gen Physiol 136: 101-116.

Zahradnikova A, Zahradnik I, Gyorke I, Gyorke S. 1999. Rapid activation of the cardiac ryanodine receptor by submillisecond calcium stimuli. J Gen Physiol 114: 787-798.

Zahradnikova A, Dura M, Gyorke I, Escobar AL, Zahradnik I, Gyorke S. 2003. Regulation of dynamic behavior of cardiac ryanodine receptor by Mg2+ under simulated physiological conditions. Am J Physiol Cell Physiol 285: C1059-1070.

Zhang J, Liu Z, Masumiya H, Wang R, Jiang D, Li F, Wagenknecht T, Chen SR. 2003. Three-dimensional localization of divergent region 3 of the ryanodine receptor to the clamp-shaped structures adjacent to the FKBP binding sites. J Biol Chem 278: 14211-14218.

Zhao M, Li P, Li X, Zhang L, Winkfein RJ, Chen SR. 1999. Molecular identification of the ryanodine receptor pore-forming segment. J Biol Chem 274: 25971-25974.

Zimanyi I, Pessah IN. 1991. Comparison of [3H]ryanodine receptors and Ca++ release from rat cardiac and rabbit skeletal muscle sarcoplasmic reticulum. J Pharmacol Exp Ther 256: 938-946.

17

Identifying Enzyme Knockout Strategies on Multiple Enzyme Associations

Bin Song[1], I. Esra Büyüktahtakın[2], Nirmalya Bandyopadhyay[1],
Sanjay Ranka[1] and Tamer Kahveci[1]
[1]CISE Department, University of Florida, Gainesville
[2]Systems and Industrial Engineering, University of Arizona, Tucson
USA

1. Introduction

Many biochemical engineering applications in drug discovery, food generation and cosmetic production, aim to modify the metabolism of a given organism to increase or decrease the production of a specific compound or a set of compounds. For example:

1. Fatty acid biosynthesis pathway converts fatty acids that are used in the cosmetic industry in creams and lotions.

2. Butanoate metabolism produces poly-β-hydroxybutyrate which is essential for producing plastics.

3. Mevalonic acid pathway and MEP/DOXP pathway produce carotenoid that are often used as anti-oxidant in food industry. The metabolisms of many organisms, such as bacteria, algae and plants naturally produce these compounds. A common practice is to extract them from these organisms.

Enzymes play a significant role in metabolism. They catalyze the chemical reactions that transform a set of substrates (i.e., input compounds) into products (i.e., output compounds). Metabolic engineering techniques often aim to manipulate a small set of genes to alter the speed of the targeted enzymatic reactions. Their eventual goal is to reach a desired level of compound concentrations produced or consumed by these reactions. One way to alter the speed of the reactions dramatically is to knockout a set of enzymes. When an enzyme is knocked out, it cannot catalyze a subset of the reactions, resulting in changes to the productions of compounds.

When detailed *in silico* models are available, computational methods can be successfully used to determine the enzyme set to knockout. These methods, when applicable, have much lower time and cost requirements as compared to *in vitro* or *in vivo* experiments conducted in wet labs. Wet-lab experiments often require substantial effort and time of the domain experts and overall time requirements may be hours to several days. Moreover, the cost of wet-lab experimentation significantly increases when the number of enzymes that needs to be knocked out is more than one. Manipulations that involve four to six enzymes are not uncommon. As a result, biologists often employ computational methods as a preprocessing step to filter out less promising compounds.

A number of heuristic *in silico* solutions exist to find a promising set of enzymes. However, finding the set of enzymes whose knockout leads to achieving the optimal compound production rate is a computationally difficult problem. The number of possible subsets of enzymes that can be considered for manipulation grows exponentially with the number of enzymes in the pathway. Even if the size of each potential subset is limited to at most four, the number of possible subsets for a pathway consisting of 500 enzymes is more than 2.5 billion. Therefore, efficient methods that avoid inspecting the entire search space are necessary.

In order to find a promising set of enzymes to knock out, we first need to provide a computational method to evaluate the metabolic system after some enzymes are knocked out. There are several models to simulate the steady state of a metabolic network. We categorize these methods into three different groups named, boolean models, linear models and non-linear models. Boolean models can be an oversimplification of the metabolic network, especially if the number of reactions and their connectivity increase. Non-linear models require additional information about the network, which may not be available. *Flux Balance Analysis, (FBA)* is a popular linear model which is widely used to compute the flux distribution on the steady state of metabolic networks (Bonarius et al., 1997; Forster et al., 2003; Kauffman et al., 2003). Segre et al. presented a quadratic programming method, named minimization of metabolic adjustment(MOMA) (Segre et al., 2002). Shlomi et al. described a MIP method, called regulatory on/off minimization (ROOM) for predicting the metabolic steady states after the gene or enzyme knockouts (Shlomi et al., 2005).

It is easy to use these models to determine the impact on the metabolism, when a given set of genes are knocked out. However, as discussed earlier, we are interested in finding the subset of enzymes that lead to a desired impact. Optknock (Burgard et al., 2003), OptReg (Pharkya & Maranas, 2006) and OptStrain (Pharkya et al., 2004) are three MIP based methods for identifying the enzymes to be knocked out for the FBA model. All these methods make the simplifying assumption that each reaction can be catalyzed by only one enzyme. This simplification allows a quick conversion of the underlying variables using linear constraints, where MILP or quadratic programming can be used to solve the problem. However, in real metabolic networks, more than one enzyme can be involved in catalyzing a reaction. In particular, more than two enzymes can substitute each other or work collaboratively to catalyze a reaction. Figure 1 illustrates this on a real example we adopted from Reed et al. (Reed et al., 2003). Here we describe these two kinds of enzyme collaborations in brief.

- **Collaborative enzymes:** Some reactions require the presence of two or more proteins or enzymes simultaneously. We call such enzymes as *collaborative enzymes*. In this case, absence of even one of these enzymes is sufficient to slow down or stop the reaction. Logically, there is an Boolean *AND* relation among these enzymes. In Figure 1 (top portion), D-Xylose ABC Transporter is responsible for exporting/importing a variety of molecules to and from bacteria. To carry out this function the genes XylF, XylG and XylH jointly work to catalyze the reaction XYLabc.

- **Substitute enzymes:** Two or more enzymes can substitute each other in catalyzing a reaction. We call such enzymes as *substitute enzymes*. In this case, the presence of one of the substitute enzymes suffices to carry out that reaction. Logically, there is a Boolean *OR* relation among these enzymes. In Figure 1 (bottom portion), Glyceraldehyde 3-Phosphate Dehydrogenase works in a number of metabolic pathways such as the Glycolysis / Gluconeogenesis pathway or biosynthesis of phenylpropanoids. In a number of organisms such as *Arabidopsis thaliana* (*A. thaliana*) this can be done by GapA or GapC with *OR* association.

One can easily generalize the notion of collaborative and substitute enzymes. Thus, a complex topology consisting of multiple enzymes connected by a combination of *OR* and *AND* may catalyze a reaction.

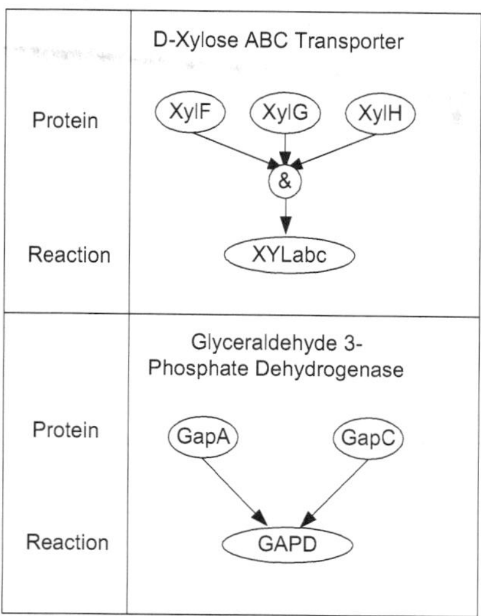

Fig. 1. The figure depicts two examples of reactions catalyzed by multiple enzymes. In the top portion, D-Xylose ABC Transporter is responsible for exporting/importing a variety of molecules to and from bacteria. To carry out this function the genes XylF, XylG and XylH jointly work to catalyze the reaction XYLabc with *AND* association. In the other portion, Glyceraldehyde 3-Phosphate Dehydrogenase works in a number of metabolic pathways such as the Glycolysis / Gluconeogenesis pathway or biosynthesis of phenylpropanoids.

Our goal aims to find the optimal set of enzymes in the presence of multiple enzymes jointly catalyzing the same reaction to knock out so that the production of the system is optimal. In summary, the main contributions of this chapter are as follows:

- We prove that the problem of finding the optimal enzyme set to knockout using MIPL-based approaches is NP-hard even when only one enzyme catalyzes each reaction. This proof is also corroborated by the fact that when the network size increases, the execution time of Optknock framework increases exponentially.

- We develop two solutions to deal with multiple enzyme association along with linear constraints. Our solutions eliminate the limitation that each reaction is catalyzed by a single enzyme. In our model, we allow multiple substitute and collaborative enzymes. Our first solution uses a small number of binary variables in the underlying MILP formulation. The second method increases the number of binary variables but requires a smaller number of constraints. Inclusion of multiple enzymes significantly extends the applicability of our methods, as in real networks, multiple enzymes can catalyze a reaction.

Our experiments using the synthetic and real datasets demonstrate that allowing multiple enzymes to catalyze a reaction increases the computational cost of the solution as compared to the cases when all reactions are catalyzed by a single enzyme. In our experiments, we observe that our second method that introduces extra binary variables is significantly superior to our first method in terms of execution time. These results also demonstrate that the enzyme topology can have a substantial influence on the performance of the MILP solution.

The rest of the chapter is organized as follows. Section 2 discusses the related work for this chapter. Section 3 proves that finding the optimal set of enzymes to knock out using MILP is NP-hard even when we allow only one enzyme to catalyze each reaction. Section 4 describes the proposed methods when a reaction is catalyzed by multiple enzymes. Section 5 discusses experimental results. We conclude our discussion in Section 6.

2. Related work

In order to identify a promising set of enzymes to knock out, we first require a computational method to evaluate the state of the metabolic system after multiple knockouts. There are several models to simulate the steady state of a metabolic network. These methods can be classified into three categories named Boolean models, linear models and non-linear models.

- **Boolean Models:** Boolean models consider each enzyme as a boolean variable. Each variable can take a either true or false value representing whether the corresponding enzyme is active or inactive. Each reaction is a boolean predicate that depends on these variables. A reaction takes place only if its predicate evaluates to true. Sridhar et al. and Song et al. propose a boolean model of the enzyme knockout strategy (Song et al., 2007; Sridhar et al., 2007; 2008). These methods require the user to supply a list of *targeted compounds* along with a metabolic network. The goal is to identify the set of enzymes whose deletion stop producing all the targeted compounds while causing minimum *damage*. Here, we define damage as the number of non-targeted compounds that are eliminated because of the knockouts. Minimum damage is defined as the minimum number of non-targeted compounds eliminated from the metabolism while eliminating the targeted compounds given all possible ways of eliminating the targeted compounds. Sridhar et al. propounds an optimal algorithm for this model (Sridhar et al., 2008). Song et al. discusses a heuristic algorithm for finding the knockout enzyme strategy (Song et al., 2007). Klamt et al. finds the enzymes for knockout by finding a minimal set of reactions whose deletion leads to an infeasible balanced flux distribution. It employs a minimum cut approach to solve the problem (Klamt & Gilles, 2004).

- **Linear models:** Boolean models can be an oversimplification of the metabolic network, specially when the number of reactions and their connectivity increase. *Flux Balance Analysis, (FBA)* is a popular technique used to analyze the steady state of metabolic networks (Bonarius et al., 1997; Forster et al., 2003; Kauffman et al., 2003). FBA describes a metabolic network as a set of linear equations. FBA finds an optimal steady-state flux distribution that maximizes growth rate under constraints such as mass balance and capacity. FBA achieves a successful description of the metabolic state system by predicting growth rate and by-products of the metabolism (Edwards & Palsson, 2000a;b; Kauffman et al., 2003). However, FBA may not be able to predict an accurate metabolic state after gene or enzyme knockouts. Segre et al. presents a quadratic programming method named minimization of metabolic adjustment (MOMA) for simulation of the resultant state after knockouts (Segre et al., 2002). MOMA attempts to minimize the changes between the flux distribution after a knockout. MOMA uses linear constraints such as mass balance, capacity, and knockout constraints, which are the same set of constraints used by FBA.

Shlomi et al. describes a mixed integer programming method, named regulatory on/off minimization (ROOM), for predicting the metabolic steady states after gene or enzyme knockouts (Shlomi et al., 2005). ROOM finds the flux distribution which minimizes the number of significant flux changes from the wild-type flux distribution. Experiments demonstrate that MOMA and ROOM are superior to FBA in their ability to predict the resultant states after gene or enzyme knockouts. Optknock is an enzyme knockout strategy based on the FBA model (Burgard et al., 2003). It uses a bi-level programming framework for identifying the enzymes to be knocked out. In the inner level, the optimization finds the flux distribution for a given cellular objective such as maximization of biomass yield or minimization of metabolic adjustment (MOMA) (Alper et al., 2005; Segre et al., 2002) etc). In the outer level, the optimization finds the enzymes to be knocked out to optimize a biological objective (e.g., chemical production). OptReg is another bilevel programming method for the enzyme knockout strategy (Pharkya & Maranas, 2006). The difference between Optknock and OptReg is that Optknock framework considers only two states (knockout vs non-knockout) for each reaction which are controlled by enzymes. However, OptReg considers three sets of binary variables for each reaction. These correspond to knockout or non-knockout and down regulation or up regulation. Thus, OptReg provides more candidate manipulation solutions for enzymes. OptStrain, a MILP based method, identifies desired phenotypes by adding or deleting genes or enzymes (Pharkya et al., 2004). All of the above methods use a MILP or a quadratic programming method. Although the objective function of these methods may not be linear, the constraints are linear.

- **Non-linear models:** Although less prevalent, these methods are also used to describe metabolic networks. These methods incorporate further details about the network and thus can simulate the cell system better than the linear model. S-systems (Savageau & Voit, 1987; Voit, 2000) and GMA model (Peschel & Mende, 1986; Voit, 2000) are two examples of non-linear models for metabolic networks. Song et al. proposes methods for these non-linear models (Song et al., 2011). Patil et al. presents an evolutionary programming method which can be applied to non-linear models (Patil et al., 2005). These heuristic solutions use non-linear models with non-linear constraints. They are not guaranteed to produce optimal solutions. Also, the non-linear constraint models require additional information about the network, which may not be available. Therefore, in this chapter we still focus on the linear constraint model.

The methods described in this chapter use a linear model. Our major contribution, as discussed already, is to allow multiple enzymes to catalyze a reaction. This significantly extends the usability of such methods, as in real networks more than one enzymes can catalyze a reaction.

3. Problem formulation

Given a metabolic network and an objective function, one standard way to find the optimal set of enzyme knockouts is to solve the problem as an MILP which is modeled using FBA. In this section, we focus on the MILP formulation of the enzyme knockout problem and prove that the problem is NP-hard even when a single enzyme catalyzes each reaction.

3.1 Formulation

Given a set $N = \{1, ..., \bar{N}\}$ of N metabolites and a set $M = \{1, ..., \bar{M}\}$ of M metabolic reactions, our goal is to determine the maximum yield of the desired products in a metabolic network while minimizing the enzyme knockout costs. We summarize the decision variables as follows:

v_j : the flux of reaction j;
y_j : binary variable which equals to 0 if an enzyme in reaction j is knocked out, and 1 otherwise.

Other relevant parameters used in this problem are:

S_{ij} : stoichiometric matrix coefficient of metabolite i in reaction j;
l_j : minimum possible flow corresponding to flux j;
u_j : maximum possible flow corresponding to flux j;
h_j : cost of blocking the enzyme corresponding to reaction j;
w_j : weight corresponding to the value of flux j.

Here, l_j and u_j are estimated by minimizing and maximizing every reaction flux subject to the constraints from the *enzyme knockout flux balance model (EKFB)* framework given below.

Let I be a set of external metabolites that are imposed on the pathway, and J be the set of metabolites that will not be used within the pathway once they are produced. We denote the flux of the source metabolites in the metabolic pathway by b_i and the flux of the sink metabolites by c_i.

Given these variables and parameters, we represent the integer programming formulation for EKFB as follows:

$$\max \sum_{j \in M} w_j v_j - \sum_{j \in M} h_j (1 - y_j) \tag{1}$$

$$\text{s.t.} \quad \sum_{j \in M} S_{ij} v_j = \begin{cases} -b_i & \text{if } i \in I; \\ c_i & \text{if } i \in J; \\ 0 & \text{if } i \in N \setminus \{J \cup I\}. \end{cases} \tag{2}$$

$$l_j y_j \leq v_j \leq u_j y_j \quad j \in M \tag{3}$$

$$\sum_{j \in M} (1 - y_j) \leq K, \quad \forall j \in M \tag{4}$$

$$y_j \in \{0, 1\} \quad \forall j \in M. \tag{5}$$

The objective function (1) maximizes weighted flux less fixed charge corresponding to the enzyme knockouts. Constraint (2) provides flux balance equations defined by the stoichiometric matrix. Constraint (3) includes the fixed charge variable y_j. If the enzyme corresponding to reaction j is knocked out, the value of the flux is set to zero and a fixed charge h_j for knocking out the enzyme is imposed. If the fixed charge variable y_j takes value 1, then the lowest flux value is l_j while the highest possible flux value is u_j. Constraint (4) imposes the condition that the maximum number of knockouts is K. Constraints (5) enforce integrality on the fixed charge variables. Similar formulations are provided in Burgard et al. (Burgard et al., 2003), Cover et al. (Covert et al., 2001) and Palsson (Palsson, 2000).

3.2 NP completeness

To prove that finding the enzymes to knockout by EKFB is NP-hard, we show that the uncapacitated fixed charge network flow problem, which is NP-hard, is a special case of the EKFB (Ng & Rardin, 1996). Let $G = (V, A)$ be a directed graph, where V is the set of nodes, A is the set of arcs, $s \in V$ is the single source node, $T \subseteq V$ is a collection of sink vertices and $d_t > 0$ is the demand for node t. Let x_{ij} denote the flow on arc (i, j) with a cost c_{ij}. Let the variable z_{ij} be equal to 1 if arc (i, j) is selected with a fixed cost f_{ij} and 0 otherwise. We then define the *uncapacitated fixed charge network flow problem (UFNF)* as the problem of finding a set of arcs that allow a supply node to send resources to a set of demand nodes, such that the sum of fixed and variable costs are minimized. UFNF can be formulated using the following mixed-integer program:

$$\min \sum_{(i,j) \in A} f_{ij} z_{ij} + \sum_{(i,j) \in A} c_{ij} x_{ij} \tag{6}$$

$$\text{s.t.} \quad \sum_{(i,k) \in A} x_{ik} - \sum_{(k,j) \in A} x_{kj} = \begin{cases} -\sum_{t \in T} d_t & \text{if } k = s; \\ d_k & \text{if } k \in T; \\ 0 & \text{if } k \in V \setminus \{T \cup s\}. \end{cases} \tag{7}$$

$$x_{ij} \leq \lambda z_{ij} \qquad \forall (i,j) \in A \tag{8}$$

$$x_{ij} \geq 0 \qquad \forall (i,j) \in A \tag{9}$$

$$z_{ij} \in \{0, 1\} \qquad \forall (i,j) \in A. \tag{10}$$

The objective function (6) minimizes the sum of the fixed costs associated with selecting arc (i, j) and variable costs for sending flow through (i, j). Constraints (7) are classical flow conservation constraints. Constraints (8) ensure that there can not be any flow if z_{ij} is 0. Also, the maximum flow can be at most λ if z_{ij} is 1. Constraints (9) and (10) ensure that x_{ij} is nonnegative and z_{ij} is binary respectively.

Theorem 1. *Finding the enzyme knockout strategy by EKFB is NP-Hard.*

Proof: Let N' be the set of the metabolites and M' be the set of the reactions in a special case metabolic pathway in EKFB. We model it as a network graph $G' = (N', M')$, where each node represents a metabolite $i \in N'$ and each arc represents a reaction $k \in M'$ using metabolite i to produce metabolite j.

For $i \in N'$ and $k \in M'$, we redefine the stoichiometric matrix S_{ik} as S'_{ij} $(i, j \in N')$ such that (i, j) represents reaction k as follows:

$$S'_{ij} = \begin{cases} 1 & \text{if } (i, j) \in M'; \\ -1 & \text{if } (j, i) \in M'; \\ 0 & \text{otherwise.} \end{cases} \tag{11}$$

Note that S'_{ij} has entries 1, -1, and 0, and thus is a special case of S_{ik}. We also define a new variable $\bar{v}_{ij}$ as the flux corresponding to reaction $k \in M'$. Let $I' \subseteq I$ be a set of external metabolites that are imposed to the pathway, and $J' \subseteq J$ be the set of metabolites that will not be used within the pathway after they are produced. Let us define a parameter $\bar{b}_i$ such that $b_i = \bar{b}_i$ and $c_i = \bar{b}_i$ for each $i \in N'$. By using the stoichiometric matrix S'_{ij} and the new variables $\bar{v}_{ij}$, the constraint (2) can be written as,

$$\sum_{(i,l)\in M'} \bar{v}_{il} - \sum_{(l,j)\in M'} \bar{v}_{lj} = \begin{cases} -\bar{b}_l & \text{if } l \in I'; \\ \bar{b}_l & \text{if } l \in J'; \\ 0 & \text{if } l \in N'\setminus\{I'\cup J'\}. \end{cases} \tag{12}$$

We now define a binary variable $\bar{z}_{ij}$ for each variable y_k, which assumes value 1 if the arc (i,j) is selected and 0 otherwise. We define costs $\bar{c}_{ij}$ and $\bar{f}_{ij}$ such that $\bar{c}_{ij} = -w_k$, $\bar{f}_{ij} = h_k$. Finally, we define a constant $\bar{\lambda}$ as $\bar{\lambda} = u_k$, and set $l_k = 0$ for each reaction $k \in M'$, which is defined by the arc (i,j). Then, the constraint (3) can be written as,

$$0 \le \bar{v}_{ij} \le \bar{\lambda}\bar{z}_{ij} \qquad \forall\, (i,j) \in M' \tag{13}$$

with an objective function,

$$\min \sum_{(i,j)\in M'} \bar{c}_{ij}\bar{v}_{ij} + \sum_{(i,j)\in M'} \bar{f}_{ij}\bar{z}_{ij} \tag{14}$$

Thus, a special case of EKFB with an objective function (14) and constraints (11), (12), (13) and $\bar{z}_{ij} \in \{0,1\}$ is a UFNF and hence EKFB is NP-Hard.   ■

4. Methods for multiple enzymes

In this section, we develop a more general version of EKFB where we allow multiple enzymes to catalyze a reaction. This extension improves the applicability of our methods as in real networks more than one enzymes can catalyze a reaction. In particular, we focus on the constraints (3) and model the possible interactions between enzymes regarding the reactions they catalyze.

Let E_i be a Boolean variable that denotes whether the ith enzyme is active (i.e., $E_i = true$) or inhibited (i.e., $E_i = false$). As discussed earlier, in EKFB, we assume that a reaction can be catalyzed only by a single enzyme. We use the Boolean variable y_i which is equal to 1 if an enzyme is active, and 0 otherwise.

Let us denote the set of variables for the enzymes that are involved in catalyzing the ith reaction with $\mathcal{E}_i \subseteq \{E_1, E_2, \cdots, E_M\}$. For simplicity, we will use the notation $\mathcal{E}_i = \{E_{ij}|\, E_{ij} \in \{E_1, E_2, \cdots, E_M\}\}$ to denote this set. Let F_i be a function on $\{0,1\}^{|\mathcal{E}_i|}$ representing the relationship between the enzymes for the ith reaction. This function takes $\mathcal{E}_i$ as input and produces an integer. It evaluates to 1 if the ith reaction takes place according to the values of the variables in $\mathcal{E}_i$. It evaluates to 0 otherwise. Also, let the constants l_i and u_i represent the minimum and the maximum flux values. We write the second set of constraints as:

$$l_i F_i \le v_i \le u_i F_i. \tag{15}$$

Depending on association between the enzymes that catalyze a reaction, we formulate F_i for three different scenarios.

- A topology consisting only of substitute enzymes that catalyze any reaction. Each reaction may be catalyzed by a single enzyme or a set of enzyme based on the *OR* association i.e., only one of the enzymes need be present to catalyze the reaction (Section 4.1).

- A topology consisting only of collaborative enzymes that catalyze any reaction. Each reaction may be catalyzed by a single enzyme or a set of enzymes based on the *AND* association i.e., all of the enzymes need to be present to catalyze the reaction (Section 4.2).

- A complex topology consisting of multiple enzymes related by a combination of *OR* and *AND* may catalyze a reaction (Section 4.3).

Shlomi et al. presents a way of replacing Boolean expressions that contains two Boolean variables with linear inequalities (Shlomi et al., 2007). However, as the number of Boolean variables grows, the number of additional variables required by this method grows rapidly making the problem nontrivial. In the following sections we discuss two alternative strategies to deal with each of these three scenarios. We name these strategies the *Binary Method* and *Continuous Method*. The former one introduces additional Boolean variables. The second one avoids the addition of Boolean variables, but comes at the expense of additional constraints. We discuss these in detail in the following sections.

4.1 MILP solution in the presence of substitute enzymes

In this section, we consider the case when all the enzymes that catalyze the same reaction can substitute each other. In this case, the presence of at least one of the substitute enzymes is sufficient to carry out the corresponding reaction. Let $\mathcal{E}_i = \{E_{ij}|\ E_{ij} \in \{E_1, E_2, \cdots, E_M\}\}$ denote a set of variables representing the substitute enzymes for reaction i (i.e., flux v_i). Then we write the function F_i that governs the relationship between the variables in $\mathcal{E}_i$ as:

$$F_i = \max_{E_{ij} \in \mathcal{E}_i} \{E_{ij}\}$$

Thus the constraint (15) becomes:

$$l_i \max_{E_{ij} \in \mathcal{E}_i} \{E_{ij}\} \leq v_i \leq u_i \max_{E_{ij} \in \mathcal{E}_i} \{E_{ij}\}. \tag{16}$$

We address the problem of nonlinearity in constraint (16) by performing a variable transformation, which leads to a set of linear constraints. We solve them using traditional MILP solution techniques such as simplex method.

Our linearization technique considers lower and upper bounds separately. We linearize lower bounding constraints given by the inequality $l_i \max_{E_{ij} \in \mathcal{E}_i} \{E_{ij}\} \leq v_i$ as follows,

$$l_i E_{ij} \leq v_i \qquad \forall\ E_{ij} \in \mathcal{E}_i. \tag{17}$$

Linearization of the upper bounding constraints given by the inequality $v_i \leq u_i \max_{E_{ij} \in \mathcal{E}_i} \{E_{ij}\}$ is more complex compared to that of the lower bound. For the linearization, we consider two approaches, namely binary and continuous methods.

Binary method: In this method, we propose the following linear constraints in order to enforce binary restrictions on F_i (i.e., $F_i \in \{0, 1\}$):

$$F_i \geq \frac{\sum_j E_{ij}}{n} \qquad\qquad \forall i \tag{18a}$$

$$F_i \leq \sum_j E_{ij} \qquad\qquad \forall i \tag{18b}$$

$$F_i \in \{0, 1\} \qquad\qquad \forall i \tag{18c}$$

Continuous method: In this method, we define F_i using a continuous variable that takes value in the real domain. We replace the upper bound constraint $v_i \leq u_i \max_{E_{ij} \in \mathcal{E}_i} \{E_{ij}\}$ with the following linear constraints:

$$F_i \leq \sum_j E_{ij} \qquad \qquad \forall i \qquad \qquad (19a)$$

$$F_i \leq 1 \qquad \qquad \forall i \qquad \qquad (19b)$$

$$F_i \geq E_{ij} \qquad \qquad \forall i,j \qquad \qquad (19c)$$

The constraints (19b)- (19c) enforces F_i to assume a binary value, even though we do not directly impose binary restrictions on it.

4.2 MILP solution in the presence of collaborative enzymes

In this section, we consider the case where multiple enzymes collaborate with each other to catalyze the same reaction. In this case, all the enzymes are necessary for the reaction to initiate. Let $\mathcal{E}_i = \{E_{ij} | \ E_{ij} \in \{E_1, E_2, \cdots, E_M\}\}$ denote a set of variables representing the substitute enzymes for reaction i (i.e., flux v_i). We write the function F_i that governs the relationship between the variables in $\mathcal{E}_i$ as:

$$F_i = \min_{E_{ij} \in \mathcal{E}_i} \{E_{ij}\}$$

Thus, we write constraint (15) as,

$$l_i \min_{E_{ij} \in \mathcal{E}_i} \{E_{ij}\} \leq v_i \leq u_i \min_{E_{ij} \in \mathcal{E}_i} \{E_{ij}\}. \qquad \qquad (20)$$

As we discussed in Section 4.1, constraint (20) is nonlinear. We linearize this constraint using additional variables. We address lower and upper bounds separately.

First, we focus on the upper bound constraints given by the inequality $v_i \leq u_i \max_{E_{ij} \in \mathcal{E}_i} \{E_{ij}\}$. We linearize this part without introducing new variables as follows:

$$v_i \leq u_i E_{ij} \qquad \forall \ E_{ij} \in \mathcal{E}_i \qquad \qquad (21)$$

The linearization of the lower bound constraints given by the inequality $l_i \min_{E_{ij} \in \mathcal{E}_i} \{E_{ij}\} \leq v_i$ is more complicated. Analogous to the substitute enzyme case, we develop both binary and continuous methods presented in the following two sections.

Binary method: We have already assumed that $F_i \in \{0, 1\}$. We linearize the nonlinear constraint $l_i \min_{E_{ij} \in \mathcal{E}_i} \{E_{ij}\} \leq v_i$ under this assumption as follows:

$$F_i \leq \frac{\sum_j E_{ij}}{n} \qquad \qquad \forall i \qquad \qquad (22a)$$

$$F_i > \frac{\sum_j E_{ij}}{n} - 1 \qquad \qquad \forall i \qquad \qquad (22b)$$

$$F_i \in \{0,1\} \qquad \qquad \forall i \qquad \qquad (22c)$$

Continuous method: For the continuous method, we replace the lower bound constraint $l_i \min_{E_{ij} \in \mathcal{E}_i} \{E_{ij}\} \leq v_i$ with the following linear constraints:

$$F_i \leq E_{ij} \qquad\qquad \forall i \qquad\qquad (23a)$$

$$F_i \geq \sum_j E_{ij} - (n-1) \qquad\qquad \forall i \qquad\qquad (23b)$$

$$F_i \geq 0 \qquad\qquad \forall i \qquad\qquad (23c)$$

4.3 MILP solution in the presence of complex association of enzymes

In this subsection, we generalize the methods described in the previous two subsections in order to allow associations with arbitrary forms. We consider the case when the reaction can be catalyzed by a set of enzymes such that some of them can substitute for each other and others need to work collaboratively.

For example, assume that ith reaction can be catalyzed by two alternative enzyme complexes that can substitute each other. Also assume that the first and the second of these complexes are formed from two and three enzymes, respectively. These two or three enzymes in the complexes collaborate with each other. We formulate this relationship as $F_i = \max \{ \min \{E_{i1}, E_{i2}\}, \min \{E_{i3}, E_{i4}, E_{i4}\} \}$.

Using standard rules from Boolean algebra, all Boolean equations can be written into disjunctive or conjunctive normal forms. Thus, we transform the equation for each reaction into the following form:

$$F_i = \max_{\mathcal{E}_i^k} \{ \min_{E_{ij} \in \mathcal{E}_i^k} \{E_{ij}\} \}. \qquad\qquad (24)$$

In this equation, $\mathcal{E}_i^k$ denotes the kth set of collaborative enzymes required by the ith reaction. Thus, we have $\bigcup_k \mathcal{E}_i^k = \mathcal{E}_i$. We define a new binary variable $Z_i^k \in \{0, 1\}$ corresponding to each $\mathcal{E}_i^k$ and rewrite Equation (24) as,

$$F_i = \max_{\mathcal{E}_i^k} Z_i^k. \qquad\qquad (25)$$

where,

$$Z_i^k = \min_{E_{ij} \in \mathcal{E}_i^k} \{E_{ij}\}. \qquad\qquad (26)$$

The methods in Section 4.1 and Section 4.2 are used for constraints (26) and (25) respectively to linearize the constraint (15).

5. Experiments

In this section, we evaluate the performance and the limitations of our methods on real and artificially generated metabolic networks. The synthetic datasets provide us a controlled simulation environment that allows us to determine the impact of different characteristics of the network on the performance of our algorithms. We evaluate the performance of our methods quantitatively in terms of their execution time (in seconds).

5.1 Datasets

In our experiments, we used the following real and synthetic datasets.

- **Synthetic datasets:** We randomly generated ten networks of different sizes (given by the number of compounds and the number of reactions). In order to simulate the real networks accurately, we generated these networks so that the number of reactions that involve a compound is distributed according to the power law distribution (Voit, 2000). In other words, the probability of the number of reactions that each compound involves in decreases exponentially with the number of reactions.

  In order to evaluate the impact of multiple enzymes for catalyzing a reaction, on the performance of the algorithms, we generated two types of datasets:

  Single enzyme dataset: In this dataset, each reaction is catalyzed by only one enzyme. Thus, the number of enzymes is equal to the number of reactions.

  Multiple enzyme dataset: In this dataset, all the reactions are catalyzed by at least one enzyme. The number of enzymes attached to a reaction is based on the power law distribution: *the probability that a reaction is catalyzed by k enzymes decreases exponentially with k.* Roughly, 40% of the reactions are catalyzed by at least two enzymes; 30% of the reactions are catalyzed by at least three enzymes; 23.5% of reactions are catalyzed by at least four enzymes; 18.5% of reactions are catalyzed by at least five enzymes and 5% of reactions are catalyzed by at least nine enzymes. Based on these probabilities, we build ten synthetic networks for each network size. Section 5.2.1 describes the results for the synthetic datasets.

- **Real dataset:** We use the metabolic pathways of *Homo sapiens* (*H. sapiens*) from KEGG (Kanehisa & Goto, 2000). The entire *H. sapiens* metabolism consists of 640 enzymes, 1176 reactions and 1067 compounds. Section 5.2.2 provides the results for these real datasets.

Experiment platform: We implemented our algorithms in C++. We applied ILOG CPLEX 11.2 to find the integer linear programming solutions. We executed our experiments on a system with two Pentium 4 3.2Ghz and 1M cache processors, 6 gigabytes of RAM, and a Linux operating system.

5.2 Results

In this section, we evaluate the performance of our algorithms on the synthetic (Section 5.2.1) and real datasets (Section 5.2.2).

5.2.1 Evaluation on synthetic datasets

Our goal in this section is to evaluate the performance of our algorithm for a variety of network parameters using synthetic datasets. These experiments can be decomposed into two sets as described in the previous subsection, namely, single enzyme dataset and multiple enzyme dataset. For an effective comparison, we use identical topology of reactions and compounds for both multiple and single enzyme set. We consider two cases for the multiple enzyme set: a) All multiple enzymes substitute each other. b) All multiple enzymes collaborate with each other.

Performance analysis on single enzyme set: Section 3 proves that finding the enzyme knockout strategy using MILP is NP-Hard. Consider the case when only one enzyme

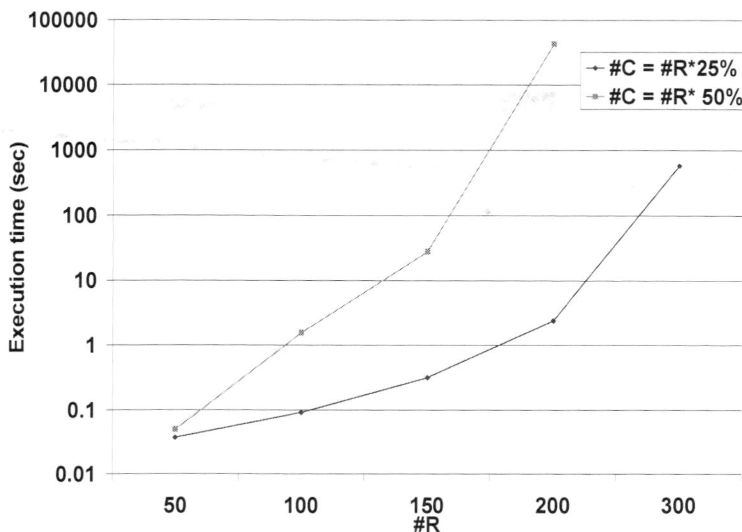

Fig. 2. The average execution time (in seconds) for the networks on single enzyme set. #R denotes the number of reactions and #C denotes the number of compounds in the network. The execution time grows exponentially as the number of reactions increases for both the cases and can be prohibitive even for a few hundred reactions.

catalyzes a reaction. We conduct our experiments using the MILP formulation for two different settings. In the first setting, the number of compounds is 25% of that of the reactions, while for the second setting, it is 50%. Figure 2 plots the average execution times for networks with different number of reactions.

The execution time grows exponentially as the number of reactions increases for both the cases and can be prohibitive even for a few hundred reactions. This time constraint necessitates the advent of heuristic methods for large networks. Also, we observe a steep increase in execution time for larger number of compounds. For the same number of reactions, doubling the number of compounds leads to an overall time increase by several orders of magnitude. It can be concluded that, heuristic methods which can reduce the number of compounds from the constraint set, can have the potential to improve the execution time of the MILP solutions.

Performance analysis for multiple enzymes set: The results in the previous section (along with the NP-hardness of the problem) show that the MILP solution has exponential execution time complexity in terms of the network size. We now study performance of our two solutions with multiple enzymes per reaction. In this experiment, we study the running time requirements in the presence of multiple substitute and collaborative enzymes. We compare these times to those of single enzymes. Note that, the comparison against single enzyme favors the single enzyme dataset as it has fewer variables. This, however, should serve as a lower bound for execution time for the multiple enzyme cases. We summarize the result as follows:

1. Binary method: Figure 3 depicts the results of our binary method for variable number of compounds and reactions. The results demonstrate that the presence of multiple enzymes

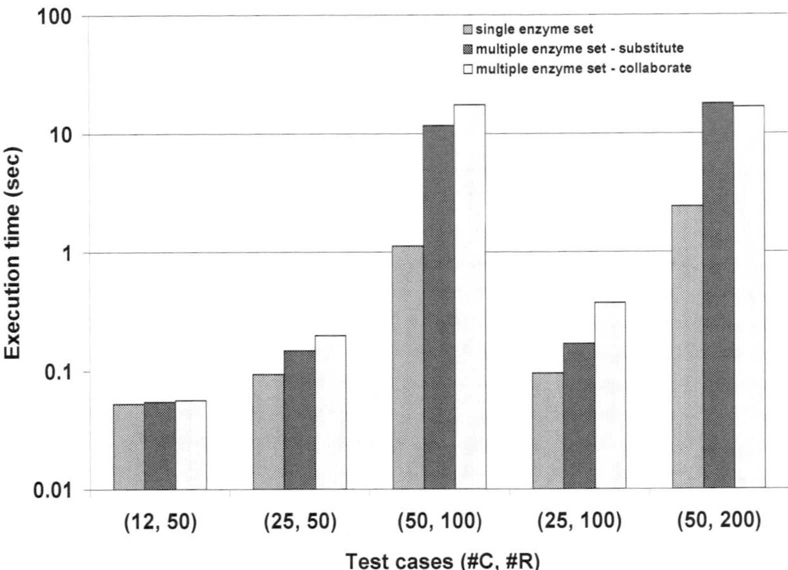

Fig. 3. The average execution time (in seconds) for the networks with single and multiple enzymes. All multiple enzymes cases are either all substitutions or all collaborations. For multiple enzymes set, we use binary method. The results demonstrate that the presence of multiple enzymes increases the execution time significantly as compared to the case when only a single enzyme catalyzes a reaction.

increases the execution time significantly as compared to the case when only single enzyme catalyzes a reaction. This improvement holds true for both substitute and collaborative enzymes. The running time for multiple enzymes is two to 16 times that of the single enzyme case. In most of the test cases, collaborative enzymes resulted in a higher increase in execution time.

2. Continuous method: Figure 4 shows the execution time of multiple enzymes set by continuous method and that for the single enzyme set. Similar to the binary method, multiple enzymes set requires much more time than that of the single enzyme set. As the network size increases, the gap between the execution time of the multiple enzymes set and that of the single enzyme set increases exponentially. This suggests that the presence of multiple enzymes necessitates heuristics solutions for large networks. Also, collaboration among enzymes requires relatively higher execution time as compared to that of the substitution between enzymes in majority of the experiments.

3. Comparison of the two methods: Recall that the binary method introduces additional binary variables to linearize the constraints. The continuous method only generates additional continuous variables. However, it requires additional constraints. Our experiments (see Figures 3 and 4) demonstrate that the Binary method executes twice or more faster than the continuous method for the case when all multiple enzymes cases are substitutions. When the multiple enzymes collaborate with each other, the gap between

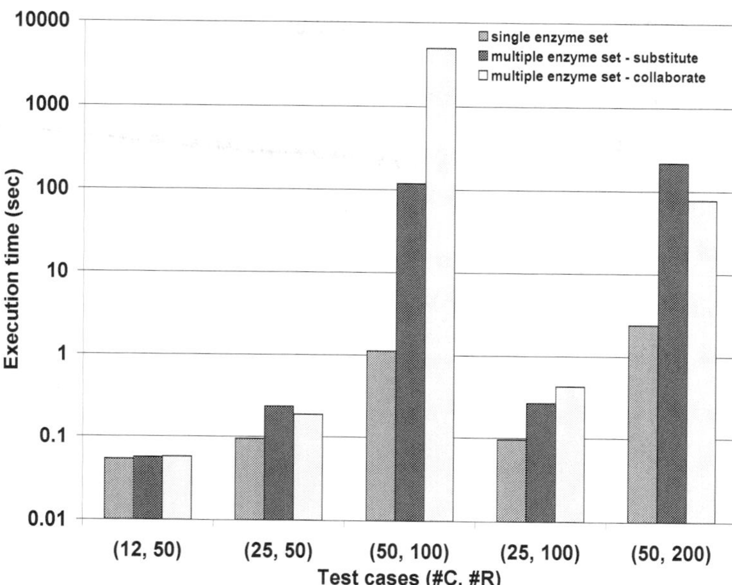

Fig. 4. The average execution time (in seconds) for the networks with single and multiple enzymes. All multiple enzymes cases are either all substitutions or all collaborations. For multiple enzymes set, we use continuous method. As the network size increases, the gap between the execution times of the multiple enzymes set and the single enzyme set increases exponentially.

the running time of the binary and continuous method increases further. Therefore, for the large networks, binary method is the preferred choice.

5.2.2 Evaluation on the real dataset

In this section, we evaluate the performance of our algorithm on real metabolic networks taken from the KEGG database. We use the metabolisms of *H. sapiens*. Given, the superior performance of the binary method over continuous method (as described in the previous subsection), we limit ourselves to the binary method on the real dataset. We execute the binary method for purine metabolism, metabolism of cofactors and vitamins, amino acid metabolism and the entire metabolism. However, the KEGG database does not provide the details of enzyme association information. Thus, we consider two alternative cases: a) all the enzymes are collaborations, b) all the enzymes are substitutions. Table 1 demonstrates the running time using the binary method. These results show that our method requires less than one second of execution time and hence, are scalable to practical network sizes for both cases. Even for the entire metabolism of *H. sapiens*, the execution time is less than half a second. This makes our methods of great practical importance.

It is worth mentioning that the execution times on the real datasets are substantially lower than that of the synthetic datasets. This is because, the topology of the real networks is much sparser than the ones we used for our synthetic experiments. Therefore, less time is required to find the flux distribution on the real networks.

Pathway	#E	#R	#C	Collaborative	Substitute
Purine metabolism	52	92	65	0.07	0.13
Metabolism of cofactors and vitamins	90	132	122	0.04	0.05
Amino acid metabolism	195	317	305	0.05	0.06
the entire metabolism	640	1176	1067	0.38	0.28

Table 1. Execution time in seconds of our binary method for the metabolisms of *H. sapiens* from KEGG. #E, #R and #C denote the number of enzymes, reactions and compounds respectively in the metabolism. The results demonstrate that our method requires less than one second of execution time. Hence it is scalable to practical network sizes for both the cases.

6. Conclusions

Given a metabolic network and a goal, such as maximizing or minimizing the production of a set of compounds, we considered the problem of computationally determining the optimal enzyme knockouts to modify the production of compounds using the Flux Balance Analysis (FBA) model. We proved that the problem of finding the optimal enzyme set to knockout is NP-hard even when only one enzyme catalyzes a reaction.

We developed two strategies to identify the enzymes to knockout, when multiple enzymes catalyze a single reaction. We allowed multiple substitute and collaborative enzymes. In the proposed solutions, we eliminate this limitation of single enzyme. Our first solution uses a small number of binary variables in the underlying MILP formulation. The second method increases the number of binary variables but requires a smaller number of constraints.

Our experiments using synthetic and real datasets demonstrated that adding extra binary variables is significantly superior to adding additional constraints in terms of execution time. For the metabolism consisting of all the pathways of H. sapiens, our binary method requires less than one second. This makes our methods of great practical importance.

We believe that the approach presented in this chapter is not limited to MILP based strategies. It should also be applicable to other linear constraint strategies, e.g. quadratic programming, where the objective function is non-linear but the constraints are linear.

7. Acknowledgment

This work was supported partially by NSF under grants CCF-0829867 and IIS-0845439.

8. References

Alper, H., Jin, Y., Moxley, J. & Stephanopoulos, G. (2005). Identifying gene targets for the metabolic engineering of lycopene biosynthesis in E. coli, *Metab. Eng.* 7(3).

Bonarius, H. P. J., Schmid, G. & Tramper, J. (1997). Flux analysis of underdetermined metabolic networks: The quest for the missing constraints, *Trends Biotechnology* 15.

Burgard, A. P., Pharkya, P. & Maranas, C. D. (2003). Optknock: A bilevel programming framework for identifying gene knockout strategies for microbial strain optimization, *Biotechnology and Bioengineering* 84.

Covert, M. W., Schilling, C. H. & Palsson, B. (2001). Regulation of Gene Expression in Flux Balance Models of Metabolism, *Journal of Theoretical Biology* 213(1).

Edwards, J. S. & Palsson, B. O. (2000a). Metabolic flux balance analysis and the in silico analysis of Escherichia coli K-12 gene deletions, *BMC Bioinformatics* 1(1).

Edwards, J. S. & Palsson, B. O. (2000b). The Escherichia coli MG1655 in silico metabolic genotype: Its definition, characteristics, and capabilities, *Proc Natl Acad Sci U S A* 97.

Forster, J., Famili, I., Fu, P., Palsson, B. O. & Nielsen, J. (2003). Genome-scale reconstruction of the saccharomyces cerevisiae metabolic network, *Genome Research* 13.

Kanehisa, M. & Goto, S. (2000). KEGG: Kyoto encyclopedia of genes and genomes, *Nucleic Acids Res.* 28(1): 27–30.

Kauffman, K. J., Prakash, P. & Edwards, J. S. (2003). Advances in flux balance analysis, *Current opinion in biotechnology* 14(5).

Klamt, S. & Gilles, E. D. (2004). Minimal cut sets in biochemical reaction networks, *Bioinformatics* 20(2).

Ng, P. H. & Rardin, R. L. (1996). Commodity family extended formulations of uncapacitated fixed charge network flow problems, *Networks* 30(1).

Palsson, B. O. (2000). The challenges of in silico biology, *Nature Biotechnology* 18.

Patil, K. R., Rocha, I., Forster, J. & Nielsen, J. (2005). Evolutionary programming as a platform for in silico metabolic engineering, *BMC Bioinformatics* 6(308).

Peschel, M. & Mende, W. (1986). *The predator-prey model: do we live in a volterra world?*, Akademie-Verlag, Berlin.

Pharkya, P., Burgard, A. P. & Maranas, C. D. (2004). OptStrain: A computational framework for redesign of microbial production systems, *Genome Res.* 14.

Pharkya, P. & Maranas, C. D. (2006). An optimization framework for identifying reaction activation/inhibition or elimination candidates for overproduction in microbial systems, *Metab. Eng.* 8(1).

Reed, J. L., Vo, T. D., Schilling, C. H. & Palsson, B. O. (2003). An expanded genomescale model of escherichia coli k-12 (ijr904 gsm/gpr), *Genome Biology* 4(R54).

Savageau, M. & Voit, E. (1987). Recasting nonlinear differential equations as S-systems: a canonical nonlinear form, *Math. Biosci* 87.

Segre, D., Vitkup, D. & Church, G. (2002). Analysis of optimality in natural and perturbed metabolic networks, *Proc. Natl. Acad. Sci. USA* 99(23).

Shlomi, T., Berkman, O. & Ruppin, E. (2005). Regulatory on/off minimization of metabolic flux changes after genetic perturbations, *Proc. Natl. Acad. Sci. USA* 102.

Shlomi, T., Eisenberg, Y., Sharan, R. & Ruppin, E. (2007). A genome-scale computational study of the interplay between transcriptional regulation and metabolism, *Mol Syst Biol* 3.

Song, B., Buyuktahtakin, I. E., Kahveci, T. & Ranka, S. (2011). Manipulating the steady state of metabolic pathways, , *IEEE/ACM Transactions on Computational Biology and Bioinformatics (IEEE TCBB)*, 8(3).

Song, B., Sridhar, P., Kahveci, T. & Ranka, S. (2007). Double iterative optimization for metabolic network-based drug target identification, *International Journal of Data Mining and Bioinformatics*, 3(2).

Sridhar, P., Kahveci, T. & Ranka, S. (2007). An iterative algorithm for metabolic network-based drug target identification, *Pacific Symposium on Biocomputing* .

Sridhar, P., Song, B., Kahveci, T. & Ranka, S. (2008). OPMET: A metabolic network-based algorithm for optimal drug target identification, *Pacific Symposium on Biocomputing* .

Voit, E. O. (2000). *Computational analysis of biochemical systems: a practical guide for biochemists and molecular biologists*, Cambridge University Press.

Part 6

Genome Analysis

18

Using Bacterial Artificial Chromosomes to Refine Genome Assemblies and to Build Virtual Genomes

Abhirami Ratnakumar[1,2], Wesley Barris[1,3],
Sean McWilliam[1] and Brian P. Dalrymple[1]
[1]CSIRO Livestock Industries, St. Lucia, QLD
[2]now at the Department of Medical Biochemistry and Microbiology,
Uppsala University, Uppsala
[3]now at Cobb-Vantress, Siloam Springs, Arkansas
[1]Australia
[2]Sweden
[3]USA

1. Introduction

Recent years have seen an explosion in the sequencing of genomes, including those of ruminants. A number of assemblies of the sequence of the bovine genome are now available (Elsik, et al., 2009; Zimin, et al., 2009). Although the sheep genome sequence is not such a high priority, the International Sheep Genomics Consortium (ISGC_website) has a long term strategy to develop a number of tools for the application of genomics in sheep research and breeding (Archibald, et al., 2010). We have demonstrated recently how comparative genomics and Bacterial Artificial Chromosome (BAC)-libraries can be used to construct detailed virtual genomes as a framework for genome assemblies of related species (Dalrymple, et al., 2007). As new and improved genome assemblies of the genomes contributing to an initial virtual genome assembly are produced, the virtual genomes will need to be regularly updated to incorporate the latest available information. In the original analysis, three genomes (bovine, dog and human) with various levels of coverage and stages of assembly were used (Dalrymple, et al., 2007). With the availability of increasing numbers of assemblies, the benefit of using more than three genomes, or the most appropriate evolutionary distances of the genomes, is not immediately clear. Here we describe the construction of a modified version of the bovine Btau3.1 assembly using cattle and sheep BACs and the use of this assembly in the construction of an updated virtual sheep genome, combining information from the original sheep virtual genome (vsg 1.2) and the horse (Wade, et al., 2009) and dog (Lindblad-Toh, et al., 2005) genomes. The impact of inclusion of additional genome sequences is analysed. The approach described here for sheep is an example of an approach which can be applied more broadly to genomes of any source, for example for the fish species, tilapia (Soler, et al., 2010) and catfish (Liu, et al., 2009). Indeed, the same principles also apply to the detection of differences between different individuals of the same species.

2. Materials and methods

2.1 Data sources and sequence search parameters

All genome sequences, except Btau3.#x versions, were downloaded from the UCSC comparative genomics website (UCSC; Fujita, et al., 2011). The full set of BAC-end sequences (BESs) from the CHORI-243 sheep BAC library, deposited in GenBank with the following accession numbers; CL632218-CL639051, CZ920079-CZ926973 and DU169919-DU532729 (Dalrymple, et al., 2007), were filtered to remove duplicate sequences and to identify the set of high confidence BACs (Ratnakumar, et al., 2010a). The filtered set of sheep BAC-end sequences were aligned to the lower case masked versions of the bovine genome assembly (Btau3.1) and the revised bovine genome assembly (Btau3.5x) using MegaBLASTn with the following optimised parameters: -r 1 -q -1 -X 40 -W 8, as previously described (Ratnakumar, et al., 2010b). The filtered set of sheep BESs were aligned to the lower case masked versions of the dog genome sequence assembly (canFam2), the horse genome sequence assembly (equCab1) and to the human genome sequence assembly (hg17) using BLASTn with the following parameters: -W 7 -r 17 -q -21 -G 29 -E 22 -X 240 -e 1 -f 280 -F m -U T and -z 3076781887 (human) and -z 2531657226 (dog), as previously described (Dalrymple, et al., 2007). No cut offs were applied to the BLAST output except that for each sheep BAC-end sequence only the best hit from each of the genomes was used for the next steps. If two BESs hits to the same genome assembly with equal scores were obtained the hit on the same chromosome as the best hit for the BES determined from the other end of the BAC was retained. If more than two hits with equal scores were obtained the BES hit was discarded.

The BESs from the CHORI-240 cattle BAC library, GenBank accession numbers; BZ830806-BZ891831, BZ896446-BZ956676, CC447354-CC447937, CC466118-CC470858, CC470880-CC596504, CC761663-CC775995, CG917936-CG918393, CG976420-CG992944, CL603252-CL610093, CW848133-CW848163, CZ012846-CZ027312 (Snelling, et al., 2007), were aligned to the cattle and virtual sheep genome sequences using BLAT (Kent, 2002).

Bovine genome assembly Btau3.1 sequence contigs were aligned to the human, dog and horse genomes using MegaBLASTn as described above.

2.2 Genome coordinate conversion

The coordinates from the mapping of the sheep BESs to the dog and human genomes were converted to the framework of the bovine genome assembly Btau3.1 using the LiftOver utility (LiftOver; Fujita, et al., 2011) and the canFam2 to Btau3.1 and hg17 to Btau3.1 coordinate conversion chain files respectively, also downloaded from UCSC genome bioinformatics site (UCSC; Fujita, et al., 2011). If the initial application of LiftOver was not successful for a region of the genome, regions of 100 bases either side of the BAC-end sequence were taken and positioned using LiftOver (pseudoliftOver). If this was again unsuccessful the process was repeated in steps of 100 bases until a successful application of the LiftOver utility for a region was achieved, or a distance of 10kb was reached (Dalrymple, et al., 2007).

Coordinate conversion (chain) files able to be read by the LiftOver utility to convert bovine genome assembly Btau3.1 coordinates to bovine genome assembly Btau3.#x version coordinates were built based on the revised order of Btau3.1 contigs and scaffolds in Btau3.#x version. Similarly a coordinate conversion file to convert Btau3.5x coordinates to virtual sheep genome assembly coordinates was built based on the order of Btau3.5x scaffolds in the virtual sheep genome.

2.3 Assigning BACs to groups and building BAC contigs

BACs were assigned to the groups; "tail-to-tail", "tail-to-head" etc. on the basis of the relative orientations of the two BESs from each BAC on the relevant genome assembly and the distance apart of the BESs. "Outsize" BACs were those with the two BESs mapped to the same chromosome in the relevant genome assembly and less than 10 kb, or more than 200 kb, apart. Data processing was undertaken using a series of Perl scripts. BACs with both BESs mapped to the genome, but mapped to two different chromosomes, were assigned to the "breaks" group. BACs with only one BES mapped to the genome were assigned to the "unpaired" group.

BAC-comparative genomic contigs (BAC-CGCs) were constructed for the BACs from each species mapped to each genome assembly using Perl scripts to process the data (Dalrymple, et al., 2007). Starting from the beginning of each chromosome the first BAC that overlapped with a second BAC was identified, the BAC-CGC was extended until no further overlapping BACs were identified. This process was repeated along the chromosome until the last BAC mapped on the chromosome was reached. The process was repeated for each chromosome in the genome assembly.

2.4 Construction of Btau3.5x

Using Perl scripts and the data set of the mapping of the bovine BESs to the scaffolds of the Btau3.1 genome assembly an initial minimization of the number of non-tail-to-tail BACs was undertaken. The scripts started with the first scaffold on chromosome 1 of the assembly and by testing the number of BAC links between this scaffold and all other scaffolds in the assembly identified the most likely adjacent scaffold and the orientation of the scaffold based on maximising the number of tail-to-tail BACs. Two or more linking tail-to-tail BACs without overlapping BES mapping coordinates on both scaffolds were required to continue the chain. Only high confidence bovine BACs (Ratnakumar, et al., 2009) were used in the assembly. Adjacent scaffolds assigned to the same chromosome in the Btau3.1 assembly were preferred over a more highly linked scaffold assigned to another chromosome, if the preferred scaffold on the original chromosome was itself linked to an adjacent scaffold on the original chromosome. If no scaffold assigned to the same chromosome as the rest of the chain was linked into the chain by BACs, or the less strongly linked scaffold from the same chromosome terminated the chain, the most highly linked scaffold from another chromosome was incorporated. If the newly added scaffold was linked back to the original chromosome at the next step of scaffold incorporation it was retained in the chain, otherwise the chain was terminated and the chromosome changing scaffold was also removed from the scaffold chain.

For each scaffold in the chain BAC-links from both ends of the scaffold were assessed to enable to inclusion of scaffolds preceding the initiating scaffold, or located between two scaffolds in a chain, but which were only linked to an adjacent following scaffold. The scaffold chain building process was continued until it was terminated with a scaffold not linked by two or more BACs to another scaffold. The penultimate scaffold in the chain was then tested for BAC links to a second scaffold and incorporated if it met the criteria described above. The chain building process was then continued. If no second linked scaffold could be identified the scaffold chain building was terminated. The next unincorporated scaffold from the same chromosome of the Btau3.1 assembly was then used to initiate the next scaffold chain. When all scaffolds from the first chromosome had been tested the first scaffold from the next chromosome was used and the process repeated until all scaffolds assigned to a chromosome of the Btau3.1 assembly had been tested.

Once the scaffold chain assembly had been completed the scaffolds not assigned to chromosomes in the Btau3.1 assembly (the UnChr) were then linked into the scaffold chains in a similar, but separate process. The resulting scaffold chains were then ordered and oriented using the consensus of the mapping of the order of the BACs in the physical bovine BAC map (Snelling, et al., 2007) to the BACs in the bovine scaffold chains. The initial data set Btau3.1x was then displayed as a browseable genome using Gbrowse (Stein, et al., 2002) to allow the integrity of the assembly of the scaffolds to be visually assessed. Genome contigs, scaffolds, bovine BAC mapping positions were displayed as separate groups. Clusters on non-congruent BACs (i.e. not tail-to-tail) identified regions with remaining assembly problems.

Using Perl scripts and the data set of the mapping of the sheep BESs to the Btau3.1 genome assembly, including BES mapping data integrated onto the Btau3.1 assembly from the horse, dog and vsg1.2 assemblies sheep BACs were assigned to tail-to-tail etc. groups and displayed on the Btau3.1x genome browser in a series of tracks. Positions of the BESs mapped to the separate genomes were integrated on Btau3.1 as previously described (Dalrymple, et al., 2007).

The mappings of the bovine genome assembly Btau3.1 sequence contigs to the human, dog and horse genomes were displayed as separate tracks on the Btau3.1x genome browser using the UCSC chromosome colour scheme (Fujita, et al., 2011) to identify the chromosome of best match in the relevant species. Asymmetric symbols were used to represent the orientation of the mapping of the contigs to the human, dog and horse genomes relative to the bovine genome. The chromosomal coordinates of the mapping in the non-bovine genome were also readily accessible to the users of the browser using mouse-over and mouse-click display boxes. This information was used in the manual refinement of the assembly, in particular in the definition of scaffold split points for the insertion of other scaffolds and/or the inversion of small numbers of adjacent contigs within a scaffold, where extensive use was made of comparative genomics information at the level of the sequence contigs.

Subsequently four major rounds of revision and refinement of the bovine genome assembly were undertaken manually and decisions on the chromosomal assignment, order of scaffolds and orientation of scaffolds and of sequence contigs were made based on the cattle and sheep BAC mapping and the comparative genomics. Generally in cases of ambiguity parsimony was applied. For the construction of each new version of the assembly changes were recorded in an Excel spreadsheet and Perl scripts were used to convert the Excel spreadsheet into a genome assembly agp file (AGP_file_specification). The agp file was used to generate the sequence of the genome assembly, the coordinate conversion chain file (for use by the LiftOver utility) and the contig and scaffold tracks for the genome browser version for the new assembly. For each successive version of the revised assembly of the bovine genome the manual revision was undertaken interactively using the tracks on the genome browser to make decisions.

2.5 Construction of the virtual sheep genome vsg2.0

To generate the virtual sheep genome assembly the mid point between each pair of BAC-CGCs built using sheep BACs on the bovine Btau3.5x genome assembly was identified. If the mid point was located in a gene (NCBI human RefSeq mRNAs (NCBI_RefSeq) were used to define the extent of a gene) the position closest to the midpoint and not in a gene was identified. The flanking BAC-CGCs were then extended to this point, or in the case of the first and last BAC-CGCs on a chromosome to the start or end coordinate of the chromosome. Thus all nucleotides in the bovine genome sequence were included in a block and therefore the virtual sheep genome sequence is exactly the same length as the bovine Btau3.5x genome sequence.

The order and orientation of the bovine genome assembly Btau3.5x-based sheep BAC-CGCs in the vsg2.0 was determined on the location and organisation of the sheep linkage map markers (Maddox, et al., 2001) mapped to the Btau3.1 genome and converted to the Btau3.5x assembly using the Btau3.1 to Btau3.5x coordinate conversion chain file and the LiftOver utility. Using Perl scripts the agp file (AGP_file_specification) was built and used to generate the sequence of the virtual sheep genome assembly, the coordinate conversion chain file (for use by the LiftOver utility), and the contig and scaffold tracks for the virtual sheep genome browser (VSG).

Using the LiftOver utility and the Btau3.5x to virtual sheep genome coordinate conversion chain file, the BES and BAC-CGC mapping coordinates, and any other features mapped to the Btau3.5x bovine genome, were converted to the virtual sheep genome coordinates. Features were also transferred from the Btau3.1 genome assembly by first converting to Btau3.5x coordinates using the Btau3.1 to Btau3.5x coordinate conversion file and the LiftOver utility and then converting from Btau3.5x to vsg2.0 coordinates. Other features were mapped directly onto the virtual sheep genome using sequence alignment programs such as BLAST and BLAT with the vsg2.0 DNA sequence.

3. Results and discussion

3.1 Identification of problems with the Btau3.1 assembly of the bovine genome

The cow is the most closely related organism to sheep for which a genome assembly is available. When this project was commenced, an early draft of the bovine genome assembly Btau3.1 (Elsik, et al., 2009) was in the public domain. Since the sheep genome assembly would be built comparatively on the bovine genome, and sheep sequence contigs from the low coverage six animals at approximately 0.5 fold coverage each, were expected to be very small, the accuracy of the bovine genome assembly would determine the accuracy of the sheep assembly at all levels above that of the individual sequence contigs.

To assess the validity of this strategy the sheep BESs from the CHORI-243 library were mapped to the Btau3.1 genome assembly to identify the extent of segments of conserved synteny between the two genomes. The reader should keep in mind that the only BACs counted as being in the same organisation in the comparison genome as in the source genome (i. e. congruent) are the tail-to-tail BACs less than 200kb in length. Unexpectedly large numbers of sheep BACs, more than 17% of the BACs with both ends mapped, had both BESs positioned on the bovine Btau3.1 genome assembly within 200kb of each other, but not in the expected tail-to-tail organisation, i. e. many BACs had their two BESs mapped in the tail-to-head and head-to-head organisations (Table 1). In addition, large numbers of BACs had both BESs positioned on the same chromosome, but more than 200kb apart, the outsize groups (Table 1). The average insert size of the BACs in the sheep BAC library is 184kb (Dalrymple, et al., 2007).

Such a result would normally suggest a substantial number of intra-chromosomal rearrangements between the sheep and cattle genomes. However, almost as many, more than 14%, of bovine BACs were also not positioned as tail-to-tail BACs on the bovine Btau3.1 genome assembly (Table 1). The organisation of sheep BACs at the locations of these apparent rearrangements between the two genomes was compared with the organisation of bovine BACs at the same locations in the genomes. Frequently clusters of tail-to-head sheep BACs overlapped with clusters of tail-to-head bovine BACs (Fig 1), suggesting that many such occurrences were in fact due to an incorrect assembly of the bovine genome, not true differences in the structures of the two genomes themselves. However, many clusters of tail-to-head sheep BACs that did not overlap with tail-to-head bovine BACs were also observed (Fig 1). These BACs probably represent rearrangements in the sheep genome relative to the bovine genome.

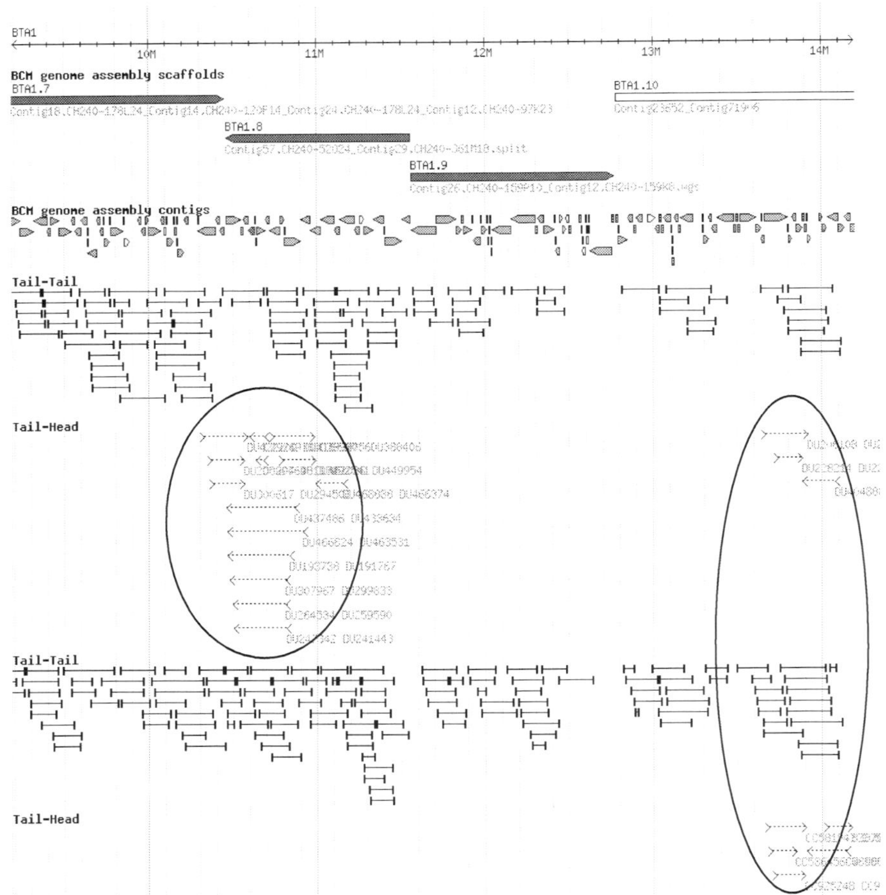

Fig. 1. Segment of chromosome one of the bovine Btau3.1 genome assembly showing the positions and orientations of sheep and cattle BACs. BCM genome assembly contigs are coloured based on the human chromosome to which they have the highest scoring match. The circles identify regions of likely inversion in the bovine and/or sheep genomes relative to the Btau3.1 genome assembly.

Genome Assembly	Btau3.1	Btau3.1	Btau3.5x	vsg2.0	vsg1.2
BAC origin	cattle	sheep	cattle	sheep	sheep
tail-to-tail (%)	86.7%	82.7%	95.63%	94.0%	89.6%
tail-to-tail outsize	2.0%	2.6%	0.4%	0.8%	1.7%
tail-to-head	3.5%	4.4%	2.6%	2.1%	2.6%
tail-to-head outsize	5.2%	7.1%	0.9%	2.1%	4.4%
head-to-head	0.4%	0.4%	0.4%	0.2%	0.3%
head-to-head-outsize	2.1%	2.8%	0.1%	0.6%	1.4%
tail-to-tail (number)	67,352	47,818	82,765	95,757	84,624
breaks		13,192		19,151	27,829
unpaired		79,172		50,142	52,663

Table 1. Mapping of cattle and sheep BACs to assemblies of the cattle and virtual sheep genomes.

3.2 Using cattle and sheep BACs to reorganise the Btau3.1 assembly of the bovine genome

The first step in the generation of the virtual sheep genome was therefore to construct the best approximation to the correct order of the bovine sequence contigs and scaffolds in the bovine genome using the bovine and sheep BACs and comparative genomics. Initially, the scaffolds in the bovine genome assembly (Btau3.1) were kept intact and scaffolds were reordered and reoriented within bovine chromosomes to minimize the number of both cattle and sheep BACs that were not in the tail-to-tail organisation. Then scaffolds apparently assigned to the wrong chromosomes on the basis of the BAC-based links to other scaffolds in the assembly were moved, including being inserted into gaps in other scaffolds guided by the mapping of the BESs. Generally these moves were also supported by the mapping of the sequence contigs to the human, dog and horse genomes (Fig. 2). In addition, scaffolds not assigned to chromosomes in Btau3.1 were included in the assembly where BACs provided unambiguous links. Finally, reordering and reorienting of contigs within the new set of ordered and reoriented scaffolds was undertaken.

Given the size of the BACs and the variation in the length of the genomic DNA contained within the BACs the correct position to insert many segments of the bovine assembly was ambiguous based solely on the BAC-end data. Throughout this process, which was mainly undertaken manually, the alignment of the bovine genome assembly contigs to the human, dog and horse genome assemblies was used in making the final decision about where exactly to insert or break scaffolds. In other words, a breakpoint between sequence contigs in an assembly scaffold was chosen that was consistent with the cattle and sheep BES data and the organisation of the human, dog and horse genomes (Fig. 2). Where conflicts between the comparative genome assemblies occurred two out of three consistent organisations were required. However, the integrity of sequence contigs was maintained throughout the process, although evidence for chimeric sequence contigs was also identified during the course of the analysis (data not shown).

To avoid ovinising the bovine genome at least one bovine BAC was required to support all reorganisations, except reordering and reorienting scaffolds within chromosomes in cases where the bovine BAC fingerprint map (Snelling, et al., 2007) also supported the

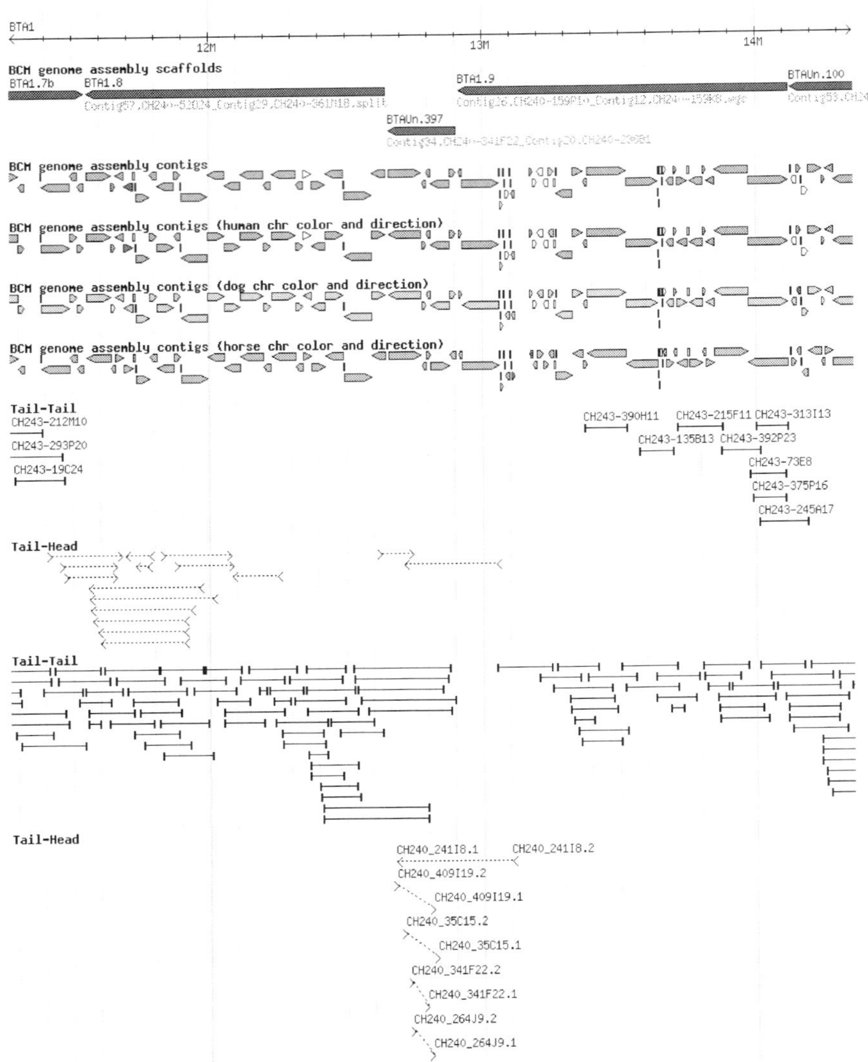

Fig. 2. Segment of chromosome one of the bovine Btau3.5x genome assembly showing the positions and orientations of sheep and cattle BACs. BCM genome assembly contigs are coloured and orientated based on the relevant species chromosome to which they have the highest scoring match The UCSC chromosome colour scheme was used (Fujita, et al., 2011).

reorganisation. This process was undertaken reiteratively to resolve any errors introduced or new links identified as the chromosome structures approached the most likely structure of the bovine genome. This revised assembly of the bovine genome based on Btau3.1 was named Btau.3.5x.

In Btau3.5x the number of bovine assembly scaffolds was reduced from 3053 scaffolds assigned to chromosomes in Btau3.1 to 537 super-scaffolds linked by the cattle and sheep BACs. Of the chromosomally assigned scaffolds in Btau3.1, 974 scaffolds were inverted, and 683 scaffolds were split into 1720 pieces, of which 710 were inverted. 14 scaffolds were moved to a different chromosome and 2192 scaffolds previously not assigned to chromosomes were incorporated into the assembly. 104 of these scaffolds were split into 233 pieces. Coverage of the genome with scaffolds assigned to chromosomes increased from 2.4 Gb to 2.77 Gb. Even after this process it is likely that there remained a number of segments of the bovine genome assembly which may not have been correctly assembled.

chromosome	scaffold	orientation	integrity
1	BTA1.1		split
1	BTAUn.418	inv	
1	BTAUn.728	inv	
1	BTA1.2		
1	BTA1.3		
1	BTA1.4		
1	BTAUn.1364	inv	
1	BTAUn.208		
1	BTA1.6		split
1	BTAUn.2125	inv	
1	BTA1.6		split
1	BTAUn.1381		
1	BTA1.5		split
1	BTAUn.1438	inv	
1	BTA1.5		split
1	BTA1.7		split
1	BTAUn.3041		
1	BTAUn.5341	inv	
1	BTA1.7		split
1	BTA1.8		

Table 2. The first twenty scaffolds of the bovine Btau3.5x assembly, scaffolds numbered BTA1.* were assigned in numerical order to chromosome 1 of the bovine genome assembly Btau3.1 build. Scaffolds numbered BTAUn.* were not assigned to a chromosome in the bovine Btau3.1 build. "inv" indicates scaffolds inverted in the Btau3.5x genome build relative to the Btau3.1 build, and "split" indicates scaffolds split in the Btau3.5x build relative to the Btau3.1 build.

3.3 Integration of the positions of sheep BESs on the Btau3.5x, dog, horse and vsg1.2 genome assemblies

We then used the virtual genome strategy (Dalrymple, et al., 2007), integrating the separate mapping of the sheep BESs to the original virtual sheep genome (v1.2), the dog and the horse genome assemblies, to maximise the positioning of sheep BESs on Btau.3.5x. There was little change in the human genome assembly over the course of the work and mapping of the sheep BACs to the human genome was captured by using the virtual sheep genome v1.2. Thus the virtual sheep genome version 2 was build on top of v1.2, rather than being a completely *de novo* version. This approach, which uses much lower specificity BLAST parameters, increased the number of sheep BACs able to be positioned on the bovine genome substantially, from 47,818 (in the initial alignments) to 95,757 in the virtual sheep genome, effectively doubling the coverage of the genome (Table 1). The number of sheep BACs able to be positioned in the tail-to-tail organisation in a genome is a complex function of the sequence coverage, assembly stage and evolutionary distance from the bovine genome. The greater distance of the dog genome appears to be partially compensated for by the more advanced state of the assembly used in this analysis. Very similar numbers of BACs were mapped in the tail-to-tail organisation to the two genomes (Table 3) with similar numbers of unique BACs (Table 4).

	bovine	horse	dog	vsg1.2
bovine	77,320			
horse	49,225	60,971		
dog	46,355	47,142	57,192	
vsg1.2	62,889	56,636	54,503	84,624

Table 3. Tail-to-tail BACs within each dataset generated by independently mapping the sheep BESs to each genome and in the intersections between each of the datasets.

genome	including vsg1.2	excluding vsg1.2
bovine	10,550	20,171
horse	701	3,035
dog	211	2,063
vsg1.2	9,204	not applicable

Table 4. Tail-to-tail BACs unique to each dataset.

The high coverage and quality of the human genome assembly and the use of the integration strategy presumably contributed to the large number of unique BACs in the tail-to-tail organisation present in vsg1.2 (Tables 3 and 4). Over and above the newer assembly of the bovine genome the inclusion of the mapping of the sheep BACs to the horse genome assembly has the biggest impact on the number of BACs assigned and on the number of BAC contigs, where fewer is better (Table 5). This is not surprising since, of the genomes used, the horse is the most closely related species to the two ruminants.

Adding the horse mapping of the sheep BESs positions to the bovine mapping of the sheep BESs positions increased the number of BACs mapped by 13,940, mainly by generating

BACs with one end directly mapped to the bovine genome and other end mapped to the bovine genome via the horse genome (Table 6). Subsequent addition of the BESs mapped via the dog genome added many fewer BACs than adding the BESs mapped via the horse genome (Table 6). The subsequent addition of the human genome data, incorporated in the vsg1.2, added slightly more BACs than the addition of the dog genome (Table 4). Thus including the dog genome had only a small impact on the improvement in the coverage of the virtual sheep genome whereas the more distant, but the better assembled/higher coverage, human genome was a useful addition to the virtual genome construction, but not unexpectedly the biggest contributions came from well assembled genomes of closely related species.

	bovine	horse	dog	vsg1.2	total
bovine	76,251				76,251
horse	13,231	709			13,940
dog	1,911	112	45		2,068
vsg1.2	3,131	284	68	55	3,538
total					95,797

Table 5. Genomes providing mapping information for the sheep BACs mapped tail-to-tail in the vsg2.0. Datasets were added in the order, bovine, horse, dog and vsg1.2.

Genome BACs positioned by	number
Both BESs vsg1.2	80,146
Both BESs bovine	13,196
One BES bovine or vsg1.2, other BES horse or dog	2431
Both BESs horse	16
One BES horse, other BES dog	5
Both BESs dog	3
	95,797

Table 6. Genomes used to position the BACs on the virtual sheep genome. Datasets were added in the order, vsg1.2, bovine, horse, and dog.

In other words, building on top of vsg1.2 and the use of a higher quality assembly of the bovine genome contributed a large number of new BACs with both ends positioned on the bovine assembly (Table 5). A large group of BACs were positioned with one end using the bovine or vsg1.2 position and the other using horse or dog. Very few BACs were positioned solely using horse and/or dog positions (Table 6). On this basis further improvement of the vsg would appear to be difficult and most likely to come from filling of gaps in the bovine genome sequence itself.

Based on the mapping of the sheep BACs to the reorganised bovine genome assembly 943 blocks of conserved synteny, defined by overlapping sheep BACs, were identified between the sheep and cattle genomes (Table 7). Assuming a genome size of 3Gb, the blocks had an average length of just over 3Mb. Although initially disappointing, even in the bovine genome assembly 537 BAC-based super-scaffolds were required to cover the complete genome. The comparison of the number of blocks of conserved synteny identified across the different combinations of datasets demonstrates that the inclusion of additional species beyond the horse has a much greater impact on the reduction in the number of blocks of conserved synteny than it has on the total number of BACs positioned tail-to-tail. Only a 25% increase in the number of BACs, but a 56% decrease in the number blocks of conserved synteny, i. e. on average every block of conserved synteny defined based on the mapping of BACs to the bovine genome has been extended to include one adjacent block of conserved synteny.

genomes	Sheep BAC contigs
dog	2,146
horse	1,470
bovine	1,411
bovine + dog + vsg1.2	1,299
bovine + horse + dog + vsg1.2	943

Table 7. Building the virtual sheep genome.

3.4 Remaining ambiguities in the build of the bovine genome

Since there were many occasions on which there was no unambiguous basis on which to identify the correct break points in the bovine genome assembly a large number of probable inversions identified by BACs remained in the final version of the bovine genome. Most of these inversions were also supported by sheep BACs (Fig 2). In addition, whilst potentially chimeric bovine genomic sequence contigs were identified during the reassembly process, their structure has not been changed in Btau3.5x.

3.5 Construction of the virtual sheep genome (vsg2.0)

The sheep markers (sheep map version 4.7) were used to reorganise the bovine genome assembly into the vsg. In the main this involved renumbering of the bovine chromosomes, with five inverted chromosomes (or segments of chromosomes), four chromosome fusions and a single chromosome breakage (Table 8). Reordering of the segments of the bovine genome defined by the BAC comparative genome contigs (CGCs) was undertaken on four chromosomes, 7, 12, 13 and X. Apart from the X chromosome, these were local changes and involved a small number of BAC CGCs covering a small region of the genome. Given the variation in the size of BACs, and the lack of comparative data from other genomes for species specific breaks, the boundaries of such breaks could not be unambiguously identified with the data currently available. Thus no attempt was made to resolve the small potential sheep specific rearrangements within chromosomes where the break points were ambiguous and there was not sufficient marker evidence to support a change in the organisation (Fig 3).

The vsg 2.0 has been used in a number of analyses of the genome organisation of sheep and in general a high level of congruence with maps determined using other approaches has been observed (Drogemuller, et al., 2008; Wu, et al., 2008; Goldammer, et al., 2009c; Wu, et al., 2009), although the vsg 2 X chromosome build appears to contain a number of significant discrepancies (Goldammer, et al., 2009a; Goldammer, et al., 2009b).

Sheep chromosome	Cattle chromosome
OAR1	BTA3 (inv) + BTA1
OAR2	BTA8 (inv) +BTA2
OAR3	BTA11 (inv) + BTA5
OAR4	BTA4
OAR5	BTA7
OAR6	BTA6
OAR7	BTA10
OAR8	BTA9 (part)
OAR9	BTA9 (part, inv) +BTA14
OAR10	BTA12
OAR11	BTA19
OAR12	BTA16
OAR13	BTA13
OAR14	BTA18
OAR15	BTA15
OAR16	BTA20
OAR17	BTA17
OAR18	BTA21
OAR19	BTA22
OAR20	BTA23
OAR21	BTA29
OAR22	BTA26
OAR23	BTA24
OAR24	BTA25
OAR25	BTA28
OAR26	BTA27
OARX	BTAX (inv)

Table 8. High level comparison of the sheep and cattle genomes based on virtual sheep genome analysis.

3.6 Construction of the virtual sheep genome (vsg2.0) genome browser

The cattle and sheep BAC and BES locations are displayed on the chromosome overview track of the virtual sheep genome browser (VSG) allowing a quick assessment of the quality of the assembly to be made (Fig 3). In addition, the sheep virtual genome assembly was annotated with the locations of the sheep markers, SNPs on the 1536 pilot sheep SNP chip (Kijas, et al., 2009) and the Illumina Ovine SNP50 BeadChip, and human and bovine mRNA RefSeqs downloaded from the NCBI (NCBI_RefSeq).

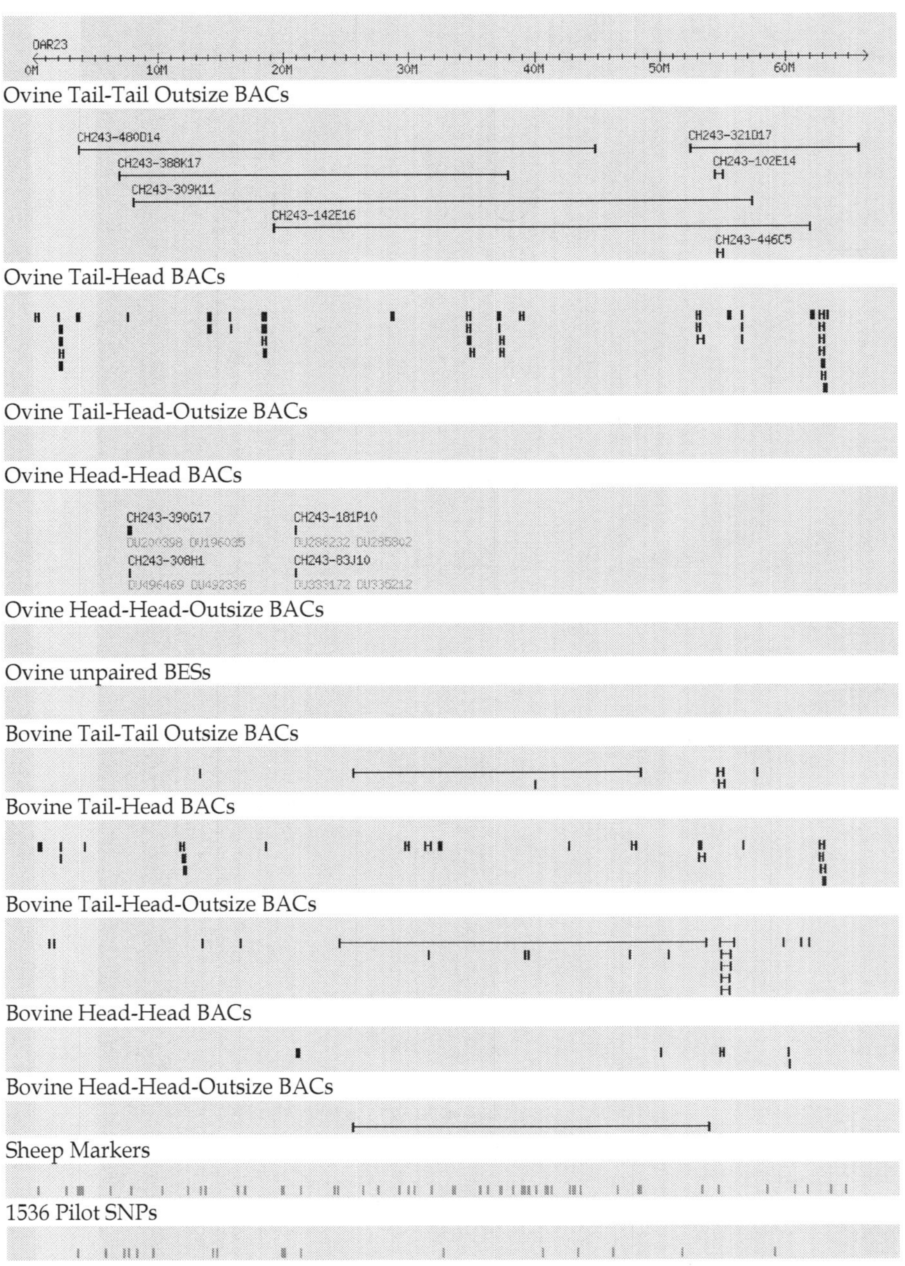

Fig. 3. Overview of chromosome OAR23 from the vsg v2 browser, displaying ovine and bovine BAC mapping, sheep linkage map markers and Pilot SNP Chip SNPs.

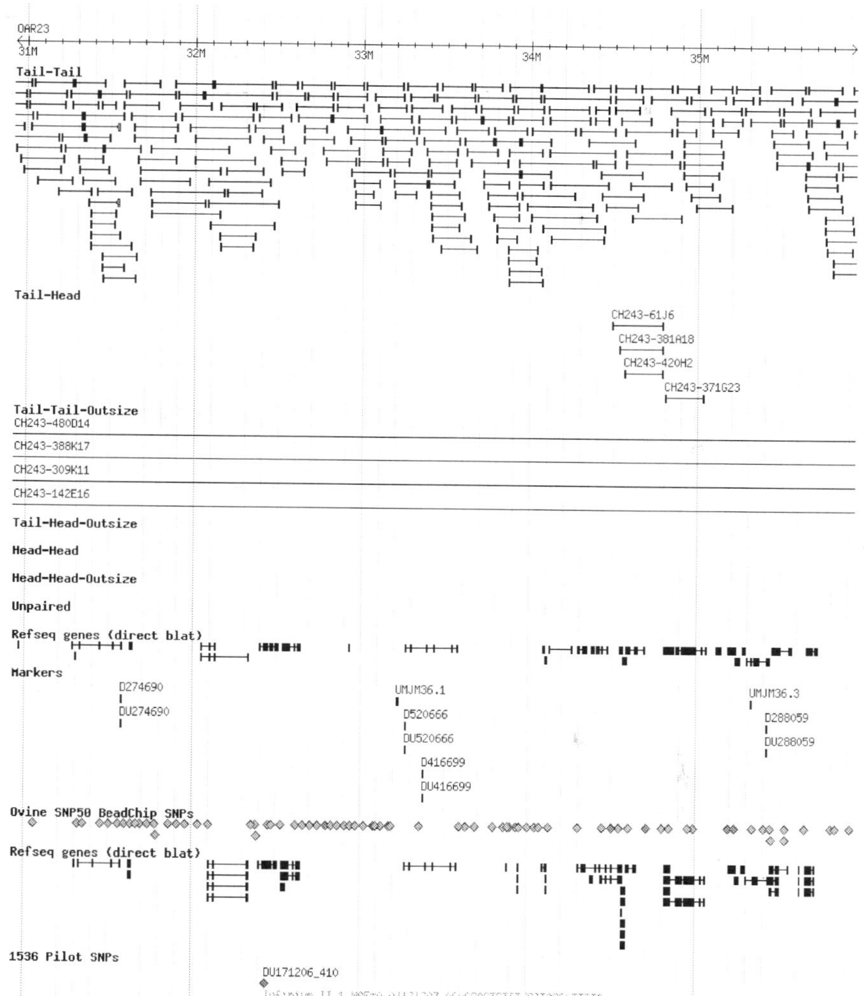

Fig. 4. A 5 Mb segment of the vsg 2 genome assembly of chromosome 23 showing the positions and orientations of sheep BACs and other tracks.

4. Conclusion

The new vsg2.0 is a significant improvement over vsg1.2, built on the human genome framework. Clearly using the genome from a closely related species and allowing the data from the species of interest to direct the process has an advantage over a very well assembled, but more distant genome. At the low resolution level down to the level of the BACs the sheep genome has a very high level of overall conserved synteny with the bovine genome structure. A number of regions of ambiguity remain, but many of these are in regions of ambiguity of the assembly of the bovine genome and therefore await further refinement of the bovine genome assembly, or a predominantly de novo assembly of the sheep genome. However, overall it is clear that the vsg 2 makes a robust framework to assemble the large number of short contigs expected from the sequencing of the sheep genome (Archibald, et al., 2010).

Two assembled genomes from closely related species is probably the optimal balance between analysis complexity and benefit, with inclusion of a more distant, but much better assembled genome, if the genomes of closely related species are not well assembled. Thus the methods that we have described are very broadly applicable.

5. Acknowledgement

The authors would like to thank the members of the International Sheep Genomics Consortium (ISGC_website) in particular Jill Maddox, John McEwan and James Kijas for useful discussions. The authors also gratefully acknowledge the early pre-publication access under the Fort Lauderdale conventions to the draft equine genome sequence provided by the Broad Institute and to the draft bovine genome sequence provided by the Baylor College of Medicine Human Genome Sequencing Center and the Bovine Genome Sequencing Project Consortium. This work was partly funded by SheepGenomics (a joint venture of Meat and Livestock Australia and Australian Wool Innovation). The work was undertaken as part of the development of sheep genomics tools by the ISGC.

6. References

AGP File Specification (v. 1.1), Available from
        http://www.ncbi.nlm.nih.gov/projects/genome/assembly/agp/AGP_Specificatio
        n.shtml
Archibald, A. L., Cockett, N. E., Dalrymple, B. P., Faraut, T., Kijas, J. W., Maddox, J. F.,
        McEwan, J. C., Hutton Oddy, V., Raadsma, H. W., Wade, C., Wang, J., Wang, W. &
        Xun, X. (2010). The sheep genome reference sequence: a work in progress. *Anim
        Genet*, Vol. 41, No. 5.pp. 449-453.
Dalrymple, B. P., Kirkness, E. F., Nefedov, M., McWilliam, S., Ratnakumar, A., Barris, W.,
        Zhao, S., Shetty, J., Maddox, J. F., O'Grady, M., Nicholas, F., Crawford, A. M.,
        Smith, T., de Jong, P. J., McEwan, J., Oddy, V. H. & Cockett, N. E. (2007). Using
        comparative genomics to reorder the human genome sequence into a virtual sheep
        genome. *Genome Biol*, Vol. 8, No. 7.pp. R152.
Drogemuller, M., Tetens, J., Dalrymple, B., Goldammer, T., Wu, C. H., Cockett, N. E., Leeb,
        T. & Drogemuller, C. (2008). A comparative radiation hybrid map of sheep
        chromosome 10. *Cytogenet Genome Res*, Vol. 121, No. 1.pp. 35-40.
Elsik, C. G., Tellam, R. L., Worley, K. C., Gibbs, R. A., Muzny, D. M., Weinstock, G. M.,
        Adelson, D. L., Eichler, E. E., Elnitski, L., Guigo, R., Hamernik, D. L., Kappes, S. M.,
        Lewin, H. A., Lynn, D. J., Nicholas, F. W., Reymond, A., Rijnkels, M., Skow, L. C.,
        Zdobnov, E. M., Schook, L., Womack, J., Alioto, T., Antonarakis, S. E., Astashyn, A.,
        Chapple, C. E., Chen, H. C., Chrast, J., Camara, F., Ermolaeva, O., Henrichsen, C.
        N., Hlavina, W., Kapustin, Y., Kiryutin, B., Kitts, P., Kokocinski, F., Landrum, M.,
        Maglott, D., Pruitt, K., Sapojnikov, V., Searle, S. M., Solovyev, V., Souvorov, A.,
        Ucla, C., Wyss, C., Anzola, J. M., Gerlach, D., Elhaik, E., Graur, D., Reese, J. T.,

Edgar, R. C., McEwan, J. C., Payne, G. M., Raison, J. M., Junier, T., Kriventseva, E. V., Eyras, E., Plass, M., Donthu, R., Larkin, D. M., Reecy, J., Yang, M. Q., Chen, L., Cheng, Z., Chitko-McKown, C. G., Liu, G. E., Matukumalli, L. K., Song, J., Zhu, B., Bradley, D. G., Brinkman, F. S., Lau, L. P., Whiteside, M. D., Walker, A., Wheeler, T. T., Casey, T., German, J. B., Lemay, D. G., Maqbool, N. J., Molenaar, A. J., Seo, S., Stothard, P., Baldwin, C. L., Baxter, R., Brinkmeyer-Langford, C. L., Brown, W. C., Childers, C. P., Connelley, T., Ellis, S. A., Fritz, K., Glass, E. J., Herzig, C. T., Iivanainen, A., Lahmers, K. K., Bennett, A. K., Dickens, C. M., Gilbert, J. G., Hagen, D. E., Salih, H., Aerts, J., Caetano, A. R., Dalrymple, B., Garcia, J. F., Gill, C. A., Hiendleder, S. G., Memili, E., Spurlock, D., Williams, J. L., Alexander, L., Brownstein, M. J., Guan, L., Holt, R. A., Jones, S. J., Marra, M. A., Moore, R., Moore, S. S., Roberts, A., Taniguchi, M., Waterman, R. C., Chacko, J., Chandrabose, M. M., Cree, A., Dao, M. D., Dinh, H. H., Gabisi, R. A., Hines, S., Hume, J., Jhangiani, S. N., Joshi, V., Kovar, C. L., Lewis, L. R., Liu, Y. S., Lopez, J., Morgan, M. B., Nguyen, N. B., Okwuonu, G. O., Ruiz, S. J., Santibanez, J., Wright, R. A., Buhay, C., Ding, Y., Dugan-Rocha, S., Herdandez, J., Holder, M., Sabo, A., Egan, A., Goodell, J., Wilczek-Boney, K., Fowler, G. R., Hitchens, M. E., Lozado, R. J., Moen, C., Steffen, D., Warren, J. T., Zhang, J., Chiu, R., Schein, J. E., Durbin, K. J., Havlak, P., Jiang, H., Liu, Y., Qin, X., Ren, Y., Shen, Y., Song, H., Bell, S. N., Davis, C., Johnson, A. J., Lee, S., Nazareth, L. V., Patel, B. M., Pu, L. L., Vattathil, S., Williams, R. L., Jr., Curry, S., Hamilton, C., Sodergren, E., Wheeler, D. A., Barris, W., Bennett, G. L., Eggen, A., Green, R. D., Harhay, G. P., Hobbs, M., Jann, O., Keele, J. W., Kent, M. P., Lien, S., McKay, S. D., McWilliam, S., Ratnakumar, A., Schnabel, R. D., Smith, T., Snelling, W. M., Sonstegard, T. S., Stone, R. T., Sugimoto, Y., Takasuga, A., Taylor, J. F., Van Tassell, C. P., Macneil, M. D., et al. (2009). The genome sequence of taurine cattle: a window to ruminant biology and evolution. *Science*, Vol. 324, No. 5926.pp. 522-528.

Fujita, P. A., Rhead, B., Zweig, A. S., Hinrichs, A. S., Karolchik, D., Cline, M. S., Goldman, M., Barber, G. P., Clawson, H., Coelho, A., Diekhans, M., Dreszer, T. R., Giardine, B. M., Harte, R. A., Hillman-Jackson, J., Hsu, F., Kirkup, V., Kuhn, R. M., Learned, K., Li, C. H., Meyer, L. R., Pohl, A., Raney, B. J., Rosenbloom, K. R., Smith, K. E., Haussler, D. & Kent, W. J. (2011). The UCSC Genome Browser database: update 2011. *Nucleic Acids Res*, Vol. 39, No. Database issue.pp. D876-882.

Goldammer, T., Brunner, R. M., Rebl, A., Wu, C. H., Nomura, K., Hadfield, T., Gill, C., Dalrymple, B. P., Womack, J. E. & Cockett, N. E. (2009a). A high-resolution radiation hybrid map of sheep chromosome X and comparison with human and cattle. *Cytogenet Genome Res*, Vol. 125, No. 1.pp. 40-45.

Goldammer, T., Brunner, R. M., Rebl, A., Wu, C. H., Nomura, K., Hadfield, T., Maddox, J. F. & Cockett, N. E. (2009b). Cytogenetic anchoring of radiation hybrid and virtual maps of sheep chromosome X and comparison of X chromosomes in sheep, cattle, and human. *Chromosome Res*, Vol. 17, No. 4.pp. 497-506.

Goldammer, T., Di Meo, G. P., Luhken, G., Drogemuller, C., Wu, C. H., Kijas, J., Dalrymple, B. P., Nicholas, F. W., Maddox, J. F., Iannuzzi, L. & Cockett, N. E. (2009c). Molecular cytogenetics and gene mapping in sheep (Ovis aries, 2n = 54). *Cytogenet Genome Res*, Vol. 126, No. 1-2.pp. 63-76.

ISGC website, Available from http://www.sheephapmap.org

Kent, W. J. (2002). BLAT--the BLAST-like alignment tool. *Genome Res*, Vol. 12, No. 4.pp. 656-664.

Kijas, J. W., Townley, D., Dalrymple, B. P., Heaton, M. P., Maddox, J. F., McGrath, A., Wilson, P., Ingersoll, R. G., McCulloch, R., McWilliam, S., Tang, D., McEwan, J., Cockett, N., Oddy, V. H., Nicholas, F. W. & Raadsma, H. (2009). A genome wide survey of SNP variation reveals the genetic structure of sheep breeds. *PLoS One*, Vol. 4, No. 3.pp. e4668.

Liftover UCSC genome coordinate conversion files, Available from http://genome.ucsc.edu/cgi-bin/hgLiftOver

Lindblad-Toh, K., Wade, C. M., Mikkelsen, T. S., Karlsson, E. K., Jaffe, D. B., Kamal, M., Clamp, M., Chang, J. L., Kulbokas, E. J., 3rd, Zody, M. C., Mauceli, E., Xie, X., Breen, M., Wayne, R. K., Ostrander, E. A., Ponting, C. P., Galibert, F., Smith, D. R., DeJong, P. J., Kirkness, E., Alvarez, P., Biagi, T., Brockman, W., Butler, J., Chin, C. W., Cook, A., Cuff, J., Daly, M. J., DeCaprio, D., Gnerre, S., Grabherr, M., Kellis, M., Kleber, M., Bardeleben, C., Goodstadt, L., Heger, A., Hitte, C., Kim, L., Koepfli, K. P., Parker, H. G., Pollinger, J. P., Searle, S. M., Sutter, N. B., Thomas, R., Webber, C., Baldwin, J., Abebe, A., Abouelleil, A., Aftuck, L., Ait-Zahra, M., Aldredge, T., Allen, N., An, P., Anderson, S., Antoine, C., Arachchi, H., Aslam, A., Ayotte, L., Bachantsang, P., Barry, A., Bayul, T., Benamara, M., Berlin, A., Bessette, D., Blitshteyn, B., Bloom, T., Blye, J., Boguslavskiy, L., Bonnet, C., Boukhgalter, B., Brown, A., Cahill, P., Calixte, N., Camarata, J., Cheshatsang, Y., Chu, J., Citroen, M., Collymore, A., Cooke, P., Dawoe, T., Daza, R., Decktor, K., DeGray, S., Dhargay, N., Dooley, K., Dorje, P., Dorjee, K., Dorris, L., Duffey, N., Dupes, A., Egbiremolen, O., Elong, R., Falk, J., Farina, A., Faro, S., Ferguson, D., Ferreira, P., Fisher, S., FitzGerald, M., Foley, K., Foley, C., Franke, A., Friedrich, D., Gage, D., Garber, M., Gearin, G., Giannoukos, G., Goode, T., Goyette, A., Graham, J., Grandbois, E., Gyaltsen, K., Hafez, N., Hagopian, D., Hagos, B., Hall, J., Healy, C., Hegarty, R., Honan, T., Horn, A., Houde, N., Hughes, L., Hunnicutt, L., Husby, M., Jester, B., Jones, C., Kamat, A., Kanga, B., Kells, C., Khazanovich, D., Kieu, A. C., Kisner, P., Kumar, M., Lance, K., Landers, T., Lara, M., Lee, W., Leger, J. P., Lennon, N., Leuper, L., LeVine, S., Liu, J., Liu, X., Lokyitsang, Y., Lokyitsang, T., Lui, A., Macdonald, J., Major, J., Marabella, R., Maru, K., Matthews, C., McDonough, S., Mehta, T., Meldrim, J., Melnikov, A., Meneus, L., Mihalev, A., Mihova, T., Miller, K., Mittelman, R., Mlenga, V., Mulrain, L., Munson, G., Navidi, A., Naylor, J., Nguyen, T., Nguyen, N., Nguyen, C., Nicol, R., Norbu, N., Norbu, C., Novod, N., Nyima, T., Olandt, P., O'Neill, B., O'Neill, K., Osman, S., Oyono, L., Patti, C., Perrin, D., Phunkhang, P., Pierre, F., Priest, M., Rachupka, A., Raghuraman, S., Rameau, R., Ray, V., Raymond, C., Rege, F., Rise, C., Rogers, J., Rogov, P., Sahalie, J., Settipalli, S., Sharpe, T., Shea, T., Sheehan, M., Sherpa, N., Shi, J., Shih, D., et al. (2005). Genome sequence, comparative analysis and haplotype structure of the domestic dog. *Nature*, Vol. 438, No. 7069.pp. 803-819.

Liu, H., Jiang, Y., Wang, S., Ninwichian, P., Somridhivej, B., Xu, P., Abernathy, J., Kucuktas, H. & Liu, Z. (2009). Comparative analysis of catfish BAC end sequences with the zebrafish genome. *BMC Genomics*, Vol. 10, No. 592.

Maddox, J. F., Davies, K. P., Crawford, A. M., Hulme, D. J., Vaiman, D., Cribiu, E. P., Freking, B. A., Beh, K. J., Cockett, N. E., Kang, N., Riffkin, C. D., Drinkwater, R.,

Moore, S. S., Dodds, K. G., Lumsden, J. M., van Stijn, T. C., Phua, S. H., Adelson, D. L., Burkin, H. R., Broom, J. E., Buitkamp, J., Cambridge, L., Cushwa, W. T., Gerard, E., Galloway, S. M., Harrison, B., Hawken, R. J., Hiendleder, S., Henry, H. M., Medrano, J. F., Paterson, K. A., Schibler, L., Stone, R. T. & van Hest, B. (2001). An enhanced linkage map of the sheep genome comprising more than 1000 loci. *Genome Res*, Vol. 11, No. 7.pp. 1275-1289.

NCBI RefSeq collection, Available from http://www.ncbi.nlm.nih.gov/RefSeq/index.html

Ratnakumar, A., Barris, W., McWilliam, S., Brauning, R., McEwan, J. C., Snelling, W. M. & Dalrymple, B. P. (2009). A multiway analysis for identifying high integrity bovine BACs. *BMC Genomics*, Vol. 10, No. 46.

Ratnakumar, A., Kirkness, E. F. & Dalrymple, B. P. (2010a). Quality control of the sheep bacterial artificial chromosome library, CHORI-243. *BMC Res Notes*, Vol. 3, No. 334.

Ratnakumar, A., McWilliam, S., Barris, W. & Dalrymple, B. P. (2010b). Using paired-end sequences to optimise parameters for alignment of sequence reads against related genomes. *BMC Genomics*, Vol. 11, No. 458.

Snelling, W. M., Chiu, R., Schein, J. E., Hobbs, M., Abbey, C. A., Adelson, D. L., Aerts, J., Bennett, G. L., Bosdet, I. E., Boussaha, M., Brauning, R., Caetano, A. R., Costa, M. M., Crawford, A. M., Dalrymple, B. P., Eggen, A., Everts-van der Wind, A., Floriot, S., Gautier, M., Gill, C. A., Green, R. D., Holt, R., Jann, O., Jones, S. J., Kappes, S. M., Keele, J. W., de Jong, P. J., Larkin, D. M., Lewin, H. A., McEwan, J. C., McKay, S., Marra, M. A., Mathewson, C. A., Matukumalli, L. K., Moore, S. S., Murdoch, B., Nicholas, F. W., Osoegawa, K., Roy, A., Salih, H., Schibler, L., Schnabel, R. D., Silveri, L., Skow, L. C., Smith, T. P., Sonstegard, T. S., Taylor, J. F., Tellam, R., Van Tassell, C. P., Williams, J. L., Womack, J. E., Wye, N. H., Yang, G. & Zhao, S. (2007). A physical map of the bovine genome. *Genome Biol*, Vol. 8, No. 8.pp. R165.

Soler, L., Conte, M. A., Katagiri, T., Howe, A. E., Lee, B. Y., Amemiya, C., Stuart, A., Dossat, C., Poulain, J., Johnson, J., Di Palma, F., Lindblad-Toh, K., Baroiller, J. F., D'Cotta, H., Ozouf-Costaz, C. & Kocher, T. D. (2010). Comparative physical maps derived from BAC end sequences of tilapia (Oreochromis niloticus). *BMC Genomics*, Vol. 11, No. 636.

Stein, L. D., Mungall, C., Shu, S., Caudy, M., Mangone, M., Day, A., Nickerson, E., Stajich, J. E., Harris, T. W., Arva, A. & Lewis, S. (2002). The generic genome browser: a building block for a model organism system database. *Genome Res*, Vol. 12, No. 10.pp. 1599-1610.

UCSC Genome Bioinformatics Website, Available from http://genome.ucsc.edu/

Virtual sheep genome browser, Available from
http://www.livestockgenomics.csiro.au/perl/gbrowse.cgi/vsheep2/

Wade, C. M., Giulotto, E., Sigurdsson, S., Zoli, M., Gnerre, S., Imsland, F., Lear, T. L., Adelson, D. L., Bailey, E., Bellone, R. R., Blocker, H., Distl, O., Edgar, R. C., Garber, M., Leeb, T., Mauceli, E., MacLeod, J. N., Penedo, M. C., Raison, J. M., Sharpe, T., Vogel, J., Andersson, L., Antczak, D. F., Biagi, T., Binns, M. M., Chowdhary, B. P., Coleman, S. J., Della Valle, G., Fryc, S., Guerin, G., Hasegawa, T., Hill, E. W., Jurka, J., Kiialainen, A., Lindgren, G., Liu, J., Magnani, E., Mickelson, J. R., Murray, J., Nergadze, S. G., Onofrio, R., Pedroni, S., Piras, M. F., Raudsepp, T., Rocchi, M., Roed, K. H., Ryder, O. A., Searle, S., Skow, L., Swinburne, J. E., Syvanen, A. C., Tozaki, T., Valberg, S. J., Vaudin, M., White, J. R., Zody, M. C., Lander, E. S. &

Lindblad-Toh, K. (2009). Genome sequence, comparative analysis, and population genetics of the domestic horse. *Science*, Vol. 326, No. 5954.pp. 865-867.

Wu, C. H., Nomura, K., Goldammer, T., Hadfield, T., Dalrymple, B. P., McWilliam, S., Maddox, J. F., Womack, J. E. & Cockett, N. E. (2008). A high-resolution comparative radiation hybrid map of ovine chromosomal regions that are homologous to human chromosome 6 (HSA6). *Anim Genet*, Vol. 39, No. 5.pp. 459-467.

Wu, C. H., Jin, W., Nomura, K., Goldammer, T., Hadfield, T., Dalrymple, B. P., McWilliam, S., Maddox, J. F. & Cockett, N. E. (2009). A radiation hybrid comparative map of ovine chromosome 1 aligned to the virtual sheep genome. *Anim Genet*, Vol. 40, No. 4.pp. 435-455.

Zimin, A. V., Delcher, A. L., Florea, L., Kelley, D. R., Schatz, M. C., Puiu, D., Hanrahan, F., Pertea, G., Van Tassell, C. P., Sonstegard, T. S., Marcais, G., Roberts, M., Subramanian, P., Yorke, J. A. & Salzberg, S. L. (2009). A whole-genome assembly of the domestic cow, Bos taurus. *Genome Biol*, Vol. 10, No. 4.pp. R42.

19

Basidiomycetes Telomeres – A Bioinformatics Approach

Lucía Ramírez, Gúmer Pérez, Raúl Castanera,
Francisco Santoyo and Antonio G. Pisabarro
*Genetics and Microbiology Research Group, Public University of Navarre, Pamplona,
Spain*

1. Introduction

1.1 The telomere: A complex nucleoprotein complex with a broad range of functions

The telomeres (from the Greek *télos* far and -*meros* part) are the genetic structures found at the physical ends of linear chromosomes. They are nucleoprotein complexes composed of DNA repeats and a myriad of telomere and non-telomere associated proteins aimed to protect the ends of eukaryotic chromosomes from being recognized as double strand breaks, and to avoid chromosome end degradation by nucleases and non-canonical chromosome end fusions. Thus, telomeres are essential for chromosome integrity (Hande, 2004; Paeschke et al., 2010; Zakian, 1995). The fascinating story about telomere biology comes from the pioneering work of Elizabeth H. Blackburn who discovered that *Tetrahymena* telomeres consisted of a short DNA sequence motif that was repeated several times at the chromosomal end (Blackburn & Gall, 1978). This pattern is conserved in lower eukaryotes and in mammalian cells (Greider, 1998). Notable exceptions are *Drosophila* and some other dipterans, which instead possess tandem arrays of retrotransposons at their chromosome ends (Abad et al., 2004).

Telomere DNA consists of tandem arrays of short repeated sequences forming a cap. Telomere length is species-specific and small cell type variations were observed. For reviews, see Fisher & Zakian, (2005) and Sanchez-Alonso & Guzman (2008). The basic telomere DNA repeat unit is the hexamer TTAGGG in which the strand running $5' \rightarrow 3'$ outwards the centromere is usually guanine-rich. This G-rich strand protrudes its complementary end and bends on itself to form a telomere DNA loop (T-loop) (Griffith et al., 1999) which protects the structure from being recognized as a double-stranded break by sequestering the 3'-overhang into a high order DNA structure. The G-rich strand also serves as an anchor for a telomere-dedicated reverse transcriptase, called telomerase, that compensates for the inability of DNA polymerases to replicate the 5' ends of linear chromosomes (Blackburn & Gall, 1978). The telomerase binds the G-rich strand by complementary pairing of the protruding DNA sequence to the telomerase RNA subunit and, as a result, telomerase elongates the overhang by adding telomere sequence repeats (Masutomi et al., 2003; Morin, 1989; Zhao et al., 2009). The T loop structure is maintained by a complex of telomere and non-telomere proteins called shelterins which repress the DNA repair machinery at telomeres, and regulate telomere length (for review see de Lange, 2005; Palm & de Lange, 2008; Rhodes et al., 2002; Vega et al., 2003; Zhao et al., 2009). The shelterin complex is formed by a core of six proteins including the Myb-type homeodomain TRF proteins in mammals, Rap1 in *Saccharomyces cerevisiae* and Taz1 in *Schizosaccharomyces pombe* which bind the duplex form of the telomere repeats, the OB-fold containing protein POT1 in mammals and *S. pombe* and Cdc13 in *S. cerevisiae* which bind the single-stranded telomere 3'overhang and by other proteins associated via protein–protein interactions with them (Rhodes et al., 2002; Vega et al., 2003; Zhao et al., 2009). This shelterin complex is evolutionary conserved although some differences between species appear in protein numbers and in its higher order structure (Linger & Price, 2009). The G-rich single stranded telomere tail is also able to form a secondary DNA order structure resulting from intra and intermolecular G-quadruplex (Fry, 2007; Maizels, 2006). G-quadruplexes are stacked associations of G-quartets, which are themselves planar assemblies of four Hoogsteen-bonded guanines, with the guanines derived from one or more nucleic acid strands (De Cian et al., 2008; Johnson et al., 2008). These structures have been observed in lower eukaryotes (Paeschke et al., 2008; Paeschke et al., 2005; Schaffitzel et al., 2001) and have the potential to regulate telomerase activity (Oganesian et al., 2006; Zahler et al., 1991).

Secondary DNA structures, G-quadruplex structures and T-loop may contribute to telomere function but pose an obstacle for semi-conservative and telomerase-mediated replication, a problem which should be solved to avoid telomere shorten. Telomeres become shortened during every cell cycle due to incomplete replication of the lagging strand (the so called "end replication problem") resulting in cumulative telomere attrition during aging. In addition, a loss of telomere DNA occurs due to post-replicative degradation of the 5′ strand that generates long 3′ G-rich overhangs (Wellinger et al., 1996; Wellinger et al., 1993). In most species, the loss of telomere DNA is counteracted by the action of telomerase that carries its own RNA template coding for the telomere repeat sequence (Chan & Blackburn, 2004). The complementary C-rich strand is then synthesized by conventional RNA-primed DNA replication (Gilson & Geli, 2007; Verdun & Karlseder, 2007). Following replication, the telomeres created by the synthesis of the leading strand are either blunt-ended or left carrying a small 50 bp overhang whereas those created by the lagging-strand synthesis have a 3′ overhang with a length determined by the position of the outermost RNA primer (de Lange, 2009). This fact supports the importance of the telomerase activity for the genome integrity. When telomeres reach a critical minimal length they become uncapped. This leads to a permanent cell cycle arrest (termed cellular senescence) or to apoptosis, depending on the cellular context in which the uncapping occurs (Aubert & Lansdorp, 2008; Blasco, 2005). Extreme telomere shortening leads to chromosome instability, end-to-end fusions, and checkpoint-mediated cell cycle arrest and/or apoptosis (reviewed in Aubert & Lansdorp (2008) and in Shore & Bianchi (2009). The whole processes are related in mammals not only to aging, but also to several age associated diseases such as tumorigenesis, coronary artery disease, and heart failure (Donate & Blasco, 2011; Ogami et al., 2004; Sherr & McCormick, 2002; Starr et al., 2007). In addition to the role of telomerase in maintaining telomere length, it has been described that homologous recombination (HR) constitute an alternative method (ALT "alternative lengthening of telomeres") to maintain telomere DNA in telomerase-deficient cells with telomeres highly heterogeneous in length. This mechanism was described in *S. cerevisiae* and consists in two pathways depending on different recombination proteins that use different telomere sequences as substrates for recombination. Cancer and immortalized cells can utilize the ALT mechanism to maintain telomere length (Lundblad & Blackburn, 1993; Teng et al., 2000; Teng & Zakian, 1999).

Telomeres were considered as regions where the transcription of structural genes is repressed (Mondoux & Zakian, 2005), although it has been recently reported that telomere repeats and subtelomere regions can be transcribed (Azzalin et al., 2007; Luke & Lingner, 2009; Luke et al., 2008; Schoeftner & Blasco, 2008). The telomere transcribed region, called TERRA (telomere repeat-containing RNA), forms an integral component of telomere heterochromatin, and produces non-coding G-rich RNAs transcribed from the telomere C-rich strand in mammals and fungi (Azzalin et al., 2007; Luke et al., 2008; Sanchez-Alonso & Guzman, 2008; Schoeftner & Blasco, 2008). TERRA transcription occurs at most or all chromosome ends and it is regulated by RNA surveillance factors and in response to changes in telomere length. The accumulation of TERRA at telomeres can also interfere with telomere replication (Azzalin & Lingner, 2007; Luke & Lingner, 2009; Schoeftner & Blasco, 2009).

The particular sequence organization of telomere makes difficult its genetic mapping and sequencing due to they are cloning recalcitrant and underrepresented in mapping and final assembled genomes. Consequently, their cloning and characterization must be made by dedicated molecular and bioinformatics strategies (Perez et al., 2009; Sanchez-Alonso & Guzman, 2008).

1.2 Subtelomere chromosome regions

Human subtelomere chromosome regions contain complex and dynamic stretches of DNA which, together with their associated proteins, are essential for genome stability and proper chromosome replication (Riethman et al., 2005). Subtelomere DNA repeats are a complex region of variable size segmentally duplicated containing low copy DNA repetitive tracts adjacent to the telomere. These duplications could be found only at the subtelomere regions, although it is common to find them also at pericentromeric and interstitial chromosomal loci (Riethman et al., 2001).

In humans, subtelomere DNA regions are operationally defined as the terminal 500 Kbp of each euchromatic chromosome arm. These regions contain subtelomere repeats (Srpts), segmental duplications, satellite sequences, and internal $(TTAGGG)_n$-like sequences (Riethman et al., 2004). The organization of the subtelomere region is structurally conserved across eukaryotes (Anderson et al., 2008; Brown et al., 1990a; Brown et al., 1990b; Chan & Tye, 1983a; 1983b; Flint et al., 1997a; Flint et al., 1997b; Karpen & Spradling, 1992; Levis, 1993; Louis, 1995; Louis & Borts, 1995; Mefford & Trask, 2002; Pryde et al., 1997; Pryde & Louis, 1997; Walter et al., 1995; Wilkie et al., 1991). This region, susceptible to hypermethylation has been recently shown to have a central function in mammalian telomere-length homeostasis (Blasco, 2007). Subtelomere repeats are characterized by their high level of polymorphism among different chromosome ends and among individuals of the same species. This polymorphism, possibly indicative of a quick and dynamic sequence turnover, leads to a lack of relationship among subtelomere repeats across species. Nonhomologous or ectopic exchange between subtelomere regions of different chromosomes has been reported as a possible reason of polymorphisms in both yeast and humans (Linardopoulou et al., 2005; Louis & Haber, 1990; Mefford & Trask, 2002). In humans, there are more re-arrangements at the sub-telomere regions than in the rest of the genome. This is also true in some lower eukaryotes such as *Plasmodium falciparum* (Freitas-Junior et al., 2000), *Magnaporthe oryzae* (Rehmeyer et al., 2006) and *Neurospora crassa* (Wu et al., 2009), among others. In all these cases genes involved in niche adaptation (species-specific genes) were found in the subtelomeric regions. It could be that the high evolutive potential of the subtelomeric regions were used by these organisms to create variability aimed to avoid the detection by the host. In fungi the genes more frequently found in subtelomere regions are transposons, telomere-linked RecQ helicases, clusters of secondary-metabolites, cytochrome oxidases, hydrolases, molecular transporters, and genes encoding secreted proteins (Perez et al., 2009). These genes could undergo transcriptional silencing (subtelomere silencing) due to its close proximity to telomeres.

1.3 Interstitial telomere repeats

The various chemical modifications occurring at the amino terminal end of the histones affect the structure of chromatin and help establishing the functional and structural domains known as euchromatin and heterochromatin. Euchromatin is an open form of chromatin that allows transcription factors access to and transcriptionally activate their target genes. It is largely occupied by housekeeping genes, condensed during metaphase and decondensed during interphase. Heterochromatin, on the contrary, differs from euchromatin in that it is condensed during interphase.

Heterochromatin has been often said to be "poor in genes" and mainly constituted by repetitive DNA sequences. Moreover, since it is highly condensed and inaccessible to transcription factors, heterochromatin is generally transcriptionally silent (Hernandez-Rivas et al., 2010). Heterochromatin appears as blocks spread over the chromosomes when they are stained with Giemsa dye. The molecular analysis of heterochromatic blocks reveals sequences similar to the telomere repeats that are called in this case interstitial telomere repeat sequences or ITRs. These sequences include those repeats located close to the centromere and those found at interstitial sites, i.e., between the centromere and the telomeres (Meyne et al., 1990; Slijepcevic et al., 1996). ITRs were described in plants, animals and humans (Bolzan & Bianchi, 2006; Uchida et al., 2002; Welchen & Gonzalez, 2005). At the chromosome level, ITRs can be detected either by using the Fluorescence *in situ* hybridization (FISH) technique with a DNA or a peptide nucleic acid (PNA) pan-telomere probe (i.e., a probe that identifies simultaneously all of the telomeres in a metaphase cell), or by the primed *in situ* labeling (PRINS) reaction using an oligonucleotide primer complementary to the telomere DNA repeated sequence (Bolzan & Bianchi, 2006).

The length and the locations of the heterochromatic blocks in chromosomes are variable (Azzalin et al., 2001; Faravelli et al., 1998; Weber et al., 1990) as well as their origin. However, the presence of ITRs in the heterochromatic blocks is interpreted as the result of tandem telomere–telomere fusions during evolution (Hastie & Allshire, 1989; Holmquist & Dancis, 1979; Meyne et al., 1990) or the insertion of telomere DNA within genome unstable sites (recombination hotspots) during the repair of double strand DNA breaks (DSB) (Azzalin et al., 2001). The presence of some relatively small ITRs flanked by unstable AT-rich DNA sequences could support this last hypothesis (Faravelli et al., 2002). On the other hand, telomere associations and fusions are common cytogenetic findings that have been implicated in the initiation of chromosome instability and tumorigenesis (Callen & Surralles, 2004; Murnane & Sabatier, 2004; Soler et al., 2005). Telomere fusions are the result of telomere dysfunction due to attrition of chromosome ends (Maser & DePinho, 2004). They are usually found in repair- and/or telomerase-deficient cells (Bailey et al., 1999; Blasco et al., 1997; Hande, 2004; Hande et al., 1999; Lo et al., 2002; Samper et al., 2000) with a variety of mutations affecting telomere function, including those occurring in proteins of the shelterin complex (Bailey et al., 1999; Goytisolo et al., 2001). Mammal cells show a high frequency of telomere fusions (end-to-end) and chromosome instability (Bailey et al., 2004; Bailey et al., 1999; Espejel et al., 2002; Hsu et al., 2000; Smogorzewska et al., 2002; Takai et al., 2003; van Steensel et al., 1998). The FISH technique allows the identification of metacentric-submetacentric and acrocentric-telocentric chromosome telomere fusions also known as Robertsonian-like configurations (Al-Wahiby et al., 2005; Hande, 2004). The occurrence of telomere–telomere associations has been suggested to play a role in nuclear organization (Nagele et al., 2001). In fact, telomere associations were seen in metaphases of human cells with shorten telomeres suggesting that a minimal telomere length is required for a proper chromosome function during mitosis.

2. Fungal telomeres - A bioinformatics approach

The basic and conserved telomere unit sequence in most filamentous fungi is TTAGGG. This sequence has been described in *Aspergillus nidulans* (Bhattacharyya & Blackburn, 1997), *Beauveria bassiana* (Padmavathi et al., 2003), *Botrytis cinerea* (Levis et al., 1997), *Cladosporium fulvum* (Coleman et al., 1993), *Fusarium oxysporum* (Inglis et al., 2000), *Glomus intraradices* (Hijri et al., 2007), *Magnaporthe grisea* (Gao et al., 2002), *Metarrhizium anisopliae* (Inglis et al., 2005), *N. crassa* (Wu et al., 2009), *Pestalotiopsis microspora* (Long et al., 1998), *Pleurotus ostreatus* (Perez et al., 2009), *Pneumocystis carinii* (Keely et al., 2001), and *Ustilago maydis* (Sanchez-Alonso & Guzman, 2008). However, variations of this sequence can be found in other fungi such as *A. oryzae* that has dodecanucleotide telomere repeats (Kusumoto et al., 2003) Incomplete and imperfect telomere units have been reported in: *A. oryzae, Candida albicans, Kluyveromyces lactis, S. cerevisiae* and *S. pombe*.

Two DNA sequence domains can be found adjacent to the telomere repeats. One of them, distal, is placed next to the telomere and contains tandem repeat motifs. The other, proximal, is interstitial, contains less repeated sequences and ferries clusters of related genes (Pryde et al., 1997). In several fungi, it has been observed an increased number of proteins involved in interactions with the environment coded for by genes mapping close to the telomeres. These genes are called 'contingency genes', they are dispensable for survival and are highly variable in populations. The accumulation of these genes near the telomeres is a strategy that allows fungi to afford new environments. In fact, it has been observed in *S. cerevisiae* that the genes located near the telomeres display variation in gene amplification and/or expression depending on the growing niche of the yeast. Some of these genes belong to the PAU family, the largest gene family in *S. cerevisiae* (23 members), whose regulation depends on the environmental growing conditions (anaerobiosis) (Rachidi et al., 2000). Other telomere associated genes in *S. cerevisiae* are MAL and MEL that participate in maltose and melibiose fermentation, used in the baking and brewing industries (Gibson et al., 1997; Teunissen & Steensma, 1995), and FLO that encodes cell-wall glycoproteins which participate in the regulation of cellular adhesion (Gibson et al., 1997; Halme et al., 2004; Teunissen & Steensma, 1995). Similarly, the TLO family unique in *C. albicans* consists of 15 members present on every chromosome, 14 of which are located at chromosome ends. Genome comparisons between *C. albicans* and *Candida dublinienesis* showed that the principal disparity in gene content between both species resides in the lack of the TLO genes in this last one. CdTLO1 null strains show a major reduction in hyphal formation in response to serum that can be reversed by complementation with either of two *C. albicans* TLO genes (Jackson et al., 2009).

In human parasites it has been described several families of well characterized or putative virulence factors at chromosome ends. In *Candida glabrata* (De Las Penas et al., 2003) nearly 24 adhesin encoding genes were located at telomere regions, and, in *P. carinii* clusters of major surface antigen genes have been bioinformatically predicted at every chromosome end (Keely et al., 2005). A similar situation was reported in *P. falciparum* and *Trypanosoma brucei* where families of antigen surface proteins inducing immune responses are encoded in telomere regions as part of a pathogen's mechanism to amplify and diversify surface antigen genes to avoid host recognition, as it has been hypothesized (Barry et al., 2003).

To determine if plant pathogenic fungi use a similar mechanism to avoid host defenses, Farman's group analyzed and characterized the telomere organization in the rice blast pathogen *M. oryzae* (Rehmeyer et al., 2006) and in *N. crassa* (Wu et al., 2009). The molecular and bioinformatics approach allowed them to identify 14 chromosomes in both of them. In *M. oryzae*, the analysis of these sequences reveals the presence of a clearly defined distal subtelomere domain that contains a telomere-linked helicase (TLH) gene. No gene duplication near the chromosome termini is observed. Thus it is impossible to detect a proximal subtelomere domain. The sequenced *N. crassa* genome (Galagan et al., 2003) contains very little intact, duplicated DNA due to the repeat-induced point mutation (RIP) process (Selker, 1990). This situation made unlikely that *N. crassa* would possess intact subtelomere domains or terminal gene duplications. The search for tandem repeats at the ends of some chromosomes whose sequences extend out of the telomere repeats shows the lack of conserved subtelomere tandem repeats. A similar situation is observed when the sequences immediately adjacent to the TTAGGG repeats were compared between strains. Consistent with the absence of distinct subtelomere elements, *N. crassa* lacks the TLH genes that are present in the subtelomere regions of diverse fungi (Gao et al., 2002; Inglis et al., 2005; Louis & Haber, 1992; Mandell et al., 2005; Perez et al., 2009; Rehmeyer et al., 2006; Sanchez-Alonso & Guzman, 1998). As in other fungi, the terminal regions of *N. crassa* chromosomes ferry genes related to secondary metabolism such as a monooyygenase (CYP450), a FAD-binding domain containing protein, a second CYP450, an O-methyltransferase, a polyketide synthase, a major facilitator superfamily efflux pump, a putative transcription factor, and an oxidoreductase. Apart from the clusters of secondary metabolite genes, there were no genes overrepresented in the chromosome ends, except those predicted to code for enzymes related to plant cell-wall degradation activity.

In basidiomycetes, despite the genomes of an ever growing number of genera involved in lignin degradation, enzyme production, and bio pulping have been sequenced and annotated, the information on the characteristics of their telomere and sub-telomere regions is rather limited. As it was discussed above, this is due to the particular characteristic of telomeres that make them refractory to cloning and difficult to sequence and assemble in whole genome sequencing projects. A consequence of the difficulty in cloning telomeres is that, for most organisms, there is limited information on the organization of chromosome ends. Data about basidiomycete telomeres are available for *U. maydis* (Sanchez-Alonso & Guzman, 1998), *M. anisopliae* (Inglis et al., 2005) and *P. ostreatus* (Perez et al., 2009). In the three cases, the conserved telomere repetitive unit is TTAGGG, and the number of tandem repetitions varies among species: 37 times in *U. maydis*, from 18 to 26 in *M. anisopliae*, and from 25 to 150 in *P. ostreatus*. In all these cases, genes coding for RecQ helicases have been found adjacent to the telomere regions.

In *P. ostreatus*, a lignin degrader edible mushroom, the analysis of telomere organization was carried out with a combination of genetic, molecular, and bioinformatics tools. This approach allowed our group to map 19 out of the 22 chromosome ends expected in its linkage map (Perez et al., 2009), as well as to study the telomere adjacent regions. Similar strategies have been described by different authors (Rehmeyer et al., 2006; Sanchez-Alonso & Guzman, 2008; Wu et al., 2009). The search for telomere regions was performed in whole genome sequence draft assemblies. These preliminary genome sequence versions appeared as incomplete, contained some genes truncated and were misassembled. The rationale for using them is that the genome final assembling strategies very often alter or eliminate the telomere and subtelomere repetitive sequences of the fully assembled genomes. We used the open-access Tandem Repeats Finder program (TRFp, http://tandem.bu.edu/trf/trf.html) to screen for repetitive telomere sequences in more than 6,200 contigs of the 4X coverage draft sequence assembly of *P. ostreatus* PC15 produced by the Joint Genome Institute (http://genome.jgi-psf.org/PleosPC15_1/PleosPC15_1.home.html). The TRFp locates and displays tandem repeats in a DNA sequence file submitted in FASTA format without need of specifying the repetitive pattern, its size or any other parameter. The TRFp output consists of two files: a repeat table and an alignment. The repeat table contains information about each repeat, its size, copy number, nucleotide content and location. Clicking on the location indices for this table's entries opens a second web browser that shows an alignment of the copies against a consensus pattern. TRFp is a very fast program that permits the analysis of up to 5 Mb sequence length. Repeats with pattern size in the range from one to 2000 bases could be detected (Benson, 1999). We identified, in each telomere sequence containing scaffold, the filtered gene models computer and manually annotated within 50 Kbp of the telomere repetitive sequence. This was done by manual inspection of each one of the predicted genes and using them as query in the non-redundant NCBI gene database using the BlastX program (Altschul et al., 1997). The BlastX results were considered significant if their expected value (e-value) was <e-20. The identified protein sequences were also used to query the online Pfam database using default parameters (Bateman et al., 2004). A similar approach has also been used by Wu et al. (2009) to search for subtelomere regions containing gene in *N. crassa*. This type of multiple analysis (genetic, molecular, and bioinformatics) allows the characterization of most of the *P. ostreatus* telomeres as well as several subtelomere regions that show high nucleotide similarity. The highly polymorphic subtelomere region of *P. ostreatus* chromosome six contains genes similar to those described in other eukaryotic organisms (RecQ helicases), apart from a species-specific laccase gene cluster (six out of 12 genes annotated in the genome (Perez et al., 2009).

In conclusion, the assemblage of telomere regions by bioinformatics strategies is a powerful tool to determine the arrangement of genomes in putative linkage groups in species with no genetic maps available, to establish synteny among different basidiomycete genomes, and to determine the presence of genes and gene clusters conserved in the subtelomere regions of different genomes.

2.1 Analysis of the basidiomycetes' telomere regions

In the following sections we will review the composition and structure of the telomere and subtelomere regions of the different basidiomycetes using the bioinformatics approach described above. We will use the genome sequence data that are publicly available at the Joint Genome Institute (DOE-JGI, http://www.jgi.doe.gov/). This institute has been developing an intensive sequencing effort on different fungi related with the biological lignocellulose degradation. Lignin is a complex recalcitrant macromolecule that hinders the access of enzymes to cellulose. The enzymatic removal of lignin will permit the access to this large carbon reservoir for its use in different energy-related applications. There are two types of fungi according to their strategy for making cellulose accessible: white rot fungi degrade lignin, and brown rot fungi minimally modify the lignin and attack the cellulose using a different chemical approach (Lundell et al., 2010; Martinez et al., 2005; Ruiz-Duenas & Martinez, 2009). Among all the sequenced basidiomycetes, we will concentrate here on the white rot degraders *Ceriporiopsis subvermispora*, *Phanerochaete chrisosporium* and *P. ostreatus*; the brown rot *Postia placenta* and the tree pathogen *Heterobasidion annosum*.

2.1.1 Analysis of the telomere regions of *Ceriporiopsis subvermispora* B

C. subvermispora is a white rot basidiomycete that rapidly depolymerizes lignin with relatively little cellulose degradation when growing on wood (Martinez et al., 2005). The chromosome number of this species has not been conclusively determined. The JGI has sequenced the strain B. Two type of sequence data (un-assembled reads and assembled scaffolds unmasked) were screened for the presence of telomere sequences in the genome of *C. subvermispora*: 297,269 unassembled and 740 assembled scaffolds. In 207 unassembled scaffolds, between five and 23 tandem repeats of the telomere motif TTAGGG were found. In most cases (82 % of these unassembled scaffolds) 17 and 19 repeats of the motif were found, and the mean repeat number was 18.7. On the other hand, 187 scaffolds carried between seven and 22 repeats of the telomere complementary sequence CCCTAA. In this case, the modal repetition number varied between 17 and 19 (84% of the scaffolds) and the mean number was 19.2. Taken together these data suggest that the average number of telomere repeats in *C. subvermispora* is 19.0.

The unmasked analysis of 740 assembled scaffolds revealed that 42 of them contained telomere sequences: 22 harbored the TTAGGG sequence and 20 the complementary CCCTAA. The telomere region TTAGGG was placed at the bottom (3′ telomere) end of the chromosome in 21 out of the 22 scaffolds. An exception to this was observed in scaffold 3. The sequence was located at an interstitial position. The telomere region CCCTAA was placed at the upper (5′ telomere) end of the chromosome in 19 out of 20 scaffolds. As it was described above, this sequence was also placed at an interstitial location in scaffold 3. This suggest a missassembling scaffold 3 because both the direct $TTAGGG_{21}$ (TTAGGG, scaffold 3: 1205371-1205497) and the reverse $CCCTAA_{21}$ (CCCTAA, scaffold 3: 1206763-1205497) telomere sequences have been found flanking a 1265 bp gap 3 (Fig. 1).

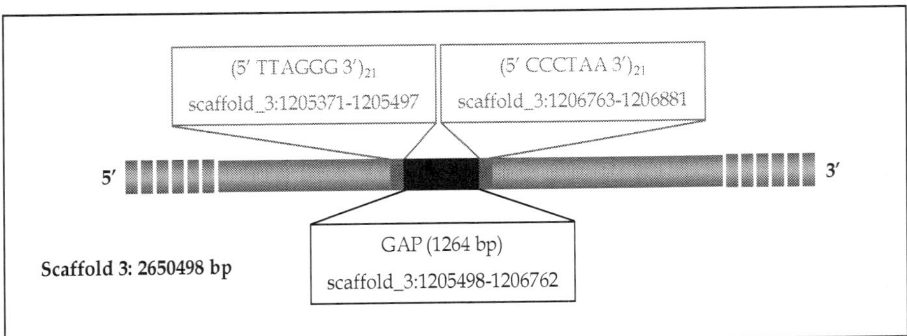

Fig. 1. Location of interstitial telomere sequences in scaffold 3 of the genome sequence of *C. subvermispora*.

The telomeres found in scaffolds 5 and 7 have a complex structure. The telomere of scaffold 5 contained 22 and 20 copies of the CCCTAA sequence separated by a gap of 193 bp. In the case of scaffold 7, 20 and 18 copies of this sequence appeared separated by a gap of 1680 bp (Fig. 2). We presume that these particular structures could reflect misassemblages of the telomere sequences in both scaffolds.

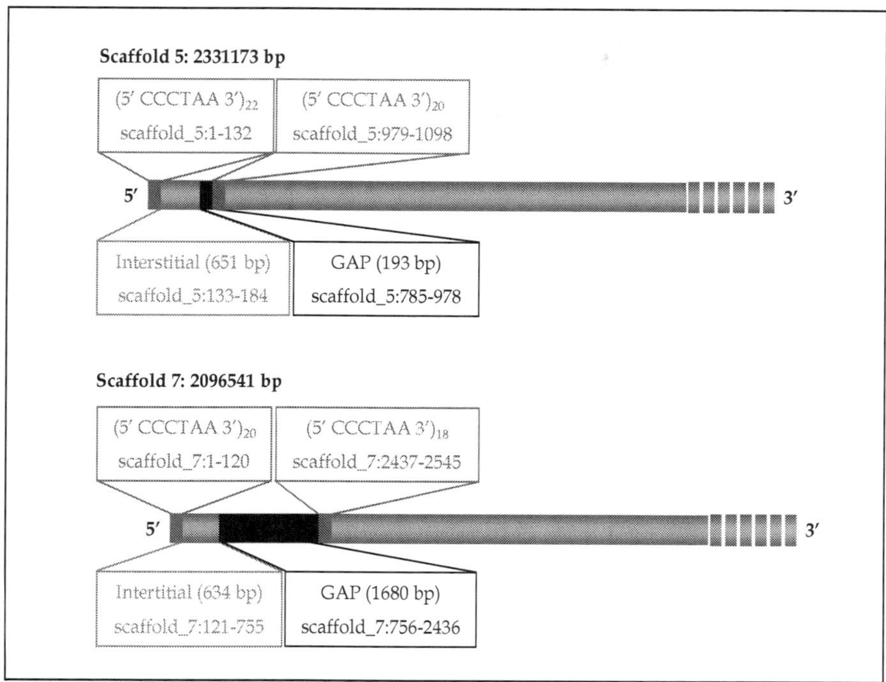

Fig. 2. Location of telomere regions in scaffolds 5 and 7 of the genome sequence of C. *subvermispora*.

In summary this analysis has allowed the identification of 42 telomere repeat containing regions. 22 out of them fit with direct telomere sequences (TTAGGG) present in 22 scaffolds and 22 reverse telomere regions (CCCTAA) present in 20 scaffolds. Taking into account that the *C. subvermispora* strain sequence was a dikaryon, these results suggest that the *Ceriporiopsis* genome would consist of 11 chromosomes. Because scaffold 7 showed telomere repeats at both ends, the sequence contained in this scaffold would be the only fully assembled chromosome of *C. subvermispora*.

2.1.2 Analysis of the telomere regions of *Phanerochaete chrysosporium* strain RP78

P. chrisosporium is a model white rot basidiomycete that has been extensively used because of it interest as lignin degrader (Kersten & Cullen, 2007; Tien, 1987). The draft genome of the homokaryotic strain of *P. chrysosporium* strain RP78 was assembled into 232 scaffolds and contains 35.1 Mbp of non-redundant sequences (Martinez et al., 2004). 90% of the assembly was found in 21 scaffolds, while 50% was found in eight scaffolds larger than 1.9 Mbp.

The screening of the telomere sequences was performed as described above using the scaffolds of the assemblage v2.0. The basic telomere unit of *P. chrysosporium* is the heptamer TTTAGGG. 16 out of the 232 scaffolds contained telomere sequences, eight of them with the TTTAGGG motif. In four of these scaffolds (numbers 7, 9, 23 y 159) the repetitive unit was located at an interstitial position at 3200 bp from the 3' end flanked by a gap. This arrangement could be the result of a wrong assemblage as it can be seen in Fig. 3.

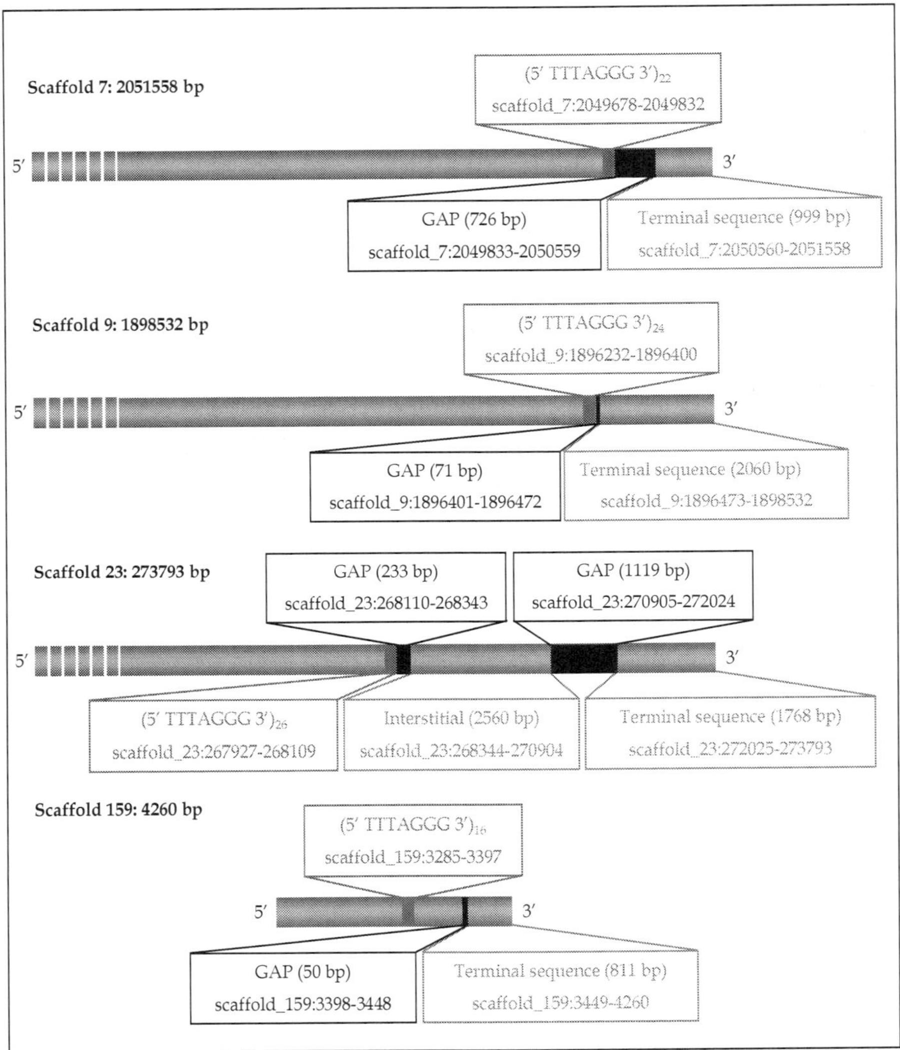

Fig. 3. Location of telomere regions in scaffolds 5, 9, 23 and 159 of the genome sequence of *P. chrisosporium*.

Another telomere-like interstitial region was found at about 300000 bp of the 3′ end of scaffold 10. The position of the interstitial telomere block within the scaffold would suggested that it could be the result of an ancestral intra-chromosomal rearrangement (inversions and/or fusions), from differential crossing-over or from the repair of double-strand break during evolution (Lin & Yan, 2008) (Fig. 4).

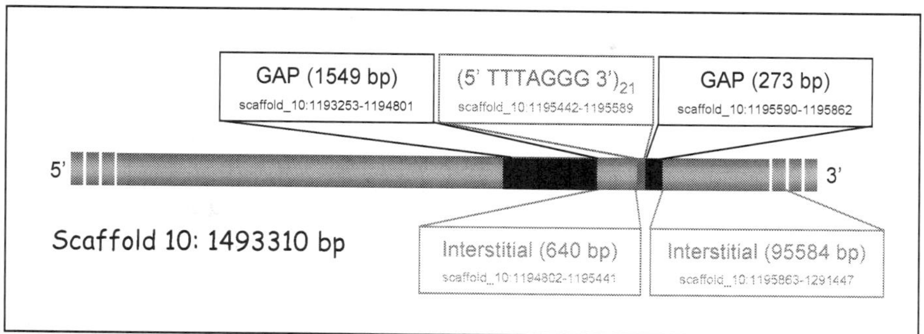

Fig. 4. Location of telomere regions in scaffold 10 of the genome sequence of
P. chrysosporium.

It was observed that in eight of the 16 telomere-containing scaffolds identified, the repetitive unit was the complementary CCCTAAA. In five of them, the heptamer unit was placed at the 5′ end. A telomere unit in an internal region at 8772 bp of the 5′ end was present in scaffold 8 while scaffold 5 ferried a telomere motif at 2123492 bp of the 3′ end and another one at 40552bp of the 3′ end (Fig. 5).

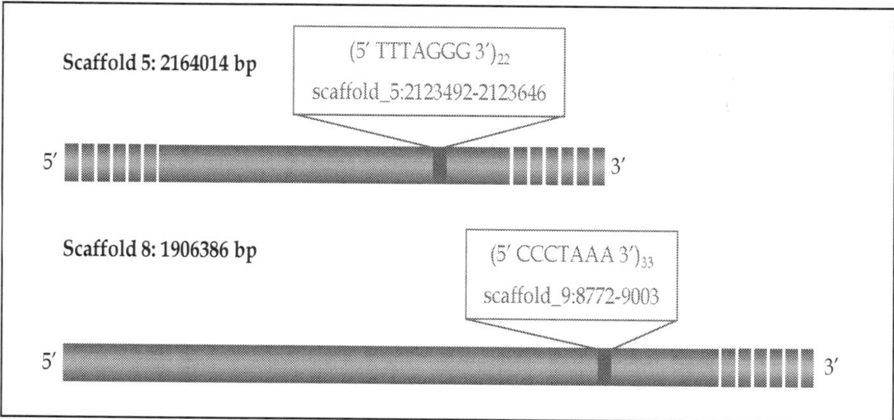

Fig. 5. Location of telomere regions in scaffolds 5 and 8 of the genome sequence of
P. chrysosporium.

The analysis of scaffold 28 revealed two arrays of interstitial copies of the heptamer CCCCTAAA (23 and 18 repeats, respectively) placed at 11417 bp and 13853 bp from the 5′

end. An interstitial fragment of 1342 bp and a gap of 933 bp were found between them suggesting the occurrence of missassemblage (Fig. 6).

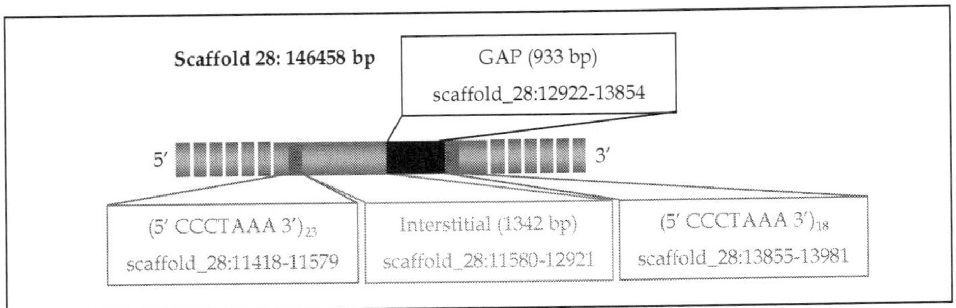

Fig. 6. Location of telomere regions in scaffold 28 of the genome sequence of *P. chrysosporium.*

In summary, the results presented here suggest that the genome of *P. chrysosporium* is arranged in at least eight linkage groups. Because scaffold 8 shows telomere repeats at both ends it is suggested that the sequence contained in this scaffold constitute the only fully assembled chromosome of *P. chrysosporium.*

2.1.3 Analysis of the telomere regions of *Pleurotus ostreatus* PC15

P. ostreatus PC15 is a monokarytic strain of an industrially-produced edible basidiomycete that has been also used as a model system for lignocellulose degradation. *P. ostreatus* differs from the other white rot model system (*P. chrysosporium*) in its enzymatic portfolio for lignin degradation. The structure of its genome was determined by linkage analysis (Larraya et al., 2000), and the complete genome of this strain has been sequenced. The assemblage v1.0 consists of 19 scaffolds of which 18 were larger than 2 Kbp. The screening of the genome for telomere sequences was carried out as described above and revealed that the elementary telomere unit of *P. ostreatus* is the hexamer TTAGGG. All scaffolds were screened for telomere regions and 19 telomere regions were recovered. In eight of them the motif TTAGGG was found, and the remaining 11 had the motif CCCTAA. The number of repetitions of the basic unit ranged from 19 to 38. As it was determined, scaffolds 1, 3, 4, 5, 6, 9, 10 and 11 show telomere repeats at both ends indicating that they are fully assembled.

2.1.4 Analysis of the telomere regions of *Postia placenta* MAD-698

P. placenta is a brown rot basidiomycete that rapidly depolymerizes the cellulose in wood without significant lignin removal. This type of decay differs sharply from white rot fungi such as *P. chrysosporium* and *P. ostreatus.* The genome of the dikaryotic strain of *P. placenta* MAD-698 revealed a genome of 90.9 Mbp assembled in 1243 scaffolds (Martinez et al., 2009). All the scaffolds of the assemblage were screened for telomere sequences as above. The basic telomere unit in this fungus is the pentamer TTAGG. The analysis of 1243 scaffolds revealed the presence of 23 regions containing telomere sequences. 12 of them carried the TTAGG sequence: in eight of them the sequence was found at the scaffold's 3' end, three scaffolds ferried the sequence in an interstitial location (Fig. 7) and in one of them two regions with the pentamer sequence appeared at the end of the chromosome but separated by 2373 bp suggesting a missassemblage of scaffold 178 at its 3' end (Fig. 8).

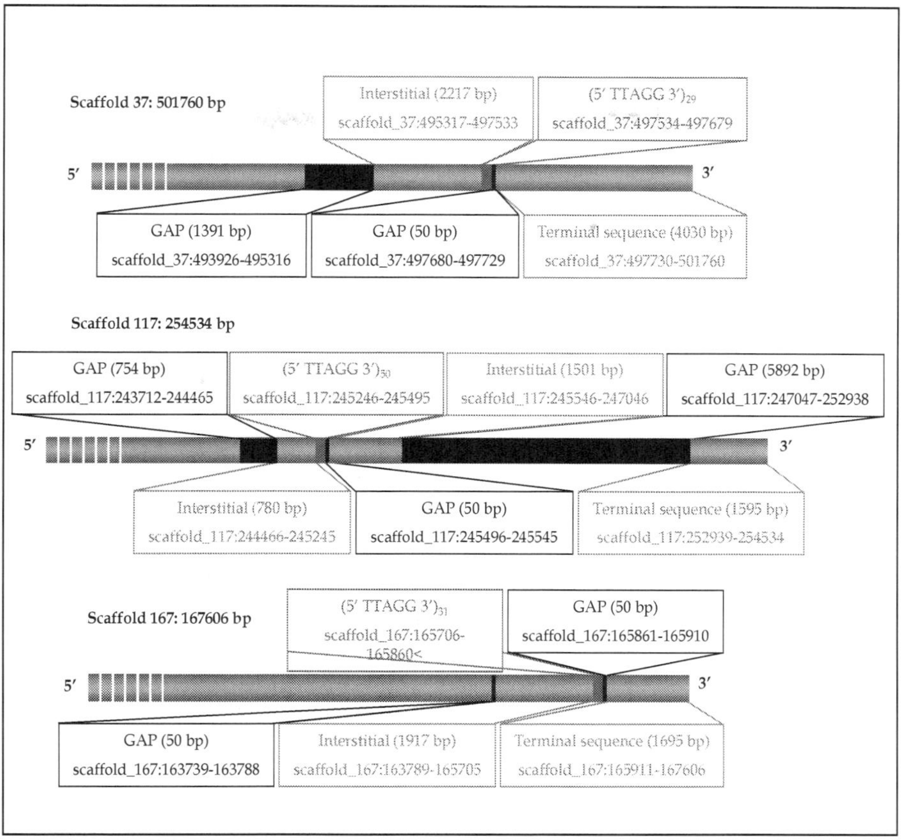

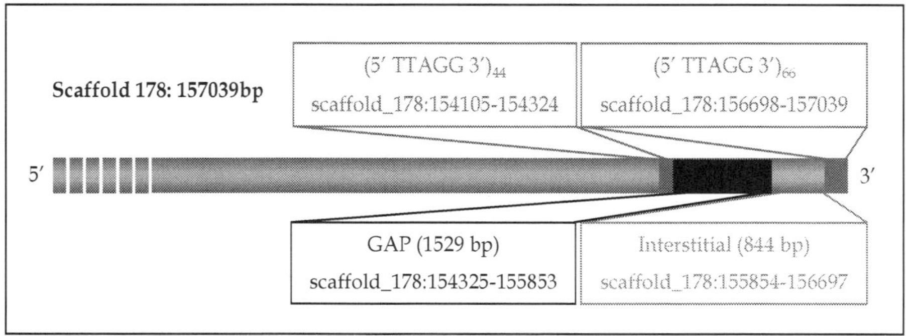

Fig. 7. Location of telomere regions in scaffolds 37, 117 and 167 of the genome sequence of *P. placenta*.

Fig. 8. Location of telomere regions in scaffold 178 of genome sequence of *P. placenta*.

The remaining 11 scaffolds carried the telomere unit CCTAA placed at the 5´end in seven of them. The scaffold 99 (Fig. 9) has a complex structure with two interstitial CCTAA regions containing the motif. One of them located towards the scaffold 5′ end, contains 40 copies of the telomere unit, and the other, located 16533 bp downstream, another interstitial region containing 19 repetitions of the unit. A gap of about 50 bp placed at the 5´end of this interstitial region suggests that this arrangement could be due to a missassemblage.

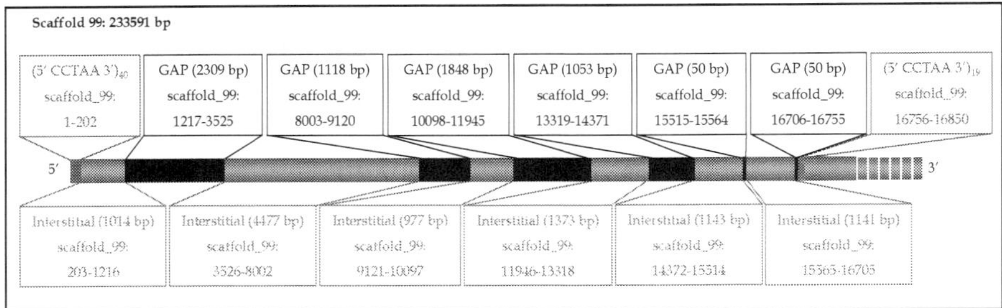

Fig. 9. Location of telomere regions in scaffold 99 of genome sequence of *P. placenta*.

The scaffold 33 also showed two interstitial regions with 40 and 30 repetitions of the of the CCTAA telomere motif. One of the regions was preceded by a gap of 701 bp suggesting that it could be a wrong assemblage. The other one (40 copies of the telomere unit) could very well represent and ITS (Interstitial Telomere Sequence) that can be produced by chromosome rearrangements as described above.

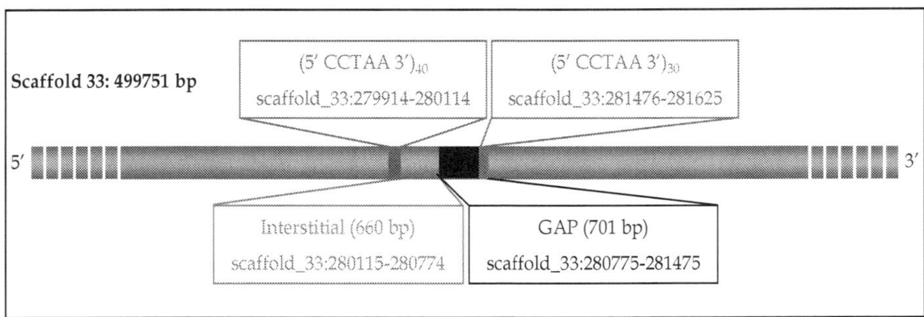

Fig. 10. Location of telomere regions in scaffold 33 of genome sequence of *P. placenta*.

Two other scaffolds with interstitial sequences were found. Scaffold 70 showed 26 repetitions of the CCTAA telomere unit at 38395 bp from the 5´ end preceded by a gap, and scaffold 144 showed 50 repetitions of the telomere unit at 181041 bp from the 5′ end preceded by another other gap of 50 bp (Fig. 11). We suggest that these structures are consequence of wrong assemblages.

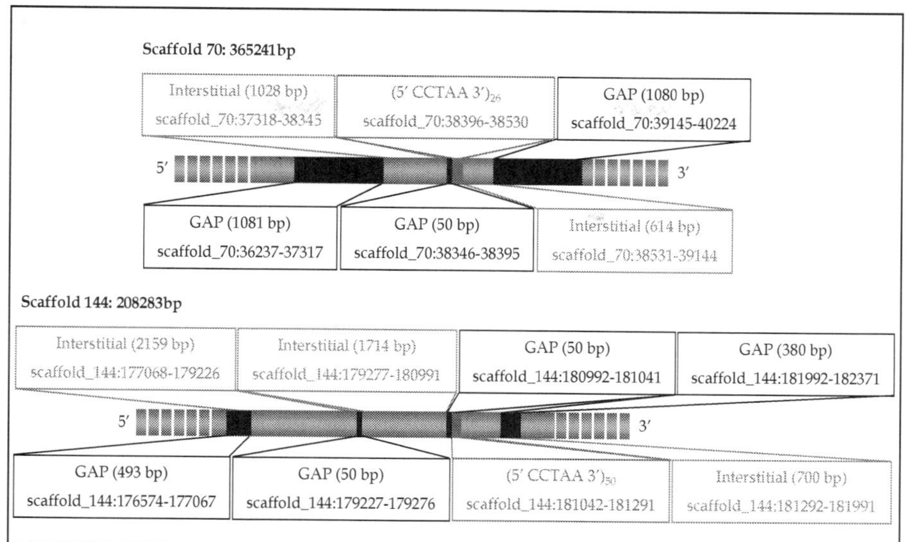

Fig. 11. Location of telomere regions in scaffolds 70 and 144 of genome sequence of
P. placenta.

In summary, *P. placenta* has a telomere pentameric (TTAGG) basic repetitive unit. The number of copies present in the assembled genome ranged from 19 to 70. The analysis of data suggests that the minimum number of linkage groups of this species could be 12.

2.1.5 Analysis of the telomere regions of *Heterobasidion annosum*

Heterobasidion annosum is a root pathogen responsible for important losses in conifer plantations and natural forests throughout the northern hemisphere (Asiegbu et al., 2005). Genetic linkage analyses of this fungus had produced maps with 19 large linkage groups and 20 smaller ones (Lind et al., 2005), but the precise chromosome number for this species has not been conclusively determined. The v2.0 of the homokaryotic *H. annosum* genome assembly consists of 33.1 Mbp sequence assembled into 15 scaffolds at least 10 of which represent nearly complete chromosomes (http://genome.jgipsf.org/Hetan2/Hetan2.home.html).
The screening of the telomere sequences was performed as it was described above. The *H. annosum* telomere repetitive sequence is a TTAGG pentamer. The screening of the 15 scaffolds rendered 19 telomere regions. Six of them corresponded to the direct repeat sequence at the 3′ end of the scaffolds, and the remaining 13 carried the reverse sequence CCTAA at the scaffold's 5′ end. These results suggest that the genome of *H. annosum* is arranged in at least 13 linkage groups. Taking into account that scaffolds 5, 6, 9, 10, 11 and 12 contained telomere repeats at both ends, it can be concluded that they could correspond to fully assembled chromosomes.

2.1.6 Summary of the telomere regions of different basidiomycetes

A summary of the structural characteristics of the telomeres studied in this paper can be found in Table 1.

Species	Genome length assembled	Scaffold number	Telomere repetition	Average number of telomere	Minimum number of linkage groups analyzed
C. subvermispora	39.0 Mb	740	TTAGGG	19 copies	11
P. chrysosporium	35.1 Mb	232	TTTAGGG	22 copies	8
P. ostreatus	34.3 Mb	12	TTAGGG	24 copies	11
P. placenta	90.0 Mb	1243	TTAGG	25 copies	12
H. annosum	33.1 Mb	15	TTAGG	25 copies	13

Table 1. Structural characteristics of the telomeres in the basidiomycetes analyzed.

2.2 Analysis of the basidiomycetes' subtelomeric regions

The analysis of the subtelomeric regions is aimed at answering two questions: are the genes sitting at the subtelomeric a representative sample of the genes of each species or is there enrichment in sub-telomere specific genes? If this were the case, which are these telomere-enriched genes and are they conserved across species? In order to address these questions, we have recorded the genes automatically annotated in 50 Kbp regions adjacent to the different telomeres identified in the species analyzed, we have checked them manually and we have recorded and classified the Gene Ontology (GO) terms related to the genes identified in these regions (Ashburner et al., 2000).

As the number of telomere-containing scaffolds differed in the various species, (from 12 in *P. ostreatus* to 1243 in *P. placenta*) the length of genomic sequence screened also varied, although in a much smaller degree (from 800 Kbp in *P. chrysosporium* to 2100 Kbp in *C. subvermispora*). The gene density of the analyzed regions was found to be related to the degree of finishing of the genome: those assembled as draft (*C. subvermispora, P. placenta* and *P. chrysosporium*) have gene densities lower than 0.20 genes per Kbp, whereas the gene density in the finished genomes is much higher (0.34 and 0.49 genes per Kbp). The gene density in the draft genomes seems to be significantly lower than the global gene density in the corresponding genomes. This can be due to deficiencies in the annotation of these draft genomes since the global gene density in all the species analyzed (with the exception of *P. placenta*) is very similar. In all cases, the most of the genes automatically annotated at the subtelomeric regions had no homology with others of the gene databases (cutoff criterion e-value<e-20 for BlastX) (Table 2).

The Gene Ontology annotation is aimed at standardizing the representation of gene and gene products in such a way that they can be compared among databases. This approach project provides a controlled vocabulary of terms for describing gene product characteristics and gene product annotation data (Ashburner et al., 2000). There are three classification categories that are provided by the consortium: Biological Process (BP), Cellular Component (CC) and Molecular Function (MF). Each identified gene product is labeled with all the GO terms in each category that can define it. By this way, a list of GO terms provides a kind of picture describing the specific condition of the gene subset that is under study. We have studied the three categories of GO annotation in the genes annotated in 50 Kbp subtelomeric regions in the five genomes studied and recorded their general statistics (Table 3). Because of the low number of gene models identified in the subtelomeric regions and because not all of them can be labeled with a GO term, the numbers of terms in the categories of Biological

Feature	C. subvermispora	P. chrysosporium	P. ostreatus	P. placenta	H. annosum
Total number of scaffolds	740	232	12	1243	15
Number of subtelomeric regions analyzed	42	16	19	23	19
Scaffolds with direct motif	22	8	8	12	6
Scaffolds with reverse motif	20	8	11	11	13
Total length analyzed (Kbp)	2100	800	950	1150	950
Total number filtered model genes	283	134	319	177	470
Unknown genes (no homology)	134 (47.3 %)	56 (41.8 %)	87 (27.3 %)	64 (36.2 %)	279 (59.4 %)
Predicted protein	104 (36.7 %)	57 (42.5 %)	182 (57.1 %)	79 (44.6 %)	131 (27.9 %)
Known/annotated/putative genes	45 (15.9 %)	21 (15.7 %)	50 (15.7 %)	34 (19.2 %)	60 (12.8 %)
Subtelomere gene density (genes / Kbp)	0.13	0.17	0.34	0.10	0.49
Whole genome gene density (genes / Kbp)	0.31	0.39	0.34	0.19	0.40

Table 2. Density and homology types in the subtelomere regions.

Processes and Cellular Component are rather low, whereas the number of Molecular Function terms is much higher and produces a clearer picture of what are the subtelomeric regions coding for (Table 3).

	C. subvermispora	P. chrysosporium	P. ostreatus	P. placenta	H. annosum
GO category					
Biological Process (BP)	46	22	24	20	48
Cellular Component (CC)	15	9	10	7	12
Molecular Function (MF)	127	88	161	65	186

Table 3. GO terms richness in the subtelomeric regions of the five basidiomycetes analyzed.

In order to determine if the genes found at the subtelomere constitute a representative sample of the genes of each species, we can perform a simple statistical analysis to calculate the numbers that would be expected for each one of the GO terms in the subtelomeric regions using the whole genome data as frequency. If we do this type of study, we conclude that the distribution of the subtelomeric GO terms for each one of the categories is not a representative sample of the total gene set for each one of the species (data not shown) and, consequently, we can conclude that there are sets of genes that are found more frequently at the telomere regions. For identifying these sets, we must discuss the GO term distribution in each one of the species.

2.2.1 Analysis of the subtelomere regions of *Ceriporiopsis subvermispora* B

The analysis of the 283 gene models annotated in the subtelomeric regions of *C. subvermispora* revealed 46 BP terms in which transport, protein amino acid phosphorylation, metabolic process, electron transport, carbohydrate metabolic process, and proteolysis are the more represented ones. The terms transport, protein amino acid phosphorylation and carbohydrate metabolism seem to be overrepresented in this region whereas the terms metabolic processes and electron transport seem to be underrepresented in comparison with the total genome. The analysis revealed 15 CC terms annotated in this region. Out of which, the terms intracellular, integral to membrane, membrane and nucleus are the most represented ones in this category. All of them, except the term nucleus, seem to be overrepresented in the subtelomeric region. Finally, out of the 127 MF terms being the more represented were ATP binding, zinc ion binding, nucleic acid binding protein, binding protein, kinase activity, protein serine/threonine kinase activity, transporter activity, oxidoreductase activity, and protein-tyrosine kinase activity. All of them seem to be overrepresented in the subtelomeric regions in comparison to the whole genome.

2.2.2 Analysis of the subtelomere regions of *Phanerochaete chrysosporium*

The analysis of the 134 gene models annotated in the subtelomeric regions of *P. chrysosporium* revealed 22 BP terms being the most represented terms proteolysis and peptidolysis, electron transport, metabolism, methionine biosynthesis, protein transport, small GTPase mediated signal transduction, and transport. The analysis revealed 9 CC terms out of which, the terms membrane, nucleus and integral to membrane are the most represented ones in this category. Finally, out of the 88 MF terms, the more represented terms are those of aspartic-type endopeptidase activity, nucleic acid binding, zinc ion binding, ATP binding, and oxidoreductase activity

2.2.3 Analysis of the subtelomere regions of *Pleurotus ostreatus*

The analysis of the 319 gene models annotated in the subtelomeric regions of *P. ostreatus* revealed 24 BP terms being the most represented terms protein amino acid phosphorylation, proteolysis, metabolic process, electron transport, and transport. The analysis revealed 10 CC terms out of which, the terms intracellular, integral to membrane, nucleus, cell wall and ribosome are the most represented ones in this category. Finally, out of the 161 MF terms, the more represented terms are those of ATP binding, nucleic acid binding, oxidoreductase activity, protein-tyrosine kinase activity and zinc ion binding.

2.2.4 Analysis of the subtelomere regions of *Postia placenta*

The analysis of the 177 gene models annotated in the subtelomeric regions of *P. placenta* revealed 20 BP terms being the most represented terms proteolysis, electron transport, protein amino acid phosphorylation and regulation of transcription DNA-dependent. The analysis revealed 7 CC terms out of which, the terms intracellular, membrane, and nucleus are the most represented ones in this category. Finally, out of the 65 MF terms, the more represented terms are those of ATP binding, nucleic acid binding and zinc ion binding.

2.2.5 Analysis of the subtelomere regions of *Heterobasidion annosum*

The analysis of the 470 gene models annotated in the subtelomeric regions of *H. annosum* revealed 48 BP terms being the most represented terms metabolic process, transport, electron transport, regulation of transcription DNA-dependent, carbohydrate metabolic process, and proteolysis. The analysis revealed 12 CC terms out of which, the terms membrane, integral to membrane, intracellular, nucleus and cytoplasm are the most represented ones in this category. Finally, out of the 186 MF terms, the more represented terms are those of zinc ion binding, oxidoreductase activity, ATP binding, binding and heme binding.

2.2.6 Comparative analysis of the subtelomere regions of the five basidiomycetes

The record of the GO terms associated to genes found in the 50 Kbp adjacent to the telomere sequences in the five basidiomycetes analyzed reveals common patterns that permit to determine some telomere-enriched GO term families. As a preliminary study, we have taken into account the terms that are always present in among the most represented ones in each of the categories and we have extracted those of them that are present in all or most of the species analyzed. If we consider the BP category, the term electron transport is among the most represented in the five species studied and the terms transport, protein aminoacid phosphorylation, metabolic process and proteolysis are present in four of the five species. So, we can conclude that the subtelomeric regions are enriched in these processes. The species *C. subvermispora*, *H. annosum*, and *P. ostreatus* have subtelomeric regions where the more abundant BP-GO terms are highly similar whereas the subtelomeric regions in *P. chrysosporium* are the most dissimilar.

If we consider the CC category, the terms nucleus and intracellular are present among the more represented ones in all the species studied, the terms membrane and integral to membrane are present in four of the species and the terms ribosome and cytoplasm are present in three of the five species. In this case the more different subtelomeric regions in terms of the CC-GO terms are those of *C. subvermispora* and *P. placenta*, being the other three species in intermediate positions.

Finally, in the case of the MF terms, as their number is much higher, a deeper comparison can be made among the species (Table 4). The five species analyzed share the most frequent MF terms associated to the genes in the subtelomere regions supporting the idea of a preference for certain gene of gene families at these chromosome locations.

Molecular function	*Ceriporiopsis subvermispora*	*Phanerochaete chrysosporium*	*Pleurotus ostreatus*	*Postia placenta*	*Heterobasidion annosum*	Presence
zinc ion binding	4,76	3,60	2,02	4,96	4,72	5
oxidoreductase activity	2,60	2,70	2,69	2,48	3,14	5
ATP binding	5,63	2,70	5,05	6,61	2,83	5
nucleic acid binding	3,90	4,50	4,38	4,96	2,20	5
catalytic activity	2,16	1,80	1,35	2,48	2,20	5
DNA binding	1,30	0,90	1,68	2,48	1,57	5
transporter activity	3,03	1,80	1,35	ND	2,20	4
iron ion binding			1,35	1,65	1,57	3
protein-tyrosine kinase activity	2,60		2,02	2,48		3

Table 4. Frequency of Molecular Function GO terms in the subtelomere regions of the studied basidiomycetes.

3. Synteny

Synteny can be defined as the conservation of the relative positions and order of genes in different chromosomes. This definition implies that the conserved genes are related by their descent from an original ancestor (homologous genes). There are two types of homology: orthology and paralogy. We can call two genes belonging to different species as orthologous if they descent from a single gene present in the last common of the two species. On the other hand, two genes are called paralogous, if they derive from gene duplication events occurred in a given species. The orthology requires that speciation has occurred, whereas this is not necessary in the case of parology, which can occur only in individuals of the same species. As the evolutionary histories of different species may differ, groups of paralogous genes can be orthologous of a single gene in a different species. The preserved co-localization of genomic regions on chromosomes of different species is called shared synteny. This may involve relationships between genes within the syntenic regions involved, such as combinations of alleles that are advantegeous when inherited together, or shared regulatory mechanisms.

The problem of identifying syntenic regions in different genomes has been addressed using different strategies including the use of FASTA (Lipman & Pearson, 1985) and Blast (Altschul et al., 1997), and different bioinformatics approaches (Catchen et al., 2009; Grabherr et al., 2010; Tang et al., 2011). We have used a method based on the identification of synteny regions at the chromosome ends by means of a BLASTP analysis of genes in the two genomes using a cut-off threshold of e-20. Later, the Vista Synteny Viewer (http://genome.lbl.gov/vista/index.shtml) integrated into the JGI Genome Portal was used in the preliminary orthologous searching of each species. This tool enables pair-wise comparative analysis of genome assemblies at three levels of resolution. The use of synteny software programs is of particular interest to see the particular changes undergone by the subtelomeric regions during evolution (Housworth & Postlethwait, 2002). For instance, the chromosome 3 in *H. annosum* maintains the synteny with *P. ostreatus* chromosome 3, but the *H. annosum* subtelomeric region aligned with a central region of *P. ostreatus* chromosome 4 suggesting the occurrence of a translocation event after the divergence of the two species.

The different basidiomycetes were used as reference genomes and *P. ostreatus* PC15 v2.0 was the query genome. Focusing in the distal 50Kbp of each chromosome, we identified the putative gene orthologous in the subtelomeric regions of each basidiomycete. Then we used that gene sequences as query in a BlastP search of the *P. ostreatus* filtered model genes as subject. Two models were considered as orthologous if their alignment had an e-value lower than e-20 and they shared a minimum 60% in identity percentage.

The synteny between the subtelomeric regions was analyzed using *P. ostreatus* chromosomes as a reference. It was observed that seven *P. ostreatus* chromosomes (chromosomes 1, 3, 4, 5, 7, 8 and 10) harbored sequences homologous to subtelomere regions of the other basidiomycetes analyzed in this study (Table 5). 47 synteny regions were uncovered when the subtelomeric regions of *C. subvermispora* were compared to those of *P. ostreatus*. The highest number (16) corresponded to those regions placed at *P. ostreatus* chromosome 7. However, it should be mentioned that 12 *C. subvermispora* gene models were found within a 30 Kbp region of the *P. ostreatus* genome (data not shown). The lowest number of synteny regions was found when the subtelomeric regions of *P. placenta* were used as query. It should be noticed that 10 out of 15 regions were placed on chromosome 5 of *P. ostreatus*. A similar situation was observed when synteny was analyzed between *H. annosum* and *P. ostreatus*. 10 out of 25 synteny regions of *H. annosum* mapped to chromosome 10 of *P. ostreatus*.

	P. ostreatus chromosome							
	Chr 1	Chr 3	Chr 4	Chr 5	Chr 7	Chr 8	Chr 10	Total
C. subvermispora	6	6	7	—	16	12	—	47
P. chrysosporium	4	—	4	—	4	—	—	12
P. placenta	—	—	5	10	—	—	—	15
H. annosum	—	—	6	9	—	—	10	25
Total	10	6	22	19	20	12	10	101

Table 5. Number of subtelomeric synteny regions in different basidiomycetes using *P. ostreatus* as reference.

The chromosome 4 of *P. ostreatus* can be defined as mosaic of modules of subtelomeres from the other basidiomycetes studied in this paper. The list below contains some gene models mapping to the subtelomeric regions in these basidiomycetes that were found at interstitial positions in *P. ostreatus* chromosome 4: from *C. subvermispora*, a cell cycle check point protein, a membrane transporter, a histone deacetylase, a histidine acid phosphatase, the ribosomal protein L1 and an ABC transporter; from *P. chrysosporium*, a haloacid dehalogenase-like hydrolase and a glycoside hydrolase; from *P. placenta*, an inositol polyphosphate phosphatase, a metal-dependent phosphohydrolase, and a monooxygenase; from *H. annosum*, a mitochondrial carrier transporter, a Golgi transporter, and zinc finger transcription factor (Fig. 12).

11 out of 12 gene models of *C. subvermispora* were syntenic to a 20 Kbp regions of *P. ostreatus* chromosome 8. These gene models corresponded to a nucleic acid binding protein, citrate synthase, a methyltransferase, an exoribonuclease, a phosphoribosyltransferase, a prenyltransferase, a homeobox transcription factor, a mitochondrial inner membrane protein importer, as DNA-J type heat shock protein, a RNA splicing protein, and a cytochrome c oxidase.

The genome of *P. falciparum* is organized in 14 compartmentalized chromosomes where the conserved regions form the central chromosomal domains and the polymorphic regions are at the terminal domains. In this way, housekeeping genes tend to be located at the central regions of the chromosomes, whereas the highly variable gene families responsible for the antigenic variation of the parasite are clustered towards the telomeres (Hernandez-Rivas et al., 2010). Our results suggest that a similar type of chromosomal organization would be expected to occur in basidiomycetes, although a larger number of genomes should be studied to fully support this hypothesis.

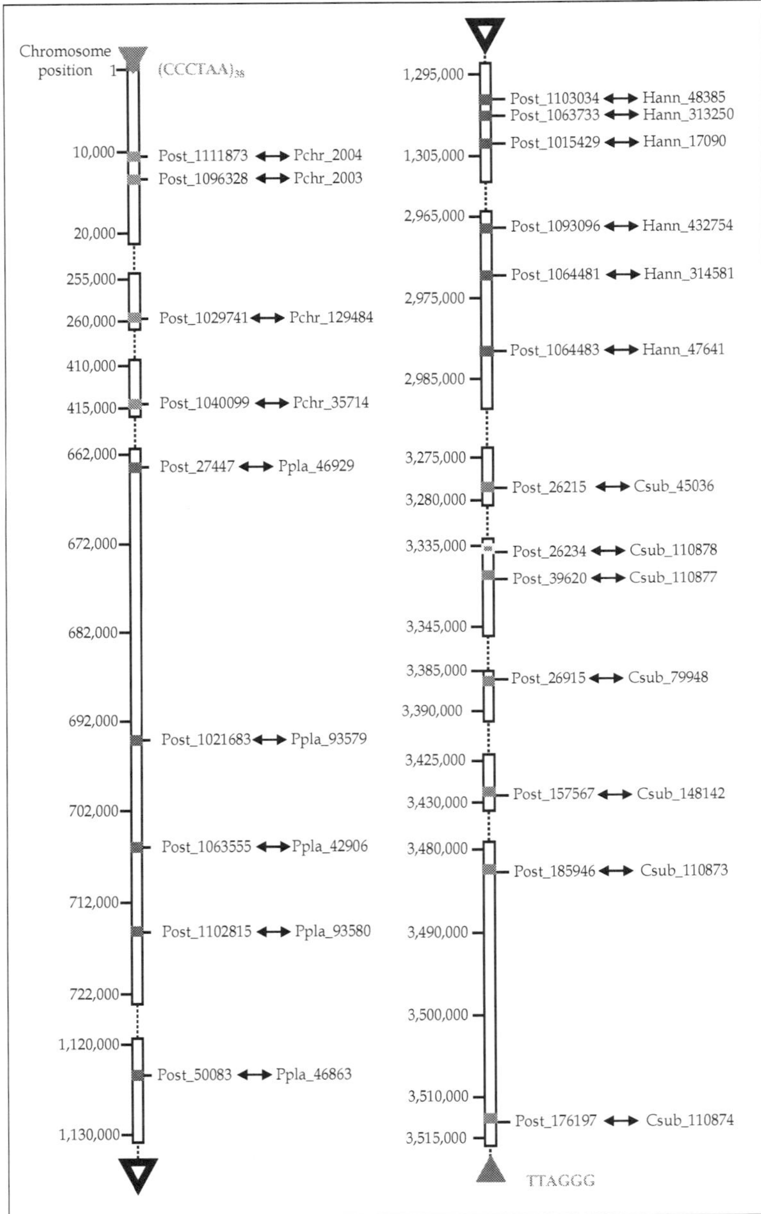

Fig. 12. Mosaic structure of *P. ostreatus* chromosome 4. The syntenic gene models of *P. ostreatus* (Post), *P. chrysosporium* (Pchr), *P. placenta* (Ppla) and *H. annosum* (Hann) are indicated along with their position on the *P. ostreatus* chromosome.

4. Conclusion

The bioinformatics analysis described in this paper allowed us to establish the type and the number of the telomere repeat unit in the basidiomycetes analyzed, to suggest the putative linkage groups in fungi where linkage maps are not available, to uncover misassembled telomere regions, and to reveal the preference for some gene models to be located at the subtelomeric regions and to uncover synteny among the subtelomere regions in the basidiomycetes analyzed.

5. Acknowledgements

This work has been supported by funds of the AGL2008-05608-C02-01 of the Spanish National Plan of Scientific Research, the Bioethanol Euroinnova project of the Goverment of Navarre (Spain), by additional institutional support from the Public University of Navarre. Some of the sequence data were produced in genome sequence projects developed at the JGI within the Community Sequence Program under the auspices of the US Department of Energy's Office of Science, Biological and Environmental Research Program, and by its associate National Laboratories Lawrence Livermore and Los Alamos.
LR led and coordinated the project, GP determined bioinformatically the telomeres and subtelomere regions in the species. RC, FS and AGP made the GO analysis of the data. The manuscript was prepared by LR, and AGP.

6. References

Abad, J. P., De Pablos, B., Osoegawa, K., De Jong, P. J., Martin-Gallardo, A. & Villasante, A. (2004). TAHRE, a novel telomeric retrotransposon from Drosophila melanogaster, reveals the origin of Drosophila telomeres. *Mol Biol Evol.*, Vol. 21, No. 9, pp. 1620-1624.

Al-Wahiby, S., Wong, H. P. & Slijepcevic, P. (2005). Shortened telomeres in murine scid cells expressing mutant hRAD54 coincide with reduction in recombination at telomeres. *Mutat Res*, Vol. 578, No. 1-2, pp. 134-142.

Altschul, S. F., Madden, T. L., Schaffer, A. A., Zhang, J., Zhang, Z., Miller, W. & Lipman, D. J. (1997). Gapped BLAST and PSI-BLAST: a new generation of protein database search programs. *Nucleic Acids Res*, Vol. 25, No. 17, pp. 3389-3402.

Anderson, J. A., Song, Y. S. & Langley, C. H. (2008). Molecular population genetics of Drosophila subtelomeric DNA. *Genetics.*, Vol. 178, No. 1, pp. 477-487.

Ashburner, M., Ball, C. A., Blake, J. A., Botstein, D., Butler, H., Cherry, J. M., Davis, A. P., Dolinski, K., Dwight, S. S., Eppig, J. T., Harris, M. A., Hill, D. P., Issel-Tarver, L., Kasarskis, A., Lewis, S., Matese, J. C., Richardson, J. E., Ringwald, M., Rubin, G. M. & Sherlock, G. (2000). Gene ontology: tool for the unification of biology. The Gene Ontology Consortium. *Nat Genet.*, Vol. 25, No. 1, pp. 25-29.

Asiegbu, F. O., Adomas, A. & Stenlid, J. (2005). Conifer root and butt rot caused by Heterobasidion annosum (Fr.) Bref. s.l. *Mol Plant Pathol.*, Vol. 6, No. 4, pp. 395-409.

Aubert, G. & Lansdorp, P. M. (2008). Telomeres and aging. *Physiol Rev*, Vol. 88, No. 2, pp. 557-579.

Azzalin, C. M. & Lingner, J. (2007). Molecular biology: damage control. *Nature.*, Vol. 448, No. 7157, pp. 1001-1002.

Azzalin, C. M., Nergadze, S. G. & Giulotto, E. (2001). Human intrachromosomal telomeric-like repeats: sequence organization and mechanisms of origin. *Chromosoma*, Vol. 110, No. 2, pp. 75-82.

Azzalin, C. M., Reichenbach, P., Khoriauli, L., Giulotto, E. & Lingner, J. (2007). Telomeric repeat containing RNA and RNA surveillance factors at mammalian chromosome ends. *Science*, Vol. 318, No. 5851, pp. 798-801.

Bailey, S. M., Cornforth, M. N., Ullrich, R. L. & Goodwin, E. H. (2004). Dysfunctional mammalian telomeres join with DNA double-strand breaks. *DNA Repair (Amst)*, Vol. 3, No. 4, pp. 349-357.

Bailey, S. M., Meyne, J., Chen, D. J., Kurimasa, A., Li, G. C., Lehnert, B. E. & Goodwin, E. H. (1999). DNA double-strand break repair proteins are required to cap the ends of mammalian chromosomes. *Proc Natl Acad Sci U S A*, Vol. 96, No. 26, pp. 14899-14904.

Barry, J. D., Ginger, M. L., Burton, P. & McCulloch, R. (2003). Why are parasite contingency genes often associated with telomeres? *Int J Parasitol.*, Vol. 33, No. 1, pp. 29-45.

Bateman, A., Coin, L., Durbin, R., Finn, R. D., Hollich, V., Griffiths-Jones, S., Khanna, A., Marshall, M., Moxon, S., Sonnhammer, E. L., Studholme, D. J., Yeats, C. & Eddy, S. R. (2004). The Pfam protein families database. *Nucleic Acids Res.*, Vol. 32, No. Database issue, pp. D138-141.

Benson, G. (1999). Tandem repeats finder: a program to analyze DNA sequences. *Nucleic Acids Res.*, Vol. 27, No. 2, pp. 573-580.

Bhattacharyya, A. & Blackburn, E. H. (1997). Aspergillus nidulans maintains short telomeres throughout development. *Nucleic Acids Res*, Vol. 25, No. 7, pp. 1426-1431.

Blackburn, E. H. & Gall, J. G. (1978). A tandemly repeated sequence at the termini of the extrachromosomal ribosomal RNA genes in Tetrahymena. *J Mol Biol.*, Vol. 120, No. 1, pp. 33-53.

Blasco, M. A. (2005). Telomeres and human disease: ageing, cancer and beyond. *Nat Rev Genet*, Vol. 6, No. 8, pp. 611-622.

Blasco, M. A. (2007). Telomere length, stem cells and aging. *Nat Chem Biol.*, Vol. 3, No. 10, pp. 640-649.

Blasco, M. A., Lee, H. W., Hande, M. P., Samper, E., Lansdorp, P. M., DePinho, R. A. & Greider, C. W. (1997). Telomere shortening and tumor formation by mouse cells lacking telomerase RNA. *Cell*, Vol. 91, No. 1, pp. 25-34.

Bolzan, A. D. & Bianchi, M. S. (2006). Telomeres, interstitial telomeric repeat sequences, and chromosomal aberrations. *Mutat Res.*, Vol. 612, No. 3, pp. 189-214.

Brown, W. R., Dobson, M. J. & MacKinnon, P. (1990a). Telomere cloning and mammalian chromosome analysis. *J Cell Sci.*, Vol. 95, No. Pt 4, pp. 521-526.

Brown, W. R., MacKinnon, P. J., Villasante, A., Spurr, N., Buckle, V. J. & Dobson, M. J. (1990b). Structure and polymorphism of human telomere-associated DNA. *Cell.*, Vol. 63, No. 1, pp. 119-132.

Callen, E. & Surralles, J. (2004). Telomere dysfunction in genome instability syndromes. *Mutat Res*, Vol. 567, No. 1, pp. 85-104.

Catchen, J. M., Conery, J. S. & Postlethwait, J. H. (2009). Automated identification of conserved synteny after whole-genome duplication. *Genome Res.*, Vol. 19, No. 8, pp. 1497-1505.

Coleman, M. J., McHale, M. T., Arnau, J., Watson, A. & Oliver, R. P. (1993). Cloning and characterisation of telomeric DNA from Cladosporium fulvum. *Gene*, Vol. 132, No. 1, pp. 67-73.

Chan, C. S. & Tye, B. K. (1983a). A family of Saccharomyces cerevisiae repetitive autonomously replicating sequences that have very similar genomic environments. *J Mol Biol.*, Vol. 168, No. 3, pp. 505-523.

Chan, C. S. & Tye, B. K. (1983b). Organization of DNA sequences and replication origins at yeast telomeres. *Cell.*, Vol. 33, No. 2, pp. 563-573.

Chan, S. R. & Blackburn, E. H. (2004). Telomeres and telomerase. *Philos Trans R Soc Lond B Biol Sci*, Vol. 359, No. 1441, pp. 109-121.

De Cian, A., Lacroix, L., Douarre, C., Temime-Smaali, N., Trentesaux, C., Riou, J. F. & Mergny, J. L. (2008). Targeting telomeres and telomerase. *Biochimie*, Vol. 90, No. 1, pp. 131-155.

de Lange, T. (2005). Shelterin: the protein complex that shapes and safeguards human telomeres. *Genes Dev*, Vol. 19, No. 18, pp. 2100-2110.

de Lange, T. (2009). How telomeres solve the end-protection problem. *Science*, Vol. 326, No. 5955, pp. 948-952.

De Las Penas, A., Pan, S. J., Castano, I., Alder, J., Cregg, R. & Cormack, B. P. (2003). Virulence-related surface glycoproteins in the yeast pathogen Candida glabrata are encoded in subtelomeric clusters and subject to RAP1- and SIR-dependent transcriptional silencing. *Genes Dev.*, Vol. 17, No. 18, pp. 2245-2258.

Donate, L. E. & Blasco, M. A. (2011). Telomeres in cancer and ageing. *Philos Trans R Soc Lond B Biol Sci*, Vol. 366, No. 1561, pp. 76-84.

Espejel, S., Franco, S., Rodriguez-Perales, S., Bouffler, S. D., Cigudosa, J. C. & Blasco, M. A. (2002). Mammalian Ku86 mediates chromosomal fusions and apoptosis caused by critically short telomeres. *Embo J*, Vol. 21, No. 9, pp. 2207-2219.

Faravelli, M., Azzalin, C. M., Bertoni, L., Chernova, O., Attolini, C., Mondello, C. & Giulotto, E. (2002). Molecular organization of internal telomeric sequences in Chinese hamster chromosomes. *Gene*, Vol. 283, No. 1-2, pp. 11-16.

Faravelli, M., Moralli, D., Bertoni, L., Attolini, C., Chernova, O., Raimondi, E. & Giulotto, E. (1998). Two extended arrays of a satellite DNA sequence at the centromere and at the short-arm telomere of Chinese hamster chromosome 5. *Cytogenet Cell Genet*, Vol. 83, No. 3-4, pp. 281-286.

Fisher, T. S. & Zakian, V. A. (2005). Ku: a multifunctional protein involved in telomere maintenance. *DNA Repair (Amst)*, Vol. 4, No. 11, pp. 1215-1226.

Flint, J., Bates, G. P., Clark, K., Dorman, A., Willingham, D., Roe, B. A., Micklem, G., Higgs, D. R. & Louis, E. J. (1997a). Sequence comparison of human and yeast telomeres identifies structurally distinct subtelomeric domains. *Hum Mol Genet.*, Vol. 6, No. 8, pp. 1305-1313.

Flint, J., Thomas, K., Micklem, G., Raynham, H., Clark, K., Doggett, N. A., King, A. & Higgs, D. R. (1997b). The relationship between chromosome structure and function at a human telomeric region. *Nat Genet.*, Vol. 15, No. 3, pp. 252-257.

Freitas-Junior, L. H., Bottius, E., Pirrit, L. A., Deitsch, K. W., Scheidig, C., Guinet, F., Nehrbass, U., Wellems, T. E. & Scherf, A. (2000). Frequent ectopic recombination of virulence factor genes in telomeric chromosome clusters of P. falciparum. *Nature.*, Vol. 407, No. 6807, pp. 1018-1022.

Fry, M. (2007). Tetraplex DNA and its interacting proteins. *Front Biosci*, Vol. 12, No., pp. 4336-4351.

Galagan, J. E., Calvo, S. E., Borkovich, K. A., Selker, E. U., Read, N. D., Jaffe, D., FitzHugh, W., Ma, L. J., Smirnov, S., Purcell, S., Rehman, B., Elkins, T., Engels, R., Wang, S., Nielsen, C. B., Butler, J., Endrizzi, M., Qui, D., Ianakiev, P., Bell-Pedersen, D., Nelson, M. A., Werner-Washburne, M., Selitrennikoff, C. P., Kinsey, J. A., Braun, E. L., Zelter, A., Schulte, U., Kothe, G. O., Jedd, G., Mewes, W., Staben, C., Marcotte, E., Greenberg, D., Roy, A., Foley, K., Naylor, J., Stange-Thomann, N., Barrett, R., Gnerre, S., Kamal, M., Kamvysselis, M., Mauceli, E., Bielke, C., Rudd, S., Frishman, D., Krystofova, S., Rasmussen, C., Metzenberg, R. L., Perkins, D. D., Kroken, S., Cogoni, C., Macino, G., Catcheside, D., Li, W., Pratt, R. J., Osmani, S. A., DeSouza, C. P., Glass, L., Orbach, M. J., Berglund, J. A., Voelker, R., Yarden, O., Plamann, M., Seiler, S., Dunlap, J., Radford, A., Aramayo, R., Natvig, D. O., Alex, L. A., Mannhaupt, G., Ebbole, D. J., Freitag, M., Paulsen, I., Sachs, M. S., Lander, E. S., Nusbaum, C. & Birren, B. (2003). The genome sequence of the filamentous fungus Neurospora crassa. *Nature.*, Vol. 422, No. 6934, pp. 859-868.

Gao, W., Khang, C. H., Park, S. Y., Lee, Y. H. & Kang, S. (2002). Evolution and organization of a highly dynamic, subtelomeric helicase gene family in the rice blast fungus Magnaporthe grisea. *Genetics*, Vol. 162, No. 1, pp. 103-112.

Gibson, A. W., Wojciechowicz, L. A., Danzi, S. E., Zhang, B., Kim, J. H., Hu, Z. & Michels, C. A. (1997). Constitutive mutations of the Saccharomyces cerevisiae MAL-activator genes MAL23, MAL43, MAL63, and mal64. *Genetics.*, Vol. 146, No. 4, pp. 1287-1298.

Gilson, E. & Geli, V. (2007). How telomeres are replicated. *Nat Rev Mol Cell Biol*, Vol. 8, No. 10, pp. 825-838.

Goytisolo, F. A., Samper, E., Edmonson, S., Taccioli, G. E. & Blasco, M. A. (2001). The absence of the DNA-dependent protein kinase catalytic subunit in mice results in anaphase bridges and in increased telomeric fusions with normal telomere length and G-strand overhang. *Mol Cell Biol*, Vol. 21, No. 11, pp. 3642-3651.

Grabherr, M. G., Russell, P., Meyer, M., Mauceli, E., Alfoldi, J., Di Palma, F. & Lindblad-Toh, K. (2010). Genome-wide synteny through highly sensitive sequence alignment: Satsuma. *Bioinformatics*, Vol. 26, No. 9, pp. 1145-1151.

Greider, C. W. (1998). Telomeres and senescence: the history, the experiment, the future. *Curr Biol.*, Vol. 8, No. 5, pp. R178-181.

Griffith, J. D., Comeau, L., Rosenfield, S., Stansel, R. M., Bianchi, A., Moss, H. & de Lange, T. (1999). Mammalian telomeres end in a large duplex loop. *Cell.*, Vol. 97, No. 4, pp. 503-514.

Halme, A., Bumgarner, S., Styles, C. & Fink, G. R. (2004). Genetic and epigenetic regulation of the FLO gene family generates cell-surface variation in yeast. *Cell.*, Vol. 116, No. 3, pp. 405-415.

Hande, M. P. (2004). DNA repair factors and telomere-chromosome integrity in mammalian cells. *Cytogenet Genome Res*, Vol. 104, No. 1-4, pp. 116-122. Epub 292010 Feb 290511.

Hande, M. P., Samper, E., Lansdorp, P. & Blasco, M. A. (1999). Telomere length dynamics and chromosomal instability in cells derived from telomerase null mice. *J Cell Biol*, Vol. 144, No. 4, pp. 589-601.

Hastie, N. D. & Allshire, R. C. (1989). Human telomeres: fusion and interstitial sites. *Trends Genet*, Vol. 5, No. 10, pp. 326-331.

Hernandez-Rivas, R., Perez-Toledo, K., Herrera Solorio, A. M., Delgadillo, D. M. & Vargas, M. (2010). Telomeric heterochromatin in Plasmodium falciparum. *Journal of Biomedicine & Biotechnology*, Vol. 2010, No., pp. 290501. Epub 292010 Feb 290511.

Hijri, M., Niculita, H. & Sanders, I. R. (2007). Molecular characterization of chromosome termini of the arbuscular mycorrhizal fungus Glomus intraradices (Glomeromycota). *Fungal Genet Biol*, Vol. 44, No. 12, pp. 1380-1386.

Holmquist, G. P. & Dancis, B. (1979). Telomere replication, kinetochore organizers, and satellite DNA evolution. *Proc Natl Acad Sci U S A*, Vol. 76, No. 9, pp. 4566-4570.

Housworth, E. A. & Postlethwait, J. (2002). Measures of synteny conservation between species pairs. *Genetics.*, Vol. 162, No. 1, pp. 441-448.

Hsu, H. L., Gilley, D., Galande, S. A., Hande, M. P., Allen, B., Kim, S. H., Li, G. C., Campisi, J., Kohwi-Shigematsu, T. & Chen, D. J. (2000). Ku acts in a unique way at the mammalian telomere to prevent end joining. *Genes Dev*, Vol. 14, No. 22, pp. 2807-2812.

Inglis, P. W., Aragao, F. J., Frazao, H., Magalhaes, B. P. & Valadares-Inglis, M. C. (2000). Biolistic co-transformation of Metarhizium anisopliae var. acridum strain CG423 with green fluorescent protein and resistance to glufosinate ammonium. *FEMS Microbiol Lett*, Vol. 191, No. 2, pp. 249-254.

Inglis, P. W., Rigden, D. J., Mello, L. V., Louis, E. J. & Valadares-Inglis, M. C. (2005). Monomorphic subtelomeric DNA in the filamentous fungus, Metarhizium anisopliae,contains a RecQ helicase-like gene. *Mol Genet Genomics*, Vol. 274, No. 1, pp. 79-90.

Jackson, A. P., Gamble, J. A., Yeomans, T., Moran, G. P., Saunders, D., Harris, D., Aslett, M., Barrell, J. F., Butler, G., Citiulo, F., Coleman, D. C., de Groot, P. W., Goodwin, T. J., Quail, M. A., McQuillan, J., Munro, C. A., Pain, A., Poulter, R. T., Rajandream, M. A., Renauld, H., Spiering, M. J., Tivey, A., Gow, N. A., Barrell, B., Sullivan, D. J. & Berriman, M. (2009). Comparative genomics of the fungal pathogens Candida dubliniensis and Candida albicans. *Genome Res.*, Vol. 19, No. 12, pp. 2231-2244.

Johnson, J. E., Smith, J. S., Kozak, M. L. & Johnson, F. B. (2008). In vivo veritas: using yeast to probe the biological functions of G-quadruplexes. *Biochimie*, Vol. 90, No. 8, pp. 1250-1263.

Karpen, G. H. & Spradling, A. C. (1992). Analysis of subtelomeric heterochromatin in the Drosophila minichromosome Dp1187 by single P element insertional mutagenesis. *Genetics.*, Vol. 132, No. 3, pp. 737-753.

Keely, S. P., Renauld, H., Wakefield, A. E., Cushion, M. T., Smulian, A. G., Fosker, N., Fraser, A., Harris, D., Murphy, L., Price, C., Quail, M. A., Seeger, K., Sharp, S., Tindal, C. J., Warren, T., Zuiderwijk, E., Barrell, B. G., Stringer, J. R. & Hall, N. (2005). Gene arrays at Pneumocystis carinii telomeres. *Genetics.*, Vol. 170, No. 4, pp. 1589-1600.

Keely, S. P., Wakefield, A. E., Cushion, M. T., Smulian, A. G., Hall, N., Barrell, B. G. & Stringer, J. R. (2001). Detailed structure of Pneumocystis carinii chromosome ends. *J Eukaryot Microbiol*, Vol. Suppl, No., pp. 118S-120S.

Kersten, P. & Cullen, D. (2007). Extracellular oxidative systems of the lignin-degrading Basidiomycete Phanerochaete chrysosporium. *Fungal Genet Biol.*, Vol. 44, No. 2, pp. 77-87.

Kusumoto, K. I., Suzuki, S. & Kashiwagi, Y. (2003). Telomeric repeat sequence of Aspergillus oryzae consists of dodeca-nucleotides. *Appl Microbiol Biotechnol*, Vol. 61, No. 3, pp. 247-251.

Larraya, L. M., Perez, G., Ritter, E., Pisabarro, A. G. & Ramirez, L. (2000). Genetic linkage map of the edible basidiomycete Pleurotus ostreatus. *Appl Environ Microbiol.*, Vol. 66, No. 12, pp. 5290-5300.

Levis, C., Giraud, T., Dutertre, M., Fortini, D. & Brygoo, Y. (1997). Telomeric DNA of Botrytis cinerea: a useful tool for strain identification. *FEMS Microbiol Lett*, Vol. 157, No. 2, pp. 267-272.

Levis, R. W. (1993). Drosophila melanogaster does not share the telomeric repeat sequence of another invertebrate, Ascaris lumbricoides. *Mol Gen Genet.*, Vol. 236, No. 2-3, pp. 440-442.

Lin, K. W. & Yan, J. (2008). Endings in the middle: current knowledge of interstitial telomeric sequences. *Mutat Res*, Vol. 658, No. 1-2, pp. 95-110.

Linardopoulou, E. V., Williams, E. M., Fan, Y., Friedman, C., Young, J. M. & Trask, B. J. (2005). Human subtelomeres are hot spots of interchromosomal recombination and segmental duplication. *Nature.*, Vol. 437, No. 7055, pp. 94-100.

Lind, M., Olson, A. & Stenlid, J. (2005). An AFLP-markers based genetic linkage map of Heterobasidion annosum locating intersterility genes. *Fungal Genet Biol.*, Vol. 42, No. 6, pp. 519-527.

Linger, B. R. & Price, C. M. (2009). Conservation of telomere protein complexes: shuffling through evolution. *Crit Rev Biochem Mol Biol*, Vol. 44, No. 6, pp. 434-446.

Lipman, D. J. & Pearson, W. R. (1985). Rapid and sensitive protein similarity searches. *Science.*, Vol. 227, No. 4693, pp. 1435-1441.

Lo, A. W., Sprung, C. N., Fouladi, B., Pedram, M., Sabatier, L., Ricoul, M., Reynolds, G. E. & Murnane, J. P. (2002). Chromosome instability as a result of double-strand breaks near telomeres in mouse embryonic stem cells. *Mol Cell Biol*, Vol. 22, No. 13, pp. 4836-4850.

Long, D. M., Smidansky, E. D., Archer, A. J. & Strobel, G. A. (1998). In vivo addition of telomeric repeats to foreign DNA generates extrachromosomal DNAs in the taxol-producing fungus Pestalotiopsis microspora. *Fungal Genet Biol*, Vol. 24, No. 3, pp. 335-344.

Louis, E. J. (1995). The chromosome ends of Saccharomyces cerevisiae. *Yeast.*, Vol. 11, No. 16, pp. 1553-1573.

Louis, E. J. & Borts, R. H. (1995). A complete set of marked telomeres in Saccharomyces cerevisiae for physical mapping and cloning. *Genetics.*, Vol. 139, No. 1, pp. 125-136.

Louis, E. J. & Haber, J. E. (1990). Mitotic recombination among subtelomeric Y' repeats in Saccharomyces cerevisiae. *Genetics*, Vol. 124, No. 3, pp. 547-559.

Louis, E. J. & Haber, J. E. (1992). The structure and evolution of subtelomeric Y' repeats in Saccharomyces cerevisiae. *Genetics.*, Vol. 131, No. 3, pp. 559-574.

Luke, B. & Lingner, J. (2009). TERRA: telomeric repeat-containing RNA. *Embo J.*, Vol. 28, No. 17, pp. 2503-2510.

Luke, B., Panza, A., Redon, S., Iglesias, N., Li, Z. & Lingner, J. (2008). The Rat1p 5' to 3' exonuclease degrades telomeric repeat-containing RNA and promotes telomere elongation in Saccharomyces cerevisiae. *Mol Cell*, Vol. 32, No. 4, pp. 465-477.

Lundblad, V. & Blackburn, E. H. (1993). An alternative pathway for yeast telomere maintenance rescues est1- senescence. *Cell*, Vol. 73, No. 2, pp. 347-360.

Lundell, T. K., Makela, M. R. & Hilden, K. (2010). Lignin-modifying enzymes in filamentous basidiomycetes--ecological, functional and phylogenetic review. *J Basic Microbiol*, Vol. 50, No. 1, pp. 5-20.

Maizels, N. (2006). Dynamic roles for G4 DNA in the biology of eukaryotic cells. *Nat Struct Mol Biol*, Vol. 13, No. 12, pp. 1055-1059.

Mandell, J. G., Goodrich, K. J., Bahler, J. & Cech, T. R. (2005). Expression of a RecQ helicase homolog affects progression through crisis in fission yeast lacking telomerase. *J Biol Chem*, Vol. 280, No. 7, pp. 5249-5257.

Martinez, A. T., Speranza, M., Ruiz-Duenas, F. J., Ferreira, P., Camarero, S., Guillen, F., Martinez, M. J., Gutierrez, A. & del Rio, J. C. (2005). Biodegradation of lignocellulosics: microbial, chemical, and enzymatic aspects of the fungal attack of lignin. *Int Microbiol.*, Vol. 8, No. 3, pp. 195-204.

Martinez, D., Challacombe, J., Morgenstern, I., Hibbett, D., Schmoll, M., Kubicek, C. P., Ferreira, P., Ruiz-Duenas, F. J., Martinez, A. T., Kersten, P., Hammel, K. E., Vanden Wymelenberg, A., Gaskell, J., Lindquist, E., Sabat, G., Bondurant, S. S., Larrondo, L. F., Canessa, P., Vicuna, R., Yadav, J., Doddapaneni, H., Subramanian, V., Pisabarro, A. G., Lavin, J. L., Oguiza, J. A., Master, E., Henrissat, B., Coutinho, P. M., Harris, P., Magnuson, J. K., Baker, S. E., Bruno, K., Kenealy, W., Hoegger, P. J., Kues, U., Ramaiya, P., Lucas, S., Salamov, A., Shapiro, H., Tu, H., Chee, C. L., Misra, M., Xie, G., Teter, S., Yaver, D., James, T., Mokrejs, M., Pospisek, M., Grigoriev, I. V., Brettin, T., Rokhsar, D., Berka, R. & Cullen, D. (2009). Genome, transcriptome, and secretome analysis of wood decay fungus Postia placenta supports unique mechanisms of lignocellulose conversion. *Proc Natl Acad Sci U S A.*, Vol. 106, No. 6, pp. 1954-1959.

Martinez, D., Larrondo, L. F., Putnam, N., Gelpke, M. D., Huang, K., Chapman, J., Helfenbein, K. G., Ramaiya, P., Detter, J. C., Larimer, F., Coutinho, P. M., Henrissat, B., Berka, R., Cullen, D. & Rokhsar, D. (2004). Genome sequence of the lignocellulose degrading fungus Phanerochaete chrysosporium strain RP78. *Nat Biotechnol.*, Vol. 22, No. 6, pp. 695-700.

Maser, R. S. & DePinho, R. A. (2004). Telomeres and the DNA damage response: why the fox is guarding the henhouse. *DNA Repair (Amst)*, Vol. 3, No. 8-9, pp. 979-988.

Masutomi, K., Yu, E. Y., Khurts, S., Ben-Porath, I., Currier, J. L., Metz, G. B., Brooks, M. W., Kaneko, S., Murakami, S., DeCaprio, J. A., Weinberg, R. A., Stewart, S. A. & Hahn, W. C. (2003). Telomerase maintains telomere structure in normal human cells. *Cell*, Vol. 114, No. 2, pp. 241-253.

Mefford, H. C. & Trask, B. J. (2002). The complex structure and dynamic evolution of human subtelomeres. *Nat Rev Genet.*, Vol. 3, No. 2, pp. 91-102.

Meyne, J., Baker, R. J., Hobart, H. H., Hsu, T. C., Ryder, O. A., Ward, O. G., Wiley, J. E., Wurster-Hill, D. H., Yates, T. L. & Moyzis, R. K. (1990). Distribution of non-telomeric sites of the (TTAGGG)n telomeric sequence in vertebrate chromosomes. *Chromosoma*, Vol. 99, No. 1, pp. 3-10.

Mondoux, M. & Zakian, V. A. (2005). Telomere position effect: silencing near the end. In: *Telomeres* T. de Lange, V. Lundblad and E. H. Blackburn, pp. (261-316), CSHL Press, Cold Spring Harbor, New York.

Morin, G. B. (1989). The human telomere terminal transferase enzyme is a ribonucleoprotein that synthesizes TTAGGG repeats. *Cell.*, Vol. 59, No. 3, pp. 521-529.

Murnane, J. P. & Sabatier, L. (2004). Chromosome rearrangements resulting from telomere dysfunction and their role in cancer. *Bioessays*, Vol. 26, No. 11, pp. 1164-1174.

Nagele, R. G., Velasco, A. Q., Anderson, W. J., McMahon, D. J., Thomson, Z., Fazekas, J., Wind, K. & Lee, H. (2001). Telomere associations in interphase nuclei: possible role in maintenance of interphase chromosome topology. *J Cell Sci*, Vol. 114, No. Pt 2, pp. 377-388.

Ogami, M., Ikura, Y., Ohsawa, M., Matsuo, T., Kayo, S., Yoshimi, N., Hai, E., Shirai, N., Ehara, S., Komatsu, R., Naruko, T. & Ueda, M. (2004). Telomere shortening in human coronary artery diseases. *Arterioscler Thromb Vasc Biol*, Vol. 24, No. 3, pp. 546-550.

Oganesian, L., Moon, I. K., Bryan, T. M. & Jarstfer, M. B. (2006). Extension of G-quadruplex DNA by ciliate telomerase. *Embo J*, Vol. 25, No. 5, pp. 1148-1159.

Padmavathi, J., UmaDevi, K., Rao, C. U. & Reddy, N. N. (2003). Telomere fingerprinting for assessing chromosome number, isolate typing and recombination in the entomopathogen Beauveria bassiana. *Mycol Res*, Vol. 107, No. Pt 5, pp. 572-580.

Paeschke, K., Juranek, S., Simonsson, T., Hempel, A., Rhodes, D. & Lipps, H. J. (2008). Telomerase recruitment by the telomere end binding protein-beta facilitates G-quadruplex DNA unfolding in ciliates. *Nat Struct Mol Biol*, Vol. 15, No. 6, pp. 598-604.

Paeschke, K., McDonald, K. R. & Zakian, V. A. (2010). Telomeres: structures in need of unwinding. *FEBS Lett*, Vol. 584, No. 17, pp. 3760-3772.

Paeschke, K., Simonsson, T., Postberg, J., Rhodes, D. & Lipps, H. J. (2005). Telomere end-binding proteins control the formation of G-quadruplex DNA structures in vivo. *Nat Struct Mol Biol*, Vol. 12, No. 10, pp. 847-854.

Palm, W. & de Lange, T. (2008). How shelterin protects mammalian telomeres. *Annu Rev Genet*, Vol. 42, No., pp. 301-334.

Perez, G., Pangilinan, J., Pisabarro, A. G. & Ramirez, L. (2009). Telomere organization in the ligninolytic basidiomycete Pleurotus ostreatus. *Appl Environ Microbiol.*, Vol. 75, No. 5, pp. 1427-1436.

Pryde, F. E., Gorham, H. C. & Louis, E. J. (1997). Chromosome ends: all the same under their caps. *Curr Opin Genet Dev.*, Vol. 7, No. 6, pp. 822-828.

Pryde, F. E. & Louis, E. J. (1997). Saccharomyces cerevisiae telomeres. A review. *Biochemistry (Mosc).* Vol. 62, No. 11, pp. 1232-1241.

Rachidi, N., Martinez, M. J., Barre, P. & Blondin, B. (2000). Saccharomyces cerevisiae PAU genes are induced by anaerobiosis. *Mol Microbiol.*, Vol. 35, No. 6, pp. 1421-1430.

Rehmeyer, C., Li, W., Kusaba, M., Kim, Y. S., Brown, D., Staben, C., Dean, R. & Farman, M. (2006). Organization of chromosome ends in the rice blast fungus, Magnaporthe oryzae. *Nucleic Acids Res*, Vol. 34, No. 17, pp. 4685-4701.

Rhodes, D., Fairall, L., Simonsson, T., Court, R. & Chapman, L. (2002). Telomere architecture. *EMBO Rep*, Vol. 3, No. 12, pp. 1139-1145.

Riethman, H., Ambrosini, A., Castaneda, C., Finklestein, J., Hu, X. L., Mudunuri, U., Paul, S. & Wei, J. (2004). Mapping and initial analysis of human subtelomeric sequence assemblies. *Genome Res.*, Vol. 14, No. 1, pp. 18-28.

Riethman, H., Ambrosini, A. & Paul, S. (2005). Human subtelomere structure and variation. *Chromosome Res*, Vol. 13, No. 5, pp. 505-515.

Riethman, H. C., Xiang, Z., Paul, S., Morse, E., Hu, X. L., Flint, J., Chi, H. C., Grady, D. L. & Moyzis, R. K. (2001). Integration of telomere sequences with the draft human genome sequence. *Nature.*, Vol. 409, No. 6822, pp. 948-951.

Ruiz-Duenas, F. J. & Martinez, A. T. (2009). Microbial degradation of lignin: how a bulky recalcitrant polymer is efficiently recycled in nature and how we can take advantage of this. *Microb Biotechnol.*, Vol. 2, No. 2, pp. 164-177. doi: 110.1111/j.1751-7915.2008.00078.x.

Samper, E., Goytisolo, F. A., Slijepcevic, P., van Buul, P. P. & Blasco, M. A. (2000). Mammalian Ku86 protein prevents telomeric fusions independently of the length of TTAGGG repeats and the G-strand overhang. *EMBO Rep*, Vol. 1, No. 3, pp. 244-252.

Sanchez-Alonso, P. & Guzman, P. (1998). Organization of chromosome ends in Ustilago maydis. RecQ-like helicase motifs at telomeric regions. *Genetics.*, Vol. 148, No. 3, pp. 1043-1054.

Sanchez-Alonso, P. & Guzman, P. (2008). Predicted elements of telomere organization and function in *Ustilago maydis*. *Fungal Genet Biol.*, Vol. 45 Suppl 1, No., pp. S54-62.

Schaffitzel, C., Berger, I., Postberg, J., Hanes, J., Lipps, H. J. & Pluckthun, A. (2001). In vitro generated antibodies specific for telomeric guanine-quadruplex DNA react with Stylonychia lemnae macronuclei. *Proc Natl Acad Sci U S A*, Vol. 98, No. 15, pp. 8572-8577.

Schoeftner, S. & Blasco, M. A. (2008). Developmentally regulated transcription of mammalian telomeres by DNA-dependent RNA polymerase II. *Nat Cell Biol*, Vol. 10, No. 2, pp. 228-236.

Schoeftner, S. & Blasco, M. A. (2009). Chromatin regulation and non-coding RNAs at mammalian telomeres. *Semin Cell Dev Biol*, Vol. 21, No. 2, pp. 186-193.

Selker, E. U. (1990). Premeiotic instability of repeated sequences in Neurospora crassa. *Annu Rev Genet*, Vol. 24, No., pp. 579-613.

Sherr, C. J. & McCormick, F. (2002). The RB and p53 pathways in cancer. *Cancer Cell*, Vol. 2, No. 2, pp. 103-112.

Shore, D. & Bianchi, A. (2009). Telomere length regulation: coupling DNA end processing to feedback regulation of telomerase. *Embo J*, Vol. 28, No. 16, pp. 2309-2322.

Slijepcevic, P., Xiao, Y., Dominguez, I. & Natarajan, A. T. (1996). Spontaneous and radiation-induced chromosomal breakage at interstitial telomeric sites. *Chromosoma*, Vol. 104, No. 8, pp. 596-604.

Smogorzewska, A., Karlseder, J., Holtgreve-Grez, H., Jauch, A. & de Lange, T. (2002). DNA ligase IV-dependent NHEJ of deprotected mammalian telomeres in G1 and G2. *Curr Biol*, Vol. 12, No. 19, pp. 1635-1644.

Soler, D., Genesca, A., Arnedo, G., Egozcue, J. & Tusell, L. (2005). Telomere dysfunction drives chromosomal instability in human mammary epithelial cells. *Genes Chromosomes Cancer*, Vol. 44, No. 4, pp. 339-350.

Starr, J. M., McGurn, B., Harris, S. E., Whalley, L. J., Deary, I. J. & Shiels, P. G. (2007). Association between telomere length and heart disease in a narrow age cohort of older people. *Exp Gerontol*, Vol. 42, No. 6, pp. 571-573.

Takai, H., Smogorzewska, A. & de Lange, T. (2003). DNA damage foci at dysfunctional telomeres. *Curr Biol*, Vol. 13, No. 17, pp. 1549-1556.

Tang, H., Lyons, E., Pedersen, B., Schnable, J. C., Paterson, A. H. & Freeling, M. (2011). Screening synteny blocks in pairwise genome comparisons through integer programming. *BMC Genomics*, Vol. 12, No., pp. 102.

Teng, S. C., Chang, J., McCowan, B. & Zakian, V. A. (2000). Telomerase-independent lengthening of yeast telomeres occurs by an abrupt Rad50p-dependent, Rif-inhibited recombinational process. *Mol Cell*, Vol. 6, No. 4, pp. 947-952.

Teng, S. C. & Zakian, V. A. (1999). Telomere-telomere recombination is an efficient bypass pathway for telomere maintenance in Saccharomyces cerevisiae. *Mol Cell Biol*, Vol. 19, No. 12, pp. 8083-8093.

Teunissen, A. W. & Steensma, H. Y. (1995). Review: the dominant flocculation genes of Saccharomyces cerevisiae constitute a new subtelomeric gene family. *Yeast.*, Vol. 11, No. 11, pp. 1001-1013.

Tien, M. (1987). Properties of ligninase from Phanerochaete chrysosporium and their possible applications. *Crit Rev Microbiol*, Vol. 15, No. 2, pp. 141-168.

Uchida, W., Matsunaga, S., Sugiyama, R. & Kawano, S. (2002). Interstitial telomere-like repeats in the Arabidopsis thaliana genome. *Genes Genet Syst*, Vol. 77, No. 1, pp. 63-67.

van Steensel, B., Smogorzewska, A. & de Lange, T. (1998). TRF2 protects human telomeres from end-to-end fusions. *Cell*, Vol. 92, No. 3, pp. 401-413.

Vega, L. R., Mateyak, M. K. & Zakian, V. A. (2003). Getting to the end: telomerase access in yeast and humans. *Nat Rev Mol Cell Biol*, Vol. 4, No. 12, pp. 948-959.

Verdun, R. E. & Karlseder, J. (2007). Replication and protection of telomeres. *Nature*, Vol. 447, No. 7147, pp. 924-931.

Walter, M. F., Jang, C., Kasravi, B., Donath, J., Mechler, B. M., Mason, J. M. & Biessmann, H. (1995). DNA organization and polymorphism of a wild-type Drosophila telomere region. *Chromosoma.*, Vol. 104, No. 4, pp. 229-241.

Weber, B., Collins, C., Robbins, C., Magenis, R. E., Delaney, A. D., Gray, J. W. & Hayden, M. R. (1990). Characterization and organization of DNA sequences adjacent to the human telomere associated repeat (TTAGGG)n. *Nucleic Acids Res*, Vol. 18, No. 11, pp. 3353-3361.

Welchen, E. & Gonzalez, D. H. (2005). Differential expression of the Arabidopsis cytochrome c genes Cytc-1 and Cytc-2. Evidence for the involvement of TCP-domain protein-binding elements in anther- and meristem-specific expression of the Cytc-1 gene. *Plant Physiol*, Vol. 139, No. 1, pp. 88-100.

Wellinger, R. J., Ethier, K., Labrecque, P. & Zakian, V. A. (1996). Evidence for a new step in telomere maintenance. *Cell*, Vol. 85, No. 3, pp. 423-433.

Wellinger, R. J., Wolf, A. J. & Zakian, V. A. (1993). Saccharomyces telomeres acquire single-strand TG1-3 tails late in S phase. *Cell*, Vol. 72, No. 1, pp. 51-60.

Wilkie, A. O., Higgs, D. R., Rack, K. A., Buckle, V. J., Spurr, N. K., Fischel-Ghodsian, N., Ceccherini, I., Brown, W. R. & Harris, P. C. (1991). Stable length polymorphism of up to 260 kb at the tip of the short arm of human chromosome 16. *Cell.*, Vol. 64, No. 3, pp. 595-606.

Wu, C., Kim, Y. S., Smith, K. M., Li, W., Hood, H. M., Staben, C., Selker, E. U., Sachs, M. S. & Farman, M. L. (2009). Characterization of chromosome ends in the filamentous fungus Neurospora crassa. *Genetics.*, Vol. 181, No. 3, pp. 1129-1145.

Zahler, A. M., Williamson, J. R., Cech, T. R. & Prescott, D. M. (1991). Inhibition of telomerase by G-quartet DNA structures. *Nature*, Vol. 350, No. 6320, pp. 718-720.

Zakian, V. A. (1995). Telomeres: beginning to understand the end. *Science*, Vol. 270, No. 5242, pp. 1601-1607.

Zhao, Y., Sfeir, A. J., Zou, Y., Buseman, C. M., Chow, T. T., Shay, J. W. & Wright, W. E. (2009). Telomere extension occurs at most chromosome ends and is uncoupled from fill-in in human cancer cells. *Cell.*, Vol. 138, No. 3, pp. 463-475.

20

SNPpattern: A Genetic Tool to Derive Haplotype Blocks and Measure Genomic Diversity in Populations Using SNP Genotypes

Stephen J. Goodswen[1,2] and Haja N. Kadarmideen[3]
[1]University of Technology Sydney, Broadway, Sydney, NSW
[2]CSIRO Livestock Industries, ATSIP, University Drive,
James Cook University Campus, Townsville, QLD
[3]Department of Basic Animal and Veterinary Sciences, Faculty of Life Sciences,
University of Copenhagen, Frederiksberg C
[1,2]Australia
[3]Denmark

1. Introduction

The aftermath of the Human Genome Project has generated new revolutionary techniques and equipment such as high throughput measurement tools for collecting biological information. One notable tool is a microarray that can be used to genotype hundreds of thousands of single nucleotide polymorphisms (SNPs) in one run. This highthroughput SNP genotypes along with phenotypic measurements can be used in fine quantitative trait loci (QTL) mapping or genome-wide association studies (GWAS). The result of fine QTL mapping or GWAS is a set of statistically significant QTL regions or genetic markers such as SNPs. See Box 1 for SNP, QTL and GWAS explanation. The significant QTLs or SNPs from QTL mapping or GWAS are used subsequently in QTL or SNP – based selection of elite animals or plants for breeding in agriculture or used to predict disease risks in humans and animals (e.g. Burton et al. 2007, Mackay et al. 2009). GWAS relies on a natural phenomenon of linkage disequilibrium (LD) between genetic (SNP) markers and causal variants or quantitative trait nucleotide (QTN). For GWAS to be applied successfully there is a need to understand the extent and distribution of linkage disequilibrium (LD) across the entire genome in a population. In particular, we need to know how LD varies from one region (or population) to another. This need to know how LD (and haplotype diversity) varies from one region or population to another provided the motivation to develop SNPpattern, a generic bioinformatic tool for finding SNP allele patterns in populations.

1.1 The principles of linkage disequilibrium (LD) and haplotypes

We are currently in a bioinformatics era. The emergence of bioinformatics is the result of two converging forces. One relates to the exponential increase in computer processing power, digital storage capacity, and digital communication. The other force is the exponential increase in biological data (Larranaga et al., 2006). Prior to the 1990s biologists could be stereotyped as being isolated in their experimental laboratories doing their poorly funded projects and recording their findings in a paper format. The Human Genome Project completely changed all of this (Collins et al., 2003). Notwithstanding the staggering $3 billion cost for the project, the scientific findings and the new revolutionary techniques and equipment have spurred on many other projects to generate an avalanche of advances in gene technologies, genomics, and molecular biology. Some of the notable developments are the high throughput measurement tools for collecting biological information; tools such as microarrays, high speed DNA sequencers, and mass spectrometers. The main outcome from all this new technology is enormous amounts of disseminated biological data in different digital formats.   One of the main challenges in bioinformatics is to transform the exponentially growing biological data into useful information. What constitutes *useful* information is of course debatable; nevertheless, information is the critical starting component to solving biological problems. Living cells are extremely complicated systems, even so, the new high throughput measurement tools have revolutionised the way we can collect biological data about these systems and begin to unravel the complexity. In the light of these advances in genomics, the bioinformatics aspiration is to provide the relevant tools to make sense of multiple sources of omics datasets or at the very least, enable the researcher to make valuable inferences, connections and predictions from the information. Kadarmideen & Reverter (2007) provided a good review of some integrative analytical framework combining multiple -omics data types specifically for livestock populations but they discuss generic issues for most species where genome sequences are being made available. For instance, Kadarmideen et al., (2006), Kadarmideen and Janss (2007) and Kadarmideen (2008), apply an integrative systems genetics approaches to map genetic variants and unravel underlying genetic networks of diabetes, stress, and reproduction, respectively in recombinant inbred strains of mouse genotyped for over 2 million SNP genetic markers and microarray expression profiled for over 20000 transcripts in various tissues. Without the relevant bioinformatics tools, it would not have been possible to integrate such large datasets and apply sophisticated statistical genetic algorithms and models.

Systematic studies of common genetic variants have shown that some combinations of polymorphisms at different loci occur more or less frequently in a population such that the alleles of these polymorphisms are associated more often than if they were unlinked. That is, there is a statistically significant difference between observed and expected allelic frequencies (expected, in this instance, refers to allelic frequencies as result of independent segregation).

This non-random and non-Mendelian association between alleles at two or more loci is referred to as linkage disequilibrium (LD) and is a departure from the Hardy-Weinberg equilibrium. SNPs (Box 1) are the most common polymorphism and are extremely dense throughout the genome which allows for an effective study of common haplotypes. For the remaining of this section, SNPs will be used when referring to variants/polymorphism in the context of LD.

Prior to the year 2004 there was little published research on LD in humans, yet from 2004 onwards an exponential release of publications commenced[1] (for instance, see patterns of human LD in Ardlie et al. 2002). It is argued that this increase in interest is mainly because of the increased applications of LD as a tool. For example, LD is the essential tool of genetic

---

[1] Based on ISI Web of Knowledge[SM] searches

BOX 1

SNP: A single-nucleotide polymorphism is a DNA sequence variation occurring when a single nucleotide — A, T, C, or G — in the genome (or other shared sequence) differs between members of a biological species or paired chromosomes in an individual. For example, two sequenced DNA fragments from different individuals, AAGCCTA to AAGCTTA, contain a difference in a single nucleotide. In this case we say that there are two alleles: C and T. Almost all common SNPs have only two alleles. (Source: http://en.wikipedia.org/wiki/Main_Pag)

QTL mapping: Quantitative trait locus (QTL) mapping means identifying genes that affects a complex phenotype like disease or explains significant proportion of genetic variation of a quantitative trait observed in mapping population. It uncovers the genetic basis of quantitative variation in a trait.

GWAS: A genome-wide association study (GWAS) is an approach that involves rapidly scanning genetic (SNP) markers across genome in hundreds of individuals to find and quantify genetic variations in a particular disease or trait associated with each SNP screened. It uses highly dense SNP marker genotype data (nearing 1 million in some animal species) to detect association with phenotypes. These study require larger sample sizes than QTL mapping and requires validations in other independent populations. GWAS techniques result in a panel of predictive markers that can predict a future phenotype of an individual. How good will be a prediction by a set of markers depends on whether or not they are linked to and/or in linkage disequilibrium with causal loci.

association studies. In genome-wide association studies (Hirschhorn et al. 2002, Pearson and Manolio 2008, Kruglyak 2008), the premise is to test for associations between the variation in a complex trait and causal mutations, however, for the most part we instead test for association between the trait and a SNP in high LD with the causal mutation. Knowledge of LD patterns has been shown to increase the power and decrease the amount of genotyping required for association studies. For example, we can use information about LD and allele frequencies across the genome to make informed decisions as to which SNPs (known as tag SNPs) should be selected for the genotyping array. That is, the number of SNPs required in GWAS can be reduced without a reduction in power if LD is extensive (Carlson et al., 2001). Linkage disequilibrium is also used in the studies of a species genetic history and origins, the detection of natural selection, and the biology of recombination from inferring the distribution of crossover events from patterns of LD Pritchard (2001). In particular for animal production, working out LD is important within breeds to determine the SNP density for GWAS, and across breeds to check whether LD based predictions are expected to persist between breeds.

To quantify the amount of LD, a variety of different statistical measures have been proposed: D, D´ and r^2. D is the basic measure for LD and the formula is $D = P_{AB} - P_A * P_B$ (where P_A and P_B are the marginal allele frequencies at two loci on a chromosome; and P_{AB} is the probability of the observed haplotype). D equates to 0 if and only if the two loci are independent. A disadvantage of D is that the range of possible values depends on the marginal allele frequencies and therefore, as there is no standardisation, it is difficult to compare D values. D´ is the standardisation of D and its formula is shown in Equation

$$D' = \frac{D}{D_{max}} \ when \ D \geq 0 \qquad \text{Where } D_{max} = \text{the smaller of } P_{Ab} \text{ and } P_{aB}$$

$$D' = \frac{D}{D_{min}} \ when \ D < 0 \qquad \text{Where } D_{min} = \text{larger of } -P_{AB} \text{ and } -P_{ab}$$

Equation 1. Measuring LD using D´ for 2 loci A and B with 2 alleles.

The most widely used measure for LD is a correlation between pairs of biallelic SNPs denoted by r^2 (refer Equation 2). Some of the properties of r^2: a value of 0 implies independence between the SNP alleles (perfect equilibrium); a value of 1 implies perfect LD. Most pairs of SNP alleles have an r^2 greater than 0 or less than 1 indicating the strength of the association between their alleles. An r^2 of 0.7 or 0.8 is considered strong LD between SNPs. For the most part, the strength of the correlation between SNPs decreases as the genetic distance between the SNP increases. The r^2 measure also has another useful property; it is claimed to be related to the power of association mapping and can consequently be used to estimate how large the sample size needs to be to capture association ($n_2 = n_1 / r^2$ where n_1 is the number of cases and n_2 is the number of controls). Currently for human genotyping arrays, tag SNPs are selected based on an r^2 concept of LD structure for their pairwise ability to predict the genotype of untyped SNPs. For species with limited knowledge of LD, the SNPs are selected evenly distributed.

$$r^2 = \frac{D^2}{P_A * P_B * P_a * P_b}$$

Equation 2. Given haplotypes for 2 loci A and B with 2 alleles. Where P = allele frequencies, and D is a basic measure of LD e.g. $D = P_{AB} - P_A * P_B$.

Population genetic factors that affect LD among specific groups of SNPs are numerous, complex, and not clearly understood. Some of the acknowledged factors are mutation, historical recombination, natural selection, founder effects, migration, population growth, random drift, gene conversion, and population admixture. Only recombination is discussed further in this chapter. It has been argued that recombination is one of the main factors affecting LD (Ardlie et al., 2002). The rate of LD decay depends on the rate of recombination and for the most part, decay in LD is affected by how close the alleles are together. Little is known about the actual molecular mechanism of recombination and why some regions of the chromosome experience more recombination than others. What we do know is that there is variation in recombination rates, and regions of recombination appear and disappear over evolutionary time. By studying the patterns of LD we can at least infer the distribution of recombination events.

In the literature LD is intertwined with the term haplotype. There are many definitions of the term haplotype in the literature, herein haplotype is used as being half of a genotype, that is, a set of ordered SNP alleles on a *single* chromosome that are transmitted as one unit from a parent to an offspring (Ardlie et al., 2002). Theoretically a haplotype, one unit, could comprise any number of SNPs from only 2 SNPs to every single SNP on the chromosome. In reality, however, recombination events result in haplotype blocks comprised of varying numbers of SNPs.

Early studies of pairwise LD (i.e. using 2-locus haplotypes) observed complex patterns of LD implying a random nature. It is now becoming clear that despite many generations of segregation from a common ancestral chromosome, certain combinations of neighbouring SNP alleles (haplotype units) have remained unchanged. In other words, there are stretches of DNA that are almost never divided during meiosis (Gibbs et al., 2003). Although we do not fully understand the biological processes that give rise to recombination in some regions of the chromosome and not in others, there still appears to be some non-random underpinning mechanism. More recently the International Hapmap Project (Gibbs et al., 2003) has shown that the underlying structure of LD in a genome could be divided into discrete haplotype blocks. Using evidence from their LD measures, a haplotype block represents a region with a few haplotypes (2-4 per block) in a population separated by a region with many haplotypes in the population. Their proposed haplotype block model of LD, from a recombination perspective, is a region of high LD separated by recombination hotspots. There are two popular methods for block definition: 1) using pair-wise disequilibrium to define regions of high LD separated by recombination hotspots, and 2) defining regions with high or low haplotype diversity.

1.2 Phasing SNP genotypes for deriving paternal and maternal haplotypes

We currently have the technology to observe genotypes but not haplotypes. That is, we do not observe individual alleles on the chromosome. This immediately presents a problem for haplotype analysis since the phase is not known when SNPs are heterozygous. For example, given the genotype of 2 SNPs with homozygous alleles at 2 different loci, "11" and "22" respectively; the haplotype on both the paternal and maternal chromosome is conclusively "12". However, given the genotype of 2 SNPs with heterozygous alleles, "12" and "12"; we do not know which allele is inherited from which parent. The possible haplotypes are shown in Figure 1.

We cannot say for certain which alleles on a haplotype go together when using genotype data with heterozygous SNP alleles. Consequently we need to determine or infer the phase from other methods. There are 3 possible methods available to the researcher: 1) use pedigree information; 2) use molecular methods to single out individual chromosomes to do genotyping (currently only possible on small regions; and 3) statistical methods to infer the haplotype given genotype data. From literature, there are several algorithms and programs for inferring haplotypes. Two of the most popular programs are called PHASE, which uses algorithms based on Bayesian coalescent models Stephens et al. (2001) and fastPHASE, which uses an EM algorithm and cluster model Scheet et al. (2006). The default PHASE and fastPHASE output format has been adopted as the format required for the input data to *SNPpattern*.

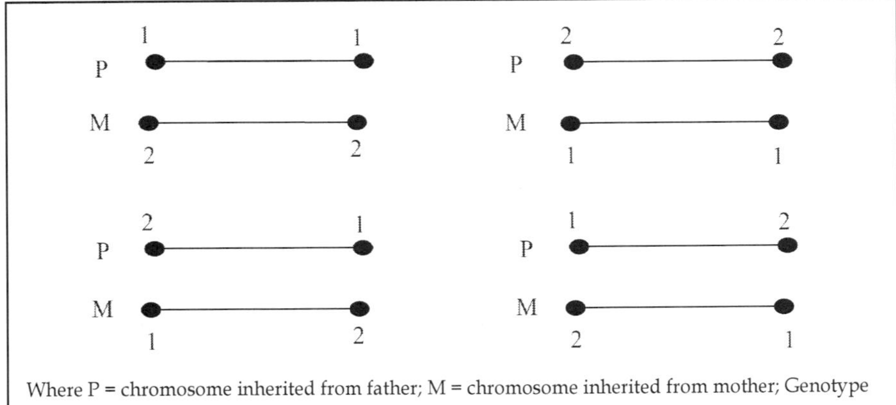

Where P = chromosome inherited from father; M = chromosome inherited from mother; Genotype for SNPs = 12)

Fig. 1. Possible haplotype when 2 SNPs have heterozygous alleles.

PHASE is a statistical method inspired from coalescent theory. The coalescent theory in essence is the tracing of alleles, shared in a sample of individuals from a population, back to the most recent common ancestor Fu et al. (1999). This theory can predict the expected patterns of haplotypes in natural populations. The PHASE method is Bayesian and uses the a priori expectation of haplotypes to inform haplotype reconstruction (see Equation 3). The phase reconstruction procedure is to evaluate the conditional distribution of the unknown haplotypes corresponding to the genotypes for the individuals from a population sample. PHASE uses Gibbs sampling (Kim, 2001) to obtain an approximate sample from the posterior distribution of unknown haplotype pairs given genotype data (e.g. Pr (H | G) is the posterior probability that the reconstruction of the haplotype pairs is correct, given the genotypes *and* knowledge of previous haplotype reconstruction states). In the most simplistic terms, the algorithm begins by estimating the haplotypes for a randomly chosen individual on the assumption all other haplotypes are reconstructed correctly. The algorithm reiterates the process enough times to result in an approximate haplotype reconstruction from the posterior probability. Stephens[38] claims that PHASE, "is sufficiently accurate that reconstructing haplotypes experimentally, or by genotyping additional family members, may be an inefficient use of resources".

$$\Pr(H \mid G) = \frac{\Pr(G \mid H)\,\Pr(H)}{\Pr(G)}$$

Equation 3. Bayes theorem.

where,
Pr(H|G) is the conditional probability that the reconstruction of the haplotype pairs is correct given the genotypes.
Pr(H) is the prior (unconditional) probability the reconstruction of the haplotype pairs is correct irrespective of genotype data.
P(G) is the total probability of observed genotypes across all possible haplotypes (acts as a normalising constant).

$Pr(G \mid H)$ is the conditional probability of obtaining the genotypes given the haplotypes. The fastPHASE software package is a statistical model that captures patterns of LD. The variation in the patterns can be applied to estimate missing genotypes and to infer haplotype phase in samples of unrelated individuals from natural populations from unphased genotype data. The fastPHASE statistical model uses an "approximate coalescent with recombination" prior manifested from the fact that over short genomic regions haplotypes in a population have been observed to cluster into groups of similar haplotypes because of recombination (Stephens et al., 2005). The model also considers each cluster of observed haplotypes to represent a common haplotype and each haplotype is assumed to have evolved from a single cluster. The membership of each cluster is allowed to change along the chromosome in accordance with a hidden Markov model (Scheet et al., 2006). An expectation-maximization (EM) algorithm (Dempster et al., 1997) is used to estimate the model parameters.

The paper presents the development of *SNPpattern* as a simple bioinformatic tool to rapidly screen the genome for haplotype structure, perform some basic descriptive genome statistics and link interesting haplotypes to functional information. We have tested our software *SNP pattern* on Ovine 60k SNPchip data (Goodswen et al., 2010). One impetus for the development of *SNPpattern* was to understand the degree of diversity in LD architecture between different livestock breeds (McKay et al. 2007). It was thought that with our increased understanding we could potentially predict effect of genome selection across breeds, which is based on SNPs being in LD with causal variants for the trait of interest. In addition, we expect *SNPpattern* be used in the comparison of LD structure in detecting and localizing genomic regions where selective sweeps[2] have occurred (Smith et al., 1974).

2. Development of *SNPpattern*

A commonly used software package for computing LD statistics and haplotype patterns for populations from genotype data is Haploview (Barrett et al., 2005). One of the interesting features of Haploview, is its ability to generate haplotype blocks. Haploview has a number of methods to partition the genome into blocks: 1) block definitions are based on D' confidence bounds e.g. SNP pairs are defined to be either "strong LD" (.i.e. no evidence of historical recombination) or "strong recombination". The algorithm is taken from Gabriel et al. (2002); 2) the block definition is based on a four gamete test of Hudson & Kaplan (1985) proposed by Wang et al (2002). In brief, for each SNP pair, the population frequencies of the 4 possible two-SNP haplotypes are computed (e.g. SNP 1 = A/a and SNP 2 = B/b. The 4 haplotypes are AB, Ab, aB, and ab). If all 4 haplotypes are observed with a frequency >= 0.01 (a user definable threshold), a recombination is assumed to have occurred. If only 3 haplotypes are observed no recombination is assumed. A block is formed when there has been no recombination for successive SNP pairs.

HaploBlock is a software package, which has as one of its capabilities the inference of haplotype block models from phased or unphased data. It primarily uses a Markov chain and can account for recombination hotspots, bottlenecks, genetic drift and mutations (Greenspan & Geiger, 2004). HapBlock (a different program to the similarly named

---

[2] A selective sweep can be caused when there is a strong directional selection for a favourable new allele that increases its frequency. Alleles in close proximity to the new allele are "swept" to fixation.

HaploBlock program) provides both a parametric dynamic programming algorithm for block partitioning with a fixed genome coverage using the minimum number of tag SNPs, and a discrete dynamic programming algorithm for block partitioning with a fixed number of tag SNPs that can cover maximum length of genome (Zhang, 2005). Finally, GERBIL is another software package that implements an algorithm for simultaneously phasing genotypes into haplotypes and block partitioning. It considers the phasing and the block partitioning as a maximum likelihood problem and uses the EM algorithm to solve it (Kimmel & Shamir, 2005). Table 1 shows a brief summary of the publicly available programs that provide functionality to define haplotype blocks from genotype data.

Program	Primary LD metric	Visualisation of LD	PHASE/ fastPHASE import[$$]	Implemen-tation	OS
Haploview	D' and r^2	Yes	No	Java	Linux Windows
HapBlock	D'	No	No	C++	Linux
HaploBlock	**	No	No	Ansi C	Linux
Gerbil	++	Yes	No	Java/C++	Linux Windows
SNPpattern	Pattern frequency in block	No	Yes	Perl	Linux Windows

Table 1. Freely available programs providing "haplotype block definition from genotype data" functionality.

LD = Linkage disequilibrium: OS = Operating System platform: ** A Bayesian Network statistical model and Markov chain at its core: ++ Uses an expectation-maximization (EM) algorithm: $$ imports genotype data in a PHASE/fastPHASE format without modification

In studies on human populations it has been shown that the human genome can be divided into haplotype blocks (Gabriel et al., 2005). A haplotype block is an ancestrally conserved region of varying size containing only a few common haplotypes in the population. The haplotype blocks have discrete boundaries defined by recombination hotspots (Wall et al., 2003) and Phillips et al., 2003) [51, 74]. *SNPpattern* implements a haplotype-block model as an empirical approach to best describe the linkage disequilibrium (LD) patterns. From a *SNPpattern* programming perspective, a haplotype block within a population is inferred from a region on the chromosome where there is a low SNP allele pattern count for a particular block size, separated by a region with a large SNP allele pattern count. It is proposed that the block with a large count relative to other counts along the chromosome is a region where more historical recombination events have occurred.

Whist the importance of pairwise measures of LD is acknowledged it may not always be the most appropriate measure of how strong LD is across an entire region that contains many SNPs. In particular, identifying precise haplotype-block boundaries may be difficult when using r^2. The r^2 measure produces for each pair of SNPs an LD strength estimate fundamentally based on probability. There is no practical evidence to explain a difference in the values of r^2 between other paired SNPs in adjacent and further away regions. Pairwise measures of LD differ from SNP to SNP and defining haplotype blocks is especially open to interpretation when r^2 values range between 0 and 1. There exists an uncertainty as to how one LD estimate in one region relates to an LD estimate in another region because SNP pairs are not necessarily independent (i.e. one region may functionally affect another region) and consequently this diminishes the certainty of which SNPs belong to which haplotype block. For example, there are cases where 2 SNPs exhibit strong pairwise LD but show different r^2 to a SNP in between, and a low strength pairwise *LD* is not necessarily indicative of high ancestral recombination. In other words, SNPs in close proximity are not always in pairwise LD and by contrast, SNPs far apart can be in pairwise LD (Phillips et al., 2003). We can also expect the haplotype block boundaries to be different depending on the sample size and SNP density used. Another limitation of r^2, particularly for marker-assisted selection in livestock, is that the r^2 can be the same between a SNP marker and a potential causal variant in different populations, and yet the phase may be different (Roos et al., 2008). Deriving clear information about the joint inheritance of alleles in a chromosome segment is also expected not to be easy from r^2 measures. It is argued instead that we can infer the joint inheritance of alleles from inferring which haplotype blocks were inherited, if we know which haplotype blocks exist in a particular population i.e. we can make inference about identity by descent (IBD) of alleles in particular regions. In light of some of these shortcomings discussed, a multiple SNP allele block approach in preference to r^2 was implemented through *SNPpattern*.

The required input data for *SNPpattern* is phased genotype data from either a single group or multiple groups of individuals (e.g. from different animal breeds or subpopulations). The premise for the multiple SNP allele block approach is to count the frequency of SNP allele blocks, of different sizes, found in the genomes of the group members. For example, a block of 5 SNPs spanning a few thousand base pairs could potentially comprise 32 different SNP allele patterns if the SNPs were totally independent and the population was of infinite size (the number of possible SNP allele patterns is 2^n where n is the number of SNPs in the block). The general process of the program is that it counts the frequency of the various SNP allele patterns found in the same chromosomal location (the same SNP allele block region) across each individual in the group sample; then repeats the process for the next SNP allele block region along the genome, and so on. From the counts we can infer the haplotype blocks after taking into account the population structure and allelic frequencies (a user of *SNPpattern* also needs to be aware that there are numerous other population genetic factors that affect LD and determine haplotypes). The inferred haplotype block represents a region with a few distinct SNP allele patterns (indicating small amount of haplotype variation) in a population separated by a region with many SNP allele patterns (indicating an excessive amount of haplotype variation) in the population. In a typical short chromosome segment, we can expect only a few distinct SNP allele patterns. Hence the larger the SNP allele block size the less likely the distinct SNP allele patterns appear by chance because of the increased probability of recombination over larger distances. It is argued that the comparison of SNP allele pattern counts can be used as a measure of genetic distance and this comparison forms the basis for a haplotype diversity analysis within and between groups.

In addition to implementing the core components for the multiple SNP allele block approach, *SNPpattern* also implements similarity scoring between individuals. We can expect that the more the SNP allele patterns between two individuals are similar the more likely they will have a similar haplotype structure. Taking this one step further, if two individuals share the same extended SNP allele patterns over the same genomic region, the chance that they carry the same causal variant allele relationship by descent is much higher.

Linkage disequilibrium mapping to identify the chromosomal region (the haplotype block) containing a QTL has proven to be a powerful tool Barrett et al., (2005) and Hayes et al., (2006). However, once the haplotype block has been identified, LD provides no further information to help localize the actual variants within the block (Rioux, 2001). It has been proposed that advantageous mutations through directional selection are more likely to occur in a region of low recombination (Wall et al., 2003). Conversely, there is evidence that there are alleles in recombination hotspots that are more likely to initiate the double-strand break associated with recombination (Jeffreys & Neumann, 2002). One of the outputs from *SNPpattern* is a list of chromosomal start and end locations of SNP allele blocks identified to have low and/or high haplotype diversity. In the program testing section of this chapter, how this output list could be used to link these identified regions to genomic annotation is demonstrated. We used the *FunctSNP* R package that we have developed earlier (Goodswen et al., 2010) .To recover the biology role of genomic regions with low haplotype diversity, a systems genetics or system biology approaches would be needed, as demonstrated in Kadarmideen et al., (2006) and Kadarmideen (2008).

3. Implementation of *SNPpattern*

SNPpattern was written in the Perl programming language. The following sections describe the methods and rationale that have shaped the development. We have tested *SNP pattern* on Ovine 60k SNPchip data and these results are based on our earlier work (Goodswen et al., 2010).

3.1 Input data

The default PHASE and fastPHASE output format has been adopted as the format required for the initial input data to *SNPpattern*. Figure 2 shows the format and is described here as it governs how the data are processed and is an aid to understanding the methods to be described later.

The genotype data for each individual is represented by 3 rows. On the first row is a unique identification of the individual. The second and third rows are the genotypes of the individual. For each consecutive locus, one allele is entered on the second row, and one on the third. *SNPpattern* expects that genotypes are phased such that the entire second row is inherited from one parent and the third row from the other parent. It is also expected that the alleles appear in the sequential order that they occur on the chromosome.

```
                    BEGIN GENOTYPES
                         # id 1
         1 2 1 2 2 2 1 2 1 2 1 2 1 2 2 2 1 1 2 1
         1 1 2 2 1 2 1 2 2 2 1 2 1 1 2 2 1 2 1 2
                         # id 2
         2 2 1 1 2 1 2 2 2 1 2 1 2 1 2 1 2 1 2 2
         1 2 1 2 2 2 1 2 1 2 1 2 1 2 2 2 1 1 2 1
                         # id 3
         2 2 1 1 1 2 2 1 2 1 2 2 2 1 2 1 2 1 2 2
         1 2 2 1 1 2 2 1 2 1 2 2 2 1 1 1 2 2 2 1
                     END GENOTYPES
```

Fig. 2. Data input format for SNPpattern.

3.2 Grouping data

In its simplest form, *SNPpattern* will accept an input, such as the one shown in Figure 2, and treat all individuals as members of the same group. The output will consequently be results for haplotype diversity within a group. The results will also be for the entire genome without any reference to the chromosomal location of the haplotypes. In spite of this, it is expected (although not mandatory) that an additional file be provided as input, which contains phenotypic information about the individual. Table 2 shows as an example the first 9 lines of a fictitious phenotype file and in this instance one specific to livestock species.

Grouping data is obviously an essential part of the evaluation of haplotype diversity *between* groups. It is also a hugely critical part to account for the count biases that may be introduced due to population structure. For example, if in a particular sire breed group the number of progeny from each sire is disproportionate then the SNP allele pattern count will be biased in favour of the progeny with the largest number of siblings. Grouping an equal number of progeny from each sire should prevent the bias. *SNPpattern* includes the functionality to group the genotype data of individuals according to user-defined criteria specific to information held in columns in a phenotypic file. Theoretically the program can create a group based on any combination of columns when using the "AND" Boolean logic. For example, group all individuals according to sire breed AND year of birth. Separate output files for each group criteria are generated containing the genotype data of the group members. The output format is the same as that shown in Figure 2. The program also allows the user to use comparison operators (=, >=, <=, >, <) on any combination of column criteria. For example, if we want to group all the female progeny in area 03 born after the year 1972 having a particular parent ID, the equivalent pseudo code is sex = F AND Area = 03 AND Year of Birth > 1975 AND parent ID = 433. The grouping of the data is of course at the discretion of the researcher to create genetically meaningful groups. Summary information about the groups can also be generated. *SNPpattern* provides the flexibility of the grouping through a configuration file in an INI file format.

Another optional file that can be provided as input is a SNP mapping file. Such a file allows the contents of a group file to be divided further into separate chromosome files. This division of the genotypes for the entire genome into their respective chromosome locations allows for the comparison of haplotype diversity of a particular chromosome in one group with the same chromosome number in another group. The fact that selective sweeps act differently in different chromosomes is one example as to why a study of haplotype diversity may be needed on a chromosome basis (Montpetit & Chagnon, 2006). It is mandatory that the SNP mapping file contains the SNP location and the chromosome number on which it resides. *SNPpattern* expects the SNPs in the file to be in the order that they are located on the chromosome. It is also an expectation that the SNP mapping file is most likely obtained from another source and will contain redundant information to *SNPpattern*. Therefore another configuration file, specific to dividing the genome into chromosomes, allows extraction of only the required SNP location and the chromosome number without the need for the researcher to modify the SNP mapping file. It may be arguable as to why a separate file is created for each group and/or each chromosome sub-group. From a programming perspective separate files are created for 3 reasons: 1) the output file format used is the same as PHASE and fastPHASE. It is envisaged that the *SNPpattern* group files could be imported into other programs that use this same format; 2) the separate files are a permanent record of the grouping that can be reused, as opposed to temporary grouping only at runtime; and 3) the data files can be extremely large and slower to parse the content if all groups are recorded separately but in the one file.

Human ID	Parent ID	Region	Sex	Parent ethnicity	Year of birth	Body Weight (kg)
1	330	01	F	American	1978	74.6
2	330	01	M	American	1971	99.0
3	405	02	F	African	1970	77.4
4	405	02	M	African	1975	63.6
5	433	03	M	Asian	1972	79.0
6	433	03	M	Asian	1971	67.0
7	433	04	F	Asian	1979	73.0
8	405	05	F	European	1974	97.4
9	405	05	M	European	1976	94.0

Table 2. Example contents of a phenotypic file.

3.3 Multiple SNP allele block approach

This section describes the multiple SNP allele block approach implemented through *SNPpattern*. We have tested *SNP pattern* on Ovine 60k SNPchip data and tables 3-6 are based on our already published work (Goodswen et al., 2010). With reference to Figure 2 the 2 rows of biallelic SNPs contained within the phased genotype file are extracted (in this instance, a single 1 or 2 constitutes a SNP allele). One row represents the SNP alleles inherited from one parent, and the second row represents the SNP alleles inherited from the other parent. So in effect, we have a representation of paternal and maternal chromosomes composed of a long serial SNP allele pattern of 1s and 2s. Without prior knowledge, the user will not know which row represents which parental chromosome. However, when the SNP allele pattern analysis progresses the identity of the row representation may become apparent as will be demonstrated in the program testing section.

The underlying unit of the multiple SNP allele block approach is of course the SNP allele block. The serial SNP allele pattern from *one* row (e.g. representing the chromosome inherited from the paternal side) is divided into block sizes of any specified number of SNP alleles at the discretion of the researcher e.g. 3, 5, 10 or 100 (or larger) SNP alleles per block. Then if required, the SNP allele pattern from the other row is divided into blocks of the same specified size. Figure 3 shows the first 40 numbers of a SNP allele pattern of 1s and 2s that represents either a paternal or maternal chromosome for one individual. In this example, the entire SNP allele pattern is divided into blocks of 3 e.g. the first 3 blocks are "112", "212", and "211". For a n SNP allele block there are 2^n possible SNP allele pattern combinations of 1 and 2. Therefore, a 3 SNP allele block has 2^3 possible patterns (111, 112, 121, 122, 211, 212, 221, and 222).

For each SNP allele block along the row that represents either the paternal or maternal chromosome, we count how many individuals in the group have the same SNP allele pattern. For example, at block location 1 (Figure 3) we count, for each of the 8 possible SNP allele combinations, how many individuals have the SNP allele pattern "111", then "112" etc. Table 3 shows an example of the SNP allele pattern count at the first 3-SNP allele block along a paternal chromosome. We could expect an equal chance of observing any one of the 8 possible SNP allele combinations (assuming the SNP allele frequencies were equal) if there was no underlying association between the 3 SNPs in the block. In reality however, we have a SNP allele pattern count profile which is a result of many generations of random and non-random SNP inheritance from a common ancestor. A challenge is to determine which of the 8 possible SNP allele combinations exist because the 3 SNPs were inherited by descent from a common ancestor and which SNP allele combinations exist by chance alone. For long SNP

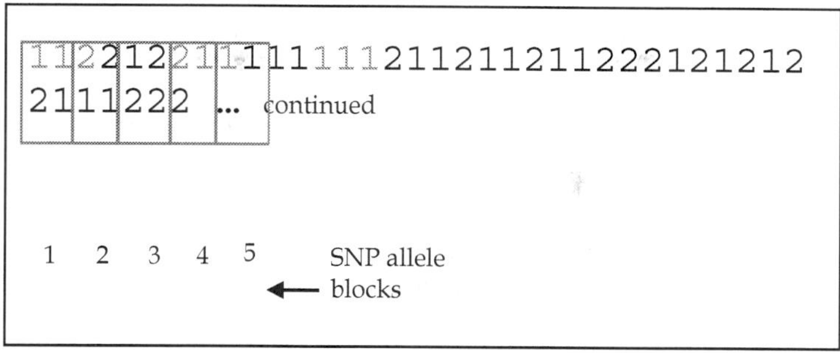

Fig. 3. Consecutive 3-SNP allele blocks along 1 row representing either a paternal or maternal chromosome.

allele patterns (e.g. 10 or more SNP alleles per block)[3] that can be inferred to be a haplotype block, identity is more likely by descent. For short SNP allele patterns (e.g. 3 SNP alleles per block) inferred to be a haplotype block, it is more likely identical by chance. Nevertheless, we can statistically test whether the observed count distribution has arisen from independently segregating SNPs. On the other hand, it *is* debatable whether the test will achieve the desired results. If SNPs are very close then we would expect SNPs not to segregate independently, and the observed counts arise more from genetic drift (i.e. some SNP allele patterns are more frequent due to limited population size and the large effect of the contribution of only some ancestors to the current population). Despite the latter concern, in an attempt to meet this challenge, expected and observed counts are still tested for statistical significance. To determine the expected SNP allele pattern count, *SNPpattern* computes the SNP allele frequencies (Table 3). For example, the expected proportion for SNP allele pattern "111" based on the allelic frequencies of each of the 3 SNPs and assuming independence is 0.072 (Pr(SNP 1 allele 1) * Pr(SNP 2 allele 1) * Pr(SNP 3 allele 1)). The expected count for SNP allele pattern "111" is therefore 72 (proportion expected * number of individuals).

Based on the allele frequencies, the null hypothesis is that we expect the observed and expected count to be the same, and as a consequence the SNPs to be independent (i.e. SNPs are segregating independently). A Fisher's Exact Test[4] for count data is applied as a statistical significance test for each SNP allele pattern. Table 5 shows an example of how the data for SNP allele pattern "111" from Table 4 is used in a 2 * 2 contingency table to compute the exact probability of observing a table with this result (Equation 4). The p-values are obtained directly using the hypergeometric distribution. The p-values (examples shown in Table 3) are used as the conditional criteria to determine which SNP allele patterns were most likely to have occurred by chance. In this example, the low p-value for pattern "111" indicates that the hypothesis is unlikely to be true and therefore the SNPs within the pattern are not independent. The success as to whether the challenge was met of distinguishing SNPs in a haplotype block from SNPs in a random pattern is reviewed in the discussion section.

From a *SNPpattern* implementation perspective, some difficulty was encountered in programming Fisher's Exact Test. A Perl module (Text::NSP::Measures::2D::Fisher2) downloaded from CPAN[5] is currently being investigated for its suitability. As an interim

---

[3] Dependent on the chromosomal distance between SNPs

[4] Used in preference to Chi-Square test since expected counts may be less than 5

[5] The Comprehensive Perl Archive Network

SNP allele pattern	Observed SNP allele pattern count	Expected SNP allele pattern count	Proportion Observed	Proportion expected	p-value[ss]
111	14	72	0.014	0.072	6.07e-11
112	32	27	0.032	0.027	0.598
121	699	652	0.697	0.650	0.097
122	241	242	0.240	0.241	1.000
211	0	1	0	0.001	-
212	0	0	0	0.000	-
221	17	7	0.017	0.007	0.062
222	0	2	0	0.002	-
Total	1003[++]	1003[++]	1.000	1.000	

[++] Number of individuals in group

[ss] p-values are obtained directly using the hypergeometric distribution following a Fisher's Exact Test

Table 3. Example of SNP allele pattern counts at the first 3-SNP allele block along a paternal chromosome based on Goodswen et al., (2010)

measure, the statistical programming language R (http://www.r-project.org/) was used. *SNPpattern* can output a file containing a list of the observed SNP allele pattern counts per block in the first column and the expected SNP allele pattern counts per block (computed from the individual SNP allele frequencies) in the second column. The output file can be read directly into R and used as input to the function fisher.test () to conduct the Fisher's Exact Test for count data.

	SNP 1			SNP 2			SNP 3		
	Count			Count			Count		
Allele	Row 2[++]	Row 3	Freq.[ss]	Row 2	Row 3	Freq.	Row 2	Row 3	Freq.
1	986	993	0.99	46	161	0.10	730	733	0.73
2	17	10	0.01	957	842	0.90	273	270	0.27
Total	1003	1003	1.00	1003	1003	1.00	1003	1003	1.00

[++] Row 2 and Row 3 are the rows that represent the genotype data for each individual (refer Figure 4-1). For genotype at SNP #1, 986 out of a total of 1003 individuals have a '1' on row 2, and 17 out of 1003 have a '2' a row 2

[ss] Freq. = Allelic Frequency. For example, the population frequency of '1' at the SNP 1 location is (986 + 993) /2006 = 0.99. Likewise the population frequency of '2' at the SNP 1 location is (17 + 10)/ 2006 = 0.01

Table 4. Example of allele frequencies for 3 sequential SNPs.

	Observed	Expected	Row totals
Pattern found	14[a]	72[b]	86[a+b]
Pattern not found	989[c]	931[d]	1920[c+d]
Column totals	1003[a+c]	1003[b+d]	2006[n]

Table 5. A 2 * 2 contingency table for SNP allele pattern "111".

$$\Pr(a,b,c,d) = \frac{(a+b)!(c+d)!(a+c)!(b+d)!}{n!a!b!c!d!}$$

Equation 4. Fisher's formula for exact probability of observing the data in a contingency table.

Table 4 shows the SNP allele pattern count for the first 6 consecutive blocks for a 10-SNP allele block size for a paternal chromosome. From the counts we can infer haplotype blocks. As per the *SNPpattern* premise for a haplotype block previously described in the introduction, it is a region with a low SNP allele pattern count separated by a region with a large SNP allele pattern count. In other words, it is expected that if a block has a large SNP allele pattern count relative to the counts within other blocks along the chromosome, it is likely to be a recombination hotspot. For each paternal or maternal chromosome, *SNPpattern* computes descriptive statistics such as the average number and standard deviation of patterns found per block. A user definable count threshold can be applied to filter large SNP allele patterns counts to infer the haplotype blocks. By default *SNPpattern* flags SNP allele patterns with counts greater than 1 standard deviation above average. Of course, the relevant count threshold to use and the interpretation of inferred haplotype blocks requires thorough knowledge of group population structure. It is therefore critically important that judicious grouping of genotypes takes place prior to the SNP allele pattern counts (refer previous section – Grouping data). Another point to note is that the chromosomal distance between SNPs is not equal and therefore the physical size of the each block of SNPs is not equal. Although *SNPpattern* computes and reports the physical block sizes, it does not adjust the SNP allele pattern counts to compensate for unequal sizes.

	SNP ALLELE BLOCKS					
	1	2	3	4	5	6
Pattern count	70	69	115	76	57	20
H/L flag [++]	L	L	H	L	L	L
Physical block size	619948	520686	437805	394152	398511	538789

[++] H indicates block with SNP allele pattern count greater than user defined threshold; L indicates block with SNP allele pattern count less than threshold

Table 6. SNP allele pattern counts per 10-SNP allele block along paternal chromosome.

In summary, for this section on the multiple SNP allele block approach, using SNP allele pattern frequency counts as a measure, we can make comparisons between individuals, groups of individuals, and groups. These comparisons then allow us to make informed decisions about the general haplotype diversity. It is also expected that processing the same genotype data several times using different block sizes, we can fine-tune the distribution of the haplotype blocks. Finding similarity between individuals.

The method presented in this section was inspired from publications [80-83] on genetic distance and similarity matrices. Two genetically identical individuals (i.e. identical DNA sequences throughout the genome) will have identical haplotype structures. It therefore could be argued that the more genetically similar two individuals are to each other, the more likely they will have the same haplotype structure. In other words, the closer two individuals are related the more the DNA sequences are expected to be in common. The genotyped SNPs are of course not as accurate a unit of comparison as genome wide nucleotide sequences. However, it is not unreasonable to assume that comparing the SNP allele patterns between two individuals will provide a guideline as to the similarity of haplotype structure. So, although this method does not show the actual haplotype structure, the overall similarity in SNP allele patterns between individuals or groups of individuals will give an indication of similarity in haplotype structure. As a simple example we take 3

```
ID:          Individual SNP allele pattern
A            1 1 2 1 2

ID:          SNP allele patterns to compare:
             Score
B            1 1 1 2 1          2
C            2 1 1 1 2          3
D            1 1 2 1 2          5

ID:          Individual SNP allele pattern
B            1 1 1 2 1

ID:          SNP allele patterns to compare:
             Score
A            1 1 2 1 2          2
C            2 1 1 1 2          2
D            1 1 2 1 2          2

etc
```

Fig. 4. Method for scoring SNPs. It shows scoring of paternal chromosome (row 1) for only 2 out of 4 individuals.

ethnic groups (EG) called A, B and C. We then compare the SNP allele patterns for the full length of the genome for each animal within each EG. From the comparisons we then determine that EG A and B share the most similar SNP allele patterns. Therefore it is proposed that there is a greater chance that EG A and EG B carry the same causal variant allele relationship by descent than EGs A and C, or B and C. The comparisons are based on similarity matrices whereby a score is incremented by 1 when a SNP allele of an individual matches that in another individual (Figure 4). Each individual is processed in turn. In the example only the paternal chromosome (row 1 in this case) is scored. The user can choose to score either row 1 or row 2, or row 1 *and* row 2 of the phased genotypes contained in the group input file(s).

ID	A	B	C	D	Total
A	5	2	3	5	16
B	2	5	2	2	11
C	3	2	5	3	14
D	5	2	3	5	15

Table 7. Example similarity matrix. Shows a simple matrix constructed from made-up data in Figure 4. Here we can see that individuals from ethnic groups A and D share the most similarity; and individuals from ethnic groups A and B, and individuals from ethnic groups B and C share the least similarity. An individuals' overall similarity to all other individuals in the group can be ranked according to its total similarity score. In this example, individuals in A is considered the most similar and individuals in B the least. In practice the similarity matrix is constructed from thousands of SNP allele pattern comparisons for hundreds of individuals.

3.4 Linking SNP allele block regions to genomic annotation

One of the output files from a *SNPpattern* Perl script is a file that contains all SNP allele blocks where the number of distinct SNP allele patterns is low or high. The script allows for a user-definable upper or lower pattern frequency threshold. For example, if a user enters a threshold of "<3" then only SNP allele blocks with a distinct SNP allele pattern frequency of less than 3 will be output. Likewise, if the user enters ">99" only SNP allele blocks with a distinct SNP allele pattern frequency of greater than 99 will be output. Figure 4-4 shows an example of the output file. The output consists of a list with 4 columns: Chromosome number of the chromosome containing the SNP allele block (the genomic region of interest); start and end genomic location of SNP allele block; the number of distinct SNP allele patterns found within the SNP allele block for a group of individuals (only lists the genomic regions where the number of patterns is below or above a user-defined threshold), and the average number of patterns per block. The intended use of the output file is to act as a starting point for a researcher to find biological meaning in regions identified to have low or high haplotype diversity. Biological meaning may help in the understanding of why in some regions and not others there is a conservation of the same alleles from generation to generation. In other words, why is there only 1 or 2 distinct SNP allele patterns existing in the same genomic region for all individuals in a group? Conversely, some regions have a large number of different SNP allele patterns implying a hotspot region for recombination. Finding the underlying biology within the hotspot region may provide clues to the mechanism of recombination. The expectation is that the output list can be used for further downstream analysis such as searching for annotation of the chromosome region within which the SNP allele block is located.

```
# Input file used: sire_31_match_10.txt
# Pattern Size: 10
# Haplotype row: paternal
# Chromosome No: Start of pattern: End of pattern: No. of Patterns:
Average No. per block
4        3000848        3170609        2        6.58
13       67400889       67687804       2        4.09
```

Fig. 5. Example output file showing genomic regions with low SNP allele pattern counts.

As an example, we could find the genes within the genomic region. In the FunctSNP R package (5) there is a function called "getGenesByRange" which returns the Gene ID for all genes located between a user-specified start and end location.

3.5 Implementation summary

In summary, three sets of Perl scripts comprise *SNPpattern*: 1) grouping data scripts – to create separate data files for further downstream comparison analysis; 2) SNP allele block scripts – to find, count, and compare the SNP allele block patterns between any group of individuals; and 3) similarity scripts - to score the similarity between individuals based on an individual's entire SNP allele pattern. Table 8 encapsulates the primary function and rationale of each script.

Perl Script Name (.pl)	Primary function	Rationale
Scripts for grouping and summarising genotype data		
Group	Genotype data is separated into files according to a grouping criterion. For example, the genotype of animals can be grouped according to their sire breed, or flock ID, or birth years.	Main purpose of dividing the data into groups is to account for population structure, facilitate the SNP-block pattern counting within a group and the comparison of the SNP-block pattern count between groups.
divide	Divide the bi-allelic SNPs in any group input file (e.g. flock, breed, and sire groups) into separate chromosome files.	Used as the main input for the SNP allele pattern analysis scripts and in particular for the multiple SNP allele block approach
Scripts for finding, counting, and comparing SNP allele block patterns		
derive_pattern	Derive all SNP allele patterns of a specified block size (e.g. 3, 100, 1000, 2000 etc.) that exist in the maternal and/or paternal chromosomes for *any* group file (e.g. either flock, breed, or sire)	Compiles all the unique SNP allele patterns found in a group into 1 file. Used as input to subsequent scripts to find and count the frequency of these unique patterns.
match	Find and count the number of matching SNP allele patterns found within a specified block size along a paternal and/or maternal chromosome for every individual in a specified group.	An essential requirement for the multiple SNP allele block approach
order_match	Similar to "match.pl" except the output is in a different format. Also creates a group consensus file containing a concatenation of the most common SNP allele pattern found at each block. In effect it creates a paternal or maternal chromosome comprising the most common SNP allele patterns in a group.	Enables a researcher to view and compare, one block at a time, the SNP allele patterns found within each block. The group consensus chromosome can be compared to the chromosomes of individuals within the group and the difference can be used as measure of dissimilarity between individuals.
score	Output the most frequent SNP allele block pattern found at each block location along the chromosome and provide additional information such as the percentage of animals with the pattern, and chromosomal start and end location of the block.	The most frequent SNP allele block pattern is deemed to be the most likely to be a haplotype. The statistics provided may enable the researcher to decide if the SNP allele pattern is a true haplotype or one occurring by chance.
Scripts used to find similarity between animals based on SNP allele patterns		
Sim	For each animal in turn, list all other animals in the same group in order of SNP allele pattern similarity. The entire chromosome is compared and individuals are scored as to how many SNP markers are the same.	Similarity matrices for individuals within flocks, breeds, or sires can be computed
Rank	Similar to "sim.pl" except rank the animals' similarity to all other animals in the group based on the summation of the scores from the similarity matrices.	Scores can be used as a measure of genetic similarity between individuals or groups. It is expected that similar individuals will have similar LD patterns.

Perl Script Name (.pl)	Primary function	Rationale
	Miscellaneous scripts	
SNP_map	Count the number of SNPs per chromosome and determine the distance between each genotyped SNP.	Knowledge of the distribution and distance between the genotyped SNPs is important for interpreting haplotype block boundaries.
pattern	Generate a file listing all the possible combinations of 1s and 2s given a pattern size	Created as a general pattern generator tool.

Table 8. The suite of Perl scripts collectively called SNPpattern.

4. Discussion

The *SNPpattern* program is a first version and is still in its development phase and the program testing was a first attempt to analyse the haplotype structure within and across populations. Nonetheless, *SNPpattern* in its current form will easily generate, with little user required effort, output files that provide a researcher with information about LD and IBD which can be used in population diversity and association studies. *SNPpattern* still has some shortcomings that need to be addressed in future releases. Accounting for the population structure of a group is currently at the discretion of the user by grouping genotypes appropriately. During the grouping of genotypes *SNPpattern* allows specified animal IDs to be excluded from the group e.g. if in a particular breed group the number of progeny from each sire is disproportionate, animal IDs can be excluded to balance the proportions. It is anticipated that knowing which animals to exclude may be difficult and the exclusions may inadvertently introduce biases. Therefore a weighted SNP allele pattern count in accordance to animal proportions may be a possible solution. Pritchard et al. propose a model-based clustering method for using genotype data to infer population structure Pritchard et al., (2000). With this method it might be possible to assign individuals to appropriate groups automatically. Another important omission that needs to be addressed is to take into account, when interpreting haplotype block locations, the varying physical distance between the SNPs within the blocks. Some SNPs are closer together in some regions and further apart in others. Also, a sliding block window would improve accuracy and needs to be implemented. For example, if we have a 3-SNP allele block the program currently uses a window of SNPs from 1 to 3, 4 to 6, 7 to 9 etc. A sliding window would encompass SNPs from 1 to 3, 2 to 4, 3 to 5 etc.

During the development of *SNPpattern* several statistical methods (in addition to Fisher's Exact Test for Count Data) were used in an attempt to determine which SNP allele pattern has occurred because there is a correlation between the SNP alleles (possible members of a haplotype block) and which SNP allele pattern occurred by chance. Despite taking allele frequencies into account, no statistical test was found to reliably prove that SNPs were inherited by descent. For example, let us suppose we have 3 SNP alleles in relative close proximity to each other on a particular chromosome in a distant ancestor. Many generations of progeny later, we have exactly the same 3 SNP alleles (the same haplotype block) in some of the progeny. The challenge is to prove that these 3 SNP alleles where inherited from the distant ancestor. The expectation is that these 3 SNP alleles have remained together on the haplotype block because they reside in a genomic region which is involved in important biological processes. That is, positive selection has ensured the survivable of the haplotype block. Consequently it is expected that in a population of descendents from the distant ancestor, the frequency of the haplotype block housing the 3 SNP alleles will be high within the population. The increased frequency of the 3 SNP alleles might be explained by the process of selective sweeps (Montpetit & Chagnon, 2006, Chevin & Hospital, 2008). A strong selective sweep can result in only 1 or 2 haplotypes existing in the same region of the genome for a population (Chevin & Hospital, 2008). Therefore, although further evidence is required, it is argued that in some instances SNP allele patterns, which are overrepresented in the population, indicate non-random SNP inheritance and could be considered a part of a haplotype block. For example, there are cases where in a particular genomic region there is only 1 out of 8 possible SNP allele patterns present in the population (i.e. 100% of individuals have the same pattern). Many of the results from the Fisher's Exact Test dispute this argument. For example, in regions on the genome where nearly all individuals have the same SNP allele pattern block and SNP allele frequencies on the block are high, Fisher's p-values indicate that the SNPs are independent.

Like all programs, the worth and accuracy of the output data from *SNPpattern* is totally dependent on the data input. For example in the program testing on sheep breeds (Goodswen et al. 2009), the frequency of SNP allele block patterns were counted and the similarity between animals scored based on only 5,494 SNPs, which were genotyped for chromosome #1. In other words, the interpretation of the LD patterns for chromosome #1 was based on the state of 5,494 nucleotides. Chromosome #1 in fact is comprised of over 299,636,549 nucleotides and, as in the case for sheep; there is an unknown number of SNPs. It is expected that as the number of SNPs increase and the distance between the SNPs decrease the more the *SNPpattern* outputs will be informative. Also it is important to know what selection criterion was used for selecting the SNPs to be genotyped before interpreting the results obtained from *SNPpattern*. For example, were the SNPs selected for even distribution across the genome and/or were the SNPs selected as tags owing to prior knowledge of the LD structure. If the purpose of using *SNPpattern* is to define haplotype blocks then it is expected that the results may be distorted if the genotyped SNPs are tag SNPs.

This chapter solely focused on SNP haplotypes in the context of LD or selective sweeps due to directional selection (natural or artificial) acting on the genetic variants affecting complex traits measured / observed on the individuals. However, the consequences of this would have been at the underlying biological level, namely the SNP haplotype diversity affecting gene expression levels or protein abundance in cells and tissues of relevance to the complex trait. This emphasises that future genetic studies on global gene expression patterns (Kadarmideen et al., 2006 and Kadarmideen 2008) should be targeted at effects of LD / expression-related SNP haplotype patterns. In fact, such studies could contribute to prediction of transcription factor binding sites, using combined SNP and gene expression datasets (Vonrohr et al., 2007). Further, identification of unique co-expression gene networks and functional gene modules distinguishing different phenotypic extremes or case/controls (e.g. Kadarmideen et al., 2011) could be speculated as being result of formation of distinct SNP haplotypes after selective sweeps.

It is expected that in the very near future SNPs will, for the most part, be superseded by entire DNA sequences due to the advent of low cost next generation sequencing (Hayden, 2009). With little modification, *SNPpattern* will handle DNA sequences in much the same way as it currently does for SNP allele sequences (although the computer performance/capability is an unknown entity). It is envisaged that varying block sizes of

DNA sequences will be compared and counted between individuals to determine the structure and distribution of LD. Also, comparing entire DNA sequences between individuals is perfect for determining genetic similarity.

Although the motivation for developing *SNPpattern* was to find patterns of LD, it is suggested that common SNP allele patterns could be used in association studies (Botstein & Risch, 2007). Common SNP allele patterns is only an interim suggestion, as it is expected that using common DNA sequences in association studies will prove to generate the most reliable results in the future.

5. Conclusions

We described the development of *SNPpattern*, which is the collective name for a suite of Perl scripts essentially designed to group, count, and compare SNP allele patterns of various block sizes. Differences in SNP allele block frequency are used as a measure of haplotype diversity within and between groups. A SNP allele pattern represents SNPs inherited from one parent and is a product from phased genotype data. The SNP allele pattern from a programming point of view is simply a line of either 2 characters (0 or 1, 1 or 2, A or B) representing 2 different states. The main factor that drove the development of *SNPpattern* was the premise that studying SNP allele patterns can reveal useful information to help understand the genetics of individuals within groups and across groups. The use of *SNPpattern* has been illustrated on sheep breeds (Goodswen et al., 2009) but it is indeed generic software meant for all species. *SNPpattern* allows researchers, given any phased genotype data in a PHASE or fastPHASE format, to analyse SNP allele patterns within any user-defined SNP allele block size. These SNP allele patterns can be compared between user-defined groups. The primary objective of the tool is to provide a researcher with useful information on SNP allele block patterns and as a major example of its usage, the information can be used to quantify haplotype diversity within and between groups. While there are similar bioinformatics tools that have a primary focus on haplotype inference and/or analysis tools (such as Haploview, HapBlock, HaploBlock, and GERBIL) we have found no tool that provides a smooth interface between a PHASE or fastPHASE output and haplotype diversity/analysis.

Two main approaches for studying the SNP allele patterns have been implemented within *SNPpattern*: a multiple SNP allele block and a pattern similarity scoring approach. For both approaches, *SNPpattern* generates various descriptive statistics of the SNP allele patterns in plaintext output files. It is not the author's intention to stipulate how a researcher should interpret or use the information. Nevertheless, in this chapter suggestions were made as to how *SNPpattern* might be used by a researcher. In particular, *SNPpattern* was proposed as a generic tool for finding the patterns of LD using a multiple SNP allele block model. We have demonstrated in another published paper how *SNPpattern* can be used to examine the patterns and extent of LD within and between 4 Australian sheep breeds (Goodswen et al., 2009). The results show that *SNPpattern* could be used to effectively evaluate overall haplotype diversity within and between groups of individuals.

In closing, *SNPpattern* is a simple pre-screening tool to rapidly screen genome for haplotype structure and provide insights on highly conserved biologically important haplotypes. SNPpattern is implemented in Perl and supported on Linux and MS Windows. We have tested *SNP pattern* on Ovine 60k SNPchip data (Goodswen et al., 2010). All scripts are freely available from: http://web4ftp.it.csiro.au/ftp4goo17a/SNPpattern/SNPpattern.zip.

SNPpattern will be made available to the public via http://systemsgenetics.dk/pages/resources.php in the future.

6. Acknowledgements

We would like to sincerely thank Julius van der Werf and Cedric Gondro for the inspiration behind this paper and help with providing sheep SNP data for program testing.

7. References

Ardlie, KG., Kruglyak, L., & Seielstad, M. (2002). Patterns of linkage disequilibrium in the human genome. *Nature Reviews Genetics*, 3(4): 299-309.

Barrett, JC., Fry, B., Maller, J., & Daly, M.J. (2005). Haploview: analysis and visualization of LD and haplotype maps. *Bioinformatics*, 21(2):263-265.

Botstein, D. & Risch, N. (2003). Discovering genotypes underlying human phenotypes: past successes for mendelian disease, future approaches for complex disease. *Nat Genet*, 33:228-237.

Burton, PR., Clayton, D.G., Cardon, L.R., Craddock, N., Deloukas, P., Duncanson, A., Kwiatkowski, D.P., McCarthy, M.I., Ouwehand, W.H., Samani, N.J. et al. (2007). Genome-wide association study of 14,000 cases of seven common diseases and 3,000 shared controls. *Nature*, 447(7145):661-678.

Carlson, C.S., Eberle, M.A., Rieder, M.J., Yi, Q., Kruglyak, L. & Nickerson, D.A. (2004). Selecting a maximally informative set of single-nucleotide polymorphisms for association analyses using linkage disequilibrium. *Am J Hum Genet*, 74(1):106-120.

Chevin, L.M. & Hospital, F. (2008): Selective Sweep at a Quantitative Trait Locus in the Presence of Background Genetic Variation. *Genetics*, 180(3):1645-1660.

Collins, F.S., Patrinos, A., Jordan, E., Chakravarti, A., Gesteland, R., Walters, L., Fearon, E., Hartwelt, L., Langley, C.H., Mathies, R.A. et al. (1998): New goals for the US Human Genome Project: 1998-2003. *Science*, 282(5389):682-689.

Dempster, AP., Laird, NM. & Rubin, DB. (1977). Maximum likelihood from incomplete data via EM algorithm. *Journal of the Royal Statistical Society Series B-Methodological*, 39(1):1-38.

Fu, YX. & Li, W.H. (1999). Coalescing into the 21st century: An overview and prospects of coalescent theory. *Theor Popul Biol*, 56(1):1-10.

Gabriel, SB., Schaffner, SF., Nguyen, H., Moore, JM., Roy, J., Blumenstiel, B., Higgins, J., DeFelice, M., Lochner, A., Faggart, M. et al. (2002). The structure of haplotype blocks in the human genome. *Science*, 296(5576):2225-2229.

Gibbs, RA., Belmont, JW., Hardenbol, P., Willis, TD., Yu, FL., Yang, HM., Chang, LY., Huang, W., Liu, B., Shen, Y. et al. (2003). The International HapMap Project. *Nature*, 426(6968):789-796.

Goodswen, SJ., Gondro, C., Watson-Haigh, NS. & Kadarmideen, HN. (2010). FunctSNP: an R package to link SNPs to functional knowledge and dbAutoMaker: a suite of Perl scripts to build SNP databases. *BMC Bioinformatics*, 11.

Goodswen, SJ. Gondro, C. Kadarmideen, HN., & van der Werf, JHJ. (2010). Evaluating haplotype diversity within and between Australian sheep breeds. *Proceedings of the 9th World Congress on Genetics Applied to Livestock Production* (WCGALP), Leipzig, Germany.

Greenspan, G. & Geiger, D. (2004). High density linkage disequilibrium mapping using models of haplotype block variation. *Bioinformatics*, 20(suppl 1):i137-i144.

Hayden, EC. (2009). Genome sequencing: the third generation. *Nature*, 457(7231):768-769.

Hayes, BJ., Gjuvsland, A. & Omholt, S. (2006). Power of QTL mapping experiments in commercial Atlantic salmon populations, exploiting linkage and linkage disequilibrium and effect of limited recombination in males. *Heredity*, 97(1):19-26.

Hirschhorn, JN., Lohmueller, K., Byrne, E. & Hirschhorn, K. (2002). A comprehensive review of genetic association studies. *Genet Med*, 4(2):45-61.

Hudson, RR. & Kaplan, NL. (1985). Statistical properties of the number of recombination events in the history of a sample of DNA-sequences. *Genetics*, 111(1):147-164.

Jeffreys, AJ.& Neumann, R. (2002). Reciprocal crossover asymmetry and meiotic drive in a human recombination hot spot. *Nat Genet*, 31(3):267-271.

Kadarmideen, HN., Von Rohr, P. & Janss, LLG. (2006). From Genetical-Genomics to Systems Genetics: Potential applications in quantitative genomics and Animal Breeding. *Mammalian Genome* 17: 548-564.

Kadarmideen, HN. & Janss, LLG. (2007). Population and Systems genetics of cortisol in pigs divergently selected for stress. *Physiological Genomics* 29: 57-65

Kadarmideen, HN. & Reverter, A. (2007). Combined genetic, genomic and transcriptomic methods in the analysis of animal traits. CAB *Reviews: Perspectives in Agriculture, Veterinary Science, Nutrition and Natural Resources*, 2(042):16.

Kadarmideen, HN. (2008). Genetical systems biology in Livestock – Application to GnRH and Reproduction. *IET Systems Biology* 2: 423-441

Kadarmideen, HN., Watson-Haigh, NS. & Andronicos, NM. (2011). Systems biology of ovine intestinal parasite resistance: disease gene modules and biomarkers. *Molecular BioSystems* 7, 235–246

Kim, SH. (2001). An evaluation of a Markov chain monte carlo method for the Rasch model. *Applied Psychological Measurement*, 25(2):163-176.

Kimmel, G. & Shamir, R. (2005). GERBIL: Genotype resolution and block identification using likelihood. *Proc Natl Acad Sci USA*, 102(1):158-162.

Kruglyak, L. (2008). The road to genome-wide association studies. *Nat Rev Genet*, 9(4):314-318.

Larranaga, P., Calvo, B., Santana, R., Bielza, C., Galdiano, J., Inza, I., Lozano, J.A., Armananzas, R., Santafe, G., Perez, A. et al: Machine learning in bioinformatics. *Briefings in Bioinformatics* 2006, 7(1):86-112.

Li, M., Chen, X., Li, X., Ma, B. & Vi. P. (2003). The similarity metric. In: *Proceedings of the fourteenth annual ACM-SIAM symposium on Discrete algorithms*. Baltimore, Maryland: Society for Industrial and Applied Mathematics;: 863-872.

Libiger, O., Nievergelt, CM. & Schork, NJ (2009). Comparison of Genetic Distance Measures Using Human SNP Genotype Data. *Hum Biol*, 81(4):389-406.

Mackay, TFC., Stone, EA. & Ayroles, JF. (2009). The genetics of quantitative traits: challenges and prospects. *Nature Reviews Genetics*, 10(8):565-577.

McKay, SD., Schnabel, RD., Murdoch, BM., Matukumalli, LK., Aerts, J., Coppieters, W., Crews, D., Dias, E., Gill, CA., Gao, C. et al. (2007). Whole genome linkage disequilibrium maps in cattle. *BMC Genet*, 8.

Montpetit, A. & Chagnon, F. (2006). The Haplotype Map of the human genome: a revolution in the genetics of complex diseases. *M S-Medecine Sciences*, 22:1061-1067.

Nei, M. & Roychoudhury, AK. (1974). Sampling variances of heterozygosity and genetic distance. *Genetics*, 76(2):379-390.

Pearson, TA. &Manolio, TA. (2008). How to interpret a genome-wide association study. *JAMA*, 299(11):1335-1344.

Phillips, MS., Lawrence, R., Sachidanandam, R., Morris, AP., Balding, DJ., Donaldson, MA., Studebaker, JF., Ankener, WM., Alfisi, SV., Kuo, FS. et al. (2003). Chromosome-wide distribution of haplotype blocks and the role of recombination hot spots. *Nat Genet*, 33(3):382-387.

Pritchard, JK. & Przeworski, M. (2001). Linkage disequilibrium in humans: Models and data. *Am J Hum Genet*, 69(1):1-14.

Pritchard, JK., Stephens, M. & Donnelly, P. (2000). Inference of population structure using multilocus genotype data. *Genetics*, 155(2):945-959.

Rioux, JD., Daly, MJ., Silverberg, MS., Lindblad, K., Steinhart, H., Cohen, Z., Delmonte, T., Kocher, K., Miller, K., Guschwan, S. et al. (2001). Genetic variation in the 5q31 cytokine gene cluster confers susceptibility to Crohn disease. *Nat Genet*, 29(2):223-228.

Roos, APW., Hayes, BJ., Spelman, RJ. & Goddard, ME. (2008). Linkage disequilibrium and persistence of phase in Holstein-Friesian, Jersey and Angus cattle. *Genetics*, 179(3):1503-1512.

Scheet, P. & Stephens, M. (2006). A fast and flexible statistical model for large-scale population genotype data: Applications to inferring missing genotypes and haplotypic phase. *Am J Hum Genet*, 78(4):629-644.

Smith, JM. & Haigh, J. (1974). Hitch-hiking effect of a favorable gene. Genet Res 1, 23(1):23-35.

Stephens, M. & Scheet, P. (2005). Accounting for decay of linkage disequilibrium in haplotype inference and missing-data imputation. *Am J Hum Genet*, 76(3):449-462.

Stephens, M., Smith, NJ. & Donnelly, P. (2001). A new statistical method for haplotype reconstruction from population data. *Am J Hum Genet*, 68(4):978-989.

Von Rohr, P., Friberg, M. & Kadarmideen, HN. (2007). Prediction of Transcription Factor Binding Sites using Results from Genetical Genomics Investigations. *J.Bioinform. Comp. Biol.*, 5: 773-793.

Wall, JD. & Pritchard, JK (2003). Haplotype blocks and linkage disequilibrium in the human genome. *Nature Reviews Genetics*, 4(8):587-597.

Wang, N., Akey, JM., Zhang, K., Chakraborty, R. & Jin L (2002). Distribution of recombination crossovers and the origin of haplotype blocks: The interplay of population history, recombination, and mutation. *Am J Hum Genet*, 71(5):1227-1234.

Witherspoon, DJ., Wooding, S., Rogers, AR., Marchani, EE., Watkins, WS., Batzer, MA. & Jorde, LB. (2007). Genetic Similarities Within and Between Human Populations. *Genetics*, 176(1):351-359.

Zhang, K., Qin, ZH., Chen, T., Liu, JS., Waterman, MS. & Sun, FZ. (2005). HapBlock: haplotype block partitioning and tag SNP selection software using a set of dynamic programming algorithms. *Bioinformatics*, 21(1):131-134.

21

Algorithms for CpG Islands Search: New Advantages and Old Problems

Yulia A. Medvedeva

*Vavilov Institute of General Genetics, Russian Academy of Sciences,
Research Institute for Genetics and Selection of Industrial Microorganisms,
Russia*

1. Introduction

CpG islands (CGIs) are regions having high GC and CpG content while generally mammalian genomes are CpG-depleted. CGIs are often located in the promoter region of the genes, mostly housekeeping but also tissue-specific. It is widely believed that CpG dinucleotides within promoters CGIs are unmethylated and are targets for specific regulatory protein binding. As a result, CGIs contain special sequence motifs for highly affinitive protein binding (transcription factor binding sites, TFBS). Methylation of cytosine in CpG context within such motifs could decrease the affinity of TF binding, increase the attraction of methyl-binding proteins, affect the histones modification and, therefore, leads to repression of genes transcription. The mechanism of local and global transcription repression via CpG methylation is used in many different normal (development, differentiation, aging, X-chromosome inactivation, imprinting) and pathological processes (cancer and other diseases). However recently it has been reported that a class of normally methylated but active promoters do exist.

Lately evidences of biological relevance of methylated CGIs or CGIs located far from gene promoters appear. Such CGIs could act as regulator for pervasive transcription, which seems to be actual genome feature rather than a side-effect of high-throughput techniques errors. Replication origins are also reported to be associated with CGIs of any location.

As a consequence of specific nucleotide content, CGIs could affect DNA or RNA secondary structures. For example, $G_{2-3}C_{2-3}$ motif common within CGIs induces significant local curiosity of DNA. Another motif, G-rich sequence (GRS) in 3′ and 5′ region of RNA, is known to form specific structures, G-quadruplexes, on both end of RNA playing important role in its stability. This motif corresponds to C-rich sequence in DNA, is likely to appear in CGIs.

Classical algorithms for CpG islands search use sliding window (SWM) or running sum (RSM) and several distinct but not independent criteria (GC content, Obs/Exp$_{CpG}$ and length). The thresholds for the criteria are rather arbitrary, unconcerned between species, and demonstrate lack of biological interpretation. SWM algorithms are rather slow, RSM algorithms are faster but tend to split large CGIs into several smaller ones and to omit CGIs with nonuniform distribution of CpG dinucleotides along the sequence. Recently, several different algorithms based on CpG dinucleotides clustering were implemented. Those algorithms have smaller number of parameters and reasonable mathematical basics. The comparison of the algorithms is tricky. Hypermutability of CpG dinucleotides lead to loss of

CGI conservation between species so comparative genomics cannot be applied for estimation of the algorithms effectiveness.

To validate the results of CGI prediction authors use different biological and mathematical properties. One of the most popular quality measures is the fraction of CGIs located near promoters of protein coding genes and avoided overlap with Alu-repeats. This measure couldn't be appropriate at least for two reasons. First, promoters of protein-coding genes are likely to be a small fraction of all promoters as it became clear recently. Second, two classes of promoters (CGI-dependent and CGI-independent) exist and their ratio is unclear. Avoiding of repetitive sequences is more or less reachable for many algorithms, but now authors prefer to remove Alu- repeats and other repetitive DNA sequences in advance.

Prediction of the methylation profile in different tissues in norm and in cancer is another idea for validation. Algorithms of CGI search *per se* fail to predict correctly the distribution of methylated cytosine in the genome. To distinguish between methylated and non-methylated CGI machine-leaning techniques (MLT) are used. Those studies include additional sequence features (di- and trinucleotide distribution, CpG and TpG frequencies, TFBS, repetitive elements and others). Machine-leaning techniques are also applicable for collecting promoter CGIs. The point that GC content and CpG frequency or density of CpG clusters is not enough to describe special types of CGIs, is highly relevant. The main problem of MLT approaches is that resulting model usually has a lot of parameters, sometimes without clear biological meaning. Consistency of the models, build up by different authors in the similar conditions is rather low, so those feastures could hardly be used for CGI validation quality in general case.

A verification problem caused by lack of universal biological properties of CGIs results in an absence of widely accepted definition. It should be mentioned that all algorithms trying to predict CGIs with one particular function (promoter or unethylated CGIs) demonstrate a high false-positive rate, probably due to the complex network of CGIs functions. It's becoming clear that many different functional elements exist within one CGI. Moreover, both methylated and unmethylated, both promoter and non-promoter CGIs seem to be functional. So, one can conclude that contemporary algorithms for CGIs search based only on GC and CpG content or on CpG clustering determine a chimeric class of objects.

2. Algorithms for CpG islands search

Nowadays, most popular algorithms for CpG islands search are still based on criteria established more than twenty years ago (Gardiner-Garden & Frommer, 1987). The DNA segment is considered to be a CpG island if it is not shorter than 200 bp, has GC content no less than 0.5 and the ratio Obs/Exp_{CpG} (1) no less than 0.6.

$$Obs/Exp_{CpG} = N_{CpG}*N/(N_C*N_G), \tag{1}$$

where N_C, N_G and N_{CpG} are numbers of C, G and CpG in the region of length N respectively. Implementations of the basic idea vary in details, mostly in methods for search of the segments having properties mentioned above.

2.1 Sliding window methods

There are several algorithms for CGIs search using sliding window methods (SWM): CpGplot (Rice et al., 2000), CpG Island Searcher (Takai & Jones, 2002), CpG Island Explorer (Wang & Leung, 2004) and CpGProD (Ponger & Mouchiroud, 2002).

CpGplot represent the simplest variant of SWM. GC content and Obs/Exp_{CpG} ratio are calculated over a window of length 100 bp moving along the sequence with 10 bp steps.

CpG Island Searcher (usually referred to as Takai-Jones algorithm) uses a window of 200 bp moving along the sequence with 200 bp steps. It has an additional threshold for minimal CpG dinucleotides in predicted CGI, equal to mathematical expectation of CpG dinucleotides in Bernoulli sequence of given length and nucleotides probabilities, multiplied by Obs/Exp_{CpG} threshold. This feature lets authors exclude "mathematical CGIs" like 300 bp sequence with 150 cytosines and one guanine in CpG context which fits standard CGI criteria. This algorithm also merges two or more CGIs if they are spaced by less than 100 bp. Takai and Jones also suggest using more strict thresholds of 500 bp for CGI length, 0.55 for GC content and 0.65 for Obs/Exp_{CpG} to find out CGIs associated with promoters of known protein-coding genes and to avoid CGIs associated with Alu-repeats.

CpG Island Explorer is a modification of CpG Island Searcher from Takai and Jones. A sliding window of CpG Island Explorer moves more slowly with a step of 10 bp. After merging of close CGIs the resulting CGI is tested ones again to fit the criteria and if it does not, one bp from each side is cutting until final CGI fits the criteria. Takai and Jones believe that CGIs predicted by CpGIE are larger in length. Closely located CGIs are merged more reasonably by CpGIE than by CpGIS.

CpGProD is a program dedicated to the prediction of promoters associated with CpG islands in mammalian genomic sequence. In every sequence found by sliding window and fitted the criteria of CGI the probability to find promoter is estimated as

$$p = \exp(Z) / (1 + \exp(Z)),\tag{2}$$

where Z is linear combination of CGI length, GC content and Obs/Exp_{CpG}. Also the probability of a strand to be a template for transcription is estimated as in (2), where Z is linear combination of AT- and GC-skews which are known properties of the nucleotide sequence around the TSS. Coefficients for Z are estimated from two generalized linear regressions trained with two datasets composed of CGIs obtaining and not obtaining TSS for protein-coding genes or two datasets with different transcription templates in human.

2.2 Running sum methods

Running sum methods (RSM) were developed as an alternative to SWM. RSM try to find segments of DNA having CpG dinucleotides more frequently comparing to the neighboring genomic sequence. RSM work faster comparing to SWM. Initially RSM did not use CGI criteria established in (Gardiner-Garden & Frommer, 1987). Most known methods from this group are CpGreport (newCpGseek) (Rice et al., 2000) and unpublished algorithm of Mikhlem and Hillier which is used in UCSC Genome Browser (http://genome.ucsc.edu) and therefore became *de facto* a standard for CGI search.

CpGreport (or newCpGseek) scores each position in the sequence using a running sum calculated from all positions in the sequence, starting with the first and ending in the last. If there is not a CpG dinucleotide at a position, the score is decremented, if there is one, the score is incremented by a constant value. If the score is higher than a threshold then a putative CGI is declared. Sequence regions scoring above the threshold are searched for recursively. It should be noticed that final CGI from predicted by this algorithm starts and ends with CpG dinucleotide and doesn't necessary reach the initial CGI criteria (Gardiner-Garden & Frommer, 1987). Authors found a lot of rather short CGI with high GC content and CpG frequency and considered such CGI as overprediction (Rice et al., 2000).

UCSC CGI (Algorithm of Mikhlem and Hillier) is based on the RSM but include additional check for CGI to fit the traditional criteria (Gardiner-Garden & Frommer, 1987). Total number of CGIs obtained by UCSC is less than those obtained by CpGplot, as not every frame is tested for fitting the criteria, but only those having score higher than a threshold on the first step. CGIs predicted by the algorithm of Mikhlem and Hillier are often shorter from both ends comparing to those predicted by CpGplot and also starts and ends with CpG dinucleotides.

2.3 CpG clustering methods

Next logical step of CpG searchers development is to implement actual CGI clustering methods (CGCM). There are several such algorithms available: CpGcluster (Hackenberg et al., 2006), CpG clusters (Glass et al., 2007), and CGI HW, an algorithm, developed by H. Wu (Irizarry et al., 2009; H. Wu et al., 2010). These algorithms are based on segmentation of the genome into regions with different frequency of CpG dinucleotides (CGI HW also uses segmentation based on GC content). Unlike methods described above this approach to CGI prediction is data-driven and allows finding CGIs in spices with different average GC-content and CpG frequency.

CpGcluster has two separate steps: a CpG cluster search and an estimation of the probability to find such a cluster by chance. Distance between neighboring CpG dinucleotides in random sequence is simulated by geometric law with CpG frequency as a parameter. Hackenberg and colleagues (Hackenberg et al., 2006) assume that within functional CpG cluster the distance between neighboring CpGs is smaller than expected in random sequence. Authors show that distances smaller than a median of the theoretical distribution is overrepresented in human genome. The median distance between neighboring CpG (23-53 bp depending of the chromosome) is used as a threshold, so each cluster consists of CpGs located no farther than the threshold. All resulting CGIs start and end with a CpG dinucleotide. Each cluster has a p-value calculated based on negative binomial distribution. Only clusters with p-value less than 1.0e-5 (1.0e-20 in (Hackenberg et al., 2010a)) are considered as CpG islands. Authors find about 200000 CpG islands in human genome (25000 CpG islands using the p-value threshold equal to 1.0e-20). A lot of such CpG islands are shorter than 200 bp. Yet, authors show functionality of some short CGIs and call them CpG islets (Hackenberg et al., 2010a).

CG clusters annotation also has two steps. The location of every CpG dinucleotide is extracted from genomic DNA sequences. Using these positions, every overlapping sequence fragment containing a fixed number of CpGs and having variable length is identified. For each number of CpGs, the frequency of each fragment length is recorded. The threshold for each maximum fragment length is defined as a local minimum in the fragment length histogram, estimated by identifying zero values of the first derivative of a cubic spline fit. Mapping the CpG-dense fragments back to the genomic sequence produces an annotation track there each annotated locus is a conglomeration of one or more overlapping fragments of variable length. As the basis for choosing the optimal track the number of overlapping fragments at a locus normalized by the maximum fragment length is used. A track with maximal fragments overlap per locus is selected based on genomic averages of this metric for different numbers of CpGs per fragment. This approach allows authors to choose the species-specific optimal number of CpGs per fragment for the final annotation.

CGI_HW (Algorithm of H. Wu) assumes that each chromosome is divided into 3 states: Alu repetitive elements, baseline, and CGI. Alu-repetitive elements are removed in advance. Hence, authors characterize the problem as that of a semi-HMM, with a known state for Alu repetitive elements, so they consider the 2-state chain conditional on being in a non-Alu state. Authors use the number of C, G, and CpG in segment of length L as parameters for the model. Hidden state Y(s) for segment is 1 for CGI and 0 for baseline. Authors assume that Y(s) is a stationary first-order Markov chain. The choice of the state is based on two HMM. One is for GC content to be high or low with assumption of the binomial distribution approximated with the normal density for baseline. The second one is for CpG number with assumption of Poisson distribution for baseline. The length L=16 for the segment was chosen based on the association of CGI with epigenetic marks. The approach summarizes the evidence for CGI status as probability scores. This provides flexibility in the definition of a CGI and facilitates CGI search in different species.

3. Validation problem

Having several methods for CGI prediction one is still unable to select the best one. The main reason is the lack of validation criteria. Su and colleagues (Su et al., 2009) propose cumulative mutual information of CpG dinucleotides as a measure of CGI's quality and show that it's a powerful criterion to avoid CGIs associated with Alu-repeats. Despite the power of this mathematical criterion, most of the authors try using biological features for CGIs validation.

3.1 Sources for biologically relevant validation: DNA methylation and protein binding
Very first work mentioned CG-rich islands (Bird, 1986) considers them as DNA regions where cytosine is unmethylated. Cytosine methylation usually appear in CpG context and increase the probability of its deamination about 10-times (Ehrlich & Wang, 1981), leading to enrichment of TpG and depletion of CpG dinucleotides in DNA. Absence (or decreased level) of cytosine methylation within CGI is usually considered as an origin of CGIs in mammalian genomes (Cross et al., 1994; Eckhardt et al., 2006). Modern research shows that methylated cytosines within CpNpG are also targets for spontaneous deamination (Cooper et al., 2010).
No doubts, that cytosine methylation plays important role in CGI functioning. During early development waves of methylation-demethylation generate tissue-specific genomic methylation profiles. These profiles are stable in somatic cells generations due to replication dependent maintenance methylation system (Brero et al., 2006). About 70-80% of cytosines in CpG context are methylated in differentiated cells (Baylin et al., 1998), recent study shows that cytosine is also methylated within CpHpN context (where H = C, A or T) especially in embryonic stem cells (Baylin et al., 1998). Cytosine methylation influence DNA structure by facilitating Z-from conformation (Behe & Felsenfeld, 1981), it also affect protein binding to DNA, so most transcription factors (TF) usually bind unmethylated DNA.
There is a class of proteins (e.g. MeCP1/2, MBD1-6, SRA, and Kaiso) binding exclusively methylated DNA (Saito & Ishikawa, 2002). MeCP1 protein complex binds methylated cytosine using MBD2 protein (Berger & Bird, 2005) and also includes chromatin remodeling complex NuRD/Mi2. MeCP2 is the key and well-studied member of methyl-binding domain (MBD) protein group (Fatemi & Wade, 2006). Besides methyl-binding domain it contains transcription repression domain (TRD) (Dhasarathy & Wade, 2008) and is involved into DNA methylation establishment with DNMT1 (Kimura & Shiota, 2003). There are evidences that both MeCP2 and MBD1/2 binds not just ^{5m}CpG but more complicated DNA motifs, MeCP2 binds ^{5m}CpG with adjacent $(A/T)_{4+}$, which is not true for MBD1/2 proteins (Klose et al., 2005). MeCP2 binds DNA with higher affinity than MeCP1 complex leading to more stable repression of transcription. For MeCP2 binding single ^{5m}CpG dinucleotide is enough whereas MeCP1 complex needs dense clusters of ^{5m}CpGs (Ng et al., 1999).

Another well-known group of methyl-binding proteins consists of Kaiso and ZBTB4/33. They obtain zinc-finger domain and bind DNA in sequence-specific manner. Data on Kaiso binding site are controversial. Van Roy and McCrea (van Roy & McCrea, 2005) believe that Kaiso binds 5mCG5mCG. Sasai and colleagues (Sasai et al., 2010) assume that 5mCG5mCG motif is a place where two Kaiso molecules bind, one on every strand. The motif also has to be in specific sequence environment. It's also known that Kaiso binds TNGCAGGA motif having non-methylated cytosine, but with 1000-times lower affinity (Daniel et al., 2002). There are some evidences that Kaiso is a global repressor of methylated genes and is essential for early embryonic development. ZBTB4 protein binds CYGCCATC motif as well as M5mCGCYAT (Sasai et al., 2010). It also has been shown that proteins of this group demonstrate affinity to half-methylated DNA (Sasai et al., 2010).

Some other proteins also bind methylated DNA. CpG methylation of the CRE-motif (TGACGTCA) enhances the DNA binding of the C/EBPα (Rishi et al., 2010). UHRF1 and UHRF2 (SET- and Ring finger-associated proteins, SRA) bind hemimethylated CpG and the tail of histone H3 in a highly methylation sensitive manner and help assemble histones and DNA into a nucleosome after replication (Hashimoto et al., 2009).

3.2 Sources for biologically relevant validation: DNA methylation and gene expression

Nowadays there are two main hypotheses explaining DNA methylation origin during evolution. Some authors believe that methylation system arose to inactivate viruses and transposons (Walsh et al., 1998). Despite some evidences in favor of this hypothesis, most of the authors nowadays suppose that main function of DNA methylation is a control of gene expression during development and cell differentiation, most likely by influence on affinity of different protein binding.

Promoter regions of many genes are unmethylated and demonstrate resistance to increasing concentration of methylating agents (Bestor et al., 1992). Yet if promoter region become methylated this usually leads to stable in cell generations and irreversible gene suppression (Razin & Riggs, 1980; Schubeler et al., 2001). However some genes demonstrate rather high expression independently to methylation level of their promoters (Shen et al., 2007) and some promoters need to have methylated cytosine to be activated (Rishi et al., 2010).

Cytosine methylation affects transcription both directly by changing the affinity of TF binding to DNA and indirectly by forming inactive chromatin domains. Both 5mC and T change DNA conformation in core positions of TFBS. For transcription repression in some cases it's enough to have one cytosine methylated, in other cases the level of expression is correlated negatively with methylation level, but is independent on the exact position of cytosine to be methylated. Inhibition of transcription caused by partial DNA methylation can be overpassed by enhancers (Hug et al., 1996), however fully methylated promoters can't be reactivated that way (Schubeler et al., 2001).

The possibility of active demethylation is still under discussion (S. C. Wu & Zhang, 2010). Cytidine deaminase AID could play a role in this process in mammals (Fritz & Papavasiliou, 2010). Recently it has been shown that elongation complex also can participate in demethylation (Okada et al., 2010). Even DNA methyl-transferases DNMT3a/b could force cytosine deamination leading to reparation of T-G mismatch pair into correct C-G pair with GC-biased reparation system (S. C. Wu & Zhang, 2010). Overexpression of MBD3 could also play a role in demethylation (S. E. Brown et al., 2008). Yet active demethylation after implantation of the embryo is very rare occasion (S. C. Wu & Zhang, 2010).

Different tissues and cell types demonstrate specific cytosine methylation patterns (Ushijima et al., 2003), those patterns in the same tissue of different individuals are similar (Lister et al., 2009), but not identical (Bock et al., 2008). Now a lot of regions with tissues-specific methylation profiles (tDMRs) are known (Rakyan et al., 2008; Brunner et al., 2009; Straussman et al., 2009; Xin et al., 2010). DMRs are likely to be involved in gene imprinting (Lopes et al., 2003). Differential activity of imprinted alleles of the gene is dependent on methylation of promoters, enhanserses or silencers of those genes (Li et al., 1993).

Females have one of the X chromosomes inactivated in somatic cells (Gartler & Riggs, 1983). The process of inactivation starts at early embryo stage with Xist activation (S. D. Brown, 1991), which leads to chromatin modification and methylation of promoters of most (Deobagkar & Chandra, 2003) but not all (Zeschnigk et al., 2009) genes. Methylation and gene repression profile of inactivated X chromosome is stable in cell generations.

Defect of normal methylation profile is a distinctive feature for different pathology conditions (Ratt syndrome, psychopathologies (Egger et al., 2004), autoimmune diseases (Richardson, 2007), hypertension (Frey, 2005)). Despite many evidences on epigenetic changes in pathologies, cancer is the most known disease having abnormalities in epigenetics, especially in DNA methylation (Jones & Baylin, 2002; Laird, 2003; Herrera et al., 2008). Tumor cells demonstrate a lot of modifications in epigenetics status: general demethylation of the genome, influencing chromatin structure, increased DNA methyl-transferase activity, and hypermethylation of promoter regions of many genes resulting in their repression. High probability of ^{5m}C to mutate into T brings about a lot of cancer-specific mutations. It's importation to notice, that pathological profiles of methylation often depend on environmental conditions and are inherited (Liu et al., 2008).

3.3 Sources for biologically relevant validation: CpG islands as promoter regions

The RNA polymerase II core promoter contains DNA motifs directing transcriptional machinery to the transcription start site (TSS). Nowadays four DNA motifs are known to be a part of core promoter: the TATA box, the TFIIB recognition element (BRE), the initiator (Inr), and the downstream promoter element (DPE) (Kutach & Kadonaga, 2000). The TATA box is an A/T-rich sequence, located about 20-30 nucleotides upstream of the TSS, that binds TFIID complex (Burley & Roeder, 1996). The BRE having the consensus SSRCGCC, is located immediately upstream of the TATA element in some promoters and increases the affinity of TFIIB binding (Lagrange et al., 1998). The Inr was originally a motif encompassing the TSS that is sufficient to direct accurate initiation in the absence of a TATA element (Smale, 1997). Inr elements are, however, present in both TATA-containing and TATA-less promoters and play a role in TFIID binding (Chalkley & Verrijzer, 1999). In mammalian promoters, the Inr consensus sequence is $RRA_{+1}NWRR$, where A_{+1} is the TSS (Bucher, 1990). The DPE acts cooperatively with the Inr helping TFIID binding and accuracy of transcription initiation in TATA-less promoters (Burley & Roeder, 1996). The DPE is located about 30 nucleotides downstream of the TSS and contains a common GWCG sequence motif.

Saxonov and colleagues (Saxonov et al., 2006) demonstrate that human genes have two different promoter types: AT-rich and GC-rich (associated with CGIs). They are easily distinguishable not only in AT- or GC content, but also in different motifs overrepresented in each promoter type. One can see that most of core promoter elements are GC-rich and could be a part of a CGI-associated promoter. CGIs are often located in 5' regions of genes, mostly overlapping with TSS (Gardiner-Garden & Frommer, 1987; Davuluri et al., 2001;

Ponger et al., 2001), and participate in regulation of transcription initiation (Rozenberg et al., 2008). Housekeeping genes tend to have CGI promoter more frequently comparing to tissue-specific genes (Zhu et al., 2008). However promoters of tissue-specific genes related to development and embryogenesis are usually located in proximity to CGIs (Robinson et al., 2004).

Many authors believe that CGIs exist since CpG dinucleotides inside them are protected from methylation. The mechanism of such protection is assumed to be protein binding at CGIs boundaries as it has been shown for Sp1 in the promoter of mouse *aprt* gene (Macleod et al., 1994). Later role of Sp1 in CGI boundaries formation has been shown for other genes (Tomatsu et al., 2002). Sp1 is often associated with CGIs as one of the key features (Macleod et al., 1994; Rozenberg et al., 2008). In one of the first works on CGI (Gardiner-Garden & Frommer, 1987) it has been shown that CGIs obtain many G/C-boxes (GGGCGG), which act as a core for Sp1 TFBS (Briggs et al., 1986). Sp1 binds both methylated and unmethylated DNA (Holler et al., 1988). Fan and colleagues (Fan et al., 2007) assume that all proteins with zinc-finger domain can play a role in CpG boundaries formation. Some other proteins, like VEZF1 (Dickson et al., 2010) and CTCF (Filippova et al., 2005; Recillas-Targa et al., 2006), also participate in this process. Naumann (Naumann et al., 2009) shows that loss of such a boundary (in fragile X-chromosome syndrome) leads to spread of methylation and gene inactivation. Moreover CGIs obtaining CTCF binding sites can themselves play a role of insulators forming boundaries of chromatin domains (Filippova et al., 2005).

Other DNA binding proteins with GC-rich binding sites can also decrease the level of DNA methylation (Lin et al., 2000; Recillas-Targa et al., 2006). It's most likely that unmethylated CpG islands form open chromatin structures simplifying the transcription (Choi, 2010). Binding sites for Cfp1 (Thomson et al., 2011), E2F (Weinmann et al., 2002), ETS, NRF-1, BoxA, CRE, E-Box (Rozenberg et al., 2008), p53 (Zemojtel et al., 2009) was found within CGIs.

Besides TFBS other DNA motifs are associated with CGI promoters. GC-skew, a feature of all unidirectional promoters, is stronger for genes starting within CGIs than for genes lacking this property (Polak et al., 2010). Tandem or simple repeats are also found within CGIs (Hutter et al., 2006). Sequence motifs $G_{2-3}C_{2-3}$, typical for CGI, induce local DNA curiosity and form G-qudruplexes at 5′ and 3′ ends of RNA molecule. G-quadruplexes in DNA restrict methylation of CpG dinucleotides genome-wide (Halder et al., 2010).

3.4 Sources for biologically relevant validation: CpG islands located far from promoter regions

At least 25% of CpG islands are located far from gene promoters (Ponger et al., 2001). Although a lot of such CGIs overlap with repeats, (Graff et al., 1997; Ponger et al., 2001), other CGIs don't (Ponger et al., 2001; Hackenberg et al., 2006). They are often located near 3′ gene region (Gardiner-Garden & Frommer, 1987) or within the gene (Hackenberg et al., 2006). Such 3′and intragenic CGIs are subject for natural selection not only on the protein level, but also on the level of nucleic acids, which confirms their functional significance (Medvedeva et al., 2010).

Many of CGIs located far from promoters of protein-coding genes perform important biological functions. For instance, a CGI within intron 10 of *KCNQ1* acting as a promoter of antisense RNA transcript is involved into imprinting regulation of the locus (Smilinich et al., 1999). Imprinting of *MAP3K12* gene is caused by differential methylation of a CGI located in its last exon (Takada et al., 2000). Many CGI around the 3′ ends of genes affect its expression in normal tissues (Appanah, Dickerson et al. 2007) and in cancer (Shiraishi et al., 2002).

Intergenic methylation plays an important role in regulation of alternative promoters (Maunakea, Nagarajan et al. 2010), modify chromatin structure (Lorincz, Dickerson et al. 2004) and influence the elongation efficiency (Jacquier, 2009).

Resenly several works show that CGIs located far from known genes in intragenic regions correspond to previously undetected promoters (Carninci et al., 2005; Medvedeva et al., 2010) playing a role during development (Illingworth et al., 2011).

CTCF insulator protein forming a boundary of chromatin active regions (Bell & Felsenfeld, 2000) often binds CCCTC core motif common within CGIs.

CpG islands and mobile elements. There are a lot of repetitive sequences in human genomes having high GC content, so many algorithms find CGI overlapping with repeats (Alu-repeat in human (Graff et al., 1997) and B1-repeat in mouse (Yates et al., 1999)). Cytosines within CGIs associated with Alu-repeats in normal cells are methylated, which in turn represses the expansion of the repeat (Xing et al., 2004). Loss of methylation in Alu-repeats is typical for tumor cells (Xie et al., 2010). Recently absence of methylation in Alu-repeats was shown for germ line (Brohede & Rand, 2006). Ullu and Tschudi (Ullu & Tschudi, 1984) believe that Alu-repeats are possessed pseudogenes of 7SL-RNA, and several Alu families still contain inner promoter of RNA polymerase III (Britten et al., 1988). One can expect that CGIs in Alu-repeats should have different DNA motifs comparing to CGIs in promoters of protein-coding genes transcribed by PolII. Nevertheless, recent studies show that pervasive PolII transcription is also a common feature for pseudogenes and transposons (Frith et al., 2006).

Alu-repeats are source of spreading DNA methylation, so unmethylated CGIs contain TFBS for Sp1 and other proteins to protect themselves from methylation (Caiafa & Zampieri, 2005). Recent studies show that Alu-repeats proximal to CpG islands could themselves form a boundary protecting CpG islands from methylation (Feltus et al., 2003).

Taking into consideration all facts mentioned above, it's obviously too early to exclude Alu- and similar repeats out of attention speaking on CGIs functionality. Most of the authors (Takai & Jones, 2002; H. Wu et al., 2010) try to build an algorithm for CGI search that avoid CGIs around Alu-repeats. There are some differences in GC content, Obs/Exp$_{CpG}$ (Takai & Jones, 2002) or in cumulative mutual information of CpG dinucleotides (Su et al., 2009) between CGIs found near Alu-repeats and around promoters of protein-coding genes. Yet most algorithms excluded *ab initio* all repetitive sequences and therefore all of the CGIs located within them, removing more than a half of CGIs in doing so. The question remains why the same sequences in repetitive elements are of no use while in unique segments are essential.

CpG islands and replication origins. Sequence properties of replication origins in mammals are not studied very well. There are some evidences that CpG islands near 3' region of the gene (Phi-van & Stratling, 1999) or in other genome regions can play a role of replication origins (Rein et al., 1997; Rein et al., 1999), it's important to know that some CpG should be methylated in those regions for success of replication (Rein et al., 1999).

3.5 Approches for validation

Taking into consideration biological properties mentioned above, DNA methylation is a logically relevant feature for CGI prediction validation. Complicated system of interactions involving CGIs makes it obvious that considering CGI as merely unmethylated region is an oversimplification. As far as DNA methylation plays important role in cell differentiation, the same DNA region can be unmethylated in early stage of development and methylated in later stages (reprogrammed DMR, rDMR), or unmethylated in one tissue and methylated in another one (tissue-specific DMR, tDMR), or unmethylated in one allele and methylated in another (allele-specific DMR, aDMR) as in case of imprinting or dosage compensation, or demonstrate cross-individual differences in methylation (individual DMR, iDMR). More appropriate way is to associate CGI with DMRs demonstrating absense (or decreased level) of cytosine methylation only in one or few conditions.

Nevertheless even methylated CGIs play a role in transcription regulation, some of them contains TSS of protein-coding (Shen et al., 2007) or non-coding genes (Medvedeva et al., 2010). Recently a mechanism of transcription activation by binding of the C/EBPα transcription factor to the methylated CRE motif (TGACGTCA) was demonstated (Rishi et al., 2010). Thus, the absence of methylation shouldn't be the only criterion for CGIs verification.

Resently a lot of works dedicated to prediction of DNA methylation status in different normal tissues ((Bock et al., 2008; Zhao & Han, 2009) and refs in them) and cancer (Feltus et al., 2006) appeared. Various machine leaning techniques (support-vector machine (Bhasin et al., 2005; Das et al., 2006), alternative decision trees (Carson et al., 2008), discriminant analysis (Feltus et al., 2003)) were used to distinguish between methylated and unmethylated regions. Authors use GC content, different di- and tri nucleotides (Das et al., 2006; Fang et al., 2006), Alu-repeat location (Das et al., 2006; Fang et al., 2006), TpG fraction, TFBS, repeats, predicted DNA structures (Bock et al., 2006) and other DNA patterns and properties (Bhasin et al., 2005; Bock et al., 2007; Oakes et al., 2007; Carson et al., 2008; Ehrich et al., 2008) as parameters for those studies. Results obtained by different authors are incomparable, as in every case the model is built on distinct set of tissues and usually not in a genome-wide manner. Features demonstrating high selectivity in one work don't do the same in other works. The consistency of features is low, so one can conclude that those models are overlearned.

Promoter proximity is another traditional key feature for CGI validation. The most popular criterion is a fraction of predicted CGIs located near promoter regions of protein coding genes. As a negative set Alu-repeats are usually used. SWM with higher thresholds for length, GC content and Obs/Exp$_{CpG}$ (Takai & Jones, 2003; Han & Zhao, 2009) and clustering algorithms (Glass et al., 2007; Hackenberg et al., 2010a; H. Wu et al., 2010) show best results. Takai-Jones algorithm predicts 40% of CGIs to be located near promoters of RefSeq genes, CpGcluster can reach the amount of 50% of all CGIs to be near promoter regions (with p-value = 1.0e-20). Wu and colleagues (H. Wu et al., 2010) believe that CGHW predicts more CGI to be located near promoters of RefSeq genes comparing to UCSC CGI and CG clusters.

Despite the fact that about half of CGIs are located near TSS of protein-coding genes the rest are not. Lately various evidences of pervasive transcription appear (Carninci et al., 2005). New high-throughput techniques (CAGE, SAGE, ets) identify at least ten times more transcriptionally active regions comparing to number of protein-coding genes. Most of those regions contain TSS for ncRNA of different types. CGIs located far from TSS of protein-coding genes can act as their promoters. Nowadays discovery of new protein-coding genes is rare occasion. Nevertheless our knowledge about ncRNA genes is extremely uncomplete. On the other side, one shouldn't forget that mammalian genomes have not only CGI-dependent promoters, but also TATA-dependent ones (Saxonov et al., 2006). The proportion of both types is still unclear. Therefore fraction of CGIs associated with protein-coding genes promoters is not an appropriate measure.

Other genomic features, like insulators, replication origins, recombination hot-spots, are also co-located with CGIs and make the whole picture more complicated. It's also becoming clear that CGI is not functionally equipotential throughout the length. CGI is not only a region with high GC content and CpG frequency. Even in very early works on CGIs (G/C)-box was mentioned as its structure element. Currently, it's obvious that not only Sp1 but also a lot of different TFs bind DNA within CGIs, so a huge fraction of them contains TFBS and their clusters. Also, at least some CGIs have boundary regions containing binding sites for Sp1, CTCF, VEZF1 or other TFs. Recently it was shown that G-quadruplex could also form a boundary of CGIs. It should be emphasized that quality of biologically relevant feature prediction is higher, if the method uses not only CGI prediction but includes other sequence properties. Therefore the concept of complex CGI definition based not only on GC or CpG content but also on other features like TFBS, repeats or DNA structure elements looks promising.

4. Unsolved problems and perspectives

Despite the huge amount of works in the area commonly accepted definition of CpG islands still doesn't exist. Most likely such situation is a result of difficulties with biological verification of predictions (Segal, 2006). Authors of SWMs and to lower extend of clustering algorithms choose the parameters arbitrarily complicating biological interpretations. Authors of machine-learning techniques usually find too many distinguishing parameters important in their models, which are not important in modeling of similar processes in other cases.

Specifically it should be emphasized that all attempts to construct CGI prediction algorithm based on simple DNA sequence properties (GC content, Obs/Exp$_{CpG}$, distance between neibouring CpG dinucleotides) having in mind prediction of complex biological feature (promoter regions, unmethylated regions and so on) bring about a high level of false positive predictions. For example, in case of promoter CGI prediction at least one third of CGIs are located far from promoters. It admits of no doubt that existing CGI searchers find a chimeric class of DNA segments, which don't have single common function. A collection of DNA motifs relevant to different biological functions could result into more adequate CGI definition. For instance, GC-skew and known core promoter elements could help to find CGI or regions within them related to TSS.

Speaking on another feature of CGIs, namely lack of DNA methylation, it should be mentioned that new high-throughput techniques show that not all CpG within CGIs are unmethylated in normal cells, as previously believed. Nowadays it became clear that not only CpGs but also CpNpGs are subject to methylation (Lister et al., 2009). Such a motif also should be included in CGI prediction model (Hackenberg et al., 2010b).

The ability of a CGI searcher to predict DMRs but not unmethylated regions seems more appropriate for quality evaluation. (Dai et al., 2008; Rakyan et al., 2008; Previti et al., 2009). Unfortunately now we are still lack of high-quality and high-resolution data on genome-wide DNA methylation in different tissues, states of developmet and conditions. High-throughput techniques, like MeDIP, MeDIP-seq (Down et al., 2008), MethylCap-Seq (Brinkman et al., 2010), bisulphyte conversion based methods (RRBS (Eckhardt et al., 2006) and Methyl-seq (Lister et al., 2009)), let us hope for a complete map of DMRs in the nearest future, which will help with CGI validation.

There is a lot of evidences that methylated cytosine also could play important functional role as sites for methyl-binding proteins. We still haven't enougth relaibale data on motif preferences for all such proteins but we expect ChIP-seq (Mardis, 2007) technique to help with the issue. There are proofs showing that it's premature to exclude Alu- and other repetitive mostly methylated sequences out of considereation speaking on CGI functions.

To resolve mentioned problems it is necessary to figure out as many biological functions associating with CGIs as possible and to find out structure elements within CGI relating to those functions or to separate CGI on several different functional groups. Such approach should result in more precise and biologically adequate CGIs definition and, therefore construction of relevant algorithm with low false positive and negative rates which in turn will improve our knowledge in genetic and epigenetic regulation of genome functioning.

5. Comparison of different algorithms

A lot of comparisons between algorithms for CGI search have been performed. This work is focused on study of various genome features potentially relates to CGIs. Three algorithms for CpG islands search participate in the comparison: UCSC CGI, CpGcluster (with p-value threshold of clusters equal to 1.0e-10, 1.0e-15, and 1.0e-20) and CGHW (the algorithm implemented by Wu and colleagues). I prefer to focus on the algorithms of a "new wave" and UCSC CGI as a reference because the last one is the most widespread now.

ENCODE regions of human genome (version hg18) were used for the study. All annotations were downloaded from http://hgdownload.cse.ucsc.edu/goldenPath/hg18/database/. Standard sensitivity (3) and specificity (4) measures for prediction quality were used.

$$Sn = L_{TP} / (L_{FP}+L_{FN}), \qquad\qquad (3)$$

$$Sp = L_{TN} / (L_{FP}+L_{TN}), \qquad\qquad (4)$$

where L_{TP} – total length (bp) of overlap of CGIs with tested annotation, L_{FP} – total length (bp) of CGIs not overlapping with tested annotation, L_{FN} - total length (bp) of tested annotation not overlapping with CGIs, L_{TN} - total length (bp) of ENCODE regions not overlapping neither with tested annotation no with CGIs.

5.1 Basic statistics

As a first step I collected the summary of statictical properties of CGIs predicted by different algorithms. CGI HW covers more then 2.2 % of total length of all ENCODE regions. CpGcluster (p-value 1.0 e-20 as recommended in (Hackenberg et al., 2010a)) demonstrate the smallest genome coverage of 0.6%. CpGcluster predicts shorter CGIs with higher average GC-content and Obs/Exp$_{CpG}$ value comparing to other algorithms. UCSC CGI obtains the largest average number of CpGs per one CGI.

	UCSC	CGI HW	CpGcluster10	CpGcluster15	CpGcluster20
#CGI	507	1124	1093	633	418
CGI total length	396722	685514	303160	222603	172676
avarage length	782	610	277	352	413
avarage GC content	0.66	0.64	0.7	0.71	0.72
avarage #CpG per CGI	71	48	29	38	46
avarage Obs/Exp$_{CpG}$	0.86	0.74	0.91	0.92	0.92
ENCODE fraction	0.0132	0.0229	0.0101	0.0074	0.0058

Table 1. Basic statistics for different CGIs.

In general one could see that CGI HW finds more "relaxed" CGIs comparing to UCSC CGI (with lower GC-content, Obs/Exp_{CpG} value and CpG frequency), whereas CpGcluster finds more "strict" CGIs comparing to UCSC CGI.

5.2 Regulatory potential

TSS prediction. It's widely accepted that a large fraction of CGIs is found around TSS of protein-coding genes. Recent studies show that total amount of TSS is about 10-times higher than the amount of protein-coding genes, so it seems more appropriate to test the CGI searchers for their ability to find TSS of any type. Several experimental techniques are able to detect any type of TSSs. Cap analysis gene expression (CAGE) is one of the most known techniques to produce a snapshot of the 5' ends of the total cellular RNA transcribed by PolII. A collection of CAGE-tags (encodeRikenCagePlus and encodeRikenCageMinus tables from UCSC) was used as a representative set of PolII TSS.

	UCSC CGI	CGI HW	CpGcluster10	CpGcluster15	CpGcluster20
CGI fraction	0.0136	0.0090	0.0130	0.0152	0.0164
CAGE fraction	0.7274	0.7909	0.4632	0.4331	0.3903
Sn	0.0136	0.0091	0.0128	0.0149	0.0158
Sp	0.9869	0.9773	0.9900	0.9927	0.9943

Table 2. CAGE-tags clusters within different CGIs.

Table 2 shows that CGI HW has the lowest sensitivity, although they obtain the highest fraction of CAGE-tags clusters. CpGcluster20 demonstrates the highest selectivity and specificity but obtain only 39% of CAGE-tags clusters. UCSC CGI has the intermediate values of Sn and Sp.

TFBS prediction. Although TFBS prediction is a classical problem for computational molecular biology, prediction of one single but highly reliable TFBS still remains tricky. I used TFBS conserved in the human/mouse/rat alignment based on Transfac Matrix Database (tfbsConsSites and tfbsConsFactors tables from UCSC). Keeping in mind that using of conserved TFBS leads to omission of all types of species-specific regulation regions, conserved TFBS are more likely to be functional comparing to other predicted TFBS.

Table 3 demonstrates that CpGcluster predicts CGI with fewer different TFs and lower sensitivity comparing to USCS CGI and CGI HW. The highest fraction of total TFBS length is covered by CGI HW, the very same algorithm shows the highest sensitivity and the lowest specificity. It's not obvious what fraction of the CGIs one should expect to be covered by TFBS but CpGcluster20 demonstrates the largest coverage (about 19 %).

	UCSC CGI	CGI HW	CpGcluster10	CpGcluster15	CpGcluster20
#TF	167	167	161	154	153
CGI fraction	0.1834	0.1347	0.1896	0.1915	0.1917
TFBS fraction	0.0860	0.1098	0.0688	0.0509	0.0393
Sn	0.0676	0.0696	0.0567	0.0443	0.0355
Sp	0.9889	0.9796	0.9916	0.9938	0.9952

Table 3. Conserved TFBS within different CGIs.

As it's difficult to estimate the expected coverage of TFBS, I compared the coverage of CGIs with the coverage of their adjacent regions of 100 bp. Results in Table 4 show that all adjacent to CGI regions contain conserved TFBS.

	UCSC CGI	CGI HW	CpGcluster10	CpGcluster15	CpGcluster20
#TF	157	167	166	162	151
CGI fraction	0.0564	0.0648	0.0871	0.0859	0.0820
TFBS fraction	0.0069	0.0177	0.0231	0.0132	0.0083
Sn	0.0063	0.0143	0.0189	0.0117	0.0077
Sp	0.9967	0.9928	0.9931	0.9960	0.9974
TFBS ratio	12.38	6.21	2.98	3.86	4.72

Table 4. Conserved TFBS within +/- 100 bp around different CGIs.

Last row of the Table 4 demonstrates the reduction of coverage in CGI adjacent regions comparing to CGI bodies. The adjacent regions of UCSC CGI and CGI HW contain more then 12 and 6 times less TFBS comparing to CGI body respectively. One should expect some TFBS around CGI which can function as CGI's boundaries. One the other hand, if we believe that CGI itself is the regulatory region, expected amount of TFBS in the adjacent regions should be dramatically lower comparing to CGI body, which is not the case for CpGcluster.

Insulators. CTCF is well known as a DNA binding protein acting both as transcriptional factor and insulator protein. To test which CGI prediction algorithm finds more CTCF binding sites I used data on CTCF binding (oregano and oreganoAttr tables from UCSC). One can see that CGI HW shows the highest sensitivity in CTCF binding prediction. It's also important to mention that CGIs from CGI HW contain more than 25% of all CTCF sites. CpGcluster10 shows the second best result, and the quality of prediction decreases in case of CpGcluster15 and CpGcluster20.

	UCSC CGI	CGI HW	CpGcluster10	CpGcluster15	CpGcluster20
CGI fraction	0.0809	0.0658	0.0503	0.0569	0.0478
CTCF fraction	0.1395	0.2517	0.1871	0.1224	0.0680
Sn	0.0267	0.0434	0.0305	0.0241	0.0157
Sp	0.9872	0.9806	0.9916	0.9939	0.9953

Table 5. CTCF binding sites within different CGIs.

DNase sensitivity regions. DNase sensitivity regions are often considered as regions of open chromatin which correspond to regulatory regions of all types. To test what algorithm predicts CGI more often associated with DNase sensitivity regions I use joined data for several tissues available in UCSC (table wgEncodeRegDnaseClustered). All CGIs demonstrate rather good association with DNase sensitivity regions, at least one third of their length is located in sensitive area. UCSC CGI shows highest sensitivity and rather good spesifisity. Vast fraction of CpGcluster CGIs are also associated with DNase sensitivity regions; althougth sensivity of the algorithm is not very good.

	UCSC CGI	CGI HW	CpGcluster10	CpGcluster15	CpGcluster20
CGI fraction	0.6047	0.3221	0.4312	0.5872	0.6040
DNase fraction	0.0768	0.0707	0.0418	0.0418	0.0334
Sn	0.0789	0.0655	0.0413	0.0424	0.0338
Sp	0.9942	0.9827	0.9936	0.9966	0.9975

Table 6. DNase sensitivity regions within CGIs predicted by different algorithms and quality of prediction.

Differently methylated regions. Data on regions differently methylated during development was downloaded from the UCSC (table rdmr). Table 7 shows that CGI HW predicts CGI located near over 43% of all rDMRs. This algorithm demonstrates also the best sensitivity in this case. It shoud be menthioned that CpGcluster20 has the lowest sensitivity and those CGIs are located near only 7% of rDMRs.

	UCSC CGI	CGI HW	CpGcluster10	CpGcluster15	CpGcluster20
#rDMR fraction	0.2500	0.4310	0.2241	0.1293	0.0776
CGI fraction	0.0170	0.0262	0.0179	0.0161	0.0137
rDMR fraction	0.0534	0.1424	0.0432	0.0284	0.0187
Sn	0.0132	0.0231	0.0130	0.0105	0.0080
Sp	0.9869	0.9776	0.9900	0.9927	0.9943

Table 7. rDMRs within different CGIs.

Replication origins. To figure out if there is any preference for replication origins to be found by one of CGI searchers data from encodeUvaDnaRepOriginsNSGM table were used. Only CGI HW and CpGcluster10 find 5 and 2 replication origins within or around (+/- 100 bp) CGI respectively. Other algorithms (and CpGcluster with more strict parameters) are unable to find any replication origins.

Polymorphic loci. Data from SNP130 were used for study of polymorphic loci within different CGIs. CGI from CGI HW contains the highest fraction of SNPs and demonstrates highest sensitivity, so one should expect more interindividual variants within those CGIs.

	UCSC CGI	CGI HW	CpGcluster10	CpGcluster15	CpGcluster20
CGI fraction	0.0072	0.0082	0.0080	0.0073	0.0066
SNP fraction	0.0140	0.0276	0.0120	0.0080	0.0056
Sn	0.0048	0.0064	0.0049	0.0038	0.0031
Sp	0.9868	0.9771	0.9899	0.9926	0.9942

Table 8. SNPs within different CGIs.

6. Conclusions

In summary, no one algorithm for CGI search predicts all biologically relevant features with appropriate accuracy. In all cases a lot of both false positives and false negatives appear.

All algorithms participating in competition have its strong sides. CpGcluster (p-value = 1.0e-15 and p-value = 1.0e-20) demonstrate the highest specificity in TSS prediction. Although such CGIs obtain the smallest fraction of CAGE-tags, this may be not a disadvantage as we don't know for sure the proportion of GC- and AT-rich promoters. The largest fraction of CGIs length is covered by TFBS in case of CGIs predicted by CpGcluster, on the other hand the largest part of their adjacent regions is also covered by TFBS. This brought me to conclusion that CpGcluster finds "cropped" promoter CGIs, espessially in case of p-value = 1.0e-20.

On the contrary CGI HW demonstrates the best sensitivity in CTCF binding sites and rDMR prediction. CGI from CGI HW are associated with at least some of origins of repliacation, thereas other algoritms (with recommended parameters) don't. They are also more prone to find diversities between humans. Also those CGIs find the highest fraction of TSS. So, CGI HW finds regions with broad regulatory potential. However all those features are related to DNA methylation, which allow me to assume that CGI HW finds DMR-associated CGIs.

UCSC CGI demonstrates moderate behavior. This algorithm has intermediate sensitivity both in TSS and rDMR prediction. Those CGIs have the highest decrease of TFBS in CGI adjasent regions and the highest sensitivity to DNase. It looks like UCSC finds CGI around promoter and also includes regulation regions, so those are promoter region CGIs.

It's quite clear that CGI is a complex object, which doesn't correspond to any single biological feature. It seems more appropriate to segregate a class of interconnected biological features: differential DNA methylation, active transcription at least in one cell type or development stage and replication. CGI HW algorithm made the first step in this direction, whereas CpGcluster (with high threshold for p-value) moves to the opposite direction and finds specific narrow class of promoters. Traditional UCSC approach still stands ground demonstrating comparable or in some points even higher quality. Hence the CpG island problem is still far from final solution.

7. Acknowledgments

Author is very grateful to N. Oparina, V. Makeev, I. Artamonova and A. Favorov for fruitful discussions on the topic of this article. This study was partially supported by RFBR grant 11-04-02016-a and by the state contract P1376 of the Federal Special Program "Scientific and educational human resources of innovative Russia" for 2009 – 2013.

8. References

Baylin, S. B., J. G. Herman, J. R. Graff, P. M. Vertino and J. P. Issa (1998). Alterations in DNA methylation: a fundamental aspect of neoplasia. *Adv Cancer Res*, Vol.72, 1998), pp. 141-96

Behe, M. and G. Felsenfeld (1981). Effects of methylation on a synthetic polynucleotide: the B--Z transition in poly(dG-m5dC).poly(dG-m5dC). *Proc Natl Acad Sci U S A*, Vol.78, No.3, (Mar, 1981), pp. 1619-23

Bell, A. C. and G. Felsenfeld (2000). Methylation of a CTCF-dependent boundary controls imprinted expression of the Igf2 gene. *Nature*, Vol.405, No.6785, (May 25, 2000), pp. 482-5

Berger, J. and A. Bird (2005). Role of MBD2 in gene regulation and tumorigenesis. *Biochem Soc Trans*, Vol.33, No.Pt 6, (Dec, 2005), pp. 1537-40

Bestor, T. H., G. Gundersen, A. B. Kolsto and H. Prydz (1992). CpG islands in mammalian gene promoters are inherently resistant to de novo methylation. *Genet Anal Tech Appl*, Vol.9, No.2, (Apr, 1992), pp. 48-53

Bhasin, M., H. Zhang, E. L. Reinherz and P. A. Reche (2005). Prediction of methylated CpGs in DNA sequences using a support vector machine. *FEBS Lett*, Vol.579, No.20, (Aug 15, 2005), pp. 4302-8

Bird, A. P. (1986). CpG-rich islands and the function of DNA methylation. *Nature*, Vol.321, No.6067, (May 15-21, 1986), pp. 209-13

Bock, C., M. Paulsen, S. Tierling, T. Mikeska, T. Lengauer and J. Walter (2006). CpG island methylation in human lymphocytes is highly correlated with DNA sequence, repeats, and predicted DNA structure. *PLoS Genet*, Vol.2, No.3, (Mar, 2006), pp. e26

Bock, C., J. Walter, M. Paulsen and T. Lengauer (2007). CpG island mapping by epigenome prediction. *PLoS Comput Biol*, Vol.3, No.6, (Jun, 2007), pp. e110

Bock, C., J. Walter, M. Paulsen and T. Lengauer (2008). Inter-individual variation of DNA methylation and its implications for large-scale epigenome mapping. *Nucleic Acids Res*, Vol.36, No.10, (Jun, 2008), pp. e55

Brero, A., H. Leonhardt and M. C. Cardoso (2006). Replication and translation of epigenetic information. *Curr Top Microbiol Immunol*, Vol.301, 2006), pp. 21-44

Briggs, M. R., J. T. Kadonaga, S. P. Bell and R. Tjian (1986). Purification and biochemical characterization of the promoter-specific transcription factor, Sp1. *Science*, Vol.234, No.4772, (Oct 3, 1986), pp. 47-52

Brinkman, A. B., F. Simmer, K. Ma, A. Kaan, J. Zhu and H. G. Stunnenberg (2010). Whole-genome DNA methylation profiling using MethylCap-seq. *Methods*, Vol.52, No.3, (Nov, 2010), pp. 232-6

Britten, R. J., W. F. Baron, D. B. Stout and E. H. Davidson (1988). Sources and evolution of human Alu repeated sequences. *Proc Natl Acad Sci U S A*, Vol.85, No.13, (Jul, 1988), pp. 4770-4

Brohede, J. and K. N. Rand (2006). Evolutionary evidence suggests that CpG island-associated Alus are frequently unmethylated in human germline. *Hum Genet*, Vol.119, No.4, (May, 2006), pp. 457-8

Brown, S. D. (1991). XIST and the mapping of the X chromosome inactivation centre. *Bioessays*, Vol.13, No.11, (Nov, 1991), pp. 607-12

Brown, S. E., M. J. Suderman, M. Hallett and M. Szyf (2008). DNA demethylation induced by the methyl-CpG-binding domain protein MBD3. *Gene*, Vol.420, No.2, (Sep 1, 2008), pp. 99-106

Brunner, A. L., D. S. Johnson, S. W. Kim, A. Valouev, T. E. Reddy, N. F. Neff, E. Anton, C. Medina, L. Nguyen, E. Chiao, et al. (2009). Distinct DNA methylation patterns characterize differentiated human embryonic stem cells and developing human fetal liver. *Genome Res*, Vol.19, No.6, (Jun, 2009), pp. 1044-56

Bucher, P. (1990). Weight matrix descriptions of four eukaryotic RNA polymerase II promoter elements derived from 502 unrelated promoter sequences. *J Mol Biol*, Vol.212, No.4, (Apr 20, 1990), pp. 563-78

Burley, S. K. and R. G. Roeder (1996). Biochemistry and structural biology of transcription factor IID (TFIID). *Annu Rev Biochem*, Vol.65, 1996), pp. 769-99

Caiafa, P. and M. Zampieri (2005). DNA methylation and chromatin structure: the puzzling CpG islands. *J Cell Biochem*, Vol.94, No.2, (Feb 1, 2005), pp. 257-65

Carninci, P., T. Kasukawa, S. Katayama, J. Gough, M. C. Frith, N. Maeda, R. Oyama, T. Ravasi, B. Lenhard, C. Wells, et al. (2005). The transcriptional landscape of the mammalian genome. *Science*, Vol.309, No.5740, (Sep 2, 2005), pp. 1559-63

Carson, M. B., R. Langlois and H. Lu (2008). Mining knowledge for the methylation status of CpG islands using alternating decision trees. *Conf Proc IEEE Eng Med Biol Soc*, Vol.2008, 2008), pp. 3787-90

Chalkley, G. E. and C. P. Verrijzer (1999). DNA binding site selection by RNA polymerase II TAFs: a TAF(II)250-TAF(II)150 complex recognizes the initiator. *EMBO J*, Vol.18, No.17, (Sep 1, 1999), pp. 4835-45

Choi, J. K. (2010). Contrasting chromatin organization of CpG islands and exons in the human genome. *Genome Biol*, Vol.11, No.7, 2010), pp. R70

Cooper, D. N., M. Mort, P. D. Stenson, E. V. Ball and N. A. Chuzhanova (2010). Methylation-mediated deamination of 5-methylcytosine appears to give rise to mutations causing human inherited disease in CpNpG trinucleotides, as well as in CpG dinucleotides. *Hum Genomics*, Vol.4, No.6, (Aug 1, 2010), pp. 406-10

Cross, S. H., J. A. Charlton, X. Nan and A. P. Bird (1994). Purification of CpG islands using a methylated DNA binding column. *Nat Genet*, Vol.6, No.3, (Mar, 1994), pp. 236-44

Dai, W., J. M. Teodoridis, J. Graham, C. Zeller, T. H. Huang, P. Yan, J. K. Vass, R. Brown and J. Paul (2008). Methylation Linear Discriminant Analysis (MLDA) for identifying differentially methylated CpG islands. *BMC Bioinformatics*, Vol.9, pp. 337

Daniel, J. M., C. M. Spring, H. C. Crawford, A. B. Reynolds and A. Baig (2002). The p120(ctn)-binding partner Kaiso is a bi-modal DNA-binding protein that recognizes both a sequence-specific consensus and methylated CpG dinucleotides. *Nucleic Acids Res*, Vol.30, No.13, (Jul 1, 2002), pp. 2911-9

Das, R., N. Dimitrova, Z. Xuan, R. A. Rollins, F. Haghighi, J. R. Edwards, J. Ju, T. H. Bestor and M. Q. Zhang (2006). Computational prediction of methylation status in human genomic sequences. *Proc Natl Acad Sci U S A*, Vol.103, No.28, (Jul 11, 2006), pp. 10713-6

Davuluri, R. V., I. Grosse and M. Q. Zhang (2001). Computational identification of promoters and first exons in the human genome. *Nat Genet*, Vol.29, No.4, (Dec, 2001), pp. 412-7

Deobagkar, D. D. and H. S. Chandra (2003). The inactive X chromosome in the human female is enriched in 5-methylcytosine to an unusual degree and appears to contain more of this modified nucleotide than the remainder of the genome. *J Genet*, Vol.82, No.1-2, (Apr-Aug, 2003), pp. 13-6

Dhasarathy, A. and P. A. Wade (2008). The MBD protein family-reading an epigenetic mark? *Mutat Res*, Vol.647, No.1-2, (Dec 1, 2008), pp. 39-43

Dickson, J., H. Gowher, R. Strogantsev, M. Gaszner, A. Hair, G. Felsenfeld and A. G. West (2010). VEZF1 elements mediate protection from DNA methylation. *PLoS Genet*, Vol.6, No.1, (Jan, 2010), pp. e1000804

Down, T. A., V. K. Rakyan, D. J. Turner, P. Flicek, H. Li, E. Kulesha, S. Graf, N. Johnson, J. Herrero, E. M. Tomazou, et al. (2008). A Bayesian deconvolution strategy for immunoprecipitation-based DNA methylome analysis. *Nat Biotechnol*, Vol.26, No.7, (Jul, 2008), pp. 779-85

Eckhardt, F., J. Lewin, R. Cortese, V. K. Rakyan, J. Attwood, M. Burger, J. Burton, T. V. Cox, R. Davies, T. A. Down, et al. (2006). DNA methylation profiling of human chromosomes 6, 20 and 22. *Nat Genet*, Vol.38, No.12, (Dec, 2006), pp. 1378-85

Egger, G., G. Liang, A. Aparicio and P. A. Jones (2004). Epigenetics in human disease and prospects for epigenetic therapy. *Nature*, Vol.429, No.6990, (May 27, 2004), pp. 457-63

Ehrich, M., J. Turner, P. Gibbs, L. Lipton, M. Giovanneti, C. Cantor and D. van den Boom (2008). Cytosine methylation profiling of cancer cell lines. *Proc Natl Acad Sci U S A*, Vol.105, No.12, (Mar 25, 2008), pp. 4844-9

Ehrlich, M. and R. Y. Wang (1981). 5-Methylcytosine in eukaryotic DNA. *Science*, Vol.212, No.4501, (Jun 19, 1981), pp. 1350-7

Fan, S., F. Fang, X. Zhang and M. Q. Zhang (2007). Putative zinc finger protein binding sites are over-represented in the boundaries of methylation-resistant CpG islands in the human genome. *PLoS One*, Vol.2, No.11, pp. e1184

Fang, F., S. Fan, X. Zhang and M. Q. Zhang (2006). Predicting methylation status of CpG islands in the human brain. *Bioinformatics*, Vol.22, No.18, (Sep 15, 2006), pp. 2204-9

Fatemi, M. and P. A. Wade (2006). MBD family proteins: reading the epigenetic code. *J Cell Sci*, Vol.119, No.Pt 15, (Aug 1, 2006), pp. 3033-7

Feltus, F. A., E. K. Lee, J. F. Costello, C. Plass and P. M. Vertino (2003). Predicting aberrant CpG island methylation. *Proc Natl Acad Sci U S A*, Vol.100, No.21, (Oct 14, 2003), pp. 12253-8

Feltus, F. A., E. K. Lee, J. F. Costello, C. Plass and P. M. Vertino (2006). DNA motifs associated with aberrant CpG island methylation. *Genomics*, Vol.87, No.5, (May, 2006), pp. 572-9

Filippova, G. N., M. K. Cheng, J. M. Moore, J. P. Truong, Y. J. Hu, D. K. Nguyen, K. D. Tsuchiya and C. M. Disteche (2005). Boundaries between chromosomal domains of X inactivation and escape bind CTCF and lack CpG methylation during early development. *Dev Cell*, Vol.8, No.1, (Jan, 2005), pp. 31-42

Frey, F. J. (2005). Methylation of CpG islands: potential relevance for hypertension and kidney diseases. *Nephrol Dial Transplant*, Vol.20, No.5, (May, 2005), pp. 868-9

Frith, M. C., L. G. Wilming, A. Forrest, H. Kawaji, S. L. Tan, C. Wahlestedt, V. B. Bajic, C. Kai, J. Kawai, P. Carninci, et al. (2006). Pseudo-messenger RNA: phantoms of the transcriptome. *PLoS Genet*, Vol.2, No.4, (Apr, 2006), pp. e23

Fritz, E. L. and F. N. Papavasiliou (2010). Cytidine deaminases: AIDing DNA demethylation? *Genes Dev*, Vol.24, No.19, (Oct 1, 2010), pp. 2107-14

Gardiner-Garden, M. and M. Frommer (1987). CpG islands in vertebrate genomes. *J Mol Biol*, Vol.196, No.2, (Jul 20, 1987), pp. 261-82

Gartler, S. M. and A. D. Riggs (1983). Mammalian X-chromosome inactivation. *Annu Rev Genet*, Vol.17, pp. 155-90

Glass, J. L., R. F. Thompson, B. Khulan, M. E. Figueroa, E. N. Olivier, E. J. Oakley, G. Van Zant, E. E. Bouhassira, A. Melnick, A. Golden, et al. (2007). CG dinucleotide clustering is a species-specific property of the genome. *Nucleic Acids Res*, Vol.35, No.20, pp. 6798-807

Graff, J. R., J. G. Herman, S. Myohanen, S. B. Baylin and P. M. Vertino (1997). Mapping patterns of CpG island methylation in normal and neoplastic cells implicates both upstream and downstream regions in de novo methylation. *J Biol Chem*, Vol.272, No.35, (Aug 29, 1997), pp. 22322-9

Hackenberg, M., G. Barturen, P. Carpena, P. L. Luque-Escamilla, C. Previti and J. L. Oliver (2010a). Prediction of CpG-island function: CpG clustering vs. sliding-window methods. *BMC Genomics*, Vol.11, pp. 327

Hackenberg, M., P. Carpena, P. Bernaola-Galvan, G. Barturen, A. M. Alganza and J. L. Oliver (2010b). WordCluster: detecting clusters of DNA words and genomic elements. *Algorithms Mol Biol*, Vol.6, pp. 2

Hackenberg, M., C. Previti, P. L. Luque-Escamilla, P. Carpena, J. Martinez-Aroza and J. L. Oliver (2006). CpGcluster: a distance-based algorithm for CpG-island detection. *BMC Bioinformatics*, Vol.7, pp. 446

Halder, R., K. Halder, P. Sharma, G. Garg, S. Sengupta and S. Chowdhury (2010). Guanine quadruplex DNA structure restricts methylation of CpG dinucleotides genome-wide. *Mol Biosyst*, Vol.6, No.12, (Dec 8, 2010), pp. 2439-47

Han, L. and Z. Zhao (2009). CpG islands or CpG clusters: how to identify functional GC-rich regions in a genome? *BMC Bioinformatics*, Vol.10, pp. 65

Hashimoto, H., J. R. Horton, X. Zhang and X. Cheng (2009). UHRF1, a modular multi-domain protein, regulates replication-coupled crosstalk between DNA methylation and histone modifications. *Epigenetics*, Vol.4, No.1, (Jan, 2009), pp. 8-14

Herrera, L. A., D. Prada, M. A. Andonegui and A. Duenas-Gonzalez (2008). The epigenetic origin of aneuploidy. *Curr Genomics*, Vol.9, No.1, (Mar, 2008), pp. 43-50

Holler, M., G. Westin, J. Jiricny and W. Schaffner (1988). Sp1 transcription factor binds DNA and activates transcription even when the binding site is CpG methylated. *Genes Dev*, Vol.2, No.9, (Sep, 1988), pp. 1127-35

Hug, M., J. Silke, O. Georgiev, S. Rusconi, W. Schaffner and K. Matsuo (1996). Transcriptional repression by methylation: cooperativity between a CpG cluster in the promoter and remote CpG-rich regions. *FEBS Lett*, Vol.379, No.3, (Feb 5, 1996), pp. 251-4

Hutter, B., V. Helms and M. Paulsen (2006). Tandem repeats in the CpG islands of imprinted genes. *Genomics*, Vol.88, No.3, (Sep, 2006), pp. 323-32

Illingworth, R. S., U. Gruenewald-Schneider, S. Webb, A. R. Kerr, K. D. James, D. J. Turner, C. Smith, D. J. Harrison, R. Andrews and A. P. Bird (2010) Orphan CpG islands identify numerous conserved promoters in the mammalian genome. *PLoS Genet*, Vol.6, No.9, (Sep 23, 2010), e1001134

Irizarry, R. A., H. Wu and A. P. Feinberg (2009). A species-generalized probabilistic model-based definition of CpG islands. *Mamm Genome*, Vol.20, No.9-10, (Sep-Oct, 2009), pp. 674-80

Jacquier, A. (2009). The complex eukaryotic transcriptome: unexpected pervasive transcription and novel small RNAs. *Nat Rev Genet*, Vol.10, No.12, (Dec, 2009), pp. 833-44

Jones, P. A. and S. B. Baylin (2002). The fundamental role of epigenetic events in cancer. *Nat Rev Genet*, Vol.3, No.6, (Jun, 2002), pp. 415-28

Kimura, H. and K. Shiota (2003). Methyl-CpG-binding protein, MeCP2, is a target molecule for maintenance DNA methyltransferase, Dnmt1. *J Biol Chem*, Vol.278, No.7, (Feb 14, 2003), pp. 4806-12

Klose, R. J., S. A. Sarraf, L. Schmiedeberg, S. M. McDermott, I. Stancheva and A. P. Bird (2005). DNA binding selectivity of MeCP2 due to a requirement for A/T sequences adjacent to methyl-CpG. *Mol Cell*, Vol.19, No.5, (Sep 2, 2005), pp. 667-78

Kutach, A. K. and J. T. Kadonaga (2000). The downstream promoter element DPE appears to be as widely used as the TATA box in Drosophila core promoters. *Mol Cell Biol*, Vol.20, No.13, (Jul, 2000), pp. 4754-64

Lagrange, T., A. N. Kapanidis, H. Tang, D. Reinberg and R. H. Ebright (1998). New core promoter element in RNA polymerase II-dependent transcription: sequence-specific DNA binding by transcription factor IIB. *Genes Dev*, Vol.12, No.1, (Jan 1, 1998), pp. 34-44

Laird, P. W. (2003). The power and the promise of DNA methylation markers. *Nat Rev Cancer*, Vol.3, No.4, (Apr, 2003), pp. 253-66

Li, E., C. Beard and R. Jaenisch (1993). Role for DNA methylation in genomic imprinting. *Nature*, Vol.366, No.6453, (Nov 25, 1993), pp. 362-5

Lin, I. G., T. J. Tomzynski, Q. Ou and C. L. Hsieh (2000). Modulation of DNA binding protein affinity directly affects target site demethylation. *Mol Cell Biol*, Vol.20, No.7, (Apr, 2000), pp. 2343-9

Lister, R., M. Pelizzola, R. H. Dowen, R. D. Hawkins, G. Hon, J. Tonti-Filippini, J. R. Nery, L. Lee, Z. Ye, Q. M. Ngo, et al. (2009). Human DNA methylomes at base resolution show widespread epigenomic differences. *Nature*, Vol.462, No.7271, (Nov 19, 2009), pp. 315-22

Liu, L., Y. Li and T. O. Tollefsbol (2008). Gene-environment interactions and epigenetic basis of human diseases. *Curr Issues Mol Biol*, Vol.10, No.1-2, pp. 25-36

Lopes, S., A. Lewis, P. Hajkova, W. Dean, J. Oswald, T. Forne, A. Murrell, M. Constancia, M. Bartolomei, J. Walter, et al. (2003). Epigenetic modifications in an imprinting cluster are controlled by a hierarchy of DMRs suggesting long-range chromatin interactions. *Hum Mol Genet*, Vol.12, No.3, (Feb 1, 2003), pp. 295-305

Macleod, D., J. Charlton, J. Mullins and A. P. Bird (1994). Sp1 sites in the mouse aprt gene promoter are required to prevent methylation of the CpG island. *Genes Dev*, Vol.8, No.19, (Oct 1, 1994), pp. 2282-92

Mardis, E. R. (2007). ChIP-seq: welcome to the new frontier. *Nat Methods*, Vol.4, No.8, (Aug, 2007), pp. 613-4

Medvedeva, Y. A., M. V. Fridman, N. J. Oparina, D. B. Malko, E. O. Ermakova, I. V. Kulakovskiy, A. Heinzel and V. J. Makeev (2010). Intergenic, gene terminal, and intragenic CpG islands in the human genome. *BMC Genomics*, Vol.11, No.1, (Jan 19, 2010), pp. 48

Naumann, A., N. Hochstein, S. Weber, E. Fanning and W. Doerfler (2009). A distinct DNA-methylation boundary in the 5'- upstream sequence of the FMR1 promoter binds nuclear proteins and is lost in fragile X syndrome. *Am J Hum Genet*, Vol.85, No.5, (Nov, 2009), pp. 606-16

Ng, H. H., Y. Zhang, B. Hendrich, C. A. Johnson, B. M. Turner, H. Erdjument-Bromage, P. Tempst, D. Reinberg and A. Bird (1999). MBD2 is a transcriptional repressor belonging to the MeCP1 histone deacetylase complex. *Nat Genet*, Vol.23, No.1, (Sep, 1999), pp. 58-61

Oakes, C. C., S. La Salle, D. J. Smiraglia, B. Robaire and J. M. Trasler (2007). A unique configuration of genome-wide DNA methylation patterns in the testis. *Proc Natl Acad Sci U S A*, Vol.104, No.1, (Jan 2, 2007), pp. 228-33

Okada, Y., K. Yamagata, K. Hong, T. Wakayama and Y. Zhang (2010). A role for the elongator complex in zygotic paternal genome demethylation. *Nature*, Vol.463, No.7280, (Jan 28, 2010), pp. 554-8

Phi-van, L. and W. H. Stratling (1999). An origin of bidirectional DNA replication is located within a CpG island at the 3" end of the chicken lysozyme gene. *Nucleic Acids Res*, Vol.27, No.15, (Aug 1, 1999), pp. 3009-17

Polak, P., R. Querfurth and P. F. Arndt (2010). The evolution of transcription-associated biases of mutations across vertebrates. *BMC Evol Biol*, Vol.10, pp. 187

Ponger, L., L. Duret and D. Mouchiroud (2001). Determinants of CpG islands: expression in early embryo and isochore structure. *Genome Res*, Vol.11, No.11, (Nov, 2001), pp. 1854-60

Ponger, L. and D. Mouchiroud (2002). CpGProD: identifying CpG islands associated with transcription start sites in large genomic mammalian sequences. *Bioinformatics*, Vol.18, No.4, (Apr, 2002), pp. 631-3

Previti, C., O. Harari, I. Zwir and C. del Val (2009). Profile analysis and prediction of tissue-specific CpG island methylation classes. *BMC Bioinformatics*, Vol.10, pp. 116

Rakyan, V. K., T. A. Down, N. P. Thorne, P. Flicek, E. Kulesha, S. Graf, E. M. Tomazou, L. Backdahl, N. Johnson, M. Herberth, et al. (2008). An integrated resource for genome-wide identification and analysis of human tissue-specific differentially methylated regions (tDMRs). *Genome Res*, Vol.18, No.9, (Sep, 2008), pp. 1518-29

Razin, A. and A. D. Riggs (1980). DNA methylation and gene function. *Science*, Vol.210, No.4470, (Nov 7, 1980), pp. 604-10

Recillas-Targa, F., I. A. De La Rosa-Velazquez, E. Soto-Reyes and L. Benitez-Bribiesca (2006). Epigenetic boundaries of tumour suppressor gene promoters: the CTCF connection and its role in carcinogenesis. *J Cell Mol Med*, Vol.10, No.3, (Jul-Sep, 2006), pp. 554-68

Rein, T., T. Kobayashi, M. Malott, M. Leffak and M. L. DePamphilis (1999). DNA methylation at mammalian replication origins. *J Biol Chem*, Vol.274, No.36, (Sep 3, 1999), pp. 25792-800

Rein, T., H. Zorbas and M. L. DePamphilis (1997). Active mammalian replication origins are associated with a high-density cluster of mCpG dinucleotides. *Mol Cell Biol*, Vol.17, No.1, (Jan, 1997), pp. 416-26

Rice, P., I. Longden and A. Bleasby (2000). EMBOSS: the European Molecular Biology Open Software Suite. *Trends Genet*, Vol.16, No.6, (Jun, 2000), pp. 276-7

Richardson, B. (2007). Primer: epigenetics of autoimmunity. *Nat Clin Pract Rheumatol*, Vol.3, No.9, (Sep, 2007), pp. 521-7

Rishi, V., P. Bhattacharya, R. Chatterjee, J. Rozenberg, J. Zhao, K. Glass, P. Fitzgerald and C. Vinson (2010). CpG methylation of half-CRE sequences creates C/EBPalpha binding sites that activate some tissue-specific genes. *Proc Natl Acad Sci U S A*, Vol.107, No.47, (Nov 23, 2010), pp. 20311-6

Robinson, P. N., U. Bohme, R. Lopez, S. Mundlos and P. Nurnberg (2004). Gene-Ontology analysis reveals association of tissue-specific 5' CpG-island genes with development and embryogenesis. *Hum Mol Genet*, Vol.13, No.17, (Sep 1, 2004), pp. 1969-78

Rozenberg, J. M., A. Shlyakhtenko, K. Glass, V. Rishi, M. V. Myakishev, P. C. FitzGerald and C. Vinson (2008). All and only CpG containing sequences are enriched in promoters abundantly bound by RNA polymerase II in multiple tissues. *BMC Genomics*, Vol.9, No.1, pp. 67

Saito, M. and F. Ishikawa (2002). The mCpG-binding domain of human MBD3 does not bind to mCpG but interacts with NuRD/Mi2 components HDAC1 and MTA2. *J Biol Chem*, Vol.277, No.38, (Sep 20, 2002), pp. 35434-9

Sasai, N., M. Nakao and P. A. Defossez (2010). Sequence-specific recognition of methylated DNA by human zinc-finger proteins. *Nucleic Acids Res*, Vol.38, No.15, (Aug, 2010), pp. 5015-22

Saxonov, S., P. Berg and D. L. Brutlag (2006). A genome-wide analysis of CpG dinucleotides in the human genome distinguishes two distinct classes of promoters. *Proc Natl Acad Sci U S A*, Vol.103, No.5, (Jan 31, 2006), pp. 1412-7

Schubeler, D., M. C. Lorincz and M. Groudine (2001). Targeting silence: the use of site-specific recombination to introduce in vitro methylated DNA into the genome. *Sci STKE*, Vol.2001, No.83, (May 22, 2001), pp. pl1

Segal, M. R. (2006). Validation in genomics: CpG island methylation revisited. *Stat Appl Genet Mol Biol*, Vol.5, Article29

Shen, L., Y. Kondo, Y. Guo, J. Zhang, L. Zhang, S. Ahmed, J. Shu, X. Chen, R. A. Waterland and J. P. Issa (2007). Genome-wide profiling of DNA methylation reveals a class of normally methylated CpG island promoters. *PLoS Genet*, Vol.3, No.10, (Oct, 2007), pp. 2023-36

Shiraishi, M., A. Sekiguchi, M. J. Terry, A. J. Oates, Y. Miyamoto, Y. H. Chuu, M. Munakata and T. Sekiya (2002). A comprehensive catalog of CpG islands methylated in human lung adenocarcinomas for the identification of tumor suppressor genes. *Oncogene*, Vol.21, No.23, (May 23, 2002), pp. 3804-13

Smale, S. T. (1997). Transcription initiation from TATA-less promoters within eukaryotic protein-coding genes. *Biochim Biophys Acta*, Vol.1351, No.1-2, (Mar 20, 1997), pp. 73-88

Smilinich, N. J., C. D. Day, G. V. Fitzpatrick, G. M. Caldwell, A. C. Lossie, P. R. Cooper, A. C. Smallwood, J. A. Joyce, P. N. Schofield, W. Reik, et al. (1999). A maternally methylated CpG island in KvLQT1 is associated with an antisense paternal transcript and loss of imprinting in Beckwith-Wiedemann syndrome. *Proc Natl Acad Sci U S A*, Vol.96, No.14, (Jul 6, 1999), pp. 8064-9

Straussman, R., D. Nejman, D. Roberts, I. Steinfeld, B. Blum, N. Benvenisty, I. Simon, Z. Yakhini and H. Cedar (2009). Developmental programming of CpG island methylation profiles in the human genome. *Nat Struct Mol Biol*, Vol.16, No.5, (May, 2009), pp. 564-71

Su, J., Y. Zhang, J. Lv, H. Liu, X. Tang, F. Wang, Y. Qi, Y. Feng and X. Li (2009). CpG_MI: a novel approach for identifying functional CpG islands in mammalian genomes. *Nucleic Acids Res*, Vol.38, No.1, (Jan, 2009), pp. e6

Takada, S., M. Tevendale, J. Baker, P. Georgiades, E. Campbell, T. Freeman, M. H. Johnson, M. Paulsen and A. C. Ferguson-Smith (2000). Delta-like and gtl2 are reciprocally expressed, differentially methylated linked imprinted genes on mouse chromosome 12. *Curr Biol*, Vol.10, No.18, (Sep 21, 2000), pp. 1135-8

Takai, D. and P. A. Jones (2002). Comprehensive analysis of CpG islands in human chromosomes 21 and 22. *Proc Natl Acad Sci U S A*, Vol.99, No.6, (Mar 19, 2002), pp. 3740-5

Takai, D. and P. A. Jones (2003). The CpG island searcher: a new WWW resource. *In Silico Biol*, Vol.3, No.3, pp. 235-40

Thomson, J. P., P. J. Skene, J. Selfridge, T. Clouaire, J. Guy, S. Webb, A. R. Kerr, A. Deaton, R. Andrews, K. D. James, et al. CpG islands influence chromatin structure via the CpG-binding protein Cfp1. *Nature*, Vol.464, No.7291, (Apr 15), pp. 1082-6

Tomatsu, S., K. O. Orii, M. R. Islam, G. N. Shah, J. H. Grubb, K. Sukegawa, Y. Suzuki, T. Orii, N. Kondo and W. S. Sly (2002). Methylation patterns of the human beta-glucuronidase gene locus: boundaries of methylation and general implications for frequent point mutations at CpG dinucleotides. *Genomics*, Vol.79, No.3, (Mar, 2002), pp. 363-75

Ullu, E. and C. Tschudi (1984). Alu sequences are processed 7SL RNA genes. *Nature*, Vol.312, No.5990, (Nov 8-14, 1984), pp. 171-2

Ushijima, T., N. Watanabe, E. Okochi, A. Kaneda, T. Sugimura and K. Miyamoto (2003). Fidelity of the methylation pattern and its variation in the genome. *Genome Res*, Vol.13, No.5, (May, 2003), pp. 868-74

van Roy, F. M. and P. D. McCrea (2005). A role for Kaiso-p120ctn complexes in cancer? *Nat Rev Cancer*, Vol.5, No.12, (Dec, 2005), pp. 956-64

Walsh, C. P., J. R. Chaillet and T. H. Bestor (1998). Transcription of IAP endogenous retroviruses is constrained by cytosine methylation. *Nat Genet*, Vol.20, No.2, (Oct, 1998), pp. 116-7

Wang, Y. and F. C. Leung (2004). An evaluation of new criteria for CpG islands in the human genome as gene markers. *Bioinformatics*, Vol.20, No.7, (May 1, 2004), pp. 1170-7

Weinmann, A. S., P. S. Yan, M. J. Oberley, T. H. Huang and P. J. Farnham (2002). Isolating human transcription factor targets by coupling chromatin immunoprecipitation and CpG island microarray analysis. *Genes Dev*, Vol.16, No.2, (Jan 15, 2002), pp. 235-44

Wu, H., B. Caffo, H. A. Jaffee, R. A. Irizarry and A. P. Feinberg (2010). Redefining CpG islands using hidden Markov models. *Biostatistics*, Vol.11, No.3, (Jul, 2010), pp. 499-514

Wu, S. C. and Y. Zhang (2010). Active DNA demethylation: many roads lead to Rome. *Nat Rev Mol Cell Biol*, Vol.11, No.9, (Sep, 2010), pp. 607-20

Xie, H., M. Wang, F. Bonaldo Mde, V. Rajaram, W. Stellpflug, C. Smith, K. Arndt, S. Goldman, T. Tomita and M. B. Soares (2010). Epigenomic analysis of Alu repeats in human ependymomas. *Proc Natl Acad Sci U S A*, Vol.107, No.15, (Apr 13, 2010), pp. 6952-7

Xin, Y., B. Chanrion, M. M. Liu, H. Galfalvy, R. Costa, B. Ilievski, G. Rosoklija, V. Arango, A. J. Dwork, J. J. Mann, et al. (2010). Genome-wide divergence of DNA methylation marks in cerebral and cerebellar cortices. *PLoS One*, Vol.5, No.6, pp. e11357

Xing, J., D. J. Hedges, K. Han, H. Wang, R. Cordaux and M. A. Batzer (2004). Alu element mutation spectra: molecular clocks and the effect of DNA methylation. *J Mol Biol*, Vol.344, No.3, (Nov 26, 2004), pp. 675-82

Yates, P. A., R. W. Burman, P. Mummaneni, S. Krussel and M. S. Turker (1999). Tandem B1 elements located in a mouse methylation center provide a target for de novo DNA methylation. *J Biol Chem*, Vol.274, No.51, (Dec 17, 1999), pp. 36357-61

Zemojtel, T., S. M. Kielbasa, P. F. Arndt, H. R. Chung and M. Vingron (2009). Methylation and deamination of CpGs generate p53-binding sites on a genomic scale. *Trends Genet*, Vol.25, No.2, (Feb, 2009), pp. 63-6

Zeschnigk, M., M. Martin, G. Betzl, A. Kalbe, C. Sirsch, K. Buiting, S. Gross, E. Fritzilas, B. Frey, S. Rahmann, et al. (2009). Massive parallel bisulfite sequencing of CG-rich DNA fragments reveals that methylation of many X-chromosomal CpG islands in female blood DNA is incomplete. *Hum Mol Genet*, Vol.18, No.8, (Apr 15, 2009), pp. 1439-48

Zhao, Z. and L. Han (2009). CpG islands: algorithms and applications in methylation studies. *Biochem Biophys Res Commun*, Vol.382, No.4, (May 15, 2009), pp. 643-5

Zhu, J., F. He, S. Hu and J. Yu (2008). On the nature of human housekeeping genes. *Trends Genet*, Vol.24, No.10, (Oct, 2008), pp. 481-4

22

Translational Oncogenomics and Human Cancer Interactomics: Advanced Techniques and Complex System Dynamic Approaches

I. C. Baianu

AFC-NMR & NIR Microspectroscopy Facility,
College of ACES, FSHN & NPRE Departments,
University of Illinois at Urbana, Urbana, IL
USA

1. Introduction

An overview of translational, human oncogenomics, transcriptomics and cancer interactomic networks is presented together with basic concepts and potential, new applications to Oncology and Integrative Cancer Biology. Novel translational oncogenomics research is rapidly expanding through the application of advanced technology, research findings and computational tools/models to both pharmaceutical and clinical problems. A self-contained presentation is adopted that covers both fundamental concepts and the most recent biomedical, as well as clinical, applications. Sample analyses in recent clinical studies have shown that gene expression data can be employed to distinguish between tumor types as well as to predict outcomes. Potentially important applications of such results are *individualized* human cancer therapies or, in general, 'personalized medicine'. Several cancer detection techniques are currently under development both in the direction of improved detection sensitivity and increased time resolution of cellular events, with the limits of single molecule detection and picosecond time resolution already reached. The urgency for the complete mapping of a human cancer interactome with the help of such novel, high-efficiency, low-cost and ultra-sensitive techniques is also pointed out.

1.1 Current status in translational genomics and interactome networks

Upon completion of the maps for several genomes, including the human genome, there are several major post-genomic tasks lying ahead such as the translation of the mapped genomes and the correct interpretation of huge amounts of data that are being rapidly generated, or the important task of applying these fundamental results to derive major benefits in various medical and agricultural biotechnology areas. Translational genomics is at the center of these tasks that are running from *transcription* through *translation* to *proteomics* and *interactomics*. The *transcriptome* is defined as the set of all 'transcripts' or messenger RNA (mRNA) molecules produced through transcription from DNA sequences by a single cell or a cell population. This concept is also extended to a multi-cellular organism as the set of all its transcripts. The transcriptome thus reflects the active part of the genome at a given instant of time. *Transcriptomics* involves the determination of mRNAs expression level in a selected cell population. For example, an improved understanding of cell differentiation involves the determination of the stem cell transcriptome; understanding carcinogenesis requires the comparison between the transcriptomes of cancer cells and untransformed ('normal) cells. However, because the levels of mRNA are not directly proportional to the expression levels of the proteins they are encoding, the protein complement of a cell or a multi-cellular organism needs to be determined by other techniques, or combination of techniques; the complete protein complement of a cell or organism is defined as the *proteome*. When the network (or networks) of complex protein-protein interactions (PPIs) in a cell or organism is (are) reconstructed, the result is called an *interactome*. This complete network of PPIs is now thought to form the 'backbone' of the signaling pathways, metabolic pathways and cellular processes that are required for all key cell functions and, therefore, cell survival. Such a complete knowledge of cellular pathways and processes in the cell is essential for understanding how many diseases -- such as cancer (and also ageing) — originate and progress through mutation or alteration of individual pathway components. Furthermore, determining human cancer cell interactomes of therapy-resistant tumors will undoubtedly allow for rational clinical trials and save patients' lives through individualized cancer therapy. Since the global gene expression studies of DeRisi et al in 1997, translational genomics is very rapidly advancing through the detection in parallel of mRNA levels for large numbers of molecules, as well as through progress made with miniaturization and high density synthesis of nucleic acids on microarray solid supports. Gene expression studies with microarrays permit an integrated approach to biology in terms of network biodynamics, signaling pathways, protein-protein interactions, and ultimately, the cell interactome. An important emerging principle of gene expression is the *temporally coordinated regulation* of genes as an extremely efficient mechanism (Wen *et al* 1998) required for complex processes in which all the components of multi-subunit complexes must be present/available in defined ratios at the same time whenever such complexes are needed by the cell. The gene expression profile can be thought of either as a 'signature/ fingerprint' or as *a molecular definition of the cell in a specified state* (Young, 2000). Cellular phenotypes can then be inferred from such gene expression profiles. Success has been achieved in several projects that profile a large number of biological samples and then utilize pattern matching to predict the function of either new drug targets or previously uncharacterized genes; this *'compendium approach'* has been demonstrated in yeast (Gray *et al* 1998; Hughes *et al* 2000), and has also been applied in databases integrating gene expression data from pharmacologically characterized human cancer lines (NCI60, http://dtp.nci.nih.gov), or to classify cell lines in relation to their tissue of origin and predict their drug resistance or chemosensitivity (Weinstein *et al*, 1997; Ross *et al* 2000, Staunton *et al* 2001). Furthermore, sample analyses in clinical studies have shown that gene expression data can be employed to distinguish between tumor types as well as to predict outcomes (Golub *et al* 1999; Bittner *et al*, 2000; Shipp et al 2002; Furteal et al., 2004). The latter approach seems to lead to important applications such as individualized cancer therapy and 'personalised medicine'. On the other hand, such approaches are complemented by studies of protein-protein interactions in the area called *proteomics*, preferably under physiological conditions, or more generally still, in *cell interactomics*. Several technologies in this area are still developing both in the direction of improved detection sensitivity and time resolution of cellular events, with the limits of single molecule detection and picosecond time resolution already attained. In order to enable the development of new applications such techniques will be briefly described in the next section, together with relevant examples of their recent applications.

1.2 Basic concepts in transcription, translation and interactome networks

The analysis of bionetwork dynamics of protein synthesis considered as a channel of information operates through the formation of protein amino acid sequences of polypeptides via *translation* of the corresponding polynucleotide sequences of (usually single –stranded, **messenger**) ribonucleic acid, that is:

DNA (gene) *transcription* → **mRNA** → *translation* **into a** polypeptide's aminoacid sequence → **protein** (quaternary) *assembly* from polypeptide subunits.

Although not shown in this scheme, several key enzymes make such processes both efficient and precise through highly-selective catalysis; moreover, the protein assembly involves both specific enzymes and ribosome 'assembly lines'. Furthermore, such processes are compartmented in the mammalian cells by selective intracellular membranes; this seems to be also important for cell cycling and the control of cell division. On the other hand, the *reverse transcription*, **RNA→ DNA**, does also occur (under certain conditions), catalized by a reverse transcriptase that contains both polypeptide chains and an RNA (master) strand. If error free, the first of these two sequence of processes — which are of fundamental biological importance-- generates true replicas of the information contained in the *sense codons* of the genes that are transcribed into mRNA *anti-codons*. Recall also that DNA stores information in the neucleotide bases A (Adenine), C (Cytosin), G (Guanine) and T (Thymine), and that a triplet of such nucleotides in the DNA sequence is called a *codon,* which may encode unambiguously just the information necessary to specify a single amino acid. Moreover, the genetic code is quasi-universal, and capable of 'reverse transcription' from certain types of RNA back into DNA. Notably also, not all nucleotide or codon sequences present in the genome (DNA) are transcribed *in vivo*. Typically only a small percentage is transcribed. The transcribed (mRNA) sequences form what is naturally called the *transcriptome;* the protein-- encoded version of the transcriptome is called the *proteome,* and upon including all protein-- protein interactions for various cellular states one obtains the (global) *interactome* network. More generally, biological interactive networks as a class of complex bionetworks consist of local cellular communities (or *'organismic sets'*) that are organized and managed by their characteristic selection procedures. Thus, in any partitioning of the organismal, or cell, structure, it is often necessary to regulate the *local* properties of the organism rather than the *global* mechanism, which explains an organism's need for specialized, 'modular constructions'. Such a modular, complex system biology approach to modeling signaling pathways and modifications of cell-cycling regulatory mechanisms in cancer cells was recently reported (Baianu, 2004); several consequences of this approach were also considered for the proteome and interactome networks in a 'prototype' cancer cell model (Prisecaru and Baianu, 2005). Note, on the other hand, that there seem to be also present in the living cell certain proteins and enzymes that are involved in *global* intra-cellular interactions which are thought to be essential to the cell survival and cell's flexible adaptation to stresses or challenge. Recent modeling techniques draw from a variety of mathematical sources, such as: topology (including graph theory), biostatistics, stochastic differential equations, Boolean networks, and qualitative system dynamics (Baianu, 1971a; de Jong *et al* 2000; 2003, 2004). Non--boolean network models of genetic networks and the interactome were also developed and compared with the results of Boolean ones (Baianu, 1977, 1984, 1987; Georgescu, 2006; Baianu, 2005; Baianu *et al.* 2006). The traditional use of comparatively rigid Boolean networks (reviewed extensively, for example in Baianu, 1987) can be thus extended through flexible, multi--valued (non--Boolean) logic algebra bionetworks with complex, *non- linear dynamic* behaviors that mimic complex systems biology (Rosen, 2000).

The results obtained with such non--random genetic network models have several important consequences for understanding the operation of cellular networks and the formation, transformation and growth of neoplastic network structures. Non--boolean models can also be extended to include *epigenetic* controls discussed in **Section 6**, as well as to mimic the coupling of the genome to the rest of the cell through specific signaling pathways that are involved in the modulation of both translation and transcription control processes. The latter may also provide novel approaches to cancer studies and, indeed, to developing 'individualized' cancer therapy strategies and novel anti-cancer medicines targeted at specific signaling pathways involved in malignant tumors resistance to other therapies.

2. Techniques and application examples

2.1 DNA microarrays

DNA microarray technology is widely employed to monitor in a single experiment the gene expression levels of all genes of a cell or an organism. This includes the identification of genes that are expressed in different cell types as well as the changes in gene expression levels caused, for example, by differentiation or disease. The terabytes of data thus obtained can provide valuable clues about the interactions among genes and also about the interaction networks of gene products. It has been reported that cDNA arrays were pioneered by the Brown Laboratory at Stanford University (Brown and Botstein, 1999; URL: http://cmgm.stanford.edu/pbrown/mguide/index.html). Several quantitative and high-density DNA array applications were then reported in rapid succession (Schena et al 1995; Chee et al 1996; Brown and Botstein, 1999). Such microarrays are generated by automatically printing double-stranded cDNA onto a solid support that may be either glass silicon or nylon. The essential technologies involved are robotics and devlopment/selection of sequence-verified and array-formatted cDNA clones. The latter ensures that both the location and the identity of each cDNA on the array is known. Sequence-verified and array-formatted cDNA clone sets are now available from companies such as Incyte Genomics (Palo Alto, CA; URL: http://www.synteni.com/) and Research Genetics (Huntsville, AL; URL: http://www.resgen.com/). In cDNA-based gene expression profiling experiments, the total RNA is extracted from the selected experimental samples and the RNA is fluorescently labeled with either cye3- or cye5-dUTP in a single round of reverse transcription. The latter have several advantages: they are readily incorporated into cDNA by reverse transcription, they exhibit widely separated excitation and emission spectra, and also they possess good photostability. Such fluorescently--labeled cDNA probes are then hybridized to a single array through a competitive hybridization reaction. Detection of hybridized probes is achieved by laser excitation of the individual fluorescent markers, followed by scanning using a confocal scanning laser microscope. The raw data obtained with a laser scanning systems is represented as a normalized ratio of cye3: cye5 and automatically color coded; thus, red color is conventionally selected to represent those genes that are transcriptionally upregulated in the test versus the reference, whereas green color represents genes that are downregulated; those genes that exhibit no difference between test and reference samples are shown in yellow. The analysis of the gene expression data obtained by such a high throughput microarray technology is quite complex and requires advanced computational/bioinformatics tools as already discussed in **Section 1.2**. Other aspects related to interactomics are discussed in **Section 3**. An alternative technology to cDNA microarrays is discussed in the next section.

2.2 Oligonucleotide arrays

By combining oligonucleotide synthesis with photolithography it was possible to synthesize specific oligonucleotides with a selected orientation onto the solid surface of glass or silicon chips (Lockhart *et al* 1996; Wodicka L, *et al* 1997), thus forming oligonucleotides arrays. The expression monitoring was then carried out by hybridization to high-density oligonucleotide arrays (Lockhart *et al* 1996; Wodicka L, *et al* 1997). Commercially available oligonucleotides array products include human, mouse and several other organisms. Each gene included on the oligonucleotides array is represented by up to 20 different oligonucleotides that span the entire length of the coding region of that gene. To reduce substantially the rate of false positives, each of these oligonucleotides is paired with a second mismatch oligonucleotide in which the central base in the sequence has been replaced by a different base. As in the cDNA approach, fluorescently labeled probes are generated from test and reference samples in order to carry out comparative gene expression profiling. After cDNA amplification, the differential fluorescent signal is detected with a laser scanning system and provides a map of the alterations in the transcriptional profile between the test and reference samples that are being compared. Dynamic analysis and further sophistication is added to such oligonucleotides array capabilities by the techniques briefly discussed in **Section 2.6.** The molecular classification of cancers is of immediate importance to both cancer diagnosis and therapy. Tumors with similar histologic appearance quite often have markedly different clinical response to therapy. Such variability is a reflection of the underlying cell line and molecular heterogeneity of almost any tumor. Gene expression profiling has been successfully employed for molecular classification of cancers. It would seem from available data that each patient has her/his own molecular identity signature or fingerprint (Mohr et al 2002). Thus, Ross *et al.* (2000) reported the gene expression analysis in 60 cancer cell lines utilized in the Developmental Therapeutics Program by the National Cancer Institute (NCI) at NIH (Bethesda, MD, USA); the report also stated that cell lines could be grouped together according with the organ type and specific expression profiles corresponded to *clusters of genes.* Similar findings were reported for ovarian and breast cancers; in the latter case, Perou *et al.* (2000) reported that specific epithelial cell line genes clustered together and are relevant in breast cancer subdivision into the basal- like and luminal groups. On the other hand, the eventual use of microarray technologies for clinical applications will involve the utilization of proteome and tissue arrays in addition to gene expression profiling by cDNA microarrays and oligonucleotides arrays. Thus, tissue markers revealed unexpected relationships, as in the case of gene expression analysis of small-cell lung carcinoma, pulmonary carcinoid tissue and bronchial epithelial tissue culture (Anbazhagan *et al* 1999). Because a single biomarker has serious limitations for clinical applications there is a need for a battery of disease biomarkers that would provide a much more accurate classification of cancers. High-density screening with microarray technologies is therefore valuable in pharmacogenomic (individualized therapy), toxicogenomic, as well as in clinical - diagnostic investigations.

2.3 Proteome arrays

In a manner similar to the transcriptome, the proteome does undergo both qualitative and quantitative changes during pathogenesis, and this is also true in carcinogenesis. Proteome array-based methodologies involve either proteins or protein-binding particles (DNA, RNAs, antibody, or other ligands). Utilizing such proteome arrays one can respectively study either differential protein expression profiling or protein-ligand interaction screening under specified, or selected, physiopathological conditions. According to Kodadek (2001), these two classes of practical applications of proteome arrays are respectively defined as protein function and protein-detecting arrays. A protein-detecting array may consist of an arrayed set of protein ligands that are employed to profile gene expression and therefore make visible 'proteosignatures' characterizing a selected cellular state or phase. In view of the potential clinical importance of a proteomic survey of cancers, the 'hunt' is now on for such proteosignatures of cancer cells but the amount of data reported to date is still quite limited. Already, the coupling of proteome arrays with high-resolution chromatography techniques followed by mass spectrometry has provided powerful analytical tools with which one can profile the protein expression in cancer cells. For example, a ProteinChip™ (Ciphergen Inc, Fremont, CA, USA) was successfully utilized to investigate the proteome of prostate, ovarian, head and neck cancer cells (von Eggeling et al 2000). Such methods identified protein fingerprints from which cancer biomarkers can also be obtained. A reverse proteome array was also reported in which many extracted proteins from a patient sample are 'printed' onto a flat, solid support (Paweletz et al 2001); this reverse system was then utilized to carry out a biochemical screening investigation of the signaling pathways in prostate cancer. Through such investigations it was found that the carcinoma progression was positively correlated with the phosphorylation state of Akt and negatively correlated with ERK pathways; furthermore, the carcinoma progression was positively correlated with the suppression of the apoptotic pathways, a finding which is consistent with the more detailed, recent reports on cyclin CDK2 and transcriptional factors affected by CDK2 that will be discussed in **Section 4.** Immunophentotyping of leukemias with antibody microarrays was also reported (Belov, de la Vega, dos Remedios, et al 2001), and does provide an increased antigen differentiation (CD) in leukemia processing.

2.4 Tissue arrays

The logical step after the identification of potential cancer markers through genomic and/or proteomic array analysis is the evaluation of such cancer markers by tissue arrays/ tissue chips for diagnostic, prognostic, toxicogenomic and therapeutic relevance. Such tissue microarrays (TMAs) were often designed to contain up to 1000 sections of 5micron thick sections, usually chemically--fixed and arrayed upon a glass slide. TMAs allow large-scale screening of tissue specimens and can be utilized, for example, for the pathological evaluation of molecular irreversible changes that are important for cancer research and treatment. Therefore, they can speed up the process of translating experimental, or fundamental, discoveries into clinical practice and improved cancer treatments.

TMAs have been utilized in cancer research in conjunction with **fluorescence** *in situ* **hybridization** (FISH), to analyze in parallel the gene amplification in multiple tissue sections thus allowing the researchers to map the distribution of gene amplification throughout an entire tumor. This also allowed the monitoring of changes in gene amplification during the cancer progression (Bubendorf et al 1999). Furthermore, utilizing immunohistochemical staining of tissue arrays it was possible to measure the protein levels in tumor specimens. Thus, topoisomerase II alpha was reported to be highly expressed in patients with the poorest prognosis in oligodendrogliomas (Miettinen et al 2000). TMAs may become a clinical validation, as well as a 'global' tool; thus, recent studies reported this technique to be highly efficient for the identification of molecular (irreversible) alterations during cancer initiation and progression (Lassus et al 2001). A pathologist might, however, object that the tissue microarray provides only a partial analysis of the tumor. The array-based technologies briefly described here provide powerful means for functional analyses of cancer and other complex diseases. Undoubtedly, much more can, and will be, done with proteome or tissue arrays combined with other state-of-the-science spectroscopic techniques as suggested in the following **Sections 2.5, 2.6, 4 and 6.2**.

The following three **Sections 2.5 and 2.6 and 6.2** will illustrate how advanced, ultra-fast and super-sensitive techniques can be used in conjunction with either nucleic acids or proteome arrays to both speed up thousand-fold the microarray data collection (for nucleic acids, proteins, ligand-binding, etc.) and also increase sensitivity to its possible limit--that of single molecule detection.

2.5 Fluorescence correlation spectroscopy and fluorescence cross—correlation spectroscopy: applications to DNA hybridization, PCR and DNA binding

In the bioanalytical and biochemical sciences Fluorescence Correlation Spectroscopy (FCS) techniques can be utilized to determine various thermodynamic and kinetic properties, such as association and dissociation constants of intermolecular reactions in solution (Thompson, 1991; Schwille, Bieschke and Oehlenschläger, 1997). Examples of this are specific hybridization and renaturation processes between complementary DNA or RNA strands, as well as antigene-antibody or receptor-ligand recognition. Although of significant functional relevance in biochemical systems, the hybridization mechanism of short oligonucleotide DNA primers to a native RNA target sequence could not be investigated in detail prior to the FCS/FCCS application to these problems. Most published models agree that the process can be divided into two steps: a reversible first initiating step, where few base pairs are formed, and a second irreversible phase described as a rapid zippering of the entire sequence. By competing with the internal binding mechanisms of the target molecule such as secondary structure formation, the rate-determining initial step is of crucial relevance for the entire binding process. Increased accessibility of binding sites, attributable to single-stranded open regions of the RNA structure at loops and bulges, can be quantified using kinetic measurements (Schwille, Oehlenschläger and Walter, 1996).

The measurement principle for nearly all FCS/FCCS applications is based so far upon the change in diffusion characteristics when a small labeled reaction partner (eg, a short nucleic acid probe) associates with a larger, unlabeled one (target DNA/RNA). The average diffusion time of the labeled molecules through the illuminated focal volume element is inversely related to the diffusion coefficient, and increases during the association process. By calibrating the diffusion characteristics of free and bound fluorescent partner, the binding fraction can be easily evaluated from the correlation curve for any time of the reaction. This principle has been employed to investigate and compare the hybridization efficiency of six labeled DNA oligonucleotides with different binding sites to an RNA target in a native secondary structure (Schwille, Oehlenschläger and Walter, 1996). Hybridization kinetics was examined by binding six fluorescently labeled oligonucleotide probes of different sequence, length and binding sites to a 101-nucleotide-long native RNA target sequence with a known secondary structure. The hybridization kinetics was monitored and quantified by FCS, in order to investigate the overall reaction mechanism. At the measurement temperature of 40°C the probes are mostly denatured, whereas the target retains its native structure. The binding process could be directly monitored through diffusional FCS analysis, via the change in translational diffusion time of the labeled 17-mer to 37-mer oligonucleotide probes HS1 to HS6 upon specific hybridization with the larger RNA target. The characteristic diffusion time through the laser-illuminated focal spot of the 0.5 µm-diameter objective increased from 0.13 to 0.20 ms for the free probe, and from 0.37 to 0.50 ms for the bound probe within 60 min. The increase in diffusion time from measurement to measurement over the 60 min could be followed on a PC monitor and varied strongly from probe to probe. HS6 showed the fastest association, while the reaction of HS2 could not be detected at all for the first 60 min. Thus, FCS diffusional analysis provides an easy and comparably fast determination of the hybridization time course of reactions between complementary DNA/RNA strands in the concentration range from 10^{-10} to 10^{-8} M. The FCS-based methodology also permits rapid screening for suitable anti-sense nucleic acids directed against important targets like HIV-1 RNA with low consumption of probes and target. Because of the high sensitivity of FCS detection, the same principle can be exploited to simplify the diagnostics for extremely low concentrations of infectious agents like bacterial or viral DNA/RNA. By combining confocal FCS with biochemical amplification reactions like PCR or 3SR, the detection threshold of infectious RNA in human sera could be dropped to concentrations of 10^{-18} M (Walter, Schwille and Eigen, 1996; Oehlenschläger, Schwille and Eigen, 1996). The method allows for simple quantification of initial infectious units in the observed samples. The isothermal Nucleic Acid Sequence-Based Amplification (NASBA) technique enables the detection of HIV-1 RNA in human blood-plasma (Winkler, Bieschke and Schwille, 1997). The threshold of detection is presently down to 100 initial RNA molecules per milliliter by amplifying a short sequence of the RNA template (Schwille, Oehlenschläger and Walter, 1997). The NASBA method was combined with FCS, thus allowing the online detection of the HIV-1 RNA molecules amplified by NASBA (Oehlenschläger, Schwille and Eigen, 1996). The combination of FCS with the NASBA reaction was performed by introducing a fluorescently labeled DNA probe into the NASBA reaction mixture *at nanomolar concentrations*, hybridizing to a distinct sequence of the amplified RNA molecule. After having reached a critical concentration on the order of 0.1 to 1.0 nM (the threshold for single-photon excitation / FCS detection is ~0.1 nm), the number of amplified RNA molecules could be determined as the reaction continued its course. Evaluation of the hybridization/extension kinetics allowed an estimation of the initial HIV-1 RNA concentration present at the beginning of amplification. The value of the initial HIV-1 RNA number enables discrimination between positive and false-positive samples (caused, for instance, by carryover contamination). This possibility of sharp discrimination is essential for all diagnostic methods using amplification systems (PCR as well as NASBA). The quantification of HIV-1 RNA in plasma by combining NASBA with FCS may be useful in assessing the efficacy of anti-HIV agents, especially in the early infection stage when standard ELISA antibody tests often display negative results. Furthermore, the combination of NASBA with FCS is not restricted only to the detection of HIV-1 RNA in plasma.

On the one hand, the diagnosis of Hepatitis (both B and C) remains much more challenging. On the other hand, the number of HIV, or HBV, infected subjects worldwide is increasing at an alarming rate, with up to 20% of the population in parts of Africa and Asia being infected with HBV. In contrast to HIV, HBV infection is not particularly restricted to the high-risk groups.

Multi-photon (MPE) NIR excitation of fluorophores--attached as labels to biopolymers like proteins and nucleic acids, or bound at specific biomembrane sites-- is one of the most attractive options in biological applications of FCS. Many of the serious problems encountered in spectroscopic measurements of living tissue, such as photodamage, light scattering and auto-fluorescence, can be reduced or even eliminated. FCS can therefore provide accurate *in vivo* and *in vitro* measurements of diffusion rates, "mobility" parameters, molecular concentrations, chemical kinetics, aggregation processes, labeled nucleic acid hybridization kinetics and fluorescence photophysics/ photochemistry. Several photophysical properties of fluorophores that are required for quantitative analysis of FCS in tissues have already been widely reported. Molecular "mobilities" can be measured by FCS over a wide range of characteristic time constants from $\sim10^{-3}$ to 10^3 ms.

Novel, two-photon NIR excitation fluorescence correlation spectroscopy tests and preliminary results were obtained for concentrated suspensions of live cells and membranes (Baianu et al, 2007). Especially promising are further developments employing multi-photon NIR excitation that could lead, for example, to the reliable detection of cancers using NIR-excited fluorescence. Other related developments are the applications of Fluorescence Cross-Correlation Spectroscopy (FCCS) detection to monitoring *DNA- telomerase interactions*, DNA hybridization kinetics, ligand-receptor interactions and HIV-HBV testing. Very detailed, automated chemical analyses of biomolecules in cell cultures are now also becoming possible by FT-NIR spectroscopy of single cells, both *in vitro* and *in vivo*. Such rapid analyses have potentially important applications in cancer research, pharmacology and clinical diagnosis.

2.6 Near infrared microspectroscopy, fluorescence microspectroscopy and infrared chemical imaging of single cells

Novel methodologies are currently being evaluated for the chemical analysis of embryos and single cells by Fourier Transform Infrared (FT-IR), Fourier Transform Near Infrared (FT-NIR) Microspectroscopy, Fluorescence Microspectroscopy. The first FT-NIR chemical images of biological systems approaching 1micron (1µm) resolution were reported (Baianu, 2004; Baianu et al 2004), and FT-NIR spectra of oil and proteins were obtained under physiological conditions for volumes as small as $2\mu m^3$. Related, HR-NMR analyses of oil contents in somatic embryos were presented with nanoliter precision. Therefore, developmental changes may be monitored by FT-NIR with a precision approaching the *picogram* level when adequately calibrated by a suitable primary analytical method.

Indeed, detailed chemical analyses are now becoming possible by FT-NIR Chemical Imaging and Microspectroscopy of single cells. The cost, speed and analytical requirements are fully satisfied by FT-NIR spectroscopy and microspectroscopy for a wide range of biological specimens. These techniques were also suggested to be potentially important in functional genomics and proteomics research (Baianu et al 2004) through the rapid and accurate detection of high-content microarrays (HCMA). Multi-photon (MP), pulsed femtosecond laser NIR Fluorescence Excitation techniques were shown to be capable of *single molecule detection* (SMD). Thus, microspectroscopic techniques allow for most sensitive and reliable quantitative analyses to be carried out both *in vitro* and *in vivo*. In particular, MP NIR excitation in FCS allows not only *single molecule detection*, but also non-invasive monitoring of molecular dynamics and the acquisition of high-resolution, *submicron* imaging of *femtoliter* volumes inside functional cells and tissues. Such ultra-sensitive and rapid NIR-FCS analyses have therefore numerous potential applications in biomedical research areas, clinical diagnosis of viral diseases, cancers and also in cancer therapy.

3. Mapping interactome networks

Mapping protein-protein interaction networks, or charting the global interaction maps, that correspond through translation to entire genomes is undoubtedly useful for understanding cellular functions, especially when such databases can be integrated into a wide collection of biologically relevant data. A prerequisite for any *'ab initio'* determination of a selected protein interactome network is to clone the open reading frames (ORFs) that encode each protein present in the selected network. Note, however, that all current analyses involve the assumption of a *model* together with some 'hidden', or implicit, *assumptions* about sampling, 'noise' levels, or uniformity/ accuracy in the database, and therefore, the *'ab initio'* claim is subject to the restrictions imposed by such additional assumptions. More than 20,000 of publicly accessible, full ORF clones have been already collected for human and mouse protein-coding genes in the Mammalian Genome Collection (MGC; http://mgc.nci.nih.gov). This community resource enables the next stages of human interactome analysis that will be directed at obtaining a reliable map of the entire human protein interactome. An additional, 12,500 ORFs are now available from the Dana Farber Cancer Institute in Boston (USA) from high-throughput, yeast two-hybrid (Y2H) analyses. A disconcerting aspect of the latest human (partial) interactome studies by different methods is the little apparent overlap of the new human interaction datasets with each other and/or with previously reported data. This aspect will be further addressed later in this section; the principal cause for the lack of overlap is likely to be caused by the low (<20%) overall coverage of the protein-protein interactions selected in such studies. A possible solution to this problem has been suggested (Warner et al 2006): several groups cooperating to produce 'networks of networks', constructed from separate—but coordinated—interaction mapping projects, 'each of which would target a specific functionality related subset of proteins and interactions'. A more effective solution would be, however, to increase the throughput, accuracy and reliability of PPI data through improved technologies (such as FCCS, or other techniques already proposed in Section 2.5, for example), reduce significantly the cost of such analyses, as well as improve the models employed for data analysis. Examples of improved modeling tools for this purpose, such as logical, ontological genetics and categorical ones, that are also appropriate for assembling the *'networks of networks...'* as in the previous approach suggested by Warner et al. (2006), were presented above in Section 1, and are described in further detail in a recent report (Baianu et al 2006) and also in two forthcoming publications (Baianu and Poli, 2011; Baianu et al 2010). Interactome network studies are currently undertaken by a number of international research teams in the US, Europe and Japan (CSH/WT, 2006; Warner et al 2006). These studies are currently undertaken only for interactome subnetworks because of both technique and funding limitations. The organisms studied were: yeast (*Saccharomyces cerevisiae*), worm (*Caenorhabditis elegans*), fruitfly (*Drosophila melanogaster*) and humans. Proteome networks were investigated for several, specific, biological processes such as: DNA degradation, ubiquitin conjugation, multivesicular formation, intracellular membrane traffick, signal transduction/ TNF☐ tumor necrosis and NF☐B mediated pathways, and early stages of T-cell signaling (for a brief summary note the recent review by Warner *et al* 2006, and references cited therein). Such challenging studies face both methodological problems such as limited sampling (Han *et al* 2006) and consideration of only pairwise ('binary') protein-protein interactions, and also the more serious technical problem of false-positive interactions in the presence of a significant 'noise' levels associated with the experimental technologies and design currently employed in such studies. Such limitations should be borne in mind (Han et al 2006) when global topology predictions are made for the whole interactome based on partial, incomplete data obtained for subnetworks that may contain less than 20% of the entire interactome network. On a more optimistic note are the recent attempts at comparing the cancer protein, human interactome (sub) networks with normal human interactome networks that involve multiple protein-protein interactions (Jonsson and Bates, 2006). The latter studies reduced the 'noise' level in the human protein interaction data by employing an orthology-based method described previously by Jonsson et al. (2006). This method claims to reduce the 'noise' level in protein-interaction (PPI) data by identifying putative interactions based on homology to experimentally determined interactions in a range of different species; both the DIP (Salwinsky et al 2004) and the MIPS, Mammalian Protein — Protein Interaction (Pagel et al 2005) databases were utilized. Furthermore, the complete interactome data set that was employed is available as Supplementary Material from *loc. cit.* The conclusions was drawn that cancer proteins have an increased frequency of protein-protein interactions in comparison with the proteins that were studied in normal cells, and this was interpreted as evidence *"indicating an underlying evolutionary pressure to which cancer genes, as genes of central importance are subjected."* It remains to be seen, however, if human interactome studies-- which occur with increasing frequency-- have indeed overcome the sampling objections raised by Han et al. (2006). The more extensive interactome data and analysis — though still quite limited- that has been reported to date is readily available and includes the following: Y2H (partial data-based) interactome maps for *C. elegans* (Li et al 2004) and *Drosophila melanogaster* (Giot et al 2003; Formstecher et al 2005), and also proteome maps obtained by co-affinity purification followed by mass spectrometry analysis in yeast-*Saccharomyces cerevisiae* (co-AP/MS: Gavin et al 2002; Ho et al 2002; Han et al 2004). The reports on the microbial transcriptional regulation network of *Escherichia coli* (Shen-Orr et al 2002) and on *Helicobacter pylori* protein complexes in the proteome map (Terradot et al 2004) are also worthile mentioning in this context. A first-draft of the human interactome has also been reported (Lehner and Fraser, 2004); although this human interactome map does not seem to have been included in the computational investigations of Han et al. (2006), it remains to be verified, or validated, by further extensive studies with improved technology and adequate models for a more comprehensive data analysis. The comprehensive two-hybrid analysis for exploring the protein interactome network was previously reported by Ito et al. (2001). Alternative interaction mapping strategies have also been developed over the last five years. An example is the tandem affinity purification (TAP) in conjunction with liquid chromatography tandem mass spectrometry (LC-MS/MS; see, for example, Gavin et al 2006). Such methods have, however, both advantages and limitations. An interesting, new approach to the determination of protein complexes has been developed that involves a combination of fluorescence spectroscopy with peptide microarrays (Stoevesandt, *cited in* Warner 2006); this methodology was then applied to investigate T-cell signaling.

4. Cell cyclins expression and modular cancer interactome networks

Carcinogenesis is a complex process that involves dynamically inter-connected biomolecules in the intercellular, membrane, cytosolic, nuclear and nucleolar compartments that form numerous inter-related pathways referred to as networks. One such family of pathways contains the cell cyclins. Cyclins are often overexpressed in cancerous cells (Dobashi et al 2004).

Our novel theoretical analysis based on recently published studies of cyclin signaling, with special emphasis placed on the roles of cyclins D1 and E, suggests novel clinical trials and rational therapies of cancer through re-establishment of cell cycling inhibition in metastatic cancer cells.

4.1 Cyclins

Cyclins are proteins that link several critical pro-apoptotic and other cell cycling/division components, including the tumor suppressor gene TP53 and its product, the Thomsen-Friedenreich antigen (T antigen), Rb, mdm2, c-Myc, p21, p27, Bax), which all play major roles in carcinogenesis of many cancers. Cyclin-dependent kinases (CDK), their respective cyclins, and inhibitors of CDKs (CKIs) were identified as instrumental components of the cell cycle-regulating machinery. CDKs are enzymes that phosphorylate several cellular proteins thus 'fueling' the sequential transitions through the cell division cycle. In mammalian cells the complexes of cyclins D1, D2, D3, A and E with CDKs are considered motors that drive cells to enter and pass through the "S" phase. Cell cycle regulation is a critical mechanism governing cell division and proliferation, and is finely regulated by the interaction of cyclins with CDKs and CKIs, among other molecules (Morgan et al 1995).

It was also reported that CDKs have another key role –the coordination of cell cycle progression with responses to possible DNA-damage that could, if unchecked or unfixed, lead to a lack of genomic integrity marking the onset of cell disease including cancers (Huang et al 2006 in *Science*). The S-phase is thought to be the most vulnerable interval of the cell cycle because during this interval all of 3 billion DNA bases of the human genome must be replicated precisely in the sense of 'carbon copies' being made of the existing DNA strands, without any breaks in the sequence or base substitutions of the copied/replicated strands. Therefore, this correct replication process controls the cell's survival, especially under genotoxic conditions such as those caused for example by mutagens or X-ray and gamma-radiation. Furthermore, Huang et al. (2006) reported that CDK mediated the phosphorylation of the FOXO1 transcriptional activator of the proapoptotic genes during the S-phase; when DNA damage occurs either before or during the S-phase, a complex network is activated in the cell which 'silences' CDK thereby either delaying or stopping/arresting the cell cycle progression. This may allow the cell to repair the DNA damage by recombination involving BRCA2 and survive. However, if this is not possible because the DNA damage was too great/irreparable, then FOXO1 would trigger apoptosis (cell death). It was proposed that during the unperturbed (normal) S-phase CDK2 phosphorylates FOXO1 at the Serine[249] residue in the cell nucleus, which then results in the transfer and sequestering of the FOXO1 in the cytoplasm, where it is well--separated from the proapoptotic genes, the 'target' of FOXO1 action.

Moreover, the CDK-mediated phosphorylation of BRCA2 during the unperturbed S-phase renders inactive the DNA recombination. On the other hand, when DNA becomes damaged, CDK2 is inhibited through the Cdc25A pathway, with the consequence of a dephosphorylated FOXO1 which then remains in the cell nucleus and is able to activate the proapoptotic genes, unless BRCA2 is able to induce DNA recombination and repair in time to prevent apoptosis. The steps that follow are then as explained above: either DNA repair and continued cell cycling, or apoptosis induced by FOXO1. There are still several important questions regarding the entire process that need to be answered before the FOXO1 and CDK2 mechanisms of action can be translated into successful clinical trials based on such knowledge.

A positive correlation has been noticed between over-expression of several cell--cycle proteins and unfavorable prognoses and outcomes in several different cancer types (van Diest et al 1995; Fukuse et al 2000). In human lung tumors and soft tissue sarcomas, it was discovered that cyclin A/cdk2 complex expression and kinase activity were reliable predictors of proliferation and unfavorable prognosis, thereby further substantiating the epidemiological factors of cyclin signaling (Dobashi et al 2003; Noguchi et al 2000).

present in the contig : NT_078088 **of Genbank**

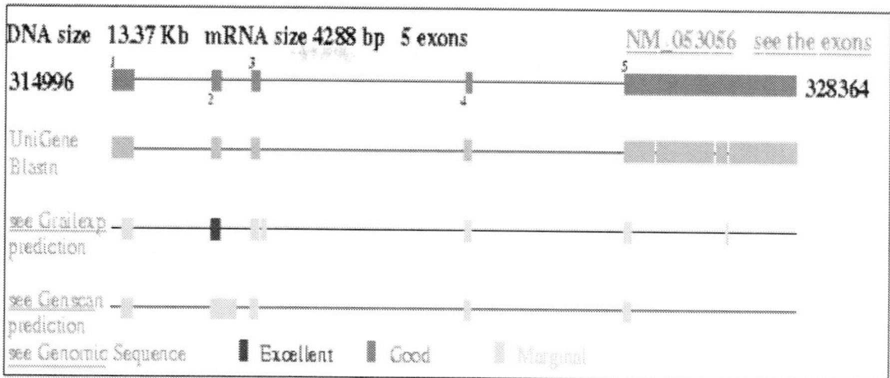

Fig. 1. Gene database of Cyclin-D1; *Source:* PBD website:
http://www.dsi.univ-paris5.fr/genatlas/fiche.php?symbol=CCND1

4.2 The p27 and p21 proteins
The proteins p27 and p21 were reported to be implicated in cyclin regulation and cancer development (**Fig. 2**). Mouse embryonic fibroblasts that were deficient for p27 and p21 were found to contain less cyclin D1 (Hashemolhosseini S, Nagamine Y, Morley SJ, et al., 1998). and D2 (Cheng et al 1999) as well as cyclin D3 (Bagui et al 2000) than controls. Similarly, mammary glands of p27-deficient mice were shown to possess decreased cyclin D1 levels (Muraoka et al 2001). It has been demonstrated *in vivo* that p27 is necessary for maintaining proper levels of cyclins D2 and D3, and this dependency on p27 is common to a wide variety of cells/tissues *in vivo*. Regarding the molecular interaction between p27 and D-cyclin, CDK4 is a clear candidate as a mediating molecule (Bryja et al 2004). Cells employ CDK4/6– cyclin D complexes to flexibly titrate p27 from the complexes containing CDK2, and thereby they control their proliferation. However, mutual dependency between cyclin D and p27 serves also some yet unidentified function in differentiation-related processes. Thus, loss of p27 not only causes unrestricted growth due to inefficient inhibition of CDK2–cyclin E/A, but may also elicit a decrease in levels of D-type cyclins, resulting in differentiation defects. Upon ablation of cyclin D, cells lose their ability to titrate p27 from CDK2–cyclin A/E complexes and proliferation is suppressed. However, defects in differentiation caused by the absence of D-cyclin are reminiscent to defects produced by the absence of p27 (Bryja et al 2004). When the changes in levels of p27 and/or D-type cyclins occur, an equilibrium alteration could result between proliferation/differentiation processes that may in the end result in tumorigenesis (Bryja et al 2004).

4.3 D1 vs. E- cyclins
The D-type and E-type cyclins control the G1 → S phase transition during normal cell cycling and are important components of steroid- and growth factor-induced mitogenesis in breast epithelial cells (Sutherland and Musgrove, 2004). Cyclin D1 null mice are resistant to breast cancer that is induced by the *neu* and *ras* oncogenes, which suggests a pivotal role for

cyclin D1 in the development of some mammary carcinomas (Sutherland and Musgrove, 2004). Cyclin D1 and E1 are usually overexpressed in breast cancer, with some association with adverse outcomes, which is likely due in part to their ability to confer resistance to endocrine therapies. The consequences of cyclin E overexpression in breast cancer are related to cyclin E's role in cell cycle progression, and that of cyclin D1 may also be a consequence of a role in transcriptional regulation (Sutherland and Musgrove, 2004). One critical pathway determining cell cycle transition rates of $G1 \rightarrow S$ phase is the cyclin/cyclin-dependent kinase (Cdk)/ p16Ink4A/ retinoblastoma protein (pRb) pathway (Sutherland and Musgrove, 2004). Alterations of different components of this particular pathway are very ubiquitous in human cancer (Malumbres and Barbacid, 2001). There appears to be a certain degree of tissue specificity in the genetic abnormalities within the Rb pathway. A model relating Rb to cyclin control in the overall scheme of pro-apoptotic behavior is shown in **Fig. 2.**

In breast cancer these abnormalities include the over-expression of cyclins D1, D3 and E1, the decreased expression of the p27Kip1 CKI and p16Ink4A gene silencing through promoter methylation. These aberrations occur with high frequency in breast cancer, as each abnormality occurs in ~40% of primary tumors. This fact implicates a major role for the loss of function of the Rb pathway in breast cancer. Cyclin D1 is the product of the *CCND1* gene and was first connected to breast cancer after localization of the gene to chromosome 11q13, a region commonly amplified in several human carcinomas, including ~15% of breast cancers (Ormandy et al 2003). The fact that cyclin D1 was overexpressed at the mRNA and protein levels in 50% of primary breast cancers have caused cyclin D1 to be considered one of the most commonly over-expressed breast cancer oncogenes (Gillett et al 1994). Although cyclin E1 locus amplification is rare in breast cancer, the protein product is overexpressed in over 40% of breast carcinomas (Loden et al 2002). Cyclin D1 is pre-dominantly overexpressed in ERC tumors, and cyclin E overexpression is confined to ER¡ tumors (Gillett et al 1994; Loden et al 2002). The overexpression of several cell cycle regulators has been strongly associated with apoptotic-like behavior, as well as frank apoptosis, in cancer cells, which include c-Myc, E2F-1 and HPV. Apoptosis and its connection to cell cycle-related proteins is of interest therapeutically, as these types therapies could ultimately lead to the cancer cell annihilation *via* apoptosis. Recently, a shift has occurred, changing the focus of chemotherapy from exploration of agents that cause cell growth arrest to those that favor apoptosis.

5. Biomedical applications of microarrays in clinical trials

5.1 Microarray applications to gene expression: identifying signaling pathways

Changes in homeostasis can be followed through various experimental strategies that monitor gene expression profiling, for example, by employing high-throughput microarray technology. This section discusses briefly the successful use of microarray technology in RNA expression studies aimed at identifying signaling pathways that are regulated by key genes implicated in carcinogenesis/ tumorigenesis. A primary objective of tumor-profiling experiments is to identify transcriptional changes that may be the cause of the transition from the normal to the tumor phenotype. Such changes may, however, occur also as a consequence of various neoplastic transformation(s). More importantly, this approach may allow the identification of molecular fingerprints that can be utilized for the classification of different tumor types, and are therefore valuable diagnostic molecular tools in cancer

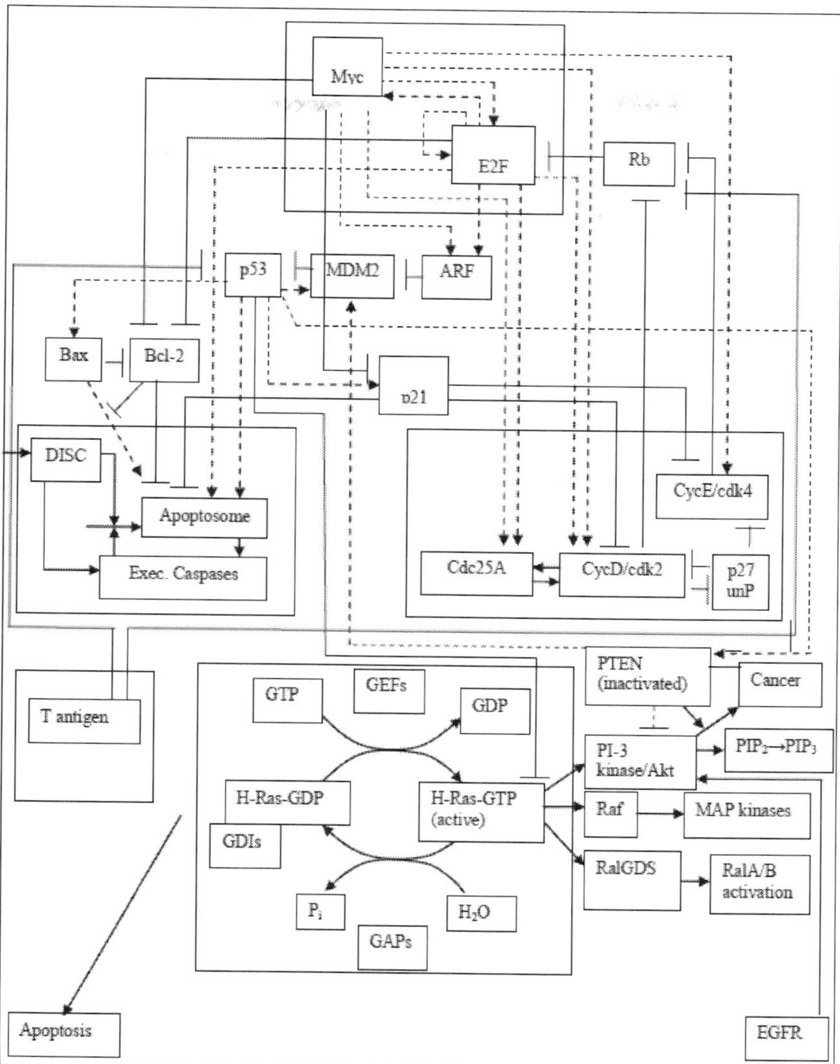

Fig. 2. Pro-Apoptotic Cancer Cycling Model: an update based on the previous model of Aguda et al. (2003).

patients. For example, Alizadeh et al. (2000) have successfully used such an approach to identify molecularly distinct subclasses of diffuse large B-cell lymphoma that could not be distinguished by conventional diagnostic tools. In another study, a molecular fingerprint comprising approximately 50 genes has been isolated from a total of over 6,000, and this fingerprint can reliably differentiate between acute myeloid leukemia and acute lymphoblastic leukemia Golub et al (1999).

5.1.1 Identification of specific transcriptional targets in cancer

The approach requires, however, multiple independent experiments with several large groups of samples in order to enable one to reliably and reproducibly separate the biologically relevant changes from false ones that may occur as a result of the genetic heterogeneity between individual samples from the same tumor, for example. The two examples quoted above were able to reproducibly identify tumor type-specific molecular determinants through multiple experiments with various tissue samples.

A different experimental approach to the one presented above is, however, needed for identifying specific targets such as defined genes that are implicated in cancer progression; this involves monitoring changes in transcriptional profile that occur as a result of modulation of the expression level of the defined gene, or genes, selected for such studies. The altered expression profile can be viewed as a 'blueprint' by which the defined gene controls its cellular function. The transcriptional profiles are thus employed to define *downstream signaling pathways* that have been previously validated through other techniques such as differential display Tanaka et al (2000) and serial analysis of gene expression Yu et al. (1999). This approach combined with microarray technology allows the simultaneous identification of all potential targets. Its only drawback is the reliance upon the prior knowledge of the selected genome for such investigations. The caveat is, however, that the investigator who employs this approach needs also to devise additional experiments in order to confirm that genes identified with the microarray are indeed *physiologically relevant* targets.

5.1.2 Identification of downstream transcriptional targets of the BRCA1 tumor-suppressor gene

The breast and ovarian cancer susceptibility gene BRCA1 is probably the most studied gene in the breast cancer field because of its clinical significance and multiple functions. BRCA1 was shown to be mutated in the germ line of women with a genetic predisposition to either breast or ovarian cancer Mikki et al (1994). Most mutations identified reported have resulted in the premature truncation of the BRCA1 protein. BRCA1 is known to encode a 1863 amino acid phosphoprotein that is predominantly localized to the nucleus, presumably with a unique function. Protein sequence analysis identified a C-terminal BRCT motif, which was then postulated to play a role in cell cycle checkpoint control in response to DNA damage Koonin EV, Altschul and Bork (1996). Consistent with this postulated role, BRCA1 becomes hyperphosphorylated in response to various agents that damage DNA such as γ/X--ray-irradiation, an effect that was reported to be partially mediated by chk2 kinases (Lee et al. 2000). Furthermore, BRCA1 has been shown to be implicated in at least three functional pathways:

- Mediating the cellular response to DNA damage,
- Acting as a cell cycle checkpoint protein, and
- Functioning in the regulation of transcription.

However, the physiological significance of such BRCA1 actions as well as their relationships with the function of BRCA1 as a tumor-suppressor gene still remain to be defined. Further details are presented next.

The BRCA1-BARD1 ubiquitin ligase

As shown above the BRCA1 gene encodes a 1863-amino-acid protein (Miki et al 1994) which consists of a RING-finger domain in its terminal N-region, a region that includes a nuclear localization signal and a domain that binds to many cellular proteins, and tandem BRCT domains in its C-terminal region. BRCA1 is associated with a diverse range of biological processes, such as DNA repair, cell cycle control, transcriptional regulation, apoptosis and centrosome duplication. Thus, a specific role has already been postulated for BRCA1 in transcriptional regulation. The C-terminal domain of BRCA1 was reported to contain a potent transactivation domain when this was fused to a heterologous DNA binding motif (Monteiro, August and Hanafusa, 1996). The oligonucleotide array-based expression profiling described above in Section 2.2 was employed by Haber (2000) in collaboration with Affymetrix Co. to identify the downstream transcriptional targets of the BRCA1 tumor-suppressor gene in order to define its function (Harkin et al 1999). A known biochemical function of BRCA1 is its E3 ubiquitin ligase activity. The following reported observations provide only indirect, additional clues to the tumor-suppressor gene function of BRCA1. Germ line mutations of BRCA1 were reported for half of breast-ovarian cancer pedigrees and for approximately 10% of women with early onset of breast cancer, uncorrelated with their family history (Fitzgerald et al 1996). It was also shown in other studies that somatic inactivation of BRCA1 is rare in sporadic breast cancers (Futreal P, Liu Q, Shattuck-Eidens D et al., 1994) and mutations were reported for approximately 10% of sporadic ovarian cancers, therefore suggesting potentially distinct genetic mechanisms for sporadic, breast and ovarian cancers (Berchuk et al 1998). The reduced BRCA1 protein expression reported for the majority of sporadic breast cancers indicates that *epigenetic mechanisms* such as those described in **Section 6** was suggested to play a significant role in regulating the BRCA1 expression (Wilson et al 1999). Furthermore, a defect was reported in the transcription-coupled repair of oxidative-induced DNA damage in mouse embryo fibroblasts with attenuated BRCA1 function (Gowen et al 1998); this observation would suggest that BRCA1 plays a more general role in mediating the cellular response to DNA damage. Thus, BRCA1 has also been reported to be involved in cell cycle checkpoint control, by becoming hyperphosphorylated during late G_1 and S cell phases, and then changing to transiently dephosphorylated early after the M phase (Ruffner and Verma, 1997). Moreover, the BRCA1 overexpression has been reported to induce a G_1/S arrest in human colon cancer cells (Somasundaram et al, 1997). By comparison with the cancer regulation model in **Figure 2**, it seems very significant for oncogenesis that BRCA1 is *physically associated* with the transcriptional regulators *p*53 (Ouichi et al 1998), CtIP (Yu et al 1998), c-Myc (Wang et al 1998), as well as the histone deacetylases HDAC1 and HDAC2 (Yarden and Brody 1999). The physical association of BRCA1 with c-Myc acquires special significance as c-Myc seems to be involved in controlling telomerase activity, whereas p53 is involved in DNA-repair, cell-cycling and apoptosis. Therefore, in the simplified model presented in Figure 3, one should add the BRCA1 links to both p53 and c-Myc in order to facilitate an understanding of the BRCA1 possible roles in oncogenesis.

5.1.3 Selecting gene expression systems

There are several related problems in studying gene function by expression profiling. For example, it has been often reported to be difficult to generate cell lines that overexpress genes such as BRCA1, or p53, because their forced overexpression can lead either to growth suppression or apoptosis (as shown for example in Figure 3, and at the end of the previous section). However, in the case of BRCA1, it was reported that the *tet-off* inducible expression system (Gossen and Bujard 1992) can be utilized to generate cell lines with highly regulated inducible expression of BRCA1 (Harkin et al, 1999). This inducible expression system introduces into the cells a chimeric transactivator; the latter consists in the *tet* repressor fused to the VP16 transactivation domain. This chimeric transactivator is inactive in the presence of tetracycline, whereas in the absence of tetracycline it can bind to promoters that contain the *tet* operator sequence; the latter sequence is then utilized to drive the expression of BRCA1. This expression system has a major advantage in that it allows the change in just one parameter involved in the induction of BRCA1. The BRCA1 induction in one population is the only difference between the genetic backgrounds of the two populations that are being compared by oligonucleotides arrays. A number of BRCA1 transcriptional targets can thus be identified with Affymetrix oligonucleotides arrays, and among these, the stress and DNA damage-inducible gene *GADD45* was the gene that exhibited the greatest degree of differential signal intensity (Harkin et al, 1999). The specific target genes thus identified were also verified by Northern blot or quantitative reverse transcriptase-PCR analysis in order to confirm induction in response to the stimulus, that is, the induction of BRCA1 (Harkin et al, 1999). Total RNA was extracted from cells in which the exogenous BRCA1 was either switched off (+ *tet*) or switched on (– *tet*). Fluorescent images were generated using the Affymetrix human cancer G110 array containing approximately 1,700 genes that were previously reported to be implicated in cancer; such fluorescent images were then scanned and analyzed. Two lanes were present in such images that corresponded to individual arrays hybridized with biotinylated cRNA probes and were generated from cells in which exogenous BRCA1 was either induced (+ *tet*) or repressed (- *tet*). Each gene on the array was represented by 16 probe pairs, one being wild-type and one containing a mismatch at the central nucleotide. In such fluorescent images, two genes, GADD45 and ATF3 were identified (and confirmed by Northern blot analysis) as being the *transcriptional targets of the BRCA1 tumor-suppressor gene*. Furthermore, in this BRCA1 study, the induction of GADD45 by BRCA1 was reported to be correlated with the BRCA1-mediated activation of the c-jun *N*-terminal kinase/stress-activated protein kinase JNK/SAPK pathway. Significantly, the activation of JNK/SAPK was then shown to be required for the BRCA1-mediated apoptotic cell death in this cell line system. This finding suggests an interesting model for the BRCA1-mediated apoptosis, as presented in some detail by Harkin et al (1999). Most significantly, the experimental approach reported by Harkin et al (1999) was indeed able to define *physiologically relevant* target genes. In another recent report, Yu et al (2001) utilized a modified version of the *tet-off* inducible expression system to define the downstream transcriptional targets of the *p*53 tumor--suppressor gene (Yu et al 1999). A total of 34 genes were identified that exhibited at least a 10-fold upregulation in response to the inducible expression of *p*53. Somewhat surprisingly, there was a marked heterogeneity of the response when it was evaluated in different cell lines derived from the same tissue of origin. Among the 33 genes studied only nine were found to be induced in a panel of five unrelated colorectal cell lines, and 17 were induced in a subset; eight were not induced at all in any of the five cell lines examined. This can be interpreted as being due to a high degree of cell type specificity. Furthermore, *p*53 was not absolutely required for induction -- for the majority of the genes identified-- in response to either adriamycin or 5-FU. Therefore, these agents do not seem to act exclusively through *p*53, suggesting that there is inherent redundancy in the majority of signaling pathways. Such inherent redundancy in signaling pathways of cancer, and untransformed, cells might be important in understanding the results of clinical trials in cancer treatment with signal transduction modulators that will be discussed in the next subsection **(5.2).**

5.2 Clinical trials with signal transduction inhibitors -- novel anticancer drugs active in chemo-resistant tumors

Recently, there is an increasing number of reports suggesting that human cancers frequently involve pathogenic mechanisms which give rise to numerous alterations in signal transduction pathways. Therefore, novel therapeutic agents that target specific signal transduction molecules or signaling pathways altered in cancer are currently undergoing clinical trials often with remarkable results in cancer treatments of patients in which chemo- and/or radio- therapy resistant tumors have become apparent. For example, several new classes of such anti-cancer drugs are:

- tyrosine/threonine kinase inhibitors, including: STI-571 ('Gleevec', or Imatinib Mesylate), ZD-1839 ('Iressa'), OSI-774, and flavopiridol, which are ATP-site antagonists and have recently completed phase I and phase II trials (see for example, Liu et al, 1999);
- several other kinase antagonists that are currently undergoing clinical evaluations, including UCN-01 and PD184352;
- other strategies for downmodulating kinase-driven signaling include 17-allyl- amino-17 demethoxygeldanamycin and rapamycin derivatives. Phospholipase-directed signaling may also be modulated by alkylphospholipids.
- Farnesyltransferase inhibitors, originally developed as inhibitors of *ras*-driven signals, may attain activity by affecting other/or additional targets (see for example, Zujewski, Horak, Bol, et al., 2000; End, Smets, Todd, et al., 2001).
- monoclonal antibodies Herceptin and C225.

Signal transduction is an efficient method for fine-tuning the development and modeling of cancer treatments (Ideker at al., 2001, 2002). There is also a detailed NCI report on clinical trial and signal transduction modulators as novel anticancer (Sausville, Elsayed, Monga and Kim, 2003).

5.3 Interactome-transcriptome analysis and differential gene expression in cancer

It has been claimed that high-throughput yeast-two-hybrid (HT-Y2H) methods will allow a systematic approach to functional genomics, by placing individual genes in the global context of cellular functions (Mendelsohn and Brent, 1999). One finds that high-throughput screening methods such as HT-Y2H have indeed allowed the mapping of the first interactomes for three eukaryotes (Giot et al 2003; Li et al 2004; Uetz et al 2000). Because of the human interactome's much larger size and its very high-degree of complexity there will be quite high costs and labor involved in obtaining the data necessary, for example, for an HT-Y2H mapping of a complete human cell interactome. Furthermore, the complete data analysis together with the assembly of the complete interactome network is likely to require both conceptual and computational advances, in addition to a significant amount of time and collective effort(s) by one or several research teams. In view of the high, potential importance of the human interactome for cancer therapy, and also for improved diagnosis and 'rational' clinical trials, such an effort should now be a top priority. Such an effort should also be coordinated with an improved mapping of the complete yeast interactome as a model, or test, system. Meantime, there have been since 2005 a few reports of 'surrogate', or partial, human cancer cell interactomes in the form of predicted maps of human protein interaction networks based on partial data and comparative analysis. Such studies emphasize even further the need and urgency for the complete mapping of several human cancer cell interactomes. Following the seminal studies of DeRisi et al (1996) that utilized cDNA microarray to analize gene expression patterns in human cancer, there have been relatively few attempts at deriving hypothetical gene expression patterns in human cancer. The first claim of such an attempt was recently made by Wachi, Yoneda and Wu (2005) for genes that were differentially expressed in squamous cell lung cancer tissues from five patients who had undergone surgical removal of the tumor(s). cRNA samples were prepared and hybridized to arrays obtained from Affymetrix® (Hg-U133A™.). These authors were able to carry out paired *t*-test analyses for each *individual* patient in order to distinguish the genes in which expression levels in their squamous lung cancer cells differed from the paired normal lung tissue (control samples) obtained from the same five individuals. The authors' prediction methodology will be briefly discussed in the next subsection as some of the details are relevant for the evaluation of these results which were the first to be reported for the (hypothetical) interactome — transcriptome analysis of human cancer cell data for a group of five patients with the same diagnosed form of (lung) cancer, and with the same treatment (tumor removal by surgery). The hypothetical human protein interaction maps are a relatively new endeavor (Brown and Jurisica, 2005; Lehner and Fraser, 2004) perhaps because they are likely to have many false positives, as well as miss a significant fraction of the relevant/real protein-protein interactions. Currently, microarray analysis still suffers inherently from relatively high noise levels and the accompanying information loss (buried in noise); although this inherent noise problem is partially eliminated through multiple replicate analyses, the number of replicates is often limited by the availability and the material cost. Another significant problem of such microarray projects is the huge amount of data that needs to be processed in order to obtain useable information (Claverie, 1999).

5.3.1 Analysis of human protein-protein interactions (HPPI) and integration of array data into a predicted protein-protein interaction network (PPIN)

Wachi, Yoneda and Wu (2005; WYU05) employed for their human cell data analysis a web-presented database (OPHID, April 25, 2005) of predicted interactions between human proteins (Brown and Jurisica, 2005) based on data for human and other four organisms which included the intensely-studied yeast and fruit fly. (OPHID is freely available to academic users at http://ophid.utoronto.ca). This protein interaction database listed 16,034 known human protein interactions obtained from various public protein interaction databases, as well as 23,889 additional, predicted interactions which are evaluated using protein domains, gene co-expression and Gene Ontology terms. The results can be visualized in OPHID using a customized, graph visualization program. The data comprises literature-derived human PPI from BIND, HPRD and MINT, "with predictions made from *Saccharomyces cerevisiae, Caenorhabditis elegans, Drosophila melanogaster* and *Mus musculus*". The genes in the WYU05 array were matched to those in OPHID using gene symbols and protein sequences. In this manner, 2137 genes in the WYU05 microarray experiments were 'matched to the protein network from OPHID'. These predictions should, however, be thought of only as 'hypotheses' until they are experimentally validated. On the other hand, there is increasing evidence that at least certain PPIs may be conserved through evolution (Pagel et al 2004; Wuchty et al 2003). Recently, Sharan et al (2005) claimed that about 50% of the protein-protein interactions predicted by using *interologs* between microorganisms are also experimentally validated. The interologs approach might play therefore a role in the partial validation of the HT-Y2H protein network mapping without, however, necessarily achieving the claimed, global validation of the predicted (hypothetical) interactome. Differentially expressed genes (DEGs) from squamous cell carcinomas (SCCs) were then identified as discussed above and their connectivity in the network graph was examined to determine their 'topological' properties, such as the edge distribution for DEGs in comparison with the surrounding graph subnetwork.

5.3.2 Differentially expressed genes –DEG- results for SCC of human lung

The genes that are upregulated in SCC were found to exhibit a positive correlation (Pearson's r-coefficient of 0.82) with the number of edges associated with them (Fig. 1a of Wachi, Yoneda and Wu 2005), which was interpreted as indicating that DEGs that are upregulated in SCC are also highly connected. However, the downregulated genes were reported also to have a positive correlation (r = 0.75) to connectivity, albeit slightly lower (Fig. 1b of Wachi, Yoneda and Wu, 2005). On the other hand, microarray probesets that matched the genes in the protein network (n =-2,137) had a negligible correlation coefficient (r =0.06) to link number, proving that the genes on the test microarrays did not contribute to bias in the number of links for DEGs in SCC.

A k-core analysis of DEGs in SCC of the human lung was also carried out *(loc. cit.)* which were reported to measure *"how close are the DEGs to the topological 'center' of the human PPI network"*. Based on the k-core analysis, it was concluded that: *"the upregulated genes are more centrally located in the protein network than the down-regulated genes"*. If duplicated and validated, such studies would be important as the 'topological centrality' of the genes in the interactome was previously reported to be associated with the *essential* functions of the genes in the yeast (Jeong et al 2001). Such essential genes, are lethal when mutated, and also tend to have high connectivity. Moreover, other genes that are not essential in this sense, but provide a vital function in toxin metabolism were reported to have a high number of edges associated with the nodes, and to be less well connected than the essential genes in yeast (Said et al 2004). Furthermore, a *k*-core analysis has also been performed on the yeast essential genes and they were reported to be global hubs, whereas the non-essential genes were not hubs (Wuchty and Almaas, 2005). It was also claimed that these essential, global hubs are conserved throughout different species; however, one notes that, thus far, there is insufficient data and evidence to prove this claim, or hypothesis. Nevertheless, one may consider as a 'working hypothesis' that *"there should be a core set of genes that needs to be maintained throughout the course of somatic evolution in the tumor microenvironment"* (Wachi, Yoneda and Wu, 2005). This hypothesis is thus consistent with the *somatic evolution model* of cancer. Such conserved genes might be the 'essential genes' in cancer cells, and they may also have somewhat analogous to the global hub, essential genes reported in yeast (Wuchty and Almaas, 2005). DEGs would thus be essential for the survival and proliferation of cancer cells in SSC of the human lung, and the upregulated genes would be centrally located in the protein network as well as have higher connectivity, perhaps suggesting their possible essential role(s) in human (SSC) lung cancer. As this is the first report of a predicted/ hypothetical human cancer interactome network one should definitely consider 'replicating' the reported studies and also evaluating such potentially important findings in the context of a complete human cancer interactome (differential) analysis. This possibility that DEGs might be essential for the survival and proliferation of cancer cells in SSC of the human lung has much too important consequences to be ignored; therefore, it must be thoroughly investigated and also tested with sufficiently extensive, translational genomics and transcriptional databases that do not seem to be currently available (Han et al. 2006). **Further supporting analyses for this conjecture made by** Wachi, Yoneda and Wu (2005) are considered in the next section.

5.4 Cancer proteins and the global topology of the human interactome network

A recent and extensive study of both cancer and non-cancer proteins (Jonsson and Bates, 2006) was integrated into a validated protein-protein interaction (PPI) network, or interactome, of human proteins. In their report, the connectivity properties were investigated for all proteins previously shown to be modified as a result of mutations leading to cancer (Furteal, et al 2004). A global protein-protein interaction network was then constructed by a homology--based method which is claimed to accurately predict protein-protein interactions. It was then suggested that human proteins that are involved in cancer, or 'cancer proteins', exhibit a network topology which is substantially different from that of other proteins which are considered not to be involved in cancer. Notably, increased connectivity was pointed out for cancer proteins involved in the following subnetworks: cell growth and apotosis-related, signal transduction (MAPK, TGF-beta, insulin, T-cell and B-cell receptor, adipocytokine, cytokine-cytokine interaction), cell motility/cytoskeleton, cell communication, adherence junction, focal adhesion, leukocyte migration, antigen processing and folding/sorting/degradation. Furthermore, it was proposed that such observations *'indicate an underlying evolutionary pressure to which cancer genes, as genes of central importance, are subjected.'* Linking these claims with previous proposals by Wuchty and Almaas (2005) that globally central proteins form an *evolutionary backbone* of the proteome and are *essential* to the organism, (and also with the conjecture made by Wachi, Yoneda and Wu, 2005, discussed here in Section 5.3.), Jonsson and Bates (2006) suggested that cancer proteins may generally be older than the non-cancer ones in evolutionary age. Furthermore, they also suggested that the somatically mutated cancer proteins may be of somewhat younger evolutionary average age in comparison with those from the germline, as a consequence of the evolutionary selection pressure postulated to affect germline mutated proteins. Note also that the previous study of (SCC) human lung cancer by Wachi, Yoneda and Wu (2005) also reported increased interaction connectivity in differentially expressed proteins in human lung cancer tissues.

6. Epigenomics in mammalian cells and multi-cellular organisms

6.1 Epigenetic controls

Upon completion of the US Human Genome Mapping Project and related studies, it became increasingly evident that a sequence of 30,000 or so 'active' genes that encode and direct the biosynthesis of specific proteins could not possibly exhaust the control mechanisms present in either normal or abnormal cells (such as, for example, cancer cells). This is even more obvious in the case of developing embryos or regenerating organs. Subsequently, more than 120,000 genes were suggested to be active in the human genome (*Nature, 2004*). Furthermore, specific control mechanisms of cellular phenotypes and processes were recently proposed that involve *epigenetic* controls, such as the specific acetylation **<=>** de-acetylation reactions of DNA-bound histones (for an overview article on epigenomics see, for example, *Scientific American* 2003, December issue). Such controls intervene from outside the genome but ultimately they also affect gene expression. Therefore, gene profiling techniques would need to be combined with epigenomic tools and analysis in order to gain an improved understanding of functional genomics and interactomics. Epigenomic tools and novel techniques begin to address the complex and varied needs of epigenetic studies, as well as their applications to controlling cell division and growth. Such tools are, therefore, potentially very important in medical areas such as cancer research and therapy, as well as for improving 'domestic' animal phenotypes *without* involving genomic modifications of the organism. This raises the interesting question if 'epigenomically controlled-growth organisms' (ECGOs) -- to be produced in the future-- would be still argued against by the same group of people who currently objects to GMOs, even though genetic modifications would be neither present nor traceable in such ECGO organisms?'

6.2 Novel tools in epigenomics: rapid and ultra-sensitive analyses of nucleic acid – protein interactions

Several novel techniques could also be applied for the highly-selective detection of epigenomic changes in mammalian cells related to diseases such as individual types of cancer (Jones and Laird, 1999; Plass, 2002) and Alzheimer disease. Such novel tools are likely to be utilized in a wide range of applications in biotechnology research related to Post-Genomics and Epigenomics. Tumor suppressor genes are transcriptionally silenced by *promoter hypermethylation* that also appears to lead to alterations in chromatin structure- a possible mechanism for such repression of the suppressor genes. In contrast to the genetic mutation or deletion mechanism of tumor suppressor gene inactivation, epigenetic inactivation of tumor suppressor genes would occur *via* methylation of specific DNA regions that could be prevented by DNA methyl-transferase or histone deacetylase inhibitors. Aberrant CpG--island methylation has non-random/tumor-type-specific patterns (Costello et al 2000). Such patterns can be identified by employing methylation--specific PCR (MS-PCR; Herman et al 1996), and can also be employed either for tumor class prediction by microarray-based DNA methylation analysis (Adorjan et al 2002) or for high-throughput microarray-based detection and analysis of methylated CpG islands (Yan et al 2002). Hypermethylation profiling is important for both accurate diagnosis and the development of optimal strategies in cancer therapy. Gene promoter hypermethylation has been reported in both tumors and serum of patients diagnosed with several types of cancer: head and neck cancers (Sanchez-Caspedes et al. 2000), nasopharyngeal carcinoma (Wong et al. 2002), non-small cell lung cancer (Belinsky et al 1998; An et al 2002), gastric carcinoma (Lee et al 2002), liver, prostate, bladder and colorectal cancers (Wong et al 1999; Jeronimo et al 2002). Substantial efforts are being made recently for the development of new methods and tools that are capable of sensitive and quantitative DNA methylation analysis, as well as early and accurate diagnosis of cancer. Among such tools are: Fluorescent methylation--specific polymerase chain reaction assay (FMS-PCR; Goessl et al 2000), SNIRF (Mahmood and Weissleder, 2003), indocyanine green-labeling (IGL) for human breast carcinomas (Ntziachristos et al 2000), ConLight-MSP (Rand et al 2002), COBRA (Xlong and Laird, 2002), Methylation-Sensitive *Single Nucleotide* Primer Extension (Ms-SnuPE; Gonzalgo and Jones, 1997), DNA microarray sensitive detection by Metal-Enhanced Fluorescence (MASD/MEF; Lakowicz, 2001; Malicka et al 2003 a, b)), and NIR Fluorescence Micro-Spectroscopy (NIRFMS), single cancer cell detection (Baianu et al 2004a). Specific molecular markers of cancer (Sidransky, 2002) hold the promise to identify those molecular signatures that are *unique* to specific types of cancer, and are essential for the *early accurate diagnosis* and treatment of cancer. Such novel molecular tools and methodologies could be employed to rapidly and accurately identify molecular signatures of cancer and aging-related diseases in mammalian cells in culture in order to determine how specific epigenomic mechanisms involved in the control of cell division and apoptosis operate throughout the cell cycle. Among the specific epigenomic control mechanisms that one could investigate with such new tools are: CpG-island methylation, p15 (INK4b) and p16 (INK4a) hyper-methylation (in synchronous hepatic carcinoma cells), GSTP1 methylation in non-neoplastic/ synchronous cells, as well as histone-deacetylation and its effects on histone- nucleic acid interactions in stable synchronous cell populations in culture. Both cancer and aging were reported to involve DNA methylation of specific genome regions (van Helden & van Helden, 1989; Ahuja et al 1998). Gene expression profiling and epigenomic testing could be carried out with both ultra-sensitive, novel human and mouse microarrays. Powerful spectroscopic and microspectrosopic techniques can be then employed for the analysis and further improvement of such tools for the investigation of nucleic acid--protein interactions.

- High-field 2D NMR of protein--protein and protein--nucleic acid interactions
- NIR Chemical Imaging of protein clusters in cells and single cancer cells in tissue; NIR-FMS; SNIRF
- MEF and FCS/FCCS/ FRET detection of single molecules amplified-ELISA; NASBA
- Ms-SnuPE; FMS-PCR; Lux ^{TM} Fluorogenic Primers*/ RT-PCR*,
- MyArray ^{TM} DNA- Human*, GeneFilters ^{R} Human Regular Arrays**.
- Specific Knock-out or silencing shRNAi's (SuperArrayTM).

**The testing of these new tools can be carried out for example with stable and synchronous mammalian (human HeLa and mouse) cells in culture.

Table 1. Techniques under Development and Related Applications that are commercially supported *,**.

7. Conclusions and discussion

Novel translational oncogenomics research is rapidly expanding with a view to the application of new technologies, findings and computational models in both pharmaceutical and clinical areas. Sample analyses in recent clinical studies have shown that gene expression data can be employed to distinguish between tumor types as well as to predict outcomes. Important, potential applications of such results are *individualized* human cancer therapy (Pharmacogenomics) and 'personalized medicine'. There is clearly a need for individualized cancer therapy strategies based on high-throughput microarray information recorded for isolated tumor cell lines from stage I through stage III cancer patients. Studies of Differential Gene Expression in human cancer cell lines are clearly required for developing new strategies for efficient cancer therapies for patients whose tumors have developed resistance to existing therapies. Such gene profiling expression, proteomic, interactomic and tissue array data is essential for improving the survival rate of stage III cancer patients undergoing clinical trials with novel signaling pathway inhibitors/ blocker medicines, such as those discussed in some detail in **Section 5**. Several technologies aimed at future applications in oncogenesis are currently under development both in the direction of improved detection sensitivity and increased time resolution of cellular events, with the limits of single molecule detection and picosecond time resolution already being reached (Sections 2.5, 2.6 and 6.2). The urgency for funding and carrying out the complete mapping of a human cancer interactome with the help of such novel, high-efficiency / low-cost and ultra-sensitive techniques is pointed out for the first time in the context of recent findings by translational oncogenomics and human cancer interactome predictions.

8. Acknowledgments

The author gratefully acknowledges receiving helpful suggestions, pertinent documentation and critical comments from: Dr. Mark Band, Director of the Genotyping/ Transcriptomics Unit at the Keck Center, Dr. Lei Liu, Director of BioInformatics Unit at the Keck Center, Professor Schuyler Korban, and Professor James F. Glazebrook of the Mathematics Dept. at UIUC and Eastern Illinois University, respectively. This research was partially supported by Renessen Co., the IMBA Consortium, an USDA Hatch Grant No. ILLU-0995362 and AES at UIUC.

9. References

[1] Adams J.; Palombella VJ; Sausville EA, et al. (1999). Proteasome inhibitors: a novel class of potent and effective antitumor agents. *Cancer Research,* Vol. 59: 2615-22.

[2] Adjei, A.A.; Erlichman C.; Davis JN; Cutler DL, Sloan JA, et al. 2000. A phase I trial of the farnesyl transferase inhibitor SCH66336: evidence for biological and clinical activity. *Cancer Res.,* 60: 1871-77.

[3] Aghajanian C.; Soignet S, Dizon DS, et al. (2001). A phase I trial of the novel proteasome inhibitor PS341 in advanced solid tumor malignancies. *Proc. Amer. Soc. Clin. Oncol.,* Vol. 20: 338 (*Abstr.*).

[4] Alle KM.; Henshall SM, Field AS, Sutherland RL. 1998. Cyclin D1 protein is overexpressed in hyperplasia and intraductal carcinoma of the breast. *Clin. Cancer Res.,* 4:847–854.

[5] Alizadeh AA.; Eisen MB, Davis RE et al. {2000). Distinct types of diffuse large B-cell lymphoma identified by gene expression profiling. *Nature,* Vol. 403: 503-11.

[6] Amundson, S.A.; et al. (2000). An Informatics Approach Identifying Markers of Chemosensitivity in Human Cancer Cell Lines. *Cancer Research,* Vol. 60: 6101-110.

[7] Andersen G, Busso D, Poterszman A, et al. (1997.) The structure of cyclin H: common mode of kinase activation and specific features. EMBO J, 16(5): 958–67.

[8] Anbazhagan, R.; Tihan, T, Bornman DM, et al.(1999). Classification of small cell lung cancer and pulmonary carcinoid by gene expression profiles. *Cancer Research,* Vol.59: 5119-22.

[9] Akinaga S; Sugiyama K, Akiyama T. (2000). UCN-01 (7-hydroxystaurosporine) and other indolocarbazole compounds: a new generation of anti-cancer agents for the new century? *Anticancer Drug Des.,* 15: 43-52.

[10] Akiyama T.; Yoshida T, Tsujita T, et al. (1997). G_1 phase accumulation induced by UCN-01 is associated with dephosphorylation of Rb and CDK2 proteins as well as

induction of CDK inhibitor p21/Cip1/WAF1/sdil in p53-mutated human epidermoid carcinoma A431 cells. *Cancer Res.*, Vol. 57: 1495-501.

[11] An, WG.; Hwang SG, Trepel JB, Blagosklonny MV. (2000). Protease inhibitor-induced apoptosis: accumulation of wt p53, p21WAF1/CIP1, and induction of apoptosis are independent markers of proteasome inhibition., *Leukemia*, 14: 1276-83.

[12] Arguello F.; Alexander M, Sterry JA, et al. (1998). Flavopiridol induces apoptosis of normal lymphoid cells, causes immunosuppression, and has potent antitumor activity in vivo against human leukemia and lymphoma xenografts. *Blood*, 91:2482-90.

[13] Ashburner M.; et al. (2000). Gene ontology: tool for the unification of biology. The Gene Ontology Consortium, *Nature Genetics*, Vol. 25: 25--29.

[14] Bagatolli LA.; Gratton, E. (2000). Two-photon fluorescence microscopy of coexisting lipid domains in giant unilamellar vesicles of binary phospholipid mixtures. *Biophys. J.*, 78: 290-305.

[15] Bagui, TK, Jackson RJ, Agrawal D, and Pledger WJ. (2000). Analysis of cyclin D3- cdk4 complexes in fibroblasts expressing and lacking p27kip1 and p21cip1. *Mol. Cell. Biol.*, 20: 8748– 57.

[16] Baianu, I. (1969). Theoretical and Experimental Models of Carcinogenesis., Medical Biophysics Dept., School of Medicine & School of Physics, Univ. Bucharest., *M.S. Thesis.* pp.1-191.

[17] Baianu, I. (1971). Organismic Structures and Qualitative Dynamics of Systems. *Bulletin of Mathematical Biophysics*, Vol. 33: 339-53.

[18] Baianu IC. (1977). A Logical Model of Genetic Activities in Łukasiewicz Algebras: The Non-linear Theory. *Bull. Mathematical Biology*, Vol.39: 249-58.

[19] Baianu IC. (1980). Natural Transformations of Organismic Structures, *Bull. Math. Biology*, Vol.42: 431-446.

[20] Baianu I.C. (1983). Natural Transformation Models in Molecular Biology, In: *Proceedings of the SIAM Natl. Meet.*, Denver, CO.; *Eprint*: Available from:
http://cogprints.org/3675/;
http://cogprints.org/3675/01/Naturaltransfmolbionu6.pdf

[21] Baianu IC. (1984). A Molecular--Set--Variable Model of Structural and Regulatory Activities in Metabolic and Genetic Networks. *FASEB Proceedings*, Vol. 43: 917.

[22] Baianu IC. (1987a). Computer Models and Automata Theory in Biology and Medicine., In: M. Witten (ed.), *Mathematical Models in Medicine*, Vol.7., New York : Pergamon Press. p.1513-77; *CERN Preprint No. EXT--2004 – 072*, Available from:
http://doc.cern.ch//archive/electronic/other/ext/ext-2004-072.pdf

[23] Baianu IC. (2004a). Interactomics and Cancer Mechanisms, *Bioline Preprint No. 00001978*. p.1- 19 Available from: http://cogprints.org/3810/;
http://bioline.utsc.utoronto.ca/archive/00001978/;

[24] Baianu I.C. (2004b). Complex Systems Analysis of Cell Cycling Models in Carcinogenesis:II. Cell Genome and Interactome, Neoplastic Non-random Transformation Models in Topoi with Łukasiewicz-Logic and MV Algebras. *CERN Preprint Archive*, EXT-2004-065. p.1-16. Available from:
http://doc.cern.ch/archive/electronic/other/ext/ext--04065/
ANeuralGenNetworkLuknTopos_oknu4.pdf

[25] Baianu IC. (2004c). Molecular Models of Genetic and Organismic Structures. *CERN Preprint Archive, EXT-2004-067*, p.1-9. Available from: http://doc.cern.ch/archive/electronic/other/ext/ext-2004-067/MolecularModelsICB3.doc

[26] Baianu IC., (Editor). (2006). Complex Systems Biology and Life's Logics, *Axiomathes*, Vol.16: 1- 243. Springer: Dordrecht, Germany.

[27] Baianu IC.; Kumosinski TF, Bechtel P.J, et al. (1988). NMR Studies of Chemical Activity and Prottein-Protein Interactions in Solutions and Hydrated Powders. In: *Proceed. 196th National Meeting of the American Chemical Society-* Division of Agricultural and Food Chemistry. American Chemical Society, p.156.

[28] Baianu IC.; Ozu EM, Wei TC, et al. (1993). Molecular Dynamics and NMR Studies of Ion-Ion Interactions in Concentrated Electrolytes with Dipoles in Water. In: *Molecular Modeling*. ACS Symp. Ser.# 576. Kumosinski TF and Liebman M, Eds. Washington, DC: American Chemical Society. p. 269-324.

[29] Baianu IC.; Costescu D, You T, et al. (2004a). Near Infrared, Fluorescence Microspectroscopy, Infrared Chemical Imaging and High-Resolution NMR Analysis of Soybean Seeds, Somatic Embryos and Single Cancer Cells. Ch.12 In: *Oil Extraction and Analysis*, Luthria DL, Ed.; AOCS Press : Champaign, Illinois, USA, pp. 241-273.

[30] Baianu IC.; Costescu D, Hoffman NE, et al. (2004). Fourier Transform Near Infrared Microspectroscopy, Infrared Chemical Imaging, High-Resolution Nuclear Magnetic Resonance and Fluorescence Microspectroscopy Detection of Single Cancer Cells and Single Viral Particles. *CERN Preprints Archive, EXT-2004-069.*, pp. 1-20. Available from: http://doc.cern.ch//archive/electronic/other/ext/ext-2004-069.pdf

[31] Baianu IC.; Brown R, Georgescu G, and Glazebrook, JF. (2006). Complex Non-Linear Biodynamics in Categories, Higher Dimensional Algebra and LM-Topos: Transformations of Neuronal, Genetic and Neoplastic Networks. *Axiomathes, Vol. 16:* 65-122.

[32] Barabasi AL.; & Oltvai ZN. (2004). Network biology: understanding the cell's functional organization. *Nature Review Genetics*, Vol. 5: 101–13.

[33] Barco, A; Alarcon, JM and Kandel, E. R. (2002). Expression of constitutively active CREB protein facilitates the late phase of long-term potentiation by enhancing synaptic capture. *Cell*, Vol. 108: 689-703.

[34] Baselga J.; Herbst R, LoRusso P, et al. (2000). Continuous administration of ZD1839 (*Iressa*), a novel oral epidermal growth factor receptor tyrosine kinase inhibitor (EGFR-TKI) in patients with five selected tumor types: evidence of activity and good tolerability. *Proceedings American Society of Clinical Oncology*, Vol. 19: 686 (Abstr.).

[35] Baselga J.; Tripathy D, Mendelsohn J, et al. (1996). Phase II study of weekly intravenous recombinant humanized anti-p185HER2 monoclonal antibody in patients with HER2/neu-overexpressing metastatic breast cancer. *Journal of Clinical Oncology*, Vol. 14: 737-44.

[36] Becker J. (2004). Signal transduction inhibitors- a work in progress. *Nature Biotechnology*, Vol. 22 (1): 15-18.

[37] Belov L.; de la Vega, O, dos Remedios CG, et al. (2001). Immunophenotyping of leukemias using a cluster of differentiation antibody microarray. *Cancer Res., Vol.* 61: 4483-89.

[38] Berchuck A.; Heron KA, Carney ME et al. 1998. Frequency of germline and somatic BRCA1 mutations in ovarian cancer. *Clin. Cancer Res*, 4: 2433-37.

[39] Bishop WR, Bond R, Petrin J, et al. (1995). Biochemical characterization and inhibition of *Ras* modification in transfected Cos cells. *J. Biol. Chem.,* 270: 30611-18.

[40] Bittner, W. et al.(2000 a,b). Gene-Expression Profiles in Hereditary Breast Cancer. *N. Engl. J. Med.,* 344 (26): 2028-29; (2001) Vol. 345 (8): 628.

[41] Blaschek, H. P. (1996). Recent Develpoments in the Genetic Manipulation of Microorganims for biotechnology applications. *In*: Baianu I.C.; Pessen H, and Kumosinski TF, Eds. *Physical Chemistry of Food Processes*. Vol 2. New York: Van Nostrand Reinhold. p. 459-74.

[42] Brown, PA; & Botstein, D. (1999). Exploring the new world of the genome with DNA microarrays. *Nature Genetics,* 21 (Suppl.): 33-37.

[43] Brown, P.; &Wouters, BG. (1999). Apoptosis, p53, and Tumor Cell Sensitivity to Anticancer Agents. *Cancer Res.,* Vol. 59: 1391-1399.

[44] Brown, K.R, and Jurisica, I. (2005). Online predicted human interaction database-(OPHID). *Bioinformatics,* 21: 2076–2082.

[45] Bryja V, Pachernik J, Faldikova L, et al. (2004). The role of p27(Kip1) in maintaining the levels of D-type cyclins *in vivo. Biochim Biophys Acta,* 3: 1691-96.

[46] Bubendorf L, Kononen J, Koivisto P, et al. (1999). Survey of gene amplifications during prostate cancer progression by high-throughput fluorescence *in situ* hybridization on tissue microarrays. *Cancer Res.,* 59: 803-6.

[47] Cheng M, Olivier P, Diehl JA, et al. (1999). The p21Cip1 and p27kip1 'inhibitors' are essential activators of cyclin D-dependent kinases in murine fibroblasts. *EMBO J,* 18: 1571– 83.

[48] Bunch RT, Eastman A. (1996). Enhancement of cisplatin-induced cytotoxicity by 7-hydroxystaurosporine (UCN-01), a new G_2-checkpoint inhibitor. *Clin. Cancer Res.,* 2:791-97.

[49] Carter P, Presta L, Gorman CM, et al. (1992). Humanization of an anti-p185HER2 antibody for human cancer therapy. *PNAS-USA,* 89: 4285-89.

[50] Carlson BA, Dubay MM, Sausville EA, et al. (1996). Flavopiridol induces G1 arrest with inhibition of cyclin-dependent kinase (CDK) 2 and CDK4 in human breast carcinoma cells. *Cancer Res.,* 56: 2973-78.

[51] Chee M, et al. (1996). Accessing genetic information with high-density DNA arrays. *Science,* 274: 610-614.

[52] Chen X, Lowe M, Keyomarsi K. (1999). UCN-01 mediated G1 arrest in normal but not tumor breast cells is pRb-dependent and p53-independent. *Oncogene,* 18: 5691-702.

[53] Ciardiello F, Caputo R, Bianco R, et al. (2000). Antitumor effect and potentiation of cytotoxic drugs activity in human cancer cells by ZD-1839 (Iressa), an epidermal growth factor receptor-selective tyrosine kinase inhibitor. *Clin. Cancer Res.,* 6: 2053-63.

[54] Clarke FC, Jee DR, Moffat AC, Hammond SV. (2001). Effective sample volume for measurements by NIR Microscopy. (Abstract), *British Pharmaceutical Conference.*

[55] Claverie JM. (1999). Computational methods for the identification of differential and coordinated gene expression. *Human Mol. Genetics*, 8: 1821–32.

[56] Compton J. (1991). Nucleic acid sequence-based amplification. *Nature,* 350: 91-92.

[57] Costello JF, et al. (2000). Aberrant CpG-island methylation has non-random and tumour-type-specific patterns. *Nature Genet.,* 24: 132-38.

[58] Decker T.; Hipp S, Schneller F, et al. (2001). Rapamycin induces G1 arrest and inhibits p70S6 kinase in proliferating B-CLL cells: cyclin D3 and cyclin E as molecular targets. *Blood,* 98: 632 (Abstr.).

[59] DeRisi, JL, et al. (1996). Use of a cDNA microarray to analyse gene expression patterns in human cancer. *Nature Genetics*, Vol. 14: 457–460.

[60] DeRisi JL; et al. (1997). Exploring the metabolic and genetic control of gene expression on a genomic scale. *Science,* 278: 680-686.

[61] de Jung H.; Gouze J-L., Hernandez, C, Page M. et al. (2004). Qualitative simulation of genetic regulatory networks using piecewise-linear models. *Bull. Math. Biology,* 66(2): 301-340.

[62] de Jung H.; and Page M. (2000). Qualitative simulation of large and complex genetic regulatory systems. In W. Horn (ed.), *Proc. 14th Europ. Conf. AI. (ECAI 2000)*, pp.141-145, IOS Press.

[63] Diaspro A.; & Robello, M. 1999. Multi-photon Excitation Microscopy to Study Biosystems. *European Microscopy and Analysis,* 5: 5-7.

[64] Dobashi Y.; Goto A, Fukayama, M, et al. (2004). Overexpression of Cdk4/Cyclin D1, a possible mediator of apoptosis and an indicator of prognosis in human primary lung carcinoma. *Intl. J. Cancer,* 110 : 532-541.

[65] Dobashi Y.; Jiang SX, Shoji M, et al. (2003). Diversity in expression and prognostic significance of G1/S cyclins in human primary lung carcinomas. *J. Pathol,* 199: 208-220.

[66] Drexler H.C. (1997). Activation of the cell death program by inhibition of proteasome function. *PNAS-USA,* 94: 855-60.

[67] Drees M.; Dengler WA, Roth T, et al. (1997). Flavopiridol (L86-8275): selective antitumor activity *in vitro* and activity *in vivo* for prostate carcinoma cells. *Clin. Cancer Res.* Vol. 3: 273-79.

[68] Dudoit S.; et al. (2003). Open source software for the analysis of microarray data. *Biotechniques*, Suppl, 45–51.

[69] Dunker AK.; et al. (2005). Flexible Nets. The roles of intrinsic disorder in protein interaction networks. *FEBS J.* 272: 5129-5148.

[70] Eigen M.; & Rigler R. (1994). Sorting single molecules: Applications to diagnostics and evolutionary biotechnology. *PNAS-USA,* 91: 5740-43.

[71] Elson E.L.; & Magde D. (1974). Fluorescence correlation spectroscopy. I: Conceptual basis and theory. *Biopolymers,* Vol. 13: 1.

[72] End D.W.; Smets, G, Todd, AV, et al. (2001). Characterization of the antitumor effects of the selective farnesyl protein transferase inhibitor R115777 in vivo and in vitro. *Cancer Res.,* 61: 131-37.

[73] Erlichman C.; Adjei AA, Thomas JP, et al. (2001). A phase I trial of the proteasome inhibitor PS-341 in patients with advanced cancer. *Proc. Am. Soc. Clin. Oncol.,* 20: 337 (Abstr.).

[74] Esteller M.; et al. (2002). CpG island hypermethylation and tumor suppressor genes: a booming present, a brighter future. *Oncogene*, 21: 5427- 40.

[75] Ferry D, Hammond L, Ranson M, et al. (2000). Intermittent oral ZD1839 (Iressa), a novel epidermal growth factor receptor tyrosine kinase inhibitor (EGFR-TKI), shows evidence of good tolerability and activity: final results from phase I study. *Proc. Amer. Soc. Clin. Oncol.*, 19: 5 (Abstr.).

[76] Formstecher E, et al. (2005). Protein interaction mapping: a *Drosophila* case study. *Genome Res.*, Vol.15: 376-384.

[77] Fraser HB et al.. (2005). Evolutionary rate in the protein interaction network. *Science*, Vol. 296: 750-52.

[78] Fukuse T, Hirata T, Naiki H, et al. (2000). Prognostic significance of cyclin E overexpression in resected non-small cell lung cancer. *Cancer Res.*, 60: 242-4.

[79] Futreal P, Liu Q, Shattuck-Eidens D et al. (1994). BRCA1 mutations in primary breast and ovarian carcinomas. *Science*, 266: 120-2.

[80] Furteal PA, et al.(2004). A census of human cancer genes. *Nature Rev. Cancer*, 4:177-183.

[81] Galfalvy HC, et al. (2003). Sex genes for genomic analysis in human brain: internal controls for comparison of probe level data extraction. *BMC Bioinformatics*, 4: 37.

[82] Gavin AC, et al. (2002). Functional organization of the yeast proteome by systematic analysis of protein complexes. *Nature,* 415: 141-147.

[83] Georgescu, G.; (2006). N-valued Logics and Łukasiewicz--Moisil Algebras. *Axiomathes*, Vol.16:123-136.

[84] Gillett C.; Fantl V, Smith R, Fisher C, et al. (1994). Amplification and over-expression of cyclin D1 in breast cancer detected by immunohistochemical staining. *Cancer Res.*, 54: 1812–17.

[85] Giot L.; et al. (2002). A Protein Interaction Map of *Drosophila melanogaster.*, *Science*, 302: 1727-36.

[86] Glass L and Kauffman, S.A. (1973). The logical analysis of continuous non-linear biochemical control networks. *J. Theor. Biology*, 39: 103-129.

[87] Golub TR.; Slonim, DK, Tamayo P, et al. (1999). Molecular classification of cancer: Class discovery and class prediction by gene expression monitoring. *Science*, Vol. 286: 531-537.

[88] Gonzalgo, M. & Jones, P. (1997). Rapid quantitation of methylation differences at specific sites using methylation-sensitive single nucleotide primer extension Ms-SnuPE). *Nucleic Acids Res.*, 25: 2529-31.

[89] Gowen L, Avrutskaya AV, Latour AM et al. (1998). BRCA1 required for transcription-coupled repair of oxidative DNA damage. *Science*, 281: 1009-12.

[90] Gray, J.W. et al (1998): High-resolution analysis of DNA copy number variation using comparative genomic hybridization to microarrays. *Nature Genetics*, 20: 207-211.

[91] Hamilton AL, Eder JP, Pavlick AC, et al. (2001). PS-341: phase I study of a novel proteasome inhibitor with pharmacodynamic endpoints. *Proc. Amer. Soc. Clin. Oncol.*, 20:336 (Abstr.).

[92] Han J-DJ, Dupuy D, Bertin N, et al. (2005). Effect of sampling on the topology predictions of protein-protein interaction networks. *Nature Biotechnology*, 23(7): 839-844.

[93] Han J-D, et al. (2004). Evidence for dynamically organized modularity in the yeast protein-protein interaction network. *Nature*, 430: 88-93.

[94] Harkin PD. (2002). Uncovering Functionally Relevant Signaling Pathways Using Microarray-Based Expression Profiling. *The Oncologist*, 5(6): 501-507.

[95] Harkin DP, Bean JM, Miklos D et al. (1999). Induction of GADD45 and JNK/SAPK-dependent apoptosis following inducible expression of BRCA1. *Cell*, 97: 575- 86.

[96] Hashemolhosseini S, Nagamine Y, Morley SJ, et al. (1998). Rapamycin inhibition of the G1 to S transition is mediated by effects on cyclin D1 mRNA and protein stability *J. Biol. Chem.*, 273: 14424-29.

[97] Herman JG, et al. (1996). Methylation-specific PCR: a novel PCR assay for methylation status of CpG islands. *PNAS-USA*, 93: 9821-26.

[98] Ho Y, et al. (2002). Systematic identification of protein complexes in *Saccharomyces cerevisiae* by mass spectrometry. *Nature*, 415: 180-183.

[99] Hughes TR, et al. (2000). Functional discovery *via* a compendium of expression profiles. *Cell*, 102: 109-126.

[100] Ideker T, et al. (2001). A new approach to decoding life: systems biology. *Annu. Rev. Genomics Human Genet.*, 2: 343–72.

[101] Ideker T, et al. (2002). Discovering regulatory and signaling circuits in molecular interaction networks. *Bioinformatics*, 18: S233-S240.

[102] Irizarry RA, et al. (2003). Summaries of Affymetrix GeneChip probe level data. *Nucleic Acids Res.*, 31: e15.

[103] Ito T, et al. (2001). A comprehensive two-hybrid analysis to explore the yeast protein Interactome., *Proc. Natl. Acad. Sci. USA.*, 98: 4569-4574.

[104] Jain KK. (2000). Applications of proteomics in oncology. *Pharmacogenomics*, 1: 385-93.

[105] Jeong H, et al. (2001). Lethality and centrality in protein networks. *Nature*, 415: 180-3.

[106] Jones PA, Laird PW. (1999). Cancer epigenetics comes of age. *Nature Genet.*, 21: 163-167.

[107] Jonsson, P.F. and Bates, P.A. (2006). Global topological features of cancer proteins in the human Interactome. *Bioinformatics*, 22 (18): 2291-97.

[108] Jonsson, P.F. et al. (2006). Cluster analysis of networks generated through homology: automatic identification of important protein communities involved in cancer metastasis. *BMC Bioinformatics*, 7: 2.

[109] Johnston SR, Ellis PA, Houston S, Hickish T, Howes AJ, et al. (2000). A phase II study of the farnesyl transferase inhibitor R115777 in patients with advanced breast cancer. *Proc. Amer.. Soc. Clin. Oncol.*, 19: 318.

[110] Jung CP, Motwani MV, Schwartz GK. (2001). Flavopiridol increases sensitization to gemcitabine in human gastrointestinal cancer cell lines and correlates with down-regulation of ribonucleotide reductase M2 subunit. *Clin. Cancer Res.*, 7: 2527-36.

[111] Kabelka EA.; Diers BW, Fehr WR, LeRoy AR, Baianu IC, et al. (2003). Identification of putative yield enhancing quantitative trait loci from exotic soybean germplasm, *Crop Sci.*, 42: 149-162.

[112] Kaur G, Stetler-Stevenson M, Sebers S, et al.(1992). Growth inhibition with reversible cell cycle arrest of carcinoma cells by flavone L86-8275. *J. Natl. Cancer Inst.*, Vol. 84 1736-40.

[113] Kawamata S., Sakaida H, Hori T, et al. (1998). The upregulation of p27Kip1 by rapamycin results in G1 arrest in exponentially growing T-cell lines. *Blood,* Vol. 91: 561-69.

[114] King R.W.; Deshaies RJ, Peters JM, Kirschner MW. (1996). How proteolysis drives the cell cycle. *Science,* 274: 1652-59.

[115] Kettling, U., Koltermann, A., Schwille, P., and Eigen, M. (1998). Real-time enzyme kinetics monitored by dual-color fluorescence cross-correlation spectroscopy. *PNAS-USA,* 95: 1416- 20.

[116] Kitano, H. (2002). Systems biology: a brief overview. *Science,* 295, 1662–1664.

[117] Klint P.; and Claesson-Welsh L. (1999). Signal transduction by fibroblast growth factor receptors. *Front. Biosci.,* 4: D165–D177.

[118] Kodadek T. (2001). Protein Microarrays: Prospects and problems. *Chem. Biol.,* Vol. 8:105- 115.

[119] Koltermann, A., Kettling, U., Bieschke, J., Winkler, T., and Eigen, M.(1998). Rapid assay processing by integration of dual-color fluorescence cross-correlation spectroscopy: High throughput screening for enzyme activity. *PNAS-USA,* 95: 1421-26.

[120] Koonin EV, Altschul SF, Bork P. BRCA1 protein products: functional motifs. (1996). *Nature Genetics,* Vol. 13: 266-68.

[121] Koziczak M, Holbro T, and Hynes NE.(2004). Blocking of FGFR signaling inhibits breast cancer cell proliferation through downregulation of D-type cyclins. *Oncogene,* 23: 3501–08.

[122] Kuenen BC.; Rosen L, Smit EF, et al. (2002). Dose-finding and pharmacokinetics study of cisplatin, gemcitabine, and SU5416 in patients with solid tumors. *J. Clin. Oncol.,* 20: 1657-67.

[123] Lakowicz JR. (2001). *Anal. Biochem.,* 298: 1-24.

[124] Lee J.S.; Collins KM, Brown AL et al. 2000. hCds1-mediated phosphorylation of BRCA1 regulates the DNA damage response. *Nature,* 404: 201-4.

[125] Lehner B and Fraser AG. (2004). A first-draft human protein-interaction map. *Genome Biol.,* 5: R63.

[126] Lewis TS, Shapiro PS, Ahn NG. 1998. Signal transduction through MAP kinase cascades. *Adv. Cancer Res.,* 74: 49-139.

[127] Li, S. et al.(2004). A Map of the Interactome Network of the Metazoan *C. elegans., Science,* 303: 540-543.

[128] Li, E. (2002). Chromatin modification and epigenetic reprogramming in mammalian development. *Nature Rev. Genet.,* 3: 662-73.

[129] Liu M, Bryant MS, Chen J, Lee S, et al. (1999). Effects of SCH 59228, an orally bioavailable farnesyl protein transferase inhibitor, on the growth of oncogene-transformed fibroblasts and a human colon carcinoma xenograft in nude mice. *Cancer Chemother. Pharmacol.,* 43:50-58.

[130] Lo YM. et al.(1999). Quantitative analysis of aberrant p16 methylation using real-time quantitative methylation-specific polymerase chain reaction. *Cancer Res.,* Vol. 59: 3899-3903.

[131] Lockhart, D.J., et al. (1996). Expression monitoring by hybridization to high-density oligonucleotide arrays. *Nat. Biotechnol.,* 14: 1675–80.

[132] Loden M., Sighall M, Nielsen NH, et al. (2002). The cyclin D1 high and cyclin E high subgroups of breast cancer: Separate pathways in tumorigenesis based on pattern of genetic aberrations and inactivation of the pRb node. *Oncogene,* Vol. 21: 4680– 90.

[133] Malicka J et al. (2003). DNA hybridization assays using metal-enhanced fluorescence. *BBRC,* 306: 213-218.

[134] Malumbres M, and Barbacid M. (2001). To cycle or not to cycle: A critical decision in cancer. *Nat. Rev. Cancer,* 1: 222–31.

[135] Matthews LR, et al. (2001) Identification of potential interaction networks using sequence-based searches for conserved protein–protein interactions or *'interologs',* *Genome Res.,* 11: 2120–26.

[136] Mendel DB, Schreck RE, West DC, et al. (2000). The angiogenesis inhibitor SU5416 has long-lasting effects on vascular endothelial growth factor receptor phosphorylation and function. *Clin. Cancer Res.,* 6: 4848-58.

[137] Mendelsohn, AR and Brent R. (1999). Protein interaction methods—toward an endgame. *Science,* 284: 1948–1950.

[138] Miettinen HE, Jarvinen TA, Kellner U, et al. (2000). High topoisomerase II-alpha expression associates with high proliferation rate and poor prognosis in oligodendrogliomas. *Neuropathol. Appl. Neurobiol.,* 26: 504-12.

[139] Mohammadi M, McMahon G, Sun L, et al. (1997). Structures of the tyrosine kinase domain of fibroblast growth factor receptor in complex with inhibitors. *Science,* Vol. 276: 955-60.

[140] Mohr S.; Leikauf GD, Keith G and Rihn BH. (2002). Microarrays as Cancer Keys: An Array of Possibilities., *J. Clinical Oncol.,* 20(14): 3165-75.

[141] Mollinedo F, Martinez-Dalmau R, Modolell M. (1993). Early and selective induction of apoptosis in human leukemic cells by the alkyl-lysophospholipid ET-18-OCH3. *Biochem. Biophys. Res. Commun.,* 192: 603-9.

[142] Monteiro ANA, August A, Hanafusa H. (1996). Evidence for a transcriptional activation function of BRCA1 C-terminal region. *Proc Natl Acad Sci USA,* Vol. 93:13595- 599.

[143] Morgan, DO. (1995). Principles of CDK regulation. *Nature,* 374:131-4.

[144] Motwani M, Delohery TM, Schwartz GK. (1999). Sequential dependent enhancement of caspase activation and apoptosis by flavopiridol on paclitaxel-treated human gastric and breast cancer cells. *Clin. Cancer Res.,* 5: 1876-83.

[145] Motwani M, Jung C, Sirotnak FM, et al. (2001). Augmentation of apoptosis and tumor regression by flavopiridol in the presence of CPT-11 in Hct116 colon cancer monolayers and xenografts. *Clin. Cancer Res.,* 7: 4209-19.

[146] Moyer JD, Barbacci EG, Iwata KK, et al. (1997). Induction of apoptosis and cell cycle arrest by CP-358,774, an inhibitor of epidermal growth factor receptor tyrosine kinase. *Cancer Res.,* 57: 4838-48.

[147] Muraoka RS, Lenferink AEG, Simpson J, et al. (2001). Cyclin-dependent kinase inhibitor p27kip1 is required for mouse mammary gland morphogenesis and function. *J. Cell Biol,* 153: 917–931.

[148] Noguchi T, Dobashi Y, Minehara H, et al. (2000). Involvement of cyclins in cell proliferation and their clinical implications in soft tissue smooth muscle tumors. *Amer J. Pathol.,* 156: 2135–47.

[149] Ohta T, Fukuda M. (2004). Ubiquitin and breast cancer. *Oncogene*, 23(11): 2079-88.

[150] Ormandy CJ, Musgrove EA, Hui R, et al. (2003). Cyclin D1, EMS1 and 11q13 amplification in human breast cancers. *Breast Cancer Res. Treat.*, 78: 323–335.

[151] Oehlenschläger F.; Schwille P, and Eigen M. (1996). Detection of HIV-1 RNA by nucleic acid sequence-based amplification combined with fluorescence correlation spectroscopy. *PNAS-USA*, 93: 1281.

[152] Ouichi T, Monteiro ANA, August A et al. (1998). BRCA1 regulates p53-dependent gene expression. *Proc Natl Acad Sci USA*, 95: 2302-06.

[153] Pagel, P.; et al. (2005). The MIPS mammalian protein-protein interaction database. *Bioinformatics*, 21: 821-34.

[154] Pandey A, Mann M. (2000). Proteomics to study genes and genomes., *Nature*, Vol. 405: 837-46.

[155] Pasini P, Musiani, M, Russo C, et al. (1998). Chemiluminescence imaging in bioanalysis. *Journal of Pharmacology and Biomedical Analysis*, 18: 555-64.

[156] Patel V, Lahusen T, Sy T, et al.(2002). Perifosine, a novel alkylphospholipid, induces p21(WAF1) expression in squamous carcinoma cells through a p53- independent pathway, leading to loss in cyclin-dependent kinase activity and cell cycle arrest. *Cancer Res.*, 62: 1401-9.

[157] Paweletz CP, Charnoneau L, Bichsel VE, et al. (2001). Reverse phase protein microarrays which capture disease progression show activation of pro-survival pathways at the cancer invasion front, *Oncogene*, 20: 1981-89.

[158] Pendergast, G.C., Orliff, A. (2000). Farnesyltransferase inhibitors: antineoplastic properties, mechanisms of action, and clinical prospects. *Semin. Cancer Biol.*, Vol. 10: 443-52.

[159] Perou, C.M.; Sorlie, T., Eisen, M.B., et al. (2000). Molecular portraits of human breast tumors. *Nature*, 406: 747-752.

[160] Peri S. et al. (2003). Development of human protein reference database as an initial platform for approaching systems biology in humans, *Genome Res.*, 13: 2363-2371.

[161] Pinkel D, Gray JW, et al. (1998). High resolution analysis of DNA copy number variation using comparative genomic hybridization to microarrays. *Nature Genetics*, 20: 207-11.

[162] Peng D, Fan Z, Lu Y, et al. (1996). Anti-epidermal growth factor receptor monoclonal antibody 225 up-regulates p27KIP1 and induces G1 arrest in prostatic cancer cell line DU145. *Cancer Res.*, 56: 3666-69.

[163] Plass C. (2002). Cancer epigenomics. *Hum. Mol. Genet.*, 11: 2479-88.

[164] Prisecaru V, and Baianu IC. (2004a). Cell Cycling Models of Carcinogenesis: A Complex Systems Analysis. *q-bio.MN/0406046 Archive*, p.1-22. Available from: http://lanl.arxiv.org/ftp/q-bio/papers/0406/0406046.pdf

[165] Prisecaru V., and Baianu IC. (2004b). Complex Biological Systems Analysis of Cell Cycling Models in Carcinogenesis: I. The essential roles of modifications in the c-Myc, TP53/p53, p27 and hTERT modules in Cancer Initiation and Progression. *CERN Archive EXT-2004-057.*, pp.1- 17. Available from: http://doc.cern.ch/archive/electronic/other/ext/ext-2004-057/ Cancersignaling_ICBval.pdf

[166] Rand M et al. (2002). Conversion-specific detection of DNA methylation using real-time polymerase chain reaction (ConLight-MSP) to avoid false positives. *Methods*, 27:114-20.

[167] Rigler R. and Widengren J. 1990. Ultrasensitive detection of single molecules by fluorescence correlation spectroscopy, *BioScience (Ed. Klinge & Owman)*. p.180.

[168] Rigler R., Mets Ü., Widengren J. and Kask P. (1993). Fluorescence correlation spectroscopy with high-count rate and low background: Analysis of translational diffusion, *Eur. Biophys J.*, 22: 69.

[169] Rippe K. (2000). Simultaneous Binding of Two DNA Duplexes to the NtrC- Enhancer Complex Studied by Two-Color Fluorescence Cross-Correlation Spectroscopy. *Biochemistry*, 39 (9): 2131-2139.

[170] Rosen L, Mulay M, Mayers A, et al. (1999). Phase I dose-escalating trial of SU5416, a novel angiogenesis inhibitor in patients with advanced malignancies. *Proc. Am. Soc. Clin. Oncol.*, 18: 618.

[171] Ross DT, Scherf U, Eisen MB, et al. (2000). Systematic variation in gene expression patterns in human cancer cell lines. *Nature Genetics*, 24: 227-235.

[172] Ruffner H, Verma IM. BRCA1 is a cell cycle-regulated nuclear phosphoprotein. 1997. *Proc Natl Acad. Sci USA*, 94: 7138-43.

[173] Saeed M.R. et al. (2006). Protein-protein interactions, evolutionary rate, abundance and age. *BMC Bioinformatics*, 7: 128.

[174] Said MR, et al. (2004). Global network analysis of phenotypic effects: protein networks and toxicity modulation in *Saccharomyces cerevisiae*. *PNAS-USA*, 101:18006-11.

[175] Salwinsky, L. et al. (2004). The Database of Interacting Proteins: 2004 update. *Nucleic acids Res.*, 32: D449-D451.

[176] Schellens JH, de Klerk G, Swart M, et al. (2000). Phase I and pharmacologic study with the novel farnesyltransferase inhibitor R115777. *Proc. Am. Soc. Clin. Oncol.*, 19: 715.

[177] Schena, M. et al. (1995). Quantitative monitoring of gene expression patterns with a complementary DNA microarray. *Science*, 270: 467-70.

[178] Schwille, P. (2001). Fluorescence Correlation Spectroscopy. Theory and applications. Rigler R and Elson ES. eds, Berlin: Springer Verlag. p. 360.

[179] Schwille, P., Bieschke, J. and Oehlenschläger F. (1997). Kinetic investigations by fluorescence correlation spectroscopy: The analytical and diagnostic potential of diffusion studies, *Biophys. Chem.*, 66: 211-228.

[180] Schwille P, Meyer-Almes F-J, and Rigler R. (1997). Dual-color fluorescence cross-correlation spectroscopy for multicomponent diffusional analysis in solution, *Biophys. J.*, 72: 1878-80.

[181] Schwille P, Oehlenschläger F and Walter, NG. (1997). Comparative hybridization kinetics of DNA-oligonucleotides to a folded RNA target in solution. *Biophys. Chem.*, Vol. 66: 211-228.

[182] Schwille P, Oehlenschläger F and Walter N. (1996). Analysis of RNA-DNA hybridization kinetics by fluorescence correlation spectroscopy, *Biochemistry*, Vol. 35: 10182.

[183] Schwille P, Haupts U, Maiti S, and Webb W. (1999). Molecular dynamics in living cells observed by fluorescence correlation spectroscopy with one- and two-photon excitation. *Biophysical Journal*, 77(10): 2251-65.

[184] Sebolt-Leopold JS, Dudley DT, Herrera R, et al. (1999). Blockade of the MAP kinase pathway suppresses growth of colon tumors in vivo. *Nat. Med.* 5:810-16.

[185] Senderowicz AM, Sausville EA. (2000). Preclinical and clinical development of cyclin-dependent kinase modulators. *J. Natl. Cancer Inst.*, 92:376-87.

[186] Senior K. (1999). Fingerprinting disease with protein chip arrays. *Mol. Med. Today*, 5: 326-327.

[187] Sekulic A, Hudson CC, Homme JL, et al. 2000. A direct linkage between the phosphoinositide 3-kinase-AKT signaling pathway and the mammalian target of rapamycin in mitogen-stimulated and transformed cells. *Cancer Res.*, 60: 3504-13.

[188] Shak S. (1999). Overview of the trastuzumab (Herceptin) anti-HER2 monoclonal antibody clinical program in HER2-overexpressing metastatic breast cancer. Herceptin Multinational Investigator Study Group. *Semin. Oncol.*, 26:71-77.

[189] Shao R, Cao C, Shimiu T, O'Connor PM, et al. (1997). Abrogation of an S-phase checkpoint and potentiation of camptothecin cytotoxicity by 7-hydroxystaurosporine (UCN-01) in human cancer cell lines, possibly influenced by p53 function. *Cancer Res.*, 57: 4029-35.

[190] Shapiro GI, Supko JG, Patterson A, et al.(2001). A phase II trial of the cyclin-dependent kinase inhibitor flavopiridol in patients with previously untreated stage iv non- small cell lung cancer. *Clin. Cancer Res.*, 7: 1590-99.

[191] Sharan R et al. (2005). Conserved patterns of protein interactions in multiple species. *PNAS-USA*, Vol. 102: 1974-1979.

[192] Sidransky, D. (2002). Emerging molecular markers of cancer. *Nature Rev. Cancer*, 2: 210-19.

[193] Silverman, L., R. Campbell, and J. R. Broach.(1998). New assay technologies for high throughput screening. *Current Opinion in Chemical Biology*, 2: 397-403. 11:825-28.

[194] Snijders, A.M. et al. (2001). Assembly of microarrays for genome-wide measurement of DNA copy number. *Nature Genetics*, 29: 263-4.

[195] Somasundaram K, Zhang H, Zeng YX et al. 1997. Arrest of the cell cycle by the tumour-suppressor BRCA1 requires the CDK-inhibitor p21 WAF1/CiP1. *Nature*, 389: 187-90.

[196] Sorlie, T., et al. (2001). Gene expression patterns of breast carcinomas distinguish tumor subclasses with clinical implications. *PNAS -USA*, 98: 10869–74.

[197] Staunton, JE, et al.(2001). Chemosensitivity prediction by transcriptional profiling. *PNAS*-USA, 98 (19): 10787-92.

[198] Sutherland RL, Musgrove EA. (2004). Cyclins and breast cancer. *J. Mammary Gland Biol. Neoplasia*, 9(1): 95-104.

[199] Tanaka H, Arakawa H, Yamaguchi T et al. (2000). A ribonucleotide reductase gene involved in a p53-dependent cell-cycle checkpoint for DNA damage. *Nature*, Vol. 404: 42-49.

[200] Terwogt JM, Mandjes IA, Sindermann H, et al. (1999). Phase II trial of topically applied miltefosine solution in patients with skin-metastasized breast cancer. *Br. J. Cancer*, 79:1158-61.

[201] Thompson NL. (1991). in *Topics of Fluorescence Spectroscopy.*, Lakowicz, J.R. ed., New York and London: Plenum Press, Vol.1. p. 337.

[202] Tortora G, Caputo R, Pomatico G, et al. (1999). Cooperative inhibitory effect of novel mixed backbone oligonucleotide targeting protein kinase A in combination with docetaxel and anti-epidermal growth factor-receptor antibody on human breast cancer cell growth. *Clin. Cancer Res.*, 5: 875-81.

[203] Uberall F, Oberhuber H, Maly K, et al. (1991). Hexadecylphosphocholine inhibits inositol phosphate formation and protein kinase C activity. *Cancer Res.*, 51: 807-12.

[204] van Diest PJ, Michalides RJ, Jannink L, et al. (1995). Cyclin D1 expression in invasive breast cancer: Correlation and prognostic value. *Amer. J. Pathol.*, 150:705-11.

[205] Velicescu, M. et al. (2002). Cell division is required for *de novo* methylation of CpG islands in bladder cancer cells. *Cancer Res.* 62: 2378-2384.

[206] Velculescu VE.; Zhang L, Vogelstein B, et al. (1995). Serial analysis of gene expression. *Science*, 270: 484-487.

[207] Velculescu, VE. (1999). Tantalizing Transcriptomes—SAGE and Its Use in Global Gene Expression Analysis. *Science*, 286 (5444): 1491-2.

[208] von Eggeling F.; Davies H, Lomas L, et al. (2000). Tissue-specific microdissection coupled with ProteinChip array technologies: Applications in cancer research. *Biotechniques*, 29: 1066-1070.

[209] Wachi S, et al. (2005). Interactome—transcriptome analysis reveals the high centrality of genes differentially expressed in lung cancer tissues. *Bioinformatics*, 21: 4205-4208.

[210] Walter N.; Schwille P. and Eigen M. (1996). Fluorescence correlation analysis of probe diffusion simplifies quantitative pathogen detection by PCR., *Proc. Natl. Acad. Sci. USA*, 93: 12805-08.

[211] Wang Q, Fan S, Eastman A, et al. (1996). UCN-01: a potent abrogator of G_2 checkpoint function in cancer cells with disrupted p53. *J. Natl. Cancer Inst.* 88: 956-965.

[212] Wang Q, Zhang H, Kajino K et al. (1998). BRCA1 binds c-Myc and inhibits its transcriptional and transforming activity in cells. *Oncogene*, 17: 1939-48.

[213] Weinstein J.N.; et al. (1997). An Information-Intensive Approach to the Molecular Pharmacology of Cancer. *Science*, 275: 343-349.

[214] Weinstein, J.N. (2000). Pharmacogenomics-Teaching Old Drugs New Tricks., *New Engl. J. Med.*, 343:1408-1409.

[215] Wilson CA, Ramos L, Villasenor MR et al. (1999). Localization of human BRCA1 and its loss in high-grade non-inherited breast carcinoma. *Nature Genet ics*, 21: 236-40.

[216] Winkler T, Kettling U, Koltermann, A, Eigen M. (1999). Confocal fluorescence coincidence analysis: An approach to ultra high-throughput screening. *PNAS-USA*, 96: 1375-1378.

[217] Winkler T, Bieschke J, Schwille P. (1997). Development of a dual-color cross-correlation system for FCS. Available from: http://www.mpibpc.gwdg.de /abteilungen/081/fcs/correlation/english.

[218] Winkler T, Schwille P, Oehlenschläger F. (1998). Detection of HIV-1 RNA by NASBA-FCS: available from: www.mpibpc.gwdg.de/abteilungen/081/fcs/nasba/english

[219] Wodicka L, Dong H, Mittmann M, et al. (1997). Genome-wide expression monitoring in *Saccharomyces cerevisiae.*, *Nature Biotechnol.*, 15: 1359-1367.

[220] Wong, IH, et al. (1999). *Cancer Res.*, 59: 71-73.

[221] Wuchty S. (2004). Evolution and topology in the yeast interaction network, *Genome Res.*, 14: 1310-1314.

[222] Xiong Z, Laird PW. (1997). COBRA: a sensitive and quantitative DNA methylation assay. *Nucleic Acids Res.*, 25: 2532-2534.

[223] Yan, PS, et al. (2002). Applications of CpG island microarrays for high-throughput analysis of DNA methylation. *J. Nutr.*, 132: 2430S-2434S.

[224] Yarden RI, Brody LC. (1999). BRCA1 interacts with components of the histone deacetylase complex. *Proc Natl Acad Sci USA*, 96: 4983-88.

[225] Yu J, Zhang L, Hwang PM et al. (1999). Identification and classification of p53-regulated genes. *PNAS -USA*, 96: 14517-14522.

[226] Yu X, Wu LC, Bowcock AM et al.(1998).The C-terminal (BRCT) domains of BRCA1 interact in vivo with CtIP, a protein implicated in the CtBP pathway of transcriptional repression *J. Biol. Chem*, 273: 25388-92.

[227] Zhu H. and Snyder M. (2001). Protein arrays and microarrays. *Curr. Opin. Chem Biol.*, 5: 40-45.

[228] Zujewski J, Horak, ID, Bol CJ, et al. (2000). Phase I and pharmacokinetic study of farnesyl protein transferase inhibitor R115777 in advanced cancer. *J. Clin. Oncol.* 18:927-34.

[229] Baianu IC, et al. (2010). Łukasiewicz -Moisil Many--Valued Logic Algebras of Highly-Complex Systems, *BRAIN-- Broad Research in Artificial Intelligence and Neuroscience*, ISSN 2067-3957, Volume 1: 1-- 15.

[230] Baianu IC, and Poli R. (2011). From Simple to Complex and Ultra-complex Systems: A Paradigm Shift Towards Non-Abelian Systems Dynamics -v. 4.0. *philoso.philica.com Article number 256:1-18.*

Part 7

Transcriptional Analysis

23

In-silico Approaches for RNAi Post-Transcriptional Gene Regulation: Optimizing siRNA Design and Selection

Mahmoud ElHefnawi[1] and Mohamed Mysara[2]
[1]National Research Center
[2]The University of Nottingham
[1]Egypt
[2]UK

1. Introduction

RNA interference (RNAi) is a naturally occurring endogenous biological post-transcriptional cellular mechanism that regulates against foreign genetic elements such as viruses and inserted gene transcripts as well as in-house gene expression regulation. Small interfering RNA (siRNA) molecules utilize this mechanism to promote homology dependent messenger RNA (mRNA) degradation.

The utilization of siRNA as a molecular target to silence gene expression has been used extensively as a research tool in functional genomics. The unprecedented advantage of siRNA molecules, which is mainly related to the ability of effective and specific inhibition of disease causing genes, elicited great expectations in therapeutic applications and drug discovery. siRNAs' potential as a drugs was investigated in viral and cancer models, and showed successful results with diseases such as HIV, HCV and several types of cancer; as most of these diseases have no cure. One advantage of siRNA-based drugs is their feasibility in clinical trials following approval of phase 1. Moreover, they do not rely on an intact immune system which give the advantage over other long double stranded RNA (dsRNA). However, several factors challenge the design of selective siRNA molecules with highly guaranteed silencing efficiency. Therefore, careful selection of siRNAs complying with all necessary properties is crucial for efficient functional performance.

This Chapter discusses RNA interference using small interfering RNS (siRNA) starting with the biological nature of mRNA and siRNA. Then it tackles factors contributing to siRNA-mRNA silencing from both biological and bioinformatics aspects that should affect siRNA effectiveness. Then, it represents step wise workflow for rational siRNA design considering state of the art tools and algorithms. By the end of this chapter, various tools are presented for siRNA evaluation phases that are used to predict siRNA efficiency and efficacy, with a practical example applying the proposed methodology.

2. Small interfering RNA

Small interfering RNAs 'siRNAs' are one of the cell defence mechanisms that act against not only exogenous genetic materials like virus genes but also against cell endogenous genes as one of the post-transcription regulation method (Ullu et al. 2002). These natural-occurring siRNAs target mRNAs (whether they are over expressed or abnormal) in a manner, so selective and potent, that they became the core of interest of many biologists in the last decade. Although siRNAs are not the only layer responsible for post-transcriptional regulation, they have the advantage of hardly invoking the innate immune response (Interferon-response) in contrast to long double stranded RNA (Stark et al. 1998) . In addition, siRNAs, have shown to be very promising new therapeutic agents in various diseases especially in Cancer, Aids and Neurodegenerative disorders as most of these diseases have no cure (Hutvágner & Zamore 2002; Surabhi & Gaynor 2002; Xia et al. 2004). That is why siRNA has been used as a drug for cancer clinical trials on human producing the efficient and specific effect on human as it was expected (Davis et al. 2010).

2.1 siRNA mechanism of action

The mechanism pathway of siRNA is as follows: long dsRNA is cleaved by "DICER" a ribonuclease III-type enzyme into the short molecules of siRNA duplexes, being homologous to the mRNA targeted for silencing, siRNA triggers the formation of RNA-induced silencing complex (RISC) in which the double stranded siRNA is incorporated cutting the long double-stranded RNA molecules to double stranded small interfering RNA (ds-siRNA), as illustrated in the [Fig. 1]. Then it is anwounded leading to single stranded siRNA that binds to the target mRNA sequence resulting in its cleavage, and according to the type of the RISC complex the RNAi action is directed through mRNA degradation, action arrest or chromatin modification. [5]. This is detailed below:

Fig. 1. Small interfering RNA formed of two short stranded RNA sequences complementary to each other.

Due to the homology (similarity) between the double stranded siRNA (ds-siRNA) and the targeted messenger RNA (mRNA), the aggregation of a complex called RNA induced silencing complex (RISC) is triggered. After binding with ds-siRNA, RISC acts to separate (unwind) the strand making the sense and the antisense strands (passenger and guide strand). After siRNA unwinding into small single strand, it could produce its action with three different mechanisms [Fig 2].

2.1.1 Direct cleavage method

The single stranded RNA together with RISC bind to the targeted mRNA and induce its degradation by the Ago-2 degradation (protein triggered by RISC-siRNA complex acts to break the targeted mRNA). The degraded mRNA is finally digested with, what is called, cellular lysosomes. This is the main mechanism by which siRNA causes selective and potent gene silencing, but this only occurs in case of high level of similarity between siRNA and the targeted mRNA region (Birmingham et al. 2006).

2.1.2 Seed-mediated translational attenuation

The complementation between the siRNA seeding region hexamer (from the second to the seventh position) and the 3'UTR (untranslated region) of the mature mRNA has been identified capable of inhibition of that mRNA's translation and causing its degradation (E. M. Anderson et al. 2008; Birmingham et al. 2006).

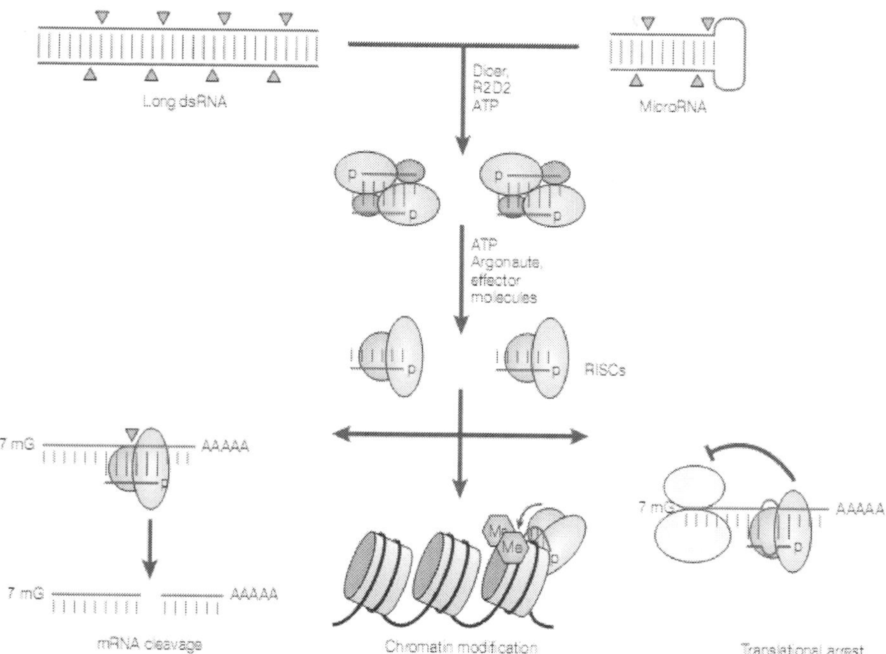

Fig. 2. Naturally occurring siRNA synthesis pathway and three its possible mechanisms of action. Endogenous (naturally occurring) siRNA are produced from either microRNA or long double strand RNA after their cleavage by the Dicer enzyme so they produce double strand siRNA. Both endogenous and exogenous (introduced by researchers) ds-siRNA pass through the activation process starting with unwinding and RNA induced silencing complex (RISC) to the lead single strand siRNA. Then RISC- single strand siRNA complex silence the targeted gene either by one of the three mechanisms: 1) Binding to the mRNA leading to their breakage through Age2 mechanism. 2) Binding to the 3' end and mediate translational attenuation of the mRNA. 3) Gene silencing through chromatin modification [Figure from the work of (Dorsett & Thomas Tuschl 2004)].

2.1.3 Chromatin modification

siRNA has another mechanism of interference by chromatin modification as illustrated by Dorsett and Tuschl in their description of Scherer work that siRNA is one of the three major nucleic-acid-based gene silencing mechanisms (Dorsett & Thomas Tuschl 2004).

3. Factors that affect siRNA design

In order to understand the interaction between siRNA and the targeted mRNA, several factors have been known to affect the design of effective and specific siRNA. These factors can be further sub classified into four major classes design as illustrated by Birmingham (Birmingham et al. 2007). Firstly, Targeted region or what is called "sequence space", this section handles the identification of regions in the mRNA to be targeted by the designed siRNA. This step is highly critical as targeting the wrong region would abolish the effect of all designed siRNAs. Sequence space is affected by several factors: Transcript region, Transcript size, mRNA multiple splicing, Orthologs consensus and Single nucleotide polymorphism. Secondly, siRNA sequence space preparation, here we discuss internal repeats, positional preferences, and other desirable/undesirable words/motifs are discussed. Thirdly, siRNA thermodynamic properties and both siRNA and mRNA target accessibility. It includes parameters like GC content, palindromes, in addition to thermodynamic stability and differential ends stability which have been identified to be highly important factors in siRNA selection. Forthly, siRNA specificity describing mechanisms through which siRNA could invoke immune reaction or has off-target effect. Each of these factors can greatly affect siRNA selection and therefore they should be studied thoroughly.

3.1 Target sequence space [Targeted region preprocessing]

Targeted regions (or what is called "sequence space") are areas of the mRNA that should be assigned for targeting by the designed siRNA. There are five factors affecting the selection of the proper sequence space summarized in (Birmingham et al. 2007).

3.1.1 Transcript regions and size

siRNA should target regions in the mRNA that is not affected by the maturation process, hence targeting 3'UTR, 5'UTR and (most importantly) open reading frame (ORF) [Fig 3]. Normally both 3'UTR and 5'UTR could be excluded from targeted sequence space, unless sequence space needs to be widened. If the mRNA length is < 500 nucleotides, 3'UTR and 5'UTR should be included in target space selection.

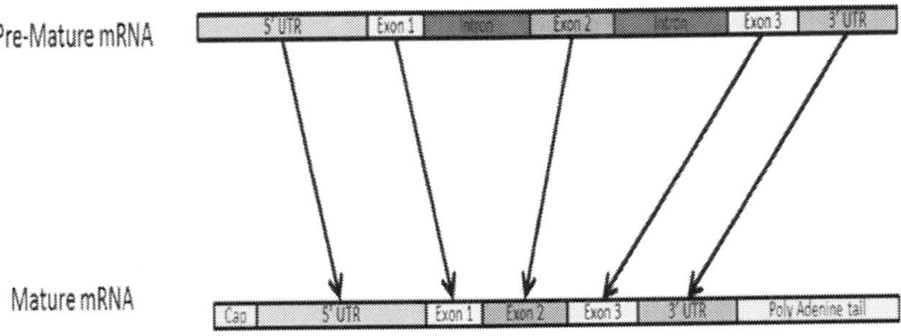

Fig. 3. Maturation process of premature to mature mRNA. This figure illustrates different regions that vary due to omission and insertion during the maturation process. In the maturation process omission of the introns (non coding areas) and addition of 5' cap and 3' tail) takes place (Mysara 2010).

3.1.2 Multiple splicing and orthologs consensus

One mRNA could be coding for several proteins as the process of splicing is accompanied by rearrangement of exons. There are several mechanisms of alternative (differential) splicing as exon insertion or deletion but the main mechanism; as described in the work of Black; is exon skipping (Black 2003). This phenomena form a huge obstacle if there is a need to target all the mRNA transcripts; therefore, regions in common among them should be recognized and targeted [Fig 4]. All the mRNA's transcripts should be included in target space selection. In case of handling multiple organisms (as in global vaccines or rapidly mutated species as virus) the consensus between different targeted mRNAs should be considered in the target space selection.

3.1.3 Single Nucleotide Polymorphism (SNPs)

Single Nucleotide polymorphism (SNP) is very crucial in siRNA design where single (several) Nucleotide(s) difference could cause dramatic shift in the produced protein (or in its regulation) or could have a non-sensible effect in this case it is named silence polymorphism. There are two main locations for SNPs existence non-coding and coding regions [Fig 5]. The first region is the **non-coding region,** where SNP existing in the Introns will not affect the mature mRNA, thus the siRNA targeting it. However, if the SNP is located in the 3′ UTR or 5′ UTR, caution should be taken in cases where the siRNA is designed to target them. The second region is **coding region,** where SNP exists in the protein coding region (ORF or Exons), there are two possibilities: SNPs will not affect the produced protein due to degeneracy of the genetic code, or it could cause changes in the produced protein, hence siRNA targeting this region should be excluded.

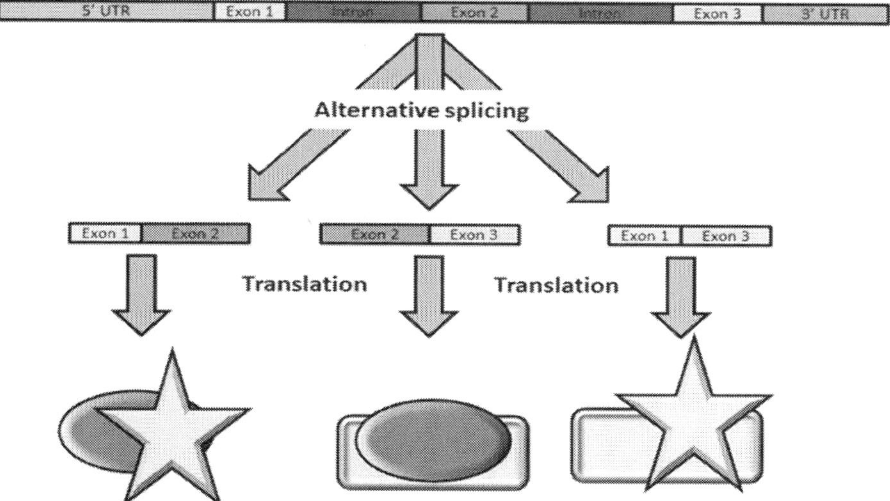

Fig. 4. mRNA alternative splicing phenomena results in several transcripts from the same gene. Each of these transcripts is later translated in a different protein. These proteins functions could be similar or non-similar to each other.

3.2 SiRNA sequence space [Positional/word preferences]

Positional/word preferences in the sense/antisense strand of the siRNA are a crucial determinant of siRNA functionality. Several position dependant preferences were identified from analysis of siRNA experimental dataset, which can affect siRNA selection process. Among those preferences within the sense strand (Ui-Tei et al. 2004): (i) A/U at the 5′ end of the antisense strand;(ii) G/C at the 5′end of the sense strand; (iii) at least five A/U residues in the 5′ terminal one-third of the antisense strand; and (iv) the absence of any GC stretch of more than 9 nt in length. (Reynolds et al. 2004): (I) At least 3 ′A/U′ bases at positions 15–19 (sense strand). (II) Absence of internal repeats. (III) An ′A′ base at position 19 (sense strand). (IV) An ′A′ base at position 3 (sense strand). (V) A ′U′ base at position 10 (sense strand). (VI) A base other than ′G′ or ′C′ at 19 (sense strand). (VII) A base other than ′G′ at position 13 (sense strand). (Mohammed Amarzguioui & Prydz 2004): asymmetry in the stability of the duplex ends (measured as the A/U differential of the three terminal basepairs at either end of the duplex) and the motifs S1, A6, and W19. The presence of the motifs U1 or G19 was associated with lack of functionality.

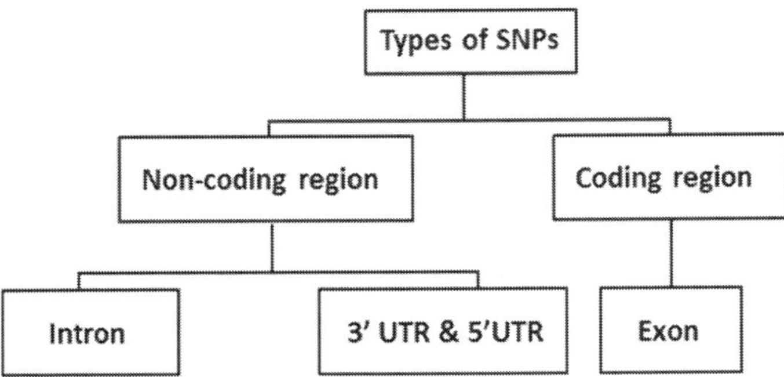

Fig. 5. Classification of SNPs according to region of occurrence in the mRNA.

Several positions in siRNA duplex that could affect their efficiency, as in (Birmingham et al. 2007), candidate duplexes with five or more of any single base in a row, should be removed. Although less detrimental than G/C stretches, repeated bases have also been shown to reduce functionality. Stretches of repeated base-containing sequences are less selective, and A or U/T stretches may additionally target regulatory motifs. Moreover, candidate duplexes with more than six consecutive G's and/or C's stretches of G's and C's have been shown to be one of the strongest negative determinants for siRNA activity that should be removed. Such regions have pronounced local stability, greatly inhibiting duplex dissociation. In addition, GC- rich stretches are not compatible with some synthetic nucleic acid chemistries utilized in vector-based expression.

3.3 The target accessibility evaluation

Several studies have been done to illustrate the structural and sequence features affection siRNA functionality, all of these aspects affect siRNA and mRNA accessibility (Patzel et al. 2005; Ladunga 2007). Target accessibility evaluation is crucial for proper designing of efficient siRNA, as mRNA tends to form secondary structure that affects its accessibility and hence reduces the capability to design siRNA targeting certain regions of mRNA. Therefore, target accessibility evaluation represents where the mRNA is more likely be accessed by short oligomers as siRNAs, it involves not only mRNA secondary structure evaluation, but also energetic calculation of siRNA and mRNA. For interaction between two RNA sequences (siRNA and mRNA) two types of energies are needed: first energy required for opening the binding site, second energy required to gain hybridization the summation of these three energies is defined as interaction energy. The energy required for opening siRNA duplex and mRNA should have lesser than the hybridization energy between siRNA and the mRNA. There are evidence based correlation between siRNA inhibition efficiency and siRNA-mRNA binding energy (Mückstein et al. 2006), that strengthens the findings of Ladunga in which target accessibility information was found to provide the most predictive feature among the 142 features studied and improves the prediction of highly efficient siRNA (Ladunga 2007). Other parameters affecting target accessibility are presented below:

3.3.1 GC content

GC content represent the percentage of Guanine and Cytosine (two of the four nucleotides types that build the mRNA) should not be too high in order not to impair the double strand siRNA unwinding and enables the ease of RISC protein entrance.

3.3.2 Palindrome

Palindrome should be addressed in target accessibility evaluationwhere region(s) in one strand binds to another region in the same strand due to reverse complementation. Therefore, palindromes should be avoided in siRNA design as they tend to make intra-molecular structure (2ry structure) which impairs RISC binding [Fig 6].

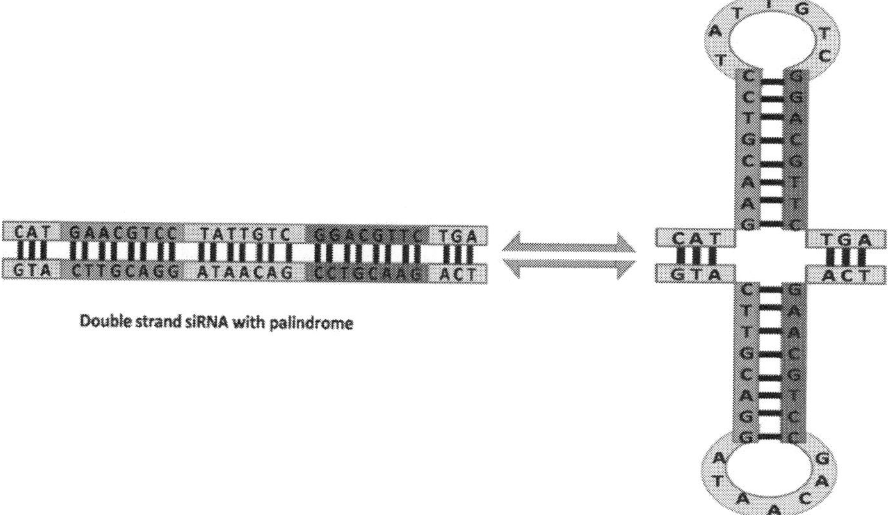

Fig. 6. Palindrome patterns and their affect on siRNA binding to RISC and the targeted mRNA. Palindromes lead to changing double stranded siRNA secondary structure which in turn affects their ability to bind to RISC and the targeted mRNA (Mysara 2010).

3.3.3 Thermodynamic stability

It is important to keep/introduce relative thermodynamic stability at both ends of the siRNA (3'UTR and 5'UTR) and low stability at the central zone as these facilitate ds-siRNA cleavage.

3.3.4 Differential end stability

Differential end stability is considered one of the most important features that affect siRNA functionality (Schwarz et al. 2003) [Fig 7]. RISC binds to either sense or the antisense strand, but with different ratio. This ratio depends on "Differential stability" between the first couple of bases ofthe 5' end from both strands. As these couple of bases affect what is called Thermo-Dynamic stability (TDS), so the lower the stability the better it binds to RISC. It has been found that only the antisense (leading) strand is capable of causing gene silencing (Dorsett & Thomas Tuschl 2004). Therefore, it is essential design siRNA with low TDS at 5' end of the antisense than TDS of the 3' end, to have a better binding with RISC and better efficiency in silencing the target mRNA.

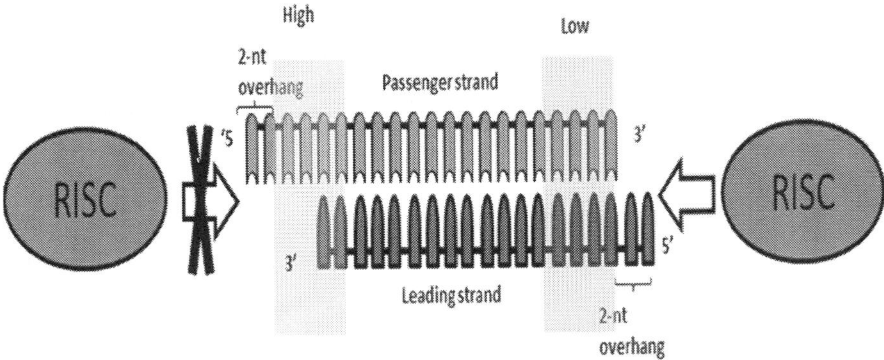

Fig. 7. RISC and Differential end stability. This figure illustrates the effect of differential end stability of RISC annealing with ds siRNA. Therefore, it is very important to ensure the 5' end of the siRNA lead-strand is less stable than the 5' end of the passenger-strand. This way RISC would form complex with only the lead-strand that is designed to bind to the targeted mRNA.

3.3.5 The number of single-stranded base pairs at the 5' and 3' ends of the target mRNA

It has recently been shown to significantly contribute to the effectiveness of siRNAs by Patzel and Kaufman in their recent (S. H. E. Kaufmann & Patzel 2008). (Patzel, Rutz et al. 2005) (Patzel, Rutz et al. 2005) (Patzel, Rutz et al. 2005) (Patzel, Rutz et al. 2005) The same conclusion was reached by Gredell and co-workers in July 2008.

3.4 siRNA specificity [The off-targeting effect]

"Ideally, the siRNA must not cause any effects other than those related to the knock down of the target gene" (Semizarov et al. 2003). It is essential that the designed siRNA affects only the

targeted mRNA. In other words, siRNA should not invoke innate immunity nor has any off-targeted mRNA.

3.4.1 Innate immunity effect

Concerning the innate immunity effect, by rational selection of appropriate length of the siRNA (21-23 nucleotides) the innate immunity will not be triggered (Birmingham et al. 2006). Although, duplexes of less than 30 nt are short enough to evade immunorecognition by cytosolic double-stranded RNA (dsRNA) receptors, but are long enough to trigger Toll-like receptor 7 sequence-dependent recognition (Patzel et al. 2005). Recognition of motifs as 5′-GUCCUUCAA-3′, 5′-UGUGU-3′ and tetrad-forming poly(G) stretches and avoidance of their presence in the sensitized siRNA, help over coming Toll-like receptor recognition. There was several works using chemical modification in order to mask the innate immunity response (interferon response) (Patzel 2007).

3.4.2 Off-target effect

Apart from that, comes the problem of off-targets which is one of the most important factors for siRNA selection and filtration. "siRNA off-target" is mainly any target that is affected by siRNA other than the assigned target. It is very common for siRNA to have a multi-target as they are only 21-23 nucleotide length; therefore, there is a good chance siRNA could match with more than one mRNA. In fact, as observed in the work of Jackson et al, both sense and antisense and know to have an off-target effect with several mRNA transcripts (Jackson et al. 2003; Jackson & Linsley 2010). There are different mechanisms through which siRNA can trigger off-targeting actions:

I) Complete or near complete off-target matches(siRNA-like effects)

This mechanism is triggered whenever the designed siRNA is completely identical (or with one mismatch) with a region in the off-targeted mRNA. This complete (near complete) matches between siRNA and mRNA leads to the destruction of that mRNA with the same mechanism that siRNA silences the targeted mRNA as described before.

II) Partial off-target (miRNA-like effects through Seed matching off-target)

If the designed siRNA seeding region (second to seventh position) matches with 3′UTR of off-targeted mRNA, this will result in affecting the off-target translation as illustrated by (E. M. Anderson et al. 2008). Therefore, these siRNAs are considered as partial off-targets and should be excluded. Chemical modifications have been applied here to reduce off-target and increase the specificity (Birmingham et al. 2007). These off-target effects (complete, near complete or partial) are responsible for loss of specificity as they make this unwanted silencing with other proteins synthesising genes. Moreover, they also cause loss of siRNA potency as the unwanted off-targeting of other mRNA could lead to unavailability of these siRNAs at the original targets (Semizarov et al. 2003; Vert et al. 2006).

In addition to those types of off-target effects, there is the protein interaction. As siRNAs are known to bind to different cellular proteins and alter them, which is known as "Aptamer Effect" as described in (Semizarov et al. 2003). Moreover, avoidance of sequence motifs interfering with RNA synthesis and purification should be considered, as Guanine-rich RNA sequences and sequences containing consecutive stretches of more than three G bases (Patzel et al. 2005).

3.5 siRNA duplex chemical modification

Several chemical modifications could be introduced to the designed siRNA in the aim of enhancing its tolerability, improving it stability, limiting its off-target effect and conjugation with tracking agent properly. There are multiple types of chemical modifications that are typically introduced into siRNAs, as summarized in the work of (Birmingham et al. 2007):

I) Sense strand disabling: it is done to increase the specificity and efficiency of siRNA designed. Various approaches were used as2′ ribose modifications including 2′-OR where R¼ fluoro, alkyl, O-alkyl40–43; LNA modifications at the 5′ end of the sense strand.

II) Stabilization: Chemical modifications of the phosphate backbone (e.g. phosphorothioate linkages), the ribose (e.g. locked nucleic acids, 2′-deoxy-2′-fluorouridine, 2′-O-ethyl),and/or the base (e.g.2′-fluoropyrimidines) increase the resistance of siRNA to nuclease. Stability of siRNAs in biological fluids needs various modifications as 2′-halogen, 2′-alkyl and/or 2′-O-alkyl modifications of one or both strands of the siRNA as well as stabilizing internucleotide modifications of the overhangs. Care should be taken when addressing those modifications not to interfere with siRNA efficiency.

III) Specificity: Chemical modifications in the aim of increasing siRNA specificity and decrease its off-target activity, include includes 2′-O-alkyl modification of unique positions of the sense and/or antisense strand. These modification patterns severely limit sense and antisense off-target effects by disrupting seed-mediated off-target activity.

IV) Conjugations: siRNAs have been conjugated with lipophilic derivatives of cholesterol, lauric acid or lithocholic acid to enhance their cellular uptake and specificity (Lorenz et al. 2004). The safest sites for conjugation are the 5′ and 3′ termini of the sense strand.

4. Guidelines for siRNA rational design

After have discussed factors influencing the siRNA efficacy,here we present our methodology and phases for efficient siRNA rational design. Originally, this methodology was inspired by the repeated Influenza pandemics, and our trials to design a novel siRNA therapy that would work for any new pandemic(ElHefnawi, Alaidi et al. 2011). There are seven phases that should be considered for proper designing of siRNA with high specificity and efficiency [Fig 8].

4.1 Targeted gene selection

"Targeted gene" selection is extremely critical for siRNA design as the purpose of gene silencing is to stop the expression of specific abnormal proteins most commonly be involved in the biological pathways as "cancer pathways". Therefore, the protein of interest should play a key role in this pathway, in order to produce the desired therapeutic effect from the silencing process. Therefore, there is a need to search the key regularity protein annotated in various biological pathway databases as "Reactome" and "KEGG" (http://www.reactome.org/ & http://www.genome.jp/kegg/pathway.html) and design siRNA capable of targeting them.

4.2 Targeted sequence specification and filtration

After selecting the gene of interest, as gene itself is not targeted but rather its transcript(s), all the available transcripts should be located. In some instance only one transcript should be targeted; in this case all other transcripts should be excluded as targeting them is considered as lack of specificity (off-target). But on the other hand, if there is a need to silence all of the gene's transcripts (which is very common), several options are available for handling such situation [Fig 9] either by mapping the transcripts on the genome, as

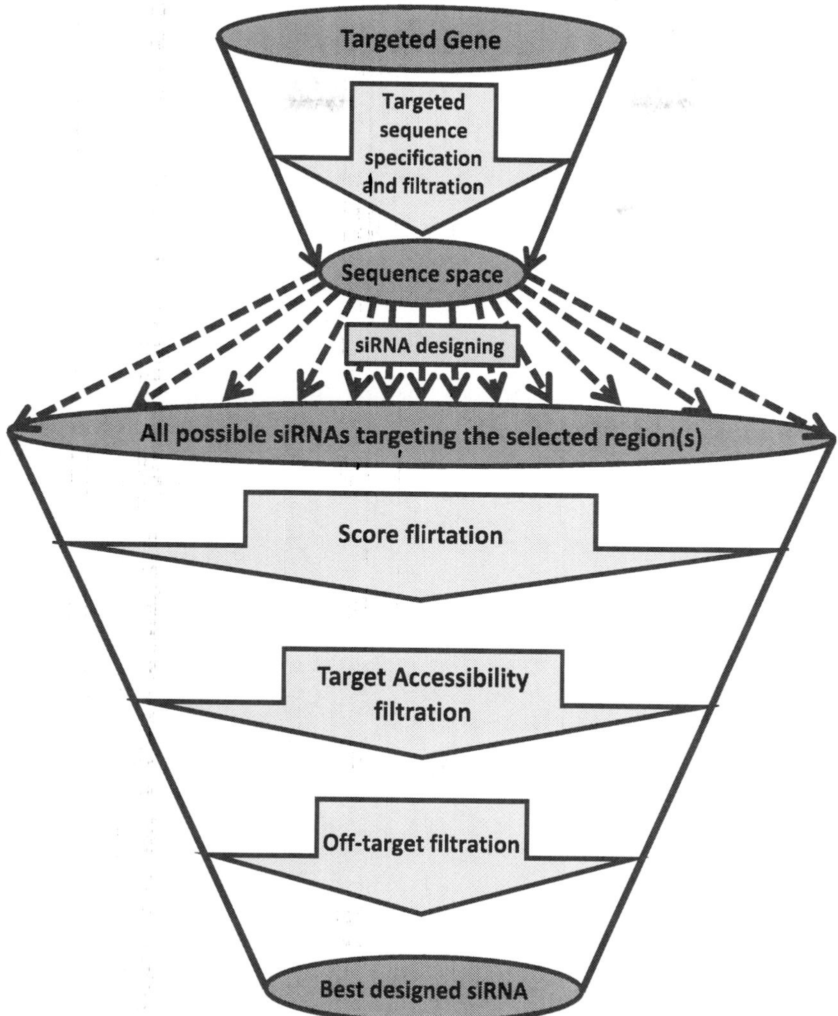

Fig. 8. Different phases for designing siRNA with high efficiency & sensitivity. There are seven distinguished phases for siRNA design: 1st choosing the targeted gene for silencing. 2nd identifying the proper target sequence space that represent all gene's transcripts and doesn't have any unstable regions. 3rd designing all possible siRNA with nineteen nucleotides length with both sense and antisense strand.4th these potential siRNAs are scored and evaluated according to several scoring mechanisms and criteria and then filter them according to produced scores. 5th siRNA are filtered according to target accessibility. 6th off-target filtration of the remaining siRNA is performed excluding siRNAs with unwanted off-target effect. 8th select the best designed siRNAs that pass all the previous filtration phases and achieve the highest predicted efficiency (Mysara 2010).

proposed in the work of (Y.-kyu Park et al. 2008), or via using multiple sequence alignment (MSA). Multiple sequence alignment is performed either by aligning different gene transcripts and selecting the transcript with the highest identity to the alignment profile, in other word; select the transcript that is more capable of representing all the other transcripts. Another manoeuvre is by considering all transcripts' regions in common (conserved).

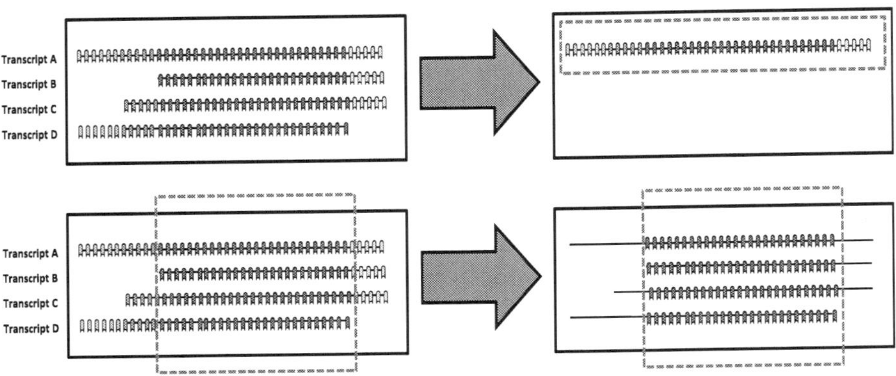

Fig. 9. Different approaches of handling multiple gene transcripts. There are two proposed approaches 1st by aligning between different gene transcripts in order to get the alignment profile and choose the closest transcript to the alignment profile. 2nd way is to get the gaped consensus between these transcripts and choose the regions that are 100% conserved between them (Mysara 2010).

The latter method ensures designing siRNA targeting all the gene's transcripts, this is very important as one mismatch between the target mRNA (transcript) and siRNA could dramatically affect siRNA efficiency (Czauderna et al. 2003) there was noticeable decrease in the efficiency of designed siRNA when induced central single nucleotide variation between the siRNA and targeted mRNA, all together with the findings in the following works (M. Amarzguioui 2003; Sayda M Elbashir et al. 2002). However, one of the main disadvantages of this approach is that it narrows the target sequence space and it is possible that no active siRNA will pass the multi-filtration phases described in [Fig 8]. In this occassion,sequence space should be widened via inclusion of (3'UTR and 5'UTR) or using the first approach.

After locating the targeted sequence space, both SNPs and unstable (highly variable) positions should be identified (if any) and any designed siRNAs targeting these residues/regions should be rejected. This way the targeted sequence space will be limited to mRNA (or the conserved region among different gene transcripts) either representing the ORF or (ORF + 3'UTR + 5'UTR) free from any SNPs or unstable regions.

4.3 Designing all possible siRNA targeting the selected regions

This section illustrates the proper siRNA length that ensures high efficiency and stability having neutral effect on host innate immunity. Then it discusses how to select siRNA from the mRNA sequence space.

4.3.1 Selection of the appropriate siRNA length

Using siRNA (with its short length) has better advantages over using long double stranded
RNAi as they do not trigger immune response and they also silence the targeted mRNA more
efficiently. However, siRNA with length equal to thirty nucleotides were found to be inactive
(S M Elbashir, Lendeckel, et al. 2001). After that the selection of proper siRNA length was
heavily studied, upper and lower limits have been assigned. It was found that shortening the
length from nineteen to seventeen affected the siRNA capability to silence the targeted gene; as
at least nineteen nucleotides are required for RISC binding. (Czauderna et al. 2003). To
establish the upper length limit, it was found that siRNAs with length from (18 to 23) are at
least eight folds more effective than other lengths. In addition the 24-25 nucleotide length
siRNAs were completely inactive (S M Elbashir, J Martinez, et al. 2001). Therefore, siRNA with
length 19-21 plus a 2-nt overhang is the appropriate length for siRNA design and any further
deviation above or below this length threshold will have a direct effect on the siRNA activity.
It was also demonstrated that using 2-3mer nucleotides dT 3' UTR overhangs increases the
efficiency of antisense strand loading to the RISC complex.

4.3.2 Picking up siRNA from sequence space

After establishing the desired siRNA length (19 nucleotides), all possible siRNA molecules
should be considered using one nucleotide shift per time [Fig 10] till reaching the end of
sequence space. Although the ideal case is that each gene would have only one transcript with
no SNPs nor highly variable regions, the vast majority of the gene's sequence space would be
separate pieces (not intact) as shown in [Fig. 9]. Therefore, the selection of the 19 nucleotide
length siRNA should only be restricted to those sequence spaces free from any gaps.

Fig. 10. Designing of all possible siRNA using fixed frame shift. After choosing the
appropriate length (most propably 19 nucleotides + 2 overhangs) the target sequence space
is scanced and all possible siRNAs with one nucleotide shift at a time(Mysara 2010).

4.4 siRNA scoring and scores filtration

This stage is the most important stage for siRNA design as proper scoring and evaluation of siRNA activity assist the time and cost consumtion. Moreover, developing siRNA scoring tools with enhanced specificity and sensitivity would also serve a lot in that regardAs normally single mRNA would produce thousand potential siRNAs, these siRNAs need to be evaluated in order to filter them to smaller number suitable for experimental testing. There are several tools have been developed to predict siRNA activity; these tools differ a lot in these prediction capabilities in the terms of specificity and sensitivity. They use several rules and trained with various datasets, therefore, careful evaluation and picking up the right tool is essential for proper siRNA scoring phase. The details regarding siRNA scoring is further explained in the next section of the chapter.

4.5 siRNAs target accessibility filtration

For interaction between two RNA sequences (siRNA and mRNA) two types of energies are needed: first energy required for opening the binding site, second energy required to gain hybridization. There are several programs that is used to calculate each energy among them *RNAduplex* is capable of calculating duplex energy and RNAplfold capable of calculating opening energy for ds-siRNA and targeted mRNA (target site accessibility energy). Both   *RNAduplex*   and   *RNAplfold*   belong   to   Vienna   RNA   package http://www.tbi.univie.ac.at/~ivo/ RNA/. There are two more tools that are able to provide better advantages, RNAup and RNAxs.

4.5.1 RNAup

RNAup (that also belongs to Vienna RNA package) is capable of calculating all the three energies required for assisting the interaction energy (Mückstein et al. 2006). *RNAup* starts with calculating the probability that the sequence intervals (after splicing the sequence in small subsequences) are unpaired. Then, it computes the interaction energy, ending with choosing the ones with the least free energy (i.e. the highest stability). However, it cannot handle sequences longer than 5000 nucleotides as it needs a lot of memory.

4.5.2 RNAxs

RNAxs program (modification of the older *RNAplfold*) is one of the programs used to evaluate siRNA efficiency according to target accessibility evaluation; it combines *RNAplfold, RNAfold and RNAduplex* (Tafer et al. 2008). *RNAxs* is able to provide two major advantages: Time reduction and single phased process, which has been shown in the work of (Hofacker & Tafer 2010) the comparative experiment done between *RNAxs* and 2 other target accessibility based programs (*OligoWalk & Sirna*). It was found that only *RNAxs* is able to identify siRNAs with inhibition efficiency >50% and to classify 50% of experiment siRNA producing prediction capability higher than the other two programs.

4.6 siRNAs off-target filtration

All the siRNAs that pass the assigned thresholds for each scoring tools are filtered by their tendency to trigger off-target effect. As described in section later (under siRNA specificity), first siRNA having complete matches (or near complete) with the off-target mRNA should be excluded (19/19 or 18/19 or 18/18). Next, the rest of the siRNAs are filtered according to the presence of partial off-target by excluding siRNAs with matches between their seeding regions (second to seventh position) and the 3' UTR of the off-targeted mRNAs. This way the selected siRNA candidates would have the required specificity [Fig 11].

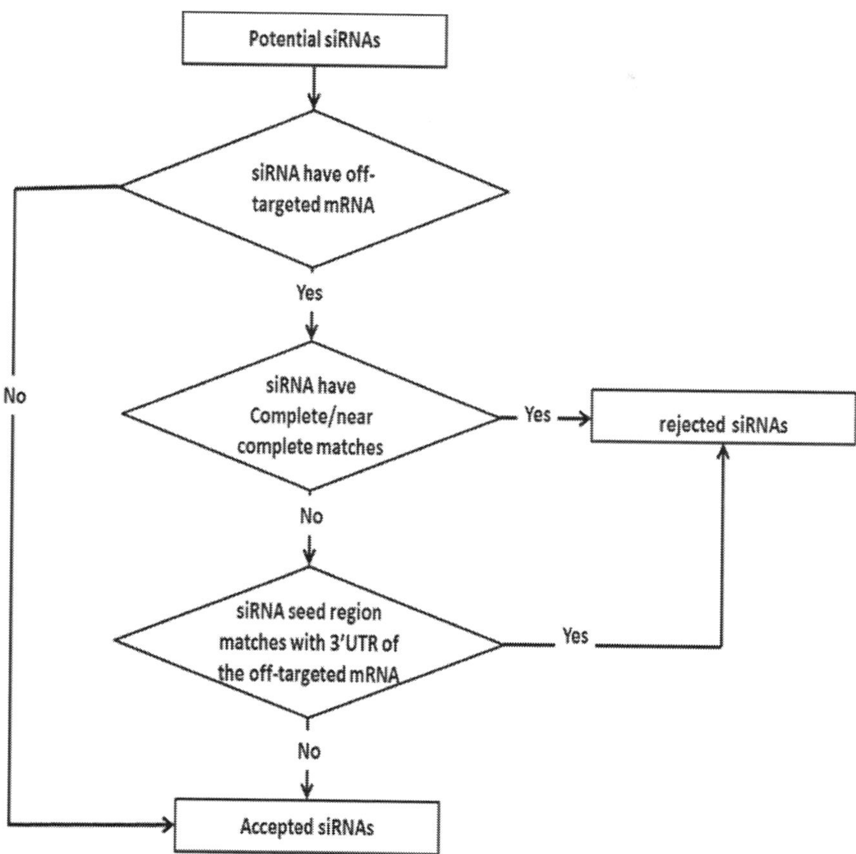

Fig. 11. Off-target filtration workflow describing decision making process for siRNAs off-target filtration.

4.7 Selecting the best designed siRNA

The final step is sorting the acceptable siRNAs candidates according to the predicted inhibition score. Taking the top 10-50 (if applicable) and order them for synthesis by adding UU or dTdT to the 3' ends. Final result is a double strand siRNAs containing leading strand and antisense strand with two 3'end overhangs. There are also several chemical modifications could be applied to the ds-siRNA would serve in increasing the stability, efficiency or neutralizing the immune response by various possible modifications (Birmingham et al. 2007).

4.8 Automation of siRNA design

This stepwise approach for designing siRNAs with acceptable target accessibility properties, passing predicted score, SNPS and off-target filtration could be automated using various programs and tools. The extend of considering those steps varies from program to another according to the used algorithm and the state of the art protocol available at its time, in our previous work, we managed to develop MysiRNA-Designer, siRNA design tool that implements all of the steps presented above [**Table 1**](Mysara, J. Garibaldi, et al. 2011).

Tools name	Multi-transcripts Consideration	Conserved Region Analysis	SNPs Evaluation	Multi-algorithms Scoring	2ry structure Evaluation	Target accessibility	Full Homology Off-target	Seed Region off-target	Server Based
MysiRNA-Designer	+	+	+	+	+	+	+	+	-
siDESIGN Center *1	+	+	+	-	-	-	+	+	+
Asi-Designer *2	+	-	+	-	+	-	+	-	+
RNAxs *3	-	-	-	-	+	+	-	-	+
siDRM *4	-	-	-	-	-	-	+	+	+

Table 1. Comparison between MysiRNA-Designer and several programs used for siRNA full automation designing. This Comparison involves tools ability to perform alignment between different transcripts, conserved regions consideration, all together with siRNA candidate evaluation using several algorithms and target accessibility. siRNAs filtration by the presence of Single Nucleotide Polymorphisms and off-targets (both full homology and seed regions)(Mysara, J. Garibaldi, et al. 2011, submitted). *1 siDESIGN Center at http://www.dharmacon.com/designcenter/DesignCenterPage.aspx. *2 Asi-Designer available at http://sysbio.kribb.re.kr:8080/AsiDesigner/menuDesigner.jsf. *3 RNAxs available at http://rna.tbi.univie.ac.at/cgi-bin/RNAxs. *4 siDRM available at http://sidrm.biolead.org/index.php.

5. Models used for predicting siRNA activity

There are several methods for scoring and predicting designed siRNA activity, some of them are more accurate than the others; however, they are classified into two groups (Ichihara et al. 2007): (i) Huesken dataset non-dependant [first generation]. (ii)Huesken dataset dependant [second generation]

5.1 Huesken dataset non dependant [First Generation]

These tool were developed to select the most efficient siRNAs, and they depend on differential ends Thermodynamic stability measures, mRNA secondary structure and base preferences specific position target uniqueness. Example of these rules: Reynolds (Reynolds et al. 2004), Amarzguioui (Mohammed Amarzguioui & Prydz 2004), Takasaki (Takasaki et al. 2004), Katoh (Katoh & Suzuki 2007), Ui-Tei (Ui-Tei et al. 2004), Hsieh (Hsieh et al. 2004). However, these first generation scoring techniques have shown to have low accuracy, as up to 65% of the siRNAs predicted as active (by these tools) failed to achieve 90% inhibition when tested experimentally and up to 20% of them were false positive, as described by (Ren et al. 2006). Therefore, there was a need for another approach that does not only take the site-specific position into consideration but also implement data mining techniques to interpret the experimentally obtained data.

5.2 Huesken dataset dependant [Second Generation]

This class has been developed mainly through experimental data observation, as the existence of dataset with fully annotated experimentally siRNAs with their different efficiency enabling sophisticated data mining handling of this data, was not available until the dataset of Novartis that was introduced by Hueshken (Hueskent et al. 2006) and used for training of several scoring tool as: *Biopredsi* (Huesken et al. 2006), *DSIR* (Vert et al. 2006), *ThermoComposition21* (S.A. Shabalina et al. 2006), *i-Score* (Ichihara et al. 2007) and *Scales* (Matveeva et al. 2007).

These scoring techniques predict siRNA efficiency more accurately than the older tools. Although they use completely different algorithms to evaluate siRNA efficiency, they have very close accuracy compared to the rest of the second generation algorithms, as described by (Ichihara et al. 2007). As in the comparative study done in the Ichihara's work all the second generation (except for Scales) and only Reynold and Katoh from the first generation achieved 90% successful prediction. Moreover, sensitivity of the second generation compared to Reynold and Karoh (which appear to have approximate accuracy) was at least 8 fold lower that the second generation sensitivity (this also supports Ren's findings mentioned earlier). Here, we handle the basicinformation of each member of this group of tools and provide comparison between them [Table 2].

5.2.1 Biopred

In Biopred, artificial neural network (ANN) was trained using huge number of records (2,182 training and 259 test), considering not only single nucleotide residue but certain patterns (as di-nucleotides). This work is considered the start of the second generation siRNA approaches and noticeable shift in the scoring accuracy. Although ANN used in this work provided ambiguity to the module and prevented further development (due to the complexity of the model), it was considered, at that time period, the best way to handle all these different parameters. The server based Biopred model was later simulated and released as Biopredsi excel-based tool together with i-Score, which is going to be illustrated later on (Ichihara et al. 2007).

5.2.2 DSIR

In DSIR, they used the exact training and test data as Biopredsi but with simplified linear regression model to give prediction based to two main sequence features and three main parameters with Pearson Correlation coefficient = 0.67. The main sequence feature is A/U presence at the first position of the 5' end guidance strand and the absence of Cytosine from both positions seven and eleven. The main parameters that have been used to build the model are: sprase21, spectra21, composition representation. These three parameters divide the siRNA by different manners and calculate the total score of all of them providing a very representative and interpretable method to evaluate a siRNA sequence, see Table 2.

Parameter	Description
Position dependant consensus	As several positions has been identified to be conserved between effective siRNA, so the are scored out of 11 for the presence of desirable residues and out of 10 (in -VE charge) for the presence of undisirable residue in specific position. 1 2 3 4 5 6 7 8 9 10 11 12 13 14 15 16 17 18 19 A/U U A/U(17-18) G/C (19)
Dinuleotide Content Index	As the occurrence of some dinucleotide combinations have exceeded the random distribution, so by combining these unique pairs with the level of effectiveness of these siRNA, it was found (or precisely confirmed) the low frequency of G/C dinucleotide pairs accompany high siRNA efficacy.
Thermodynamic Profile & Free Energy (ΔG)	It was found that the difference between 5′ and 3′ in free energy (or its oppose "stability") especially at the last 2,3,4,5 from each side plays a crucial role in not only distinguishing the sense and antisense but in efficiency evaluation.

Table 2. Description of parameters considered by ThermoComposition (Mysara 2010).

5.2.3 Thermo composition

Here a small number of parameters have been used in to train neural network using 653 siRNA-records as a training set. These parameters have been carefully selected from 18 parameters leading to this small number of parameters (three parameters), that had provided the advantage of simplicity over other neural network as no need for huge number of training dataset is required, and that opened the door for any further development. The uniqueness in this work is that it combines "the position dependant features" with "Thermodynamic features" [Table 2].

5.2.4 i-Score

In i-Score, linear regression model was built on identifying the nucleotide that is preferred in each position and calculated the inhibition score (i-score) working on Huesken dataset (2431) with Pearson correlation coefficient = 0.635. Also in this work they pointed out a very important threshold as the exclusion of Thermostable siRNA (with stacking energy (whole ΔG) < -34.6 k.cal) improved the score accuracy of not only i-Score but also DSIR, Biopredsi and ThermoComposition21 (Ichihara et al. 2007).

5.2.5 Scales

Linear regression model fitting with local stability of siRNA duplex and other parameters was the way Matveeva's team managed to score siRNA in "siRNA Scales", using Huesken dataset for training and three other dataset from various pharmaceutical companies for validation. The use of linear regression provided additional advantages over neural network, as it enabled the introduction of relevant importance to the same parameter at different positions which cannot be applied to the same node parameter in the neural network. In "scales" the linear regression was build on two sets of parameters: the first group covers the stability of siRNA ends especially the 1st and last two base pair of the siRNA the second group depends on evaluation of certain nucleotide at specific positions. A comparison between all second generation tools is provided in [**Table 3**] (Mysara 2010). However, all these models have limitations in performance. There are recent efforts to enhance the siRNA scoring functionality through applying a second artificial intelligent layer that depends on the predicted scores of other second generation tool, as in MysiRNA model. It is siRNA functionality/efficacy prediction model that was developed by combining two existing scoring algorithms (ThermoComposition21 and i-Score), together with the whole stacking energy (ΔG), in a multi-layer artificial neural network. It was found that this kind of combination increases the correlation coefficient of the prediction accuracy from (0.5 to 0.6) between scales and MysiRNA models (Mysara, M. Elhefnawi, et al. 2011, submitted).

6. Experimental section

Here we present an example about working with the previously mentioned protocol for proper siRNA design for targeting human TP53 gene that has been identified as oncogenes. We start with finding P53 mRNA, by searching the NCBI Nucleotide dataset; we will find mRNA refseq id "NM_000546.4" for Homo sapiens tumor protein p53 (TP53), transcript variant 1. Knowing that we need to target all the gene's transcripts, we should find all available transcripts. One way to do that is by blasting the mRNA refseq database, searching for mRNA sharing the same name and organism, using NCBI remote Blast. Seven different mRNAs were identified as following: NM_000546, NM_001126112, NM_001126115, NM_001126117, NM_001126116, NM_001126114, NM_001126113. All of these transcripts were later alignment together, as an approach to identify conserved regions. We used ClustalW to align those 7 transcripts with their different lengths 2586, 2583, 2271, 2331, 2404, 2719 and 2646 respectively. The resulted alignment file, was the treated with "cons" tool to find the consensus between those transcripts, using 100% conservation.

Tools	Model Technique	Training Dataset used	Tool available at	Disadvantages
Biopredsi (Huesken et al. 2006)	Neural network	2,431 records from Huesken dataset.	http://www.biopredsi.org	Possible over estimation due to over fitting of training set with test (S.A. Shabalina et al. 2006)

Tools	Model Technique	Training Dataset used	Tool available at	Disadvantages
DSIR (Vert et al. 2006)	Linear Regression	2,431 records from Huesken dataset.	http://biodev. extra.cea.fr/DS IR/DSIR.html	Too many parameters resulted in slow performance
ThermoCompsition* (S.A. Shabalina et al. 2006)	Neural network	653 records from different publications.	ftp://ftp.ncbi. nlm.nih.gov/p ub/shabalin/si RNA/Thermo Composition	Small number of parameters for ANN training. Slow due to secondary structure calculation
i-Score (Ichihara et al. 2007)	Linear Regression	2,431 records from Huesken dataset.	http://www. med.nagoya-u.ac.jp/neurog enetics/i_Score /i_score.html	Relatively low statistical accuracy
Scales (Matveeva et al. 2007)	Linear Regression	2,431 records from Huesken dataset.	http://gestela nd.genetics.uta h.edu/siRNA_ scales/	Relatively low statistical accuracy

Table 3. Comparison between different second generation scoring techniques (Mysara 2010). *In case of ThermoComposition19, however, Huesken dataset used for training ThermoComposition21 and 653 siRNA used for validation.

The resulted consensus was found as per below:

```
NNNNNNNNNNNNNNNNNNNNNNNNNNNNNNNNNNNNNNNNNNNNNNNNNNNNNNNNNNNNNN
NNNNNNNNNNNNNNNNNNNNNNNNNNNNNNNNNNNNNNNNNNNNNNNNNNNNNNNNNNNNNN
NNNNNNNNNNNNNNNNNNNNNNNNNNNNNNNNNNNNNNNNNNNNNNNNNNNNNNNNNNNNNN
NNNNNNNNNNNNNNNNNNNNNNNNNNNNNNNNNNNNNNNNNNNNNNNNNNNNNNNNNNNNNN
NNNNNNNNNNNNNNNNNNNNNNNNNNNNNNNNNNNNNNNNNNNNNNNNNNNNNNNNNNNNNN
NNNNNNNNNNNNNNNNNNNNNNNNNNNNNNNNNNNNNNNNNNNNNNNNNNNNNNNNNNNNNN
NNNNNNNNNNNNNCCANGNNATGGANGNTNNNNTGNNCTGTNNNCNNACNAN
NNTGNNCNANGNNTNANTGANAGANCNAGNNCCNNNNNNANNNNNNANAAN
NNNANAGNNNNNNNNCNCCNGNGGNNNNNNNCNCCANCNNNNNNCTANNNCGNN
NGNNNNNNTGCANNAGNNNCNTNCNNNNNNNNTGTNNNNNTTNCTGNCNNNNTNCCA
GNNNNNNNTANCNGNNCANNTNNGNNNNTNNNNTNTNNNCTNNNNTGNNTNCTNNN
NNNNNNNNNNTCNNNNNNCNTNCANGTACTCCCCTGCCCTCAACAAGATGTTTTGCC
AACTGGCCAAGACCTGCCCTGTGCAGCTGTGGGTTGATTCCACACCCCCGCCCGGC
ACCCGCGTCCGCGCCATGGCCATCTACAAGCAGTCACAGCACATGACGGAGGTTGT
GAGGCGCTGCCCCCACCATGAGCGCTGCTCAGATAGCGATGGTCTGGCCCCTCCTCA
GCATCTTATCCGAGTGGAAGGAAATTTGCGTGTGGAGTATTTGGATGACAGAAACA
```

```
CTTTTCGACATAGTGTGGTGGTGCCCTATGAGCCGCCTGAGGTTGGCTCTGACTGTAC
CACCATCCACTACAACTACATGTGTAACAGTTCCTGCATGGGCGGCATGAACCGGA
GGCCCATCCTCACCATCATCACACTGGAAGACTCCAGTGGTAATCTACTGGGACGG
AACAGCTTTGAGGTGCGTGTTTGTGCCTGTCCTGGGAGAGACCGGCGCACAGAGGA
AGAGAATCTCCGCAAGAAAGGGGAGCCTCACCACGAGCTGCCCCCAGGGAGCACT
AAGCGAGCACTGCCCAACAACACCAGCTCCTCTCCCCAGCCAAAGAAGAAACCAC
TGGATGGAGAATATTTCACCCTTCAGNNNNNNNNNNNNNNNNNNNNNNNNNNNNNN
NNNNNNNNNNNNNNNNNNNNNNNNNNNNNNNNNNNNNNNNNNNNNNNNNNNNNNNN
NNNNNNNNNNNNNNNNNNNNNNNNNNNNNNNNNNNNNNNNNNNNNNNNNNNNNNNN
NNNNNNNNNNCCGTGGGCGTGAGCGCTTCGAGATGTTCCGAGAGCTGAATGAGGC
CTTGGAACTCAAGGATGCCCAGGCTGGGAAGGAGCCAGGGGGGAGCAGGGCTCAC
TCCAGCCACCTGAAGTCCAAAAAGGGTCAGTCTACCTCCCGCCATAAAAAACTCAT
GTTCAAGACAGAAGGGCCTGACTCAGACTGACATTCTCCACTTCTTGTTCCCCACTG
ACAGCCTCCCACCCCCATCTCTCCCTCCCCTGCCATTTTGGGTTTTGGGTCTTTGAAC
CCTTGCTTGCAATAGGTGTGCGTCAGAAGCACCCAGGACTTCCATTTGCTTTGTCCCG
GGGCTCCACTGAACAAGTTGGCCTGCACTGGTGTTTTGTTGTGGGGAGGAGGATGGG
GAGTAGGACATACCAGCTTAGATTTTAAGGTTTTTACTGTGAGGGATGTTTGGGAGA
TGTAAGAAATGTTCTTGCAGTTAAGGGTTAGTTTACAATCAGCCACATTCTAGGTAG
GGGCCCACTTCACCGTACTAACCAGGGAAGCTGTCCCTCACTGTTGAATTTTCTCTA
ACTTCAAGGCCCATATCTGTGAAATGCTGGCATTTGCACCTACCTCACAGAGTGCAT
TGTGAGGGTTAATGAAATAATGTACATCTGGCCTTGAAACCACCTTTTATTACATGG
GGTCTAGAACTTGACCCCCTTGAGGGTGCTTGTTCCCTCTCCCTGTTGGTCGGTGGGT
TGGTAGTTTCTACAGTTGGGCAGCTGGTTAGGTAGAGGGAGTTGTCAAGTCTCTGCT
GGCCCAGCCAAACCCTGTCTGACAACCTCTTGGTGAACCTTAGTACCTAAAAGGAA
ATCTCACCCCATCCCACACCCTGGAGGATTTCATCTCTTGTATATGATGATCTGGATC
CACCAAGACTTGTTTTATGCTCAGGGTCAATTTCTTTTTTTCTTTTTTTTTTTTTTTTTCT
TTTTCTTTGAGACTGGGTCTCGCTTTGTTGCCCAGGCTGGAGTGGAGTGGCGTGATCT
TGGCTTACTGCAGCCTTTGCCTCCCCGGCTCGAGCAGTCCTGCCTCAGCCTCCGGAG
TAGCTGGGACCACAGGTTCATGCCACCATGGCCAGCCAACTTTTGCATGTTTTGTAG
AGATGGGGTCTCACAGTGTTGCCCAGGCTGGTCTCAAACTCCTGGGCTCAGGCGATC
CACCTGTCTCAGCCTCCCAGAGTGCTGGGATTACAATTGTGAGCCACCACGTCCAGC
TGGAAGGGTCAACATCTTTTACATTCTGCAAGCACATCTGCATTTTCACCCCACCCTT
CCCCTCCTTCTCCCTTTTTATATCCCATTTTTATATCGATCTCTTATTTTACAATAAAA
CTTTGCTGCCACCTGTGTGTCTGAGGGGTG
```

Then, we used this consensus to evaluate its target accessibility using RNAxs, finding all possible regions to be targeted by siRNA. 1033 possible siRNA were designed using RNAxs. Those siRNAs were evaluated using 10 siRNA efficiency prediction tools as Reynolds (Reynolds et al. 2004), Amarzguioui (Mohammed Amarzguioui & Prydz 2004), Takasaki (Takasaki et al. 2004), Katoh (Katoh & Suzuki 2007), Ui-Tei (Ui-Tei et al. 2004), Hsieh (Hsieh et al. 2004), *Biopredsi* (Huesken et al. 2006), *DSIR* (Vert et al. 2006), *ThermoComposition21* (S.A. Shabalina et al. 2006) and *i-Score* (Ichihara et al. 2007). Selecting siRNA passing 90% or 0.90 predicted score. 111 siRNAs passed these filtration processes, those siRNAs were searched to identify SNPs occurrence residues. All of those 111 siRNAs were found to be targeting SNPs free regions. The last step was to filter those siRNAs against mRNA dataset, to identify those having off-targets. Any siRNA with either complete or partial off-target should be excluded. 85 siRNAs were found to be off-target free candidates. Finally they were filtered and only siRNA with inhibition efficiency above 90%, according to MysiRNA model, were accepted.

siRNA position	Sense	Antisense	Predicted efficiency
800	GCGUGUGGAGUAUUUGGAU	AUCCAAAUACUCCACACGCaa	90.6%
822	AGAAACACUUUUCGACAUA	UAUGUCGAAAAGUGUUUCUgu	92.6%
883	GUACCACCAUCCACUACAA	UUGUAGUGGAUGGUGGUACag	91.5%
1330	CCCGCCAUAAAAAACUCAU	AUGAGUUUUUUAUGGCGGGag	91.4%
1842	GAAACCACCUUUUAUUACA	UGUAAUAAAAGGUGGUUUCaa	92.3%
1915	GGUGGGUUGGUAGUUUCUA	UAGAAACUACCAACCCACCga	92.1%
1919	GGUUGGUAGUUUCUACAGU	ACUGUAGAAACUACCAACCca	90%
2016	CCUUAGUACCUAAAAGGAA	UUCCUUUUAGGUACUAAGGuu	95.4%
2111	GCUCAGGGUCAAUUUCUUU	AAAGAAAUUGACCCUGAGCau	92.9%
2499	CCCUCCUUCUCCCUUUUUA	UAAAAAGGGAGAAGGAGGGga	92%
2530	CUCCCUUUUUAUAUCCCAU	AUGGGAUAUAAAAAGGGAGaa	91.5%
25030	AUAUCGAUCUCUUAUUUUA	UAAAAUAAGAGAUCGAUAUaa	93.1%

Table 4. Final siRNA candidates after all stages of design and filtration.

In ElHefnawi et. Al., other examples of optimal siRNA design and selection as silencers for difficult targets such as the Hepatitis C virus (HCV), and the Influenza a virus that have been experimentally tested for verifications of the methodology are under publication (Mahmoud ElHefnawi1 2011) (Mahmoud ElHefnawi 1 2011)).

7. Conclusion

In this chapter we provide a comprehensive foundation of the underlying bioinformatics methodology for optimal design and selection of siRNA molecules. We address factors affecting siRNA interference, covering both siRNA and mRNA sides. These factors can be classified into four major classes, **the first class of factors**, "targeted region" or "target sequence space", addresses how to identify regions in the mRNA that should be targeted by the designed siRNA; and discusses five factor affecting target sequence space: transcript region, transcript size, mRNA multiple splicing, single nucleotide polymorphism and orthologs consensus. **The second class of factors**, "siRNA sequence space", addresses positional/word preferences in the sense/antisense strand of the siRNA. siRNA sequence space is affected by several factors including nucleotide positional preferences Protocol, GC content, and palindrome. In addition, thermodynamic stability and differential ends instability have been identified to be highly important factors in siRNA functionality. **The third class of factors**, is the" **target accessibility**", and how the targeted mRNAs tend to form secondary structure that affect their accessibility hence reduce the capabilities of the designed siRNA to target certain regions of mRNA. Target accessibility is considered as the sum of the energy required to open mRNA and siRNA duplex and the energy required to stabilize siRNA-mRNA duplex. **The fourth class of factors**, "off-target matches", that influence siRNA specificity via perfect-match, and partial off targets & sequence motifs that invoke immune reaction. Each of these classes can greatly affect siRNA selection and therefore are studied thoroughly in this chapter.

We present a step wise protocol for designing siRNA with the highest specificity and sensitivity in seven different phases, Targeted gene assignment, targeted sequence specification and filtration, designing all possible siRNAs targeting the selected regions, siRNAs scoring and scores filtration, siRNAs target accessibility filtration, siRNAs off-target filtration, selecting the best designed siRNA. We cover state of the art tools for siRNA efficiency prediction, in two generation: the **first generation tools** select the most efficient siRNAs depending on differential ends thermodynamic stability measures, mRNA secondary structure and base preferences specific position target uniqueness. **The second generation tools** have been developed by applying sophisticated data mining techniques to handle huge annotated records of siRNAs with their experimental inhibition, as in *Biopredsi, ThermoComposition21 and Scales's* artificial neural network model and *DSIR and i-Score's* linear regression model. By the end of the chapter, we design siRNA targeting human P53 protein, as a practical example of the proposed protocol. Future directions would be to find additional factors that affect shRNA (siRNAs inserted into expression vectors) that further decrease the efficacy of the expressed siRNAs from them, and extending this methodology latter for miRNA target recognitionpredictions.

8. References

Amarzguioui, M., 2003. Tolerance for mutations and chemical modifications in a siRNA. *Nucleic Acids Research*, 31(2), pp.589-595.

Amarzguioui, Mohammed & Prydz, H., 2004. An algorithm for selection of functional siRNA sequences. *Biochemical and biophysical research communications*, 316(4), pp.1050-8.

Anderson, E.M. et al., 2008. Experimental validation of the importance of seed complement frequency to siRNA specificity. *RNA (New York, N.Y.)*, 14(5), pp.853-61.

Birmingham, A. et al., 2006. 3' UTR seed matches, but not overall identity, are associated with RNAi off-targets. *Nature methods*, 3(3), pp.199-204.

Birmingham, A. et al., 2007. A protocol for designing siRNAs with high functionality and specificity. *Nature protocols*, 2(9), pp.2068-78.

Black, D.L., 2003. Mechanisms of alternative pre-messenger RNA splicing. *Annual review of biochemistry*, 72, pp.291-336.

Czauderna, F. et al., 2003. Structural variations and stabilising modifications of synthetic siRNAs in mammalian cells. *Nucleic acids research*, 31(11), pp.2705-16.

Davis, M.E. et al., 2010. Evidence of RNAi in humans from systemically administered siRNA via targeted nanoparticles. *Nature*, 464(7291), pp.1067-70.

Dorsett, Y. & Tuschl, Thomas, 2004. siRNAs: applications in functional genomics and potential as therapeutics. *Nature reviews. Drug discovery*, 3(4), pp.318-29.

Elbashir, S M, Lendeckel, W. & Tuschl, T, 2001. RNA interference is mediated by 21- and 22-nucleotide RNAs. *Genes & development*, 15(2), pp.188-200.

Elbashir, S M et al., 2001. Functional anatomy of siRNAs for mediating efficient RNAi in Drosophila melanogaster embryo lysate. *The EMBO journal*, 20(23), pp.6877-88.

Elbashir, Sayda M et al., 2002. Analysis of gene function in somatic mammalian cells using small interfering RNAs. *Methods (San Diego, Calif.)*, 26(2), pp.199-213.

Hofacker, I.L. & Tafer, H., 2010. Designing optimal siRNA based on target site accessibility. *Methods in molecular biology (Clifton, N.J.)*, 623, pp.137-54.

Hsieh, A.C. et al., 2004. A library of siRNA duplexes targeting the phosphoinositide 3-kinase pathway: determinants of gene silencing for use in cell-based screens. *Nucleic acids research*, 32(3), pp.893-901.

Huesken, D. et al., 2006. Design of a genome-wide siRNA library using an artificial neural network. *Nature Biotechnology*, 23(8), pp.995-1002.

Hutvágner, G. & Zamore, P.D., 2002. A microRNA in a multiple-turnover RNAi enzyme complex. *Science (New York, N.Y.)*, 297(5589), pp.2056-60.

Ichihara, M. et al., 2007. Thermodynamic instability of siRNA duplex is a prerequisite for dependable prediction of siRNA activities. *Nucleic Acids Research*, pp.1-10.

Jackson, A.L. et al., 2003. Expression profiling reveals off-target gene regulation by RNAi. *Nature biotechnology*, 21(6), pp.635-7.

Jackson, A.L. & Linsley, P.S., 2010. Recognizing and avoiding siRNA off-target effects for target identification and therapeutic application. *Nature reviews. Drug discovery*, 9(1), pp.57-67.

Katoh, T. & Suzuki, T., 2007. Specific residues at every third position of siRNA shape its efficient RNAi activity. *Nucleic acids research*, 35(4), p.e27.

Kaufmann, S.H.E. & Patzel, V., 2008. Structures of Active Guide Rna Molecules and Method of Selection.

Ladunga, I., 2007. More complete gene silencing by fewer siRNAs: transparent optimized design and biophysical signature. *Nucleic acids research*, 35(2), pp.433-40.

Lorenz, C. et al., 2004. Steroid and lipid conjugates of siRNAs to enhance cellular uptake and gene silencing in liver cells. *Bioorganic & medicinal chemistry letters*, 14(19), pp.4975-7.

Matveeva, O. et al., 2007. Comparison of approaches for rational siRNA design leading to a new efficient and transparent method. *Access*, 35(8), pp.1-10.

Mysara, M., 2010. *MysiRNA: Automation of siRNA Design Considering Multi-score Filtration*.

Mysara, M. et al., 2011. MysiRNA: Improving siRNA Efficacy Prediction Using a Machine-Learning Model Combining Multi-tools and Whole Stacking Energy (ΔG). *Journal of Biomedical Informatics*, pp.1-23.

Mysara, M., Garibaldi, J. & Elhefnawi, M., 2011. MysiRNA-Designer : a Workflow for Efficient siRNA Design. *PLoS One*, pp.1-14.

Mückstein, U. et al., 2006. Thermodynamics of RNA-RNA binding. *Bioinformatics (Oxford, England)*, 22(10), pp.1177-82.

Park, Y.-kyu et al., 2008. AsiDesigner : exon-based siRNA design server considering alternative splicing. *Knowledge Creation Diffusion Utilization*, 36(May), pp.97-103.

Patzel, V., 2007. In silico selection of active siRNA. *Drug Discovery Today*, 12(3-4), pp.139-48.

Patzel, V. et al., 2005. Design of siRNAs producing unstructured guide-RNAs results in improved RNA interference efficiency. *Nature biotechnology*, 23(11), pp.1440-4.

Ren, Y. et al., 2006. siRecords : an extensive database of mammalian siRNAs with efficacy ratings. *Access*, pp.1-10.

Reynolds, A. et al., 2004. Rational siRNA design for RNA interference. *Nature biotechnology*, 22(3), pp.326-30.

Schwarz, D.S. et al., 2003. Asymmetry in the Assembly of the RNAi Enzyme Complex. *Cell*, 115(2), pp.199-208.

Semizarov, D. et al., 2003. Specificity of short interfering RNA determined through gene expression signatures. *Proceedings of the National Academy of Sciences of the United States of America*, 100(11), pp.6347-52.

Shabalina, S.A., Spiridonov, A.N. & Ogurtsov, A.Y., 2006. Computational models with thermodynamic and composition features improve siRNA design. *BMC bioinformatics*, 7(1), p.65.

Stark, G.R. et al., 1998. How cells respond to interferons. *Annual review of biochemistry*, 67, pp.227-64.

Surabhi, R.M. & Gaynor, R.B., 2002. RNA interference directed against viral and cellular targets inhibits human immunodeficiency Virus Type 1 replication. *Journal of virology*, 76(24), pp.12963-73.

Tafer, H. et al., 2008. The impact of target site accessibility on the design of effective siRNAs. *Nature biotechnology*, 26(5), pp.578-83.

Takasaki, S., Kotani, S. & Konagaya, A., 2004. An effective method for selecting siRNA target sequences in mammalian cells. *Cell cycle (Georgetown, Tex.)*, 3(6), pp.790-5.

Ui-Tei, K. et al., 2004. *Guidelines for the selection of highly effective siRNA sequences for mammalian and chick RNA interference.*

Ullu, E. et al., 2002. RNA interference: advances and questions. *Philosophical transactions of the Royal Society of London. Series B, Biological sciences*, 357(1417), pp.65-70.

Vert, J.-P. et al., 2006. An accurate and interpretable model for siRNA efficacy prediction. *BMC bioinformatics*, 7(1), p.520.

Xia, H. et al., 2004. RNAi suppresses polyglutamine-induced neurodegeneration in a model of spinocerebellar ataxia. *Nature medicine*, 10(8), pp.816-20.

ElHefnawi, M., O. Alaidi, et al. (2011). "Identification of novel conserved functional motifs across most Influenza A viral strains." *Virol J* 8: 44. BACKGROUND: Influenza A virus poses a continuous threat to global public health. Design of novel universal drugs and vaccine requires a careful analysis of different strains of Influenza A viral genome from diverse hosts and subtypes. We performed a systematic in silico analysis of Influenza A viral segments of all available Influenza A viral strains and subtypes and grouped them based on host, subtype, and years isolated, and through multiple sequence alignments we extrapolated conserved regions, motifs, and accessible regions for functional mapping and annotation. RESULTS: Across all species and strains 87 highly conserved regions (conservation percentage > = 90%) and 19 functional motifs (conservation percentage = 100%) were found in PB2, PB1, PA, NP, M, and NS segments. The conservation percentage of these segments ranged between 94-98% in human strains (the most conserved), 85-93% in swine strains (the most variable), and 91-94% in avian strains. The most conserved segment was different in each host (PB1 for human strains, NS for avian strains, and M for swine strains). Target accessibility prediction yielded 324 accessible regions, with a single stranded probability > 0.5, of which 78 coincided with conserved regions. Some of the interesting annotations in these regions included sites for protein-protein interactions, the RNA binding groove, and the proton ion channel. CONCLUSIONS: The influenza virus has evolved to adapt to its host through variations in the GC content and conservation percentage of the conserved regions. Nineteen universal conserved functional motifs were discovered, of which some were accessible regions with interesting biological functions. These regions will serve as a foundation for universal drug targets as well as universal vaccine design.

Mahmoud ElHefnawi1, Rania Siam3, Nafisa Hassan2 , Mona Kamar2 , Marco Sgarbanti4, Annalisa Rimoli4, Iman El-Azab5, Osama AlAidy6, Giulia Marsiliin Marco Sgarbanti4 (2011). "The design of optimal therapeutic small interfering RNA molecules targeting diverse strains of influenza A virus." *Bioinformatics* OUP under revision.

Mahmoud ElHefnawi 1, TaeKyu Kim3, Mona A. Kamar 2, Nafisa M. Hassan 2, Iman A El-Azab4, Suher Zada5, Marc P. Windisch3* (2011). "Novel DESIGN AND SELECTION OF EFFICIENT SPECIFIC UNIVERSAL SMALL INTERFERING RNA MOLECULES tested in Hepatitis C Virus replicon cell lines." *PLOS1* submitted.

Patzel, V., S. Rutz, et al. (2005). "Design of siRNAs producing unstructured guide-RNAs results in improved RNA interference efficiency." *Nat Biotechnol* 23(11): 1440-1444.

24

MicroRNA Targeting in Heart: A Theoretical Analysis

Zhiguo Wang

Research Centre, Montreal Heart Institute, Montreal, and Department of Medicine,
Universite de Montreal, Montreal,
Canada

1. Introduction

Cardiovascular disease remains the major cause of morbidity and mortality; according to statistics, heart failure, the syndrome consequential to many diseases of the cardiovascular system, is estimated to have a prevalence of 1–2% and an annual incidence of 5–10 per 1,000 in the developed countries and is the leading cause of hospitalization in the population over 50 years of age. Worse so, there is a clear tendency of increasing prevalence of cardiovascular disease in this planet particularly in the developing nations. This problem casts enormous health concern and costly socioeconomic burden worldwide.

We have entered post-genome era after the human genome project had been completed years ago. Only <2% of all transcribed bases of the entire human genome constitutes the genetic sequence encoding proteins and the rest of 98% accounting for ~70% of all genes carry the sequences for RNAs not encoding a polypeptide chain that was used to be considered for many years "junk DNA" of no physiologic function; proteins were generally assumed the sole biopolymer capable of regulatory function. Intriguinly, the proportion of transcribed non-protein-coding sequences increases with developmental complexity and is a better indicator of phylogenetic level than the number of protein-coding genes of an organism. It is now known that "junk DNA" encodes non-protein-coding RNAs (ncRNAs) that are involved in determining the expression of protein-coding genes by regulating the activity of that 2% of the genome. These ncRNAs include microRNAs (miRNAs), once ignored completely or overlooked as cellular detritus, which were discovered over a decade ago have recently taken many by surprise because of their widespread expression and diverse functions.

miRNAs are endogenous small mRNAs of ~22 nucleotide in length which act primarily to repress gene expression at the post-transcriptional level. To date, ~6400 vertebrates mature miRNAs have been registered in miRBase, an online repository for miRNA, among which ~5100 miRNAs are found in mammals which include >850 human miRNAs. These miRNAs are predicted to regulates >60% of protein–coding genes. The discovery of miRNA challenges the central dogma of molecular biology that has be hold since the latter half of the 20th century. With the recent rapid evolution of miRNA research, researchers have begun to appreciate the roles of these small non-protein-coding mRNAs in the cardiovascular system. Based on the published studies, it is now clear that miRNAs are involved in nearly all aspects of cardiac function and pathogenesis (Wang, 2010; Wang et al., 2008; Yang et al., 2008).

It known that an individual miRNA has the potential to target multiple protein-coding genes and *vice versa* a single protein-coding gene may be regulated by multiple miRNAs, implying that the action of miRNAs is not gene-specific. This fact creates an obstacle to our thorough understanding of miRNA functions and the mechanism underlying these functions. For example, we have recently found that *miR-125-5p* target GJA1 (encoding gap junction channel protein connexin43) and GJC1 (encoding another gap junction channel protein connexin40) to cause slowing of both ventricular and atrial conduction promoting arrhythmogenesis in failing heart where its expression is upregulated (Wang, 2010). However, based upon computational prediction it can also target SCN5A (encoding Nav1.5 Na$^+$ channel α-subunit). An immediate question is whether the potential repression of SCN5A also plays a role in *miR-125-5p*-induced conduction slowing. On the other hand, GJA1, GJC1 and SCN5A are predicted to be regulated by other miRNAs in addition to *miR-125-5p* (such as *miR-101, miR-125, miR-130, miR-19, miR-23, miR-26* and *miR-30*); whether these miRNAs are also involved in the deregulation of these genes in heart failure remained unknown. This same uncertainty may exist in the interactions between literally all miRNAs and protein-coding genes. Proper experimental approaches are ultimately required to clarify these issues. However, at present it is not feasible to have thorough elucidation of the complete set of target genes of a given miRNA or of the complete array of mRNAs that regulate a given protein-coding genes; computational prediction remains the best alternative for rapid identification of miRNA target genes.

This chapter aims to shed light on how to take rational uses of bioinformatics analysis to identify the miRNAs from the currently available miRNA databases which have the potential to regulate human genes related to cardiac function and pathology and to validate the analysis taking several pathological settings associated with the deregulated miRNAs in the heart. The pathological conditions to be discussed include arrhythmogenesis, apoptosis and fibrogenesis that are known to be critical to the adverse electrical, cellular and structural remodelling processes in various diseased states of heart such as myocardial infarction, cardiac hypotrophy and heart failure.

2. Ion channel genes as targets for miRNAs

Cardiac cells are excitable cells that can generate and propagate excitations; At the cellular level, excitability is reflected by cardiac action potential, which is orchestrated by transmembrane proteins like ion channels and transporters and intracellular proteins for Ca^{2+} handling. (Wang, 2010; Wang et al., 2008; Yang et al., 2008). Deregulation of miRNA expression has been implicated in a variety of diseased conditions of the heart and aberrant expression of miRNAs can render expression deregulation of ion channel genes resulting in channelopathies–arrhythmogenesis leading to sudden cardiac death. Indeed, we and others have shown the critical involvement of miRNAs, particularly the muscle-specific miRNAs *miR-1* and *miR-133*, in regulating every aspects of cardiac excitability to affect arrhythmogenesis under various pathological conditions including myocardial infarction, cardiac hypertrophy, diabetic cardiomyopathy, etc. This property of miRNAs is conferred by their ability to target ion channels and intracellular Ca^{2+} handling proteins at the post-transcriptional level, as already revealed by numerous studies. Even though, our current knowledge about miRNA regulation of cardiac ion channels is still rather preliminary with limited experimental data available in the literature. This is largely due to the limitations of our technologies and approaches to conduct thorough characterization of miRNA targeting. As a surrogate to these limitations, we have conducted a rationally designed bioinformatics analysis in conjunction with experimental approaches to identify the miRNAs which have the potential to regulate human cardiac ion channel genes and to validate the analysis with several pathological settings associated with the deregulated miRNAs and ion channel genes in the heart (Luo et al., 2010). In this way, we have been able to identify an array of miRNAs that are expressed in cardiac cells and have the potential to regulate the genes encoding cardiac ion channels, transporters and intracellular Ca^{2+} handling proteins. Our data well explain the ionic remodelling processes occurring in hypertrophy/heart failure, myocardial ischemia, or atrial fibrillation at the level of miRNA; the changes of miRNAs appear to have anti-correlation with the changes of many of the genes encoding cardiac ion channels under these pathological conditions.

2.1 *In Silico* analysis of miRNA targets

We used the miRecords miRNA database and target-prediction website for our initial analysis. The miRecords is resource for animal miRNA-target interactions developed at the University of Minnesota (Xiao et al., 2009). The miRecords consists of two separate databases. The Validated Targets database contains the experimentally validated miRNA targets being updated from meticulous literature curation. The Predicted Targets database of miRecords is an integration of predicted miRNA targets produced by 11 established miRNA target prediction programs. These algorithms include DIANA-microT, MicroInspector, miRanda, MirTarget2, miTarget, NBmiRTar, PicTar, PITA, RNA22, RNAhybrid, and TargetScan/TargetScanS.

As an initial "screening" process, we performed miRNA target prediction through the miRecords database (Xiao et al., 2009). This miRNA database integrates miRNA target predictions by 11 algorithms. Four of the 11 algorithms (microInspector, miTarget, NBmiRTar, and RNA22) were removed from our data analysis because they failed to predict; these websites require manual input of 3'UTR sequences of the genes. Thus, our data analysis was based upon the prediction from seven algorithms (TargetScan, DIANA-miT3.0, miRanda, PicTar, PITA, RNAHybrid, and miRTarget2) (Enright et al., 2003; Kertesz et al., 2007; Kiriakidou et al., 2004; Krek et al., 2005; Lewis et al., 2003 & 2005; Rehmsmeier et al., 2004; Wang & El Naqa., 2008). These prediction techniques are based on algorithms with different parameters (such as miRNA seed:mRNA 3'UTR complementarity, thermodynamic stability of base-pairing (assessed by free energy), evolutionary conservation across orthologous 3'UTRs in multiple species, structural accessibility of the binding sites, nucleotide composition beyond the seed sequence, number of binding sites in 3'UTR, and anti-correlation between miRNAs and their target mRNAs). A then-updated set of RefSeq genes and their annotations was used to define a set of human 3' UTRs. Orthologous UTRs (based on whole-genome alignments) were obtained for 22 other species from UCSC Genome Bioinformatics. Conservation of each miRNA site was evaluated using phylogenetic branch lengths of all species containing the site based on the methods by Friedman et al (2009). For all highly conserved miRNAs, the probability of preferentially conserved targeting for each site was estimated as described (Friedman et al., 2009). Predicted consequential pairing to 3' end of miRNAs was included only if the raw 3' pairing score (Grimson et al., 2007) is at least 3.0.

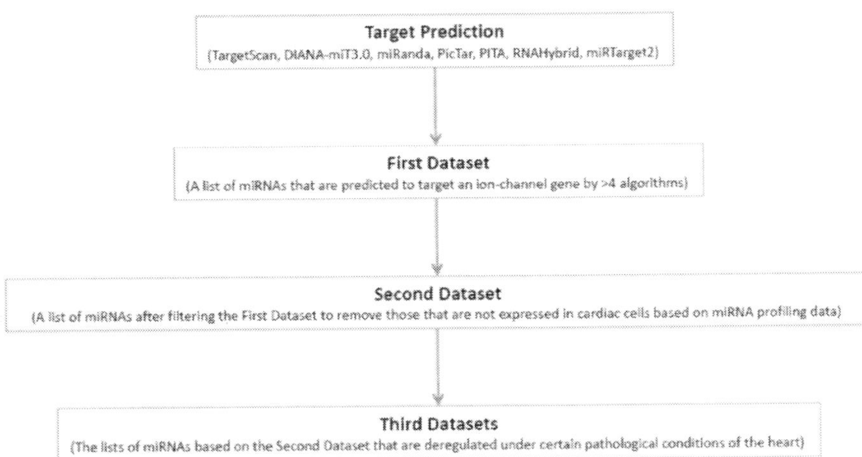

Fig. 1. Flow chart illustrating the procedures of our analysis. The First Dataset include all miRNAs in the then-updated database that have the potential to target at least an ion-channel-coding gene as predicted by at least 4 of the 7 algorithms. The Second Dataset limits the miRNAs from the First Dataset to only those that are expressed in cardiac cells. These miRNAs represent those that most likely play a role in regulating ion channel expression in the heart. The Third Datasets are the lists of miRNAs that have been shown to be deregulated in the pathological conditions under analysis, e.g. myocardial infarction, heart failure, etc. These miRNAs represent those that likely play an important role in defining ion channel expression under a given diseased state.

Each of the seven algorithms provides a unique dataset. Some of the algorithms have higher sensitivity of prediction but lower accuracy and the others weight on the accuracy in the face of reduced sensitivity. We collected all miRNAs predicted by at least four of the seven algorithms to have the potential to target any one of the selected cardiac ion channel and ion transporter genes. Meanwhile, we also collected all ion channel and ion transporter genes that contain the potential target site(s) (the binding site(s) with favourable free energy profiles) for at least one of then-registered 718 human miRNAs in the miRNA database (miRBase).

Expression of miRNAs is tightly controlled by the genetic programme to ensure certain spatial (depending on cell-, tissue-, or organ-type) and temporal (depending on developmental stage) patterns. The expression profile under a defined condition is considered the miRNA expression signature or miRNA transcriptome of a particular tissue. One way to minimize the possibility of false positive predictions and to narrow down the list of putative miRNA targets would be to compare the *in silico* target predictions to the miRNA transcriptome signatures in the biological system of interest. We therefore conducted miRNA microarray analysis of miRNAs including all 718 human miRNAs for their expression in left ventricular tissues of five healthy human individuals. Using this set of cardiac miRNA expression profiling data in conjunction with published data obtained by real-time RT-PCR by Liang et al (2007), we refined the miRNA–target prediction by filtering out the miRNAs that are not expressed in the heart and focusing on the top 20 abundant miRNAs in human heart (*miR-1, miR-133a/b, miR-16, miR-100, miR-125a/b, miR-126, miR-145, miR-195, miR-199*, miR-20a/b, miR-21, miR-26a/b, miR-24, miR-23, miR-29a/b, miR-27a/b, miR-30a/b/c, miR-92a/b, miR-99, and let-7a/c/f/g*). In this way, we generated the modified datasets for subsequent analyses and obtained an overall picture of control of expression of ion channel genes by miRNAs in heart under normal conditions.

Next, we intended to apply the theoretical prediction to explaining some established observations of the electrical remodeling related to deregulation of both miRNAs and the genes for ion channels and transporters. Three pathological conditions, cardiac hypertrophy/heart failure, ischemic myocardial injuries, and atrial fibrillation, were studied based on the expression profiles and participations of miRNAs in these conditions as previously reported. The results are presented in the section following the next.

2.2 Control of expression of Ion channel genes by miRNAs under normal conditions

The above analyses allow us to reach the following notes.

1. One hundred ninety-three out of 718 human miRNAs or out of 222 miRNAs expressed in the heart have the potential to target the genes encoding human cardiac ion channels and transporters.
2. Only two genes CLCN2 and KCNE2 were predicted not to contain the target site for miRNAs expressed in the heart.
3. It appears that the most fundamental and critical ion channels governing cardiac excitability have the largest numbers of miRNAs as their regulators. These include SCN5A for I_{Na} (responsible for the upstroke of the cardiac action potential thereby the conduction of excitations), CACNA1C/CACNB2 for $I_{Ca,L}$ (accounting for the characteristic long plateau of the cardiac action potential and excitation-contraction coupling), KCNJ2 for I_{K1} (sets and maintains the cardiac membrane potential), SLC8A1 for NCX1 (an antiporter membrane protein which removes Ca^{2+} from cells), GJA1/GJC1 (gap junction channel responsible for intercellular conduction of excitation), and ATP1B1 for Na^+/K^+ pump (establishing and maintaining the normal electrochemical gradients of Na^+ and K^+ across the plasma membrane). Each of these genes is theoretically regulated by >30 miRNAs.
4. The atrium-specific ion channels, including Kir3.4 for I_{KACh}, Kv1.5 for I_{Kur}, and CACNA1G for $I_{Ca,T}$, seem to be the rare targets for miRNAs (<5 miRNAs).
5. All four genes for K^+ channel auxiliary β-subunits KCNE1, KCNE2, KCHiP, and KCNAB2 were also found to have less number of regulator miRNAs (<10).
6. Intriguingly, 16 of these top 20 miRNAs are included in the list of the predicted miRNA-target dataset; the other four cardiac-abundant miRNAs miR-21, miR-99, miR-100 and miR-126 are predicted unable to regulate the genes for human cardiac ion channels and transporters.
7. There is a rough correlation between the number of predicted targets and the abundance of miRNAs in the heart. It appears that the miRNAs within top 8 separate from the rest 12 less abundant miRNAs in their number of target genes. The muscle-specific miRNA miR-1 was predicted to have the largest number of target genes (9 genes) among all miRNAs most abundantly expressed in the heart, followed by miR-30a/b/c, miR-24 and miR-125a/b that have 6 target genes each. The muscle-specific miRNA miR-133 has four target genes and three of them (KCNH2, KCNQ1 and HCN2) have been experimentally verified (Luo et al., 2008; J Xiao et al., 2007; L Xiao et al., 2008).

8. Comparison of the target genes of the three muscle-specific miRNAs miR-1, miR-133 and miR-208 revealed that they might play different role in regulating cardiac excitability. It appears that miR-1 may be involved in all different aspects of cardiac excitability: cardiac conduction by targeting GJA1 and KCNJ2, cardiac automaticity by targeting HCN2 and HCN4, cardiac repolarization by targeting KCNA5, KCND2 and KCNE1, and Ca^{2+} handling by targeting SLC8A1. By comparison, miR-133a/b mainly controls cardiac repolarization through targeting KCNH2 (encoding HERG/I_{Kr}) and KCNQ1 (encoding KvLQT1/I_{Ks}), the two major repolarizing K^+ channels in the heart. miR-208 was predicted to target only KCNJ2 (encoding Kir2.1 for I_{K1}). The non-muscle-specific let-7 seed family members seem to regulate mainly cardiac conduction by targeting SCN5A (Nav1.5 for intracellular conduction) and GJC1 (Cx45 for intercellular conduction). miR-30a/b/c and miR-26a/b, miR-125a/b, miR-16, and miR-27a/b were predicted to be L-type Ca^{2+} channel "blockers" through repressing α1c- and/or β1/β2-subunits.

2.3 Application of our bioinformatics analysis to heart failure

The mechanisms for arrhythmogenesis in failing heart involve (Nattel et al., 2007): (1) Abnormalities in spontaneous pacemaking function (enhanced cardiac automaticity) as a result of increases in atrial and ventricular If due to increased expression of HCN4 channel may contribute to ectopic beat formation in CHF; (2) Slowing of cardiac repolarization thereby prolongation of APD due to reductions of repolarizing K^+ currents (including I_{K1}, I_{Ks}, and I_{to1}) provides the condition for occurrence of early afterdepolarizations (EADs) leading to triggered activities; (3) Delayed afterdepolarizations (DADs) due to enhanced Na^+-Ca^{2+} exchanger (NCX1) activity in cardiac hypertrophy/CHF is a consistent finding by numerous studies. Upregulation of NCX1 expression is the major cause for the enhancement; (4) Reentrant activity due to slowing of cardiac conduction velocity.

To date, there have been seven published studies on role of miRNAs and cardiac hypertrophy (Carè et al., 2007; Cheng et al., 2007; Sayed et al., 2008; Tatsuguch et al., 2007; Thum et al., 2007; van Rooij et al., 2006, 2007). The common finding of these studies is that an array of miRNAs is significantly altered in their expression, either up- or down-regulated, and that single miRNAs can critically determine the generation and progression of cardiac hypertrophy. The most consistent changes reported by these studies are up-regulation of miR-21 (6 of 6 studies), miR-23a (4 of 6), miR-125b (5 of 6), miR-214 (4 of 6), miR-24 (3 of 6), miR-29 (3 of 6) and miR-195 (3 of 6), and down-regulation of miR-1, miR-133, miR-150 (5 of 6 studies) and miR-30 (5 of 6). These miRNAs were therefore included in our analysis of target genes encoding ion channel and transporter proteins. Our analyses suggest the following.

1. It is known that cardiac myocytes are characterized with re-expression of the funny current (or pacemaker current) If that may underlie the increased risk of arrhythmogenesis in hypertrophic and failing heart (Luo et al., 2008), which is carried by HCN2 channel in cardiac muscles. We have previously verified that downregulation of miR-1 and miR-133 caused upregulation of HCN2 in cardiac hypertrophy (Luo et al., 2008). This may contribute to the enhanced abnormal cardiac automaticity and the associated arrhythmias in CHF.

2. The NCX1 is upregulated in cardiac hypertrophy, ischemia, and failure. This upregulation can have an effect on Ca^{2+} transients and possibly contribute to diastolic

dysfunction and an increased risk of arrhythmias (Flesch et al., 1996; Nattel et al., 2007; Pogwizd & Bers, 2002). Our target prediction indicates that SLC8A1, the gene encoding NXC1 protein, is a potential target for both miR-1 and miR-30a/b/c. The downregulation of miR-1 and miR-30a/b/c in hypertrophy/failure is deemed to relieve the repression of SLC8A1/NCX1 since a strong tonic repression miR-1 and miR-30a/b/c is anticipated considering the high abundance of these miRNAs. On the other hand, upregulation of miR-214 tends to repress NCX1, but the expression level of miR-214 is of no comparison with those of miR-1 and miR-30a/b/c; its offsetting effect should be minimal. Our prediction thus provides a plausible explanation for the upregulation of NCX1 through the miRNA mechanism.

3. A variety of Na^+ channel abnormalities have been demonstrated in heart failure. Several studies suggest that peak I_{Na} is reduced which can cause slowing of cardiac conduction and promote re-entrant arrhythmias (Zicha et al., 2004). It has been speculated that post-transcriptional reduction of the cardiac I_{Na} α-subunit protein Nav1.5 may account for the reduction of peak I_{Na}. In this study, we found that the only miRNA that can target Nav1.5 and is upregulated in cardiac hypertrophy/CHF is miR-125a/b. As an abundantly expressed miRNA, upregulation of miR-125a/b could well result in repression of SCN5A/Nav1.5.

4. The gap junction channel proteins connexin43, connexin45 and connexin40 are important for cell-to-cell propagation of excitations. Downregulation of connexin43 expression is associated with an increased likelihood of ventricular tachyarrhythmias in heart failure (Kitamura et al., 2002). Other connexins, including connexin45 (Yamada et al., 2003) and connexin40 (Dupont et al., 2001), are upregulated in failing hearts, possibly as a compensation for connexin43 downregulation. Our analysis indicates that the upregulation of miR-125a/b and miR-23a/b should produce repression of connexin43 and connexin45 and the down regulation of miR-1, miR-30a/b/c and miR-150 should do the opposite. These two opposing effects may cancel out each other.

5. Prolongation of ventricular APD is typical of heart failure to enable the improvement of contraction strength, thereby supporting the weakened heart. However, APD prolongation consequent to decreases in several repolarizing K^+ current (I_{to1}, I_{Ks}, and I_{K1}) in failing heart often results in occurrence of early afterdepolarizations (EADs) (Beuckelmann et la., 1993; Tsuji et al., 2000). Our prediction failed to provide any explanation at the miRNA level: None of the upregulated miRNAs may regulate the genes encoding repolarizing K^+ channels. On the contrary, downregulation of miR-1 and miR-133 predict upregulation of KCNE1/minK and KCNQ1/KvLQT1, respectively.

6. A majority of published studies showed a decrease in I_{K1} in ventricular myocytes of failing hearts (Beuckelmann et la., 1993; Rose et al., 2005). But whether KCNJ2/Kir2.1, the major subunit underlying I_{K1}, is downregulated remained controversial in previous studies and the mechanisms remained obscured. One study noted decreased KCNJ2 mRNA expression but unaltered Kir2.1 protein level (Rose et al., 2005). With our prediction, the upregulated miRNAs (miR-125, miR-214, miR-24, miR-29, and miR-195) predict reduction of inward rectifier K^+ channel subunits including KCNJ2/Kir2.1, KCNJ12/Kir2.2, KCNJ14/Kir2.4, and KCNK1/TWIK1, whereas the downregulated miRNAs (miR-1 and miR-30a/b/c) predict increase in KCNJ2/Kir2.1.

In summary, our analysis of target genes for deregulated miRNAs in hypertrophy/CHF may explain at least partly the enhanced cardiac automaticity (relief of HCN2 repression and increased NCX1 expression) and reduced cardiac conduction (repression of Nav1.5). But the data suggest that miRNAs are hardly involved in the abnormality of cardiac repolarization in cardiac hypertrophy and heart failure since the genes for the repolarizing K^+ channels were not predicted as targets for the upregulated miRNAs. The prediction of NCX1 upregulation as a result of derepression from miRNAs may be of particular importance aberrantly enhanced NXC1 activity has also been noticed in atrial fibrillation occurring in CHF.

2.4 Application of our bioinformatics analysis to myocardial infarction (MI)

MI is manifested as cascades of electrical abnormalities and even lethal arrhythmias as a result of deleterious alterations of gene expression outweighing adaptive changes (Carmeliet, 1999). Ischemic myocardium demonstrates characteristic sequential alterations in electrophysiology with an initial shortening of APD and QT interval during the early phase (<15min) of acute ischemia and subsequent lengthening of APD/QT after a prolonged ischemic period and chronic myocardial ischemia (Carmeliet, 1999; Nattel et al., 2007). To exploit if miRNAs could be involved in the remodelling process, several original studies have been published. We first identified upregulation of *miR-1* in acute myocardial infarction and the ischemic arrhythmias caused by this deregulation of *miR-1* expression (Yang et al., 2007). Subsequently, miRNA expression profiles in the setting of myocardial ischemia/reperfusion injuries were reported by four groups (Dong et al., 2009; Luo et al., 2010; Ren et al., 2009; Roy et al., 2009).

Based on these published data, we made an analysis to exclude that miRNAs that were found deregulated by a study but not by others and that were found deregulated in rat heart but was not expressed in human heart. In this way, we identified an array of miRNAs that are likely deregulated in the setting of myocardial ischemia. The MI-upregulated miRNAs include *miR-1, miR-23, miR-29, miR-20, miR-30, miR-146b-5p, miR-193, miR-378, miR-181, miR-491-3p, miR-106, miR-199b-5p,* and *let-7f*; and the downregulated miRNAs include *miR-320, miR-185, miR-324-3p,* and *miR-214.* Interesting to note is that some of the miRNAs demonstrated the opposite directions of changes in their expression between ischemic myocardium and hypertrophic hearts. For example, *miR-1, let-7, miR-181b, miR-29a* and *miR-30a/e* are upregulated in ischemic myocardium, but downregulated in hypertrophy. Similarly, *miR-214, miR-320* and *miR-351* are down-regulated in ischemic myocardium, but up-regulated in hypertrophy. This fact further reinforces the notion that different pathological conditions are associated with different expression profiles: miRNA signatures. Our analysis yielded the following notions.

1. Six upregulated miRNAs (*miR-1, miR-29, miR-20, miR-30, miR-193* and *miR-181*) were predicted to target several Kir subunits (KCNJ2, KCNJ12, KCNJ, and KCNK1), but none of the downregulated miRNAs can target these genes (Fig. 4). This is in line with the previous finding that I_{K1} is reduced and membrane is depolarized in ischemic myocardium (Carmeliet, 1999; Nattel et al., 2007; Yang et al., 2007).

2. The cardiac slow delayed rectifier K^+ current (I_{Ks}) is carried by co-assembly of an α-subunit KvLQT1 (encoded by KCNQ1) and a β-subunit mink (encoded by KCNE1). Loss-of-function mutation of either KCNQ1 or KCNE1 can cause long QT syndromes, indicating the importance of I_{Ks} in cardiac repolarization. In ischemic myocardium, persistent decreases in minK with normalized KvLQT1 protein expression have been observed which may underlie unusual delayed rectifier currents with very rapid

activation (Sanguinetti et al., 1996; Dun & Boyden, 2005), resembling currents produced by the expression of KvLQT1 in the absence of minK. We have experimentally established KCNE1 as a target for *miR-1* repression [Luo et al., 2007], which was also predicted in the present analysis. Moreover, no other miRNAs were predicted to target KCNQ1. This finding is coincident with the observations on the diminishment of minK alone without changes of KvLQT1 in ischemic myocardium.

3. It has been observed that cells in the surviving peri-infarct zone have discontinuous propagation due to abnormal cell-to-cell coupling (Gardner et al., 1985; Peters, 1995; Spear et al., 1983). This is largely due to decreased expression and redistribution of gap junction protein connexins (Cxs). In this study, seven out of 12 upregulated miRNAs were predicted to target Cxs including GJA1/Cx43, GJC1/Cx45, and GJA5/Cx40, but only one downregulated miRNA *miR-185* may regulate GJA5/Cx40. This result clearly points to the role of miRNAs in damaging cardiac conduction in ischemic myocardium. Indeed, repression of GJA1/Cx43 to slow conduction and induce arrhythmias in acute myocardial infarction has been experimentally verified by our previous study (Yang et al., 2007).

4. In ischemic myocardium, fast or peak sodium current (I_{Na}) density is reduced, which may also account partly for the conduction slowing and the associated re-entrant arrhythmias (Friedmanet al., 1975; Pu & Boyden, 1997; Spear et al., 1983). Our analysis showed that *let-7f* and *miR-378* may target SCN5A/Nav1.5 and upregulation of these miRNAs is anticipated to cause reduction of I_{Na} via downregulating SCN5A/Nav1.5 in myocardial infarction. By comparison, none of the downregulated miRNAs may repress SCN5A/Nav1.5 based on our target prediction.

5. Transient outward K$^+$ current (I_{to1}) is reduced in myocardial ischemia and in rats, I_{to1} decreases correlate most closely with downregulation of KCND2-encoded Kv4.2 subunits. *miR-1* is predicted to repress KCND2/Kv4.2, and *miR-29* may target KCHiP2 that is known to be critical in the formation of I_{to1}.

6. L-type Ca^{2+} current ($I_{Ca,L}$) is diminished in border-zone cells of dogs. *miR-30* family has the potential to target CACNA1C/Cav1.2 and CACNB2/Cavβ2, and *miR-124*, *miR-181*, *miR-320* and *miR-204* to target CACNB2. Upregulation of *miR-30*, *miR-124* and *miR-181* therefore would decrease CACNA1C/Cav1.2 and CACNB2/Cavβ2 expression, but downregulation of *miR-320* and *miR-204* tends to increase the expression of these genes. Considering the relative abundance of these miRNAs, it seems that the decreasing force overweighs the increasing force with a balance towards a net inhibition of $I_{Ca,L}$.

7. Na$^+$/K$^+$ ATPase is a sarcolemmal ATP-dependent enzyme transporter that transports three intracellular Na$^+$ ions to the extracellular compartment and moves two extracellular K$^+$ ions into the cell to maintain the physiological Na$^+$ and K$^+$ concentration gradients for generating the rapid upstroke of the action potential but also for driving a number of ion-exchange and transport processes crucial for normal cellular function, ion homeostasis and the control of cell volume. It is electrogenic, producing a small outward current I_P. We noticed that the ischemia-induced upregulation of *miR-29* and *miR181* expression might render inhibition of Na$^+$/K$^+$ ATPase activity as they possibly target the ATP1B1 β-subunit of the enzyme. This may contribute to the electrical and contractile dysfunction in the ischemic/reperfused myocardium due to the ischemia-induced inhibition of the Na$^+$/K$^+$ ATPase and the failure of intracellular Na$^+$ to recover completely on reperfusion [Fuller et al., 2003].

In a whole, it appears that the expression signature of miRNAs in the setting of myocardial ischemia and the predicted gene targeting of these miRNAs coincide with the ionic remodelling process under this pathological condition. The miRNAs seem to be involved in all aspects of the abnormalities of cardiac excitability during ischemia, as manifested by the slowing of cardiac conduction due to reduced I_{Na} and Cx43, the depolarized membrane potential to adversely affect cardiac conduction due to reduced I_{K1}, the impaired excitation-contraction coupling and contractile function due to reduced $I_{Ca,L}$ and Na^+/K^+ ATPase, and the delayed cardiac repolarization due to reduced I_{Ks} and I_{to1}.

3. Apoptosis-related genes as argets for miRNAs

It has been nearly 40 years since Kerr named the novel death process "apoptosis," from the Greek word meaning "falling of the leaves", an active process that leads to cell death (Kerr et al., 1972). The human body destroys ~60×10^9 cells/day through an apoptotic process in response to various stresses such as physiological, pathogenic, or cytotoxic stimuli (Reed, 2002). Unlike necrosis, apoptosis is a complex endogenous gene-controlled event that requires an exogenous signal–stimulated or inhibited by a variety of regulatory factors, such as formation of oxygen free radicals, ischemia, hypoxia, reduced intracellular K^+ concentration, and generation of nitric oxide. Progressive cell loss due to apoptosis is a pathological hallmark implicated in a wide spectrum of degenerative diseases such as heart disease, atherosclerotic arteries and hypertensive vessels, Alzheimer's disease, etc (Jaffe et al., 1997; Palojoki et a., 2001; Sabbah et a., 1998). Apoptosis as an early and predominant form of cell death has been detected in human acute myocardial infarcts and it was shown to increase in reperfused myocardium. Apoptosis is also believed to account for the loss of cell mass in failing heart. Evidence for the role of miRNAs in cardiomyocytes apoptosis has been rapidly accumulating. My group documented the first of such evidence; the muscle-specific miRNAs miR-1 and miR-133 produce opposing actions on cardiomyocyte apoptosis with the former being proapoptotic while miR-133 being antiapoptotic (Xu et al., 2007). miR-21 is also an antiapoptotic miRNA. It has been shown to produce beneficial effects against H_2O_2-induced injury on cardiac myocytes and ischemia/reperfusion injury via antiapoptosis through its target Programmed Cell Death 4 (PDCD4). Based on our computational prediction, many other miRNAs, such as the miR-17~92 cluster and its two paralogs miR-106a~363 and miR-106b~25 clusters, also have the potential to regulate cardiomyocyte apoptosis by targeting the related genes in the signalling pathways (unpublished observations).

Following similar procedures we used to predict ion channel genes as targets for miRNAs described in section 2.1, we analyzed the genes known to be crucial for cell survival and death for miRNA regulation.

3.1 Control of cardiomyocyte apoptosis by miRNAs under normal conditions

Our analyses allowed us to have an overall picture on how the cardiomyocyte homeostasis may be maintained by miRNAs and to divide miRNAs roughly into two groups: pro-apoptotic miRNAs and anti-apoptotic miRNAs, though there is no clear-cut distinction as each miRNA may simultaneously target both survival and apoptotic genes. This property indicates that cardiomyocyte survival and death is tightly controlled and delicately balanced. Any changes of expression of miRNAs can shift the balance leading to alterations of cell fate.

1. Among the top 20 most abundant miRNAs in the heart, only miR-99 and miR-100 have no predicted target genes relevant to apoptosis and others have 1 to 27 targets.
2. The let-7 family, miR-16, miR-20a/b, miR-125a/b, and miR-29a/b were predicted to some major survival genes including BCL2, BCL2L2, AKT2, AKT3, STAT3, IGF0-1 and MCL1. Thus, they are more likely to be pro-apoptotic miRNAs. Indeed, miR-29 has

been experimentally proven to be pro-apoptotic (Ye et al., 2010). And our unpublished observations indicate a strong promotion of cardiomyocyte apoptosis by miR-20a/b. The studies conducted in cancer cells support our notion that miR-16 induces apoptosis (Cimmino et al., 2005; Tsang & Kwok, 2010), though its effects on cardiac cells have not yet determined.

3. The miR-30 family, miR-24, miR-23a/b, miR-26a/b, miR-27a/b, miR-145, miR-92a/b, and miR-199a/b may be anti-apoptotic miRNAs as they were predicted to target many important cell death genes, such as CASP3 (encoding caspase 3), CASP7, BCL2L11, BAK1, BAX, FOS, etc. Among these miRNAs, miR-199 and miR-24 have been shown to produce cardioprotective effects against apoptosis (Qian et al., 2011). miR-145 is known to mediate inhibition of proliferation and induction of apoptosis of cancer cells (Ostenfeld et al., 2010; Sachdeva & Mo, 2010).

4. Several miRNAs were predicted to target both survival and apoptotic genes; these include the muscle-specific miRNAs miR-1, miR-133, miR-21, miR-195. In theory, these miRNAs are neutral without affecting ell death or can produce either pro-apoptotic or anti-apoptotic effect depending on particular cellular context: expression of particular target genes for a particular miRNA. Indeed, miR-1 and miR-133 do not affect cardiomyocyte apoptosis under normal conditions, but when many survival and death genes are increased in their expression in response to oxidative stress, miR-1 promotes cardiomyocyte apoptosis by targeting heat shock protein 60 whereas miR-133 protects against apoptosis by repressing caspase 9 (Xu et al., 2007). miR-21 has been commonly believed to elicit cardioprotective effects in myocardial ischemia and ischemia/reperfusion injuries (). But in tumor cells it has been reported to be pro-apoptotic, anti-apoptotic or neutral. For example, knockdown of miR-21 in cultured glioblastoma cells resulted in a significant drop in cell number. This reduction was accompanied by increases in enzyme activity of caspases 3 and 7, as well as terminal deoxyribonucleotidyl transferase-mediated dUTP – digoxigenin nick end-labelling (TUNEL) staining (Chan et al., 2005; Corsten et al., 2007). In MCF-7 human breast cancer cells, miR-21 elicits anti-apoptotic effects (Si et al., 2007; Zhu et al., 2007). However, in neuroblastoma cells, miR-Lat was reported to protect against apoptotic cell death (Gupta et al., 2006). This property of miR-21 in cancer cells is in line with our prediction.

5. The cardiac-specific miRNAs miR-208a/b and miR-499 do not seem to have significant role in regulating apoptosis since they were predicted to target only a small number of genes involved apoptosis signalling: CDKN1A and E2F6 whose expression levels are low in heart. Moreover, the expression levels of these cardiac-specific miRNAs are also in the low range.

3.2 Control of cardiomyocyte apoptosis by miRNAs in ischemic myocardium

Myocardial infarction (MI), a typical situation of metabolic stress, is presented as cascades of cellular abnormalities as a result of deleterious alterations of gene expression outweighing adaptive changes. MI can cause severe cardiac injuries and the consequences are contraction failure, electrical abnormalities and even lethal arrhythmias, and eventual death of the cell. Apoptosis is an important mechanism for the cell death occurring in ischemic myocardium. Previous work on miRNAs and apoptosis has been mostly limited to the context of cancer, while studies on apoptosis regulation by miRNAs in non-cancer cells have been sparse. The first evidence for the role of miRNAs in cardiomyocyte apoptosis was obtained in 2007 from my laboratory demonstrating the proapoptotic effect of miR-1 and anti-apoptotic effect of miR-133 in response to oxidative stress (Xu et al., 2007), with miR-1 causing proapoptotic effects confirmed by other groups (Yu et al., 2008; Tang et al., 2010). Subsequent studies in 2009 and 2010 revealed the involvement of other miRNAs such as miR-21, miR-24, miR-29, miR-199a, and miR-320 in ischemic myocardial injury (Cheng et al., 2010; Qian et al., 2011; Rane et al., 2009; Ren et al., 2009; Ye et al., 2010; Yin et al., 2008).

Extracting of the overlapping results from different laboratories and filtering with the cardiac expression profile verified by real-time RT-PCR in human hearts allowed us to identify an array of miRNAs that are likely deregulated in the setting of myocardial ischemia. The upregulated miRNAs include miR-1, miR-23, miR-29, miR-20, miR-30, miR-146b-5p, miR-193, miR-378, miR-181, miR-491-3p, miR-106, miR-199b-5p, and let-7f; the downregulated miRNAs include miR-320, miR-185, miR-324-3p, and miR-214. We then applied our procedures to these miRNAs and our analyses yielded the following notions.

1. Among the upregulated miRNAs, only miR-99 and miR-100 have no predicted target genes relevant to apoptosis and others have 1 to 27 targets related to cell survival and death. Notably, a majority of these miRNAs are predicted to be pro-apoptotic: let-7f, miR-1, miR-20, miR-29, miR-106, miR-181, miR-193, miR-378 and miR-491-3p, leaving the other four (miR-23, miR-30, miR-146b-5p and miR-199b-5p) being anti-apoptotic.

2. Among the downregulated miRNAs, except for miR-185 which is expressed with extremely low abundance, miR-214, miR-320 and miR-324 are supposed to be neutral as they were predicted to target both survival (AKT3, STAT3 and MCL1) and apoptotic (CASP3, BAX, CDK6, etc) genes. Their downregulation therefore may not cause significant impact on cell death in MI. However, it has been reported that overexpression of miR-320 in cultured adult rat cardiomyocytes enhanced apoptotic cell death, whereas knockdown produced cytoprotective effect against apoptosis, on simulated ischemia/reperfusion injuries, through targeting HSP20 (Ren et al., 2009), which is not within the list of our present theoretical prediction.

3. Taken together, it appears that the pro-apoptotic force is enhanced more than the anti-apoptptoic force, being in agreement with the fact that apoptosis is increased in the setting of MI.

4. Fibrosis-related genes as targets for miRNAs

In tissues composed of post-mitotic cells, like heart, new cells cannot be regenerated; instead, fibroblasts proliferate to fill the gaps created due to removal of dead cells. In the normal heart, two thirds of the cell population is composed of nonmuscle cells, the majority of which are fibroblasts (Maisch, 1995; Manabe et al., 2002). Cardiac fibroblasts, along with cardiomyocytes, play an essential role in the progression of cardiac remodelling. Damaging insults evoke multiple signalling pathways that lead to coordinate and sequential gene regulation; the initial events lead to the activation of cardiac fibroblasts. Cardiac fibrosis is the result of both an increase in fibroblast proliferation and extracellular matrix (ECM) deposition. Cardiac myocytes are normally surrounded by a fine network of collagen fibres. Myocardial fibrosis is an established morphological feature of the structural myocardial remodelling that is a characteristic of all forms of cardiac pathology (Berk et al., 2007; Khan & Sheppard, 2006). A growing body of evidence indicates that, along with cardiomyocytes hypertrophy, diffuse interstitial fibrosis is a key pathologic feature of myocardial remodelling in a number of cardiac diseases of different (e.g. ischemic, hypertensive, valvular, genetic, and metabolic) origin. Acute myocardial infarction due to coronary artery occlusion represents a major cause of morbidity and mortality in humans (Fox et al., 2007). The loss of blood flow to the left ventricular free wall of the heart after MI results in death of cardiomyocytes and impaired cardiac contractility. Scar formation at the site of the infarct and interstitial fibrosis of adjacent myocardium prevent myocardial repair, diminish coronary reserve and contribute to loss of pump function, and predisposes individuals to ventricular dysfunction and arrhythmias, which, in turn, confer an increased risk of adverse cardiovascular events (Swynghedauw, 1999). Elucidation of the precise mechanisms responsible for the actions of these factors could forge new frontiers in both risk identification and prevention of fibrosis-derived clinical complications in patients with cardiac disease.

A subset of miRNAs is enriched in cardiac fibroblasts compared to cardiomyocytes. A number of studies have demonstrated the involvement of miRNAs in regulating myocardial fibrosis in the settings of myocardial ischemia or mechanical overload. In this conceptual framework, the investigation of miRNAs might offer a new opportunity to advance our knowledge of the pathogenesis of fibrosis. Characterization of individual miRNAs or miRNA expression profiles that are specifically associated with myocardial fibrosis might allow us to develop diagnostic tools and innovative therapies for fibrogenic cardiac diseases. The identification of miRNAs as potential regulators of myocardial fibrosis has clinical implications; the search for a miRNA expression pattern specific to fibrosis might provide a novel diagnostic approach. Yet, the molecular mechanisms that lead to a fibrogenic cardiac phenotype are still being elucidated.

4.1 Control of cardiac fibrogenesis by miRNAs under normal conditions

Our analysis revealed that 19 of the 20 most abundant miRNAs in the heart have the potential to repress multiple genes known to be involved in fibrogenesis including various types of collagens (COL), CTGF (connective tissue growth factor), FBN1/2/3 (fibrillin1/2/3), ASPN (asporin), MMP2 (matrix metallopeptidase 2), FN1 (fibronectin 1), and various types of TRP channels (transient receptor potential). miR-126 is the only one among the 20 most abundant miRNAs that was not predicted to regulate any fibrosis-relevant genes. The cardiac-specific miRNAs miR-208a and miR-208b seem to have minimal effects on fibrosis sine they have only two target genes OMG (oligodendrocyte myelin glycoprotein) and TTN (titin). Another cardia-specific miRNA miR-499 is likely an anti-fibrotic miRNA as it was predicted to target 12 profibrotic factors including collagens, LAMA1 (laminin 1), FBN2, FN1, OMG, SLN (sarcolipin), TTN, etc. It should be noted that all these target genes encode profibrotic proteins. Our data therefore indicate that the heart is evolved with a super-strong epigenetic program to prevent fibrogenesis or to suppress fibrosis under normal conditions.

Experimentally, several miRNAs including miR-29, miR-30, miR-133 and miR-590 were all found to produce anti-fibrotic effects (Duisters et al., 2009; Shan et al., 2009; van Rooij et al., 2008), whereas evidence exists for miR-208 (van Rooij et al., 2007) and miR-21 as pro-fibrotic miRNAs (Roy et al., 2009; Thum et al., 2008; van Rooij et al., 2008;). The former can be explained based on our prediction that miR-29, miR-30, miR-133 and miR-590 all have the potential to target profibrotic genes. The latter, however, seems not quite straightforward. Surprisingly, a murine genetic miR-21 knockout model failed to show an antifibrotic phenotype after cardiac stress suggesting differences in pharmacological and genetic miR-21 knockdown (Patrick et al., 2010). Indeed, the various miR-21 inhibitor chemistries have different effects on cardiac fibrosis (Thum et al., 2011). It is likely that other genes not included in our analysis may be the targets for miR-208 and miR-21 to produce pro-fibrotic actions.

4.2 Control of atrial fibrogenesis by miRNAs during atrial fibrillation

Atrial fibrillation (AF) is the most commonly encountered clinical arrhythmia that causes tremendous health problems by increasing the risk of stroke and exacerbating heart failure. It is characterized by a process termed atrial structural remodelling with increased atrial fibrosis. Indeed, atrial fibrosis has been strongly associated with the presence of heart diseases/arrhythmias, including congestive heart failure (CHF) and AF (Pellman et al., 2010; Tan & Zimetbaum, 2010).

To determine if miRNAs are involved in atrial structural remodelling, we first conducted expression profiling to identify deregulated miRNAs in the atrial tissues of a canine model of tachypacing-induce chronic AF, using miRNA microarray analysis comparing the differential expressions of miRNAs between control and AF dogs. Four miRNAs miR-223, miR-328, miR-664 and miR-517 were found increased by >2 folds, and six were decreased by at least 50% including miR-101, miR-133, miR-145, miR-320, miR-373 and miR-499. Real-time quantitative RT-PCR (qRT-PCR) analysis confirmed the significant upregulation of miR-223, miR-328 and miR-664 (miR-517 was undetectable), and the significant downregulation of miR-101, miR-320, and miR-499. Intriguingly, none of these deregulated miRNAs are within the list of top 20 most abundant miRNAs. But miR-223 and miR-328 are among the cardiac-enriched miRNAs. This notion would suggest that altered miRNA expression in this AF model tends to favour fibrogenesis; however, miRNAs are definitely not the major determinant for atrial structural remodelling associated with fibrosis.

In a recent study reported by Chen's group (Xiao et al., 2011), it was found that miRNA expression undergoes tremendous alterations in atrial tissues from AF patients with mitral stenosis. Intriguingly, out of 20 most abundant miRNAs in the heart, only let-7b/i and miR-30d were found significantly upregulated but 9 of 20 including miR-29, miR-133, miR-24, miR-26, miR-126, miR-125, miR-99, miR-20, and miR-23 were downregulated. Based on our computational prediction, these changes are expected to result in reduction of the anti-fibrotic force to promote atrial fibrogenesis.

5. Conclusion

The theoretical analyses in conjunction with experimental demonstration of miRNA expression profiles under various conditions performed presented here allowed us to establish a matrix of miRNAs that are expressed in cardiac cells and have the potential to regulate the genes encoding cardiac ion channels and transporters, proteins responsible for cell survival and death, and proteins involved in fibrogenesis in heart. These miRNAs likely play an important role in controlling cardiac excitability, cardiomyocyte homeostasis and cardiac fibrosis of the heart. In other words, the genes determining these processes may normally be under the post-transcriptional regulation of a group of miRNAs. Indeed, some of the predicted targets have already been demonstrated experimentally. Also we were able to link a particular remodeling process in hypertrophy/heart failure, myocardial ischemia, or atrial fibrillation to the corresponding deregulated miRNAs under that pathological condition; the changes of miRNAs appear to have anti-correlation with the changes of many of the genes responsible for cardiac electrophysiology, cardiomyocyte apoptosis and cardiac fibrosis under these situations. The present study should aid us to pinpoint the individual miRNAs that can most likely take part in the electrical and structural remodelling processes through targeting particular genes.

It should be noted, however, that the present computational study is in no way to replace experimental approaches for understanding the role of miRNAs in regulating expression of genes; rather it merely presents a prediction of the odds of miRNA:mRNA interactions under normal situation and in the context of electrical/ionic remodeling under the selected circumstances of the heart. This theoretical analysis like all other computational studies needs to be eventually verified with the bench-top work and should not be considered original results. Nonetheless, with sparse experimental data published to date and the anticipated difficulties to acquire complete experimental data using the currently available techniques, the analytical procedures described here can well serve as first-hand information, providing a framework and guideline for future experimental studies.

The second limitation of the study is the possibility of underestimating the number of miRNAs that could regulate ion channels, apoptosis and fibrosis due to the stringent criterion for inclusion of miRNAs with positive prediction of targets by at least four out of seven algorithms; in the past, we had been able to experimentally verified nearly all the target genes predicted by only one algorithm miRanda for our pre-experiment analysis. However, the fact that our prediction includes all 20 most abundant miRNAs and other highly expressed miRNAs in the myocardium suggests that this limitation might not have significant negative impact on the accuracy of our analysis and inclusion of more miRNAs by more permissive criteria does not guarantee their physiological function if they are scarcely expressed in the heart. Yet it should be noted that the miRNA expression profiles were obtained from myocardium that also includes fibroblasts and caution needs to be taken when interpreting the expression data.

Another important notion is that despite that our prediction of miRNA targeting coincides with the changes of expression of relevant genes under the pathological conditions, it does not imply that miRNAs are necessarily the important or even the only determinant of the electrical remodeling processes. Our data to the most indicate the potential contribution of miRNAs to such conditions; other molecules like transcription factors must also be involved in the regulation of expression of ion channel genes under these conditions.

Finally, it is also difficult to predict the net outcome when two miRNAs target a same gene but alter in their expression in the opposite directions. Yet, with deepened and broadened understanding of miRNA targeting and action, these possible limitations should eventually be worked out.

6. Acknowledgment

The work presented was supported by the Canadian Institute of Health Research (CIHR).

7. References

Berk, B.C., Fujiwara, K., & Lehoux S (2007). ECM remodeling in hypertensive heart disease. *J Clin Invest* 117, 568–575.

Beuckelmann, D.J., Nabauer, M., & Erdmann, E. (1993). Alterations of K^+ currents in isolated human ventricular myocytes from patients with terminal heart failure. *Circ Res* 73, 379–385.

Carè, A., Catalucci, D., Felicetti, F., Bonci, D., Addario, A., Gallo, P., Bang, M.L., Segnalini, P., Gu, Y., Dalton, N.D., Elia, L., Latronico, M.V., Høydal, M., Autore, C., Russo, M.A., Dorn, G.W 2nd., Ellingsen, O., Ruiz-Lozano, P., Peterson, K.L., Croce, C.M., Peschle, C., & Condorelli, G. (2007). MicroRNA-133 controls cardiac hypertrophy. *Nat Med* 13: 613–618.

Carmeliet, E. (1999). Cardiac ionic currents and acute ischemia: from channels to arrhythmias. *Physiol Rev* 79, 917–1017.

Chan, J.A., Krichevsky, A.M., & Kosik, K.S. (2005). MicroRNA-21 is an antiapoptotic factor in human glioblastoma cells. *Cancer Res* 65, 6029–6033.

Cheng, Y., Ji, R., Yue, J., Yang, J., Liu, X., Chen, H., Dean, D.B., & Zhang, C. (2007). MicroRNAs are aberrantly expressed in hypertrophic heart. Do they play a role in cardiac hypertrophy? *Am J Pathol* 170, 1831–1840.

Cheng, Y., Zhu, P., Yang, J., Liu, X., Dong, S., Wang, X., Chun, B., Zhuang, J., & Zhang, C. (2010). Ischemic preconditioning-regulated miR-21 protects the heart from ischemia/reperfusion injury via anti-apoptosis through its target PDCD4. *Cardiovasc Res* 87(3), 431–439.

Cimmino, A., Calin, G.A., Fabbri, M., Iorio, M.V., Ferracin, M., Shimizu, M., Wojcik, S.E., Aqeilan, R.I., Zupo, S., Dono, M., Rassenti, L., Alder, H., Volinia, S., Liu, C.G., Kipps, T.J., Negrini, M., & Croce, C.M. (2005). miR-15 and miR-16 induce apoptosis by targeting BCL2. *Proc Natl Acad Sci USA.* 102(39), 13944–13949.

Corsten, M.F., Miranda, R., Kasmieh, R., Krichevsky, A.M., Weissleder, R., & Shah, K. (2007). MicroRNA-21 knockdown disrupts glioma growth in vivo and displays synergistic cytotoxicity with neural precursor cell delivered S-TRAIL in human gliomas. *Cancer Res* 67, 8994–9000.

Dong S, Cheng Y, Yang J, Li J, Liu X, Wang, X., Wang, D., Krall, T.J., Delphin, E.S., Zhang, C. (2009). MicroRNA expression signature and the role of microRNA-21 in the early phase of acute myocardial infarction. *J Biol Chem* 284, 29514–29525.

Duisters, R.F., Tijsen, A.J., Schroen, B., Leenders, J.J., Lentink, V., van der Made, I., Herias, V., van Leeuwen, R.E., Schellings, M.W., Barenbrug, P., Maessen, J.G., Heymans, S., Pinto, Y.M., & Creemers, E.E. (2009). miR-133 and miR-30 regulate connective tissue growth factor: implications for a role of microRNAs in myocardial matrix remodeling. *Circ Res* 104, 170–178.

Dun, W., & Boyden, P.A (2005). Diverse phenotypes of outward currents in cells that have survived in the 5-day-infarcted heart. *Am J Physiol* 289, H667–H673.

Dupont, E., Matsushita, T., Kaba, R.A., Vozzi, C., Coppen, S.R., Khan, N., Kaprielian, R., Yacoub, M.H., & Severs, N.J. (2001). Altered connexin expression in human congestive heart failure. *J Mol Cell Cardiol* 33, 359–371.

Enright, A.J., John, B., Gaul, U., Tuschl, T., Sander, C., & Marks, D.S. (200). MicroRNA targets in Drosophila. *Genome Biology* 5, R1.

Flesch, M., Schwinger, R.H., Schiffer, F., Frank, K., Südkamp, M., Kuhn-Regnier, F., Arnold, G., & Böhm, M. (1996). Evidence for functional relevance of an enhanced expression of the Na$^+$-Ca^{2+} exchanger in failing human myocardium. *Circulation* 94, 992–1002.

Fox, C.S., Coady, S., Sorlie, P.D., D'Agostino, R.B. Sr, Pencina, M.J., Vasan, R.S., Meigs, J.B., Levy, D., & Savage, P.J. (2007). Increasing cardiovascular disease burden due to diabetes mellitus: The Framingham Heart Study. *Circulation* 115, 1544–1550.

Friedman, P.L., Fenoglio, J.J., & Wit, A.L. (1975). Time course for reversal of electrophysiological and ultrastructural abnormalities in subendocardial Purkinje fibers surviving extensive myocardial infarction in dogs. *Circ Res* 36, 127–144.

Friedman, R.C., Farh, K.K-H., Burge, C.B., & Bartel, D.P. (2009). Most mammalian mRNAs are conserved targets of microRNAs. *Genome Res* 19, 92–105.

Fuller, W., Parmar, V., Eaton, P., Bell, J.R., & Shattock, M.J. (2003). Cardiac ischemia causes inhibition of the Na/KATPase by a labile cytosolic compound whose production is linked to oxidant stress. *Cardiovasc Res* 57, 1044–1051.

Gardner, P.I., Ursell, P.C., Fenoglio, J.J. Jr., & Wit, A.L. (1985). Electrophysiologic and anatomic basis for fractionated electrograms recorded from healed myocardial infarcts. *Circulation* 72,: 596–611

Grimson, A., Farh, K.K-H., Johnston, W.K., Garrett-Engele, P. Lim, L.P., & Bartel, D.P. (2007). MicroRNA targeting specificity in mammals: determinants beyond seed pairing. *Molecular Cell* 27, 91–105.

Gupta, A., Gartner, J.J., Sethupathy, P., Hatzigeorgiou, A.G., & Fraser, N.W. (2006). Anti-apoptotic function of a microRNA encoded by the HSV-1 latencyassociated transcript. *Nature* 442, 82–85.

Jaffe, R., Flugelman, M.Y., Halon, D.A., & Lewis, B.S. (1997). Ventricular remodelling: from bedside to molecule. *Adv Exp Med Biol* 430, 257–266.

Kerr, J.F., Wyllie, A.H., & Currie, A.R. (1972). Apoptosis: A basic biological phenomenon with wide-ranging implications in tissue kinetics. *Br J Cancer* 26, 239–257.

Kertesz, M., Iovino, N., Unnerstall, U., Gaul, U., & Segal, E. (2007). The role of site accessibility in microRNA target recognition, *Nature Genet* 39, 1278–1284.

Khan, R., & Sheppard, R. (2006). Fibrosis in heart disease: understanding the role of transforming growth factor-beta in cardiomyopathy, valvular disease and arrhythmia. *Immunology* 118, 10–24.

Kiriakidou, M., Nelson, P.T., Kouranov, A., Fitziev, P., Bouyioukos, C., Mourelatos, Z., & Hatzigeorgiou, A. (2004). A combined computational-experimental approach predicts human microRNA targets. *Genes Dev* 18, 1165–1178.

Kitamura, H., Ohnishi, Y., Yoshida, A., Okajima, K., Azumi, H., Ishida, A., Galeano, E.J., Kubo, S., Hayashi, Y., Itoh, H., & Yokoyama, M. (2002). Heterogeneous loss of connexin43 protein in nonischemic dilated cardiomyopathy with ventricular tachycardia. *Cardiovasc Electrophysiol* 13, 865–870.

Krek, A., Grün, D., Poy, M.N., Wolf, R., Rosenberg, L., Epstein, E.J., MacMenamin, P., da Piedade, I., Gunsalus, K.C., Stoffel, M., & Rajewsky, N. (2005). Combinatorial microRNA target predictions. *Nat Genet* 37, 495–500.

Lewis, B.P., Burge, C.B., & Bartel, D.P. (2005). Conserved seed pairing, often flanked by adenosines, indicates that thousands of human genes are microRNA targets. *Cell* 120, 15–20.

Lewis, B.P., Shih, I.H., Jones-Rhoades, M.W., Bartel, D.P., & Burge, C.B. (2003). Prediction of mammalian microRNA targets. *Cell* 115, 787–798.

Liang, Y., Ridzon, D., Wong, L., & Chen, C. (2007). Characterization of microRNA expression profiles in normal human tissues. *BMC Genomics* 8, 166.

Luo, X., Lin, H., Lu, Y., Li, B., Xiao, J., Yang, B., & Wang, Z. (2007). Transcriptional activation by stimulating protein 1 and post-transcriptional repression by muscle-specific microRNAs of I$_{Ks}$-encoding genes and potential implications in regional heterogeneity of their expressions. *J Cell Physiol* 212, 358–367.

Luo, X., Lin, H., Pan, Z., Xiao, J., Zhang, Y., Lu, Y., Yang, B., & Wang, Z. (2008). Downregulation of miRNA-1/miRNA-133 contributes to re-expression of pacemaker channel genes HCN2 and HCN4 in hypertrophic heart. *J Biol Chem* 283, 20045–20052.

Luo, X., Zhang, H., Xiao, J., & Wang, Z. (2010). Regulation of human cardiac ion channel genes by microRNAs: Theoretical perspective and pathophysiological implications. *Cell Physiol Biochem* 25, 571–586.

Maisch, B. (1995). Extracellular matrix and cardiac interstitium: restriction is not a restricted phenomenon. *Herz* 20, 75–80.

Manabe, I., Shindo, T., & Nagai, R. (2002). Gene expression in fibroblasts and fibrosis involvement in cardiac hypertrophy. *Circ Res* 91, 1103–1113.

Nattel, S., Maguy, A., Le Bouter, S., & Yeh, Y-H. (2007). Arrhythmogenic ion-channel remodeling in the heart: heart failure, myocardial infarction, and atrial fibrillation. *Physiol Rev* 87, 425–456.

Ostenfeld, M.S., Bramsen, J.B., Lamy, P., Villadsen, S.B., Fristrup, N., Sørensen, K.D., Ulhøi, B., Borre, M., Kjems, J., Dyrskjøt, L., & Orntoft, T.F. (2010). miR-145 induces caspase-dependent and -independent cell death in urothelial cancer cell lines with targeting of an expression signature present in Ta bladder tumors. *Oncogene* 29(7), 1073–1084.

Palojoki, E., Saraste, A., Eriksson, A., Pullkki, K., Kallajoki, M., Voipio Pulkki, L.M., & Tikkanen, I. (2001). Cardiomyocyte apoptosis and ventricular remodeling after myocardial infarction in rats. *Am J Physiol Heart Circ Physiol* 280, H2726–H2731.

Patrick, D. M. Montgomery, R.L., Qi, X., Obad, S., Kauppinen, S., Hill, J.A., van Rooij, E., & Olson, E.N. (2010) Stress-dependent cardiac remodeling occurs in the absence of microRNA-21 in mice. *J Clin Invest* 120, 3912–3916.

Pellman, J., Lyon, R.C., & Sheikh, F. (2010). Extracellular matrix remodeling in atrial fibrosis: mechanisms and implications in atrial fibrillation. *J Mol Cell Cardiol* 48(3), 461–467.

Peters, N.S. (1995). Myocardial gap junction organization in ischemia and infarction. *Microsc Res Tech* 31, 375–386.

Pogwizd, S.M., & Bers, D.M. (2002). Na/Ca exchange in heart failure: contractile dysfunction and arrhythmogenesis. *Ann NY Acad Sci* 976, 454–465.

Pu, J., & Boyden, P.A. (1997). Alterations of Na$^+$ currents in myocytes from epicardial border zone of the infarcted heart. A possible ionic mechanism for reduced excitability and postrepolarization refractoriness. *Circ Res* 81, 110–119.

Rane, S., He, M., Sayed, D., Vashistha, H., Malhotra, A., Sadoshima, J., Vatner, D.E., Vatner, S.F., & Abdellatif, M. (2009). Downregulation of miR-199a derepresses hypoxia-inducible factor-1alpha and Sirtuin 1 and recapitulates hypoxia preconditioning in cardiac myocytes. *Circ Res* 104, 879–886.

Rehmsmeier, M., Steffen, P., Hochsmann, M., & Giegerich, R. (2004). Fast and effective prediction of microRNA/target duplexes. *RNA* 10, 1507–1517.

Ren, X.P., Wu, J., Wang, X., Sartor, M.A., Qian, J., Jones, K., Nicolaou, P., Pritchard, T.J., & Fan, G.C. (2009). MicroRNA-320 is involved in the regulation of cardiac ischemia/reperfusion injury by targeting heat-shock protein 20. *Circulation* 119, 2357–2366.

Reed, J.C. (2002). Apoptosis-based therapies. *Nat Rev Drug Discov* 1, 111–121.

Rose, J., Armoundas, A.A., Tian, Y., DiSilvestre, D., Burysek, M., Halperin, V., O'Rourke, B., Kass, D.A., Marbán, E., & Tomaselli, G.F. (2005). Molecular correlates of altered expression of potassium currents in failing rabbit myocardium. *Am J Physiol* 288, H2077–H2087.

Roy, S., Khanna, S., Hussain, S.R., Biswas, S., Azad, A., Rink, C., Gnyawali, S., Shilo, S., Nuovo, G.J., & Sen, C.K. (2009). MicroRNA expression in response to murine myocardial infarction: miR-21 regulates fibroblast metalloprotease-2 via phosphatase and tensin homologue. *Cardiovasc Res* 82:21-29.

Qian, L., Van Laake, L.W., Huang, Y., Liu, S., Wendland, M.F., & Srivastava, D. (2011). miR-24 inhibits apoptosis and represses Bim in mouse cardiomyocytes. *J Exp Med* 208(3), pp549–560.

Sabbah, H.N., Sharov, V.G., & Goldstein, S. (1998). Programmed cell death in the progression of heart failure. *Ann Med* 30, S33–S38.

Sachdeva, M., & Mo, Y.Y. (2010). miR-145-mediated suppression of cell growth, invasion and metastasis. *Am J Transl Res* 2(2), 170–180.

Sanguinetti, M.C., Curran, M.E., Zou, A., Shen, J., Spector, P.S., Atkinson, D.L., & Keating, M.T. (1996). Coassembly of KvLQT1 and minK (IsK) proteins to form cardiac I_{Ks} potassium channel. *Nature* 384, 80–83.

Sayed, D., Hong, C., Chen, I.Y., Lypowy, J., Abdellatif, M. (2007). MicroRNAs play an essential role in the development of cardiac hypertrophy. *Circ Res* 100, 416–424.

Shan, H., Zhang, Y., Lu, Y., Zhang, Y., Pan, Z., Cai, B., Wang, N., Li, X., Feng, T., Hong, Y., & Yang, B. (2009). Downregulation of miR-133 and miR-590 contributes to nicotine-induced atrial remodelling in canines. *Cardiovasc Res* 83, 465–472.

Si, M.L., Zhu, S., Wu, H., Lu, Z., Wu, F., & Mo, Y.Y. (2007). miR-21-mediated tumor growth. *Oncogene* 26, 2799–2803.

Spear, J.F., Michelson, E.L., & Moore, E.N. (1983). Reduced space constant in slowly conducting regions of chronically infarcted canine myocardium. *Circ Res* 53, 176–185.

Swynghedauw, B. (1999). Molecular mechanisms of myocardial remodeling. *Physiol Rev* 79, 215–262.

Tan, A.Y., & Zimetbaum, P. (2010). Atrial Fibrillation and Atrial Fibrosis. *J Cardiovasc Pharmacol* 2010 Dec 4. [Epub ahead of print]

Tang, Y., Zheng, J., Sun, Y., Wu, Z., Liu, Z., & Huang, G. (2009). MicroRNA-1 regulates cardiomyocyte apoptosis by targeting Bcl-2. *Int Heart J* 50, 377–387.

Tatsuguchi, M., Seok, H.Y., Callis, T.E., Thomson, J.M., Chen, J.F., Newman, M., Rojas, M., Hammond, S.M., & Wang, D.Z. (2007) Expression of microRNAs is dynamically regulated during cardiomyocyte hypertrophy. *J Mol Cell Cardiol* 42, 1137–1141.

Thum, T., Galuppo, P., Wolf, C., Fiedler, J., Kneitz, S., van Laake, L.W., Doevendans, P.A., Mummery, C.L., Borlak, J., Haverich, A., Gross, C., Engelhardt, S., Ertl, G,. & Bauersachs, J. (2007). MicroRNAs in the human heart: a clue to fetal gene reprogramming in heart failure. *Circulation* 116, 258–267.

Thum, T., Gross, C., Fiedler, J., Fischer, T., Kissler, S,. Bussen, M., Galuppo, P., Just, S., Rottbauer, W., Frantz, S., Castoldi, M., Soutschek, J., Koteliansky, V., Rosenwald, A., Basson, M.A., Licht, J.D., Pena, J.T., Rouhanifard, S.H., Muckenthaler, M.U., Tuschl, T., Martin, G.R., Bauersachs, J., & Engelhardt, S. (2008). MicroRNA-21 contributes to myocardial disease by stimulating MAP kinase signalling in fibroblasts. *Nature* 456, 980–984.

Thum, T. Chau, N., Bhat, B., Gupta, S.K., Linsley, P.S., Bauersachs, J., & Engelhardt, S. (2011). Comparison of different miR-21 inhibitor chemistries in a cardiac disease model. *J Clin Invest* 121, 461–462.

Tsang, W.P., & Kwok, T.T. (2010). Epigallocatechin gallate up-regulation of miR-16 and induction of apoptosis in human cancer cells. *J Nutr Biochem* 21(2), 140–146.

Tsuji, Y., Opthof, T., Kamiya, K., Yasui, K., Liu, W., Lu, Z., & Kodama, I. (2000). Pacing-induced heart failure causes a reduction of delayed rectifier potassium currents along with decreases in calcium and transient outward currents in rabbit ventricle. *Cardiovasc Res* 48, 300–309.

van Rooij, E., Sutherland, L.B., Liu, N., Williams, A.H., McAnally, J., Gerard, R.D., Richardson, J.A., & Olson, E.N. (2006). A signature pattern of stress-responsive microRNAs that can evoke cardiac hypertrophy and heart failure. *Proc Natl Acad Sci USA* 103, 18255–18260.

van Rooij, E., Sutherland, L.B., Qi, X., Richardson, J.A., Hill, J., & Olson, E.N. (2007). Control of stress-dependent cardiac growth and gene expression by a microRNA. *Science* 316, 575–579.

van Rooij, E., Sutherland, L.B., Thatcher, J.E., DiMaio, J.M., Naseem, R.H., Marshall, W.S., Hill, J.A., & Olson, E.N. (2008). Dysregulation of microRNAs following myocardial infarction reveals a role of miR-29 in cardiac fibrosis. *Proc Natl Acad Sci USA* 105, 13027–13032.

Wang, X., & El Naqa, I.M. (2008). Prediction of both conserved and nonconserved microRNA targets in animals. *Bioinformatics* 24, 325–332.

Wang, Z. (2010). MicroRNAs and cardiovascular disease. *Bentham Science.* doi: 10.2174/97816080518471100101 (eISBN: 978-1-60805-184-7).

Wang, Z., Luo, X., Lu, Y., & Yang, B. (2008). miRNAs at the heart of the matter. *J Mol Med* 86, 772–783.

Xiao, F., Zuo, Z., Cai, G., Kang, S., Gao, X., & Li, T. (2009). miRecords: an integrated resource for microRNA-target interactions. *Nucleic Acids Res* 37, D105–D110.

Xiao, J., Liang, D., Zhang, Y., Liu, Y., Zhang, H., Liu, Y., Li, L., Liang, X., Sun, Y., & Chen, Y.H. (2011). MicroRNA expression signature in atrial fibrillation with mitral stenosis. *Physiol Genomics* 2011 Feb 15. [Epub ahead of print].

Xiao, J., Luo, X., Lin, H., Zhang, Y., Lu, Y., Wang, N., Zhang, Y., Yang, B., & Wang, Z. (2007). MicroRNA miR-133 represses HERG K⁺ channel expression contributing to QT prolongation in diabetic hearts. *J Biol Chem* 282, 12363–12367.

Xiao, L., Xiao, J., Luo, X., Lin, H., Wang, Z., & Nattel, S. (2008). Feedback remodeling of cardiac potassium current expression. A novel potential mechanism for control of repolarization reserve. *Circulation* 118, 983–992.

Xu, C., Lu ,Y., Pan, Z., Chu, W., Luo, X., Lin, H., Xiao, J., Shan, H., Wang, Z., & Yang, B. (2007). The muscle-specific microRNAs miR-1 and miR-133 produce opposing effects on apoptosis by targeting HSP60, HSP70 and caspase-9 in cardiomyocytes. *J Cell Sci* 120, 3045–3052.

Yamada, K.A., Rogers, J.G., Sundset, R., Steinberg, T.H., & Saffitz, J.E. (2003). Up-regulation of connexin45 in heart failure. J *Cardiovasc Electrophysiol* 14, 1205–1212.

Yang, B., Lin, H., Xiao, J., Lu, Y., Luo, X., Li, B., Zhang, Y., Xu, C., Bai, Y., Wang, H., Chen, G., & Wang, Z. (2007). The muscle-specific microRNA miR-1 regulates cardiac arrhythmogenic potential by targeting GJA1 and KCNJ2. *Nat Med* 13, 486–491.

Yang, B., Lu, Y., & Wang, Z. (2008). Control of cardiac excitability by microRNAs. *Cardiovasc Res* 79, 571–580.

Ye, Y., Hu, Z., Lin, Y., Zhang, C., & Perez-Polo, J.R. (2010). Down-regulation of microRNA-29 by antisense inhibitors and a PPAR-{gamma} agonist protects against myocardial ischemia-reperfusion injury. *Cardiovasc Res* 87(3), 535–544.

Yin, C., Salloum, F.N., & Kukreja, R.C. (2009). A novel role of microRNA in late preconditioning: upregulation of endothelial nitric oxide synthase and heat shock protein 70. *Circ Res* 104, 572–575.

Yu, X.Y., Song, Y.H., Geng, Y.J., Lin, Q.X., Shan, Z.X., Lin, S.G., & Li, Y. (2008). Glucose induces apoptosis of cardiomyocytes via microRNA-1 and IGF-1. *Biochem Biophys Res Commun* 376, 548–552.

Zhu, S., Si, M.L.,Wu, H., & Mo, Y.Y. (2007). MicroRNA-21 targets the tumor suppressor gene tropomyosin 1 (TPM1). *J Biol Chem* 282, 14328–36.

Zicha, S., Maltsev, V.A., Nattel, S., Sabbah, H.N., & Undrovinas, A.I. (200). Post-transcriptional alterations in the expression of cardiac Na⁺ channel subunits in chronic heart failure. *J Mol Cell Cardiol* 37, 91–100.

25

Genome-Wide Identification of Estrogen Receptor Alpha Regulated miRNAs Using Transcription Factor Binding Data

Jianzhen Xu[1], Xi Zhou[2] and Chi-Wai Wong[3]
[1]College of Bioengineering, Henan University of Technology, Zhengzhou,
[2]Guangzhou Institute of Biomedicine and Health, Chinese Academy of ScienceGuangzhou,
[3]NeuMed Pharmaceuticals Limited, Hong Kong,
China

1. Introduction

MicroRNAs (miRNAs) are one class of endogenous non-coding RNA which can repress protein translation or cause target mRNA degradation(Bartel 2004). Currently 15,172 entries, including 1,048 human miRNAs, are recorded in a major miRNAs database miRbase (Release 16: Sept 2010) (Kozomara and Griffiths-Jones 2011). MiRNAs reside reside in protein-coding, intronic and intergenic regions throughout the genome. MiRNAs are mainly transcribed into long primary miRNAs (pri-miRNAs) by RNA polymerase II(Lee et al. 2004). Since mammalian miRNA genes are often clustered along the genome, the pri-miRNA can contain one single miRNA gene or multiple clustered miRNA genes. In the nucleus, pri-miRNAs, which are both capped and polyadenylated, are processed by RNase III enzymes Drosha into about 70-nucleotide hairpins called pre-miRNAs(Lee et al. 2002). The transporter protein exportin-5 then exports pre-miRNAs to the cytoplasm, where they are cleaved by another RNase III Dicer to generate mature miRNA duplexes. One strand of miRNA duplex preferentially enters into miRNA-induced silencing complexes (miRISCs) and guides the complex to recognize its target genes. Previous studies indicated that this target inhibition of miRNAs mainly function via imperfect base pairing with the targeting sequences on the 3' untranslated region(3'UTR) and the first 2–8 bases of a particular mature miRNA sequence referred to the "seed" region. MiRNAs play essential regulatory roles in diverse biological processes. For example, we recently found that miRNA-153, the expression level of which is significantly repressed in glioblastoma (GBM), could inhibit cell proliferation and induce apoptosis via targeting B-cell lymphoma 2 (Bcl-2), myeloid cell leukemia sequence 1 (Mcl-1) and insulin receptor substrate-2 (Irs-2) in glioblastoma cell lines(Xu, Liao, and Wong 2010; Xu et al. 2011).

In the past few years, computational approaches have played an important role in miRNA studies, for example, dozens of prediction tools used for miRNA gene finding and miRNA target prediction were developed. These tools have greatly facilitated experimental discovery. However, knowledge about the regulation of these essential regulators is at its early stage(Schanen and Li 2010; Li et al. 2010). Transcriptional regulations mediated by specific transcriptional factors (TFs) have only been intensively studied on a small number of miRNAs(Lee et al. 2004; Houbaviy et al. 2005). Importantly, certain "oncogenic miRNAs" and "tumour suppressor miRNAs" are inappropriately expressed in cancers. However, our understanding as to the TFs or chromatin modifications responsible for governing the expression levels of these essential miRNAs remains limited.

At the transcriptional level, gene expression is governed by interactions among TFs and cis-elements such as promoters and enhancers. Chromatin immunoprecipitation (ChIP) experiment discovers specific protein-DNA interactions in a given cell type and is regarded as a major tool for investigating interactions between TFs and their binding sites. Based on the pairing of ChIP with DNA microarray and high-throughput sequencing technologies (ChIP-chip and ChIP-seq), genome-wide maps of TF binding sites can now be readily produced. Many groups have used ChIP-chip and ChIP-seq assays to globally study direct targets of TFs and provided significant insights into gene regulation networks (Farnham 2009). Together with mRNA-based expression microarrays, vast amounts of data are publicly available for analysis by bioinformatics. Indeed, networks of gene expression (or systems biology) are gaining popularity to help uncover the physiology regulation underneath and interpret the biological meaning behind these networks.

In principle, one can use the genome-wide binding map of a specific TF (or a chromatic modifying factor) to search for its putative target miRNAs, i.e. locate putative binding sites inside miRNA regulatory regions (such as promoter or enhancer) according to genomic coordinates. In the following section, we present a procedure which uses published ChIP-chip data to predict candidate miRNAs regulated by a specific TF. Specifically, based on one genome-wide estrogen receptor (ER) binding map, we found 59 miRNA regulatory regions in which there is at least one ER binding site. Several putative ER-regulated oncogenic and tumour suppressor miRNAs were further confirmed in a breast cancer cell model.

2. Methods

2.1 Prediction of ER-regulated miRNAs

Accessing and analyzing the genomic sequence and functional annotations were based on the UCSC Genome Browser(Rhead et al. 2010) and Galaxy platform(Goecks, Nekrutenko, and Taylor 2010). UCSC Genome Browser is a web tool for convenient displaying and accessing the genome sequences, together with rich annotation tracks. Galaxy platform is an interactive system that combines existing multiple genome resources via a simple web portal. Users can manipulate remote resources and perform flexible operations such as intersections, unions, and subtractions. Currently, 718 miRNAs have been annotated in human genome (hg18). Their regulatory regions (50 Kb upstream from the pre-miRNAs) were collected from UCSC Genome Browser. The original ChIP-chip data were produced by Carroll et al. (Carroll et al. 2006). Totally 3,665 estrogens receptor binding regions, which were considered with high confidence, were used in this study. Since the original coordinates were annotated in hg17, a web-based liftOver utility with default settings was used to convert the genomic coordinates to the hg18 version of the human genome (http://genome.ucsc.edu/cgi-bin/hgLiftOver). Overlapping regions were searched in Galaxy platform.

2.2 Motif analysis

The ER binding regions which overlapped with miRNA regulatory sequences were download from UCSC Genome Browser and further analyzed by TOUCAN 2, a widely used regulatory sequence analysis suite (Aerts et al. 2005). It screened the input sequences against a precompiled library of motifs to find the statistically over-represented motifs. TRANSFAC is a database storing eukaryotic transcription factors and the transcription regulating DNA sequence elements(Matys et al. 2006). Position weight matrixes (PWMs) were obtained from the TRANSFAC 7.0 database. The Eukaryotic Promoter Database (EPD) collected annotated eukaryotic RNA polymerase II promoters sequences around the experimentally determined transcription start site(Schmid et al. 2006). The human promoter sequence (-499,100 around TSS) from EPD were used as background sequences. The 0th order of the Markov model with prior 0.1 was chosen to compute both the background sequences and the actual sequence frequencies. The p-value and significance value indicate the probability that the observed over-representation of the motif is achieved by random selection for a single or multiple TFs, respectively.

2.3 Cells culture, cell counting and qRT-PCR

MCF-7 cell line was from American Type Culture Collection (Manassas, VA). Cells were grown with phenol red-free D-MEM supplemented with 0.5% charcoal stripped FBS for 3 Days. The estrogen-deprived MCF-7 cells were treated with 10 nM 17β-estradiol (E2, Sigma-Aldrich Co.) or DMSO as a control. At the indicated time points, cells were rinsed with PBS and counted manually under the microscope. Total RNA was collected and extracted with Trizol reagent (Invitrogen). Reverse transcription of mature miRNAs and quantitative real-time PCR analysis were performed as previously reported(Xu, Liao, and Wong 2010). Primers specific for the indicated miRNAs were available upon request.

3. Results

3.1 Identifying putative miRNAs regulated by ERs

Estrogen receptor alpha (ERα) and beta (ERβ) are members of the nuclear receptors super-family which are ligand-regulated transcription factors. Estrogen (17β-estradiol, E2) is a potent ligand for both ERs. ERs either directly interact with cis-regulatory elements of target genes by binding to estrogen-response elements (EREs) or indirectly tether to transcription factors such as AP1 and SP1 (Ali and Coombes 2002). By transcriptional control of a large number of target genes, ERs regulate a wide variety of cellular processes including development and differentiation (Deroo and Korach 2006). In particular, ERα is thought to be involved in the progression of breast cancer. Depending on the status of ERα expression, breast cancer is classified into ERα+ and ERα- subtypes. Differential anti-hormone treatments are prescribed in conjunction with anti-cancer drugs to manage these breast cancer subtypes. Therefore, understanding how ER affects the expressions of oncogenic and tumour suppressor miRNAs may assist better development of anti-cancer therapy.

Carroll et al. previously used ChIP-chip technology to analyze ER binding regions genome-wide. They found that the majority of ER binding regions are located outside of the classical promoter-proximal regions, suggesting distal regulation by ER (Carroll et al. 2006). To account for the possible bias when only focusing on promoter-proximal regions, we regarded 50 Kb upstream of all known pre-miRNAs as possible regulatory regions. Besides, setting a wider candidate region should be beneficial at this exploring step. Totally 59 miRNA regulatory regions were found that overlapped with 65 Carroll's ER binding regions (Table 1). As shown in Figure 1, there are three representative patterns of ER binding regions relative to specific miRNAs. For example, the promoter of hsa-miR-342 contains both promoter-proximal and distal ER binding regions, whereas the promoter of hsa-miR-21 is characterized by two proximal ER binding regions. In contrast, there is only one distal ER binding region within the miR-143~145 cluster upstream regulatory region.

chromosome	chrStart	chrEnd	miRNA regulatory regions	strand
chr1	149734895	149784895	hsa-mir-554_up_50000_chr1_149734896_f	+
chr1	160528959	160578959	hsa-mir-556_up_50000_chr1_160528960_f	+
chr1	154656845	154706845	hsa-mir-9-1_up_50000_chr1_154656846_r	-
chr1	153381591	153431591	hsa-mir-92b_up_50000_chr1_153381592_f	+
chr10	14468580	14518580	hsa-mir-1265_up_50000_chr10_14468581_f	+
chr10	134911115	134961115	hsa-mir-202_up_50000_chr10_134911116_r	-
chr10	98578511	98628511	hsa-mir-607_up_50000_chr10_98578512_r	-
chr10	29931281	29981281	hsa-mir-938_up_50000_chr10_29931282_r	-
chr11	74723878	74773878	hsa-mir-326_up_50000_chr11_74723879_r	-
chr11	2112015	2162015	hsa-mir-483_up_50000_chr11_2112016_r	-
chr11	64918504	64968504	hsa-mir-612_up_50000_chr11_64918505_f	+
chr12	96431720	96481720	hsa-mir-135a-2_up_50000_chr12_96431721_f	+
chr12	52621788	52671788	hsa-mir-196a-2_up_50000_chr12_52621789_f	+
chr12	63252555	63302555	hsa-mir-548c_up_50000_chr12_63252556_f	+
chr12	12910029	12960029	hsa-mir-614_up_50000_chr12_12910030_f	+
chr12	52664000	52714000	hsa-mir-615_up_50000_chr12_52664001_f	+
chr14	99595744	99645744	hsa-mir-342_up_50000_chr14_99595745_f	+
chr15	60853208	60903208	hsa-mir-190_up_50000_chr15_60853209_f	+
chr15	61950271	62000271	hsa-mir-422a_up_50000_chr15_61950272_r	-
chr15	78921469	78971469	hsa-mir-549_up_50000_chr15_78921470_r	-
chr15	68158861	68208861	hsa-mir-629_up_50000_chr15_68158862_r	-
chr15	73433079	73483079	hsa-mir-631_up_50000_chr15_73433080_r	-
chr16	84332807	84382807	hsa-mir-1910_up_50000_chr16_84332808_r	-
chr16	2211748	2261748	hsa-mir-940_up_50000_chr16_2211749_f	+
chr17	43469612	43519612	hsa-mir-152_up_50000_chr17_43469613_r	-
chr17	55223408	55273408	hsa-mir-21_up_50000_chr17_55223409_f	+
chr17	26876542	26926542	hsa-mir-365-2_up_50000_chr17_26876543_f	+
chr19	10473797	10523797	hsa-mir-1238_up_50000_chr19_10473798_f	+
chr19	58817033	58867033	hsa-mir-1323_up_50000_chr19_58817034_f	+
chr19	10789172	10839172	hsa-mir-199a-1_up_50000_chr19_10789173_r	-
chr19	58811744	58861744	hsa-mir-512-1_up_50000_chr19_58811745_f	+
chr19	58814222	58864222	hsa-mir-512-2_up_50000_chr19_58814223_f	+
chr2	232236267	232286267	hsa-mir-1244_up_50000_chr2_232236268_f	+
chr20	48664729	48714729	hsa-mir-1302-5_up_50000_chr20_48664730_r	-
chr20	48585729	48635729	hsa-mir-645_up_50000_chr20_48585730_f	+
chr20	61971237	62021237	hsa-mir-941-1_up_50000_chr20_61971238_f	+
chr20	61971544	62021544	hsa-mir-941-2_up_50000_chr20_61971545_f	+
chr20	61971656	62021656	hsa-mir-941-3_up_50000_chr20_61971657_f	+
chr22	36570324	36620324	hsa-mir-658_up_50000_chr22_36570325_r	-
chr22	36573727	36623727	hsa-mir-659_up_50000_chr22_36573728_r	-
chr3	187937154	187987154	hsa-mir-1248_up_50000_chr3_187937155_f	+
chr3	129513697	129563697	hsa-mir-1280_up_50000_chr3_129513698_f	+
chr3	50135762	50185762	hsa-mir-566_up_50000_chr3_50135763_f	+
chr3	113264337	113314337	hsa-mir-567_up_50000_chr3_113264338_f	+
chr4	8058008	8108008	hsa-mir-95_up_50000_chr4_8058009_r	-
chr5	167920556	167970556	hsa-mir-103-1_up_50000_chr5_167920557_r	-
chr5	41461490	41511490	hsa-mir-1274a_up_50000_chr5_41461491_f	+
chr5	132791297	132841297	hsa-mir-1289-2_up_50000_chr5_132791298_r	-
chr5	153656858	153706858	hsa-mir-1294_up_50000_chr5_153656859_f	+

chromosome	chrStart	chrEnd	miRNA regulatory regions	strand
chr5	148738673	148788673	hsa-mir-143_up_50000_chr5_148738674_f	+
chr5	148740401	148790401	hsa-mir-145_up_50000_chr5_148740402_f	+
chr6	166842911	166892911	hsa-mir-1913_up_50000_chr6_166842912_r	-
chr6	135551990	135601990	hsa-mir-548a-2_up_50000_chr6_135551991_f	+
chr6	107288692	107338692	hsa-mir-587_up_50000_chr6_107288693_f	+
chr7	101833307	101883307	hsa-mir-548o_up_50000_chr7_101833308_r	-
chr8	128827389	128877389	hsa-mir-1204_up_50000_chr8_128827390_f	+
chr8	128992060	129042060	hsa-mir-1205_up_50000_chr8_128992061_f	+
chr8	129181543	129231543	hsa-mir-1208_up_50000_chr8_129181544_f	+
chr8	1702803	1752803	hsa-mir-596_up_50000_chr8_1702804_f	+
chr1	154656845	154706845	hsa-mir-9-1_up_50000_chr1_154656846_r	-
chr1	153381591	153431591	hsa-mir-92b_up_50000_chr1_153381592_f	+
chr10	14468580	14518580	hsa-mir-1265_up_50000_chr10_14468581_f	+
chr10	134911115	134961115	hsa-mir-202_up_50000_chr10_134911116_r	-
chr10	98578511	98628511	hsa-mir-607_up_50000_chr10_98578512_r	-
chr10	29931281	29981281	hsa-mir-938_up_50000_chr10_29931282_r	-
chr11	74723878	74773878	hsa-mir-326_up_50000_chr11_74723879_r	-
chr11	2112015	2162015	hsa-mir-483_up_50000_chr11_2112016_r	-
chr11	64918504	64968504	hsa-mir-612_up_50000_chr11_64918505_f	+
chr12	96431720	96481720	hsa-mir-135a-2_up_50000_chr12_96431721_f	+
chr12	52621788	52671788	hsa-mir-196a-2_up_50000_chr12_52621789_f	+
chr12	63252555	63302555	hsa-mir-548c_up_50000_chr12_63252556_f	+
chr12	12910029	12960029	hsa-mir-614_up_50000_chr12_12910030_f	+
chr12	52664000	52714000	hsa-mir-615_up_50000_chr12_52664001_f	+
chr14	99595744	99645744	hsa-mir-342_up_50000_chr14_99595745_f	+
chr15	60853208	60903208	hsa-mir-190_up_50000_chr15_60853209_f	+
chr15	61950271	62000271	hsa-mir-422a_up_50000_chr15_61950272_r	-
chr15	78921469	78971469	hsa-mir-549_up_50000_chr15_78921470_r	-
chr15	68158861	68208861	hsa-mir-629_up_50000_chr15_68158862_r	-
chr15	73433079	73483079	hsa-mir-631_up_50000_chr15_73433080_r	-
chr16	84332807	84382807	hsa-mir-1910_up_50000_chr16_84332808_r	-
chr16	2211748	2261748	hsa-mir-940_up_50000_chr16_2211749_f	+
chr17	43469612	43519612	hsa-mir-152_up_50000_chr17_43469613_r	-
chr17	55223408	55273408	hsa-mir-21_up_50000_chr17_55223409_f	+
chr17	26876542	26926542	hsa-mir-365-2_up_50000_chr17_26876543_f	+
chr19	10473797	10523797	hsa-mir-1238_up_50000_chr19_10473798_f	+
chr19	58817033	58867033	hsa-mir-1323_up_50000_chr19_58817034_f	+
chr19	10789172	10839172	hsa-mir-199a-1_up_50000_chr19_10789173_r	-
chr19	58811744	58861744	hsa-mir-512-1_up_50000_chr19_58811745_f	+
chr19	58814222	58864222	hsa-mir-512-2_up_50000_chr19_58814223_f	+
chr2	232236267	232286267	hsa-mir-1244_up_50000_chr2_232236268_f	+
chr20	48664729	48714729	hsa-mir-1302-5_up_50000_chr20_48664730_r	-
chr20	48585729	48635729	hsa-mir-645_up_50000_chr20_48585730_f	+
chr20	61971237	62021237	hsa-mir-941-1_up_50000_chr20_61971238_f	+
chr20	61971544	62021544	hsa-mir-941-2_up_50000_chr20_61971545_f	+
chr20	61971656	62021656	hsa-mir-941-3_up_50000_chr20_61971657_f	+
chr22	36570324	36620324	hsa-mir-658_up_50000_chr22_36570325_r	-
chr22	36573727	36623727	hsa-mir-659_up_50000_chr22_36573728_r	-
chr3	187937154	187987154	hsa-mir-1248_up_50000_chr3_187937155_f	+

chromosome	chrStart	chrEnd	miRNA regulatory regions	strand
chr3	129513697	129563697	hsa-mir-1280_up_50000_chr3_129513698_f	+
chr3	50135762	50185762	hsa-mir-566_up_50000_chr3_50135763_f	+
chr3	113264337	113314337	hsa-mir-567_up_50000_chr3_113264338_f	+
chr4	8058008	8108008	hsa-mir-95_up_50000_chr4_8058009_r	-
chr5	167920556	167970556	hsa-mir-103-1_up_50000_chr5_167920557_r	-
chr5	41461490	41511490	hsa-mir-1274a_up_50000_chr5_41461491_f	+
chr5	132791297	132841297	hsa-mir-1289-2_up_50000_chr5_132791298_r	-
chr5	153656858	153706858	hsa-mir-1294_up_50000_chr5_153656859_f	+
chr5	148738673	148788673	hsa-mir-143_up_50000_chr5_148738674_f	+
chr5	148740401	148790401	hsa-mir-145_up_50000_chr5_148740402_f	+
chr6	166842911	166892911	hsa-mir-1913_up_50000_chr6_166842912_r	-
chr6	135551990	135601990	hsa-mir-548a-2_up_50000_chr6_135551991_f	+
chr6	107288692	107338692	hsa-mir-587_up_50000_chr6_107288693_f	+
chr7	101833307	101883307	hsa-mir-548o_up_50000_chr7_101833308_r	-
chr8	128827389	128877389	hsa-mir-1204_up_50000_chr8_128827390_f	+
chr8	128992060	129042060	hsa-mir-1205_up_50000_chr8_128992061_f	+
chr8	129181543	129231543	hsa-mir-1208_up_50000_chr8_129181544_f	+
chr8	1702803	1752803	hsa-mir-596_up_50000_chr8_1702804_f	+

Table 1. miRNA regulatory regions overlapped with ER binding regions. Each miRNA regulatory region was annotated with chromosome, start and end position and the strand it resides.

a

b

c

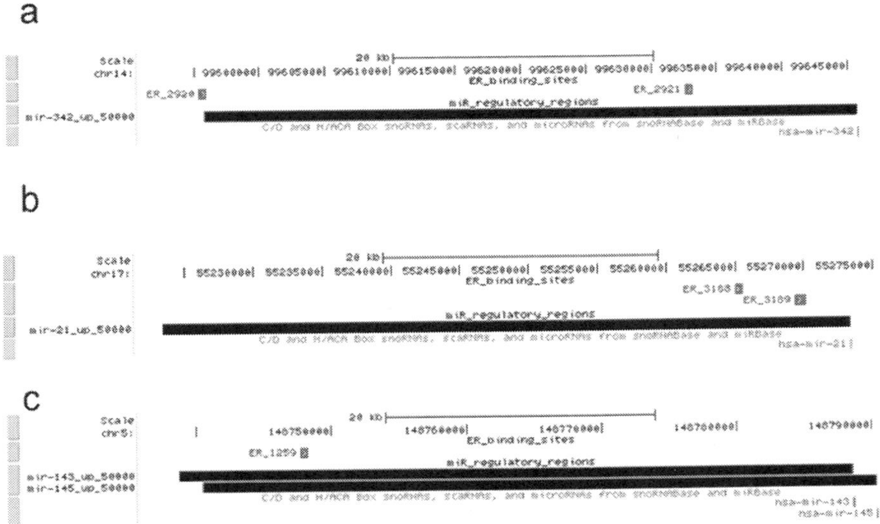

Fig. 1. ER binding sites relative to specific miRNAs. The blue boxes represent ER binding regions and the black blocks represent upstream 50 Kbp of miRNAs. The pre-miRNAs, miR-342, miR-21, miR-143~145 were represented by red colour. To note, there are two ER binding regions within miR-342 and miR-21 regulatory regions. Correspondingly, miR-143 and miR-145 share the same ER binding region.

We then used TOUCAN 2 to see whether there are TFs binding sites over-represented in these miRNA-related ER-binding regions. The top 10 significant binding motifs are listed in Table 2. Not surprisingly, we identified the consensus ERE (AGGTCANNNTGACC) as the most common TF binding motif presented in these miRNA regulatory regions bound by ER. In addition, we also observed enrichments of activator protein 1(AP-1) and forkhead (FKH) motifs among the miRNA-related ER-binding regions. The AP-1 family consists of proteins belonging to the JUN, FOS and ATF subfamilies. These subunits can hetero-dimerize and bind to their DNA target genes. AP-1 complex modulates a variety of cellular processes in response to environmental stimuli. Specially, AP-1 complex is an important regulator in tumour development since its target genes are involved in oncogenic transformation, tumour suppression, invasive growth and angiogenesis(Wagner 2001; Jochum, Passegue, and Wagner 2001). FKH proteins are a super-family of transcription factors that participate in regulating the expression of genes involved in cell growth, proliferation and differentiation. Many FKH proteins are important to embryonic development, glucose homeostasis, tumourigenesis and even vocal learning (Hannenhalli and Kaestner 2009). In previous analysis of mRNA targets, these two binding motifs were also shown to enriched in ER binding regions, suggesting their role in ER–regulated mRNAs transcription (Carroll et al. 2006). Our findings further implied that AP-1 and forkhead family members are cooperating transcription factors to regulate ER responsive miRNAs in combinatorial fashions.

In our result, p53 motif is the fourth most significant enriched binding sites in ER binding regions. p53 is an essential tumour suppressor because mutations or aberrations in the expression of p53 gene were frequently observed in a variety of cancer cell lines and clinical tumour samples(Nigro et al. 1989). Liu et al. also found that ERα can bind directly to p53 and repress its target genes (Liu et al. 2006). This important finding has profound translational implications because the same group of investigators recently demonstrated that (1) Ionizing radiation disrupts the ERα-p53 interaction in breast tumours, functionally leads to p53 restoration in breast tumours subjected to radiation therapy and elucidates a novel mechanism underlying the anti-tumour effect of radiation therapy(Liu et al. 2009); (2) The presence of wild-type p53 is an important determinant for responsiveness to anti-estrogen therapy since anti-estrogens could reactivate p53 by disrupting the ERα–p53 interaction and subsequently p53 activates many tumour suppressor genes(Konduri et al. 2010). Similar with the situation for mRNA target regulation, we therefore hypothesize that ERα–p53 interaction may also involve in modulating the transcription of "oncogenic miRNAs" and "tumour suppressor miRNAs" although the exact mechanism needs further analysis. Except for co-regulator of ERα, there is also possible interaction between the enriched TFs. For example, cross-talk between glucocorticoid receptor (GR) and AP-1 has been well established (Herrlich 2001). In our result, both GR and AP-1 are also enriched in the binding region, whether such interactions are involved in miRNAs target regulation warrants further investigation.

In the original analysis of binding sites in mRNA promoters, Carroll et al. found there is a strong correlation among ERα, Forkhead, Oct, Ap-1 and C/EBP(Carroll et al. 2006). In our analysis of miRNA promoter regions, we did not find significant enrichment for Oct and C/EBP. But interestingly, several novel TF binding sites (v-Maf, Meis-1, p53, GR-α, RORα1, Hand1) are over-represented in miRNA-related ER-binding regions. This observation perhaps reflect the similar (in the case of common TFs, i.e. ERα, FHK and AP-1) and distinct modes of ERα modulation in miRNA and mRNA gene regulation.

TRANSFAC Motif	N	P-value	Sig value	TFs
M00191	33	1.76E-13	10.338	ER-α
M00035	21	1.52E-7	4.401	v-Maf
M00419	28	1.22E-6	3.498	Meis-1
M00272	21	2.32E-5	2.217	P53
M00192	34	4.13E-5	1.967	GR-α
M00199	28	5.54E-5	1.84	AP-1
M00156	16	7.24E-5	1.723	RORα1
M00291	16	8.48E-5	1.655	FOXC1(Forkhead box protein C1)
M00222	22	1.86E-4	1.313	E47(Hand1)
M00269	24	2.14E-4	1.254	Xenopus fork head domain factor 3

Table 2. Top 10 enriched motifs in the miRNA-related ER-binding sites. N: number of times TF site appears in the input sequences. Note that TF binding site might appear more than once in one sequence. P-value: probability to find even more occurrences than N in the input sequences. Sig value: a significance coefficient used to select the most overrepresented patterns among the distinct motifs. When analyzing only one TF site, a P-value smaller than 0.05 could be considered as being over-represented. In case of multiple TF sites, sig-value is used to select the significant result. Generally, positive sig values mean significant.

3.2 Confirmation of ER-regulated miRNA in a breast cancer cell model

MCF-7 is a well established ERα+ cell line that reflects hormone-dependent breast cancer; namely, E2 increases MCF-7 cell proliferation. In our hand, the cell number significantly increased after four days of treatment with 10 nM E2 compared to DMSO control while a late phase increase in cell number was observed starting on day 9 (Figure 2a). Among the predicted E2-regulated miRNAs, we randomly selected 8 miRNAs and used qRT-PCR to detect the time-dependent changes in their expression levels during cell proliferation. Compared to DMSO control, miR-342, miR-21, miR-422a, miR-124, and miR-181c were generally found to be up-regulated by E2 treatment; whereas miR-143, miR-145, and miR-483 were down-regulated (Figure 2b and 2c), suggesting that they are under the respective influences of positive and negative EREs. Intriguingly, the down-regulated miRNAs exhibit wave patterns of expression, i.e., significantly suppressed on day 4 with differential levels of restoration on day 7 followed by another round of suppression and partial rebound. Other than miR-124 which displays a wave pattern of induction, the rest of the E2-induced miRNAs show a gradual pattern of induction. The determinants and regulatory networks that dictate these patterns of expression await comprehensive investigations.

Of those up-regulated miRNAs, miR-342 was induced to the highest extent by E2. MiR-342 is encoded in an intron of the gene EVL and commonly suppressed in human colorectal cancer (Grady et al. 2008). Over-expression of miR-342 in the colorectal cancer cell line HT-29 induced apoptosis, pointing towards a pro-apoptotic tumour suppressor function (Grady et al. 2008). On the other hand, miR-342 expression level in breast tumours is more complicated with highest level in ER and HER2/neu-positive luminal B tumours but lowest level in ER, PR and HER2/neu triple-negative tumours (Lowery et al. 2009). Adding to the uncertainty regarding its role, miR-342 is down-regulated in tamoxifen-resistant MCF-7 cells (Miller et al. 2008). Consistent with these findings, Cittelly et al. compared miRNA expression profiles between MCF-7/pcDNA (tamoxifen-sensitive) and MCF-7/HER2Δ16 (tamoxifen-resistant) cells when both cell lines were treated for 24 hr with 100 pM 17-β-estradiol (E2) and 1μM 4-hydroxytamoxifen (TAM). They found that miR-342 was the most dramatically down-regulated miRNA in the tamoxifen resistant MCF-7/HER2Δ16 cells. They further proved that other tamoxifen resistant cell lines such as TAMR1 and LCC2, all exhibited dramatically suppressed levels of miR-342 whereas another tamoxifen sensitive MCF-7/HER2 cell lines also expressed high levels of miR-342, indicating that loss of miR-342 was a common feature of tamoxifen resistance(Cittelly et al. 2010).

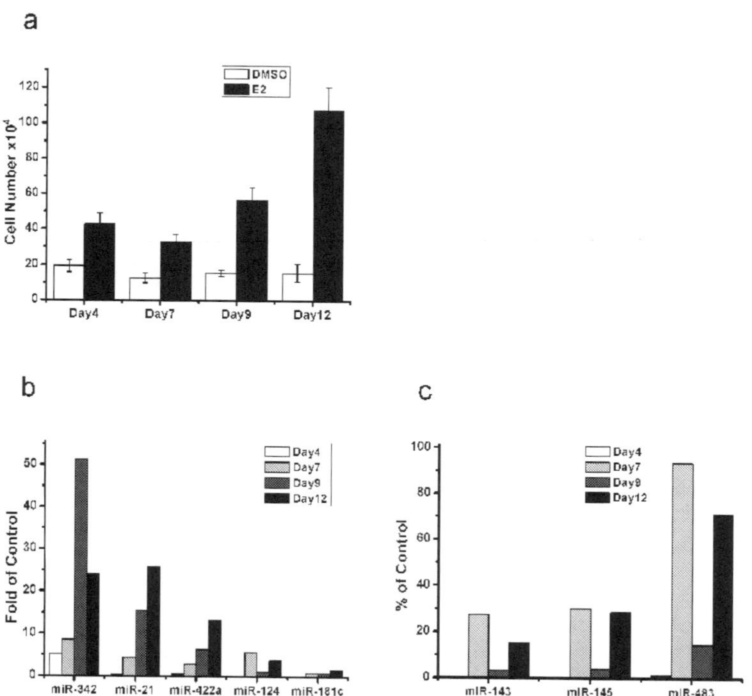

Fig. 2. ER binding sites relative to specific miRNAs. (a) The effects of E2 (10 nM) on MCF-7 cell number over the course of 12 days are shown. (b-c) E2 induces expression of miR-342, miR-21, miR-422a, miR-124 and miR-181c; whereas, decreases expression of miR-143, miR-145 and miR-483 in MCF-7 cells. Cells were treated with E2 (10 nM) for indicated time and miRNAs were subjected to qRT–PCR analysis.

The expression level of miR-21 was previously found to be significantly changed in various cancers; especially, it is higher in ERα+ than ERα– breast tumour (Mattie et al. 2006; Volinia et al. 2006). However, inconsistent results were reported regarding the effect of E2 on miR-21 expression in MCF-7. Wickramasinghe et al. reported that E2 inhibited miR-21 expression after 6 hr (Wickramasinghe et al. 2009). In contrast, another group found that miR-21 was induced after a 4 hr E2 treatment (Bhat-Nakshatri et al. 2009). In our investigation, we found that initially miR-21 was repressed after 4 days on E2. However, miR-21 was up-regulated by E2 upon long term treatments. MiR-21 is thought to be an oncogenic miRNA (oncomiR) and several confirmed endogenous targets such as PDCD-4 and PTEN are important tumor suppressers (Asangani et al. 2008; Folini et al. 2010; Meng et al. 2007). Consistent with its proposed role as an oncomiR, our results showed that miR-21 expression progressively increased from day 7 to day 12 in parallel with the late phase increase in cell number.

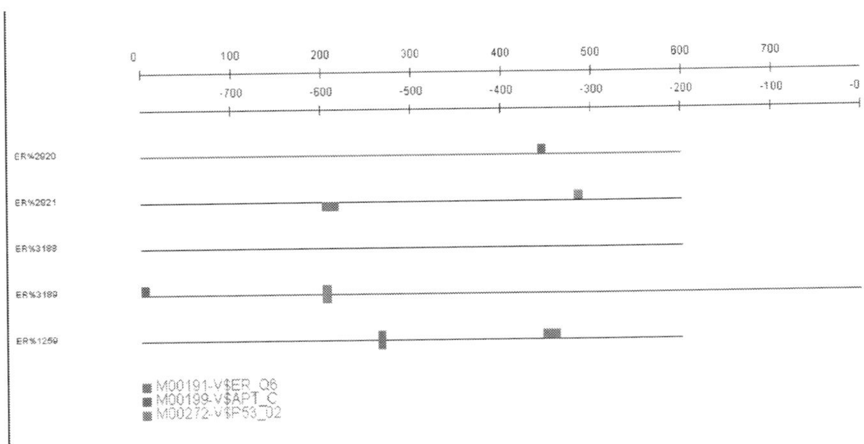

Fig. 3. ER,AP-1 and p53 binding motifs relative to miR-342,miR-21 and miR-143~145. The red, blue and pink boxes represent ER, AP-1 and p53 binding sites respectively. ER_2920 and ER2921 located in miR-342 upstream region; ER_3188 and ER_3189 located in miR-21 regulatory region; ER_1259 located in miR-21 upstream region (please referring to Figure 1).

MiR-143 and miR-145 are clustered miRNAs with their expression levels co-ordinately down-regulated in multiple forms of cancer (Akao et al. 2007; Michael et al. 2003; Sevignani et al. 2007; Wang et al. 2008). They can function as important tumour suppressers by targeting multiple key genes in apoptosis, proliferation, and metastasis signalling pathways (Chen et al. 2009; Chiyomaru et al. 2010; Sevignani et al. 2007; Zaman et al. 2010). However, whether miR-143 and miR-145 are regulated by E2 in MCF-7 breast cell is unclear. In this study, we found that both were repressed by E2 in a long term treatment. Importantly, we also observed that ectopic expression of miR-145 repressed MCF-7 cell proliferation (data not shown). These observations are consistent with previous studies in other cancers, indicating that miR-145 is repressed in cancers compared to the normal control.

Analyzing the miR-342, miR-21 and miR-143~145 regulatory regions, we found AP-1 binding motifs in all of them, supporting the role of AP-1 as a basal activator (Figure 3) (Wagner 2001). In addition, there are both ER and p53 motifs in the miR-342 upstream region, therefore miR-342 may be a dual target of these two TFs and the expression of miR-342 perhaps depends on both the integrity of estrogen signalling pathway but also the status of p53. Estrogen-response elements were detected in both miR-342 and miR-143 promoter regions, indicating direct estrogen receptor binding. However, ERE is not present in miR-21 upstream regulatory region and it is possible that transcriptional activation of miR-21 may be mediated via estrogen receptor tethered to AP-1 motifs.

Except for miR-342, miR-21, miR-143, and miR-145, little is known for the other miRNAs regarding their roles in breast cancer development. Since our analysis has already implicated several oncogenic and tumour suppressor miRNAs to be regulated by ER, we believe that this strategy can provide promising miRNAs candidates for additional functional exploration.

4. Discussion

Understanding gene regulation is crucial to elucidating the mechanisms of development, differentiation and signaling response. Over the past three decades, advances in technologies such as genomic sequencing and expression profiling by microarray have paved ways to more thorough investigations into gene regulatory networks. These advances also necessitated the development of bioinformatics. Namely, analytical tools and methods are continuingly being invented for processing the vast amount of information generated and mining the corresponding datasets; hence, new discoveries are observed and novel concepts are developed for hypothesis building and testing. Nonetheless, the accumulation of datasets sometimes outpaces the development of bioinformatics and a certain amount of valuable information is left un-mined. In this chapter, we present a case of utilizing developed bioinformatics tools to learn more about gene regulation network based on published transcriptional factor binding datasets.

We used a previous published ER ChIP-chip data to find a set of putative ER-regulated miRNAs. This concept and method can be extended to other aspects. Firstly, several ChIP based techniques, such as ChIP-PET (paired-end tag), ChIP-DSL (DNA selection and ligation), were developed to map TFs binding sites. The genome-wide TF binding sites generated from these variations of ChIP-chip techniques could also be used to map the miRNAs promoters. Secondly, our methods can be extended to other nuclear hormone receptors (NHRs) and TFs providing that corresponding genomic coordinates of TFs binding are available. Importantly, the specificity of TF binding sites could be investigated by comparing different but related TF binding data. For example, recently by comparison of ER and estrogen-related receptor (ERR) binding data in breast cancer cell line MCF-7, Deblois et al. showed that ERR and ER display strict binding site specificity while a small number of binding sites were shared by both transcriptional factors(Deblois et al. 2009).Another prominent feature of this versatile procedure lies in its easy application and low cost. In recent years, ChIP based techniques are popular assays to study direct targets of TFs genome-wide. For example , many NHR binding maps have been published (Deblois and Giguere 2008). Surprisingly, few miRNAs regulated by a specific NHR were mined from these valuable datasets. The directly targeted miRNAs by a specific NHR or TF can be readily discovered through our procedure if the genome-wide binding sites for this TF have been produced by others. Thus, it avoids redundant experiments and greatly facilitate rapid discovery.

MiRNAs microarray is a common practice to identify miRNA expression changes upon a specific treatment. However, there are some limitations inherited in microarray platform. For instance, microarray data is usually mixed with primary, secondary, and even tertiary gene expression changes, making it difficult to dissect which TFs are responsible for these different levels of regulation. Our procedure directly links the candidate TFs with putative target miRNAs through analyzing ChIP-chip and ChIP-seq binding data. Uniquely, our analysis also allows investigation into the relationships between mRNAs and miRNAs co-ordinately regulated by a specific TF in a given cell type upon a particular treatment, providing an entirely new set of information not revealed by mircroarray analysis alone. However, it should be noted that not all regulatory regions are included in the original design of ChIP-chip platform. Thus, our analysis can only provide a partial picture that is dependent on the completeness of ChIP-chip design. As more comprehensive technology such as ChIP-seq analysis is used in investigation, the genomic coverage will be significantly improved. Besides, TF binding sites may be located outside of the 50 kb upstream regulatory region defined in our analysis. Therefore, it is best to complement ChIP data analysis with microarray studies to obtain comprehensive information on TFs and miRNAs regulation networks.

5. Conclusion

Understanding the relationships between transcriptional factors and their target mRNAs is greatly facilitated by genome-wide analysis based on the pairing of chromatin immunoprecipitation with DNA microarray. However, few miRNAs regulated by transcription factors have been mined from these data. Our bioinformatics procedure efficiently utilize genome-wide binding data to screen upstream regulatory regions of all human miRNAs and hunt for miRNA targets modulated by a specific transcription factor. As an example, we predicted 59 putative estrogen-responsive miRNAs based on a published genome-wide ER binding dataset. Several ER-regulated miRNAs were further confirmed in a breast cancer cell model. Among these, miR-342, miR-21, miR-422a, miR-124, and miR-181c were generally found to be up-regulated by estrogen treatment; whereas miR-143, miR-145, and miR-483 were down-regulated. This example demonstrated the power and efficiency of this novel analysis method. Furthermore, this example also indicated miRNA target of a specific TF can be equally detected from ChIP-chip based binding data, which are usually produced for identifying mRNA targets. Integrating our method with routine analysis procedure will gain a full picture of gene regulation network by simultaneously elucidating the miRNAs and mRNAs targets of a specific TF.

6. Acknowledgment

We are in debt to Ms. Xuemei Liao for assistance on graphic preparation. The research is supported by the science foundation of the education department of Henan province (Grant No. 2011A180009) and a start-up grant from Henan University of Technology (#2009BS040).

7. References

Aerts, S., P. Van Loo, G. Thijs, H. Mayer, R. de Martin, Y. Moreau, and B. De Moor. 2005. TOUCAN 2: the all-inclusive open source workbench for regulatory sequence analysis. Nucleic Acids Res 33 (Web Server issue):W393-6.

Akao, Y., Y. Nakagawa, Y. Kitade, T. Kinoshita, and T. Naoe. 2007. Downregulation of microRNAs-143 and -145 in B-cell malignancies. Cancer Sci 98 (12):1914-20.

Ali, S., and R. C. Coombes. 2002. Endocrine-responsive breast cancer and strategies for combating resistance. Nat Rev Cancer 2 (2):101-12.

Asangani, I. A., S. A. Rasheed, D. A. Nikolova, J. H. Leupold, N. H. Colburn, S. Post, and H. Allgayer. 2008. MicroRNA-21 (miR-21) post-transcriptionally downregulates tumor suppressor Pdcd4 and stimulates invasion, intravasation and metastasis in colorectal cancer. Oncogene 27 (15):2128-36.

Bartel, D. P. 2004. MicroRNAs: genomics, biogenesis, mechanism, and function. Cell 116 (2):281-97.

Bhat-Nakshatri, P., G. Wang, N. R. Collins, M. J. Thomson, T. R. Geistlinger, J. S. Carroll, M. Brown, S. Hammond, E. F. Srour, Y. Liu, and H. Nakshatri. 2009. Estradiol-regulated microRNAs control estradiol response in breast cancer cells. Nucleic Acids Res 37 (14):4850-61.

Carroll, J. S., C. A. Meyer, J. Song, W. Li, T. R. Geistlinger, J. Eeckhoute, A. S. Brodsky, E. K. Keeton, K. C. Fertuck, G. F. Hall, Q. Wang, S. Bekiranov, V. Sementchenko, E. A. Fox, P. A. Silver, T. R. Gingeras, X. S. Liu, and M. Brown. 2006. Genome-wide analysis of estrogen receptor binding sites. Nat Genet 38 (11):1289-97.

Chen, X., X. Guo, H. Zhang, Y. Xiang, J. Chen, Y. Yin, X. Cai, K. Wang, G. Wang, Y. Ba, L. Zhu, J. Wang, R. Yang, Y. Zhang, Z. Ren, K. Zen, J. Zhang, and C. Y. Zhang. 2009. Role of miR-143 targeting KRAS in colorectal tumorigenesis. Oncogene 28 (10):1385-92.

Chiyomaru, T., H. Enokida, S. Tatarano, K. Kawahara, Y. Uchida, K. Nishiyama, L. Fujimura, N. Kikkawa, N. Seki, and M. Nakagawa. 2010. miR-145 and miR-133a function as tumour suppressors and directly regulate FSCN1 expression in bladder cancer. Br J Cancer 102 (5):883-91.

Cittelly, D. M., P. M. Das, N. S. Spoelstra, S. M. Edgerton, J. K. Richer, A. D. Thor, and F. E. Jones. 2010. Downregulation of miR-342 is associated with tamoxifen resistant breast tumors. Mol Cancer 9:317.

Deblois, G., and V. Giguere. 2008. Nuclear receptor location analyses in mammalian genomes: from gene regulation to regulatory networks. Mol Endocrinol 22 (9):1999-2011.

Deblois, G., J. A. Hall, M. C. Perry, J. Laganiere, M. Ghahremani, M. Park, M. Hallett, and V. Giguere. 2009. Genome-wide identification of direct target genes implicates estrogen-related receptor alpha as a determinant of breast cancer heterogeneity. Cancer Res 69 (15):6149-57.

Deroo, B. J., and K. S. Korach. 2006. Estrogen receptors and human disease. J Clin Invest 116 (3):561-70.

Farnham, P. J. 2009. Insights from genomic profiling of transcription factors. Nat Rev Genet 10 (9):605-16.

Folini, M., P. Gandellini, N. Longoni, V. Profumo, M. Callari, M. Pennati, M. Colecchia, R. Supino, S. Veneroni, R. Salvioni, R. Valdagni, M. G. Daidone, and N. Zaffaroni. 2010. miR-21: an oncomir on strike in prostate cancer. Mol Cancer 9:12.

Goecks, J., A. Nekrutenko, and J. Taylor. 2010. Galaxy: a comprehensive approach for supporting accessible, reproducible, and transparent computational research in the life sciences. Genome Biol 11 (8):R86.

Grady, W. M., R. K. Parkin, P. S. Mitchell, J. H. Lee, Y. H. Kim, K. D. Tsuchiya, M. K. Washington, C. Paraskeva, J. K. Willson, A. M. Kaz, E. M. Kroh, A. Allen, B. R. Fritz, S. D. Markowitz, and M. Tewari. 2008. Epigenetic silencing of the intronic microRNA hsa-miR-342 and its host gene EVL in colorectal cancer. Oncogene 27 (27):3880-8.

Hannenhalli, S., and K. H. Kaestner. 2009. The evolution of Fox genes and their role in development and disease. Nat Rev Genet 10 (4):233-40.

Herrlich, P. 2001. Cross-talk between glucocorticoid receptor and AP-1. Oncogene 20 (19):2465-75.

Houbaviy, H. B., L. Dennis, R. Jaenisch, and P. A. Sharp. 2005. Characterization of a highly variable eutherian microRNA gene. Rna 11 (8):1245-57.

Jochum, W., E. Passegue, and E. F. Wagner. 2001. AP-1 in mouse development and tumorigenesis. Oncogene 20 (19):2401-12.

Konduri, S. D., R. Medisetty, W. Liu, B. A. Kaipparettu, P. Srivastava, H. Brauch, P. Fritz, W. M. Swetzig, A. E. Gardner, S. A. Khan, and G. M. Das. 2010. Mechanisms of estrogen receptor antagonism toward p53 and its implications in breast cancer therapeutic response and stem cell regulation. Proc Natl Acad Sci U S A 107 (34):15081-6.

Kozomara, A., and S. Griffiths-Jones. 2011. miRBase: integrating microRNA annotation and deep-sequencing data. Nucleic Acids Res 39 (Database issue):D152-7.

Lee, Y., K. Jeon, J. T. Lee, S. Kim, and V. N. Kim. 2002. MicroRNA maturation: stepwise processing and subcellular localization. Embo J 21 (17):4663-70.

Lee, Y., M. Kim, J. Han, K. H. Yeom, S. Lee, S. H. Baek, and V. N. Kim. 2004. MicroRNA genes are transcribed by RNA polymerase II. Embo J 23 (20):4051-60.

Li, L., J. Xu, D. Yang, X. Tan, and H. Wang. 2010. Computational approaches for microRNA studies: a review. Mamm Genome 21 (1-2):1-12.

Liu, W., M. M. Ip, M. B. Podgorsak, and G. M. Das. 2009. Disruption of estrogen receptor alpha-p53 interaction in breast tumors: a novel mechanism underlying the anti-tumor effect of radiation therapy. Breast Cancer Res Treat 115 (1):43-50.

Liu, W., S. D. Konduri, S. Bansal, B. K. Nayak, S. A. Rajasekaran, S. M. Karuppayil, A. K. Rajasekaran, and G. M. Das. 2006. Estrogen receptor-alpha binds p53 tumor suppressor protein directly and represses its function. J Biol Chem 281 (15):9837-40.

Lowery, A. J., N. Miller, A. Devaney, R. E. McNeill, P. A. Davoren, C. Lemetre, V. Benes, S. Schmidt, J. Blake, G. Ball, and M. J. Kerin. 2009. MicroRNA signatures predict oestrogen receptor, progesterone receptor and HER2/neu receptor status in breast cancer. Breast Cancer Res 11 (3):R27.

Mattie, M. D., C. C. Benz, J. Bowers, K. Sensinger, L. Wong, G. K. Scott, V. Fedele, D. Ginzinger, R. Getts, and C. Haqq. 2006. Optimized high-throughput microRNA expression profiling provides novel biomarker assessment of clinical prostate and breast cancer biopsies. Mol Cancer 5:24.

Matys, V., O. V. Kel-Margoulis, E. Fricke, I. Liebich, S. Land, A. Barre-Dirrie, I. Reuter, D. Chekmenev, M. Krull, K. Hornischer, N. Voss, P. Stegmaier, B. Lewicki-Potapov, H. Saxel, A. E. Kel, and E. Wingender. 2006. TRANSFAC and its module TRANSCompel: transcriptional gene regulation in eukaryotes. Nucleic Acids Res 34 (Database issue):D108-10.

Meng, F., R. Henson, H. Wehbe-Janek, K. Ghoshal, S. T. Jacob, and T. Patel. 2007. MicroRNA-21 regulates expression of the PTEN tumor suppressor gene in human hepatocellular cancer. Gastroenterology 133 (2):647-58.

Michael, M. Z., O' Connor SM, N. G. van Holst Pellekaan, G. P. Young, and R. J. James. 2003. Reduced accumulation of specific microRNAs in colorectal neoplasia. Mol Cancer Res 1 (12):882-91.

Miller, T. E., K. Ghoshal, B. Ramaswamy, S. Roy, J. Datta, C. L. Shapiro, S. Jacob, and S. Majumder. 2008. MicroRNA-221/222 confers tamoxifen resistance in breast cancer by targeting p27Kip1. J Biol Chem 283 (44):29897-903.

Nigro, J. M., S. J. Baker, A. C. Preisinger, J. M. Jessup, R. Hostetter, K. Cleary, S. H. Bigner, N. Davidson, S. Baylin, P. Devilee, and et al. 1989. Mutations in the p53 gene occur in diverse human tumour types. Nature 342 (6250):705-8.

Rhead, B., D. Karolchik, R. M. Kuhn, A. S. Hinrichs, A. S. Zweig, P. A. Fujita, M. Diekhans, K. E. Smith, K. R. Rosenbloom, B. J. Raney, A. Pohl, M. Pheasant, L. R. Meyer, K. Learned, F. Hsu, J. Hillman-Jackson, R. A. Harte, B. Giardine, T. R. Dreszer, H. Clawson, G. P. Barber, D. Haussler, and W. J. Kent. 2010. The UCSC Genome Browser database: update 2010. Nucleic Acids Res 38 (Database issue):D613-9.

Schanen, B. C., and X. Li. 2010. Transcriptional regulation of mammalian miRNA genes. Genomics 97 (1):1-6.

Schmid, C. D., R. Perier, V. Praz, and P. Bucher. 2006. EPD in its twentieth year: towards complete promoter coverage of selected model organisms. Nucleic Acids Res 34 (Database issue):D82-5.

Sevignani, C., G. A. Calin, S. C. Nnadi, M. Shimizu, R. V. Davuluri, T. Hyslop, P. Demant, C. M. Croce, and L. D. Siracusa. 2007. MicroRNA genes are frequently located near mouse cancer susceptibility loci. Proc Natl Acad Sci U S A 104 (19):8017-22.

Volinia, S., G. A. Calin, C. G. Liu, S. Ambs, A. Cimmino, F. Petrocca, R. Visone, M. Iorio, C. Roldo, M. Ferracin, R. L. Prueitt, N. Yanaihara, G. Lanza, A. Scarpa, A. Vecchione, M. Negrini, C. C. Harris, and C. M. Croce. 2006. A microRNA expression signature of human solid tumors defines cancer gene targets. Proc Natl Acad Sci U S A 103 (7):2257-61.

Wagner, E. F. 2001. AP-1--Introductory remarks. Oncogene 20 (19):2334-5.

Wang, X., S. Tang, S. Y. Le, R. Lu, J. S. Rader, C. Meyers, and Z. M. Zheng. 2008. Aberrant expression of oncogenic and tumor-suppressive microRNAs in cervical cancer is required for cancer cell growth. PLoS One 3 (7):e2557.

Wickramasinghe, N. S., T. T. Manavalan, S. M. Dougherty, K. A. Riggs, Y. Li, and C. M. Klinge. 2009. Estradiol downregulates miR-21 expression and increases miR-21 target gene expression in MCF-7 breast cancer cells. Nucleic Acids Res 37 (8):2584-95.

Xu, J., X. Liao, N. Lu, W. Liu, and C. W. Wong. 2011. Chromatin-modifying drugs induce miRNA-153 expression to suppress Irs-2 in glioblastoma cell lines. Int J Cancer.

Xu, J., X. Liao, and C. Wong. 2010. Downregulations of B-cell lymphoma 2 and myeloid cell leukemia sequence 1 by microRNA 153 induce apoptosis in a glioblastoma cell line DBTRG-05MG. Int J Cancer 126 (4):1029-35.

Zaman, M. S., Y. Chen, G. Deng, V. Shahryari, S. O. Suh, S. Saini, S. Majid, J. Liu, G. Khatri, Y. Tanaka, and R. Dahiya. 2010. The functional significance of microRNA-145 in prostate cancer. Br J Cancer 103 (2):256-64.

Part 8

Gene Expression and Systems Biology

26

Quantification of Gene Expression Based on Microarray Experiment

Samane F. Farsani and Mahmood A. Mahdavi
Department of Chemical Engineering, Ferdowsi University of Mashhad,
Azadi Square, Pardis Campus, Mashhad,
Iran

1. Introduction

Gene expression is a common process in all forms of living cells including eukaryotes, prokaryotes and viruses to generate the macromolecular requirements for life. The study of gene expression provides a systemic comprehension of the cell function for addressing specific biological questions. This process comprises replication, transcription, RNA splicing, translation and post translational modification of a single protein. At first, DNA serves as a template to replicate itself and the production of RNA (transcription), a copy from the DNA, is mediated by RNA polymerase. In prokaryotes, transcription creates messenger RNA (mRNA) which doesn't need any additional processing for translation but this stage in eukaryotes produces a primary transcript of RNA, which needs further processing prior to becoming a mature mRNA. This step is referred to as RNA splicing that in the proper context, involves the removal of certain sequences called intervening sequences, or introns. Hence, the final mRNA contains the remaining sequences, called exons, which are spliced together (Knapp et al., 1978). In the next stage, so called translation, mRNA separates from DNA strand and serves as a template for protein production that such a process is assisted by ribosomes. Proteins are modified after translation in variety of processes i.e. they are altered at structural level to achieve the final 3D conformation. These modifications are essential for all aspects of biology and can be performed spontaneously or driven by enzyme mediation. Common post-translational modifications include phosphorylation, glycosilation, dimerization or tetramerizaion, etc. (Doyle & Mamula, 2001). Therefore, the transfer of genetic information, from DNA to RNA and to proteins, ending up with the expression of genes in all cells makes up the central dogma of molecular biology (Figure 1) (Crick, 1970).

Genomics information is delivered to the cells in three biochemical datasets including the complete set of mRNA species that result in generating proteins (transcriptomics), the complete collection of proteins (proteomics), and the complete series of metabolites produced in the cell (metabolomics) (Figure 2)(Karakach et al., 2010; van der Werf et al., 2005).

Transcriptomics provides a complete profile of RNAs that appear within the cells, tissues and biological fluids at a specific time. The mRNA levels do vary over time, among diverse cell types and within cells under different conditions while DNA is more or less unchanged over the life cycles. Thus, gene expression based on mRNA mediates cellular function and specifies genes that are turned on or off in different status of cells. As transcriptome

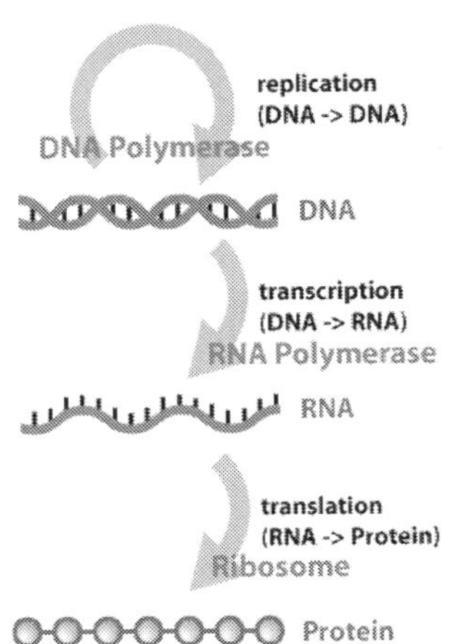

Fig. 1. Central dogma of molecular biology.

represents small percentage of the genome and much more complexity, information carried in the transcriptome has no substantial direct relation to information from the genome (Frith et al., 2005; Tsiridis & Giannoudis, 2006). Proteomics assists to comprehensively characterize quantity, structure and activity of the entire complement of expressed proteins (proteome) in large scale within a cell or tissue at a particular time. In addition, this approach provides the studies of protein-protein interactions and detailed understanding of the complex responses of a living system to stimuli (Beranova-Giorgianni, 2003; Hirsch et al., 2004). However, genome is relatively static while the dynamic proteome changes constantly in response to environmental signals. This is due to many reasons, including different amino acid sequences, alternative splicing of mRNAs and post-translational protein modifications that often give rise to more than one protein per a single gene. Proteomics, therefore, produce large high dimensional datasets that require powerful tools to handle and analyze the data effectively (Hegde et al., 2003; Tsiridis & Giannoudis, 2006).

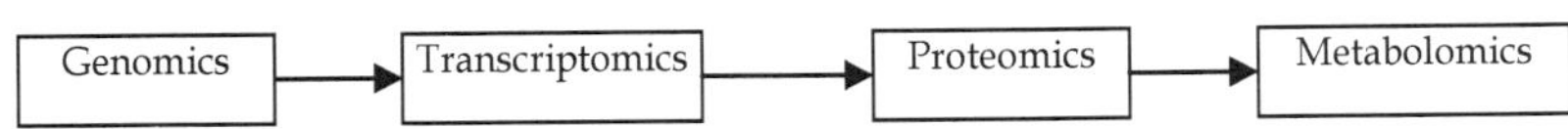

Fig. 2. Biochemical levels of information in gene expression study.

Metabolomics is the study of the entire set of metabolites, low-molecular-weight organic compounds, in the cell (metabolome) assisting the inference of biological functioning (Schaub et al., 2009; van der Werf et al., 2005). It involves the large-scale analysis of changes in metabolites in response to environmental or cellular changes. Metabolomics aims at quantifying every single metabolite and is one step further than metabolic profiling that only elucidates an inventory of the metabolites present in the cell (van der Werf et al., 2005). The transcriptome, proteome and metabolome can change considerably depending on various environmental conditions and directly represent the status of cellular physiology. Hence, these sources are so beneficial in understanding biological performance. Although omics technologies have been advancing over the years, they still contain some drawbacks. Proteomics and metabolomics offer the holistic and complementary insights into cells because transcriptomics cannot always reflect corresponding protein or metabolite profiling. They are, however, limited in lack of standardized methodologies and poor reproducibility (Pinet, 2009). This is partly due to the heterogeneous characteristics of the compounds identified. In proteomic analysis, the wide range of proteins makes it difficult to design standard protocols for identification of compounds. Likewise, metabolomics suffers from the diverse collection of chemical properties of different metabolites (Karakach et al., 2010). Scientists are not well trained to cope with the large data and limited availability of commercial metabolites. Despite these limitations, going from one biochemical level to the next, information is acquired or lost by regulatory events such as post-transcriptional and post-translational modifications that occur between these levels. Metabolomics, however, is valuable as it is the closest to the function of a cell i.e. the phenotype (Tsiridis & Giannoudis, 2006; van der Werf et al., 2005; Zhang et al., 2010).

Compared to proteomics and metabolomics, transcriptomics is a more robust, large-scale, moderate cost technology of simultaneously measuring thousands of mRNA levels, but most transcriptomic analysis platforms are not routinely set up to systematically detect changes in spliced species as nearly 50% of human genes may undergo alternative splicing (Hegde et al., 2003). Also in some cases mRNA levels are a reasonable proxy for protein abundance, allowing one to make a rational inference regarding the level of protein expression based on the levels of mRNA expression. But, sometimes some caution seems necessary where protein expression is controlled post-transcriptionally by other factors. Since mRNA molecules are relatively more homogeneous than metabolites and proteins, and capture methods based on complementary DNA have been developing, the field of transcriptomics has been more associated with gene expression studies using microarray technology (Karakach et al., 2010).

In conclusion, the study of omics sciences plays an important role in understanding different perspectives of cells to gain knowledge about cellular pathways, mechanisms and functions that eventually make up an expression cycle. The transcriptome is more crucial in expression measurements while the proteome and the metabolome together assist in determining the functionality of expressed genes (van der Werf et al., 2005). Thus, effective integration of omics datasets provides a broader view of systematic changes in expression levels. However, this integration still remains one of the challenges of systems biology and functional genomics.

2. Methods to quantifying mRNA level

Composition and differences of various transcriptomes is specified through mRNA level measurements. There are a number of methods to quantitatively determine this factor including northern blotting, reverse transcriptase polymerase chain reaction (RT-PCR) and DNA microarray. These techniques are briefly discussed in the following.

Northern blotting is a standard method for studying the expression profile of specific genes in mRNA level. It can detect alternatively spliced transcripts and transcript size. In Northern blot analysis, mRNAs are extracted from sample then separated based on size in gel electrophoresis (targets). Probes are a complementary sequence to all or a part of interested mRNAs. Afterwards, targets are transferred to a solid support from an agarose gel to hybridize with radio-labeled probes. If the probe has complemented sequence to an mRNA, then it will bind to the location of that mRNA on the gel (Trayhuru, 1996). Degree of radiation gives an indication of expression level in gene of interest. This method is a semi-quantitative detection because the amount of radioactivity depends to some extent on the amount of the probe which in turn depends on the amount of mRNA in the sample (Perdew et al., 2006; Trayhuru, 1996). Northern blotting is an appropriate assay especially for laboratories which are limited with the lack of specialized equipments and expertise in molecular biology (Trayhuru, 1996). One of the pitfalls in northern blotting is often sample degradation through the action of RNases, which can be overcome by proper sterilization of glassware and reagents and the employment of RNase inhibitors. Also the used chemicals can be a risk to the researcher.

Polymerase chain reaction (PCR) is an enzymatic assay which produces large amount of a specific DNA sequence from even a small and complex mixture. Also reverse transcriptase (RT)-PCR is a rapid and flexible approach for mRNA examination and quantification. In this method, first the mRNA must be converted to a double-stranded molecule by using the enzyme reverse transcriptase (Perdew et al., 2006). Since small variations of amplification efficiencies between samples can result in significant differences in product yield, quantification of mRNA by RT-PCR is difficult, therefore modified methods have been developed such as quantitative competitive (QC)-PCR, relative RT-PCR and real time RT-PCR. The QC-PCR measures the absolute level of a particular mRNA sequence in a biological sample. It relies on using dilutions of a synthetic RNA called competitors. These competitors compete with the target cDNA for co-amplification. Since competitor molecule differs in size from the target one, the two PCR products can be separated by gel electrophoresis. Although this method provides an accurate result, the design and construction of competitor for each gene is technically complicated. Validation of the results of the technique is also labor intensive (Breljak et al., 2005). Relative or semi-quantitative RT-PCR measures mRNA level using a co-amplified internal control with the gene of interest. Results are reported as ratios of the gene-specific signal to the internal control signal. Although this method requires only common laboratory equipment, it suffers from poor dynamic range of the quantification and being time consuming as well as labor intensive (Lipshutz et al., 1999). A novel approach of PCR, real-time PCR, is the combination of the best features of both relative and competitive PCR. It is much faster, higher throughput and less labor-intensive assay than current quantitative PCR. Furthermore, it combines amplification and detection in one step. Unlike other quantitative PCR methods, real-time PCR does not need preventing carryover contamination of PCR products and PCR processing such as electrophoresis. This approach is carried out through dual labeled fluorogenic probes. The amount of fluorescence emitted is directly proportional to the amount of product produced in each PCR cycle (Breljak et al., 2005; Heid et al., 1996). In spite of outstanding advances performed in the area of real-time RT-PCR, competitive and semi-quantitative RT-PCR may still utilize for relative mRNA quantification especially for small number of samples (Breljak et al., 2005). RT-PCR is much more sensitive, rapid with a large dynamic range of quantification. It requires specialized expensive equipment and ingredient which may be restrictive to some researchers (Perdew et al., 2006; Trayhuru, 1996). Since undesirable primer–primer interactions may happen, RT-PCR is limited in the number of genes to be analyzed each time. Some sources of variation such as template concentration and amplification efficiency make difficult quantification based on RT-PCR (Trayhuru, 1996).

Microarray experiment is an emerging technique as such, based on determining expression levels of thousands of genes simultaneously. This approach can be considered as a massive parallel Northern blotting. DNA microarray gives a holistic picture of gene expression within the cell or the sample in different environmental conditions at a specific time (Tarca et al., 2006). Practically, such high throuput method utilizes an inert surface containing a certain number of spots. Each spot contains a single species of a nucleic acid representing the genes of interest (probe). Hybridization between labeled biological sample (target) and probes creates a signal that represents the level of expression of a gene in a biological sample. The microarrays have become important because they are easier to use and do not require large-scale DNA sequencing. However these studies are still limited by lack of universally accepted standards for data collection, analysis and validation (Bilban et al., 2002; Russo et al., 2003). Microarrays are quite user friendly and usually consistent with results produced from northern blotting and PCR; although, these approaches can measure small levels in gene expression that microarrays cannot. The main advantage of microarrays is visualizing thousands of genes at a time, while other methods are usually quantifying one or a small number of genes (Bilban et al., 2002; Trayhuru, 1996).

Some features of the above mentioned methods have been summarized in Table 1. Regarding the advantages and limitations of each technique, it is concluded that even though the all methods can measure mRNA levels, they differ on their special attributes.

Method	Pros	Cons
Northern blotting	-Detecting alternatively spliced transcripts -Detecting transcript size -Straightforward -Inexpensive	-Insensitive -RNase contamination -Low throughput -Use of hazardous reagents -Low quality quantification -Needs large quantity of RNA -High background on solid supports
RT-PCR	-High sensitive -Rapid -Wide dynamic range (Real time RT-PCR) -Sensitive and robust -Nearly high throughput -needs small sample	-Expensive equipment -needs expertise in molecular biology -The ease with which minor contamination may yield false-positive results -Post-PCR manipulation except real time PCR

Microarray	-The parallel quantification of thousands of genes from multiple samples
	-Rapid
	-Robust
	-Convenient for directed and focussed studies
	-Cost effective
	-Easy to use
	-do not require large-scale DNA sequencing
		-needs verification
		-Difficult to correlate with absolute transcript number
		-Sensitive to alternative splicing
		-many factors can affect microarray result:
		  • chip type
		  • sample preparation
		  • data analysis
		-Requires bioinformatics for data analysis.
		-Lack of standard preprocessing methods
		-Low sensitivity of microarray detection technology

Table 1. Features of conventional techniques to quantifying mRNA level.

Therefore, the selection of methods is performed based on required characteristics in experimental design. It should be noted that although traditional techniques of gene expression analysis provide valuable biological insights into the living cells, they are probably limited in some ways such as scale, economy, and sensitivity. As a result, compared to the other commonly used techniques, quantification based on microarray is remarkable because of high throughput and cost effective features.

3. Microarray technology

Microarray technology has become one of the most commonly used high-throughput techniques to query a large variety of biological issues. It enables the simultaneous analysis of thousands of parameters within one single experiment. Such miniaturized binding technology is typically divided into DNA, protein, tissue, cellular and chemical compound microarrays (Templin et al., 2002). Some of the arrays such as protein array and tissue array will be described in detail with a special emphasis on DNA arrays.

Protein microarrays assist in characterizing of thousands of proteins in a parallel format. Proteome chips afford researchers a way to address true level of gene function by studying the pair-wise interactions such as protein-protein, protein-DNA, protein-lipid, protein-drug, protein-receptor and antigen-antibody (Hall et al., 2007). In this technique, probes such as aptamers, engineered antibody fragments, affibodies, full-length proteins or protein domains can be spotted on a microscope slide. The array is then probed with a target solution and binding detected using the analytical approaches. Antibody microarray is the most powerful type of protein microarray. Figure 3 shows the detailed view of the steps taken to carry out antibody microarray experiment (Angenendt, 2005). Tissue microarray (TMA) technology was developed in order to evaluate the difference of molecular targets (in the DNA, RNA or protein level) in several thousands of tissue samples at the same time (Kononen et al., 1998; Singh & Sau, 2010). TMA is constructed from paraffin embedded material, frozen tissue, paraffin embedded cell lines or cell blocks (Parsons & Grabsch, 2009). Totally, TMA is made of tissue core samples taken with a precision punching instrument from donor paraffin blocks. These cores of tissue are arrayed into an empty recipient block, TMA block (Figure 4). Afterwards, the TMA block is sectioned by using a device called microtome. The sections are placed on a microscope slide and then analyzed by any standard histological procedure. From a TMA block, approximately 200–300 5-μm sections can be cut and used at independent tests (Parsons & Grabsch, 2009).

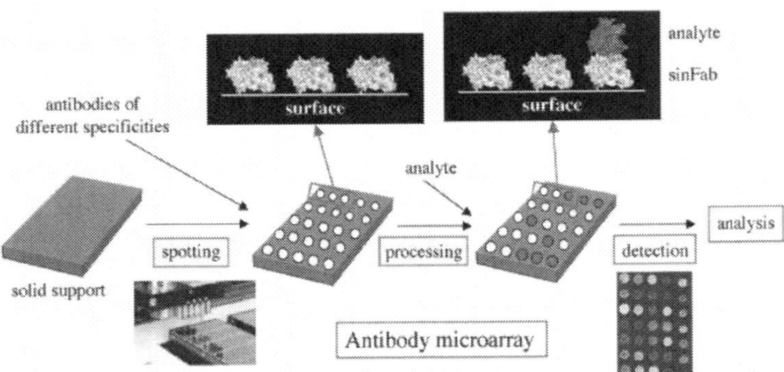

Fig. 3. Schematic diagram of an antibody microarray technology.

DNA microarray is the most popular type of microarray technology that uses nucleic acid–nucleic acid interactions. It allows measuring the amount of mRNA transcripts for thousands of genes in different combinations of sample derived from normal and diseased or treated and non-treated tissues, time courses of treated cells and stages of cell differentiation or development (Karakach et al., 2010). It has been proved that DNA microarrays are extremely valuable in studying of expression profiling, sequence identification and location of transcription factor binding sites (Hall et al., 2007).

4. The DNA microarray experiment

DNA microarrays are currently manufactured using two main techniques: in-situ synthesis and deposition of pre-synthesized probes (spotted arrays). There are various platforms or types of DNA microarrays that are commercially available. Figure 5 summarizes some of these platforms based on different fabrication methods. The two most commonly micarrays are the affymetrix oligonucleotide chips (Lockhart et al., 1996) and spotted cDNA arrays (Schena et al., 1995). Experimental steps and construction process of these arrays are discussed in this section.

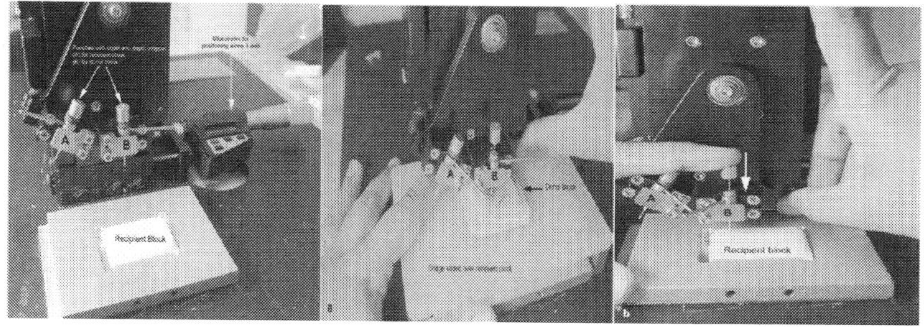

Fig. 4. **a.** Tissue arrayer instrument, **b.** Extraction of the donor core, **c.** Insertion into recipient block (Gulmann & O'Grady, 2003).

4.1 Affymetrix Gene Chips
4.1.1 Fabrication of Affymetrix Gene Chip

The in situ synthesis of oligonucleotides (Affymetrix Gene Chip) can be achieved using a photolithographic method (Fodor et al., 1991). This approach involves adding of adenine (A), cytosine (C), guanine (G) and thymine (T) nucleotides step by step through a set of designed masks. In fabrication process, solid substrate, usually quartz wafer, is washed to provide uniform hydroxylation of the surface and is then placed in a silane bath. Silane molecules are capable to directly react with the hydroxyl groups of the quartz. Therefore starting points are formed to synthesize new oligonucleotide strands. In the following steps, synthetic linkers are attached to silanes and coated with a light-sensitive protecting group (Figure 6). The first mask is placed over the surface which then exposed to the light source. Masks selectively direct light toward specific areas on the substrate. Afterwards linker molecules are activated at the unprotected position. Next, the first of a series of nucleotides, linked to the light-sensitive agent, is incubated on the surface. Thus, the nucleotides are chemically coupled to the activated sites. Photo labile agents block further nucleotide binding to linkers until light subsequently activates them through a new mask. This chemical cycle is repeated until several hundred thousands of oligonucleotides (probes) with desired lengths and sequences are synthesized at each of sites on the surface of the chip (Lipshutz et al., 1999).

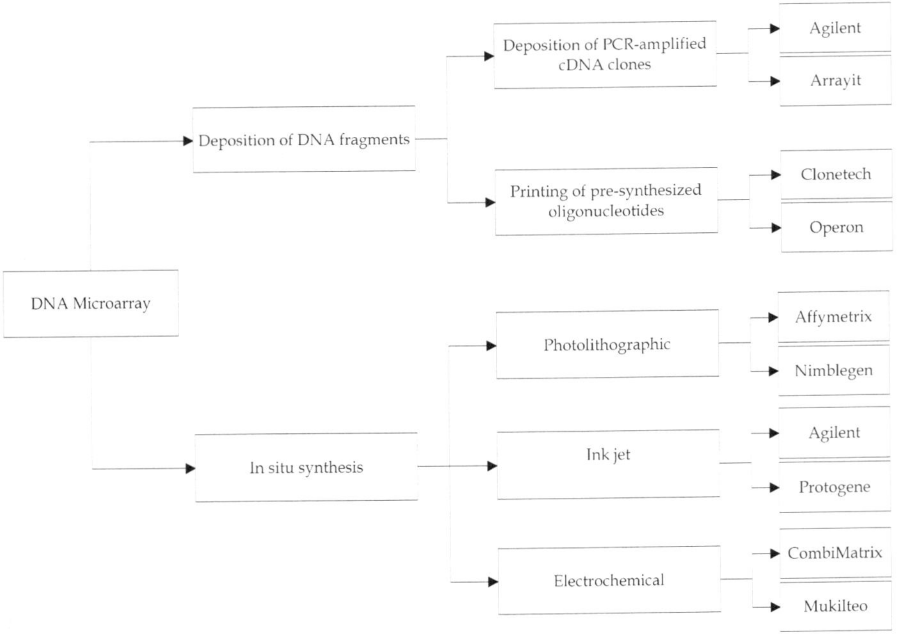

Fig. 5. Different microarray platforms and their fabrication methods.

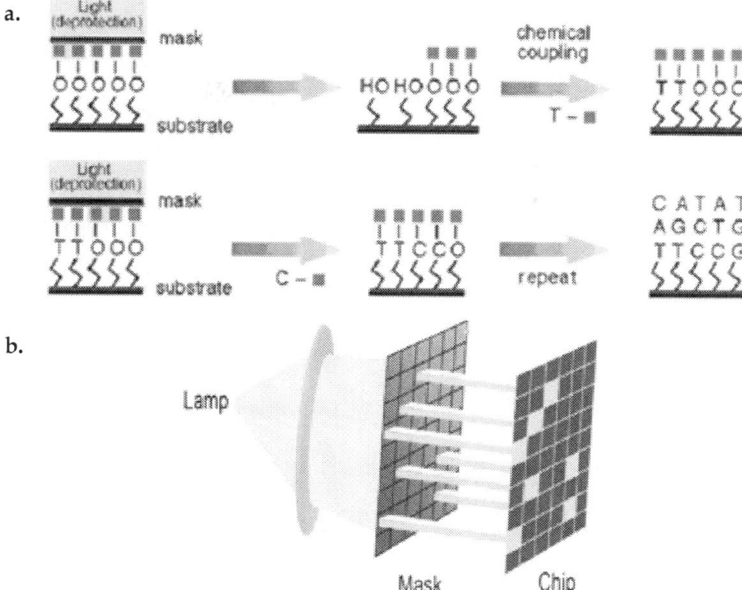

Fig. 6. **a.** Schematic overview on photolithographic fabrication of Gene Chip. **b.** Drawing of the lamp, mask and chip (Lipshutz et al., 1999).

4.1.2 Experiment of Affymetrix Gene Chip

Microarrays use various approaches based on uniqueness and composition design rules to select the 25-nucleotide-length (25mer) probes (Lipshutz et al., 1999). They utilize the Perfect Match/Mismatch probe strategy (Figure 7). Each gene sequence (or expressed sequence tag (EST)) is represented by typically 12-20 different probe pairs. The collection of probes for each gene is referred to as a probeset. Each pair includes a perfect match (PM) oligonucleotide and a mismatch (MM) oligonucleotide. A PM probe is perfectly complementary to the gene sequence of interest (Barrett & Kawasaki, 2003; Lipshutz et al., 1999) while the MM probe has a one-base mismatch in the central base position (the 13th base). The MM probe is used as an internal control to estimate the signal of any non-specific hybridization or contaminating fluorescence within measurement (Lipshutz et al., 1999; Tarca et al., 2006). These probesets are made on array through in situ synthesis and the microarray will be ready to carry out the experiment.

The basic steps in this single-dye experiment are as follows. Total RNA (or mRNA) is extracted from the biological sample, called target. The total RNA is then reversed transcribed to generate double-stranded cDNA. Then, biotin-labeled cRNA is produced from cDNA using *in vitro* transcription. Next, biotin-labeled cRNA is fragmented into smaller segments and hybridized on the array. After a series of washing for removing non-hybridized material, the array is incubated with appropriate fluorescent dyes linked to the biotins on the cRNAs. The array is placed in a scanner and emission of fluorescent staining agent is quantified (Schadt et al., 2001). Measurement of the florescent agent intensity provides an estimate of the level of mRNA within each gene of interest on the chip.

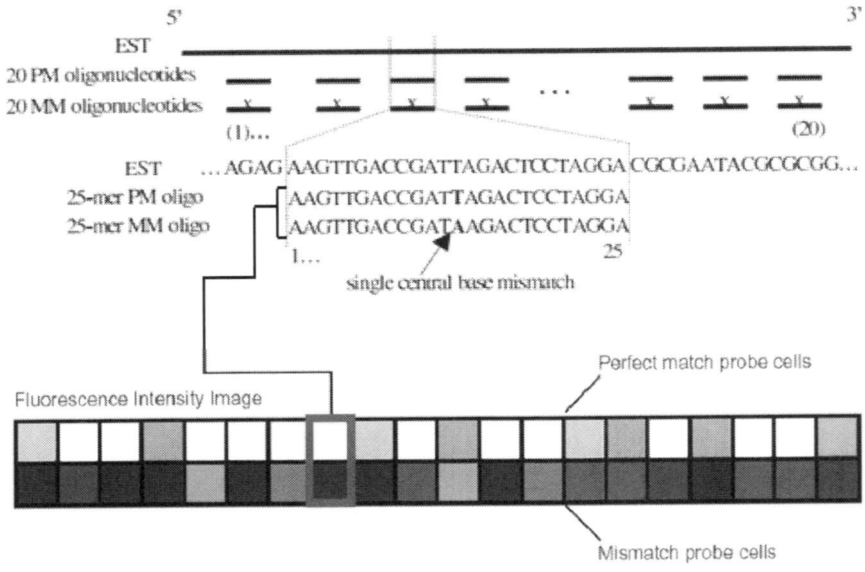

Fig. 7. Design of Affymetrix Gene Chip technology.

4.2 Spotted cDNA array

In spotted technology, probe sequences are synthesized separated from the array. In this technique, the probes correspond to specific genes, expressed sequence tag i.e. a stable cDNA fragment, or cDNAs from libraries of interest (Bilban et al., 2002). If the quantity of available probes is limiting, PCR amplification is performed to make sufficient probes. The PCR products are then analyzed by gel electrophoresis, quantified and eventually spotted using a robotic printing on the microarray surface. Probes are immobilized or attached at fixed locations onto the slides electrostatically, through cross-linking by heat or ultraviolet irradiation and via amines or other active groups on modified slides (Barrett & Kawasaki, 2003). Therefore, the location of each spot on the array can also assist researchers to identify a desired gene sequence.

Since the cDNA probes are double stranded the array is then heated (or alkali treated) until the DNA is separated and hybridized to its complementary strand. In this two color approach there are two samples, a test sample and a reference sample. In order to prepare the targets, cDNAs are synthesized using reverse transcript of mRNAs in the samples. Targets are labeled through variety of labeling methods. The most common approach is labeling with a red and green fluorescent dye, called Cy5 and Cy3, respectively. The labeled targets are combined and deposited on the array. If a gene is present in one or both samples, it will bind to its complementary probe according to the complementary base pairing property of nucleic acids. After washing the array to remove the non-hybridized targets, a

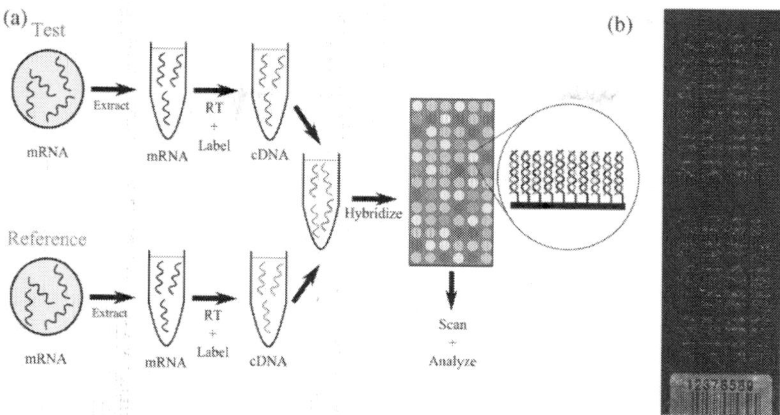

Fig. 8. **a.** Spotted cDNA microarray experiment consists of the following: preparation of target genes, labeling of the targets, hybridizing, scanning, **b.** Scanned image of a cDNA microarray (Karakach et al., 2010).

laser scanner assists to quantify the emission from Cy3 and Cy5 dyes (Figure 8). A green spot indicates that the corresponding gene is more strongly expressed in the reference sample compared to the test sample, while a red spot shows the opposite. A yellow spot reveals a gene in both samples is expressed in the same levels while a black spot shows that the gene is not express in either sample. The fluorescent spot intensity directly gives an estimate of the amount of mRNA concentration at specific condition and cell type. Details of each experimental step have been reviewed elsewhere (Bilban et al., 2002; Karakach et al., 2010). Characteristics of the two discussed microarrays are summarized in Table 2. This table provides a comparative view of cDNA and affymetrix oligonucleotide microarrays. Selection of desired platform is based on biological question which determines aims of the experiment. In the remainder of the chapter, we will focus mainly on the spotted cDNA microarray because of limited space even though some of the discussions can be generalized to other platforms such as affymetrix oligonucleotide array.

Platforms	Pros	Cons
cDNA microarray	-Low cost -More flexible -Easier to customize and analyse -Wide availability -No sequence information required	-More variability in system -Cross-hybridization -Intensive labour requirement -Frequent failure of array or individual spots
Affymetrix oligonucleotide chip	-More reliable -Easier to use - Speed and specific -Reproducible -Low failure rate -Ability to differentiate between splice variants -Detection of mutant sequences	-More difficult to analyze -Expensive array and reagents -Exact sequence information necessary -Lack of flexibility

Table 2. A comparison between cDNA and oligonucleotides arrays.

5. Image processing

In the microarray experiment, as mentioned earlier, hybridized slides are inserted into a scanner to prepare fluorescent images arranged into a matrix of spots. The next step is processing these images to quantify level of gene expression based on the intensity of each spot and obtain background estimates and quality measures (Istepanian, 2003, Yang et al., 2002a). Accuracy of analysis in this phase has remarkable effect on downstream analyses such as clustering, classification or the identification of differentially expressed genes (Yang et al., 2001). Generally, laser scanning confocal microscopy acquires fluorescent signals emitted by fluorescently labelled targets on the array. Scanners detect and record the signals using photomultiplier tubes (PMT) or charge coupled device (CCD) cameras (Figure 9). These signals are stored in two 16-bit tiff (tagged image file format) images for further analysis (Karakach et al., 2010). Images contain information about each fluorescent dye, typically Cy3 and Cy5. Most of the softwares create a composite image by overlaying the two images corresponding to the individual channels for visualizing different status of genes.

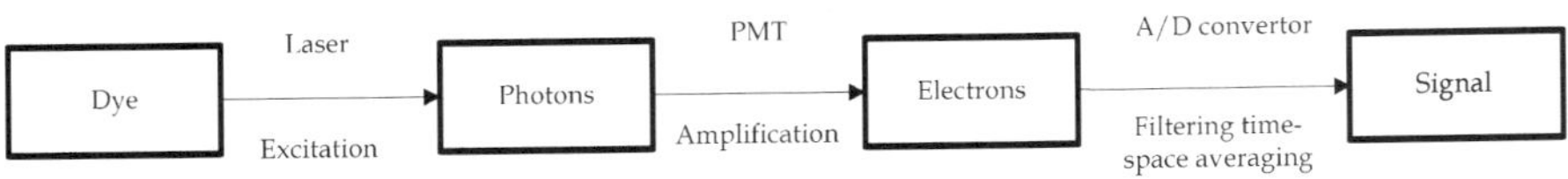

Fig. 9. Photons emit from a fluorescent samples through excitation, enter into a PMT, resulting in the release of electrons. Analogue signals from PMT are converted into digital signals by an analog-to-digital (A/D) converter. (More details in Schena, 2003).

Image processing techniques can be divided into the following steps: gridding, segmentation, quantification and spot quality assessment (Istepanian, 2003; Yang et al., 2001). Over the last years, a number of commercial and free softwares have been developed which can perform each step of image processing in a particular approach. These steps are discussed in more details in following sections.

5.1 Image gridding

The basic layout of a microarray image is determined by the robotic printing devices (arrayers) as it is known in advance (Figure 10). The arrayer itself consists of a series of pins arranged as a print tip (also referred to as sub-arrays or grids). The pins pick up reagents and deposit them on the array. Hence, the spots on array are organized in several print tips that each one is composed of spots printed with one pin (Karakach et al., 2010). Gridding (addressing) is the process of finding location of the spots on images. This is carried out using a simple model based on layout of scanned image. In order to enhance the reliability, manual intervention is utilized in association with automatic procedures (semi-automatic) (Yang et al., 2001). However, this can probably make the process very time consuming and introduce user bias and loss of consistency. At first, the user manually specifies the positions of spots on the image. Then, a suitable grid pattern is automatically provided from the indicated positions (Gjerstad et al., 2009; Yang et al., 2002a).

5.2 Image segmentation

Grid spots are partitioned into foreground (within printed spot) and background regions through a process referred to as segmentation. Foreground pixels represent the true signal while pixels in the background area correspond to signals not due to hybridization of target molecules (noise or artifacts) (Yang et al., 2001; Yang et al., 2002a). The most common segmentation methods are classified based on whether they place restrictions on the spot geometry. Fixed circle and adaptive circle segmentation methods assume circular spot shapes, while the histogram and adaptive shape segmentation approaches apply no restrictions on the shapes of the spots in the estimation of the spot masks. Each segmentation method generates a spot mask which consists of a set of foreground pixels for each spot (Karakach et al., 2010; Yang et al., 2001). The simplest method is fixed circle that assigns a circle with constant diameter to all spots. It characterizes the pixels within the circle as true signal and the pixels out of the circle as background pixels. Adaptive circles segmentation estimates the circles' diameters separately for each spot (Yang et al., 2002a; Yang et al., 2001). Since this approach requires the user to adjust spot sizes, it can be time-consuming for an array with thousands of spots. Furthermore it will be hard to distinguish a transition between the foreground and background if the signal strength is low (Yang et al., 2002a). Although most spot shapes are expected to be circular, in practice non-commercial arrayers rarely print the perfect circular shapes of spots resulting in poor estimates of fluorescent intensities for hybridized targets. Thus, novel approaches known as "adaptive shape segmentation" methods has been developed which try to find the best shape of the spot (Yang et al., 2001; Yang et al., 2002a). These methods are commonly based on the watershed transform (Beucher & Meyer, 1993) and the seeded region growing algorithm (SRG) (Adams & Bischof, 1994) which successfully detect different sizes and shapes of segmented spots (Karakach et al., 2010).

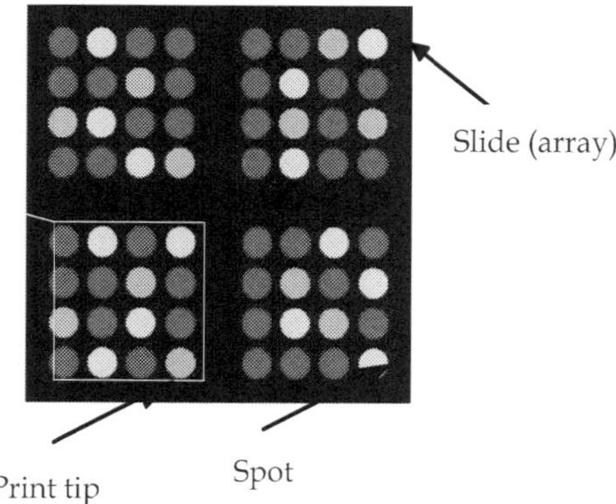

Fig. 10. Common structure of a cDNA microarray slide.

The most widely used method for segmenting spots, without restricting to particular shapes, is the histogram-based technique (Yang et al., 2001). It defines a target spot mask whose size is larger than any other spot. Foreground and background intensities of each spot are estimated from histogram of the pixels within this mask in various ways (Yang et al., 2002a). This technique directly quantifies values and needs no spot quantification stage. The discussed segmentation methods are implemented in most softwares to perform primary level processing of microarray images (Table 3) (Yang et al., 2001).

Segmentation method	Software Implementing Method
Fixed Circle	ScanAnalyze, GenePix, QuantArray
Adaptive Circle	QuantArray, GenePix, Dapple, Agilent Feature Extraction
Histogram	ImaGene, QuantArray and DeArray
Adaptive shape	Spot

Table 3. Different segmentation methods in different image processing softwares.

5.3 Image quantification

After detecting the location of spot and classifying pixels, it is necessary to compute red and green foreground intensities as well as red and green background fluorescent values for each spot on the array (Yang et al., 2002a).

5.3.1 Foreground quantification

In fact, the aim of the spot quantification is estimating a quantitative measure which is a combination of pixel intensity values (Yang et al., 2001). There are different statistics to compute this measure. Simple sum of pixel intensities is not a good statistic because it dependent on the size of the spot. Thus, values obtained from spots with different densities cannot be compared directly. Most microarray imaging softwares estimate the foreground intensity as the mean or median of pixel values within the segmented spot mask (Yang et al., 2002a). The median value is more robust to possible outlier pixels; hence it is preferable over the mean. Also interquartile range (IQR) (i.e., the difference between the 25th and 75th percentiles) of foreground may be computed for each channel as pixel variation estimation.

5.3.2 Background quantification

Background estimation is generally considered necessary for the aim of performing background correction (Yang et al., 2002a). Background estimation methods can be classified into four categories: local, morphological, constant and no adjustment background (Yang et al., 2001). In the first category, background intensities are computed by focusing on small regions around the spot mask. Different softwares utilize variety of shapes for these areas such as square, diamond-shape (referred to as the valley) and circles with different diameters. Usually, the background measure is estimated by the median of pixel values within these specific regions; however, it is possible to calculate mean, standard deviation, and interquartile range of pixels (Yang et al., 2001). Also, there are two types of morphological filters. The first one corresponds to a non-linear filter called morphological opening that is obtained by applying a form of local minimum filter (an erosion process) followed by a local maximum filter (a dilation process) with the same window for each image (for more details, see (Soli, 1999)). The second one corresponds to a combination of a closing followed by an opening that removes small dark regions as a better estimate (Wang, 2007; Yang et al., 2001). Constant background is a global method which estimates the mean or median intensity of the whole image background as a constant background for all spots. The fourth option is possibility of no background correction (Yang et al., 2001).

5.4 Spot quality assessment

The quality assessment step facilitates to diagnose possible quality problems or even mistakes that occurred during microarray fabrication and experiment. If this step does not report any serious irregularities, it will allow performing the following preprocessing steps.

After calculation of foreground and background intensities, quality measures are estimated to assess spot quality and reliability. These include variability of pixel values within each spot, spot area, a circularity measure, relative signal to background intensity (signal to noise ratio) and flag (Yang et al., 2001; Yang et al., 2002a). Each quality measure can be interpreted as follows. In most arrays the spots should be of the same size, thus very large or very small spots may be an indication of problems (Wang, 2007). Eliminating or marking of poor-quality and low-intensity spots is called flagging. This is zero if the spot is good, but will take different values if the spot has problems. Different image processing software uses different flag values for different problems, but the typical flagged spots are:

1. Bad spot: The pixel standard deviation is considerably higher than the pixel mean.
2. Dark spot: The signal of the spot is very weak.
3. Negative spot: The signal of the spot is less than the background value.
4. Manually flagged spot: The user has flagged the spot using the image processing software (Stekel, 2003).

Performing the four steps of image processing, quantitative parameters are generated in an output file of the software as shown in Table 4. These measures exhibit some of the location information, foreground and background quantifications and quality measures in a microarray experiment.

6. Preprocessing of cDNA microarray data

Prior to identification of DEGs, the data collected from image processing step needs to be preprocessed. This important step in microarray data analysis removes non-biological variations, makes data more meaningful, transforms data into an appropriate scale for analysis and enhances the quality of subsequent analysis. There are a number of approaches for preprocessing such as background correction, logarithm transformation and normalization of microarray data. It should be mentioned that spot quality assessment (section 5.4) in image processing could also be considered as a preprocessing step.

6.1 Background correction

Background correction is a necessary step in preprocessing of cDNA microarray data since the quantified fluorescence intensity of a spot contains background noise which does not reflect the true hybridization of the target to the probe. Background noise results from several sources such as non-specific hybridization of labeled target to the array surface, autofluorescence from the array surface or detection instrument, spatial heterogeneity across the arrays (Ritchie et al., 2007; Tarca et al., 2006). For the purpose of background correction, it is conventionally assumed that the background signals are additive to the foreground signals (Ritchie et al., 2007). Also, the standard approach for correction is subtracting an estimate of the local background intensity from the foreground intensity. Despite spread implementation of this approach in different software packages, it may cause problems. It generates negative corrected intensities resulting in missing log ratios, if the background intensity is larger than the foreground intensity. Even when there is no missing, it results highly variable log-ratios for low intensity spots (Kooperberg et al., 2002). Also it may cause some difficulties in the identification of differentially expressed genes (Yang et al., 2001). To overcome aforementioned limitations, alternative approaches have been proposed such as subtractive correction using an estimate of the global instead of the local background and

Index	grid.r	grid.c	spot.r	spot.c	Area	Gmean	Gmedian	GIQR	bgGmean
1	1	1	1	1	95	22028.26	23219	0.564843	372.6964
2	1	1	1	2	85	25613.2	20827	0.672128	928.8974
3	1	1	1	3	77	22652.39	17498	0.939413	1371.86
4	1	1	1	4	21	8929.286	5270	1.975485	250.5417
5	1	1	1	5	21	8746.476	7396	2.518724	262.0417
6	1	1	1	6	112	37010.08	41539	0.943238	499.1722

bgGmed	bgGSD	Valley	morphG	morphG.erode	morphG.close.open	Logratio	Perimeter	Circularity	Badspot
307	0.252131	306	182	153	289	-0.17171	40	0.746128	0
299	0.390198	280	171	153	278	-0.16341	36	0.824183	0
339	0.820078	275	153	136	278	-0.15408	34	0.837033	0
244	0.270411	258	153	132	271	0.80675	16	1.030835	0
235	0.275412	244	153	132	216	-0.10662	16	1.030835	0
304	0.740031	244	139	120	224	-0.44679	44	0.72698	0
381	1.05041	243	138	120	224	-0.21073	34	0.739198	0

Table 4. Partial output file from Spot software for green (Cy3) channel: Location information (spot index, grid row, grid column, spot row and spot column), Area: the number of foreground pixels for each spot, Gmean: the average of foreground pixel values, Gmedian: the median of foreground pixel values, GIQR: the interquartile range of foreground pixel, bgGmean: the average of background pixel values, bgGmed: the median of background pixel values, bgGSD: the standard deviation of background pixel values , valleyG: the background intensity estimate from the local background valley method, morphG: background estimate using morphological opening, morphG.erode: green background estimate using morphological erosion, morphG.close.open: green background estimate using morphological closing-opening, Logratio: the log-ratio for each spot is calculated as $\dfrac{\log_2(Rmean - bgmedR)}{\log_2(Gmean - bgmedG)}$, Circularity: Shape of spot defined as $\dfrac{4 \times \pi \times Area}{primeter^2}$, Badspot: If the spot has problem, it equals to 1, otherwise 0.

morphological opening filters which provide less variable log ratios (Ritchie et al., 2007; Yang et al., 2001). Some methods utilize statistical models, other than subtraction, to adjust the background estimate. A simpler background correction method was proposed to avoid negative corrected values. This model adjusts the foreground intensities by subtracting the background when the difference between the foreground and background is larger than a threshold value. However, when the difference is less than the threshold, subtraction is replaced by a smooth monotonic function. Kooperberg et al., 2002 proposed an empirical bayes model to correct background noise. A remarkable feature of this method is only the use of the mean, median and standard deviation statistics for each spot that are provided through the scanning software. In other methods, the models based on variance stabilizing transformations were proposed for incorporating additive components which prevent negative intensities. The Models use an arcsinh function instead of the logarithm transformation of the data. Also background correction and normalization are simultaneously performed on all the arrays together (Kooperberg et al., 2002; Ritchie et al., 2007). It is notable that no background correction has been recommended. Sometimes, local background methods show greater variability around the low intensity spots rather than no background adjustment (Yang et al., 2001).

6.2 Logarithm transformation

Before normalization, a logarithmic transformation is often performed on microarray data. This transformation is successful at reducing some of the variations, and makes the multiplicative noise of the data additive. Also data is transformed into a symmetrical and normal data distributed around zero through taking log transformation. This means that up- and down-expressed genes are treated in identical way (Quackenbush, 2002). However, the log transformed ratios limit subsequent analyses and the amount of information gained from the data (Zhao et al., 2007). The ratios do not provide information about the absolute expression levels. Also, the use of the ratios remarkably dependents on the choice of the reference sample, which is uncharacterized and not accurately reproduced. This will make it difficult to compare between data sets that use different reference samples (Zhao et al., 2007).

6.3 Normalization

There is variety of variations from the beginning of the experimental process through generation of raw data in microarray experiment. Two sources of variations are biological variations and procedural variations. Biological variations are the consequence of environmental changes or biological differences of the studied genes on the array. These are desired variations and represent the true changes in expression cycle. Procedural variations can be attributed to many sources such as microarray fabrication, mRNA preparation, reverse transcription, labelling, amplification, pin geometry, fluctuations in target volumes, target fixation, hybridization parameters, overshining, and image analysis. Detail description of each variation source is presented elsewhere (Schuchhardt et al., 2000; Yang et al., 2002b). Procedural variations can be removed (or minimized) using statistical approaches, so that biological variations are more accurately detected. The processes and transformations for the purpose of adjusting data are referred to as normalization. Hence, normalization is a crucial step in microarray data preprocessing, since data interpretation and identification of DEGs depends on the choice of normalization method (Yang et al., 2002b).

Different biases arise from variations in the microarray data. The most common is dye bias i.e. imbalance between the two channels due to differences between physical properties of dyes and detection efficiencies between the fluorescent dyes. Other biases such as print tip bias and spatial bias may arise from variation between spatial positions on the array due to differences between the print-tips on the arrayer (Smyth & Speed, 2003). In order to remove biases, numerous normalization approaches have been proposed. These algorithms can be applied either globally to an entire data set or locally to a subset of the data. For cDNA spotted microarray, local normalization is often applied to each print tip (Quackenbush, 2002). Normalization methods can be divided into two main categories: within-array normalizations and between-array normalizations. Within-array normalization has to be performed to adjust procedural variations for each single microarray. Some of more common approaches are as follows.

6.3.1 Global normalization

Global normalization is the simplest and most common within-array normalization method. It assumes the red and green intensities are related by a constant factor k, namely R=kG. The log-ratios are corrected by subtracting a constant c to get normalized values. $(\log R, \log G)$ are background corrected red and green intensities and then:

$$\left[\log_2\left({R_i}/{G_i}\right)\right]_{normalized} = \log_2\left({R_i}/{G_i}\right) - c = \log_2\left({R_i}/{G_i}\right) - \log_2(k) \tag{1}$$

The global constant c is usually estimated from the mean or median log ratios over a subset of the genes assumed to be not differentially expressed, although variety of strategies have been proposed for estimating this global constant (Quackenbush, 2002; Smyth & Speed, 2003). Global method is limited in adjusting intensity-dependent dye bias and spatial bias.

6.3.2 Intensity-dependent linear normalization

In most cases, the dye bias appears to be dependent on spot intensity linearly or nonlinearly. Linear normalization assumes the relation between M and A is linear based on model $M = \beta_0 + \beta_1 A$, where (β_0, β_1) can be estimated by least squares estimation. The most common method to visualize behavior of two channels is MA plot which uses log intensity ratios (M) and log intensity averages (A) where M and A are usually defined for each gene as

$$M_i = \log_2\left({R_i}/{G_i}\right) \quad \text{and} \quad A_i = \frac{1}{2}\times\log_2(R_i \times G_i)$$

6.3.3 Intensity dependent nonlinear normalization

The most efficient and widely used nonlinear normalization approach was proposed by Yang et al., 2002b. It considers the relation between M and A as a function of A i.e. M = c(A), instead of a linear relation. The estimation of c(A) is made by using a loess (locally weighted scatter plot smoother) function to operate a local scatter plot smoothing to the MA plot. The scatter plot smoother performs local linear fits in overlapping windows on the data and then combines the regressions to produce a smooth curve. This method can be divided into three categories based on the type of the treatment performed on the data. These categories include: global loess, print tip loess, and two-dimensional loess. Global Loess (Gloess) normalization method uses the loess function to perform a local A-dependent analysis:

$$\left[\log_2\left({R_i}/{G_i}\right)\right]_{normalized} = \log_2\left({R_i}/{G_i}\right) - c(A) = \log_2\left({R_i}/{G_i}\right) - \log_2(k(A)) \tag{2}$$

Where c(A) is the loess fit to the MA plot for all printed genes (Smyth & Speed, 2003).
Print tip loess (PTloess) is performed within each of the print tip groups separately as follows:

$$\left[\log_2\left({R_i}/{G_i}\right)\right]_{normalized} = \log_2\left({R_i}/{G_i}\right) - c_p(A) = \log_2\left({R_i}/{G_i}\right) - \log_2(k_p(A)) \tag{3}$$

Where $c_p(A)$ is the loess fit as a function of A for the pth print tip. By fitting separate loess lines for each group and correcting the intensity by its corresponding loess lines, not only the dye bias will be removed, but it can also correct the print tip bias. Two dimensional loess (twoDloess) method fits a smooth two-dimensional surface to the data which is a function of overall row position r and column position c of the spot on the array. The intensity-based trend is assumed to be global rather than varying across the array as for print-tip loess normalization.

$$\left[\log_2(R_i/G_i)\right]_{normalized} = \log_2(R_i/G_i) - loess(r,c) \tag{4}$$

Where loess(r,c) is a loess fit calculated based on the position of the spots. The three techniques remove different biases arose from the experiment. Gloess removes the dye bias dependent to spot intensity. PTloess removes spatial bias introduced from print tips and twoDloess removes the spatial bias on the overall slide.

The above normalization methods are applied to a single microarray. But in order to be able to facilitate comparison and integration of different microarrays, it is required to remove the variability caused by using multiple microarrays. It can be performed through the following approaches. Differences between arrays may arise from differences in print quality or from differences in ambient conditions when the plates are processed (Smyth & Speed, 2003).

6.3.4 Scale normalization

This method is a simple scaling of the data on multiple arrays so that each array has identical median absolute deviation (MAD). It aims to remove scale differences in the data and assumes that the log ratios on the array follow a normal distribution with mean zero and variance $a_j^2\sigma^2$ where σ^2 is the variance of the true log ratios and a_j is the scale factor for array j with n denoting the total number of arrays (Yang et al., 2002b).

$$a_j = MAD_j \Big/ \sqrt[n]{\prod_{j=1}^{n} MAD_j} \tag{5}$$

Where MAD_j denote the median absolute deviation for array i. Then

$$MAD_j = median_j\left\{\left\|M_j - median(M_j)\right\|\right\} \tag{6}$$

Finally, all log ratios are scaled through dividing by the same scale factor for each array. It is notable that scale normalization can also be applied to data within a microarray locally at the print tip level.

6.3.5 Quantile normalization

Quantile normalization was initially developed for the Affymetrix single channel chip, and then extended for two color cDNA microarrays. The goal of this method is to produce the same empirical distributions of expression levels on all arrays analyzed. It relies on the assumption that the probe intensities among arrays are always exactly the same, regardless of biology or study design. Clearly the situation where all samples have equal amounts of expressed genes is the exception, not the rule, making it the rare case where quantile normalization will normalize data without introducing errors. Quantile normalization is carried out through the following steps: Suppose that we have the (log base 2 transformed) probe level expression values from p genes and n arrays in a p × n matrix $X = \{X_{1j}\}$ with i = 1,2,...,p and j = 1,2,...,n. First, each column of X separately is ranked to generate a p × n matrix $Y = \{Y_{1j}\}$. Next, the average of each row of Y is computed and generated X_m. X_m is assigned to each column of Y to get a matrix denoted as X_{sort}. Finally, the normalized genes for each array is provided by rearranging each column of X_{sort} to have the same ordering as the corresponding column of the matrix X so that empirical distributions of the normalized genes are the same across arrays. Because the algorithm consists of only sorting and averaging operations, it runs quickly, even with large data sets (Bolstad et al., 2003). (More details in (Stafford, 2008))

All above normalization methods utilize certain critical biological and statistical assumptions about data distribution which may not be valid in practice. The main assumption is that the most genes on the array are non-differentially expressed between the two samples and the number of up-regulated genes approximately equals the number of down-regulated genes. In such cases, above-mentioned normalization methods may yield unreliable results. Xiong et al., 2008 proposed a novel statistical method based on the Generalized Procrustes Analysis (GPA) algorithm free of assumption (Xiong et al., 2008).

7. Differentially gene expression

Once the data is normalized, further analysis is necessary to obtain biologically meaningful results. In fact, the main purpose of microarray experiment is to identifying genes that are significantly differentially expressed under different biological, and/or clinical conditions. A growing number of approaches have been presented to fulfill this purpose that can be divided in three categories: marginal filters, wrappers, and embedded methods. The wrapper and embedded methods are a type of search algorithms by which subsets of genes that are useful to define a good predictor are generated. Evaluation of a specific subset of genes is provided by running a specific classification model on the subset. The filter approaches are scalable and fast methods and independent of the classification algorithm including t-tests and nonparametric tests and analysis of variance (ANOVA) (Saeys et al., 2007). We will provide a brief overview on some of the popular statistical differential expression methods. It is notable that various methods usually identify different ordered list of significant genes since each approach is based on a specific set of assumptions, and takes certain features of dataset into account.

Fold Change (FC) cutoff is one of the early approaches for DEG identification that is still widely used to rank genes in microarray assays. In this method, when ratio of two color intensities from each gene exceeds a pre-set threshold is said to be differentially expressed. Usually a threshold of twofold up- or down-regulation is considered as cutoff value in most biological studies. This method ranks genes based on the ratio of average gene expression under two different groups or conditions. Simplicity is a main reason for popularity of fold change approach. Also a major drawback is that it does not consider variance of the expression values quantified. Hence, in order to cope with this problem, it will be used in combination with other statistical methods (Tarca et al., 2006). There also exists variety of statistical tests instead of using a fold change cutoff, for a correct selection of deferentially expressed genes. A simple but popular method is the t-test and its variants (Cui & Churchill, 2003). The t-test performs according to the simple estimation of the population variance for a gene through the sample variance of its expression levels. It typically compares the difference between the mean expression levels among the two groups, considering the variability of genes in their ranking (Tarca et al., 2006). T-test depends on the type of distribution of the gene expression data. Thus, may not properly perform when data exhibit a strong departure from the normal distribution. Also the performance of t-test will be poor when sample sizes are small, because variance estimation is more challenging (Yan et al., 2005).

The ANOVA approach is a generalization of the t-test that can be used when more than two conditions are compared. The idea underlying ANOVA is to make a model that considers the variation sources that affect measurements. Then variance of each individual variable in the model is computed using expression data (Tarca et al., 2006). In order to improve the performance of the ordinary t-test and produce more stable results, modified t-statistics are alternatively proposed. The main difference between an ordinary t-statistic and these novel statistics is that the latter estimate variability regarding to information not only from the gene tested, but also from other genes displaying a similar magnitude of expression level (Smyth, 2004). Two commonly used approaches, i.e. the modified t-statistic methods (empirical Bayes and SAM), will be described in more detail as fallows.

7.1 The empirical Bayes t-test LIMMA

This empirical Bayes t-tset has been implemented in the limma R statistical package. In this approach, gene-wise linear models are separately made to represent the design of a microarray experiment. Next, the coefficients of each linear model are estimated through the expression data. After quantification of coefficients of model and standard errors, moderate t, F and B (log-odds) statistics of differential expression are computed using empirical Bayes approach. It is equivalent to reduction of the gene-wise sample variance towards a pooled estimate producing more stable result when the number of measurements is small in experiments. Finally, genes can be ranked based on one of the chosen statistics. A more detailed derivation can be found in (Smyth, 2004).

7.2 Significance analysis of microarrays (SAM)

SAM is a statistical technique, proposed by Tusher et al., 2001. It utilizes a non-parametric statistics, since the expression data may not be normally distributed. Modified t-statistic used in this method is essentially similar to the moderated t-statistic used in limma but have no associated distributional theory. Also the empirical bayes method provides a more complex model of the gene variance. SAM assigns a score to each gene based on change in gene expression relative to the standard deviation over repeated measurements for that gene (Smyth, 2004). Genes with scores greater than a threshold are considered differentially expressed. The threshold significance is determined by the user based on the FDR. The proportion of such genes identified by chance (false positives) is the false discovery rate (FDR). To estimate the FDR, nonsense genes are specified using random permutations of the repeated measurements (Tusher et al., 2001; Yan et al., 2005).

8. R and bioconductor packages

Microarray experiments produce large and highly complex datasets. Access to an efficient statistical computing environment is a critical aspect of the analysis of these gene expression datasets. There are a lot of free and commercial software. In most cases, the microarray kits come with the software that adequately analyses microarray data. One of the best options for data analysis is the R statistical programming environment (www.rproject.org) where the open-source Bioconductor R packages (www.bioconductor.org) are resourceful and effective in dealing with these microarray data.

There are plenty of packages such as limma, marray and arrayQuality for two-color spotted arrays or affy, affyPLM, affyPara and gcrma for Affymetrix array and Agi4x44PreProcess and AgiMicroRna for Agilent chips. The complete documentation of Bioconductor packages can be found on the Bioconductor project web site at: http://www.bioconductor.org/help/bioc-views/release/bioc/. Bioconductor packages remove noise from measurements of microarray experiments through preprocessing of data. Also they specialize in various related tasks in handling microarray data. Some packages are dedicated to facilitation and automation of array data input and applied to detection of spatial and dye effects on arrays via a variety of diagnostic plots and graphs. In addition to the primary fluorescence intensity data, these packages also extract textual information on probe sequences and target samples, such as gene annotations, layout array, target sample descriptions and hybridization conditions, etc.

Limma package implements tools for data quality assesment, background correction, normalization and identification of DEGs in microarray experiments. Marray package also provides alternative functions for reading microarray data into R, normalization data and diagnostic plots of different measurements. Limma and marray packages share some features (Smyth & Speed, 2003; Yang et al., 2002b).

In the following, in a case study, we will demonstrate a microarray analysis flow using Bioconductor R packages in experimental design, data preprocessing, and differential expression detection. This analysis is performed using Bioconductor Release 2.7 based on R Version 2.9.

8.1 Step by step microarray analysis

The publicly available dataset from Swirl zebra fish two-color spotted microarray experiment was used as a typical example in this analysis. Swirl is a point mutant in the BMP2 gene that affects the dorsal/ventral body axis. In this experiment, two sets of dye-swap were prepared. On the first array, the wild type and mutated samples were labelled with Cy5 and Cy3 dyes, respectively. On the second array, the Cy5 and Cy3 dyes were swapped for the samples. The next two arrays were replicates of the first two arrays, respectively (Table 5). Thus, four arrays were prepared. Each array consisted of 16 print tips (4 by 4) and each print tip comprised 22 by 24 spots. Therefore, each array accounted for 8448 spots. Once the experimental steps were carried out, each array was scanned and then analyzed by SPOT software (Buckley, 2000). The main purpose of the Swirl experiment is to find genes with altered expression in the swirl mutant compared to wild type zebra fish.

Date	FileName	Slide number	Conditions
2001/9/20	Swirl.1.spot	81	Swirl(Cy3), wild type (Cy5)
2001/9/20	Swirl.2.spot	82	Swirl(Cy5), wild type (Cy3)
2001/11/8	Swirl.3.spot	93	Swirl(Cy3), wild type (Cy5)
2001/11/8	Swirl.4.spot	94	Swirl(Cy5), wild type (Cy3)

Table 5. All experiments for the study of Swirl mutant.

In order to analyze the microarray data, a directory of all the image processing output files should be created (.spot files). This directory includes a file containing experiment description (SwirlSamples.txt file) and a file describing information on probe sequences, such as gene names, spot ID (fish.gal). Then R is started in the desired working directory. The following command will load Limma and marray packages for preprocessing swirl data.

```
>library (limma)
>library (marray)
```

Information about the hybridizations and the raw fluorescent intensities data are provided through the following commands

```
>targets <- readTargets ("SwirlSamples.txt")
>RG <- read.maimages (targets$FileName, source="spot")
```

In order to identify gene names the following command may be used,

```
>Genes <- readGAL("fish.gal")
```

and the layout information of slides uses this command,

```
>Layout <- getLayout (Genes)
```

Qualitative assessment of arrays can be performed using different plots and graphs in microarray experiments. Therefore, serious quality problems and sources of artifacts will be identified in the data. In this step, the background signal, different biases such as dye bias and spatial bias are evaluated using visualization techniques. According to the results of the quality assessment, the need for each preprocessing method is clearly revealed. Firstly, the background signal distribution is evaluated to identify whether there is any region with non-uniformity distribution.

```
>imageplot (log2(RG$Rb[,1]), Layout, low="white", high="red")
>imageplot (log2(RG$Gb[,1]), Layout, low="white", high="green")
```

Figure 11 shows that the background signals in both red and green channels are unreliably high in some region of array. It can be concluded as that there is spatial non-uniformity.

Fig. 11. Image of green and red channel background intensities for slide 1.

Therefore background correction is performed on swirl data. Since data have no negative value, subtractive methods can be carried out. Background corrected M and A-values are generated through subtraction method as follows

```
>MA <- normalizeWithinArrays (RG, method="none")
```

Secondly, we visualize the intensity range of M-values for each individual microarray using MA-plots. The signals include both background signals and foreground signals. These plots are generated using the following commands:

```
> plotMA (MA[,1], main="slide 1", ylim=c(-3,3))
> plotMA (MA[,2], main="slide 2", ylim=c(-3,3))
```

Figure 12 shows MA-plots of raw data of two slides of swirl experiment. Swirl experiment satisfies major assumption in microarray experiment i.e. a small percentage of genes are expected to be differentially expressed. Therefore, the majority of the points on the y axis (M-value) would be located at 0, since log (1) is 0. The shape of the curve on slide 1 shows more non–linear dependence on the overall spot intensity than slide 2. Therefore, normalization will attempt to remove the curvature of the spread and centralize the data around zero axis.

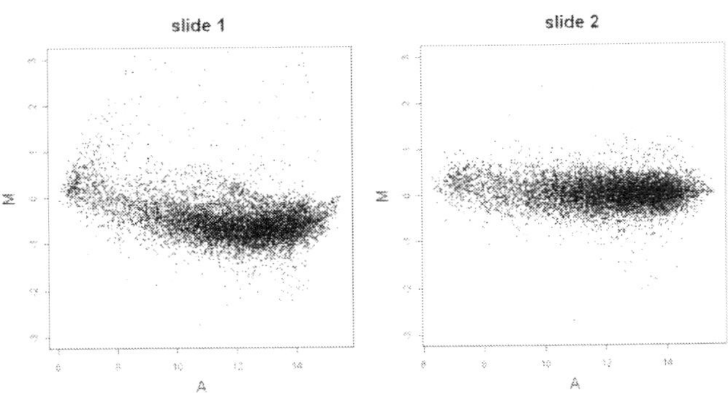

Fig. 12. MA plots for slide 1 and slide 2 in swirl experiment.

Another diagnostic plot is boxplot which can be useful for comparing M-values and homogeneity between print tip group and slides. Boxplot in different print tip is plotted using marray package after generation background corrected data by maNorm function.

```
>swirl.norm <- maNorm (swirl, norm="none")
>boxplot (swirl.norm[,1], xvar="maPrintTip", yvar="maM", main="slide
1")
```

The following command also produces a boxplot of the pre–normalization M-values for all four arrays in the swirl experiment.

```
>boxplot (MA$M~col (MA$M), xlab="slides", ylab="M")
```

A boxplot shows graphically 5-number summary of data, the median, the upper and lower quartiles, the range, and individual extreme values. The central box in the plot represents the interquartile range (IQR), which is specified as the difference between the 75th percentile and 25th percentile. The width of a box represents the variability of the data and solid line in the middle of the box represents the median. Extreme values, greater than 1.5×IQR above the 75th percentile and less than 1.5×IQR below the 25th percentile, are plotted individually (54).

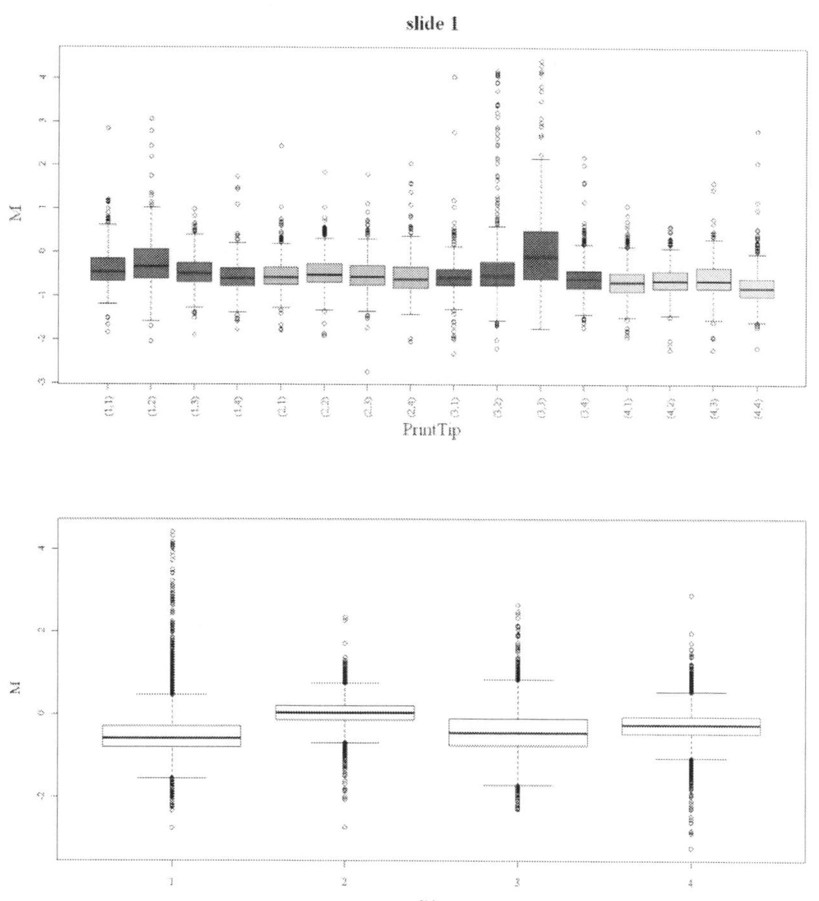

Fig. 13. Boxplots in different slides and print tips of slide 1.

In the next step, we can normalize data through different within and between array normalization using both marray and limma packages. The pre-normalization MA–plot and boxplot for slide 1 in Figures 12 and 13 illustrate the non–linear dependence of the M-value on the overall spot intensity A and the existence of spatial biases. We thus perform PTloess normalization on this data. In the following scale normalization will be performed on the swirl data because four slides have different spread of M-values (Figure 14).

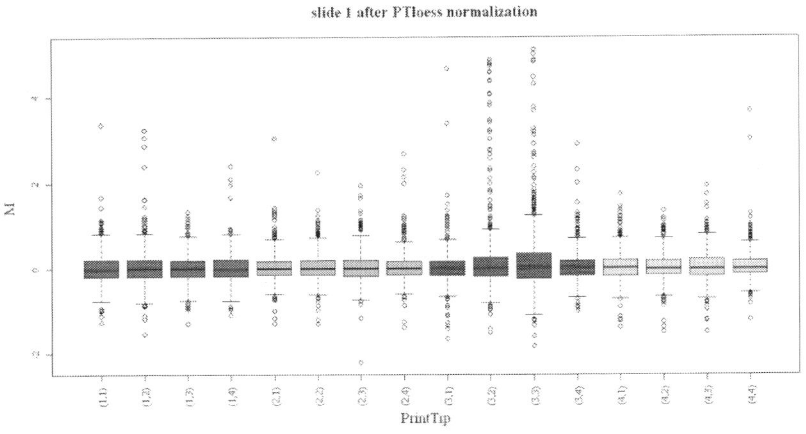

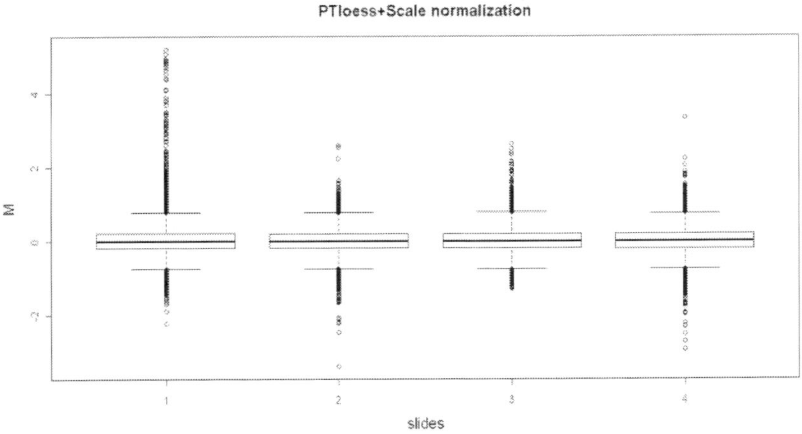

Fig. 14. Swirl data after PTloess normalization and PTloess fallowing Scale normalization.

```
>MA <- normalizeWithinArray(RG)
>MA <- normalizeBetweenArrays (MA, method="scale")
```

The closer the solid line to zero line in Figure 14 the more centrality of the data after normalization. In boxplot plotted between arrays when the width of the rectangles are approximately the same the distribution of the spots on replicate arrays are the most similar that means between-array normalization method has been selected appropriately.
In order to detect genes with differential expression between wild type and mutant samples, linear model and empirical bayes methods in limma package are used (Smyth, 2004). Dye swap samples are specified using the design matrix, which allows calculating of the average M- values across multiple arrays.

```
>design <- c(-1,1,-1,1)
```

M-values are estimated between these two samples using the lmFit function.

```
>fit <- lmFit(MA,design)
```

Moderated t-statistics and log–odds (B-statistics) of expression data are calculated using empirical Bayes methods

```
> fit <- eBayes (fit)
```

A summary table of some statistics for the top genes will be obtained using the following command.

```
>topTable(fit, number=10, adjust="fdr", sort.by="t")
```

ID	Name	M-value	Moderated-t	B	Adj.P.val
Control	BMP2	-2.205288	-21.06952	7.960750	0.0003572816
Control	BMP2	-2.296045	-20.28697	7.778330	0.0003572816
Control	Dlx3	-2.184900	-20.01066	7.710959	0.0003572816
Control	Dlx3	-2.180471	-19.63599	7.710959	0.0003572816
fb94h06	20-L12	1.271119	14.08467	7.617005	0.0020666932
fb40h07	7-D14	1.347207	13.52924	5.535983	0.0020666932
fc22a09	27-E17	1.266129	13.41339	5.483567	0.0020666932
fb85f09	18-G18	1.275686	13.39543	5.475386	0.0020666932
fc10h09	24-H18	1.195126	13.23722	5.402676	0.0020666932
fb85a01	18-E1	-1.287128	-13.07059	5.324819	0.0020666932

Table 6. Top 10 genes from the Swirl data.

The moderated t-statistic with adjusted p-values can identify differentially expressed genes. As seen in Table 6, it can sort both copies of the gene BMP2 knocked out and both copies of Dlx3, which is a known target of BMP

9. Conclusion

Gene expression is a common process in all forms of living cells to generate the macromolecules which are necessary for life. Systemic comprehension of the cell function is provided using study of gene expression. Investigation of molecular dynamics of the cell can be performed in three biochemical levels, transcriptomics, proteomics, metabolomics. Compared to others, transcriptomics is a more robust, large-scale, moderate cost technology of simultaneously measuring thousands of mRNA level. There are various techniques for quantifying gene expression based on mRNA. However gene expression traditional techniques provide valuable biological information, they are limited in some ways such as scale, economy and sensitivity. Therefore, compared to the other commonly used techniques, quantification based on microarray is really remarkable because of being high throughput and cost effective. It enables the simultaneous analysis of thousands of genes within one single experiment. Such miniaturized binding technology is typically divided into DNA, protein, tissue, cellular and chemical compound microarrays. DNA microarrays are the most popular type of this technology which currently manufactured through two main approaches: in situ synthesis and deposition of pre-synthesized probes (spotted arrays). We focused mainly on the spotted cDNA microarray. After microarray experiment, slides are inserted into scanner. The output data are fluorescent images arranged into a matrix of spots. Then, images are processed to quantify level of gene expression based on the intensity of each spot and obtain background estimates and quality measures. It is performed in gridding, segmentation, quantification and spot quality assessment stages. The output data from image processing stage needs to be preprocessed to eliminate non-biological variations, transform data into a suitable scale and improve the quality of downstream analysis. These are performed using background correction, logarithm transformation and normalization of microarray data. Finally, identification of genes that are significantly differentially expressed under different conditions can be carried out using marginal filters, wrappers, and embedded methods. We pointed some of the filter approaches such as t-test and its variants such as moderated t-test and SAM approach and analysis of variance (ANOVA). In summary, in order to analyze microarray data, the R statistical programming environment is chosen where the Bioconductor R packages such as limma and marray are effective in processing these microarray data. These packages address data input, production of diagnostic plots to detection of different biases, the statistical methods of removing experimental noises and errors on the spots within and between arrays. Finally, limma package is also used as a powerful tool to identification of differentially expressed genes.

10. References

Adams, R., & Bischof, L. (1994). Seeded region growing. *IEEE transactions on pattern analysis and machine intelligence*, Vol.16, No.6, pp. 641–647

Angenendt, P. (2005). Progress in protein and antibody microarray technology. *DDT.*, Vol.10, No.7, pp. 503-511

Barrett, J.C., & Kawasaki, E.S. (2003). Microarrays: the use of oligonucleotides and cDNA for the analysis of gene expression. *DDT.*, Vol.8, No.3, pp. 134-141

Beranova-Giorgianni, S. (2003). Proteome analysis by two-dimensional gel electrophoresis and mass spectrometry: strengths and limitations. *Trends in Analytical Chemistry*, Vol.22, No.5, pp. 273-281

Beucher, S., & Meyer, F. (1993). The morphological approach to segmentation: the watershed transformation. *Processing of mathematical morphology in image*, NewYork, pp. 433–481

Bilban, M., Buehler, L.K., Head, S., Desoye, G., & Quaranta, V. (2002). Normalizing DNA Microarray Data. *Curr. Issues Mol. Biol.*, Vol.4, pp. 57-64

Bolstad, B.M., Irizarry, R.A., Astrand, M., & Speed, T.P. (2003). A comparison of normalization methods for high density oligonucleotide array data based on variance and bias. *Bioinformatics*, Vo.19, No.2, pp. 185-193

Breljak, D., Ambriović-Ristov, A., Kapitanović, S., Čačev, T., & Gabrilovac, J. (2005). Comparison of Three RT-PCR Based Methods for Relative Quantification of mRNA. *Food Technol. Biotechnol*, Vol.43, No.4, pp. 379–388

Buckley, M.J. (2000). Spot User's Guide, CSIRO Mathematical and Information Sciences, Sydney, Australia, Available from:
<http://www.cmis.csiro.au/iap/Spot/spotmanual.htm>

Crick, F. (1970). Central dogma of molecular biology. *Nature*, Vol.227, pp. 561–563

Cui, X., & Churchill, G.A. (2003). Statistical tests for differential expression in cDNA microarray experiments. *Genome Biol*, Vol.4, pp.210–219

Doyle, H.A., & Mamula, M.J. (2001). Post-translational protein modifications in antigen recognition and autoimmunity. *TRENDS in Immunology*, Vol. 22, No.8, pp. 443-449

Fodor, S.P.A., Read, J.L., Pirrung, M.C., Stryer, L., Lu, A.T., & Solas, D. (1991) Light-directed, spatially addressable parallel chemical synthesis. *Science*, Vol.251, pp. 767–773

Frith, M.C., Pheasant, M., & Mattick, J.S. (2005). The amazing complexity of the human transcriptome. *European Journal of Human Genetics*, Vol.13, pp. 894–897

Gjerstad, Ø., Aakra, Å., Snipen, L., & Indahl, U. (2009). Probabilistically assisted spot segmentation-with application to DNA microarray images. *Chemometrics and Intelligent Laboratory Systems*, Vol.98, pp. 1–9

Gulmann, C., & O'Grady, A. (2003). Tissue microarray: an overview. *Current Diagnostic Pathology*, Vol.9, pp. 149 -154

Hall, D.A., Ptacek, J., & Snyder, M. (2007). Protein Microarray Technology. *Mech Ageing Dev*, Vol.128, No.1, pp. 161–167

Hegde, P.S., White, I.R., & Debouck, C. (2003). Interplay of transcriptomics and proteomics. *Current Opinion in Biotechnology*, Vol.14, No.6, pp. 647–651

Heid, C.A., Stevens, J., Livak, K.J., & Williams, P.M. (1996). Real Time Quantitative PCR. *Genome Research*, Vol.6, pp. 986-994, ISSN 1054-9803/96

Hirsch, J., Hansen, K.C., Burlingame, A.L., & Matthay, M.A. (2004). Proteomics: current techniques and potential applications to lung disease. *Am J Physiol Lung Cell Mol Physiol*, Vol. 287, No.1, pp. L1–L23

Istepanian, R.S.H., (2003). Microarray Image Processing: Current Status and Future Directions. *IEEE Trans. Nanobioscience*, Vol.2, No.4, pp. 173-175

Karakach, T.K., Flight, R.M., & Douglas, S. (2010). An introduction to DNA microarrays for gene expression analysis. *Chemometrics and Intelligent Laboratory Systems*, Vol.104, No.1, pp. 28–52

Knapp, G., Beckwith, J.S., Johnson, P.F., Fuhrman, S.A., & Abelson, J. (1978). Transcription and processing of intervening sequences in yeast tRNA genes. *Cell 14*, pp. 221–236

Kononen, J., Bubendorf, L., Kallioniemi. A., Barlund, M., Schraml, P., Leighton. S., Torhorst. J., Mihatsch, M.J., Sauter, G., & Kallioniemi, O.P. (1998). Tissue microarrays for high-throughput molecular profiling of tumor specimens. *Nat Med*, Vol.4, pp. 844–847

Kooperberg, C., Fazzio, T.G., Delrow, J.J., & Tsukiyama, T. (2002). Improved Background Correction for Spotted DNA Microarrays. *Journal of computational biology*, Vol.9, No.1, pp. 55-66

Lipshutz, R.J., Fodor, S.P.A., Gingeras, T.R., & Lockhart, D.J. (1999). High density synthetic oligonucleotide arrays. *Nature genetics supplement*, Vol.21, pp. 20-24

Lockhart, D.J., Dong, H., Byrne, M.C., Follettie, M.T., Gallo, M.V., Chee, M.S., Mittmann, M., Wang, C., Kobayashi, M., Norton, H., & Brown, E.L. (1996). DNA expression monitoring by hybridization of high density oligo-nucleotide arrays. *Nature Biotechnology*, Vol.14, pp. 1675–1680

Parsons, M., & Grabsch, H. (2009). How to make tissue microarrays. *Diagnostic histopathology*, Vol.15, No.3, pp. 142-150

Perdew, G.H., Vanden Heuvel, J.P., & Peters, J.M. (2006). Regulation of Gene Expression: Molecular Mechanisms. *Humana Press*, pp. 11-30

Pinet, F. (2009). Identifying patients at risk of progressive left ventricular dysfunction. *Heart Metab*, Vol. 42, pp. 10–14

Quackenbush, J. (2002). Microarray data normalization and transformation. *Nature genetics supplement*, Vol.32, pp. 496–501

Ritchie, M.E., Silver, J., Oshlack, A., Holmes, M., Diyagama, D., Holloway, A., & Smyth, G.K. (2007). A comparison of background correction methods for two-colour microarrays. *Bioinformatics*, Vol.23, No.20, pp. 2700–2707

Russo, G., Zegar, C., & Giordano, A. (2003). Advantages and limitations of microarray technology in human cancer. *Oncogene*, Vol.22, pp. 6497–6507

Saeys, Y., Inza, I., & Larranaga, P. (2007). A review of feature selection techniques in bioinformatics. *Bioinformatics*, Vol.23, No.19, pp. 2507–2517

Schadt, E.E., Li, C., Su, C., & Wong, W.H. (2001). Analyzing High-Density Oligonucleotide Gene Expression Array Data. *Journal of Cellular Biochemistry*, Vol.80, pp. 192–202

Schaub, M.C., Lucchinetti, E., & Zaugg, M. (2009). Genomics, transcriptomics, and proteomics of the ischemic heart. *Heart Metab*, Vol.42, pp. 4–9

Schena, M., Shalon, D., Davis, R., & Brown, P.O. (1995). Quantitative monitoring of gene expression patterns with a complementary DNA microarray. *Science*, Vol.270, pp. 467-470

Schena, M. (2003). *Microarray analysis*. John Wiley & Sons, New Jersey

Schuchhardt, J., Beule, D., Wolski, E., Eichhoff, H., Leharch, H., & Herzel, H. (2000). Normalization strategies for cDNA microarrays. *Nucleic Acids Research*, Vol.28, No.10, pp. e47

Singh, A., & Sau, A. K. (2010). Tissue Microarray: A powerful and rapidly evolving tool for high-throughput analysis of clinical specimens. *IJCRI*, Vol.1, No.1, pp. 1-6

Stekel, D. (2003). *Microarray Bioinformatics*. Cambridge University Press, Cambridge

Smyth, G.K., & Speed, T. (2003). Normalization of cDNA microarray data. *Methods*, Vol.31, pp. 265-273

Smyth, G.K. (2004). Linear Models and Empirical Bayes Methods for Assessing Differential Expression in Microarray Experiments. *Statistical Applications in Genetics and Molecular Biology*, Vol.3, No.1, Article 3

Soli, P. (1999). *Morphological image Analysis: Principles and Applications*. Springer-Verlag Berlin, Heidelberg, New York

Stafford, P. (2008). *Methods in microarray normalization*. Taylor and Francis CRC Press, 978-1-4200-5278-7, Boca Raton, London, NewYork

Tarca, A.L., Romero, R., & Draghici, S. (2006). Analysis of microarray experiments of gene expression profiling. *American Journal of Obstetrics and Gynecology*, Vol.195, pp. 373-388

Templin, M.F., Stoll, D., Schrenk, M., Traub, P.C., Vöhringer, C.F., & Joos, T.O. (2002). Protein microarray technology. *TRENDS in Biotechnology*, Vol.20, No.4, pp. 160-166

Trayhuru, P., (1996). Northern blotting. *Proceedings of the Nutrition Society*, Vol.55, pp. 583-589

Tsiridis, E., & Giannoudis, P.V. (2006). Transcriptomics and proteomics: Advancing the understanding of genetic basis of fracture healing. *Injury, Int. J. Care Injured*, Vol. 37S, pp. S13–S19

Tusher, V.G., Tibshirani, R., & Chu, G. (2001). Significance analysis of microarrays applied to the ionizing radiation response. *Proceedings of the National Academy of Sciences*, Vol.98, No.9, pp. 5116-5121

van der Werf, M.J., Jellema, R.H., & Hankemeier, T. (2005). Microbial metabolomics: replacing trial-and-error by the unbiased selection and ranking of targets. *J Ind Microbiol Biotechnol*, Vol. 32, pp. 234-252

Wang, D. (2007). Spot: cDNA Microarray Image Analysis Users Guide. CSIRO Mathematical and Information Sciences, Australia, Available from: < http://spot.cmis.csiro.au/spot/doc/Spot.pdf>

Xiong, H., Zhang, D., Martyniuk, C.J., Trudeau, V.L., & Xia, X. (2008). Using Generalized Procrustes Analysis (GPA) for normalization of cDNA microarray data. *BMC Bioinformatics*, Vol.9, No.25

Yan, X., Deng, M., Fung, W.K., & Qian, M. (2005). Detecting differentially expressed genes by relative entropy. *Journal of Theoretical Biology*, Vol.234, pp. 395-402

Yang, Y.H., Buckley, M.J., & Speed, T.P. (2001). Analysis of cDNA microarray images. *Briefings in bioinformatics*, Vol.2, No.4, pp. 341-349

Yang, Y.H., Buckley, M.J., Dudoit, S., & Speed, T.P. (2002a). Comparison of methods for image analysis on cDNA microarray data. *J. Comput. Graph. Statist.*, Vol.11, pp. 108-136

Yang, Y.H., Dudoit, S., Luu, P., Lin, D.M., Peng, V., Ngai, J., & Speed, T.P. (2002b). Normalization for cDNA microarray data: a robust composite method addressing single and multiple slide systematic variation. *Nucleic Acids Research*, Vol.30, No.4, pp. e15

Zhang, L., Zhang, X., Ma, Q., Ma, F., & Zhou, H. (2010). Transcriptomics and Proteomics in the Study of H1N1 2009. *Genomics Proteomics Bioinformatics*, Vol.8, No.3, pp. 139-144

Zhao, H., Engelen, K., De Moor, B., & Marchal, K. (2007). CALIB: a BioConductor package for estimating absolute expression levels from two-color microarray data. *Bioinformatics*, Vol.23, No.13, pp. 1700-1701

27

On-Chip Living-Cell
Microarrays for Network Biology

Ronnie Willaert and Hichem Sahli
Vrije Universiteit Brussel,
Belgium

1. Introduction

The recently developed field of systems biology creates a new framework for understanding the molecular basis of physiological or pathophysiological states of cells. Screening modalities that can be used on single cells are needed to study cellular systems biology. The recent development of cellular microarrays has provided a method for the complex molecular analysis of living, single cells (Chen & Davies, 2006). Unlike other high-throughput systems, such as gene expression profiling microarrays or protein microarrays, cellular microarrays use a printed pattern of geographically distinct spots to probe living cells, rather than cell lysates, or other non-viable samples. Among the most powerful tools to assay gene function on a genome-wide scale in the physiological context of intact living cells are fluorescence microscopy and related imaging techniques (Pepperkok & Ellenberg, 2006). To enable these techniques to be applied to functional genomics experiments, fluorescence microscopy is making the transition to a quantitative and high-throughput technology.

The combination of time-lapse microscopy, quantitative image analysis and fluorescent protein reporters has enabled observation of multiple cellular components over time in individual cells (Locke & Elowitz, 2009). In conjunction with mathematical modelling, these techniques are now providing powerful insights into genetic and proteomic behaviour in diverse microbial systems. Recently, a quantitative system-wide analysis of mRNA and protein expression in individual cells with single-molecule sensitivity using a yellow fluorescent protein fusion library for *E. coli* has been realised (Taniguchi *et al.*, 2010).

2. Microfluidic chips for cell microarrays

2.1 Cell assays and cell microarrays

A cell assay is defined here as a measurement and analysis of the cellular response, at a given level, to a chemical and/or physical stimulus (Barbulovic-Nad & Wheeler, 2008). Cellular responses are diverse, e.g. alterations of intracellular and extracellular biochemistry, cell morphology, motility and (de)adhesion, survival and apoptosis, and proliferation properties. These responses characterise single aspects of cell phenotype, and are typically monitored in a culture dish or a multiwell plate, while more recently microfluidic devices have been employed. While culture dishes require millilitre volumes of media and reagents, multiwell plates contain microliter volumes and enable simultaneous analysis of multiple cell types or stimuli. Experiments with multiwell plates are typically integrated in a robotic analysis platform. Two major drawbacks of robotic platforms are the expense of the instrumentation, and the cost of experimental consumables.

The use of microarrays was first reported in 1989 (Ekins *et al.*, 1989). The variety and diversity of microarrays has become impressive. Three main types of microarrays have been developed: DNA microarrays, protein microarrays, and cell microarrays (Barbulovic-Nad *et al.*, 2006). Several different approaches to cell microarrays have been explored to investigate gene expression, cell-surface interactions, extracellular matrix composition, cell migration and proliferation, the effects of drugs on cellular activity and many other areas (Angres, 2005). There are two fundamental methods to produce cell microarrays: the indirect and the direct method. The indirect method – i.e. the "reverse transfection" method – was developed by Ziauddin and Sabbatini (2001). In the direct method, the cells are printed onto a substrate. In few cases contact-based microarrayers are used, but more often non-contact-based devices are used.

Miniaturisation of cellular assays via cell microarrays increases assay throughput while reducing reagent consumption and the number of cells required, making these systems attractive for a wide range of assays in drug discovery, toxicology, and stem cell research (Fernandes *et al.*, 2009). Cell microarrays have been developed for highly parallel, high-throughput analyses of cell phenotypes (Narayanaswamy *et al.*, 2006), assessing cell proliferation and morphology (Bochner *et al.*, 2001; Xu, 2002), protein expression levels (Schwenk *et al.*, 2002), and imaging of tissues (Kononen *et al.*, 1998; Radhakrishnan *et al.*, 2008) and single cells (Biran *et al.*, 2003). In these initially developed living-cell microarrays, microbial cells were printed on an agar growth medium and could grow as microcolonies, or cells were grown in multiwell plates and printed on a glass slide for imaging, or only short time analyses on living cells were performed. High-throughput experiments on a library of cells require on-chip cell culture. Microchip 2- or 3-D cell cultivation techniques can provide many advantages for cell culture systems because the scale of the cultivated environment inside the microchip is fitted to the size of the cells. Table 1 gives some examples of developed mammalian cell microarrays/wells.

2.2 Cell assays in microfluidics

Microfrabrication technology originated from the electronics industry, where 3D micro-features for electronic devices were manufactured in the sub-centimeter to sub-micrometer range using lithography techniques (Franssila, 2010). Microfluidics emerged as an extension of MEMS (Micro Electro Mechanical Systems) technology at the beginning of the 1980s. Microfluidics is a technology that is characterised by devices containing networks of micrometer-dimension channels (Whitesides, 2006). It involves the manipulation of very small fluid volumes, enabling the creation and control of µl to nl volume reactors. Microsystems create new opportunities for the spatial and temporal control of cell proliferation and stimuli by combining surfaces that mimic complex biochemistries and geometries of extracellular matrix with microfluidic channels that regulate transport of fluids and soluble factors (West *et al.*, 2008). Further integration with bioanalytic microsystems results in multifunctional platforms for basic biological insights into cells and tissues, as well as for cell-based sensors with biochemical, biomedical and environmental functions. Highly integrated microdevices show great promise for basic biomedical and pharmaceutical research, and for drug discovery (Dittrich & Manz, 2006). Microfluidic "lab

Cell type	Batch/ micro-fluidics	Array size (wells, spots)	Characteristics	References
Carcinoma cells	Microfluidics	1	Cells immobilised with peptide gel	Kim *et al.*, 2007
Hepatocytes	Batch microarray	512	Dynamic monitoring of fluorescet probes in single cells	Roach *et al.*, 2009
Fibroblast	Microfluidics	4	Ligand labeling and cell binding analysis	Sui *et al.*, 2007
Fibroblast 3T3	Microfluidics	96	Response of single cells to different concentration of signalling molecule (TNF)-α	Tay *et al.*, 2010
Fibroblast 3T3	Microfluidics	16	Perfusion culture for 3 days	Kim *et al.*, 2006
Fibroblast 3T3	Microfluidics	32	Quantitative interrogation of signalling networks	Cheong *et al.*, 2009
H 35 cells	Microfluidics	64/100	8x8 array with individually addressable rows/10x10 array	Hung *et al.*, 2005; Lee *et al.*, 2006
Hela-NF	Microfluidics	40	8x5 array: row with 5 wells is individually addressed; GFP-based gene expression	Thompson *et al.*, 2004
Hela-NF	Microfluidics	256	16x16 array; GFP-based gene expression	Wieder *et al.*, 2005
Human stem cells	Batch microarray	1700	Interaction of biomaterials with cells	Anderson *et al.*, 2004
Human stem cells	Microfluidics	96	Transient stimulation schedules on proliferation, differentiation and motility	Gómez-Sjöberg *et al.*, 2007
Human neural SC	Microfluidics	1	Growth and differentiation	Chung *et al.*, 2005
mESC	Microfluidics	16	Proliferation is flow rate dependent, 4 days culture	Chin *et al.*, 2004
mESC	Batch microarray	280	Cells immobilised in alginate gel spots	Fernandes *et al.*, 2010
Rat stem cells	Batch microarray	10000	Dimensions of the wells are tunable, diameter: 20 to >500µm, height: 10-500 µm	Chin *et al.*, 2004

Table 1. Examples of mammalian and stem cell microarrays/wells.

on a chip" technologies have been used to track gene expression changes in individual cells, enabling large populations of cells to be monitored, and allowing precise control of the cell microenvironment (Breslauer *et al.*, 2006; Charvin *et al.*, 2009).

Conventional methods of fabricating microfluidic devices have centered on etching in glass and silicon (Pisani & Tadigadapa, 2010). Polymers have assumed the leading role as substrate materials for microfluidic devices in recent years (Becker & Gärtner, 2008). They offer a broad range of material parameters as well as material and surface chemical properties, which enable microscopic design features that cannot be realised by any other class of materials. Today, the most preferred material for biocompatible microfluidic devices is poly(dimethylsiloxane) (PDMS) (Velve-Casquillas *et al.*, 2010), which was introduced as soft lithography by Whitesides (Anderson *et al.*, 2000). PDMS is soft, transparant, permeable to gasses, for most, impermeable to liquids, biocompatible, nontoxic, and has a low electrical conductivity, making it a very suitable material for biological applications in microfluidic devices. Fabrication of microfluidic devices in PDMS by soft lithography provides faster, less expensive routes than these conventional methods to devices that handle aqueous solutions. Soft lithography refers to a collection of techniques for creating microstructures and nanostructures based on printing, moulding and embossing (Weibel *et al.*, 2007). It is based on rapid prototyping and replica molding. In rapid prototyping, a computer-aided design program is used to create a design for channels, which are printed at high resolution onto transparency film. The transparency film then serves as the photomask. The master molds are generated by using the photomask in contact lithography to produce a positive relief of photoresist. In replica molding, PDMS is poured over the master and heat cured to generate a negative replica of the master. The PDMS is then removed from the mold and sealed against a glass coverslip to form the device features and channels. Flows in microfluidic devices are mainly pressure-driven by using syringe pump, rotary pump, or electro-osmotic flow.

Microfluidic devices are advantageous for cell assays for various reasons. The most obvious one is the similarity in dimensions of cells and microchannels (10-100 µm widths and depths). Another important advantage is flow: fluid flow in these small channels is laminar. Consequently, convection only exists in the direction of the applied flow, whereas in the direction perpendicular to the applied flow, diffusion contributes to mass transport. Although diffusion-based transport is slow across long distances, in microchannels diffusion enables rapid reagent delivery. In addition, the combination of laminar flow and diffusion makes the formation of highly resolved chemical gradients across small distances. This feature is particular useful for cell assays as such gradients are common in living systems (but difficult to implement in macroscale setups). Another advantage is the increased surface-to-volume ratio, which facilitates favourable scaling of heat and mass transfer, as well as favourable scaling of electrical and magnetic fields that are used in electromagnetic cell analysis. Another consequence of the size regime lies in the concentration of analytes: as cells in microchannels are confined in sub-microliter volumes, relevant analytes do not become too dilute and can thus be more readily detected. A limitation of the high surface-to-volume ratio of microchannels is the adsorption of molecules onto channel walls that are generally hydrophobic. However, surfaces can be chemically treated to prevent adsorption of biomolecules (Velve-Casquillas *et al.*, 2010). Automated high-throughput experiments may be performed in a large number of repeating functional microstructures fabricated on a single chip. These microsystems can also monitor the time course of the release, which is difficult to measure by conventional batch cell culture methods. Microfluidic devices can be made transparant and the cells monitored in real time by imaging, using fluorescence markers to probe cell functions and cell fate.

In a microfluidic device for cell-based assays, adequate culture conditions must be maintained for the duration of the experiment, which can span several days. While being cultured, cells must be continuously perfused with nutrients and oxygen; in addition, constant temperature and pH must be maintained. In contrast to traditional batch cultures, miniaturised perfusion systems provide precise control of medium composition, long-term unattented cultures and tissue-like structuring of cultures (Heiskanen *et al.*, 2010). Adherent cells must be detached from culture flasks and seeded or spotted into a microfluidic device while sufficient time has to be allowed to achieve proper cell attachment and reduction of stress induced by the transfer. Mobile cells in suspension are easier to handle and require less time to adapt to the new environment.

2.3 Single-cell analysis/monitoring in microfluidic devices

A fundamental goal of cell biology is identifying how cell behaviour arises from the dynamic collection of environmental stimuli to which the cell is exposed (Lee & Di Carlo, 2009). From a biosystems science and engineering perspective, there is great interest in how the cell behaves as a system that processes time-dependent input signals into output behaviour(s). Ideally, with knowledge of the history of the ensemble of environmental stimuli, one would be able to predict the precise behaviour that a particular cell would exhibit under a given stimulus. Unfortunately, cells under seemingly identical environmental conditions often display a distribution of heterogeneous behaviour(s) (Lidstrom & Meldrum, 2003). This appears to be partly due to probabilistic behaviour in the "decision" processes that connect input and output (Raser & O'Shea, 2005; Mettetal et al., 2006). Underlying the links between inputs and outputs are systems of interconnected molecular interactions (signalling pathways). Signalling within one pathway as well as cross-signalling between pathways, localisation of reactions and the sometimes small molecule numbers involved in signalling contribute to stochastic behaviour in these systems (Raser & O'Shea, 2005; Kholodenko et al., 2010), which in the case of stem cells may very well be an essential and necessary feature of their biology and enables them to transit from one state to another. Because of the meanwhile well-documented heterogeneity within such cell population, increased emphasis has been put on analysing a large number of single cells and determining distributions of responses (Cai et al., 2006; Mettetal et al., 2006; Yu et al., 2006). New tools, based on microfabrication and microfluidic technologies, are now allowing improved dynamic control of environmental variables for high-throughput single-cell analysis. These experimental technologies combined with systems analysis of signalling pathways are expected to lead to an improved quantitative description of single-cell function (Lee & Di Carlo, 2009).

Several single-cell analysis techniques have been developed, which may be classified in terms of information content (number of elements capable of being studied simultaneously) and throughput (number of cells studied in a give time). The simplest and most widely used forms of single-cell analysis are fluorescence microscopy and flow cytometry. Automated microscopy techniques, often termed high-content screening (HCS) or "cellomics", recently provided also quantitative insight into cellular behaviour and in most cases are applied to observe the response of the cells, e.g. to drug candidate molecules.

The utility of single-cell measurements with high temporal resolution has been demonstrated by bacterial studies, which used optical microscopy to observe *Escherichia coli* over long time periods and reveal interesting temporal fluctuations and cell-to-cell variability that would otherwise be masked by population-wide measurements (Pedraza & van Oudenaarden, 2005). A microfluidic microchemostat has been constructed and used to acquire single-cell fluorescence data from *Saccharomyces cerevisiae* over many cellular generations (Charvin et al., 2009; Rowat et al., 2009). One way in which cells can rapidly respond to environmental stimuli is to alter the localisation and abundance of proteins (Charvin et al., 2009). In a microfluidic device, these aspects can be studied on the same cells under various growth conditions or in response to environmental insults.

2.4 Localisomics

Localisomics seeks to identify the subcellular location of all proteins in the cell, which can provide key insights into the cellular function of the individual proteins a well as their probable interacting partners (Joyce & Palsson, 2006). Protein localisation has to be described in intracellular compartments, e.g. the nucleus or cytoplasm, and also in organelles, as specialisation of cellular organelles defines the functional roles of proteins (Souchennytskyi, 2005). The most informative is data about protein localisation and its dynamics in a single, living cell.

Mostly fluorescence microscopy techniques have been used to monitor green fluorescent protein (GFP)-tagged- or yellow fluorescence protein (YFP)-tagged proteins in *E. coli* (Taniguchi *et al.*, 2010), *S. cerevisiae* (Huh *et al.*, 2003) and human cells (Shariff *et al.*, 2010). Visual interpretation of the fluorescent images, and more recently, automated image analysis, have been used to extract dynamic protein localisation data (Schubert *et al.*, 2006; Conrad *et al.*, 2011). Images from many studies are publicly available (Table 2).

Species (cell type)	Number of proteins	Tagging method	Website	Reference
Human (U-2 OS, A-431, U-251 MG)	> 6000	Immuno-fluorescence, immunochemistry	www.proteinatlas.org	Berglund *et al.*, 2008
Mouse (3T3)	>100	Internal GFP fusion	cdtag.bio.cmu.edu	Jarvik *et al.*, 2002
Human (HeLa) Monkey (Vero)	>1000	cDNA terminal GFP fusion	gfp-cdna.embl.de	Liebel *et al.*, 2004
Human (HeLa) Mouse (3T3)	>100	Immunofluorescence and genomic internal GFP fusion	murphylab.web.cmu.edu	Huang *et al.*, 2002
Human (H1299 carcinoma)	> 2000	YFP CD tagging	www.dynamicproteomics.net	Frenkel-Morgenstern *et al.*, 2010
Yeast	> 4000	cDNA C-terminal GFP fusion	yeastgfp.yeastgenome.org	Huh *et al.*, 2003
Human (brain) Various	Various	Various	ccdb.ucsd.edu	Martone *et al.*, 2008

Table 2. Publicly available microscopy images concerning protein localisation in cells (adapted from Newberg *et al.*, 2009).

3. Computational methods for quantitative image analysis

Quantitative information from live cell microscopy can be obtained. To reach this goal, image analysis methods have to be used. These methods can provide quantified geometric, intensity, and motion properties, and these quantitative parameters can be used as input parameters for predictive systems biology models (Pepperkok & Ellenberg, 2006; Megason & Fraser, 2007; Bakal *et al.*, 2007; Verveer & Bastiaens, 2008).

Advances in imaging technology provide a huge amount of digital image data. A manual analysis is hardly possible. Additionally, 3D images over time are difficult to interpret manually and the result suffers from subjectivity. Therefore, computer-based image analysis is required to cope with the enormous amount of image data and to extract reproducible as well as quantitative information (Peng, 2008; Zhou & Wong, 2008; Hamilton, 2009; Swedlow *et al.*, 2009; Rohr *et al.*, 2010).

Automatic analysis of multidimensional live cell microscopy images requires different computational methods. A general workflow for quantitative analysis of live cell microscopy images is composed of the following steps: (i) preprocessing, (ii) segmentation, (iii) registration, (iv) tracking and (v) classification (Rohr *et al.*, 2010).

3.1 Preprocessing

The goal of image preprocessing is to improve the quality of raw images prior to image segmentation and feature extraction. Applications include denoising for reducing the image noise, elimination of artifacts, intensity normalisation, contrast enhancement, and deconvolution for reducing the image blur introduced by the imaging process. Denoising methods use either linear or nonlinear filters to reduce noise in images and improve the signal-to noise ratio. For denoising images, a Gaussian filter is often applied (Rohr *et al.*, 2010). Filters that are not based on convolution are called nonlinear filters. A nonlinear filter that is often used to remove the pepper-noise generated by CCD detectors in optical fluorescent microscopy is the median filter (Zhou & Wong, 2008). This median filter can preserve high frequency information describing cell edges in high content microscopy images.

Deconvolution methods to reduce the image blur are relevant for both wide-field and confocal light microscopes (Cannell *et al.*, 2006). It is often assumed that the blurring of an image is caused by a linear process and thus can be presented by convolution with a point spread function (PSF). The aim of deconvolution is to reconstruct the original (true) image by reversing the effect of convolution and thus improving the resolution and contrast of the image (Rohr *et al.*, 2010). Examples of such approaches are the inverse filter, the Wiener filter, and the constrained least-squares filter.

3.2 Segmentation

Image segmentation is one of the most basic processing steps in many bioimage informatics applications. The goal is to segment out meaningful objects of interest in the respective image. In the case of microscopy images, one main task is to identify cells and to distinguish them from the background. Another task is to detect and localize particles in the image. Because particles are much smaller than cells and corresponded to spot-like image structures, different segmentation methods are required for cells and particles (Rohr *et al.*, 2010). Segmentation is a prerequisite for quantifying geometric properties of objects as well as for quantifying the corresponding signal intensities. Additionally, segmentation is often the basis for subsequent image analysis steps, i.e. for tracking.

3.2.1 Cell segmentation

Cell segmentation can be categorised into two classes, i.e. nucleic segmentation and cytoplasm (or whole cell) segmentation. In recent years, there has been significant effort towards the development of automated methods for cell nuclei image and 3D cell segmentation have been developed (Ortiz de Solorzano *et al.*, 1999; Sarti *et al.*, 2000; De Solorzano *et al.*, 2001; Umesh Adiga & Chaudhuri, 2001; Malpica *et al.*, 1997; Belien *et al.*, 2002; Wählby *et al.*, 2004; Lin *et al.*, 2005; Lindblad *et al.*, 2004; Dufour *et al.*, 2005; Li *et al.*, 2007, 2008; Dorn *et al.*, 2008; Ko *et al.*, 2009). The main methods for cell segmentation can be classified as: threshold-based segmentation, edge-based segmentation, region-based segmentation, and deformable models (reviewed in Rohr *et al.*, 2010).

3.2.2 Particle localisation

Often it is assumed that the intensities representing a fluorescently labelled particle resemble a 2D Gaussian function in which the peak intensity value of the particle differs significantly from that of the local background. A bottom-up or a top-down strategy is used to address the problem of particle localisation.

Bottom-up localisation schemes for fluorescent particles typically comprise three consecutive steps: image preprocessing, particle detection, and particle localisation (Rohr *et al.*, 2010). A common technique is to apply a threshold on the intensities of a (preprocessed) image to determine image regions that correspond to particles (Ponti *et al.*, 2003; Sbalzarini & Koumoutakos, 2005). Automatic schemes for determining an optimal threshold is required since manual determination is often impractical and can give inconsistent results.

Top-down approaches use model-driven strategies in which hypotheses regarding the possible configuration of the models are tested against the information found in the images. A 2D Gaussian function is typically used as a model for the shape and appearance of fluorescently labelled particles (Godinez *et al.*, 2007; Cortes & Amit, 2008).

3.3 Registration

The task of finding an optimal geometric transformation between corresponding image data is known as registration. Bioimage registration is essential in many applications that need to compare multiple image subjects of different conditions. Registration approaches can be classified based on the type of transformation model and image information used (Rohr *et al.*, 2010). The transformation model defines the degrees of freedom for geometrically matching two images, and a main distinction is made between rigid, affine, and nonrigid schemes.

Many of the 2D and 3D image registration methods proposed for medical image analysis, such as the mutual information registration (Viola & Wells, 1997), spline-based elastic registration (Rohr *et al.*, 2003), invariant moment feature-based registration (Shen & Davatzikos, 2002), congealing registration (Miller, 2006; Zollei *et al.*, 2005), etc., can be extended to align the molecular and cellular images (Peng, 2008). Nonrigid or elastic registration approaches are required to cope with the shape changes of live cells (Rohr *et al.*, 2010). An intensity-based nonrigid registration approach for cell microscopy images, which relies on an optic flow scheme and uses segmented images, has been developed recently (Yang *et al.*, 2008). An intensity-based approach has been used to register segmented 2D static images of different cell nuclei (Rohde *et al.*, 2008), and a biomechanical model has been used to register 3D segmented images of cell nuclei (Gladilin *et al.*, 2008). An intensity-based nonrigid registration approach that directly analyses the intensity information without requiring a segmentation step has been developed (Kim *et al.*, 2007). This approach relies on optic flow estimation and has been applied to register 2D and 3D time-lapse images of live cells for accurate analysis of protein particle movement.

3.4 Tracking and motion analysis

Dynamic cell population studies are becoming more and more important in understanding pathways and networks (Glory and Murphy, 2007). Live cell fluorescent video microscopy offers a wealth of information on the dynamic organisation of proteins and subcellular structures that is unavailable in static 2D and 3D imaging. With the addition of time, organelle dynamics as proteins are recruited, transported and expelled can be viewed in detail and the passage through a cell of proteins and the structures that they interact with can be readily observed (Hamilton, 2009). Additionally, the addition of temporal parameters such as the change of size and size of nuclei and the duration between the different stages are important indicators of the cell division cycle (Zhou and Wong, 2006). There is also extensive work on analysing the behaviour of specific labelled proteins by tracking individual objects in time series images (Meijering *et al.*, 2006).

Tracking denotes the repeated localisation of objects in successive images. The aim is to establish temporal correspondences between objects to analyse object motion (Rohr *et al.*, 2010). Although finding correspondences is largely simplified when there is only one object in the images, this task is generally quite challenging when there are several or a large number of moving objects. Therefore, sophisticated multiple target tracking methods are required.

Object tracking from fluorescent video microscopy present many challenges (Hamilton, 2009). Objects viewed may join, split, disappear, change direction or substantially change their morphology, and there are technical challenges such as photobleaching and compromises between spatial and temporal resolution. Tracking algorithms developed in other research areas and adapted to fluorescent video microscopy tend to perform poorly and considerable research has gone into designing algorithms specific to fluorescent imaging (reviewed in Kalaidzidis, 2009).

3.5 Classification

A last step in image analysis is to distinguish objects into different classes. Automatic classification methods can be divided into supervised and unsupervised learning methods (Glory & Murphy, 2007). Supervised learning methods allow classification into predefined classes and require training of the classifier with a set of annotated examples. In unsupervised learning methods, the classes do not need to be known in advance. Supervised learning methods are used for cell microscopy since the classes are known in advance. Common used classifiers are artificial neural networks (Boland & Murphy, 2001), *k*-nearest-neighbour classifiers (Chen *et al.*, 2006), and support vector machines (Conrad *et al.*, 2004; Huang & Murphy, 2004; Harder *et al.*, 2008).

4. Biological network analysis

4.1 Network modelling

Network modelling is a key step for processing dynamic proteomics data, because a network model provides: (i) a means of understanding how detected proteins are associated with underlying network operations, and (ii) a platform into which other useful information, (such as protein abundances and localisation) can be integrated.

A cell is an enormous complex entity made up by myriad interacting molecular components that perform the biochemical reactions that maintain life. A cell can be described through the set of interconnections between its component molecules according to the network hypothesis (De Los Rios & Vendruscolo, 2010). The central dogma in molecular biology describes the way in which a cell processes the information required to produce the molecules necessary to maintain life and reproduce (Crick, 1970). In order to obtain a more complete description of the functioning of a cell, a deeper understanding of the manner in which the sets of interconnections between these molecules are defining the identity of the cell itself is needed (De Los Rios & Vendruscolo, 2010). Therefore, it is important to investigate whether the genetic makeup of an organism does not only specify the rules for generating proteins, but also the way in which these proteins interact among themselves and with the other molecules in a cell. Networks provide a way to organise and regulate efficiently complex systems. In an effective network different parts are linked by reducing at a minimum the number of interconnections. A network is also a powerful method to represent the data in one object and to enable the quantitative assessment of the fragility or robustness of the system. The biological molecules in a cellular system are individual molecules, which affect each other by pairwise interactions (Chen *et al.*, 2009). A cascade of those pairwise interactions forms a local structure (i.e. a linear pathway or a subnetwork), which transforms local perturbations into a functional response. All linear pathways or subnetworks are assembled into a global biomolecular network, which eventually generates global behaviours and holds responsability for complicated life in a living organism.

Gene products, such as mRNA and proteins, are produced through the transcription and translation processes. Gene, mRNA, and protein are known as biological molecules or basic components (Chen *et al.*, 2009). The complicated relations and interactions between these components are responsible for diverse cellular functions. Transcription factors (TFs) are DNA-binding proteins that can activate or inhibit the transcription of genes to synthesise mRNAs by regulating the activities of genes. Since these TFs themselves are products of genes, the final effect is that genes regulate each other's expression as part of a transcription (or translational) regulatory network (TRN) or gene regulatory network (GRN). At the proteome level, proteins participate in diverse posttranslational modifications of other proteins or form protein complexes and pathways together with other proteins. Such local associations between proteins molecules are called protein-protein interactions (PPIs), which form a protein interaction network. The biochemical reactions in cellular metabolism can likewise be integrated into a metabolic network whose fluxes are regulated by enzymes that catalyse the reactions. In many cases, these interactions at different levels are integrated into a signaling network.

Multiple proteins in a cell are in dynamic interaction with each other, and these interactions provide functioning and behaviour of living cells (Terentiev *et al.*, 2009). Reversible protein-protein interactions are among other dynamic processes that proceed in a cell and contribute to cell functioning. The whole set of protein-protein interactions of a given organism is referred to as the "interactome". Structural organisation of interactomes and the total number of interactions in them are important factors that determine complexity of biological systems. The number of copies of a certain protein per cell can vary from several tens to millions (Ghaemmaghami *et al.*, 2003). Interactomes even of simple organisms can be formed by a rather large number of interactions. The determination of physically interacting protein pairs makes it possible to design interactome maps as graphs consisting of nodes, in which a particular protein is located, and of links between them that indicate paired interactions. The interactome maps are considered as keys to obtain knowledge on protein functioning (Rual *et al.*, 2005).

4.2 Integration of biological networks
4.2.1 Network visualisation and analysis
Many tools exist for visually exploring networks and network analysis, including examples such as Cytoscape (Shannon *et al.*, 2003), VisANT (Hu *et al.*, 2009), Osprey (Breitkreutz *et al.*,

2003), CellDesigner (Kitano *et al.*, 2005), BioLayout (Goldovsky *et al.*, 2005), GenMAPP (Dahlquist *et al.*, 2002), PIANA (Aragues *et al.*, 2006), ProViz (Iragne *et al.*, 2005), and Patika (Demir *et al.*, 2002). These systems play a key role in the development of integrative biology, systems biology and integrative bioinformatics. The trend in the development of these tools is to go beyond static representations of cellular states, towards a more dynamic model of cellular processes through the incorporation of gene expression data, subcellular localisation information and time-dependent behaviour (Suderman & Hallett, 2007).

Cytoscape is an open source software project for integrating biomolecular interaction networks with high-throughput expression data and other molecular states into a unified conceptual framework (Shannon *et al.*, 2003). In Cytoscape, nodes representing biological entities, such as proteins or genes, are connected with edges representing pairwise interactions, such as experimentally determined protein–protein interactions. Nodes and edges can have associated data attributes describing properties of the protein or interaction. A key feature of Cytoscape is its ability to set visual aspects of nodes and edges, such as shape, color and size, based on attribute values. This data-to-visual attribute mapping allows biologists to synoptically view multiple types of data in a network context. Additionally, Cytoscape allows users to extend its functionality by creating or downloading additional software modules known as "plugins".

VisANT is a web-based software framework for visualising and analysing many types of networks of biological interactions and associations (Hu *et al.*, 2005). Given user-defined sets of interactions or groupings between genes or proteins, VisANT provides: (i) a visual interface for combining and annotating network data, (ii) supporting function and annotation data for different genomes from the Gene Ontology and KEGG databases, and (iii) the statistical and analytical tools needed for extracting topological properties of the user-defined networks. The new VisANT (v3.5) functions can be classified into three categories (Hu *et al.*, 2009). (i) Visualisation: a new tree-based browser allows visualisation of GO hierarchies. GO terms can be easily dropped into the network to group genes annotated under the term, thereby integrating the hierarchical ontology with the network. This facilitates multi-scale visualisation and analysis. (ii) Flexible annotation schema: in addition to conventional methods for annotating network nodes with the most specific functional descriptions available; VisANT also provides functions to annotate genes at any customized level of abstraction. (iii) Finding over-represented GO terms and expression-enriched GO modules: two new algorithms have been implemented as VisANT plugins. One detects over-represented GO annotations in any given sub-network and the other finds the GO categories that are enriched in a specified phenotype or perturbed dataset. Both algorithms take account of network topology (i.e. correlations between genes based on various sources of evidence).

Osprey is a Java-based network visualisation and analysis tool for protein-protein and genetic interaction networks (Breitkreutz *et al.*, 2003). Osprey builds data-rich graphical representations that are color-coded for gene function and experimental interaction data. Mouse-over functions allow rapid elaboration and organisation of network diagrams in a spoke model format. User-defined large-scale datasets can be readily combined with Osprey for comparison of different methods.

GenMAPP is a free computer application designed to visualise gene expression and other genomic data on maps representing biological pathways and groupings of genes (Dahlquist *et al.*, 2002). Integrated with GenMAPP are programs to perform a global analysis of gene expression or genomic data in the context of hundreds of pathway MAPPs and thousands of

Gene Ontology Terms (MAPPFinder), import lists of genes/proteins to build new MAPPs (MAPPBuilder), and export archives of MAPPs and expression/genomic data to the web. The main features underlying GenMAPP are: (i) draw pathways with easy to use graphics tools, (ii) color genes on MAPP files based on user-imported genomic data, (iii) query data against MAPPs and the GeneOntology.

CellDesigner is a structured diagram editor for drawing gene-regulatory and biochemical networks (Kitano *et al.*, 2005). Networks are drawn based on the process diagram, with graphical notation system proposed by Kitano, and are stored using the Systems Biology Markup Language (SBML), a standard for representing models of biochemical and gene-regulatory networks. Networks are able to link with simulation and other analysis packages through Systems Biology Workbench (SBW). CellDesigner supports simulation and parameter scan by an integration with SBML ODE Solver and Copasi. By using CellDesigner, you can browse and modify existing SBML models with references to existing databases, simulate and view the dynamics through an intuitive graphical interface.

BioLayout uses a general approach for the representation and analysis of networks of variable type, size and complexity (Goldovsky *et al.*, 2005). The application is based on the original BioLayout program (C-language implementation of the Fruchterman-Rheingold layout algorithm), entirely re-written in Java to guarantee portability across platforms. BioLayout(Java) provides broader functionality, various analysis techniques, extensions for better visualisation and a new user interface.

PIANA (Protein Interactions And Network Analysis) facilitates working with protein interaction networks by (i) integrating data from multiple sources, (ii) providing a library that handles graph-related tasks and (iii) automating the analysis of protein-protein interaction networks (Aragues *et al.*, 2006). PIANA can also be used as a stand-alone application to create protein interaction networks and perform tasks such as predicting protein interactions and helping to identify spots in a 2D electrophoresis gel.

ProViz is a tool for the visualisation of protein-protein interaction networks, developed by the IntAct European project (Iragne *et al.*, 2005). It provides facilities for navigating in large graphs and exploring biologically relevant features, and adopts emerging standards such as GO and PSI-MI.

Patika (Pathway Analysis Tool for Integration and Knowledge Acquisition) is based on an ontology for a comprehensive representation of cellular events (Demir *et al.*, 2002). The ontology enables integration of fragmented or incomplete pathway information and supports manipulation and incorporation of the stored data, as well as multiple levels of abstraction. Patika is composed of a server-side, scalable, object-oriented database and client-side editors to provide an integrated, multi-user environment for visualising and manipulating network of cellular events. This tool features automated pathway layout, functional computation support, advanced querying and a user-friendly graphical interface.

4.2.2 Subcellular localisation

Interesting tools that take into account the subcellular localisation are (Suderman & Hallett, 2007): the Cytoscape plugin Cerebral (Barsky *et al.*, 2007), Patika (Demir *et al.*, 2002; see 4.2.1), and Cell Illustrator (Nagasaki *et al.*, 2010). Cerebral (Cell Region-Based Rendering and Layout) is an open-source Java plugin for the Cytoscape biomolecular interaction viewer. Given an interaction network and subcellular annotation, Cerebral automatically generates a view of the network in the style of traditional pathway diagrams, providing an intuitive interface for the exploration of a biological pathways or system. The molecules are separated into layers according to their subcellular localisation. Potential products or outcomes of the pathway can be shown at the bottom of the view, clustered according to any molecular attribute data-protein function, for example. Celebral scales well to networks containing thousands of nodes.

Patika partitions the drawing space into regions corresponding to the subcellular localisations and then search for layouts where nodes are forcibly constrained to their respective locations (Demir *et al.*, 2002). It makes use of a modified force-directed algorithm to achieve this.

Cell Illustrator is a software platform for systems biology that uses the concept of Petri net for modeling and simulating biopathways (Nagasaki *et al.*, 2010). It is intended for biological scientists working at bench. The recent version of Cell Illustrator 4.0 uses Java Web Start technology and is enhanced with new capabilities, including: automatic graph grid layout algorithms using ontology information; tools using Cell System Markup Language (CSML) 3.0 and Cell System Ontology 3.0; parameter search module; high-performance simulation module; CSML database management system; conversion from CSML model to programming languages (FORTRAN, C, C++, Java, Python and Perl); import from SBML, CellML, and BioPAX; and, export to SVG and HTML. Cell Illustrator employs an extension of hybrid Petri net in an object-oriented style so that biopathway models can include objects such as DNA sequence, molecular density, 3D localisation information, transcription with frame-shift, translation with codon table, as well as biochemical reactions.

4.2.3 Network integration for cellular microarray data using Cytoscape

Data from cellular microarray experiments include a list of differentially expressed proteins, i.e. changed fluorescence intensity (protein abundance), as a function of time and localisation in the cell. Integration of these data with other available biological network data for a specific organism can be performed using the above listed software platforms (see 4.2.1), e.g. by using Cytoscape supplemented with the available plugins.

The cellular microarray data can be mapped to the protein interactome. Network data related to these proteins can be imported into Cytoscape using three options: querying interaction databases using cPath (Cerami *et al.*, 2006), building an association network through text mining using Agilent Literature Search plugin (Vailaya *et al.*, 2005), and loading own network data from a text file. Additionally, pathways from repositories, such as KEGG (Wixon & Kell, 2000), Reactome (Joshi-Tope *et al.*, 2005) via the PSI-MI, BioPAX, or SBML data exchange formats (Strömbäck *et al.*, 2006), can be imported.

Networks can be analysed further using topologic information, and using combined information of various types, such as GO annotations and known pathways. Network modules enriched by GO terms and pathways (functional enrichment) can be identified. Therefore, the Cytoscape plugins BiNGO (Maere *et al.*, 2005) and DAVID (Dennis *et al.*, 2003; Huang da *et al.*, 2009) can be employed. GO Biologic Process (GOBP) trees with nodes corresponding to GOBP terms is generated using the BiNGO plugin. GOBP terms that differ in terms of their degrees of enrichment can be identified, as can sets of network nodal proteins belonging to such GOBP terms. Pathways enrichment analysis can be performed for network nodal proteins using DAVID.

Network structures and active subnetworks can be explored using the Cytoscape plugins MCODE (Bader *et al.*, 2003) and jActiveModules (Ideker *et al.*, 2002). The MCODE-plugin can be used to generate network clusters within which proteins are densely connected, whereas proteins across different network clusters loosely interact. Both the core network modules and their dynamic relationships can be identified by integrating time-dependent protein abundance information. In addition, active networks can be identified among network modules using jActiveModules, which select networks with high collective abundances.

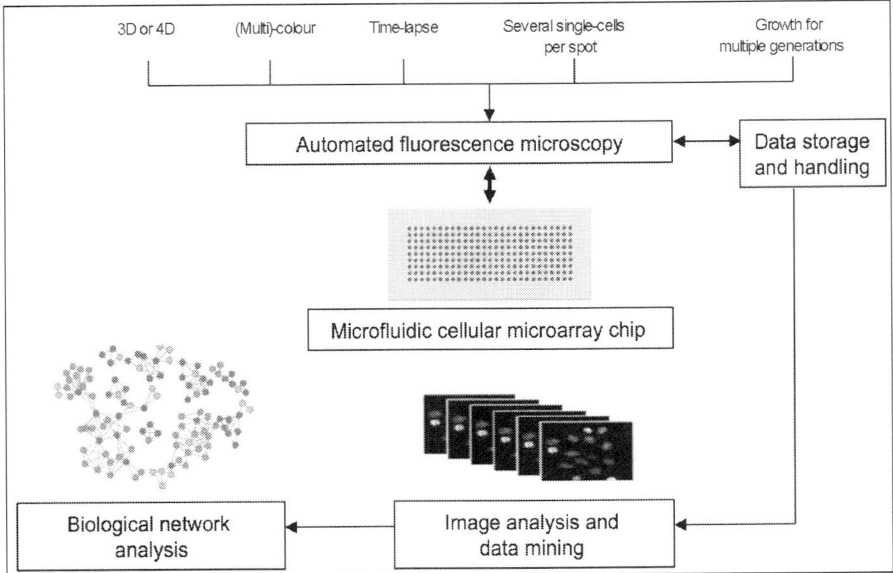

Fig. 1. Work scheme for on-chip cellular microarray screening and biological network analysis.

5. Summary

In this chapter, on-chip living-cell microarrays to study network biology is reviewed. A general work scheme is shown in Figure 1. Microfluidic technology holds great promise for the creation of advanced cell culture models. It can be used — in combination with time-lapse fluorescent microscopy, and image analysis and data mining — to observe multiple cellular components over time in individual cells, i.e. dynamics of a FP-tagged protein. Integration of dynamic localisomics data with other avialable biological network data allows performing a quantitative system-wide analysis for a particular cell.

Cell assays in microfluidic chips that have been used for cellular microarrays are discussed in detail in this chapter. Next, image analysis algorithms to extract dynamic proteomics data from cellular microarray experiments are reviewed. In the last part, the integration of the cellular microarray data into a network model, as well as network analysis options are discussed.

6. Acknowledgment

R. Willaert is supported by the Belgian Federal Science Policy Office and European Space Agency (ESA) PRODEX program, the Institute for the Promotion of Innovation by Science and Technology in Flanders (IWT) and the Research Council of the VUB.

7. References

Anderson, J.R., Chiu, D.T., Jackman, R.J., Cherniavskaya, O., McDonald, J.C., Wu, H., Whitesides, S.H., & Whitesides, G.M. (2000) Fabrication of topologically complex three-dimensional microfluidic systems in PDMS by rapid prototyping. *Anal. Chem.*, Vol. 72, pp. 3158-3164.

Anderson, D.G., Levenberg, S., & Langer, R. (2004) Nanoliter-scale synthesis of arrayed biomaterials and application to human embryonic stem cells. *Nature Biotechnol.*, Vol. 22, pp. 863-866.

Angres, B. (2005) Cell microarrays. *Expert. Rev. Mol. Diagn.*, Vol. 5, pp. 769-779.

Aragues, R., Jaeggi, D., & Oliva, B. (2006) PIANA: protein interactions and network analysis. *Bioinformatics*, Vol. 22, pp. 1015-1017.

Bader, G.D., & Hogue, C.W. (2003) An automated method for finding molecular complexes in large protein interaction networks. *BMC Bioinformatics*, Vol. 4, pp. 2.

Bakal, C., Aach, J., Church, G., & Perrimon, N. (2007) Quantitative morphological signatures define local signaling networks regulating cell morphology. *Science*, Vol. 316, pp. 1753-1756.

Barbulovic-Nad, I., Lucente, M., Sun, Y., Zhang, M., Wheeler, A.R., & Bussmann, M. (2006) Bio-microarray fabrication techniques - a review. *Crit. Rev. Biotechnol.*, Vol. 26, pp. 237-259.

Barbulovic-Nad, I., & Wheeler, A.R. (2008) Cell assays in microfluidics. In: *Encyclopedia of microfluidics and nanofluidics*. D. Li (Dd.), 209-216, Springer, New York, USA.

Barsky, A., Gardy, J.L., Hancock, R.E., & Munzner, T. (2007) Cerebral: a Cytoscape plugin for layout of and interaction with biological networks using subcellular localization annotation. *Bioinformatics*, Vol. 23, pp. 1040-1042.

Becker, H., & Gärtner, C. (2008) Polymer microfabrication technologies for microfluidic systems. *Anal. Bioanal. Chem.*, Vol. 390, pp. 89-111.

Belien, J.A.M., Ginkel, H.A.H.M., Tekola, P., Ploeger, L.S., Poulin, N.M., Baak, J.P.A., & Diest, P.J. (2002) Confocal DNA Cytometry: A Contour-Based Segmentation Algorithm for Automated Three-Dimensional Image Segmentation. *Cytometry*, Vol. 49, pp. 12-21.

Berglund, L., Björling, E., Oksvold, P., Fagerberg, L., Asplund, A., Al-Khalili Szigyarto, C., Persson, A., Ottosson, J., Wernérus, H., Nilsson, P., Lundberg, E., Sivertsson, A., Navani S., Wester K., Kampf C., Hober S., Pontén F., & Uhlén M. (2008) A gene-centric human protein atlas for expression profiles based on antibodies. *Mol. Cell Proteomics*, Vol. 7, pp. 2019-2027.

Biran, I., Rissin, D.M., Ron, E.Z., & Walt, D.R. (2003) Optical imaging fiber-based live bacterial cell array biosensor. *Anal. Biochem.*, Vol. 315, pp. 106-113.

Bochner, B.R., Gadzinski, P., & Panomitros, E. (2001) Phenotype microarrays for high-throughput phenotypic testing and assay of gene function. *Genome Res.*, Vol. 11, pp. 1246-1255.

Breitkreutz, B.J., Stark, C., & Tyers, M. (2003) Osprey: a network visualization system. *Genome Biol.*, Vol. 4, pp. R22.

Breslauer, D.N., Lee, P.J., & Lee, L.P. (2006) Microfluidics-based systems biology. *Mol. BioSyst.*, Vol. 2, pp. 97-112.

Cai, L., Friedman, N., & Xie, S. (2006) Stochastic protein expression in individual cells at the single molecule level. *Nature*, Vol. 440, pp. 358-362.

Cannell, M.B., McMorland, & A. Soeller, C. (2006) Emage enhancement by deconvolution. In: Handbook of biological confocal microscopy. J.B. Pawley (Ed.), 488-500, Speinger Science+Business Media, LCC, New York, ISBN 987-0387-25921-5.

Cerami, E.G., Bader, G.D., Gross, B.E., & Sander, C. (2006) cPath: open source software for collecting, storing, and querying biological pathways. BMC Bioinformatics, Vol. 7, pp. 497.

Charvin, G., Cross, F.R., & Siggia, E.D. (2009) Forced periodic expression of G1 cyclins phase-locks the budding yeast cell cycle. *Proc. Natl. Acad. Sci. USA*, Vol. 106, pp. 6632-6637.

Chen, D.S., & Davis, M.M. (2006) Molecular and functional analysis using live cell microarrays. *Curr. Opin. Chem. Biol.*, Vol. 10, pp. 28-34.

Chen, L., Wang R.-S., & Zhang, X.-S. (2009) Biomolecular networks: methods and applications in systens biology. John Wiley & Sons, ISBN 978-0-470-24373-2, Hoboken, New Jersey.

Chen, X., Zhou, X., & Wong, S.T. (2006) Automated segmentation, classification, and tracking of cancer cell nuclei in time-lapse microscopy. *IEEE Trans Biomed. Eng.*, Vol. 53, pp. 762-766.

Cheong, R., Wang, C.J., & Levchenko, A. (2009) Using a microfluidic device for high-content analysis of cell signaling. *Sci Signal.*, Vol. 2, pp. pl2.

Chin, V.I., Taupin, P., Sanga, S., Scheel, J., Gage, F.H., & Bhatia, S.N. (2004) Microfabricated platform for studying stem cell fates. *Biotechnol. Bioeng.*, Vol. 88, pp. 399-415.

Chung, B.G., Flanagan, L.A., Rhee, S.W., Schwartz, P.H., Lee, A.P., Monuki, E.S., & Jeon, N.L. (2005) Human neural stem cell growth and differentiation in a gradient-generating microfluidic device. *Lab Chip*, Vol. 5, pp. 401-406.

Conrad, C., Erfle, H., Warnat, P., Daigle, N., Lörch, T., Ellenberg, J., Pepperkok, R., & Eils, R. (2004) Automatic identification of subcellular phenotypes on human cell arrays. *Genome Res.*, Vol. 14, pp. 1130-1136.

Conrad, C., Wünsche, A., Tan, T.H., Bulkescher, J., Sieckmann, F., Verissimo, F., Edelstein, A., Walter, T., Liebel, U., Pepperkok, R., & Ellenberg, J. (2011) Micropilot: automation of fluorescence microscopy-based imaging for systems biology. *Nature Methods*, Vol. 8, pp. 246-249.

Cortés, L, & Amit, Y. (2008) Efficient annotation of vesicle dynamics video microscopy. *IEEE Trans. Pattern Anal. Mach. Intell.*, Vol. 30, pp. 1998-2010.

Crick, F. (1958) On protein synthesis. *The Symposia of the Society for Experimental Biology, Vol.* 12, pp. 138-163.

Crick, F. (1970) Central dagma of molecular biology. *Nature*, Vol. 227, pp. 561-563.

Dahlquist, K.D., Salomonis, N., Vranizan, K., Lawlor, S.C., & Conklin, B.R. (2002) GenMAPP, a new tool for viewing and analyzing microarray data on biological pathways. *Nat. Genet.*, Vol. 31, pp. 19-20.

De Los Rios, P. & Vendruscolo, M. (2010) Network views of the cell. In: *Networks in Systems Biology*, M. Buchanan, G. Caldarelli, P. De Los Rios, F. Rao & M. Vendruscolo, (Eds.), 4-13, Cambridge University Press, ISBN 978-0-521-88273-6.

Demir, E., Babur, O., Dogrusoz, U., Gursoy, A., Nisanci, G., Cetin-Atalay, R., & Ozturk, M. (2002) PATIKA: an integrated visual environment for collaborative construction and analysis of cellular pathways. *Bioinformatics*, Vol. 18, pp. 996-1003.

Dennis, G. Jr, Sherman, B.T., Hosack, D.A., Yang, J., Gao, W., Lane, H.C., & Lempicki, R.A. (2003) DAVID: Database for Annotation, Visualization, and Integrated Discovery. *Genome Biol.*, Vol. 4, pp. P3.

De Solorzano, C.O., Malladi, R., Lelievre, S.A., & Lockett, S.J. (2001) Segmentation of nuclei and cells using membrane related protein markers. *J. Microsc.*, Vol. 201, pp. 404-415.

Dittrich, P.S., & Manz, A. (2006) Lab-on-a-chip: microfluidics in drug discovery. *Nat. Rev. Drug Discov.*, Vol. 5, pp. 210-218.

Dorn, J.F., Danuser, G., & Yang, G. (2008) Computational processing and analysis of dynamic fluorescence image data. *Methods Cell Biol.*, Vol. 85, pp. 497-538.

Dufour, A., Shinin, V., Tajbakhsh, S., Guillen-Aghion, N., Olivo-Marin, J.C., & Zimmer, C. (2005) Segmentation and Tracking Fluorescent Cells in Dynamic 3-D Microscopy with Coupled Active Surfaces. *IEEE Trans Image Processing*, Vol. 14, pp. 1396-1410.

Ekins, R., Chu, F., & Biggart, E. (1989) Development of microspot multi-analyte ratiometric immunoassay using dual fluorescent-labelled antibodies. *Anal. Chim. Acta*, Vol. 227, pp. 73-96.

Fernandes, T.G., Diogo, M.M., Clark, D.S., Dordick, J.S., & Cabral, J.M. (2009) High-throughput cellular microarray platforms: applications in drug discovery, toxicology and stem cell research. *Trends Biotechnol.*, Vol. 27, pp. 342-349.

Fernandes, T.G., Kwon, S.J., Bale, S.S., Lee, M.Y., Diogo, M.M., Clark, D.S., Cabral, J.M., & Dordick, J.S. (2010) Three-dimensional cell culture microarray for high-throughput studies of stem cell fate. *Biotechnol. Bioeng.*, Vol. 106, pp. 106-118.

Franssila, S. (2010) Introduction to microfabrication. Second edition. John Wiley & Sons, Chichester, UK.

Frenkel-Morgenstern, M., Cohen, A.A., Geva-Zatorsky, N., Eden, E., Prilusky, J., Issaeva, I., Sigal, A., Cohen-Saidon, C., Liron, Y., Cohen, L., Danon, T., Perzov, N., & Alon, U. (2010) Dynamic Proteomics: a database for dynamics and localizations of endogenous fluorescently-tagged proteins in living human cells. *Nucleic Acids Res.*, Vol. 38(Database issue), pp. D508-512.

Ghaemmaghami, S., Huh, W.K., Bower, K., Howson, R.W., Belle, A., Dephoure, N., O'Shea, E.K., & Weissman, J.S. (2003) Global analysis of protein expression in yeast. *Nature* Vol. 425, pp. 737-741.

Gladilin, E., Goetze, S., Mateos-Langerak, J., Van Driel, R., Eils, R., & Rohr, K. (2008) Shape normalization of 3D cell nuclei using elastic spherical mapping. *J. Microsc.*, Vol. 231, pp. 105-114.

Glory, E., & Murphy, R.F. (2007) Automated subcellular location determination and high-throughput microscopy. *Dev. Cell.*, Vol. 12, pp. 7-16.

Godinez, W.J., Lampe, M., Worz, S., Muller, B., Eils, R., & Rohr, K. (2007) Tracking of virus particles in time-lapse fluorescence microscopy image sequences. *Proc. IEEE Int. Symp. Biomed. Imaging*, pp. 272-299.

Goldovsky, L., Cases, I., Enright, A.J., & Ouzounis, C.A. (2005) BioLayout(Java): versatile network visualisation of structural and functional relationships. *Appl. Bioinformatics*, Vol. 4, pp. 71-74.

Gómez-Sjöberg, R., Leyrat, A.A., Pirone, D.M., Chen, C.S., & Quake, S.R. (2007) Versatile, fully automated, microfluidic cell culture system. *Anal. Chem.*, Vol. 79, pp. 8557-8563.

Hamilton, N. (2009) Quantification and its applications in fluorescent microscopy imaging. *Traffic.*, Vol. 10, pp. 951-961.

Harder, N., Eils, R., & Rohr, K. (2008) Automated classification of mitotic phenotypes of human cells using fluorescent proteins. *Methods Cell Biol.*, Vol. 85, pp. 539-554.

Heiskanen, A., Emnéus, J., & Dufva, M. (2010) In: *Microfluidic based Microsystems: fundamentals and applications*. S. Kakac, B. Kosey, D. Li, Pramuanjaroenkij (Eds.), 427-452, Spinger Science + Business Media B.V., Dordrecht, The Netherlands.

Hu, Z., Hung, J.H., Wang, Y., Chang, Y.C., Huang, C.L., Huyck, M., & DeLisi, C. (2009) VisANT 3.5: multi-scale network visualization, analysis and inference based on the gene ontology. *Nucleic Acids Res.*, Vol. 37(Web Server issue), pp. W115-121.

Huang, K., Lin, J., Gajnak, J.A., & Murphy, R.F. (2002) Image Content-based Retrieval and Automated Interpretation of Fluorescence Microscope Images via the Protein Subcellular Location Image Database. *Proc 2002 IEEE Intl Symp Biomed Imaging* (ISBI 2002), pp. 325-328.

Huang da, W., Sherman, B.T., & Lempicki, R.A. (2009) Systematic and integrative analysis of large gene lists using DAVID bioinformatics resources. *Nat. Protoc.*, Vol. 4, pp. 44-57.

Huang, K., & Murphy, R.F. (2004) Boosting accuracy of automated classification of fluorescence microscope images for location proteo- mics. *BMC Bioinformatics*, Vol. 5, pp. 78.

Huh, W.K., Falvo, J.V., Gerke, L.C., Carroll, A.S., Howson, R.W., Weissman, J.S., & O'Shea, E.K. (2003) Global analysis of protein localization in budding yeast. *Nature*, Vol. 425, pp. 686-691.

Hung, P.J., Lee, P.J., Sabounchi, P., Lin, R., & Lee, L.P. (2005) Continuous perfusion microfluidic cell culture array for high-throughput cell-based assays. *Biotechnol. Bioeng.*, Vol. 89, pp. 1-8.

Ideker, T., Ozier, O., Schwikowski, B., & Siegel, A.F. (2002) Discovering regulatory and signalling circuits in molecular interaction networks. *Bioinformatics*, Vol. 18 Suppl 1, pp. S233-240.

Iragne, F., Nikolski, M., Mathieu, B., Auber, D., & Sherman, D. (2005) ProViz: protein interaction visualization and exploration. *Bioinformatics*, Vol. 21, pp. 272-274.

Jarvik, J.W., Fisher G.W., Shi C., Hennen L., Hauser C., Adler S., & Berget P.B. (2002) *In vivo* functional proteomics: Mammalian genome annotation using CD-tagging. *BioTechniques*, Vol. 33, pp. 852-866

Joshi-Tope, G., Gillespie, M., Vastrik, I., D'Eustachio, P., Schmidt, E., de Bono, B., Jassal, B., Gopinath, G.R., Wu, G.R., Matthews, L., Lewis, S., Birney, E., & Stein, L. (2005) Reactome: a knowledgebase of biological pathways. *Nucleic Acids Res.*, Vol. 33(Database issue), pp. D428-432.

Joyce, A.R. & Palsson, B.Ø. (2006). The model organism as a system: integrating ‚omics' data sets. *Nature Reviews Molecular Cell Biology*, Vol.7, No.4, pp. 198-210.

Kalaidzidis, Y. (2009) Multiple objects tracking in fluorescence microscopy. *J. Math. Biol.*, Vol. 58, pp. 57-80.

Kholodenko, B.N., Hancock, J.F., & Kolch, W. (2010) Signalling ballet in space and time. *Nat. Rev. Mol Cell. Biol.*, Vol. 11, pp. 414-426.

Kim, L., Toh, Y.C., Voldman, J., & Yu, H. (2007) A practical guide to microfluidic perfusion culture of adherent mammalian cells. *Lab Chip*, Vol. 7, pp. 681-694.

Kim, I., Yang, S., Le Baccon, P., Heard, E., Chen, Y.-C., Spector, D., Kappel, C., Eils, R., & Rohr, K. (2007) Non-rigid temporal registration of 2D and 3D multi-channel microscopy image sequences of human cells. *Proc. IEEE Int. Symp. Biomed. Imaging,* pp. 1328-1331.

Kim, L., Vahey, M.D., Lee, H.Y., & Voldman, J. (2006) Microfluidic arrays for logarithmically perfused embryonic stem cell culture. *Lab Chip*, Vol. 6, pp. 394-406.

Kitano, H., Funahashi, A., Matsuoka, Y., & Oda, K. (2005) Using process diagrams for the graphical representation of biological networks. *Nat. Biotechnol.*, Vol. 23, pp. 961-966.

Ko, B., Seo, M., & Nam, J.Y. (2009) Microscopic cell nuclei segmentation based on adaptive attention window. *J. Digit. Imaging.* Vol. 22, pp. 259-274.

Kononen, J., Bubendorf, L., Kallioniemi, A., Bärlund, M., Schraml, P., Leighton, S., Torhorst, J., Mihatsch, M.J., Sauter, G., & Kallioniemi, O.P. (1998) Tissue microarrays for high-throughput molecular profiling of tumor specimens. *Nat. Med.*, Vol. 4, pp. 844-847.

Lee, P.J., & Di Carlo, D. (2009) In: *Single cell analysis: technologies and applications.* D. Anselmetti (ed.), 135-160, Wiley-VCH Verlag GmbH & Co., Weinheim.

Lee, P.J., Hung, P.J., Rao, V.M., & Lee, L.P. (2006) Nanoliter scale microbioreactor array for quantitative cell biology. *Biotechnol. Bioeng.*, Vol. 94, pp. 5-14.

Li, G., Liu, T., Nie, J., Guo, L., Chen, J., Zhu, J., Xia, W., Mara, A., Holley, S., & Wong, S.T. (2008) Segmentation of touching cell nuclei using gradient flow tracking. *J. Microsc.*, Vol. 231, pp. 47-58.

Lidstrom, M.E., & Meldrum, D.R. (2003) Life-on-a-chip. *Nat. Rev. Microbiol.*, Vol. 1, pp. 158-164.

Liebel, U., Starkuviene, V., Erfle, H., Simpson, J.C., Poustka, A., Wiemann, S., & Pepperkok, R. (2003) A microscope-based screening platform for large-scale functional protein analysis in intact cells. *FEBS Letters*, Vol. 554, pp. 394-398.

Lin, G., Chawla, M.K., Olson, K., Guzowski, J.F., Barnes C.A., & Roysam B. (2005) Hierarchical, model-based merging of multiple fragments for improvoed three-dimensional segmentation of nuclei. *Cytometry*, Vol. 63A, pp. 20-33.

Lindblad, J., Wählby, C., Bengtsson, E., & Zaltsman, A. (2004) Image analysis for automatic segmentation of cytoplasms and classification of Rac1 activation. *Cytometry A.* Vol. 57, pp. 22-33.

Locke, J.C., & Elowitz, M.B. (2009) Using movies to analyse gene circuit dynamics in single cells. *Nat. Rev. Microbiol.*, Vol. 7, pp. 383-392.

Maere, S., Heymans, K., & Kuiper, M. (2005) BiNGO: a Cytoscape plugin to assess overrepresentation of Gene Ontology categories in biological networks. *Bioinformatics*, Vol. 21, pp. 3448-3449.

Malpica, N., de Solórzano, C.O., Vaquero, J.J., Santos, A., Vallcorba, I., García-Sagredo, J.M., & del Pozo, F. (1997) Applying watershed algorithms to the segmentation of clustered nuclei. *Cytometry.* Vol. 28, pp. 289-297.

Martone, M.E., Tran, J., Wong, W.W., Sargis, J., Fong, L., Larson, S., Lamont, S.P., Gupta, A., & Ellisman, M.H. (2008) The Cell Centered Database project: An update on building community resources for managing and sharing 3D imaging data. *J. Struct. Biol.*, Vol. 161, pp. 220-231.

Megason, S.G., & Fraser, S.E. (2007) Imaging in systems biology. *Cell*, Vol. 130, pp. 784-795.

Meijering, E., Smal, I., & Danuser, G. (2006) Tracking in biomolecuar imaging. *IEEE Signal Process. Mag.*, Vol. 23, pp. 46-53.

Mettetal, J.T., Muzzey, D., Pedraza, J.M., Ozbudak, E.M., & van Oudenaarden, A. (2006) Predicting stochastic gene expression dynamics in single cells. *Proc. Natl. Acad. Sci. USA*, Vol. 103, pp. 7304-7309.

Miller, E. (2006) Data driven image models through continuous joint alignment. *IEEE Trans. Pattern Anal. Mach. Intell.*, Vol. 28, pp. 236-250.

Nagasaki, M., Saito, A., Jeong, E., Li, C., Kojima, K., Ikeda, E., & Miyano, S. (2010) Cell Illustrator 4.0: A computational platform for systems biology. *In Silico Biol.*, Vol. 10, pp. 0002.

Narayanaswamy, R., Niu, W., Scouras, A.D., Hart, G.T., Davies, J., Ellington, A.D., Iyer, V.R., & Marcotte, E.M. (2006) Systematic profiling of cellular phenotypes with spotted cell microarrays reveals mating-pheromone response genes. *Genome Biol.*, Vol. 7, pp. R6-9.

Newberg, J., Hua, J., & Murphy, R.F. (2009) Location proteomics: systematic determination of protein subcellular location. In: *Methods in Molecular Biology, Systems Biology*, I.V. Maly, (Ed.), 313-332, Humana Press, ISBN 987-1-934115-64-0, New York, NY, USA.

Ortiz de Solorzano, C., Garcia Rodriguez, E., Jones, A., Pinkel, D., Gray, J.W., Sudar, D., & Lockett, S.J. (1999) Segmentation of confocal microscope images of cell nuclei in thick tissue sections. *J. Microsc.*, Vol. 193, pp. 212-226.

Pedraza, J.M., & van Oudenaarden, A. (2005) Noise propagation in gene networks. *Science*, Vol. 307, pp. 1965-1969.

Peng, H. (2008) Bioimage informatics: a new area of engineering biology. *Bioinformatics* Vol. 24, pp. 1827-1836.

Pepperkok, R., & Ellenberg, J. (2006) High-throughput fluorescence microscopy for systems biology. *Nat. Rev. Mol. Biol.*, Vol. 7, pp. 690-696.

Pisani, M.B., & Tadigadapa, S.A. (2010) Microfabrication techniques for microfluidic devices. In: *Methods in Bioengineering: Biomicrofabrication & biomicrofluidics.* J.D. Zahn (Ed), 1-57, Artech House, Boston, USA.

Ponti, A., Vallotton, P., Salmon, W.C., Waterman-Storer, C.M., & Danuser, G. (2003) Computational analysis of F-actin turnover in cortical actin meshworks using fluorescent speckle microscopy. *Biophys J.*, Vol. 84, 3336-3352.

Radhakrishnan, R., Solomon, M., Satyamoorthy, K., Martin, L.E., & Lingen, M.W. (2008) Tissue microarray - a high-throughput molecular analysis in head and neck cancer. *J. Oral Pathol. Med.*, Vol. 37, pp. 166-176.

Raser, J.M., & O'Shea, E.K. (2005) Review: Noise in gene expression: origins, consequences, and control. *Science*, 309, pp. 2010-2013.

Roach, K.L., King, K.R., Uygun, B.E., Kohane, I.S., Yarmush, M.L., & Toner, M. (2009) High throughput single cell bioinformatics. *Biotechnol. Prog.*, Vol. 25, pp. 1772-1779.

Rohde, G.K., Ribeiro, A.J., Dahl, K.N., & Murphy, R.F. (2008) Deformation-based nuclear morphometry: capturing nuclear shape variation in HeLa cells. *Cytometry A.*, Vol. 73, pp. 341-350.

Rohr, K., Godinez, W.J., Harder, N., Wörz, S., Mattes, J., Tvarusko, W., & Eils, R. (2010) Tracking and quantitative analysis of dynamic movement of cells and particles. In: *Live cell imaging: a laboratory manual.* R.D. Goldman, Swedlow, J.R., Spector, D.L. (eds.), 239-256, Cold Spring Harbor Laboratory Press, New York, ISBN 978-0-87969-893-5.

Rohr, K., Fornefett, M., & Stiehl, H.S. (2003) Spline-based elastic image registration, integration of landmark errors and orientation attributes. *Comput. Vis. Image Underst.*, Vol. 90, pp. 153-168.

Rowat, A.C., Bird, J.C., Agresti, J.J., Rando, O.J., & Weitz, D.A. (2009) Tracking lineages of single cells in lines using a microfluidic device. *Proc. Natl. Acad. Sci. USA*, Vol. 106, pp. 18149-18154.

Rual, J.F., Venkatesan, K., Hao T., *et al.* (2005) Towards a proteome-scale map of the human protein-protein interaction network. *Nature*, Vol. 437, pp. 1173-1178.

Sarti, A., de Solorzano, C.O., Locket, S., & Malladi, R. (2000) A Geometric Model for 3-D Confocal Image Analysis. *IEEE Trans Biomedical Engineering*, Vol. 47, pp. 1600-1609.

Sbalzarini, I.F., & Koumoutsakos, P. (2005) Feature point tracking and trajectory analysis for video imaging in cell biology. *J. Struct. Biol.*, Vol. 151, pp. 182-195.

Schubert, W., Bonnekoh, B., Pommer, A.J., Philipsen, L., Böckelmann, R., Malykh, Y., Gollnick, H., Friedenberger, M., Bode, M., & Dress, A.W. (2006) Analyzing proteome topology and function by automated multidimensional fluorescence microscopy. *Nature Biotechnology*, Vol. 24, pp. 1270-1278.

Shannon, P., Markiel, A., Ozier, O., Baliga, NS., Wang, J.T., Ramage, D., Amin, N., Schwikowski, B., & Ideker, T. (2003) Cytoscape: a software environment for integrated models of biomolecular interaction networks. *Genome Res.*, Vol. 13(11), pp. 2498-2504.

Shariff, A., Kangas, J., Coelho, L.P., Quinn, S., & Murphy, R.F. (2010) Automated image analysis for high-content screening and analysis. *J. Biomol. Screen.*, Vol. 15, pp. 726-734.

Shen, D., & Davatzikos, C. (2002) HAMMER: heirarchical attribute matching mechanism for elastic registration. *IEEE Trans. Med. Imaging*, Vol. 21, pp. 1421-1439.

Souchelnytskyi, S. (2005) Bridging proteomics and systems biology: what are the roads to be traveled? *Proteomics*, Vol. 5, pp. 4123-4137.

Strömbäck, L., Jakoniene, V., Tan, H., & Lambrix, P. (2006) Representing, storing and accessing molecular interaction data: a review of models and tools. *Brief Bioinform.*, Vol. 7, pp. 331-338.

Suderman, M, & Hallett, M. (2007) Tools for visually exploring biological networks. *Bioinformatics*, Vol. 23, pp. 2651-2659.

Sui, G., Lee, C., Kamei, K., Li, H., Wang, J-Y., Wang, J., Herschman, H.R., & Tseng, H. (2007) A microfluidic platform for sequential ligand labeling and cell binding analysis. Biomed. *Microdevices*, Vol. 9, pp. 301-305.

Swedlow, J.R., Goldberg, I.G., & Eliceiri, K.W. (2009) OME Consortium. Bioimage informatics for experimental biology. *Annu. Rev. Biophys.* Vol. 38, pp. 327-346.

Taniguchi, Y., Choi, P.J., Li, G.W., Chen, H., Babu, M., Hearn, J., Emili, A., & Xie, X.S. (2010) Quantifying *E. coli* proteome and transcriptome with single-molecule sensitivity in single cells. *Science*, Vol. 329, pp. 533-538.

Tay, S., Hughey, J.J., Lee, T.K., Lipniacki, T., Quake, S.R., & Covert, M.W. (2010) Single-cell NF-kappaB dynamics reveal digital activation and analogue information processing. *Nature*, Vol. 466, pp. 267-271.

Terentiev, A.A., Moldogazieva, N.T., & Shaitan, K.V. (2009) Dynamic proteomics in modeling of the living cell. Protein-protein interactions. *Biochemistry (Mosc)*, Vol. 74, pp. 1586-607.

Thompson, D.M., King, K.R., Wieder, K.J., Toner, M., Yarmush, M.L., & Jayaraman, A. (2004) Dynamic gene expression profiling using a microfabricated living cell array. *Anal. Chem.*, Vol. 76, pp. 4098-4103.

Schwenk, J.M., Stoll, D., Templin, M.F., & Joos, T.O. (2002) Cell microarrays: an emerging technology for the characterization of antibodies. *Biotechniques*, Dec, Suppl, pp. 54-61.

Taniguchi, Y., Choi, P.J., Li, G, Chen, H., Babu, M., Hearn, J., Emili, A., & Xie, X.S. (2010) Quantifying *E. coli* proteome and trancriptome with single-molecule sensitivity in single cells. *Science*, Vol. 329, pp. 533-538.

Umesh Adiga, P.S., & Chaudhuri, B.B. (2001) An efficient method based on watershed and rule-based merging for segmentation of 3-D histo-pathological images. *Pattern Recognition*, Vol. 34, pp. 1449-1458.

Vailaya, A., Bluvas, P., Kincaid, R., Kuchinsky, A., Creech, M., & Adler, A. (2005) An architecture for biological information extraction and representation. Bioinformatics, Vol. 21, pp. 430-438.

Velve-Casquillas, G., Le Berre, M., Piel, M., & Tran, P.T. (2010) Microfluidic tools for cell biological research. *Nano Today*, Vol. 5, pp. 28-47.

Verveer, P.J., & Bastiaens, P.I. (2008) Quantitative microscopy and systems biology: seeing the whole picture. *Histochem. Cell Biol.*, Vol. 130, pp. 833-843.

Viola, P., & Wells, W.M. (1997) Alignment by maximization of mutual information. *Int. J. Comput. Vis.*, Vol. 24, pp. 137-154.

Wählby, C., Sintorn, I.M., Erlandsson, F., Borgefors, G., & Bengtsson, E. (2004) Combining intensity, edge and shape information for 2D and 3D segmentation of cell nuclei in tissue sections. *J. Microsc.*, Vol. 215, pp. 67-76.

Weibel, D.B., DiLuzio, W.R., & Whitesides, G.M. (2007) Microfabrication meets microbiology. *Nat. Rev. Microbiol.*, Vol. 5, pp. 209-218.

West, J., Becker, M., Tombrink, S., & Manz, A. (2008) Micro total analysis systems: latest achievements. *Anal. Chem.*, Vol. 80, pp. 4403-4419.

Whitesides, G.M., Ostuni, E., Takayama, S., Jiang, X., & Ingber, D.E. (2001) Soft lithography in biology and biochemistry. *Annu. Rev. Biomed. Eng.*, Vol. 3, pp. 335-373.

Whitesides, G.M. (2006) The origins and the future of microfluidics. *Nature*, Vol. 442, pp. 368-373.

Wieder, K.J., King, K.R., Thompson, D.M., Zia, C., Yarmush, M.L., & Jayaraman, A. (2005) Optimization of reporter cells for expression profiling in a microfluidic device. *Biomed. Microdevices*, Vol. 7, pp. 213-222.

Wixon, J., & Kell, D. (2000) The Kyoto encyclopedia of genes and genomes--KEGG. *Yeast*, Vol. 17, pp. 48-55.

Xu, C.W. (2002) High-density cell microarrays for parallel functional determinations. *Genome Res.*, Vol. 12, pp. 482-486.

Yang, S., Kohler, D., Teller, K., Cremer, T., Le Baccon, P., Heard, E., Eils, R., & Rohr, K. (2008) Nonrigid registration of 3-d multichannel microscopy images of cell nuclei. *IEEE Trans Image Process*, Vol. 17, 493-499.

Yu J., Xiao J., Ren X., Lao K., & Xie S. (2006) Probing gene expression in live cells, one protein molecule at a time. *Science*, Vol. 311, pp. 1600-1603.

Zhou, X., & Wong, S.T.C. (2006) High content cellular imaging for drug development. *IEEE Signal Process. Mag.*, Vol. 23, pp. 170-174.

Zhou, X., & Wong, S.T.C. (2008) A primer on image informatrics of high content screening. In: *High Content Screening*. S. Haney (Ed.), 43-84, John Wiley & Sons, Hoboken, ISBN 978-0-470-03999-1.

Ziauddin, J., & Sabatini, D.M. (2001) Microarrays of cells expressingdefined cDNAs. *Nature*, Vol. 411, pp. 107-110.

Zollei, L., Learned-Miller, E., Grimson, E., Wells, W. (2005) Efficient population registration of 3D data. 2005. In *ICCV Workshop on Computer Vision for Biomedical Image Applications: Current Techniques and Future Trends*.

28

Novel Machine Learning Techniques for Micro-Array Data Classification

Neamat El Gayar, Eman Ahmed and Iman El Azab
Faculty of Computers and Information,
Cairo University,
Egypt

1. Introduction

Machine learning, data mining and pattern recognition have been quite often used in various contexts of medical and bioinformatics applications. Currently computational methods and tools available for that purpose are quite abundant. The main aim of this chapter is to outline to the practitioners the basic concepts of the fields focusing on essential machine learning tools and highlighting their best practices to be successfully used in the medical domain. We present a case study for DNA microarray classification using ensemble methods and feature subset selection techniques.

The background section will begin by introducing the reader to the fields of pattern recognition, machine learning and data mining. It will then focus on some of the most important concepts related to machine learning.

In particular in section 2 we review the most popular machine learning models for classification used in the context of the medical domain. We then describe one of the most powerful and widely used classifiers for high dimensional feature spaces; the support vector machines (SVM). We cover the area of classifier evaluation and comparison to provide practitioners with essential understanding of how to test, validate and select the appropriate models for their applications. Finally, we summarize the main advances in the field of ensemble learning, feature subset selection and feature subset ensembles.

Section 3 presents a review of using machine learning in various fields of bioinformatics.

In section 4, a recent case study on DNA microarray data that uses an ensemble of SVMs coupled with feature subset selection methods is presented. We show how the proposed model can alleviate the curse of dimensionality associated with expression-based classification of DNA data in order to achieve stable and reliable results.

Section 5 describes the data used and the experiments conducted, while section 6 presents results and a comparative analysis for the proposed models.

Finally in section 7 we summarize the main contributions of this chapter and review the main guidelines to effectively use machine learning tools. We end this section by highlighting a set of challenges that need to be addressed and propose some future research directions in the field.

2. Background

2.1 Pattern recognition, machine learning and data mining

Pattern recognition can be defined as the categorization of the input data into identifiable classes via the extraction of significant features or attributes of the data from a background of irrelevant detail (Duda et al, 2000). The task of pattern recognition is also viewed as the transformation from the measurement space to the feature space and finally to a decision space.

Machine learning techniques aim at producing a system that can learn and adapt from the environment and hence exhibits a kind of intelligence essential for applications that lack known solutions (Alpydin, 2004). Machine learning models very often attempt to optimize a criterion function through exploiting information from training examples.

Data mining, on the other hand, can be thought of as a collection of statistical, machine learning, pattern recognition and artificial intelligence tools that help uncover and extract 'hidden' knowledge from data. Particularly in the medical domain data mining refers often to techniques and methods that analyze large amounts of data. These techniques include among many others classification, clustering, association rule mining and regression or prediction.

Cluster analysis usually addresses segmentation problems. The objective of this analysis is to separate data with similar characteristics from the dissimilar ones. Cluster analysis is frequently the first required task of the mining process. Cluster analysis can also be used for outlier detection to identify samples with peculiar behavior. Among the most simple and efficient clustering techniques are K-means, fuzzy K-means, Self Organizing maps; in addition to more advanced clustering methods like evolving clustering techniques and distributed clustering.

The purpose of *association rule mining*, on the other hand, is to search for the most significant relationship across large number of variables or attributes. Sometimes, association is viewed as one type of dependencies where affinities of data items are described (e.g., describing data items or events that frequently occur together or in sequence). Some techniques for association analysis are nonlinear regression, rule induction, Apriori algorithm and Bayesian networks.

Time Series prediction is also an important aspect in data mining whereby the temporal structure and ordering of the data is utilized to estimate some future value based on current and past data samples. Time-series prediction encompasses a wide variety of applications.

As mentioned earlier, the purpose of this chapter is to provide a broad introduction to the fundamentals of machine learning suitable for bioinformatics. The rest of the chapter will mainly focus on the classification problem.

2.2 Machine learning models for classification

Classification is usually referred to as the process of devising models that can predict categorical (discrete, unordered) class labels. Often machine learning models are used for these purposes that learn the class functions using a set of given training examples.

Popular machine learning classification models are decision tree classifiers, Bayesian classifiers, Bayesian belief networks, rule based classifiers and Backpropagation- Multi layer neural network (Hand et. al, 2001). More recent approaches to classification include support vector machines and ensemble methods. In addition, other approaches are frequently encountered in the literature like *k*-nearest-neighbor classifiers, case-based reasoning, genetic algorithms, rough sets and fuzzy logic techniques.

According to a recent ranking (KDnuggets : Polls, 2006) common classification models used in the data mining community are decision trees, decision rules, logistic regression, artificial neural networks, support vector machines, the naïve Bayesian classifier and Bayesian networks.

It is worth mentioning at this point that particularly in medical applications sometimes models are preferred that are more interpretable. Such models posses some characteristics like being able to make knowledge discovered from data explicit and communicable to domain experts, the provision of an explanation when deploying and using the knowledge with new cases, in addition to the ability to encode and use the domain knowledge in the data analysis process (Bellazi & Zupan 2008). Decision trees and Bayesian networks are among the models that are easily explainable. Decision Trees are sometimes preferred over more accurate classifier because of their descriptive power; i.e. the ability interpret classification rule produced by the model. This is particularly important for 'safety critically' medical applications where results are required to be understood by domain experts.

Moreover, the fact that medical data can often be imperfect is complemented in practice by exploiting domain knowledge. Building classification models using background knowledge is very useful in order to take into account information which is already known and should not be rediscovered from data. Background knowledge can be expressed using different models like Bayesian models, decision rules and fuzzy rules.

From another perspective, in the bioinformatics applications and in particular for the DNA microarray data classification; more powerful tools are needed to deal with the challenges posed by the low sample size, high dimensionality, noise and large biological variability present in the data.

We therefore devote the next subsections for reviewing Support Vector Machines (SVMs), ensembles methods and feature subset selection techniques. These techniques are known to be robust tools for classification in noisy, high-dimensional and complex domains.

2.3 Support vector machines

This section is devoted to review one of the most powerful and widely used classifiers for high dimensional feature spaces; the support vector machines (SVM).

SVMs are binary classifiers that aim to produce an optimal classifier that lies in midway between the nearest data points of the 2 classes of the problem at hand.

In case of linearly separable problem, SVMs discriminate between two classes by fitting an optimal separating hyper-plane in the midway between the closest training samples of the opposite classes in a multi-dimensional feature space. This is done by maximizing the margin which is the distance between the closest training samples and the classifier.

Given Z a training dataset with N samples in d-dimensional feature space R^d.

Each x_i has class $y_i = \pm 1$.

The objective is to find the linear hyper-plane represented by:

$$f(x) = wx + b \tag{1}$$

Where w is the weight vector and b is the bias that maximizes the margin under the constraint of correct classification. It was found that minimizing w maximizes the margin. This forms the following optimization problem:

$$\min\left(\frac{w^2}{2} + C\sum_{i=1}^{N}\theta_i\right) \tag{2}$$

With C as regularization parameter and θ as slack variables.

In case of non-linearly separable classes, the input samples are mapped to a high dimensional feature space using a kernel function. Thanks to kernel trick, it is possible to work within the newly transformed feature space without having to map every sample explicitly.

The training of the SVM requires getting optimal parameter values for the regularization parameter C.

The final SVM function for non-linearly separable case is represented by:

$$f(x) = \sum_{i=1}^{N} \alpha_i y_i k \langle x, x_i \rangle + b \tag{3}$$

Where α_i are Lagrange multipliers.

Further detailed explanation can be found in (Abe, 2005).

2.4 Ensemble learning

Ensemble classifiers - also called Multiple Classifier Systems (MCS) - are based on the design of several classifiers separately then joining the final classification decision. MCS are a preferred solution to recognition problems because it allows simultaneous use of different feature descriptors of many types, corresponding measures of similarity and many classification procedures. Examples of these techniques include bagging, boosting, and mixtures of experts and others. Refer to (Roli & Giacinto 2002) (Kuncheva, 2004) (MCS series) for a good review on methods and research in that area.

Perhaps the most obvious motivation for classifier ensembles is the possibility to boost the classification accuracy by combining classifiers that make different errors or by combining local experts. The fact that the best individual classifier for the classification task at hand is very difficult to identify unless deep prior knowledge is available is also a motivation for using multiple classifiers. Another reason is when the features of a sample may be presented in very diverse forms, making it impossible to use them as input for one single classifier. Another rationale is the desire to boost efficiency by using simple and cheap classifiers that operate only on a small set of features. These are all cases that can be found in medical and bioinformatics data.

Classifier combination can fall under one of the following taxonomies according to the type of outputs produced by the classifiers (Kittler et al. 1998). Classifier outputs can be crisp outputs (also called abstract level), ranked list of data classes or measurement level outputs. For abstract level, a classifier outputs a unique label for every pattern to be classified. The combination of such classifiers is usually done by voting strategies, such as majority vote, weighted majority vote or by trained fusion rules such as Behavioural Knowledge Space (Kuncheva, 2004).

For rank level classifiers, the output is a ranked list of labels for every pattern. Borda Count is the common technique to combine these rankings. The rankings from all classifiers are combined by ranking functions assigning votes to the classes based on their positions in the classifiers' rankings. The final decision is taken as the minimum of the sum of these rankings. Finally, at the measurement level, the classifier output represents the degree of belongingness in each class. For this type of output various combination rules can be applied like product, sum, mean, etc. These combination rules are derived mainly from Bayesian decision rule. Non-Bayesian combinations can also be applied such that a weighted linear combination of classifiers is learnt using optimization techniques.

In our model described in section 4, we present a combiner based on a SVM trainable classifier that works on measurement level outputs of the base classifiers.

2.5 Feature subset selection and feature subset ensembles

A common way to build base classifiers for further combination is by randomly selecting different subsets of features and training classifiers on those subsets. Feature subset selection should enforce diversity among classifiers created and hence lead to more robust ensembles.

In applications that are characterized by having a huge number of features, feature subset ensembles can be used in order to make use of all the features.

The way this method works is by sub-sampling the features such that the base classifiers in the ensemble can be built on different subsets of features, either disjoint or overlapping. So instead of over-whelming a single classifier with all the features, individual classifiers can be built on groups of feature then their decisions are combined to get the final decision.

The choice of features for each subset depends on the problem at hand. The features may be naturally grouped forming the feature subsets. They can also be selected by any available feature selection method. The random subspace methods (Ho, 1998) work well when there is redundant information dispersed across all the features (Kuncheva, 2004).

Also, various heuristic search techniques such as genetic algorithms, tabu search and simulated annealing are used for feature subset selection. The feature subsets can be selected one at a time or all at the same time in one run of the algorithm by optimizing some ensemble performance criterion function (Kuncheva, 2004).

Random selection is the intuitive way for selecting samples and is the simplest method available. It assumes a uniform distribution for all the samples.

There are two types of random selection: *Random selection without replacement* in which the samples are randomly selected then removed so that they cannot be chosen again and *Random selection with replacement* where the samples are randomly selected then placed back so that they can be chosen again.

In our case study presented later, we use *Random selection without replacement*. We also propose a feature subset selection method based on the K-means clustering algorithm. K-means is a typical partition-based clustering method. Given a pre-specified number K, the algorithm iteratively partitions the data set till it gets K disjoint subsets. In these iterations, K-means tries to minimize the sum of the squared distances of the samples from their cluster centres. It is a simple and fast algorithm. In our proposed approach the genes are the objects of interest to be clustered and they are characterized by their expression values among the samples in the microarray dataset.

2.6 Classifier testing and evaluation

As follows we present main concepts for classifier evaluation and comparison. We start by reviewing cross validation and then discuss main performance measures that can be used to evaluate classification results.

2.6.1 Cross validation

A classifier usually learns from the available data. The problem is that the resulting classifier may fit on the training data, but might fail to predict unseen data.

Cross validation is a technique for assessing the generalization performance of a given classifier. It can be used for estimating the performance of a given classifier as well as for tuning the model parameters.

Methods of cross validation include *Re-substitution Validation*, *Hold-Out Validation*, *K-Fold Cross Validation*, and *Leave-One-Out Cross Validation* as will be described next.

In *Re-substitution Validation* all the available dataset is used for training the classifier. Then, it is tested on the same dataset. This makes it liable to overfitting. Thus, the classifier might perform well on the available data yet poorly on future unseen test data. However in the *Hold-Out Validation* the available dataset is split into 2 sets: one for training and the other for testing the model, such that the model can be tested on unseen data. For this approach the results are highly dependent on the choice for the training / test split. The instances in the test set may be too easy or too difficult to classify and this can skew the results. On the other hand, the instances in the test set may be valuable for training and when they are held out, the prediction performance may suffer leading to skewed results.

To overcome this drawback in *K-Fold Cross Validation*, the available data is divided into k equally sized folds. Subsequently, k iterations of training and validation are performed such that, within each iteration a different fold of the data is held-out for validation while the remaining (k-1) folds are used for training the classification model. Data is usually stratified prior to being split into k folds i.e. data is rearranged to ensure that each fold contains instances of all the classes in the problem at hand.

Leave-One-Out Cross Validation (LOOCV) is a special case of k-fold cross validation where k equals the number of instances in the data. In other words, in each iteration, all the data except for a single instance are used for training the model and the model is tested on that single instance. An accuracy estimate obtained using LOOCV is known to be almost unbiased but it has high variance.

To obtain more reliable performance estimates, multiple runs of k-fold cross validation can be applied. The data is reshuffled and re-stratified before each round. This is referred to as *Repeated K-Fold Cross Validation*.

2.6.2 Performance measures

In this section we review some of the most important measures to calculate classifier performance. In particular we discuss the accuracy, sensitivity, specificity and precision measures.

A classifier is tested by applying it to unseen test data with known classes and comparing the predicted classes resulted from the classifier with the target classes.

The confusion matrix summarizes the correct and incorrect classifications resulted from a given classifier. It displays both the actual target classes and the predicted classes. The matrix dimension is $M \times M$, where M is the number of classes of the problem at hand. The entry m_{ij} of such a matrix denotes the number of samples whose actual class is w_i, and which are assigned by the classifier to class w_j.

Usually, in medical diagnosis, there are two classes, the positive class that indicates infection/sickness and the negative class that indicates being healthy. For assessing the performance of a given classifier, there are other important measures that need to be considered in addition to accuracy. Among them are the sensitivity and the specificity. Sensitivity is the proportion of correctly classified samples for being positive of all the samples that are actually positive, while specificity is the proportion of correctly classified samples for being negative of all the samples that are actually negative.

In the confusion matrix, in figure 1, 'A' represents the number of samples that actually belong to the positive class and are predicted to belong to the positive class. This is also

Confusion Matrix		Predicted Classes	
		+ve	-ve
Actual Target Classes	+ve Class	A	B
	-ve Class	C	D

Fig. 1. Confusion matrix.

quite often referred to as the *true positive (TP)*. For medical application this would indicate the number of patterns found to be sick; while they are really sick. *'B'* on the other hand represents the *false negatives (FN)*; i.e the number of sick people (positive samples) who have been falsely classified to be healthy (or negative). Similarly *'C'* is referred o as the *false positive (FP)* while *'D'* indicates the *true negative (TN)*.

Accuracy is the percentage of correctly classified samples. It can also be formulated as in equation 4 using TP, TN, FP and FN.

$$\text{Accuracy} = \frac{TP + TN}{TP + FP + TN + FN} \times 100\% \tag{4}$$

Sensitivity measures the ability of a classifier to recognize the positive class (in our application to detect sick people). It is also known as *True Positive Rate (TPR)* or *recall*.

$$\text{Sensitivity} = \frac{TP}{TP + FN} \times 100\% \tag{5}$$

On the other hand **Specificity** measures the ability of a classifier in detecting the negative class (i.e healthy samples). This is also known as *True Negative Rate (TNR)*.

$$\text{Specificity} = \frac{TN}{TN + FP} \times 100\% \tag{6}$$

The relationship between sensitivity and specificity, as well as the performance of the classifier, can be visualized and studied using a receiver operating characteristic *(ROC)* Curve. It is a graphical plot of the *sensitivity (TPR)* versus *false positive rate (FPR)* which is (1 − *specificity*), for a binary classifier as its discrimination threshold is varied.

The ROC space is defined by two axes which are *FPR* and *TPR* representing the x-axis and the y-axis, respectively. This depicts relative trade-offs between true positive representing benefits and false positive representing costs. A point in the ROC space represents a prediction of the classifier.

A prefect classification would yield a point in the upper left corner or coordinate (0, 1) of the ROC space where there is 100% sensitivity (no false negatives) and 100% specificity (no false positives). The point (0, 0) represents a classifier that predicts all cases to be negative, while the point (1, 1) corresponds to a classifier that predicts every case to be positive. Point (1, 0) is the classifier that is incorrect for all classifications as it means 100% false negatives and 100% false positives. The diagonal divides the ROC space. Generally, the points above the diagonal represent good classification results while the points below the line poor results.

Precision is the proportion of the true positives against all the positive results.

$$\text{Precision} = \frac{TP}{TP + FP} \times 100\% \tag{7}$$

F_1 score (also **F-score** or **F-measure**) is a measure that considers both the precision and the recall of the test to compute the score.

$$F = 2 \cdot \frac{\text{Precision} \times \text{Recall}}{\text{Precision} + \text{Recall}} \tag{8}$$

This is also known as the F_1 measure, because recall and precision are evenly weighted. It is a special case of the general F_β measure (for non-negative real values of β).

$$F_\beta = \left(1 + \beta^2\right) \cdot \frac{\text{Precision} \times \text{Recall}}{\beta^2 \cdot (\text{Precision} + \text{Recall})} \tag{9}$$

Two other commonly used F measures are the F_2 measure, which weights recall higher than precision, and the $F_{0.5}$ measure, which puts more emphasis on precision than recall. Usually the measure chosen for performance evaluation is application dependent. In medical applications usually precision and recall – in addition to accuracy- are very important. In our case study presented in section 4 we use accuracy, sensitivity, specificity and precision to evaluate the proposed model for DNA microarray data classification.

3. Machine learning techniques in bioinformatics

Due to the availability of huge amounts of data delivered by high-throughput biotechnologies, data management procedures are required to provide the ability to store and retrieve biological information efficiently (Valentini, 2008)(Goble & Stevens,2008); this is in addition to the need of methods to extract and model biological knowledge from the data (Baldi & Brunak, 2001).

Machine learning techniques deal with a wide range of bioinformatics problems in genomics, proteomics, gene expression analysis, biological evolution, systems biology, and other relevant bioinformatics domains (Valentini, 2008) (Larranaga et.al., 2005). As follows we briefly review the use of machine learning in each of the previously mentioned fields of bioinformatics. However, the rest of the chapter will focus on micro-array data classification. The state of a cell consists of all those variables-both internal and external-which determine its behaviour. According to the Central Dogma of molecular biology, the activity of a cell is determined by which of its genes are expressed i.e., which genes are ``turned on", resulting in the active production of the respective proteins. When a particular gene is expressed, its DNA is first transcribed into the complementary messenger RNA (mRNA), which is then translated into the specific protein this gene codes for. We can measure the level of expression of each gene (i.e. how much each gene is ``turned on") by measuring how many mRNA copies are present in the cell (Lander, 1996).

Genomics is one of the most important domains in bioinformatics. It studies biological sequences at genome level such as DNA and RNA. (Mathe´ et al., 2002) provide a review on some important applications which are locating the genes in a genome and identifying its function. Ensemble methods have been applied to predict gene function in comparison with single classifier as in (Re & Valentini, 2010), where several data sources are integrated then input to SVM base classifiers and combined using weighted average and decision templates. The ensembles outperform the single SVM classifier. Sequence information is also used for gene function and RNA structure prediction (Freyhult, 2007) as well as many other relevant genomics problems.

Gene expression data analysis is a well-established bioinformatics domain where Machine Learning methods for classification and clustering have been widely applied. *DNA gene expression microarrays* allow biologists to study genome-wide patterns of gene expression in any given cell type, at any given time, and under any given set of conditions (Baldi & Brunak, 2001). Gene expression data is arranged into a matrix where, columns represent genes and rows represent the samples. Each element in the matrix represents the expression level of a gene under a specific condition and it is represented by a real number.

The use of these arrays produces large amounts of data, potentially capable of providing fundamental insights into biological processes ranging from gene function to development, cancer, aging and pharmacology (Baldi & Brunak, 2001). However the data needs to be pre-processed first, i.e. modified to be suitably used by machine learning algorithms. Then the data is analyzed to look for useful information.

Clustering techniques such as *k*-means, hierarchical clustering (Eisen et al., 1998) and self-organizing maps (SOMs) (Tamayo et al., 1999) have been applied to identify genes according to their function similarities. These methods assume that related genes have similar expression patterns across all samples and hence divide the set of genes into disjoint groups. Accordingly, identifying local patterns with subset of genes that are similarly expressed over a subset of samples is difficult using traditional clustering techniques. (AboHamad et al., 2010) propose a bi-clustering technique which is based on clustering similarly expressed genes set over a subset of samples simultaneously. On the other hand, many classification techniques are used. The majority of papers published in the area of machine learning for genomic medicine deal with analyzing gene expression data coming from DNA microarrays, consisting of thousands of genes for each patient, with the aim to diagnose (sub) types of diseases and to obtain a prognosis which may lead to individualized therapeutic decisions (Bellazi & Zupan, 2008). The published papers are mainly related to oncology, where there is a strong need for defining individualized therapeutic strategies (Mischel & Cloughesy, 2006). A seminal paper from this area is that of (Golub et al., 1999) and focuses on the problem of the early differential diagnosis of acute myeloid leukemia (AML) and acute lymphoblastic leukemia (ALL). Several classification techniques have been applied on different benchmark datasets, among these are decision trees, naïve bayes classifier, multilayer perceptron and SVMs which have proved to be very effective in such applications. The mentioned classification approaches are usually coupled with feature (gene) selection methods to improve the performance. To avoid removing some features, the use of ensembles has emerged with different ways of distributing features among subsets as explained in section 2.

Proteomics is the field that studies proteins. Proteins transform the genetic information into actions performed in life. The prediction of the secondary and tertiary structure of proteins represents one of the main challenges for Machine Learning methods in bioinformatics. Neural networks have been applied to predict protein secondary structure (Baldi & Brunak, 2001). This is due to the fact that proteins are very complex macromolecules with thousands of atoms and bounds so there are huge number of possible structures. This makes protein structure prediction a very complicated combinatorial problem where optimization techniques are required. Machine learning is also applied for protein function prediction, fold recognition as well as other relevant proteomics problems (Valentini, 2008).

Systems biology is an emerging bioinformatics area where Machine Learning techniques play a central role (Kitano, 2002). It is concerned with modelling biological processes inside the cell. Mathematical models and learning methods are required to model the biological networks ranging from genetic networks to signal transduction networks to metabolic pathways (Bower et al., 2004).

Phylogenetic trees are schematic representations of organisms' evolution. Machine Learning is applied for phylogenetic tree construction by comparisons made by multiple sequence alignment where many optimization techniques are used (Larranaga et al., 2005).

As follows we present a novel machine learning model for micro-array data classification. Experiments and comparative results demonstrate the efficiency of these models to deal with high-dimensional DNA data.

4. A case study of an SVM ensemble using feature subset selection for DNA classification

In this section, we present a case study of a SVM ensemble that uses SVM base classifiers and another SVM classifier for combining the results of the base classifiers to get the final classification. The proposed ensemble uses k-means clustering for grouping the features into subsets. The ensemble is referred to as k-means-SVM fusion throughout the rest of this chapter.

The flow charts in figures 2, 3 and 4 illustrate the main phases used for building the ensemble. A dataset consisting of a set of labelled examples is initially given. Each example is characterized by a set of features and a label indicating its class. The dataset is divided into a training set, a validation set and a test set. For clustering, the features are grouped into k feature subsets and k-means clustering is applied to the training set. Then, each of the SVM base classifiers is trained using the training set characterized by features of a single feature subset. The SVM classifier responsible for fusion is trained using the validation set and then the ensemble is ready to be tested on the test set.

Figure 5 presents the steps of the algorithm for building the ensembles that use an SVM classifier for fusion in more details. Initially, the available data set Z containing all features is divided into training Z_{Train}, validation Z_{Valid} and testing set Z_{Test}. The training set Z_{Train} is used for building the base SVM classifiers and determining their parameters through cross validation by further splitting the training set into training part and validation part, applying grid search using range of values for the parameters and selecting the parameter values that resulted in the best accuracy among the validation set. The validation set Z_{Valid} is used to train the combiner SVM, while the test set Z_{Test} is used to evaluate the overall ensemble.

Before any of the data parts are applied, we first perform a feature subset selection procedure to choose k subsets to be used as an input for each base classifier. The input to any base SVM classifier i is hence the training samples with features in the cluster i. After the base classifiers are trained using the training portion Z_{Train}, the combiner is trained using the validation set Z_{Valid} as follows:

The outputs of the k SVMs are collected to form a new feature-sample training matrix for the SVM combiner where each sample is characterized by the base SVM outputs as features and its label is the same as its original labels.

In the test phase, the overall accuracy of the ensemble is tested using the remaining samples of Z_{Test} reserved.

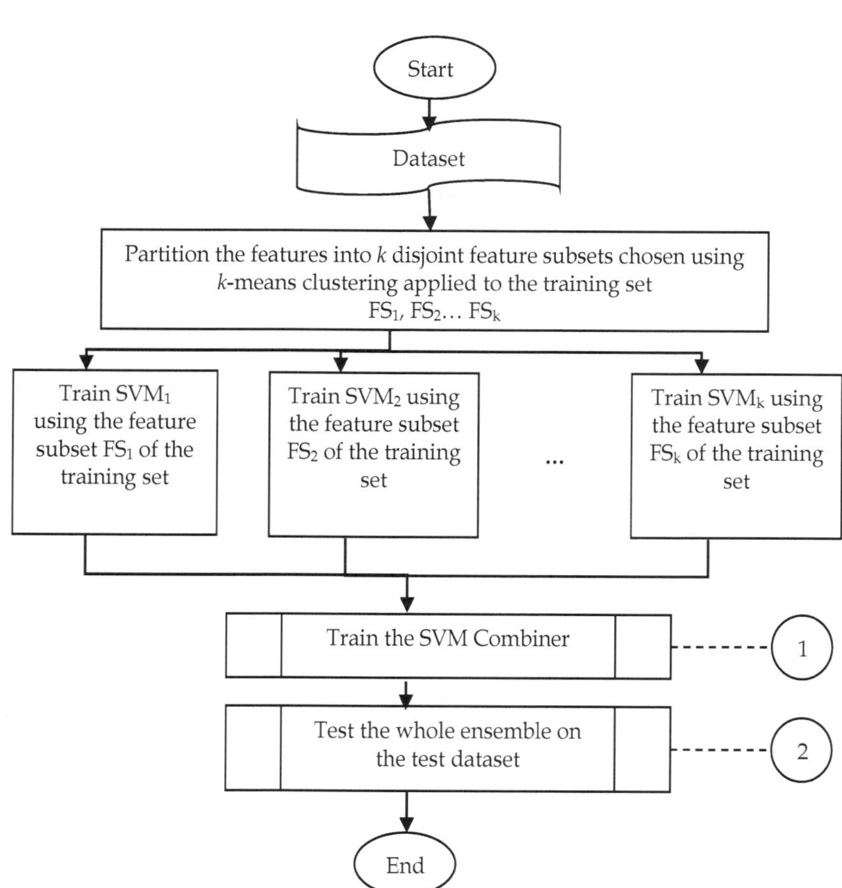

Fig. 2. Ensembles using SVM fusion.

Cross validation is used to evaluate the proposed model using different partitions of Z for training and validation.

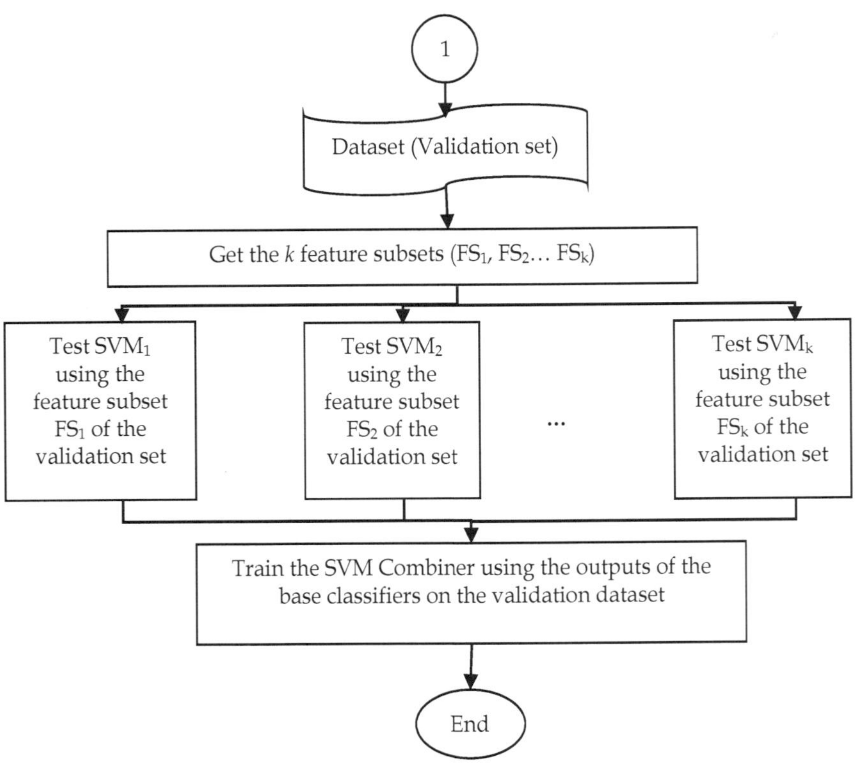

Fig. 3. Training the SVM Combiner in the Ensemble.

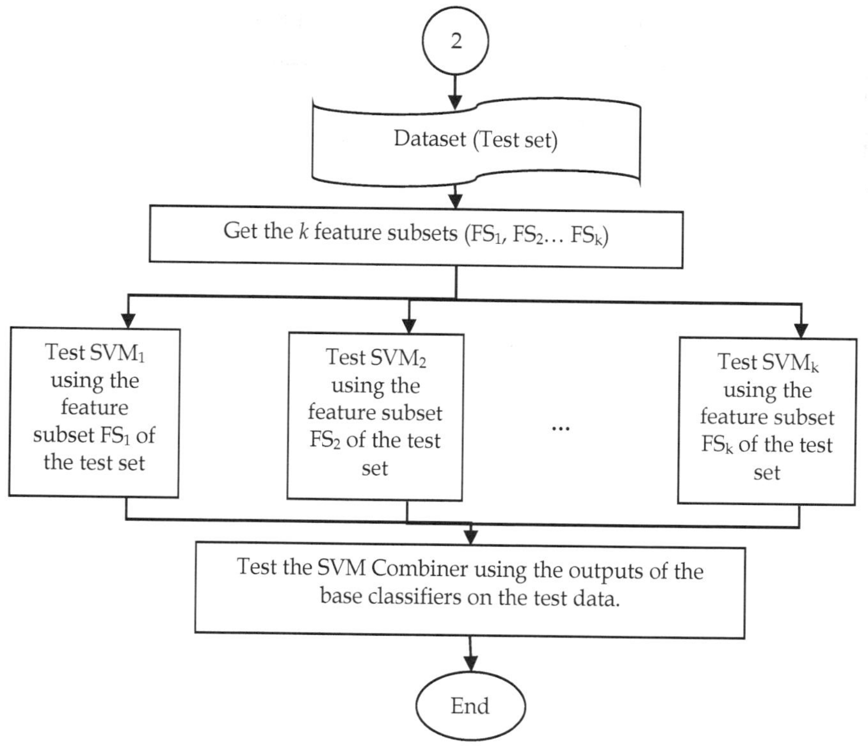

Fig. 4. Testing the ensemble with SVM fusion.

5. Data and experimental setup

In this section, we describe the experiments conducted to test and evaluate the proposed the k-means-SVM fusion ensemble on the Leukaemia data set. Refer to (Ahmed et al., 2010) for more experiments on other data sets.

The Leukemia dataset is a benchmark micro-array dataset which consists of 72 samples, 7129 features and 2 classes (AML and ALL). The 72 samples consist of 47 samples of Acute Lymphoblastic Leukemia (ALL) and 25 samples of Acute Myeloblastic Leukemia (AML). The training and test samples in (Chang & Lin, 2001), (Golub et al., 1999) are merged then normalized as indicated in (Shevade & Keerthi, 2003).

The proposed k-means-SVM fusion ensemble is compared to a single SVM classifier as well as three different SVM ensembles: the *random-majority vote* ensemble, the *k-means-majority vote* ensemble and the *random-SVM fusion* ensemble. The *random-majority vote* ensemble uses the random subspace method to select feature subsets and distribute them among base classifier in the ensembles. A fixed fusing rule –majority vote- is used to combine the output of the base classifiers. In contrast, the *k-means-majority vote* ensemble uses feature subsets resulting from k-means clustering as described in section 4 but still uses majority voting for classifier fusion. Alternatively, the *random-SVM fusion* ensemble uses Random subspace method for feature subset selection and a trainable SVM classifier as a combination rule.

Given:
- Z, a set of N crisp labelled samples x.
- $FS: (1 \rightarrow n)$, a set containing all n features.

Step 1: Choose feature subsets using k-means clustering
- k-means on dataset Z_{Train}
  - Initialize k, the number of clusters and the number of the base classifiers.
  - Cluster analysis on features using Z_{Train} using k-means algorithm.
  - Get k disjoint feature subsets $FS_1, FS_2, \dots , FS_K$.

Step 2: Train the Base Classifiers
- Train the base classifiers using Z_{Train} such that each base classifier SVM_i is trained with feature subset FS_i.

Step 3: Train the Combiner
- Test every SVM $(1 \rightarrow k)$ base classifiers using Z_{Valid} with the corresponding feature subset $FS(1 \rightarrow k)$.
- Train the SVM(combiner) using the outputs of the $SVM(1 \rightarrow k)$ on the validation data set Z_{Valid}.

Step 4: Test the ensemble
- Test the ensemble using the Test data set Z_{Test} as follows:
  - Z_{Test} is passed through the SVM $(1 \rightarrow k)$ base classifiers.
  - Z_{Test} with the outputs of the SVM base classifiers as features is given to the SVM(combiner).
  - SVM(combiner) classifies the samples of Z_{Test}.

Fig. 5. Ensembles using SVM fusion.

The suggested ensembles are tested for different number of feature subsets, i.e different number of base classifiers. Experiments are repeated for number of feature subsets $k = 2^n$-1 where $n = 2, 3, 4, 5, 6$. Results are compared using different measures of performance including accuracy, sensitivity, specificity and precision. For the sake of brevity we only present results based on accuracy and sensitivity.

Cross validation is used to obtain different training, test and validation sets. Since DNA microarrays are characterized by having a very small number of samples, the training and validation sets are overlapped with 1/3 of the samples.

The usage of cross validation differs according to the ensemble model. For the ensembles that use majority vote combiner, the dataset is divided into a training set and a test set. The training set is used to train the base classifiers while the test set is used to test the base classifiers then the majority vote is applied to their outputs. For tuning the parameters of the base classifiers, the training set is further split into a training set and a validation set on which the classifier is validated. Grid search using range of values for the parameters is applied and the parameter values that get the best performance on the validation set are chosen for the base classifiers.

For the ensembles that use a SVM for fusion, the dataset is divided into a training set, validation set and a test set using k-fold cross validation. The training set is used to train the base classifiers then the validation set is used to test the base classifiers. The outputs of the base classifiers are then used in the training of the SVM combiner. The test set is then used to test the whole ensemble.

All experiments are performed using LibSVM (Chang & Lin, 2001) using 5 fold cross validation for training the base classifiers and the combiner. K-means is applied with values for k ranging from 3 to 63 with increment of 2. Linear kernels are chosen for the SVM base classifiers as well as for the SVM combiner as it was found in literature that they are suitable for the high dimensional microarray datasets (Chang & Lin, 2001), (Bertoni et al., 2005). For each SVM with linear kernel, parameter C requires to be optimized. This is done using grid search by 5 fold cross validation.

We experimented with exponentially growing sequences of C in the rage of -15 to 15 to identify a good value for the parameter.

6. Results and discussions

Figure 6 compares the accuracy of the *k-means-SVM fusion* ensemble to the *random-majority vote* ensemble, the *k-means-majority vote* ensemble and the *random-SVM fusion* ensemble for different number of feature subsets (i.e. different number of base classifier or ensemble sizes).

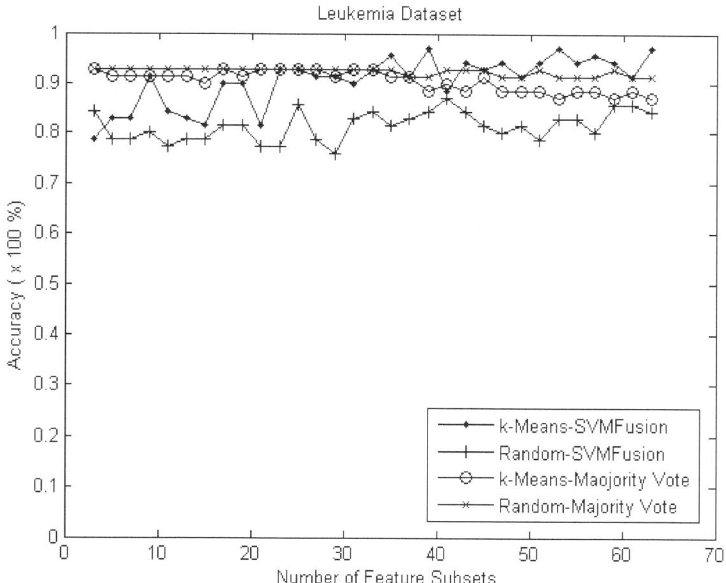

Fig. 6. Test accuracies of the four ensembles with respect to the number of feature subsets.

The accuracy of the K-Means-SVM fusion ensemble seems to outperform the other models with growing number of feature subsets (i.e. with increased number of base classifiers). Also, the accuracy of random-SVM fusion increases with higher number of feature subsets. However, it still has the lowest accuracy among the four ensembles.

On the other hand, for the *k-Means-majority vote* ensemble, increasing the number of feature subsets results in a drop of the accuracy; while for *random-majority vote* ensemble results are not affected by the change of the number of feature subsets.

Table 1 summarizes the best results obtained for each ensemble across the different number of feature subsets in addition to those obtained using a single SVM classifier. The number of feature subsets at which the best results are obtained is mentioned for each ensemble. It can be noticed that the ensembles that use majority vote combiner work well only with small number of feature subsets while those that use an SVM classifier for fusion need a large number of feature subsets.

Results reveal that the *k-means-SVM fusion* ensemble outperforms *k-means-majority vote* ensemble as well as *random-SVM fusion* and *random-majority vote* ensembles. *K-means-SVM fusion ensemble* also shows to have a high sensitivity with respect to the other ensembles in the comparison.

Since for the leukemia dataset, both classes are patients, there is no *positive* or *negative* class. Accordingly, the sensitivity is calculated twice; at first, considering AML as the *positive* class and then considering ALL as the *positive* class. The average of both is then calculated.

Classifier/Ensemble	Accuracy	Sensitivity (Average)
Single SVM classifier	92.86 ± 15.97	81.68
Random-Majority Vote (3)	92.86 ± 15.97	90.00
Random-SVM Fusion (41)	87.14 ± 19.17	84.67
K-Means-Majority Vote (3)	92.86 ± 15.97	90.00
K-Means-SVM Fusion (63)	**97.14 ± 3.92**	**96.89**

Table 1. Best classification accuracy and sensitivity measures obtained by applying the ensembles and the single SVM classifier to the leukemia dataset. The number of feature subsets at which the best results are obtained are mentioned between brackets.

Figures 7-10 illustrate for each ensemble the improvement of the combined model over the average performance of the base classifiers. The figures show the average accuracies of the base classifiers of each ensemble compared to the ensemble accuracies. In addition the ratio of the ensemble accuracies to those of the base classifiers are depicted. It is obvious that the *k-means-SVM fusion* has the best ratio among the four ensembles.

Figure 7 shows the results for the *k-means-majority vote* ensemble. It can be noticed that the ensemble improves the performance of the base classifiers but its accuracy drops with higher number of the feature subsets. So, it works better with small number of feature subsets. Figure 8 demonstrates the performance of the *k-means-SVM fusion ensemble*. Clearly the ensemble enhances the performance of the base classifiers except when using 3 feature subsets. Unlike the *k*-means-majority vote ensemble, its performance does not drop with increased number of feature subsets. *K-means-SVM fusion* ensemble achieves the best accuracy among the four ensembles when using 63 feature subsets. Figure 9 summarizes the performance of the *random-majority vote* ensemble. It is noticed that it has a slight improvement over the average performance of the base classifiers resulting in a nearly constant behaviour. Figure 10 demonstrates that *random-SVM fusion* ensemble does not work well on using a small number of feature subsets but as the number of feature subsets increase, it improves the performance and become better than the average performance of the base classifiers.

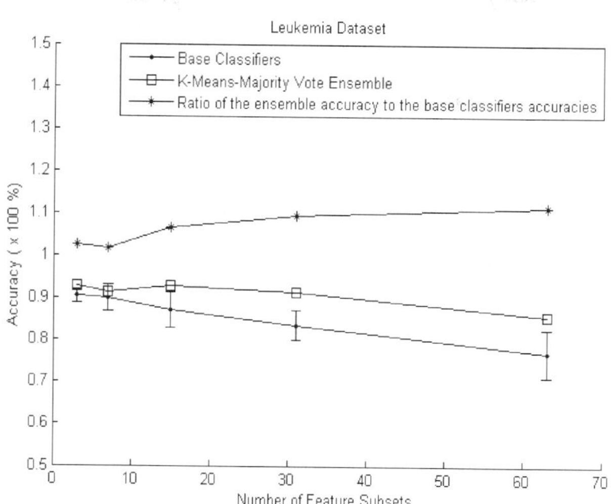

Fig. 7. Results of the k-means-majority vote ensemble.

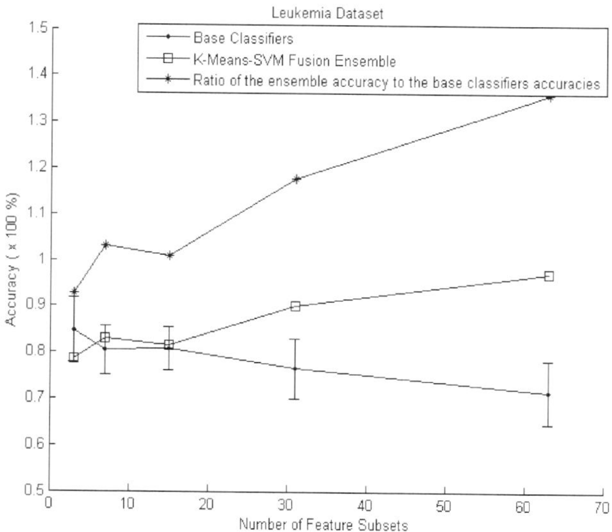

Fig. 8. Results of the k-means-SVM fusion ensemble.

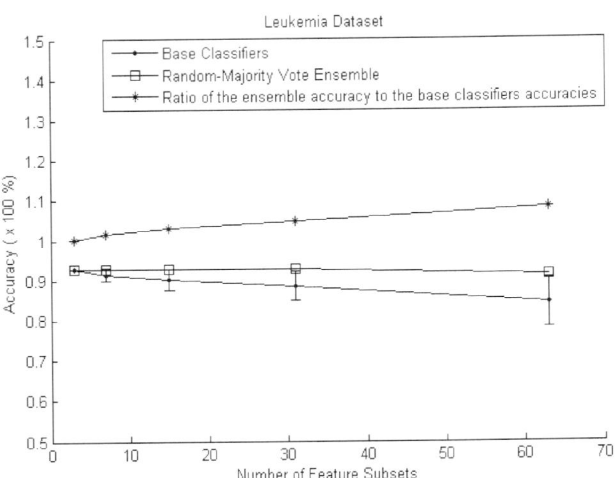

Fig. 9. Results of the random-majority vote ensemble.

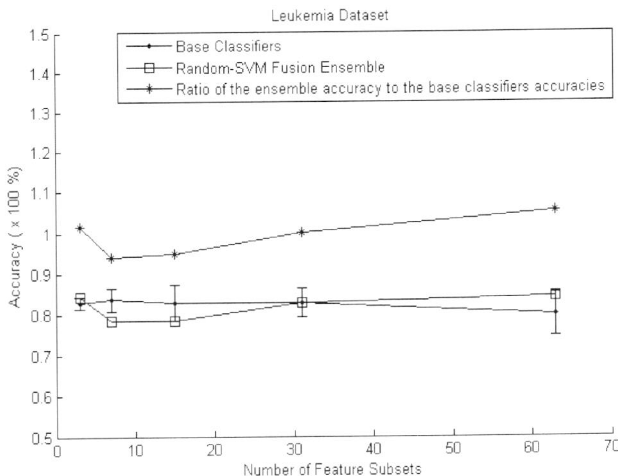

Fig. 10. Results of random-SVM fusion ensemble.

As a general conclusion of the previous experiments we can state that the ensembles with SVM classifier as base classifiers generally improve the classification accuracy over single classifiers. Ensembles that use an SVM classifier for fusion outperform those that use majority vote as a combiner when using a reasonably large number of feature subsets and base classifiers.

According to the study on the leukemia dataset, k-means-SVM fusion ensemble performs the best among the four ensembles with regards to both accuracy and sensitivity. More results to confirm this conclusion are reported in (Ahmed et al., 2010).

7. Conclusions and future directions

This chapter presents a broad introduction to machine learning and focuses on the classification problem in bioinformatics. In particular we cover main terminologies from the pattern recognition, machine learning and data mining fields. We try to review main models used for classification and to elaborate on classifier testing and evaluation techniques. We devote a special attention to SVM, ensemble techniques and feature subset ensembles as they are the base of our proposed DNA micro-array data classification model. The proposed classification model exploits the use of powerful machine learning models such as SVMs and ensemble methods coupled with feature subset selection. The proposed approach proves to be able to deal with data challenges that are imposed by this application which is mainly the huge number of features and the small samples size.

Results are shown on the leukemia dataset and compared to four different models. The study concludes that the use of ensembles is very fruitful in such applications. The way of distributing the features among subsets affects the performance of the ensemble. K-means is a systematic way that proved to be suitable for clustering the features into subsets especially when used with a SVM classifier for combination. For the leukemia dataset, k-means-SVM fusion ensemble performed the best with respect to accuracy and sensitivity. The study confirms the importance of ensembles in bioinformatics applications and highlights that the coupling between the method of distributing the features among subsets and the combination method is crucial for obtaining good results.

Different method can be investigated for distributing the features among subsets. Higher numbers of base classifiers / numbers of feature subsets can be experimented with. Time complexity of the proposed models need to be calculated and accessed. The use of other combiners especially classifiers are worth investigating. In addition, the use of the proposed models can be extended to other data sets and other domains in the bioinformatics field.

8. Acknowledgment

This work was supported by DFG (German Research Society) grants SCHW 623/3-2 and SCHW 623/4-2.

9. References

Abe,S. (2005). Support Vector Machines for Pattern Classification, *Springer*, ISBN 1-85233-929-9.

Abohamad, W., Korayem, M. & Moustafa,K. (2010), Biclustering of DNA Microarray Data Using Artificial Immune System, *Proceedings of International Conference on Intelligent Systems Design and Applications (ISDA)*, pp. 1223-1228, Cairo, Egypt.

Ahmed, E., El-Gayar, N. & El-Azab, I.A. (2010). Support Vector Machine Ensembles Using Features Distribution among Subsets for Enhancing Microarray Data Classification, *Proceedings of International Conference of Systems and Design (ISDA)*, Cairo, Egypt, December, 2010.

Alpydin , E. (2004). *Introduction to Machine Learning*. The MIT Press, ISBN 0-262-01211-1.

Baldi,P.& Brunak,S. (2 ed). (2001). *Bioinformatics The Machine Learning Approach*. MIT Press, ISBN 0 – 262 – 02506 – X.

Bellazi, R. & Zupan, B. (2008). Predictive data mining in clinical medicine: Current issues and guidelines, *INTERNATIONAL JOURNAL OF MEDICAL INFORMATICS*, Vol. 7, pp. (81 – 97).

Bernal, A., Crammer, K., Hatzigeorgiou, A. & Pereira, F., (2007). Global discriminative learning for higher-accuracy computational gene prediction, *PLoS Computational Biology*, Vol. 3, No. 3.

Bertoni, A., Folgieri, R. & Valentini, G. (2005). Bio-molecular cancer prediction with random subspace ensembles of support vector machines, *Neurocomputing*.

Bower, J. & Bolouri, H. (2004). Computational Modeling of Genetic and Biochemical Networks, *MIT Press*.

Brent, M. & Guigo, R. (2004). Recent advances in gene structure prediction, *Current Opinion in Structural Biology*. Vol. 14, No. 3, pp.(264–272).

Chang, C.-C. & Lin, C.-J. (2001). *LIBSVM: a library for support vector machines*. Available from http://www.csie.ntu.edu.tw/_cjlin/libsvm.

Duda, R. O., Hart, P. E. & Stork, D. G. (2nd ed). (2000). *Pattern Classification*, John Wiley & Sons.

Eisen, M. B., Spellman, P. T., Brown, P. O. & Botstein, D.(1998).Cluster analysis and display of genome-wide expression patterns, *in Proc. Natl. Acad. Sci, National Acad Sciences*, Vol. 95, No. 25., pp. (14 863–14 868), USA.

Freyhult, E. (2007). *A Study in RNA Bioinformatics, Identication, Prediction and Analysis*. PhD thesis, ACTA Universitatis Upsaliensis Uppsala.

Goble, C. & Stevens, R. (5 August 2008). State of the nation in data integration for bioinformatics. *Journal of Biomedical Informatics (in press)*, available on line at http://www.sciencedirect.com

Golub, T.R., Slonim, D.K., Tamayo, P., Huard, C. Gaasenbeek, M., Mesirov, JP., Coller, H., Loh, M.L., Downing, J.R.,Caligiuri, M.A., Bloomfield, C.D. & Lander, E. (1999). Molecular classification of cancer: class discovery and class prediction by gene expression monitoring, *Science*, pp. (531 – 537).

Hand, D., Mannila, H. & Smyth, P. (2001). *Principles of Data Mining*, MIT Press.

Handl, J., Kell, D. & Knowles, J. (2007). Multiobjective optimization in bioinformatics and computational biology, *IEEE/ACM Trans. Comput. Biol. Bioinformatics*, Vol. 4, No. 2, pp. (279–292).

Ho, T. K. (1998).The random space method for constructing decision forests. *IEEE Transactions on Pattern Analysis and Machine Intelligence*, Vol. 20, No. 8, pp. (832–844).

Holloway, D., Kon, M. & DeLisi, C. (2007). Machine learning for regulatory analysis and transcription factor target prediction in yeast, *Systems and Synthetic Biology*, Vol. 1, No. 1, pp. (25–46).

KDnuggets , Polls, *Data Mining Methods* (Apr 2006) Available from: http://www.kdnuggets.com/polls/2006/data_mining_methods.htm

Kitano, H. (2002). Systems biology: A brief overview, *Science*. Vol. 295, No. 5560, pp.(1662 – 1664).

Kittler, J., Hatef, M., Duin, R.P.W. & Matas, J. (1998). On Combining Classifiers. *IEEE Trans. on Pattern Analysis and Machine Intelligence*, Vol. 20, No. 3, pp. (226-239).

Krallinger, M., Erhardt, R.A. & Valencia, A. (2005). Text-mining approaches in molecular biology and biomedicine. *Drug Discovery Today*, Vol. 10, No.6, pp. (439–45).

Kuncheva, L. I. (2004). *Combining Pattern Classifiers: Methods and Algorithms*. John Wiley Sons, Inc, ISBN 0-471-21078-1.

Lander, E.S. (1996). The new genomics global views of biology. *Science*, Vol. 274, No. (5287), pp.(536 – 539), (October 1996).

Larranaga,P., Calvo, B., Santana, R., Bielza, C., Galdiano, J., Inza, I., Lozano, J. A., Armananzas, R., Santafe, G., Perez, A. & Robles, V. (2005). Machine learning in bioinformatics, *Briefings in bioinformatics*, Vol. 7, No. 1, pp. (86-112).

Lopez-Bigas, N. & Ouzounis, C. (2004). Genome-wide identification of genes likely to beinvolved in human genetic diseases, *Nucleic Acid Research*, Vol. 32, No. 10, pp. (3108 – 3114).

Mathe´, C., Sagot, M-F and Schlex, T. (2002). Current methods of gene prediction, their strengths and weaknesses. *Nucleic Acids Research*. Vol. 30, No. 19, spp. (4103–4117).

(MCS series) Multiple Classifier Systems. Lecture Notes in Computer Science, *Springer Verlag*, Vols. 1857 (2000), 2096 (2001), 2364 (2002), 2709 (2003), 3077 (2004), 3541 (2005), 4472 (2007), 5519 (2009), 5997 (2010), 6713 (2011).

Mischel, P.S., Cloughesy, T. (2006). Using molecular information to guide brain tumor therapy, *Nat. Clin. Pract. Neurol.* Vol.2, pp. (232–233).

Pomeroy, S.L., Tamayo, P., Gaasenbeek, M., Sturla, L.M., Angelo, M., McLaughlin, M.E., Kim, J.Y., Goumnerova, L.C., & et al. (2002). Prediction of central nervous system embryonal tumour outcome based on gene expression, *Nature*, Vol. 415, pp. (436 - 442).

Ratsch, G., Sonnenburg, S., Srinivasan, J., Witte, H., Mller, K.-R., Sommer, R.-J. & Scholkopf, B. (2007). Improving the Caenorhabditis elegans genome annotation using machine learning, *PLoS Computational Biology* , Vol. 3, No. 2.

Re, M. & Valentini, G. (2010). Prediction of Gene Function Using Ensembles of SVMs and Heterogeneous Data Sources. Applications of supervised and unsupervised ensemble methods, *Computational Intelligence Series*, Springer, Vol.245, pp. (79-91).

Ritchie, M., White, B.C., Parker, J.S., Hahn, L.W. & Moore, J.H. (2003). Optimization of neural network architecture using genetic programming improves detection and modelling of gene-gene interactions in studies of human diseases, *BMC Bioinformatics*, Vol. 4, No. 28.

Roli, F. & Giacinto, G. (2002). *Design of Multiple Classifier Systems, HYBRID METHODS IN PATTERN RECOGNITION* , H Bunke and A Kandel (Eds.) , World scientific.

Shevade, S. K. & Keerthi, S. S. (2003). A simple and efficient algorithm for gene selection using sparse logistic regression, *Bioinformatics*, Vol. 19, No.17, pp. (2246 – 2253).

Shipp, M.A., Ross, K.N., Tamayo, P., Weng, A.P., Kutok, J.L., Aguiar, R.C., Gaasenbeek, M., Angelo, M. & et al. (2002). Diffuse large B-cell lymphoma outcome prediction by gene expression profiling and supervised machine learning, *Nat. Med.* Vol. 8, pp. (68–74).

Tamayo, P., Slonim, D., Mesirov, J., Zhu, Q., Kitareewan, S., Dmitrovsky, E. , Lander, E. S. & Golub, T. R. (1999). Interpreting patterns of gene expression with self-organizing maps: Methods and application to hematopoietic differentiation, *in Proc. Natl. Acad. Sci. USA, National Acad Sciences*, Vol. 96, No. 6, pp. (2907–2912).

Valentini, G. (August 2008). Guest editorial computational intelligence and machine learning in bioinformatics, *Preprint submitted to Elsevier*.

Van't Veer, L.J., Dai, H., van de Vijver, M.J., He, Y.D., Hart, A.A., Mao, M., Peterse, H.L. & van der Kooy, K., et al., (2002). Gene expression profiling predicts clinical outcome of breast cancer, Nature, Vol. 415, pp. (530–536).

Won K. -J, Pru¨gel-Bennet A. & Krogh A. (2004). Training HMM structure with genetic algorithm for biological sequence analysis. *Bioinformatics*;Vol. 20, No. 18, pp.(3613–3619).

Part 9

Next Generation Sequencing

29

Deep Sequencing Data Analysis: Challenges and Solutions

Ofer Isakov and Noam Shomron
Sackler Faculty of Medicine,
Tel Aviv University,
Israel

1. Introduction

Ultra high throughput sequencing, also known as deep sequencing or Next Generation Sequencing (NGS), is revolutionizing the study of human genetics and has immense clinical implications. It has reduced the cost and increased the throughput of genomic sequencing by more than three orders of magnitude in just a few years, a trend which is guaranteed to rapidly accelerate in the near future (Metzker, 2010). Using deep sequencing, for example, it is now possible to discover novel disease causing mutations (Ley et al., 2008) and detect traces of pathogenic microorganisms (Isakov et al., 2011). For the first time, research fields such as personalized medicine for patient treatment are becoming tangible at genomic levels given advances in deep sequencing data integration.

The amount of data produced by a single ultra high throughput sequencing run is often tremendous and can reach hundreds of millions of reads in various lengths per experiment (Mardis, 2008). The storage, processing, querying, parsing, analyzing and interpreting of such an incredible amount of data is a significant task that holds many obstacles and challenges (Koboldt et al., 2010). In this chapter we will address some of the possibilities, potentials and questions raised during ultra high throughput sequencing data analysis. We will mainly focus on common pre-analysis concepts and crucial advanced considerations for alignment, assembly and variation detection. Currently, the deep sequencing user is faced with an abundance of deep sequencing data analysis tools, both publicly and commercially available. For each of the aforementioned analysis types, we will point out the various aspects to be considered when choosing a tool, and emphasize the relevant challenges and possible limitations in order to assist the user in picking the most suitable one. Since deep sequencing data analysis is a rapidly evolving field, our focus will be on fundamental concepts of the analysis process and the its challenges, allowing this read to be relevant amid additional published software.

Our first part will encompass a brief overview of current leading deep sequencing technologies with special attention to their features, strengths and possible drawbacks in regards to the different preliminary questions that one might ask when using ultra high throughput sequencing. The second part of the chapter introduces pre-analysis processes. These are common quality control and assurance methods that alleviate deep sequencing derived biases and improve the overall results of any down-stream analysis. In the third part of the chapter, we will go over the different aspects of the post-sequencing analysis, specifically deep sequencing data alignment, assembly and variant detection. For each section we will cover leading methods and tools, quality evaluation and filtration and address the requirements, capabilities and limitations of these tools. The section on variation detection will cover both common variant detection considerations, variant specific challenges and currently available solutions.

2. Sequencing technologies

Sequencing technologies are evolving rapidly, with an overwhelming increase in efficiency and throughput (Mardis, 2008). This expeditious rate of change and improvement is accompanied by a variety of different sequencing platforms, with both great similarities and differences alike. Without going into the technology underlying each sequencing platform in detail, we will specify advantages and limitations both general and specific, that are relevant for deep sequencing experiment design. For this purpose, we will refer to the leading commercially available platforms produced by Roche/454 (Margulies et al., 2005a), Illumina/Solexa (Bentley et al., 2008), Life/APG (SOLiD) (McKernan et al., 2009) and Pacific Biosciences (Eid et al., 2009).

The initial step in the sequencing process is random fragmentation of the nucleotide sequence of interest, in order to increase throughput by simultaneously sequencing millions of fragments. These template fragments can then either undergo clonal amplification, in which they are ligated with adapters and amplified using common PCR (Polymerase Chain Reaction) primers (Roche; Illumina; Life), or they can be used as the sequencing templates themselves (single molecule templates; Pacific Biosciences). Clonal amplified template preparation requires a higher amount of initial DNA material. Since this technique relies on PCR amplification, errors might be introduced to the target before the sequencing process begins. The amount of introduced errors is related to the fidelity of the polymerase utilized in the reaction (Chan, 2009). These potential background errors could be considered actual sequence variants in the down stream analysis. PCR utilization might also result in amplification bias, misrepresenting high GC content areas. Such is the case in a recent study in which PCR introduced expression biases for GC rich chromosomes required additional assessment, hampering the uniformity of the results (Chiu et al., 2010). Simultaneously sequencing clonal amplified templates is further complicated by potential different extension rates that cause asynchronous sequencing (phasing), resulting in a higher background noise. Single molecule template sequencing (Schadt, Turner, & Kasarskis, 2010) does not require PCR amplification thus circumventing its derived amplification and clonal sequencing biases making it an appropriate tool to be used in quantification experiments (e.g RNA-seq, Chip-seq etc.) and in cases where the initial sample DNA content is scarce. Because sequencing is performed on a single molecule and sequences are inferred from extremely weak signals, the correcting effect of simultaneous same-sequence template sequencing is lost resulting in a higher error rate (Schadt et al., 2010). Therefore a higher sequencing fidelity is required (Metzker, 2010).

In addition to the aforementioned general template preparation and sequencing method associated biases, one needs to consider the inherent benefits and shortcomings of each sequencing technology. Pyrosequencing, for example, employed by the Roch 454's GS FLX platform, generates long reads (~400nts) and presents relatively unbiased coverage, enhancing de-novo genome assembly and improving alignment capabilities, thus making it an appropriate tool for SNP and structural variations discovery, demonstrating low false positive rates (Margulies et al., 2005a; Nothnagel et al., 2011). However, the technology's susceptibility to insertion and deletion errors and higher rate of homo-polymer (e.g contiguous run of the same base pair) sequencing errors should be considered when performing a variation oriented research (Chan, 2009). Current reverse termination (Illumina's Genome Analyzer or HiSeq 2000) and sequencing by ligation (Life's SOLiD) technologies produce shorter reads (<200nts) but at a much higher throughput and are considered optimal for small scale variants detection (e.g SNPs and indels) due to very high detection resolution owed to massive read overlap and high coverage. However, short reads' inherent problems of ambiguous mapping and complicated assembly can result in higher false positive rates in variant discovery (Nothnagel et al., 2011), that could be alleviated by higher throughput and employment of paired-end sequencing (e.g sequencing both ends of a fragment template) (Medvedev et al., 2009; Metzker, 2010). Sequencing by ligation technology, employed by Life's SOLiD, reads the colors of fluorescently marked ligated primers and converts them into the template sequence. SOLiD is less susceptible to phasing errors and the unique conversion of color to sequence results in an inherent error correction and thus a more accurate SNP detection process. However, this reduced error rate requires utilization of a reference genome in the color conversion process (Kircher & Kelso, 2010). We also note that error rate increases across all platforms towards the end of a sequenced read (Dohm et al., 2008), due to reduced enzyme efficiency, loss of enzymes, increased phasing effect or incomplete dye removal. The different attributes of the variety of platforms can result in significantly different output data and performance, and it was demonstrated that the combination of more than one platform is potentially more cost effective and could yield higher fidelity and accuracy (Dalloul et al., 2010; Nothnagel et al., 2011). We will now discuss how to alleviate some of these inherent and general difficulties using pre-analysis processing.

3. Pre-analysis processing

In this section we will discuss the processing performed on deep sequencing output data prior to the specific experimental analysis. Mentioned above are examples of the vast cross platform differences that could affect the downstream analysis and thus the biological conclusions derived. These differences accompany the inherent bias in deep sequencing experiments (Dohm et al., 2008; Schwartz et al., 2011). In order to reduce these possibly confounding effects, platform manufacturers and developers provide the end-user with a sequencing quality scale for both automated and recommended manual quality based data filtration and refinement (Bentley et al., 2008; Harris et al., 2008; Margulies et al., 2005a; K. J. McKernan et al., 2009). We will suggest quality confirmation methods for the text based output end-users face after a sequencing run, and discuss common necessary pre-analysis processing steps that ensure data validity and proper utilization. For each platform's inherent quality assurance and control measures, one should address the specific platform's technical support and annotation.

The most common initial form of output format is either a sequence FASTA file accompanied by a numerical quality QUAL file, describing the per-base probability of incorrect sequencing based on the PHRED quality score (Ewing and Green, 1998; Ewing et al., 1998), or the FASTQ format (Cock et al., 2010), containing sequences coupled with their quality stored as ASCII characters. Currently, Sanger FASTQ files use ASCII 33–126 to encode PHRED qualities from 0 to 93 (i.e. PHRED scores with an ASCII offset of 33), marking an error probability between 10^0 and 10^{-93}. Up until the Genome Analyzer v1.3,

Illumina utilized a different scoring scale in their sequencing output, described in (Cock et al., 2010). Currently Illumina encodes PHRED scores with an ASCII offset of 64, and so can hold PHRED scores from 0 to 62 (ASCII 64-126). Life's SOLiD produce a color based FASTQ file (CSFASTQ) that utilizes the digits 0-3 to mark the sequenced color, the processing of which we will not cover in this section. Though these different scoring methods potentially contribute to misinterpretation and confusion, they can be easily converted and conformed (Cock et al., 2009; Goto et al., 2010; Holland et al., 2008; Stajich et al., 2002). Most current analysis tools are able to handle both scoring methods, though some require specific parameters to be set for dealing with each. When employing these analysis tools, one should mind the appropriate quality score is used.

Quality control of deep sequencing data refers to an overview on the base and quality distribution between lanes, tiles and cycles, and correlating the initial sequence data with expected length, GC content, ambiguous bases, sequence complexity and alignment ensuing location distributions which can hold information regarding possible sequencing bias, contamination or artifacts. Platform specific quality control tools.

(Cox et al., 2010; Dolan and Denver, 2008; Martinez-Alcantara et al., 2009) and more general quality assessment software (Dai et al., 2010; Schmieder and Edwards, 2011) can help circumvent such biases, by both raising awareness to implicating irregularities with textual and graphical data representation and by removing such low quality or aberrant sequences prior to the downstream analysis. The need for careful quality control is exemplified by deep sequencing data with a tile specific A base bias, leading to over-expression of the base in the sequences derived from that tile. When searching for rare sequence variants, such base over-expression should be considered when sequences supporting an A variant are derived from the aforementioned tile. A more common example is sequence duplication (Gomez-Alvarez et al., 2009),usually an artifact of PCR amplification and other library preparation processes, that cause over-representation of certain sequences. This creates a skewed coverage distribution that may subsequently bias the error model and thus substantially increase the number of false-positive SNP discoveries and tilt expression and metagenomic analysis results. Available quality control software allow the user to completely remove these duplicates (*FASTX - toolkit*; Li et al., 2009) or mark them for downstream analysis consideration (*PICARD*). Recently various algorithms utilizing suffix tree data structures were developed for sequencing error correction (Kelley et al., 2010; Zhao et al., 2010).

A common procedure in the pre-analysis process, following initial quality control, and prior to sequence duplication removal, is the compulsory tag / adapter removal (Lassmann et al., 2009; Schmieder et al., 2010) and optional quality trimming. Tags are used during the library preparation phase for amplification or differentiation processes (e.g multiplexing; Galan et al., 2010). If they are sequenced, they can profoundly affect the downstream analysis unless removed (e.g clipping). The clipping process, removes any tag remnants from the sequence reads, ridding the data from reads composed mainly or even solely of the tags. The user must set the minimal read length to be retained (according to the sequenced sample and experimental question) and consider possible sequence similarities between the sample and the adapters. Trimming, refers to the sequence removal from either the 5' or the 3' ends of a read where either the sequence complexity or quality does not pass user settings. It is often used for poly-A or poly-T removal, or removal of bases with significantly lower, bias introducing quality scores. Unlike clipping, which is mandatory for valid downstream analysis, trimming is only recommended to improve accuracy and performance in subsequent analysis steps such as alignment and assembly. Following both clipping and trimming, the researcher may review the sequence data for size distribution, and verify concordance with the experimental context. For example, when performing microRNA sequencing experiments, one would expect the sequence size composition to be approximately 20-24 nts in length. If the majority of the data deviates from this range, a more careful examination of the information is in order and library preparation bias should be considered.

We urge the user to consider the sequencing data in the appropriate experimental context and utilize the aforementioned quality control and assurance methods prior to the downstream analysis to increase the experimental validity and accuracy and to ensure better, more reliable results.

4. Data analysis pathways

In the previous sections, we covered common deep sequencing data considerations and refinement, crucial and beneficial for all types of down stream analysis. In this section, we will go over the common data analysis pathways and possibilities, covering their appropriate utilization, the benefits and limitations of each pathway, and familiarizing the user with some of the common available analysis tools.

4.1 Alignment

Most of the analysis pathways specified below involve an initial step of mapping the deep sequencing reads against a reference genome of either the sequenced species, or a related organism with sufficient genetic resemblance. This step presents a computational challenge due to the sheer amount of short reads produced in deep sequencing experiments. It is further complicated by nucleotide and structural variance, sequencing errors, RNA editing and epigenetic modifications. When deep sequencing was initially introduced, established early-generation sequence alignment tools (Altschul et al., 1990; Kent, 2002) more suited for the query of a limited number of sequences were less appropriate for high throughput sequencing's millions of short sequence fragments mapping (Trapnell and Salzberg, 2009), requiring novel alignment algorithms and tools to be specifically designed. Current short read alignment tools.

(Langmead et al., 2009; Li and Durbin, 2009; Li et al., 2008; Li et al.,2009; Lin et al., 2008; *Novoalign*), utilize various heuristic techniques for alignment of millions of short sequences within an acceptable time requirement (Flicek and Birney, 2009). This section will not cover the underlying algorithms for each tool (Li and Homer, 2010). Instead, we will address a few imperative features to be considered when initiating data analysis and alignment.

When choosing an alignment tool, one needs to consider the memory and time requirements and limitations and the appropriateness of the tool to the exploratory question at hand. Some important features to be considered include:

Quality utilization and control - As we mentioned before, sequencing quality provides the user with initial assessment of the data. Some alignment tools, utilize these quality scores (Langmead et al., 2009; Li et al., 2008; *Novoalign*) and it was shown that such employment greatly improves the mapping performance (Frith et al., 2010; Li and Homer, 2010). Most common alignment software generate the alignment output in the Sequence Alignment Map (SAM) format (Li et al., 2009), with a multitude of supporting downstream analysis tools. This common format provides users with a simple and flexible common ground to evaluate alignment results and easily extract and utilize data for further analysis. As for the sequencing output, so does the alignment output contain a PHRED based quality score for each of the aligned reads, describing the probability of per-base false alignment. Combination of this quality score together with other alignment parameters such as mismatches could and should be further assessed using specialized tools (Lassmann et al., 2011) in order to characterize mapped and unmapped reads for potential alignment improvement. These alignment quality scores can be re-assessed using currently available tools (McKenna et al., 2010; *Novoalign*), so that they better denote the probability of a mismatch between the aligned base and the reference sequence. This quality recalibration takes into account the given base and its quality score, the position within the read and the adjacent nucleotides to account for sequencing chemistry biases (Li, Li et al. 2009), and was shown to reduce the effect of sequencing technology derived biases and improve overall variant detection fidelity (DePristo et al., 2011).

Gapped alignment – An important feature one should be mindful of when choosing an alignment tool is whether the tool utilizes the gapped alignment algorithm. Since gapped alignment only mildly increases alignment sensitivity, it is not crucial to pick a supporting tool for many general purposes. However it is especially crucial for variant calling, specifically insertions and deletions (indels) detection (Krawitz et al., 2010) and it is highly recommended to choose a tool that implements gapped alignment (Li and Durbin, 2009; Li et al., 2008; *Novoalign*), when venturing on variant detection experiments, or when targeting known indel abundant areas.

Mismatches and Gap penalties – Most alignment tools allow the user to set the number of allowed mismatches between the read and a reference location and the scoring scale for gap opening and extension. Allowing more mismatches results in a higher portion of mapped reads but at the cost of increased ambiguity and reduced confidence of these alignments. Mismatch allowance should be set while considering the specific experiment at hand. For example, when undergoing microRNA expression profiling, one will want an accurate estimate of the abundance of each microRNA , and should not allow a high mismatch rate if any. On variant calling experiments however, the user should consider the possible expected size range of the variants before setting the allowed mismatch and gap penalty parameters (e.g, if one aims to find a >5nt long deletion, the mismatch limitation should allow it).

Multiple mapping - In theory, unique alignment, mapping a read to a single unique loci on the reference genome is expected by most reads longer than 30 nts when aligning against a large human scale reference. Usually, a portion of the reads will remain unmapped due to contaminant origin or sequencing errors, or more commonly, they will ambiguously map to several different locations (multiple mapping) due to sequence homology and repetitiveness. Different alignment tools flag these multiply mapped reads, and provide the user with the option to either randomly assign them to one loci (Li and Durbin, 2009) or just output all of them (*Novoalign*). Researchers may choose to incorporate only uniquely mapped reads into their downstream analysis, or set a maximal number of different mapping locations for incorporated reads. Discarding multiply mapped reads results in loss of a substantial portion of the data, with potential crucial effects on the following analysis. Currently, there are several approaches for allocation of these multiply mapped reads. One method is to count each read as if originating from each of the mapped loci, potentially over-estimating the expression or coverage of some, since the same read could not have originated from more than one loci. Another method is to divide each read count between all its mapped loci, adding a small equal portion to each. This could have the opposite effect of under-estimating expression and coverage, especially for low complexity loci. Several methods utilize heuristics for dividing these reads amongst their mapped loci according to the uniquely mapped reads in those regions (Hashimoto et al., 2009; Mortazavi et al., 2008). A fairly novel approach utilizes probabilistic models such as maximum likelihood to compute the most likely origin of each read greatly improving the results of quantitative deep sequencing experiments and differential expression (Paşaniuc et al., 2011).

Since each parameter can greatly affect various performance attributes, considering the aforementioned features is crucial when initiating deep sequencing data alignment. The user should always mind the alignment tool's inherent limitations and implement parameters settings according to the experiment at hand and the expected possible downstream analysis, picking an appropriate tool and tuning necessary features for optimal alignment results.

4.2 Assembly

Assembly refers to the process of piecing together short DNA/RNA sequences into longer ones (e.g contigs) which are then grouped to form scaffolds for computationally reconstructing a sample's genetic component. When the assembly process is performed with the assistance of a reference genome, it is referred to as mapping assembly, if no reference is available it is called *de novo* assembly. Original computational assembly tools were designed to use capillary-based sequencing's 800 base pairs long sequences in order to deduce the original full sequence through examination of overlapping segments. Deep sequencing data presents a more compound assembly problem due to higher amounts of sequences that are significantly shorter. Though it adds complexity to the process, this significant increase in throughput enables the successful realization of whole mammalian genome *de novo* assembly as shown in (Li, Fan, et al., 2010; Li, Zhu, et al., 2010). Sequencing errors, uneven genome coverage and reads too short to be informative in repeated regions required a new breed of assembly tools designed specifically for short reads (Butler et al., 2008; Chaisson and Pevzner, 2008; Dohm et al., 2007; Jeck et al., 2007; Li, Zhu, et al., 2010; Margulies et al., 2005b; Simpson et al., 2009; Treangen et al., 2011; Zerbino and Birney, 2008). These tools mainly rely on two algorithms, and differ mostly in the way they deal with sequencing errors and inconsistencies and sequence repeats. Since tools utilized today could be either deprecated or significantly changed in the near future, we will not address the underlying advantages and disadvantages for each specific tool. We will, however, cover some of the more general inherent challenges of deep sequencing data assembly and recommended optimization methods.

Assembly Algorithms - Currently there are two main models for deep sequencing data assembly, Overlap-Layout-Consensus (OLC) (Myers, 1995) which calculates overlaps by (computationally expensive) pairwise alignments, and de Bruijn graph-based (DBG) which creates a shared k-mer dictionary for the assembly process. K is often set by the user and it is recommended that it be set large enough so that most overlaps are true and do not occur by chance, and short enough so as to allow overlap between related sequences. Since comprehensive reviews are available on these algorithms (Miller et al., 2010), we will focus more on specific algorithm related considerations for tool selection. A recent overview comparing the performance of a variety of tools for assembly under different conditions (Zhang et al., 2011), recommended the use of OLC based assemblers (Hernandez et al., 2008; Margulies et al., 2005b) for small scale (e.g microorganisms) genome assemblies While reserving the use of the less computationally demanding DBG based tools for the assembly of large (eukaryote) genomes (Butler et al., 2008; Li, Zhu, et al., 2010; Simpson et al., 2009; Zerbino and Birney, 2008). Another consideration is the read size, with OLC being most appropriate for a limited number of fairly long reads (~100-800 bp) and DBG more suited for the assembly of millions of short reads (25-100 bp) (Miller et al., 2010). One should note that DBG based tool's implementation of specific heuristics reduces CPU demand but at the cost of higher sensitivity to sequencing errors that could result in a much higher memory requirement. We therefore urge the user to run a more strict quality assessment and filtration when embarking on DBG based assembly. We also note that some of the assembly challenges such as identical repeat regions longer than the sequenced reads length, remain insurmountable by computational and algorithmic improvements and must be alleviated by technical means such as longer reads or paired-end sequencing (Cahill et al., 2010).

Quality Assessment - An assembly's quality is measured by it's contiguity and cumulative size and the accuracy of the assembly. The contiguity is assessed using length statistics such as contig and scaffold maximal and average length, combined total length and N50 (The length of the smallest contig in the set that contains the fewest (largest) contigs whose combined length represents at least 50% of the assembly (Miller et al., 2010)). An assembly's accuracy is more difficult to assess and external data is usually needed to reveal both miss-assembly (e.g sequences that are inaccurately joined) and per base accuracy (e.g contigs with nucleotide mismatches). One way to estimate fidelity is by utilizing paired end reads, re-aligning them against the assembled contigs to reveal discrepancies in insert size which probably indicate wrong assembly. When there are available reference sequences they should be utilized for further validation of the assembled contigs, matching sequences and marking possible mismatches and chimeras (non-related sequences assembled into one contig). If no reference sequence is available, it has been shown that the sequence of available closely related organism (e.g comparative assembly (Pop et al., 2004)) could be utilized for the same purpose and for contig adjacency assessment (Gnerre, et al., 2009; Husemann and Stoye, 2010; Meader et al., 2010). A crucial aspect of assembly quality assurance is the sequence quality. Erroneous sequence reads result in higher computer memory requirements (especially in DBG based tools (Miller et al., 2010)) and either no assembly output or wrong inaccurate contigs. As part of the assembly related quality assurance, it is recommended to discard all reads with ambiguous bases (e.g N) and reads composed entirely of homo-polymer sequences to alleviate this increase in computational demand (Paszkiewicz and Studholme, 2010). It is also good practice to trim low quality bases from read edges and of course remove adapters prior to assembly.

Assembly represents one of the more challenging computational tasks at present and it is further complicated when implemented on deep sequencing data. General considerations mentioned in this chapter will help the user to both better understand the challenges inherent in the sequence data and to match a selected tool's underlying implemented algorithm with the data at hand and the assembly goals. Moreover, assembly quality could now be better assessed using the aforementioned parameters, such as N50 and fidelity, in order to compare assembly tools performance for both existing and future software.

4.3 Variant calling

Variant calling refers to the identification of single nucleotide polymorphisms (SNPs), insertions and deletions (indels), copy number variations (CNVs) and other types of structural variations (e.g inversions, translocations etc.) in a sequenced sample (Durbin et al., 2010). Detection of these variants from deep sequencing data requires in most cases both a reference genetic sequence to compare the sequence data against (Li, Li, et al., 2009), and a specialized variant calling software that utilizes probabilistic methods for correctly inferring variants. The process is complicated by areas of low coverage, sequencing errors, misalignment caused by either low complexity and repeat regions or adjacent variants and library preparation biases (e.g PCR duplicates) (Chan, 2009). Variant calling depends on an efficient combination between an accurate alignment and sophisticated inference of variance from it. Since alignment optimization was already discussed in a previous section, in this section our focus will be more on aspects of variant deduction. We will cover the basic common challenges and difficulties both general and specific for each variant type, Present leading bioinformatic tools and databases and their contributions to the field and provide the user with critical considerations and solutions for some of the aforementioned challenges.

After initial alignment, certain factors can critically alter the results of variant detection. One should consider them prior to downstream analysis and implement the appropriate modifications if necessary.

Depth of coverage – Previous studies demonstrated positive correlation between variant calling sensitivity and increased read depth (Krawitz et al., 2010). Depth can be increased by either reducing the size of the selected or enriched target region, performing a higher number of sequencing cycles to produce longer reads to cover the target region or simply assigning more sequencing lanes. Each method has its benefits and drawbacks. For example, assigning an additional lane to sequence the same sample requires a higher financial investment but allows better noise filtration and sequencing errors recognition. Targeting a specific region increases the coverage and sensitivity at the selected segment, but at the cost of information loss at the areas outside. After the sequencing process is complete, upper and lower depth thresholds should be applied on the sequencing data before variant calling is performed. Setting a lower coverage limit removes erroneous mismatches caused by sequencing errors and thus supported by very few reads (Durbin et al., 2010; Li, Li, et al., 2009). Although it is recommended on most tools, setting a lower limit has been shown to reduce sensitivity without increasing specificity in some tools (Goya et al., 2010) and therefore should be considered in the context of the utilized tool. Setting an upper limit removes mismatches caused by copy number variations, PCR duplicates introduced by library preparation (Gomez-Alvarez et al., 2009) and reads mapping to paralogous sequences. The limit should be set according to the initial coverage and we recommend setting the limit to ~10 times the average coverage. PCR duplicates should be further assessed, removed and marked using specialized tools (Li et al., 2009; *PICARD*) as mentioned in the pre-analysis processing section.

Mapping quality and Quality recalibration – Some reads mapping to under represented regions in the genome, especially low complexity and repetitive regions will be inaccurately mapped with a low mapping quality. SNPs derived from these reads have higher chance of being false-positives (Durbin et al., 2010) and should be more carefully examined, setting a more strict quality and coverage threshold if possible. As mentioned in the prior section of alignment considerations, quality recalibration increases the validity of the alignment qualities so that they better denote the probability of a mismatch between the base and the reference. Naturally, these re-calibrated qualities improve the efficiency of variant detection tools that incorporate alignment qualities into their calling algorithms (Koboldt et al., 2009; Li, Li, et al., 2009; McKenna et al., 2010; Qi, et al., 2010).

Cross-lane comparison – It is good practice, when different-lane same-sample sequences are available, to compare the amount of SNPs, insertions and deletions detected for each lane. If one of the lanes has a significantly higher amount of detected variants, it is probable that it will introduce false-positives to the analysis and exclusion of that lane from downstream variant calling is recommended. Another possible data validation option is comparison against a SNP chip if available (Koboldt et al., 2010). Going over each annotated SNP provides the user with more than a million checkpoints to ascertain both the validity and fidelity of the sequencing process, and the chromosomal representation (e.g haploid or diploid).
We will now address a few more variant specific considerations and applications.

4.3.1 Single nucleotide polymorphisms

After aligning deep sequencing reads against a reference genome, SNPs can be naively inferred from the results by simply denoting each base that is inconsistent between reference and read as a SNP. This straightforward inference of mismatches results in a massive amount of alleged SNPs, many of which suffer from some sort of inaccuracy such as: calling a mismatch in the wrong location, homozygousity and heterozygousity discrepancies and even calling a mismatch in the correct location but with the wrong base. Currently most SNP calling tools (Koboldt et al., 2009; Li et al., 2009; 2008; Li, Li, et al., 2009; McKenna et al., 2010; Qi et al., 2010) apply different probabilistic based considerations and heuristics such as quality assessment and recalibration, SNP filtration, local realignment, coverage assessment, prior probability based on known SNPs, genotype based likelihood and even cancer genomics (Goya et al., 2010) to elucidate SNPs from alignment results. The user should be familiar with these considerations and be aware of the tools that apply each when performing SNP calling. We will go over some of them and discuss their effects and benefits.
Local realignment – Current mapping tools align reads independently of the alignment region context. If a read's beginning or end maps to a region containing an indel, a mismatch will be called instead of an indel due to alignment scoring considerations. Adding a secondary, local alignment that considers reads that support the presence of an indel in the vicinity of either detected SNPs or known SNP sites retrieved from dbSNP (Day, 2010), results in a significant reduction in false positive SNPs (Durbin et al., 2010; McKenna et al., 2010). This local realignment is highly recommended prior to SNP analysis and is either performed inherently in some tools (Qi et al., 2010) or can be specifically performed using other available tools (McKenna et al., 2010).
Base Alignment Quality – Since local realignment is a computationally intensive process that depends on correctly denoting insertions and deletions, another method for increased SNP detection accuracy is purposed (Li, 2011). Implementing a per-base alignment quality recalibration for re-evaluation of misalignment probability using profile hidden markov models. This quality recalibration can be performed using SAMtools (Li et al., 2009).
Transition / Transversion Ratio (Ti/Tv) – The expected ratio between transitions (e.g purine purine substitutions) and transversions (e.g purine pyrimidine substitutions) can be elucidated from empirical data retrieved from the 1000 Genomes project Durbin et al., 2010). This ratio could be utilized as an initial quality assessment standard. Currently the expected Ti/Tv ratio is ~2.3 for whole-genome sequencing and around 3.3 for whole-exome sequencing (coding regions only) (DePristo et al., 2011). When detected SNPs demonstrate a ratio closer to the expected ratio for random substitutions, with transversions twice as

common as transitions (e.g ~0.5), low quality variant calling or data is implied and quality thresholds should be reassessed.

dbSNP validation – After producing a list of detected SNPs, it is highly recommended to compare it against dbSNP, the largest repository of SNP data found within the National Center for Biotechnology Information database. Detected SNPs present in the database are considered as known, and the ones not found are considered novel (Li and Stockwell, 2010). The portion of novel SNPs detected in a deep sequencing experiment should range between 1 and 10 percent (DePristo et al., 2011). If this proportion is higher, a high rate of false positive variants is suggested and we recommended reevaluating the detection process and possibly implementing a more strict variation inclusion criteria.

4.3.2 Insertions and deletions (Indels)

Indels are the second most common type of polymorphism and the most common structural variant, in this sub-section we will address only short indels as the next section will deal with the larger (>1000kb) structural variants. Most indels range between 2-16 bases in length (Mullaney, et al.,2010) (also referred to as micro-indels) and their frequency has been shown to vary across the genome with lower rate in conserved and functional regions and an increased rate in hot spots for genetic variation. The average indel rate is approximately one indel in 5.1 to 13.2 kb of DNA (Mills et al., 2006). Their presence implicates on the pathogenesis of disease, gene expression and functionality, viral disease forms identification and they can be used as genetic markers in natural populations. Indels occur in an estimated rate that is eight-fold lower than SNPs (Durbin et al., 2010). This rate varies extensively between sequenced individuals, usually due to variability between mapping and detection tools. Reads covering an indel are generally more difficult to map since their correct alignment either involves complex gapped alignment or paired-end sequencing inference. Optimal indel detection is performed by combining application of an appropriate alignment software and variant detection tool (Albers et al., 2010; Koboldt et al., 2009; Li et al., 2009; McKenna et al., 2010; Qi et al., 2010; Kai et al., 2009), and careful adjustment of their parameters according to the suspected variants. As mentioned before in the alignment section, it is highly recommended to perform indel calling with alignment tools that implement gapped alignment (Krawitz et al., 2010; Li and Durbin, 2009; Li et al., 2008; *Novoalign*). A few considerations when addressing insertion-deletion detection:

Read length – Increasing the read length has been shown to improve the ability to map and detect insertion related reads. Sequence reads 36 bases long, such as the ones produced by the Illumina GAIIx, have been shown to be inefficient for detection of insertions longer than 3 bases with a complete inability to detect insertions longer than 7 bases. Hence the length of the sequenced reads should be considered according to the insertion size range suspicion and adjusted appropriately. Naturally, when insertion size is expected to surpass the read length it is impossible to detect them using single-end sequencing. Increasing the read length has also been shown to improve micro-indel (<10 bases) detection sensitivity without significantly affecting specificity, demonstrating a more efficient method for increasing coverage than simply producing more reads.

Paired-end reads – Indel detection greatly improves when based on paired end reads deep sequencing data (Mullaney et al., 2010). Both alignment (Li and Durbin, 2009; Li et al.,2008) and variant detection tools (Kai Ye et al., 2009) utilize paired-end reads so that one of the reads is used to pinpoint the pair's loci in the reference while the other read can be subjected to gapped alignment and indel inference. Furthermore, the insert (e.g the unsequenced gap between a read pair) can also be used to deduce the presence of an indel (discussed in the next section).

4.3.3 Structural variants

Structural variants (Feuk et al., 2006) are defined as genomic alterations that involve segments of DNA that are larger than 1 kb. They include: (1) Copy number variations (CNV), which are sections in the DNA with a variable copy number when comparing to a reference genome. Insertions, deletions and duplications are types of CNVs. (2) Segmental duplications, several copies of DNA segments that are almost identical (>90%) that can appear in a variable number of copies, also considered a type of CNV. (3) Inversions, segments in the DNA that are reversed in orientation. (4) Translocations, an intra or inter chromosomal location shift in a DNA segment without changing the total DNA content. (5) Segmental uniparental disomy, where a diploid individual's pair of homologous chromosomes originated from a single parent. Since current deep sequencing platforms do not produce reads that span the length of structural variants, utilization of paired end mapping is necessary for their exact elucidation. The quality of structural variation detection using deep sequencing can be assessed by the accuracy of break point localization, copy number count and variation size estimation (Medvedev et al., 2009).

Paired-end mapping (PEM) - Paired-end sequencing refers to the process of sequencing a cloned DNA fragment on both ends, resulting in two associated sequence reads with an unsequenced insert between them. The insert length varies between several bases to several thousands of bases and thus appropriate for the detection process of the aforementioned large scale structural variants. Structural variants are often detected indirectly through associated paired-end deep sequencing data patterns (Bashir et al., 2008; Korbel et al., 2009; Medvedev et al., 2009). Some of these patterns approximate the location of the structural breakpoints, and some provide an exact localization. For example, the signature of an insertion or deletion can be easily inferred by comparing the expected read pair distance according to the reference with the expected insert size, if the reference distance is longer or shorter than the insert size, the presence of a deletion or insertion can be inferred respectively but the deduction of the exact location of the indel from these signatures is more difficult. However, in an "anchored split mapping" signature, when one read from a pair is perfectly aligned against the reference and its pair cannot be aligned against its designated reference location, the unaligned read can be utilized in order to pinpoint the exact location of existing large deletions or small insertions (Medvedev et al., 2009). SV PEM signatures improve all aspects of SV detection quality and so PEM is highly recommended for this purpose.

Insert size - insert size, set by the size of the DNA fragments introduced by library preparation can affect the outcome of SV detection. If the experimental goal is to detect as many structural variants as possible, a larger insert length is suggested. If however, a more precise localization of the variants is necessary, a shorter insert length is recommended, though resulting in an overall lower variant discovery sensitivity (e.g if you find the variant, there is a greater probability of precise localization) (Bashir et al., 2008).

Depth of coverage - Coverage can also be utilized for SV elucidation, specifically large scale deletions and duplications (Yoon et al., 2009). As we expect reads mapping to each region to follow a Poisson distribution, deviations from the expected coverage suggest the presence of a duplication or deletion. SV detection benefits from combining increased coverage with abundance of paired-end reads with a significant increase in specificity (Bashir et al., 2008). Coverage cannot be utilized however to elucidate the exact location of these SVs, only to suggest the expected region in some cases. Coverage biases, as mentioned in previous sections, can also misconstrue the SV detection process.

Clustering methods – After SV signatures have been detected, a calculated inference process is crucial. Most methods utilize some sort of clustering for all the pairs supporting a variant, and deduce variant information from that cluster. Since most methods rely on PEM and coverage for SV detection, they differ mainly on their clustering methods. It is important to familiarize with these methods since some are more suited for certain variation types. Since describing each clustering method is beyond the scope of this chapter, we will only point out certain aspects that are both easy to implement and have significant effects on detection quality. The standard clustering method (Korbel et al., 2009) utilizes only uniquely mapped read pairs, and discards the ones mapped to multiple loci. It also utilizes a set standard deviation limit for the difference between known insert size range and the observed mapped reference distance. These "hard" filters reduce the effectiveness of both homozygousity/heterozygousity inference and small scale variation detection (Medvedev et al., 2009). Soft (Hormozdiari et al., 2010) and Distribution (K. Chen et al., 2009; McKernan et al., 2009) based clustering methods consider multiply mapped reads and assigns them according to their supporting context, thus increasing sensitivity for the presence of small indels and heterozygousity and should be considered when experimentally relevant.

Validation by assembly – It is recommended to combine *de novo* assembly with structural variant detection in order to validate detected variants. Once the assembly process is complete, a search for supporting and conflicting sequence contigs should be performed (Koboldt et al., 2010).

We note that the field of structural variation deduction from deep sequencing data is still in its infancy and both false-positive and false-negative rates are far from satisfactory (Hormozdiari et al., 2009). As both sequencing technology improves, raising coverage and read length, and the algorithmic utilization of such improvements continues, we expect greater utilization of deep sequencing for SV detection.

4.3.4 Variant classification

Calling variants using deep sequencing data often results in a multitude of detected variations, even after strict and effective quality filtration as denoted earlier, deep sequencing data reveals thousands to millions of different variations (Imelfort et al., 2009). These variations can result in biological effects through introduction of different amino acids into protein sequences, early termination of coding sequences and alteration of regulatory elements and splice sites. A natural step following the variant calling process is annotating the detected variants and elucidating their effect and biological significance, separating clinically, scientifically and medically relevant variations from neutral, non functional ones. In a large list spanning this many variants, manual annotation of each variant effect is neither feasible or accurate. We will therefore cover currently leading principles for computational classification and prioritization of detected variants.

Initial prioritization - The first step in variation characterization is basic variation properties deduction. Variant properties such as it's location, whether in a known coding sequence, non coding transcript, promoter, splice site etc. Once a variation is localized in a coding sequence, a subsequent analysis of it's frame effect and whether its synonymous (e.g changing an amino acid) or non-synonymous should be performed. These basic properties allow initial prioritization of the variation list, considering that coding sequence non-sense mutations are more likely to be functionally relevant than mutations in an unexpressed genomic sequence. When dealing with an annotated genome, computational tools should be utilized for this purpose (Conde et al., 2006; Li and Stockwell, 2010; McLaren et al., 2010; Yuan et al., 2006). We recommend checking the dbSNP version utilized by chosen annotation tools and strive to employ the most up-to-date version available so as to increase the availability of variant annotations.

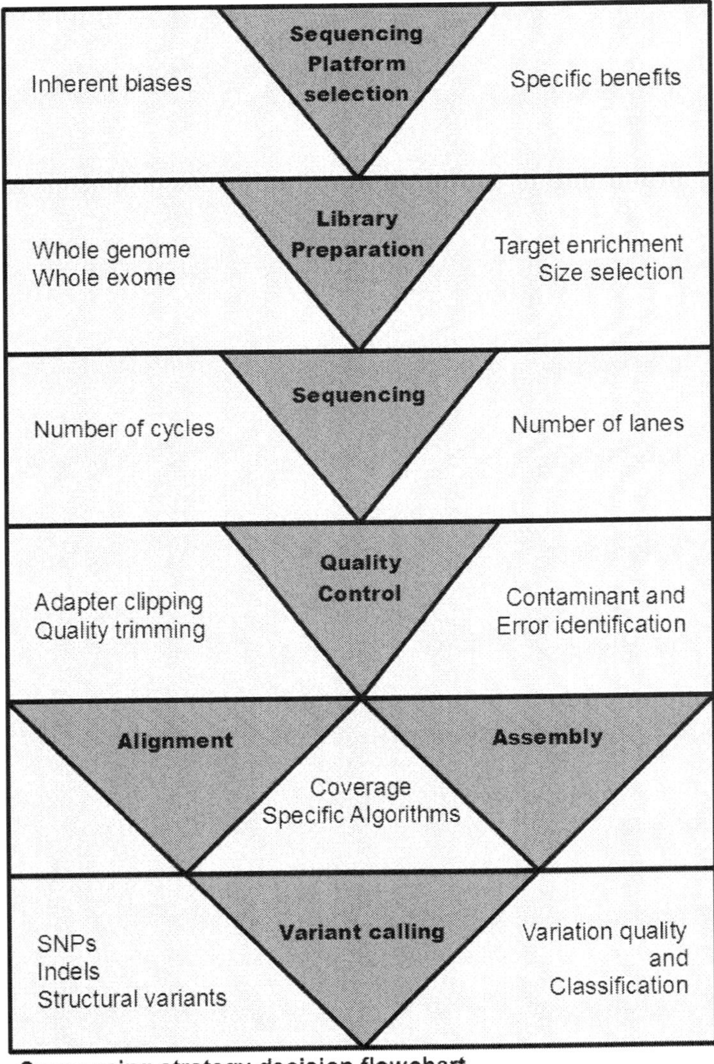

Sequencing strategy decision flowchart

Coding sequence variants - In order to ascertain the most likely phenotype affiliated coding sequence variation from a given list, current variation profiling methods utilize biochemical and physical properties of both amino acids and proteins considering both structure (Ramensky et al., 2002) and function (Bromberg and Rost, 2007; Calabrese et al., 2009) and utilizing various probability algorithm (Mi, et al., 2007). Possible incorporated characteristics include: molecular mass, polarity, acidity, basicity, aromaticity, conformational flexibility and hydrophobicity of amino acids (Ng and Henikoff, 2006) and hydrogen bond breaks, introduction of a buried polar residue, loss of salt bridge, insertion of proline into α-helix, and the breaking of disulfide bonds in proteins (Wang and Moult, 2001). Some available tools (Ashkenazy et al., 2010; Kumar et al., 2009; Li et al., 2009) utilize the fact that functionally crucial amino acids are evolutionary conserved, by employing multiple sequence alignment based conservation scores in order to prioritize given variations. Utilizing orthologous sequences for this purpose demonstrates higher efficiency than incorporation of paralogous, since the latter represents proteins with slight differences in both sequence and function and is less informative for conservation analysis. It was shown that conservation degree is in fact the most reliable method for predicting possible pathogenicity of a missense variant (Flanagan et al., 2010).

For the purpose of both prioritization and functional analysis optimization, we recommend combining available annotation tools that employ a variety of prioritization features (George et al., 2008; Lee and Shatkay, 2008). A recent study implemented some of these variation classification methods on recorded SNPs in a target gene, in order to elucidate possible cancer causing mutations, reducing the initial number of suspected SNPs from thousands to less than 30 (Choura and Rebai, 2009). Another study utilized bioinformatic tools to classify known non synonymous mutations in colon cancer and was able to pinpointed four SNPs already known as related to increased cancer risk (Doss and Sethumadhavan, 2009). However, a recent comprehensive review (Karchin, 2009), implemented and compared leading variant classification tools on three different studies (Doecke et al., 2008; Fatemi et al., 2008; Van Deerlin et al., 2008) associating both exonic and intronic, novel and known SNPs with a variety of disease, and demonstrated that a combination of several tools can possibly result in conflicting annotations and functional effects deduction. Another comparison (Thusberg et al., 2011), that tested the performance of several of the aforementioned tools in predicting pathogenicity using test data retrieved from dbSNP, demonstrated the sensitivity characterizing these tools to range between 0.59 to 0.9, with the preferred tools for their analysis to be SNPs&GO and MutPred (Calabrese et al., 2009; Li et al., 2009). Both studies agree that inference of functionality and pathogenicity is not a fully automatic pathway and educated interpretation of the results must be conducted.

5. Conclusion

Deep-sequencing data analysis is a growing field with many computational challenges. A normal deep sequencing run outputs a massive amount of data which require complex computational processing and interpretation. The overflow of available bioinformatic tools and software for each of the optional analysis steps presents a challenge for the researcher aiming to evaluate and interpret deep sequencing data. In this chapter we familiarized the reader with crucial concepts and considerations for preparation, refinement, analysis and elucidation of valid and accurate conclusions. The field is rapidly evolving both in hardware and sequencing platform technology and in computational techniques, algorithms, software and tools. It is crucial to understand the various challenges involved in deep sequencing experiments, and the current available solutions, both in concept and in practice. The concepts presented in this chapter are aimed towards optimizing deep sequencing experiments, concentrating on initial steps of data preparation and quality refinement and covering several possible analysis pathways while denoting some of the currently available and leading tools, and some of their underlying methods.

The first section of this chapter, introduced deep sequencing technology's available platforms in regards to their advantages and limitations, emphasizing that although they are all considered high throughput sequencing platforms, they present different capabilities and proficiencies. When a choice between platforms is available, one can improve data retrieval and validity simply by matching the most appropriate platform with the specific experimental needs.

The second section covered the concept of deep sequencing data quality control. Using bioinformatic tools, based on both empirical and probabilistic deduction, sequencing derived errors can be reduced which otherwise would be incorporated into downstream analysis. We described current quality scales, with methods for their assessment and their relevance for improved data retrieval. Employment of these quality control and assurance methods can assist in uncovering biased sequencing lanes and recurring errors and contaminants that could significantly alter deep sequencing results. We therefore strongly urge users to utilize them prior to any following experimental evaluation, making their incorporation a standard in deep sequencing experiments.

The third and subsequent sections covered specific and very common analysis pathways: alignment, assembly and variant calling. The chapter introduced basic challenges faced in each type of analysis, their current limitations and considerations pivotal for preferential experimental planning. A description of each challenge was accompanied by delineation of current methods, tools and solutions when available. Familiarized with these challenges, the user can now conduct better analytic decisions and employ the most appropriate tools and techniques. Understanding the exact edge of each analytic pathway can help the user to perform their deep sequencing experiments in the most effective manner employing both current and future software for optimal variant calling.

6. References

Albers, C. A., Lunter, G., Macarthur, D. G., McVean, G., Ouwehand, W. H., & Durbin, R. (2010). Dindel: Accurate indel calls from short-read data. *Genome Research.* doi:10.1101/gr.112326.110

Altschul, S. F., Gish, W., Miller, W., Myers, E. W., & Lipman, D. J. (1990). Basic local alignment search tool. *Journal of Molecular Biology, 215*(3), 403-410. doi:10.1006/jmbi.1990.9999

Ashkenazy, H., Erez, E., Martz, E., Pupko, T. & Ben-Tal, N. ConSurf 2010: calculating evolutionary conservation in sequence and structure of proteins and nucleic acids. Nucleic Acids Res 38, W529-533 (2010).

Bashir, A., Volik, S., Collins, C., Bafna, V., & Raphael, B. J. (2008). Evaluation of paired-end sequencing strategies for detection of genome rearrangements in cancer. *PLoS Computational Biology, 4*(4), e1000051. doi:10.1371/journal.pcbi.1000051

Bentley, D. R., Balasubramanian, S., Swerdlow, H. P., Smith, G. P., Milton, J., Brown, C. G., Hall, K. P., et al. (2008). Accurate whole human genome sequencing using reversible terminator chemistry. *Nature, 456*(7218), 53-59. doi:10.1038/nature07517

Bromberg, Y., & Rost, B. (2007). SNAP: predict effect of non-synonymous polymorphisms on function. *Nucleic Acids Research, 35*(11), 3823-3835. doi:10.1093/nar/gkm238

Butler, J., MacCallum, I., Kleber, M., Shlyakhter, I. A., Belmonte, M. K., Lander, E. S., Nusbaum, C., et al. (2008). ALLPATHS: de novo assembly of whole-genome shotgun microreads. *Genome Research, 18*(5), 810-820. doi:10.1101/gr.7337908

Cahill, M. J., Köser, C. U., Ross, N. E., & Archer, J. A. C. (2010). Read length and repeat resolution: exploring prokaryote genomes using next-generation sequencing technologies. *PloS One, 5*(7), e11518. doi:10.1371/journal.pone.0011518

Calabrese, R., Capriotti, E., Fariselli, P., Martelli, P. L., & Casadio, R. (2009). Functional annotations improve the predictive score of human disease-related mutations in proteins. *Human Mutation, 30*(8), 1237-1244. doi:10.1002/humu.21047

Chaisson, M. J., & Pevzner, P. A. (2008). Short read fragment assembly of bacterial genomes. *Genome Research, 18*(2), 324-330. doi:10.1101/gr.7088808

Chan, E. Y. (2009). Next-generation sequencing methods: impact of sequencing accuracy on SNP discovery. *Methods in Molecular Biology (Clifton, N.J.), 578*, 95-111. doi:10.1007/978-1-60327-411-1_5

Chen, K., Wallis, J. W., McLellan, M. D., Larson, D. E., Kalicki, J. M., Pohl, C. S., McGrath, S. D., et al. (2009). BreakDancer: an algorithm for high-resolution mapping of genomic structural variation. *Nat Meth, 6*(9), 677-681. doi:10.1038/nmeth.1363

Chiu, R. W. K., Sun, H., Akolekar, R., Clouser, C., Lee, C., McKernan, K., Zhou, D., et al. (2010). Maternal Plasma DNA Analysis with Massively Parallel Sequencing by Ligation for Noninvasive Prenatal Diagnosis of Trisomy 21. *Clin Chem, 56*(3), 459-463. doi:<p>10.1373/clinchem.2009.136507</p>

Choura, M., & Rebaï, A. (2009). Applications of computational tools to predict functional SNPs effects in human ErbB genes. *Journal of Receptor and Signal Transduction Research, 29*(5), 286-291. doi:10.1080/10799890902911948

Cock, P. J. A., Antao, T., Chang, J. T., Chapman, B. A., Cox, C. J., Dalke, A., Friedberg, I., et al. (2009). Biopython: freely available Python tools for computational molecular biology and bioinformatics. *Bioinformatics (Oxford, England), 25*(11), 1422-1423. doi:10.1093/bioinformatics/btp163

Cock, P. J. A., Fields, C. J., Goto, N., Heuer, M. L., & Rice, P. M. (2010). The Sanger FASTQ file format for sequences with quality scores, and the Solexa/Illumina FASTQ variants. *Nucleic Acids Research, 38*(6), 1767-1771. doi:10.1093/nar/gkp1137

Conde, L., Vaquerizas, J. M., Dopazo, H., Arbiza, L., Reumers, J., Rousseau, F., Schymkowitz, J., et al. (2006). PupaSuite: finding functional single nucleotide polymorphisms for large-scale genotyping purposes. *Nucleic Acids Research, 34*(Web Server issue), W621-625. doi:10.1093/nar/gkl071

Cox, M. P., Peterson, D. A., & Biggs, P. J. (2010). SolexaQA: At-a-glance quality assessment of Illumina second-generation sequencing data. *BMC Bioinformatics, 11*, 485. doi:10.1186/1471-2105-11-485

Dai, M., Thompson, R. C., Maher, C., Contreras-Galindo, R., Kaplan, M. H., Markovitz, D. M., Omenn, G., et al. (2010). NGSQC: cross-platform quality analysis pipeline for deep sequencing data. *BMC Genomics, 11 Suppl 4,* S7. doi:10.1186/1471-2164-11-S4-S7

Dalloul, R. A., Long, J. A., Zimin, A. V., Aslam, L., Beal, K., Blomberg, L. A., Bouffard, P., et al. (2010). Multi-platform next-generation sequencing of the domestic turkey (Meleagris gallopavo): genome assembly and analysis. *PLoS Biology, 8*(9). doi:10.1371/journal.pbio.1000475

Day, I. N. M. (2010). dbSNP in the detail and copy number complexities. *Human Mutation, 31*(1), 2-4. doi:10.1002/humu.21149

DePristo, M. A., Banks, E., Poplin, R., Garimella, K. V., Maguire, J. R., Hartl, C., Philippakis, A. A., et al. (2011). A framework for variation discovery and genotyping using next-generation DNA sequencing data. *Nat Genet, advance online publication.* doi:10.1038/ng.806

Doecke, J., Zhao, Z. Z., Pandeya, N., Sadeghi, S., Stark, M., Green, A. C., Hayward, N. K., et al. (2008). Polymorphisms in MGMT and DNA repair genes and the risk of esophageal adenocarcinoma. *International Journal of Cancer. Journal International Du Cancer, 123*(1), 174-180. doi:10.1002/ijc.23410

Dohm, J. C., Lottaz, C., Borodina, T., & Himmelbauer, H. (2007). SHARCGS, a fast and highly accurate short-read assembly algorithm for de novo genomic sequencing. *Genome Research, 17*(11), 1697-1706. doi:10.1101/gr.6435207

Dohm, J. C., Lottaz, C., Borodina, T., & Himmelbauer, H. (2008). Substantial biases in ultra-short read data sets from high-throughput DNA sequencing. *Nucleic Acids Research, 36*(16), e105. doi:10.1093/nar/gkn425

Dolan, P. C., & Denver, D. R. (2008). TileQC: a system for tile-based quality control of Solexa data. *BMC Bioinformatics, 9,* 250. doi:10.1186/1471-2105-9-250

Doss, C. G. P., & Sethumadhavan, R. (2009). Investigation on the role of nsSNPs in HNPCC genes--a bioinformatics approach. *Journal of Biomedical Science, 16,* 42. doi:10.1186/1423-0127-16-42

Durbin, R. M., Abecasis, G. R., Altshuler, D. L., Auton, A., Brooks, L. D., Durbin, R. M., Gibbs, R. A., et al. (2010). A map of human genome variation from population-scale sequencing. *Nature, 467*(7319), 1061-1073. doi:10.1038/nature09534

Eid, J. et al. Real-Time DNA Sequencing from Single Polymerase Molecules. Science 323, 133 -138 (2009).

Ewing, B., & Green, P. (1998). Base-calling of automated sequencer traces using phred. II. Error probabilities. *Genome Research, 8*(3), 186-194.

Ewing, B., Hillier, L., Wendl, M C, & Green, P. (1998). Base-calling of automated sequencer traces using phred. I. Accuracy assessment. *Genome Research, 8*(3), 175-185.

FASTX - toolkit. (n.d.). Retrieved from http://hannonlab.cshl.edu/fastx_toolkit/

Fatemi, S. H., King, D. P., Reutiman, T. J., Folsom, T. D., Laurence, J. A., Lee, S., Fan, Y.-T., et al. (2008). PDE4B polymorphisms and decreased PDE4B expression are associated with schizophrenia. *Schizophrenia Research, 101*(1-3), 36-49. doi:10.1016/j.schres.2008.01.029

Feuk, L., Carson, A. R., & Scherer, S. W. (2006). Structural variation in the human genome. *Nature Reviews. Genetics, 7*(2), 85-97. doi:10.1038/nrg1767

Flanagan, S. E., Patch, A.-M., & Ellard, S. (2010). Using SIFT and PolyPhen to predict loss-of-function and gain-of-function mutations. *Genetic Testing and Molecular Biomarkers, 14*(4), 533-537. doi:10.1089/gtmb.2010.0036

Flicek, P., & Birney, E. (2009). Sense from sequence reads: methods for alignment and assembly. *Nature Methods, 6*(11 Suppl), S6-S12. doi:10.1038/nmeth.1376

Frith, M. C., Wan, R., & Horton, P. (2010). Incorporating sequence quality data into alignment improves DNA read mapping. *Nucleic Acids Research, 38*(7), e100. doi:10.1093/nar/gkq010

Galan, M., Guivier, E., Caraux, G., Charbonnel, N., & Cosson, J.-F. (2010). A 454 multiplex sequencing method for rapid and reliable genotyping of highly polymorphic genes in large-scale studies. *BMC Genomics, 11*, 296. doi:10.1186/1471-2164-11-296

George Priya Doss, C., Sudandiradoss, C., Rajasekaran, R., Choudhury, P., Sinha, P., Hota, P., Batra, U. P., et al. (2008). Applications of computational algorithm tools to identify functional SNPs. *Functional & Integrative Genomics, 8*(4), 309-316. doi:10.1007/s10142-008-0086-7

Gnerre, S., Lander, E. S., Lindblad-Toh, K., & Jaffe, D. B. (2009). Assisted assembly: how to improve a de novo genome assembly by using related species. *Genome Biology, 10*(8), R88. doi:10.1186/gb-2009-10-8-r88

Gomez-Alvarez, V., Teal, T. K., & Schmidt, T. M. (2009). Systematic artifacts in metagenomes from complex microbial communities. *The ISME Journal, 3*(11), 1314-1317. doi:10.1038/ismej.2009.72

Goto, N., Prins, P., Nakao, M., Bonnal, R., Aerts, J., & Katayama, T. (2010). BioRuby: bioinformatics software for the Ruby programming language. *Bioinformatics (Oxford, England), 26*(20), 2617-2619. doi:10.1093/bioinformatics/btq475

Goya, R., Sun, M. G. F., Morin, R. D., Leung, G., Ha, G., Wiegand, K. C., Senz, J., et al. (2010). SNVMix: predicting single nucleotide variants from next-generation sequencing of tumors. *Bioinformatics (Oxford, England), 26*(6), 730-736. doi:10.1093/bioinformatics/btq040

Harris, T. D., Buzby, P. R., Babcock, H., Beer, E., Bowers, J., Braslavsky, I., Causey, M., et al. (2008). Single-molecule DNA sequencing of a viral genome. *Science (New York, N.Y.), 320*(5872), 106-109. doi:10.1126/science.1150427

Hashimoto, T., de Hoon, M. J. L., Grimmond, S. M., Daub, C. O., Hayashizaki, Y., & Faulkner, G. J. (2009). Probabilistic resolution of multi-mapping reads in massively parallel sequencing data using MuMRescueLite. *Bioinformatics (Oxford, England), 25*(19), 2613-2614. doi:10.1093/bioinformatics/btp438

Hernandez, D., François, P., Farinelli, L., Osterås, M., & Schrenzel, J. (2008). De novo bacterial genome sequencing: millions of very short reads assembled on a desktop computer. *Genome Research, 18*(5), 802-809. doi:10.1101/gr.072033.107

Holland, R. C. G., Down, T. A., Pocock, M., Prlić, A., Huen, D., James, K., Foisy, S., et al. (2008). BioJava: an open-source framework for bioinformatics. *Bioinformatics (Oxford, England), 24*(18), 2096-2097. doi:10.1093/bioinformatics/btn397

1000 Genomes Project, http://www.1000genomes.org/

Hormozdiari, F., Alkan, C., Eichler, E. E., & Sahinalp, S. C. (2009). Combinatorial algorithms for structural variation detection in high-throughput sequenced genomes. *Genome Research, 19*(7), 1270-1278. doi:10.1101/gr.088633.108

Hormozdiari, F., Hajirasouliha, I., Dao, P., Hach, F., Yorukoglu, D., Alkan, C., Eichler, E. E., et al. (2010). Next-generation VariationHunter: combinatorial algorithms for transposon insertion discovery. *Bioinformatics (Oxford, England), 26*(12), i350-357. doi:10.1093/bioinformatics/btq216

Husemann, P., & Stoye, J. (2010). Phylogenetic comparative assembly. *Algorithms for Molecular Biology: AMB, 5*, 3. doi:10.1186/1748-7188-5-3

Imelfort, M., Duran, C., Batley, J., & Edwards, D. (2009). Discovering genetic polymorphisms in next-generation sequencing data. *Plant Biotechnology Journal, 7*(4), 312-317. doi:10.1111/j.1467-7652.2009.00406.x

Isakov O, Modai S, Shomron N. Pathogen detection using short-RNA deep sequencing subtraction and assembly. *Bioinformatics*. 2011 Aug 1;27(15):2027-30.

Jeck, W. R., Reinhardt, J. A., Baltrus, D. A., Hickenbotham, M. T., Magrini, V., Mardis, E. R., Dangl, J. L., et al. (2007). Extending assembly of short DNA sequences to handle error. *Bioinformatics (Oxford, England), 23*(21), 2942-2944. doi:10.1093/bioinformatics/btm451

Karchin, R. (2009). Next generation tools for the annotation of human SNPs. *Briefings in Bioinformatics, 10*(1), 35-52. doi:10.1093/bib/bbn047

Kelley, D. R., Schatz, M. C., & Salzberg, S. L. (2010). Quake: quality-aware detection and correction of sequencing errors. *Genome Biology, 11*(11), R116. doi:10.1186/gb-2010-11-11-r116

Kent, W. J. (2002). BLAT--the BLAST-like alignment tool. *Genome Research, 12*(4), 656-664. doi:10.1101/gr.229202. Article published online before March 2002

Kircher, M., & Kelso, J. (2010). High-throughput DNA sequencing--concepts and limitations. *BioEssays: News and Reviews in Molecular, Cellular and Developmental Biology, 32*(6), 524-536. doi:10.1002/bies.200900181

Koboldt, D. C., Chen, K., Wylie, T., Larson, D. E., McLellan, M. D., Mardis, E. R., Weinstock, G. M., et al. (2009). VarScan: variant detection in massively parallel sequencing of individual and pooled samples. *Bioinformatics (Oxford, England), 25*(17), 2283-2285. doi:10.1093/bioinformatics/btp373

Koboldt, D. C., Ding, L., Mardis, E. R., & Wilson, R. K. (2010). Challenges of sequencing human genomes. *Briefings in Bioinformatics, 11*(5), 484 -498. doi:10.1093/bib/bbq016

Korbel, J. O., Abyzov, A., Mu, X. J., Carriero, N., Cayting, P., Zhang, Zhengdong, Snyder, M., et al. (2009). PEMer: a computational framework with simulation-based error models for inferring genomic structural variants from massive paired-end sequencing data. *Genome Biology, 10*(2), R23. doi:10.1186/gb-2009-10-2-r23

Krawitz, P., Rödelsperger, C., Jäger, M., Jostins, L., Bauer, S., & Robinson, P. N. (2010). Microindel detection in short-read sequence data. *Bioinformatics (Oxford, England), 26*(6), 722-729. doi:10.1093/bioinformatics/btq027

Kumar, P., Henikoff, S., & Ng, P. C. (2009). Predicting the effects of coding non-synonymous variants on protein function using the SIFT algorithm. *Nature Protocols, 4*(7), 1073-1081. doi:10.1038/nprot.2009.86

Langmead, B., Trapnell, C., Pop, M., & Salzberg, S. L. (2009). Ultrafast and memory-efficient alignment of short DNA sequences to the human genome. *Genome Biology, 10*(3), R25. doi:10.1186/gb-2009-10-3-r25

Lassmann, T., Hayashizaki, Y., & Daub, C. O. (2009). TagDust--a program to eliminate artifacts from next generation sequencing data. *Bioinformatics (Oxford, England), 25*(21), 2839-2840. doi:10.1093/bioinformatics/btp527

Lassmann, T., Hayashizaki, Y., & Daub, C. O. (2011). SAMStat: monitoring biases in next generation sequencing data. *Bioinformatics (Oxford, England), 27*(1), 130-131. doi:10.1093/bioinformatics/btq614

Lee, P. H., & Shatkay, H. (2008). F-SNP: computationally predicted functional SNPs for disease association studies. *Nucleic Acids Research, 36*(Database issue), D820-824. doi:10.1093/nar/gkm904

Ley TJ, Mardis ER, Ding L, Fulton B, McLellan MD, et al., DNA sequencing of a cytogenetically normal acute myeloid leukaemia genome. *Nature.* 2008 Nov 6;456(7218):66-72.

Li, Biao, Krishnan, V. G., Mort, M. E., Xin, F., Kamati, K. K., Cooper, D. N., Mooney, S. D., et al. (2009). Automated inference of molecular mechanisms of disease from amino acid substitutions. *Bioinformatics (Oxford, England), 25*(21), 2744-2750. doi:10.1093/bioinformatics/btp528

Li, H. (2011). Improving SNP discovery by base alignment quality. *Bioinformatics, 27*(8), 1157-1158. doi:10.1093/bioinformatics/btr076

Li, H., & Durbin, R. (2009). Fast and accurate short read alignment with Burrows-Wheeler transform. *Bioinformatics (Oxford, England), 25*(14), 1754-1760. doi:10.1093/bioinformatics/btp324

Li, H., Handsaker, B., Wysoker, A., Fennell, T., Ruan, J., Homer, N., Marth, G., et al. (2009). The Sequence Alignment/Map format and SAMtools. *Bioinformatics (Oxford, England), 25*(16), 2078-2079. doi:10.1093/bioinformatics/btp352

Li, H., & Homer, N. (2010). A survey of sequence alignment algorithms for next-generation sequencing. *Briefings in Bioinformatics, 11*(5), 473-483. doi:10.1093/bib/bbq015

Li, H., Ruan, J., & Durbin, R. (2008). Mapping short DNA sequencing reads and calling variants using mapping quality scores. *Genome Research, 18*(11), 1851-1858. doi:10.1101/gr.078212.108

Li, K., & Stockwell, T. (2010). VariantClassifier: A hierarchical variant classifier for annotated genomes. *BMC Research Notes, 3*(1), 191. doi:10.1186/1756-0500-3-191

Li, R., Fan, W., Tian, G., Zhu, H., He, L., Cai, J., Huang, Q., et al. (2010). The sequence and de novo assembly of the giant panda genome. *Nature, 463*(7279), 311-317. doi:10.1038/nature08696

Li, R., Li, Y., Fang, X., Yang, H., Wang, Jian, Kristiansen, K., & Wang, Jun. (2009). SNP detection for massively parallel whole-genome resequencing. *Genome Research, 19*(6), 1124-1132. doi:10.1101/gr.088013.108

Li, R., Yu, C., Li, Y., Lam, T.-W., Yiu, S.-M., Kristiansen, K., & Wang, Jun. (2009). SOAP2: an improved ultrafast tool for short read alignment. *Bioinformatics (Oxford, England), 25*(15), 1966-1967. doi:10.1093/bioinformatics/btp336

Li, R., Zhu, H., Ruan, J., Qian, W., Fang, X., Shi, Z., Li, Y., et al. (2010). De novo assembly of human genomes with massively parallel short read sequencing. *Genome Research, 20*(2), 265-272. doi:10.1101/gr.097261.109

Lin, H., Zhang, Zefeng, Zhang, M. Q., Ma, B., & Li, M. (2008). ZOOM! Zillions of oligos mapped. *Bioinformatics (Oxford, England), 24*(21), 2431-2437. doi:10.1093/bioinformatics/btn416

Mardis, E. R. (2008). The impact of next-generation sequencing technology on genetics. *Trends in Genetics: TIG, 24*(3), 133-141. doi:10.1016/j.tig.2007.12.007

Margulies, M., Egholm, M., Altman, W. E., Attiya, S., Bader, J. S., Bemben, L. A., Berka, J., Braverman, M. S., Chen, Y.-J., & Chen, Z. (2005a). Genome sequencing in microfabricated high-density picolitre reactors. *Nature, 437*(7057), 376-380. doi:10.1038/nature03959

Margulies, M., Egholm, M., Altman, W. E., Attiya, S., Bader, J. S., Bemben, L. A., Berka, J., Braverman, M. S., Chen, Y.-J., & Chen, Z. (2005b). Genome sequencing in microfabricated high-density picolitre reactors. *Nature, 437*(7057), 376-380. doi:10.1038/nature03959

Martínez-Alcántara, A., Ballesteros, E., Feng, C., Rojas, M., Koshinsky, H., Fofanov, V. Y., Havlak, P., et al. (2009). PIQA: pipeline for Illumina G1 genome analyzer data quality assessment. *Bioinformatics (Oxford, England), 25*(18), 2438-2439. doi:10.1093/bioinformatics/btp429

McKenna, A., Hanna, Matthew, Banks, E., Sivachenko, A., Cibulskis, K., Kernytsky, A., Garimella, K., et al. (2010). The Genome Analysis Toolkit: a MapReduce framework for analyzing next-generation DNA sequencing data. *Genome Research, 20*(9), 1297-1303. doi:10.1101/gr.107524.110

McKernan, K. J., Peckham, H. E., Costa, G. L., McLaughlin, S. F., Fu, Y., Tsung, E. F., Clouser, C. R., et al. (2009). Sequence and structural variation in a human genome uncovered by short-read, massively parallel ligation sequencing using two-base encoding. *Genome Research, 19*(9), 1527-1541. doi:10.1101/gr.091868.109

McKernan, K. J., Peckham, H. E., Costa, G. L., McLaughlin, S. F., Fu, Y., Tsung, E. F., Clouser, C. R., et al. (2009). Sequence and structural variation in a human genome uncovered by short-read, massively parallel ligation sequencing using two-base encoding. *Genome Research, 19*(9), 1527-1541. doi:10.1101/gr.091868.109

McLaren, W., Pritchard, B., Rios, D., Chen, Y., Flicek, P., & Cunningham, F. (2010). Deriving the consequences of genomic variants with the Ensembl API and SNP Effect Predictor. *Bioinformatics, 26*(16), 2069 -2070. doi:10.1093/bioinformatics/btq330

Meader, S., Hillier, L. W., Locke, D., Ponting, C. P., & Lunter, G. (2010). Genome assembly quality: assessment and improvement using the neutral indel model. *Genome Research, 20*(5), 675-684. doi:10.1101/gr.096966.109

Medvedev, P., Stanciu, M., & Brudno, M. (2009). Computational methods for discovering structural variation with next-generation sequencing. *Nature Methods, 6*(11 Suppl), S13-20. doi:10.1038/nmeth.1374

Metzker, M. L. (2010). Sequencing technologies - the next generation. *Nature Reviews. Genetics, 11*(1), 31-46. doi:10.1038/nrg2626

Mi, H., Guo, N., Kejariwal, A., & Thomas, P. D. (2007). PANTHER version 6: protein sequence and function evolution data with expanded representation of biological pathways. *Nucleic Acids Research, 35*(Database issue), D247-252. doi:10.1093/nar/gkl869

Miller, J. R., Koren, S., & Sutton, G. (2010). Assembly algorithms for next-generation sequencing data. *Genomics, 95*(6), 315-327. doi:10.1016/j.ygeno.2010.03.001

Mills, Ryan E, Luttig, C. T., Larkins, C. E., Beauchamp, A., Tsui, C., Pittard, W Stephen, & Devine, Scott E. (2006). An initial map of insertion and deletion (INDEL) variation in the human genome. *Genome Research, 16*(9), 1182-1190. doi:10.1101/gr.4565806

Mortazavi, A., Williams, B. A., McCue, K., Schaeffer, L., & Wold, B. (2008). Mapping and quantifying mammalian transcriptomes by RNA-Seq. *Nature Methods, 5*(7), 621-628. doi:10.1038/nmeth.1226

Mullaney, J. M., Mills, R. E., Pittard, W. S., & Devine, S. E. (2010). Small insertions and deletions (INDELs) in human genomes. *Human Molecular Genetics, 19*(R2), R131-R136. doi:10.1093/hmg/ddq400

Myers, E. W. (1995). Toward simplifying and accurately formulating fragment assembly. *Journal of Computational Biology: A Journal of Computational Molecular Cell Biology*, 2(2), 275-290.

Ng, P. C., & Henikoff, S. (2006). Predicting the effects of amino acid substitutions on protein function. *Annual Review of Genomics and Human Genetics*, 7, 61-80. doi:10.1146/annurev.genom.7.080505.115630

Nothnagel, M., Herrmann, A., Wolf, A., Schreiber, S., Platzer, M., Siebert, R., Krawczak, M., et al. (2011). Technology-specific error signatures in the 1000 Genomes Project data. *Human Genetics*. doi:10.1007/s00439-011-0971-3

Novoalign. (n.d.).. Retrieved from http://www.novocraft.com/main/page.php?s=novoalign

Paşaniuc, B., Zaitlen, N., & Halperin, E. (2011). Accurate Estimation of Expression Levels of Homologous Genes in RNA-seq Experiments. *Journal of Computational Biology: A Journal of Computational Molecular Cell Biology*, 18(3), 459-468. doi:10.1089/cmb.2010.0259

Paszkiewicz, K., & Studholme, D. J. (2010). De novo assembly of short sequence reads. *Briefings in Bioinformatics*, 11(5), 457-472. doi:10.1093/bib/bbq020

PICARD. (n.d.).. Retrieved from http://picard.sourceforge.net/index.shtml

Pop, M., Phillippy, A., Delcher, A. L., & Salzberg, S. L. (2004). Comparative genome assembly. *Briefings in Bioinformatics*, 5(3), 237-248.

Qi, J., Zhao, F., Buboltz, A., & Schuster, S. C. (2010). inGAP: an integrated next-generation genome analysis pipeline. *Bioinformatics (Oxford, England)*, 26(1), 127-129. doi:10.1093/bioinformatics/btp615

Ramensky, V., Bork, P., & Sunyaev, S. (2002). Human non-synonymous SNPs: server and survey. *Nucleic Acids Research*, 30(17), 3894-3900.

Schadt, E. E., Turner, S., & Kasarskis, A. (2010). A window into third-generation sequencing. *Human Molecular Genetics*, 19(R2), R227-240. doi:10.1093/hmg/ddq416

Schmieder, R., & Edwards, R. (2011). Quality control and preprocessing of metagenomic datasets. *Bioinformatics (Oxford, England)*, 27(6), 863-864. doi:10.1093/bioinformatics/btr026

Schmieder, R., Lim, Y. W., Rohwer, F., & Edwards, R. (2010). TagCleaner: Identification and removal of tag sequences from genomic and metagenomic datasets. *BMC Bioinformatics*, 11, 341. doi:10.1186/1471-2105-11-341

Schwartz, S., Oren, R., & Ast, G. (2011). Detection and removal of biases in the analysis of next-generation sequencing reads. *PloS One*, 6(1), e16685. doi:10.1371/journal.pone.0016685

Simpson, J. T., Wong, K., Jackman, S. D., Schein, J. E., Jones, S. J. M., & Birol, I. (2009). ABySS: a parallel assembler for short read sequence data. *Genome Research*, 19(6), 1117-1123. doi:10.1101/gr.089532.108

Stajich, J. E., Block, D., Boulez, K., Brenner, S. E., Chervitz, S. A., Dagdigian, C., Fuellen, G., et al. (2002). The Bioperl toolkit: Perl modules for the life sciences. *Genome Research*, 12(10), 1611-1618. doi:10.1101/gr.361602

Thusberg, J., Olatubosun, A., & Vihinen, M. (2011). Performance of mutation pathogenicity prediction methods on missense variants. *Human Mutation*, 32(4), 358-368. doi:10.1002/humu.21445

Trapnell, C., & Salzberg, S. L. (2009). How to map billions of short reads onto genomes. *Nature Biotechnology*, 27(5), 455-457. doi:10.1038/nbt0509-455

Treangen, T. J., Sommer, D. D., Angly, F. E., Koren, S., & Pop, M. (2011). Next Generation Sequence Assembly with AMOS. *Current Protocols in Bioinformatics / Editoral Board, Andreas D. Baxevanis... [et Al, Chapter 11*, Unit11.8. doi:10.1002/0471250953.bi1108s33

Van Deerlin, V. M., Leverenz, J. B., Bekris, L. M., Bird, T. D., Yuan, W., Elman, L. B., Clay, D., et al. (2008). TARDBP mutations in amyotrophic lateral sclerosis with TDP-43 neuropathology: a genetic and histopathological analysis. *Lancet Neurology, 7*(5), 409-416. doi:10.1016/S1474-4422(08)70071-1

Wang, K., Li, M. & Hakonarson, H. ANNOVAR: functional annotation of genetic variants from high-throughput sequencing data. *Nucleic Acids Res 38*, e164 (2010).

Wang, Z., & Moult, J. (2001). SNPs, protein structure, and disease. *Human Mutation, 17*(4), 263-270. doi:10.1002/humu.22

Ye, Kai, Schulz, M. H., Long, Q., Apweiler, R., & Ning, Z. (2009). Pindel: a pattern growth approach to detect break points of large deletions and medium sized insertions from paired-end short reads. *Bioinformatics (Oxford, England), 25*(21), 2865-2871. doi:10.1093/bioinformatics/btp394

Yoon, S., Xuan, Z., Makarov, V., Ye, Kenny, & Sebat, J. (2009). Sensitive and accurate detection of copy number variants using read depth of coverage. *Genome Research, 19*(9), 1586 -1592. doi:10.1101/gr.092981.109

Yuan, H.-Y., Chiou, J.-J., Tseng, W.-H., Liu, C.-H., Liu, C.-K., Lin, Y.-J., Wang, H.-H., et al. (2006). FASTSNP: an always up-to-date and extendable service for SNP function analysis and prioritization. *Nucleic Acids Research, 34*(Web Server issue), W635-641. doi:10.1093/nar/gkl236

Zerbino, D. R., & Birney, E. (2008). Velvet: algorithms for de novo short read assembly using de Bruijn graphs. *Genome Research, 18*(5), 821-829. doi:10.1101/gr.074492.107

Zhang, W., Chen, J., Yang, Y., Tang, Y., Shang, J., & Shen, B. (2011). A practical comparison of de novo genome assembly software tools for next-generation sequencing technologies. *PloS One, 6*(3), e17915. doi:10.1371/journal.pone.0017915

Zhao, X., Palmer, L. E., Bolanos, R., Mircean, C., Fasulo, D., & Wittenberg, G. M. (2010). EDAR: an efficient error detection and removal algorithm for next generation sequencing data. *Journal of Computational Biology: A Journal of Computational Molecular Cell Biology, 17*(11), 1549-1560. doi:10.1089/cmb.2010.0127

30

Whole Genome Annotation: In Silico Analysis

Vasco Azevedo et al.*
*Federal University of Minas Gerais (UFMG) and Federal University of Pará (UFPA),
Brazil*

1. Introduction

After a genome is assembled, the next step is genomic annotation, which can generate data that will allow various types of research of the model organism. Complete DNA sequences of the organism are then mapped in areas pertinent to the research objectives. In this chapter, we explore relevant ongoing research on genes and consider the gene as a basic mapping unit. Gene prediction is the first hurdle we come across to begin the extensive and intensive work demonstrated in first item, which deals with assembly of the genome. Gene prediction can be made with computational techniques for recognizing gene sequences, including stop codons and the initial portions of nucleotide sequences; it involves empirical rules concerning minimum coding sequences (CDS's) and is limited due to overlapping sequences coding forward and reverse.

Finishing gene prediction step by a computer initiates the functional annotation stage. Functional annotation, item 3, can be done initially by computer, using similarity in sequence alignment. However, no software is capable of generating a functional annotation without many false positive results, since conserved protein domains with varied functions make gene sequence alignment difficult. In this case, after automatic annotation, the predicted genes need to be revised manually. In manual curation, item 4, an expert can more accurately locate frameshifts in the DNA strand. Depending on the number of errors found, genomic annotation may be postponed, requiring a return to the previous stage of genome assembly. In manual curation, the principal contributions are usually correction of the start codon position, gene name, gene product and, finally, identification of frameshifts.

When functional annotation is completed, the genome should subsequently be submitted. It occurs after the assembly and annotation steps making the data generated available in public-access databanks. Submission is a pre-requisite for publication in scientific journals. Another advantage of genome publication in public-access sites is that it permits use of various genome analysis tools. For example, searches for genomic plasticity, pangenomic study, exported antigens and evaluation of innate and adaptive immune responses. The pangenome approach, item 5, concepts of species can be used as a filter for targeting candidates for vaccines, diagnostic kits and drug development. For drug development, the

* Vinicius Abreu, Sintia Almeida, Anderson Santos, Siomar Soares, Amjad Ali, Anne Pinto, Aryane Magalhães, Eudes Barbosa, Rommel Ramos, Louise Cerdeira, Adriana Carneiro, Paula Schneider, Artur Silva and Anderson Miyoshi
Federal University of Minas Gerais (UFMG) and Federal University of Pará (UFPA), Brazil

core set of proteins is a more likely source of useful information, for developing both vaccines and diagnostic materials for a unique pangenome set of a species of interest.

Genomic plasticity, item 6, is the dynamic property of genomes, involving DNA gains, losses, and rearrangement; it allows bacteria to adapt to new hosts and environments. There are several mechanisms that can drive these changes, including point mutations, gene conversions, rearrangements (inversion or translocation), deletions and DNA insertions from other organisms (through plasmids, bacteriophages, transposons, insertion elements and genomic islands). Gene acquisition and loss by all these mechanisms influences bacterial lifestyles and physiological versatility. Analyses of HGT regions in silico has become feasible due to the introduction of next–generation sequencing technologies, which allows sequencing of prokaryotic genomes at a faster rate than the earlier Sanger method and at a considerably lower operational cost. Consequently, the number of complete genome sequences available for analysis has grown and continues to grow rapidly.

In post-genomics, study of Reverse Vaccinology (RV), item 7, can provide predictions of the sub cellular locations of an entire predicted proteome. Additionally, these previous annotations, prediction of peptides with high affinity for class I and II MHC proteins is another in silico analysis that increases the probability of selecting antigens that can promote immune responses in organisms infected by a pathogen. The field of research referred to as immunoinformatics, item 8, is giving us the opportunity to analyze antigens with greater selectivity and increase the likelihood of developing a successful vaccine.

2. Gene prediction

The development of modern sequencing technology has resulted in an exponential increase in the number of available genome sequences. To illustrate, in 1997 there were 10 complete genome sequences of bacteria available in the NCBI (Lukashin & Borodovsky, 1998); by 2011, this number had sharply increased to 1,538 http://www.ncbi.nlm.nih.gov/genomes/lproks.cgi. This enormous increase in the quantity of available information stimulated the development of tools for gene prediction. The development of these tools is a tremendous challenge, and it is a major contribution of Bioinformatics to the field of genomics.

2.1 Gene prediction strategies

Gene prediction programs can be divided into two categories: an empirical category, which relies on sequence similarity; and ab initio, which uses signal and content sensors. Empirical gene predictors search for similarity in the genome; they predict genes based on homologies with known databases, such as genomic DNA, cDNA, dbEST and proteins. This approach facilitates the identification of well–conserved exons. Ab initio gene finders use sequence information of signal and content sensors. Usually, these programs are based on Hidden Markov Models. Ab initio can be organized into categories based on the number of genome sequences used in gene analysis; it includes single, dual and multiple–genome predictors. Integrated approaches couple the extrinsic methodology of empirical gene–finders and intrinsic ab initio prediction. This technique significantly improves gene prediction protocols (Allen et al., 2004).

2.2 Eukaryotes

The complexity of the challenge faced by Bioinformatics is only completely understood when we look at the complexity of the eukaryotic genome. Within genomes, genes are not organized in a continuous cluster. Instead, the coding regions (exons) are often widely interspersed with non–coding intervening sequences (introns). Furthermore, in many cases the intronic region is much larger than the exonic region. These low–density coding sequences are evident in the human genome, in which only approximately 3% of the DNA generates proteins. The exon and intron issue can be compared to trying to read a non-continuous article in a journal. In an analogy, one must first identify in which part of the journal (genome) the article (gene) of interest is; then, as the DNA sequences are read, it is necessary to identify which part is informative (exon) and which part contains random information (intron). Also, genes can be altered by alternative splicing, which is a process that generates multiple protein sequences from the same gene sequence template (Schellenberg et al., 2008).

Gene prediction methodology for eukaryotes involves two distinct aspects; the first focuses on the information utilized for gene recognition, basically recognizing signal functions in the DNA strand; the second uses algorithms implemented by prediction programs for accurate prediction of gene structure and organization. The signal function search can be divided into two mechanisms utilized for locating genes. One classifies the content of the DNA strand and the other searches for functional signals in the genome:

(i) The content sensor classifies the DNA regions into coding and non-coding segments (introns, intergenic regions and untranslated regions). This mechanism involves two approaches, intrinsic and extrinsic. The extrinsic approach relies on the assumption that coding regions are evolutionarily more conserved than non–coding regions. Consequently, this methodology employs local alignment tools, like BLAST (Johnson et al., 2008) ; this makes it possible to make comparisons within the genome and between closely-related species. However, one important flaw in this approach involves the necessity of identifying homologies within the database in order to extract results. If none is found, this methodology is unable to determine if a region "codes" for a protein (Sleator, 2010). (ii) The functional sensor approach searches the genome for consensus sequences. Consensus sequences are extracted from multiple alignments of functionally-related documented sequences. The functional signals involve transcription, translation and splice sites. Transcriptional signals includes the CAP signal at the transcriptional start site and the polyadenylation signal located 20 to 30 bp downstream of the coding region. Another important signal to identify is the translation initiation site, although this feature has limitations due to a lack of knowledge concerning initiation sites in eukaryotes (Mathé et al., 2002).

2.3 Prokaryotes

Unlike eukaryotes, the archaeal, bacterial and virus genomes are highly gene-dense. The protein coding regions usually represent more than 90% of the genome. Therefore the accuracy of gene predictors depends primarily on determining which of the six frames contains the real gene. The simplest approach in gene prediction is to look for Open Reading Frames (ORFs). An ORF is a DNA sequence that initiates at a start codon and ends at a stop codon, with no other intervening stop codon. One way to locate genes is to look for ORFs with the mean size of proteins (roughly 900 base pairs) (Allen et al., 2004). Therefore, long ORFs indicate possible genes, although this methodology fails to predict small genes.

The major problem in simply applying this technique is the possibility of ORF overlap in the different DNA strains. This approach must be used along with guidelines to avoid overlapping, choosing the more likely candidates. Also, numerous false positives are found in non-coding regions. Due to the high gene density, it is difficult to confidently state that any gene predicted in a non–coding region is false. This problem can be minimized by searching for homologies in closely-related organisms. If we do not find a conserved sequence in related species, it is assumed that the prediction (of a gene) is false.

Another problem faced by prediction programs in prokaryotes is how to determine the start codon of a sequence. The first initiation site in a sequence is not necessarily the true one. To solve this problem, programs can employ ribosome binding sites (RBS), which provide a strong signal, indicating the position of the true start site. In conclusion, there is a drop in prediction accuracy in high–GC–content genomes. Rich GC genomes contain fewer stop codons and more spurious ORFs. These false ORFs are often chosen by prediction programs instead of the real ones in the same DNA region. Additionally, the longer ORFs in GC–rich genomes contain more potential start codons, leading to a drop in the accuracy of translation initiation site prediction (Hyatt et al., 2010).

2.4 Tools
2.4.1 Glimmer
The first version of Glimmer (Gene Locator and Interpolated Markov ModelER) was released in 1998 ; the 3.02 version was released in 2006. Glimmer is a system for finding genes in microbial DNA, especially the genomes of bacteria, archaea, and viruses. Glimmer uses interpolated Markov models (IMMs) to identify coding regions and distinguish them from noncoding DNA. Glimmer was the primary microbial gene finder used at The Institute for Genomic Research (TIGR), where it was first developed, and it has been used to annotate the complete genomes of over 100 bacterial species from TIGR and other labs. Like other gene prediction programs, Glimmer can be installed and run locally and has a web-based platform (Salzberg et al., 1998). All one needs for online gene prediction of a genome is the fasta version of the sequence and access to the site:

http://www.ncbi.nlm.nih.gov/genomes/MICROBES/glimmer_3.cgi.

2.4.2 FgenesB
FgenesB is a package developed by Softberry Inc. for automatic annotation of bacterial genomes. The gene prediction algorithm is based on Markov chain models of coding regions and translation and termination sites. The package includes options to work on sets of sequences, such as scaffolds of bacterial genomes or short sequencing reads extracted from bacterial communities. For community sequence annotation, it includes ABsplit program, which separates archebacterial and eubacterial sequences. FGENESB was used in the first published bacterial community annotation project (Tyson et al., 2004).

2.4.3 Prodigal
Prodigal (Prokaryotic Dynamic Programming Genefinding Algorithm) is a microbial (bacterial and archaeal) gene finding program developed at Oak Ridge National Laboratory and the University of Tennessee. Prodigal focuses specifically on three goals: improved gene structure prediction, improved translation initiation site recognition, and reduced false positives (Hyatt et al., 2010). The source code is freely available under the General Public License and the program can be accessed at http://compbio.ornl.gov/prodigal/.

2.4.4 GeneMarkTM

GeneMark is a public access program for gene prediction in eukaryotes. It is a family of gene prediction programs developed at Georgia Institute of Technology, Atlanta, Georgia, USA. GeneMark can operate in two ways: the first one is online, where one can make predictions, using for comparison one of the many available models; the second option is for novel genomes, in this way one can install and run the program locally. The web–based version of GeneMark is available at http://exon.biology.gatech.edu/.

For gene prediction in eukaryotes, GeneMark combines two programs, GeneMark–E* and GeneMark.hmm–E. The GeneMark-E program determines the protein-coding potential of a DNA sequence (within a sliding window) by using species-specific parameters of the Markov models of coding and non-coding regions. This approach allows delineating local variations with coding potential. The GeneMark graph shows details of the protein-coding potential distribution along a sequence, while the GeneMark.hmm-E program predicts genes and intergenic regions in a sequence as a whole. The Hidden Markov models take advantage of the "grammar" of gene organization. The GeneMark.hmm programs identify the most likely parse of the whole DNA sequence into protein coding genes (with possible introns) and intergenic regions.

The statistical model employed in the GeneMark.hmm algorithm is a hidden Markov model. It includes hidden states for initial, internal and terminal exons, introns, intergenic regions and single exon genes. It also includes hidden states for start site (initiation site), stop site (termination site), and donor and acceptor splice sites. The protein-coding states (initial, internal, terminal exons and single exon genes) emit nucleotide sequences modeled by inhomogeneous 3–periodic fifth–order Markov chains. The non-coding states (intron and intergenic regions) emit sequences modeled by homogeneous Markov chains (Lukashin & Borodovsky, 1998).

3. Automated functional annotation

Automated functional annotation of genomes can be quite efficient because it is a computational process based on the alignment of ORF sequences of the organism with sequences from various other organisms (Kislyuk et al., 2010). Public domain databases contain full annotations of thousands of prokaryotic organisms (Benson et al., 2008). Automatic functional annotation takes advantage of knowledge concerning ORFs of homologous organisms, saving considerable time in manual curation (Li et al., 2010). However, care must be taken with fully automated functional annotation, since similarity of sequences can easily incur false positives (Lorenzi et al., 2010). In this section we discuss the advantages and dangers of using fully-automated functional annotation, and we explore some features of tools and services for this purpose.

3.1 Massive sequence alignments must be planned

Algorithms for alignment of biological sequences are intensively used in automatic functional annotation (Aparicio et al., 2006; Meyer et al., 2003). Alignments of ORFs from a newly assembled genome with counterpart ORFs can provide the first hints about the new genome. For an organism with about 2,000 ORFs, analysis of similar sequences against a database of non-redundant (NR) proteins from NCBI can consume several processing hours. For example, assuming that this analysis is done on a computer isolated from the internet, hardware with 24 Gb RAM and eight processors, totaling 24 GHz CPU, this task will consume approximately eight hours of processing time.

Though it is a completely automated computer process, the user has considerable responsibility to set conditions to be utilized in the computation in order to obtain good quality data. These conditions define the quality criteria that best fit the type of organism, for example, the cut–off value for a significant alignment with sequences of other organisms in the NCBI, the number of homologous sequences to be returned as a result and the file format of the output alignment. An additional parameter is required if the sequence search (query) and the targeted search sequences (subject) are in different formats (nucleotides versus amino acids). This parameter determines the most adequate table for translation of codons of the organism in question so that the alignment algorithm of sequences is able to interpret the correspondence between the query sequences and the subject. The number of parameters of an algorithm for aligning sequences can be quite large, justifying training with a heavy workload for optimal utilization. Our objective here is not to explore possible situations, but to alert users that the results of these algorithms can improve these alignments by reading the manual algorithm and consequently adjusting it to a particular situation concerning a query organism or subject. Thus, when beginning a massive alignment sequences project involving a novel genome, with an analysis that will take hours and create high expectations, it is advisable to use not just the basic configurations in these alignment algorithms. It would be useful to take time to weigh and incorporate options that will determine the success or failure of these alignments.

3.2 Knowledge reapplication and time saving

There has been significant growth in the number of DNA sequences available in public databases, because of new genome sequencing technologies, which have made it simpler, more efficient and cheaper to obtain complete genomes (Zhao & Grant, 2010). Fully assembled and annotated genomes of various forms of bacterial life are available to facilitate the processing and inclusion of a newly assembled genome. This wide range of genomes provides the opportunity for new research into large-scale SNPs, DNA methylation and mRNA expression profiles, and resequencing data (Datta et al., 2010). It also allows comparison of annotations from different research groups working with different organisms, some of which may be homologous to a newly-sequenced genome. Just as one can take advantage of knowledge about the function of genes from different organisms, it is also advisable to use the personal knowledge of a researcher on a specific organism in order to accelerate the process of automatic annotation. Based on evidence about a high degree of evolutionary proximity between a newly-assembled genome and a particular organism homolog that already has a fully-assembled and annotated genome, we can choose to use only the annotation of such an organism as a resource for a first automatic annotation.

The problems a researcher would normally encounter when utilizing annotations from various genomes could be resolved by comparison with the annotation of a homologous organism. This situation is common when one examines the pangenome of a species, as it is expected that most of the coding sequences of different strains of bacteria are not very different (Trost et al., 2010). In this case, it appears to be advantageous to identify a small set of target organisms (subject) in a sequence similarity search, with the objective of providing a first genome annotation (query); this may even be a set with only one organism.

3.3 Error propagation: Automated versus manual annotation

It is important to bear in mind that the GenBank is not a fully curated database (Benson et al., 2008); many genomes may have been deposited only as automatic annotations. With current technology, it is not possible to dispense with manual curation of an automatic annotation, or even experimental evidence concerning gene prediction and annotation based on sequence similarities (Poptsova & Gogarten, 2010). Although it is not normally feasible to initially include experimental verification of gene prediction, it seems reasonable to take advantage of expert human annotation of genomes to help determine the outcome of automatic annotation. Assuming one is working on the pangenome of an organism, such a measure can not only reduce false positives in comparisons of sequence similarities, but also determination of homologous genomes based on a particular annotation. During automatic annotation, a measure that has the potential to minimize error propagation would be allocating different weights for the results of sequence similarity to genes from organisms for which there is evidence of expert manual curation.

3.4 Tools

The following are some tools for automatic annotation of entire genomes, with brief descriptions of their core functionality and instructions on how to use them.

3.4.1 GenDB

One of the reasons that GenDB is included among a select set of tools for automatic annotation of genomes is the fact that it was developed for the web platform (Meyer et al., 2003). Geographically dispersed research groups can benefit from web interfaces using standard tools and a centralized database. Version 2.4 of GenDB has three modules: core, web, and gui. The core module has programs written in perl that allow creation of an annotation project, importation of data in fasta / EMBL format, execution pipeline automatic annotation, display of circular genomic maps, data export and annotation project deletion. Implementation of the programs in the module allows a team of curators to work on the web and edit diverse features of various genes. The gui module has editing features that are more sophisticated than those of the web module, allowing execution of tasks performed by the core module, but with a graphical interface. The GenDB program performs sequence alignments using the program Blast (Altschul et al., 1997) and allows incorporation of predictions of conserved domains of protein families based on InterPro-Scan (Hunter et al., 2009),as well as transmembrane domains based on TMHMM (Krogh et al., 2001), and indications of export to the extracellular medium through SignalP (Bendtsen et al., 2004).

3.4.2 BLAST2GO (B2G)

This tool was designed as an interface for Gene Ontology (GO); additional features have transformed it into a more comprehensive annotation platform (Aparicio et al., 2006). The program menus include various steps initiating annotation, with an automatic alignment of genome sequences against a protein-based non-redundant (NR) NCBI database, through prediction of conserved domains (InterPro–Scan), GO annotation ratings against the enzymatic English Enzymatic Code (EC) and subsequent visualization of molecular interactions in a genome by means of maps in the format of the Kyoto Encyclopedia of Genes and Genomes (KEEGO). Being a visually oriented tool, it has graphical tools to help analyze the vast amount of data generated in the predictions. A user of B2G does not necessarily have to perform all the steps of analysis that are offered, but in order to advance to the next phase of analysis it is imperative that the previous phase be performed beforehand. Processing of an entire genome with approximately two thousand ORFs can take several days, as the first step is always sequence alignment against the NCBI NR base. Fortunately, B2G is designed to be a modular analysis tool. If a B2G user has computational resources that are more efficient than the shared resources on the public server, the user can perform alignment of sequences on his own hardware to generate an output in HTML format and continue the alignment processes following annotation with B2G. Should the user be dissatisfied with the efficiency of processes of annotating GO terms of the server's common B2G, there is a version of B2G than he can run separately with his superior hardware. The results generated in the offline mode can be uploaded to the online tool to continue the review process using a variety of tools, including statistical comparisons between two genomes. B2G was developed with Sun Java technology, which can be run on any operating system; however, the B2G offline module is designed to run on the Linux platform.

3.4.3 CpDB relational schema: a practical example

This tutorial has approximately 100 steps, including software installation and configuration, edition of files by Linux commands or through interfaces with biological sequence manipulation programs. The tutorial presumes that the programs Artemis, Java (Sun) and Blast version 2.2.20 or previous were locally installed. Many editions of files are made with the "sed" program of Linux, which is included in most Linux versions. All of the steps in this manual can be automated in order to develop an automatic pipeline for annotation, allowing the *Corynebacterium pseudotuberculosis* DataBase (CpDB), a relational database schema and tools for bacterial genomes annotation and pos-genome research, to become another web-based automatic annotation environment. For now, this tutorial has an instructional character, to help make a student aware of the necessities and difficulties involved in the process of automatic annotation of genomes. In order to obtain the tutorial files, type the following command in Linux, Ubuntu 10.10 or later:

svn   checkout   svn://150.164.37.20/genomes/autoannotation   --username=student   --password=bioinfo

After finalizing the verification of all of the files, this tutorial continues in the document "Tutorial.pdf", which will be in the folder "autoannotation".

4. Manual curation

Genome annotation is a process that consists of adding analyses and biological interpretations to DNA sequence information. This process can be divided (Stein, 2001), into three main categories: annotation of nucleotides, proteins and processes. Annotation of nucleotides can be done when there is information about the complete genome (or DNA segments) of an organism. It involves looking for the physical location (position on the chromosome) of each part of the sequence and discovering the location of the genes, RNAs, repeat elements, etc. In the annotation of proteins, which is done when there is information about the genes (obtained by genome or cDNA sequencing) of an organism, there is a search for gene function. Besides general predictions about gene and protein function, other information can be found in an annotation, such as biochemical and structural properties of a protein, prediction of operons, gene ontology, evolutionary relationships and metabolic cycles (Stothard & Wishart, 2006). Consequently, functional annotation or manual curation is a fundamental part of the process of assembling and annotating a genome, in which the curator is the person responsible for validating the elements. In manual curation, all of the predicted genes will be validated and their products named (Stein, 2001). A more detailed description of the gene or gene family product is obtained through similarity analyses using protein data banks that contain well-characterized and conserved proteins (Overbeek et al., 2005).

4.1 Technical terms used in manual annotation

In functional annotation done with Artemis, several fields should be filled out to increase knowledge about particular genome elements. It is necessary to use annotation terms, which involve an official nomenclature developed for this purpose. Some of these terms and respective examples are given below: "LOCUS-TAG" is the term used to identify all of the genome elements, except for the feature "misc". Generally, one uses an abbreviation to identify the particular species, followed by an underline (_) and numbers, for example: Cp1002_0001 (*Corynebacterium pseudotuberculosis*, strain 1002). For tRNAs, the nomenclature is the abbreviation, followed by underline, a "t" and numbers, with a specific count, which is not included in the total CDS count, among others; for example: Cp1002_t001. For rRNAs, the nomenclature is the symbol followed by underline, an "r" and numbers, with specific counts, not included in the total CDS count; for example: Cp1002_r001. "PROTEIN_ID" is used to designate all of the elements of the genome, except for the feature "misc". It is a standardized form for NCBI to identify e proteins; for example: gnl | gbufpa | Cp1002_0001. "GENE" is one of the most important topics to be informed in manual annotation, indicating the gene symbol of the protein; fore example: pld. The field "SIMILARITY" corresponds to information obtained from the best similarity search result – BLASTp. Various types of information should be entered into this field, such as similarity among organisms, size of the amino-acids sequence analyzed, e-value and also the percentage identity between its own protein and the protein found in the data bank; for example: similar to *Corynebacterium pseudotuberculosis* 1002, hypothetical protein Cp1002_00047 (345 aa), e–value: 0.0, 98% ID in 344 aa. In "PRODUCT", there is a description of the gene product, for which similarity was found in the public domain data bank; for example: Phospholipase D. The tag "PSEUDO" should be added whenever a protein presents one or various breaks, due to insertion of a premature stop codon. These are the famous proteins that have frameshifts or probable pseudogenes. Consequently, the manual annotation window has this pattern:

/gene="dnaA"

/product="Chromosomal replication initiation protein"

/locus_tag="Cp1002_0001"

/protein_id="gnl | ufmg | Cp1002_0001"

/colour=3

/similarity="Similar to *Corynebacterium pseudotuberculosis* FRC41,

Chromosomal replication initiation protein (603 aa), e value: 0.0, 98% id in 599s aa"

4.2 Steps for manual curation

Manual curation is a very complex task and is subject to errors for various reasons. One of these is a lack of padronization in the interpretation of BLAST results. Another problem is propagation of errors, which involves prediction of protein function based on proteins that were also predicted but could have imprecise or even incorrect annotation (Gilks et al., 2002). For these reasons, some criteria are suggested in order to obtain reliable functional annotation. The fundamental step for doing this well is mining data obtained from similarity analyses of BLASTp data banks. It is recommended to give greater value to annotation of proteins of individuals of the same species or of species that are phylogenetically close to the organism under study, the protein of which one wants to infer the function of, decreasing in this way the possibility of annotation errors. Another parameter is to observe if there is any consensus among the first 10 hits (the same protein is identified among various). In this case, even if the best hit is not identified as such, it is preferable to identify the sequence as similar to that of an organism that appears various times in the BLASTp results and is within the consensus. In cases where there is no consensus or when the e-value of the best hit (first BLAST result and which corresponds to the best alignment within the data bank that is being researched) is significantly larger than that of the following sequences, it is preferable to transfer the annotation of the best hit (Prosdocimi, 2003), or if necessary, in cases of non-significant alignments, always also run a similarity search at the nucleotide level (BLASTn). Other criteria are also analyzed, such as percentage identity between the sequence being analyzed and the sequence in the data bank, score value and e-value, as well as pair-by-pair alignment evaluation. This evaluation consists of checking the texture of the alignment (evaluating the number of gaps, size of the gaps, and the number of conserved substitutions of amino acids). If doubts remain, research of domain data banks and protein classification are also commonly utilized.

4.3 Frame shifts (Pseudogenes)

Comparisons between non-coding regions of genomes of various prokaryotic species has aided in the identification and characterization of genome segments with regulatory roles (Pareja et al., 2006), contributing to the elucidation of genetic circuits of transcriptional regulation. These non-coding regions, known as pseudogenes, are DNA sequences that are highly similar to functional genes but do not express a functional protein, probably because of deleterious mutations. These degraded genes contain one or more inactivating mutations, such as a nonsense mutation that introduces a premature stop codon, resulting in an incomplete protein and a later change in the open reading frame (Lerat & Ochman, 2005). When found in the genome, the break region is checked with Artemis, and the quality of the bases in that region is also evaluated. Whenever possible, addition or removal of erroneous bases can restore the reading frame. If there is no data that justifies addition or removal of bases, the genes should be classified as pseudogenes (tag /pseudo).

4.4 Tools

4.4.1 Artemis

The program Artemis, (Berriman & Rutherford, 2003), available for download at http://www.sanger.ac.uk/Software/Artemis is a freely-distributed algorithm developed for visualization of genomes and for annotation and manual curation. Artemis allows the curator to visualize various characteristics of the genome sequences, such as: product coded by the predicted gene; presence of tRNAs and rRNAs; search for protein and nucleotide similarity in biological data banks; visualization of probable domains and conserved protein families; visualization of GC / AT content, and misplaced codon use; and various other functions. These data can be visualized in the six phases of translating DNA reads into proteins (Rutherford et al., 2000). Also, the program provides a visualization of BLAST visits between two complete genome sequences, allowing rapid analysis of the degree of synteny (conservation at the level of genes), the main genomic rearrangements and integration of new genomic islands (Field et al., 2005). This algorithm is written in the Java language and is available for the following operating systems: UNIX, Macintosh and Windows. Artemis is capable of processing data in the formats EMBL and GENBANK, or even sequences in the format FASTA.

4.5 Sequence similarity searches
4.5.1 BLAST (Basic Local Alignment Search Tool)
BLAST (Altschul et al., 1990) is a tool that is widely used for the characterization of products coded by genes that are identified by gene prediction. It is able to identify a great majority of the alignments that attend the desired criteria, with a significant gain in performance (Gibas & Jambeck, 2001). This program is available on the NCBI - National Center for Biotechnology Information site http://www.ncbi.nlm.nih.gov (Stein, 2001), which is considered the central databank for genome information. As shown in the figure, BLAST has programs for alignment of protein and nucleotide sequences, among others, according to the needs of the work that is to be undertaken:

Program	Entry sequence	Type of sequence target
BLASTp	Protein	Protein
BLASTn	Nucleotide	Nucleotide
BLASTx	Translated nucleotide	Protein
TBLASTn	Protein	Translated nucleotide
TBLASTx	Translated nucleotide	Translated nucleotide

Table 1. Types of BLAST – NCBI programs.

Through this type of algorithm, we can compare any DNA sequence or protein (query) with all of the genome sequences in the public domain (subject) (Altschul et al., 1997). It is important to note that the program BLAST does not try to make a comparison of the full extension of the molecules that are being compared, but rather it identifies in the data bank a sequence that is sufficiently similar to that of the sequence that is being studied.

4.5.2 Interpreting blast results
In the manual annotation of genomes, analysis of BLAST parameters, such as the number of points obtained (score), gap opening/extension penalties, number of expected alignments in the case of scores equal to or superior to the alignment that is being investigated (expectation value), and the normalized score (bitscore), are indispensible for the interpretation of the results. The smaller the value of "E", the smaller the chance of such a comparison being found merely by chance, consequently inferring a greater homology between the sequence being investigated and the data base (Baxevanis & Ouellette, 2001). Among the sequences with identity above 50%, a general approach is to characterize the function of the known sequence and transfer this annotation to the new sequence. Though annotation transfer is a common practice, a high rate of error has been reported when this is done without due caution (Liberman, 2004). Based on this principle, we consider that for sequences with identity above 80%, a simple alignment or a comparison with a protein that has been experimentally characterized using BLAST can be sufficient to infer function, as long as the pair being compared has similar lengths and align end to end without large

deletions or insertions. For pairs with identity in the range of 50-80%, the general approach for attributing function includes evaluation of databanks with homologous protein and protein domain families.

4.5.3 PFAM

Proteins generally are composed of one or more functional regions, or domains. Different combinations of domains result in the large variety of proteins found in nature. Identification of the domains that are found in proteins can, therefore, provide insight about protein function (Sanger Institute, 2009). In sequences with an identity of less than 70%, without end to end similarity, the approach that is used is to evaluate the protein domains through a search of the Pfam database, which gives very extensive coverage (Mazumder & Vasudevan, 2008). The Pfam database is accessible via the Web http://pfam.sanger.ac.uk and is available in various formats for download. This databank is contains two complementary groupings; Pfam-A is composed of high-quality protein domains that have been manually verified, while Pfam-B contains data that has been generated automatically from the ProDom databank (Finn et al., 2010). Pfam-B is generally lower in quality, though it can suggest new domains that can be added to the manual annotation, if they are not available in Pfam-A. Basically, in Pfam, the sequences that are in full alignment are identified through a search for a hidden profile using the algorithm Hidden Markov Model (HMM), which is later generated using the software HMMER, based on the UniProt database (UniProt, 2007). These HMMs are statistical models that capture specific information about how much each alignment column is conserved and indicates the residuals in this evaluation.

5. Genomics

A genome is the complete set of DNA sequences of a living organism; it consists of coding and non-coding sequences. Genomics is a discipline of genetics that deals with genomes or DNA sequences. Simply put, genomics is the study of genomes. Computational genomics derives knowledge from genome sequences and related data, including both DNA and RNA sequences as well as experimental data. Computational biology mainly deals with whole genome analysis to understand the DNA mechanisms and molecular biology of a species. As biological datasets are extremely large, computational biology has become an important part of modern biology.

5.1 Pangenomics

The efficient and low cost sequencing technologies that are currently available provide complete genome sequences of pathogenic, industrially useful, and other economically-important organisms. Genome sequences, and information that is coded in these sequences, can help identify pathogenicity and other important genes.

Complete genomic sequences of various strains of a species are important to help us understand pathogenesis mechanisms and to determine how genetic variability affects pathogenesis; it would be difficult to extract such useful information from a single genome (Lefébure & Stanhope, 2007).

A pangenome consists of a "core genome", which contains the gene or sequences present in all strains. In other words, genes that are found in all the genomes in a species of bacteria are called the core genome. A "dispensable genome or accessory genome" consists of genome sequences present in more than two strains but are not part of the core genome. "Unique genomic sequences" or "unique genes" are strain-specific genes. These genes are limited to single strain. The pangenome is important for identification and for designing effective vaccines and drug targets (Mira et al., 2010).

There are many web tools and softwares available to manage and efficiently extract data from genomes of various strains of the same species. These tools recognize the accession numbers allotted to complete genomes submitted to NCBI and to other databanks. Online tools developed by the Computational Genomics group of Bielefeld University, Germany, EDGAR – "Efficient Database framework for comparative Genome Analyses using BLAST score Ratios" http://edgar.cebitec.uni-bielefeld.de are efficient web tools to determine the core genome, along with dispensable and unique genes in the form of colored graphs and tables (Blom et al., 2009)

For example, we analyzed the core genome, dispensable genes and unique genes, using "EDGAR", of three different *Corynebacterium pseudotuberculosis* strains, *C. pseudotuberculosis* Cp–I19, *C. pseudotuberculosis* Cp1002 and *C. pseudotuberculosis* CpC231.

This core genome consists of 1,862 genes, with 48 dispensable genes between Cp–I19 and Cp1002, 52 dispensable genes between Cp-I19 and CpC231, and 103 dispensable genes between Cp1002 and CpC231. There were 208, 46 and 36 unique genes in strains Cp-I19, Cp1002 and CpC231, respectively.

6. Genome plasticity

The high degree of adaptability of bacteria to a wide range of environments and hosts is long known to be influenced by genome plasticity, a dynamic property that involves DNA gain, loss and rearrangement (Maurelli et al., 1998). Various mechanisms can drive these changes, including point mutations, gene conversions, rearrangements (inversion or translocation), deletions and DNA insertions from other organisms (plasmids, bacteriophages, transposons, insertion elements and genomic islands) (Schmidt & Hensel, 2004).

6.1 Plasmids

Plasmids contribute to genomic plasticity through their transfer capability. They are also able to mobilize co-resident plasmids and integrate into the chromosome. Plasmids may harbor antibiotic resistance genes and other genes associated with pathogenicity (Dobrindt & Hacker, 2001); e.g., Rhodococcus equi harbors a virulence plasmid that codes for surface-associated proteins (vap genes) that is absent in avirulent strains (Takai et al., 2000).

6.2 Bacteriophages

Bacteriophages are viruses that infect bacteria and which influence genome plasticity through transduction mechanisms. Functional phages inject DNA from one bacterium into another one without causing damage to the acceptor organism; the DNA can incorporate into the acceptor genome leading to adaptive changes. Additionally, prophages (viral DNA incorporated in the bacterial chromosome) confer protection against lytic infections and they can harbor virulence genes that may be acquired by the acceptor bacterium and directly affect its pathogenicity; this has been reported from various species, including Clostridium botulinum, Streptococcus pyogenes, Staphylococcus aureus, Escherichia coli and C. diphtheriae (Brüssow et al., 2004).

6.3 Genomic islands

Genomic islands (GEIs) affect genome plasticity because of their mobility and their capability of carrying a large number of genes as a single block, including operons and groups of coding genes with related functions. These GEIs can cause dramatic changes that lead the acceptor bacterium to evolve very rapidly compared to wild-type counterparts. GEIs are characterized as large DNA regions acquired from other organisms. They vary in size (10-200 kb), and can harbor sequences derived from phages and/or plasmids, including integrase genes; GEIs are flanked by tRNA genes or direct repeats, which help produce their characteristic instability (Hacker & Carniel, 2001). The instability of GEIs is exemplified by rapid gene acquisition and/or loss and changes in gene composition, as seen in different strains of Burkholderia pseudomallei (Tumapa et al., 2008). Additionally, GEIs can be classified into several classes according to gene content. These include Symbiotic Islands, which are involved in the association of bacterium with Leguminosae hosts (Barcellos et al., 2007); Resistance Islands, which harbor genes related to antibiotic resistance (Krizova & Nemec, 2010); Metabolic Islands, which contain genes associated with secondary metabolite biosynthesis (Tumapa et al., 2008); and Pathogenicity Islands (PAIs), which have a high concentration of virulence genes. PAIs are associated with pathogenic bacteria and have been implicated in the reemergence of various pathogens as causes of serious disease problems (Dobrindt et al., 2000). The first description of a PAI was made in 1990, in vitro (Hacker et al., 1990),. The identification was based on the observation of a close relation between deletion of hemolysin and fimbrial adhesin coding regions and non pathogenic strains of E. coli. This was investigated by gene cloning technique, pulse field electrophoresis and Southern hybridization. Using these procedures, they showed that the hemolysin and fimbrial adhesin coding genes are located in the same chromosomal region in several wild-type strains of E. coli and that they go through deletion events both in vivo and in vitro (Hacker et al., 1990).

6.4 "Black Holes"

Additionally, it is important to keep in mind that gene deletion is just as important as gene acquirement in some organisms. One example of this event is the so called "Black Holes" or deletion events of "antivirulence" genes, i.e. genes whose expression in pathogenic organisms is incompatible with virulence. The concept of evolution through deletion of "antivirulence" genes is based on the premise that genes required for adaptation of one organism in a specific niche may inhibit adaptability in another niche, a potential host, for example (Maurelli, 2007). In E. coli, loss of cadA, the lysine decarboxylase (LDC) coding gene, and ompT, which synthesizes an outer membrane protein, may confer virulence (Suzuki & Sasakawa, 2001). The mechanism of action of cadaverine, produced by decarboxylation of lysine by LDC, is still unknown. However, there are two hypotheses: cadaverine inactivates the synthesized toxin, or cadaverine acts directly on the target cell to protect it. Maurelli et al. (1998) demonstrated that when rabbit mucous cells are pre-treated with cadaverine and then washed, they are protected from enteroxin effects. Absence of Omp-T in Shigella strains and enteroinvasive E. coli strains is crucial for maintaining VirG on the cell surface, a pre-requisite for mobility on mammal cells, including bacterial dispersion through epithelial cells (Suzuki & Sasakawa, 2001).

6.5 Software to identify horizontal gene transfer (HGT) events

Gene acquisition and loss through HGT influence bacterial lifestyles and their physiological versatility (Dobrindt & Hacker, 2001). The increasing number of complete genome sequences available for analysis has stimulated in silico research in an effort to identify HGT events. Horizontally–acquired regions can be identified based on observation G+C content and codon usage patterns, which differ among species and species groups. Sets of genes acquired by HGT events show deviations in these patterns that reflect the genomic signature of the donor genome (Langille et al., 2008). Various softwares can be used to identify HGT events based on base composition patterns (wavelet analysis of G+C content, cumulative GC profile, P-web, IVOM, IslandPath and PAI-IDA) and codon usage deviation (SIGI-HMM and PAI-IDA). However, due to adaptations in codon usage (Karlin et al., 1998), which tend towards homogenous base composition distributions (Hershberg & Petrov, 2009), identification of mobile regions based on genomic signature is only possible for regions that have recently been acquired from phylogenetically distant organisms, i.e. those that have a discrepant genomic signature when compared to the acceptor genome.

Additionally, identification of HGT events may be aided by concentrating on regions that are flanked by tRNA genes, which are "hot spots" for transfer elements since they possess 3'-terminal insertion sequences that are recognized by various integrases (Hou, 1999). The integration of PAIs into these insertion sequences is responsible for their instability, since a single integrase may cause excision of the entire region. Insertion/deletion events have been demonstrated in PAIs I and II of E. coli strain 536, which are flanked by selC and leuX tRNA genes (Blum et al., 1994), and in high pathogenicity islands (HPIs) of several *Yersinia pseudotuberculosis* and *Y. pestis* strains (Lesic et al., 2004), which frequently insert into ASN3 tRNA genes.

However, although efficient in the identification of HGT events, approaches based on genomic signature and flanking tRNAs are not aimed at classification of GEIs, since they do not consider the overall gene content of the region. Additionally, horizontally acquired regions may deviate only in G+C content or codon usage alone, which would be a problem for the identification process if only one of these features is used to identify the event. However, there are tools designed to identify a specific class of GEIs, pathogenicity islands, through a multi-pronged strategy that overcomes such constraints. These tools are named PredictBias (Pundhir et al., 2008), IslandViewer (Waack et al., 2006) and PIPS (unpublished); they perform analyses based on genomic signature deviations that are not found in closely-related organisms and finding of genes coding for virulence factors. Although all of these programs use similar strategies and are complementary, PIPS deserves special attention since it surpasses the others in accuracy and is easy to install.

In analysis of C. diphtheriae strain NCTC 13129, PIPS outperformed the other approaches, identifying 12 out of the 13 PAIs of the reference strain, compared to 10 by IslandViewer and six by PredictBias. In the identification of PAIs of uropathogenic E. coli strain CFT073, PIPS had an overall accuracy of 93.9% (unpublished) against 89.5% for IslandViewer and 88.1% for PredictBias.

7. Reverse vaccinology

Reverse Vaccinology (RV) (Rappuoli, 2000) starts from the genomic sequence of a pathogen, which is an expected coded sequence for all the possible genes expressed during the life cycle of the pathogen. All open reading frames (ORF's) derived from the genome sequence can be evaluated with a computer program in order to determine their aptitude as vaccine candidates. Special attention is given to exported proteins because they are essential in host-pathogen interactions. Examples of this interaction can be cited: (i) adherence to host cells, (ii) invasion of compliant cells, (iii) damage to host tissues, (iv) resistance to environmental stress by the machinery defense of the cell being infected and finally, (v) mechanisms for subversion of the host immune response (Sibbald & van Dij, 2009). The word "Reverse" in RV can be explained by the reverse genetics (RG) technique. Before the dawn of genomics, there were attempts to discover the genes responsible for each phenotype. With Crick's central dogma (DNA > RNA > Protein) the research path was reversed. In possession of the likely gene sequence, several techniques have been developed to identify changes in the phenotype of an organism derived from sequence changes in genes. The principle of Crick's dogma is also used by RV; when a gene sequence is found, one can determine whether a probable protein encoded by this sequence can be an antigen capable of stimulating an immune response in a host organism.

Long before the creation of the term RV, a number of approaches had been considered to determine exported proteins in order to move to the next step of the production of a subunit vaccine (Diaz Romero & Outschoorn, 1994). For example, research on exported proteins was advanced as an alternative to subunit vaccines based on the polysaccharide capsule of meningococci. Vaccines produced with such antigens had a low capacity to induce a satisfactory immune response. This research effort on exported proteins includes almost two decades of work searching for a vaccine against meningococcal serogroup B, which now gives good results. This vaccine currently is the best RV alternative for the production of a subunit vaccine for Neisseria meningitidis serogroup B. Meningitis caused by serogroup B (Men B) is responsible for approximately half of the worldwide incidence of this disease (Diaz Romero & Outschoorn, 1994), and this research result for targeted vaccination is commonly used as a demonstration of the usefulness of RV, because of the excellent results.

Currently, a subunit vaccine against Men B created with antigens targeted by RV is being tested in phase-2 clinical trials (Bambini & Rappuoli, 2009). The advantages of RV continue to be attractive, enabling vaccine research for organisms whose cultivation in the laboratory is difficult or impossible. Reducing the time needed to select target proteins could allow investigation of different species or strains at the same time, for selecting vaccine candidates that can elicit adaptive immune responses. To achieve these benefits all we need is to have a sequenced genome, a personal computer and core software widely available to the scientific community. These conditions demonstrate another advantage of using RV, the low cost. What we call core software is a set of tools for identifying well-known motifs, such as, for example, SignalP, TMHMM, LipoP, and HMMSEARCH. There is still room for innovation in the use of core software; the choice of software strategies can be directed to the identification of vaccine candidates specific to an organism, such as in the case of gram-negative (bilayer) or gram positive (monolayer) bacteria, or also according to heuristics for selection of vaccine candidates with specific characteristics. For example, membrane or exported to the extracellular environment (Barinov et al., 2009).

The concept of RV was adapted to fit a new reality of widespread availability of genomic data (Rinaudo et al., 2009). Instead of researching vaccine targets for a single strain or subspecies of an organism, we can do it simultaneously in dozens of genomes, exploring potential joint antigens or those exclusive to multiple genomes (Lapierre & Gogarten, 2009). The possibility of having a large number of genomes available to implement RV leads to the emergence of the concept of pangenomics RV (PGRV) (Bambini & Rappuoli, 2009). PGRV can also apply the concepts of core, extended, and character genomes. The core genome in PGRV is composed of exported genes (genes that transcribe exported proteins) that are common to all strains, genes that could be candidates for a universal vaccine, while the extended genome consists of genes that are absent in at least one of the strains of the studied species, while the character genome consists of genes that are specific to a strain (Lapierre & Gogarten, 2009). From the standpoint of vaccines, the core and character genomes would be good candidates to develop a vaccine that is suitable for all strains, without losing sight of the particularities of specific genes in each strain.

8. Immunoinformatics

The immune system has considerable diversity in its components, such as, for example, immunoglobulin receptors of lymphocytes, or cytokines, with the principle cell types being B- and T-cells, which have important roles in inflammation, infection and protection (Evans, 2008). Immunoinformatics is very complex and can be characterized as a combinatory science, since it has a great complexity of regulatory cycles and network type interactions, which allows the utilization of computational models to resolve problems that can be converted into biological significant responses (Brusic & Petrovsky, 2003). This leads us to immunoinformatics, which is the application of informatics techniques to immune system molecules, with the main objective of helping develop vaccines through the prediction of immunogenic epitopes (Flower & Doytchinova, 2002).

8.1 Immunological databases

The immunological databases are a source of data used to explore, refine and develop new tools and algorithms (Salimi et al., 2010). There is a large variety of databases that group information relevant to the immune system. The Nucleic Acids Research Molecular Biology Database Collection http://www3.oup.co.uk/nar/database/c/ included 29 immunological databases in March 2011. The International ImMunoGeneTics information system (IMGT), the world reference databank for immunogenetics and immunoinformatics, was created by Marie-Paule Lefranc in 1989 (Lefranc et al., 2009). This databank is specialized in immunoglobulins or antibodies, T-cell receptors (TCR), MHCs, and others. The IMGT is constituted of a variety of databanks, including: structure, monoclonal antibody, sequence and genome databanks. All of these databanks are curated manually and daily by a team that works fulltime, which helps maintain high-quality annotation and standardization of the information. Other databases that house information related to epitopes, such as AntiJen (Toseland et al., 2005) and FIMM (Schonbach et al., 2000), have not been maintained and their data has migrated to other websites. Among these, the most promising epitope database seems to be the Immune Epitope Database (IEDB) (Peters et al., 2005), which is a curated database that has information based on experimental data associated with the target epitope; consequently, it is hoped that all of the information in the various existing databanks also migrates to IEDB within the next few years.

8.2 Epitope prediction

The principal goal of immunoinformatics is the development of algorithms that can both help develop vaccines and analyze the gene products of pathogens, such as viruses and bacteria. This is why it is very important to understand antigen-antibody interactions. Macallum et al. (1996) made a detailed analysis of 26 antigen–antibody complexes; they found that binding between molecules is very complex, and that there are different antibody-antigen classes for different types of molecules. A later study of 59 antigen–antibody interactions (Almagro, 2004) found results similar to those of Macallum. These studies show that tools that can identify molecules and predict their interactions with other molecules need to be very accurate and sensitive.

8.2.1 B cell epitope prediction

Epitopes of B cells are antigenic regions that are recognized by antibodies of the immune system, specifically those that interact with B cell receptors. These epitopes can be continuous or discontinuous (Kumagai & Tsumoto, 2001). B-cell epitopes can be used to design vaccines and new diagnostic tests (Larsen et al., 2006). As with T cells, there are also numerous methodologies to model and predict B-cell epitopes. The classic system to predict B-cell epitopes (Hopp & Woods, 1981) uses propensity scale methods (Parker et al., 1986; Levitt, 1978). This method attributes a propensity value to each amino acid, based on studies of the physical-chemical properties. A combination of various scales can improve the prediction results (Pellequer et al., 1991). This work used hydrophilicity scales (Parker et al., 1986), as well as secondary structure (Levitt, 1978; Chou & Fasman, 1978) and accessibility (Emini et al., 1985). The Immune Epitope Database and Analysis Resource, IEDB (Peters et al., 2005), utilizes parameters such as hydrophilicity, flexibility, accessibility, turns, exposed surface, polarity and antigenic propensity of polypeptides chains, which have been correlated with the location of continuous epitopes. All of the prediction calculations are based on propensity scales. Another methodology that can be used to predict continuous B-cell epitopes combines hidden Markov model (HMM) and propensity scale methods (Parker et al., 1986; Levitt, 1978); it is called Bepipred http://www.cbs.dtu.dk/services/BepiPred/ (Larsen et al., 2006). This methodology has given increased prediction accuracy. Prediction of discontinuous B-cell epitopes has also improved, due to an increase in the number of three-dimensional (3D) structures of antibody–antigen complexes available in PDB and in IMGT/3Dstructure-DB (Kaas et al., 2004) and in the Epitome database (Schlessinger et al., 2006).

8.2.2 T cell epitope prediction

There are two classes of T cells: (1) CD8+ T cytotoxic (Tc) cells, which produce cytotoxins responsible for cell lysis, recognize peptides presented by class I MHCs and (2) CD4+ T helper (Th) cells, which recognize proteins associated with MHC class II. Interferon γ (IFN-γ) and tumor necrosis factor β (TNF-β) are produced by Th1 cells. Th2 cells produce interleukin 4 (IL-4), IL-5, IL-10 and IL-13. Eptitopes that bind to MHC de class I generally are 8-10 amino acids long, with a mean of nine amino acids (Reche et al.., 2002), while epitopes that bind to MHC class II are 13-17 amino acids long (Sercarz & Maverakis, 2003; Chicz et al., 1992). There are various online tools for predicting T-cell epitopes on the basis of MHC class I and class II binding. Prediction of MHC binding is based on motifs associated with epitopes or binders for specific alleles. SYFPEITHI is a tool that is widely used for prediction of T-cell epitopes and MHC binding; however, these predictions have been found to be of low quality (Ruppert et al., 1993). More sophisticated tools that use quantitative matrixes, artificial neural network decision trees, hidden Markov models

(HMM), support vector machines (SVM), homology modeling, protein threading and docking techniques have been developed. The NetMHC 3.2 server http://www.cbs.dtu.dk/services/NetMHC/ predicts binding of peptides to a series of different HLA alleles using artificial neural networks (ANNs) and weight matrixes. All of the previous versions are available online, for comparison and reference. ANNs were trained with 57 different human MHCs (HLA), representing all of the 12 HLA alleles, supertypes A and B (Lund et al., 2004). Also predictions are available for 22 animal alleles (monkey and rat). ANN prediction values are given in nM IC50 values. Weight prediction matrixes use an aptitude score, with a high aptitude score indicating strong binding. Predictions can be made for sizes from 8 to 11 for all of the alleles using an ANNs algorithm trained with 9mer peptides. Probably because of the limited quantity of 10mer data available, this method has better prediction value when an ANNs algorithm is trained with 10mer data. However, one should be careful with 8mer predictions, since some alleles do not link to 8mer to a significant degree. Binding peptides are indicated at output as strongly binding (SB) and weakly binding (WB). The allele for each HLA supertype is indicated in the selection window for HLA alleles (Lundegaard et al., 2008).

The NetMHCII 2.2 server http://www.cbs.dtu.dk/services/NetMHCII/ predicts peptides that bind to MHC classe II alleles HLA-DR, HLA-DQ, HLA-DP and mouse alleles, using ANNs. Predictions can be obtained for the 14 HLA-DR alleles, including the nine HLA-DR, six HLA-DQ, and six HLA-DP supertypes and two H2 class II alleles in mice. The prediction values are given in nM IC50 values, and in %-Rank for a random set of 1,000,000 natural peptides. Strongly and weakly binding peptides are indicated in the output file (Nielsen et al., 2007).

Without a doubt, there is a great variety of predictors, which when they are combined can be quite precise in the prediction of T-cell epitopes; however, this is only possible when well-characterized alleles are available, which is true for some alleles that have been predicted as MHC class I alleles, but much less so for those predicted as MHC class II. This is even more of a problem in the prediction of B cell proteins, for which it is often necessary to have prior knowledge of the structure and sequence of the protein. Nevertheless, it is known that no method can go further than the data used to train it, and only through extensive compilation and by obtaining high quality data, will it be possible to create excellent models that will can be generally applied (Flower & Doytchinova, 2002).

9. References

Allen, J. E., Pertea, M. Salzberg, S. L. 2004. Computational gene prediction using multiple sources of evidence, *Genome Res* 14(1): 142–8.

Almagro, J. C. 2004. Identification of differences in the specificity-determining residues of antibodies that recognize antigens of different size: implications for the rational design of antibody repertoires, *J Mol Recognit* 17(2): 132–43.

Altschul, S. F., Gish, W., Miller, W., Myers, E. W. Lipman, D. J. 1990. Basic local alignment search tool, *J Mol Biol* 215(3): 403–10.

Altschul, S. F., Madden, T. L., Schäffer, A. A., Zhang, J., Zhang, Z., Miller, W. Lipman, D. J. 1997. Gapped blast and psi-blast: a new generation of protein database search programs, *Nucleic Acids Res* 25(17): 3389–402.

Aparicio, G., Götz,, S., Conesa, A., Segrelles, D., Blanquer, I., García, J. M., Hernandez, V., Robles, M. Talon, M. 2006. Blast2go goes grid: developing a grid-enabled prototype for functional genomics analysis, *Stud Health Technol Inform* 120: 194–204.

Bambini, S. Rappuoli, R. 2009. The use of genomics in microbial vaccine development, *Drug Discov Today* 14(5-6): 252–60.

Barcellos, F. G., Menna, P., da Silva Batista, J. S. Hungria, M. 2007. Evidence of horizontal transfer of symbiotic genes from a bradyrhizobium japonicum inoculant strain to indigenous diazotrophs sinorhizobium (ensifer) fredii and bradyrhizobium elkanii in a brazilian savannah soil, *Appl Environ Microbiol* 73(8): 2635–43.

Barinov, A., Loux, V., Hammani, A., Nicolas, P., Langella, P., Ehrlich, D., Maguin, E. van de Guchte, M. 2009. Prediction of surface exposed proteins in streptococcus pyogenes, with a potential application to other gram-positive bacteria, *Proteomics* 9(1): 61–73.

Baxevanis, A. D. Ouellette, F. F. 2001. A practical guide to the analysis of genes and proteins, *Wiley* (2): 260–2.

Bendtsen, J. D., Nielsen, H., von Heijne, G. Brunak, S. 2004. Improved prediction of signal peptides: Signalp 3.0, *J Mol Biol* 340(4): 783–95.

Benson, D. A., Karsch-Mizrachi, I., Lipman, D. J., Ostell, J. Wheeler, D. L. 2008. Genbank, *Nucleic Acids Res* 36(Database issue): D25–30.

Berriman, M. Rutherford, K. 2003. Viewing and annotating sequence data with artemis, *Brief Bioinform* 4(2): 124–32.

Blom, J., Albaum, S. P., Doppmeier, D., Pühler, A., Vorhölter, F.-J., Zakrzewski, M. Goesmann, A. 2009. Edgar: a software framework for the comparative analysis of prokaryotic genomes, *BMC Bioinformatics* 10: 154.

Blum, G., Ott, M., Lischewski, A., Ritter, A., Imrich, H., Tschäpe, H. Hacker, J. 1994. Excision of large dna regions termed pathogenicity islands from trna-specific loci in the chromosome of an escherichia coli wild-type pathogen, *Infect Immun* 62(2): 606–14.

Brown, T. A. 1999. Genes e expressÃ£o gênica., *Genética – um enfoque molecular* 1(2): 124–132.

Bru, C., Courcelle, E., Carrère, S., Beausse, Y., Dalmar, S. Kahn, D. 2005. The prodom database of protein domain families: more emphasis on 3d, *Nucleic Acids Res* 33(Database issue): D212–5.

Brusic, V. Petrovsky, N. 2003. Immunoinformatics–the new kid in town, *Novartis Found Symp* 254: 3–13; discussion 13–22, 98–101, 250–2.

Brüssow, H., Canchaya, C. Hardt, W.-D. 2004. Phages and the evolution of bacterial pathogens: from genomic rearrangements to lysogenic conversion, *Microbiol Mol Biol Rev* 68(3): 560–602.

Chicz, R. M., Urban, R. G., Lane, W. S., Gorga, J. C., Stern, L. J., Vignali, D. A. Strominger, J. L. 1992. Predominant naturally processed peptides bound to hla-dr1 are derived from mhc-related molecules and are heterogeneous in size, *Nature* 358(6389): 764–8.

Choi, G.-E., Eom, S.-H., Jung, K.-H., Son, J.-W., Shin, A.-R., Shin, S.-J., Kim, K.-H., Chang, C. L. Kim, H.-J. 2010. Cysa2: A candidate serodiagnostic marker for mycobacterium tuberculosis infection, *Respirology* 15(4): 636–42.

Chou, P. Y. Fasman, G. D. 1978. Prediction of the secondary structure of proteins from their amino acid sequence, *Adv Enzymol Relat Areas Mol Biol* 47: 45–148.

Cole, S. T., Eiglmeier, K., Parkhill, J., James, K. D., Thomson, N. R., Barrell, B. G. 2001. Massive gene decay in the leprosy bacillus, *Nature* 409(6823): 1007-11.

Datta, S., Datta, S., Kim, S., Chakraborty, S. Gill, R. S. 2010. Statistical analyses of next generation sequence data: A partial overview, *J Proteomics Bioinform* 3(6): 183-190.

Diaz Romero, J. Outschoorn, I. M. 1994. Current status of meningococcal group b vaccine candidates: capsular or noncapsular? , *Clin Microbiol Rev* 7(4): 559-75.

Dobrindt, U. Hacker, J. 2001. Whole genome plasticity in pathogenic bacteria, *Curr Opin Microbiol* 4(5): 550-7.

Dobrindt, U., Janke, B., Piechaczek, K., Nagy, G., Ziebuhr, W., Fischer, G., Schierhorn, A., Hecker, M., Blum-Oehler, G. Hacker, J. 2000. Toxin genes on pathogenicity islands: impact for microbial evolution, *Int J Med Microbiol* 290(4-5): 307-11.

Emini, E. A., Hughes, J. V., Perlow, D. S. Boger, J. 1985. Induction of hepatitis a virus-neutralizing antibody by a virus-specific synthetic peptide, *J Virol* 55(3): 836-9.

Evans, M. C. 2008. Recent advances in immunoinformatics: application of in silico tools to drug development, *Curr Opin Drug Discov Devel* 11(2): 233-41.

Field, D., Feil, E. J. Wilson, G. A. 2005. Databases and software for the comparison of prokaryotic genomes, *Microbiology* 151(Pt 7): 2125-32.

Finn, R. D., Mistry, J., Schuster-Böckler, B., Griffiths-Jones, S., Hollich, V., Lassmann, T., Moxon, S., Marshall, M., Khanna, A., Durbin, R., Eddy, S. R., Sonnhammer, E. L. L. Bateman, A. 2006. Pfam: clans, web tools and services, *Nucleic Acids Res* 34(Database issue): D247-51.

Finn, R. D., Mistry, J., Tate, J., Coggill, P., Heger, A., Pollington, J. E., Gavin, O. L., Gunasekaran, P., Ceric, G., Forslund, K., Holm, L., Sonnhammer, E. L. L., Eddy, S. R. Bateman, A. 2010. The pfam protein families database, *Nucleic Acids Res* 38(Database issue): D211-22.

Flower, D. R. Doytchinova, I. A. 2002. Immunoinformatics and the prediction of immunogenicity, *Appl Bioinformatics* 1(4): 167-76.

Gibas, C. Jambeck, P. 2001. Developing bioinformatics computer skills, *O'Reilly* 1(1): 21-22.

Gilks, W. R., Audit, B., De Angelis, D., Tsoka, S. Ouzounis, C. A. 2002. Modeling the percolation of annotation errors in a database of protein sequences, *Bioinformatics* 18(12): 1641-9.

Hacker, J., Bender, L., Ott, M., Wingender, J., Lund, B., Marre, R. Goebel, W. 1990. Deletions of chromosomal regions coding for fimbriae and hemolysins occur in vitro and in vivo in various extraintestinal escherichia coli isolates, *Microb Pathog* 8(3): 213-25.

Hacker, J. Carniel, E. 2001. Ecological fitness, genomic islands and bacterial pathogenicity. a darwinian view of the evolution of microbes, *EMBO Rep* 2(5): 376-81.

Hershberg, R. Petrov, D. A. 2009. General rules for optimal codon choice, *PLoS Genet* 5(7): e1000556.

Hopp, T. P. Woods, K. R. 1981. Prediction of protein antigenic determinants from amino acid sequences, *Proc Natl Acad Sci U S A* 78(6): 3824-8.

Hou, Y. M. 1999. Transfer rnas and pathogenicity islands, *Trends Biochem Sci* 24(8): 295-8.

Hunter, S., Apweiler, R., Attwood, T. K., Bairoch, A., Bateman, A., Yeats, C. 2009. Interpro: the integrative protein signature database, *Nucleic Acids Res* 37(Database issue): D211-5.

Hyatt, D., Chen, G.-L., Locascio, P. F., Land, M. L., Larimer, F. W. Hauser, L. J. 2010. Prodigal: prokaryotic gene recognition and translation initiation site identification, *BMC Bioinformatics* 11: 119.

Johnson, M., Zaretskaya, I., Raytselis, Y., Merezhuk, Y., McGinnis, S. Madden, T. L. 2008. Ncbi blast: a better web interface, *Nucleic Acids Res* 36(Web Server issue): W5–9.

Kaas, Q., Ruiz, M. Lefranc, M. P. 2004. Imgt/3dstructure-db and imgt/structuralquery, a database and a tool for immunoglobulin, t cell receptor and mhc structural data, *Nucleic Acids Res* 32(Database issue): D208–10.

Karlin, S., Mrázek, J. Campbell, A. M. 1998. Codon usages in different gene classes of the escherichia coli genome, *Mol Microbiol* 29(6): 1341–55.

Kendrew, J. 1999. In: The encyclopedia of molecular biology, *in* B. Science (ed.), *Gene*, Porto Alegre, pp. 343–401.

Kislyuk, A. O., Katz, L. S., Agrawal, S., Hagen, M. S., Conley, A. B., Jayaraman, P., Nelakuditi, V., Humphrey, J. C., Sammons, S. A., Govil, D., Mair, R. D., Tatti, K. M., Tondella, M. L., Harcourt, B. H., Mayer, L. W. Jordan, I. K. 2010. A computational genomics pipeline for prokaryotic sequencing projects, *Bioinformatics* 26(15): 1819–26.

Krizova, L. Nemec, A. 2010. A 63 kb genomic resistance island found in a multidrug-resistant acinetobacter baumannii isolate of european clone i from 1977, *J Antimicrob Chemother* 65(9): 1915–8.

Krogh, A., Larsson, B., von Heijne, G. Sonnhammer, E. L. 2001. Predicting transmembrane protein topology with a hidden markov model: application to complete genomes, *J Mol Biol* 305(3): 567–80.

Kumagai, I. Tsumoto, K. 2001. Antigen-antibody binding, *Encyclopedia of Life Sciences - Nature Publishing Group* pp. 1–7.

Langille, M. G. I. Brinkman, F. S. L. 2009. Islandviewer: an integrated interface for computational identification and visualization of genomic islands, *Bioinformatics* 25(5): 664–5.

Langille, M. G. I., Hsiao, W. W. L. Brinkman, F. S. L. 2008. Evaluation of genomic island predictors using a comparative genomics approach, *BMC Bioinformatics* 9: 329.

Lapierre, P. Gogarten, J. P. 2009. Estimating the size of the bacterial pan-genome, *Trends Genet* 25(3): 107–10.

Larsen, J. E., Lund, O. Nielsen, M. 2006. Improved method for predicting linear b-cell epitopes, *Immunome Res* 2: 2.

Lefranc, M. P., Giudicelli, V., Ginestoux, C., Jabado-Michaloud, J., Folch, G., Bellahcene, F., Wu, Y., Gemrot, E., Brochet, X., Lane, J., Regnier, L., Ehrenmann, F., Lefranc, G. Duroux, P. 2009. Imgt, the international immunogenetics information system, *Nucleic Acids Res* 37(Database issue): D1006–12.

Lefébure, T. Stanhope, M. J. 2007. Evolution of the core and pan-genome of streptococcus: positive selection, recombination, and genome composition, *Genome Biol* 8(5): R71.

Lerat, E. Ochman, H. 2005. Recognizing the pseudogenes in bacterial genomes, *Nucleic Acids Res* 33(10): 3125–32.

Lesic, B., Bach, S., Ghigo, J.-M., Dobrindt, U., Hacker, J. Carniel, E. 2004. Excision of the high-pathogenicity island of yersinia pseudotuberculosis requires the combined actions of its cognate integrase and hef, a new recombination directionality factor, *Mol Microbiol* 52(5): 1337–48.

Levitt, M. 1978. Conformational preferences of amino acids in globular proteins, *Biochemistry* 17(20): 4277–85.

Li, L., Shiga, M., Ching, W.-K. Mamitsuka, H. 2010. Annotating gene functions with integrative spectral clustering on microarray expressions and sequences, *Genome Inform* 22: 95–120.

Liberman, F. 2004. *Análise dos fatores determinantes para a qualidade da anotação genÃ´mica automática*, Master's thesis, Universidade Católica de Brasília.

Lorenzi, H. A., Puiu, D., Miller, J. R., Brinkac, L. M., Amedeo, P., Hall, N. Caler, E. V. 2010. New assembly, reannotation and analysis of the entamoeba histolytica genome reveal new genomic features and protein content information, *PLoS Negl Trop Dis* 4(6): e716.

Lukashin, A. V. Borodovsky, M. 1998. Genemark.hmm: new solutions for gene finding, *Nucleic Acids Res* 26(4): 1107–15.

Lund, O., Nielsen, M., Kesmir, C., Petersen, A. G., Lundegaard, C., Worning, P., Sylvester-Hvid, C., Lamberth, K., Roder, G., Justesen, S., Buus, S. Brunak, S. 2004. Definition of supertypes for hla molecules using clustering of specificity matrices, *Immunogenetics* 55(12): 797–810.

Lundegaard, C., Lamberth, K., Harndahl, M., Buus, S., Lund, O. Nielsen, M. 2008. Netmhc-3.0: accurate web accessible predictions of human, mouse and monkey mhc class i affinities for peptides of length 8-11, *Nucleic Acids Res* 36(Web Server issue): W509–12.

Macallum, R. M., Martin, A. C. R. Thornton, J. M. 1996. Antibody-antigen interactions: Contact analysis and binding site topography, *Journal of Molecular Biology* 262: 732–45.

Mathé, C., Sagot, M.-F., Schiex, T. Rouzé, P. 2002. Current methods of gene prediction, their strengths and weaknesses, *Nucleic Acids Res* 30(19): 4103–17.

Maurelli, A. T. 2007. Black holes, antivirulence genes, and gene inactivation in the evolution of bacterial pathogens, *FEMS Microbiol Lett* 267(1): 1–8.

Maurelli, A. T., Fernández, R. E., Bloch, C. A., Rode, C. K. Fasano, A. 1998. "black holes" and bacterial pathogenicity: a large genomic deletion that enhances the virulence of shigella spp. and enteroinvasive escherichia coli, *Proc Natl Acad Sci U S A* 95(7): 3943–8.

Mazumder, R. Vasudevan, S. 2008. Structure-guided comparative analysis of proteins: principles, tools, and applications for predicting function, *PLoS Comput Biol* 4(9): e1000151.

Meyer, F., Goesmann, A., McHardy, A. C., Bartels, D., Bekel, T., Clausen, J., Kalinowski, J., Linke, B., Rupp, O., Giegerich, R. Pühler, A. 2003. Gendb–an open source genome annotation system for prokaryote genomes, *Nucleic Acids Res* 31(8): 2187–95.

Mira, A., Martín-Cuadrado, A. B., D'Auria, G. Rodríguez-Valera, F. 2010. The bacterial pan-genome:a new paradigm in microbiology, *Int Microbiol* 13(2): 45–57.

Nielsen, M., Lundegaard, C. Lund, O. 2007. Prediction of mhc class ii binding affinity using smm-align, a novel stabilization matrix alignment method, *BMC Bioinformatics* 8: 238.

Overbeek, R., Begley, T., Butler, R. M., Choudhuri, J. V., Chuang, H.-Y., Cohoon, M., de Crécy-Lagard, V., Diaz, N., Disz, T. Edwards, e. a. 2005. The subsystems approach to genome annotation and its use in the project to annotate 1000 genomes, *Nucleic Acids Res* 33(17): 5691–702.

Pareja, E., Pareja-Tobes, P., Manrique, M., Pareja-Tobes, E., Bonal, J. Tobes, R. 2006. Extratrain: a database of extragenic regions and transcriptional information in prokaryotic organisms, *BMC Microbiol* 6: 29.

Parker, J. M., Guo, D. Hodges, R. S. 1986. New hydrophilicity scale derived from high-performance liquid chromatography peptide retention data: correlation of predicted surface residues with antigenicity and x-ray-derived accessible sites, *Biochemistry* 25(19): 5425–32.

Pearson, W. R. Lipman, D. J. 1988. Improved tools for biological sequence comparison, *Proc Natl Acad Sci U S A* 85(8): 2444–8.

Pellequer, J. L., Westhof, E. Van Regenmortel, M. H. 1991. Predicting location of continuous epitopes in proteins from their primary structures, *Methods Enzymol* 203: 176–201.

Peters, B., Sidney, J., Bourne, P., Bui, H. H., Buus, S., Doh, G., Fleri, W., Kronenberg, M., Kubo, R., Lund, O., Nemazee, D., Ponomarenko, J. V., Sathiamurthy, M., Schoenberger, S., Stewart, S., Surko, P., Way, S., Wilson, S. Sette, A. 2005. The immune epitope database and analysis resource: from vision to blueprint, *PLoS Biol* 3(3): e91.

Poptsova, M. S. Gogarten, J. P. 2010. Using comparative genome analysis to identify problems in annotated microbial genomes, *Microbiology* 156(Pt 7): 1909–17.

Prosdocimi, F. 2003. Bioinformática: manual do usuário., *Biotecnologia Ciência & Desenvolvimento* 2(29): 2.

Pundhir, S., Vijayvargiya, H. Kumar, A. 2008. Predictbias: a server for the identification of genomic and pathogenicity islands in prokaryotes, *In Silico Biol* 8(3-4): 223–34.

Rappuoli, R. 2000. Reverse vaccinology, *Curr Opin Microbiol* 3(5): 445–50.

Retter, I., Althaus, H. H., Munch, R. Muller, W. 2005. Vbase2, an integrative v gene database, *Nucleic Acids Res* 33(Database issue): D671–4.

Rinaudo, C. D., Telford, J. L., Rappuoli, R. Seib, K. L. 2009. Vaccinology in the genome era, *J Clin Invest* 119(9): 2515–25.

Ruppert, J., Sidney, J., Celis, E., Kubo, R. T., Grey, H. M. Sette, A. 1993. Prominent role of secondary anchor residues in peptide binding to hla-a2.1 molecules, *Cell* 74(5): 929–37.

Rutherford, K., Parkhill, J., Crook, J., Horsnell, T., Rice, P., Rajandream, M. A. Barrell, B. 2000. Artemis: sequence visualization and annotation, *Bioinformatics* 16(10): 944–5.

Salimi, N., Fleri, W., Peters, B. Sette, A. 2010. Design and utilization of epitope-based databases and predictive tools, *Immunogenetics* 62(4): 185–96.

Salzberg, S. L., Delcher, A. L., Kasif, S. White, O. 1998. Microbial gene identification using interpolated markov models, *Nucleic Acids Res* 26(2): 544–8.

Schellenberg, M. J., Ritchie, D. B. MacMillan, A. M. 2008. Pre-mrna splicing: a complex picture in higher definition, *Trends Biochem Sci* 33(6): 243-6.

Schlessinger, A., Ofran, Y., Yachdav, G. Rost, B. 2006. Epitome: database of structure-inferred antigenic epitopes, *Nucleic Acids Res* 34(Database issue): D777-80.

Schmidt, H. Hensel, M. 2004. Pathogenicity islands in bacterial pathogenesis, *Clin Microbiol Rev* 17(1): 14-56.

Schonbach, C., Koh, J. L., Sheng, X., Wong, L. Brusic, V. 2000. Fimm, a database of functional molecular immunology, *Nucleic Acids Res* 28(1): 222-4.

Sercarz, E. E. Maverakis, E. 2003. Mhc-guided processing: binding of large antigen fragments, *Nat Rev Immunol* 3(8): 621-9.

Servant, F., Bru, C., Carrère, S., Courcelle, E., Gouzy, J., Peyruc, D. Kahn, D. 2002. Prodom: automated clustering of homologous domains, *Brief Bioinform* 3(3): 246-51.

Setúbal, J. Meidanis, J. 1997. *Introduction to Computational Molecular Biology*, Pacific Grove.

Sibbald, M. J. J. B. van Dij, J. M. l. 2009. Secretome mapping in gram-positive pathogens. in karl wooldridge (ed.), bacterial secreted protein: Secretory mechanisms and role in pathogenesis, *Caister Academic Press* pp. 193-225.

Sleator, R. D. 2010. An overview of the current status of eukaryote gene prediction strategies, *Gene* 461(1-2): 1-4.

Smith, T. F. Waterman, M. S. 1981. Identification of common molecular subsequences, *J Mol Biol* 147(1): 195-7.

Stein, L. 2001. Genome annotation: from sequence to biology, *Nat Rev Genet* 2(7): 493-503.

Stothard, P. Wishart, D. S. 2006. Automated bacterial genome analysis and annotation, *Curr Opin Microbiol* 9(5): 505-10.

Suzuki, T. Sasakawa, C. 2001. Molecular basis of the intracellular spreading of shigella, *Infect Immun* 69(10): 5959-66.

Takai, S., Hines, S. A., Sekizaki, T., Nicholson, V. M., Alperin, D. A., Osaki, M., Takamatsu, D., Nakamura, M., Suzuki, K., Ogino, N., Kakuda, T., Dan, H. Prescott, J. F. 2000. Dna sequence and comparison of virulence plasmids from rhodococcus equi atcc 33701 and 103, *Infect Immun* 68(12): 6840-7.

Trost, B., Haakensen, M., Pittet, V., Ziola, B. Kusalik, A. 2010. Analysis and comparison of the pan-genomic properties of sixteen well-characterized bacterial genera, *BMC Microbiol* 10: 258.

Tumapa, S., Holden, M. T. G., Vesaratchavest, M., Wuthiekanun, V., Limmathurotsakul, D., Chierakul, W., Feil, E. J., Currie, B. J., Day, N. P. J., Nierman, W. C. Peacock, S. J. 2008. Burkholderia pseudomallei genome plasticity associated with genomic island variation, *BMC Genomics* 9: 190.

Tyson, G. W., Chapman, J., Hugenholtz, P., Allen, E. E., Ram, R. J., Richardson, P. M., Solovyev, V. V., Rubin, E. M., Rokhsar, D. S. Banfield, J. F. 2004. Community structure and metabolism through reconstruction of microbial genomes from the environment, *Nature* 428(6978): 37-43.

UniProt 2007. The universal protein resource (uniprot), *Nucleic Acids Res* 35(Database issue): D193-7.

Waack, S., Keller, O., Asper, R., Brodag, T., Damm, C., Fricke, W. F., Surovcik, K., Meinicke, P. Merkl, R. 2006. Score-based prediction of genomic islands in prokaryotic genomes using hidden markov models, *BMC Bioinformatics* 7: 142.

Zhao, J. Grant, S. F. A. 2010. Advances in whole genome sequencing technology, *Curr Pharm Biotechnol*.

Part 10

Drug Design

31

Designing of Anti-Cancer Drug Targeted to Bcl-2 Associated Athanogene (BAG1) Protein

Amit Kumar, Kriti Verma and Amita Sinha
Department of Bioinformatics and MolecularBiology,
Bioaxis DNA Research Centre, Hyderabad,
India

1. Introduction

Cancer is a disease of uncontrolled cell growth in tissues. This growth may lead to metastasis, which is the invasion of adjacent tissue and infiltration beyond the site of initiation. Cancer is initiated by activation of oncogenes or inactivation of tumor suppressor genes. Nearly 10-30% of all adenocarcinomas are due to the mutations in the *K-ras* proto-oncogene. [1] Function and regulation of Bcl-2 proteins depends upon their interaction with other non-family member proteins, including NIP1, NIP2, NIP3, p53 BP2, Raf-1, CED-4, calcineurin, R-Ras and Bag-1 to form homo and hetero dimmers.[21] Bag1 belongs to the Bcl-2 associated athanogene (BAG) family of multifunctional proteins. This widely expressed protein interacts with a number of signalling molecules (including Bcl2, HGF receptor and Raf1) as it regulates signalling molecules in pathways involving cell survival, growth and differentiation. [13] Bcl2 associated athanogene (BAG1) protein is involved in regulation of the Ras/Raf signal transduction pathway. Of particular relevance to tumour cells, BAG-1 interacts with the anti-apoptotic BCL-2 protein, various nuclear hormone receptors the 70 kDa heat shock proteins, Hsc70 and Hsp70; and serine/threonine kinase. Raf-1 which plays an important role in MAPK pathway.[2][3][4] Recent studies have shown that BAG-1 expression is frequently altered in malignant cells, and BAG-1 expression may have clinical value as a prognostic or predictive marker for various cancer types including breast cancer, prostate cancer and lung cancer.[6][7][8] (Fig 1) Interaction with chaperones may account for many of the pleiotropic effects associated with BAG-1 over expression. The finding that BAG-1 can independently associate with Raf-1 or Bcl-2 provides at least two mechanisms by which BAG-1 promotes cell survival. [20]

Bcl2-associated athanogene (BAG) family proteins participate in a wide variety of cellular processes to regulate growth control pathways, including cell survival (stress response), proliferation, migration, signalling and apoptosis (Fig 2).[2][5][18] This family of co-chaperones functionally regulates signal transduction proteins Raf/MEK/ERK and transcription factors important for cell stress responses, apoptosis, proliferation, cell migration and hormone action. In response to stress, they bind to heat shock proteins HSP70/HSC70 coordinating cell growth signals, by down-regulating the activity of serine/threonine kinase, Raf-1, which plays an important role in MAPK pathway. [5][9] The proteins show anti-apoptotic activity and increase the anti-cell death function of BCL-2 induced by various stimuli. Over expression of BAG-1 suppresses activation of caspases and apoptosis induced by a very broad range of agents in different cell types, for example chemotherapeutic agents, radiation and growth factor withdrawal. Therefore, in addition to contributing to reduced cell death in cancer development, BAG-1 may also contribute to resistance to important therapeutic modalities.

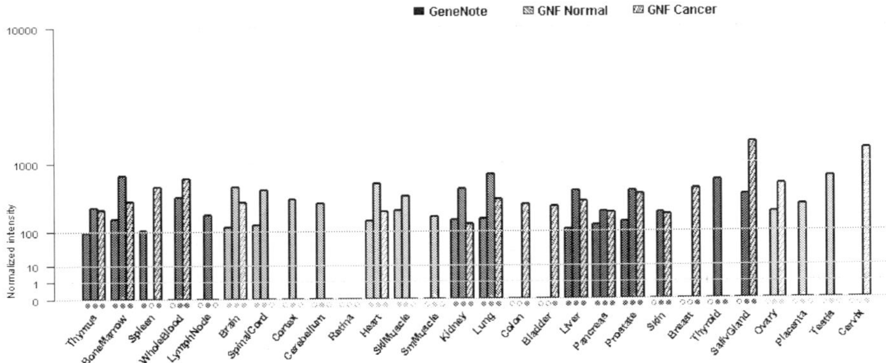

Fig. 1. BAG1 expression in normal and diseased human tissues.

BAG-1 proteins are expressed as multiple isoforms generated by alternate translation initiation from a single mRNA. Translation of the major human BAG-1 isoform, BAG-1S, initiates at an internal AUG codon, whereas of the larger BAG-1L (p50) and BAG-1M proteins translation begins upstream at CUG and AUG codons, respectively.[6][9] Hence, the proteins share a common C-terminus. However, the larger isoforms have additional N-terminal sequences. Various domains have been identified within BAG-1 proteins. [14] A potential nuclear localisation signal (NLS) within the unique N-terminal domain of BAG-1L has been identified. However, BAG-1S and BAG-1M lack this sequence. BAG-1S is largely located in the cytoplasm in contrast to BAG-1M which partitions between the nucleus and cytoplasm. [8]

At the carboxy terminal of all BAG-1 isoforms there is a conserved region of about 110 amino-acids, named as the '**BAG domain**', which binds and regulates Hsp70/Hsc70 molecular chaperones. [8][23] BAG domains are present in Bcl-2-associated athanogene 1 and silencer of death domains.

The crystal structure of the BAG domain revealed that it consists of three anti-parallels α helices. In the BAG domain the first and the second α-helices interact with the serine/threonine kinase Raf-1 and the second and third α-helices interact with the ATP-binding pocket of Hsc70/Hsp70. Therefore, Raf-1 and Hsp70/Hsc70 have partially overlapping sites and their binding is competitive. [2] [8]

BAG-1 promotes cell growth by binding to and stimulating Raf-1 activity. The binding of Hsp70 to BAG-1 diminishes Raf-1 signalling and inhibits subsequent events, such as DNA synthesis, as well as arrests cell cycle. When cellular levels of Hsp70 are elevated during stress, or in cells conditionally over expressing Hsp70, Bag1-Raf-1 is displaced by Bag1-Hsp70, and DNA synthesis is arrested.[5][10] Thus, BAG-1 has been suggested to function as a molecular switch that controls cells to proliferate in normal conditions but become quiescent under a stressful environment.[16]

The C-terminus of the BAG domain is also a site of interaction with Bcl-2 which provides a supra-additive anti-apoptotic effect. The BAG-1 protein shares no significant homology with Bcl-2 or other Bcl-2 family proteins, which can form homo- and heterodimers. [11]

All BAG-1 isoforms also contain an ubiquitin-like domain (ULD), similar to ubiquitin and ubiquitin-like proteins that appears to be essential for at least some biological effects[8][7][15]. Although the precise function of the ULD in BAG-1 is unknown, BAG-1 isoforms are very stable proteins suggesting that they are not generally targets for degradation by the ubiquitin/proteasome system and are not covalently attached to other proteins.

2. Role of BAG1 and Bcl2 in apoptosis

Bcl-2 is an anti-apoptotic protein located mainly on the outer membrane of mitochondria. It has been found that over-expression of Bcl-2 inhibits cells from undergoing apoptosis in response to a various stimuli. [12] The members of the Bcl-2 family share one or more of the four characteristic domains of homology entitled the Bcl-2 homology (BH) domains (named BH1, BH2, BH3 and BH4).[11][13] The BH domains are known to be crucial for its function, as deletion of these domains via molecular cloning affects survival/apoptosis rates. The anti-apoptotic Bcl-2 proteins, such as Bcl-2 and Bcl-xL, conserve all four BH domains. Bcl-2 interacts with pro-apoptotic proteins BAX and BAK. The hydrophobic unit of Bcl-2 forms a heterodimer with the amphipathic unit of BAX and BAK. This heterodimer formation inhibits release of cytochrome c from the mitochondria and prevents activation of caspases. The protein encoded by BAG1 gene binds to BCL2 and is referred to as BCL2-associated athanogene. It enhances the anti-apoptotic effects of BCL2. [12][13]

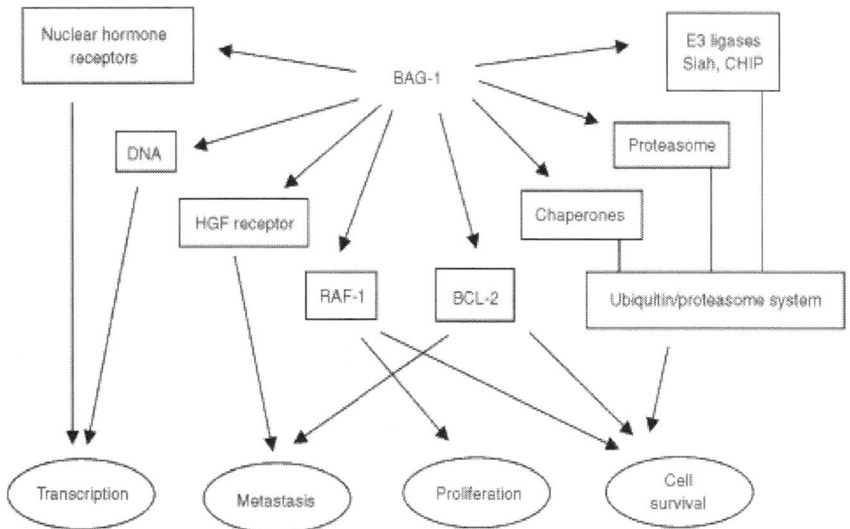

Fig. 2. Interaction of BAG1 protein with other proteins and cellular components. [8]

3. Role of Raf-1/ MAPK pathway in cancer

The pathways regulated by BAG-1 play key roles in the development and progression of cancer and determining response to therapy. The extracellular signal-related kinase (ERK), among the MAPK pathways, plays a key role in promotion of cellular proliferation, survival, and metastasis, this pathway directly affects the initiation and progression of human tumors. This pathway has been found to be activated in numerous cancer types without obvious genetic mutations. Cell lines derived from various organs such as pancreas, colon, lung, ovary and kidney have been reported to show a high degree of MAP kinase activation as observed in 50 tumor cell lines. However, it ihas been found that the constitutive activation of MAP kinases in tumor cells is not due to the disorder of MAP kinases themselves, but is due to the disorder of Raf-1, Ras, or some other signaling molecules upstream of Ras.[3]

The Ras/Raf/MEK/ERK pathway also interacts with the p53 pathway thereby regulating the activity and subcellular localization of BCl2 family proteins (Bim, Bak, Bax, Puma and Noxa). Thus the Raf/MEK/ERK pathway has different effects on growth, prevention of apoptosis, cell cycle arrest and induction of drug resistance in cells of various lineages.[3][4]

4. Methodology used in present study

The strategy used in this project is to target the first alpha helix of the BAG domain. Binding of a ligand to the first alpha helix provides two simultaneous scenarios i.e. firstly it blocks the site for Raf1 binding and thus blocks the MAPK pathway. Secondly, it makes the second and third alpha helix available for Hsp70 binding. Binding of Hsp70 to BAG1 protein renders the heat shock protein inactive as BAG1 has been found to have inhibitory effect on Hsp proteins. This shall produce pseudo stress conditions and attenuate DNA synthesis and cellular proliferation.

Thus, the aim of the present study is to design a drug, targeted to the first alpha helix of 'BAG Domain' of BAG1 protein that binds to the competitive binding site of Raf1 and Hsp70 thereby blocking the binding site of Raf1, making it available for Hsp70 binding and hence suppressing its anti-apoptotic activity. The therapeutic goal is to arrest further tumor progression and trigger tumor-selective cell death by disrupting the balance between pro-apoptotic proteins and anti-apoptotic proteins (Fig 3).

5. Important tools and databases

NCBI is a primary database majorly used for sequence retrieval and similarity based searches. We used NCBI for our sequence retrieval of query protein sequence. BLAST is the most widely used sequence similarity search programme. It finds regions of local similarity between sequences. In this study protein blast has been extensively used. PubMed database was primarily used for literature search including journals, abstracts, full text articles and other sources related to the research. PDB is repository for the 3-D structural data of large biological molecules, such as proteins and nucleic acids which is obtained by X-ray crystallography and NMR spectroscopy. PDB was used to retrieve the 3D structure of the protein. Biology Workbench is a web based tool integrated with access to a wide variety of analysis and modeling tools. This tool has been used for phylogenetic analysis of the Bag1 protein sequences.

Clustalw is a multiple sequence alignment program that calculates the best match for the selected DNA or protein sequences and then lines them up so that the identities, similarities and the differences can be seen. Boxshade works by global alignment of all sequence. Conserved and similar residues are emphasized by various degrees of shading. KEGG database was used for pathway analysis for this Bag1 protein. Genecards has been used in this work to get various expression and sequence related information pertaining to proteins of the Bag1 protein. In this work all the above programs have been used to obtain the peptide recognition pattern for the interpretation of results.

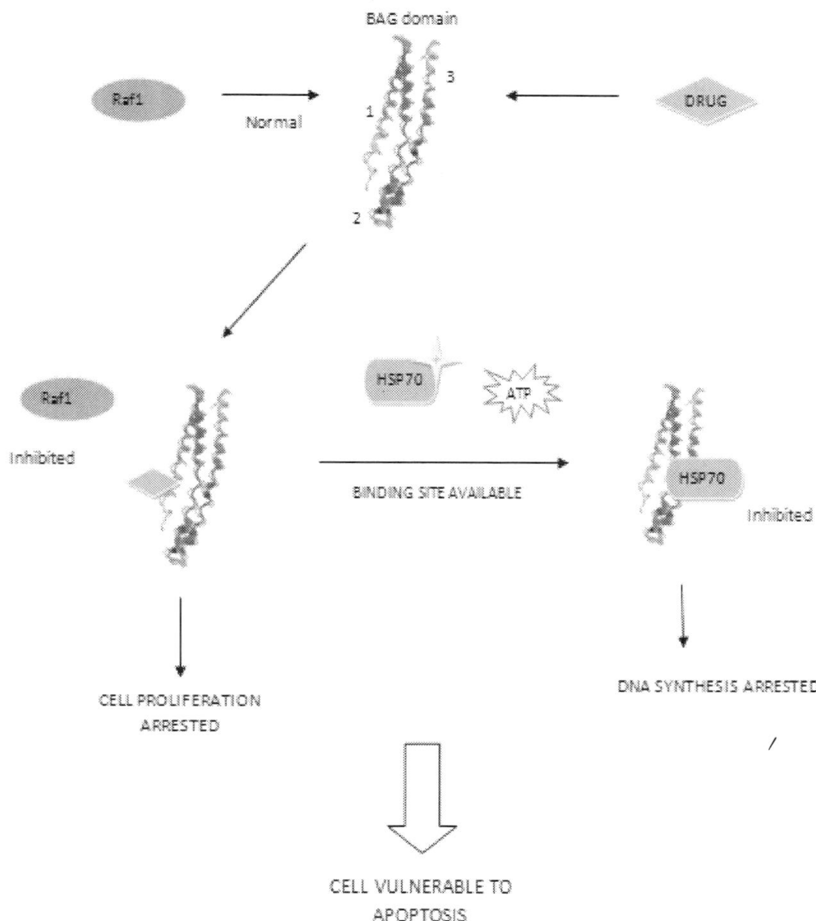

Fig. 3. Flowchart depicting the drug targeted strategy.

6. Structure analysis tools

ProtParam is a tool which allows the computation of various physical and chemical parameters for a protein sequence. The computed parameters include the molecular weight, theoretical pI, amino acid composition, atomic composition, extinction coefficient, estimated half-life, instability index, aliphatic index and grand average of hydropathicity (GRAVY).

The HNN method was used for secondary structure prediction for Bag1 protein. CPHmodels is a web server predicting protein 3D structure by use of single template homology modeling. The CPHmodels server predicts protein structure from amino acid sequence with respect to distance constraints. CPHmodels is a collection of methods and databases consisting of the following tools: CPHmodels was used for tertiary structure prediction of Bag1 protein.

The 3d structure obtained as a pdb file format was viewed using RasMol.

PRODOM and PROSITE is a comprehensive database of protein domain and families. PROSITE offers tools for protein sequence analysis and motif detection.

STRING is a database of known and predicted protein interactions.

CASTP (Computed Atlas of Surface Topography of Proteins) is a server that provides identification and measurements of surface accessible pockets as well as interior inaccessible cavities for proteins and other molecules.

7. Drug discovery tools

Drugbank, Pubchem, therapeutic target database (TTD), Tocris are the various databases which were searched for potential drug candidates.

ArgusLab was used as a molecular modelling program to optimize the target receptor protein and design a drug targeted to the BAG1 protein. The quantum mechanical calculations were performed using the Argus compute server.

HEX5.1 is an interactive protein docking and molecular superposition program. HEX5.1 was used for docking of the selected drug candidate with the BAG1 target protein.

8. Results and discussion

BAG1 isoform 1-L sequence was retrieved from NCBI. The protein BAG1-L is 345 amino acids in length. Sequence analysis by BLASTp shows that Bag1-L protein showed maximum identities with *Bos Taurus* (83%) followed by *Mus musculus* (80%). BLAST results of BAG1 protein compared with other model organisms is shown in Table 1.

Evolutionary relationship of BAG1 protein among various species was obtained in the form of a dendrogram (Fig.4) The query protein was seen to be most closely related to *Mus musculus* and showed a distinct evolutionary relationship with *Suberites domuncula*. The highly conserved regions in the amino acid sequence of BAG1 in protein among various model organisms were analysed using Boxshade (Fig. 5). The amino acids Glycine and Glutamine were found to be the maximum conserved regions among all the species analysed.

The structural analysis of BAG1-L protein was done by using ProtParam, HNN & CPH. Since the GRAVY value is negative (-0.905) it can be inferred from the results that the protein is a hydrophobic molecule present at the cell surface. It is an unstable protein. It consists of 40.00% alpha helices and no beta bridges or turns are present. (Fig. 6) Using CPH model, the 3D structure of the protein was retrieved in the form of a PDB ID. The PDB ID with the maximum score i.e. 1HX1 was chosen and viewed in Rasmol. (Fig. 7) The PDB ID 1HX1 shows the 3D structure for two molecules Hsp70 and Bag domain as Chain A (400aa) and Chain B (114aa) respectively. The Chain B i.e. Bag domain (receptor) was isolated and its energy was optimized to 3734.78 au using ArgusLab. The molecule converged at 298.92 kcal\mol.

CASTP was used to find the active pocket in the receptor protein. The amino acid Lysine in Chain B (receptor molecule) at position 172 is selected as the target residue for Arguslab docking as it is the most hydrophilic residue in the active pocket.

A number of small molecules that bind to the target were searched by screening libraries of potential drug compounds. The toxic effects and pharmacodynamics of the compounds was tested by ADME/Tox. The compound Carmustine was chosen out of the drug library as it followed the Lipinski's rule of five and had the best combination of required properties for a potential drug candidate. (Table 2)

The molecule Carmustine was designed in ArgusLab and geometry optimization of the drug got converged at energy of 22.2 Kcal\mol. Total energy of the compound converged at -101.413 au.

The drug was docked to the target residue using Arguslab and Hex5.1. In Hex, the drug docked to the receptor with an Emax value (Energy) of -94.68 kcal\mol and Emin value of -166.49 kcal\mol. (Fig. 9) In Arguslab, the drug docked to the target receptor with energy of -5.51 kcal\mol.

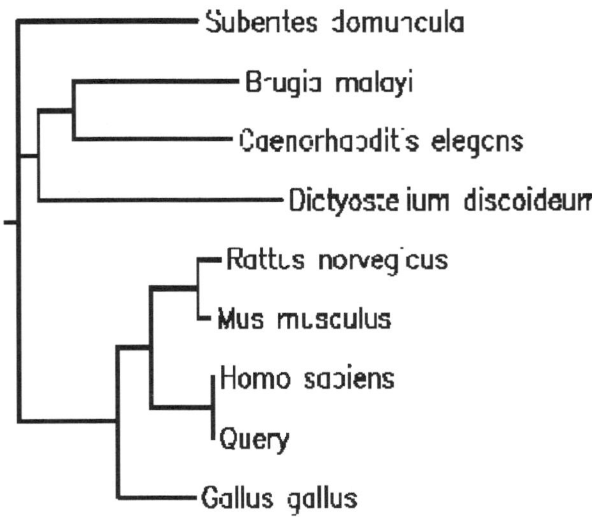

Fig. 4. Dendogram depicting the phylogenetic relationship of Bag1 (Query) protein in Homo sapiens with Bag1 protein of other model organisms (humans).

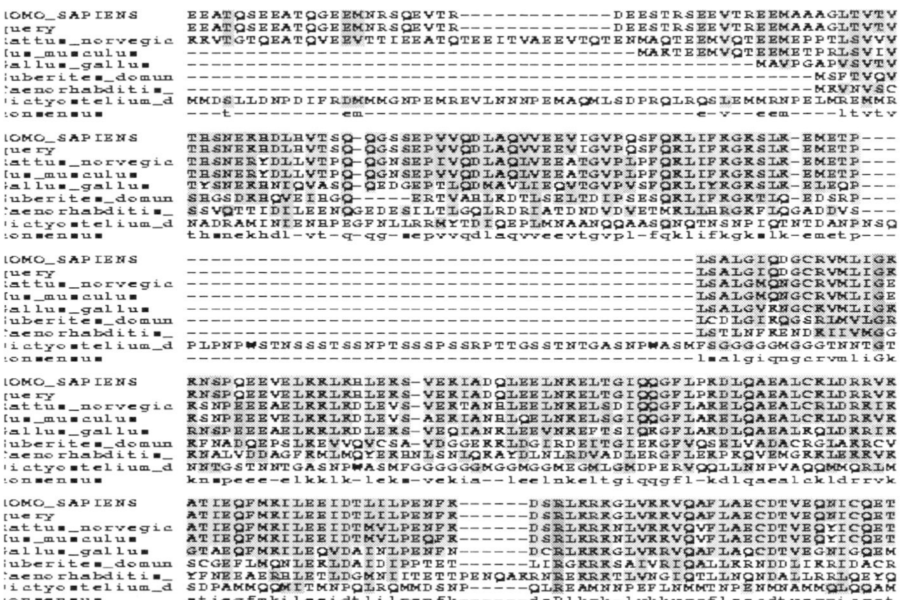

Fig. 5. Boxshade showing some of the highly conserved (green) and similar (cyan) pattern for Bag1 protein in different model organisms.

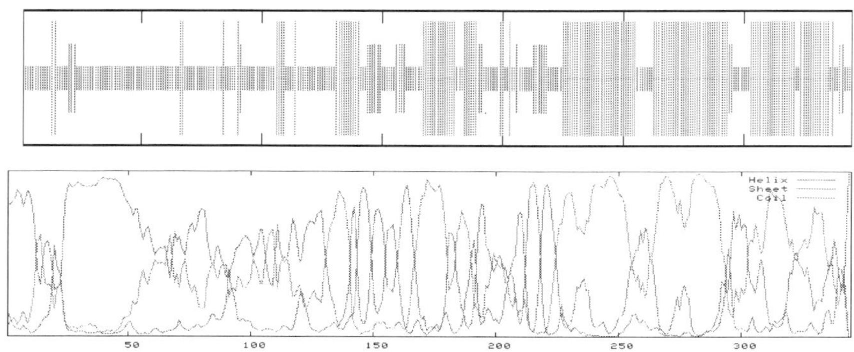

Fig. 6. The secondary structure analysis result of Bag1 by HNN tool. The alpha helices are shaded blue, beta sheets are shaded red.

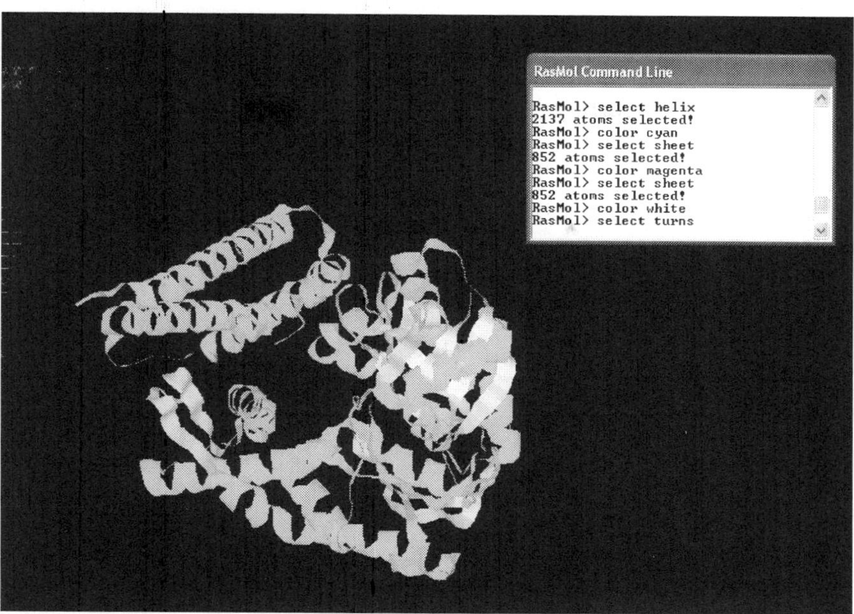

Fig. 7. Visualization result of Bag1protein using the tool RASMOL showing the 3D structure details.

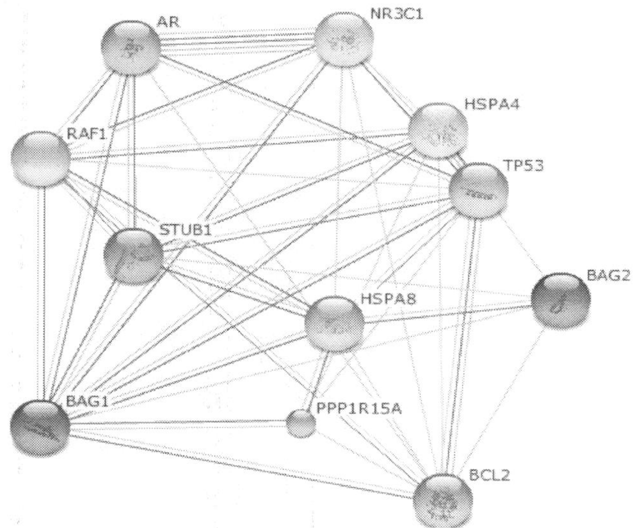

Fig. 8. STRING analysis of BAG1 protein showing its interaction with other proteins in the human. The number of lines represents the strength of interaction.

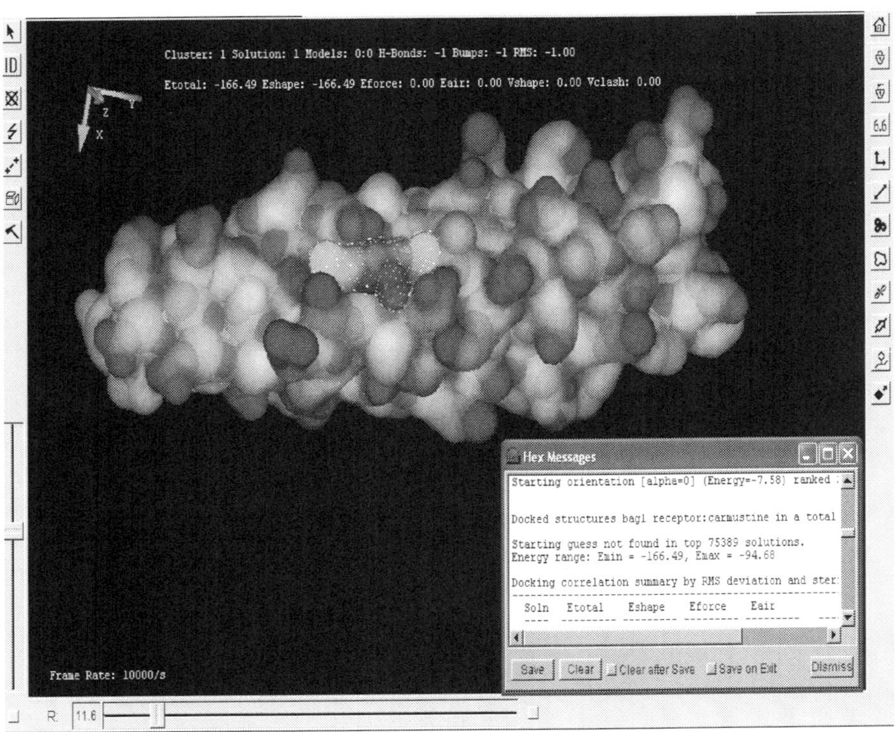

Fig. 9. Docking analysis result of Bag1 protein with the drug Carmustine in Hex5.1.

Model Organism Name	BLAST Results
Homo sapiens	GENE ID: 573 BAG1 | BCL2-associated athanogene [Homo sapiens] (Over 10 PubMed links) Score = 724 bits (1671), Expect = 0.0, Method: Compositional matrix adjust. Identities = 345/345 (100%), Positives = 345/345 (100%), Gaps = 0/345 (0%)
Bos taurus	GENE ID: 613855 BAG1 | BCL2-associated athanogene [Bos taurus] Score = 413 bits (950), Expect = 1e-115, Method: Compositional matrix adjust. Identities = 198/236 (83%), Positives = 214/236 (90%), Gaps = 1/236 (0%)
Mus musculus	GENE ID: 12017 Bag1 | BCL2-associated athanogene 1 [Mus musculus] (Over 10 PubMed links) Score = 362 bits (831), Expect = 1e-99, Method: Compositional matrix adjust. Identities = 172/214 (80%), Positives = 188/214 (87%), Gaps = 0/214 (0%)
Gallus gallus	GENE ID: 420967 BAG1 | BCL2-associated athanogene [Gallus gallus] (10 or fewer PubMed links) Score = 310 bits (712), Expect = 8e-85, Method: Compositional matrix adjust. Identities = 144/209 (68%), Positives = 179/209 (85%), Gaps = 2/209 (0%)
Rattus norvegicus	GENE ID: 297994 Bag1 | BCL2-associated athanogene [Rattus norvegicus] (Over 10 PubMed links) Score = 497 bits (1145), Expect = 9e-141, Method: Compositional matrix adjust. Identities = 250/358 (69%), Positives = 286/358 (79%), Gaps = 13/358 (3%)
Dictyostelium discoideum	GENE ID: 8616246 sonA | UAS domain-containing protein [Dictyostelium discoideum AX4] (10 or fewer PubMed links) Score = 34.5 bits (102), Expect = 0.053, Method: Compositional matrix adjust. Identities = 17/49 (34%), Positives = 29/49 (59%), Gaps = 1/49 (2%)
Caenorhabditis elegans	GENE ID: 172373 bag-1 | BAG1 (human) homolog [Caenorhabditis elegans] (10 or fewer PubMed links) Score = 51.5 bits (160), Expect = 8e-07, Method: Compositional matrix adjust. Identities = 44/145 (30%), Positives = 81/145 (55%), Gaps = 8/145 (5%)

Model Organism Name	BLAST Results
Suberites domuncula	emb|CAJ65915.1| BAG family molecular chaperone regulator 1 [Suberites domuncula] Length=258 Score = 99.5 bits (324), Expect = 4e-19, Method: Compositional matrix adjust. Identities = 63/186 (33%), Positives = 110/186 (59%), Gaps = 4/186 (2%)
Brugia malayi	GENE ID: 6105907 Bm1_55120 | BAG domain containing protein [Brugia malayi] (10 or fewer PubMed links) Score = 47.1 bits (145), Expect = 5e-06, Method: Compositional matrix adjust. Identities = 57/199 (30%), Positives = 92/199 (46%), Gaps = 8/199 (4%)

Table 1. Showing the result of query sequence BLAST with different model organisms.

Drug Name	MW[gm/mol]	LogP	H-Doner	H-Accepter	Hex Docking Value Emin	Emax	Arguslab Docking Value[Kcal/mol]
Carmustine	214.04986	1.53	1	3	-166	-94.68	-5.7995
Benzoyloxy-MAB	331.36	4.75	0	5	-236	-76.51	-9.21813
THIOFLAVIN	226.336	4.59	0	0	-219.48	-94.56	-9.2251
nchembio	283.4116	4.77	0	1	-234.89	-106.75	-8.12071
Disperse Red 53	357.357	2.63	2	7	-245.67	-107.41	-6.99146
Honokiol	266.334	4.95	2	2	-256.14	-92.45	-8.41591
progesterone	314.461	3.89	0	2	-225.06	-80.55	-8.42643
Spectrum_000864	314.4617	3.89	0	2	-226.55	-91.26	-7.82574
CCRIS 4309	373.5289	4.97	3	3	-228.10	-97.30	-7.49083
Methotrexate	432.373601	-1.45	5	4	-288.88	-103.99	-6.4956
Fludarabine	285.231783	<-2	4	9	-198.91	-76.86	-6.4956
2-Fluoroadenosine	285.2317	<-2	4	9	-201.19	-80.10	-6.13115
dexamethasone	392.461063	1.80	3	6	-236.89	-90.34	-7.25208
CID1150209	392.461	1.80	3	6	-223.98	-92.86	-6.94276
Decadronal	434.497713	1.93	2	7	-253.85	-105.54	-7.56959

Table 2. List of various potential drug candidates for binding with Bag domain of Bag 1 protein.

The BAG proteins having anti-apoptotic activity promotes cell growth by binding to and stimulating Raf-1 activity. BAG-1 binds to the serine/threonine kinase Raf-1 or Hsc70/Hsp70 in a mutually exclusive interaction. The binding of Hsp70 to BAG-1 diminishes Raf-1 signalling and inhibits subsequent events, such as DNA synthesis, as well as arrests the cell cycle. Hence Bag1 plays an important role in the progression of cancers when over expressed. The 345 amino acid long protein sequence of BAG1-L was obtained from NCBI and a BLASTp was performed to analyze its evolutionary relationships with other counterparts in various model organisms. This was confirmed by the phylogenetic analysis done using SDSC workbench. The dendrogram presents that Bag1 had close evolutionary relationship with *Mus musculus.*

From the primary structure analysis it was concluded that BAG1 protein is a surface protein which is hydrophilic in nature. Its secondary structure analysis confirmed that it contains more alpha helices and no beta sheets. Its 3D structure was obtained in the form of PDB id and viewed in Rasmol. The chain B of PDB structure represents the BAG domain. Various confirmatory tools were used for validation of the results. The geometry and energy of the BAG domain was optimized in Arguslab. Using Castp, the active pocket in the BAG domain was identified and the most hydrophilic residue in the first alpha helix of the BAG domain i.e. LYS at position 242 of BAG1-L protein sequence obtained from NCBI (or position 172 in the Chain B of pdb id 1HX1) was selected as the target receptor.

A drug library was maintained of possible lead compounds that follow the Lipinski rule of five and their toxicity and disposition was checked using ADME/TOX. These candidate drugs were docked to the target receptor. The drug CARMUSTINE showed the best docking result with docking Energy of -5.51kcal/mol. As the docking (Fig 9) was successful in both HEX5.1 and Arguslab it can be concluded that Carmustine can be a potential drug for BAG1 binding and arresting tumor progression. Further analysis must be performed on this drug for use in treatment of cancer.

9. Acknowledgements

The work was done by worthwhile efforts of the staff and the research associates of the Department of Molecular Biology Bioaxis DNA Research Centre, Hyderabad, India. In addition, the authors would like to thank all the technical staff of instrumental section in developing and maintaining the various databases and tools mentioned in this article.

10. References

[1] Downward J. Targeting RAS signalling pathways in cancer therapy. *Nat Rev Cancer.* (2003) 3(1):11-22.

[2] Klára Briknarová1, Shinichi Takayama, Lars Brive, Marnie L. Havert, Deborah A. Knee1, Jesus Velasco1, Sachiko Homma, Edelmira Cabezas1, Joan Stuart, David W. Hoyt, Arnold C. Satterthwait, Miguel Llinás, John C. Reed & Kathryn R. Ely. Structural analysis of BAG1 cochaperone and its interactions with Hsc70 heat shock protein. *Nature Structural Biology,* (2001) 8(4):349-52.

[3] Sebolt-Leopold JS. Oncovera Therapeutics, Ann Arbor. Advances in the development of cancer therapeutics directed against the RAS-mitogen-activated protein kinase pathway. *Clin Cancer Res* (2008) 14:3651-3656

[4] Hoshino R, Chatani Y, Yamori T, Tsuruo T, Oka H, Yoshida O, Shimada Y, Ari-i S, Wada H, Fujimoto J, Kohno M. Constitutive activation of the 41-/43-kDa mitogen-activated protein kinase signaling pathway in human tumors. *Oncogene.* (1999) 18(3);813-22

[5] Sharp A, Crabb SJ, Townsend PA, Cutress RI, Brimmell M, Wang XH, Packham G. BAG-1 in carcinogenesis. *Expert Rev Mol Med.* (2004) 6(7):1-15.

[6] Rudolf Götz, Boris W Kramer, Guadalupe Camarero and Ulf R Rapp. BAG-1 haploinsufficiency impairs lung tumorigenesis. *BMC Cancer* (2004) 24; 4:85.

[7] HE Maki, OR Saram''aki, L Shatkina, PM Martikainen, TLJ Tammela, WM van Weerden, RL Vessella, ACB Cato2 and T Visakorpi1. Overexpression and gene amplification of BAG-1L in hormone-refractory prostate cancer. *J Pathol* (2007) 212: 395–401

[8] R I Cutress, P A Townsend, M Brimmell, A C Bateman, A Hague and G Packham. BAG-1 expression and function in human cancer. *British Journal of Cancer* (2002) 87; 834 – 839.

[9] Jaewhan Song, Masahiro Takeda & Richard I. Morimoto. Bag1–Hsp70 mediates a physiological stress signalling pathway that regulates Raf-1/ERK and cell growth. *Nature Cell Biology* (2001) 3: 276 – 282.

[10] Ellen A. A. Nollen,1 Jeanette F. Brunsting,1 Jaewhan Song,2 Harm H. Kampinga,1 and Richard I. Morimoto2 . Bag1 Functions In Vivo as a Negative Regulator of Hsp70 Chaperone Activity. *Mol Cell Biol.* (2000) 20(3):1083-8

[11] Ruth M. Kluck, Ella Bossy-Wetzel, Douglas R. Green, Donald D. Newmeyer. The Release of Cytochrome c from Mitochondria: A Primary Site for Bcl-2 Regulation of Apoptosis. *Science.* (1997) 275(5303):1132-6.

[12] Yang J, Liu X, Bhalla K, Kim CN, Ibrado AM, Cai J, Peng TI, Jones DP, Wang X. Prevention of apoptosis by Bcl-2: release of cytochrome c from mitochondria blocked. *Science.* (1997) 275(5303);1129-32.

[13] Wang, HG, Takayama S, Rapp UR, Reed JC. Bcl-2 interacting protein, BAG-1, binds to and activates the kinase Raf-1. *Proc. Natl. Acad. Sci. U.S.A* (1996). 93(14):7063-8

[14] Takayama S, Xie Z, Reed JC. An evolutionarily conserved family of Hsp70/Hsc70 molecular chaperone regulators. *The Journal of Biological Chem.* (1999) 274 (2); 781–786.

[15] Takayama S, Krajewski S, Krajewska M, Kitada S, Zapata JM, Kochel K, Knee D, Scudiero D, Tudor G, Miller GJ, Miyashita T, Yamada M, Reed JC.. Expression and location of Hsp70/Hsc-binding anti-apoptotic protein BAG-1 and its variants in normal tissues and tumor cell lines. *Cancer Res.* (1998) 15; 58(14):3116-31.

[16] Sondermann H, Scheufler C, Schneider C, Hohfeld J, Hartl FU, Moarefi I. Structure of a Bag/Hsc70 complex: convergent functional evolution of Hsp70 nucleotide exchange factors. *Science.* (2001) 291(5508):1553-7.

[17] Sharp A, Crabb SJ, Johnson PW, Hague A, Cutress R, Townsend PA, Ganesan A, Packham G. Thioflavin S (NSC71948) interferes with Bcl-2-associated athanogene (BAG-1)-mediated protein-protein interactions. *J Pharmacol Exp Ther.* (2009); 331(2): 680–689.

[18] Takahashi N, Yanagihara M, Ogawa Y, Yamanoha B, Andoh T. Down-regulation of Bcl-2-interacting protein BAG-1 confers resistance to anti-cancer drugs. *Biochem Biophys Res Commun.* (2003) 14; 301(3):798-803.

[19] Rorke S, Murphy S, Khalifa M, Chernenko G, Tang SC. Prognostic significance of BAG-1 expression in nonsmall cell lung cancer. *Int J Cancer.* (2001) 20; 95(5):317-22.

[20] Shinichi Takayama, David N.Bimston1, Shu-ichi Matsuzawa, Brian C.Freeman1,2, Christine Aime-Sempe, Zhihua Xie, Richard I.Morimoto1 and John C.Reed3. BAG-1 modulates the chaperone activity of Hsp70/Hsc70. *The EMBO Journal* (1997) 16 ;4887–4896.

[21] Graham P, Matthew B and John LC. Mammalian cells express two differently localized Bag-1 isoforms generated by alternative translation initiation. *Biochem. J.* (1997) 328; 807-813

[22] Yang X, Pater A, Tang SC. Cloning and characterization of the human BAG-1 gene promoter: upregulation by tumor-derived p53 mutants. *Oncogene.* (1999) 12; 18 (32):4546-53.

[23] Zeiner M, Gehring U. A protein that interacts with members of the nuclear hormone receptor family: identification and cDNA cloning. *Proc Natl Acad Sci U S A.* (1995) 5;92(25):11465-9.

[24] Moriyama T, Littell RD, Debernardo R, Oliva E, Lynch MP, Rueda BR, Duska LR. BAG-1 expression in normal and neoplastic endometrium. *Gynecol Oncol.* (2004) 94(2):289-95.

[25] Clemo NK, Collard TJ, Southern SL, Edwards KD, Moorghen M, Packham G, Hague A, Paraskeva C, Williams AC. BAG-1 is up-regulated in colorectal tumour progression and promotes colorectal tumour cell survival through increased NF-kappaB activity. *Carcinogenesis.* (2008) 29(4):849-57

[26] Clemo NK, Arhel NJ, Barnes JD, Baker J, Moorghen M, Packham GK, Paraskeva C, Williams AC. The role of the retinoblastoma protein (Rb) in the nuclear localization of BAG-1: implications for colorectal tumour cell survival. *Biochem Soc Trans.* (2005) 33(Pt 4):676-8.

[27] Townsend PA, Cutress RI, Sharp A, Brimmell M, Packham G. BAG-1 prevents stress-induced long-term growth inhibition in breast cancer cells via a chaperone-dependent pathway. *Cancer Res.* (2003) 15; 63(14):4150-7.

[28] Kikuchi R, Noguchi T, Takeno S, Funada Y, Moriyama H, Uchida Y. Nuclear BAG-1 expression reflects malignant potential in colorectal carcinomas. *Br J Cancer.* (2002) 4; 87(10):1136-9.

[29] Liu HY, Wang ZM, Bai Y, Wang M, Li Y, Wei S, Zhou QH, Chen J. Different BAG-1 isoforms have distinct functions in modulating chemotherapeutic-induced apoptosis in breast cancer cells. *Acta Pharmacol Sin.* (2009) 30(2):235-41.

[30] Vora HH, Mehta SV, Shah KN, Brahmbhatt BV, Desai NS, Shukla SN, Shah PM. Cytoplasmic localization of BAG-1 in leukoplakia and carcinoma of the tongue: correlation with p53 and c-erbB2 in carcinoma. *Int J Biol Markers.*(2007) 22(2):100-7.

[31] Pusztai L, Krishnamurti S, Perez Cardona J, Sneige N, Esteva FJ, Volchenok M, Breitenfelder P, Kau SW, Takayama S, Krajewski S, Reed JC, Bast RC Jr, Hortobagyi GN. Expression of BAG-1 and BcL-2 proteins before and after

neoadjuvant chemotherapy of locally advanced breast cancer. *Cancer Invest.* (2004);22(2):248-56.

[32] Tang SC. BAG-1, an anti-apoptotic tumour marker. *IUBMB Life.* (2002) Feb; 53(2):99-105.

[33] Brive L, Takayama S, Briknarová K, Homma S, Ishida SK, Reed JC, Ely KR. The carboxyl-terminal lobe of Hsc70 ATPase domain is sufficient for binding to BAG1. *Biochem Biophys Res Commun.* (2001) 21; 289(5):1099-105.

[34] Nadler Y, Camp RL, Giltnane JM, Moeder C, Rimm DL, Kluger HM, Kluger Y. Expression patterns and prognostic value of Bag-1 and Bcl-2 in breast cancer. *Breast Cancer Res.* (2008) 10(2):R35.

[35] Lüders J, Demand J, Höhfeld J. The ubiquitin-related BAG-1 provides a link between the molecular chaperones Hsc70/Hsp70 and the proteasome. *J Biol Chem.* (2000) 275(7):4613-7.

[36] McCubrey JA, Steelman LS, Chappell WH, Abrams SL, Wong EW, Chang F, Lehmann B, Terrian DM, Milella M, Tafuri A, Stivala F, Libra M, Basecke J, Evangelisti C, Martelli AM, Franklin RA. Roles of the Raf/MEK/ERK pathway in cell growth, malignant transformation and drug resistance. *Biochim Biophys Acta.* (2007). 1773(8):1263-84.